Concepts of
MARKETING

Gilbert D. Harrell

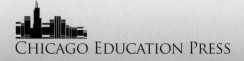

CHICAGO EDUCATION PRESS

This book was previously published by: Pearson Education, Inc.
The work contained here is the 2009 edition produced by Chicago Education Press, LLC.

Printed in the United States of America

10 9 8 7 6 5 4 3 2

ISBN 13: 978-0-9798304-3-3

ISBN 10: 0-9798304-3-5

CHICAGO EDUCATION PRESS

Chicago Education Press, LLC
27 N. Wacker Drive, Suite 390
Chicago, IL 60606-2800
USA

www.chicagoeducationpress.com

**To Susanna, Rachael,
Nicholas and Katherine**

contents

ABOUT THE AUTHOR   XI
PREFACE   XIII

SECTION 1: VALUE ORIENTATION 2

CHAPTER 1
CONCEPTS OF MARKETING: CREATING & CAPTURING VALUE
CONCEPTS OF MARKETING 6
MARKETING IS   6
   THE ACTIVITY 7
   SET OF INSTITUTIONS 9
   PROCESSES 10
   CREATING, COMMUNICATING, (&) DELIVERING 11
   AND EXCHANGING OFFERINGS THAT HAVE VALUE 11
   FOR CUSTOMERS, CLIENTS, PARTNERS & SOCIETY 14
THE EVOLUTION OF MARKETING 15
   THE PRODUCTION ERA 16
   THE SALES ERA 16
   THE CUSTOMER MARKETING ERA 17
THE MARKETING STRATEGY PROCESS 18
   MARKETING MIX DECISIONS 19
FORCES IMPORTANT TO CREATE AND CAPTURE VALUE 21
   CREATING AND CAPTURING VALUE THROUGH TECHNOLOGY AND E-COMMERCE 21
   CREATING AND CAPTURING VALUE THROUGH RELATIONSHIPS 23
   CREATING AND CAPTURING VALUE GLOBALLY 24
   CREATING AND CAPTURING VALUE THROUGH DIVERSITY 25
   CREATING AND CAPTURING VALUE ETHICALLY 26
   CREATING AND CAPTURING VALUE THROUGH SUSTAINABILITY 27
MARKETING: YOUR INVOLVEMENT 28
   CHAPTER SUMMARY 29

CHAPTER 2
THE MARKETING STRATEGY & PLANNING PROCESS
THE CONCEPT OF THE STRATEGIC MARKETING PLANNING PROCESS 36
THE ORGANIZATION VISION 37
   CORE VALUES: THE ETHICAL FOUNDATION 37
   BUSINESS DEFINITION (MISSION) 39
   STRATEGIC DIRECTION (INTENT) 40
   STRATEGIC INFRASTRUCTURE 40
THE STRATEGIC MARKETING PLAN 46
   THE PLANNING TEAM 46
   WHAT IS STRATEGY? 46
   COMPONENTS OF THE STRATEGIC MARKETING PLAN 48
   OBJECTIVES 48
   SITUATION ANALYSIS 48
   TARGET MARKETING 49
   POSITIONING 49
   INTEGRATED MARKETING MIX PLANS 50
   THE MARKETING CONTROL PROCESS 54
CONNECTING GLOBALLY: ENTERING WORLD MARKETS TO CAPTURE VALUE 55
   GEOGRAPHIC SCOPE 55
   STRATEGIES FOR FOREIGN MARKET ENTRY 56
   CHAPTER SUMMARY 58

CHAPTER 3
THE GLOBAL MARKETING ENVIRONMENT & E-COMMERCE
THE CONCEPT OF THE MARKETING ENVIRONMENT 66
THE MICROENVIRONMENT 67
   RELATIONSHIPS WITH STAKEHOLDERS 67
   INDUSTRY COMPETITION 69
THE GLOBAL MACROENVIRONMENT 70
   TECHNOLOGICAL ENVIRONMENT 70
   ECONOMIC ENVIRONMENT 71
   DEMOGRAPHIC ENVIRONMENT 74
   CULTURAL ENVIRONMENT 76
   LEGAL/REGULATORY ENVIRONMENT 79
   ETHICAL ENVIRONMENT 82

MARKETING E-COMMERCE 83
   THE STRUCTURE OF INTERNET MARKETING 84
   VALUE OF THE INTERNET TO BUYERS AND SELLERS 85
   CHAPTER SUMMARY 88

SECTION 2: DISCOVER VALUE *94*

CHAPTER 4
MARKETING INFORMATION & RESEARCH
THE CONCEPT OF MARKETING INFORMATION SYSTEMS AND
   MARKETING RESEARCH 98
MARKETING INFORMATION SYSTEMS AND DATA 99
   TURNING DATA INTO INFORMATION 99
   INFORMATION IS FOR DECISION MAKING 101
THE MARKETING RESEARCH PROCESS 103
   DEFINING THE PROBLEM 103
   RESEARCH DESIGN 104
   EXPLORATORY RESEARCH 104
   QUANTITATIVE RESEARCH 106
   SAMPLING 109
   INTERPRETING AND REPORTING SURVEY FINDINGS 110
   WHO DOES MARKETING RESEARCH? 112
TECHNOLOGY'S EFFECT ON MARKETING RESEARCH 113
   INTERNET SEARCHES 113
GLOBAL MARKETING RESEARCH 114
ETHICS IN MARKETING RESEARCH AND INFORMATION
   USE 115
   CHAPTER SUMMARY 116

CHAPTER 5
UNDERSTANDING CONSUMER BEHAVIOR
THE CONCEPT OF CONSUMER BEHAVIOR 122
CONSUMER INVOLVEMENT AND DECISION MAKING 122
   CONSUMER INVOLVEMENT 122
   CONSUMER DECISION MAKING 124
PSYCHOLOGICAL FACTORS THAT INFLUENCE CONSUMER
   DECISIONS 125
   MOTIVATION 125
   PERCEPTION 127
   LEARNING 129
   ATTITUDES 130
   INFORMATION PROCESSING 131
SOCIAL FACTORS THAT INFLUENCE CONSUMER DECISIONS 132
   CULTURE 132
   SUBCULTURE 133
   SOCIAL CLASS 135
   REFERENCE GROUPS 137
   THE FAMILY 138
USING TECHNOLOGY TO TRACK CONSUMER BEHAVIOR 140
THE ETHICS OF INFLUENCING CONSUMER BEHAVIOR 142
   CHAPTER SUMMARY 143

CHAPTER 6:
UNDERSTANDING BUSINESS MARKETING

THE CONCEPT OF BUSINESS-TO-BUSINESS MARKETING 150
   DERIVED BUSINESS MARKET DEMAND 150
   TYPES OF MARKETS 151
   LARGE PURCHASES IN B2B MARKETS 154
   BUSINESS MARKET LINKAGES: THE SUPPLY CHAIN 154
   GLOBALIZATION OF BUSINESS MARKETS 154
ORGANIZATIONAL BUYING 154
   BUYING DECISIONS 154
   STEPS IN THE ORGANIZATIONAL BUYING PROCESS 157
   RELATIONSHIPS BETWEEN BUYERS AND SELLERS 158
   FUNCTIONS INVOLVED IN BUSINESS PURCHASES 161
   INFLUENCES ON ORGANIZATIONAL BUYING BEHAVIOR 164
   CHAPTER SUMMARY 166

SECTION 3: FOCUS RESOURCES ON VALUE *172*

CHAPTER 7
CREATING CUSTOMER SATISFACTION & LOYALTY
THE CONCEPTS OF CUSTOMER SATISFACTION, LOYALTY, AND
   QUALITY 176
   CUSTOMER SATISFACTION AND CUSTOMER LOYALTY 176
   WHY SATISFACTION AND LOYALTY ARE IMPORTANT 176
   CUSTOMER EXPECTATIONS 178
   CUSTOMER DEFECTIONS AND COMPLAINING BEHAVIOR 178
   SATISFACTION RATINGS AND MEASUREMENT 179
RELATIONSHIPS BUILD SATISFACTION AND LOYALTY 180
   CREATING A PERSONAL RELATIONSHIP 181
   DIVERSITY AND SATISFACTION 183
   GLOBAL COMPETITION AND SATISFACTION 184
ORGANIZATIONAL SYSTEMS AND ACTIONS THAT DELIVER
   QUALITY 184
   QUALITY 184
   TOTAL QUALITY MANAGEMENT 186
   QUALITY AWARDS 188
DELIVERING VALUE TO IMPROVE SATISFACTION 190
   INTEGRATED SUPPLY CHAIN 190
   ETHICAL BEHAVIOR IN FULFILLING COMMITMENTS 191
   EMPLOYEE AND CUSTOMER INVOLVEMENT 191
   CHAPTER SUMMARY 193

CHAPTER 8:
SEGMENTATION, TARGETING & POSITIONING
THE CONCEPT OF SEGMENTATION, TARGETING, AND POSITIONING
   200
MARKET SEGMENTATION 202
   SEGMENTATION VERSUS MASS MARKETING 202
   SEGMENTATION VERSUS PRODUCT DIFFERENTIATION 203
   SEGMENTATION VARIABLES 203
   BUSINESS MARKET SEGMENTATION 213
   TWO COMMON SEGMENTING METHODS 214
TARGET MARKETING 215
   SELECTING TARGET SEGMENTS 215
   FINDING NEW MARKETS TO TARGET 217
   TARGET MARKETING STRATEGIES 217
   ETHICAL DIMENSIONS OF TARGETING 220

GLOBAL TARGETING 221
POSITIONING STRATEGIES 221
THE POSITIONING MAP 221
POSITIONING BUSINESS PRODUCTS 222
STEPS FOR POSITIONING 222
BASES FOR POSITIONING 223
REPOSITIONING 225
CHAPTER SUMMARY 225

SECTION 4: CREATE VALUE 230

CHAPTER 9:
BRAND MANAGEMENT & PRODUCT DECISIONS

THE CONCEPT OF PRODUCTS 234
CORE PRODUCTS 234
BRANDED PRODUCTS 235
AUGMENTED PRODUCTS 235
CONSUMER PRODUCT CLASSIFICATION 236
BUSINESS PRODUCT CLASSIFICATION 238
PRODUCT LINE DECISIONS 239
GLOBAL PRODUCTS 240
BRAND MANAGEMENT 241
TRADEMARKS 242
TRADEMARK PIRACY 243
BRAND STRATEGIES 244
BRAND EQUITY: CONNECTING WITH A SUCCESSFUL BRAND 246
MAINTAINING BRAND VALUE 249
DEVELOPING A SUCCESSFUL BRAND NAME 249
JOINT MARKETING OF BRANDS 250
PACKAGING AND LABELING 250
ETHICAL ISSUES SURROUNDING PRODUCT SAFETY AND
LIABILITY 251
PRODUCT WARRANTIES 251
PRODUCT RECALLS 252
CHAPTER SUMMARY 253

CHAPTER 10:
GOODS, SERVICES & NON PROFIT MARKETING

THE CONCEPT OF SERVICES 260
GLOBAL FORCES CREATING GROWTH IN SERVICES 261
TECHNOLOGY 261
QUALITY OF LIFE 262
GOVERNMENT DEREGULATION OF SERVICES 262
COMPETITION IN PROFESSIONAL SERVICES 263
PRIVATIZATION 264
THE NEED FOR SPECIALIZATION 264
ACCESS TO KNOWLEDGE 264
GROWTH OF FRANCHISING 265
SERVICE CHARACTERISTICS THAT AFFECT MARKETING
STRATEGY 265
CONTRASTS BETWEEN GOODS AND SERVICES 265
THE SERVICE-GOODS CONTINUUM 268
CONSUMER EVALUATION OF SERVICES 269
SERVICE QUALITY 271
DEVELOPING THE SERVICE MIX 273
CORE, AUGMENTED, AND BRANDED SERVICES 273
DEVELOPING NEW SERVICES 273
AN EXPANDED CONCEPT OF SERVICES 274
PERSON MARKETING 274
ENTERTAINMENT AND EVENT MARKETING 276
PLACE MARKETING 276
POLITICAL MARKETING 276
CAUSE MARKETING 277
INTERNAL MARKETING 277
THE MARKETING OF NONPROFIT SERVICES 278
TYPES OF NONPROFIT SERVICE PROVIDERS 278
THE NEED FOR EXCESS REVENUES 278
FUND-RAISING AND REVENUE GENERATION 279
PROVIDING POSITIVE SOCIAL BENEFITS 282
ETHICAL ISSUES SURROUNDING NONPROFIT ORGANIZATIONS 282
CHAPTER SUMMARY 283

CHAPTER 11:
PRODUCT INNOVATION & MANAGEMENT

THE CONCEPTS OF PRODUCT DEVELOPMENT AND PRODUCT
MANAGEMENT 290
PRODUCT PLANNING AND TYPES OF INNOVATION 291
PRODUCT PLANNING 291
TYPES OF PRODUCT INNOVATION 292
WHY INNOVATIONS SUCCEED 293
THE NEW-PRODUCT DEVELOPMENT PROCESS 294
NEW-PRODUCT STRATEGY 295
IDEA GENERATION 295
IDEA SCREENING 297
BUSINESS ANALYSIS 297
PROTOTYPE PRODUCT DEVELOPMENT 298
MARKET TESTING 298
COMMERCIALIZATION 299
THE ETHICS OF PRODUCT IMITATION 299
ORGANIZATIONAL STRUCTURES AND PRODUCT
MANAGEMENT 300
RECENT ORGANIZATIONAL TRENDS 300
FUNDAMENTAL STRUCTURES 301
PRODUCT LIFE CYCLES 302
STAGES IN THE PRODUCT LIFE CYCLE 303
VARIATIONS IN PRODUCT LIFE CYCLES 306
EXTENDING THE PRODUCT LIFE CYCLE 307
THE PRODUCT LIFE CYCLE IN INTERNATIONAL MARKETS 308
CONSUMER ACCEPTANCE OF INNOVATION 308
ADOPTION PROCESS 308
DIFFUSION PROCESS 309
CHAPTER SUMMARY 311

SECTION 5: COMMUNICATE VALUE 316

CHAPTER 12:
INTEGRATED MARKETING COMMUNICATIONS
THE CONCEPT OF INTEGRATED MARKETING
    COMMUNICATIONS 320
OBJECTIVES OF INTEGRATED MARKETING
    COMMUNICATION 321
    PROVIDE INFORMATION 321
    CREATE DEMAND FOR PRODUCTS 322
    COMMUNICATE VALUE 322
    COMMUNICATE PRODUCT UNIQUENESS 322
    CLOSE THE SALE 323
    BUILD RELATIONSHIPS AND LOYALTY 323
THE COMMUNICATION PROCESS 323
    THE MESSAGE SENDER 324
    PRESENTATION CREATION: ENCODING 325
    MESSAGE CHARACTERISTICS 326
    MEDIA 328
    INTERPRETATION BY RECEIVERS: DECODING 329
    CONSUMER FEEDBACK 329
THE COMMUNICATION MIX 329
    TYPES OF COMMUNICATION ACTIVITIES 329
    FACTORS AFFECTING THE COMMUNICATION MIX 333
    DEVELOPING THE IMC PLAN 335
    SELECTING AND UNDERSTANDING TARGET AUDIENCES 335
    DETERMINING OBJECTIVES AND SELECTING THE IMC MIX 336
DEVELOPING THE COMMUNICATION BUDGET 336
    IMPLEMENTATION 338
    MEASURING IMC RESULTS 338
ISSUES IN COMMUNICATION 339
    DIVERSITY 339
    ETHICS 339
    TECHNOLOGY THAT BUILDS RELATIONSHIPS 339
    CHAPTER SUMMARY 340

CHAPTER 13:
MASS COMMUNICATION: ADVERTISING, SALES
PROMOTIONS, & PUBLIC RELATIONS
THE CONCEPT OF MASS COMMUNICATIONS: ADVERTISING,
    SALES PROMOTION, AND PUBLIC RELATIONS 346
    TECHNOLOGICAL PERSPECTIVE 346
    GLOBAL MASS COMMUNICATIONS 347
    ETHICAL ISSUES IN ADVERTISING, SALES PROMOTION, AND PUBLIC
        RELATIONS 348
ADVERTISING 348
    THE MULTIPLE PURPOSES AND ROLES OF ADVERTISING 348
    ADVANTAGES OF ADVERTISING 350
    CATEGORIES OF ADVERTISING 351
    ADVERTISING AGENCIES 352
THE ADVERTISING PLAN 352
    SETTING OBJECTIVES 352
    DEVELOPING THE ADVERTISING BUDGET 353
    DEVELOPING THE THEME AND MESSAGE 353
    SELECTING AND SCHEDULING MEDIA 355

    CREATING ADS 359
    ASSESSING ADVERTISING EFFECTIVENESS 359
SALES PROMOTION 360
    TYPES OF SALES PROMOTION 361
    THE SUCCESS OF SALES PROMOTION 362
    CREATING CUSTOMER RELATIONSHIPS AND LOYALTY THROUGH SALES
        PROMOTION 362
    BUSINESS-TO-BUSINESS PROMOTIONS 363
    TRADE PROMOTIONS 364
    RETAILER PROMOTIONS 365
    CONSUMER PROMOTIONS 365
PUBLIC RELATIONS AND PUBLICITY 367
    PUBLIC RELATIONS 367
    PUBLICITY 368
    CHAPTER SUMMARY 370

CHAPTER 14
PERSONAL SELLING & SALES FORCE MANAGEMENT
THE CONCEPTS OF PERSONAL SELLING & SALES MANAGEMENT
    378
PERSONAL SELLING 378
    TYPES OF SALES PERSONNEL AND SELLING SITUATIONS 378
    RELATIONSHIP AND OTHER SELLING APPROACHES 382
    THE RESPONSIBILITIES OF A SALESPERSON 385
    THE STEPS IN PERSONAL SELLING 387
    CHARACTERISTICS OF STRONG SALESPEOPLE 392
    ORGANIZING THE SALES FORCE 393
    DEVELOPING THE SALES TEAM 395
    SALES FORECASTING AND BUDGETING 396
    IMPLEMENTING SALES ACTIONS 398
    OVERSEEING SALES FORCE ACTIVITIES 401
    SALES FORCE AUTOMATION 401
    CHAPTER SUMMARY 402
SECTION 6: DELIVER VALUE 408

CHAPTER 15
SUPPLY CHAIN MANAGEMENT & CHANNELS
THE CONCEPT OF SUPPLY CHAIN MANAGEMENT AND
    MARKETING CHANNELS 412
SUPPLY CHAIN MANAGEMENT, LOGISTICS, AND PHYSICAL
    DISTRIBUTION 412
    SUPPLY CHAIN MANAGEMENT 413
    LOGISTICS 414
    PHYSICAL DISTRIBUTION 415
    GLOBAL PHYSICAL DISTRIBUTION 421
MARKETING CHANNELS 422
    CHANNEL STRUCTURE, DYNAMICS AND FUNCTIONS 422
    CHANNEL ALIGNMENT 425
    EXTENSIVE, SELECTIVE AND EXCLUSIVE DISTRIBUTION 426
    STRATEGICALLY MANAGING CHANNEL RELATIONSHIPS 427
    LEGAL AND ETHICAL ISSUES IN CHANNEL MANAGEMENT 429
    CHAPTER SUMMARY 431

CHAPTER 16
RETAILING, DIRECT MARKETING & WHOLESALING
THE CONCEPTS OF RETAILING, DIRECT MARKETING, &
   WHOLESALING 438
RETAILING 438
   THE IMPORTANCE OF RETAILERS 438
   RETAIL STRATEGY 439
   TYPES OF RETAILERS 443
   ISSUES IN RETAILING 445
DIRECT MARKETING 446
   DIRECT-MARKETING DATABASES 447
   DIRECT-MARKETING MEDIA 447
   ETHICS IN DIRECT MARKETING 453
WHOLESALING 454
   THE IMPORTANCE OF WHOLESALERS 455
   TYPES OF WHOLESALERS 456
   WHOLESALING RELATIONSHIPS 457
   CHAPTER SUMMARY 458

SECTION 7: CAPTURE VALUE 462

CHAPTER 17
PRICING OBJECTIVES & INFLUENCES
THE CONCEPT OF PRICING 466
PRICE AS PART OF THE MARKETING MIX 466
OBJECTIVES OF PRICE SETTING 467
   PROFIT OBJECTIVES 467
   VOLUME (SALES) OBJECTIVES 468
   COMPETITIVE OBJECTIVES 468
   RELATIONSHIP (CUSTOMER) OBJECTIVES 468
MAJOR FACTORS INFLUENCING PRICE 468
   ECONOMIC FACTORS: DEMAND AND SUPPLY 468

LEGAL AND ETHICAL INFLUENCES ON PRICING 472
COMPETITIVE FACTORS THAT INFLUENCE PRICE 476
COST FACTORS THAT INFLUENCE PRICE 478
INTERNATIONAL PRICING 481
   GLOBAL MARKET FACTORS 481
   GRAY MARKETING 483
   GLOBAL COST FACTORS 483
   GLOBAL FINANCIAL FACTORS 485
   CHAPTER SUMMARY 485

CHAPTER 18
PRICING STRATEGIES
THE CONCEPT OF PRICE STRATEGY 492
VALUE AS THE BASIS FOR PRICING 492
   SOURCES OF VALUE 493
   CUSTOMER VALUE IN PRICING 493
CUSTOMER, COMPETITOR, AND GLOBAL PRICING 495
   CUSTOMER-ORIENTED PRICING 495
   COMPETITOR-ORIENTED PRICING 499
   GLOBAL PRICING 500
IMPLEMENTING THE PRICING STRATEGY 501
   SETTING PRICES 501
   PRODUCT LINE PRICING STRATEGIES 504
   COMMUNICATING PRICE 505
   UNETHICAL PRICING PRACTICES 507
   CHAPTER SUMMARY 507

PHOTO AND AD CREDITS C-1
INDEX I-1

about the author

Gilbert D. Harrell, Ph.D.

Gilbert D. Harrell, Ph.D., is Professor of Marketing, Eli Broad College of Business and Graduate School of Management, Michigan State University. Professor Harrell is featured by Business Week as one of the top American educators in leading business schools. He has received the John D. and Dorthea Withrow Award, as the top teacher/scholar in The Eli Broad College of Business; the Phi Chi Theta Professor of the Year Award; and, the Golden Key National Honor Society Teaching Excellence Award, as the top teacher at Michigan State University. His activities include the Undergraduate, MBA, Executive MBA and Ph.D. programs, where over 30,000 students have taken his classes. His teaching, research, and consulting activities focus on competitive advantage; building business value; customer value management; consumer loyalty; and strategic business, marketing and sales planning systems.

Dr. Harrell's publications have appeared in many journals, including The Journal of Long Range Planning, Journal of Marketing Research, Journal of Consumer Research, Journal of Marketing, Journal of Consumer Affairs, Journal of Industrial Marketing Management, Journal of Consumer Satisfaction, Journal of Services Marketing, Journal of Retailing, Business Topics, Journal of Logistics Information Management, Journal of Advertising, Journal of Health Care Marketing, Journal of International Marketing, Journal of the Academy of Marketing Science, and others. He has authored several books and has contributed chapters to several editions. He has been or is a member of the University Graduate Council, the University Graduate Professional Judiciary, the University Automotive Industry Advisory Board, Committee on Executive Development, and others.

Professor Harrell has consulted in over 20 countries and he maintains an active multinational clientele. He has received wide acclaim as a leading marketing strategist and consultant and has developed strategic business and marketing systems for many Fortune 500 corporations. Dr. Harrell is founder of Harrell & Associates, Inc., a professional consulting group, which specializes in services regarding strategic business, marketing, technology and sales. His firm has developed StrategyPaths®, a planning system utilized by several leading corporations.

Dr. Harrell's doctorate degree is from Pennsylvania State University, where he was elected to the Phi Kappa Phi Honorary and the American Marketing Association Consortium. Both his Bachelor's and Master's degrees are from Michigan State University. He lives with his wife, Susanna, in Okemos, Michigan. They have 3 grown children residing in California.

preface

Marketing is so dynamic that examples relevant a year ago seem "old hat" to many students. Actions taken only a couple of years ago might no longer be applicable. A challenge for educators is to continue to evolve and align marketing concepts to prepare students to deal with complex marketing phenomenon in ways that are ethical, technological, diversity sensitive, global, relationships oriented and synchronous with green-sustainable actions. At the same time, great marketing practice is founded on strong conceptual underpinnings. This book has these issues in mind.

In 2008, the American Marketing Association created a revised definition of Marketing. That definition is highlighted in the first chapter as a foundation for the text. A second new force is the recognition by leading edge organizations that sustainablility (green marketing) is a critical ingredient in business practice. Therefore, each chapter provides examples of current organizations that are benefiting customers and themselves through sustainable practices.

The book has many features designed to make it enjoyably relevant to read and study – including the following explicitly noted features in each chapter: opening stories of leading edge organizations; web links to green best practices; The Marketing Gazette™; Web and E-commerce stars; Career Tips; a global marketing project; and, a short practice case. The opening chapter stories are about great organizations that are currently deploying the marketing concepts in insightful ways. Each chapter has several web links to organizations that have exemplary green marketing practices. The Marketing Gazette™ feature openly addresses major issues faced by marketers. The Web and E-commerce Stars features identify the 18 (one for each chapter) premier web sites developed by top organizations. Inspired students can find career tips highlighted in short notes with links for additional information. Each chapter also has a short global project that utilizes globalEDGE™, the leading knowledge portal in international business as ranked by all major search engines. Finally, chapters end with a short case pertaining to the chapter's core subjects.

The book's theme, "creating and capturing value" provides insight into the dynamic world of marketing. The ability to creating and capture value is a the common thread among the top performers. Here is how that theme is featured in the text:

CREATING AND CAPTURING VALUE THROUGH TECHNOLOGY AND E-COMMERCE

Technology's effect on marketing is featured seamlessly in every chapter. Chapter 1 introduces the use of the Internet in such areas as scanning, communication, distribution, and research. Internet connections to more than 300 leading-edge companies are provided in opening stories, highlighted in text examples, The Marketing Gazette™ and cases. The Web and E-commerce feature is notable, because it provides access to the world's greatest marketing web-sites.

CREATING AND CAPTURING VALUE THROUGH RELATIONSHIPS

Relationship marketing is central to outstanding marketing, and for good reason. Relationship marketing is introduced early in the book to emphasize the tremendous importance of satisfied, loyal customers. Meaningful relationships with customers happen when all employees within the organization develop the sensitivity, agility, and desire to satisfy customers' needs and wants.

CREATING AND CAPTURING VALUE GLOBALLY

Global marketing is covered in each chapter and is integrated throughout. International aspects of marketing are so important for today's business that coverage only in a separate chapter would not be adequate. We live in a world in which the international theme is increasingly recognized as important in all aspects of business. Marketing nearly always takes place in the international arena, so the global connection is woven into numerous principles and examples. You will find headings and references on this subject throughout.

CREATING AND CAPTURING VALUE THROUGH DIVERSITY

Diversity among organizations and customers is a source of enormous economic strength and opportunity. Understanding diversity is needed by all marketers, even those who do not specifically target diverse segments. Clearly, progressive companies better understand and appreciate the similarities and differences among various populations. Like no other marketing text, each chapter addresses diversity and it is the subject of several chapter-opening vignettes.

CREATING AND CAPTURING VALUE ETHICALLY

Ethics are critical in all aspects of business, but particularly in marketing, because decisions in this area can affect many groups of people in very different ways. Marketers often face ethical issues. Every chapter of this book identifies ethical dilemmas marketers encounter. In each situation material is provided to help you think about the implications of marketing decisions and resolve inconsistencies. Real-life situations are discussed, and outcomes are identified.

CREATING AND CAPTURING VALUE THROUGH SUSTAINABILITY

Sustainable development and green initiatives is a growing trend that provides a tremendous opportunity for organizations. Leading edge marketers understand that consumers are focusing more and more on an organization's environmental policies and the purchasing of green products is on the rise. Throughout this book, you will find references to and examples of organizations that are leaders in environmental sustainability.

ACKNOWLEDGMENTS

I want to thank many people who have made outstanding contributions to this book. Without their help it would not have been produced.

Special thanks go to the following marketing faculty members from over 50 different schools who contributed in-depth reviews of this and/or other editions. Many have adopted the text for their students. Their excellent suggestions have been incorporated into the production of this book:

David Andrus	*Kansas State University*
Bob Balderstone	*Western Melbourne Institute of TAFE (Australia)*
Richard Brand	*Florida State University*
Jim Brock	*Susquehanna University*
Bruce Buskirk	*Pepperdine University*
William Carner	*University of Texas–Austin*
George Chrysschoidis	*University of Wales*
Howard Combs	*San Jose University*
John Cronin	*Western Connecticut State University*
Bernard Delagneau	*University of Wales*
Peter Doukas	*Westchester Community College*
Jim Dupree	*Grove City College*
John Durham	*San Francisco State University*
William Flatley	*Principia College*
James S. Gould	*Pace University*
Joyce Grahn	*University of Minnesota-Duluth*
Robert F. Guinner	*Arizona State*
Pola Gupta	*University of Northern Iowa*
Lynn Harris	*Shippensburg University*
Benoit Heilbrunn	*Le Groupe ESC Lyon/Lyon Graduate School of Business (France)*
George Kelley	*Erie Community College*
Stephen Koernig	*California State University, Fullerton*
Rex Kovacevich	*University of Southern California*
Frank Krohn	*Suny, Fredonia*
Felicia G. Lassk	*Western Kentucky University*
Ken Lawrence	*New Jersey Institute of Technology*
Chong S. K. Lee	*California State University–Hayward*
Marilyn Liebrenz-Himes	*George Washington University*
Elizabeth Mariotz	*Philadelphia College of Textiles and Science*
Mike Mayo	*Kent State University*
Gary McCain	*Boise State University*
G. Stephen Miller	*St. Louis University*
Herbert Miller	*University of Texas–Austin*
Mark Mitchell	*University of South Carolina*
David Mothersbaugh	*University of Alabama*
Robert O'Keefe	*DePaul University*
Cliff Olson	*Southern State College of SDA*
Stan Paliwoda	*University of Calgary*
Eric Pratt	*New Mexico State University*
Abe Qastin	*Lakeland College*

Zahir Quaraeshi — *Western Michigan University*
Mohammed Rawwas — *University of Northern Iowa*
Deborah Reed Scarfino — *William Jewell College*
A.J. Taylor — *Austin Peay State University*
David Urban — *Virginia Commonwealth University*
Anthony Urbaniak — *Northern State University*
Simon Walls — *Western Washington University*
Mike Welker — *Franciscan University*
Ken Williamson — *James Madison University*
Mark Young — *Winona State University*
George Zinkham — *University of Houston*

Literally every aspect of the project from planning to production has been aided by an exceptional team, which dedicated its time and talent to this project. Troy Miller, Executive Director, Chicago Education Press, managed the production of this book with great imagination, spirit and insight. An outstanding team comprised of Jenna Comstock, Collin Middleton and others worked with him to create graphics, complete conversion of text to files for printing, make editorial additions, find or take photographs and track down relevant sources. I can't thank Troy and this team enough for their positive energy, creativity and dedication.

I also want to thank colleagues at Michigan State University for ideas, content, and support including Al Arens, Don Bowersox, Roger Calantone, Forest Carter, Dave Closs, Bix Cooper, David Frayer, Regina McNally, Rich Spreng and Dewey Ward, to name a few. Due to prior commitments, Gary Frazier was unable to participate in this edition. I thank him for his wonderful contributions to the earlier edition. Also, appreciation goes to Tamer Cavusgil and Tomas Hult for the support of Michigan State University CIBER which sponsored the globalEDGE™ material and to Brian Chabowski, now at University of Tulsa, for creating globalEDGE™ projects. Elizabeth Johnston carefully edited the first draft of the manuscript, focusing material, and sculpting the sentences to communicate what was intended. Peter Fontano, Rachael, Nicholas and Katherine Harrell, Martin Ku, Mathew Struger-Fritz, Maureen VanGlabbeek and others enthusiastically did extra library research, checked sources and found insightful examples. Special thanks goes to Peter Bennett (The Pennsylvania State University), my valued mentor, who contributed greatly to my enthusiasm for the subject.

Thank you all so much!

A work of this magnitude is truly a team enterprise. Excellent ideas in this text are the product of collaboration with all of the previously mentioned people and others. Any errors or weaknesses are solely my responsibility.

Finally, my heartfelt thanks for their support and encouragement go to my family: to my wife Susanna and our children Rachael, Nicholas, and Katherine.

Gil Harrell
East Lansing, Michigan

SECTION

1

Value Orientation

In this section of Concepts of Marketing: Creating & Capturing Value, you will learn the value orientations of customers, organizations and society across the globe. Value orientation is the foundation on which marketing activities are built. The following chapters are included in this section:

Chapter 1 The Concepts of Marketing: Creating and Capturing Value
Chapter 2 Marketing Strategy & Planning Process
Chapter 3 The Global Marketing Environment & E-Commerce

Concepts of Marketing: Creating & Capturing Value

General Electric Company's Ecomagination develops and markets alternative sources of energy. The company markets high efficiency offshore wind turbines that provide power for coastal populations.

Courtesy of GE

Learning Objectives

1. Understand the concept of marketing, including its definition, purpose, and role in creating exchanges.

2. Contrast the periods of marketing evolution from its early history through the eras of production, sales, and customer marketing, leading up to today.

3. Learn what is involved in the marketing strategy process in making marketing decisions, including examples of product, price, promotion, and place decisions to create a marketing mix.

4. Understand the six key forces that are dramatically influencing how organizations create and capture value.

5. Determine how marketing pertains to you.

From household appliances to aircraft engines, General Electric has a portfolio that extends through a variety of businesses. GE Money, GE Commercial Finance, GE Healthcare, GE Infrastructure, GE Industrial and NBC Universal comprise the six industries lines in which GE engages.

When the current CEO, Jeff Immelt, replaced business icon Jack Walch, he announced a new corporate strategy focused on the environment. Naturally, there was skepticism that a company once criticized for dumping 1.3 million pounds of toxic waste into New York's Hudson River would be able to commit to going green. However, "Ecomagination," as Immelt called it, would radically change the direction of the company and launch an entire marketing campaign aimed at informing customers of environmental issues and GE's green products.

The Ecomagination initiative is comprised of four commitments: Doubling investment of alternative energy research and technology, increasing revenue from Ecomagination products, reducing greenhouse gas emissions, and keeping the public informed. To coincide with the Ecomagination commitments, GE has launched a series of commercials to connect with customers about its green campaign. Whether it is fisherman netting bottles of fresh water to promote GE's water desalination program or walking trees to promote green household appliances like solar panels and high efficiency washers and dryers, the clever commercials certainly catch the eye of customers.

However, Ecomagination goes far beyond commercials. The company has committed $6 billion of investments in renewable energies and hopes for $20 billion in revenues from green products by 2010. Emerging economies represent the fastest-growing segment of the company's revenues. As a result of rapid international growth, General Electric has made a substantial effort to connect with customers abroad, most notably through the internationally recognized event, The Olympic Games. The company partnered with the Olympic Games and has become a key contributor in the 2008 Beijing and 2012 London Olympic Games. "GE's contribution to the building of the Beijing Games has been significant in many areas from venue construction to city infrastructure," said Gerhard Heiberg, Marketing Commission Chairman of the International Olympic Committee. "As a global leader in environmental solutions, GE is helping the Olympic Movement address its goals for sustainable building by implementing many of its clean technologies." Furthermore, since General Electric lacks brand awareness outside of the United States, the Olympic Games is the perfect platform for gaining recognition among international customers.

The Olympic Games is only one way in which the company is connecting with international customers. Most of GE's commercials use voice-overs instead of dialogue, making it easy to translate into other languages. The company has also called on its longtime advertising agency, BBDO New York, to incorporate foreign sensibilities into advertisements. The result has been a series of print and commercial advertisements in China featuring goldfish, a ubiquitous symbol in Chinese culture, to promote desalination techniques and a lotus flower holding a light bulb to promote solar energy. In the Middle East, GE's water purification systems ads state, "A camel can go without water for 30 days. A growing economy can't." Judy

CONCEPTS OF MARKETING

Nike, Coca-Cola, and Apple seem to have the uncanny ability to fit into your world. They use the latest technologies to serve you; they are there when you need them—at home or abroad; they understand and accommodate diversity; and they are ethically and socially responsible. They work hard to understand what you want. They provide outstanding value to you as a valued customer. They take every possible action to relate to you in order to form a lasting connection with you. In turn, perhaps you will connect with them. That's what they want. These organizations know you have plenty of choices, so they practice marketing at its highest level.

Ideally, organizations are created, grow, and continue to grow. In reality, many decline, and some die. For one reason or another, declining organizations fall out of favor with customers who replace them with more vibrant organizations. The common link: Winning organizations do an exceptional job of creating and capturing value for customers. They are extraordinary marketers. They understand the marketing concept and use a full range of marketing tools and techniques. They help customers experience the tremendous satisfaction that occurs when products precisely match their needs and wants. Every time satisfaction occurs, value is created.

Today's business environment is global, diverse, and ethically challenging. It is based on technologies that serve customers in ways only imagined a short time ago. Therefore, marketing plays a critical role in determining where, when, and how these technological advances will be applied. Marketing is about much more than just selling a product. It is about providing value to customers in ways that are deeply rewarding for them. Marketing is also about serving the needs of society and accomplishing the goals of the organization. It includes researching potential customers' needs and wants; developing appropriate goods and services; communicating with the market; creating, selecting, and managing channels to reach customers; and pricing to deliver superior customer value. It is about satisfying customers so they will reward the business with the loyalty necessary to reach organizational objectives. And, it's about capturing value from customers so organizations can grow and prosper.

This chapter introduces marketing. As ideas are presented, chapters are referenced to provide a brief overview of the book. We begin by defining marketing and discussing its purpose including how marketing creates and facilitates economic exchanges. This is followed by a short discussion of how marketing has evolved. Then a section on the marketing strategy process introduces the basic elements used to build a marketing plan. We then describe how six key factors are shaping the ways in which organizations will connect with customers. Finally, the chapter ends with a note on the personal perspective you bring to marketing.

MARKETING IS...

How do you view marketing? Is your impression positive or negative? Because marketing is a broad subject that can be viewed from many perspectives, it can be described in many ways. Most people have been exposed to advertising, point-of-purchase displays, and personal selling, so marketing is often seen strictly as the promotion and sale of existing products. However, marketing is much more extensive. Excellent marketing begins long before a product exists. This allows all marketing decisions—including promotion—to be made with customer needs and wants in mind. Marketing extends far beyond a purchase to ensure customer satisfaction and loyalty. You can gain a good idea about the extent of marketing by understanding each element in its definition.

The American Marketing Association (AMA), an organization of professionals interested in furthering the marketing discipline, developed the following definition. **Marketing** is the activity, set of institutions, and processes for creating, communi-

www.ge.com

Visit General Electric's Web site to learn more about Ecomagination products that you can use to make your home green.

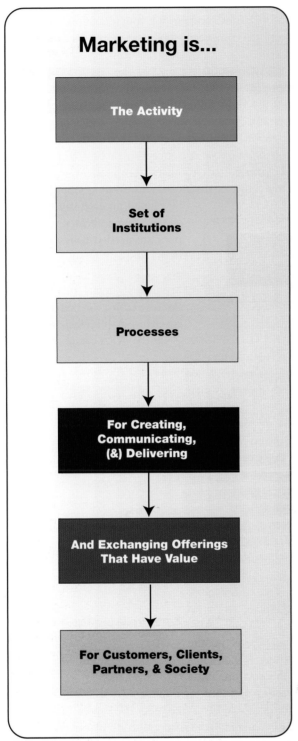

Marketing is...

The Activity

↓

Set of Institutions

↓

Processes

↓

For Creating, Communicating, (&) Delivering

↓

And Exchanging Offerings That Have Value

↓

For Customers, Clients, Partners, & Society

Figure 1.1   Key Elements of the Marketing Definition (Source: American Marketing Association, 2008)

cating, delivering, and exchanging offerings that have value for customers, clients, partners, and society at large.[2] Figure 1.1 highlights key elements of the marketing definition. As an introduction to the subject, the first part of this chapter discusses the definition in depth.

THE ACTIVITY

Marketing activity centers on understanding the needs and wants of customers and engaging in competitive behavior to satisfy those needs and wants. Organizations that do this activity well tend to grow and prosper. Overall the quest to understand and satisfy customers provides the basis for an awesomely competitive system that dramatically benefits society. Because needs and wants are numerous, diverse, and dynamic, there are unlimited opportunities for marketing.

Understand the Needs and Wants of Customers

Understanding customer needs and wants is central to marketing activities. It is not possible to implement appropriate marketing without this understanding. Marketers use a **customer orientation**, an organizational philosophy that focuses on satisfying customer needs and wants.

Needs and wants are not the same. **Needs** are fundamental requirements—meeting them is the ultimate goal of behavior. Of course, there are many needs, ranging from those that allow life to exist to those that produce personal enrichment. A need becomes apparent when there is a gap between a desired state and an actual state. For example, you need proper nutrition on a regular basis to have a healthy and energetic body. When nutrition drops below the desired state, your body signals the deprivation—you feel hungry. When the need is satisfied, the hunger goes away. Needs represent what people and organizations must have to survive and thrive. The degree to which needs are satisfied determines the quality of life for all people and organizations.

A **want** is the specific form of consumption desired to satisfy a need. Therefore, a want is simply one of many desires a person may have to help fulfill a particular need. For instance, hunger can be satisfied with a candy bar, an orange, or a chicken sandwich. Needs produce many wants.

Like people, organizations have objectives that must be met. For-profit companies must make a siz-

Marketing Vocabulary

MARKETING
The activity, set of institutions, and processes for creating, communicating, delivering, and exchanging offerings that have value for customers, clients, partners, and society at large.

CUSTOMER ORIENTATION
An organizational philosophy that focuses on satisfying consumer needs and wants.

NEEDS
Fundamental requirements the meeting of which is the ultimate goal of behavior.

WANT
A specific form of consumption desired to satisfy a need.

able return on the owners' investment or they will go out of business. Nonprofit companies have other needs: The Red Cross, for example, must help increasing numbers of disaster victims if it is to meet its organizational objectives. Every organization needs customers or clients—the people they serve. There are many ways to obtain them, as well as specific types of suppliers, characteristics of employees, and profit objectives. Boeing addresses the need of United Airlines for aircraft by designing planes the airline will want with attributes that satisfy United's needs. Figure 1.3 shows the relationship between needs and wants.

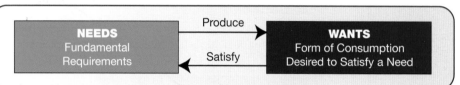

Figure 1.3   Needs and Wants

Potential customers continuously search to satisfy wants in such a way as to produce the greatest amount of need satisfaction. Therefore, customers are dynamic. Marketing leaders facilitate and adjust to change rapidly by learning how to serve customers in new and creative ways. Marketers that learn how to best serve customers can gain tremendous competitive advantages. Because needs and wants are numerous, diverse, and dynamic, the concept points toward unlimited opportunities for marketing.

Competitive Behavior Strong marketers compete, and they measure success by the way their customers judge them, especially relative to competitors. Competition is the key to our economic system. You see aggressive global competition occurring every day: Coke versus Pepsi, McDonald's versus Burger King, and American Airlines versus British Airways. Phil Knight, founder of Nike, has challenged its marketing team to take competition to a new level—replace Coca-Cola as the most recognized brand in the world. Since Coke and Nike don't compete head to head with the same products, this competition is unique. It will be interesting to see whether Nike, Coke, or another company has the number-one position in the next few years.

Don't think that only for-profit companies compete. Even nonprofit groups compete. Mail-order catalogs from the Art Institute of Chicago, the Metropolitan Museum of Art, the Smithsonian Institution, and Boston's Museum of Fine Arts all compete for your purchases. The

United Way competes for your discretionary income, and political parties compete for your donations. Marketers outperform competitors by being more effective, efficient and agile.

Effectiveness means that the organization's activities produce results that matter to consumers. It means doing the right things. **Efficiency** means doing these things with minimal waste of time and money. Baxter International, a hospital products company with over $10 billion in annual sales, is successful on both counts.[3] First, it recognized that customers—hospitals—were spending too much money storing and distributing supplies. Baxter developed an electronic ordering system that indicates what supplies are needed daily and where in the hospital the supplies should go. This system is effective because it meets the wants of Baxter's customers better than the competition. It is efficient because it saves both the hospitals and Baxter substantial amounts of money and time. In many cases hospitals choose Baxter as their only supplier, which leads to higher sales and profits for Baxter.

Agility is the anticipation of market dynamics and speed of response to changing customer desires and competitor's actions. Organizations that possess agility continually sense and explore marketplace opportunities. For example, organizations at the forefront of considering the environmental impact of decisions are more agile than competitors that lag in this area. Over five years IBM spent $165 million to build, maintain and upgrade its plants and labs to make them environmentally friendly. The company esti-

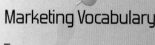

Marketing Vocabulary

EFFECTIVENESS
How well an organizations activities produce results that matter to consumers.

EFFICIENCY
The ability of an organization to execute activities with minimal waste of time and money.

AGILITY
The flexibility and speed with which organizations can identify or create new wants and take action to satisfy them.

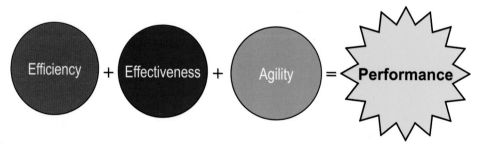

mates that the cost savings from energy, material and water reduction over the same time was double its investment. IBM can in turn invest more money in other areas of the business making it more agile than its non-green competitors.

SET OF INSTITUTIONS

Value is exchanged within markets. A **market** consists of all the organizations and individuals with the potential to have the desire and the ability to acquire value, that is to own a particular idea, good, or service. Generally, we talk about marketing products, which are usually goods that are manufactured or services that are performed. Marketing can also be applied to any idea that can be used in an exchange of value. These include, for example, marketing events, causes, people, and places. Ideas, goods, and services are exchanged in consumer markets, business-to-business markets, nonprofit markets, and internal markets.

Nearly every type of organization, large or small, public or private has the need for marketing. That is why marketing professionals find a vast array of career opportunities. Peter Drucker, renowned educator and author, says the two critical functions of an organization are innovation and marketing. All other functions, such as finance, accounting and personnel management support these two key functions. To him innovation involves rearranging what currently exists or creating something entirely new. These innovations provide the "raw-materials" that can be used by organizations to advance the standard of living for people. From a societal point of view, marketing is the function that, in total, creates exchanges that allow those innovations to be delivered and consumed by society. Looking at marketing from a societal point of view is often called **macro-marketing.**

From an organizational point of view, marketing is so important that it is often seen as a function of the entire business or the responsibility of a department or of several departments. When marketing is viewed in this way, from the perspective of a single organization, it is called **micro-marketing.** Professionals in these marketing roles often have titles such as chief marketing officer, marketing manager, director of marketing research and so forth. Most leading organizations have marketing departments that report directly to the leader of the organization or to the head of major sections of the organization. In a great number of cases the top executive of the organization has very strong background and experience in marketing.

Consumer Marketing Literally millions of products are marketed to many diverse consumers. **Consumer marketing** occurs when organizations sell to individuals or households that buy, consume, and dispose of products. Leading consumer marketers include such companies as Procter & Gamble, Johnson & Johnson, General Mills, Hewlett-Packard, and Nike.

You know the products of these companies very well. You have probably already purchased or used many of them and will continue to do so over the years. Because you buy, consume, and dispose of products such as these daily, you are an important part of consumer marketing. We will learn more about consumer marketing throughout this book.

Business-to-Business Marketing **Business-to-business marketing** occurs when a business purchases goods or services to produce other goods, to support daily operations, or to resell at a profit. Although there are many more consumers than companies, business-to-business purchases far outweigh the consumer market in dollar amount.

Organizations belong either to the public or private sector. The public sector consists of federal, state, and local government organizations. The private sector includes industrial firms, professionals, retailers, and service organizations. Utility companies, which provide water, electricity, gas, and waste disposal, fall between the public and private sectors because they are regulated by the government but may be privately owned. All these organizations rely on business-to-business marketing to purchase goods and support their operations. For example, Procter & Gamble, a producer of some 400 brands of packaged consumer products, spends $26 billion on goods and services purchased from other companies each year. Procter & Gamble and 50 other members of the Grocery Manufacturers of America (GMA) have a massive Internet marketplace to streamline their supply chains and do much of their business-to-business purchasing online.[4] In

Marketing Vocabulary

MARKET
All the individuals and organizations with the desire or potential to have the desire and the ability to acquire a particular good or service.

MACRO-MARKETING
Viewing marketing from a societal point of view, marketing is the function that creates exchanges that facilitates the delivery of the standard of living to society.

MICRO-MARKETING
Marketing from the point of view of the firm or organization – (the definition of marketing described in detail in this book)

CONSUMER MARKETING
When organizations sell to individuals or households that buy, consume, and dispose of products.

BUSINESS-TO-BUSINESS (B2B) MARKETING
When a business purchases goods or services to produce other goods, to support daily operations, or to resell at a profit.

Chapter 6 we will explore many of the topics and issues involved in business-to-business marketing.

Nonprofit Marketing **Nonprofit marketing** occurs when an organization does not try to make a profit but instead attempts to influence others to support its cause by using its service or by making a contribution. It is generally used to benefit a particular segment of society. Marketing has many applications in the not-for-profit sector. Churches, museums, hospitals, universities, symphonies, and municipalities regularly create marketing plans in an effort to be more consumer oriented. The National Fish and Wildlife Foundation uses such marketing tools as fundraisers and conferences to create partnerships with government agencies, universities, individuals, and corporations that will support its cause, which is to solve environmental problems.[5] The U.S. Postal Service competes with private companies, such as Federal Express and United Parcel Service (UPS), to attract consumers, and the U.S. Army, Navy, Air Force, and Marines use their large marketing budgets for recruiting purposes. Sometimes companies work with not-for-profit organizations for mutual benefit. Gatorade Co. partnered with the nonprofit Women's Sport Foundation to promote its line of sports drinks while encouraging the athletic participation of women and girls.[6]

Like businesses that seek profit, many of these organizations want to please their constituents, and they have competition. Although they may not be motivated by profit, many are interested in obtaining revenues that equal or exceed expenses. A full range of marketing decisions is often required. We will learn in chapter 9 that, in making these decisions, many not-for-profit groups seek the same quality of marketing talent as for-profit companies.

Internal Marketing **Internal marketing** occurs when managers of one functional unit market their capabilities to other units within their own organization. This type of marketing addresses the needs and wants of internal customers, the employees of the firm, so these people can ultimately contribute to the external customers, who are the end users of a company's products or services. For example, Dr. Lew Dotterer, director of learning and organizational development at Sparrow Health System is responsible for maintaining the knowledge and skills of employees in all units of the system. Applying marketing techniques, he first identified the key customers—doctors, nurses, administrators, and so forth. Next, he researched each group to determine its learning needs. He then created

educational programs to address the learning needs of each group and promoted these programs throughout the organization. Through internal marketing, One functional unit was able to help employees better serve Sparrow's external customers (patients).

PROCESSES

Marketing is comprised of many ongoing processes. Processes are used to manage complex phenomena that undergo change. New competitors enter the market, customers change, and the economic climate shifts. What works today may be totally wrong tomorrow. Consequently, those who practice marketing must take a long view of events and see the world over time. They must not focus on a single transaction at one moment but on the enduring, systematic management of change. Marketers look for patterns, trends, and surprises that signal what is likely to happen in the future. In fact, later it will be apparent that marketing has its greatest value when it helps guide organizations in highly dynamic environments.

Consider the dynamic computing field, in which the marketing plan is crucial. In 1978, the world's fastest computer processed 160 MHz and cost about $20 million. It occupied the space of a small room and required special cooling to function properly. Today, most personal computers cost less than $1,000, and many use inexpensive, and rapid processing microchips. In the next 20 years, speed compression and cost reduction for computing power will be even more pronounced, and the number of new products and services will be staggering. In 2001, Apple released a industry-breaking portable MP3 music player called the iPod that could hold 1,000 songs, weighed just 6.5 ounces, and cost $400. Today, iPods are

Nonprofit groups such as the Smithsonian Institution compete for customers.

available in many different models ranging between $49 - $499 and can hold up to 40,000 songs, 50,000 digital photos, or 200 hours of video. The Apple iPod revolutionized the music industry by combining both form and function to produce a superior MP3 player and the worlds largest online MP3 music download store containing millions of songs, podcasts, movies, and TV shows.[7] No company today can enter a major market expecting that a single product and strategy will sustain it for long. Rather, it is the ability to change that separates great marketers from others.

Apple's introduction of the iPhone integrates media, global positioning, satellite and communication technologies to bring consumers the most advanced personal communication device to date. 2008 models allow consumers to organize all of their personal data, calendars, songs, games, pictures, work projects and digital tools to communicate and collaborate globally using every possible media including the vast resources of the World Wide Web.[8]

Marketing is concerned with the process of planning and providing the guidance system for companies. Planning sets direction before action takes place. It addresses what is to be accomplished and how to accomplish it. Competition forces marketing plans to be strategic, to address ways to satisfy customer needs and wants better than competitors. Later we will see that plans are created for a whole organization as well as for select products. No matter what is being planned, marketing involves a broad range of people in order for plans to be relevant. Consequently, marketing usually means working in groups rather than working alone. Many marketing processes help groups of people work together to build strategies and plans.

Marketing is also responsible for processes involved in executing or carrying out the plan. Marketing manages people and events in line with the plan, which serves as a guide. To carry out plans, marketing must acquire and develop many of the organization's human resources. Marketers are managers and do-ers. Marketing processes guide actions.

FOR CREATING, COMMUNICATING, (&) DELIVERING

Years ago, Professor James Culliton described the business executive as a "decider" and "artist"—a "mixer of ingredients" who sometimes follows a recipe as he or she goes along, sometimes adapts a recipe to the ingredients immediately available, and sometimes experiments with or invents ingredients no one else has tried. This description gave Neil Borden, another noted professor, the idea that there is a list of elements the marketer mixes together. He called these elements the **marketing mix**.[9] Today they are known as the four Ps—product, price, promotion, and place. Several other elements are incorporated within this list. For example, product development, branding, packaging, and service are included in the product area. Leasing, credit terms, and price are all part of pricing. Advertising, personal selling, and sales promotion are included in promotion. Distribution, logistics, retailing, and direct marketing are part of place.

It is through the mixing process that organizations arrive at unique ways of addressing customers. In the process of mixing, marketing creativity and imagination play a key role. For example, Jimmy Au's for men 5'8" and under, a specialty clothing store chain, found a market among the estimated 30 percent of all men between 20 and 60 that are under 5-foot-8. By introducing a line of clothing tailored for the men shorter than 5-foot-8, Jimmy Au's for Men 5'8" and Under broke into one of the fastest growing segments in the retail men's wear market. Jimmy Au's for Men 5'8" and Under, located in Woodland Hills, CA reaches these consumers over the Internet.[10] A dramatic shift in the mix produces a huge winner and minor shifts create day-to-day competition.

AND EXCHANGING OFFERINGS THAT HAVE VALUE

Value occurs for customers and for the organization only when an exchange is created. Thus, marketing creates valuable exchanges. An **exchange** is a process in which two or more parties provide something of value to one another. At the most

---

Marketing Vocabulary

NONPROFIT MARKETING
When an organization does not try to make a profit but instead attempts to influence others to support its cause by using its service or by making a contribution.

INTERNAL MARKETING
When managers of one functional unit market their capabilities to other units within their own organization.

MARKETING MIX
The four controllable variables - product, price, promotion, and place (distribution) - that are combined to appeal to the company's target markets.

EXCHANGE
A process in which two or more parties provide something of value to one another.

basic level, an exchange generally involves a seller who provides a good or service to a buyer for money or some other item. Most exchanges are much more complex than that. They involve several parties in a social system exchanging all kinds of items.[11]

Relationship marketing is the development and maintenance of successful relational exchanges. It involves interactive, ongoing, two-way connections among customers, organizations, suppliers, and other parties for mutual benefit. DWS Scudder Investment Services, a financial firm, teamed with AARP to create the only investment program geared to the over-50 market. Realizing that aging baby boomers were especially active and wealthy, Scudder tailored its portfolio programs to meet the particular needs of this segment.[12]

Courtesy of Jimmy Au's For Me 5'8" and Under

Jimmy Au's For Men 5'8" and Under Creatively Markets to A Fast Growing Segment

Emotion is a key ingredient in relationships, so in addition to providing logical reasons for buyers to prefer particular brands, marketers involve customers by being trustworthy, supportive and a part of their lives. Coca-Cola Worldwide President of Marketing, Mary Minnick, captured this idea - "Historically, we thought 'enjoyment' was great taste. But it's a very complex 'need' state... We don't just want to entertain customers, we want Coke (brands) to be more relevant, an integral part of consumers' everyday lives. We want to build a relationship with consumers, not hold a mirror up to them."[13] Relationship marketing builds customer loyalty, a critical goal of marketing that dramatically improves business performance. As we will see, leading organizations have many loyal customers.

Not all customers are looking for strong relationships in all exchanges. Marketers need to be sensitive to this fact. However, there is a clear trend. In recent years, mar-

keting has evolved from transaction-based exchanges toward relationship-based exchanges. The change goes far beyond the interaction between an organization and its customers. It includes suppliers and other parties who are dependent on the customer. These relationships range from informal to contractual or even ownership. On the informal level, incentives make it difficult or inconvenient for customers to switch to a new organization. For example, Land Rover has a club for customers that publishes a newsletter and sends invitations to off-road rallies. Service managers call customers to see how their Land Rover Discovery is performing.

Marketing brings the many parties together and facilitates exchanges. This provides utility. When marketers create utility, value is created. Utility is a term economists use to describe the want-satisfying potential of a good or service. There are four fundamental types of utility—form, place, time, and ownership.

Form, Place, Time, and Ownership Utility
Form utility occurs when knowledge and materials are converted into finished goods and services. Marketing provides form utility when it guides decisions about what products to create and the attributes those products should possess. When McDonald's created Grilled Chicken Salads with low-fat salad dressing alternatives for health-conscious consumers, the specific grilled chicken salads provided form utility. Quicken.com provides form utility by combining personal finances, including stock tracking, analyst alerts, bank account tracking, financial news, and bill paying into one convenient Web site.[14] Humm Foods created LÄRABAR with the belief that,

We Deliver For You.

www.usps.com

United States Postal Service uses place utility by providing mail service to the entire country.

"the foundation of a healthy mind, body, spirit is derived from what you eat."[15] LÄRABAR is able to offer natural nutritional value in a raw or uncooked form to health conscious individuals embracing a special diet. Generally, the marketing function is responsible only for specifying what form utility the final product should possess; research and development (R&D), engineering, manufacturing, and other units are responsible for actually building it.

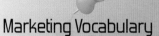

This bar provides form utility.

Place utility makes goods and services conveniently available. Fresh bananas on a remote tree are not nearly as want satisfying as those at a local supermarket, convenience store, or restaurant. They are worth many times more at those locations than where they are grown. Marketing brings products to customers for the sake of convenience. When DHL, operator of the world's premiere global delivery network, delivers shipments to over 220 countries and territories, it is providing place utility.[16] Place utility can be extremely valuable. Shopping malls provide utility by grouping stores and products together, making it convenient and sometimes fun to shop. For example, Amazon.com has brought together a huge selection of products and services to make shopping by brand or product convenient.

Time utility makes goods and services available when they are wanted. DVD's can be watched at your convenience, which is one reason for their tremendous popularity. UPS, Federal Express, DHL, and other overnight carriers offer outstanding time utility. L. L. Bean now receives an order one day and has the item at your home the next, 15 times faster than the Sears, Roebuck & Co. mail orders that dominated the 1970s and earlier. General Motor's e-commerce site, www.gm.com, allows customers to choose a car's make, model, trim, and options and then pinpoints the nearest dealership with that particular model in stock.[17]

Ownership utility makes it possible to transfer the title of goods and services from one party to another. The most obvious way is through cash transactions, but credit card purchases and leasing are other means. Later we will learn about this function internationally. Even airplane travel is a form of ownership utility. By leasing a seat (buying a ticket), you can possess the vast resources of the air transportation system during the time required to reach nearly any destination on the planet. Marketing has progressed by finding better ways to produce increasing amounts of utility.

Marketing Vocabulary

RELATIONSHIP MARKETING
The development and maintenance of successful relational exchanges through interactive, ongoing, two-way connections among customers, organizations, suppliers, and other parties for mutual benefit.

FORM UTILITY
A want-satisfying value that is created when knowledge and materials are converted into finished goods and services.

PLACE UTILITY
A want-satisfying value that is created by making goods and services conveniently available.

TIME UTILITY
A want-satisfying value that is created when goods and services are made available when they are wanted.

OWNERSHIP UTILITY
A want-satisfying value that is created by making it possible to transfer the title of goods and services from one party to another.

FedEx, UPS, and DHL provide time utility to customers all over the world.

FOR CUSTOMERS, CLIENTS, PARTNERS & SOCIETY

For Customers & Clients

Customer value refers to what consumers perceive they gain from owning or using a product over and above the cost of acquiring it—a topic we will consider in more detail in chapter 6. **Satisfaction** refers to the consumer's overall rating of his or her experience with a company and its products. **Loyalty** is a measure of how often, when selecting from a product class, a customer purchases a particular brand. In combination, satisfaction and customer value help create customer loyalty. Loyal customers provide a continuous revenue stream through repeated purchases of a product. They tell others about their satisfaction, which is one of the most effective and inexpensive forms of promotion. To increase customer satisfaction, Xerox's Total Satisfaction Guarantee allows unsatisfied customers to return any equipment and Xerox will replace it without charge.[18] Assurz recently launched a satisfaction guarantee program for online merchants. The 100 percent Satisfaction Guarantee enables online stores to offer a 90-day evaluation period with a full refund of merchandise and shipping charges as well as free return shipping and packaging. Assurz pays all costs and procedures related to the guarantee, including the consumer's refund. This industry-first program works to overcome insecurities about unfamiliar Web sites and possible product dissatisfaction.[19]

Southwest Airlines is increasing customer loyalty by simplifying its online ticket ordering. Southwest Ding! application allows customers to book flights, cars, hotels, and cruises in just a few clicks. It also delivers headlines for specials, discounts, and flight information directly to your desktop.[20] Sears allows customers to request a repair online. These organizations are responding to a request from customers to make their lives easier, thereby adding customer value. Organizations that strive to implement marketing activities that benefit the company develop satisfied and loyal customers. A level of satisfaction strong enough to create product loyalty requires an organizational commitment to customer value in every aspect of the business.

Partners (Organization and its Stakeholders)

All organizations have objectives. Many organizations generally focus on financial measures such as profit margins and return on investment to evaluate performance.

Profit generated by other operations allows GE to pursue innovations like these water desalination filters.

Courtesy of GE

Companies must make money when they fulfill consumer needs. Profit provides the financial fuel that allows companies to innovate and grow. Nonprofit organizations, in contrast, use measures such as donation levels, membership, and services provided to evaluate performance. Although nonprofit organizations must be effective and efficient, by definition they do not seek profit as a primary goal. Still, even nonprofit organizations strive to satisfy their constituents in a cost-effective way. For example, the national organizations for Boy Scouts and Girl Scouts have rigorous financial goals. They often strive for growth in sales and in number of members as well as certain levels of customer satisfaction relative to competitors.

An organization increases its own value by creating value for customers and society. Organizations that do

Xerox's Total Satisfaction Guarantee Increases Customer Satisfaction

the best job of competing have profits required to grow and prosper. These profits are used to further innovate and deliver innovations to waiting customers. In turn, society, employees and owners benefit. The organization grows and the process continues.

Both private and public companies strive to increase the value of the organization to its stakeholders. Stakeholders of an organization include customers, suppliers, stockholders, and employees. The single most important role of the marketing effort is to increase the value to the stakeholders by establishing and implementing an effective marketing strategy. Many strategies can be developed. For example, it can involve focusing on a new set of customers or focusing on the types of customers that the company has targeted in the past.

Increasing the value of the organization can also be done by introducing an entirely new product. For example, Smith Klein Beecham created a vaccine for Lyme disease in an attempt to limit new cases of the disease. The organization was able to increase the value to all stakeholders: its employees, its customers, its suppliers, and society as a whole. Creating value for the organization and its share holders is part of the activities of marketing.

Society

Marketing offers great value to society. It stimulates demand, promotes innovation and improves life by providing an array of goods and services that benefit every citizen. And, a significant percentage of the population is employed in marketing. Additional marketing decisions ultimately contribute to the profit of firms which in turn fuels economic growth. Today, leading edge companies also accomplish their objectives through the concept of sustainability.

Sustainability is the steps and processes organizations undertake to manage growth without detrimentally affecting the resources or biological systems of the earth. It is the fundamental concept of meeting the needs of today without compromising the ability of future generations to meet their needs.[21] As consumer awareness of environmental sustainability increases, organizations have focused on marketing their sustainable initiatives. Some organizations are doing this by offering green products to consumers. Green products provide energy saving options or inflict minimal damage on the surrounding environment. Other organizations may focus on reducing waste and emissions.

An example of involvement in environmental causes is Aveda, a skin and hair care company committed to protection of the environment, animals, and humans. Using organic ingredients, plant-based alternatives to chemicals, and responsible packaging are just a few of the ways Aveda reflects their commitment to their environmental sustainability policy.[22] The Marketing Gazette feature in this chapter, "Aveda - Makes The Earth A More Beautiful Place," highlights Aveda's commitment to our natural and cultural environment.

Many organizations have made sustainability a top priority and have implemented proactive plans. For example, S.C. Johnson & Sons, the maker of popular household cleaning products such as Windex, implemented a sustainability process titled Greenlist. Through Greenlist, the company searches for the most environmentally friendly inputs and raw materials.[23] Ikea Group, the producer of household furnishings, found that sustainable product packaging methods not only reduce pollution emissions, it permits the company to deliver its products to customers at lower prices.[24]

THE EVOLUTION OF MARKETING

Marketing activities, in the broadest sense, can be traced to the trading and barter that occurred thousands of years ago. The ancient Egyptians had vending machines as early as 200 B.C.! But it wasn't until the 1500s in England and the 1600s in Germany and North America that modern marketing began. Most people lived in rural areas and produced all necessary goods themselves. Nevertheless, enterprising business people, who were actually early marketers, discovered they could make money by providing luxury items to the upper class and more practical goods to others in the population.

Although large trading companies had been around for centuries, many merchants and craftsmen built their businesses by satisfying individual customers. You often bought your shoes from a cobbler who knew the exact dimensions of your feet, your preferred shoe style, and your ability to pay. Even if the cobbler had competition, why would you go elsewhere?[25] During the late 1700s and early 1800s, major improvements in production and transportation, along with growing urbanization, fostered the development of mass marketing. **Mass marketing** is the mass production, mass distribution, and mass promotion of a product to all buyers. A free enterprise system based on competition began to develop. Starting in the late 1800s, advertising, marketing research, improved physical distribution methods, and retailing were used to help find and develop markets for mass production. Unlike the days when the consumer came into direct contact with the producer, more goods began to be purchased through an intermediary. The producer had no contact with the end user. During this twentieth century, the economy moved through three basic eras in terms of the focus of business: the production era, the sales era, and the customer marketing era as depicted in Figure 1.4.

Ford Model T

Salespeople were more interested in helping the manufacturer take orders than in helping the customer. Demand for these new lower-priced products was often greater than supply, which led to the growth of large manufacturing organizations.

Henry Ford's approach is a prime example of production orientation. Until Ford came along, automobiles were made one at a time in small factories. Often each car was unique; perhaps a few of each type were made. Ford standardized the design of the Model T and mass-produced it on an assembly line. This dramatically reduced costs and made cars affordable to more people. Visualizing a ready demand for this cheap form of transportation, he remarked that people "can have any color they want, as long as it's black."

THE SALES ERA

As production methods improved and more firms entered markets, competition increased. Eventually, the supply of many products outpaced demand. Since businesses had more goods than their regular customers could buy, the need for personal selling and advertising arose. The sales era focused on ways to sell more effectively. This period was marked by the Great Depression of the 1930s when spending power was drastically reduced. Consumers resisted purchasing nonessential goods and services. Sales forces and sales tactics were developed to overcome their resistance.

The **sales orientation** emphasized that consumers must be convinced to buy. Consumer tastes, preferences, and needs did not receive much consideration. Rather, companies tried to shape consumers' ideals to fit the attributes of the products offered.

After World War II, a vastly different economic environment emerged in the United States. The country was moving from the **seller's market**, in which scarcity of products lets the seller control the market, to a **buyer's market**, in which abundance of products lets the buyer control the market. With the emergence of the buyer's market came rewards to organizations that gave customers a prominent place in their business thinking.

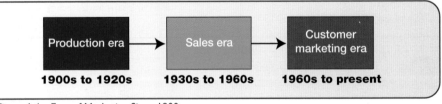

Figure 1.4   Eras of Marketing Since 1900

THE PRODUCTION ERA

During the production era, which lasted until about 1925, companies focused on ways to make products in mass quantities. They achieved production economies that often led to lower prices. This **production orientation** emphasized new products and the efficiency of production. Businesses were primarily concerned with ways to speed physical production. Manufacturers did not address the consumer until after the goods had been made. They assumed a good product would sell itself.

THE CUSTOMER MARKETING ERA

A company with a sales philosophy focuses internally. Emphasis is placed on making the product, then on selling it. The sales force has to push existing products to the consumer through increased promotion and personal selling. In contrast, the customer marketing concept emphasizes customer satisfaction, value. and loyalty After an organization determines consumer needs, it coordinates its activities so that the product will satisfy customer needs and wants.

During the past 50 years marketing has evolved into a tremendously important business function. Figure 1.5 illustrates this evolution from the viewpoint of top executives. Before the 1960s, the prevailing economic philosophy in the United States was caveat emptor—"Let the buyer beware." In other words, consumers had to be cautious when purchasing a product. Once they did, they were stuck with it—and any injuries that might result. It didn't matter if the product was defective.

Led by the efforts of President John F. Kennedy, legislators began to be more responsive to consumer rights. Throughout the 1960s and 1970s, government agencies and private consumer protection groups advanced this cause. Successful companies realized they could gain a competitive edge by treating customers fairly. They also became keenly aware that a loyal repeat buyer is more profitable than a one-time buyer (which you will learn more about in Chapter 7). Businesses began to realize that customer satisfaction was paramount.

In the early 1980s, executives turned their attention to competitors. For the first time in U.S. history, foreign rivals seriously threatened the dominance enjoyed for years by U.S.-based global companies. Competition,

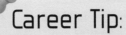

Career Tip:

Most companies hope to find college graduates with experience directly related to the career they seek. Summer internships are the perfect opportunity to gain such experience. Ford Motor Company offers summer internships at locations throughout the country. Visit Ford Motor Company's Web site at www.mycareer.ford.com to view internship opportunities in your area.

beyond mere price and promotion, was developed and refined in many ways. During the 1980s, strategic planning became widely accepted. The role of marketing was elevated from understanding consumer behavior to assessing customer expectations, learning about competitors' practices, and determining how to make the organization an industry leader in a continuously changing world.

In the early 1990s, business executives began building teams designed to focus all of the organization's resources on customer satisfaction. Achieving customer satisfaction depends on the entire organization and on how well the various parts work together. A business is like any other team; success is determined not only by individual talents but also by the ability to do well as a unit. The organization that can form fast, flexible, powerful teams is capable of competing in global markets. It is clear that an organization must be designed to maximize both the speed of its responsiveness to customers and its ability to work as a team.

Marketing Vocabulary

MASS MARKETING
The mass production, mass distribution, and mass promotion of a product to all buyers.

PRODUCTION ORIENTATION
Historical marketing period that emphasized new products and the efficiency of production.

SALES ORIENTATION
Historical marketing period that emphasized that consumers must be convinced to buy.

SELLER'S MARKET
The marketing environment in which scarcity of products lets the seller control the market.

BUYER'S MARKET
The marketing environment in which an abundance of product lets the buyer control the market.

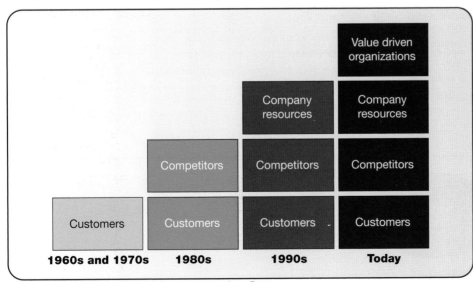

Figure I.5 Marketing's Recent Past and Immediate Future

Today, **value-driven organizations** are implementing the marketing concept by ensuring that all parts of the organization made the maximum possible contribution toward creating value for the customer. They make sure that every part of the organization has a clear line of sight to the customer. This often involves using research tools to study customers, their satisfaction, and their loyalty to the company as well as competitors. Value-driven organizations also make sure that all the costs they incur over the long run provide at least as much value in customer want satisfaction. For example, Microsoft is value driven. It brings software to market that creates huge amounts of want satisfaction. Its products use the latest technology, such as the latest version of Microsoft Windows Media software. Windows Media Player, standard with Windows Vista operating systems, integrates Urge, a music software service based on MTV Networks that features thumbnail and album art during music playback and has improved library management.[26]

Microsoft willingly supports millions of users, one at a time, with customer service and 800 numbers to ensure that its products can be used as intended. Customers have rewarded Microsoft with loyalty that yields enormous profits. These, in turn, fuel additional change in Microsoft, making it one of the most competitive companies in the world. Companies such as Microsoft are using their value-driven approaches to produce outstanding value for customers.

Today, organizations want lasting relationships so customers become assets of the organization, not just one-time buyers. How do marketers create value for customers? They go through the steps of target marketing, positioning, and development of the marketing mix. Then they can get personal with customers in the target market. Personal attention occurs when organizations are value-driven. That means being responsible by capturing value through actions that sustain and in some cases even renew the environment - a top highlighted throughout this book.

THE MARKETING STRATEGY PROCESS

The marketing concept is implemented through the marketing strategy process, the series of steps the organization takes to interface with the rest of the world. Chapter 2 defines the elements of that process in depth. Figure 1.6 illustrates the steps of the marketing strategy process.

Situation Analysis Situation analysis includes all the marketing activities required to understand the global marketing environment, the customer's needs and wants, and the competition. It predicts future marketing conditions for the period covered by the strategic marketing plan and gives a good idea of the issues an organization must address. It provides the context around which plans are created, altered, and adjusted. It includes analysis of the marketing environment (covered in Chapter 3), an assessment of customer needs and behaviors covered in Chapters 5, 6, and 7, and the competition. Understanding the situation requires a thorough knowledge of consumer behavior or, in business-to-business marketing, of organizational buying behavior. Understanding consumer behavior gives marketers insight into why buyers respond to goods and services as they do. As we will see in Chapter 6, consumer behavior involves not only their purchase behavior but also the ways in which consumers perceive and use information and how they arrive at feelings of satisfaction and dissatisfaction. Organizational buying behavior is more complex in terms of the functions and personnel involved in the buying decision, and marketer relationships with these buyers are often more direct. Chapter 6 covers organizational buying in the context of business-to-business marketing. An important function of the situation analysis is to provide the information needed to select certain customers for emphasis—targeting—which is covered next.

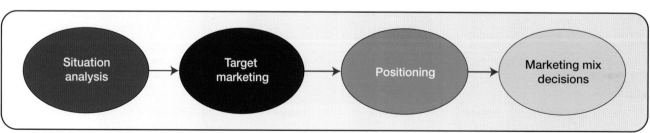

Figure I.6   Steps in the Marketing Strategy Process

Target Marketing Markets usually have several types of potential customers with many different needs and wants. It is impractical to attempt to satisfy all customers. Consequently, leading marketers divide customers into groups with similar characteristics. They then select one or several unique groups to address. A **target market** is a group of potential customers with similar characteristics that the company tries to satisfy better than the competition. Leading edge companies do an excellent job of identifying potential market segments by using marketing research and information covered in Chapter 4. Nike has used target marketing to focus attention on college sport teams. Most leading college basketball teams wear the Nike swoosh in clear view on their uniforms. Chapter 8 covers target marketing in depth.

Positioning **Positioning** is the process of creating an image, reputation, or perception of the company or its goods and services relative to competitors in the consumer's mind. Although the idea exists in the buyer's mind, it is formed by very specific actions of the marketing organization. Nike says "Just Do It," reinforcing the image of an aggressive, action-oriented company. It's no accident that amateur as well as professional athletes perceive Nike as producing high-quality shoes that help athletes perform to their maximum potential. Everything Nike does is designed to create this impression, including the use of outstanding athletes such as Tiger Woods to spread its promotional message. Chapter 9 examines positioning strategies in more detail.

MARKETING MIX DECISIONS

Once the target market is selected, marketing mix decisions have to be made. How do you go about blending the elements into an appealing mix? Clearly, there needs to be a focus and a purpose. That's where the target market enters the picture. Since it is composed of similar customers, it is possible to address them with one marketing mix. Adjustments to individual customers then can be made within this framework. Figure 1.7 illustrates elements of the marketing mix and target marketing. The Marketing mix is based on product, place, promotion, and pricing decisions.

Product A **product** is any physical object, service, idea, person, event, place, or organization offered to satisfy consumers' needs and wants. Product strategy includes decisions about which products to develop, how to manage current products, and which products to phase out. It thereby determines the portfolio of goods and services the organization provides to the market. Equally important for many companies is the establishment of brands and the creation of brand equity, the value associated with a brand. Brands

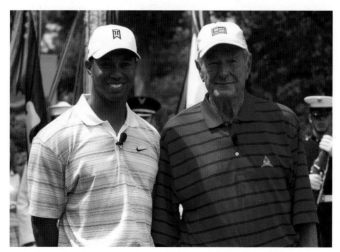

Tiger Woods and former President George H.W. Bush during the inaugural Earl Woods Memorial Pro-Am Tournament. Woods wears only Nike golf products when making appearances.

Figure 1.7 The Marketing Mix and Target Marketing

send messages to consumers about the unique qualities of products. A great deal of care must be taken to establish brand names and protect their reputation. For example, Coca-Cola introduced Coca-Cola Zero, a soft drink with 0 calories while preserving the original Coca-Cola flavor. Vitamin Water, another Coca-Cola company product, is offering many different flavors of water. While a shift away from soda and toward healthier alternatives may account for the new beverages, these new products keep Coca-Cola current in the changing environment. Both products are a part of the company's product strategy. Techniques for making product decisions will be discussed in Chapter 11, "Product Innovation and Management."

Coca-Cola's Vitamin Water offers a healthy alternative to soda.

Place **Place** strategy is developed to serve customers by providing products where and when they are needed, in the proper quantities, with the greatest appeal, and at the lowest possible cost. The first task is to determine which distribution channels to use. A **distribution channel** is a set of independent organizations that make a good or service available for purchase by consumers or businesses. Some companies sell directly, such as your local dry cleaner, whereas others use longer channels with more members. For example, a company may sell to wholesalers, who sell to retailers, who sell to you. Imagine how complicated this becomes in global markets, when numerous channel members are required to move products to customers around the world. **Physical distribution** is the movement of products through the channels to consumers. Companies need order entry systems, transportation, and shipping and inventory storage capacity. Sophisticated information systems are creating some extremely innovative ways of serving customers better.

Retailing and direct marketing provide direct contact with customers. Retailing involves selling products directly to end users, often in retail outlets such as McDonald's or Kmart. Chapter 15, "Supply Chain Management, and Channels," and Chapter 16,

"Retailing, Direct Marketing and Wholesaling," address the place strategy.

Promotion **Promotion** involves communicating with customers in a variety of ways. The promotion strategy includes determining the objectives to be attained, as well as creating messages and the forms they will take. In addition, the communication mechanism or media must be selected. Will two-way communication be used, such as personal selling, the phone, or Internet, or will one-way radio, television, or other media carry the message? Since many messages are carried by numerous media, these decisions can be complex and tremendously interesting. Marketers have a vast number of options when developing promotions, such as training and managing a sales force or creating advertising. Because these mechanisms work together, coordination is vital. The promotion strategy is addressed in Chapter 12, "Integrated Marketing Communications"; Chapter 13, "Mass Communications: Advertising, Sales Promotions, and Public Relations"; and Chapter 14, "Personal Selling and Sales Force Management."

Price **Price** strategy affects nearly every part of a business. The objective is to set prices to reflect the value received by customers and to achieve the volume and profit required by the organization. When prices are too high, customers are dissatisfied and refuse to buy or switch to a competitor. When prices are too low, companies don't have money to cover costs, invest in new development, and provide a fair return to owners. So pricing strategy is extremely important. Pricing must focus on determining value, which is based on what customers expect and desire, what competitors charge, and the unique qualities of the products. Marketers must also determine how their prices will influence the volume sold relative to the competition, and what competitors are likely to do with their prices. Prices not only need to be set but also must be communicated and administered. Will warranty charges be extra? What is charged for the base product or add-on? What financing is available? These questions must be answered and factored in. Pricing strategy is covered in Chapter 17, "Pricing Approaches" and Chapter 18, "Pricing Strategy."

FORCES IMPORTANT TO CREATE AND CAPTURE VALUE

The future will center around better ways of creating value for customers. How marketers create and capture value for customers is embodied in the five supporting themes of this book. They are:

- Technology and e-commerce
- Relationships
- Globally
- Diversity
- Ethics
- Sustainability

These supporting themes were carefully selected to describe how marketers build lasting connections. These five key forces, depicted in Figure 1.8, will reappear throughout the book.

CREATING AND CAPTURING VALUE THROUGH TECHNOLOGY AND E-COMMERCE

New technology is all around us, but three types are particularly noteworthy: (1) product technology that spawns new goods and services, (2) mass customization, which is customization of a product for a specific customer by means built into a process, (3) the Internet, which facilitates two-way global connectivity with customers. Additionally, we will discuss the concept of a marketspace that is bringing many of these technological forces into a single focus.

Product Technology and Mass Customization **Product technology** is technology that spawns the development of new goods and services. Product technology provides the raw material that fuels improvements in our standard of living. Examples of

innovative technology that has produced radically new goods and services are everywhere. Olympic swimmers use advanced bodysuits such as the Speedo Fastskin LZR Racer because the product's tiny V-shaped ridges allow swimmers to reduce drag by 4 percent and increase speed.[27] Cellular systems support telephone calls, fax, and data transmissions, as well as global positioning from moving vehicles everywhere. Digital television and flat-screen technology support in-home theater systems that rivals today's best movie theaters. Although there are many practical and ethical issues, we can clone the "best" sheep, tomatoes, and viruses.

Mass customization occurs when customizing a product for a specific customer is built into a process. Mass customization gives companies the opportunity to produce affordable, high-quality goods and services—but with a shorter cycle time and the lower costs associated with mass production.[28] One form of mass customization occurs at the time of use. When an automobile is programmed to recognize one or several drivers and automatically adjust the seat, radio, and ride, customization occurs. Today, mapping systems hooked to satellites provide customized direction finding. Voice-recognition technology will soon make it possible to mass-customize a broad range of items, connecting customers with products that adjust automatically, and with direct verbal links to companies everywhere.[29]

Customization can also occur in conjunc-

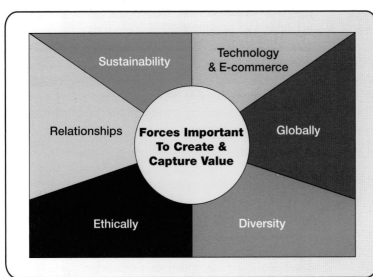

Figure 1.8   Marketing in the 21st Century

Marketing Vocabulary

PLACE
Providing products where and when they are needed, in the proper quantities, with the greatest appeal, and at the lowest possible cost.

DISTRIBUTION CHANNEL
A set of independent organizations that make a good or service available for purchase by consumers or businesses.

PHYSICAL DISTRIBUTION
The movement of products through the channels to consumers.

RETAILING & DIRECT MARKETING
Selling products directly to end users.

PROMOTION
Setting objectives to be attained, creating messages and forms they will take.

PRICE
Setting prices to reflect the value received by customers and to achieve volume and profit required by the organization.

PRODUCT TECHNOLOGY
Technology that spawns the development of new goods and services.

MASS CUSTOMIZATION
The customization of a product for a specific customer by means built into a process.

tion with manufacturing. For example, customers can visit Volkswagen's Web site and fully customize a vehicle to your specifications. Customers can then request a quote for purchase from a local dealership.[30] Direct marketer L. L. Bean links a publisher's subscription list with its customer list placing ads for customers in certain magazine issues and ads for noncustomers in others. In other words, you may receive the same magazine as your next-door neighbor but with different ads targeting each of you.

Not long ago, the challenge was to forecast the styles and quantity of goods to be produced and have them ready for customers when needed. Today, flexible manufacturing is changing all that. This type of manufacturing is often called agile production systems, which describes its versatility. These systems make it possible to respond to customers in a virtual environment—to build a product they request immediately in real time.

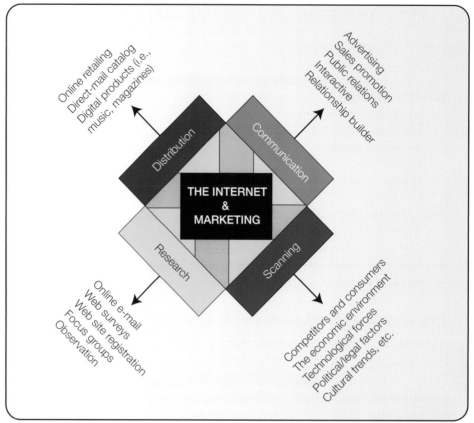

Figure 1.9   The Internet as a Marketing Tool

E-commerce and the Internet

Of the many technological advances that have assisted marketers in their work, perhaps the most significant to date is the Internet. It is a tremendous asset in many ways: Global, interactive, and fully integrated, it creates the opportunity to establish one-to-one relationships with customers. An estimated 6.5 billion people use the Internet worldwide, with nearly 18 percent in located in North America.[31] The Internet is home to content providers, advertisers, and you—the audience.

The **Internet** is a global network of computers that has been around since the 1960s, when it was first deployed by the Department of Defense as a means to send messages in case of a nuclear attack. Until the 1990s, the network was accessed primarily by researchers, who shared the capacity of supercomputers as well as electronic mail capabilities. The Web itself, with the use of hypertext, which allowed people to click on text on their screens in order to link to another computer, was introduced in the mid-1990s. The World Wide Web of today—which provides graphics, sound, color, and video—is made possible by graphical browsers, such as the widely popular Microsoft Internet Explorer and Mozilla Firefox. Today, people can connect to the inter-

net and consequently communicate with nearly any person or organization on the planet via numerous types of computers and wireless devices. The structure of the Internet as it pertains to marketing is described in Chapter 3.

Throughout this textbook you will learn many ways in which the Internet serves as a tool for marketers—including scanning, research, communication, and distribution. Figure 1.9 highlights a few of the various uses. As a scanning tool, the Internet can be used to evaluate trends, the environment, customers, competitors, and other forces. As a research tool, the Internet can be used to conduct Web surveys, focus groups, observation, and so forth. The Internet is also a fantastic means of distributing products such as magazines, music, and video clips.

Online retailing has become a very popular form of distribution. Marketers communicate with customers through interactive and relationship-building promotions. The Internet is a medium for advertising and public relations, as well.

Marketplace and Marketspace

We tend to think of marketing as activities that occur in a physical marketplace. With the amazing new developments in technology it is possible to market goods and services in **marketspace**, an electronic space where business occurs.

Marketspace transactions take place via the Internet, interactive television or CDs, ATM machines, online services, shopping channels, 800 numbers, and others. You can visit your local record store and buy music or movies. In contrast, you can visit iTunes online and purchase digital music, television shows, and even movies. Some marketspaces encourage you to explore new artists and sounds by providing their music free of charge.

Numerous marketspaces available on the Internet are ideal for searching for nearly every good or service. Browsing capabilities on Web sites are outstanding. Typing the name of a favorite artist can turn up obscure recordings not easily found in a store. You can even experience music from around the world, including Russian, Pakistani, or Chinese selections. Other Internet marketspaces provide information about nearly every other type of purchase. For instance, while you're browsing the Internet you can listen to your favorite music by artist, by genre, or by radio station. You can also find out what musical events are happening in your area and online, listen to interviews, download RealPlayer for free, and buy and review CDs. Live365.com offers over 30 different genres of music and thousands of radio stations representing over 150 countries, 24 hours per day, 7 days per week.[32] Even the social networking Web site Facebook is now open to all its users to market their goods. For just a few dollars per day, the goods a person has for sale are shown to millions of other users.

Some predict that the growth of marketspace will eventually result in the eradication of marketplaces. Indeed, online retail sales are expected to reach $144 billion by 2010.[33] Although this is a significant growth, the eradication of marketplaces altogether is unlikely for several reasons. Technology does not offer the social dimension of shopping in a marketplace where consumers can interact with store personnel and other shoppers. In addition, in a store consumers can physically touch, test, compare, and try on products. Shopping in a marketplace also gives some consumers greater reassurance that their credit card transactions will remain confidential.

CREATING AND CAPTURING VALUE THROUGH RELATIONSHIPS

Before the production era, marketers embraced the customer orientation. They created products on demand for specific customers. Relationships were built on a personal level. Consumers dealt directly with manufacturers. With mass production began the separation of manufacturers and consumers. As more levels of distribution channels were added—including retailers and wholesalers—the consumer's voice was heard less and less. In an effort to get closer—to become more connected—organizations today are enthusiastically embracing rela-

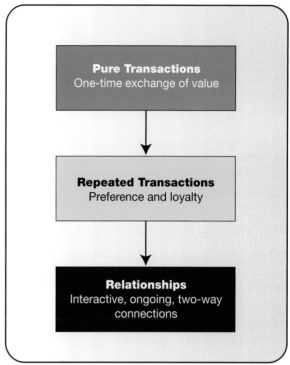

Figure 1.10 Types of Marketing Exchange

tionship marketing. Figure 1.10 describes a continuum of marketing exchanges from pure transactions to repeated transactions to relationships.[34]

A pure transaction occurs only once. When it is finished, both parties go their separate ways. Repeated transactions occur when customers have strong preferences. Many times they become loyal customers. Relationships create an even stronger connection. In business markets, suppliers develop computerized systems that are tied to a customer's manufacturing processes. If the customer selects a new supplier, the computer system will also need alterations. In some cases, these relationships are based on long-term contracts and partnerships.

Strategic alliances occur between firms in which each commits resources to achieve a common set of objectives. For example, credit card companies often ally with airlines or automotive companies. American Express has marketed a card - the IN:NYC card - in partnership with multiple New York City establishments. Users earn points that can be redeemed for dining,

Marketing Vocabulary

INTERNET
A global network of computers that enables the transmission of data through the use of a personal computer.

MARKETSPACE
An electronic space where business occurs

STRATEGIC ALLIANCE
A partnership formed by two or more organizations which commit resources to achieve a common set of goals.

drinking and entertainment rewards.[35]

Some alliances may involve actual ownership arrangements. In these cases, several parties form an organization that is owned jointly. For example, America Online, Inktomi Corp., and Adero Inc. formed a global alliance known as "Content Bridge" to compete in the billion-dollar Internet content delivery business. According to their agreement, Inktomi will deliver the content, Adero will update it and oversee transactions, while AOL will provide the network.[36] Since ownership is involved, these relationships strengthen the connections between the parent organizations.

CREATING AND CAPTURING VALUE GLOBALLY

Marketers are connecting globally like never before. The global marketplace is tremendously important for U.S. companies, as the United States reigns as the world's leading exporter, shipping approximately $1 trillion in goods and services per year.[37] Marketers should not ignore or lose sight of the importance of a global organization. Compared to domestic firms, global companies have an increased customer reach and a better understanding of diversity and competition. They also offset economic downturns with the implementation of appropriate strategies.

The global marketplace can be very complex. Marketers evaluate many considerations and implement well-planned strategies to ensure their success. The Internet has had a tremendous impact on global marketing. Experts predict that the number of brands around the globe will actually decrease, as companies use the same brand name to market a product regardless of its location. For example, Mars markets 3 Musketeers in the United States, but the same candy bar is called Mars Bar in the United Kingdom. With global marketing empha-

The Marketing Gazette™

CREATING & CAPTURING VALUE THROUGH SUSTAINABILITY

Aveda - Makes The Earth a More Beautiful Place

Founded in 1978 and purchased by Estee Lauder in 1997, Aveda is known for their ecologically friendly cosmetics, perfumes, hair care and skin care products. Aveda conducts business in a way that will help protect the earth for future generations. In 2007, Aveda was named one of the top 20 green brands in the U.K.

Aveda's annual Earth Month Candle is packaged in a box made from cardboard usually discarded during the printing process, and labeled by soy ink. Each April the company holds an Earth Month campaign featuring themes such as halting deforestation, habitat protection, and global warming. The proceeds benefit various environmentally focused nonprofit groups such as Greenhouse Network and Gulf Coast Restoration Network. To date, the company has raised over $8 million dollars through its Earth Month campaigns.

In addition to raising money to protect the environment, Aveda uses green ingredients in its products and packaging whenever possible. Many of the ingredients are naturally-derived from sustainable plant sources. The company utilizes eco-friendly product containers made from materials such as recycled plastic and cornstarch. Using post-consumer recyclable plastics is also a priority when selecting packaging.

Aveda not only looks for ways to protect our natural environment, but also our cultural environment. Aveda has worked with the Yawanawa tribe of the Brazilian Amazon rain forest since the early 1990s, when it partnered with them to procure a red pigmented color called "annatto" from the urukum plant, which the tribal people used to paint their bodies. The Yawanawa leadership said its culture had been on a steep decline prior to Aveda's involvement, but the company helped them create a business model and provided resources such as education and advanced mapping technology. In the future, Aveda will have nine partnerships with those indigenous communities around the world.

Barbie. Style

Girls dress Barbie. Barbie dresses girls.

Recognizing the diversity of its market, Mattel uses ethnic models to market its Barbie toy line.

sized, it is quite likely that Mars will use only one name for the same candy bar. Additionally, Procter & Gamble has chose to decrease the number of its brands from 600 to 400, to focus more on global marketing, especially via the Internet.[38] Throughout this book, you will learn that differences need to be researched and accommodated at many levels. These include language, culture, currency, infrastructure, laws and regulations, consumer preferences, and differences in negotiating style. Marketers also need to understand the varying tastes and needs of global customers.

CREATING AND CAPTURING VALUE THROUGH DIVERSITY

Professor Warren Plunkett teaches what he calls the "new golden rule." The traditional golden rule states that you should do unto others as you would have them do unto you, but that assumes all people are the same. In an increasingly diverse society, you must be able to see others' point of view. People from different cultures or backgrounds don't necessarily have the same perceptions, needs, and wants. Plunkett's new rule is: Do unto others as they would have you do unto them. In other words, as a marketer you must remember to satisfy your customer

on the basis of your customer's desires and social norms—not your own.[39]

As marketers move to a more personalized, one-to-one connection with customers, it is imperative to understand and respect diversity among customers because no two are alike. As you will learn in the consumer behavior chapter, some commonalties exist within the various subcultures and social classes. But marketers today are much more sensitive to the needs of a diverse population. It is important to understand that cultural diversity refers to far more than just ethnic groups. U.S. West Airlines, which recognizes diversity as part of its corporate culture, distinguishes among the following categories: race/color, gender, age, sexual orientation, religion, cultural heritage, veteran status, marital status, liberal/conservative, and national origin. The companies you will work for may have even more distinguishing factors. According to Marsha Farnsworth Riche, director of the U.S. Bureau of the Census, "We're all minorities now. If you count men and women as separate groups, all Americans are now members of at least one minority group."[40]

When marketing to ethnic groups, it is important to distinguish between ethnic background and ethnicity. A person's **ethnic background** is usually determined by birth and related to one or more of four elements: country of origin, native language, race, and religion. Hispanics are an ethnic group, but members have diverse interests and beliefs depending on country of origin, length of time in the United States, geographic placement, and other factors. **Ethnicity** refers to the amount of identification an individual feels with a particular ethnic group. According to Lafayette Jones, president and CEO of Segmented Marketing Services, Inc., marketers should, "look at the market not in terms of black and white, but in terms of true ethnicity. We use terms like 'African American' because these terms really describe what we're talking about, without the social and political implications of race. . . . Every culture has its own food, music, and religious practices. They're diverse in competition, flavorings, attitudes, and expressions."[41] In the chapter on consumer behavior, we'll look more specifically at various ethnic markets. Applying what you learn can help you as a marketer cultivate and satisfy customers from varied ethnic backgrounds.

Marketers recognize that there is

Marketing Vocabulary

ETHNIC BACKGROUND
Subculture membership usually determined by birth and related to one or more of four elements: country of origin, native language, race, and religion.

ETHNICITY
The amount of identification an individual feels with a particular ethnic group.

tremendous diversity in marketing. They also recognize the immense spending power of diverse groups. African Americans, Hispanic Americans, and Asian Americans will spend in excess of $1.7 trillion a year by 2010, more than triple its level of $454 billion in 1990.[42] Mature customers (age 50 and older) control half the U.S. buying power. Young adults spend $153 billion annually, whereas women reportedly buy 85 percent of all consumer goods.[43] These are just a few of the many diverse customers you will be learning about in this book. It is both profitable and rewarding for marketers to connect and build relationships with every type of customer. By acknowledging, understanding, and accommodating the needs of diverse groups, marketers can create a loyal base of customers for future business.

globalEDGE™

http://globaledge.msu.edu
Visit globalEDGE™ Online for the ultimate international marketing research tool!

Marketers have many resources to gain insights about global marketing opportunities. One of the most useful is globalEDGE™. Developed by MSU-CIBER as the ultimate international marketing research tool, it has up-to-date information on 200 countries, including maps, key statistics, history, economic, government, stock market, country specific marketing resources and news. Web-based computer software programs incorporate research knowledge in easily usable formats. Each chapter of the text has a globalEDGE™ exercise tied to its content.

CREATING AND CAPTURING VALUE ETHICALLY

After emerging from the profit-oriented 1980s, marketers began to rediscover the importance of social responsibility and ethical behavior to a company's performance. In fact, ethical initiatives by businesses have more than doubled in the last five years. Responsible marketers make decisions with a clear code of ethics in mind. They must make important decisions about the standards of conduct for an organization. A worldwide poll conducted by Environics International asked 25,000 people in 23 countries to name the factors that most affected their impressions of individual companies. A majority mentioned factors related to social responsibility (i.e., labor practices, business ethics, and the like) and felt that companies should go beyond the traditional goals of "making a profit, paying taxes, and providing employment. . . ."[44] Thus, ethics and social responsibility go hand in hand. We will examine each of these forces more closely in the following sections.

Ethics Ethics are the values or standards that govern professional conduct. **Marketing ethics** deal specifically with the application of moral standards to marketing decisions, behaviors, and institutions.[45] Nearly every area of marketing has significant ethical dimensions that raise difficult questions.[46]

Throughout this book, we will evaluate many different ethical situations, including issues of fairness, equity, conflict of interest, privacy, confidentiality, product safety, and others. You will also find that every area of marketing can present an ethical dilemma, including product development, promotion, distribution, and pricing.

In order to promote ethical behavior in each area of marketing, both large and small businesses implement a code of conduct, sometimes referred to as value statements or management integrity statements. These may provide a wide range of guidelines, depending on the beliefs and values of a particular organization. For example, Johnson & Johnson established one of the first codes in 1947. It embodies a commitment to ethical business practices as well as a responsibility to consumers, employees, the community, and shareholders. You will learn more about Johnson & Johnson in Chapter 2.

Aside from implementing a code of ethics, organizations try to build an ethical culture by communicating standards to employees and ensuring that ethics remain a priority. An ethical organization requires the support of top management, and many companies aim to manage beyond compliance by exceeding the standards defined by federal, state and local rules and regulations. Microsoft was recently awarded top honor by WE Magazine, a disability lifestyle publication, for hiring, accommodating and creating accessible technologies for people with disabilities. Each year, WE Magazine recognizes 10 companies that go beyond what is required by the Americans with Disabilities Act (ADA) to recruit and accommodate employees with disabilities. Microsoft received top honor not only for its workplace policies and accommodation strategies, but also for the company's efforts in creating accessible technologies and as a founding member of the Able to Work Consortium.[47]

Because the marketing function within an organization relies heavily on interaction with customers, it is often subject to public scrutiny. This emphasizes the power of ethics as a force in making business decisions. Over the long run, it is likely that organizations with a strong ethical culture and code of conduct will be better equipped to handle ethical dilemmas.

Social Responsibility Many people believe that a socially responsible business must satisfy the needs of customers in ways that provide profits to the owners or meet other requirements outlined by the owners. Some argue that profits represent the response of consumers to businesses that best serve their needs. As mentioned previously, social responsibility and ethics are closely related. The **societal marketing concept** seeks to balance customer satisfaction against corporate profits and the well-being of the larger society. It extends the marketing concept to include satisfying the citizen as well as the customer. Social responsibility reflects "the consequences of a person or firm's acts as they might affect the interest of others."[48]

Many companies are well known for their commitment to social causes and for acting in the best interest of the citizen as well as the consumer. Consider Ben & Jerry's, which contributes 7.5 percent of its pretax profits to charitable causes.[49] Ben & Jerry's is well known for its environmental initiatives, including innovative recycling, energy saving, and waste reduction. The company incorporated its dedication to societal marketing into this part of its mission statement: "To operate the company in a way that actively recognizes the central role that business plays in the structure of society by initiating innovative ways to improve the quality of life of a broad community: local, national, and international."

Marketers have many opportunities to correct questionable behavior. Today, television shows often resort to sex, violence, and outrageousness in order to command market share. Procter & Gamble (P&G) and AT&T are taking the lead in cleaning up televised trash, hoping producers will understand that positive topics are more economically viable with advertisers than salacious topics.[50]

www.benjerry.com

Learn more about the actions Ben & Jerry's is taking to promote sustainable agriculture, efficient packaging and more. Be sure to check out the new ice cream flavors too!

CREATING AND CAPTURING VALUE THROUGH SUSTAINABILITY

It is often believed that sustainability pertains strictly to environmental issues. However, the World Commission on Environment and Development outlined in its classic report *Our Common Future* that sustainable development is a complex process involving three components: the environment, economy, and society. It is important to understand that these elements are highly linked. The environment is where we live while economic and social development is the actions we take to improve our conditions within the environment.[51] How does this relate to creating and capturing value? Increased environmental concerns among consumers lead them to assess an organization's value not only by its products but how its products and processes affect the environment.

The result of consumer environmental consciousness has been the creation of green marketing campaigns by many organizations. Green marketing is the mar-

Ben & Jerry's contributes to charitable causes.

Courtesy of Ben & Jerry's

© Ben & Jerry's Homemade, Inc. - www.benjerry.com
© Woody Jackson - www.holycowinc.com

Marketing Vocabulary

ETHICS
Standards or values that govern professional conduct.

MARKETING ETHICS
The ethics that deal specifically with how moral standards are applied to marketing decisions, behaviors, and institutions.

SOCIETAL MARKETING CONCEPT
The marketing concept extended to include satisfying the citizen as well as the consumer.

keting of eco-friendly products or processes. It can also be marketing using eco-friendly methods. For example, S.C. Johnson and Sons markets how its manufacturing facilities use waste methane gas, a byproduct of decomposition in landfills, for energy. Marketers must weight the importance of sustainability to its customers and implement a strategy accordingly. Throughout this book, you will learn of different companies undertaking environmental initiatives in order to create and capture value for customers.

MARKETING: YOUR INVOLVEMENT

By now it should be clear that marketing affects you in many ways. Your exploration of marketing begins from many angles—the prospective marketer, member of a target market, customer, and citizen. Each of these roles gives you a slightly different slant, which can lead to the development of valuable marketing skills. Throughout this text we will highlight opportunities in the Career Tip feature. One in three of you will be in a job that directly involves marketing. Your career may involve strategic marketing planning, personal selling, promotion or advertising, retailing, product development, getting products to market (distribution), or establishing pricing criteria. No matter what career you choose—working for a political campaign, a not-for-profit organization, a religious organization, or a Fortune 500 company—your job will require an understanding of marketing. Many of the ideas we will explore in this book can be applied to your personal actions.

In a sense, you are already a marketer through your everyday actions. You market yourself when you apply to schools or pursue a scholarship. You are a marketer when you seek election to an organization or attempt to influence its members. You are a marketer when you interview for an internship or job. In all likelihood, you will be applying marketing in a professional sense in the future. Since marketing is so important, this is true no matter what your college major happens to be.

You also belong to a target market, which makes you tremendously important to other marketers. You are part of a target

market when political candidates on MTV ask for your votes, when the Fox network produces a television show designed to appeal to you, and when sports teams, theme parks, and movies compete for your entertainment dollars. You'll also meet various marketers and learn from their experiences.

Marketing affects you through your role as a customer. You are a customer every time you purchase. You are a loyal customer when you have a strong preference that results in your repeated purchase of a company's good or service. You are part of a marketing relationship when a company that knows you by name wants to customize its actions to fit your desires precisely.

Finally, marketing pertains to you as a citizen. You are affected by marketing when McDonald's selects paper over styrofoam packaging to reduce pollution. You are affected when Mothers Against Drunk Driving (MADD) reduces your chance of a serious injury from a traffic accident. You are affected when General Motors designs a Cadillac that is completely recyclable.

Marketing is a relevant, fun subject. It is filled with examples that you see every day. It touches your life directly in a million ways.

Web and E-commerce Stars
Coca-Cola - www.coke.com

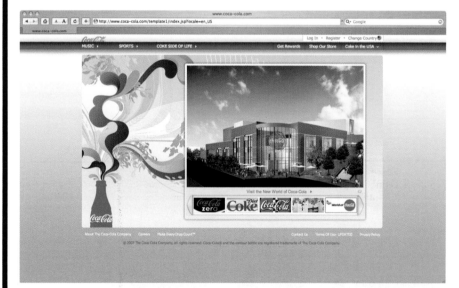

The Coca-Cola Company has created a website that combines practical product information with a fun and interactive experience. To coincide with the launch of their new marketing platform, 'Coke side of life', the Coca-Cola Company renovated their website to allow consumers to play a more comprehensive role in the creative process. Along with product information, the website includes unique features such as 'create your own Coke artwork' and articles about hydration and health. The Coca-Cola Web site also allows users to download music from unsigned artists, shop the Coke store and take virtual tours of The World of Coke in Atlanta, Georgia.

Chapter Summary:

Objective 1: Understand the concept of marketing, including its definition, purpose, and role in creating exchanges.

Marketing is an organizational function and a set of processes for creating, communicating, and delivering value to customers and for managing customer relationships in ways that benefit the organization and its stakeholders. The purpose of marketing is to identify the needs and wants of customers within markets and creates customer value in ways that will ensure the long-run success of the organization by making connections between companies and customers. Many people refer to the purpose as the marketing concept. Marketing works by creating valuable exchanges that provide utility. Utility is produced when products are created or adjusted, when goods and services are placed so consumers can discover and acquire them, when products are delivered at the right time, and when the transfer of ownership is facilitated.

Objective 2: Contrast the periods of marketing evolution from its early history through the eras of production, sales, and customer marketing, leading up to today.

Marketing has progressed through three eras—the production era, the sales era, and the customer marketing era. As the names suggest, the production era focused on ways to efficiently mass-produce new products while the sales era focused on getting people to buy products. The customer marketing era moved management's attention toward satisfying customer needs and wants.

Objective 3: Learn what is involved in making marketing decisions, including examples of product, price, promotion, and place decisions to create a marketing mix.

The marketing strategy process has four steps—situation analysis, targeting, positioning, and marketing mix decisions. Situation analysis provides information about the marketing environment and specific company elements. It is based on insights gained from the use of marketing information systems and marketing research. Targeting occurs when groups of customers with identifiable characteristics are selected for attention. Targeting helps focus resources. The best marketing strategies do an excellent job of addressing the needs and wants of customers within these targets. Positioning is used to determine what image or impression the marketer wants customers within a target segment to possess regarding the organization or its products. By blending the marketing mix—product, price, promotion, and place—marketing decisions are made to support the positioning strategy. These decisions can be blended into a vast array of combinations, each producing different results.

Objective 4: Understand the five key forces that are dramatically influencing how organizations will connect with customers in the future.

Marketing is influenced by relationships, technology, ethics, diversity, and globalization. Today, more organizations are implementing the marketing concept by forging relationships with valued customers. These are creating loyalty and repeat business that help the organization to achieve its objectives. Product technology develops radically new goods and services, and process technology makes it possible to be more responsive to customers by altering how marketing occurs. The Internet is a particularly noteworthy technological advance because it brings us new distribution, communication, scanning, and research capabilities. The global economy has an impact on all customers and competitors. Consequently, global factors must be considered when making marketing decisions. Ethics and social responsibility are also important forces because they help guide many marketing decisions. Ethics involve making decisions based on what is right and wrong. Social responsibility involves decisions that affect citizens as well as customers.

Objective 5: Determine how marketing pertains to you.

You are intimately involved in marketing—as a marketer, as a member of a target market, as a customer, and as a citizen. Marketing pertains to you personally and you begin your study of the subject having already experienced many of its facets. Professionally, marketing is important no matter what major or career you choose. In a sense, you are often a marketer when you attempt to advance yourself or your views. Along with other people similar to yourself, you are part of a target market toward which certain marketers direct their attention. As a customer, you experience the actions of marketers. As a citizen, you are impacted positively and negatively by organizations whether or not you purchase their products.

Review Your Understanding

1. What is marketing? What are the key elements in its definition?
2. What are the four basic areas (types of markets) in which marketing is typically applied?
3. What is utility? What are the four types of utility involved in marketing exchanges?
4. What is the difference between a need and a want? Give examples of each.
5. What is the marketing concept? What are its three key aspects?
6. What are the stages in marketing evolution? Describe each of the three marketing eras.
7. What is a marketing strategy? Describe each of its four steps.
8. How do product, place, promotion, and price decisions form the marketing mix? Give examples of each decision.
9. What are the five key forces shaping marketing as we enter the 21st century? Describe each.
10. How does marketing relate to you? List four ways.

Discussion of Concepts

1. Describe marketing, highlighting examples from your daily life that illustrate each of its four aspects.
2. Identify one company with which you are familiar and describe four ways in which it provides utility.
3. Discuss the activities involved in implementing the marketing concept. How do they pertain to customers, competitors, and the marketing organization?
4. Describe the steps in developing a marketing strategy. Why is it important to target prior to positioning? Why is positioning important prior to marketing mix decisions?
5. Compare and contrast the various eras of marketing, assessing the role each era played in reaching the current relationship era.
6. Discuss the five forces shaping marketing by showing how they help implement the marketing concept.

Key Terms And Definitions

Business-To-Business marketing: When a business purchases goods or services to produce other goods, to support daily operations or to resell at a profit.

Buyer's market: The marketing environment that exists when an abundance of product lets the buyer control the market.

Consumer marketing: When organizations sell to individuals or households that buy, consume, and dispose of products.

Consumer orientation: An organizational philosophy that focuses on satisfying consumer needs and wants.

Customer value: What consumers perceive they gain from owning or using a product over and above the cost of acquiring it.

Distribution channel: A set of independent organizations that make up a good or service available for purchase by consumers or business.

Effectiveness: The degree to which an organization's activities produce results that matter to consumers.

Efficiency: The degree to which activities are carried out without waste of time or money.

Ethics: Standards or values that govern professional conduct.

Ethnic background: Subculture membership usually determined by birth and related to one or more of four elements: country of origin, native language, race, and religion.

Ethnicity: The amount of identification an individual feels with a particular ethnic group.

Exchange: A process in which two or more parties provide something of value to one another.

Form utility: A want-satisfying value that is created when knowledge and materials are converted into finished goods and services.

Internal marketing: When managers of one functional unit market their capabilities to other units within their own organization.

Internet: A global network of computers that enables the transmission of data through the use of a personal computer.

Loyalty: A measure of how often, when selecting from a product class, a customer purchases a particular brand.

Macro-marketing: Viewing marketing from a societal point of view, marketing is the function that creates exchanges that facilitates the delivery of the standard of living to society.

Market: All the individuals and organizations with the desire or potential to have the desire and the ability to acquire a particular good or service.

Marketing: The process of planning and executing the conception, pricing, promotion, and distribution of ideas, goods, and services to create exchanges that satisfy individual and organizational objectives.

Marketing concept: Holds that the purpose of marketing is to identify the needs and wants of customers within markets and satisfy them in ways that ensure the long-run success of the organization.

Marketing ethics: The ethics that deal specifically with how moral standards are applied to marketing decisions, behaviors, and institutions.

Marketing mix: The four controllable variables—product, price, promotion, and place (distribution)—that are combined to appeal to the company's target markets.

Marketspace: An electronic space where business occurs.

Mass customization: The customization of a product for a specific customer by means built into a process.

Mass marketing: The mass production, mass distribution, and mass promotion of a product to all buyers.

Micro-Marketing: Marketing from the point of view of the firm or organization

Needs: Fundamental requirements the meeting of which is the ultimate goal of behavior.

Nonprofit Marketing: When an organization does not try to make a profit but instead attempts to influence others to support its cause by using its service or by making a contribution.

Ownership utility: A want-satisfying value that is created by making it possible to transfer the title of goods and services from one party to another.

Physical distribution: The movement of products through the channels to consumers.

Place: Providing products where and when they are needed, in the proper quantities, with the greatest appeal, and at the lowest possible cost.

Place utility: A want-satisfying value that is created by making goods and services conveniently available.

Positioning: The process of creating an image, reputation, or perception of the company or its goods and services in the consumer's mind.

Price: Setting prices to reflect the value received by customers and to achieve volume and profit required by the organization.

Process technology: Technology used to make goods and services.

Product: Any physical object, service, idea, person, event, place, or organization offered to satisfy consumers' needs and wants.

Product technology: Technology that spawns the development of new goods and services.

Production orientation: Historical marketing period that emphasized new products and the efficiency of production.

Promotion: Setting objectives to be attained, creating messages and forms they will take.

Relationship marketing: The development and maintenance of successful relational exchanges; it involves interactive, ongoing, two-way connections among customers, organizations, suppliers, and other parties for mutual benefit.

Retailing & direct marketing: Selling products directly to end users.

Sales orientation: Historical marketing period that emphasized that consumers must be convinced to buy.

Satisfaction: The customer's overall rating of his or her experience with a company's products.

Seller's market: The marketing environment that exists when scarcity of products lets the seller control the market.

Societal marketing concept: The marketing concept extended to include satisfying the citizen as well as the consumer.

Strategic alliances: A partnership formed by two or more organizations for a new venture.

Sustainability: The steps and processes organizations undertake to manage growth without detrimentally affecting the resouces or biological systems of the earth.

Target market: A group of potential customers with similar characteristics that a marketer is trying to satisfy better than the competition.

Time utility: A want-satisfying value that is created when goods and services are made available when they are wanted.

Value-Driven organization: An organization that implements the marketing concept by ensuring that all parts of the organization make the maximum contribution toward creating value for the customer.

Want: A specific form of consumption desired to satisfy need.

References

1. Claudia H. Deutsch, "To G.E., a Chinese Olympics Is Just Made for a Global Message," New York Times Late Edition. February 28, 2008; Francesco Guerrera, "GE Boosts 'Green' Energy Plans," Financial Times US Edition, January 14 2008; Hoovers Company Records, General Electric Company, www.hoovers.com, site visited March 10, 2008; www.ge.com, site visited March 10, 2008.

2. www.ama.org, Web site visited April 20, 2008.

3. Hoover's Company Records. April 15, 2008. Baxter International Inc.

4. "Moving Procter & Gamble into E-procurement," Purchasing, June 15, 2000, p. 5149.

5. www.nfwf.org, Web site visited May 23, 2008

6. www.womenssportsfoundation.org, Web site visited April 21, 2008

7. www.apple.com, Web site visited May 15, 2007

8. www.apple.com/iPhone, Web site visited April 21, 2008

9. James W. Culliton, The Management of Marketing Costs (Boston: Division of Research, Graduate School of Business Administration, Harvard University, 1948), cited in Neil H. Borden, "The Concept of the Marketing Mix," Journal of Advertising Research, June 1964, pp. 2–7.

10. "Measuring Up In a World Where Bigger is Better, Short Men Have Few Fashion Alternatives", The New York Times, June 9, 2005.

11. Richard P. Bagozzi, "Marketing as Exchange," Journal of Marketing, October 1975, pp. 32–39.

12. Kathleen Sampey, "Coke Unveils Global Strategy," Adweek, December 7, 2005.

13. "The Joy of Empty Nesting," American Demographics, May 2000, pp. 48–53.

14. www.quicken.com, site visited May 3, 2008

15. www.larabar.com, site visited April 25, 2008

16. www.dhl-usa.com,Web site visited April 21, 2008

17. www.GM.com, site visited June 3, 2008

18. www.xerox.com, site visited April 23, 2008

19. "Assurz Launches Satisfaction Guarantee Program for Online Merchants," Press Release, April 3, 2007; www.assurz.com, site visited April 13, 2007.

20. www.southwest.com, site visited April 13, 2007

21. The President's Council on Sustainable Development

22. www.aveda.com, Web site visited April 14, 2007

23. www.scjohnson.com Web site visited July 1, 2008

24. www.ikea-group.com Web site visited July 1, 2008

25. Don Peppers and Martha Rogers, The One To One Future (New York: Doubleday, 1993), pp. 21–22.

26. www..microsoft.com, Web site visited April 21, 2008

27. www.speedo.com, site visited April 20, 2008

28. Christopher Hart, "Mass Customization: Conceptual Underpinnings, Opportunities and Limits," International Journal of Service Industry Management 6, no. 2 (1995): 36–45.

29. Peppers and Rogers, The One to One Future, p. 2.

30. www.vw.com, Web site visited April 28, 2008.

31. www.internetworldstats.com , site visited May 20, 2008

32. http://www.live365.com/, site visited May 11, 2008

33. Devin Comiskey, "2006 Online Retail Sales to Hit $100 Billion," www.ecommerce-guide.com, April 11, 2006

34. See Frederick E. Webster, Jr., "The Changing Role of Marketing in the Corporation," Journal of Marketing, October 1992, pp. 1–17.

35. www.americanexpress.com/cards, site visited May 10, 2008

36. "3-Way Web Pact," Los Angeles Times, August 24, 2000, p. C-8.

37. CIA - World Factbook, March 15, 2007.

38. Kathleen Schmidt, "Outlook 2000: Globalization," Marketing News, January 17, 2000, pp. 9–12.

39. Warren Plunkett, Instructor's Manual for Supervision, 7th ed. (Boston: Allyn & Bacon, 1993), pp. 6–7.

40. Marcia Mogelonsky, Everybody Eats: Supermarket Consumers in the 1990s (Ithaca, NY: American Demographic Books, 1995), p. 185.

41. Ibid., p. 163.

42. Jeffrey M. Humphreys, "The Multicultural Economy 2005: America's Minority Buying Power," Georgia Business and Economic Conditions, Third Quarter 2005.

43. www.marketresearch.com, site visited April 14, 2007; www.sba.gov, site visited May 20, 2007.

44. "Great Expectations," Across the Board, January 1, 2000.

45. Gene R. Laczniak and Patrick E. Murphy, Ethical Marketing Decisions: The Higher Road (Boston: Allyn & Bacon, 1993), p. 3.

46. See John R. Boatright, Ethics and the Conduct of Business (Upper Saddle River, NJ: Prentice Hall, 1997), pp. 284–315.

47. "Microsoft Receives Top Honor for Hiring, Accommodating and Creating Accessible Technologies for People With Disabilities," www.microsoft.com, Web site visite April, 21, 2008.

48. Peter D. Bennett, ed., Dictionary of Marketing Terms (Chicago: American Marketing Association, 1995), p. 267.

49. "Ben & Jerry Hope Social Mission Won't Fade; Unilever Sees It as Marketing Tool," Associated Press Newswire, May 2, 2000, www.wire.ap.org.

50. Joe Mandese, "Talk Show Stalwart P&G Cans 'Trash,'" Advertising Age, November 20, 1995, p.1

51. Our Common Future: Report of World Commission on Environment and Development. United Nations. 1987.

The Marketing Gazette:
   "Landor Survey Reveals Confusion about Greenness," Design Week, May 17, 2007, p.7; Ellen Groves, "Package Mentality; Beauty Companies Lessen Their Environmental Impact With Recycled and Renewable Packaging," WWD, Apr 10, 2007, 193(76), p.17s; Michelle Edgar, "Aveda Campaign Pushes Clean Water Effort," WWD, Apr 13, 2007, 193(79), p.9; Julie Naughton, "Aveda's New Masculine Mandate" WWD, May 25, 2007, 193(113), p.6; www.aveda.com, site visited June 17, 2008.

CASE 1

Starbucks

Wake up and smell the coffee! Starbucks is everywhere. According to the company whose largest competitor is less than half its size, coffee is not a trend—it is a lifestyle. Starbucks has been "elevating the coffee experience" since 1971, when three men opened a gourmet coffee shop in Seattle, Washington. Many are unaware that Starbucks has been around for so many years. In fact, it was not long ago that latté, cappuccino, and espresso were not part of America's everyday vocabulary.

Starbucks' success can be attributed greatly to marketing efforts. In 1982, the company hired Howard Schultz as its marketer. After visiting Italy the following year, Schultz was inspired. The relationship he saw between coffee and people in Italy awakened him to the untapped markets in America. In 1987, Schultz added six Starbucks stores and planned to go national with his ideas. The corporation is now the leading retailer and roaster of specialty coffee, with 10,000 Starbucks stores in over 20 markets around the world. Starbucks supplies fine dining, food service, travel, and restaurant accounts with both coffee and equipment. Yet Starbucks remains ambitious: The company plans to ultimately reach 30,000 coffeehouses worldwide.

Considered one of the top 100 companies in the US to work for, approximately 100,000 employees known as "partners," undergo multiple sessions of rigorous training. They are taught to educate customers about coffee making, to remind them to purchase new beans weekly, to explain the various blends and beverages, and most importantly to serve only the highest-quality drinks. Employees learn to make drinks in an eight-hour seminar that includes lectures, demonstrations, and hands-on experience. They taste beverages that do not meet quality standards so they can be more sensitive to an unsatisfied customer.

Starbucks has the best success in its top markets—Seattle, Los Angeles, and Chicago. Traditionally located in urban areas and college towns, Starbucks has also ventured into alliances with other companies. It has paired up with Minneapolis-based Target Corp. in a deal that will place Starbucks coffee shops in the new Target Supercenters opening across the country. The demographics of a Starbucks and Target customer cross and the companies have both created an upscale image. Its extended line of products includes a coffee-flavored ice cream from Dreyer's Grand, a coffee-flavored beer from Redhook Ale Brewery, and a bottled version of its Frappuccino developed with PepsiCo. Consistent with its target customer base, every Barnes & Noble Bookseller and Borders Bookstore with a coffee shop serves Starbucks coffee.

Global expansion has been a large success as well. When Starbucks was introduced in Japan, as many as 200 customers lined up at a time. The company provides informational pamphlets in Japanese and posts menus in both English and Japanese. The world's fourth largest consumer of coffee, Japan is a potential $7 million market for Frappuccino alone.

Despite its rapid growth, Starbucks refuses to compromise quality. The company will not franchise, will not artificially flavor its coffee, and is very selective about business alliances. However, a recent Consumers Report taste test ranked Starbucks coffee behind the less expensive McDonalds. Fierce competition and concerns about the economy has lead Starbucks to lower its 2008 projected earnings. According to Mr. Schultz, the company has implemented a strategy called "segmentation" to look at how it can appeal to price-conscious consumers. "We're not going to get into any price-value discounting that would dilute the premium place we occupy," the CEO said. However, the chain is testing a $1 cup of brewed coffee at test locations in Seattle and testing free brewed-coffee refills.

Not only has the company made its logo visible through its products, accounts, and locations, but Starbucks also has received a significant amount of press for community involvement, charity work, and progressive employee policies. Amazingly, traditional advertising has not played a major role in the company's success.

Starbucks seems to have found its way into coffee cups everywhere. Never tried it? There are fewer and fewer people that have not tasted Starbucks coffee. Those who have not yet sampled Starbucks' brew can easily find someone to tell you what you are missing.

1. *The definition of marketing describes four types of decisions made by marketers: product, price, promotion, and place. Identify a place and promotion decision Starbucks has made.*

2. *Based on the types of retail locations selected by Starbucks, what customer characteristics form its target markets?*

3. *The marketing concept holds that the purpose of marketing is to understand the needs and wants of customers and create customer value through satisfaction and quality more effectively and efficiently than competitors. Given the information provided in this case, summarize how Starbucks implements the marketing concept.*

4. *Starbucks opens several new stores every business day. This includes global expansion into new markets. What factors must Starbucks consider as it continues to pursue global opportunities?*

Sources: www.hoovers.com; Barbra Murray, Starbucks Corporation, July 19, 2005; Starbucks.com visited July 8, 2005; Starbucks Coporation Fiscal 2004 Annual Report, March 31, 2005; Jeff Miers "New label gives McCartney a jolt: Former Beatle's latest effort backed by Starbucks is sweetened by layers of emotion and beauty," Knight Ridder Tribune Business News. Washington: June 2, 2007; Wireless News. Coventry: May 17, 2007; www.consumersreport.org Starbucks Wars March 2007, site visited February 25, 2008. Earnings Digest: Starbucks Slows Expansion, Seeks New Customer Segment. Janet Adamy. The Wall Street Journal. 31 January 2008.

CHAPTER 2

The Marketing Strategy & Planning Process

The iconic Spaceship Earth at Epcot Walt Disney World Resort houses a 13-minute ride that explores the progression of human communications from cavemen to the dawn of the Internet and beyond.

Learning Objectives

1. Understand how the strategic marketing planning hierarchy fits together to provide a complete planning system.

2. Describe the four elements of an organization's vision that provide guidance for all actions.

3. Integrate components of the strategic marketing plan with the vision.

4. Understand why elements of the marketing mix must be integrated and outline the steps of the marketing control process.

5. Identify the four major ways that organizations enter and cultivate global markets.

Over 80 years ago, Walt Disney founded his company based on three principles: Tell a great story, tell it with great characters, and push the technological boundaries. His characters formed the basis of the movies, cartoons, theme parks, and merchandise that would propel Disney to the forefront of entertainment. His creative vision was easily summed up: Demand the impossible! His marketing vision for the Disneyland theme park, opened in 1955, was far ahead of its time.

On the one hand, Walt's visionary zeal created a number of businesses—movies, cartoons, television shows, theme parks, and merchandise—held together by the Disney brand. On the other hand, the company lacked any real marketing strategy. Walt's autocratic leadership and unchallenged control in every detail of the operation simply did not focus on the long term. When Walt Disney died in 1966, the company floundered. As one senior employee put it, "Everyone looked to the past, asking, 'What would Walt have done?' No one looked to the future and asked the visionary question, 'What if . . . ?'"

It was not until the mid-1980s that a new team of executives began strategic and marketing planning for the Walt Disney Company. The organization was divided into strategic business units (theme parks and resorts, filmed entertainment, and consumer products) so each part could focus on what it did best. Instead of short-term planning, long-range strategic marketing plans became the norm. It is not unusual for a Disney division to have 5-, 10-, and 15-year plans to help it stay focused. While the business press was writing off Euro Disney (now called Disney Paris) when it first opened, Disney officials could see that they were actually ahead of their 30-year plan!

Disney's global strategy continues to expand through diversifying itself in international media, tourism, and entertainment industries. Walt Disney Parks and Resorts operates or licenses 11 theme parks on three continents. Five of those theme parks remain the most visited tourist destination on three continents. Beyond theme parks, Disney operates Disney Cruise Line, Disney Vacation Club and Disney Regional Entertainment (which runs eight ESPN Zone Sports Dining and Entertainment Locations).

Disney consumer products range from apparel, toys, home decor and books to interactive games, foods and beverages, electronics and fine art. Businesses under the Disney name make up an impressive group. Disney cable networks include ABC, Disney Channel, ESPN, A&E, the History Channel, E! Entertainment and many more. Production companies include Walt Disney Pictures, Touchstone Pictures, Hollywood Pictures, Pixar, and Miramax Films.

Disney Direct Marketing (DDM) online sales now represent the primary method of order placement. Disney Online is a spectacular Web site offering Disney's vacation, shopping, entertainment, and consumer products information. As the top-ranked family entertainment destination on the World Wide Web, the site offers visitors a virtual-theme-park experience complete with "all things Disney." The intuitive site allows children and parents alike to explore the magic of Disney right from your own home.

And Disney continues to recognize diversity. The Disney Store recruiting brochure maintains that it is "committed to supporting cultural diversity in the workplace because . . . 'It's a Small World After All.'"

Animated films have moved away from the exclusively Caucasian characters: Pocahontas celebrates Native Americans, Lilo and Stich spreads the Hawaiian culture across the world and the year 2009 will mark the release of The Frog Princess featuring Maddy, an animated Black princess.

The "Magic Kingdom" did not become successful through magic. Rather, Disney developed a strategic marketing plan aimed at exceeding customer expectations. Along the way, it also developed short-term tactics to keep the plan in focus.[1]

THE CONCEPT OF THE STRATEGIC MARKETING PLANNING PROCESS

Connecting with customers to create and capture value requires a sustained effort by organizations over the long and short term. Long-run plans concentrate on developing the resources an organization needs to win. Short-run plans describe how these resources will be deployed. An effective planning system addresses both the development and use of resources. The strategic marketing plan provides the guidance necessary to build relationships, develop and use technology, court diversity, and ensure ethical behavior in domestic as well as global markets.

Marketing can be described as philosophy, as strategy, and as tactics. Leading-edge businesses such as Disney, Eli Lilly, and Johnson & Johnson develop marketing plans that address each of these aspects to help them connect with customers. Figure 2.1 outlines the type of planning that corresponds with each aspect of marketing, including the people who usually implement each.

Marketing as philosophy can be viewed as the organization's marketing concept. It is embodied within the organization's vision statement, which articulates what customer value will be delivered, the codes of conduct guiding organizational behavior, and the resources that will be developed and deployed to build value. The vision describes the fundamental contributions the business intends to make to society, its position relative to competitors, and the attributes that make the organization unique from others. The vision is usually developed by top executives. In many organizations, this often includes the board of directors. Input from all organizational levels may be sought as well.

Marketing Aspect	Type of Planning	Responsibility
Marketing as philosophy	Vision	Top executive and top management team
Marketing as strategy	Strategic marketing plan	Marketing executive and other members of the strategic marketing team
Marketing as tactics	Marketing mix plans	Managers responsible for product, price, promotion, and place programs

Figure 2.1 Strategic Marketing Planning Hierarchy

Marketing as strategy is formalized in the **strategic marketing plan**, a document describing the company's objectives and how to achieve them in light of competitive activities. Essentially, this plan outlines the decisions executives have made about how the vision will be accomplished. The strategic marketing plan generally requires input and guidelines from marketing executives and a planning team of top- and middle-level personnel.

Marketing as tactics refers to precisely how each part of the marketing mix (product, price, promotion, place, and customer service) will be managed to meet requirements of the strategic marketing plan. Marketing mix plans are developed by specialists in each component, such as product managers, advertising executives, and sales personnel.

In a small company, the owner may perform all these planning roles whereas several hundred people may be involved in companies such as Johnson & Johnson or General Electric, two global giants known for exceptional marketing planning. You will find that companies tend to blend philosophy, strategy, and tactics into a range of planning appropriate for the organization. Still, all three aspects are found within leading organizations. The hierarchy shown in Figure 2.2 describes what takes place as companies develop plans to address the three aspects of marketing: philosophy, strategy, and tactics. Each of the major components of the vision,

www.corporate.disney.go.com

Visit Disney's corporate Web site to learn about what it's doing to help the environment. Explore green Disney events in your area and take the *How Green are You?* quiz for insight on your own environmental impact.

Figure 2.2   Marketing Planning as Philosophy, Planning, Tactics

strategic marketing plan, and marketing mix plans depicted here is examined in detail in the following sections. The final section of the chapter focuses on the strategies companies use to enter and build strength in foreign markets.

THE ORGANIZATION VISION

Outstanding performers have a vision that focuses marketing efforts purposefully. The vision provides an umbrella to help everyone maintain consistent direction despite volatile market environments. When President John F. Kennedy said, "We will put a man on the moon and return him safely to the earth," he created an effective vision. He provided a picture that inspired the U.S. space program, largely because the vision was simple, clear, and easy to remember. If Kennedy had described the enormity of the challenge in detail (how many people were needed, what talents they must possess, what type of equipment would be required), it's doubtful the venture would have succeeded. Instead, Kennedy's vision was fulfilled in 1969, when Neil Armstrong took "one small step for man, one giant leap for mankind," and walked on the moon.

Take a few minutes to visualize your life now and in five years, 15 years, and beyond. You are forming a personal vision. To make that vision a reality, what values will guide your behaviors? What will you contribute to people around you? What is your idea of excellence? What skills and attributes do you possess or will you develop? These

same questions must be answered by organizations. This is the visioning process. Discovering the vision is critical for companies (or people) who wish to deliver superior value.

The corporate vision provides a common understanding of what the organization is trying to accomplish in the broadest sense. Most company visions are composed of four parts: a set of core values, a business definition, the strategic direction of the company, and the strategic infrastructure.

CORE VALUES: THE ETHICAL FOUNDATION

Core values describe the type of behavior expected from a company's employees. They are the articulation of ethics and social responsibility, which were discussed in chapter 1. Everyone must live them everyday. Whole Foods Market considers its values the underpinning of its company culture. The company commits to selling the highest quality natural and organic products available, satisfying and delighting customers, supporting

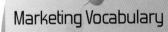

Marketing Vocabulary

STRATEGIC MARKETING PLAN
The document describing the company's objectives and how to achieve them in light of competitive activities.

CORE VALUES
A set of statements describing the type of behavior expected of the company and its employees.

team member excellence and happiness, creating wealth through profits and growth, and caring about communities and our environment. By sustaining these core values, Whole Foods believes it will preserve what has made it special since its beginning, regardless of how large the company becomes.[2] Employees believe that if they do this, business will take care of itself. Core values often express the company's philosophy about societal well-being, good corporate citizenship, and treatment of employees.

Top leaders today know that in order for values to work, they must be described and lived. Eli Lilly executives have clearly articulated the organization's core values. Notice that each of the many stakeholders of the organization is explicitly addressed.

Eli Lilly Core Values

Long established core values guide us in all that we do as we implement our strategies and pursue our mission

- Respect for the people that includes our concern for the interests of all the people worldwide who touch—or are touched by—our company: customers, employees, shareholders, partners, and communities.
- Integrity that embraces the very highest standards of honesty, ethical behavior, and exemplary moral character.
- Excellence that is reflected in our continuous search for new ways to improve the performance of our business in order to become the best at what we deliver.

A first step in their strategic planning process, a team of top executives and managers from Zappos gathered to undertake the difficult task of developing their core values. The result is shown in Figure 2.3.[3] A

www.lilly.com

Eli Lilly invites you to learn more about its global research-based pharmaceutical corporation. Download its *Corporate Citizenship Report* and read about its response to environmental issues being faced by the pharmaceutical industry.

self-proclaimed "service company that happens to sell," online retailer Zappos is known for its exceptional customer service. The company embraces these values to make Zappos a better place and to better serve its customers.

Core values provide an ethical guide that may be particularly useful in a crisis. It is possible Johnson & Johnson would not be around today if it had not adhered to its core values when Tylenol capsules laced with cyanide were linked to several deaths. The company's values are described in a credo, outlined in the early 1940s, which today reads in part: "We believe our first responsibility is to the doctors, nurses, and patients, to mothers and all others who use our products and services. In meeting their needs, everything we do must be of high quality."[4] That credo represents the organization's main purpose: to produce products responsibly with consumer safety in mind.

The tragic Tylenol situation in 1982 is one that few companies could withstand. By following the guidelines set forth in its credo, however, Johnson & Johnson did not just survive, but it emerged stronger. This ethics issue, one of the most heavily covered of this type by the Wall Street Journal, provides a fascinating classic example of core values.[5] Johnson & Johnson owns McNeil Consumer Products Company, the maker of Tylenol, which in 1982 generated $500 million in annual sales and contributed 8 percent of Johnson & Johnson's annual revenues. It was outselling Bayer aspirin, Bufferin, Excedrin, and Anacin combined.

On September 30, 1982, when Extra-Strength Tylenol capsules laced with cyanide were reportedly linked with five deaths and one serious illness, McNeil immediately and voluntarily withdrew from the market the lot of 93,000 units from which the two bottles came. That same day, 500 sales agents were sent to remove the product from store shelves. By midafternoon, the company had sent half a

Zappos.com Core Values:

1. Deliver WOW Through Service
2. Embrace and Drive Change
3. Create Fun and A Little Weirdness
4. Be Adventurous, Creative, and Open-Minded
5. Pursue Growth and Learning
6. Build Open and Honest Relationships With Communication
7. Build a Positive Team and Family Spirit
8. Do More With Less
9. Be Passionate and Determined
10. Be Humble

Figure 2.3 Zappos.com Core Values

million messages to physicians, hospitals, and distributors notifying them of the deaths and indicating the lot number.

Tougher times were ahead. Another death occurred in April that was linked to poisonous Tylenol. The company removed from the market all 22 million bottles of Tylenol capsules, valued at $79 million. To offset the loss in consumer goodwill, the marketing focus shifted to selling Tylenol tablets and voluntarily exchanging these for bottles of capsules. Nevertheless, by October 25, 1982, sales of all Tylenol products had slipped more than 25 percent. A letter was sent to approximately 61,000 doctors nationwide in which McNeil's Dr. Thomas N. Gates outlined the steps taken in response to the product tampering. In addition, 2 million pieces of literature were sent to doctors, dentists, nurses, and pharmacists emphasizing that the company was not the source of the poison. A special promotion offered coupons for Tylenol, and customers who had thrown away their bottles following the scare could have them replaced for free by calling an 800 number. Investor confidence improved and Johnson & Johnson stock, which had fallen 17 percent immediately after the first deaths were reported, bounced back on the New York Stock Exchange. Johnson & Johnson had all stores restocked with tamper-proof capsules by January 1, 1983.

Tylenol's comeback can best be attributed to Johnson & Johnson's early management decision to both stand by its credo and not let the brand die. The credo concludes: "We are responsible to the communities in which we live and work and to the world community as well. . . . We must experiment with new ideas. Research must be carried on, innovative programs developed, and mistakes paid for."

BUSINESS DEFINITION (MISSION)

The **business definition**, also referred to as the company mission, describes the fundamental contributions the organization provides to customers. The mission of clothing company Patagonia is, "to build the best product, cause no unnecessary harm, and use business to inspire and implement solutions to the environmental crisis."[6] Google's mission is "to organize the world's information and make it universally accessible and useful."[7]

Noted scholar Ted Levitt has had a tremendous influence on how companies develop their business definition. In a classic Harvard Business Review article, "Marketing Myopia,"

he explains why a customer orientation is absolutely critical to a company's business definition. **Marketing myopia** occurs when executives focus on their company's current products and services rather than on benefits to consumers. Levitt uses U.S. railroads as an example. They didn't stop growing because the need for passenger and freight transportation declined; in fact it grew. They got into trouble because they saw themselves in the railroad business rather than the transportation business. They were product oriented, not benefit oriented. Trucking and airline companies took customers away from railroads because they better met their needs. In addition, the railroads' failure to focus on customer needs created a situation whereby they also failed at making railroads themselves as competitive as could be. If the railroads had defined their business as transportation, then maybe Penn Central or some other company would have invented the truck or the airplane or served customers' transportation needs in other innovative ways with the railroads themselves. Levitt adds that "the entire corporation must be viewed as a customer-creating and customer-satisfying organization. Management must think of itself not as producing products but as providing customer-creating value satisfactions."

L.L.Bean's philosophy toward providing customer-creating value satisfactions has withstood the test of time. The following definition of a customer is critical to L.L.Bean's success today:

What is a Customer?
- A customer is the most important person ever in this company - in person or by mail.
- A customer is not dependent on us, we are dependent on him/her.
- A customer is not an interruption of our work, he/she is the purpose of it.
- We are not doing a favor by serving him/her, he/she is doing us a favor by giving us the opportunity to do so.
- A customer is not someone to argue or match wits with. Nobody ever won an argument with a customer.
- A customer is a person who brings us his/her wants. It is our job to handle them profitably to him/her, and to ourselves.[8]

> ### Marketing Vocabulary
>
> **BUSINESS DEFINITION**
> Describes the contributions the business makes to customers and society; also called the company mission.
>
> **MARKETING MYOPIA**
> A focus on company products rather than on how the products benefit consumers.

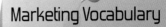

www.jnj.com

Johnson & Johnson is well known for its adherence to core values set forth by the company. Visit the *Our Caring* section of its site to learn about its green accomplishments, *healthy planet goals,* and environmental partnerships.

THE BUSINESS MISSION
"WHAT IS OUR REAL BUSINESS?"

Myopic Definition	Customer-Centered Definition
Medical Care	Health
Screws	Fasteners
Industrial controls	Productivity
Cars and trucks	Transportation
Computers	Problem solving
Industrial coatings	Protection and aesthetics
Nuclear power	Energy
Cosmetics	Hope
Telephones	Communication

Figure 2.4 The Business Definition

The organization's business definition should be stated in basic, benefit-rich terms and should focus on consumer benefits, not product features. It should always answer this question: "What business are we really in?" For example, is a cereal company in the "food" business (product focused) or the "nutrition" business (focused on consumer needs)? Benefits are based on what customers receive, not on the work companies do. Microsoft has grown dramatically and received substantial profit because of the benefits its software provides. Customers don't care how much raw material Microsoft uses or what it costs to produce the software. Basketball stars, Dwayne Wade and Lebron James make hundreds of millions of dollars because of the entertainment they provide, not just the points they score. Figure 2.4 contrasts myopic business definitions with customer-centered business definitions.

STRATEGIC DIRECTION (INTENT)

Strategic direction is the desired leadership position of an organization and the measures used to chart progress toward reaching this position. Strategic intent is another term for strategic direction: "Strategic intent captures the essence of winning."[9] Strategic direction addresses the competitiveness of the organization and often sets specific growth, profit, share, or scope goals relative to the competition and market opportunities. Eli Lilly's strategic direction is "to be a leading innovation-driven pharmaceutical corporation." It plans to focus primarily on three strategic dimensions: achieving a global presence, using its critical capabilities, and concentrating its resources to be a leader in the five disease categories in which the company believes it can achieve market leadership.[10]

Strategic direction may identify competitors by name

or by type. Fuji's strategic direction is aimed at overtaking Kodak, and Toyota has recently surpassed General Motors - its intent set over a decade ago. Strategic direction may guide organizations toward becoming one of the largest in an industry. General Electric wants to be either a leader or close follower in each venture it pursues. Mozilla and Microsoft's strategic direction involves a battle for dominance of the Web. While Microsoft's Internet Explorer holds about 80 percent of the market, Firefox continues in pursuit with advanced new releases. In Finland, Firefox controls more than 45 percent of the market and continues to grow.[11]

STRATEGIC INFRASTRUCTURE

Executives must develop and organize the company's **strategic infrastructure**, the corporate configuration that produces the company's distinctive or core competencies and provides the resources necessary to satisfy customer wants. This often means dividing the business into functional units and determining which core competencies to develop. The idea is to focus energy on specific

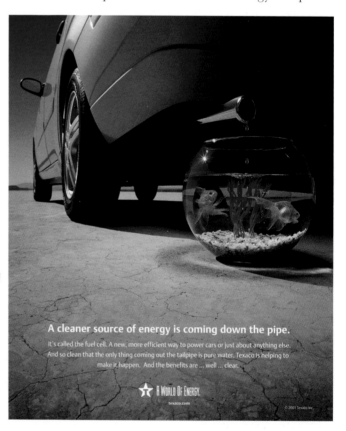

A cleaner source of energy is coming down the pipe.
It's called the fuel cell. A new, more efficient way to power cars or just about anything else. And so clean that the only thing coming out the tailpipe is pure water. Texaco is helping to make it happen. And the benefits are ... well ... clear.

A WORLD OF ENERGY.
texaco.com
© 2001 Texaco Inc.

Texaco's strategic direction involves a commitment to a cleaner environment.

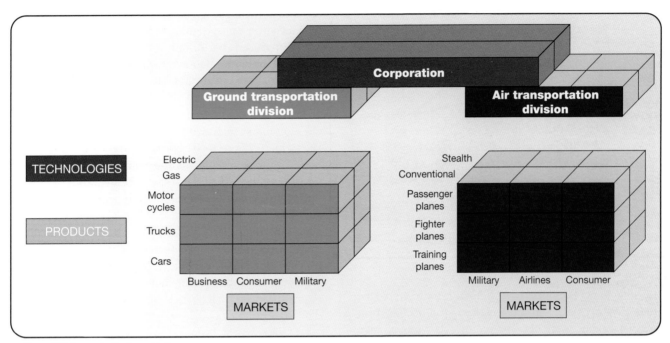

Figure 2.5 Strategic Business Units

goods, services, and talents necessary to create customer value in specific market segments.

Strategic Business Units (SBUs)
Most medium-sized and large companies have several strategic departments or units. A **strategic business unit (SBU)** is a part of the firm that can be managed separately for marketing purposes; it may be a division within the company, a separate product or product line, a distinct group of customers, or a unique technology. Johnson & Johnson has three SBUs: pharmaceuticals, consumer and medical devices, and diagnostics. The consumer SBU concentrates its efforts on marketing consumer products such as Band-Aids, No More Tears shampoo, and Tylenol. The pharmaceutical SBU mainly markets prescription drugs to the health care industry. The diagnostic SBU produces sutures, surgical equipment, and medical supplies for physicians, dentists, and others. The Walt Disney Company has four SBU's: Studio Entertainment, Parks and Resorts, Media Networks and Consumer products.[12]

Consider the corporation illustrated in Figure 2.5. It has two divisions: ground transportation and air transportation. The ground transportation division can be divided into SBUs according to products (motorcycles, trucks, and cars), types of markets (business, consumer, and military), and technology (electric and gas). The air transportation division can be divided similarly (products are passenger planes, fighter planes, and training planes; markets are military, airlines, and consumers; and technologies are conventional and stealth).

The total SBUs possible for this company is 36, but not all combinations would make sense (such as an SBU that produces stealth passenger planes for consumers). There are several ways to structure the SBUs in

Marketing Vocabulary

STRATEGIC DIRECTION
The desired leadership position of an organization as well as the measures used to chart progress toward reaching that position.

STRATEGIC INFRASTRUCTURE
The corporate configuration that produces the company's distinctive or core competencies and provides the resources necessary to satisfy customer wants.

STRATEGIC BUSINESS UNIT (SBU)
A part of the firm that can be managed separately for marketing purposes; it may be a division, a product or product line, a distinct group of customers, or a unique technology.

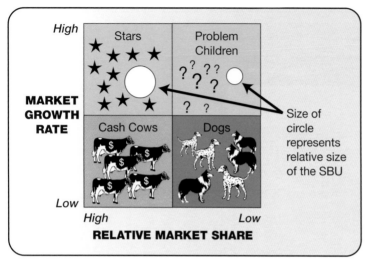

Figure 2.6 Boston Consulting Group Growth-share Matrix

this company. Grouped by technology, there would be four (electric, gas, conventional, and stealth); based on products there would be six (motorcycles, trucks, cars, passenger planes, fighter planes, and training planes); according to type of market, there would be four (airlines, other businesses, consumers, and the military). Many companies, lacking a customer focus, form SBUs by product line. In market-oriented companies, SBUs often address specific segments. That's why UPS Logistics Group is organized by the industries it serves: automotive, pharmaceuticals, computer, and so forth.[13]

Typically, an SBU is managed by a team from several different functional areas, such as marketing, accounting, and manufacturing. The corporate executives are responsible for managing the collection of SBUs—often called a portfolio—that makes up the organization. The general health of the company depends on how well the SBU portfolio does. **Portfolio planning tools** measure the contribution each SBU makes to the overall performance of the company. We will discuss two tools that are widely used: the growth-share matrix developed by the Boston Consulting Group (BCG) and the attractiveness-strength matrix developed by General Electric.

Assessing SBUs: The Growth-Share Matrix
Marketers need to understand market opportunities and the strength of their organization's resources relative to competitors. The growth-share matrix, shown in Figure 2.6, uses market growth as a measure of opportunity and the company's market share as the measure of resource strength. SBUs are placed in a matrix according to their scores on these two dimensions. Different actions are recommended, depending on the category into which the SBU falls.

In the low-share/high-growth category are SBUs called question marks. Although they are in a market that is growing fast, most have not yet achieved competitive

advantage or begun generating substantial revenues. A new airborne transportation vehicle, dubbed "SkyCat," was introduced by Britain's Advanced Technologies Group. Combining the better qualities of airplanes and hovercraft, the SkyCat can land or fly virtually anywhere. Though SkyCat may have potential to revolutionize global air transport, it has not received wide adoption. Since question marks such as the SkyCat are indeed risky, marketers may choose to (1) invest a little in the SBU and hope for the best; (2) spend time, energy, and patience on developing the SBU; (3) invest everything and keep their fingers crossed; or (4) get more information before doing anything.

Stars (high-share/high-growth SBUs) are a lot like movie personalities—give them lots of attention and expect a lot of success. Because they're growing, stars require a high investment, but it can result in a high return. Products such as the Nintendo Wii and the Apple iPod are examples.

Cash cows (high-share/low-growth SBUs) require a relatively small investment but should yield fairly substantial returns. Although the market is growing at a very low rate, the SBU has enough share to generate substantial cash flow. Companies want at least one product in this category and often have more, since revenues from these products can support the development of others. Two huge cash cows are Microsoft Office and Ivory soap for Procter & Gamble.

Dogs (low-share/low-growth SBUs) typically provide less than desirable returns. They're often considered competitively disadvantaged and unlikely to generate profits. They may actually consume resources, becoming cash drains that create negative value for the company. An example is Playboy magazine. It loses lots of money, so why keep it? Because it's the cornerstone of the profitable activities of Playboy Enterprises. The astoundingly profitable playmate videos (an SBU star) and other Playboy businesses are possible largely because of the magazine.

Assessing SBUs: The Attractiveness-Strength Matrix
The growth-share matrix just described says nothing about competitive behavior or market characteristics, and for this reason most marketing strategists use the attractiveness-strength matrix. As illustrated in Figure 2.7, the marketer first examines such factors as market size, market growth, competi-

Marketing Vocabulary

PORTFOLIO PLANNING TOOLS
Tools that measure the contribution each SBU makes to the overall performance of the company.

CORE COMPETENCIES
The unique resources a company develops and employs to create superior customer value; the fundamental building blocks of competitive advantage.

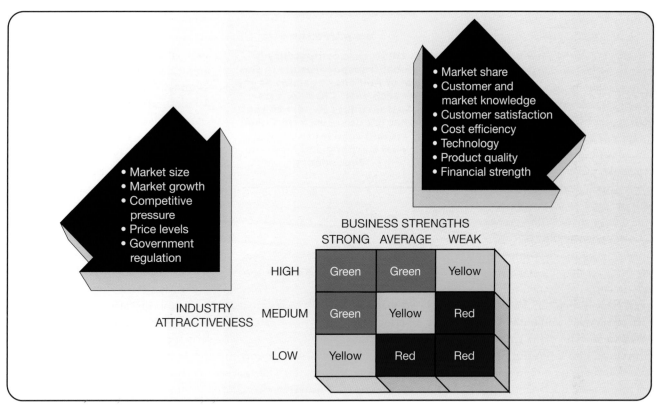

Figure 2.7 The General Electric Attractiveness-Strength Matrix

tive pressure, price levels, and government regulation to develop a composite industry attractiveness score. Next, the business strengths of each SBU are assessed based on estimates of the company's market share, customer and market knowledge, customer satisfaction with the company, cost efficiency, level of technology, product quality, and financial strength. Each SBU is then graphed in the matrix based on these several measures.

The attractiveness-strength matrix uses colors to signal whether executives should stop (red), be cautious (yellow), or go ahead (green) with the SBU. Unfortunately, during the 1960s and 1970s, "red" SBUs were sometimes categorically denied the resources required to compete, dooming them to failure. At the same time, "green" SBUs were allowed to charge ahead, irrespective of the vision of the company. All that was important was the amount of investment required and the SBU's potential return.

Today, portfolio planning tools are considered useful indicators, not predictors. Even SBUs that fall in the same category may need vastly different strategies. Portfolio techniques are helpful in iden-

tifying the current business situation, but they are inappropriate for making resource allocations. These, as we shall see later, should be made only after the strategic marketing plan has been developed. Because portfolio techniques say little about strategy, they should be used only as a first step in strategic marketing.

Core Competencies As shown in Figure 2.2, core competencies are the other important aspect of strategic infrastructures. **Core competencies** are the unique resources a company employs to create superior customer value. They are the fundamental building blocks of competitive advantage.

McDonald's core competencies in food distribution and preparation give it the ability to reproduce precisely the same taste, texture, and service millions of times a day, anywhere in the world.

UPS exhibits core competencies in specialized transportation and logistics services.

Recently, McDonald's has added competencies in coffee based drinks in order to compete with Starbucks. FedEx has developed a core competency in computerized information and tracking system technology so it can determine the location of any package worldwide within seconds.

Core competencies underlie the success of any one SBU and also span several SBUs or corporate divisions. Core competencies allow new products to grow. Marketing's role is to interpret market forces so that the proper core competencies can be developed to provide maximum benefit to consumers in the marketplace. When this role is performed well, companies are rewarded with the profit necessary to support continued improvement and growth.

An understanding of core competencies is necessary to comprehend how technology is shaping marketing practices. Through the rapid growth of technologies, companies build the millions of products and services that produce superior customer value. The many types of core competencies can be grouped into five categories: (1) base technologies, (2) process technologies, (3) product technologies, (4) people systems, and (5) information systems.

Base Technologies The research and development skills of companies can be applied to an endless array of product areas. For example, one of Canon's core

---

www.UPS.com

UPS's core competency in global transport results in the use of millions of gallons of gas each year. Check out its Sustainability Report to see what it's doing with its 95,000 ground vehicles to combat global warming and fossil fuel dependency.

---

competencies, vision optics, can be used to deliver outstanding cameras, copiers, and numerous inventive products. DuPont, known for basic chemistry, has developed multitudes of industrial and consumer products. General Dynamics is skilled in the wave technology necessary for radar and other types of vision systems. General Electric has spent billions of dollars developing its extensive knowledge of physics. Base technologies can be applied simultaneously to a number of diverse industries and product areas.

Process Technologies Process technologies allow the firm to produce quality products in the most effective and flexible manner possible. Marketing's job is to make sure that the development of processes is consistent with market trends and is in the customer's best interest. In efforts to improve customer wait-time, McDonald's has selected InfoLogic PC as a wireless device for inputting orders during peak hours. The device has significantly reduced the amount of time customers wait in drive-thru lines.[14] This improvement requires extensive changes in employee training, as well as the technologies used to process food. ARAMARK set out to serve a record-breaking 2 million meals in 17 days using its superior process technologies. Between 24,000 and 55,000 meals a day were served to athletes, coaches, and officials from 201 countries at the 2004 Olympic Games in Athens, Greece.[15] ARAMARK's Work Apparel and Uniforms division designs thousands of new products each year for the custom clothing market. An order for a shirt with a company logo or Little League team name can be received over the phone and shipped within 24 hours. In fact, ARAMARK maintains a tracking system on its Web site for checking the status and location of a customers order 24 hours a day.[16] Its production is tied so closely to the customer order process that no time is spent without contributing value to the customer.

Product Technologies The company's ability to create new goods and services is supported by product technologies. Many organizations have worked hard to develop competency in moving quickly from the idea stage through a series of well-defined steps to commercialization. Others follow the leader, copying competitors' products, possibly improving upon them slightly. Followers benefit from the innovation of leaders without having to invest substantially in developing their own product technology.

DuPont's core competencies in chemistry have enabled it to develop a number of industrial and consumer products.

The music industry, for instance, has been dramatically affected by changes in technology. Thanks to the advent of digital music recording, MP3 players have found a wide and expanding market. Music can be downloaded straight from the Internet onto many brands of players like the Apple iPod. These players are a result of the desire of companies like Apple to expand into a new product line from its formally core group of products that included computer hardware and software. Apple developed a venture with AT&T to acquire the communication technology to support it's iPhone product.[17] Motorola, formerly the market leader in the cell phone industry, is losing market share to competitors. Nokia now holds the top spot with a market share of more than 35 percent. This can be partly explained by the companies' research and development investments

Courtesy of Nokia

Nokia's nanotechnology concept Morph demonstrates the functionality that nanotechnology could potentially deliver: flexible materials, transparent electronics, self-cleaning surfaces, ability to observe local environment and harvest energy.

in recent years. In the past, Nokia spent less than half what its rivals invested in R&D, and trailed Motorola in market share. Today, it spends approximately 25 percent more than Motorola and has emerged as the market leader.[18] Eli Lilly also invests heavily in research and development to retain its status as an innovation-driven corporation committed to developing a growing portfolio of best-in-class and first-in-class pharmaceutical products that help people live longer, healthier and more active lives.[19]

People Systems The procedures that provide the human connection between companies and consumers are called people systems. Jan Carlzon from Scandinavian Airlines said the "moment of truth" occurs each time an employee has contact with a customer. He meant that the encounter results in either a good or bad impression being formed. Therefore, Carlzon invested in employee training to ensure that the moment of truth resulted in a positive experience for customers. He pulled his company into a leadership position by using people systems that provide outstanding customer service.

The Walt Disney Company has always placed high value on its team of employees. Walt once said: "The whole thing here is the organization. Whatever we

accomplish belongs to our entire group, a tribute to our combined effort. I feel that there is no door with which the kind of talent we have cannot be opened." Today Disney has updated those sentiments: "The Disney name—and the image it conveys—is one of our greatest assets, second only to the people who have contributed their talents and dreams toward the achievement of the goals we have set for ourselves."[20] The importance of Disney's employees is reflected in the organization's retail operation. To foster a spirit of teamwork, employees are called cast members. On the retail floor, they are on stage; in the storeroom they are backstage. Customers are guests. Such role-playing helps employees keep the desired goal in mind: Exceed guests' expectations.[21]

Information Systems An exceptional information system can be a core competency. Historically, companies were located close to their customers, so information about them was easy to obtain firsthand. Even executives talked directly with customers. Today, the situation is vastly different because of the increasing diversity of products, customers, and competitors. Especially important in global marketing, information-processing technologies put vast amounts of data at our fingertips rapidly. Companies that don't possess this core competency will be at a dramatic competitive disadvantage.

FedEx has satellite technology that enables it to track packages instantaneously. Route drivers are equipped with scanning devices, which provide information on exactly when a package is picked up or delivered. If you want to know where your package is, simply get on the Web and go to the FedEx home page. This information benefits not only the customer but also FedEx. Management teams determine what types of services are used most often, which destinations are most common, where more drivers may be needed, and so forth.

Basing the marketing strategy on core competency gives companies the longer-term flexibility required for sustained leadership. Technological advances can be shared throughout the company. SBUs should be treated as relatively temporary reservoirs of competencies that may be phased in, phased out, or adjusted radically in accord with strategic marketing conditions. According to Prahalad and Hamel, noted educators, "The real sources of advantage are to be found in management's ability to consolidate corporate wide technologies and production skills into competencies that empower the individual business to adapt quickly to changing opportunities."[22]

TITLE	RESPONSIBILITY
Marketing	Development of strategic plan and team leader
Engineering	Technological product development
Manufacturing	Efficient manufacturing
Finance	Financial modeling of strategies
Marketing Intelligence	Estimate competitor strengths, vulnerabilities
Marketing Research	Customer and consumer requirements
Sales	Potential sales strategies
Promotion and Advertising	Support program development
Procurement	Available supply partners and costs
Human Resources	Union and employee relations
Logistics	Distribution systems approaches
Accounting	Analysis of cost data

Figure 2.8 A Cross-Functional Strategic Planning Team

Marketing Vocabulary

CROSS-FUNCTIONAL PLANNING TEAM
Employees from several areas responsible for developing the company's strategic marketing plan.

STRATEGY
The development and/or deployment of resources with the intent of accomplishing goals and objectives in a competitive arena.

STRATEGIC WINDOW
The time during which market needs and the competencies of the firm fit together to create a significant opportunity.

THE STRATEGIC MARKETING PLAN

As we have mentioned, implementing the marketing concept is the responsibility of everyone in the organization. Consequently, many people are involved in developing and executing strategic marketing plans. Marketing isn't conducted only within a marketing department. As noted scholar and business consultant Frederick Webster, Jr. says: "Everyone in the firm must be charged with responsibility for understanding customers and contributing to developing and delivering value to them."[23] Marketing is so pervasive in customer-focused, competitively driven companies that it's often carried out by marketers in coordination of teams from diverse areas of the firm, such as accounting, finance, engineering, and manufacturing.

THE PLANNING TEAM

In the past, the planning process included only marketing personnel. Today, strong marketers generally assemble a **cross-functional planning team**. This team works together with a total understanding of the market and the organization's capabilities.[24] Just as relationships with stakeholders outside the company are important, so are internal relationships. Since each member of the planning team brings a unique perspective, these people must bring all parts of the picture together. Figure 2.8 gives each person's functional area and a short description of his or her main responsibility.

WHAT IS STRATEGY?

Before we talk about strategic marketing plans, we need to discuss one of the most overused and misused terms in business. The military defines strategy as "the art of meeting the enemy in battle under advantageous conditions." Although there are several "correct" definitions of strategy, we will use the following: A **strategy** is the development and/or deployment of resources with the intent of accomplishing goals and objectives in competitive arenas. Executives must determine how best to use companies with limited resources to accomplish organizational goals. Note that "competitive arena" implies the presence of competitors. They are striving to achieve their own goals, perhaps the same ones set by your company. Certainly, their actions affect your ability to achieve your goals. Japanese companies tend to be acutely aware of competitors. Consider Honda's public statement, "Yamaha No Tsubusu" "We will crush, squash, and slaughter Yamaha." But beating competitors with the intent of hurting them is not really what strategy is all about. The idea is to win outright by serving customers better—by connecting better—through relationships and technology, with attention to diversity, global dimensions and ethics.

Strategy is not just about meeting competitors fact to face. It's also about seizing the moment to create change in a timely manner. Hang around any group of planners and you're sure to hear someone refer to the **strategic window**. Derek Abell, noted business strategist, coined the term strategic window to describe the moment when requirements of the market and competencies of the firm fit together to create a significant opportunity.[24] Now, more than ever, the strategic window is important. Products and technologies are changing so rapidly that organizations late to introduce advances are likely to spend millions in product development only to see it go

Known for its use of low-cost strategy, Wal-Mart now offers a wide range of organic products.

miniaturization.

- *Consolidation of the value chain.* Combine several steps in the value chain into one.
- *Low-cost suppliers.* Lower costs by purchasing materials and other inputs more cheaply.
- *Location.* Put facilities in low-wage areas or nearby markets to lower distribution costs.
- *Economies of scale and scope.* Produce more and market in a larger area so costs are spread over more units and customers.[27]

Differentiation Strategy A **differentiation strategy** involves delivering customer value in a way that clearly distinguishes the product from its competitors. Differentiation works through effectiveness by giving superior benefits or reducing customer cost rather than price. There are several ways to achieve differentiation.

- *New functional capabilities.* Create products that do new things.
- *Improved performance.* Make products that work better
- *Product tailoring.* Make products that more closely suit the needs of select groups.
- *Lower Costs.* Make products more energy efficient, have less maintenance, or are cheaper to operate.

Customer Intimacy Strategy A **customer intimacy strategy** is based on delivering value through superior empathy for customers and solutions tailored to specific customer needs. Intimacy requires developing close relationships with the customer. There are several ways to achieve intimacy:

- Take on more responsibilities normally assumed by customers. Automatically update and support products at the customer's site.
- Mass customization. Use a process that creates products precisely to the specifications of individual customers.
- Information. Collect and maintain databases regarding customer product usage.
- Product Bundling. Develop product configurations specifically suited for individual customers.

Sustainable Competitive Advantage Sustainable competitive advantage is the strategy that competitors cannot easily duplicate or surpass. These various strategies are meant to create sustainable competitive advantages for the company. Once it is

down the drain. Competitors who get there first will obtain the sales, while the late product sits on the shelf.

For example, AT&T and Apple launched the iPhone, a highly advanced mobile device by Apple. Seizing the strategic window, Cingular, which had been recently acquired by AT&T, accelerated its rebranding to accommodate the projected sales of the highly anticipated device. Utilizing the best technologies among these two companies, impressive sales were anticipated.[26] Savvy marketers AT&T and Apple know that the strategic window is open for a relatively short period as consumers reconsider their dated mobile devices. Even though strategic windows may open only for a short time, the objective is to create a sustainable strategy.

Low-Cost Strategy A **Low-cost strategy** focuses on winning through efficiency. The objective is to be the low-cost leader, which allows the company to have higher margins than competitors and to pass some savings on to customers through lower prices. There are many ways to gain a favorable cost position:

- *Process technology.* Invent a low-cost way to create and deliver a product.
- *Product design.* Create a product that provides the same level of functionality with lower cost, often through new materials or

Marketing Vocabulary

LOW COST STRATEGY
Strategy whose objective is to be the low-cost leader, thereby allowing the company to have higher margins than competitors and pass some savings on to customers through lower prices; works through efficiency.

DIFFERENTIATION STRATEGY
Strategy based on delivering customer value in a way that clearly distinguishes the product from competitors; works through effectiveness.

CUSTOMER INTIMACY STRATEGY
Strategy based on delivering value through superior empathy for customers and solutions tailored to specific customer needs.

SUSTAINABLE COMPETITIVE ADVANTAGE
The strategy that competitors cannot easily duplicate or surpass.

attained, competitors generally try to copy it or develop their own advantages. Organizations that create sustainable advantages have less volatility and better long-run performance.

COMPONENTS OF THE STRATEGIC MARKETING PLAN

Guided by the corporate vision, the strategic marketing plan essentially describes how to accomplish that vision. Keep in mind that many organizations are complex and may have many strategic marketing plans. Similar planning steps are used for the entire company or for parts within a company. General Electric has a strategic marketing plan for the company itself and additional ones for selected parts of the organization such as aircraft engines and lighting. It also developed a separate plan for its participation in the 2008 Olympics.

The planning team has to address several areas: objectives, situation analysis, target markets, positioning, and integration of the marketing mix. The first step is to state the objectives the business will pursue and the specific goals it expects to obtain. The second step usually is a situation analysis, which describes the current business environment and how well the company will be able to compete in it. The third step is to determine target markets, or which customers the organization plans to serve. The fourth step is to decide positioning relative to competitors, that is, the image the organization wants customers to have about it and its products. The fifth step is to develop plans for each aspect of the marketing mix and integrate these into the overall strategic plan. We will discuss each step in detail following this logical order, but as actual plans are developed, the various steps usually interact with one another. For example, objectives are stated first but may later be changed to reflect information uncovered during the situation analysis. Finally, like a baseball pitch, a good strategic marketing plan needs follow-through or control measures that provide feedback on how well the plan is working.

OBJECTIVES

The strategic marketing plan must support the business definition laid out in the organization's vision. Since the objectives are an outgrowth of the vision, they tend to be stated up front. But, they must take into account all of the remaining parts of the plan as well, so objectives might be recast as strategies emerge during subsequent steps in the planning process. Companies usually set objectives in terms of desired profit, market share, or total sales. Profit is the most common choice and may be stated in various ways, such as return on investment, cash flow (amount of cash returned to the business), or profit margins. Market share refers to a proportion relative to competitors that the company captures: the percentage of customers within a given market, the percentage of dollars spent on similar products, or the percentage of all similar product units that are sold (unit sales). Finally, businesses determine a total sales objective, defined as either a dollar amount or a product quantity sold. Most organizations state objectives in these ways, but many may add others: number of loyal customers, customer retention rates, and customer satisfaction scores.

A company's market share, profit, and sales objectives are important because managers from various functional areas (such as production and distribution) often base their activities on them. Falling far short of objectives can spell disaster. The objectives stated up front usually are reviewed when the entire plan is completed and adjustments may be made. This makes sense, since implementing a realistic plan is important.

Often, it's appropriate to state very specific objectives such as "Forty-four percent market share by 2012." Notice that objectives always provide a time frame and must be verifiable. Verifiable means that it will be possible to determine precisely whether the objective has been met or not. You will see why this is important when we talk later about the marketing control process.

SITUATION ANALYSIS

All marketing activities required to understand the marketing environment, customer needs and wants, and the competition are examined in the situation analysis. This analysis predicts market conditions for the period that the strategic marketing plan is in effect. If the plan extends through 2012, for example, then predictions should be made up to that time. Developing possible scenarios generally requires bringing together data and expertise from different parts of the company to provide an accurate picture.

The situation analysis can be very elaborate or fairly simple, depending on the circumstances. At a minimum, it should give the planning team a general idea about the future, including potential size of the market, types of customers, competitors, technology, channels of distribution, economic conditions, governmental regulations, and the resources the company will have at its disposal, both globally and in individual countries.

As a final step in the situation analysis, the planning team must determine how well the company's skills and resources match the predicted market opportunities. This is typically called a **SWOT analysis**, which is an acronym for strengths, weaknesses, opportunities, and threats. An example is shown in Figure 2.9. Strengths and weaknesses are defined by such measures as market share, number of loyal customers, level of customer satisfaction,

Strengths

Assess good use of competencies and results in the market:
- Share increase
- High loyalty and satisfaction ratings
- Excellent sales force
- Unique products, services

Opportunities

Assess areas where advantage may be gained:
- Add a new product
- Promote to new segment
- Sell more to existing customers
- Use a new form of distribution to reach new markets

Weaknesses (Constraints)

Assess poor use of competencies and results in the market:
- Share decrease
- Disloyal customers
- Not enough salespeople
- Product launch delays

Threats (Vulnerability)

Assess external forces that may prevent the company from accomplishing its objectives:
- Competitor with a new technology
- New government regulations
- Changing customer preferences

Figure 2.9 An Example of SWOT Analysis

and rate of product introduction success. Strengths describe the unique resources or circumstances that can be used to take advantage of opportunities. Weaknesses suggest aspects of the organization or product that need improvement or, if that is not possible, ways to minimize any negative effects. The opportunities portion proposes advancements that can be made in new or existing markets and identifies areas in which competitive advantages can be gained. The threats section describes how the competition, new technology, the business environment, or government possibly may impede the company's development.

Companies are constrained by their weaknesses and are vulnerable to threats. When the government eliminated the use of certain environmentally hazardous resins in the manufacture of recreational boats, irate customers complained that colors faded in the sun. Many stopped purchasing designer-style boats for that reason. White didn't fade, but the lack of color reduced much of the excitement of new models and designs. Today, technological breakthroughs in environmentally friendly but stable colors have eliminated this threat.

TARGET MARKETING

Once the situation analysis is complete, the planning team determines the characteristics of customer groups on whom to focus attention. Businesses cannot be "all things to all people"; given their competencies, they must choose which segments have the greatest potential. **Target marketing** is the process of selecting which market segments the firm will emphasize in attempts to satisfy customers better than its competitors. Many consumer businesses target the Generation Y customers (born in the 1980's and 1990's). As marketers are well

aware, Gen Y teens spend an average of $150 billion a year and represent about a quarter of the American population.[28] Many companies are targeting Generation Y by using names and ads with the word "Extreme," or simply "X-." Extreme products include Right Guard's X-treme Sport deodorant, Flavor Blasted Goldfish Xtreme, Schick's X-treme III razor, and D-Link's Xtreme G Wireless Router. This market is getting a lot of attention from companies like Toyota, Honda, Ford, Volkswagen, and Saturn. Ford was one of the first to target this market with the Focus in the United States. Ford specifically aimed at winning Generation Y customers by providing a vehicle with a Sony stereo system, affordable pricing, and fashionable design. Other companies followed suit with blaring factory stereo systems, faster designs, and sporty interiors.

POSITIONING

Planning teams often decide to pursue different positioning strategies with different target market segments. **Positioning**, as you recall, refers to creating a perception in the minds of consumers about the company and/or its products relative to competitors. A common

Marketing Vocabulary

SWOT ANALYSIS
An analysis of strengths, weaknesses, opportunities, and threats to determine how well the company's skills and resources match the predicted market opportunities.

TARGET MARKETING
The process of selecting which market segments the organization will emphasize in attempts to satisfy customers better than its competitors.

POSITIONING
Creating an image or perception in the minds of consumers about the organization or its products relative to the competition.

word for positioning is image, often evoked by the brand name. For example, the Ralph Lauren Company wants to convey an image of high quality and status. If consumers see the company that way, then the marketing team has been successful in its positioning efforts.

Positioning is closely related to the **value proposition** which is the compelling reason customers should select your brand. For example, the value proposition for Advanced Micro Devices Inc. (AMD) is simple: AMD offers superior products at competitive costs and industry-standard products at lower costs. In today's competitive business world, positioning is extremely important. "Everyone is after everyone's business. The mind of your customer or prospect is the battleground and that's where you win or lose," says Jack Trout, author of numerous marketing books and president of Trout & Partners, Ltd. According to him, "just as each product needs to be positioned in the mind [of consumers] against competitors, so does a company need to be positioned. Customers want to know where you're going. So do your employees."

INTEGRATED MARKETING MIX PLANS

Once the desired positioning is established, the marketing mix—product, place, promotion, and price—must be integrated to make the strategy happen. Taken alone, each mix element does not represent a strategy. A strategy combines all the mix elements to create a unified effect on customers in the market.

There are numerous excellent examples of companies that have integrated all elements of the marketing mix into an effective strategy. As previously mentioned, Disney offers multiple products—amusement parks, MGM Studios, Epcot Center, Blizzard Beach, Discovery Island, and others. Each provides a high-quality experience, whether for vacations, weddings, or business meetings. And new products are constantly added, closely related to current consumer lifestyles. Disney carefully chooses theme park locations (place) that are easily accessible to consumers. It also makes information about its products readily available through Web sites and thousands of travel agents around the world. The variety of pricing options—deluxe, moderate, or economy—makes it easy for customers from all walks of life to purchase. And Disney takes care to promote its products to a variety of customers. Some are aimed directly at children, others at young singles, yet others at married couples whose children have left home. This communicates to consumers that Disney parks are for everyone. Clearly, the integrated strategy is paying off as Disney's annual sales are over $35 billion and continue to rise.[29]

A plan is needed for each part of the company's marketing mix: product, place, promotion, and price. The plan for each element often is developed within specific

Disney has had a long history of movie success.

functional areas of marketing, such as the product development department. In some cases, all these plans are combined into one. Each marketing mix element will be covered in depth in future chapters, but a brief discussion of the issues is provided here. Figure 2.10 illustrates some of the questions marketers face when developing plans for each aspect of the marketing mix. There are many, many more, some of which will be covered in later chapters.

Each plan for an element of the marketing mix deals with both strategies and tactics. For example, the decision to enter a new product area or distribution channel is strategic. Changes to an existing product or the addition of a new retailer in distribution are tactical. Tactics are used to achieve strategies. Strategies are long term and broad in scope; **tactics** are short-term, well-defined actions suited to specific market conditions. Strategies describe how we will compete to serve customers, whereas tactics describe who will do what and when.

Companies usually employ several tactics to accomplish a given strategy. McDonald's strategy is to provide high-quality, moderately priced food and friendly, fast

Marketing Mix Element	Types of Decisions
Product/Service	What new products/services should we introduce? Which ones should we drop? What are our objectives with each product or service? Are any new technologies available to improve our product/service? What type of service do our customers expect or desire? What policies should we implement in terms of product returns, spare parts, or repairs?
Place	Where do our customers shop? Should our product/service be available at all these places or just a few? Should we sell directly to our customers or through middlemen, such as retailers, wholesalers, or dealers? How should we ship the product—by rail, truck, air, ship, or others? How should we handle customer complaints?
Promotion	What are our promotion objectives? Are we trying to create awareness, encourage purchases, or others? What medium should we use: television or radio advertising, coupons, free trials, personal selling, public relations campaign, or a combination of these?
Price	What type of message do we want to send out? What is our overall pricing philosophy? Do we want to exceed, meet, or underprice our competitors? Is our price consistent with the amount of value we deliver to our customers? Should we change our prices? How will this affect demand for our product or service? Do our prices allow the organization to make a profit and invest in improved performance?

Figure 2.10 Examples of Marketing Mix Decisions

Marketing Vocabulary

VALUE PROPOSITION
The compelling reason customers should select your brand.

TACTICS
Short-term actions and reactions to specific market conditions through which companies pursue their strategy.

PRODUCT LINE
Closely related products marketed by the organization.

service to families. One tactic is to have a mini playground at some of its restaurants. Another is colorful packaging of children's meals and personal appearances by the popular Ronald McDonald clown. McDonald's strategy involves the use of major cartoon stars, such as Shrek.[30] Subway, which targets a more adult audience, pursues a strategy of preparing customized sandwiches quickly. Its assembly-line tactic allows patrons to build their own sandwiches. A Subway strategy focuses on providing healthy alternatives to other fast-food restaurants. Their tactic is to preassemble the meat element of the sandwich, leaving only the toppings to be added, which speeds the process but maintains patron selection. It would be tactically inconsistent for McDonald's to add gourmet items to its menu or for Subway to offer complicated full-course meals.

Product Plans A company may sell physical goods (such as automobiles or textbooks) or intangible services (a college education, legal counsel, or health care). Many companies sell both. In the business world, the word product has come to mean services as well as physical goods, and when marketers refer to product decisions, they are also referring to services. Unless specified otherwise, we shall use product to mean either goods or services. Product decisions are critical for most companies and they are among the most difficult to make. Marketers must help determine which products or product lines to develop and which ones to drop. Because products go through a life cycle, product strategy decisions are ongoing. Most organizations use systematic processes to develop new products and manage products over their life cycles, including decisions regarding product attributes, warranties, package design, and customer service features.

A **product line** consists of several closely related products marketed by an organization. For example, Nabisco offers many different types of snack foods, including Oreos, Fig Newtons, Chips Ahoy!, and Ritz crackers; each of these is a separate product line. Items are constantly being added, such as Nabisco's Ritz Bitz crackers, a product designed to fulfill customer demand for a smaller snack.

Marketers must take consumers into account when making product decisions. Each year, Coach, the maker of handbags and fine accessories, interviews more than 60,000 customers through Internet questionnaires, phone surveys and face-to-face encounters with shoppers. The information has helped executives spot trends and to extend its brand beyond their traditional leather bags. After hearing customers complain that they couldn't find

Nabisco's product line includes types of cookies and crackers..

decent carry-on luggage for weekend getaways, Coach launched its successful Signature Stripe travel bags.[31]

Technological product plans challenge marketers to continuously monitor, assess, and make decisions based on the ever-changing technological environment (and other factors). Technological products are developed, introduced, and dropped rapidly. This requires marketers to make frequent and sometimes difficult product decisions. In the console game industry, the leading companies have changed often, from Atari and Coleco to Sega and Nintendo to Playstation and Xbox. The Microsoft Xbox was of the first to debut with its own individual hard drive. "It is possible to leapfrog the competition in the video game market," said one analyst. "Sony was the last one to do it. But when they came out with the Playstation, they were considered a long-shot. They were coming from the stereo business, but now they are the ones to beat." Apple's success with the video market through its video iPod and iTV has potentially opened the door for them to enter the video game market. With the video consoles of today packing enough features to drive your home entertainment, not entering the market could adversely impact Apple's iTunes Movie download business, along with iTV and video iPod sales. With superiority in design and a well-recognized brand name, should Apple choose to enter the market, perhaps it will be the next to leapfrog competition.[32]

Place Plans **Physical distribution** (or logistics) involves getting the right product, in the right condition, to the right customer, at the right time, for the minimum cost. This is one of the fastest growing and most important areas of marketing. Globally, $3 trillion is spent on supply-chain logistics services annually, and is increasing at a rate of 10 percent each year. Approximately 10 percent of U.S. GDP is related to transportation.[33]

Physical distribution decisions can greatly affect the profitability of the company. For example, excess inventory in the channel increases storage costs. It is marketing's job to help ensure that an optimal amount of inventory moves through the channel. Of course, some companies are more successful at this than others. Bob Willett, CEO of Best Buy International, is helping shape Best Buy's model for inventory control. Through its "Customer Centricity" program, Best Buy uses agility, responsiveness, and accuracy to meet the specific needs of customers. The company is focused on increasing delivery frequency, reducing shipment size, and generating more effective forecasts. Companies, Willett explains, must take a holistic view, looking back in the supply chain as Best Buy does, to functions such as sourcing product from component manufacturers, assembling finished product, consolidation, shipping, reconsolidation, cross-docking, and distribution to stores.[34]

Distribution channels are the set of independent organizations involved in making the product available for purchase. A channel describes the route a product follows as it moves from manufacturer to consumers. First, marketers must determine where target customers shop: malls, shopping centers, downtown areas, discount outlets, drive-thrus, or at home via mail or telephone. People also shop in many different types of stores: supermarkets, merchandise marts, hyperstores, specialty shops, and outdoor markets. In each area of the world, consumer shopping patterns are unique. Parisians buy bread baked daily at small shops located throughout the city. The Japanese prefer to purchase fresh fish, caught within hours of eating, from small neighborhood retailers. Suburban Americans often shop once a week and freeze many items for use days or even weeks later. They like one-stop supermarkets and are willing to drive to them. Obviously, it's important for marketers to know where consumers prefer

---

Marketing Vocabulary

PHYSICAL DISTRIBUTION
The movement of finished products through channels of distribution to customers.

DISTRIBUTION CHANNELS
A set of independent organizations involved in making the product available for purchase.

to shop for the types of products or services that their company makes.

Promotion Plans The third element of the marketing mix, promotion, provides information about a company's product or service in an effort to encourage purchase. Marketers develop integrated marketing communications by coordinating advertising, sales promotion, personal selling, and public relations to get consistent messages to all types of customers. These messages provide information necessary for the choice process. Promotion also

increases demand for products, describes unique product characteristics, and helps build customer loyalty by creating expectations and reinforcing buying decisions. For example, Wyndham Worldwide launched a sweepstakes and ad campaign featuring Arnold Palmer. The integrated promotion is built around the Title Sponsor of a PGA Tour event. A national TV campaign featuring golf legend Arnold Palmer, and the Wyndham Foursome Sweepstakes are designed to introduce consumers to its unparalleled range of accommodations.[35]

Broadway shows, once only promoted in theater

The Marketing Gazette™

CREATING & CAPTURING VALUE THROUGH RELATIONSHIPS

Kraft Foods - Growing a Better Future for Agriculture

As one of the nation's largest food and beverage companies, Kraft is committed to reducing the environmental impact of its activities through different ways year by year. The company recently develops a five-year Kraft Environmental Roadmap to provide an improved framework for global environmental activities, but what makes Kraft different from its competitors may be that they understand the impact the supply chain, especially that the agriculture supply base has on the environment.

Kraft's philosophy is to promote the principle of sustainability in its agricultural supply base, and one of the major commodities it purchases is coffee. Since 1993, the company began to support projects of sustainable coffee, which is produced in a way that conserves wildlife, protects farm workers, and helps them improve their incomes and quality of life. In Ethiopia, where coffee accounts for 60 percent of the value of the country's total exports, Kraft introduced a quality laboratory and a quality control system at the farms, which improves washing process. In turn, the quality of coffee has improved and farmers have learned techniques to minimize water use and soil erosion. In addition, the company invests in long-term social projects for

local people, such as education programs and healthcare initiatives.

Kraft, along with other organizations, has made an ongoing commitment to farmers in Vietnam. The project introduces sustainable farming practices that help safeguard the environment, including waste water treatments, composting waste and environmental monitoring systems.

Moreover, Kraft teams up with Rainforest Alliance, a leading international conservation organization, to market sustainably produced coffee. Rainforest Alliance provides certification for producers of sustainable coffee, and Kraft has made a commitment to financially support Rainforest Alliance's work to expand the number of farms that are able to meet the criteria for producing sustainable coffee. Kraft then purchases this certified coffee and blends it into its mainstream coffee brands.

The partnership between Kraft and Rainforest Alliance has helped more than 140,000 coffee planters in improving their lives, and the Rainforest Alliance certification has saved more than 27,820 hectares of native forests and other ecosystems around the world.

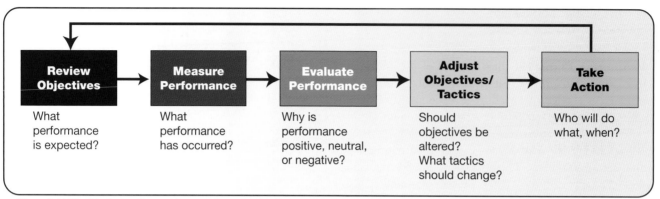

Figure 2.11. The Marketing Control Process: Assessing the Strategic Marketing Plan

directories, use several forms of promotion today. Marketing a Broadway show has taken on a new importance. Today ads appear on water towers and subways, while many consumers are reached by direct mail. Jeffrey Seller, a producer of the Broadway show Rent, says, "You have to get the word into the consciousness of many different people and that involves many different outlets, like magazines, radio, outdoor, print, publicity." Rent used a unique promotional strategy. A major subway advertising campaign was designed to reach teenagers and consumers in their twenties. This market was considered the "non-Broadway-going public." Print ads explained the show's story line and how to purchase tickets. Radio spots were also used on the integrated marketing mix plan to reach consumers.[36] Sometimes other products are marketed in conjunction with Broadway shows. For instance, New World Coffee, a chain of coffee stores on the east coast, introduced a Triple Berry Darkness frozen drink, which is sold as a tie-in to the show Jekyll and Hyde.[37]

Pricing Plans When Reebok aerobic shoes were first introduced into the women's market segment, demand was disappointing. The product was priced incorrectly, in this case too low. When prices were raised, demand increased. Prices send strong signals to buyers. Consumers often equate low price with poor quality, whereas higher prices signal unique and positive characteristics as well as higher quality. Raising price to increase demand is not unusual. Porsche did it in the United States. Ralph Lauren found it worked with men's and women's clothing. The perfume industry has used this technique since its inception.

In other cases, price increases can be devastating to sales volume. Think about the airline industry, with many

Marketers are taking new approaches to promoting Broadway shows like Rent.

different providers offering service between the same cities. What do you think would happen to ticket sales at United Airlines if it raised its prices above those of Delta or Northwest? Demand for travel on United Airlines would start dropping. That's why a price shift in one airline triggers shifts in most others.

THE MARKETING CONTROL PROCESS

Once a strategic marketing plan is implemented, results seldom occur precisely as expected. The **control process** provides feedback on how well the strategy is working. In a typical **control review meeting**, members of the planning team assemble to see whether objectives are being met. As described in Figure 2.11, the team reviews the original objectives, including sales volume projections, order quantities, customer loyalty rates, customer satisfaction rates, and market share projections. These numbers for each target market segment and in total are compared to actual results. This procedure is often called metrics, which connotes metering what actually happened. This process gives a picture of what has occurred.

By comparing actual results to the stated objectives, the team can assess the organization's performance. During these reviews, trends can be spotted. For example, sales and market share may be higher than expected because competitors were late in launching a new product, or sales may be low because the company's price was too high in relation to competitors. If it's not apparent what caused the results, additional marketing research may be needed.

Next, the team may decide to adjust objectives or plans. If results are strong, then objectives may be elevated. If not, objectives can be lowered, but the team usually resists this step because it can be viewed as a sign of weakness.[38] Adjustments to the plans usually are tactical rather than strategical, done through changes in the marketing mix elements. If a change in overall strategy is required, then a more involved and lengthy process starts. Sometimes teams go back to ground zero and start fresh. In either case, time is critical. One executive says that adjusting plans and taking action can be "like changing a flat tire on a moving automobile." It happens rapidly in companies that are flexible, efficient, and competitive.

CONNECTING GLOBALLY: ENTERING WORLD MARKETS TO CAPTURE VALUE

Once the domain of a few corporate giants, global marketing is fast becoming a requirement for most companies. Why? First, world markets offer tremendous opportunities. Many foreign market segments are larger and growing more rapidly than segments in the United States. Second, like it or not, U.S. business is no longer safe from global competitors. In comparison with other countries, the United States has few restrictions on foreign entry. Most U.S. companies must deal with some form of global competition, even within local markets. Third, a company intent on becoming an industry leader must operate globally or be placed at a severe competitive disadvantage.

GEOGRAPHIC SCOPE

World trade has skyrocketed in recent years. U.S. exports exceed $1.1 trillion annually. The United States also imports a large amount of foreign goods and services - almost $2 trillion annually.[39] From a planning standpoint, marketers must identify the **geographic scope** of the strategy, which is the extent of a company's international activities. Generally, geographic scope is divided into four categories, as outlined in Figure 2.12.

International Scope When a company conducts business in one or a very few foreign countries, it has an international scope. Generally, international companies treat foreign business as a supplement to their domestic operations rather than as a strategic necessity. Yet expansion in even one country can provide useful experience for further global activity at a later date. For example, Forestry Systems, Inc., of Greensboro, North Carolina, began international operations by selling its handheld computer inventory systems to lumber and logging companies in Canada and Mexico and has recently added markets in South America.[40]

Regional Scope Operations in several adjacent countries give a company regional scope. In essence, regional companies are competing within one large market that crosses national borders and generally only in one area of the world. Regional operations tend to be efficient because the markets are close together. The benefits of large market size can be combined with localized production and distribution to provide a viable strategy. This was the approach of Starbucks Corporation, the specialty coffee chain, as it expands outside the United States. The company opened its first Pacific Rim outlet in Tokyo and from there expanded into other regional parts of the Asian-Pacific region, including Singapore, Hong Kong, Taiwan, and Indonesia. Today, Starbucks is a global company with nearly 3,000 stores in 37 countries outside the U.S. It targets a long-term potential of 30,000 stores worldwide with 15,000 in the U.S. and 15,000 in international markets.[41]

Multinational Scope When companies operate in several countries around the world, their scope is multinational.

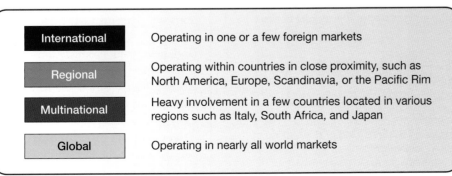

International	Operating in one or a few foreign markets
Regional	Operating within countries in close proximity, such as North America, Europe, Scandinavia, or the Pacific Rim
Multinational	Heavy involvement in a few countries located in various regions such as Italy, South Africa, and Japan
Global	Operating in nearly all world markets

Figure 2.12 Geographic Scope

The markets are not concentrated in one region. For example, Westinghouse Process Control sells services to electric utilities in the United States and several selected countries in many regions of the world. However, Westinghouse has decided to avoid marketing to certain countries in several areas. Multinational companies carefully pick their target areas and choose not to enter many countries. They tend to operate differently within each area of the world.

Global Scope   Operations in nearly all countries around the world constitute a global scope. Kenichi Ohmae, previous global consultant for McKinsey & Company, describes global scope with the mental image of hovering like a satellite over the earth.[42] Global businesses develop totally integrated strategies that maximize competitiveness worldwide over the long term. The Quaker Oats Company has committed to this type of integrated global strategy. Its Quaker International Branding Program is designed to ensure that the Quaker name means "healthy," no matter where you live. The company has a basic advertising, packaging, and promotion plan that is tailored to meet local conditions. This helps keep the Quaker image consistent around the globe.

A global market reaches nearly all countries. Differences among market areas are recognized, but so are similarities, so that similar segments of buyers within the various regions can be targeted.[43]

This helps marketers achieve vast economies of scale, especially in advertising, packaging, and distribution. Consider Gillette, which claims 1 billion people each day use a Gillette product worldwide. The company has always had a worldwide focus. In 1926, King C. Gillette said of the company's safety razor that "There is no other article for individual use so universally known and widely distributed. In my travels, I have found it in the most northern town in Norway and in the heart of the Sahara Desert." However, today, travelers can find Gillette products in far greater places than the founder ever imagined. The company is the global market leader in eight product categories and 62 percent of its sales are generated outside of the North America.[44]

Global marketing is based on the notion that consumers around the world are growing more alike and that modern technology has created a degree of commonality. Travel and communication have exposed more and more people to the same types of goods and services. Global companies appreciate the differences in consumer preferences, shopping behavior, cultural institutions, and promotional media, but they believe that these preferences and practices can and will become more similar.[45]

STRATEGIES FOR FOREIGN MARKET ENTRY

There are several different approaches for entering and developing markets. Small companies may use only one or two methods, whereas larger companies may use several simultaneously. Figure 2.13 outlines the most important approaches.

Exporting and Importing   Exporting and importing are the least risky and most common forms of international marketing. Exporting sends domestically manufactured products into foreign countries for resale. Importing brings products from foreign countries for resale within the home market, usually as part of another product. Exporting and importing are relatively easy ways to enter foreign trade because the investment is lower than for most other methods. In addition, most governments offer support and expertise to help domestic companies with these activities.

Because foreign trade can involve many complicated details, most firms use **export and import intermediaries**, which are firms with specialized expertise in exporting or importing. There are two types. **Indirect export intermediaries** are located in the domestic market and help send products abroad. They specialize in knowledge about foreign customs, regulations affecting businesses and products, laws, and market conditions. **Direct export intermediaries** are located in the foreign market. Since they are very familiar with the local business environment,

Export—Import	Send products abroad for resale (exporting) or purchase products from foreign companies for resale, usually as part of another product, within the home market (import)
Foreign Licensing and Franchising	Agreements that permit foreign companies to produce and distribute merchandise, often using trademarks and/or selected merchandising and customer delivery approaches
Overseas Marketing and Manufacturing	A marketing infrastructure and/or manufacturing facilities abroad
Joint Ventures and Strategic Alliances	The shared ownership of operations by two or more local and foreign companies (joint venture) or the pooling of resources by two or more companies for the purpose of competing as one entity (strategic alliance)

Figure 2.13 Approaches for Entering and Building Foreign Markets

they can help clients in special ways, such as offering unique government contacts. Intermediaries can be very beneficial because they assume many of the risks involved with distribution. At the same time, the exporting company must give up a significant amount of control over how its product is distributed.

Trading companies are large intermediaries that facilitate the movement of goods in and out of countries. For example, Koch is an international trading company that facilitates the sale of goods to and from a variety of regions, such as crude oil, petroleum products and other commodities. In order to provide customers a diverse array of products and commodities, Koch companies have access to major international trading regions in the United States, Europe, Asia and the Middle East.[46]

Foreign Licensing and Franchising

Foreign licensing assigns the rights to a patent, trademark, or manufacturing process to a foreign company for a fee, often called a royalty. Licensing allows companies to gain entry into a foreign market at almost no cost or risk, but control of the marketing strategy is turned over to the licensee. **Franchising** is a special type of licensing arrangement whereby the marketer provides not only the product, technology, process, and/or trademark but also most of the marketing program. In nearly any major city around the world, you are likely to find McDonald's, Burger King, and Kentucky Fried Chicken, or Holiday Inn, Hilton, and Marriott. They are there because local entrepreneurs have bought the franchise. Franchising allows companies to maintain marketing control while passing along many of the costs, risks, and responsibilities to the foreign licensees. These often function quite autonomously from the parent company but benefit from being part of a large corporation.

Overseas Marketing and Production

Also called subsidiaries, overseas marketing and production operations are owned by a parent company in foreign countries, whether a small sales office or something more elaborate. A subsidiary operation may simply assemble finished goods or may function as an independent business, responsible for product development, manufacturing, marketing, and so on. For example, General Motors operates assembly plants for automotive components in Mexico, while its German and British subsidiaries produce entire automobiles. Subsidiaries can be very costly to establish and very risky to operate, since the owner is liable for any mishaps. Foreign operations also are subject to a host of circumstances beyond the company's control. For example, several oil companies lost billions of dollars when their Iranian subsidiaries were closed after invasion of Kuwait. The major advantage of a subsidiary is that the parent company retains control and can carry out its own strategy.

Foreign Strategic Alliances

Strategic alliances involve partnering. A **joint venture** occurs when two companies combine resources for a new venture. They are formed to provide products and services more competitively than a single organization could do independently. Typically, a foreign joint venture has one company in each of two countries, but more partners or countries are possible. National laws often require any business to have a certain percentage

globalEDGE™
The Marketing Strategy & Planning Process

http://globaledge.msu.edu

Visit globalEDGE™ Online for the ultimate international marketing research tool!

An element of having a successful marketing strategy both domestically and globally is to offer innovative products and/or services to customers. After referring to a magazine of innovation, which three firms in the automotive industry may be considered the most innovative? Which three may be referred to as least innovative? From which countries are each of these firms? What does this mean about the automotive industry for the near future?

Marketing Vocabulary

EXPORT INTERMEDIARIES
Domestic or foreign firm that assists with exporting activity.

IMPORT INTERMEDIARIES
Firm set up to help guide importing actions.

INDIRECT EXPORT INTERMEDIARIES
Firm located in a domestic market which specializes in knowledge about foreign customs, regulations affecting businesses and products, laws, and market conditions.

DIRECT EXPORT INTERMEDIARIES
Firm located in a foreign market which specializes in knowledge about foreign customs, regulations affecting businesses and products, laws, and market conditions.

TRADING COMPANIES
Large intermediaries that facilitate the movement of goods in and out of countries.

FOREIGN LICENSING
Assigning the rights to a patent, trademark, or manufacturing process to a foreign company for a fee, often called a royalty.

FRANCHISING
A special type of licensing arrangement whereby the marketer provides not only the product, technology, process, and/or trademark but also the entire marketing program.

JOINT VENTURE
An alliance of two companies that combine resources to provide products and services more competitively than either could do independently.

of domestic ownership. Sony develops many of its innovative computer and communications products through strategic alliances and ventures with companies in the United States. When the Soviet bloc dissolved, joint ventures were formed rapidly as foreign firms attempted to gain access to these markets. Often, the first strategy was to buy ownership, which Volkswagen did in the Czech Republic. The Germans beat out other contenders, such as Renault of France, and acquired a significant percent of the Czech auto leader Skoda.

Global strategic alliances are joint ventures that involve actions taken internationally by two or more companies contributing an agreed amount of resources. The arrangement often resembles a well-funded start-up operation. This approach may be preferred when competition is tough or technology and capital requirements are relatively large for one partner. General Motors has global alliances with Suzuki, Isuzu, and Fiat. Ford has allied with Volkswagen and Nissan, Daimler-Chrysler with Mitsubishi and Honda. General Mills created an alliance with Nestlé in Europe, called Cereal Partners Worldwide (CPW), to compete against Kellogg's growing global share. General Mills and Nestlé agreed to pool part of their product lines and distribution system.

A global strategic alliance may be formed between or among companies that compete in some regions of the world but decide to cooperate in others. Toshiba, for example, has allied with a number of firms in the United States (United Technologies, Apple, Sun Microsystems, Motorola, and National Semiconductor) as well as a number of firms in Europe (Olivetti, Seimens, Rhore-Poulenc Ericcson, and SGS Thomson). Notice that many of these are rivals in various markets, but each works with Toshiba.

Whether its scope of operations is global or local, the company needs in-depth knowledge of its targeted markets in order to shape the strategic plan and meet its goals. In the next chapter we will look at the importance of E-commerce and it's role in the global marketing environment.

Web and E-commerce Stars
The Walt Disney Company - www.disney.com

The Walt Disney Company designed their web site with their customers in mind. The unique interface allows visitors to explore everything Disney offers from one convenient site. Disney.com has links to customized pages based on age, gender and specifically for families. This distinct feature creates a fun and friendly experience for all users. On the Web site, customers can watch movie trailers, preview Disney channel shows, listen to music, and play games. Customers can also plan Disney vacations, shop the Disney store and Disney mobile and learn about live events such as The Lion King on Broadway.

Chapter Summary:

Objective 1: Understand how the strategic marketing planning hierarchy fits together to provide a complete planning system.

Strategic marketing proceeds from a company's vision, to the strategic marketing plan, to the marketing mix plans. The vision describes what the organization is trying to accomplish in the broadest sense. It includes the organization's marketing philosophy. The strategic marketing plan is developed in line with the vision by a cross-functional team representing several business areas, such as manufacturing, accounting, finance, and engineering. The plan describes the company's goals and states how the company will achieve them. Specialists in each component of the marketing mix

prepare a plan for that area.

Objective 2: Describe the four elements of an organization's vision that provide guidance for all actions.

The vision statement expresses the company's core values, business definition, strategic direction, and strategic infrastructure. Core values reflect the company's beliefs about the types of behavior acceptable from employees and the company as a whole as well as its relationship to employees, customers, and society in general. A business definition describes the contributions a company seeks to make to customers and society. It is important to avoid marketing myopia when developing a mission statement. Marketing myopia occurs when executives focus on the company's goods and services rather than on the benefits these goods and services provide to consumers. Strategic direction is the desired leadership position of an organization as well as the measures used to chart progress toward reaching that goal. It captures the "essence of winning" and addresses the competitiveness of the organization. A company's strategic infrastructure consists of both strategic business units and core competencies. SBUs can be managed using portfolio planning tools, such as the growth-share matrix or the attractiveness-strength matrix. Core competencies are the unique resources a company develops and employs to create superior customer value. They are the fundamental building blocks of competitive advantage and can be developed in one or more of the following areas: base technologies, process technologies, product technologies, people systems, or information systems.

Objective 3: Integrate components of the strategic marketing plan with the vision.

The strategic marketing plan describes how to accomplish the vision for a particular part of the business. It has five components: objectives, situation analysis, target marketing, positioning, and integration of the marketing mix. Objectives are developed in line with the vision and the situation analysis. They state aims regarding profit, market share, and total sales as well as customer satisfaction and loyalty. The situation analysis describes the marketing environment for the period that the plan is in effect. It gives all the information required to estimate possible business scenarios, including market size, customer characteristics, competitors, and technology. A key part of the situation analysis is to examine strengths, weaknesses, opportunities, and threats (SWOT). The target marketing phase of strategic marketing planning focuses the organization on select groups of customers. In the positioning phase, the image of the organization relative to the competition is developed. The final step is to integrate the marketing mix plans to accomplish the overall strategy. It is important to look at the total effect of the marketing mix, rather than a single element, on the market.

Objective 4: Understand why elements of the marketing mix must be integrated and outline the steps of the marketing control process.

Plans for each part of the marketing mix are usually developed by specialists in the respective areas. Often a separate plan is created for product, place, promotion, and price, but sometimes these plans are combined. Plans for any of these elements are both strategic and tactical. Strategies are long term and broad in scope, whereas tactics are short-term actions suited to specific market conditions. Several tactics may be used to carry out a single strategy.

To determine whether the strategic marketing plan is accomplishing the intended objectives, a marketing control process is needed. It has five steps. First, the original performance objectives are reviewed. Second, measures indicate what performance has occurred. Third, performance is evaluated by interpreting the results obtained and looking for any trends. Fourth, it is decided whether actions or objectives should be altered. Fifth, the strategy proceeds as planned or another course is developed and implemented.

Objective 5: Identify the four major ways that organizations enter and cultivate global markets.

Organizations enter and cultivate global markets through exporting and importing, foreign licensing and franchising, overseas marketing and manufacturing, and joint ventures and strategic alliances. Exporting involves sending domestically manufactured products into foreign markets. It is usually the low-risk and low-cost way to enter markets. There are many forms of help for companies just getting started in exporting or importing. Foreign licensing and franchising simply assign the rights to a patent, trademark, or process to a foreign company. Overseas marketing and production involve setting up operations in a foreign country. This requires the commitment of direct investment in a foreign country. Strategic alliances and joint ventures involve sharing resources with a partner to enter markets. Often the partner has strong contacts in the country or region where the venture takes place. Joint ventures can simply involve contracts between companies or shared ownership of new organizations. In some cases these can involve huge investments and substantial risks.

Review Your Understanding

1. What are the elements of the marketing planning hierarchy?
2. What are the components of a vision?
3. What is marketing myopia? How is the company's mission related to myopia?
4. In what ways can strategic business units be structured?
5. What are portfolio planning tools and how are they used?
6. What are core competencies? Give examples of five types.
7. Which people in an organization create the strategic marketing plan?

8. What is the difference between a strategy and a tactic? How do they work together?
9. What are the components of the strategic marketing plan? Describe each.
10. What are the elements of a SWOT analysis?
11. How are marketing mix plans strategic and tactical?
12. What is the marketing control process, and what are its steps?
13. In what four ways can foreign markets be entered? Describe each.

Discussion of Concepts

1. Define strategy. Define tactics. How is strategy related to tactics? What strategy do you think Coca-Cola is following? What tactics is it using to support this strategy?
2. How are a company's core values, business definition, strategic infrastructure, and strategic direction interrelated? Do you think it is important for a company to develop an explicit statement about each of these?
3. Imagine that the following companies describe their business as shown: (a) Black & Decker: drills and sanders; (b) Sherwin-Williams: paint; (c) Schwinn: bicycles; (d) U.S. Post Office: mail delivery. Do you think these companies are suffering from marketing myopia? How may they better define their business?

4. Why is it important for a company to have a well-defined strategic direction? In your opinion, what may happen to a company that lacks strategic direction?
5. How would you assess the contribution made by each strategic business unit? Do you think it is important for technology to be shared among SBUs? Why or why not?
6. Who should be involved in the development of a strategic marketing plan? Why?
7. What is the purpose of a situation analysis? What type of information should be included?
8. Why do most companies engage in some type of target marketing? Whom do you think Nintendo is targeting with its Game Boy product line?

Key Terms And Definitions

Business definition: Describes the contributions the business makes to customers and society; also called the company mission.

Control process: Procedures designed to provide feedback on how well the marketing strategy is working.

Control review meeting: Meeting of members of the planning team to see whether objectives are being met.

Core competencies: The unique resources a company develops and employs to create superior customer value; the fundamental building blocks of competitive advantage.

Core values: A set of statements describing the type of behavior expected of the company and its employees.

Cross-functional planning team: Employees from several areas responsible for developing the company's strategic marketing plan.

Differentiation strategy: Strategy based on delivering customer value in a way that clearly distinguishes the product from competitors; works through effectiveness.

Direct export intermediary: A firm located in a foreign market which specializes in knowledge about foreign customs, regulations affecting businesses and products, laws, and market conditions.

Distribution channel: A set of independent organizations involved in making the product available for purchase.

Export intermediary: Domestic or foreign firm that assists with exporting activity.

Foreign licensing: Assigning the rights to a patent, trademark, or manufacturing process to a foreign company for a fee, often called a royalty.

Franchising: A special type of licensing arrangement whereby the marketer provides not only the product, technology, process, and/or trademark but also the entire marketing program.

Geographic scope: The extent of a company's international activities.

Import intermediary: Firm set up to help guide importing actions.

Indirect export intermediary: Firm located in a domestic market which specializes in knowledge about foreign customs, regulations affecting businesses and products, laws, and market conditions.

Joint venture: An alliance of two companies that combine resources to provide products and services more competitively than either could do independently.

Low-cost strategy: Strategy whose objective is to be the low-cost leader, thereby allowing the company to have higher margins than competitors and pass some savings on to customers through lower prices; works through efficiency.

Marketing myopia: A focus on company products rather than on how these products benefit consumers.

Physical distribution: The movement of finished products through channels of distribution to customers.

Portfolio planning tools: Tools that measure the contribution each SBU makes to the overall performance of the company.

Positioning: Creating an image or perception in the minds of consumers about the organization or its products relative to the competition.

Product line: Closely related products marketed by the organization.

Strategic business unit (SBU): A part of the firm that can be managed separately for marketing purposes; it may be a division, a product or product line, a distinct group of customers, or a unique technology.

Strategic direction: The desired leadership position of an organization as well as the measures used to chart progress toward reaching that position.

Strategic infrastructure: The corporate configuration that produces the company's distinctive or core competencies and provides the resources necessary to satisfy customer wants.

Strategic marketing plan: The document describing the company's objectives and how to achieve them in light of competitive activities.

Strategic window: The time during which market needs and the competencies of the firm fit together to create a significant opportunity.

Strategy: The development and/or deployment of resources with the intent of accomplishing goals and objectives in a competitive arena.

Sustainable competitive advantage: The strategy that competitors cannot easily duplicate or surpass.

SWOT analysis: An analysis of strengths, weaknesses, opportunities, and threats to determine how well the company's skills and resources match the predicted market opportunities.

Tactics: Short-term actions and reactions to specific market conditions through which companies pursue their strategy.

Target marketing: The process of selecting which market segments the organization will emphasize in attempts to satisfy customers better than its competitors.

Trading companies: Large intermediaries that facilitate the movement of goods in and out of countries.

References

1. "The Walt Disney Company 2005 Annual Report"; www.disney.com, Web site visited on April 15, 2007; "Disney First: Black Princess in Animated Film," MSNBC News Services, March 12, 2007.

2. Whole Foods Market Company Philosophy: Core Values, www.wholefoodsmarket.com, site visited April 21, 2008.

3. Zappos.com Core Values - www.zappos.com/core-values.zhtml, site visited May 29, 2008.

4. www.jnj.com/our_company/our_credo/, site visited April 21, 2008.

5. Michael Waldholz and Dennis Kneale, "Tylenol's Maker Tries to Regain Good Image in Wake of Tragedy," Wall Street Journal, October 8, 1982; "Johnson & Johnson to Scrap All Capsules in Its Effort to Save the Brand Name," Wall Street Journal, October 8, 1982; "It Could Have Been Anyone," Wall Street Journal, October 8, 1982; Michael Waldholz, "Johnson & Johnson Officials Take Steps to End More Killings Linked to Tylenol," Wall Street Journal, October 4, 1982, p. 16; "Johnson & Johnson Pulls Tylenol Lot from Market in Wake of Five Cyanide Deaths," Wall Street Journal, October 1, 1982; "Authorities Say Cyanide-Laced Tylenol Likely Was Planted at Individual Stores," Wall Street Journal, October 4, 1982, p. 3; Michael Waldholz, "Johnson & Johnson Can Weather Tylenol Storm—If It Hurries," Wall Street Journal, October 5, 1982, p. 22; "Tylenol Containing Strychnine Is Found in California as Consumer Fears Mount," Wall Street Journal, October 6, 1982, p. 2; "J&J Tries Ads to Revive Sales of Tylenol," Wall Street Journal, October 25, 1982, p. 20; Michael Waldholz, "Drop in Johnson & Johnson Shares Is Linked to Belief That Fears Over Tylenol Will Linger," Wall Street Journal, October 29, 1982; Michael Waldholz, "Tylenol Maker Mounting Campaign to Restore Trust of Doctors, Buyers," Wall Street Journal, November 12, 1982, p. 33; Michael Waldholz, "Johnson & Johnson Plans to Reintroduce Tylenol Capsules in More Secure Package," Wall Street Journal, November 12, 1982, p. 4; and Michael Waldholz, "Tylenol Regains Most of No. 1 Market Share, Amazing Doomsayers," Wall Street Journal, December 24, 1982, p. 1.

References

6. "Patagonia Company Information: Our Reason for Being," www.patagonia.com/usa/patagonia.go?assetid=2047, site visited April 21, 2008.

7. www.google.com/corporate, site visited April 21, 2008.

8. Craig Altschul "Customer Credo Defines Who You Are L.L. Bean Exec Tells CNL Resort GMs," October 18, 2007. http://industryreport.mountainnews.com/2007/10/an_ir_exclusive_part_two_custo_1.shtml, site visited April 21, 2008.

9. "Strategic Intent," Harvard Business Review, May–June 1989, p. 64.

10. www.lilly.com, site visited April 21, 2008.

11. Ryan Paul, "Firefox Share Up Over 20 Percent in Europe, Mostly at Expense of IE," January 29, 2008. www.arstechnica.com, site visited April 21, 2008.

12. http://corporate.disney.go.com/corporate/sourcing.html, site visited April 23, 2008.; www.jnj.com, site visited April 23, 2008.

13. www.upslogistics.com, site visited April 23, 2008.

14. www.infologixsys.com/products/, site visited April 22, 2007

15. "ARAMARK: Providing Food Service for 2004 Olympic Games in Athens, Greece," www.aramark.com, site visited April 23, 2008.

16. www.aramark-uniform.com, site visited April 23, 2008.

17. Kloer, Phil, "Me, myself & iPod; Music lovers gush about pocket-size hip, hot jukebox," The Atlanta Journal-Constitution, March 26, 2004, p. 1B.

18. John Walko, "Europe Continues to Lag US Companies' R&D Spend," Nov. 12, 2007. www.dspdesignline.com/news/202805484, site visited April 23, 2008; W. David Gardner, "Nokia, Samsung Gain Cell Phone Market Share, Putting Pressure On Motorola," August 23, 2007. Information Week.

19. www.lilly.com site visited April 23, 2008.

20. Recruiting brochure for the Disney Store.

21. Ibid.

22. "The Core Competence of the Corporation," Harvard Business Review, May/June 1990, p. 81.

23. "The Changing Role of Marketing in the Corporation," Journal of Marketing, October 1992, p. 14.

24. Jeffery B Schmidt, Mitzi M Montoya-Weiss, & Anne P. Massay, "New Product Development Decision Making Effectiveness: Comparing Face-to-Face Teams and Virtual Teams," Decision Sciences, Fall 2001.

25. Derek F. Abell, "Strategic Windows," Journal of Marketing, July 1978, p. 21.

26. "iPhone prompts accelerated Cingular rebranding", Reuters, CNET News.com, May 5, 2007.

27. Based on Michael Porter, Competitive Advantage: Creating and Sustaining Superior Performance (New York: The Free Press, 1985).

28. Jane L. Krotz, "Tough Customers: How to Reach Gen Y," www.microsoft.com/smallbusiness, site visited April 23, 2008.

29. www.hoovers.com, site visited April 23, 2008.

30. "McDonald's Brings the Joy of Shrek to Customers Around the World," May 8, 2007, www.prnewswire.com.

31. "The 50 best stocks of the S&P 500," BusinessWeek, April 30, 2007

32. "Computing Column," Houston Chronicle, August 18, 2000; Prince McLean, "Apple rumored to be eyeing video game market," Apple Insider, December 6, 2006.

33. www.ita.doc.gov/investamerica/logistics.asp, site visited April 23, 2008.

34. William Atkins, "Bob Willett: Just a Simple Shopkeeper," Inboundlogistics.com, January 2007.

35. "Wyndham Worldwide Launches Sweepstakes, Ad Campaign Featuring Arnold Palmer," Wyndham Worldwide Corporate News Release, May 28, 2007.

36. Pamela Ellis-Simmons, "Broadway Means Business," Special Advertising Section, Fortune, June 9, 1997, pp. 49–56.

37. "New World Coffee Tie-In Has a Split Personality," Nation's Restaurant News, July 24, 2000.

38. Jeffery Schmidt, Ph.D. dissertation, Michigan State University, 1996.

39. CIA World Factbook, www.cia.gov/library/publications/the-world-factbook/index.html, site visited April 23, 2008.

40. www.forestrysystems.com, Web site visited April 23, 2008.

41. www.starbucks.com, site visited April 23, 2008.

42. Kinichi Ohmae, The Borderless World (New York: Harper Business, 1990), pp. 17–31.

43. Roger J. Calantore, Daekwan Kim, Jeffery B. Schmidt, S. Tamer Clavusgil, "The Influence of Internal and External Firm Factors on International Product Adoption Strategy and Export Performance," Journal of Business Research, April 19, 2004.

44. Gillette Investor Factsheet, http://media.corporate-ir.net/media_files/irol/10/106746/factsheet/factsheet_0205.pdf, site visited April 23, 2008.

45. David A. Erickson, "Standardized Approach Works Well in Establishing Global Presence," Marketing News, October 7, 1996, p. 9.

46. www.kochoil.com, site visited April 23, 2008.

The Marketing Gazette:
"Growing a Better Future for Coffee," Kraft brochures, www.kraft.com,; "Rainforest Alliance – A New Approach to Marketing Sustainably Produced Coffee," "Coffee – From the Farm to the Cup," "Reducing Our Environment Impact," sites visited June 13, 2007.

CASE 2

Martha Stewart

Revitalizing a business is not easy. The "dominatrix of domesticity," the New York Times once called her. Some abhor her; some adore her. Like it or not, Martha Stewart's brilliant sense of publicity has people thinking about her—regularly. As with all great marketers, she saw a need, filled it with her formidable presence, and created an empire. It ranges from home improvement to interior design, gardening, cooking, entertainment, and more.

"Stewart is one of the best self-marketers in the industry," says Steve Cohn, editor of Media Industry Newsletter. "She's amazing—she appeals to ordinary women as well as upscale types." According to Mike McGrath, a fellow magazine editor, "In the great anonymous era, she connects with people." The president and CEO of Time, Inc., Don Logan, credits both the magazine Stewart created and her "tireless marketing, promotion, and publicity efforts" for her success.

Stewart's past successes includes 37 books, a daily Emmy Award–winning "how to" domestic arts television show, a daily culinary arts cable television program, a syndicated newspaper column entitled "Ask Martha," a daily radio spot, a mail-order business called Martha By Mail, a line of $110-a-gallon paints, three magazines, and marthastewart.com, which includes material from all other channels. She established other strategic merchandising relationships by distributing Martha Stewart products through Kmart, Sears, Zellers, and P/Kaufmann. In 1999, her company, Martha Stewart Living Omnimedia became publicly traded.

However, Stewart's success and image was marked by scandal in 2005 when she was sentenced to 5 months in prison and another 5 months of house arrest due to the sale of her ImClone Systems stock in late 2001 based on insider information. Consumers and fans were quick to forgive her and in 2006, Martha Stewart Living Omnimedia posted a 36 percent increase in revenue from the previous year. The resurgence of Martha Stewart Living Omnimedia has allowed the company to grow and leverage new ideas. The company has strategically created an integrated plan that is the envy of the industry. Each division is used to cross-promote the others which drastically reduces the cost of gaining new customers.

Kmart continues to be the company's most profitable merchandising relationship but recent expansions to other merchandising outlets is proving quiet beneficial. A broad range of the Martha Stewart Home Collection products are available exclusively at Macy's stores. Michael's craft stores now carry the Martha Stewart Crafts line which includes scrapbook and paper products. Also, a line of fresh, refrigerated and frozen foods called Kirkland Signature by Martha Stewart became available at Costco Wholesale stores in early 2008. "We are strategically expanding our merchandise assortments to new distribution channels in categories where we have strong brand equity. Our goal is to provide out customers with everything they need to decorate their homes in their own way with beautifully styled, higher-quality, Martha Stewart designs," said Robin Marino, President of Merchandising for Martha Stewart Living Omnimedia.

1. A differentiation strategy is based on delivering customer value in a way that clearly distinguishes the product from its competitors. Using what you've learned in this case, describe the differentiation strategy.

2. There are several ways to construct strategic business units. How does Martha Stewart Living Omnimedia structure its business units? What portfolio planning tools can be used to asses the effectiveness of the company's SBU's?

3. What low-cost strategies does Martha Stewart Omnimedia use to deliver savings to their customers?

Sources: Martha Stewart Omnimedia 2006 Annual Report, www.marthastewart.com ,February 25, 2008; James Mammarella, "Martha Stewart Aims for Profitability With New Programs.(Martha Stewart Living Omnimedia Inc.)(Financial report)," Home Textiles Today, InfoTrac OneFile, March 12, 2007: p6.; Krysten Crawford, "Martha: I cheated no one," CNN/Money www.cnnmoney.com, July 20, 2004.

CHAPTER 3

The Global Marketing Environment & E-Commerce

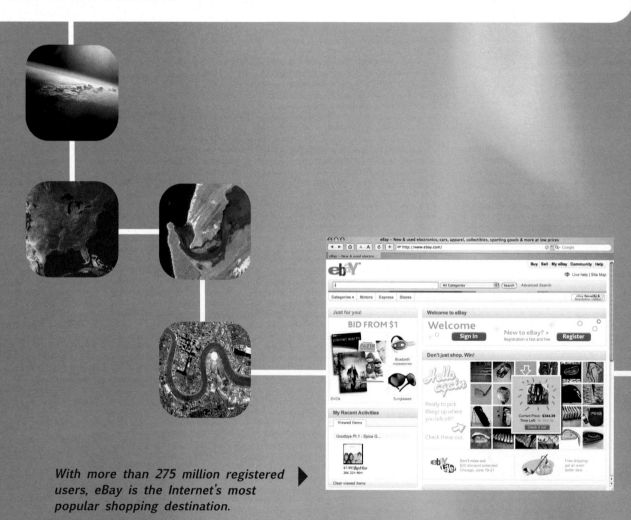

With more than 275 million registered users, eBay is the Internet's most popular shopping destination.

Learning Objectives

1. Describe the marketing environment and the use of environmental scanning.

2. Understand how the roles that stakeholders play influence the accomplishment of marketing objectives. Know why marketing must address stakeholder desires when making decisions.

3. Be able to integrate an understanding of industry competition into environmental analysis.

4. Synthesize aspects of the global macroenvironment, including technological, economic, demographic, cultural, and legal/regulatory elements in order to be in step with long-term trends

5. Recognize the importance of ethics and guides to ethical behavior.

6. Understand the impact that e-commerce is making on the global business environment and understand the structure of Internet marketing.

There was a time when finding an out-of-print Spice Girls Japanese import album was much more difficult, if not impossible. Today, nearly 300 million eBay users find what they're looking for in a matter of seconds. Users can find anything from out-of-print recordings and books, vintage car parts, and designer clothés to vampire killings kits, real shrunken heads, and pretzels shaped like the Virgin Mary.

Shortly after writing the code for what would become eBay, Founder Pierre Omidyar placed a broken laser pointer up for auction in late 1995 on the then-called AuctionWeb site. To his amazement, the item sold for nearly $15. Upon auction close, Omidyar contacted the buyer to ensure he understood that it was a broken laser pointer. When the buyer replied that he was a collector of broken laser pointers, Omidyar knew he was on to something big.

From the time of its first auction, eBay was built around core values that remain with the company today; the ideas that people are basically good, that everyone has something to contribute, and that an open environment brings out the best in people.

With more than 275 million registered users, eBay is the Internet's most popular shopping destination. Present in nearly 40 markets across the globe, more than $2,000 of goods is exchanged on eBay every second. At any given time, there are approximately 110 million items listed for auction, including almost anything you can think of. Thousands of items every day sell for $1 or less, while some sell for far more like a private business jet that was auctioned off for $4.9 million.

eBay is best known for its auctions, but many items sell at fixed prices. These fixed-price items account for more than 40 percent of gross merchandise volume. Many of these fixed-price items are sold by its more than 500,000 eBay stores across the world.

In the early days of eBay, payments to sellers were carried out primarily through money orders and personal checks. Mailing payments and waiting for checks to clear drastically slowed the transaction process. The invention of Web sites like Billpoint and PayPal that facilitate online payments and money transfers made paying sellers faster and easier. eBay acquired PayPal in 2002, and it has since become the preferred payment for eBay transactions.

With more than 160 million accounts around the world, PayPal allows users to make payments in 17 currencies using credit cards, bank accounts, buyer credit or account balances without sharing personal financial information. It offers no liability for unauthorized transactions, buyer protection on purchases up to $2,000, and a free dispute resolution process. This faster, easier, safer payment option has contributed to eBay's growing success.[1]

THE CONCEPT OF THE MARKETING ENVIRONMENT

Change abounds. It can be your friend or enemy depending on how it is handled. Some organizations are reactive—they do not adjust strategies until environmental changes have occurred. That can be dangerous, since it may be too late to construct a successful new strategy. Other organizations are proactive—they anticipate environmental changes and adjust ahead of time. A few organizations are so agile that they make appropriate changes precisely when environmental factors call for change. Agile organizations quickly take advantage of new opportunities and minimize or eliminate damage from negative changes. Connecting with customers is best accomplished with a agile philosophy because the forces that affect your organization are the same that affect customers. In fact, agile companies connect best. They are in step with their customers by being in step with the marketing environment. The **marketing environment** is the sum of all factors that affect a business. Figure 3.1 depicts the marketing environment surrounding our theme: connecting with customers. First is the microenvironment, then the all-encompassing global macroenvironment. You will learn about both in the following sections.

An organization does not operate in a vacuum. Many factors can have a dramatic influence. These create opportunities, but they can also prevent the company from pursuing its desired strategy. An organization must be sensitive to its surroundings. **Environmental scanning** collects and analyzes information in order to detect any trends that may affect a company's strategy. It can be performed by the company itself, by professional or industry associations, or by one of the numerous consulting organizations that special-

Figure 3.1 The Marketing Environment

(Global Macro Environment / Micro Environment / Creating & Capturing Value)

---

www.uspto.gov

Have an idea for a new green product or invention? Visit the U.S. Patent Office Web site for information on patenting your idea.

---

ize in forecasting.

Through scanning the environment, AT&T monitors technology capabilities and trends in order to deploy state of the art advances at precisely the time advances are ready for market application. AT&T is building a strategy around "three screens," which focus on delivering content in an integrated and familiar way to the three communication devices consumers value most - TV, PC and wireless phones. With cutting-edge technology, a TV show that you start watching at home can be continued on wireless devices on the train and in the office.[2] The Internet is an extraordinary environmental scanning tool. It enables marketers to investigate press releases, news stories, online magazines, journals, newspapers, and company Web sites highlighting product offerings, as well as technical and financial data. Even company strategies can be gathered from this public information by a skilled marketing analyst.

Getting information about competitors is much faster and easier on the Internet. The U.S. Bureau of the Census Web site (www.census.gov) provides demographic information, and online magazines such as American Demographics (www.demographics.com) identify cultural trends. When scanning for legal/regulatory information, marketers can check government sites for relevant material. For example, data on pending designs can be found at the U.S. Patent Office Web site (www.uspto.gov). The most authoritative sources for economic and demographic information about foreign countries are globalEdge™ (www.globaledge.msu.edu), the CIA (www.cia.gov) and Economist Intelligence Unit (www.eiu.com) Web sites. The Internet also offers research, surveys, and other means for studying Web user behavior and surfing habits. All this is used extensively to collect marketing information, which we will discuss in Chapter 4.

If you want help scanning,

Courtesy of Panera Bread

Panera's rapid growth in sales exceeded shareholders' expectations and drove the stock price higher.

plenty is available. Companies that specialize in competitive intelligence even offer subscriptions to access data they have assembled. GE Information Services (Global Exchange) and Factiva (a Dow Jones & Reuters Company) are two leading providers of these services.[3]

THE MICROENVIRONMENT

The **microenvironment** is made up of the forces close to the company that influence how it connects with customers. As you'll notice in Figure 3.2, stakeholders and industry competition are part of the microenvironment. Stakeholders, as the name suggests, have a stake in an organization. Companies deal with stakeholders daily. Marketers need to understand stakeholders, recognizing that marketing decisions affect them and are affected by their influence. Marketers need to have other parties' needs in mind. Competition is also a daily phenomenon. Competitors challenge your organization—sometimes you win, and sometimes they win. In either case, healthy competition is good because it stimulates change. Competitors, like stakeholders, must be considered in nearly every major marketing decision.

RELATIONSHIPS WITH STAKEHOLDERS

Any group or individual, other than competitors, who can influence or be influenced by an organization's actions is a **stakeholder**, including customers, owners, employees, suppliers, intermediaries, action groups, and many others. In the previous chapter we stressed the importance of building relationships with customers. In this chapter we stress building relationships with other stakeholders. Marketers form interactive, ongoing, two-way connections with stakeholders. They build these lasting relationships so that stakeholders will be a positive influence on the organization. Stakeholders can help serve customer needs and wants as well as help accomplish the objectives of the organization. Consequently, marketers try to act in the best long-term interest of all the firm's stakeholders. Because stakeholders have conflicting objectives, this can be difficult. Balanced score cards are used to set objectives that address the needs of all stakeholders. Let's examine some of these stakeholders.

Owners and Employees Whether public or private, an organization operates to benefit its owners, who establish its objectives. For companies, these objectives usually stress increasing the value of the business—making substantial profit. In nonprofit organizations, the objectives usually relate to benefiting constituents. For example, the beneficiaries of Greenpeace are people concerned about the environment. Shareholders have purchased, been given, or inherited a share of the business. Typically, owners either represent themselves or are represented by a board of directors, which is charged with the responsibility to speak for all the owners. Marketers need to understand the goals, risks, and reward levels acceptable to owners, who only invest in a company that continues to reach its objectives.[4] For example, Panera Bread Company had a 100 percent increase in stock price in a single year. It took an aggressive and somewhat risky market approach by introducing several new menu items and announcing plans to open 500 new stores. Panera continues to grow at an impressive rate and now operates over 1,000 bakery-cafes.[5] These actions produced results in line with shareholders' expectations so they were willing to pay more for the stock.

Employees are also key stakeholders. Their livelihood depends on the company. Since every employee helps create and deliver value to the end consumer, each

---

MICROENVIRONMENT

RELATIONSHIPS WITH STAKEHOLDERS
• Owners
• Employees
• Suppliers
• Intermediaries
• Action groups
• Others

COMPETITIVE INDUSTRY
• Competitors
• Competitive groups

Figure 3.2 The Microenvironment

employee has a very important influence on the organization. Companies that have happy employees are often rewarded with satisfied customers. It is hard to imagine a disgruntled employee being pleasant to customers. W. L. Gore & Associates, Inc., a top 100 company to work for, encourages hands-on innovation by involving those closest to a project in decision making. The founder, Bill Gore, created an organization with no chains of command nor pre-determined channels of communication. Employees are called "associates," which communicate directly with each other and are accountable to fellow members of multi-disciplined teams. Instead of bosses, "sponsors" guide associates to reach team objectives in an environment that combines freedom with cooperation and autonomy with synergy. "We work hard at maximizing individual potential, maintaining an emphasis on product integrity and cultivating an environment where creativity can flourish," says Terri Kelly, the company's new president and CEO. "A fundamental belief in our people and their abilities continues to be the key to our success, even as we expand globally."[6]

Suppliers and Intermediaries

Suppliers are stakeholders who provide a company with necessary services, raw materials, and components. Very few organizations can exist without suppliers, who also can be a major factor in creating customer satisfaction. For example, Ford relies on more than 2,000 production suppliers to provide many of the parts that are assembled into Ford vehicles. Another 9,000 suppliers provide a wide range of non-production goods and services, from production equipment to computers to advertising.[7] If you like the dashboard, seats, or electronics on the new Ford Flex, chances are a supplier worked with Ford to design it. Suppliers manufacture many of the components that go into vehicles—no matter what brand.

Since they specialize, suppliers are an excellent source of new technology and are likely to speed the introduction of the latest designs and techniques. They often provide expertise that helps companies compete in ways that would be impossible if they had to rely on their own resources. For example, until 1987, DuPont sold only adhesives to Reebok. Then DuPont technicians suggested that Reebok use a plastic tube technology, originally designed for the automobile industry. The tubes made Reebok shoes "bouncier" and were a hit with consumers. Chances are that Reebok never would have developed this technology on its own at the time. This single idea dramatically influenced the entire industry.

Companies rely on suppliers. When they have their own problems, it can mean trouble. Failure to develop and maintain good working relationships with suppliers can have consequences. Mattel recalled over 20 million toys in 2007 for hazardous levels of lead paint found on it's toys. If the company had more visibility with it's suppliers, the recall may have been avoided.[8]

Intermediaries are independently owned organizations that act as links to move products between producers and end users. They have an important influence on organizations because they dramatically extend the ability of marketers to reach customers at home and abroad. Book wholesalers and campus bookstores help publishers sell textbooks to students. Beverage manufacturers such as Gatorade, Dole, and Ocean Spray use intermediaries to deliver their goods to outlets that sell them to the final consumer. Chris-Craft, 4Winns, and Sea Ray market their watercraft through dealerships.

Some intermediaries specialize in international markets, using their unique skills and capabilities to give a company global reach. For example, an intermediary with special expertise in an emerging market may provide access to channels necessary to reach select customers. Companies that want to expand into untapped markets find intermediaries invaluable in delivering their product to the consumer. It is very beneficial for companies to establish solid working relationships with their intermediaries.

Leonardo DiCaprio is a strong advocate for global warming issues, and attended the Live Earth concert in support of the cause.

Action Groups

Action groups are stakeholders that support some cause in the interest of consumers or environmental safety. They act as "watchdogs," making sure that companies keep the interests of people and the environment in balance with those of profit. There are hundreds of action groups. A vocal and well-known environmental advocate, former Vice President Al Gore, is fighting to stop global warming and is calling for action through his Web site, AlGore.com. By signing a virtual postcard, you could help Al Gore take the message to congress. He is also the Chairman of the Board for the Alliance For Climate Protection which is on mission to persuade the the world of the importance and urgency of implementing comprehensive solutions for the climate crisis.[9] Many movie and television personalities lend their names and celebrity status to consumer or environmental causes like global warming. StopGlobalWarming.org has an impressive list of celebrity supporters including Jon Bon Jovi, Kobe Bryant, Reggie Bush, Sheryl Crow, Leonardo DiCaprio, Tony Hawk, Arnold Schwarzenegger, and Shaun White.[10] In July 2007, Al Gore introduced the "Live Earth - the Concerts for a Climate in Crisis" supported by many of the world's greatest entertainers and attended by millions on stages simultaneously synchronized globally.

Marketers are very aware of consumer groups that frequently criticize the pursuits of business. A marketer may have to make difficult decisions when there is a conflict between the desires of action groups and other stakeholders. When the Washington D.C. Center for Gay, Lesbian, Bisexual and Transgender People was found to be a member of Wal-Mart's affiliate program, The American Family Association initiated a national boycott, claiming that the deal suggests Wal-Mart executives believe "the homosexual agenda is worthy of their support." Nevertheless, Wal-Mart did not give in to protesters and said it forges business partnerships with many minority organizations to help it attract a diverse array of suppliers. While stressing its support for diversity and nondiscrimination, Wal-Mart said in its statement that it "will not make corporate contributions to support or oppose highly controversial issues unless they directly relate to our ability to serve our customers." In response to Wal-Mart's comments, The American Family Association later abandoned the boycott.[11]

Action groups can also help marketers gain positive publicity and may help business make a greater contribu-tion to society. Avon has gained publicity for it sponsors with action groups to fight breast cancer throughout the United States. For example, Avon supports a walk for breast cancer in many major cities each year. Along with the Avon Foundation, many other businesses support action groups intent on wiping out breast cancer in your lifetime.

INDUSTRY COMPETITION

The word *competition* brings to mind an image of two giant companies vying against each other; however, competition also involves companies of differing types and sizes. These companies, along with potential new companies, suppliers, and customers, form an industry structure that dictates the intensity of competition. Competitors may be individual companies or the industry as a whole.

The competitive environment can be marked by intense change, making it difficult to successfully launch a new product.[12] It is important companies assess the risks and ask the following questions: Who are the existing rivals? What new competitors may emerge? What is the relative strength of suppliers and buyers within the industry? Finally, what substitutes are likely to appear? The answers give a complete picture of the overall nature of competition within an industry. Figure 3.3 depicts the forces that shape the competitive environment.

Existing Firms As a marketer, you need a thorough understanding of each major competitor. This includes how each competes against your company and every other in the industry. You should examine each rival's strategy in terms of current and potential products, pricing, promotion, and distribution. You also should identify key customers and suppliers, the types of technologies used, current performance, and strengths and weaknesses. From all this information,

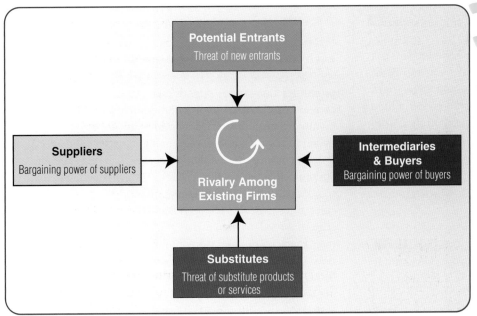

Figure 3.3 Forces Driving Industry Competition
Source: The Free Press, a division of Simon & Schuster, from Competitive Strategy: Techniques for Analyzing Industries and Competitors, by Michael Porter, Copyright 1980.

Marketing Vocabulary

SUPPLIERS
Organizations that provide a company with necessary services, raw materials, or components.

INTERMEDIARIES
Stakeholders who move products from the manufacturer to the final user.

ACTION GROUP
A number of people who support some cause in the interest of consumers or environmental safety.

the marketing manager attempts to determine the plans of every competitor and how every competitor will react to the marketer's actions.

Potential Competitors At any time a company may enter an industry with similar products. This is nothing new. Each year nearly a thousand new confectionery products debut in the candy industry, including about 200 for snack bars alone.[13] Competitors such as Snickers, Mars, and Almond Joy are clearly unhappy to see such an increase in competition; however, one advantage is that aggressive marketing by several companies will often draw attention to the product category and cause industry-wide sales to increase. Microsoft's entry into the MP3 market has required new strategies by the leader Apple (iPod), which responded with the iPhone. With its huge financial base and outstanding technological capabilities, Microsoft is now iPod's biggest rival.

Substitutes A **substitute product** is any good or service that performs the same function or provides the same benefit as an existing one. For example, who competes with Federal Express for overnight delivery of letters? If you said United Parcel Service (UPS), the U.S. Postal Service, Airborne Express, or other overnight delivery companies, then you are correct, but you probably left out two important ones: the fax machine and electronic mail.

Marketers should not limit their analysis to the same industry. Companies in other industries that make or develop substitutes may be an even greater competitive threat. For example, JPMorganChase, a successful marketer of financial services, faces such industry rivals as Merrill Lynch and Paine Webber but also experiences tough competition from insurance companies, banks, brokers, and others. Often information about substitutes can be found on the World Wide Web.

The Bargaining Power of Buyers and Suppliers Marketers must also ask which group—buyers or suppliers—has the most power in an industry. The answer affects both company strategy and competition. Generally, when there are many suppliers, buyers are the most powerful. Buyers can be more demanding when there are several competing suppliers. For example, Wal-Mart is powerful because there are fewer retailers than in the past and many, many small suppliers. Wal-Mart spends more than $200 billion annually on mer-

chandise through its 61,000 vendors.[14] If a vendor does not go along with Wal-Mart's policies, there are many others from which it can select.

When buyers are extremely plentiful, suppliers tend to be more powerful. Since demand is great, suppliers can negotiate contracts on their terms and generally command higher prices. A supplier has the most power when it offers a unique and superior good or service that buyers are clamoring to purchase.

THE GLOBAL MACROENVIRONMENT

Like stakeholders and industry forces in the microenvironment, the global macroenvironment also influences the company but indirectly. The **global macroenvironment** consists of large external influences considered vital to long-term decisions but not directly affected by the company itself. It is critical for marketers to identify, anticipate, and plan for the effect of those factors. Larger forces—each of which constitutes an environment in itself—tend to shift slowly, so they have long-term implications for the organization. Yet, they also affect day-to-day operations. Figure 3.4 lists the most important forces or environments—technological, economic, demographic, cultural, legal/regulatory, and ethical—that make up the global macroenvironment.

Constituents of the Global Macroenvironment
- Technological environment
- Economic environment
- Demographic environment
- Cultural environment
- Legal/regulatory environment
- Ethical environment

Figure 3.4 - The Global Macroenvironment

TECHNOLOGICAL ENVIRONMENT

As you know, technology is one of the five key elements in connecting with customers. The **technological environment** is the total body of knowledge available for use in developing, manufacturing, and marketing products. Companies spend huge sums each year to increase this body of knowledge. Merck Pharmaceutical Company, an industry leader, annually invests about $4 billion in research and development activities.[15] The government also plays a role. When the U.S. government announced a war against AIDS, it included federally sponsored studies on the disease. Several pharmaceutical companies used this research as the fundamental knowledge required to make patentable products. On their own, many companies would not make the uncertain and risky investment in AIDS research and development (R&D). Basic research is expensive and so time-consuming that it is often years or even decades before any revenue is received from product users.

A huge technological effect has resulted from microprocessor R&D. U.S. companies were the first to realize the importance of computers and made large investments in them. Today, leading computer companies spend several billion dollars on research and development annually! For instance, Intel Corporation spends over $6 billion on R&D alone.[16]

R&D has accelerated the rate of technological change. Products quickly become obsolete. The personal computer (PC) is an example. First introduced on a broad scale by Steve Jobs and Steve Wozniak in 1977, the PC is still evolving rapidly. Many of the first models used the same cassette technology for memory that were once used to record your favorite music. This quickly gave way to floppy disks, then hard disks, then compact discs, DVDs and USB flash drives. The world's first gigabyte disk drive, built in 1980, was the size of a refrigerator and cost $40,000. Today Apple easily packs a gigabyte into a MP3 player the size of a matchbook and sells it for less than $100. Processing capability is also growing phenomenally. At the end of the 1980s, Intel's 20 MHz chip offered state-of-the-art speed. Intel has now producing speeds of 2.93GHz with the evolutionary Intel Core 2 — which packs the power of two processor cores inside a single chip.[17] Obviously, changes such as these create great opportunities and challenges for companies.

"With new processes and technologies, you want to replace [your own product] instead of letting someone else do it," says Gary Tooker, former CEO of Motorola, adding that "success comes from a constant focus on renewal."[18] The rapid rate of change has important implications for businesses today. First, investment in R&D is critical to ensure you're not left behind by the competition. If a computer company cannot build a

www.motorola.com
Visit Motorola's Web site to learn how to recycle your old cell phone. You can also learn about how going green is affecting its global community, business units and products.

machine that processes information quickly and accommodates future additions, it will soon be as obsolete as its products. Second, companies must be creative in looking for future technologies. Microsoft Research (MSR) Asia, Microsoft's fundamental research arm in Asia Pacific, conducts fundamental curiosity driven research which cultivates groundbreaking technologies at the cusp of innovation. [19]

ECONOMIC ENVIRONMENT

The **economic environment** refers to financial and natural resources that are available to consumers, businesses, and countries. An understanding of consumer economic factors such as income, spending behavior, spending power, and wealth dispersion is essential in assessing opportunities that may emerge. Global marketers must also be familiar with the economic features of the world's major trading blocs.

Income and Spending Behavior It is said that only two things are certain in life: death and taxes. **Disposable income** is the money consumers have left after paying taxes, and many marketers prefer to use this as the measure of consumer wealth. People spend some of their disposable income on necessities, such as food, clothing, and shelter; anything left over is called **discre-**

Courtesy of Walmartfacts.com
Wal-Mart is a powerful buyer

Marketing Vocabulary

SUBSTITUTE PRODUCT
Any good or service that performs the same function or provides the same benefit as an existing one.

GLOBAL MACROENVIRONMENT
The large external influences considered vital to long-term decisions but not directly affected by the company itself.

TECHNOLOGICAL ENVIRONMENT
The total body of knowledge available for development, manufacturing, and marketing of products and services.

ECONOMIC ENVIRONMENT
The financial and natural resources available to consumers, businesses, and countries.

DISPOSABLE INCOME
The income consumers have left after paying taxes.

tionary income. Consumers may choose to spend all their discretionary income or may choose to save part of it. Marketers of nonessentials, such as vacation packages, jewelry, and stereos, focus on discretionary income, because that is how much consumers have available to purchase nonessential items.

No less important than the amount of income is the willingness, or propensity, to spend. The typical middle-income American family is spending more on luxury goods. According to the U.S. Bureau of the Census, the average income of the top fifth of households rose 38 percent in the last 10 years. Marketers have seized this opportunity to promote purchases of nonessential items, especially over the Internet.

Spending Power and Wealth Dispersion

Marketers must be careful not to equate a large population with a large marketing opportunity. An important consideration is **spending power**, or the ability of people to purchase goods and services. A common measure of spending power is the gross domestic product of a country. **Gross domestic product (GDP)** is the total market value of all final goods and services produced for consumption during a given period by a particular coun-

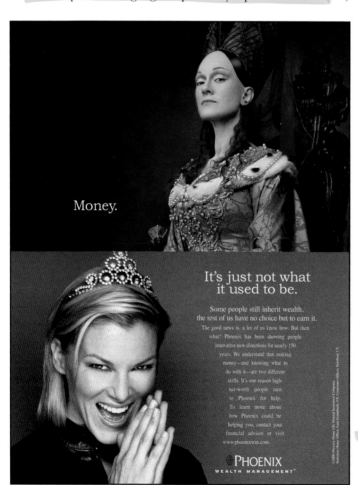

Consumers with high net worth are the target market for Phoenix Wealth Management Company.

try. The U.S. GDP is approximately $13.1 trillion followed closely by the European Union at $13.0 trillion. The next closest GDP is China ($10 trillion), followed by Japan ($4.2 trillion), and India ($4.1 trillion)[20]

When the GDP of every nation is added together, the gross world product (GWP) today is about $66 trillion. That figure is not spread equally among countries, however. India accounts for about 6 percent of GWP, China for about 15 percent, and the United States for about 20 percent. This figure is high, considering that the United States has only about 5 percent of the world's population. With 38 percent of the world's population, China and India contribute about 21 percent to GWP.[21]

Many marketers do not look solely at GDP because it does not indicate how much each person in the country has to spend. For example, Mexico and Sweden have approximately the same GDP, but we know that the standard of living is lower in Mexico than in Sweden. Because the population of Mexico is large, a smaller portion of GDP can be allocated to each inhabitant. Consequently, many marketers use GDP per capita (which means "per person") to assess the standard of living. It tells how well off, on average, each citizen of a country is.

Even GDP per capita has limitations because it ignores the dispersion of wealth within a country. Often there are a few rich people and many, many poor ones. In Brazil, for example, 46 percent of the wealth goes to the richest 10 percent of the population, whereas only 14 percent of the wealth goes to the poorest 50 percent. In the United States, approximately 28 percent is owned by the richest 10 percent, whereas 4.2 percent goes to the poorest 20 percent. In Japan and Poland, the dispersion of wealth is much more even.[22]

Trading Blocs The world's three major trading blocs—Europe, Pacific Rim, and North America—are shown in Figure 3.5. Often called the world's economic superpowers, they will compete for the mastery of international markets well into the 21st century. Combined, these three regions are responsible for about 80 percent of the world's economic activity. For example, customers in the superpower triad buy a great majority of all computers and consumer electronics. The triad contains over half a billion consumers with converging preferences. Among others, IBM, Motorola, and Gucci are found nearly everywhere in the triad. Today, each of these blocs is basically equal in terms of economic activity, but this will not be true if current trends hold. The Pacific Rim is growing the fastest, Europe next, then North America.

Despite their collective power, the triad's constituent economies are not without difficulties. Many of these countries have a mature economy, rising social welfare costs, an aging population, and escalating research and

NORTH AMERICA	EUROPE		PACIFIC RIM
Canada USA Mexico	France Spain Germany Denmark Great Britain Italy Austria Sweden Cypress Czech Republic Estonia Hungary Slovenia	Portugal Greece Ireland Luxembourg Belgium Netherlands Finland Latvia Lithuania Malta Poland Slovakia	South Korea Singapore Japan China
Combined GDP: $15.3 Trillion Combined population: 443,231,000 NAFTA (North American Free Trade Agreement)	Combined GDP: $13.0 Trillion Combined population: 490,426,000 EU (European Union)		Combined GDP: $15.5 Trillion Combined population: 1,502,883,000

Figure 3.5 The Three Superpower Trading Blocks

development costs.[23] Let's look at each of the trading blocs in more detail.

North America When the United States, Canada, and Mexico entered into the North American Free Trade Agreement (NAFTA), they created the largest single market in the world. The objective of this economic alliance is to make all three nations more competitive globally by combining their strengths. The United States and Canada have capital, skills, technology, and natural resources; Mexico has low-cost labor. Proponents of NAFTA believe efficient North American companies will be able to offer lower-priced products to consumers. Over all, the open market means removal of tariffs and other trade barriers, increased investment opportunities, stronger protection of intellectual property, and more environmentally sound business practices. Today the North American Free Trade Area boasts a total gross domestic product of over $13.7 trillion.[24]

NAFTA is not without critics. Companies will be more mobile, and some will go where labor is cheapest. If U.S. technology does not create enough high-paying jobs at home, U.S. workers will ultimately be fighting for low-paying jobs with fewer benefits.

Pacific Rim The Pacific Rim (PAC Rim), which comprises much of East Asia, is named for the ocean it borders. It is made up of Japan and the four "dragons"— South Korea, Singapore, Taiwan, and China, including Hong Kong—known for enormous manufacturing potential. Soon, depending on economic reform, Thailand, Malaysia, and Indonesia could also be included. Economic integration in the PAC Rim is based pure-ly on market forces, not a formal agreement such as NAFTA. Much of the growth in East Asia has been spurred by Japanese investors, such as Matsushita Electric, which has established 10 major operations in Southeast Asia since 1961.

East Asia has undergone explosive economic growth, although it has had a difficult economic period in the recent past. In their classic book, Megatrends 2000, authors Naisbitt and Aburdene call it the greatest economic expansion in world history—five times the rate of the Industrial Revolution. These economies, driven by export sales, have been growing three times faster than economies in the rest of the world, although today, with the exception of China, these economies are experiencing slower growth. Yet, China is having growth as its economy benefits from deregulation, the import of new technology, and a shift from farm labor to industrial jobs.[25] China is predicted to experience a 7 to 8 percent annual growth rate to 2010, making it the fastest-growing area in the region. Over all, experts project that the average income of Chinese citizens will double by 2010.[26]

These Asian nations are feeding their home markets with the net gain in money received from other economies, which is possible when a country exports more than it imports. The domestic markets are increasing in size as companies and workers earn more money. With cash reserves of several hundred billion dollars and personal wealth, large amounts of goods can be bought from other countries. In Japan, for instance, annual household savings amount to a hefty $6.6 trillion.[27] As a result, U.S. companies such as Starbucks, Toys "R" Us, and Gap are eager to expand into a Japanese market.[28]

Europe The European Union (EU) has occupied much of the news in Europe and has tremendous economic relevance in Europe and around the world. The European Union has the goal of eliminating barriers to the flow of people, goods, services, and money within the union. The objective is to restructure Europe economically so that it can better compete against the United States, Japan, and other developed nations. The EU members include Belgium, Bulgaria, Cyprus, France, Germany, Italy, Luxembourg, The Netherlands, Denmark, Romania, Ireland, The United Kingdom, Greece, Portugal, Spain, Austria, Finland, Sweden, Czech Republic, Estonia, Hungary, Latvia, Lithuania, Malta, Poland, Slovakia, and Slovenia, which outlines key EU directives.[29]

The **Maastricht Treaty** consists of 282 directives that eliminate border controls and customs duties; strengthen external borders; establish a single European currency; coordinate defense and foreign policy; unify product standards and working conditions; protect intellectual property; and deregulate many industries, including telecommunications, airlines, banking, and insurance. This will make it much easier to move products from one region to another. Eventually, a company will be able to create a more unified marketing strategy for all of the EU, whereas today its different market environments still have to be addressed.

General Agreement on Tariffs and Trade and the World Trade Organization In 1947, the General Agreement on Tariffs and Trade (GATT) was founded under the United Nations. GATT is responsible for many of the current trade agreements among its 132 members. This organization has successfully negotiated significant reductions in trade restrictions and import duties that countries would otherwise impose in their own self-interest. GATT has been successful in reducing import duties and tariffs from more than 40 percent in 1947 to less than 5 percent today. Today there are challenges in many areas of foreign trade such as foreign investment and intellectual property rights. In 1995, GATT was absorbed by the World Trade Organization (WTO), which will carry out the traditional role of GATT. The WTO deals with a broad range of issues, including pollution, tariffs, trade agreements, and trade disputes.

Natural Resources The availability of natural sources of wealth (such as timber or oil) within a given region or nation is an important economic factor. For example, the U.S. Pacific Northwest provides a rich source of timber for the paper and construction industries. Similarly, countries in the Middle East control approximately 65 percent of the world's crude oil. In both cases, natural resources provide income to the area's inhabitants. Natural resources also include minerals, plants, wildlife, water, salt, fish, and many others.

Resource availability affects a marketer's pricing strategy. If a company operates a large plant in an area where energy or raw materials are expensive, the cost of producing the product will be high, and its price must be set accordingly.

Marketers in quest of natural resources must balance these efforts against preservation of the environment. An example is the long struggle over drilling for oil in the Arctic National Wildlife Refuge. Environmentalists and locals claim that drilling in the refuge will destroy natural habitats, drive species to extinction and endanger the ancient traditions of the Inupiat Eskimos, while proponents of drilling argue it will boost the local economy, create jobs, and lessen our dependence on foreign oil.[30]

Environmental regulations also must be considered by marketers, since these may threaten current business practices or create new opportunities. For example, the Strategic Environment Initiative (SEI) recommends that the government provide tax breaks to companies using environmentally friendly technologies and levy high taxes on those using older, unsafe methods. Product and process innovations often enable companies to comply with environmental regulations. In the product area, for example, companies can retrofit antipollution devices or engineer more environmentally friendly designs. Many marketers are developing strategies with the environment in mind. When it became known that the chlorofluorocarbons (CFCs) released from aerosol cans were thinning the ozone layer, many companies switched to pump spray bottles. Due to environmental concerns, McDonald's discontinued its use of styrofoam sandwich containers.

DEMOGRAPHIC ENVIRONMENT

The **demographic environment** consists of the data that describe a population in terms of age, education, health, and so forth. Marketers examine such information to gain an understanding of current opportunities and discover trends that may indicate future opportunities. Some frequently studied demographics include population size and density, urbanization, and age structure.

Population There are about 6.4 billion people in the world, and there are expected to be over 9 billion by 2050.[31] If marketing opportunities were defined solely by population size, then the prospects would be bright indeed. Other opportunity indicators must be evaluated, however, such as the income available.

Population growth depends on the number of live births plus the number of immigrants entering a country. The birthrate, which is measured as the number of live births per 1,000 people, is increasing throughout the world, but the rate of increase has begun to slow. It's estimated that about 85 million people are added to the world population each year. This translates into about 233,000 births a day.[32] At the same time, advances in medicine and technology mean that people are healthier, and the number of deaths per 1,000 people is decreasing. The longer life spans combined with births result in an even larger world population.

Movement from one country to another redistributes the world's population, and the United States is gaining considerable numbers this way. Although U.S. laws have become more restrictive, immigration is still expected to contribute as much to U.S. population growth as will natural births. This will further diversify the ethnic makeup of the country. Experts predict that by 2010 the multicultural population will climb to one-third of the total U.S. population.[33]

The U.S. population is expected to grow to 338 million in 2025 and to 404 million in 2050. Nevertheless, the average annual growth rate is expected to decrease by nearly half from 1.1 percent in the 1990s to around .54 percent by 2045. This would be the lowest rate ever. The predicted decline is attributed to numerous factors, including the general aging of the population, increased age at first marriage, delayed childbearing, a growing proportion of childless couples, and the greater participation of women in the labor force.[34]

Density A country with a large population may seem to offer a large marketing opportunity, but it is important to know where those people live. **Population density** refers to the number of people within a standard measurement unit, such as a square mile. Canada has more than 32 million people but only 9.2 people, on average, per square mile. Yet, because 77 percent of Canadians live in a few large cities, such as Quebec and Toronto, large areas of the country are quite sparsely populated. Singapore's population of 3.5 million is highly concentrated, with an average of almost 6,000 people per square kilometer. Where people are located within a country is also important. When they are concentrated, it's easier and more cost-effective to reach them with advertising campaigns and products. When they are spread out, marketing can be difficult, time-consuming, and expensive. Consider the Pacific Rim countries, where many more people live in the coastal regions than inland. Much the same is true of Australia with its sparsely populated Outback. Imagine the task of delivering products to consumers in these areas. Organizations are likely to focus marketing efforts on densely populated areas.

Urbanization **Urbanization** refers to the population shift from rural areas to cities. Many countries have a high proportion of urban population. About half of the world's population lives in an urban area. This is higher in some countries than in others. In Germany, for example, 86 percent of the population lives in urban areas; in Singapore, 100 percent.[35] In the United States, four out of five people live in or near a city. Nearly 40 percent of the U.S. population is concentrated in the 20 largest metropolitan areas. At the top are New York City (8.08 million), Los Angeles (3.7 million), and Chicago (2.8 million).[36] Urbanization is significant to marketers for three important reasons. First, as noted earlier,

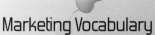

Marketing Vocabulary

MAASTRICHT TREATY
Consists of 282 directives that eliminate border controls and customs duties among members of the European Union.

DEMOGRAPHIC ENVIRONMENT
The statistical data used to describe a population.

POPULATION DENSITY
The concentration of people within some unit of measure, such as per square mile or per square kilometer.

URBANIZATION
The shift of population from rural to urban areas.

Atlanta is an example of a city experiencing rapid urban growth.

©iStockphoto.com/Jeremy Edwards

it is easier to reach a concentrated population. Second, as a group, people in cities tend to have enough income to purchase luxuries and support the arts, such as opera or theater. Third, people in urban areas tend to demand a wider variety of products than do rural inhabitants.

When the city population spills into the suburbs, neighboring cities may eventually join together. The U.S. Bureau of the Census uses the following to categorize urban concentrations. A **Metropolitan Statistical Area (MSA)** is a stand-alone population center, not linked to other cities, with more than 50,000 people. Examples are San Antonio, Texas; Montgomery, Alabama; and Spokane, Washington. A **Consolidated Metropolitan Statistical Area (CMSA)** is two or more overlapping urban communities with a combined population of at least 1 million. An example is the area that includes New York City, northern New Jersey, and southwestern Connecticut, with 20.1 million people.

Age Structure   Because generations differ in their tastes, age-related marketing research has become popular. An **age cohort** is a group of people close in age who have been shaped by their generation's experience with the media, peers, events, and the larger society. Often these cohorts are divided into four groups. "Matures" were born between 1909 and 1945, "baby boomers" between 1946 and 1964, "Generation Xers" between 1965 and 1976, and those of "Generation Y" thereafter. Research reveals substantial differences among them in values, tastes, and needs.

Globally, the average age is less than 25 years and declining. For example, because the Mexican population is growing rapidly, it is getting younger on average. In many industrialized nations, however, the picture is different. Children constitute a declining proportion of the German population, which is aging slowly but is older than the U.S. population. In less than 25 years, over one-fourth of all Japanese will be over age 65. Today the median age in the United States is 36.27; by 2030, the average age will be more than 40 years, and about 20 percent of the population will be age 65 or older. This is partly due to the baby boom after World War II, which will affect U.S. demographics for many years. The U.S. age distribution varies according to race. About 80 percent of Americans are Caucasian, but that percentage increases with age. Among the 12.9 percent of all Americans who are African American, nearly 15 percent are under age 10. Fourteen percent of Americans are Hispanic, and 20 percent of them are under age 10.[37]

Now that U.S. baby boomers are migrating into sen-ior-life status, when spending power is substantial, marketers are focusing on older consumers. Thousands of products already are being marketed to help them look and feel their best—such as Oil of Olay moisturizing cream, Just for Men hair coloring, Centrum Silver multivitamins, NordicTrack cardiovascular fitness equipment, and Weight Watcher foods. In fact, Just for Men based an entire promotional campaign on this concept. Targeting men 35 to 54 years old, Just for Men unveiled a new ad campaign with former Washington Redskins quarterback Joe Theismann as its spokesman. Theismann pitched the product in men's lifestyle and sports magazines such as *Men's Health, Sports Illustrated, and Playboy*. "We've been marketing to baby boomers for 40 years," says Dominic Demain, a company spokesman. "We recognize this generation of men is different from their fathers."[38]   In the years ahead, marketers will face the growing task of serving an aging market and addressing its unique concerns.

CULTURAL ENVIRONMENT

The **cultural environment** consists of the learned values, beliefs, language, symbols, and behaviors shared by people in a society and passed on from one generation to the next. Culture includes morals, values, customs, traditions, folkways, myths, and norms. It also includes religion, laws, economics, history, family structure, knowledge, food customs, art, music, and technology. These and other characteristics distinguish one society from another. They define the way we think about ourselves and the world, what we want, and how we behave. Marketers must be in step with the cultural environment because it helps them to make stronger connections with diverse customers.

Most people are socialized to be part of the culture in which they grow up. The socialization process is so strong that marketers may rely unconsciously on their own values when trying to understand another culture. This is called the **self-reference criterion**. But what we do may not be acceptable elsewhere. For example, most people in the United States would not think twice about eating a candy bar as they walk down the street, but in Japan this is bad manners. In China, when people approach a bus, the first person is expected to buy tickets for the group. It is easy to embarrass yourself and others in a foreign culture unless you take the time to understand it.

Because of people's tendency to use the self-reference criterion, it's often difficult to assess opportunities in other countries—but global success requires precisely

©iStockphoto.com/David Freund

Xtreme sporting events often attract advertisers wanting to appeal to the Generation X and Y cohorts.

that. McDonald's targets the same audience around the world—young families with children—but the basic concept must be "translated" into local conditions. Beer is on the German menu. In India, where cows are considered sacred, McDonald's markets the Maharaja Mac made of two all-mutton patties plus the usual toppings. Understanding different cultures has helped McDonald's establish itself in the new global market.

In a classic article, Edward Hall notes that perceptions of time, space, things, friendships, agreements, and negotiations cause the greatest misunderstanding between people of different cultures.[39] If you do not recognize these differences and address them, then you will almost certainly fail to connect in the global marketplace.

Perceptions of Time It's extremely important to consider a culture's perception of time, which communicates several subtle points. For example, in some cultures the most significant decisions are given the greatest amount of time. In contrast, Americans tend to operate within deadlines, and time is a scarce resource to be used efficiently. In the United States, if visitors are kept waiting, then they infer that they are unimportant. In a Latin culture, this is not the case; schedules are not rigid, and time is seen as a resource that can be used more flexibly. More recently, many Latin American countries have redefined time for business. In some cultures, a very long time may pass between customer awareness of a product and the actual purchase. Marketers need to plan a longer time frame for recapturing the investment in new-product development. In cultures in which decisions are made quickly, this time frame may be much shorter.

Size and Space In the United States, size is equated with importance; the larger and taller a building, the

www.mcdonalds.com

Learn more about what McDonald's restaurants around the world are doing to manage energy use, combat litter and promote recycling.

greater the degree of status represented. The dean of a college of business is likely to be located in a spacious office on the top floor; the university president is likely to have a larger office in a taller building. In contrast, the French try to place important executives close to the scene of action, where their influence can be most strongly felt. Thus, a remote office is not equated with high status, but quite the opposite.

The distance between people during conversations also can be culturally related. In many Latin cultures, people stand close and even touch while talking. To communicate friendship, they may come to within two or three inches of one another, whereas an interpersonal space of three to five feet is considered acceptable to most people in the United States. To Latins, that great a distance could be a sign of rejection. Marketers must be sensitive to space. For example, in promotional materials, the wrong interpersonal distance among the actors or models could deliver the wrong message.

Negotiations and Agreements Business agreements may have different meanings in various parts of the world. In highly legalistic cultures, they must be written and signed prior to acceptance. In other cultures, legal documents are viewed as inconveniences; more important is a meeting of the minds, sealed with a handshake. When people in the United States consult a lawyer, visit a

Marketing Vocabulary

METROPOLITAN STATISTICAL AREA (MSA)
A stand-alone population center, unlinked to other cities, that has more than 50,000 people.

CONSOLIDATED METROPOLITAN STATISTICAL AREA (MSA)
Two or more overlapping urban communities with a combined population of at least 1 million.

AGE COHORT
A group of people close in age who have been shaped by their generation's experience with the media, peers, events, and society at large.

CULTURAL ENVIRONMENT
The learned values, beliefs, language, symbols, and patterns of behavior shared by people in a society and passed on from generation to generation.

SELF-REFERENCE CRITERION
The unconscious reliance on values gained from one's own socialization when trying to understand another culture.

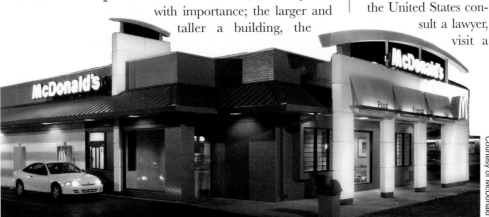

Courtesy of McDonald's

McDonald's has established itself in the global market by understanding different cultures.

doctor, or take a taxi, they assume the charge will be at the going rate. This is not the case in many cultures. For example, in the Middle East, it's best to settle the charge in advance or the person providing the service is likely to set an arbitrary price. This can be important knowledge when developing a pricing strategy for your products. Whereas a predetermined price is expected in the United States, bartering is part of the social process elsewhere, and a preset price upsets or offends consumers.

The Marketing Gazette™

CREATING & CAPTURING VALUE THROUGH GLOBAL RELATIONSHIPS

McDonald's Is Global

Imagine this scenario. After a long day of work or play, a grumbling in your stomach draws your car into the nearest McDonald's. Relishing the familiar McDonald's atmosphere, you choose a supersized Big Mac value meal or another favorite. The crewmember passes you your food and change, and you find a booth to enjoy your meal. It's a typical scene that we've all been through, but now you can replay it in over 119 countries around the world and on every continent but Antarctica. The hamburger is no longer simply an American food.

McDonald's has forged relationships with the world built on the enduring images of Big Macs, Ronald, and the Golden Arches. How do you make a hamburger a global icon?

McDonald's believes that the customers' experience is critical to business success and growth. In a recent statement to shareholders, Michael R. Quinlan, chairman and chief executive officer of McDonald's, admits that "by focusing on adding restaurants, we took our eye off the basics that made us famous—quality, service, cleanliness, and value." So now McDonald's has three priorities. The first is to improve restaurant operations. The second is to reopen the value gap against competitors by offering the best prices for the total dining experience. The third is to strengthen relationships with franchisees and energize employees. These are all part of a strategy to improve customer satisfaction and enhance loyalty.

McDonald's is a global corporation, and almost half of its 30,000 franchises are located outside the United States. Internationally, service consistency is maintained while modifying products to meet local needs and tastes. In India, the Maharaja Mac replaces the traditional Big Mac's two all-beef patties with mutton, out of respect for the Hindu faith. Also, vegetarian items are offered on a separate menu that is color-coded for simplicity. In Malaysia and many Middle Eastern countries, food is prepared within Muslim guidelines, and in China customers can enjoy localized tastes such as Szechuan-style spicy chicken wings, seafood soup, rice, oriental sauces, and taro and red bean desserts. Many restaurants have decided to follow McDonald's lead into the global eatery environment. Rivals Burger King, Wendy's, and Subway have branched out into foreign countries, and even the "all-American" Applebee's has chosen to alter its menu and strategy to accommodate locations in Kuwait and on the Nile River! "A global strategy is imperative if corporations want to increase revenue bases and defend competitive positions against domestic and foreign-owned [rivals]," says Paul Hazlinger, president of a globally focused Phoenix consulting firm. McDonald's used the global advertising opportunity of a lifetime at the Millennium Olympic Games in Sydney, Australia, to promote its product to customers all over the world. Now as the "Official Restaurant" of the Olympic games, McDonald's has a goal of operating 1,000 restaurants in China before the 2008 Olympics in Beijing.

McDonald's activities, both within its restaurants and in communities around the world, are focused on creating customer satisfaction. This emphasis on customer value and satisfaction has provided McDonald's with a competitive advantage and a way to make a hamburger not just a hamburger, but an institution.

Consumer Products Safety Commission (CPSC)
• Enforces regulations to protect consumers from being harmed by products.
Environmental Protection Agency (EPA)
• Regulates business actions to prevent damage to the environment.
Federal Communication Commission (FCC)
• Regulates communications on telephone, radio, television, and other aspects including allocations of frequencies.
Federal Trade Commission (FTC)
• Enforces laws to prevent unfair or deceptive marketing practices.
Food and Drug Administration (FDA)
• Enforces laws to maintain safety in food and drug products.

Figure 3.6   Federal Agencies Regulating Marketing

Marketing Vocabulary

LEGAL/ REGULATORY ENVIRONMENT
International, federal, state, and local regulations and laws, the agencies that interpret and administer them, and the court system.

CARTEL
A group of businesses or nations that work together to control the price and production of a particular product.

LEGAL/REGULATORY ENVIRONMENT

The **legal/regulatory environment** is composed of international, federal, state, and local regulations and laws, the agencies that interpret and administer them, and the court system. It also includes the ethical standards and theories that guide marketing decisions. This environment reflects long-standing political and economic philosophies and varies dramatically from one country or region to another. It indicates the general outlook of government toward business practices and ethical issues as well as how cooperative it is likely to be in meeting the requests of business. It also includes the effect that legal/regulatory decisions can have on an organization, individuals, and society as a whole.

In the United States, several agencies are charged with the responsibility of regulating businesses to conform with the intentions of major laws. Among the most important are those listed in Figure 3.6. These agencies must interpret laws and develop policies and procedures to gain compliance. In some cases, the agency gives guidelines so businesses can self-regulate. Those businesses that step out of line may be taken to court by the agency. In other cases, the agency provides approval prior to marketing actions. For example, the Food and Drug Administration (FDA) must approve all drugs prior to their release in the United States.

Although the U.S. legal and regulatory sphere covers hundreds of specific practices, for our purposes these can be divided into four basic types: laws promoting competition, laws restricting big business, laws protecting consumers, and laws protecting the environment.

U.S. Laws Promoting Competition During the 1800s and early 1900s, a few U.S. enterprises grew to the point of monopoly. Companies such as Standard Oil and Pennsylvania Railroad could exercise economic control over smaller firms, in many cases forcing them into bankruptcy by temporarily lowering prices. In 1890, due to a strong political movement led by midwestern farmers, Congress passed the Sherman Antitrust Act, which prohibits business practices designed to create monopolies or restrict trade across state lines or internationally. The Sherman Antitrust Act is extremely important because it laid the foundation for many laws that followed. The premise behind the legislation is that fair competition allows more companies to serve the market, which in turn keeps prices down and provides a greater number of choices to consumers. As you can see from Figure 3.7, many laws since 1890 are designed to ensure fair competition.

Sherman Antitrust Act (1890)
Outlaws monopolies and any business practice that restricts interstate or international commerce.
Federal Trade Commission Act (1914)
Declares as unlawful "unfair methods of competition in or affecting commerce, and unfair or deceptive acts or practices in or affecting commerce."
Clayton Act (1914)
Prohibits mergers and acquisitions that may "substantially lessen competition or tend to create a monopoly"; outlaws tie-in and exclusive dealing arrangements; allows violators to be held criminally liable.
Robinson-Patman Act (1936)
Developed primarily to protect small retailers. Amends the Clayton Act. Makes it illegal to sell "commodities of like grade and quality" to competing buyers at different prices if it will restrict competition. Also makes it illegal knowingly to receive an illegal price break.
Miller-Tydings Act (1937)
Protects interstate fair-trade (price fixing) agreements from antitrust prosecution.
Wheeler-Lea Act (1938)
Outlaws the pursuit of unfair or deceptive practices or actions.
Antimerger Act (1950)
Prevents corporate acquisitions or mergers that may substantially reduce competition.

Figure 3.7 U.S. Laws Promoting Competition

U.S. Laws Affecting Company Size The U.S. approach to competition has tended to restrict company size and power. The Federal Trade Commission (FTC) has explored numerous accusations of monopolistic control. For example, Electronic arts, the software company behind many popular video games, proposed an acquisition of Take-Two, another video game maker. The proposal underwent review by the FTC for possible monopolistic activity in the video game market.[40]

Some countries promote monopoly. Many have laws that favor cartels, which are outlawed in the United States. A **cartel** is a group of businesses or nations working together to control the price and output of a particular product. The U.S. government has recognized that laws intended to provide a fair environment for domestic competition may hamper U.S. companies competing globally. Put simply, they may be too small and lack the competitive strength to take on global rivals. In the late 1970s, the Department of Justice began to change its enforcement of traditional antitrust laws. It now permits business cooperation that would have been outlawed in the past.

U.S. Laws Protecting Consumers Recall that the early economic philosophy in the United States was typically caveat emptor, "Let the buyer beware." Essentially, consumers were responsible for protecting themselves against the unscrupulous acts of sellers. The Pure Food and Drug Act (1906) and the Meat Inspection Act (1906) were the first attempts to protect consumers. For four decades, regulations concentrated on making the food supply safe. Laws then were extended to other products, such as automobiles and toys. Eventually, laws were passed to protect consumers from misleading advertising and deceptive labeling.

By 1960, the consumer movement was so powerful

Pure Food and Drug Act (1906)
Regulates the manufacture and labeling of food and drugs.

Meat Inspection Act (1906)
Permits federal inspection of companies selling meat across state line and allows for enforcement of sanitary standards.

Lanham Trademark Act (1946)
Outlaws misrepresentation of goods and services sold across state lines; forces trademarks to be distinctive.

Automobile Information Disclosure Act (1958)
Forces auto manufacturers to disclose the suggested retail price of their new cars, which keeps car dealers from inflating prices.

National Traffic and Safety Act (1958)
Provides a set of automobile and tire safety standards.

Fair Packaging and Labeling Act (1966)
Permits the FTC and FDA to create standards for packaging and labeling content.

Child Protection Act (1966)
Makes illegal the sale of dangerous toys and children's articles as well as products creating a thermal, mechanical, or electrical danger.

Federal Cigarette Labeling and Advertising Act (1967)
Requires cigarette manufacturers to label cigarettes as dangerous. Outlaws use of television media for cigarette advertisements.

Truth-in-Lending Act (1968)
Also called the Consumer Credit Protection Act. Forces lenders to disclose in writing, before the credit transaction: (1) the actual cash price, (2) the required down payment, (3) how much cash is being financed, (4) how much the loan will actually cost, (5) estimated annual interest rate, and (6) penalty for late payments or loan default.

Fair Credit Reporting Act (1970)
Allows consumers to see free of charge a copy of their credit report. Forces credit reporting agencies to remove any false information. Protects the confidentiality of the consumer.

Consumer Product Safety Act (1972)
Created the Consumer Product Safety Commission. It collects and disperses information on all consumer goods except automobiles, food, and a few others. It also has the authority to develop and enforce product standards, when deemed necessary.

Consumer Goods Pricing Act (1975)
Prevents retailers and manufacturers from entering into certain types of price maintenance agreements.

Magnuson-Moss Warranty/FTC Improvement Act (1975)
Requires the company or individual who offers a warranty to explain fully what the warranty covers and what its limitations are. This information allows consumers to file a lawsuit if the warranty is breached.

Equal Credit Opportunity Act (1975)
Forces creditors to disclose the reason for any credit denial. Credit connot be denied on the basis of sex, marital status, race, national origin, region, age, or receipt of public assistance.

Fair Debt Collection Practice Act (1978)
Prohibits debt collectors from using harassment, abuse, or deceit when collecting a debt.

Toy Safety Act (1984)
Allows the government immediately to remove dangerous toys from the market.

Figure 3.8 Consumer Protection Laws

that President Kennedy issued the Consumer Bill of Rights, which guaranteed consumers

1. The right to choose freely from a variety of goods and services.
2. The right to be informed about specific products and services so that responsible purchase decisions can be made.
3. The right to be heard when voicing opinions about products and services offered.
4. The right to be safe from defective or harmful products and services when used properly.

The idea was to impress upon marketers that consumers were not solely responsible for assessing the quality of a product, its safety, and the honesty of the marketer's claim. In 1959, the FTC held a landmark conference at which consumer action groups and businesses discussed harmful practices. This activity led to the FTC assuming responsibility for the enforcement of truth-in-packaging and truth-in-lending laws. The FTC tackled tobacco advertising, forcing manufacturers to include a strong warning about the dangers of cigarette smoking in ads and on packages. Shortly thereafter, the Supreme Court ruled it illegal to create advertising gimmicks that would mislead the public or exaggerate product benefits.

Today the FTC and the FDA aggressively focus on the tobacco industry. In the late 1990s, the FTC investigated the R. J. Reynolds Tobacco Company for unfair advertising with its Joe Camel campaign, allegedly aimed at minors. The campaign was part of the industry's $4.8 billion annual expenditure on ads and promotions.[41] R. J. Reynolds agreed to drop the Joe Camel cartoon figure from such items as hats, lighters, bags, and T-shirts. In addition, R. J. Reynolds will not use Joe Camel in billboard advertising or in the sponsorship of entertainment events. Recently two other tobacco companies, Phillip Morris and Brown & Williamson, agreed to reduce cigarette advertising in magazines read by teens. All told, the companies pulled ads from 42 magazines with more than 2 million readers under 18 years of age.[42] The FTC also examines the Internet for tobacco and alcohol Web sites that may violate advertising guidelines.

There are numerous consumer protection laws, and marketers need to know the ones affecting their company. Consumer safety legislation has a direct effect on important marketing decisions, such as product design, label information and design, and advertising claims. Interest in consumer safety has resulted in the development of seat belts, air bags, shatterproof windshields, antilock brakes, food labels, air quality standards, gasoline restrictions, and others. Consider the effect of air bags on marketing in the auto industry. Although air bags have saved approximately 17,000 lives

since 1990, they have caused at least 256 deaths, 135 of whom were children.[43] As a result, Ford Motor Company was the first to introduce less forceful air bags in 1998. Starting in the 2006 model year, all passenger cars and light-duty trucks must be equipped with sensors that identify children and very small adults and deploy the airbag with less force or not at all. The new Buick Lucerne has new airbag technology that deploys the front airbags not just with less force but also in a smaller size depending on the size and location of the occupant.[44] Figure 3.8 lists several of the most important consumer protection laws.

U.S. Laws Protecting the Environment By the early 1960s, it was clear that the world's natural resources were being consumed as if the supply were endless. The most basic resources—air and water—were often so polluted that they were unfit to sustain life. Although little was done internationally, the U.S. Congress enacted the National Environmental Policy Act in 1969 to direct environmental protection activities. The following year, the Environmental Protection Agency (EPA) was formed so that one agency would be responsible for enforcing all federal environmental regulation.

U.S. companies are required to make adequate disclosure of potential environmental liabilities. The EPA maintains that those responsible for environmental contamination must pay for the cleanup and subsequently protect citizens' health. The EPA's Water Alliances for Volunteer Efficiency (WAVE) seeks to encourage commercial businesses and institutions to reduce water consumption while simultaneously increasing efficiency, profitability, and competitiveness. WAVE is a part of EPA's long-standing effort to prevent pollution and reduce demand on America's water and energy infrastructure.[45]

Environmental groups such as the Audubon Society, Greenpeace, and the Sierra Club have drawn attention to

Organizations like Greenpeace increase awareness of the need to protect our environment.

©iStockphoto.com/Elianet Ortiz

numerous environmental disasters and are active participants in finding remedies and developing legislation.

ETHICAL ENVIRONMENT

Questions of ethics are not always straightforward. What is acceptable in one part of the world may not be in another. In many countries bribery is regarded as highly unethical, but in others it is considered standard business practice. There is an important difference between what is legal and what is ethical. To determine legality, you must examine the relevant law. If the meaning is unclear, then a court may have to interpret it. Without a precedent, you may have to assess whether the action would be deemed legal or illegal.

Ethical issues are not so easily defined. Is it ethical for a pharmaceutical company to charge a price for a new drug that is much higher than the cost to produce it? After all, the company has poured millions into R&D and is trying to recoup its investment. Yet the high price makes the drug unaffordable to many people who desperately need it. Is the drug company acting unethically?

The matrix in Figure 3.9 shows that marketing decisions may fall into one of four categories: legal and ethical, illegal and ethical, legal and unethical, or illegal and unethical.

The appropriate behavior is easy to assess when the proposed action is clearly legal and ethical or clearly illegal and unethical. In the first case you do it, in the second you do not. However, neither legality nor ethics are always clear. What is legal and ethical may also be open to different interpretations. So marketers must be sensitive to both legal and ethical issues.

Perhaps the most difficult circumstances occur when legal and ethical standards conflict. Some people place more weight on the ethical side ("Should we do it?"), while others emphasize

	Legal	**Illegal**
Ethical	Market FDA-approved cold medicine	Market a safe AIDS vaccine not yet approved by the FDA
Unethical	Market a harmful drug banned by the FDA in a country with no drug review agencies	Market contraband drugs

Figure 3.9   Ethics Situations

the legal ("Can we do it?"). Many people believe it is best to avoid altogether any actions that are either potentially illegal or unethical. Most laws that affect business are interpreted in the courts, which set precedents to be followed. Every legislative session creates new laws that lead to new regulations, which often require new court decisions to set new precedents. So even legal and illegal issues may stretch along a continuum.

Many companies have developed written guidelines

Members of the American Marketing Association (AMA) are committed to ethical professional conduct. They have joined together in subscribing to this Code of Ethics embracing the following topics:

Responsibilities of the Marketer
Marketers must accept responsibility for the consequences of their activities and make every effort to ensure that their decisions, recommendations, and actions function to identify, serve, and satisfy all relevant publics: customers, organizations, and society.

Marketers' professional conduct must be guided by:
1. The basic rule of professional ethics: not knowingly to do harm;
2. The adherence to all applicable laws and regulations;
3. The accurate representation of their education, training, and experience; and
4. The active support, practice, and promotion of this Code of Ethics.

Honesty and Fairness
Marketers shall uphold and advance the integrity, honor, and dignity of the marketing profession by:
1. Being honest in serving consumers, clients, employees, suppliers, distributors, and the public;
2. Not knowingly participating in conflict of interest without prior notice to all parties involved; and
3. Establishing equitable fee schedules, including the payment or receipt of usual, customary, and/or legal compensation for marketing exchanges.

Rights and Duties of Parties in the Marketing Exchange Process
Participants in the marketing exchange process should be able to expect that:
1. Products and services offered are safe and fit for their intended uses;
2. Communications about offered products and services are not deceptive;
3. All parties intend to discharge their obligations, financial and otherwise, in good faith; and
4. Appropriate internal methods exist for equitable adjustment and/or redness of grievances concerning purchases.

It is understood that the above would include, but is not limited to, the following responsibilities of the marketer.

Continued

Figure 3.10 American Marketing Association Code of Ethics
Source: Courtesy of the American Marketing Association.

for employees. This helps ensure that everyone in the company is following the same set of ethical standards. The American Marketing Association also has a code of ethics, shown in Figure 3.10. Notice that the code goes beyond stating simply "Follow the law." It impresses upon marketers the importance of being honest and acting with integrity. It covers basic responsibilities, including a code of conduct and the importance of fairness. It describes what a customer should be able to expect from an exchange. It also describes ethical dimensions in the areas of product, promotion, place, and price—as well as in marketing research and relationships with others.

MARKETING E-COMMERCE

Internet marketing can be divided into two sectors. **Business-to-consumer (B2C) e-commerce** is trade involving businesses selling to consumers over the Internet. Business-to-business (B2B) e-commerce is trade involving Internet sales in which businesses sell to other businesses, including governments and organizations. Marketing is extremely important to both sectors.

Although purchasing on the Web was nonexistent in 1993, within ten years online sales reached nearly $1.7 trillion. The business-to-business sector has posted the largest gains and today consists of 94 percent of all e-commerce. Today this kind of e-commerce totals nearly $2 trillion, which is 19 percent of the U.S. business-to-business market and is growing each year. Before long, a very large percentage of all business-to-business trade in the world will involve e-commerce in some way.

The U.S. consumer retail e-commerce sales (e-sales) has soared to $86 billion and increasing at a rate of about 25 percent a year. Although retail e-sales account for only about two percent of total retail sales, the rate of increase is strongly outpacing the total retail sales growth of four percent.[46] Online shopping, especially during the holiday seasons, is expected to continue to see a sizeable growth. Fueling this growth is the expansion of high-speed internet access. Today, over 60 percent percent of U.S. Internet users now have broadband access at

---

In the Area of Product Development and Management:
- Disclosure of all substantial risks associated with product or service usage;
- Identification of any product component substitution that might materially change the product or impact on the buyer's purchase decision;
- Identification of extra-cost added features.

In the Area of Promotions:
- Avoidance of false and misleading advertising;
- Rejection of high pressure manipulations, or misleading sales tactics;
- Avoidance of sales promotions that use deception or manipulation.

In the Area of Distribution:
- Not manipulating the availability of a product for purpose of exploitation;
- Not using coercion in the marketing channel;
- Not exerting undue influence over the reseller's choice to handle a product.

In the Area of Pricing:
- Not engaging in price fixing;
- Not practicing predatory pricing;
- Disclosing the full price associated with any purchase.

In the Area of Marketing Research:
- Prohibiting selling or fund raising under the guise of conducting research;
- Maintaining research integrity by avoiding misrepresentation and omission of pertinent research data;
- Treating outside clients and suppliers fairly.

Organizational Relationships
Marketers should be aware of how their behavior may influence or impact on the behavior of others in organizational relationships. They should not demand, encourage, or apply coercion to obtain unethical behavior in their relationships with others, such as employees, suppliers, or customers.
1. Apply confidentiality and anonymity in professional relationships with regard to privileged information;
2. Meet their obligations and responsibilities in contracts and mutual agreements in a timely manner;
3. Avoid taking the work of others, in whole, or in part, and representing this work as their own or directly benefit from it without compensation or consent of originator or owner;
4. Avoid manipulation to take advantage of situations to maximize personal welfare in a way that unfairly deprives or damages the organization of others.
Any AMA members found to be in violation of any provision of this Code of Ethics may have his or her Association membership suspended or revoked.

Figure 3.10 Continued

Marketing Vocabulary

BUSINESS-TO-CONSUMER (B2C) E-COMMERCE
Trade involving businesses selling to consumers over the Internet.

Type of Player	Role	Business-to-Consumer	Business-to-Business
Web Portals	Bring together information for consumers or businesses and direct them to the Web sites of product-service providers and intermediaries	America Online (AOL) Yahoo! MSN.com	ZDNet Marketsite.net
Web Market Makers	Facilitate transactions between buyers and sellers by providing information about each party and by helping to ensure secure, low-cost exchanges	Ebay.com Priceline.com Travelocity.com	Bloomberg ChemConnect NetBuy.com
Web Product-Service Providers	Deal directly with consumers in an Internet transaction and customize processes to accommodate online customers	Amazon.com Barnes&Noble.com Toys-R-Us.com	Cisco Dell Compaq

Figure 3.11   The Structure of E-Commerce
Source: Based on California Management Review, Vols. 1 & 2, No. 4, Summer 2000.

home and it reaches 99 percent at the workplace.[47] With connection speeds on the rise, both B2B and B2C markets demands serious attention.

Globally, the United States represents about 41 percent of e-commerce trade. The Asia Pacific area accounts for about 20 percent. Western Europe represents about 19 percent, and the rest of the world makes up about 20 percent.[48] The United States is expected to hold the lead as e-commerce continues to grow, but its percentage of the total will decline slightly.

THE STRUCTURE OF INTERNET MARKETING

Some organizations and individuals benefit from the Internet merely by setting up a Web site. You may have an e-mail address, and nearly every progressive organization can be reached via the Web. Only organizations that are set up to conduct commercial transactions over the Internet are part of e-commerce, which we term the **Internet marketing economy**.[49]

As shown in Figure 3.11, the Internet marketing economy has three components, each with a different role: portals, market makers, and product-service providers.[50] Each contributes to the overall functioning of e-commerce. Together they provide a market space that is globally expansive and personalized.

Web Portals   The purpose of **Web portals** is to direct consumers or businesses to Web sites of product providers or intermediaries. They offer information and Web linkages that enable consumers and businesses to connect with the right commercial sites for their needs. Portals are valuable because they help with this sorting and matching process. Web sites change frequently, and good portals must work constantly to remain current and timely.

Portals allow users to sort information so that companies, products, and messages can be accessed in useful ways. To help with this process, marketers must classify their Web site with appropriate key words, descriptors, and categories. That begins by selecting a domain name that labels an organization's Internet presence, much like branding is used to identify products. Each domain has a numerical address, and a company may use the same address for several domain names or split them up. For example, Coke can be reached at www.cocacola.com, www.coca-cola.com, www.coke.com or by specifying the numerical ip address (216.64.210.28) directly.

Good portals are powerful search engines that help users reach the sites they want. A search engine like Yahoo! can guide consumers to sites they want to explore in depth. These sites are usually owned by Web market makers or by Web product service providers, both of which are described next.

Web Market Makers   The purpose of **Web market makers** is to help buyers and sellers obtain information about each other and to facilitate secure, low-cost exchanges. Market makers have a great deal of knowledge about domains. In many cases they specialize in certain types of products or exchanges. They also add an element of security and trust to the business transaction. For example, eBay brings consumers together for auctions. It specifies the rules, communicates the auction itself, and provides information about past activities of sellers and buyers, including feedback from each party regarding the other.

In the business-to-business arena, market makers include Chendex (chemicals), HoustonStreet.com (electricity), FastParts (electronic components), and BigBuyer.com (small business products). Experts expect business-to-business market makers to experience tremendous growth. They can organize auctions, set up exchanges, and integrate product and service catalogs from several suppliers.[51] In addition, they can offer **virtual trade shows**, that is, online sites that display new products and technologies from several suppliers to current or potential customers. Industry associations, trade associations, or companies sponsor these trade shows.

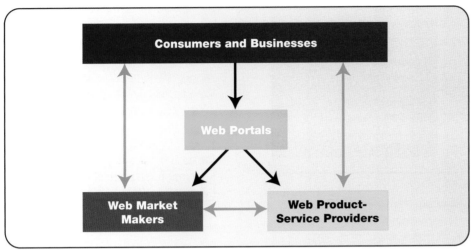

Figure 3.12   Participation in E-Commerce

Web Product-Service Providers Because they deal directly with customers, **Web product-service providers** customize processes to accommodate online transactions. They go to great lengths to make online buying a major aspect of their business. Minor adjustments to accommodate a small percentage of online orders do not count. Instead, these companies adjust their infrastructure so that Web-based business can become an extensive part of their marketing strategy. These providers connect directly with customers, and the Internet becomes a business channel. Popular organizations in this category are Amazon.com for consumers and Dell for both businesses and consumers.

How the Structure Interacts Figure 3.12 shows how consumers and businesses interact with the three major parts of the Internet marketing economy. Market makers and product-service providers gain the attention of customers by working with portals as well as through traditional efforts, such as advertising, personal selling, and word of mouth. The revenue stream of a portal depends on how well it supports the Web market makers and product-service providers. At the same time, market makers depend on product-service providers for items to sell, and product-service providers depend on market makers for many of their customers. All parties are roughly interdependent.

New marketing companies have been established just because the benefits of the Internet economy are so great, but the dangers are also high. Thousands of dot-com companies that boomed in the late 90's flopped soon after the turn of the century. Some companies like Google, Yahoo!, and Amazon emerged victoriously, but many simply failed.[52] Yet, Michael Krauss, a regular columnist for Marketing News, notes that traditional bricks-and-mortar firms are increasingly aware of the Internet marketing economy. "The dinosaurs are starting to dance," he says, mentioning such alliances as Wal-Mart Stores and America Online, Kmart and Yahoo!, and Best Buy and Microsoft.[53]

VALUE OF THE INTERNET TO BUYERS AND SELLERS

E-commerce is gaining ground because, as Figure 3.13 indicates, both buyers and sellers receive great value from it. Compared to traditional channels, buyers get better information, greater convenience, wider and customized selection, and better prices. Marketers have access to more customers, reduced supply chain costs, efficient two-way communication with customers, and the ability to personalize messages and products. These advantages are described next.

Value to Buyers   Better Information The Internet enables buyers to obtain a great deal of information about products, including availability, costs, attributes, and use instructions, as well as information about manufacturers and sellers of particular brands. Some Internet services perform the difficult task of comparison shopping to find the right product configurations at the lowest prices. In many cases, before selecting an item, potential buyers can even obtain other customers' reactions to products: "If you want to hear how other readers evaluate "Harry Potter and The Deathly Hallows" by J.K. Rowling, just contact Amazon.com."

Greater Convenience Shopping at home or in the office via computer reduces the amount of travel and time associated with in-store purchases. This is particularly useful for buyers in rural areas or more remote commu-

Marketing Vocabulary

INTERNET MARKETING ECONOMY
All organizations that are set up to conduct commercial transactions with business partners and buyers over the Internet.

WEB PORTALS
Organizations that direct consumers or businesses to the Web sites of product-service providers and intermediaries.

WEB MARKET MAKERS
Organizations that help buyers and sellers by providing information about each party and by facilitating secure, low-cost exchanges.

VIRTUAL TRADE SHOWS
Online sites that display new products and technologies from several suppliers to current and potential customers.

WEB PRODUCT- SERVICE PROVIDERS
Companies that customize processes to accommodate online customers.

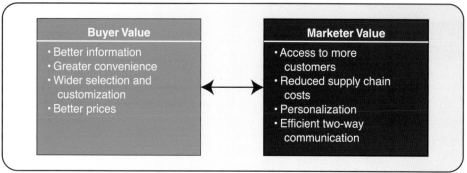

Figure 3.13   Internet Marketing Benefits Buyers and Sellers

nities around the world. In urban and suburban settings, traffic congestion is high, and consumers may save many hours each week otherwise spent waiting in traffic or on long checkout lines. In addition, savings in gasoline and other vehicle costs can be substantial, not to mention the social benefits of less auto pollution and congestion.

Wider Selection and Customization Online buyers can choose from a wide selection as well as customized products. Retail outlets may carry only certain brands and sizes, but online sources offer all possible configurations. Buyers can compare many more brands and price points. Even unique and scarce products can be sourced quickly. If you need a particular book on some obscure medical topic, contact Amazon.com. Amazon.com will find it if it's in print. At the same time, more customization is possible because buyers can interface with a seller's manufacturing facilities, which in turn are networked with suppliers, so sellers can build or manufacture on demand.

Better Prices Due to the competitive nature of the Internet marketing economy and the efficiency saving, shoppers may benefit from lower prices. One company asks: "Would you like to buy this camera [a popular brand is shown] at $169 or $149 or at $129? Shop at MySimon.com." Internet retailers tend to be driven by price because many buyers go online specifically to obtain price savings. Companies that pioneered in e-commerce used a low-price strategy to attract business and this strategy has continued because online shoppers have become accustomed to the competitive prices.

Values to Marketers Access to More Customers On the seller side of the market, Internet businesses have access to a world of customers. A firm in Chicago can communicate with a potential customer in India as easily as with one next door. And communications can be tailored to each party. E-commerce

has grown by leaps and bounds, which means that more businesses and customers are being brought together in more uniquely personal ways than could be imagined a decade ago. Internet sellers have access to vastly more customers than their bricks-and-mortar rivals. Even if such marketing forms as retail outlets and catalogs are combined, more potential customers can be reached through the Internet.

According to Computer Industry Almanac, there are over 1 billion people around the world with Internet access. The proportion of users is highest in the North America - estimated at nearly 75 percent of the population, compared to 48 percent in Europe.[54] Obviously, not all users make Web purchases. In fact, online holiday sales are only about one-tenth of total. Many shoppers go online to do research, but still prefer to go to shops in order to purchase. "Not everyone trusts they could get a good fit of jeans and shoes online," said Vikram Sehgal of Jupiter's Research in New York. Retailers are increasingly recognizing the value of their Web sites to drive the high volume of consumer contacts to their brick-and-mortar stores.[55]

Personalized and Customized Products E-commerce makes it easier for sellers to cater to customer needs. This can be done through product representation and product configuration.[56] Product representation refers to how the product is presented to customers. With the Web it is possible to use the customer's name in a communication or arrange information about the product to reflect more closely the potential buyer's preferences. A more complex customization occurs with product configuration, which promotes selected products or brands directly to a consumer or adjusts attributes to user specifications. In addition, buyers themselves can make adjustments online. For example, computer marketers

such as Dell or Compaq allow purchasers to specify precisely what computer configuration they want. Levi-Strauss and other clothing manufacturers can store consumers' personal measurements and manufacture items for each unique body. Broad Vision is a company that helps marketers develop this kind of site.

Reduced Supply-Chain Costs E-commerce reduces not only the **supply chain costs** associated with procuring goods and services from suppliers but also the costs of distributing products to consumers. Savings occur throughout the supply chain, including lower inventory costs, due to better demand forecasting, streamlined manufacturing, warehousing, and transportation. Better communication among all members of the value chain reduces errors. Dell has been successful in the computer server market by integrating its supply chain through the Internet. All members of Dell's supply chain are connected online and are given intensive information linked to customer demand. This allows each supplier to operate efficiently while supplying precisely what Dell customers want. Not just part of the supply chain, the Web itself is a marketing channel. What makes this channel unique is that so many customers are within a few keystrokes of a shopping experience. Because many e-commerce companies take advantage of the latest technologies, their supply chains tend to be very efficient.

Two-Way Communication A significant benefit of the Internet for marketers is how efficiently it allows two-way communication and customization to take place. It costs less than telephone or mail contact and is significantly less expensive than face-to-face communication. This technology is as revolutionary for communication today as the telephone, radio, and television were when they were introduced. The Web began as a way to present and send information, such as online newspapers or reports. Then it allowed access on demand to all sorts of data, a library function that helped users find information among the most widely ranging sources imaginable. In the most significant communication advance to date, however, the Web can personalize contact. It facilitates dialogue between two parties or among thousands. This two-way, multiple-person communication enables marketers to create dialogues among consumers quickly and inexpensively, so marketers can learn consumers' views on products and issues in real time.

Web communication also facilitates personalization and customization of both products and messages. Marketers can easily collect opinions and test reactions to marketing activities. Also, data on past purchases reveal a lot about what people will buy in the future.

Customers can order and pay for items online. Perhaps even more important, there are opportunities for two-way dialogue about product attributes, ordering, and customer service. The Web even facilitates product customization. The amount and type of communication, including product options and pricing, can be personalized. This kind of contact helps marketers develop and maintain customer loyalty. Connect with Nike (www.nike.com/nike_id/) to build a personal pair of shoes. You can select colors, add a personalized set of initials, and basically design a pair of Nikes just to your taste for approximately an additional $10.

Marketing Vocabulary

SUPPLY CHAIN COSTS
Costs associated with procuring goods and services from suppliers and with distributing products from businesses to consumers.

Web and E-commerce Stars
eBay -www.ebay.com

"Whatever it is... you can get it on eBay" - eBay.com, is one of the most popular Web sites on the Internet. It revolutionized the online auction concept and has been a hit with millions of people since its inception. With more than 233 million members and 10 million products at any point in time, it generates approximately $6 billion annually and is growing rapidly. A 30 percent increase in revenue each year is not uncommon to this internet powerhouse. eBay allows people to participate in E-Commerce locally and nationally by including links to other sites such as Paypal, Skype, Kijiji, Rent.com, and Shopping.com to facilitate relationships between millions of buyers and sellers every day. Moreover, to keep pace in the global market, you can shop in 26 countries around the world.

Chapter Summary:

Objective 1: Describe the marketing environment and the use of environmental scanning.

The marketing environment comprises all factors that affect a business. The factors are divided into two groups—the microenvironment and the global macroenvironment. The microenvironment includes factors that marketers interact with regularly. Consequently, the microenvironment influences and is influenced by marketing. The global macroenvironment includes factors that marketers must take into account when making decisions. However, marketers seldom influence these factors. Together, the environments can facilitate or inhibit organizations from reaching their objectives. Proactive organizations anticipate changes in the marketing environment and plan accordingly. Organizations use environmental scanning in order to keep up with environmental changes. The Web is a great technological tool to help maintain currency in knowledge of the environment.

Objective 2: Understand how the roles that stakeholders play influence the accomplishment of marketing objectives. Know why marketing must address stakeholder desires when making decisions.

Stakeholders are important parts of the microenvironment and directly participate in accomplishing the organization's goals. They include owners, employees, suppliers, intermediaries, and action groups. Stakeholders participate with the organization in order to accomplish their own goals; consequently, marketers must take their desires into consideration when making decisions. Because owners are entitled to a fair return on their investment, companies need to make a substantial profit, and nonprofit organizations must accomplish the goals their owners (sponsors) intend. Employees are also important; happy employees produce happy customers. Suppliers provide necessary services, raw materials, and components. They also provide technology in specialized areas. Suppliers have a dramatic influence on your customers. Intermediaries help move products between you and your customers. They often contact customers directly. Since they represent your organization, you must carefully interface with them. Action groups are "watchdogs" that keep the interests of the environment and people in balance with profit seeking. They can help marketers interface better with society. Marketers must address stakeholders' desires because stakeholders support marketers in order to attain their goals. In turn, marketers depend on stakeholders to accomplish their organization's objectives.

Objective 3: Be able to integrate an understanding of industry competition into environmental analysis.

An understanding of industry competition provides an integrated picture about the major forces that determine competitive intensity. Competition involves single competitors and groups of company types that compete. We look at the rivalry among existing firms to understand one-on-one competition. Potential competitors are also viewed because firms enter and exit industries. At the same time, substitute products can play a role especially when new technologies bring new ways to perform old functions. The bargaining power of buyers and suppliers determines how a company competes. Suppliers have more power when there are few

suppliers and many buyers. All of these aspects of industry competition need to be understood in order to build appropriate marketing strategies.

Objective 4: Synthesize aspects of the global macroenvironment, including technological, economic, demographic, cultural, and legal/regulatory elements, in order to be in step with long-term trends.

The global macroenvironment is being influenced by many forces. The technological environment provides knowledge and tools that companies can acquire to produce better products. By phasing in new technology, progressive companies stay abreast of the best ways to create customer value. Economic factors are also important. Changes in income and spending power and other factors help determine which countries have the ability to purchase. The world has three major trading areas. The regions offer large markets, but they also compete against one another. The natural resources environment also comes into play. It provides raw materials and must be protected. Global demographics are changing. Shifts in population density and dispersion are important, as are age shifts. It is important to grasp the cultural environment and to view things from the other's perspective. The values, beliefs, and behaviors of others may differ from your own. Finally, the legal/regulatory environment is complex. Laws must be interpreted and followed. They help promote competition, influence business size, protect customers, and protect the environment.

Objective 5: Recognize the importance of ethics and guides to ethical behavior.

Marketers often face ethical dilemmas, particularly when legal and ethical standards conflict. Many companies have developed codes of ethics for their employees to help ensure that everyone in the company is following the same standards. The American Marketing Association has a code of ethics that covers the basic responsibilities of marketers in each of the areas in which they are likely to be active. It stresses the importance of fairness and integrity.

Objective 6: Understand the impact that e-commerce is making on the global business environment and understand the structure of Internet marketing.

Both business-to-consumer and business-to-business organizations are using the Internet increasingly. However, the business-to-business sector is growing faster. The Internet marketing economy is comprised of three structural elements. Web portals direct consumers or businesses to Web sites of product providers or intermediaries. Web market makers help buyers and sellers enter into transactions on the Web by providing information and making arrangements for selling and buying between parties. Web product-service providers deal directly with customers utilizing special technologies developed to facilitate sales over the Internet. These three entities interact to provide a viable infrastructure to conduct marketing over the Internet in several types of marketspaces, including virtual shopping malls and virtual trade shows. The Internet marketing economy is growing because it offers great value for buyers as well as marketers.

Review Your Understanding

1. What is environmental scanning and what technology is being used for it today?
2. What is the microenvironment and what are its elements?
3. What is the global macroenvironment and what are its elements?
4. Who are stakeholders and why are they important? List five different types of stakeholders.
5. What are the elements of industry competition? Describe each.
6. Why is the technological environment important?
7. What are the elements of the economic environment? List three aspects that are influencing global marketing.
8. What are the three major trading blocs in the world economy?

9. What demographic trends are influencing marketing?
10. What is the self-reference criterion? What are some cultural differences to be aware of?
11. What are the types of laws that affect marketing?
12. What is the difference between unethical and illegal behavior?

Discussion of Concepts

1. Suppose that IBM and Microsoft announced plans to merge into one company. Would U.S. laws allow this to happen? Do you think that other countries around the world would have the same reaction?
2. What is culture, and how does it affect marketing? Can you think of any products that are successful in the United States but would fail in Japan because of cultural differences?
3. In the 1980s, McDonald's discontinued the use of styrofoam containers for its sandwiches. What other changes have occurred recently in the natural resources environment? What types of legislation do you expect in the future? How would that legislation affect marketing?
4. Do you think that General Motors should invest a significant amount of money in research and development projects? Why or why not?
5. Recently, discount stores such as Wal-Mart and Kmart have become extremely large and powerful. How does this affect industry structure and competitive intensity?
6. As the director of marketing for Dow Chemical Company, you are required to interact regularly with a number of different publics. List these publics, the concerns that each might have, and how you would address each of those concerns.
7. What effect do you expect the new European currency to have on trade among the three superblocs? Which trading relationships will be most affected? In what ways?
8. Which do you feel is more important—ethics or the law? Why?

Key Terms And Definitions

Action group: A number of people who support some cause in the interest of consumers or environmental safety.

Age cohort: A group of people close in age who have been shaped by their generation's experience with the media, peers, events, and society at large.

Business-to-business (B2B) e-commerce: Trade involving Internet sales in which businesses sell to other businesses, including governments and organizations.

Business-to-consumer (B2C) e-commerce: Trade involving businesses selling to consumers over the Internet.

Cartel: A group of businesses or nations that work together to control the price and production of a particular product.

Consolidated Metropolitan Statistical Area (CMSA): Two or more overlapping urban communities with a combined population of at least 1 million.

Cultural environment: The learned values, beliefs, language, symbols, and patterns of behavior shared by people in a society and passed on from generation to generation.

Demographic environment: The statistical data used to describe a population.

Discretionary income: The amount of money consumers have left after paying taxes and purchasing necessities.

Disposable income: The income consumers have left after paying taxes.

Economic environment: The financial and natural resources available to consumers, businesses, and countries.

Environmental scanning: Collecting and analyzing information about the marketing environment in order to detect important changes or trends that can affect a company's strategy.

Global macroenvironment: The large external influences considered vital to long-term decisions but not directly affected by the company itself.

Gross domestic product (GDP): The total market value of all goods and services produced by a country in a single year.

Intermediaries: Stakeholders who move products from the manufacturer to the final user.

Internet marketing economy: All organizations that are set up to conduct commercial transactions with business partners and buyers over the Internet.

Legal/regulatory environment: International, federal, state, and local regulations and laws, the agencies that interpret and administer them, and the court system.

Maastricht Treaty: Consists of 282 directives that eliminate border controls and custom duties among members of the European Union.

Marketing environment: The sum of all the factors that affect a business.

Metropolitan Statistical Area (MSA): A stand-alone population center, unlinked to other cities, that has more than 50,000 people.

Microenvironment: The forces close to a company that influence how it connects with customers.

Population density: The concentration of people within some unit of measure, such as per square mile or per square kilometer.

Self-reference criterion: The unconscious reliance on values gained from one's own socialization when trying to understand another culture.

Spending power: The ability of the population to purchase goods and services.

Stakeholder: A group who can influence or be influenced by the firm's actions.

Substitute product: Any good or service that performs the same function or provides the same benefit as an existing one.

Suppliers: Organizations that provide a company with necessary services, raw materials, or components.

Supply chain costs: Costs associated with procuring goods and services from suppliers and with distributing products from businesses to consumers.

Technological environment: The total body of knowledge available for development, manufacturing, and marketing of products and services.

Urbanization: The shift of population from rural to urban areas.

Virtual trade shows: Online sites that display new products and technologies from several suppliers to current and potential customers.

Web market makers: Organizations that help buyers and sellers by providing information about each party and by facilitating secure, low-cost exchanges.

Web portals: Organizations that direct consumers or businesses to the Web sites of product-service providers and intermediaries.

Web product-service providers: Companies that customize processes to accommodate online customers.

References

1. John Lippman, "News Corp.'s Profit Jumped in Period, Aided by Purchase," Wall Street Journal Interactive Edition, May 8, 1997; Joshua Levine, "Luke Skywalker Is Back. Let Us Pray," Forbes, December 30, 1996, www.forbes.com; Randall Lane, "The Magician," Forbes, March 11, 1996, pp. 122–128; "Starman," Inc. Technology, 1995, no. 2, p. 44; Joseph Garber, "Virtual Superstar," Forbes, March 13, 1995, p. 152; Jeff Jensen, "Star Wars' Empire Shows New Strength," Advertising Age, December 5, 1994, p. 33; Thomas Jaffe, ed., "Telephone Assault," Forbes, December 5, 1994, p. 20; A.D., "LucasArts Entertainment," Fortune, July 11, 1994, pp. 129–130; interview with Jeanne Cole, Lucasfilms, May 1998; Dan Fost, Marin Independent Journal, December 29, 1977, p. D5; Philip Van Munching, "The Devil's Adman," Brandweek, January 31, 2000, p. 70; "Lucasfilm THX Unveils Now Optimode," Emedia, August 2000, p. 22; John Jimenez, "Star Wars Trilogy" to Be Re-Released with Bonus Footage of 'Episode II' Preview," Video Store, September 3–September 9, 2000, p. 10; Marco R. della Cava, "Lucas: The Titan of Tech," USA Today, February 23, 2001, p. E1, 2; "Closing the Circle of Star Wars, CNN.com, May 20, 2005; www.lucasarts.com, site visited June 13, 2007.
2. www.att.com/corporate Web site visited April 14, 2008
3. www.factiva.com and www.gegxs.com, sites visited June 22, 2007.
4. Gene R. Laczniak and Patrick E. Murphy, Ethical Marketing Decisions: The Higher Road (Boston: Allyn & Bacon, 1993), pp. 14–15.
5. www.panerabread.com/about/company, Web site visited May 20, 2008.
6. Patrick J. Kiger, "Small Groups, Big Ideas," Workforce Management, February 27, 2006, p. 1, 22-27.
7. Ford Sustainability Report, 2006-07. http://www.ford.com/aboutford. Web site visited April 14, 2008.
8. Business: Pleny of blame to go around; Chinese manufacturing. The Economist. London. September 29, 2007.
9. www.allianceforclimateprotection.org, site visited May 2, 2007; www.algore.com, site visited May2, 2007.
10. www.stopglobalwarming.com, site visited May2, 2007.
11. Marilyn Geewax, "Gay link prompts call for Wal-Mart boycott," The Austin American-Statesman, November 11, 2006; David Crary, "Conservatives abandon planned boycott of Wal-Mart over outreach to gay groups," Associated Press, November 22, 2006.
12. C. Anthony, D. Bendetto, Roger Calantone, Jeffrey Schmidt, "New Product Activities and Performance: The Moderating Role of Environmental Hostility," J Product Innovation Management, 1997.
13. www.candyusa.org/Classroom/Trends/default.asp, site visited May 22, 2007.
14. "Corporate Fact Sheet," www.walmartfacts.com, April, 2008.
15. "Merck Annual Report," www.merck.com, site visited May 1, 2007.
16. Intel 2007 10-K http://www.intc.com Web site visited April 14, 2008.
17. www.intel.com, site visited May 1, 2007.
18. Terrence E. Deal and Allan A. Kennedy, Corporate Cultures: The Ethics and Rituals of Corporate Life (Reading, MA: Addison-Wesley Publishing, 1982), p. 8.
19. www.research.microsoft.com/aboutmsr/labs/asia/innovationday/MSRAsia.aspx, site visited May 1, 2007.
20. www.cia.gov/cia/publications/factbook/rankorder/2001ran k.html, site visited May 16, 2007.
21. www.cia.gov/cia/publications/factbook/, site visited May 25, 2007.
22. "Gap Between Rich and Poor as Wide as Ever in Latin America," Associated Press Newswires, September 4, 2000.
23. "Becoming a Triad Power: The New Global Corporation," International Marketing Review, Autumn 1986.
24. http://www.cia.gov/cia/publications/factbook/rankorder/2001rank.html, site visited May 12, 2007.
25. Andrew Tanzer, "Stepping Stones to a New China?" Forbes, January 27, 1997, p. 78–83.
26. "China to Continue with More Reforms to Boost Growth," Asia Pulse, January 14, 2000.
27. Japan's household savings, deposits fall for 1st time since 1964 – report," AFXNEWS.com, January 5, 2007.
28. "Japan Rising," Adweek, May 1, 2000, p. 58-64.
29. http://europa.eu/abc/european_countries/index_en.htm, site visited May 9, 2007.
30. Justin Blum, "Alaska Town Split Over Drilling in Wildlife Refuge; Oil Money Tantalizes, but Many Fear Effect on Way of Life," The Washington Post, April 23, 2007.
31. www.prb.org/Content/NavigationMenu/PRB/Educators/Human_Population/Population_Growth/Population_Growth.htm, Web site visited September 9, 2006.
32. www.bartleby.com/151/in.html, site visited May 29, 2007.
33. Lisa Yorgey Lester, "America's Changing Face," Target Marketing. Philadelphia: Apr 2004.Vol.27, Iss. 4; pg. 26, 6 pgs.
34. Claudette Bennett, Current Population Reports (Washington, DC: Bureau of the Census, U.S. Department of Commerce, January 1995), p. 2.0
35. www.atlapedia.com, site visited September 29, 2006.
36. www.city-data.com/top1.html site visited August 23, 2006.
37. www.census.gov/population/projections/nation/summary/np-t4-b.txt, site visited April 23, 2007; www.census.gov/ipc/www/usinterimproj/natprojtab01a.xls, site visited April 23, 2007.
38. Mercedes M. Cardona, "Just for Men's New Ad Formula: Take Quarterback, Add Color," Advertising Age, July 24, 2000, p 12.
39. Edward T. Hall, "The Silent Language in Overseas Business," Harvard Business Review, May–June 1960, p. 87.
40. FTC information request recieved by EA in connection with Take-Two takeover. Telecomworldwire. April 18, 2008.
41. "FTC and FDA Team Up Against Tobacco," Wall Street Journal Interactive Edition, May 1, 1997.
42. Wendy Melillo, "PM Claims Withdrawal of Ads Was Voluntary," AdWeek East, June 12, 2000.
43. www.iihs.org/safety_facts/airbags/stats.htm, site visited April 21, 2008.
44. http://www.buick.com/lucerne/index.jsp Web site visited April 21, 2008.
45. www.epa.gov/nscep/, site visited May 12, 2007.
46. US Census Bureau, E-Stats, www.census.gov/estats, site visited May 12, 2007.
47. www.ecommerce-guide.com/news/trends/article.php/3524581, site visited May 11, 2007.
48. Forester Research, www.cyberatlas.internet.com/bigpicture/demographics/article/0,1323,5911348161,00.html, January 15, 2000, p.1.
49. See definitions by B. Mahadevan, "Business Models for Internet-Based E-Commerce," California Management Review, 42 Summer 2000, p.56.
50. Ibid.
51. B. Mahadevan, "Business Models," p. 57.
52. Thomas L. Friedman, "The World Is Flat," (New York: Farrar, Straus and Giroux, 2006).
53. Ibid.
54. www.internetworldstats.com/stats.htm, site visited July 10, 2008.
55. Andria Cheng, Bloomberg News, "Online shopping isn't death knell for real-life retail; Many need to see items in person or enjoy social aspects of a trip to the mall," The Houston Chronicle, December 4, 2006.
56. Hansen, Principles of Internet Marketing, p. 197.

The Marketing Gazette
Janice Matsumoto, "Passport to Expansion," Restaurants and Institutions, July 15, 2000, pp. 143–144; Mark Kleinman, "Sydney 2000 Hailed as Ad Success," Marketing, October 5, 2000, p.7.; www.mcdonalds.com/corp/about.html, site visited June 13, 2007.; "McDonald's Corp.(NEWS IN A MINUTE)(Brief Article)." The Food Institute Report 19, May 16, 2005: 7.; InfoTrac OneFile. Thomson Gale. Michigan State University Libraries. June 13, 2007.

CASE 3

The National Basketball Association

Picture an NBA team in 2008, such as the Chicago Bulls, playing for a half-empty arena. Or image the league's premier event—the championship games—being shown on tape delay against The Tonight Show due to a lack of interest from fans. Seem impossible? Amazingly, the NBA has not always been the worldwide phenomenon we know today. According to Sales and Marketing Management, about 20 years ago the NBA was "a product about as appealing as a week-old banana." How did it become an international success? Many attribute the transformation to the marketing savvy of Commissioner David Stern. He expanded the league from 24 to 29 teams, gross revenues increased from $181.1 million to about $1 billion, and average attendance per game has grown from 11,141 in 1985 to more than 17,000 in 2008. Pat Williams, senior executive vice president of the NBA's Orlando Magic, indicated that "David Stern has a tremendous marketing mind, and he is one of the great sports stories of the twentieth century."

During the 1970s and 1980s, marketing efforts by most NBA teams were minimal. Today, kids are wearing Chicago Bulls T-shirts in Casablanca, Phoenix Suns caps in Punta del Este, and Los Angeles Lakers jackets in London. NBA stars such as Steve Nash, Dwayne Wade and Kobe Bryant are recognized around the globe. And worldwide sales of NBA merchandise amount to more than $1 billion a year.

The NBA has spent more than a decade creating a global brand and has emerged as the first truly global sports league. Commissioner Stern, said, "We're okay in Melbourne, Tokyo, and Hong Kong, but we've got to beef up our operations in Singapore, Jakarta, and Kuala Lumpur." When Stern became commissioner in 1984, he immediately saw the NBA's global potential. In addition to worldwide requests for more games to telecast, Stern noted a number of environmental changes: the collapse of communism and the growth of market economies, the globalization of U.S. consumer products, and a worldwide television revolution that created new cable and satellite channels. A more recent development is the growth of the global Internet, where the NBA has an official Web site. The NBA also offers twelve international Web sites including China, Brazil, Japan and Germany and draws over 50 percent of its traffic from outside the United States.

How has this vast international opportunity been exploited? Television is the number-one tool. The opening game of the 2008 NBA Finals between the Boston Celtics and the Los Angeles Lakers was broadcasted on stations across the globe. The NBA also sells television rights to local broadcasters, even in countries where it does no other business. In such countries as Spain, France, Mexico, and Japan, the NBA collects more than $1 million in rights fees. Given the intensity of media competition, these numbers are expected to grow. In 1970, the NBA sold cable rights for $400,000. Today, it commands an astounding $660 million just in the United States. Add to that the NBA games that are currently being broadcast to over 200 countries. Each week over 10 hours of NBA games and coverage are broadcast to foreign countries.

A number of factors have facilitated the worldwide growth of the NBA, including electronic media, sports marketing, and foreign-born players. David Stern wants the NBA to be a part of pop culture in "every global medium that matters." He believes "the real-time delivery of data and statistics about the NBA on a global basis via the Web is about as exciting as it gets." Stern himself has participated in online chat sessions. In addition to the popularity of interactive media, sports marketers such as Nike have complemented the NBA's global presence. According to Stern, "They have enormous marketing, distribution and manufacturing capability that we borrow. And to the extent that that's associated with their brand, it makes our brand stronger. We're sort of borrowing each other's equity." Cultural diversity in the league has also facilitated the NBA's global growth. Foreign players intensify the media coverage in their own countries. For example, Yao Ming brings NBA popularity to China, Emanuel Ginobili to Argentina, and Darko Milicic to Serbia.

Managing the NBA is a dynamic role demanding job. It requires interfacing with apparel companies, licensees, U.S. and global media companies, and corporate giants such as McDonald's, Coca-Cola, Nike, and Disney. The NBA is not just a provider of sports programming; it is also in the sporting goods, sponsorship, consumer products, and trading card businesses, among others. With these relationships comes the need to defend property rights, and the NBA has been the most active league in that regard. This includes even digital rights. Stern says: "I just want to be standing with this big bundle of carefully protected rights . . . I had owners in 1979 that didn't want me to get involved with cable, but if you can be part of the growth pattern, you will always do better."

Growth often brings difficult management decisions. Stern tries to incorporate ethical choices into the league's expansion. "You must be on the ground in every continent exploiting your brand with sensibility towards local issues. But there's nothing easy about that," he says. "We want to play into the existing infrastructure, not supplant it. We do not wish to injure or disrupt the Italian League, Spanish League, or any other league."

Stern predicts that one-third of the NBA's revenues could come from abroad within the next 10 years. Today's staff of 800 is almost eight times the number that ran the league in the 1980s. The game is played nearly everywhere and is easily understood. The phenomenal popularity and worldwide presence of the NBA are all about marketing. As the league continues to grow, fans will continue to cheer for The Mate in Latin America, the Trofsla in Iceland, and the Smash in France. And the Chinese will continue to root for the Bulls, better known as the "Red Oxen."

1. *The global macroenvironment consists of large external influences vital to long-term decisions but not directly affected by the company itself. Identify these influences and note several ways each has affected or may affect the NBA's global expansions.*

2. *What considerations does the NBA need to address before entering a particular country or region? Suggest several adjustments that may be required to serve customers successfully in those markets.*

3. *Stakeholders include groups such as owners, employees, suppliers, intermediaries, and action groups. Identify the groups with a stake in the NBA, making assumptions as necessary. How may each of these influence marketing decisions?*

Sources: Hoover's Online, "National Basketball Association, www.hooversonline.com, visited June 19, 2000; Daniel Roth, "The NBA's Next Shot," Fortune, www.fortune.com, February 21, 2000; Marc Gunther, "They All Wanna Be Like Mike," Fortune, July 21, 1997 www.fortune.com; Jeff Jensen, "Experiential Branding Makes It to the Big Leagues," Advertising Age, April 14, 1997, pp. 20, 24; Terry Lefton, "At Age 50, Stern Looks Ahead," Brandweek, October 28, 1996, pp. 34–38; Bob Ryan, "Hoop Dreams," Sales and Marketing Management, December 1996, pp. 48–53; and Michael Schrage, "David Stern," Adweek, May 26, 1997, pp. 24–26. Michael Wallace, Knight Ridder Tribune Business News, Washington: June 8, 2007. pg. 1; http://sports.espn.go.com/nba/attendance, site visited June 20, 2008; The National Basketball Association Web site, www.nba.com, June 23, 2008

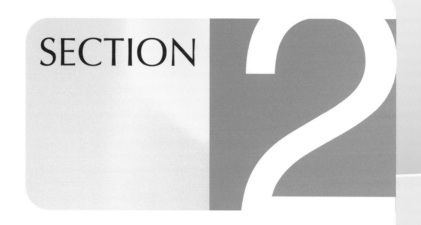

SECTION

2

Discover Value

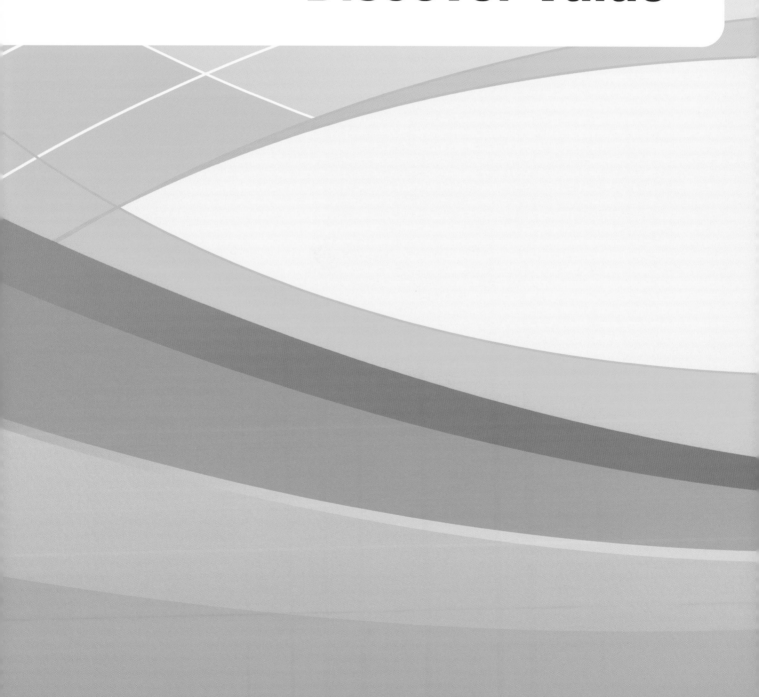

Discovering value is the process of evaluating markets, customers, and competitors. Gathering and using marketing information to further understand consumers and other businesses is a fundamental marketing process. The following chapters are included in this section:

Chapter 4 Marketing Information and Research
Chapter 5 Understanding Consumer Behavior
Chapter 6 Understanding Business Marketing

Marketing Information & Research

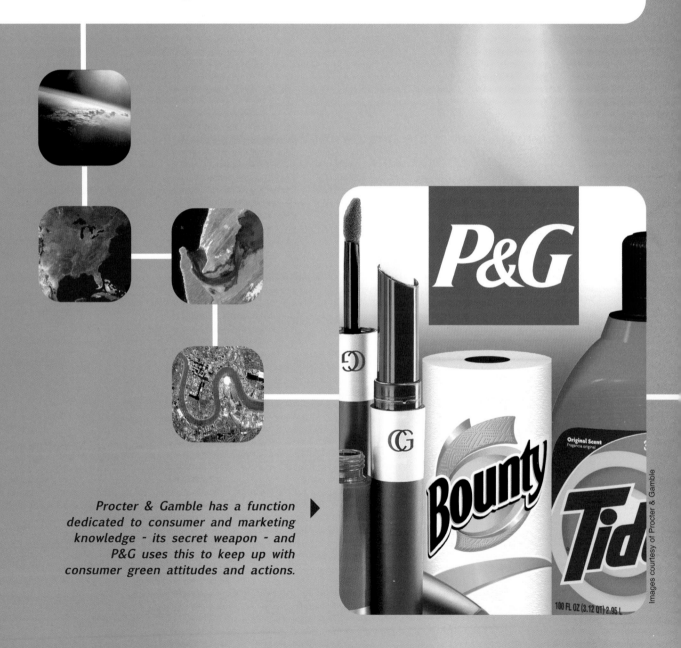

Procter & Gamble has a function dedicated to consumer and marketing knowledge - its secret weapon - and P&G uses this to keep up with consumer green attitudes and actions.

Learning Objectives

1. Understand the roles that marketing information systems (MIS) and research play in marketing decision making.

2. Recognize how data are transformed into information to be used in a variety of marketing decisions.

3. Understand the types of research and the steps of a typical marketing research process.

4. Describe widely used marketing research techniques.

5. Explore how marketing information is being influenced by technology and is obtained globally.

6. Understand that ethical issues surround the use and dissemination of research.

What began as a small, family operated business in the 1830s has grown into one of the largest corporations in the world. Today, Cincinnati, Ohio-based Procter & Gamble employs nearly 140,000 employees in 80 countries and features more than 20 brands that generate $1 billion or more each in annual sales. The company makes many brands you probably use everyday, including Tide, Bounty, Folgers, Pringles and Pampers. Its commitment to product innovation and the environment landed Procter & Gamble a 2007 spot among Fortune's 10 Most Admired Corporations.

With hundreds of scientists and engineers responsible for assuring the environmental safety of products and operations, P&G is truly dedicated to the protection of the environment. For seven consecutive years, P&G has been named the Dow Jones Sustainability Index Super Sector Leader in the non-durable household products market. Rather than developing a separate line of green products, compromising the reputation of non-green ones, Procter & Gamble holds all of its products to high environmental standards.

Procter & Gamble is one of the few companies with a function dedicated solely to consumer and marketing knowledge and considers this division its "secret weapon." These employees explore what consumers think and want, influencing company decisions and direction. They develop strategies for brands entering new markets and analyze market trends to predict future customer behavior.

It acquires e-mail and mailing addresses when customers call a product line or submit a request for information on a P&G website, as well as from reputable mailing list companies. It uses these mailings and e-mails to inform consumers of new products, offer free samples, and conduct surveys. Customers are offered vouchers for gift certificates or other incentives for taking surveys. These surveys are of great value to its Consumer and Marketing Knowledge division. It uses the information generated by surveys to analyze trends, target customers, adjust advertising campaigns, and generate ideas for new products.

With customers in 140 countries, Procter & Gamble is truly a global company. To gain insight on customers, particularly in foreign markets, P&G uses a method called immersion research. Instead of using focus groups, marketers visit customers in their homes or other local settings to help understand the roles its products play in their lives. This research method provides valuable information in markets where consumers act differently than American consumers. "When I was in China the last time, I wanted to visit a very poor consumer and a very wealthy one, just to look at the differences in how they thought about brands, how they thought about media, what was important in their life," said James Stengel, Global Marketing Officer for Procter & Gamble.

For students interested in pursuing a career in marketing information, Procter & Gamble offers a free workshop to gain insight on what it's like to work in its Consumer and Marketing Knowledge division. Its Consumer Strategy Workshop is a five day seminar that offers college students a hands-on experience using consumer and marketing infor-mation to influence business strategy. Students that qualify for the program spend a week working as part of a business team with top students from across the country. They learn how to tap into consumer marketing insights and apply for a chance at a 12 week summer internship with Procter & Gamble.[1]

THE CONCEPT OF MARKETING INFORMATION SYSTEMS AND MARKETING RESEARCH

Connecting with customers requires vast amounts of information. You can't connect if you can't locate, understand, and respond to customers. That's where marketing information systems and marketing research enter the picture. Technology has changed the way the business world views marketing information. Data gathering and dissemination occur at the speed of light. Information is at the fingertips of anyone with a personal computer and an Internet connection. The director of strategic planning at a large midwestern hospital commented recently: "We have access to more information than we can possibly use. The trick is to determine which information will be useful to us in making decisions that positively affect our future."[2]

In fact, a major problem for executives today is data overload—access to so much that their minds simply can't process all of it. To help decision makers, most companies carefully structure the way data are collected, stored, and made available through marketing information systems and marketing research.

Marketing information systems (MIS) are computerized systems that collect and organize marketing data on a timely basis to provide information for decision making. The results become part of the MIS so that executives have constant feedback. Note that the abbreviation MIS can be confusing because many organizations have a **management information system**, also called an MIS. Many times the marketing information system is considered part of that larger system. Management information systems usually contain additional data, such as employee records and various internal documents.

Marketing research is the formal assembly and analysis of data about specific issues surrounding a marketing strategy. It is called for when managers face a complex marketing situation for which little or no information is available. All the data gathered focus on the problem at

www.greenguarantee.com

Procter & Gamble utilizes its consumer and marketing knowledge division to identify consumer trends, like the desire for green products. Visit its Green Guarantee Web site for information on the P&G Pro Line.

hand. For example, Tantau Software Inc., a developer of computer programs for the wireless Internet, hired IntelliQuest Research to provide marketing data on the attitudes of current and potential wireless users. IntelliQuest discovered that financial-based transactions showed the most promise of creating a market for the wireless Internet. However, it also found that customers were most concerned with the security of their transactions, and, thus, were hesitant to invest in or use the medium. As a result, Tantau was able to use IntelliQuest's research to better focus on e-commerce and wireless security software, something that consumers obviously needed.[3]

The type of research just described addresses a specific issue with a clearly identified objective regarding marketing strategy. Once the research is completed, it's typically saved as part of the MIS. Figure 4.1 depicts the relationships of the MIS and marketing research to marketing decision making. This chapter starts with an examination of marketing information systems and their role in marketing decisions. This is followed by a discussion of the marketing research process, which is also key in decision making. The chapter concludes with sections on the all-important technological, global, and ethical dimensions of information generation and usage.

Marketing Vocabulary

MARKETING INFORMATION SYSTEM (MIS)
A computerized system used to collect and analyze the data needed for management decision making. The marketing information system is often considered a part of this system.

MANAGEMENT INFORMATION SYSTEM (MIS)
A computerized system used to collect and analyze the data needed for management decision making. The marketing information system is often considered a part of this system.

MARKETING RESEARCH
The formal assembly and analysis of information about specific issues surrounding the marketing of goods and services.

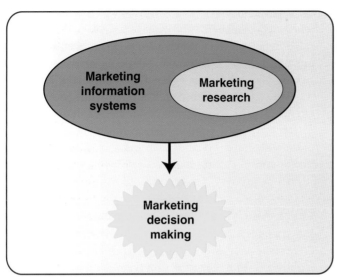

Figure 4.1   Marketing Information and Decision Making

MARKETING INFORMATION SYSTEMS AND DATA

Marketing information systems often include a **marketing decision support system (MDSS)**, which allows decision makers to access raw data from the MIS and manipulate it into a useful form. A typical MDSS consists of a computer database, data retrieval and modeling software, and a user-friendly graphical interface. Let's say that a marketing manager wants to know how the price of the company's downhill skis compares to that of a competitor. The information is probably in the MIS on a store-by-store basis. It would be difficult for the manager to wade through all the raw data and draw any conclusions. Instead the manager may sit down at a computer and access the company's MDSS. A user-friendly display appears and, through interactive directions, helps the user determine how to manipulate the raw data. The marketing manager may want to compare average prices across the entire country or for one region or state. Once that is decided, the MDSS software retrieves and models the relevant data. Now the manager is able to interpret the data and make an informed decision.

A **transaction-based information system (TBIS)** is a specialized type of MIS which is an electronic link between a firm and its customers, distributors, and suppliers. Originally designed for ordering, billing, shipping, and inventory control, these systems are now designed to provide data on customer preferences, loyalty, sales trends, and an array of marketing issues. As part of an initiative to streamline communications, Wal-Mart requires all of its suppliers to adopt Applicability Statement 2 (AS2), a company-created connectivity standard designed to standardize trading and facilitate data interchange over the Internet.[4]

To develop an excellent MIS and design a useful MDSS, the organization needs to assess its marketing information needs. This assessment begins by identifying the types of executive decisions, what information will help make them, and the best formats and timetables for presenting it. Figure 4.2 describes the types of questions used to assess marketing information needs.

TURNING DATA INTO INFORMATION

In order to comprehend marketing information systems and marketing research, you must understand how data becomes information useful for decision making. Keep in mind that data and information are not the same. Data are simply facts. **Information** is data that have been analyzed and put in useful form, as depicted in Figure 4.3. Data in simple tabular form is often not very useful. Today's executives need information in formats that are easily understood. In other words, market analysts and researchers need to interpret data—turn then into information—to assist upper-level managers and executives in making quick, informed decisions.

Types of Data

Data provides the starting point from which marketing information is derived. **Data** can be any set of facts or statistics obtained from outside (external) or inside (internal) the

> ### Marketing Vocabulary
>
> **MARKETING DECISION SUPPORT SYSTEM (MDSS)**
> A two-way communication bridge between the people who collect and analyze information and the executives who use it.
>
> **TRANSACTION- BASED INFORMATION SYSTEM (TBIS)**
> A computerized link between a firm and its customers, distributors, and suppliers.
>
> **INFORMATION**
> Data that has been analyzed and put into useful form.
>
> **DATA**
> Facts or statistics obtained from inside or outside the company.

1. What decisions are made, with what frequency?
2. What information helps make those decisions?
3. What information is currently supplied?
4. What additional information is required?
5. What information do you get now that is unnecessary?
6. How would you like the information displayed?
7. What sources of information would you like to receive on a regular basis?

Figure 4.2   How to Determine Marketing Information Needs

company. Usually the data are stored in a **database**, which is a collection of material that can be retrieved by a computer.

External data come from outside the company. Popular external databases include LEXIS®-NEXIS®, Dow Jones Interactive, Hoover's Online, and Dialog. They provide raw data as well as articles, newsletters, breaking news stories, financial reports on companies, and nearly any other type of data imaginable. For specific needs, you can use sources such as Forrester Research Group's Technographic Data, which provides continuous surveys of 260,000 households in North America and Europe. Technographic Data gives valuable survey information on how consumers think about, buy, and use technology in the categories of devices and media, healthcare, financial services, retail, and travel- survey information that many companies need.[5]

To track competitors, one approach is the source in the Nexis® service, which analyzes specific industries and companies. If you're interested in business customers, Dun & Bradstreet can provide information on 92 million businesses in 200 countries.[6] It can give in-depth financial and operational reports on most of the companies. The databases generally have a cost. Companies charge either for time online or for each piece of data, such as a name or news release.

for a particular issue being addressed. As a result, they tend to take longer and be more expensive to collect than other types of data. **Secondary data** are those that already have been collected. Nearly all marketing information falls into this category. For example, the National Trade Data Bank, with data from numerous government agencies, is a wonderful resource for international research. While secondary data is much easier to obtain and considerably cheaper than primary data, it can still be expensive, costing thousands of dollars for access to studies by primary researchers.

Data Analysis Data analysis transforms material into a usable form, so insights can be developed. It usually involves data sorting, statistics, and models. Data sorting uses several tools for grouping data. For example, Burger King may want to know sales by time of day to determine whether certain items are more popular at certain times.

Statistics help describe data in more detail or tell us how representative certain occurrences are relative to overall patterns. Most information systems have readily available statistical packages that can easily be applied to the data. In some cases they simply count frequencies of occurrence or describe using cross-tabulations or averages. For example, Gannett Co, a leading international

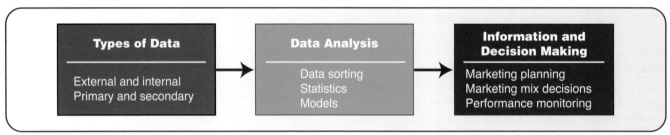

Figure 4.3   How Data Become Information

Internal data are found within a company. Sales data, accounting records, and sales force call reports are examples. Internal data are likely to reside in several different departments. For example, the accounting department has detailed records of sales costs and how much cash is generated by each product. In some cases these figures are available for each market segment. The manufacturing and shipping departments track production schedules, amount of capacity utilized, shipping dates, and inventory levels. In many companies, the supply chain management department provides detailed records of the flow of goods into the company and out to each customer, including the frequency of orders, stock levels, and purchase rates. The marketing department will usually have such data as type and frequency of sales calls, orders received from each location, and advertising schedules.

Primary data are those gathered for the first time

news and information company receives 65 percent of its revenues from advertising. However, 43 percent of that comes from local advertising alone. Awareness of such statistical data helps Gannett Co. focus its time and resources on that pivotal 43 percent.[7]

Models are miniature representations of marketing phenomena. They simplify complex situations by presenting key facts and ignoring unnecessary details. Marketers need models for the same reasons that architects need blueprints. With a blueprint, the architect can visualize various parts of the building without actually being there. Marketing models describe which variables are important for specific marketing situations. For example, General Electric evaluates consumer satisfaction in order to predict loyalty. Its model indicates that satisfaction leads to customer loyalty. The important thing is that the data analysis should be insightful, so that it will lead to innovative marketing decisions, and easy to use, so executives will be more inclined to incorporate it into their decision making.

INFORMATION IS FOR DECISION MAKING

Using information is not easy; however, it's absolutely critical to have good information if you expect to develop a good marketing strategy. Marketers have historically relied on their own intuition. Although experience is still important, the world is more complex today. So experience must be supplemented with marketing information. Good information helps executives make key marketing decisions. As was illustrated in Figure 4.3, marketing information is generally used in three key areas: marketing planning, marketing mix decisions, and performance monitoring. Let's take a look at each of these in more detail.

Marketing Planning Marketing planning requires information at nearly every stage of the process. The situation analysis needs input about customers, competitors, market trends, technology, channels of distribution, and economic conditions. Marketing information also helps marketers make better decisions about which segments to target and how to position the organization. Often, marketing information affects the competitive thrust of the company and data about competitors is critical. Marketing planning should always be fact based rather than opinion based. This places priority on having objective and complete data. Most marketing planning teams have a marketing information specialist who makes relevant information available.

Marketing Mix Decisions Marketing mix decisions are another area in which marketing information is required. In fact, it is so critical to decisions about product, place, promotion, and price that expertise has evolved in each area. For example, Booz, Allen & Hamilton, a large consulting firm, has a department that focuses primarily on product research. The University of Tennessee funds the Center for Logistics Research, which concentrates on distribution channels. The way marketing information aids each of the marketing mix decisions is discussed next.

Product Decisions Marketing information on new products is essential. Marketing information monitors test markets, helps monitor customer satisfaction with good and services, forecasts technology trends, and indicates when to introduce new products or phase out old ones. J.C. Penney conducted an in-depth research in order to find out the needs for "the missing middle" defined as middle-income married women aged between 35 and 54. The company did a telephone survey of 900 women asking them about casual clothes; videotaped interviews with 30 women for up to six hours, recording their feelings about fashion and shopping preferences. The research shows the target women have a more casual lifestyle, want to look trendy with good quality, and crave something suitable for relaxed office dress codes, parties, luncheons and their children's school events. As a result, Penney launched two lines of moderately priced casual clothes with one by designer Nicole Miller. [8]

Place Decisions Marketing information helps with place decisions such as determining the appropriate distribution channel, either directly to consumers or through intermediaries, such as wholesalers and retailers. It can be used to identify specific distributors or the inventory requirements for selected channels. One form of marketing information tracks every item sold in every store. "It captures the entire retail marketing area," says Donald Stuart, partner at Cannondale Associates. "Manufacturers are able to identify the stores that are most important to their category, least important to their category, or that hold the best opportunities for brand or category development." Marketers can identify similar consumer clusters in individual stores and determine which products do better in particular stores. Information such as this "gives manufacturers a definitive read on their business in any account," says Joe Battoe, president of sales and retail services at IRI Research.[9] Once executives gain a good understanding of market phenomena, they are able to make quality decisions regarding the distribution of their products and services.

Marketing Vocabulary

DATABASE
A collection of data that can be retrieved by a computer.

EXTERNAL DATA
Data obtained outside the company.

INTERNAL DATA
Data obtained within the company.

PRIMARY DATA
Information collected for the first time.

SECONDARY DATA
Information that already has been collected.

J.C. Penney uses primary data to aid in product decisions.

Courtesy of JCPenney

Staples, the world's largest office products company, recently relaunched it's Web site with help from qualitative and quantitative customer research. Through every step beginning with the Web site design, feedback from thousands of customers was used. Some additions to the Web site now include timesaving features such as the easy reorder option and the "necessary and recommended products" tool.[10]

Promotion Decisions Vast amounts of information are necessary in the area of promotions. Executives determine the budget required to accomplish desired objectives by delivering the proper combination of advertising, personal selling, or other promotion approaches. For advertising, they need to determine the most effective amounts of Internet, print, television, and radio ads to reach targeted consumers. Information is available regarding the number of target audience members that can be reached by each media, including variations by type of programming, time of day and region of the country. A.C. Nielsen provides data to help decide whether to advertise during particular programs and time slots for several groups of targeted customers. Data even tells the cost for each exposure/ likelihood that a consumer will see a promotion. Data is available to judge the potential effectiveness of sales promotions such as the use of in-store coupons on point of sales discounts.[11]

Pricing Decisions Because prices send strong signals to the market about the value of a product, information on pricing is critical for almost every marketing decision. In many cases, pricing is specific to a region. Wal-Mart and Toys "R" Us advertise that they will meet or beat competitors' prices. They monitor these locally, feeding the information into a centralized MIS. They also collect ads that consumers bring in. Automobile companies look not only at the prices of major competitors but also at finance and leasing terms. Information is collected about the effectiveness of cash discounts and rebates as well as the likelihood of buyers switching from one brand to another at various price points. The airline industry, whose profits are highly sensitive to volume, continually monitors how price affects demand in local, national, and international markets. Internet ticket sellers such as

www.staples.com

Staples used qualitative and quantitative research to design the best Web site for its customers. Visit its corporate responsibility page for information on its nearly 3,000 products comprised of post-consumer recycled materials.

Travelocity.com are especially helpful in this regard, as commercial Web sites are an excellent source of consumer information.

Monitoring Performance

The third area supported by marketing information is performance monitoring. This helps managers make sure that plans and programs are moving ahead on target. Information is required to track progress, identify unsuspected obstacles, and make corrections to accomplish objectives. For British Columbia-based Robeez Footwear, a manufacturer of children's soft-soled leather footwear, customer input is not an occasional goal, it's a way of life. "We have a very loyal group of customers who love to give us feedback," explains Tricia Burton, Robeez's Internet marketing manager. Robeez launched a post purchase online survey to gauge the effectiveness of a redesign its website underwent the previous month. The survey, which appears as a popup includes eight questions on the quality of the content, ease of navigation and the ordering process. So far, the survey has both validated the site redesign and given Robeez a strong direction for the future.[12]

Marketing information also provides valuable feedback. "Without indicators like increased sales or market share gain, we really have no way of knowing how effective our plan for a brand really is," says Dana Anderson, media buyer for United Airlines at Leo Burnett Company, Inc., a major advertising agency. "Marketing information also tells us how well an advertising plan meets specific marketing objectives, like an increase in company or product awareness or an improved image of a brand ... We also evaluate the effects of our promotional campaign on competitors."[13]

Today, nearly every organization monitors customer service levels. Marketing information provides data on customer expectations and how well the company meets them. Witness Systems, a leading global provider of workforce optimization software and services, recently implemented its contact center quality monitoring solution in the DaimlerChrysler Customer Assistance Center (CAC). Using Witness Systems, DaimlerChrysler captures entire

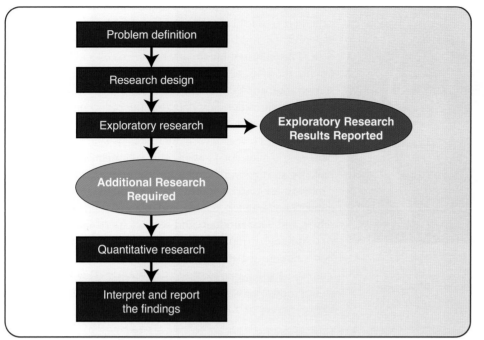

Figure 4.4   The Marketing Research Process

THE MARKETING RESEARCH PROCESS

Marketing research is a key aspect of the organization's ability to make good marketing decisions. It starts with a clear understanding of the problem to be addressed and ends with an interpretation of findings that will aid in decision making. Each step is shown in Figure 4.4.

DEFINING THE PROBLEM

A highly respected marketing research executive for Pharmacia Corporation said, "Never begin a research process with a search for market information. Always start by understanding the decisions to be made and the managerial circumstances surrounding those decisions." This isn't as easy as it sounds, but it's a critical step in the research process. As Albert Einstein said, "The formulation of a problem is often more essential than its solution."[16]

The marketing researcher and key decision makers should work together to specify the problem. The researcher usually must ask probing questions to identify objectives. What is the environment of the problem? When must it be solved? What resources will be committed to the final course of action? It does no good to recommend a remedy clearly beyond the capacity of the company.

Care must be taken to isolate the symptoms from the actual problem. Imagine that Pepsi sales decline rapidly. This sounds like a problem, but it's only a symptom. The

customer interactions - including voice conversations and agent desktop activities - which are analyzed for a complete quality assessment. DaimlerChrysler CAC uses the captured interactions to supplement its e-learning and training programs, as well as to provide input into the company's key performance indicators. "Quality-driven customer service is a core DaimlerChrysler value..." commented DaimlerChrysler CAC's General Manager Marketing and Sales, Roland Staehler. "We knew that implementing a quality monitoring solution would help us increase the quality of our customer service and make it more transparent and consistent."[14]

Outside rating services can provide unbiased information on how consumers evaluate performance. You're probably familiar with the Nielsen ratings, which usually appear weekly in publications such as USA Today. Nielsen Media Research, the leading international television information services company, monitors approximately 5,100 homes. A Nielsen People Meter is installed on each television to record tuning records for every channel: the time of day, duration of tuning, and which household members are watching. The company retrieves the information through the phone lines. The result is television show rankings, weekly ratings, and season to date rankings.[15]

> "The formulation of a problem is often more essential than its solution."

real problem may be a new promotional campaign by Coca-Cola that Pepsi has failed to address. Or perhaps many Pepsi customers are switching to bottled water. Just as a fever is a sign of the flu, declining sales usually indicate a deeper problem. Once it is isolated,

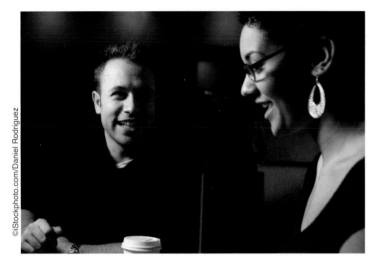

Depth Interviews cover all aspects of participant's attitudes, opinions, or motivations.

the variables or factors causing it can be identified. This helps define the problem before any marketing research begins.

RESEARCH DESIGN

A **research design** is an outline of what data will be gathered, what sources will be used, and how the data will be collected and analyzed. The research design is, in effect, a master plan for the research project as shown in Figure 4.4.

Most designs call for two types of research: exploratory and quantitative. **Exploratory research** clarifies the problem and searches for ways to address it. **Quantitative research** provides the information needed to select the best course of action and forecast the probable results. Research generally starts with an exploratory study, may include a pilot phase, and ends with quantitative research. A **pilot study** is a small-scale project that allows the researcher to refine and test the approaches that ultimately will be used.

EXPLORATORY RESEARCH

Exploratory research enables investigators to obtain a better understanding of the issues. Specifically, it helps:
- determine the exact nature of the problem or opportunity,
- search for causes or explanations for the problem,
- define the magnitude of the problem,
- create hypotheses about underlying causes,
- describe why or how the causes may affect the situation,
- understand competitors' actions and reactions to company strategies, and
- estimate how courses of action may affect the market.

Exploratory research seeks information that will enlighten marketers in the decision-making process. It generally begins by finding and reviewing secondary data. This information already has been collected, so it's usually the quickest and most cost-effective way to get started. Sometimes the entire research question can be answered with secondary data, but the collection of primary data usually is required. A simple Google search for sports sites reveals 81.7 million homepages for basketball, 81.6 million for football, and 108 million for baseball. By starting with exploratory research, companies can learn a lot about sports, such as how fans follow the game, how leagues, teams, and players market themselves, and what products and services sports fans buy.[17]

Although exploratory research seldom quantifies the best solution, it helps define the problem and suggests options. Exploratory research is conducted with focus groups, interviews, projective techniques, observation, and case analysis. Each is discussed next.

Focus Groups A **focus (focused) group** usually involves eight to twelve people whose opinions provide qualitative insights into a problem. This approach is particularly useful in clarifying problems with a company's products, services, advertising, distribution channels, and the like. It's possible to gather a wide range of information about customers' feelings on these subjects and discover the reasons for their attitudes or purchase behaviors. Techniques are used that probe into thoughts and feelings. Researchers ask questions and encourage participants to interact with one another to uncover unexpected attitudes, behaviors, and ideas that may suggest innovative marketing strategies. In a sense, the group interviews itself. The social interaction often yields insights that could not be obtained through one-on-one interviews.

Focus groups have been used for a variety of purposes. Although most focus groups are conducted in person with a facilitator, other formats can be used, such as videoconferencing through tele-

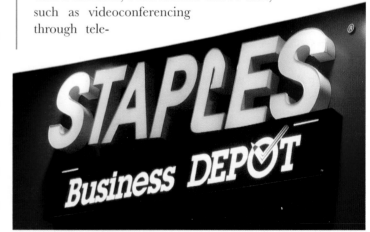

Staples used qualitative and quantitative research to create the most fitting Web site for its customers.

To get a lead on the buying habits of teens and 20-somethings market researchers are now talking to kids and young adults in nontraditional research settings such as the streets.

Projective Techniques **Projective techniques** enable respondents to project their thoughts onto a third party, or through some type of contrived situation. This is often done using word associations, sentence completion, and role-playing. Because projective approaches do not require respondents to provide answers in a structured format, people are more likely to interpret the situation creatively and in the context of their own experiences and emotions. When asked directly why they purchase a particular item, they may describe a far more rational process than the one that actually occurs. For example, if a recent college graduate is asked why she purchased a Saturn or Pontiac Solstice, she may cite performance, gas mileage, and overall value of the product. But if asked to project the feelings of a person who purchases this kind of automobile, she may focus on status, self-esteem, and the need to be noticed.

vision monitors, remote control cameras, and digital transmission. The Internet has become an excellent—and cost-effective—tool for focus group research. The Atlanta-based ActiveGroup has emerged as one of the leading providers of Internet-based focus group technology. This emerging technology is allowing marketing specialists to conduct focus groups from their homes, hotels and boardrooms. Lately, ActiveGroup has focused on Web site and computer-usability testing by placing a camera above the computer monitor. By doing so, ActiveGroup can record consumer facial expressions of satisfaction, confusion, like, or dislike.[18] You'll learn more about this unique format in the technology section.

When selecting participants for a focus group, it's generally best to choose those with similar demographics, since common experiences provide the basis for more in-depth discussion. Most exploratory research calls for more than one focus group. In fact, a single session is likely to produce erroneous information. The researcher should use several groups to ensure that the findings are somewhat representative. Even though many individuals may be involved, the unit of analysis is the group and not the individual. Six groups with eight people each, in effect, yields six interviews, not 48.

Depth Interviews **Depth interviews** are relatively unstructured conversations that allow researchers to probe into a consumer's thought processes. Often they are used to investigate the mechanisms of purchase decisions. Although the discussion may appear casual to the participant, the skilled researcher exerts a great deal of control. Often the interview is designed to cover all aspects of the participant's attitudes, opinions, or motivations. The marketer uses these results both as individual case studies and as comparative data to examine commonalities among respondents.

Observation **Observation** is a technique whereby the participants are simply watched. In one classic study, researchers stationed themselves in both crowded and uncrowded supermarkets to discover whether buying behavior differed. In uncrowded stores shoppers tended to use the information on labels and shelves, whereas in crowded conditions they tended to make decisions more hastily. This exploratory observation was followed by a more formal survey that enabled conclusions to be drawn about buyer behavior in crowded situations.[19]

Marketing Vocabulary

RESEARCH DESIGN
An outline of what data will be gathered, what sources will be used, and how the data will be collected and analyzed.

EXPLORATORY RESEARCH
Research designed to clarify the problem and suggest ways to address it.

QUANTITATIVE RESEARCH
Research designed to provide the information needed to select the best course of action and estimate the probable results.

PILOT STUDY
A small-scale project that allows the researcher to refine and test the approaches that eventually will be used.

FOCUS GROUP
A group, usually composed of eight to twelve people, whose opinions are elicited by an interviewer to provide exploratory insights into a problem.

DEPTH INTERVIEW
A relatively unstructured conversation that allows the researcher to probe deeply into a consumer's thoughts.

PROJECTIVE TECHNIQUES
A technique that enables respondents to project their thoughts onto a third party or object or through some type of contrived situation.

OBSERVATION
A research technique whereby researchers simply watch the participants they are studying.

Structured observation is made through mechanical means. Galvanometers record electrical resistance in the skin, associated with sweating and other responses. Tachistoscopes measure visual stimuli. Special cameras often are used to study eye movement as a subject reads advertising copy. By observing pupil dilation and blinking responses, it is possible to judge what receives attention in ads or on packaging.[20]

Case Analysis **Case analysis** is the in-depth study of a few examples. This technique is particularly appropriate for complex buying and competitive situations. For example, how industrial companies make decisions for particular components or capital goods is often studied this way. A single researcher may spend several days interviewing a firm's employees who purchase and use the product in question. In addition, buying policies, documents, and actual purchase history are investigated. When a few (perhaps as many as 10) companies are examined in this way, researchers obtain a more complete understanding of why and how certain suppliers are selected. The information can help suppliers determine the appropriateness of various marketing approaches.

Case analysis can also be used to study the competition. Researchers may select two or three activities of key competitors and examine them in depth. By knowing all aspects of the strategies used to introduce a couple of products, researchers can assess competitors' strengths and weaknesses and also predict how they might behave in the future with other products. Benchmarking is also a form of case analysis. Even individual departments can benchmark their expense costs and productivity with those of other companies' departments.

Quantitative research played an enormous role in the successful positioning and launch of Kimberly-Clark's Expressions facial tissue line. In the face of increasing competition from products, the company began looking for an innovative way to increase market share for its Kleenex brand. Nearly 37 percent of buyers said they disliked the look of tissue boxes and often hid them in closets or bathrooms, where they wouldn't clash with household decor. The Expressions line introduced packaging with about 18 different motifs that range from Native American animal drawings to Amish quilts to an impressionistic Manhattan skyline. Product testing in eight U.S. cities revealed consumer preferences for six styles: traditional, country, southwestern, contemporary, Asian, and Victorian. Expressions was ultimately a great success, partly because marketers took the time to learn the opinions of consumers.[21]

Quantitative research usually follows the **scientific method** to ensure that faulty conclusions are not drawn. The scientific method is a systematic way to gather, analyze, and interpret data in order to confirm or disconfirm a prior conception. Essentially, it is a two-step procedure. First, researchers develop a **hypothesis** about an issue based on a limited amount of information. A hypothesis is a tentative assumption about a particular event or issue. Second, rigorous tests are conducted to determine whether the hypothesis is supported by the information.

Let us say we have an idea that more men and women shop in malls on the weekend because they're not working, so we hypothesize that greater sales volumes will be obtained on Saturday and Sunday than on weekdays. We then gather information to test the hypothesis. The key is for researchers to state beforehand what they believe the results may be and why. This enables appro-

QUANTITATIVE RESEARCH

Quantitative research provides information that helps decision makers select the best course of action and estimate the probable results. As the name suggests, numbers are involved. Rigorous statistical procedures allow researchers to estimate how confident they can be about their conclusions. Since quantitative research uses widely accepted methods, duplicating the study should arrive at approximately the same results. Certain techniques also indicate how closely the findings represent the views or attitudes of the whole population at large, not just the sample studied.

INSTRUCTIONS: Please put an X in the space that indicates how strongly you agree or disagree with the following statements about MTV.

	Strongly Disagree	Disagree	Neither Agree Nor Disagree	Agree	Strongly Agree
Watching MTV programs is enjoyable	___	___	___	___	___
MTV is less educational than most evening programming	___	___	___	___	___
MTV appeals more to those with higher income	___	___	___	___	___

Figure 4.5   A Typical Likert Scale

INSTRUCTIONS: Please put an X in the space that most appropriately indicates your feelings about shopping at Gap.

	Very	Moderately	Slightly	Neither One nor the Other	Slightly	Moderately	Very	
Inexpensive	—	—	—	—	—	—	—	Expensive
Helpful Salespeople	—	—	—	—	—	—	—	Unhelpful Salespeople
High-quality Products	—	—	—	—	—	—	—	Low-quality Products

Figure 4.6   A Typical Bipolar Adjective Scale

priate data to be gathered and analyzed to assess whether the hypothesis is true.

Data Collection Methods   Two of the most common methods for collecting quantitative data are experiments and surveys. **Experiments** usually take place either where the marketing problem occurs or in a laboratory setting that is contrived to match research needs. To test new packaging for a pain reliever, for example, the manufacturer may invite consumers to "shop" in a simulated supermarket. In that way shopping patterns can be observed to see whether the packaging is eye-catching. Experiments are often used for causal research. Causal research attempts to show a cause-and-effect relationship between two events. One of the most important forms of **causal research** is test marketing. A test market provides a limited trial of a product strategy under realistic conditions.

Surveys are the most popular way to collect data. When researchers want to ensure that each subject is asked for the same information, they prepare a written survey questionnaire. It is a measurement device, much like a thermometer or a ruler. Two common units of measure for questionnaire items are the points along Likert scales and bipolar adjective scales.

Likert scales are simple to develop and easy to interpret. **Likert scales** allow the intensity of feelings to be expressed and tend to provide information about a person's attitude toward something. Subjects are asked to indicate the extent to which they agree or disagree with each statement in the survey. The Likert scale shown in Figure 4.5 has five points (units of measure). A seven-point scale often is used, adding "somewhat disagree" and "somewhat agree" on either side of the middle point.

Bipolar adjective scales allow respondents to choose along a range between two extremes. Figure 4.6 shows a typical bipolar adjective scale. In general, there are three, five, or seven points in the scale. Many dimensions can be measured in a relatively short questionnaire. Perhaps that is why this scale is so frequently used in marketing research.

The wording of an item can make quite a difference. A classic example occurred in the 1980s during the battles between Burger King and McDonald's. Burger King asked respondents: "Do you prefer your hamburgers flame-broiled or fried?" The three-to-one preference for flame-broiled was touted extensively by Burger King in an ad campaign. The results were completely different when McDonald's researchers asked: "Do you prefer a hamburger that is grilled on a hot stainless-steel grill or cooked by passing the warmed meat through an open-gas flame?" McDonald's frying method received a clear majority. When the question was modified to include the fact that the gas-flame burgers were warmed in a microwave oven prior to serving, McDonald's won seven to one.[22]

Administering Surveys   A survey can be administered through personal interviews, mall intercepts, telephone, mail or the Internet. Each technique has benefits and disadvantages, as shown in Figure 4.7. The researcher needs to select the method

Marketing Vocabulary

CASE ANALYSIS
The in-depth study of a few examples.

SCIENTIFIC METHOD
A systematic way to gather, analyze, and interpret data in order to confirm or disconfirm a prior conception.

HYPOTHESIS
A tentative assumption about a particular event or issue.

EXPERIMENT
A test conducted under controlled conditions in order to prove or disprove a marketing hypothesis.

CAUSAL RESEARCH
Research that attempts to show a cause-and-effect relationship between two phenomena.

LIKERT SCALE
A scale that measures the respondent's intensity of agreement with a particular statement.

	Personal Interviews	Mall Intercepts	Telephone	Mail	Internet
Speed of Completion	Slowest	Fast	Fast	Moderate	Fastest
Response Rate	High	Moderate	Moderate	Low	Moderate
Quality of Response	Excellent	Good	Good	Limited	Good
Interviewer Bias	High	Moderate	Moderate	Low	Low
Geographic Reach	Limited	Limited	Excellent	Excellent	Excellent
Cost	Very expensive	Moderate	Moderate	Inexpensive	Inexpensive

Figure 4.7   Comparative Advantages of Interviews, Mall Intercepts, Telephone Surveys, Mail Questionnaires and Internet Surveys

most appropriate for the current project.

Personal Interviews Personal interviews require face-to-face, two-way communication between the interviewer and the respondent. This method is particularly useful in probing complex answers or observing the respondent's behavior. The setting usually is comfortable, and the respondent is given undivided attention. Gen-X Press is a leading full-service consulting group that helps companies to better market to Generations X and Y, usually collecting through face-to-face interviews with members of these generations. Questions are asked about motivation, the relationship between pay and happiness, and empowerment in the workplace. Marketers believe that the opinions of individuals can be used to predict future actions among mainstream members of Generations X and Y.[23]

One benefit of personal interviews is the high participation rate. It's unlikely that any questions will go unanswered, and props or visual aids can be used. But there are several disadvantages. Subjects may be influenced by the interviewer, and they give up anonymity when meeting face-to-face, so they may withhold information or answer in unnatural ways. Interviewing is expensive, since professionals must be trained and then sent to the various locations. The cost can range from $25 per average consumer to thousands of dollars per top executive, surgeon, legislator, or others.

Mall Intercepts Mall intercepts, as the name implies, occur at a shopping mall, and the interviewer chooses respondents on some objective basis, such as every fifth person encountered. Mall intercepts are simple to conduct, and data can be collected quickly and cost-effectively. Questions can be asked about actual purchases during some specified period. This helps the researcher determine actual behaviors as well as opinions and attitudes. One variation of this method is a shopping basket study, or simply looking at what a consumer purchases during a particular trip to the store. Grocery stores often want this kind of information in order to identify which products are purchased together, the total amount of spending, and the shopping patterns of individuals while in the store.

Telephone Surveys Telephone surveys offer speed and relatively low cost. Using banks of telephones, marketers can contact a large number of people at approximately the same time. This method is particularly effective with professionals, who tend to be articulate and willing to discuss things over the telephone. By prearranging the call, it's possible to gain considerable cooperation from respondents. Now that fax machines and the Internet are so prevalent, a common procedure is to call ahead, fax the information or ask respondents to get it from a Web site, and obtain reactions over the telephone. This enables interviewers not only to probe for thoughts and ideas but also to elicit responses to printed materials. Another advantage of the telephone is that a second call can be arranged easily if the individual cannot respond at that moment. Today, computer-assisted technology allows respondents to register their answers using the touch-tone pad, which works particularly well with a large panel of subjects. Also, computerized systems that are voice activated save on telephone charges and make online data analysis possible.

The major drawback of telephone interviews is the increase in unlisted numbers, which makes it very difficult to obtain a valid sample. In some cities more than half

©iStockphoto.com/Lajos Répási

Telephone surveys can reach a large number of people in a short time frame, at relatively low cost.

the population has an unlisted number. Many young consumers have done away with land-lines, using their cell phones, numbers which are rarely listed, as their primary phone line. One way to overcome this is through random digit dialing by a computer, although many consumers are adding Caller ID service to screen out unwanted surveys. In addition, phone surveys have an obvious limitation if respondents are required to see something, as in evaluating ads or product renderings.

Mail Surveys In mail surveys, a questionnaire is sent directly to the respondent's home or place of business. An advantage is that people can answer at their own pace and at a convenient time. Mailed questionnaires can be extremely useful for surveying professionals, who have a high response rate and tend to give thoughtful answers. Publishers regularly survey professors by mail concerning textbooks they have adopted, teaching methods, and their ideas about innovative materials that can be created. Associations often obtain good response quality and return rates from membership surveys by mail.

Many techniques are used to encourage people to answer mail questionnaires. Often a cover letter explains the purpose of the study and why it will be beneficial to them. A little gift or a small amount of money can improve return rates. Research also reveals that the rate can be boosted considerably by multiple prior notification, while sending only one has no influence. Mailing a second survey has a significant effect on response rates as well.[24]

It helps to have the surveys sponsored by a legitimate organization, such as a professional association. A study reported in *Industrial Marketing Management* examined this effect. The mean response rates for the questionnaires from a university and an honor society sponsor were significantly higher than for those sponsored by a marketing research firm and an unidentified source.[25] Despite every effort to improve the percentage of responses, many people refuse to answer mail questionnaires. This is a serious problem, since those who do respond may differ from the rest of the population. For example, they may be motivated to answer because they intensely like or dislike a product.

Internet Surveys Many researchers use the Internet to gain individuals' participation in surveys. The main advantage of using the Internet instead of traditional methods is that the information is available very quickly. Additionally, researchers can survey a greater number of people with less costs compared to written and mailed surveys, and data can be analyzed as they are collected.

There are four main types of online surveys:

1. Pop-Up Surveys - When an Internet surfer leaves a Web site, another window, containing a questionnaire, pops up on the screen. Internet users have the option of either completing the survey or closing the browser window. The response rate for this type of survey ranges from 15 to 45 percent.

2. E-Mail or Web Surveys - Via e-mail, a company can invite someone for his or her participation in an online questionnaire. The response rates for these surveys range from 25 to 50 percent and are usually completed by the user in two to three days.

3. Online Groups - A research company can organize what is essentially a focus group discussion on the Internet. These discussions are held in chat rooms on the Internet.

4. Moderated E-Mail Groups - Researchers can carry on long discussions with individuals by communicating through e-mail. Online bulletin boards are an example of this type of research.[26]

Marketers also observe discussions among Web users to gather information about current and prospective customers. Many companies encourage customers to fill out a Web site registration form. The participant is usually asked to volunteer some personal information in exchange for a free gift, coupon, or some other incentive. The information helps the marketer to understand Internet behavior and habits. The New York Times, for example, has a Web site registration form that profiles customer interests. Not only can the information be used for research but also relevant e-mail can be automatically forwarded to those who want it.[27]

Procter & Gamble uses pop-up surveys to gain customer feedback.

SAMPLING

Surveys are conducted to draw insights about the people being studied. The **population (universe)** is comprised of all the individuals or organizations relevant to the marketing

Marketing Vocabulary

POPULATION (UNIVERSE)
All the individuals or organizations relevant to the marketing research project.

research project. For example, if the government wants to know the average number of jobs a U.S. resident holds during the first 10 years out of high school, the relevant population is all U.S. residents age 28 or older. There are millions in this age group. The government could attempt to interview all of them, but that would be impractical, if not impossible, and far too costly. Researchers have developed methods for surveying a subset of people from whom they draw inferences about the larger population.

The first step is to obtain a **sampling frame**, which is a list of people in the universe who potentially could be contacted. From this, researchers select the sample. A **sample** is the group of people who are asked to participate in the research. Since focus groups usually are very small, it is difficult to determine whether the opinions expressed truly represent those of the larger population.

There are two categories of samples: probability and nonprobability. In a **probability sample**, the chance of selecting a given individual can be calculated. One popular method is **simple random sampling**, whereby each individual has an equal chance of being chosen (say, every third name is selected). Another is **stratified random sampling**, whereby each individual within a selected subgroup of the sample has a known chance of selection (say, every third household with income of $50,000+). This method is often used in marketing since much research focuses on market segments. If some form of random sampling is adopted, then statistics can be used to determine the likelihood that responses from the sample will be similar to the responses of the larger population.

When using **nonprobability samples**, the researcher does not know the likelihood of selecting a particular respondent. The two most common types are judgment and convenience samples. **Judgment samples** are chosen by the researcher based on the belief that these people represent a majority of the study population.

Convenience samples are people who happen to come along, such as shoppers in a given store at a certain time or travelers passing through an airport. Convenience samples are relatively inexpensive, and the selection can be purposely unrepresentative, such as interviewing only females. In general, this method does not provide data reliable enough for quantitative research. Even probability samples can become like convenience samples if care is not taken regarding the smallest details, such as when interviews are conducted. Tom Brokaw, renowned broadcast anchor, once remarked that election polls could not

---

www.ford.com

Learn how you can conserve fuel while driving by exploring the Eco-Driving Tips at the Ford Web site.

---

be taken on Friday night. It seems the results would be skewed because so many Republicans go out that evening.

INTERPRETING AND REPORTING SURVEY FINDINGS

Once the research is completed, the results must be reported to the appropriate decision makers. No matter how sophisticated or reliable, marketing research is of little use unless it can be easily understood by the people who act upon it. Most managers and executives have little experience with research techniques and little interest in learning about them. Thus, presentation of understandable research results is an important skill for marketers. Good research moves from data to information to insigh. Unfortunately, to demonstrate the hard work that has gone into a project, many researchers give too much extraneous information. A report that describes each table in detail instead of using the information to reach conclusions is not likely to meet the needs of executives.

Experience pays off in interpreting research. When the Museum of Fine Arts (MFA) in Boston held focus groups on an upcoming exhibition of Winslow Homer, the researchers found that the public did not know much about the artist and might not attend. A museum executive used her experience, including the MFA shop's sales records of items linked to Homer, to indicate that while the public may not know his

---

Marketing Vocabulary

SAMPLING FRAME
A list of people in the universe who potentially could be contacted.

SAMPLE
The group participating in a research project that represents the entire population of potential respondents.

PROBABILITY SAMPLE
A sample in which the chance of selecting a given individual from the sampling frame or population can be calculated.

SIMPLE RANDOM SAMPLING
A sampling technique in which each member of the study population has an equal and known chance of being chosen.

STRATIFIED RANDOM SAMPLING
A sampling technique in which each member of a selected subgroup of the population has an equal chance of selection.

NONPROBABILITY SAMPLE
A sample in which the likelihood of selecting a particular respondent from the sampling frame cannot be calculated.

JUDGMENT SAMPLE
A sample selected by the researchers or interviewers based on their belief that those chosen represent a majority of the study population.

CONVENIENCE SAMPLE
A sample composed of people who happen to come along, such as shoppers in a store at a given time, whoever answers the doorbell, or travelers passing through an airport.

name, it knows his pictures and would turn out for the show. Because the museum relied on the executive's experience, to help interpret the focus group, it was able to create a blockbuster event. Yet, sometimes research is right when the experts are wrong. Ford didn't listen to

marketing research in the mid-1950s. The Edsel was built with features that consumers said they wanted, but the car itself did poorly in several rounds of consumer testing. Ford went ahead anyway, believing it could push the car with a strong sales force. The mistake cost about $350

The Marketing Gazette™

CREATING & CAPTURING VALUE THROUGH RELATIONSHIPS

J.D. Power & Associates

A common blind spot of marketers is to look for research that confirms what they think, not research that points up what they don't know. This was certainly the case when independent researcher John David Power presented his data to the automotive industry about 30 years ago. Power approached the nation's automakers with extensive independent surveys on customer satisfaction. Instead of embracing Power and his work with open arms, the Big Three gave him the cold shoulder. The surveys highlighted America's dissatisfaction with U.S. made cars, and Detroit didn't want to hear about it. Ironically, it was Power's insistence on maintaining an arm's-length relationship with the auto industry that finally brought Detroit around. Today, the J. D. Power & Associates Customer Satisfaction rating is the most coveted, and credible, seal of approval in the business.

A former financial analyst at Ford Motor Company, Power struck out on his own in 1968. His idea was to pay for his own customer surveys of the automotive industry and later sell the results. Says J. Ferron, a former Power executive and now partner-in-charge of Coopers & Lybrand's auto practice, "Dave's genius was not to depend on companies to finance proprietary studies, but to do independent studies and publish the results." Detroit turned a blind eye, but the Japanese were only too happy to see what the surveys had to say about their competitors. Power's data were a crucial step in their campaign to break into the U.S. auto market, which they did.

By the mid-1980s, Japanese cars were overtaking U.S. models in sales, and the Big Three were forced to listen to

Power. "Our goal has always been to improve the quality of cars," says Power. Today, automakers whose cars receive a top rating are happy to fork over the large licensing fee that Power requires when they advertise his results. It's actually a small price to pay, since a J. D. Power & Associates number-one rating has been known to double sales of a particular model.

Drawing on the success of his car ratings, Power is taking his multimillion-dollar company in some exciting new directions. He extended his arm's-length handshake to the nation's 21,000 new car dealerships, giving them the chance to compete for their own J. D. Power awards. The Power Information Network (PIN) is a computerized program that collects details of every transaction made by participating dealers. PIN gives carmakers and dealers an accurate picture of what cars are selling where and at what price. It's a far cry from tabulating survey results at the kitchen table, which is what Power and his wife did when he first started out.

Over the years, J. D. Power has added several other markets for which it conducts market research. Instead of only focusing on the automotive industry, J. D. Power also does work in finance, travel, housing, and telecommunications. In the area of finance, J. D. Power publishes ratings for online broker and credit card ratings. It also publishes ratings for other industries including airlines, home builders, wireless providers, and Internet service providers.

The Edsel is an example of a marketing mistake.

million (in 1950s dollars)!

There is some debate about whether marketing researchers should recommend action. Whether marketing researchers make recommendations must depend on the total data available, the inclinations of the researcher, and the desires of decision makers. In keeping with the team spirit, most executives would like knowledgeable people to provide as many insights as possible. If recommendations are made, then all the underlying assumptions should be clearly stated.

WHO DOES MARKETING RESEARCH?

The first commercial research department was founded in 1911 at the Saturday Evening Post, when Charles C. Parlin completed his now famous study of Campbell's soup users. He undertook the research because Campbell's executives refused to purchase advertising in the Post, believing that its working-class readership did not represent a significant market for the company. The soup sold at 10 cents a can, a cost they believed only wealthy consumers could afford. By counting cans in the garbage from different neighborhoods, Parlin proved they were wrong. He showed that canned soup was bought mainly by the time-constrained working class, whereas the wealthy enjoyed homemade soup prepared by ser-

vants. Campbell's became a big advertiser in the magazine and one of the top brand names in the United States.

In-Company Research An American Marketing Association (AMA) survey indicates that three out of four large companies have a formal in-company marketing research department. In fact, nearly all consumer products manufacturers, retailers, wholesalers, advertising agencies, and publishers have such a department. Most were created within the last decade.

Most in-company marketing research departments are headed by experienced personnel who report to top executives. The research staff usually includes project directors, analysts, and specialists. The project director is responsible for designing projects, which may be conducted within the department or by outside agencies. The position of analyst is an entry-level job with the function of interpreting specific types of data for select decisions. Analysts usually are part of a marketing team from several units or divisions, although they report directly to the head of their department. Marketing research specialists have expertise in one aspect of a project, such as survey design, data collection, statistics, modeling, or marketing science.

Marketing research has become so sophisticated that few organizations are willing to rely entirely on their internal capabilities. Consequently, research is conducted by both in-house personnel and outside agencies, who may or may not work together. Often it's not cost-effective for companies to hire employees with all the different skills required to conduct a broad range of research. This is especially true regarding data collection. Numerous companies offer field services in that area. Even if external agencies are used, however, most companies still need internal staff to help identify the research problem and interface with the outside agency.

External Research Companies often hire out marketing research. As you can see from Figure 4.8, conducting research can be a very lucrative business.

Outside agencies include consulting companies, full-service research firms, specialty research firms, and syndicated data companies. Such consulting companies as Deloitte & Touche and Electronic Data Systems (EDS) often conduct all phases of marketing research but only for clients

Rank	Organization	Headquarters	Total Research Revenue (Millions)
1	VNU Inc.	New York, NY	$1,794.4
2	IMS Health Inc.	Fairfield, CT	$ 571.0
3	Westat Inc.	Rockville, MD	$ 397.8
4	TNS U.S.	New York, NY	$ 396.0
5	Information Resources Inc.	Chicago, IL	$ 379.6
6	The Kantar Group	Fairfield, CT	$ 365.7
7	Arbitron Inc.	New York, NY	$ 284.7
8	NOP World US	New York, NY	$ 213.0
9	Ipsos	New York, NY	$ 193.9
10	Synovate	Chicago, IL	$ 193.5

Figure 4.8 Top 10 U.S. Research Organizations
Source: : "Top 50 U.S. Research Organizations," Marketing News, June 15, 2005, p4

with whom they have an ongoing relationship. Full-service firms focus on all aspects of data collection and analysis, and their personnel can handle the entire project. Specialty research firms concentrate on certain aspects of a project. There are more than 180 research firms in the United States, and U.S. companies spend more than $7 billion annually on external research.[28] Some only conduct surveys, relying on others to supply questionnaires and yet others to perform data analysis. Certain specialty research firms help marketers better understand diversity or particular segments. Companies such as VNU Inc., IMS Health Inc. and Westat earn hundreds of millions of dollars in research revenue each year.[29] Syndicated data companies also research one type of information or a single industry. For example, the Bureau of the Census and the Bureau of Labor Statistics are experts on census data and use the data to model various scenarios for clients. Neurocommunication Research Laboratory specializes in customized information about how broadcast and print advertisements trigger the maximum responses in viewers.

Because marketing research is critical for good decision making but expensive to conduct, most companies build a long-term association with one or more outside sources. This enables the agency to become familiar with the typical problems faced by the organization and to establish a good working relationship with in-company marketing research staff.

TECHNOLOGY'S EFFECT ON MARKETING RESEARCH

Technology has brought many changes to marketing research. Today's marketers can acquire and analyze more information faster than ever before. Technology also has made it easier for them to connect with an increasing number of customers and information sources. In the past, marketing research was a relatively static process in the face of constantly changing markets. Now marketers can know in real time what is happening in the marketplace. Data are quickly converted to information that can be used in a specific decision.

Technology has not merely sped up the research process. Advances in computerized 3-D modeling make it easy to simulate retail stores on computer

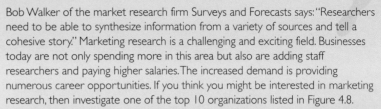

Career Tip:

Bob Walker of the market research firm Surveys and Forecasts says: "Researchers need to be able to synthesize information from a variety of sources and tell a cohesive story." Marketing research is a challenging and exciting field. Businesses today are not only spending more in this area but also are adding staff researchers and paying higher salaries. The increased demand is providing numerous career opportunities. If you think you might be interested in marketing research, then investigate one of the top 10 organizations listed in Figure 4.8.

screens. Virtual shopping is inexpensive to create when compared to the cost of setting up an actual store. Consumers can make product selections as they scroll through the computer image. You can change brand assortment or features in minutes. The virtual store gives marketers a no-risk way to exercise their imagination early in the product development process.[30] For an example, virtual tours of the hotel room became an important feature of online travel website such as Travelocity, Expedia, and Orbitz.[31] Technology helps reduce the cost as well as the risk of marketing innovations.

INTERNET SEARCHES

The Internet's World Wide Web can be an excellent source of marketing data. In fact, it is sometimes referred to as the world's largest resource library. It contains information on literally millions of topics and is updated instantly. The trick is to sift through all of it to find what you need. Marketers do this through the use of a search engine such as Google, Yahoo!, America Online, WebCrawler, Ask.com, or Mozilla. You type a key word into the search engine, and it scans all the Web sites to which it's linked, providing you with a list of available information matching the keyword. Google is expanding its search capabilities to include offline library content in online search results. All 11 universities of the Big Ten consortium have joined Google's efforts; over 10 million volumes of material will be added to Google's current volume of 78 million. Books are scanned and digitized,

Visitors to Ask.com can choose from different customizable background skins.

http://globaledge.msu.edu

Visit globalEDGE™ Online for the ultimate international marketing research tool!

Marketers have many resources to gain insights about global marketing opportunities. One of the most useful is globalEDGE™. Developed by MSU-CIBER as the ultimate international marketing research tool, it has up-to-date information on 200 countries, including maps, key statistics, history, economic, government, stock market, country specific marketing resources and news. Web-based computer software programs incorporate research knowledge in easily usable formats. Each chapter of the text has a globalEDGE™ exercise tied to its content.

and when a user searches a key word, the Google results will show information about the book and a few sentences that display that search term within the book.[32]

GLOBAL MARKETING RESEARCH

Global marketing research involves the same process as any other kind—from research design to the interpretation and presentation of results. And usually the same techniques are employed—interviews, focus groups, and surveys. The big difference is that global marketing research is very difficult.

It is not easy to locate secondary data in foreign countries. Sometimes it simply isn't collected in a country. For example, Ethiopia and Chad don't gather population statistics.[33] Many developing countries lack mechanisms for collecting data about retail and wholesale activities. And even if secondary data are available, they may be incomplete or their accuracy questionable. The data may be manipulated by the government for political reasons - for instance, some countries report a lower than accurate inflation rate. Industrialized nations usually have sophisticated collection procedures, at least for basic statistics on population and economic activity. In developing countries, data are likely to be based on estimates or outdated processes.[34]

Because secondary data are difficult to find, global research often requires the collection of primary data. This, too, presents many challenges.

One of the most obvious is that of language. It's very hard to ensure an exact translation, especially when slang is used. Many researchers use a technique called back translation: The research question is translated into the foreign language by one person, and then it is put back in the original language by a second person. This helps catch any errors. It certainly helped an Australian soft-drink company hoping to market its product in Hong Kong. Its slogan, "Baby, it's cold in here," translated into Chinese as: "Small mosquito, on the inside it is very cold."[35] Needless to say, that would have been an embarrassing marketing blunder!

Once the survey instrument is translated, participants must be found. Again, this isn't easy. In Mexico, there are only 15 phones lines per 100 citizens, compared to 61 phones per 100 people in the United States. And the phone service in Mexico is extremely unreliable. In Brazil, nearly 30 percent of all mail is never delivered. Postal service is equally poor in other developing countries. Even if the mail gets through, literacy can be another barrier. Sometimes even individual interviews present challenges. In many cultures, it's considered embarrassing to discuss personal hygiene, such as which shampoo or soap you use. The Germans tend to avoid conversations about personal finances and the Dutch would rather talk about sex than money.[36]

Nevertheless, companies that avoid global marketing research find themselves in trouble. When Gerber started selling baby food in Africa, they used the same packages they did in the U.S., picturing the beautiful baby on the

Global Marketing Research uses maps and aerial photos to identify population locations and estimate sizes in remote places.

front. What they did not realize was that because the primary language was not English in every African country, companies routinely put pictures on the label to represent what's inside. The packaging of Gerber's product was misinterpreted, and people refused to buy the product. In Taiwan, the Pepsi slogan "Come alive with the Pepsi Generation" was translated as "Pepsi will bring your ancestors back from the dead."[37] Proper marketing research would have caught these mistakes.

Global marketing research is becoming more and more prevalent as companies expand their scope of operations. The time it takes to conduct worldwide research has been reduced by computer-based interviews via the Internet, the spread of telephones and fax machines, and express delivery services. For example, one software company conducted a worldwide survey of more than 80 clients in only three weeks. This amazing feat, which would have been virtually impossible without use of the Internet, involved modeling tasks, computer programming, list development, respondent recruiting, and data retrieval, analysis, and reporting. As a result of the research, the company was able to improve its pricing strategy.

ETHICS IN MARKETING RESEARCH AND INFORMATION USE

J. D. Power is paid by automakers to provide research on customer satisfaction. This information is then used in publications to promote autos. Some magazine editors receive "consulting fees" from auto companies and write reviews of car performance. These are certainly legal practices, but are they ethical? With the information explosion comes an increasing amount of potentially deceptive research that can be used to alter consumers' opinions. Historically, studies were sponsored by scientists, the federal government, and academic institutions. Today, with government and universities on tight budgets, private companies fill the void with so-called objective research for hire. Corporations, litigants, political candidates, trade associations, lobbyists, and special-interest groups can buy research to use as they like.[38]

A study by the Boston Center

for Strategy Research revealed that some marketing managers believe market research is likely to reflect biases rather than present objective information. They also believe much of it is conducted to confirm a preconceived conclusion or validate a client's position. In other words, it arrives at the desired answer, no matter what the facts may indicate. Research of this nature is confirmatory, not exploratory.[39]

The scientific method is supposed to prevent this type of bias because anyone duplicating a study or experiment should come up with the same results. More and more of the information available to consumers is created to sell a product or advance a cause. Buying and selling information to advance a private agenda demonstrates how the modern sense of truth may be warped.[40] Privately sponsored research tends to emphasize positive results and downplay negative ones. Companies obviously want their products to look good.[41] If study results contradict the sponsor's agenda, then they may be suppressed. Yet, if the information indicates potential harm to consumers, then ethical and possibly legal issues arise.

Although consumers are increasingly suspicious about "facts," they often have little basis for questioning them. The average consumer does not have enough personal knowledge to dispute the research that almost daily shapes our beliefs about social, political, economic, and

Web and E-commerce Stars
Amazon.com - www.amazon.com

Amazon.com is well known for its large inventory of products and ease of searchability. From books and magazines to homewares and electronics, users can shop online with Amazon yet still receive personal attention. Visitors are encouraged to log on with each visit, so Amazon can access the user's previous purchases and create a recommended product list to help cross sell based on previous likes. Attention to customization and personalization keeps Amazon.com on the leading edge and customers coming back.

environmental issues. That is why many groups exist to assist and protect consumers. Interested in truth, objectivity, and accuracy, these groups consist of representatives from industry, individual companies, academia, and the government. They have taken action to regulate the content of information and to defend the average consumer from distorted messages. Some industries have collectively formulated policies in order to reduce litigation, prevent mandatory regulation, and increase consumer trust. Still, questionable information finds its way to consumers.

Consider a study sponsored by Procter & Gamble, the leading maker of disposable diapers. For several years, the company had been fighting a public relations battle against environmentalists and the cloth diaper industry. Environmentalists pushed cloth diapers, and their sales skyrocketed; more than a dozen state legislatures were considering various regulations for disposable diapers. Under pressure, Procter & Gamble decided to finance a public policy study. The researchers found that disposable and cloth diapers were environmentally equivalent, when factors such as energy and water use were taken into account. The media disseminated the results and the sale of disposables improved. Gerber Products, the largest supplier of cloth diapers, closed three plants and laid off 900 workers. Gerber's CEO said: "There was

a dramatic change in the cloth diaper market caused by reduced environmental concern about disposable diapers."[42] Procter & Gamble won back lost market share and gained, at least temporarily, acceptance of disposables.

Although a marketer may occasionally benefit from biased information, those who connect ethically are more likely to create a profitable long-term relationship based on trust and loyalty. Often, as companies seek to build such relationships, the first question they must answer is: What customers are we trying to reach and how do we go about it? One concern for parents is the ethical use of information about children under the age of 18. The Children's Online Privacy Act of 1998 covers targeting children. In response, Kibu.com has promised to keep all information regarding its 13- to 18-year-old target market private.[43]

Another dimension of the ethical use of marketing research information lies in information obtained about the Internet. Privacy is an important issue for most Internet users. The Online Privacy and Disclosure Act of 2003 passed in California, requires all commercial entities that collect personal information online to clearly post a privacy policy and makes it unlawful for an online entity to violate its posted privacy policy.[44]

Chapter Summary:

Objective 1: Understand the roles that marketing information systems (MIS) and research play in marketing decision making.

You can't connect with customers if you can't locate, understand, and respond to them. MIS are critical in making informed decisions about nearly every aspect of marketing. They are used to systematically collect and analyze data to support decision making. An MIS often includes a marketing decision support system (MDSS), which puts information in convenient form for executives to use. MIS are ongoing and encompass all information. Marketing research is conducted to address a particular opportunity, problem, or issue. Marketing information is used in planning, marketing mix decisions, and performance monitoring.

Objective 2: Recognize how data are transformed into information to be used in a variety of marketing decisions.

Data and information are not the same. Data must be translated into information before they are useful for decision making. External data come from outside the firm, and internal data originate inside the firm. Both types are stored in databases so they can be retrieved through a computer. Primary data are collected for the first time to address a specific issue. Secondary data already exist and can be accessed immediately by a broad range of users. Once data are assembled, they must be analyzed through data sorting, the use of statistics, and models. All of this is done with particular issues and decision areas in mind.

Objective 3: Understand the types of research and the steps of a typical marketing research process.

The marketing research process starts with the problem definition, which focuses on the needs of decision makers to ensure that the research will be useful. The research design is then based on what decisions need what information, what data and data sources will provide that information, and how the data will be collected and analyzed. Next, exploratory research helps investigators better understand issues by defining problems, searching for possible explanations, and creating hypotheses. Quantitative research yields information to help decision makers select the best course of action. Because it is quantitative, estimates usually can be made of the likely results of actions. This requires appropriate measurement and sampling. The last steps are to interpret and report findings. Experience and insight are useful at this stage because the same information can be interpreted in various ways.

Objective 4: Describe widely used marketing research techniques.

Exploratory research techniques include focus groups, depth interviews, projective techniques, observation, and case analysis. A focus group usually has eight to twelve people. Several sessions must be used since the group, not individuals, provide the data. Depth interviews are one-on-one conversations. Researchers spend a lot of time probing a few respondents about their opinions and actions. With projective techniques, subjects are asked to analyze contrived situations or to give opinions about how they believe others may respond. Observation provides insights by watching consumers in a range of situations. Finally, case analysis is the study of a few situations in depth. It is particularly useful for benchmarking. Quantitative research often involves using the scientific method. Surveys and test markets are common in this type of research. Survey data are usually collected from a sample of the population. Questionnaire design is important. Likert scales or bipolar adjective scales frequently are used in questionnaires.

Objective 5: Explore how marketing information is being influenced by technology and is obtained globally.

Both internal and external marketing research is being dramatically influenced by technology. It facilitates the faster collection and analysis of greater quantities of information than was possible in the past. The Internet is a revolutionary way of interacting with customers. Research in global markets is complicated because secondary data may be scarce. Surveys must be carefully translated, and data collection is often difficult. Still, global research is becoming more and more important.

Objective 6: Understand that ethical issues surround the use and dissemination of research.

There are many ethical issues surrounding marketing research. One problem is that it sometimes can reflect the biases of marketers. When research is conducted to confirm a preconceived conclusion or validate a position, the results are not likely to be objective. The scientific method can eliminate this type of bias. A number of groups exist to prevent the manipulation of marketing research. They are interested in accuracy and want to protect consumers.

Review Your Understanding

1. What is a marketing information system (MIS)? What is a marketing decision support system (MDSS)? What is a transaction-based information system (TBIS)?
2. What is marketing research? How is it different from an MIS?
3. How are data transformed into information? What are the three steps?
4. What are the differences between primary and secondary data? Give examples.
5. What are the three major uses of marketing information? Explain.
6. What are the steps in a typical marketing research project?
7. What is exploratory research? List five exploratory research methods.
8. What is quantitative research? Name two quantitative methods.
9. Give two challenges associated with global marketing research.
10. What are the pros and cons of each type of survey data collection?

Discussion of Concepts

1. How is an MIS used? What are the two components of a typical MIS? Describe them.
2. What is the difference between data and information? Why is it important for marketers to provide executives with information rather than data?
3. Explain the objective of the marketing decision support system.
4. List and describe the four types of information an MIS provides. What is the importance of each type for decision making?
5. Describe each step of the marketing research process. Why is it so important to lay out each step in detail prior to beginning any research project?
6. Select a marketing problem and design a marketing research approach suitable to address it.
7. After completing an exploratory research study, how would you decide whether quantitative research is in order?
8. What would be the major considerations in developing a marketing research capability for a small company?
9. Under what circumstances would you consider it to be ethical to withhold marketing research from interested consumers? When would it be unethical?

Key Terms And Definitions

Case analysis: The in-depth study of a few examples.

Causal research: Research that attempts to prove a cause-and-effect relationship between two phenomena.

Convenience sample: A sample composed of people who happen to come along, such as shoppers in a store at a given time, whoever answers the doorbell, or travelers passing through an airport.

Data: Facts or statistics obtained from outside or inside the company.

Database: A collection of data that can be retrieved by a computer.

Depth interview: A relatively unstructured conversation that allows the researcher to probe deeply into a consumer's thoughts.

Experiment: A test conducted under controlled conditions in order to prove or disprove a marketing hypothesis.

Exploratory research: Research designed to clarify the problem and suggest ways to address it.

External data: Data obtained outside the company.

Focus group: A group, usually composed of eight to twelve people, whose opinions are elicited by an interviewer to provide exploratory insights into a problem.

Hypothesis: A tentative assumption about a particular event or issue.

Information: Data that has been analyzed and put in useful form.

Internal data: Data obtained within the company.

Judgment sample: A sample selected by the researchers or interviewers based on their belief that those chosen represent a majority of the study population.

Likert scale: A scale that measures the respondent's intensity of agreement with a particular statement.

Management information system (MIS): A computerized system used to collect and analyze the data needed for management decision making. The marketing information system is often considered a part of this system.

Marketing decision support system (MDSS): A two-way communication bridge between the people who collect and analyze information and the executives who use it.

Marketing information system (MIS): A computerized system used to collect and analyze marketing data.

Marketing research: The formal assembly and analysis of information about specific issues surrounding the marketing of goods and services.

Nonprobability sample: A sample in which the likelihood of selecting a particular respondent from the sampling frame cannot be calculated.

Observation: A research technique whereby researchers simply watch the participants they are studying.

Pilot study: A small-scale project that allows the researcher to refine and test the approaches that eventually will be used.

Population (universe): All the individuals or organizations relevant to the marketing research project.

Primary data: Information collected for the first time.

Probability sample: A sample in which the chance of selecting a given individual from the sampling frame or population can be calculated.

Projective technique: A technique that enables respondents to project their thoughts onto a third party or object or through some type of contrived situation.

Quantitative research: Research designed to provide the information needed to select the best course of action and estimate the probable results.

Research design: An outline of what data will be gathered, what sources will be used, and how the data will be collected and analyzed.

Sample: The group participating in a research project that represents the entire population of potential respondents.

Sampling frame: A list of people in the universe who potentially could be contacted.

Scientific method: A systematic way to gather, analyze, and interpret data in order to confirm or disconfirm a prior conception.

Secondary data: Information that already has been collected.

Simple random sampling: A sampling technique in which each member of the study population has an equal and known chance of being chosen.

Stratified random sampling: A sampling technique in which each member of a selected subgroup of the population has an equal chance of selection.

Transaction-based information system (TBIS): A computerized link between a firm and its customers, distributors, and suppliers.

References

1. www.pg.com, site visited May 01, 2008; Geoff Colvin, "Selling P&G," Fortune Magazine, Sep. 18, 2007, www.money.cnn.com/magazines/fortune, site visited May 01, 2008; "America's Most Admired Companies 2007," www.money.cnn.com/magazines/fortune, site visited May 01, 2008; www.greenguarantee.com, site visited May 29, 2008.

2. Personal interview with Olga Dazzo, Sparrow Health System, Lansing, MI.

3. "IntelliQuest Research Identifies Key Concerns About Mobile eCommerce," Canadian Corporate Newswire, August 14, 2000.

4. Dave Fusaro, "Meeting Wal-Mart's mandates," www.foodprocessing.com, site visited April 16, 2008.

5. www.forrester.com, site visited April 16, 2008.

6. www.dnb.com, site visited April 16, 2008.

7. www.gannett.com, site visited April 16, 2008.

8. Ellen Byron, "New Penney: Chain Goes for 'Missing Middle'," The Wall Street Journal, Feb 14, 2005, p. B1.

9. Lean haran, "Grocery Category management made Better by Census Data," Advertising Age, May 6, 1996, p. 16.

10. www.prnewswire.com, site visited April 16, 2008.

11. www.acnielsen.com, site visited April 16, 2008.

12. Tracy A Gill, "Online Survey Facilitates Customer Feedback," Target Marketing. Philadelphia: Jul 2005.Vol.28, Iss. 7; pg. 13

13. Personal interview with Dana Anderson, Leo Burnett Company, Inc., Chicago, July 3, 1996.

14. "DaimlerChrysler Customer Assistance Center to Implement Witness Systems' Quality Monitoring Software", Business Wire, June 13, 2005

15. www.nielsenmedia.com, site visited April 16, 2008.

16. A. Einstein and L. Infeld, The Evolution of Physics (New York: Simon & Schuster, 1942), p. 95.

17. www.google.com visited April 16, 2008.

18. www.activegroup.net, site visited April 16, 2008.

19. Gilbert D. Harrell, Michael D. Hutt, and James C. Anderson, "Path Analysis of Buyer Behavior under Conditions of Crowding," Journal of Marketing Research, February 1980, p. 47.

20. For a discussion of human mechanical observation techniques, see Gilbert A. Churchill, Jr., Marketing Research, 5th ed. (Chicago: Dryden Press, 1991), p. 349.

21. Raju Narisetti, "Plotting to Get Tissues into Living Rooms," Wall Street Journal, May 3, 1996, p. B1.

22. Christy Marshall, "Have It Your Way with Research," Advertising Age, April 4, 1983, p. 18.

23. "Fusing the Generational Gap," Business Wire, April 4, 2000.

24. Jeffery B. Schmidt, Roger J. Calantone, Abbie Griffin, Mitzi M. Montoya-weiss, "Do Certified Mail Third-wave Follow-ups Really Boost Response Rates and Quality?," Marketing Letters 16:2, p129-141, 2005.

25. Peter Girard, "Alloy's Online/Offline Dividends," Catalog Age, May 2000, p. 12.

26. Richard Cross, "Real-Time and Online Research Is Paying Off," Direct Marketing, May 2000, p. 61.

27. www.nytimes.com, site visited April 16, 2008.

28. Jack Honomichl, "Strong Progress, U.S. research firms see healthy growth in '04", Marketing News, June 15, 2005, p3.

29. Source: "Top 50 U.S. Research Organizations," Marketing News, June 15, 2005, p4.

30. "Tru Dynamics Launches E-Commerce Virtual Mall," Business Wire, June 20, 2000.

31. Len Lewis, "Paddle Surfing", Stores Vol88., November 2006, p136.

32. Bowdeya Tweh, "Google deal will add books: MSU libraries next in project," Knight Ridder Tribune Business News, June 7, 2007, p1.; http://books.google.com/googlebooks/library.html, site visited in April 16, 2008.

33. Jeannet Henessey, Global Marketing Strategies, 3rd ed. (Boston: Houghton Mifflin, 1995), p. 202.

34. "The Good Statistics Guide," Economist, September 11, 1993, p 34.

35. Sak Onkvisit and John J. Shaw, International Marketing, 2nd ed. (Upper Saddle River, NJ: Prentice Hall, 1993), p. 398.

36. www.cia.gov/cia/publications/factbook/, site visited April 16, 2008.

37. Ian Bush, Rachelle Damminger, Lisa Marie Daniels and Elizabeth Laoye, "Communication Strategies: Marketing to the 'Majority Minority'," Villanova University Publications, 2005.

38. Cynthia Crossens, Tainted Truth: The Manipulation of Fact in America (New York: Simon & Schuster, 1994), p 19.
39. "Respondents Assail Quality of Research," Marketing News, May 8, 1995, p. 14.
40. Crossens, Tainted Truth, p 14.
41. Ibid., p. 19
42. Jeffery Kluger, "Poll Vaulting," Discover, May 1995.
43. "They Know What Girls Want," Marketing News, March 27, 2000, p. 3.

44. Nikki Swartz, "California Passes Online Privacy Bill," Information Management Journal. Lemexa: Sep/Oct 2004.Vol.38, Iss. 5; pg. 11, 1 pgs

The Marketing Gazette
Larry Armstrong, "Rating J. D. Power's Grand Plan," Business Week, September 2, 1996, pp. 75–76; David Carnoy et al., "Know Your Customer," Success, February 1997, pp. 36–38; and J. D. Power & Associates, http://www.jdpower.com/ Web site visited June 7, 2007.

CASE 4

Google

Need an answer? Just Google it. Google, the leading internet search engine, began in 1996 when Larry Page and Sergey Brin joined forces to create a new search engine named BackRub. After a few years and gaining a small but loyal user base, the company changed its name to Google. Playing off the word googol, which is a mathematical term for a number represented by 1 followed by 100 zeros, Google represented Brin and Page's mission to organize the vast amount of information on the internet. The company went public in 2004 and has since undergone rapid expansion. In the year 2007, the company boasted over $16 million in sales, up 56.6 percent from the previous year.

Search engine services and advertising make up Google's core business but the company also provides Webmail (Gmail), blogging, and photo sharing. The majority of Google's revenues however, come from its advertising system. The company only sells discrete text ads placed near search results and does not place pop-up or banner ads on its Web site. Google uses two programs, AdWords and AdSense to help clients achieve their advertising goals. AdWords allows advertisers to create ads independently or with the assistance of Google marketing teams to appear alongside Google search results. Google marketing specialists can provide vital information on the advertiser's customers and ways to target new segments. Google then charges the advertiser a cost-per-click and measures the effectiveness of the advertisement through performance reports. AdWords comes with integrated marketing information features, such as conversion tracking, that measure the effectiveness of an advertiser's campaign. AdSense allows content-relevant Google test ads to appear on pages in Google Network Websites. Both AdWords and AdSense facilitate marketing effectiveness and marketing information.

While Google itself is an expert in search engine marketing, it also is a provider of information and research to other marketers. A few years back, technology writer and founder of Wired magazine, John Battelle, observed that when people typed words into a search engine, they were, "announcing their intentions." The result is a database of information full of the needs and wants of the massive number of search engine users. Google harnessed this information to create a product called Google Trends. Rankings and relative popularity of search terms are displayed by graphs and can be broken down into geographical areas. For now, Google has kept Google Trends a relatively detail-less tool with information about a month out-of-date in order to maintain a competitive advantage over other online advertisers but the potential of this product could start a marketing phenomenon. Google intends on enhancing the Trends tool and eventually companies will be able to get advertising feedback from an enormous online customer base.

Aside from revolutionizing advertising and marketing information, Google announced in June 2007 that it was expanding its environmental initiatives. The company, along with 30 other organizations, formed the Climate Savers Computing Initiative aimed at using more energy-efficient computers. Recognizing that clean and affordable energy will impact its future operations, Google has invested in an initiative called Renewable Energy Cheaper Than Coal. The company has assembled its own internal research and development group designated to create 1 gigawatt of renewable energy from alternative energy sources such as geothermal and hydro systems. Google also applied power saving technologies to its own facilities by installing evaporative cooling systems and solar panels.

Since its inception, Google has experience phenomenal growth and has become one of the most widely recognized companies in the world. From environmental sustainability initiatives to marketing information, Google is using its unique position as a link between advertisers and customers to revolutionize how we access information.

1. How does the information provided by Google through Google Trends enhance marketing mix decisions?

2. Outline ethical guidelines in which Google should abide when providing information to advertisers and other companies.

Sources: www.google.com/corporate Web site visited March 13, 2008; David Leonhardt, "The Internet Knows What You'll Do Next," New York Times, July 5, 2006.

Understanding Consumer Behavior

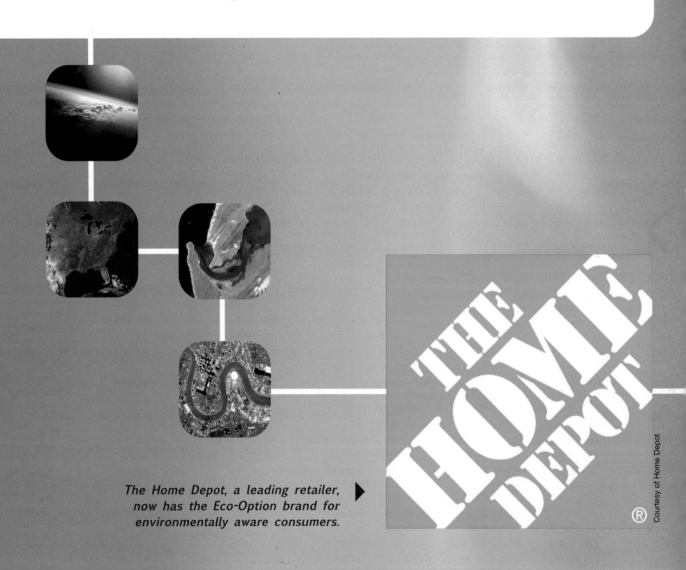

The Home Depot, a leading retailer, now has the Eco-Option brand for environmentally aware consumers. ▶

Learning Objectives

1. Appreciate the importance of involvement in the decisions consumers make.

2. Evaluate the effect on consumer behavior of such psychological factors as motivation, perception, learning, attitudes, and information processing.

3. Explain how social factors such as culture, subculture, social class, reference groups, and family help explain consumer behavior.

The do-it-yourself home improvement industry was revolutionized when Bernie Marcus and Arthur Blank opened the first The Home Depot in 1978. As the fastest growing retailer in U.S. history, The Home Depot has captured the spirit of customers looking to improve their homes. Through trained associates, The Home Depot provides the tools and knowledge on how to lay tile, install faucets and use power tools to the ordinary home owner. At The Home Depot, customers will find up to 40,000 top of the line products including building materials, home improvement supplies, and lawn and garden products. Each store is tailored to the local market, offering products based on climate needs.

Understanding the needs of its different customers has made The Home Depot the success it is today. The company acknowledges that for many people, their home is the biggest financial investment they make and improvements can be costly and stressful. The company strives to make home improvements as easy as possible for all of its customers. As a result, the company divides it's customers into three categories. The first category is the do-it-yourself customers. For these customers, the company provides free "how-to" clinics every Saturday and Sunday for common household projects. The second customer category it the do-it-for-me customers. These customers generally purchase the materials themselves but hire a third party for installations. The Home Depot readily provides installation for a variety of projects through independent contractors. Lastly, The Home Depot provides for the needs of professional customers through will-call services, expanded credit programs, and merchandise selection.

Today, the company is transforming the home improvement industry through the aggressive introduction of the Eco-Option brand. Realizing increased customer awareness of the environment, the company has labeled every product that benefits sustainable forestry, energy efficiency, healthy homes, clean air and water conservation. Fluorescent light bulbs, natural insect killers, and bamboo flooring are just a few of the 3,000 environmentally friendly products the company is offering in its stores. By 2009, the company hopes to extend its Eco-Option's product line to include 6000 products and 12 percent of sales. Educating customers and helping them find green products is likely to promote sales of the Eco-Option brand. "One study we did shows 84 percent of consumers are interested in using eco-friendly products and that 30 percent actively look for them," said Sheila McCuskey, an analyst for Information Resources Inc. "And 50 percent of the people who actively seek them are young adults." She also noted that eco-friendly products are expanding into new product categories including green cleaning products, which accounted for only 1 percent of the market in 2006 but saw sales increase by 52 percent the following year.

While The Home Depot is influencing its customers to buy green products, it is also encouraging its suppliers to do the same. As the world's largest buyer of building materials, The Home Depot has promoted suppliers who earn the Eco-Option label through prominent shelf space and marketing in weekly advertisements. The company's dedication to make positive environmental product purchasing decisions is realized through policies such as wood purchasing. The Home Depot researched every wood containing product it sells from building lumber to broom handles to understand where it was harvested. The company then pledged preference to wood that has come from managed forests, meeting strict sustainable guide-

THE CONCEPT OF CONSUMER BEHAVIOR

More than ever there is vastly greater diversity among a growing number of consumers in expanding global markets. The challenge leading-edge organizations face is to enhance the life experiences of consumers with products that live up to their expectations. Every action must contribute in some way toward consumer well-being. This doesn't happen with wishful thinking or intuition. It requires a thorough knowledge of consumer decision making and the forces that influence it. To connect with customers, we must understand the societal and psychological factors that determine their decisions. Leading-edge organizations are bundling their knowledge of all these factors into systematic ways of influencing customer satisfaction, loyalty, and relationships. Discovering and delivering value requires a thorough understanding of consumer behavior.

Consumer behavior involves the actions and decision processes of individuals and households in discovering, evaluating, acquiring, consuming, and disposing of products. Consider the key parts of that definition. First, it looks at both actions—what people do—and decision processes—how they think and feel. Marketers want to know how often the shopping occurs and for what reasons. Second, the definition refers to individuals and households. Usually an individual makes the purchase, but those decisions are often related to household considerations. When a mother shops, she may buy Pepsi for one person, Coke for another, bottled water for a third, and so forth. Third, evaluating, acquiring, and consuming products are important parts of the process, but we need to remember that consumer behavior starts with discovery and proceeds through disposal.

Figure 5.1 provides an overview of the main topics covered in this chapter. We begin with the relationship between consumer involvement and decision making.

Since involvement can be low or high, decision making can be relatively passive or very active. Next we deal with five psychological factors that influence consumer behavior: motivation, perception, learning, attitudes, and information processing. The third major section on social influences describes how culture, subculture, social class, reference groups, and family members affect the decisions of individual consumers. In the last sections, we look at ways in which technology is used to track consumer behavior, as well as ethical issues related to attempts to persuade consumers.

CONSUMER INVOLVEMENT AND DECISION MAKING

Decision making and involvement are closely related processes. Knowledge about them provides insight into how and why consumers behave as they do. Involvement is a function of how important, complex, and/or time-consuming a purchase may be. Decision making varies with the degree of involvement. For high-involvement purchases, the consumer is likely to devote time and attention to each of five steps in the decision process.

CONSUMER INVOLVEMENT

Think about the difference between buying a box of breakfast cereal and a new home. Which purchase would you spend more time researching and generally care more about? Not all purchases have the same importance; some mean more to us than others. **Low-involvement purchases** require only simple decision making. Cereal, soap, soft drinks, and similar items don't require much thought. Many people purchase the same brand every time they shop, which underscores the importance of brand awareness. **High-involvement purchases**

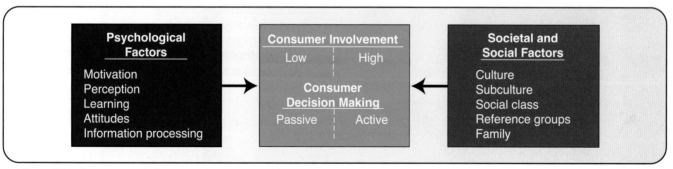

Figure 5.1   Connecting with Customers: Understanding Consumer Behavior

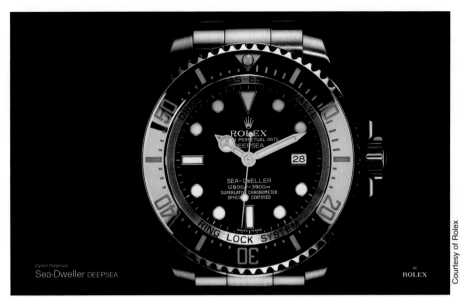

Oyster Perpetual
Sea-Dweller DEEPSEA

ROLEX

Courtesy of Rolex

Rolex luxury timepieces are an example of a purchase in The Robb Report magazine, which specializes in high-involvement purchases.

demand more extensive and complex decision making. Buying a car, a computer, or even a television set requires a good deal of thought. The product is expensive, and you probably will have to live with it for a long time. Nontraditional products often fall in this category. An extreme example of high involvement purchases involves Curtco Robb Media LLC, which publishes magazines such as *The Robb Report* and *Showcase*. These magazines advertise such nontraditional products as Philip Johnson's glass house in New Canaan, CT, a Mississippi Grand Manor built in the late Renaissance period, and a Rodriquez WideBody yacht priced at $4.2 million. These magazines tout themselves as a one-stop resource for the luxury lifestyle. However, many high involvement products are frequently purchased items like jeans, jewelry and autos and what is high involvement for one person might be low involvement by another.[2]

Figure 5.2 shows how involvement influences decision making. The level of involvement with any product depends on its perceived importance to the consumer's self-image. High-involvement products tend to be tied to self-image, whereas low-involvement products are not. A middle-aged consumer who feels (and wants to look) youthful may invest a great deal of time in her decision to buy a sport-utility vehicle instead of a station wagon. When purchasing an ordinary light bulb, however, she buys almost without thinking because the purchase has nothing to do with self-image. On the other hand, if she sees herself as a "green" consumer, her desire for energy conservation might get her

to think a lot about which type of light bulb to buy. Generally, but not always, the more visible, risky, or costly the product, the higher the level of involvement.

Involvement also influences the relationship between product evaluation and purchasing behaviors. With low-involvement products, consumers generally will try them first and then form an evaluation. With high-involvement products, they first form an evaluation (expectation), and then purchase. One reason for this behavior is that consumers do not actively search for information about low-involvement products. Instead, they acquire it while engaged in some other activity, such as watching television or chatting with a friend. This is called **passive learning,** which characterizes the passive decision-making process. Only when they try the product do they learn more about it. In contrast, high-involvement products are investigated through **active learning**—part of an active decision-making process—in order to form an opinion

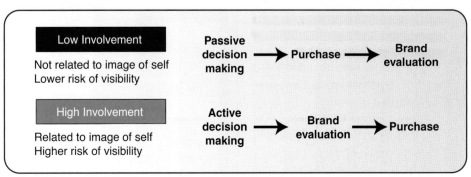

Figure 5.2   Low/High Involvement and Passive/ Active Decision Making

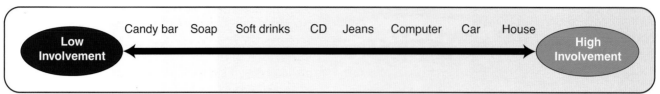

Figure 5.3 Examples of Products on an Involvement Continuum

about which product to purchase.

Figure 5.3 shows that products fall on a continuum between low and high involvement. Moving toward the high end, decisions are made about more expensive, permanent, and complex products that also are more related to self-concept. Consumers give these purchases more thought.

CONSUMER DECISION MAKING

For a better understanding of consumer buying behavior, marketers have broken the decision process into the five steps described next. These are shown in Figure 5.4, along with a description of how one consumer, Erin, made a high-involvement purchase. For low-involvement purchases, the first three steps may be skipped. As involvement increases, each step takes on greater importance, and more active learning occurs.

Problem recognition occurs when a consumer becomes aware of an unfulfilled desire. In a low-involvement situation, such as the purchase of a song, you might immediately go to a place such as iTunes and casually select recordings by two or three of your favorite artists. Or, if you're thirsty, you may simply run out and buy a soft drink. In a high-involvement purchase the recognition of a need may arise long before it is acted upon. In the case of a house, the cost may prevent you from acting on your need for several years.

The **information search** consists of thinking through the situation, calling up experiences stored in memory (internal search), and probably seeking information from friends, salespeople, advertisements, online services, and other sources (external search). Each source has its benefits and drawbacks. Experience is a good teacher, but you may not have enough information in memory. External search is beneficial, but friends may have preferences different from yours, salespeople may push the product that earns them

the highest commission, and ads are often incomplete.

Alternatives evaluation is based on decision rules about which product or service is most likely to satisfy goals. These rules are personal; that is, they vary according to what the individual consumer considers important. At this point, complex thinking is likely to occur. Using the results of the information search, the consumer weighs the pros and cons of each choice.

The **purchase decision** emerges from the evaluation of alternatives. The consumer may decide not to buy and save the money or spend it on a different item altogether. Or he or she may want to play it safe by deciding to purchase a small amount for trial purposes, or by deciding to lease rather than buy. The decision to buy often occurs some time before the actual purchase. The **purchase** is a financial commitment to make the acquisition. It may take time to secure a mortgage or car loan, or the dealer may be temporarily out of stock.

The **purchase evaluation** stage results in satisfaction or dissatisfaction. Buyers often seek assurance from others that their choice was correct. Positive assurance reinforces the consumer's decision, making it more likely

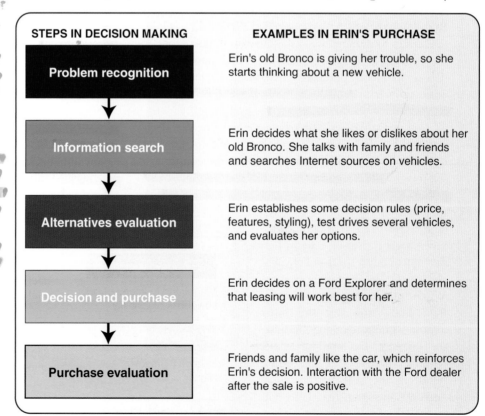

STEPS IN DECISION MAKING	EXAMPLES IN ERIN'S PURCHASE
Problem recognition	Erin's old Bronco is giving her trouble, so she starts thinking about a new vehicle.
Information search	Erin decides what she likes or dislikes about her old Bronco. She talks with family and friends and searches Internet sources on vehicles.
Alternatives evaluation	Erin establishes some decision rules (price, features, styling), test drives several vehicles, and evaluates her options.
Decision and purchase	Erin decides on a Ford Explorer and determines that leasing will work best for her.
Purchase evaluation	Friends and family like the car, which reinforces Erin's decision. Interaction with the Ford dealer after the sale is positive.

Figure 5.4 The Consumer Decision-Making Process

that such a purchase will be made again. Positive feedback confirms the buyer's expectations.

PSYCHOLOGICAL FACTORS THAT INFLUENCE CONSUMER DECISIONS

Although the decision-making process appears straightforward, it is influenced by many psychological factors. We will look at the most important ones: (1) motivation, (2) perception, (3) learning, (4) attitudes, and (5) information processing.

MOTIVATION

Marketers first conducted "motivation research" during the 1950s and early 1960s in an attempt to identify buyers' subconscious reasons for purchasing various products. This work has since been discredited because it was based on a very limited theory and poor research techniques. Early motivation researchers depended on the ideas of Sigmund Freud. This pioneering psychoanalyst suggested that most human behavior is determined not by conscious thought but by unconscious urges, passions, repressed feelings, and underlying desires. Based on these beliefs, motivation researchers declared that men purchase a convertible as a substitute for a mistress, and women make cakes as a symbol of giving birth. About the best that can be said for this early work is that it inspired marketers to develop new concepts of motivation. Today, motivation theories are much sounder, and they provide several basic insights for marketers.

Motivation is an internal force that directs behavior toward the fulfillment of needs. It involves the needs (or goals) a person has and the energy that is triggered to drive the person to action. The needs that underlie motivation can be classified as either biological or psychological. Biological needs have been called primary or innate needs because they seem to exist in all people, regardless of environment. Needs in this category include food, water, shelter, fresh air, and at least some degree of comfort. Products such as Evian spring water, Kellogg's Special K, and various brands of bedding were developed in direct response to this type of need. **Psychological needs** are often called secondary or learned needs because they result from socialization. Needs in this category include friendship, a sense of self-worth, and achievement or self-fulfillment. The U.S. Army slogan "Be all that you can be" appeals directly to psychological needs.

Maslow's Hierarchy of Needs Abraham Maslow's famous classification is often used by marketers to help categorize consumer desires. According to Maslow, five basic needs underlie most human goals. He ranked them in a hierarchy to indicate that higher-level needs tend to emerge only after lower-level needs are satisfied. Figure 5.5 illustrates Maslow's hierarchy in the form of a pyramid.

At the base of the pyramid are physiological needs essential to survival such as food, clean air and water, warmth, and sleep. Evian produces bottled spring water to fulfill the need for clean, unadulterated water.

On the next level is the need for safety, which includes basic security and freedom from physical abuse. These needs are both biological and psychological. Insurance companies appeal to them with such slogans as "You're in good hands with Allstate" and "Get a piece of the rock" (Prudential).

The third level of

Marketing Vocabulary

PROBLEM RECOGNITION
Becoming aware of an unfulfilled need or desire.

INFORMATION RESEARCH
Thinking through a situation by recalling information stored in memory or obtaining it from external sources.

ALTERNATIVES EVALUATION
Use of decision rules that attempt to determine which product would be most likely to satisfy goals.

PURCHASE DECISION
The decision of whether or not to buy and which competing product to buy, which is made after carefully weighing the alternatives.

PURCHASE
A financial commitment to acquire a product.

PURCHASE EVALUATION
The process of determining satisfaction or dissatisfaction with a buying choice.

MOTIVATION
An internal force that directs behavior toward the fulfillment of needs.

PSYCHOLOGICAL NEEDS
A need that arises in the socialization process.

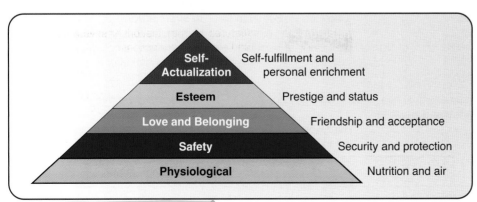

Figure 5.5   Maslow's Hierarchy of Needs

Source: Adapted from Abraham H. Maslow, Motivation and Personality, 2nd ed. Copyright 1970 by Abraham H. Maslow. Reprinted by permission of Harper & Row Publishers, Inc.

the pyramid is the need for love and belonging. Humans seek out companionship to fulfill this psychological need. Family and friends are extremely instrumental in satisfying it. Advertisements for Hallmark cards and FTD florists play on our need for human interaction, love, and belonging.

The fourth level is the need for esteem, which comes from prestige, status, and self-respect. Many consumers maintain and exhibit their social status through high-visibility products. Designer labels or symbols on clothing and recognizable automobile designs are two ways marketers have attempted to fulfill this need.

The final level of Maslow's hierarchy is the need for self-actualization. As people begin to feel physically satisfied, safe and secure, accepted, and esteemed by others, they may need a higher level of personal satisfaction. They are motivated by a desire to develop themselves and use their abilities. Education is directed toward this need by helping people attain knowledge and experiences that improve self-worth, sharpen talents, and promote personal growth. Self-actualization also may come from coaching youth soccer or playing in a basketball league. Backpacking, writing, skiing, painting, and composing are other examples. The Adidas ad campaign, "Impossible is nothing" is aimed at consumers who are motivated by self-actualization. The Peace Corps offers a challenge as well as a reward: "The toughest job you'll ever love."

Motivational Conflict   People are motivated to attain some ends and avoid others. In marketing terms, consumers approach activities that help them attain desired outcomes but avoid activities that have negative consequences. Yet, because human needs and wants are so varied, consumers may be faced with outcomes that combine both desirable and undesirable features. Three types of such motivational conflict have been identified: approach-approach, avoidance-avoidance, and approach-avoidance. These are summarized in Figure 5.6.

Approach-approach conflict occurs when a consumer desires two objectives but cannot have both. Suppose George wants sports-car performance but sport-utility vehicle carrying capacity in a new car.   Unless he can afford to buy a Viper and a Durango, he will have to buy one or the other.   Dodge promotes its 340 Horsepower Magnum RT car by stating, "Style, with room for life."   This type of promotion is aimed at consumers who want to combine style and storage capacity in one vehicle.[3]

Avoidance-avoidance conflict results when a choice must be made between two undesirable alternatives. Elaine's car has a bad muffler. The noise draws disapproving looks from strangers, and her friends are starting to make jokes about it. But the repair will deplete Elaine's savings account. She will have to resolve this conflict by selecting the least adverse choice. Midas Muffler offers a Midas Lifetime Guarantee option for mufflers for as long as a vehicle is owned. The appeal is to consumers

Type	Description	Sample Situation	Possible Marketing Response
Approach-Approach	Two objectives are desired, but the consumer cannot have both	Toothpaste ↙ ↘ Health with fluoride / Sex appeal with breath freshener	*Provide both benefits:* Toothpaste with fluoride and a breath freshener.
Avoidance-Avoidance	The consumer must choose between two undesirable alternatives	Muffler repair ↙ ↘ Depleted savings / Bothersome exhaust noise	*Stress unpleasantness of one alternative to get desired action:* Muffler ads that emphasize how embarrassing a defective muffler can be or that offer financing or delayed payments.
Approach-Avoidance	The consumer's goal has both positive and negative aspects	College education ↙ ↘ Hard work and expense / Greater earnings opportunities	*Emphasize positive benefits of desired action:* A college ad campaign that illustrates how long-term earnings compare for a college graduate and a nongraduate.

Figure 5.6   Types of Motivational Conflict

who don't want engine problems yet also don't want to spend extra money on maintenance.

Approach-avoidance conflict occurs when a consumer desires an alternative that has positive and negative qualities. If Jim works out on his NordicTrack, then his body will be stronger but at the cost of time-consuming strenuous exercise. Many types of purchases cause approach-avoidance conflict because they have drawbacks, side effects, or other undesirable features. In a way, all purchases can be considered a mixed blessing, since the buyer must forfeit some money sooner or later. Consider the Army National Guard, which may offer tuition assistance and enlistment bonuses but requires training obligations and a period of service.[4] The approach-avoidance conflict for people who join up involves positive rewards in exchange for hard work and sacrificed time.

By understanding motivational conflicts, marketers can respond with new products as well as advertising, pricing, and distribution plans that help minimize these buyer conflicts.

PERCEPTION

Human beings use their sensory organs to see, hear, smell, taste, and touch an almost infinite variety of sensations. The sensations are caused by stimuli—the sound of a jackhammer, the fragrance of a flower, the texture of material, and so on. **Perception** is the process of recognizing, selecting, organizing, and interpreting these stimuli in order to make sense of the world around us.

We constantly receive so many stimuli that only a limited number can be processed. Therefore, consumers must select—either consciously or subconsciously—the stimuli on which to focus. Typically, this selection occurs in four stages: selective exposure, selective attention, selective comprehension, and selective retention. At each stage, a product or message may be screened out, disregarded, misinterpreted, or forgotten by the consumer. Figure 5.7 illustrates the perception process.

Selective Exposure U.S. companies spend more than a billion dollars every day in the hope of communicating messages to consumers. However, a large portion of these messages are screened out in the first stage, when consumers choose whether to ignore or receive the message. How often do you reach for the remote and channel surf whenever an ad appears on television? Marketers call the consumer's ability to seek out or avoid information **selective exposure**. For example, Soloflex advertises extensively on television, but you can choose to watch, tune out mentally, or change the channel. You decide whether to be exposed to Soloflex information. This happens to you hundreds of times a day with other media—billboards, radio, newspapers, and so on.

Selective Attention Consumers do not pay attention to very many messages. Noticing every one of them would lead to mental exhaustion from information overload. So consumers are extremely skilled at screening out irrelevant messages.

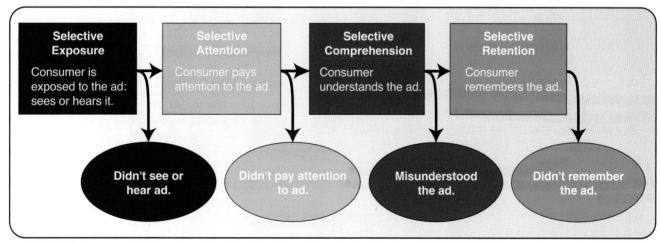

Figure 5.7   Process of Perception

Through **selective attention,** people have a strong tendency to heed information that supports their current views. Democrats listen more often to Democratic than Republican politicians, and vice versa. Similarly, consumers attend to advertising for products they have already purchased or intend to purchase. They screen out much of the information that conflicts with their experience or goals because it is irrelevant and distracting. One of the most important challenges faced by any marketer is gaining the consumer's attention. Without it, no matter how well crafted, the message will have no effect on the intended target.

©iStockphoto.com

Selective attention is common when it comes to politics.

A good example is the ineffectiveness of smoking prevention campaigns. Forty-four million American adults continue to smoke, despite millions of dollars spent in anti-smoking campaigns trying to dissuade them. Even with warnings from the U.S. Surgeon General and proof that each year 440,000 American die prematurely from a tobacco-related illness, tobacco use remains the leading preventable cause of death in the United States.[5] Smokers may tune into advertisements about their brand but ignore prevention ads. This selective attention reinforces the likelihood that they will continue to smoke, since the negative messages about health implications do not get through.

To help gain attention, a marketer should initiate the message in a way relevant to the consumer—by using a known sports figure, a common activity, an attractive person, or humor. Then the brand name can be related to that attention-getter. Next, it is important to maintain attention by keeping the ad meaningful or interesting to the consumer. Shimano does an excellent job of attracting attention with its mountain bike ads. The logo is eye-catching and the simple, direct ads have unusual visuals.

Selective Comprehension Marketers must take care to ensure that their products and messages are understood by consumers in the way intended. **Selective comprehension** refers to consumers' tendency to interpret messages based on their biases. If a message runs counter to a consumer's strong beliefs, then it is perceived as being farther from the buyer's point of view than is really the case. Consumers are likely to reject any information that contradicts their current beliefs or past behaviors. That is why many ads keep it simple and avoid controversial images. A notable exception is political ads, since selective comprehension can work in the marketer's favor.

Selective Retention **Selective retention** means that consumers remember some messages and forget others. The way information is understood determines how well it is remembered. People tend to recall what agrees with their own beliefs, desires, or behaviors.

Once information is retained, it is held until replaced or altered. Old information may be forgotten when new, conflicting messages are received, or it may be reshaped if the new information is more consistent with the person's beliefs or goals. Joan wants a Macintosh laptop computer but has heard it will be very expensive. She reads an ad comparing the cost of laptops and sees that Macintosh is not the highest. As a result, she discards the idea that Macintosh laptops are expensive and retains the information that other brands cost more. The "Nobody Beats Midas—Nobody" advertisement was designed by the muffler giant to achieve such an effect.

Subliminal Perception Since our conscious perceptions selectively and routinely filter messages, is it possible to bypass that level and market to the consumer's subconscious? The belief in subliminal persuasion began in 1957 in a New Jersey movie theater. Market researcher Jim Vicary claimed to flash messages such as "Drink Coca-Cola" and "Eat Popcorn" on the screen too fast to be recognized by the naked eye. According to him, the messages still registered in the brain, resulting in sales increases of 18 percent for Coke and almost 60 percent for popcorn. Vicary then coined the term subliminal advertising. Researchers were never able to replicate his study, and there is no evidence to support his claim.[6]

We do have evidence that subliminal messages do not work. A 1991 psychology study set out to determine whether self-improvement tapes really help people lose weight, improve memory, raise self-esteem, or quit smoking. Researcher Anthony Greenwald found that roughly half the people who listened to the audio tapes claimed improvement in the area specified on the label. But the labels had been deliberately switched, so any effect has to be attributed to the power of suggestion, not the tapes themselves.[7] It is still debated whether subliminal messages are effective in changing the minds of consumers.

LEARNING

Consumers learn how to acquire and use products. The process starts at an early age and continues throughout life. It is through learning that consumers select the patterns of behavior that determine when, where, and how they purchase, consume, and discard goods. **Learning** is any change in consumers' behavioral tendencies caused by experience. There are two basic types of learning: cognitive and behavioral. Cognitive learning emphasizes perception, reason, and problem solving. It focuses on knowledge, insights, ideas, opinions, and goals. High-involvement and challenging purchases incorporate active learning that focuses attention on problem-solving behavior. The five decision steps outlined in Figure 5.4 dealt with this type of learning. Behavioral learning occurs through either classical or operant (sometimes called instrumental) conditioning when consumers react to external events. Behavioral learning primarily concerns what consumers do, not what they are thinking.

Classical Conditioning Classical conditioning gets its name from an early (and, therefore, classical) experiment by the Russian physiologist Ivan Pavlov in the 1920s. He presented meat paste to a dog, and the dog salivated. He then presented the paste while ringing a tuning fork. Again, the dog salivated. Pavlov repeated this several times. Eventually, when the tuning fork was rung without the meat paste, the dog still salivated.[8] The basic idea behind **classical conditioning** is that people can learn to respond to one stimulus in the same way they respond to another if the two stimuli are presented together.

Classical conditioning is used extensively in marketing.[9] Think for a minute about the ad that featured young people on a hot day drinking Mountain Dew and jumping off a steep cliff into a river. Marketers were trying to get consumers to associate the soft drink with excitement and refreshment in summer weather, in much the same way that Pavlov's dogs associated the tuning fork with meat paste. Then, when a hot day comes along (stimulus), you will want to drink Mountain Dew.

Consumer preferences are often influenced by advertising features (stimuli) rather than the product itself. Marketers say that music often helps define the emotional appeal of a certain brand. Classical music is often used

to convey comfort, luxury, and distinctive taste.[10] Chevrolet developed an advertising campaign for trucks around Bob Seger's "Like a Rock," which now is identified with the reliability and strength of Chevy trucks.

Marketers need to understand that consumers may generalize stimuli or discriminate among them. **Generalization** occurs when people make the same response to different stimuli. **Discrimination** occurs when consumers make different responses to different stimuli. For instance, when oat bran cereals were first found to reduce cholesterol levels, the oat bran image was generalized to other bran cereals, such as Raisin Bran. With experience, however, consumers began to discriminate, aided by advertisers. The Quaker Oats Company says "Oats contain soluble fiber that binds with and helps remove some of the cholesterol which can clog your arteries and lead to heart disease."[11]

To take advantage of a strong brand name, marketers establish visual consistency across categories. The various products in ConAgra's Healthy Choice line, including pasta sauces, cereals, breakfast bars, frozen dinners, and ice cream, are branded under the distinctive green Healthy Choice label. Consumers can readily identify the brand and are able to generalize the health benefits of Healthy Choice products even across product categories.

Marketers also try to take advantage of a buyer's ability to discriminate among brands. For example, McDonald's names its products "Mc," as in the case of the Egg McMuffin and the McFlurry, to ensure that its food is associated only with McDonald's.

Operant Conditioning Even before Pavlov gained fame, Thorndike, a noted psychologist, published work showing how rewards encourage certain responses and punishment discourages others. Behavior that is intermittently rewarded (positive or negative

Marketing Vocabulary

SELECTIVE ATTENTION
The tendency to heed information that supports current views and behaviors.

SELECTIVE COMPREHENSION
The tendency to interpret products and messages according to current beliefs.

SELECTIVE RETENTION
The tendency to remember some and forget other information.

LEARNING
Any change in consumer behavior caused by experience.

CLASSICAL CONDITIONING
After two stimuli are presented together repeatedly, people learn to respond to one in the same way as the other.

GENERALIZATION
Making the same response to different stimuli.

DISCRIMINATION
Making different responses to different stimuli.

reinforcement) will be repeated in the expectation of eliciting the reward. Behavior that is punished will be avoided and, thus, will diminish in frequency. Psychologist B. F. Skinner later termed this type of conditioning operant because the learning occurs as the subject responds to or "operates on" the environment. Thus, **operant conditioning** is the use of reinforcement or punishment to shape behavior. Today, marketers know that consumers associate positive and/or negative consequences with the items they consume.

There are several ways positive reinforcement can occur. The first is through a product satisfying a need or want. If you drink Lipton's iced tea and your thirst disappears, then that behavior is reinforced. The next time you are thirsty, you are likely to reach for Lipton's. The second reinforcer is information or knowledge. Many organizations publish magazines to support their business: Delta Airlines has *Sky Magazine*, the National Football League issues *NFL Insider*, and AARP publishes *Modern Maturity*.[12] These offer information that will reinforce purchases and stimulate new interests while maintaining brand loyalty. A third way consumer behavior can be reinforced is by seeing results. For example, EAS nutrition products promote "before and after" body-building programs. "It took Michelangelo three years to sculpt a masterpiece" reads one testimonial; "It took me only three months."[13] The 20-minute daily workout required to see results actually becomes a reinforcer because consumers know they are making progress toward getting in shape. Yet another way companies reward purchasers and encourage repeat purchases is the frequent-customer card promotion. Punishment may result from such things as a product that fails to perform as advertised; a service agent who acts in a curt, unfriendly manner; or even news stories that cast the corporation in a bad light and undermine the consumer's pride in owning its products.

ATTITUDES

An **attitude** is a state of readiness with cognitive, emotional, and behavioral components, which reflects the beliefs of the consumer with regard to messages, brands, products, product characteristics, or other aspects of life. Attitudes are often described as consumer preferences—a like or dislike for products or their characteristics. Marketers usually think of attitudes as having three dimensions: cognitive, affective, and behavioral. The **cognitive** aspect refers to knowledge about product attributes that is not influenced by emotion. The **affective** component relates to the emotional feelings of like or dislike. The **behavioral** element reflects the tendency to act positively or negatively. In other words, attitudes toward purchasing a product are a composite of what consumers know about its attributes; whether they like or dislike them; and how positively or negatively they feel about the purchase.

Figure 5.8 shows how attitude can affect the purchase of a mountain bike. Attitudes are important because they help us understand why a particular action is taken. And notice that attitudes are not the same as beliefs. A **belief** is a descriptive thought or conviction that expresses an opinion about the characteristics of something. For example, a consumer may believe that rapid-fire shifters are a feature of a Specialized brand bicycle. Beliefs may help shape attitudes but don't necessarily imply like or dislike. Attitudes also influence beliefs: If rapid-fire shifters increase the price, then a consumer who dislikes high cost may believe they are not a very useful feature.

Consumers frequently form attitudes to help evaluate whether products and brands fit into their lifestyle. These attitudes are drawn from a broad range of ideas, not just the characteristics of a product.

Generally, marketers use their knowledge of consumer attitudes to make sure that strategies are consistent with

Product Attribute	ATTITUDE COMPONENT		
	Cognitive (Does the bike have this attribute?)	Affective (Do I like this attribute?)	Behavioral (Am I likely to buy this bike?)
Rapid-fire shifters	Yes	Like very much	Very positive
Light weight	Yes	Like very much	Very positive
Rigid frame	Yes	Neither like nor dislike	Neutral
Durability	No	Like somewhat	Somewhat negative
Vibration absorption	Yes	Like somewhat	Somewhat positive
High cost	Yes	Dislike somewhat	Somewhat negative

Figure 5.8 Attitudes About a Mountain Bike Purchase

To overcome the behavioral aspect of consumer attitudes, Merle Norman C.S. offered this promotion.

consumer tastes and preferences. From time to time, marketers attempt to change consumer attitudes, usually by influencing one of the three components. A common approach is to use promotion to influence the cognitive component. This may involve claims of product superiority such as the Calloway Golf Club claim "a better game by design."

Marketers also try to influence the affective component of consumer attitudes. For example, as the health and fitness craze swept the United States, many people developed a dislike for beef, believing it to be high in fat and cholesterol. The industry launched a campaign showing that beef is nutritional and easy to prepare, hoping to make consumers feel good about eating it. "Beef. It's what's for dinner" became a recognizable slogan for millions of Americans in the 1990s. Today, the promotion of Atkins type low carb dieting which places a greater emphasis on beef has resulted in a dramatic increase in the consumption of pounds of beef consumed per person, which now approaches nearly 94 pounds per year.[14]

To change the behavioral aspect of consumer attitudes, often a coupon or free sample is offered. Research indicates that once a product is purchased or used—even if only a free sample—the likelihood of future purchase

is greater.

INFORMATION PROCESSING

Information processing refers to ways in which consumers acquire, store, and evaluate the data they use to make decisions. The human mind has a remarkable ability to process (understand and apply) the information it takes in. Perception, motivation, behavioral learning, and attitudes are integrated into the human thought system, which acquires, stores, and analyzes data to arrive at goal-directed behaviors. Key to information processing is the encoding of information and its use in memory.

Encoding   **Encoding** is the process of converting information to knowledge. The brain is sometimes described as having two relatively distinct ways of encoding information.[15] These enable it to handle pictorial, geometric, and nonverbal information as well as verbal, symbolic, and analytical thinking. The mind combines all this information and produces integrated perceptions.

The mental images encoded are thoughts held in "picture" form called episodes. Episodes are not like pictures taken with a camera, and they can be felt and known without words. Aesthetics, tastes, and symbolic meaning are represented this way. Ads and other phenomena are also likely to be retained as episodes.[16] Nike traditionally uses a highly visual format for its advertisements. These images capitalize on consumer emotions and attempt to link personal value to the wide array of Nike products. Advertising is never just about Nike, the brand. Nike uses a variety of ways to draw in the consumer, and relates to them in many "every day" ways, such as showcasing famous athletes' competition wounds. By relating professional athletes to its customers, Nike connects its own prod-

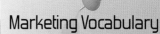

Marketing Vocabulary

OPERANT CONDITIONING
The use of reinforcement or punishment to shaper behavior.

ATTITUDE
A state of readiness with cognitive, emotional, and behavioral components, which reflects the beliefs of the consumer with regard to messages, brands, products, product characteristics, or other aspects of life.

COGNITIVE
Knowledge about a product's attributes not influenced by emotion.

AFFECTIVE
Emotional feeling of like or dislike.

BEHAVIORAL
Tendency to act positively or negatively.

BELIEF
A conviction that something is true or that descriptive statements are factual.

INFORMATION PROCESSING
The process whereby consumers acquire, store, and evaluate the data they use in making decisions.

ENCODING
The process of converting information to knowledge.

ucts with the physical and emotional side of athletic competition. The Nike swoosh symbol is a highly recognized trademark that elicits these desired effects because it is an episode encoded in the consumer's brain.

Verbal encoding occurs when words or symbols are stored in semantic memory. General knowledge, facts, and principles gleaned from experience are held there. Many believe that information such as package size, the meaning of brand names, prices, and so forth are stored this way. For example, advertisements for Johnson & Johnson's baby products use facts to appeal to concerned mothers. One ad states that Johnson's Baby Wash is the number one choice of hospitals.[17] Many mothers may form an impression in their semantic memory based on this information and call upon it later to make a purchase decision.

Marketers must remember that consumers encode both verbal and pictorial information about the world.[18] In the early stage of information processing, the pictorial tends to dominate. In later stages, verification and more analytical thoughts dominate. Therefore, visual, musical, creative, and pictorial elements of ads catch the consumer's attention. Then facts, reasoning, and details of product messages are likely to be picked up.

Memory **Memory** is the brain function that stores and recalls encoded information (knowledge). There are three types of memory: sensory, short term, and long term. Each operates differently and can be considered a separate step in the process of memory formation.

The first and most basic stage is sensory memory, which takes in an almost unlimited amount of encoded information. These sensory impressions decay (are forgotten) within a fraction of a second. But when attention is focused on a few stimuli, sensory information about them is transferred to short-term memory, where it can be coded and interpreted.

Short-term memory interprets what is sent from sensory memory. It usually can hold information for only a short time, and its capacity is much smaller than that of sensory memory—about four to seven chunks of information at once.[19] A chunk is a unit of organized information that can be recalled to solve specific problems of short duration. A chunk may vary greatly among persons focusing on the same object. A first-time buyer of a used car is likely to have a more difficult time than a person who has purchased several. For example,

www.nike.com

Learn how Nike has integrated sustainable designs and materials into your shoes. Visit the locker room and have a look at all Nike products.

Hippocampus

The hippocampus is the brain area responsible for short-term memory.

the experienced buyer probably will ask for past service receipts to learn about repair history, whereas the novice may not think of it.

In long-term memory, a vast amount of information may be held for years or even indefinitely. It remains there until replaced by contradictory information through a process called interference. For example, you go to your favorite restaurant and receive a poor meal or poor service. This interferes with your positive memory of the place, and you then reclassify it to a lower status. Once a brand is stored in long-term memory, consumers can add relevant information to help with future choices. Makers of ChapStick often associate their product with the elements (sun, wind, dryness). That way, when outdoor enthusiasts need lip protection from the elements, they often think of ChapStick.

SOCIAL FACTORS THAT INFLUENCE CONSUMER DECISIONS

Social factors have a great influence on how individual consumers and households behave. Consider something as simple as a pair of earrings. In some societies, children's ears are pierced at birth; other societies frown on ear piercing altogether. Some social groups regard earrings as a symbol of wealth and refinement; others consider them showy and in poor taste. Some people wear them to indicate membership in a group, others to enhance status, yet others to make a fashion statement. Some people have many sets and change earrings almost daily; others wear the same pair forever. Many different social influences affect our purchase decisions, but for marketers the most notable ones are culture, subculture, social class, reference groups, and the family.

CULTURE

Perhaps the most pervasive influence on human beings is culture. **Culture** is the learned values, beliefs, language, symbols, and patterns of behavior shared by people in a society and passed on from generation to generation. It produces manners and actions that are often taken for granted as the "appropriate" way.

Culture changes very slowly unless outside forces intervene. Historically, such forces have included political and religious wars and natural disasters. Today, global economics and technology are having an enormous effect. They have made the world much smaller and culture more uniform. Take television, for instance. The hugely popular NBC comedy *The Office* was first broadcast in the UK and ran for two series on BBC. It did not take long for the the program's success to spread beyond the UK and America. The original stories have already been sold in 80 countries worldwide, making it the most successful BBC comedy export of all time.[20] However, globalization extends beyond just entertainment. Banks, investment firms, and credit card companies exchange capital and important knowledge-based information 24 hours a day, thus taking advantage of this emergent world culture.

By taking cultural values into account, companies adjust to the particular customs of people in different societies. **Values** are the shared norms about what is right to think and do. They reflect what society considers to be worthy and desirable. Marketers need to understand values so their actions are not counter to what consumers in a given market consider acceptable. For a company like Whirlpool, where many of its products can be found in kitchens around the world, it would be important to know how different societies view and utilize their kitchens. In Sweden, for example, the cooking area and facilities are more prized areas of the house as indicated by the fact that utensils are often given as gifts and subsequently shown proudly to guests. On the other hand, in India, the kitchen is probably not somewhere that guests would see, but rather a simple functional area for cooking. Thus, while Swedes might be interested in more up-scale kitchenware and appliances, people in India might prefer space-saving, more practical items.[21]

SUBCULTURE

Understanding a culture provides marketers with an overall picture, but they also need more specific information. A **subculture** is a group of people with shared values within a culture. In the United States, these groups may be defined by ethnicity, age, religion, geographic location, and national origin. In this section we will focus on ethnicity and look at three groups: Hispanic, Asian, and African American consumers.

It should be noted that an ethnic subculture can be a very broad category. For example, the U.S. Hispanic community includes Cubans, Puerto Ricans, Mexican Americans, Tejanos, and Chicanos, among others. Within such groups are further distinctions—low or high ethnicity, length of time in the United States, immigrant or native-born, and place of residence, to name a few. A marketer may want to target Cubans with high ethnicity living in New York City—as Miller beer does.

Marketers know that ethnic subgroups are much more likely to buy branded products and spend more for what they perceive as quality. Immigrants are often perplexed by the wide variety of choices, so they tend to stick with the major brands they knew at home. Gary Berman, president of Miami-based Market Segment Research, says that "these groups define nationally advertised brands as being quality products and are more likely to select quality over price."[22]

Groups with strong ethnicity form some of the most important subcultures. You will learn that marketers are interested in identifying segments of the population with common needs, wants, and buying behaviors. Marketing strategies can then be developed to appeal directly to these segments. Therefore, it's critical for marketers to identify people of high ethnicity—who identify strongly with their ethnic subculture—rather than simply those with a certain skin color or national origin. A thorough understanding of ethnic backgrounds can lead to the formation of homogeneous segments. Figure 5.9 illustrates the spending power, income, and population percentages of several ethnic groups in the United States.

With the increase in ethnic populations, companies that produce, sell, and market ethnic products may see a considerable growth. Use your knowledge of diversity to your advantage in interviews and by writing targeted cover letters. Remember that companies in growth areas may offer you better opportunities for advancement.

Hispanic Consumers   Hispanics are a booming subculture. Their number is growing rapidly due to births and immigration. Research shows that there were over 42 million Hispanics in the U.S. in 2006, and Hispanic buying power reaching over $800 billion. These numbers make the Hispanic community a very important target for marketers.[23]

Because Hispanics share Spanish as a common language (except for Brazilians who speak Portuguese), radio or television stations that program in Spanish are obvious media choices for promotional messages. Although many

---

Marketing Vocabulary

MEMORY
The brain function that stores and recalls encoded information; includes sensory, short-term, and long-term capacities.

CULTURE
The learned values, beliefs, language, symbols, and patterns of behavior shared by people in a society that are passed on from generation to generation.

VALUES
The shared norms about what is right to think and do; what culture considers to be worthy and desirable.

SUBCULTURE
A subset of people with shared values within a culture.

	All Groups	White	African American	Hispanic	Asian
Percentage of U.S. Population	100%	67.6%	12%	12%	4%
Average Household Income	$46,326	$50,784	$30,858	$35,967	$61,094
Annual Spending Power	$9,710 billion	$7,811 billion	$760 billion	$736 billion	$396 billion

Figure 5.9   Subculture Spending Power in the United States
Source: 2005 Census Race and Hispanic Data, www.census.gov., U.S. Census Bureau.

Hispanics are fluent in English, most marketers believe that it is better to sell in Spanish. According to a pilot study by Skunkworks of New York, advertisers can gain a 20 percent increase in sales among Hispanics simply by advertising on Spanish-language network television. The National Association of Hispanic Publications is even seeking to aid advertisers wishing to reach Hispanics and has begun a "one-stop shopping program" called the Latino Print Network.[24]

Grocery store chains are weighing the benefits of separate labels for Hispanic products besides salsa, such as sardines in tomato sauce and canned spaghetti, with private-label products being offered mainly in areas such as Texas and California where the concentration of Hispanics is high. Difficulties arise, however, because Hispanics are not a homogeneous group. Food preparation as well as vocabulary, for example, vary among Hispanics of different origins.[25]

Asian American Consumers   Imagine a market segment that's highly educated, affluent, and geographically concentrated. That describes the 10 million Asian Americans whose numbers are growing at a rapid rate. The Census Bureau estimates that the Asian American population will grow to 33.4 million or 8 percent of the population by 2050.[26] Moreover, they generally spend more than other ethnic groups, particularly in categories such as computers and insurance.

However, just as with other ethnic groups, marketers must pay careful attention to cultural and language differences. For example, when an airline briefly used the number 1-800-FLY-4444, it failed to recognize that it was offending many in the Asian American community to whom the number 4 implied death. This one instance symbolizes the potential embarrass-

ment and problems that many companies are shying away from as they continue to neglect targeting Asian Americans. Because Asian Americans represent only 4.5 percent of America's populations and are highly diverse

Sponsoring the Mexican Football Federation is one way that Allstate, an insurance company, markets to Hispanic consumers.

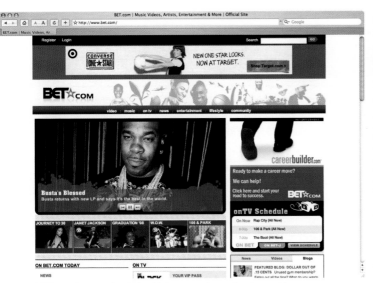

BET.com has received the highest number of unique visitors among sites designed specifically for African Americans

as a group, many companies may not consider the risk worth the effort.[27]

Cultural differences can pay off when used for profit, however, and some companies are focusing their attention on Asian Americans during important cultural holidays such as the Asian Lunar New Year as a means of recognizing Asian culture and getting paid for it. Hallmark Cards, for example, has developed a line of Lunar New Year products such as greeting cards. According to Kim Newton, marketing manager for Hallmark's Ethnic Business Center, "We wanted to make sure we chose cards that are appropriate for the domestic market but still tie ethnic consumers to who they are. Our goal is to help them keep *cultural* traditions alive during the holidays that are important to them." Whereas Hallmark's advertising is a large-scale effort, Honest Tea is also realizing the value of the Asian American market and is currently planning to market its products during the Lunar New Year.[28]

Through future studies, marketers hope to learn more about the desires of Asian Americans, making advertising to them a more feasible task. Organizations like the Association of Asian-American Advertising Agencies seek to increase the information available to advertisers about this relatively unstudied group.

African American Consumers African Americans represent about 13.4 percent of the total U.S. population and will have an annual buying power of over $1 trillion by 2012.[29] According to the Buying Power of Black America, a study conducted by Target Market News, African Americans are increasing their expenditures in various areas, from books to automobiles, making them an even more important market. In addition, though they have traditionally been the least active ethnic

group in Internet use and buying, they are now the fastest-growing group of Internet users, making their importance to marketers significant in a number of areas.[30] Demonstrating the power of the Internet in reaching ethnic groups, BET.com has received the highest number of unique visitors among sites designed specifically for African Americans since it began in February 2000. The site even had over 45 percent more visitors than the next two most visited sites, BlackPlanet.com and BlackVoices.com. The site, which provides information for African Americans between the ages of 18 and 44, runs nine content channels, including news, careers, romance, and entertainment. President of BET's Digital Media Group, Scott Mills says, "BET's cable viewers are digital media super-consumers - they want BET's brands and content on every platform."[31]

Some companies are seeking to market goods directly to African Americans by focusing on African American culture, much like Hallmark has done through its cards and e-cards celebrating Kwanzaa. However, some consumers are concerned about the lack of major advertising to African Americans outside of January and February, when Martin Luther King, Jr.'s Birthday and Black History Month are celebrated, arguing that advertising only during this time is patronizing. As Clifford Franklin stated in a *St. Louis Post* editorial, "I would hope these companies and their ad agencies realize it will take more than advertising during Black History Month to build a relationship with the African-American community."[32]

Many marketers pay careful attention to cultural issues. Marketing techniques should support cultural traditions in a sensitive manner. The African American community is distinct and "marketers should develop advertising and promotions specifically targeted to the African-American community, rather than assuming general-market advertising is enough because this ethnic group speaks English."[33]

SOCIAL CLASS

The third major social influence on consumer behavior is social class. A **social class** is a relatively homogeneous grouping of people based on similarities in income and occupation. Members tend to share values, interests, and behaviors. How would you rank the following occupations by status: salesperson, high school teacher, and accountant? What about a physician, a professor, or a lawyer? Your views agree with research findings if, in both groups, you

Marketing Vocabulary

SOCIAL CLASS
A relatively stable division of society based on education, income, and occupation.

Social Class	Percentage of U.S. Population	Description	Examples of Purchases
Upper Upper	Less than 1%	Often called the "old rich," upper-upper class families have been wealthy for generations and are born into wealth. People in this group do not have to work for a living.	Jewelry, fine wine, luxury cruises, yachts
Lower Upper	About 2%	Often called the "new rich" because their fortunes are not inherited, these self-made millionaires tend to be executives, athletes, consultants, movie stars, and high-technology entrepreneurs.	Highly visible products such as cars
Upper Middle	12%	Comprised of doctors, professors, lawyers, veterinarians, state politicians, and business executives, this class is upwardly mobile and success oriented.	Condominiums, skiing, travel, home computers, outdoor furniture, camcorders, cellular phones
Middle	32%	In addition to white- and blue-collar workers, the middle class includes such professions as clerk, bank teller, public school teacher, and nearly all nonmanagerial office positions and other such occupations.	Brand-name clothing, family vacations
Working Class	38%	Largely blue collar, the working class has jobs that can be defined as fairly routine and not requiring advanced education. Many in this class are union members.	Used trucks and motorcycles
Upper Lower	9%	Living standards are just above poverty. Work is predominantly unskilled and low wage. The members of this class are often poorly educated.	Fundamental necessities: food, rental housing, medical care
Lower Lower	7%	At the bottom of the social class system are the visibly poor, many of whom are third-generation welfare recipients. Typically underemployed or unemployed, they rely on public aid or charity to survive.	Food, used clothing, minimum necessities

Figure 5.10 A Breakdown of Social Classes

ranked them from highest to lowest in the order presented. Feelings about the relative prestige of these occupations reflect the tendency in most cultures to make social class distinctions. Figure 5.10 describes various social classes and gives examples of purchases for each.

Global Social Class Dimensions Marketers increasingly look at social class from a global perspective. In some societies—such as India, South Africa, and Brazil—class distinctions are clear, and status differences are great. In others—such as Australia, Denmark, and Canada—differences are less extreme. In countries with strong class differences, where people

www.whymilk.com

Learn how to maintain a healthy lifestyle through diet, exercise and drinking milk at the Why Milk Web site.

live, the cars they drive, the restaurants they frequent, the sports in which they participate, the types of clothing they wear, how much they travel, and where (or whether) they go to college are largely determined by social class.

Commercial activity, particularly interpersonal relations, also can be greatly influenced by class associations. For example, the president of a French company expects to deal only with the top executives of another firm. More than once, U.S. companies have failed at marketing in France because they did not know or ignored this. In some cases, the French were offended when the Americans sent lower-level managers to important meetings. In other cases, the Americans lost status when high-ranking executives communicated with middle-level French managers. In a country with a more homogeneous class structure, such as Sweden or Denmark, it is not uncommon for executives from all levels to work as a team, so Americans of various rank are accepted as well.

Marketers study global social class dimensions in order to understand consumer profiles, habits, interests, and purchasing behavior. For example, three national surveys costing more than $30 million were mailed to more than 24 million British homes by ICD Marketing Services. The research was designed to give insight into consumer preferences for cars, finance, travel, and other purchases.[34]

REFERENCE GROUPS

Another major influence on consumer behavior is reference groups. We all live with, depend on, and are nurtured by other people. We influence and are influenced by those with whom we have frequent contact—friends, coworkers, and family members. We also are influenced by people we know only indirectly through the mass media. Research shows that groups have an immense effect on the purchasing behavior of their members, including their search for and use of information, their response to advertisements, and their brand choices.[35]

Reference groups are people whose norms and values influence a consumer's behavior. Consumers depend on them for product information, purchase comparisons, and rules about correct or incorrect buying behavior. College fraternities and sororities are examples of reference groups. Although each member is unique, each adheres to certain group norms and standards.

Marketers distinguish between two types of reference groups. **Associative reference groups** are those to which people want to belong, although they may be prevented by income, occupation, or education. In contrast, **disassociative reference groups** are those to which people do not want to belong. The same reference group can be associative to some people and disassociative to others. For example, a widely publicized concern about the world of some rock 'n' roll artists is the use of drugs. There is a possibility that teens who are drawn to some rock artists may become more accepting of drugs despite the obvious hazards. Well-known artists such as Nirvana's Kurt Cobain, Shannon Hoon of Blind Melon, and Sublime frontman Brad Nowell died of overdoses. Many other musicians and groups are known to be current or past users, including members of the Rolling Stones and Red Hot Chili Peppers, Scott Weiland, and Amy Winehouse. Teens may choose these bands as associa-

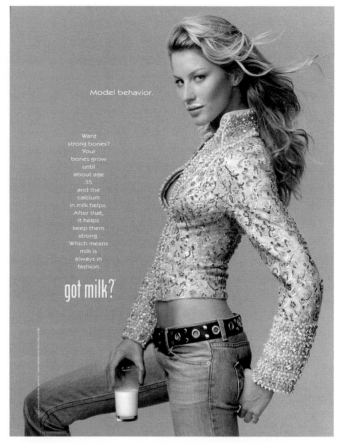

Model behavior.

Want strong bones? Your bones grow until about age 35 and the calcium in milk helps. After that, it helps keep them strong. Which means milk is always in fashion.

got milk?

The "milk mustache" ads use a diverse collection of celebrities to bring success to the campaign.

tive or disassociative reference groups.

Advertisers capitalize on the human tendency to rely on groups. In one form or another, groups are a part of almost all mass media advertisements and are used in many personal selling presentations. One Revlon campaign used a diverse collection of celebrities to create an atmosphere of intrigue playing to the characteristics of each celebrity. Revlon spokespeople included Halle Berry, Jessica Alba and Julianne Moore to target a number of different reference groups.[36]

Promotions that appeal to associative tendencies command a good deal of attention. Ads in youth-oriented magazines often depict people who belong to admired groups. Because consumers are full of hopes and dreams for the future, the use of associative reference groups is very effective.

Amy Winehouse

Marketing Vocabulary

REFERENCE GROUP
A set of people whose norms and values influence a consumer's behavior.

ASSOCIATIVE REFERENCE GROUP
A group with which people want to identify.

DISASSOCIATIVE REFERENCE GROUP
A group with which people do not want to identify.

http://globaledge.msu.edu

Visit globalEDGE™ Online for the ultimate international marketing research tool!

Marketers have many resources to gain insights about global marketing opportunities. One of the most useful is globalEDGE™. Developed by MSU-CIBER as the ultimate international marketing research tool, it has up-to-date information on 200 countries, including maps, key statistics, history, economic, government, stock market, country specific marketing resources and news. Web-based computer software programs incorporate research knowledge in easily usable formats. Each chapter of the text has a globalEDGE™ exercise tied to its content.

Marketing Vocabulary

HOUSEHOLD
Family members (and occasionally others) who share the same housing unit; for marketers, the standard purchase and consumption unit.

Consider the number of advertisers that use famous spokespersons to tout their messages about products. Professional athletes are often seen as being members of associative reference groups. A survey by Advertising Age and Knowledge Networks found that Michael Jordan is the leading sports celebrity endorser in terms of influencing consumer purchasing decisions. In terms of popularity with advertisers and income earned annually, Tiger Woods topped the ranks, bringing in $87 million in 2006 from appearances and endorsements alone.[37]

THE FAMILY

How much has your family influenced the way you behave, speak, or dress? Often the family in which you grow up—known as your family of orientation—teaches you certain purchase habits that continue throughout your life. Many consumers buy the same brand of soap, toothpaste, mayonnaise, laundry detergent, or gasoline that their mother or father did. Later people start their own family, called the family of procreation, and it also influences purchase habits.

The family is especially important to marketers because it forms a **household,** which is the standard purchase and consumption unit. If you do not already have a household, chances are great that someday you will purchase or rent a home, buy appliances and durable goods, and require banking and insurance services. In other words, your household will be a consumption unit.

Not all households consist of a mother, a father, and children. Many have only one person, or several nonrelatives, or a single parent with children. This section, however, focuses on the traditional nuclear family. Marketers generally look at three important aspects:

- How do families make decisions as a group?
- What roles can various members play in a purchase decision?
- How does family purchase behavior change over time?

Family Decision Making

Family decision making is "one of the most under researched and difficult areas to study within all of consumer behavior."[38] How does your family make buying decisions? Most purchases are probably conceived and carried out by one member with little influence from the others. These are called autonomous decisions. In other cases, several family members may be involved. These are called joint decisions.

Marketers must remember that gender roles affect how family decisions are made. Decisions are termed *syncratic* when both spouses are jointly and equally involved; *autonomous* when either one of them makes the decision independently; and *husband- or wife-dominant* depending on which one has the influence. Research has found that gender especially affects financial decisions and that men and women approach finances differently. In general, men perceive themselves as advisors, active in business and in influencing their friends' financial decisions. Men are more likely to take independent financial risks, and they often place value on ego-gratifying opportunities. Women are more likely to discuss finances with friends and others before making a decision. They are less likely to take risks and are more open to advice. Directing marketing activities to the wrong person in the household could be as wasteful as directing them to the wrong market segment.[39] For this reason, it's important for marketers to understand the decision-making roles within a family.

Family Purchasing Roles

When children ask a parent to buy a certain type of cereal, they are influencing the purchase, but the parent still makes the final decision. In contrast, when teenagers go to the mall to buy clothing, while they certainly may be influenced by their parents, they usually make the final decision. Family members play certain roles in certain purchases and play different roles for different products. There are five key roles:

- Initiator - First suggests that a particular product be purchased.
- Influencer - Provides valuable input to the decision-making process.
- Decision maker - Makes the final buying deci-

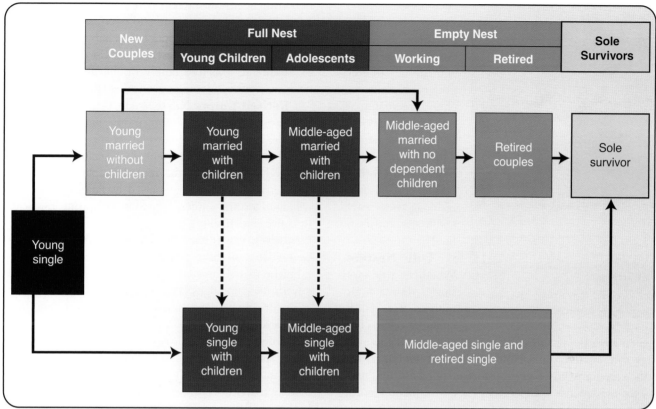

Figure 5.11   The Family Life Cycle

sion.

- Purchaser - Physically goes out and makes the purchase.
- User - Uses the product.

The role a consumer plays is not always obvious. For example, women no longer rely on a husband or boyfriend to take care of home repair and construction. Retailers, such as Home Depot are now actively targeting this segment that spends $50 billion a year on hand tools, power tools and other equipment.[40]

Children have a significant effect on family decisions. In fact, for certain products, the marketer may decide to focus on them rather than parents. The Coleman Company, maker of outdoor equipment such as tents, sleeping bags, and lanterns, is among the many companies that have formed a club targeting kids. The Coleman Kids' Club offers information on camping and outdoor gear for youths as well as outdoor news, campfire tales, and the like. Kids identify with "their" brand, and the next time a parent purchases camping equipment for them Coleman can be assured it has developed a young influencer in the purchasing decision.[41] Cereal manufacturers also recognize the important role young children play. Eye-catching boxes and cartoon characters are designed to appeal directly to children. The influence of children continues as they grow but usually for a different set of products—clothes, video or computer games, and such services as family vacations or video rentals.

Family Life Cycle   As families age, they progress through a series of predictable stages, called the family life cycle. At each point, unique problems and life situations must be addressed. An understanding of each stage gives marketers powerful insight into the needs and expectations of families.

Only a few decades ago, everyone was expected to move in orderly progression from youth, to marriage, to childrearing, to retirement. Today, the picture is more complex because of widespread divorce and single parenting, as shown in Figure 5.11. As you can imagine, a family's needs and purchase decisions vary at each stage. Let's look at these in more detail.

Young Singles Young singles are in the process of setting up their first household. Items they buy tend to be easily transportable from one location to another as living arrangements change or they find a new job. During this stage, courtship activities make social events, recreation, and entertainment important. Advanced education and training also may be purchased to further a career. This market category, when combined with middle-aged singles and sole survivors, has shown high growth from 18 percent of all households in 1970 to 25 percent in 1990. The U.S. Bureau of the Census predicts the figure will be 27 percent by 2010.

New Couples Young married people without children generally try to build an economic foundation for

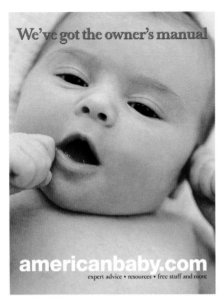

We've got the owner's manual

americanbaby.com
expert advice • resources • free stuff and more

AmericanBaby.com markets to young parents, the young nesters cohort.

later responsibilities. By combining resources, a new couple may have enough discretionary income to enjoy recreational activities while still saving for the future. This group spends more than other households on furnishings, new cars and trucks, and alcohol.

Full Nesters Whether you are single, divorced, or married, a great deal changes once children enter the picture. They are expensive and consume great amounts of time. Household budgets for full nesters increase for nearly every category of purchase, and new expenses emerge—diapers, day care, toys, piano lessons, and so forth. As children reach adolescence, their sports activities may cost from several hundred to several thousand dollars per year. Many families prepare for the cost of college, which can consume over 41 percent of annual household income for each child in lower middle income families.[42]

Of course, purchase behavior will differ according to family structure—traditional family, divorced or widowed parent, or single parent. The latter group often has very limited spending power. A divorced or widowed parent may have some child support or death benefits to ease the burden a little, but often he or she must work long hours to make ends meet and has very little free time. In traditional families, both parents usually work to provide for their children. Their earnings tend to increase over time as they become well established in a career.

Working Empty Nesters This category consists of three types of consumers: middle-aged singles, married couples with no children, and married couples with grown children who have left home. These households are in their prime wage-earning years. According to the U.S. Census Bureau, the median income of people aged 45 to 54 was $62,424 in 2005, the highest income bracket of any one group. Some 75 percent of Americans in their fifties still work, whereas the baby boomers who were born between 1946 and 1964 are the largest segment of the U.S. popula-

tion with nearly 80 million people.[43] Without children around, empty nesters are free to travel, pursue hobbies, and explore new lifestyle options. As baby boomers turn 50, this market will grow even more. For details on how to capture it—whether empty or full nesters—see the diversity feature, "Boomers Don't Act Like Seniors."

Retired Empty Nesters Americans aged 65 and over are worth considerably more than the average American and over the next 20 years, this market is expected to grow by 30 percent. This wealthier group has changed the image of the retired couple over the last decade. Retirees are now viewed as financial investors willing to assume some risk, mobile and daring, physically active and health conscious, and willing to pamper themselves. It was once thought that advertising dollars were wasted on this segment but no longer; it's a powerful niche that is targeted in television programming and advertising campaigns. The wealthy elderly are the focus of luxury cruise lines, automobile manufacturers, and land developers.

Sole Survivors Sole survivors are men and women whose spouse has died as well as older single people who never married. Their net worth and buying power have increased over the past two decades due to the stock market boom of the mid-1980s and mid-1990s and the rise in home values. A number of sole survivors are senior citizens, who today are targeted heavily by marketers. The growing number of goods and services designed to appeal to seniors include home health care as well as Internet sites such as CareScout.com, which are devoted to senior needs.[44] Television fitness programs are also targeted to the elderly, as well as a variety of diet supplements.

USING TECHNOLOGY TO TRACK CONSUMER BEHAVIOR

Technology not only helps marketers better understand consumers but also is having a direct influence on how companies build relationships. As computer usage rises in the classroom and at home, younger generations have increasing exposure to the Internet. Likewise, many seniors have begun using the Internet as an alternative to shop and

JC Penney's online gift registry is an example of how technology can be used to track consumer behavior.

The Marketing Gazette™

CREATING & CAPTURING VALUE THROUGH DIVERSITY

Boomers Don't Act Like Seniors

Call them young at heart, in their prime, or maybe even mature. Just don't call them seniors. Marketers who treat the aging baby boomers like previous generations of seniors are in for a shock. Defined as the 80 million people born between 1946 and 1964 in the United States, baby boomers are fast approaching traditional retirement age but aren't acting the way retired people traditionally act. With one person turning 50 every 9 seconds, 68.2 million people—one-third of the adult population—are above 50 and this number will jump to 115 million in the next 25 years. These boomers are reinventing senior citizenship in their own young image, and their numbers are too great to be ignored.

The marketing community needs to be reminded that there's gold in those golden years. Baby-boomers already consume more than $1.7 trillion a year and they are known as a richer group than any other group in the past. After all, 50-plus households control 41 percent of all discretionary income and $169 billion is nothing for the business world to ignore. This generation is not buying just hearing aids and prescription medicine, but is the leading age group of online purchasers, comprising 48 percent of online shoppers. They also travel more than any other age group, taking approximately 259 million trips annually. It seems as though founder and president of Age Wave Ken Dychtwald is right, "A phenomenal economic opportunity is about to unfold for those that are ready."

Companies that are ready are recognizing the different needs of baby boomers from the needs their parents had. But boomers do seem to have one common denominator: denial of aging. Formerly the American Association of Retired Persons, for example, the organization is now referring to itself simply as AARP to remove the traditional connotations of retirement. Moreover, its monthly publication Modern Maturity is now divided into one section for the retired and one for those still working, and covers such diverse topics as grandparenting, dating, midlife career changes, and the 50 greatest adventures in the world. The age group formerly associated with golfing is even becoming interested in sports such as biking, jogging, and in-line skating, and in activities such as yoga and pilates in its quest for greater health and fitness. Del Webb, a company with 40 years of experience in advertising to adults, recognizes these changes in lifestyles and has altered its advertising campaign to appeal to the subsequent buying habits. Its "Live On" campaign appeals to baby boomers seeking to live as actively as possible. Myprimetime.com, visited by 2.2 million unique visitors monthly, aids baby boomers in making positive changes in their lives through its five content areas—Family, Money, Health, Work, and Play.

But the future for boomers won't be all fun in the sun. According to a Del Webb survey, more than 60 percent of boomers plan to work at least 20 hours per week after they retire. Others plan to volunteer for charities or their communities. Perhaps the most surprising, however, are the 28 percent of boomers who plan to go back to school after they retire. In Sun City, Texas, 350 residents participate in Senior University, learning and discussing topics from foreign policy to French Impressionism. Perhaps companies should also begin rethinking their back-to-school sales.

stay in touch with others.

What implications does this have for marketing? Dozens of Internet survey groups such as CyberAtlas, Nua, and Jupiter Communications maintain up-to-date databases and news sites with information on Internet demographics, advertising rates, and industrywide Web spending and usage. These groups allow marketers to effectively track consumer behavior. For instance, American web surfers visited an average of 56 unique domains at home and 94 at work. The average length of time spent by Americans online is nearly 15 hours per month.[45] Currently the NPD Group maintains an "Online Panel" of consumers, demographically selected, who participate in continuous surveys of the Web. For a fee, companies can access Online Panel reports, including attitude and usage studies, longitudinal tracking, as well as product and concept reviews. Together with names, addresses, and other data requested when a Web site is accessed, such research provides a reservoir of information about consumers.[46]

Marketers also make use of Web-tracking software that allows marketers to track every Web site a surfer visits and to compile information based on criteria such as purchases made and sites visited. The resulting silhouette, or profile, provides the kind of precision targeting that marketers so eagerly desire.

Ultimately, the growing use of new technologies will provide marketers with greater insight into consumer behavior. Categorizing user behavior as well as providing consumers with easy Web access enables marketers to reach many of their targeted audiences. This will benefit both consumers seeking information and the companies supplying it.

THE ETHICS OF INFLUENCING CONSUMER BEHAVIOR

For a long time, marketers have used sexual themes to heighten brand awareness and influence consumers. Today, ethical questions are being raised about some of these promotions, which many people find offensive. Procter & Gamble set up a "sex task force" to examine its policy toward sexually suggestive magazine articles and cover headlines. With nearly $500 million in magazine advertising per year, Procter & Gamble was concerned that it was overly connected with sexually risqué content in magazines such as *Cosmopolitan* and *Glamour*.[47]

Controversial promotion risks losing consumers in the selective comprehension phase of perception. Some people screen out ads altogether that conflict with their values. At the same time, controversy generates free publicity, which can result in positive or negative impacts to a company. Ben & Jerry's liberal political view was controversial enough for three angry conservatives to launch their own brand of ice cream in 2005, Star Spangled Ice Cream, to target conservative consumers. Their flavors include Iraqi Road, I Hate the French Vanilla and Smaller GovernMINT.[48] Italian shoe company Geox S.p.A. donated several pairs of their antifoot-sweat system shoe to the Pope, hoping that they might be able to capitalize on a photograph of the pope wearing the company's shoes. Although the Pope does not receive money for endorsing products, his use has created marketing

Web and E-Commerce Stars
www.priceline.com

This Web site offers valuable information on flights, hotels, car rentals, vacation packages, and cruises. As one of the first online discount travel sites, its popularity skyrocketed and it continues to be a staple for those looking for affordable travel arrangements. Visitors can easily make an account by entering an email address to start your search. Search results results with high speed, practical convenience, and big savings. The PriceBreakers section contains great travel deals delivered by "deal experts" every day. Priceline.com also offers information on non-travel related items such as low interest mortgages and free web banking. Special seasonal promotions are also a big draw. For instance, each summer they have a special summer promotion - no booking fees, flights on sale, and so on - to help their customers save more

opportunities. The Pope also owns Bushnell sunglasses and a specially engraved Apple iPod. These kinds of endorsement pursuits are seen as being unethical by some consumers and may result in backlash from the Pope's followers.[49]

Although consumers are free to seek out or avoid information, people often feel that children should not be exposed to objectionable images. When these are plastered on billboards or the side of a bus, it is hard to avoid them. Marketers face a challenge when deciding whether to promote a product with a sexual theme or shock tactics. They must weigh the risk of losing customers and crossing ethical boundaries against the advantages of gaining attention and strongly influencing purchase behavior.

Many of the factors that influence consumer decision making also play a role in the buying decisions of businesses because businesspeople are, after all, individuals with psychological motivations, perceptions, and attitudes. Over all, however, the buying behavior of businesses is quite different from consumer buying behavior. Business-to-business transactions follow formalized procedures, involves many persons and functions, and requires more personalized communication with the selling firm.

Chapter Summary:

Objective 1: Appreciate the importance of involvement in the decisions consumers make.

Marketers know that an understanding of consumer behavior lies at the heart of nearly every successful strategy for connecting with customers. Consumer behavior is the actions and decision processes of individuals and organizations in discovering, evaluating, acquiring, consuming, and disposing of products. Consumers behave differently in low- and high-involvement purchasing situations. When involvement is high, they use an elaborate five-step decision process, and their attitudes are learned actively. When involvement is low, they make choices without much effort, and learning is passive.

Objective 2: Evaluate the effect on consumer behavior of such psychological factors as motivation, perception, learning, attitudes, and information processing.

The five important psychological factors influencing consumer behavior are motivation, perception, learning, attitudes, and information processing. Motivation is an internal force that directs behavior toward the fulfillment of needs. Marketers often use Maslow's hierarchy to categorize needs. Consumers may experience one of three forms of motivational conflict: approach-approach, avoidance-avoidance, or approach-avoidance. Perception is the process of recognizing, selecting, organizing, and interpreting stimuli in order to make sense of the world around us. It occurs in four stages: selective exposure, selective attention, selective comprehension, and selective retention. Learning is any change in behavioral tendencies due to previous experience. The two basic types of learning are cognitive learning and behavioral learning. Behaviors can be learned (conditioned) by classical conditioning and operant conditioning. Attitudes have cognitive, affective, and behavioral components. Information processing involves encoding and memory processes. The human brain encodes information differently depending on the type of data. It processes nonverbal, emotional, and visual concepts in one way, while it handles general knowledge, facts, and justifications in another. Memory consists of sensory, short-term, and long-term memory.

Objective 3: Explain how social factors such as culture, subculture, social class, reference groups, and family help explain consumer behavior.

Subcultures are groups that display homogeneous values and behaviors that diverge from the surrounding culture. Social class is a relatively stable division into groups based on such factors as education, income, and occupation. Reference groups provide norms and values that become the perspectives that influence a consumer's behavior. Associative groups are ones with which people want to be associated, whereas disassociative groups are ones with which people do not want to identify. Families have a profound influence on consumer behavior.

Review Your Understanding

1. What is involvement? How does it influence passive and active learning?
2. Describe the five steps in decision making.
3. What is motivation? Describe Maslow's hierarchy of needs.
4. Describe the four elements of the perception process.
5. What is learning? Describe cognitive learning and two types of behavioral learning.
6. What are attitudes? What are their three components? How does knowledge of the components help in creating attitude change strategies?
7. What is information processing and how does it work?
8. What social influences are most important to marketers? List and define each.
9. How is social class measured?

Discussion of Concepts

1. Name several subcultures in the United States. Which companies have target-marketed to them?
2. Why must marketers distinguish between a person's ethnic background and ethnicity?
3. How does social class affect consumer behavior? Which social classes exist in the United States?
4. What are the different ways families make purchase decisions? How do these affect marketing?
5. Imagine that you are the marketing manager for the Pontiac Firebird sports car. What product features would you include to meet each of the five types of needs described by Maslow's hierarchy? (For example, air bags might fulfill the safety need.)
6. What types of motivational conflict might be associated with the purchase of this Pontiac Firebird? How would you try to resolve the conflict?
7. You are in charge of marketing for a major league baseball team. How might you apply the principles of cognitive learning to your job? Could you also apply the principles of classical conditioning or reinforcement learning? How?

Key Terms And Definitions

Active learning: Learning in which substantial energy is devoted to thinking about and elaborating on information.

Affective (component of attitude): Emotional feeling of like or dislike.

Alternatives evaluation: Use of decision rules that attempt to determine which product would be most likely to satisfy goals.

Approach-approach conflict: Motivational conflict that occurs when a consumer desires two objectives but cannot have both.

Approach-avoidance conflict: Motivational conflict that occurs when a consumer desires an alternative that has positive and negative qualities.

Associative reference groups: A group with which people want to identify.

Attitude: A state of readiness with cognitive, emotional, and behavioral components, which reflects the beliefs of the consumer with regard to messages, brands, products, product characteristics, and so forth.

Avoidance-avoidance conflict: Motivational conflict that occurs when consumers must choose between two undesirable alternatives.

Behavioral (component of attitude): Tendency to act positively or negatively.

Belief: A conviction that something is true or that descriptive statements are factual.

Classical conditioning: After two stimuli are presented together repeatedly, people learn to respond to one in the same way as the other.

Cognitive (component of attitude): Knowledge about a product's attributes not influenced by emotion.

Consumer behavior: The actions and decision processes of individuals and households in discovering, evaluating, acquiring, consuming, and disposing of products.

Culture: The learned values, beliefs, language, symbols, and patterns of behavior shared by people in a society that are passed on from generation to generation.

Disassociative reference groups: A group with which people do not want to identify.

Discrimination: Making different responses to different stimuli.

Encoding: The process of converting information to knowledge.

Generalization: Making the same response to different stimuli.

High-involvement purchase: A complex buying decision made after extensive thought.

Household: Family members (and occasionally others) who share the same housing unit; for marketers, the standard purchase and consumption unit.

Information processing: The process whereby consumers acquire, store, and evaluate the data they use in making decisions.

Information search: Thinking through a situation by recalling information from stored memory or obtaining it from external sources.

Learning: Any change in consumer behavior caused by experience.

Low-involvement purchase: A routine buying decision.

Memory: The brain function that stores and recalls encoded information; includes sensory, short-term, and long-term capacities.

Motivation: An internal force that directs behavior toward the fulfillment of needs.

Operant conditioning: The use of reinforcement or punishment to shape behavior.

Passive learning: Learning in which little energy is devoted to thinking about or elaborating on information.

Perception: The process of recognizing, selecting, organizing, and interpreting stimuli in order to make sense of the world.

Problem recognition: Becoming aware of an unfulfilled need or desire.

Psychological needs: A need that arises in the socialization process.

Purchase: A financial commitment to acquire a product.

Purchase decision: The decision of whether or not to buy and which competing product to buy, which is made after carefully weighing the alternatives.

Purchase evaluation: The process of determining satisfaction or dissatisfaction with a buying choice.

Reference groups: A set of people whose norms and values influence a consumer's behavior.

Selective attention: The tendency to heed information that supports current views and behaviors.

Selective comprehension: The tendency to interpret products and messages according to current beliefs.

Selective exposure: The tendency to seek out or avoid information sources.

Selective retention: The tendency to remember some and forget other information.

Social class: A relatively stable division of society based on education, income, and occupation.

Subculture: A subset of people with shared values within a culture.

Values: The shared norms about what is right to think and do; what a culture considers to be worthy and desirable.

References

1. www.homedepot.com, site visited June 5, 2008; Doug Desjardins, "Hardware's New Shade of Green," Retailing Today, May 7, 2007, Vol. 46, Iss. 7, pg. 23; www.thehomedepot.com/ecooptions site visited February 15, 2008.
2. www.robbreport.com,Web site visited April 11, 2008.
3. http://www.dodge.com/en/2008/magnum. Web site visited April 11, 2008.
4. The Army National Guard Recruiting Homepage, www.1800go-guard.com, site visited May 13, 2007.
5. Admiral John Agwunobi, remarks at a press conference to launch "The Health Consequences of Involuntary Exposure to Tobacco Smoke: A Report of the Surgeon General," www.surgeongeneral.gov/news/speeches/, June 27, 2006.
6. John Vivian, The Media of Mass Communication (Boston: Allyn & Bacon, 1993), p. 296.
7. Eric R. Spangenberg and Anthony G. Greenwald, "A Field Test of Subliminal Self-Help Audiotapes: The Power of Expectancies," Journal of Public Policy & Marketing, Fall 1992, Vol. 11 Issue 2, 26-36.
8. Ivan Pavlov, Conditioned Reflexes: An Investigation of the Physiological Activity of the Cerebral Cortex, trans. G. V. Anrep (London: Oxford University Press, 1927).
9. For further discussions, see Walter R. Nord and J. Paul Peter, "A Behavior Modification Perspective on Marketing," Journal of Marketing 44(2) (1980): 36–47; and J. Paul Peter and Walter R. Nord, "A Clarification and Extension of Operant Conditioning Principles in Marketing," Journal of Marketing 46(3) (1982): 102.
10. "Stand by Your Fans," Advertising Age, April 29, 1996, p. M1.
11. www.quakeroatmeal.com/qo_hearthealthy/oatmealandhearthealth/index.cfm, Web site visited April 12, 2008.
12. www.delta-sky.com, www.nfl.com/insider, www.aarp.org/mmaturity, sites visited May 13, 2007.
13. EAS advertisement, Muscle Media, September 2000, pp. 12–13.
14. http://www.ers.usda.gov/news/BSECoverage.htm site visited May 26, 2007; http://www.census.gov/popest/states/tables/NST-EST2004-01.pdf site visited May 26, 2007
15. Flemming Hansen, "Hemispherical Lateralization: Implications for Understanding Consumer Behavior," Journal of Consumer Research 8 (June 1981): 23–36; and Sidney Weinstein, "A Review of Brain Hemisphere Research," Journal of Advertising Research 22 (1982): 59.
16. Morris B. Holbrash and William L. Moore, "Feature Interactions in Consumer Judgments of Verbal versus Pictorial Presentations," Journal of Consumer Research 8 (1981): 103.
17. http://www.johnsonsbaby.com Web site visited APril 11, 2008.
18. Allan Piave, "A Dual Coding Approach to Perception and Cognition," in Herbert L. Pich, Jr. and Elliot Saltzma, Modes of Perceiving and Processing Information (Hillsdale, NJ: Laurence Erlbaum, 1978), p. 16.
19. Herbert A. Simon, "How Big Is a Chunk?" Science, February 8, 1974, p. 183.
20. "The Office remade for French TV," http://news.bbc.co.uk, February 9, 2006.
21. Michael Fielding, "In One's Element", Marketing News, Feb 2006, Vol. 40, Iss. 2, pg. 15.
22. Leah Richard, "Minorities Show Brand Loyalty," Advertising Age, May 9, 1994, Vol 60, Issue 20, pg. 29.
23. http://www.census.gov/ Web site visited April 11, 2008.
24. Dwight Cunningham, "One Size Does Not Fit All."
25. Nancy Brumback, "Salsa Savvy," Supermarket News, March 22, 1999, supermarketnews.com.
26. www.census.gov site visited May 2, 2007.
27. State & Country QuickFacts, US Census Bureau, http://wuickfacts.census.gov/qfd/states/ site visited May 7, 2007.
28. Kelly Gates, "Marketers Tie into Asian Lunar New Year," Brandmarketing, May 2000.
29. Black Buying Power to Reach $1.1 Trillion by 2012. Washington Informer. Washington D.C. February-March 2008.
30. "The Buying Power of BLACK America," Target Market News, 2006.

31. William Garth Sr., "BET Networks Finance Chief Promoted to Head New Digital Media Business Unit" Chicago, IL, Vol.42, Iss. 1; pg. 6, 1 pgs, April 4, 2007.
32. Clifford Franklin, "Why Do Companies Only Pay Attention to Black Consumers in January and February?," St. Louis Post.
33. Nancy Brumback, "Ethnic Markets Are Growing Up," Brandmarketing, July 2000.
34. "Giant Lifestyle Survey to Hit U.K.," December 4, 1996, www.adage.com.
35. J. Paul Peter and Jerry C. Olson, Consumer Behavior and Marketing Strategy, 3rd ed. (Homewood, IL: Richard D. Irwin, 1993).
36. http://www.revlon.com Web site visited April 11, 2008.
37. Anonymous, "Payoff Pitches." Advertising Age (Midwest Region Edition), October 27, 2003, Volume 74 Issue 43, pg. 6; Rick Horrow, "Athlete Dramas, Scandals, Suspensions: How do Corporations Respond?" August 9, 2006, http://sportsline.com.
38. William L. Wilkie, Elizabeth S. Moore-Shay, and Amardeep Assar, Family Decision Making for Household Durable Goods (Cambridge, MA: Marketing Science Institute, 1992), p. 1.
39. Richard E. Plank, Robert C. Greene, Jr., and Joel M. Greene, "Understanding Which Spouse Makes Financial Decisions," Journal of Retail Banking, Spring 1994, Vol 16, Issue 1, pg. 21-26.
40. Andrew Baroch, "American Women Flock to Home Improvement Stores for Do-It-Yourself Classes," www.voanews.com, March 16, 200; Women take on home improvement projects, big and small. Jane Kwiatkowski. McClatchy Tribune Business news. Washington: March 8, 2008.
41. "Coleman Kids' Club," www.colemanforkids.com, Web site visited April 11, 2008.
42. "Changes in the Cost of College across Income Classes", www.economistsview.typepad.com, October 23, 2005.
43. Carmen DeNavas-Walt, Bernadette D. Proctor and Cheryl Lee Hill, "Income, Poverty and Health Insurance Coverage in the United States: 2005," US Census Bureau, August 2006; "Facts for Features: Oldest Baby Boomers Turn 60!" US Census Bureau, January 3, 2006.
44. www.carescout.com, Web site visited April 11, 2008.
45. ClickZ Stats staff, "November 2003 Internet Usage Stats," December 29, 2003, http://www.internetnews.com/stats/article.php/3293491; Sean Michael Kerner, "Report: U.S. Internet Usage Thins Out" March 18, 2005, http://www.internetnews.com/stats/article.php/3491366.
46. www.internetnews.com site visited May 12, 2007.
47. Anne Marie Kerwin and Jack Neff, "Too Sexy? P&G 'Task Force' Stirs Magazine Debate," Advertising Age, April 10, 2000, www.adage.com.
48. "Companies in the Crossfire," BusinessWeek, April 17, 2006, Iss. 3980, pg. 30.
49. Stacy Meichtry, "Does the Pope Wear Prada? Marketers Pray for Day Pontiff Is Seen Using Their Brand; Even Better than a Movie Star", Wall Street Journal, April 25, 2006, pg. B1.

The Marketing Gazette
Laurie Tarver, "Businesses, Marketers Can Earn from Boomers' Plans," Memphis Business Journal, June 16, 2000, p. 33; "Myprimetime.com Surges into Top 300 of All Internet Sites; Dominates Baby Boomer Online Category with More Than 2 Million Unique Monthly Site Visitors," PR Newswire, July 24, 2000; Becky Edenkamp and Gina Czark, "Buy Buy Baby Boomer," Brandweek, June 26, 2000, p. 18; "TIA 2000 Report: Baby Boomers Prime Movers in Travel Market," Travel Weekly, July 20, 2000, p. 10; Marianne Wilson. Money, New Opportunity," Chain Store Age, June 2000, p. 136; and Paul Temple, "No Retirement for Boomers," Workforce, July 2000, p. 6; "BoomerEyes Study Finds That Boomers are redefining the role of aging Americans", Wireless News, April 10, 2007, p1; Rance Crain, "Boomer boon: 'Crazy aunts and uncles' spend $1.7 thrillion' ", Advertising Age Vol 78, April 2, 2007, p15.

CASE 5

Viacom

It may not be a household name but Viacom is a leading global entertainment company that operates many brands watched on our televisions daily. MTV, BET, VH1, Nickelodeon, Comedy Central and Paramount Pictures all produce huge profits for Viacom by catering to a broad target market ranging from toddlers to music-loving baby boomers. Viacom operates through film, television, and digital media to deliver globally recognized brands. The company believes that its strong connection with audiences sets it apart from the competition and the driving force behind that is its creative culture. The company has seen steady growth in operating income.

While the company prides itself on its brands, Nickelodeon, operated by the MTV networks, has been a remarkable success. Started in 1979, Nickelodeon has become cable's most watched network. Targeted at 2-to-11 year olds, it is in the desirable position of being able to extend its brand name to everything from kids' toys to macaroni and cheese. Ad spots sell out almost two seasons ahead. Despite a lot of new competition, Nickelodeon has maintained its top-rated position, reaching nearly 92 million U.S. households and has expanded into feature films, consumer products, music, online recreation and publishing.

Nickelodeon's philosophy of putting kids first has led to quality programming and entertainment for children. The company launched Nick Jr. in 1994 designed to inspire 2-to-5 year olds' understanding of the world and themselves through playful entertainment. Its award winning programs include Dora the Explorer, Blue's Clues, and The Wonderful Pets!

Nickelodeon has also been connecting kids and families through movies since 1996. In partnership with Paramount Pictures, another one of Viacom's company's, Nickelodeon has created successful films based off of its television programs, and classic children's novels. When Charlotte's Web, a film based off the classic children's novel, starring Dakota Fanning, Julia Roberts and Oprah Winfrey, was released, box office sales grossed almost $82 million. Furthermore, the top-rated network connects to kids through the top-rated internet site for parents with young children. Nick.com and NickJr.com connects kids to each other through online games and activities. The Web sites also offer parents tips and activities to do with their children.

While Viacom uses Nickelodeon to target young viewers, MTV is geared toward teenagers and young adults. Originally designed as a music video network, its programming has expanded to fashion, lifestyle, sports, politics and trends with shows such as The Hills, The Real World, and Life of Ryan. Nearly 91 million viewers in the United States tune into MTV, whose corporate philosophy is "Think Globally but Act Locally." The Network stays in tune with a staff of young executives whose success depends on pleasing young viewers much like themselves. In MTV's free flowing corporate culture, ideas count more than traditions, and even interns get heard. However, a common complaint from viewers is that it is hard to find music on MTV. The problem with music videos is that viewers surf them so rapidly that the ratings don't pick the up, ultimately hurting the network. It was then up to the creative employees to devise a solution. The result has been shows such as Direct Effect and Total Request Live. These live shows have music content, but less channel surfing than the video hours and offer viewer interaction through online voting. Despite the lack of music videos, ad rates have grown steadily around 10 percent because sponsors are willing to pay a premium to connect with hard-to-reach consumers ages 13-34.

Viacom continues to strengthen the size and diversity of its audiences. Both Nickelodeon and MTV partnered with the Arabian Television Network and Arab Media Group to launch the channels across the Middle East via satellite television in 2008. MTV also celebrated the first anniversary of MTV Tr3s, the Hispanic version of the channel, in late 2007. BET is continually ranked the number one cable network among Black adults with excellence awards from the National Association of Black Journalists. By constantly keeping a connection with the mindset of each core market segment, Viacom's conglomerate of outstanding entertainment media has become a pop culture icon in cultures across the United States and the globe.

1. How are the stages of family life cycle used by each of the Viacom networks in order to reach viewers successfully?

2. List three possible viewer reference groups for each Viacom network. How do they networks use reference groups to influence consumer behavior?

3. Discuss why advertisers would select each of the Viacom networks and how attitudes, learning, and perception about the sponsor's brand might be influenced by the network.

Sources: www.viacom.com site viewed February 18, 2008; Viacom Third Quarter Report, PULSE, viewed February 18, 2008; Hoovers Company Records, www.hoovers.com, site viewed June 5, 2008.

Understanding Business Marketing

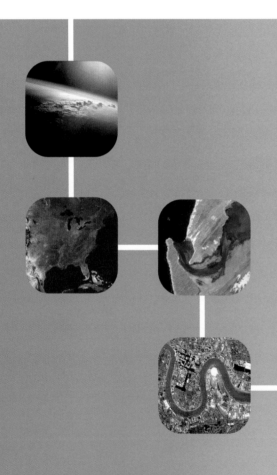

Construction of the 2008 Olympic stadium in Beijing, China. ARAMARK has a long history of supplying services to the Olympics.

Learning Objectives

1. Describe the types of organizations and products involved in business-to-business marketing and understand the importance of this market.

2. Understand the link between consumer demand and business-to-business marketing.

3. Describe the organizational buying process.

4. Know how buyer–seller relationships work, including informal and contractual partnerships.

5. Learn what functions and roles within organizations influence the purchase of a broad range of products.

Without ever knowing it, most of you have been served by ARAMARK. The company sells to thousands of colleges, schools, corporations, convention centers, hospitals, parks, and sports arenas, providing food and support services and uniform apparel. It is principally owned by its employee managers who have worked to produce annual revenues of $7 billion. Every day its 240,000 employees connect with more than 15 million people throughout 18 countries in more than 500,000 worldwide locations.

You may not have heard of the name, however, because ARAMARK partners with businesses to provide expertise on-site. ARAMARK's best-known partnership, for example, is with the Olympic Games. When ARAMARK was appointed to provide catering services for the 2008 Olympic Games in China, it marked the 14th time the company has been selected to serve at the Olympics since the 1968 Mexico City Games.

ARAMARK believes it is qualified to perform a task as lofty as managing the food service of the Olympics. Because of its history with the Olympic Games, almost half of the team has previously worked at an Olympics. This experience allows ARAMARK employees to successfully prepare and present the more than 600 international recipes offered, all of which represent a wide variety of cultural, religious, and ethnic backgrounds.

Chairman and CEO Joseph Neubauer says, "We take our accountability to the athletes and the countries they represent very seriously. Consider how important the moment is to young athletes who have waited their entire lives for one single event. Their preparation—including how they train and what they eat—in the days leading up to the defining moment of their careers is critical."

Together with its partner Beijing Tourism Group, ARAMARK will manage the design and construction of the kitchen and dining facilities for the 2008 Olympic catering venues; it is expected to provide catering services for the Athletes' Village, Media Villages, International Broadcast Center and the Main Press Center. That is to say, the company will serve more than 3.5 million meals over the two-month duration of the summer games.

ARAMARK's unique position as a business-to-business retailer allows the company to have a substantial impact on its upstream and downstream supply chain. The company has used this position to develop environmental stewardship programs that include sustainable food and agriculture, eco-friendly procurement, energy management and waste management. ARAMARK teams have helped many of its clients, including Delta Air Lines, universities, sports arenas, and hospitals, implement aggressive recycling programs and the results have been remarkable.

ARAMARK makes its people responsible to its customers as part of its efforts to ensure customer satisfaction. Each client has an "unlimited partnership" with the company and receives a specially designed program that will work with its own existing infrastructure instead of a prepackaged corporate relationship. The company has even developed "World Class Patient Service," a training program that establishes customer service standards for hourly staff members who have direct contact with the patients of hospital clients.

ARAMARK is an excellent example of an organization dedicated to helping its customers excel in their own businesses. Although the company seldom sells directly to consumers, its own consumers do. Like many business marketers, the company forms lasting relationships with its clients and plays a major role in how well they compete. This chapter describes the challenges of business-to-business marketing and shows its importance to the world economy.[1]

THE CONCEPT OF BUSINESS-TO-BUSINESS MARKETING

Dow Chemical Company, Sun Microsystems, and General Electric, like thousands of other companies market directly to other companies. They connect with customers, one customer at a time, and each customer buys huge amounts of their products. Business-to-business (B2B) marketing is the marketing of goods and services to other businesses, governments, and institutions. It includes everything except marketing by companies with products which are sold to consumers.

Total B2B sales are much greater than total business to consumer (B2C) sales. It is safe to assume that the B2B area is more than five times greater than B2C. On the surface, this seems paradoxical because most goods and services ultimately benefit consumers who pay for them. Consumer products are made from a variety of components and processes. The products are marketed from one organization to another, until the one at the end of the chain sells to the final consumer. Think about a product like an Apple iPod. Dow Chemical, for example, purchases petroleum to create a special plastic used for the case. A plastics manufacturer purchases the Dow raw material to use in its manufacture of the case. The computer chips and communication components are manufactured by other suppliers to Apple. Each of those business suppliers have 10 or more suppliers selling sub-components and services. Each manufacture adds some value to the process and eventually Apple has a finished product to sell to consumers in the B2C arena. At each B2B step, money, time, and effort are spent on marketing, and value is created. What the first party in the chain contributes is charged to the next party, which is included in the price to the next party as it moves along the chain. So prices get double, triple and multiple counted.

In other cases of business-to-business marketing, a finished product is simply sold and re-sold along the line until it reaches the end consumer. For example, a deck of playing cards is purchased by a wholesaler, who resells it

www.ARAMARK.com

Visit the ARAMARK Web site and learn how the world's largest managed services company supports small and sustainable farmers.

to a retailer such as Kmart, who then sells it to the final consumer. Again, time, money, and effort are expended at each step. In still other cases, one company sells products directly to another for its own internal use—whether copy machines, laptop computers, or paper tablets.

Many types of organizations buy business products. For example, General Motors (a B2C company) purchases nearly $200 million worth each day from outside organizations and Ford has several thousand suppliers that support its auto divisions. Other for-profit and nonprofit organizations—from the Fortune 500 to small private firms—do the same and add to this total volume. Finally, the government market makes purchases nearly as large as all private organizations combined, ranging from country road repairs to army boots to toothbrushes. The business market offers tremendous opportunities and upon graduation most business students enter the B2B arena.

Key aspects of the business-to-business market are depicted in Figure 6.1. The first half of this chapter discusses the nature of B2B markets, while the second half deals with business buyer behavior.

This section begins by describing how B2B markets are formed from derived demand. Next we will look at the industries that comprise the overall market. Then we will see that supply linkages between companies create a supply chain reaching from raw materials extractors to neighborhood retailers. This is followed by the globalization of business markets.

DERIVED BUSINESS MARKET DEMAND

The demand for business products is not based solely on what happens in the business sector. It is dependent largely on what happens to consumers.

Derived Demand **Derived demand** means that the amount of sales for business-to-business products ultimately depends on (is derived from) the demand for products by consumers. For example, when iPod sales increase, so does the need for materials, components, and sub-assemblies. The first (original) demand occurs among consumers and is reflected in the business-to-business market. This ripple effect is felt all along the supply chain, and it drives economic growth.

Inelastic Demand Certain products are so essential that they are less responsive than others to changes in the economy. **Inelastic demand** refers to products so necessary that a change in price has relatively little effect on the quantity demanded. If the price of sugar or another cola ingredient rises, it's doubtful that Coke or Pepsi will use less of it in making their product. The cost has little to do with their decision about what to buy, although it may affect the price charged to consumers.

Fluctuating Demand: The Accelerator Principle Some business products are highly sensitive to changes in consumer demand. We see the accelerator principle operating when a small fluctuation (increase or decrease) in consumer demand has a larger effect on busi-

ness demand. Suppose that the economy is sluggish. In an effort to save money, consumers are closely watching their energy consumption—turning off lights when not in use, running the air conditioner as little as possible, and so forth. Obviously, this will affect the revenues of local power plants. A few dollars saved by each customer quickly mount when multiplied by thousands of people in the utility's service area. Even a small drop in consumer demand may be enough to force the plant to postpone the purchase of multimillion-dollar equipment. Of course, if consumer demand exceeds expectations by only a little, the result may be blackouts, power outages, or the need to buy energy from outside the system.

TYPES OF MARKETS

The business market is divided into the seven categories shown in Figure 6.2, commercial market, extract industries, trade industries, institutions, utilities, transportation and telecommunications, and government. Each category is comprised of organizations with similar business circumstances and general purchasing requirements.

Commercial Market The **commercial market** category consists of organizations that acquire goods and services that are then used to produce other goods and services. Many of these products are used in finished products purchased by consumers. For example, Pulte, the nation's largest home builder, has hundreds of suppliers of construction products used to build houses. These, in turn, have other suppliers. All the marketing activities leading up to and including the sale of goods and services to Pulte are part of the commercial market.

Extractor Industries The **extractor industries** category includes organizations that obtain and process raw materials, as in forestry or mining. Extractor companies are separated from the commercial segment because they acquire much of their supply from the earth.

Marketing Vocabulary

DERIVED DEMAND
A demand, such as the demand for business-to-business products, which depends ultimately on the demand of end customers.

INELASTIC DEMAND
Demand that is influenced little by price changes.

COMMERCIAL MARKET
Organizations and individuals that acquire goods and services to produce other goods and services sold to an end consumer for profit.

EXTRACTOR INDUSTRIES
Industries that obtain and process raw materials.

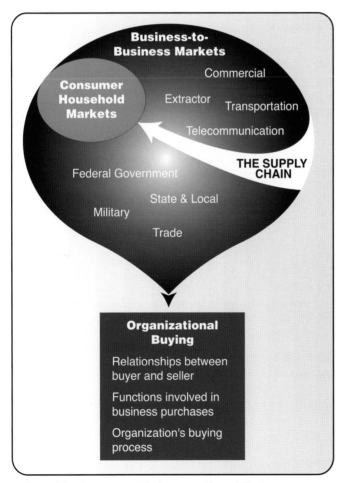

Figure 6.1   Connecting with Customers Through Business-to-Business Marketing

Category	Examples of Organizations	Purchase Examples
Commercial	Fabricators Component manufacturers Processors Original equipment manufacturers Designers	Raw materials Component parts Processing equipment Transportation Consulting services
Extractor	Agriculture Forestry Mining Drilling Water	Fertilizer and pesticides, seeds Heavy- and light-duty equipment Pipe Aircraft and transportation Real estate, mining rights Products for resale Loading equipment
Trade	Retailers Wholesalers Dealerships	Computer systems Buildings/real estate Advertising Transportation Warehousing Pharmaceuticals Equipment
Institutions	Hospitals Schools Day care centers Banks and finance organizations Insurance Churches Charities	Food Consulting Health care Suppliers Computer systems
Utilities	Electric utilities Gas utilities Water and waste disposal plants	Nuclear fuel Power generation equipment Electric components Motors Computers Chemicals Testing equipment
Transportation and Telecommunications	Airlines Trucking Rail companies Telephones Cellular	Fuel Equipment Computers Real estate
Government *Federal*	Senate and House Judicial Agencies Military	Consulting Offices Forms Computers Energy Aircraft Radar communications
State and Local	Highway commissions Health and social services Schools and universities Prisons Police Libraries Parks and recreation Museums	Health care items Food Logistics Equipment Energy Books Sports equipment Restoration

Figure 6.2 Types of Business-to-Business Markets

They require expensive equipment such as drilling rigs and instrumentation. These industries are huge consumers of nearly every product imaginable. Many of the companies in this category have global operations, such as Exxon-Mobil.

There are often unique demands on extractor organizations to be environmentally sensitive. An agency of the U.S. Department of the Interior, the Bureau of Land Management, has initiated the Director's Excellence Awards program to recognize environmental sensitivity in the production of fluid materials. Two winners include River Gas Corporation of Utah, which has substantially reduced the impacts of coal bed methane development, and Cross Timbers Operating Company of Wyoming, which has designed facilities that minimize surface disturbance and contamination, preventing the need for surface containment pits.[2] There are numerous opportunities in this category for marketing ecological products. EnviroGroup is a firm that provides both consulting and testing services. Its expertise in vapor intrusion evaluation and mitigation helps clients deal with the technical, regulatory, and risk communication challenges presented by vapor intrusion — an emerging focus of environmental agencies. With its expertise and advanced equipment, EnviroGroup manages environmental issues for clients worldwide.[3]

Trade Industries The **trade industries** category is made up of organizations that acquire or distribute finished products to businesses or to consumers. It includes retailers, wholesalers, and other intermediaries. These companies play an important role in the "place" component of the marketing mix. The importance of **resellers**, companies that purchase a product and sell it in the same form for profit, has been gaining more and more recognition recently. The computer industry, for example, is now emphasizing the role of resellers in distribution and increasingly relies on them to install and service products. Customers can, for instance, buy Apple computers through any number of resellers. Apple realizes the benefits of reselling and expanded its offerings to resellers by extending its build-to-order (BTO) capabilities to them, now allowing customers to order custom-built computers from their preferred reseller.[4]

In many cases, resellers repackage products to suit the needs of particular market segments. For example, Kroger buys meat in bulk and cuts it into sizes and forms for household use. The Cappuccino Café buys coffee in 100-pound units and sells it by the pound or freshly brewed.

Institutions

Institutions The **institutions** category covers public and private organizations that provide health, education, and welfare services to consumers. It includes universities, hospitals, churches, nursing homes, and museums. Institutional buyers purchase a broad range of products with funds of their own or from third parties, such as donors, insurance companies, and government grants.

Because of third-party funding, institutions may have unique purchasing requirements. Consequently, companies often establish very specific strategies for marketing to these organizations. For example, most pharmaceutical firms have separate units that market to hospitals. ARAMARK has a separate food service division that markets specifically to universities. Its expertise in nutrition, understanding of the college-age population, and knowledge of how universities make decisions combine to create unique, highly targeted marketing programs.

Utilities

Utilities The **utilities** category is comprised of companies that distribute gas, electricity, and water. Once highly regulated by the government, utilities are being given the opportunity to operate more like private organizations. Public service commissions continue to provide oversight, however, because even private utilities are considered to be part of the public sector to some degree. Consolidated Edison and Florida Power & Light are huge buyers of business products. General Electric sells billions of dollars in nuclear fuel, power generation equipment, and design services to both public and privately owned utilities.

Transportation and Telecommunications

Transportation and telecommunications make up another business market category. The transportation portion is comprised of companies that provide passenger and freight service such as Union Pacific Railroad and United Airlines. Telecommunications companies supply local and long-distance telephone service as well as cable and broadcasting. CBS, AOL Time Warner, Northwest Airlines, AT&T, and Ameritech are somewhat like utilities. This category was once subject to extensive government regulation that has been relaxed in recent years.

Although there are relatively few companies in this category, their purchases are huge. In one year, Boeing will purchase more than $37 billion worth of parts, components, and systems from more than 30,000 suppliers located in 46 states and 37 countries.[5] The cable and broadcast companies purchase satellite capacity, equip-

Principal Financial Group targets business-to-business companies.

ment, and a huge range of services necessary to develop state-of-the-art telecasting.

Government Markets In the United States, the subdivisions in the government market category are (1) the federal government, (2) the 50 state governments, and (3) 8,700 local units. Together, they make more purchases than any other group in the United States. The U.S. government spends more than $2.5 trillion each year. The national military is by far the largest purchaser of goods and services, accounting for over $500 billion of U.S. spending.[6]

LARGE PURCHASES IN B2B MARKETS

Unlike B2C marketers who sell a relatively small amount to a large number of buyers, business marketers choose to sell a large amount to a few customers. Often the price of a single item is high, like the cost of a corporate jet or a new information technology system for a company. In other cases, the buyer purchases a huge number of a lower priced item that adds up to a large amount. For example if EDS wins an order to replace computer work stations for a client, each work station might be just over $1,000, but the total price tag could easily be several hundred million dollars. In some cases these sales amounts are great enough to affect the companies stock price. For example when FedEx canceled its order to purchase several planes from Boeing's competitor Airbus and instead decided to buy 15 Boeing 777 aircraft for $3.5 billion dollars, Boeing's stock price increased by 5 percent in a single day. This was a huge win for Boeing's marketing team.[7]

BUSINESS MARKET LINKAGES: THE SUPPLY CHAIN

The **supply chain** links organizations involved in the creation and delivery of a product. Figure 6.3 is a simplified diagram of the supply chain for automobiles. The original equipment manufacturer (OEM), such as Toyota, is in the middle of the chain. There are supply activities both upstream and downstream. In B2B marketing, the word "**tier**" refers to the degree of contact between sup-

Timken, a worldwide leader in bearings and steel, is a part of the commercial market

pliers and the OEM. For example, there are third-tier suppliers (extractors who process steel from ore), second-tier suppliers (manufacturers of components such as wiring), and first-tier suppliers (makers of computer chips). The first-tier is a direct supplier to the OEM.

Supply chain management involves establishing or improving linkages to maximize efficiency and effectiveness. Marketers view the supply chain in terms of activities that need to be coordinated to provide the greatest value to the consumer, who is at the end of the chain. UPS, for example, works with many companies to improve supply chain management. Its experts help clients with systems design, transportation, information systems, and other services.

GLOBALIZATION OF BUSINESS MARKETS

Business-to-business marketing opportunities overseas abound. Strong business marketers support their customers' business efforts globally. Companies such as International Data Group (IDG), a global leader for marketing publications, information technology solutions and conference management, is capable of providing multi-country coverage. IDG currently has over 3,000 business clients in 85 countries.[8] Global brand identity is as important in B2B marketing as in consumer marketing. JP Morgan, a highly recognized financial services firm in the United States, launched a global branding campaign to expand its customer base to include younger, high-tech, and Web-based firms.[9]

ORGANIZATIONAL BUYING

BUYING DECISIONS

Businesses decide whether to buy from suppliers or make the product in-house. When suppliers are used, a variety of people are involved on behalf of the purchaser. So, if you are a supplier, there are many factors to consider in

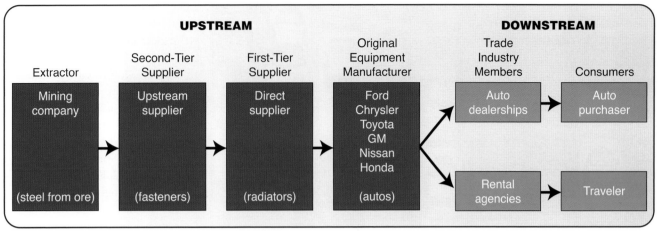

Figure 6.3   An Example of the Supply Chain in Automotives

selecting a marketing program that works to satisfy business customers – make or buy decisions, steps in the buying process and relationships inside the customer's firm.

The Make or Buy Decision

The **make or buy decision** occurs when an organization determines whether to supply products or services in-house (the make decision) or to buy them from other businesses (the buy decision). The buy decision results in outsourcing from a supplier. Outsourcing helps companies focus investments on their core business. An organization must evaluate its need for direct control over production or quality, and the costs associated with supplying internally versus externally. Other issues include supplier reliability, design secrecy, and workforce stability.

The Outsourcing Decision

Outsourcing has become widely popular—of the 300 largest global companies, about three quarters use it as a strategy. For instance, in a single year, IBM Japan was awarded over $3 billion in outsourcing contracts to run the data centers and sales offices of Mitsubishi Trust (a bank), and Meiji Seika Company, a pharmaceuticals firm. Flextronics, a global printed circuit board and plastics fabrication supplier, has a $30 billion outsourcing agreement to manufacture Motorola cellular phones, pagers, and various other communication devices. As for the Internet, AOL turns to Google to provide the backbone of their search engine for its customers. AOL spokesperson David Theis says "Having the most popular search company power our search, so popular that 'googling' has entered the lexicon, increases member loyalty."[10] Outsourcing reduces

straight rebuy is a routine purchase with which the organization has had a great deal of experience. For example, an exclusive furniture manufacturer may purchase leather for its sofas from only one supplier, which has a reputation for the highest quality. The two organizations have done business for years, and the manufacturer has made hundreds of purchases. In this case, a buying decision may take less than a week and

need for in-house expertise and cuts costs, allowing companies to focus resources on primary business activities. Essentially, this allows B2B buyers to extend their enterprise by using the specialized talents and resources of suppliers.

Outsourcing may involve the purchase of a product on a routine basis, changes in suppliers, or purchase of a product for the first time. These three kinds of situations straight rebuy, modified rebuy, and new task situations are summarized in Figure 6.4. A

Marketing Vocabulary

SUPPLY CHAIN
The linkage of organizations involved in the creation and delivery of a product.

TIER
The degree of contact between the supplier and the OEM.

MAKE OR BUY DECISION
The decision whether to supply products in-house, or to purchase them from other businesses.

OUTSOURCING
Purchasing products and services from other companies.

STRAIGHT REBUY
A routine purchase with which the organization has considerable experience.

CNF takes a look at the distribution side of supply chain management in this advertisement.

than establish long-term relationships with suppliers. Most government purchases must be made this way by law. Many companies, such as General Motors, have purchasing rules that require a minimum number of bids—usually three—for certain types of purchases. Often exceptions can be made so long as the rationale for noncompliance with the bidding policy is documented. In straight rebuy situations in the private sector, competitive bids are seldom required. They are likely in modified rebuys that involve the evaluation of alternative suppliers and are common in new task situations. In any of these cases, if the amount is very large, then the bidding procedure will probably be used.

Competitive bids may be sealed or negotiated. For the sealed bids, each seller is given a request for quotation (RFQ), which describes all the product and purchase specifications. The responses are due on a given date, when envelopes are opened, and the lowest bidder is awarded the order. Negotiated bids differ in that suppliers may be invited to comment on the specifications, modifications are possible, and the two or three most appropriate bids are then negotiated to determine the best choice—not necessarily the lowest bidder.

Web Auctions For competitive bidding, the auctions need to have an enough bidders in the same place at the same time. The Internet has solved this problem, as there is no need for bidders to meet together physically; just the need to be online while the auction is in process. **Web auctions** are conducted online and match buyers and sellers around the world. They are powerful and efficient to both buyers and sellers on two levels. The first is informa-

involve only one or two people from each organization. In fact, it's normal for a purchasing agent to handle the entire transaction.

Suppose that the furniture manufacturer is dissatisfied with the leather supplier or doesn't want to depend on only one. A **modified rebuy** situation involves purchasing a familiar product from an unfamiliar supplier or a new or different product from a familiar supplier. Usually more people will be involved in a modified rebuy decision, and more time and energy will be expended. Finally, let us say the furniture manufacturer decides to add a line of fabric sofas. This **new task situation** involves purchasing an unfamiliar product from an unfamiliar supplier. Because there is a great deal at risk, many people will likely provide input to the decision process, which may take several weeks, months, or even years.

Competitive Bidding Some organizations use competitive bidding, especially for purchases over a certain amount. They want to obtain the lowest price rather

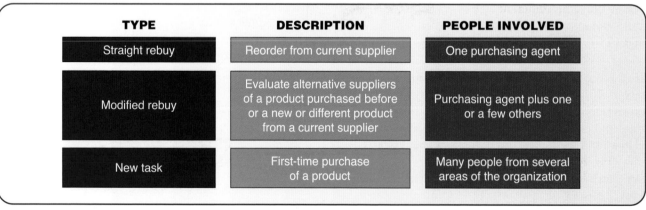

TYPE	DESCRIPTION	PEOPLE INVOLVED
Straight rebuy	Reorder from current supplier	One purchasing agent
Modified rebuy	Evaluate alternative suppliers of a product purchased before or a new or different product from a current supplier	Purchasing agent plus one or a few others
New task	First-time purchase of a product	Many people from several areas of the organization

Figure 6.4   Organizational Buying Situations

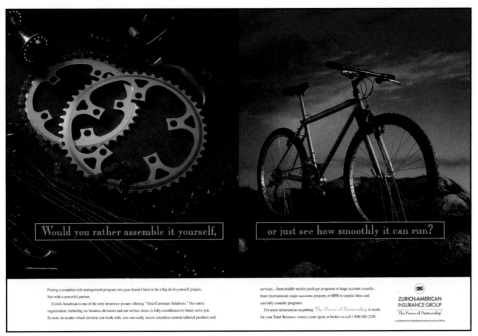

Approximately 86 percent of major corporations use outsourcing so they can focus on their core business.

Marketing Vocabulary

MODIFIED REBUY
Purchase of a familiar product from an unfamiliar supplier or a new or different product from a familiar supplier.

NEW TASK SITUATION
Purchase of an unfamiliar product from an unfamiliar supplier.

WEB AUCTIONS
Online auctions that match buyers and sellers around the world.

tion. In-depth information enhances bidders' understanding of the products. Buyers are more comfortable and feel that they can properly assess the products when they have adequate time to research. The comfort level will be revealed by their bid. On average, sellers will obtain higher winning bids and bidders will more often acquire products that they truthfully evaluate. The second is that the web can increase the numbers of bidders. This helps the seller, leading to a higher winning bid. It also aids to evade an action failure; when bids do not meet a designated price, the seller can later agree to accept a lower bid.[11]

STEPS IN THE ORGANIZATIONAL BUYING PROCESS

An organization may go through eight different stages when making a buying decision, but every purchase does not require all of them. New task situations may involve all eight, modified rebuys fewer, and straight rebuys the fewest. The eight possible steps in the organizational buying process are shown in Figure 6.5: problem recognition, general need description, product specifications, supplier search, proposal solicitation, order routine specifications, purchase and use of product, and performance review and feedback.

Problem recognition occurs when the buying organization realizes that a situation can be improved by acquiring a good or service. Potential problems include unsatisfactory materials, machine failure, or development of a new product that requires new equipment. A general need description is developed that identifies the basic characteristics of what is wanted, such as reliability, price, range, and durability. Next, the organization prepares product specifications, which usually are technical and

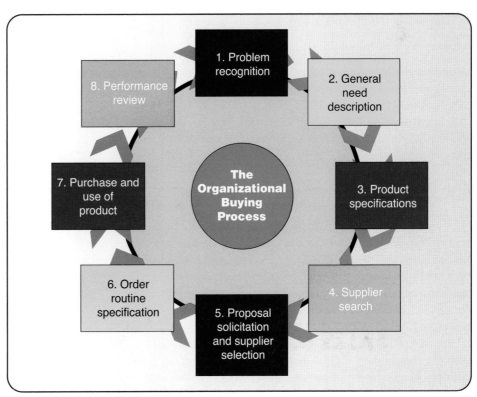

Figure 6.5   Steps in the Buying Process

very detailed: Precise dimensions, tolerances, quantity, or the objectives of a consultant's study are examples.

Unless it has been decided to make the product in-house, the search for suppliers now begins. Some may have been involved in the previous stages, but the organization usually looks for more to be certain no options are missed and to encourage price competition. New products may require a lengthy search, and straight rebuys may involve a very limited one. During the proposal solicitation and supplier selection stage, the buying organization invites bids and assesses these according to the criteria set forth in the specifications. The lowest price usually wins, especially in the government sector, but such considerations as a reputation for quality and reliability may enter as well.

When a supplier has been selected, the buying organization negotiates the final terms of the agreement, called order routine specifications. Some fine-tuning may occur, now that a particular supplier has been chosen. During the purchase and use of product stage, the buyer signs the contract, takes the delivery, and begins to evaluate whether the product does the job as anticipated. At this point, follow-through by the seller is critical to resolve any problems that may arise. The final step is performance review and feedback. After making a formal analysis, the buyer lets the supplier know how well the product meets the needs of the organization.

As the buying organization moves through this process repeatedly, creeping commitment may occur. If there is consistent satisfaction with a seller's products, the two parties may begin to build a lasting relationship. In that case, the buying process becomes simpler for both organizations, as modified or straight rebuys are more likely.

RELATIONSHIPS BETWEEN BUYERS AND SELLERS

Relationships grow in phases as the buying and selling organizations learn to work together. A marketer that understands the buyer's strategies, problems, and opportunities can help the company become more competitive. "With knowledgeable professional buyers, multiple decision makers, and fewer overall customers to choose from, B2B marketers have a more complex task than many realize," commented Nick Kaczmarek of Dow Chemical. Marketers that do a good job of understanding buying organizations are seen as valued members of

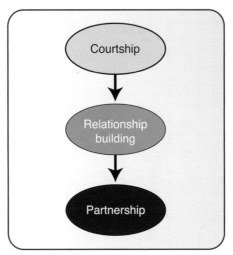

Figure 6.6   Building Business-to-Business Partnerships

their customer's supply chain.

Relationships in business do not occur overnight. It may take weeks, months, or even years for the companies to understand and trust each other. The typical sequence is the courtship phase, the relationship-building phase, and the partnership phase. Figure 6.6 illustrates these steps. For example, when UPS supplies warehousing and shipping services, first a customer begins by purchasing only a few services. As the business comes to realize that UPS services are core aspects of the buyer's ability to satisfy its own customers, more services are purchased. Over time it is not unusual for UPS to supply all of a customer's warehousing and transportation needs. UPS's high-technology information systems are not the only reason; UPS works to understand each customer's business thoroughly. This means that strategies and plans must be shared freely, and the client must trust UPS to keep them confidential. In many cases, UPS even helps customers develop the strategies and plans.

The Courtship Phase During courtship, purchasers express their desires to sellers. This phase often begins when a seller is placed on the buyer's approved supplier list, which means it meets at least minimum standards. The criteria usually include financial health, size, licensing qualification, and delivery capabilities.

Unlike many people, businesses tend to look before they leap. Often courtship takes a good deal of time. Each company is trying to understand the other's requirements, so there are many dis-

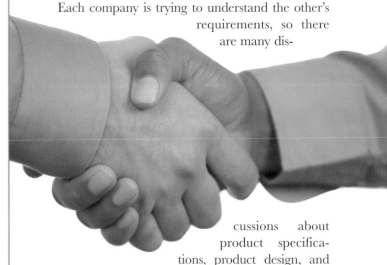

cussions about product specifications, product design, and order routines. Eventually, the social distance begins to narrow. Often the buyer will grant the supplier a small order to test the waters, including the response to any problems that occur. In addition, the effectiveness of a solution depends on a customer's willingness to adapt to a supplier's offerings, and share relevant internal operations and political considerations with a supplier.[12]

The Relationship-Building Phase

The buyers and sellers work together for the first time in the relationship-building phase, which strengthens the bond between them. Unlike consumer marketing, business-to-business marketing tends to involve customizing the product, its delivery, and its terms and conditions to each individual buyer. Buyers often grow to rely on suppliers for additional expertise, especially regarding new technologies. That is why trust, loyalty, and compromise become so important in organizational buying activities. Due to the complexity and technical nature of most organizational purchasing, buyers and sellers must learn to work together. Each party may even adjust its internal practices to better satisfy the other's needs. Understanding the customer—and its customers—is critical.

During the relationship-building phase, the purchasing organization does not always have the upper hand. In fact, the relationship is sometimes said to be symmetrical—that is, the buyer and the seller may have equal power.[13] Both frequently feel a very strong need to interact in order to explore all options before signing a contract. This is particularly the case if a formal partnership is being considered. Sellers generally offer information to help buyers formulate ideas about the purchase decision. Buyers provide information that helps the sellers do a better job of matching products to needs. Dell once manufactured only computer hardware but now provides an array of customized products and services to help companies improve business performance. Its focused portfolio of seven service suites wins customers by evaluating what services they need, then customizing entire infrastructures to meet those needs.[14]

The Partnership Phase

After numerous purchases have been completed satisfactorily and long-term agreements are reached, the partnership phase begins. Because the buyer and seller have extensive experience with each other, they spend less time on the relationship itself and more time on ways to improve the productive aspects of the exchange. The buying process becomes routine. The seller may become an exclusive supplier or blanket orders may guarantee that the buyer will purchase a certain amount within a certain period.

www.searsholdings.com

Learn more about how the parent company of Kmart and Sears maintains strong business relationships. Also explore how the company gives preference to suppliers that practice sustainable forestry.

The seller can commit resources to the buyer because the business relationship will continue. Chrysler, for example, gets 70 percent of the value of its vehicles from its regular suppliers. Jeffrey Trimmer, director of operations and strategy, says that the company's challenge is how to continue with its suppliers while using the Internet to facilitate that relationship and to identify and foster technology developments.[15] In many cases, computerized order entry systems are developed to link the buyer with the seller's manufacturing facilities. Nearly all Kmart suppliers have such a link. Known as the Co-Managed Inventory Program, or CMI, Kmart's order entry system allows its suppliers to monitor its inventory and replenish its stock without prior approval from Kmart. Through this close relationship with its suppliers, Kmart can keep costs down and speed product distribution to avoid lost

Siemens VDO Viewline instrument series is a B2B product marketed to boat builders and engine manufacturers.

Courtesy of Siemens

sales.[16]

Partnerships can be informal or contractual. Informally, each party may work without any guarantee of long-term business. A good example is an advertising agency and its client. Both invest a lot of time and energy and share important information, so it's costly for either party to end the relationship.

A contractual partnership is formed when the buyer

The Marketing Gazette™

CREATING & CAPTURING VALUE THROUGH RELATIONSHIPS

Computer Discount Warehouse - CDW

Building relationships between buyers and sellers is critical in business-to-business marketing. One savvy company found that customer relationships are profitable, year after year. However, it is perhaps this online and catalog company's humble beginnings that have ensured its success.

CDW (Computer Discount Warehouse) began in 1982 when Chairman and CEO Michael P. Krasney put a $3 classified ad in the Chicago Tribune to sell his personal computer. When the calls kept coming long after he had sold the machine, he realized the need for a computer business and began selling directly to customers. He soon had so many customers that he began employing technicians. His home-based business has since developed into a billion-dollar company, providing customized computer products, software, accessories, and computing solutions for businesses, the government, and educational institutions throughout the country.

CDW has much to be proud of—its net income, net sales, and Direct Web sales have all greatly increased. In the second quarter of 2007, the company generated sales of over $2 Billion, a 24 percent increase from the same quarter in the previous year. Besides, it is the Gold Winner of "2007 Logistics Management Best Practices Award", was named "100 Best Companies to Work for in America" by Fortune magazine, and this year it is ranked 342 on the Fortune 500 list.

CDW calls its focus on customer satisfaction its "clicks and people" strategy and believes that it is the key to its overall mission. Though a leading source of technology products and services for large companies such as Compaq, Hewlett-Packard, IBM, and Microsoft, CDW strives to treat each of its customers in an individual manner. Its CDW@work Web site program is customized for each customer and is a model for businesses seeking to combine e-business with one-on-one customer relationships. The customers can access their account information anytime and anywhere, view special contract pricing, track inventory, customize purchasing and product standards, as well as optimize time through real-time order status.

Recently, CDW offered a seminar focusing on technology innovations for small- and medium-sized businesses. By bringing together experts from Compaq, Microsoft, Cisco, and IDC, the seminar follows the company's mission to make itself a better provider of computer solutions and demonstrates dedication to its customers.

Each major company that CDW works with is assigned its own account manager who works with that company and understands its own particular needs. In addition, though much of the company's work is done via the Internet, CDW does not attempt to fully automate the sales process. Believing that customers still want to be satisfied with their service, the company continues to hire sales account managers while Internet sales continue to increase. When phone calls are heavy, it is even common for the CEO to step out of his office and help answer queries. New coworkers at CDW are trained at CDW University, where they learn Krasney's vision of ensuring customer satisfaction. Coworkers are even viewed as part of the satisfaction project because the company believes that happy coworkers lead to happy customers. For example, employees are called coworkers rather than employees. They receive free breakfast on Tuesdays and Thursdays, and have fitness and child care centers at CDW's Vernon Hills, Illinois base.

signs an agreement with a supplier for a specified period, usually three to five years. The trend in purchasing today is toward fewer suppliers, the use of programs that certify the qualifications of suppliers, and long-term contracts. Close relationships with suppliers help ensure quality. Many buying organizations find that contractual partnerships have considerable advantages. The long-term relationship with suppliers allows the buying organization to concentrate energy on its customers. The buyer and supplier work as a team, each contributing its own expertise to provide products that better meet consumer needs. The longer the relationship, the better are the results in terms of cooperation, efficiency, quality control, and profits. Contractual partnerships were a major part of Toyota's campaign to enhance its competitive position in global automobile markets.

Many suppliers also find contractual partnerships advantageous, but there are risks. The organizations often share highly secret market and technological information as well as sensitive strategic marketing plans. Contracts safeguard a supplier against an unethical buyer that might reveal those secrets to the supplier's competitors in an attempt to receive price reductions. When this occurs, most strong suppliers will refuse to market their newest technology to unethical buyers or in some cases refuse to sell to them altogether. Partnerships can have other hazards. Strong relationships mean greater dependence. If one partner experiences downsizing, strikes, or financial failure, then the other party feels the consequences.

Sometimes the partnership phase results in strategic alliances, including joint R&D, licensing agreements, joint ventures, and others. Typically, alliances are formed because each company can offer something of value to the other. Suppose a Frito-Lay supplier has an idea for making chips stay fresh longer but lacks the money to conduct the necessary research. A joint R&D project might benefit both organizations.

Ethics and Business Relationships

Unethical decisions can have a destructive effect on business relationships. Purchasing agents are often very familiar with the trade secrets, production plans, and technologies of sellers. Misuse of this information has both ethical and legal implications. Consider former employees of Coca-Cola that conspired to sell trade secrets to rival Pepsi for $1.5 million. The employees offered Pepsi confidential Coca-Cola documents as well as a sample of a newly developed Coke product. Suspicious Pepsi employees informed Coke, who in turn contacted the FBI. The Coke employees were discovered and exposed in an undercover sting by the FBI and ultimately sentenced to federal prison terms and to pay fines in excess of $40,000.[17]

Turning over trade secrets to a competitor is a serious breech of ethics with numerous repercussions. The image of both the company and its individual executives may be tarnished. Legal disputes consume large amounts of money as well as management's time and energy. A long-running dispute also can hinder normal business practices and competitive relationships between the companies involved. An individual who steals and betrays company information may face serious criminal charges. In 2007, Joya Williams and Ibrahim Dimson, the unethical Coca-Cola employees, were sentence to serve eight and five-year federal prison sentences respectively, for conspiring to steal and sell trade secrets.[18]

Career Tip:

John A. Edwardson, Chairman and CEO of CDW, says the culture of the company is more than great perks and benefits, and it is built on mutual respects. According to Edwardson, "Happy coworkers lead to happy customers, and that is fundamental in what shapes our business and help us continue to grow." Therefore, the company is willing to listen to its workers, and give them the tools they need to succeed and celebrate in their success. As one of the "100 Best Companies to Work for in America," CDW states in its Web site that it is a great place to work, and people do business with people they like.

FUNCTIONS INVOLVED IN BUSINESS PURCHASES

Many employees are important to the purchasing process. Because of their different functions, they do not have the same motives for purchasing and do not use the same criteria. This section highlights functions most often involved in organizational buying: purchasing agents, functional managers, and the buying center.

Laterally, people at about the same level of management but from different functional areas (such as purchasing, engineering, production, sales, and marketing) may take part in a purchasing decision. Although their status is roughly similar, their influence on a particular purchase can vary considerably. Imagine that several vice presidents meet to select a strategic marketing consultant. Comments by the vice presidents of manufacturing and purchasing are certainly valuable, but the vice president of marketing probably will have the most influence on the final decision.

Vertically, people at different management levels within one functional area may participate in a buying decision. For example, the need for a new piece of equipment may be pointed out by a production floor worker to the foreman, who relays this to the production manager. The production manager seeks approval from the plant manager. If the purchase is costly, then the vice president of manufacturing or even the company president might be involved. If not, then the production engineer may have authority to approve the purchase.

Purchasing Agents   Purchasing agents help buy a broad range of products most effectively. They establish and enforce procedures that help maintain consistent purchase arrangements with all suppliers. They interact with many suppliers and gain a good deal of experience in negotiations. Through training programs, purchasing agents can learn how to obtain the best delivery schedules, prices, and financing, while still meeting product specifications.

Purchasing agents are extremely important executives in some major corporations. In others, they simply process procurement requests. This function has received more attention in recent years, partly because of restricted supply in some industries and a greater general recognition of the cost savings from effective purchasing. College programs emphasizing the buying function have been developed, and graduates with this specialized education are finding increasing opportunities in global purchasing.

Functional Managers Functional managers have a position in a specific operational area of the buying organization. At one time or another in their career,

most will be involved in negotiations to buy equipment or supplies. Typically, they come from the following areas:

- Administration (including accounting and finance): Help evaluate the cost effectiveness of projects.
- Design engineering: Buy equipment and material for products the company is marketing.
- Research and development: Look at basic materials and supplies rather than specific applications.
- Manufacturing: Often responsible for production equipment and processing approaches.
- Technical specialists: Advise others regarding the best brands and suppliers for a particular product type.

The Buying Center   A group of people in the organization who make a purchase decision are said to form the **buying center**. These people may play one of six important roles: gatekeeper, information seeker, advocate, linking pin, decision maker, or user. It's important to note that buying center membership changes, depending on the type of purchase being considered. Often the selling organization that wins the order is the one that has made contact with each of the buying influencers. Figure 6.7 depicts the buying center roles.

Gatekeepers A **gatekeeper** controls the flow of commercial (outside) information into the buying organization. Purchasing agents have been referred to as gate-

Marketing Vocabulary

BUYING CENTER
The group of people from the buying organization who make a purchase decision.

GATEKEEPER
A person within the buying center who controls the flow of commercial (outside) information into the buying organization by screening all potential sellers and allowing only the most qualified to have access to decision makers.

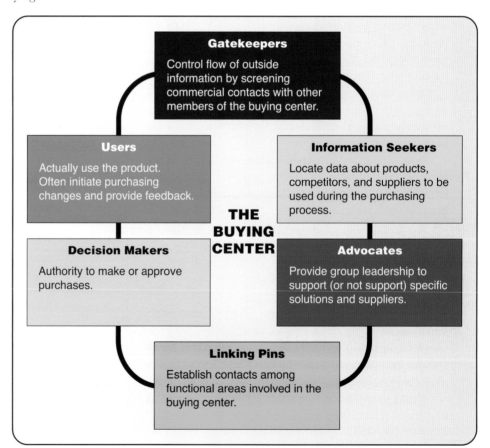

Figure 6.7 The Buying Center Roles

keepers because they are often the first people that sales representatives contact. They are responsible for screening all potential sellers and allowing only the most qualified to gain access to key decision makers. When the purchasing department is very small and unusual or complicated products are being purchased (such as high-tech parts), the gatekeeper may be a specialist outside the purchasing area. For example, the head of engineering may recommend that only suppliers with which the company has a working relationship should be contacted for engineering consulting services.

Clearly, a skilled salesperson is one who succeeds in working around and through the gatekeeper. Generally, gatekeepers understand the roles played by various people in the organization. When they are cooperative, they can direct salespeople to the appropriate decision maker.

Information Seekers A great deal of information about products, competitors, and suppliers is required for major purchases. **Information seekers** locate data that they or others can use during the purchasing process. Often the purchasing department is responsible for obtaining lists of firms or alternative types of products, but this task can also be performed by others. Think about the fundamental changes technology has brought to business-to-business marketing. Virtually every company in the world maintains a Web site to provide information about itself. The Web can satisfy some of an information seeker's needs in only seconds.

The role of information seeking differs from that of gatekeeper. The former looks for sources of information, whereas the latter tends to reject sources of information and limits the number of people and companies allowed access to the buying firm. Naturally, marketers can make the job of the information seeker easier by clearly presenting relevant product data in an accessible way.

Advocates The **advocate** exercises a powerful influence over buying center decisions. Advocates participate the most in group discussions, have high status, and play a leadership role. They often obtain their power from the amount of interaction they have with outside organizations and from their expertise on particular topics. Advocates sometimes use their position to inhibit the communications (or recommendations) of less powerful people in the organization. Thus, they may support one seller's offering while restricting the influence of competitors' presentations. Consequently, sellers often seek high-status, knowledgeable, and articulate people within the buying organization to help promote their products. If salespeople are to succeed, then one or more advocates must take their side during purchase deliberations.

Linking Pins Contact among the functional areas involved in a buying center is provided by **linking pins**. They are particularly important to marketers of products that affect several parts of the buying company, such as electronic data-processing and telecommunications equipment. Linking pins communicate with one another both formally and informally. In many cases, information from the seller to one linking pin is then spread throughout the buying organization. A cooperative linking pin makes the seller's job easier.

Users Users actually will use the product being purchased. In manufacturing firms, for example, they are the employees who operate or service production equipment. When components are purchased, the **users** assemble the parts. In hospitals and other health care facilities, users may be nurses, physicians, or the technicians who operate medical equipment. In other professional organizations, they may be programmers or technical support staff who interface with computers. There are almost as many types of users as there are job descriptions, and their influence on the purchasing process varies.

Users with a high degree of expertise may help develop product specifications. They are especially important in the last phase of the buying process, follow-through. They can provide valuable feedback to sales representatives about how well the product performs. The sophisticated salesperson seeks out such feedback, in turn providing users with information to make the product function as smoothly as possible.

Decision Makers Sometimes it is difficult for the seller to identify **decision makers**, the persons with authority to make or at least approve the purchase decision. It is also hard to determine when the decision is actually made. Often the selling organization solidifies its relationship with the buying center over time, which is called creeping commitment. The seller gradually wins enough support to obtain the order. In competitive bidding situations, the decision to purchase occurs when the envelopes are opened. In these cases, however, much depends on how the specifications are drawn up in the first place. Some salespeople work closely with the buying organization at that stage to tilt the specs and ultimate

Marketing Vocabulary

INFORMATION SEEKER
A person within the buying center who locates data that can be used during the purchasing process.

ADVOCATE
A person within the buying center who exercises a powerful influence over group decisions.

LINKING PIN
A person within the buying center who establishes contact among functional areas formed within the buying organization.

USER
A person within the buying center who actually uses the product.

DECISION MAKER
A person within the buying center who has the authority to make or approve a purchase decision.

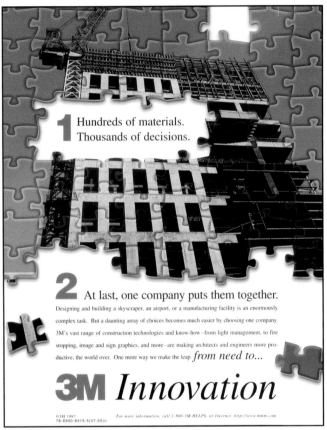

1 Hundreds of materials.
Thousands of decisions.

2 At last, one company puts them together.

Designing and building a skyscraper, an airport, or a manufacturing facility is an enormously complex task. But a daunting array of choices becomes much easier by choosing one company. 3M's vast range of construction technologies and know-how—from light management, to fire stopping, image and sign graphics, and more—are making architects and engineers more productive, the world over. One more way we make the leap *from need to...*

3M *Innovation*

©3M 1997
78-6900-8315-5(47.55)ii   *For more information, call 1-800-3M-HELPS, or Internet, http://www.mmm.com*

To reduce perceived risk, 3M creates products that meet business needs.

decision in their favor.

In many cases the salesperson can identify exactly who will make the buying decision. In some organizations the decision maker is the purchasing agent. In most cases, however, the choice is made by a buying center or by someone who has budgetary authority and long-term experience with the product. Retail organizations often use a buying committee. Salespeople are invited to make a presentation or to supply information so that a committee member can decide.

INFLUENCES ON ORGANIZATIONAL BUYING BEHAVIOR

The buying process is seldom the same from one firm to the next, or even from one purchase to the next within a given firm. In each case, the decision-making process of the buying organization is affected by a number of factors.[19]

Background of Buying Center Members

The background of the buying center members affects the buying process. Purchasing agents, engineers, users, and others in the organization have expectations that are formed largely by their experiences. These expectations, in turn, influence the criteria used for decision making. Specialization has a great deal to do with the way people look at problems. Engineers see things differently from financial professionals. Engineers are highly trained in technical areas and are likely to judge a product accordingly. Financial managers are inclined to evaluate products on the basis of profitability.

Role orientation, which refers to the way people see themselves, is also a factor. Position or rank within the organization obviously can have an effect—one vice president among several lower-level managers has a stronger say in buying center decisions.

Finally, personal characteristics play a role. The lifestyles, interests, activities, and general opinions of buying center members affect the buying process.

Information Sources
Organizational buying is influenced by the sources of information—salespeople, exhibitions and trade shows, direct mail, press releases, journal advertising, professional and technical conferences, trade news, word of mouth, and others. Like direct selling, exhibitions provide one-on-one contact with a company's target audience. Although sales calls generally reach only a small number of potential customers per day, exhibitions can reach dozens more per hour.

The Internet is playing an increasing role in business-to-business marketing. Web sites enable organizations to promote brand values, reduce printing costs, attract and qualify prospects and leads, and foster customer loyalty. Sites also can expand the customer database, provide customer service, and showcase and sell products.

Product Factors: Time and Risk
Product and company factors tend to influence the organizational buying process. **Product factors** include time pressure and perceived risk. Time pressure relates to the speed with which a purchase must be made. When more members of the buying organization are involved in the decision, more time is required to make it. Perceived risk refers to what can be lost rather than gained when making the purchase.

Five types of uncertainty or risk aversion have been identified among buying organizations:

1. *Acceptance uncertainty*: Buyers are not sure of their need for a product.
2. *Need uncertainty*: The buying organization has not yet established product specifications
3. *Technical uncertainty*: Buyers are unsure about the performance of a product in their own particular environment.
4. *Market uncertainty*: Buyers are unsure of the possible offerings from which they can select.
5. *Transaction uncertainty*: Buyers are unsure about the terms of the sale and product delivery.

When uncertainty is high, buyers strive to reduce perceived risk by either purchasing less or learning more.

http://globaledge.msu.edu

Visit globalEDGE™ Online for the ultimate international marketing research tool!

globalEDGE™
Understanding Business Marketing

Business-to-business (B2B) marketing requires managers to develop and maintain relationships between large organizations. Currently, your firm is a leading US manufacturing company in fabricated metal products. You have recently discovered that strategic plans are in place to enter the South African market. Survey the latest ranking of the largest manufacturing companies and determine which firm(s) would be suitable to partner with in a joint venture prior to market entry.

Decreasing the amount at stake means smaller orders or a reluctance to pay top prices. When much is at stake, others in the organization may be included in the purchase decision, thus spreading the personal risk.

Company Factors Three company factors have particular influence on the purchasing process: the organization's orientation, its size, and its degree of centralization. An organization's orientation, or dominating function, is very important. Some companies are production oriented, whereas others are marketing oriented. In still others, finance or accounting controls the decisions. When marketing dominates, sales factors tend to be very important in making purchase decisions. In production-oriented organizations, production factors are most important. In finance-oriented organizations, decisions are likely to be made on the basis of cost and other financial concerns. The seller must understand the organization's orientation in order to determine the basis for purchasing decisions and which members of the buying center are most influential.

The size of the organization is also likely to influence the number of people involved in purchasing. In very small companies, the purchasing process tends to be informal. Decisions are often made by a key executive at the top. Very large organizations use a formal purchasing process, and decisions often are made by members lower in the managerial structure.

Finally, highly decentralized organizations are likely to give various departments or divisions the autonomy to make their own purchases. Nevertheless, owing to the need for accountability, even these companies have formal buying procedures that can involve red tape.

Joint Decisions and Conflict Resolution
Whenever several people are involved in decision making, there is a potential for conflict. Purchase decisions are no exception and can be affected by how conflict is handled. When it occurs, members of the buying organization negotiate with one another to arrive at a solution. These negotiations can be shaped by task or nontask motives. Task motivation refers to solving the organization's problem, whereas nontask motivation refers to the personal needs of the buying group members. Organizations usually attempt to resolve conflicts through problem solving and persuasion. The objective of this task-oriented and constructive approach is to make the best decision for the company. Nontask-oriented approaches to conflict involve bargaining and politicking. Each party is attempting to "get its own way" without considering the organization's goals or engaging in open communication. Sellers who are sensitive to the prevailing negotiating

The American Arbitration Association provides conflict resolution services.

Web and E-commerce Stars
www.alibaba.com

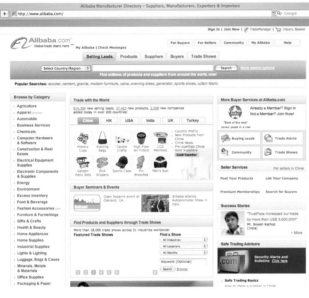

Alibaba.com is the world's largest online business-to-business marketplace for global trade, with over 500,000 people visiting the site every day. Based in China, Alibaba.com has more than 300,000 registered users from over 200 countries and territories, most of whom are global buyers and importers looking to find and trade with sellers in China and other major manufacturing countries.

Alibaba.com has been awarded the "Best of the Web" for seven years in a row by Forbes.

Marketing Vocabulary

PROBLEM SOLVING
A task-oriented method of conflict resolution whereby all parties agree to put the organization's goals first.

PERSUASION
A task-oriented mode of handling conflict in which persons with different goals attempt to convince the others that their goal should take precedence.

BARGAINING
A non task-oriented mode of handling conflict in which one person obtains his or her goal by agreeing to allow the other's goal to prevail at another time.

POLITICKING
A non task-oriented mode of handling conflict in which personal ego needs take precedence over problem solving.

---

mode can plan their approach accordingly.

Problem solving in the buying context occurs when all decision makers agree on the goals of the particular purchase. Sellers address those goals and show how their product can help meet them. This is very straightforward.

Persuasion occurs when buying center members do not agree on purchase goals, and each tries to convince the others that his or her own goals should take precedence. In the case of buying a computer, for example, the purchasing agent may consider cost most important, whereas a user may put software compatibility first. When the two discuss the merits of the various trade-offs, they are engaging in persuasion. The seller needs to understand both parties and address both sets of goals.

Bargaining occurs when people in the buying center cannot arrive at a solution. Through dialogue, one person may try to obtain his or her preferred product by agreeing that someone else can choose the supplier for a different product. The supplier needs to make sure to address all individuals who might ultimately be in a good bargaining position.

Politicking occurs when buying center members of the organization have strong ego needs. In their search for power or self-esteem, they place their own goals before those of the organization as a whole. Such people are looking for support rather than the most functional purchase choice. What usually results is a "pecking order" within the buying firm, in which an employee's influence on the purchase is proportional to his or her status in the company. The seller's claims about product superiority will go unnoticed because personalities are more important. Sellers must be very sensitive to personalities if they wish to conduct business under this circumstance.

Chapter Summary:

Objective 1: Describe the types of organizations and products involved in business-to-business marketing and understand the importance of this market.

A large number of companies sell most of their products to other companies, which is known as business-to-business marketing. In total volume, business-to-business marketing is much larger than consumer marketing. Types of business markets include the commercial market, extractor industries, trade industries, institutions, utilities, transportation and telecommunications, and government markets. These markets can be segmented according to company demographics, geographic scope, buying approach, and product/technology. Multiple steps bring the final product to consumers as businesses sell materials and processes to each other along the supply chain.

Objective 2: Understand the link between consumer demand and business-to-business marketing.

Business markets rely on derived demand to create opportunities for their products. When consumers purchase more, businesses buy more in order to produce more. The demand for business goods and services tends to be inelastic, which means that a price change does not greatly affect the types of products purchased. The accelerator principle recognizes that some business goods and services are highly sensitive to changes in consumer demand.

Objective 3: Describe the organizational buying process.

Organizations make purchases to support their production requirements and business needs. Buying decisions often start with the make or buy decision. Decisional situations in outsourcing include straight rebuy, modified rebuy, and new task situations. The buying process can involve as many as eight steps: problem recognition, need description, product specification, supplier search, proposal solicitation and supplier selection, order routine specification, purchase and use, and performance review and feedback. Good buyer–seller relationships are key to facilitating the process.

Objective 4: Know how buyer–seller relationships work, including informal and contractual partnerships.

The buyer–seller relationship between businesses develops over time, usually in three sequential phases: courtship, relationship building, and partnership. During courtship, buyers express their desires to sellers, who propose products to satisfy the purchaser's needs. In relationship building, the two parties work together for the first time, customizing the product, its delivery, and conditions. In the partnership phase, long-term agreements are reached either informally or contractually, and closer cooperation develops lasting relationships.

Objective 5: Learn what functions and roles within organizations influence the purchase of a broad range of products.

Different functional areas may be involved in business purchases, ranging from operational units to a purchasing department. The group of people who make a purchase decision forms the buying center. Having different backgrounds and functions in the company, they have different buying motives and use different criteria in evaluating products. Purchase decisions may be made laterally, through the interaction of people from different functional areas, or vertically, at one or more levels in the corporate hierarchy. Various buying center members play different roles: gatekeeper, information seeker, advocate, linking pin, decision maker, and user. It is important that the salesperson identify exactly who will make the purchase decision, whether the purchasing agent, a buying committee, or someone with budgetary authority.

Review Your Understanding

1. What is business-to-business marketing? How does it differ from consumer marketing?
2. List the types of business-to-business markets.
3. What is the supply chain? Give an example.
4. What is derived demand? Inelastic demand? How do they apply to business markets?
5. What are two ways that globalization affects business marketing?
6. What is a make or buy decision?
7. What are three types of decisional situations in outsourcing?
8. What are the steps in the organizational buying process?
9. List the phases in buyer–seller relationships.
10. List six functions performed in the buying center.
11. What are purchasing agents? Functional managers?
12. List and explain five types of purchase uncertainty.

Discussion of Concepts

1. Why is business-to-business marketing larger than consumer marketing? Explain the process of business-to-business marketing.
2. The private sector is composed of several classes of organizations. List examples of these classes, along with companies in each, and explain their importance within business-to-business marketing.
3. Explain the accelerator principle and how it relates to business-to-business marketing. Give an example.
4. When making a purchase, an organization generally goes through a number of steps. Describe these and explain why some purchases require more than others.
5. Describe an informal partnership and a contractual partnership. What are the advantages and disadvantages to both buyer and seller of each type? How does price-only purchasing come into play?
6. Why are many employees within a buying organization essential to the purchasing process? Explain the different levels of involvement in business purchases. What roles do purchasing agents and functional managers play?
7. Several roles that people play within the buying center are essential to the purchasing process. Define these and explain why they are necessary. Is one more important than the other? Which has the most influence on the purchase decision?
8. Numerous factors influence the buying process. Explain the relevance of each in purchase decisions.

Key Terms And Definitions

Advocate: A person within the buying center who exercises a powerful influence over group decisions.

Bargaining: A nontask-oriented mode of handling conflict in which one person obtains his or her goal by agreeing to allow the other's goal to prevail at another time.

Business-to-business marketing: Marketing goods and services to other producers of goods and services.

Buying center: The group of people from the buying organization who make a purchase decision.

Commercial market: Organizations and individuals that acquire goods and services to produce other goods and services sold to an end consumer for profit.

Decision maker: A person within the buying center who has the authority to make or approve a purchase decision.

Derived demand: A demand, such as the demand for business-to-business products, which depends ultimately on the demand of end consumers.

Extractor industries: Industries that obtain and process raw materials.

Gatekeeper: A person within the buying center who controls the flow of commercial (outside) information into the buying organization by screening all potential sellers and allowing only the most qualified to have access to decision makers.

Government markets: The federal, state, and local governments in their role as purchasers of goods and services.

Inelastic demand: Demand that is influenced little by price changes.

Information seeker: A person within the buying center who locates data that can be used during the purchasing process.

Institutions: Public and private organizations that provide services to consumers.

Linking pin: A person within the buying center who establishes contact among functional areas formed within the buying organization.

Make or buy decision: The decision whether to supply products in-house or to purchase them from other businesses.

Modified rebuy: Purchase of a familiar product from an unfamiliar supplier or a new or different product from a familiar supplier.

New task situation: Purchase of an unfamiliar product from an unfamiliar supplier.

Outsourcing: Purchasing products and services from other companies.

Persuasion: A task-oriented mode of handling conflicts in which persons with different goals attempt to convince the others that their goals should take precedence.

Politicking: A nontask-oriented mode of handling conflict in which personal ego needs take precedence over problem solving.

Problem solving: A task-oriented method of conflict resolution whereby all parties agree to put the organization's goals first.

Product factor: A factor such as time or perceived risk that influences the organizational buying process.

Reseller: A company that purchases a product and sells it in the same form for profit.

Straight rebuy: A routine purchase with which the organization has considerable experience.

Supply chain: The linkage of organizations involved in the creation and delivery of a product.

Tier: The degree of contact between the supplier and the OEM.

Trade industries: Industries comprised of organizations that acquire finished products and distribute them to others.

User: A person within the buying center who actually uses the product.

Utilities: Companies that distribute gas, electricity, or water.

References

1. "Grub for the Games; ARAMARK Feeds Athletes At Olympics 24/7," Philadelphia Daily News, August 18, 2004; "Aramark Scores 2008 Summer Games," Philadelphia Business Journal, May 29, 2007.
2. "Bureau of Land Management Presents Excellence Awards to Industry Leaders in Fluid Minerals Production," M2 Presswire, July 25, 2000.
3. www.envirogroup.com, site visited April 13, 2008.
4. www.apple.com, site visited April 13, 2008.
5. "Boeing to Forge 21st Century Partnership with Suppliers," September 22, 1999, www.boeing.com, site visited April 13, 2008.
6. https://www.cia.gov/cia/publications/factbook/print/us.html, site visited April 13, 2008.
7. Laurence Frost/Associated Press, "National-World Business," The Albuquerque Tribune, November 8, 2006.
8. www.idg.com, site visited April 13, 2008.
9. www.jpmorgan.com, site visited April 13, 2008.
10. Danny Sullivan, "AOL Renews With Google," October 8, 2003 http://searchenginewatch.com, visited February 14, 2007.
11. Ward Hanson & Kirthi Kalyanam, "Internet Marketing & e-Commerce," 2007, p. 410; Paul Milgrom, "Auction and Bidding : A primer," Journal of Economic Perspectives 3 (3), Summer 1989, p. 3.
12. Kapil R. Tuli, Ajay Kohil, Sundar G. Bharadway, "Rethinking Customer Solutions: From Product Bundles to Relational Processes," Journal of Marketing, Vol. 71, No. 3, July 2007.
13. Hakan Hakanson and Bjorn Wootz, "A Framework of Industrial Buying and Selling," International Marketing Management 8 (1979): 39–49.
14. www.dell.com, site visited April 13, 2008.
15. Gail Kachadourian, "DCX Relies on Supplier Innovations," Automotive News, June 19, 2000, p. 28.
16. www.kmartcorp.com/corp/business/vendor/general/cmi.stm, site visited April 13, 2008.
17. Kathleen Day, "Three Accused in Theft of Coke Secrets," July 6, 2006, Washington Post.
18. "Two Sentenced in Coke Trade Secret Case," May 23, 2007. www.money.cnn.com, site visited April 14, 2008.
19. Jagdish N. Sheth, "A Model of Industrial Buyer Behavior," Journal of Marketing 37 (October 1973): 50–58.

The Marketing Gazette
"CDW in Top Five on Catalog Age 100 List," PR Newswire, August 7, 2000; "CDW Computer Centers, Inc. Reports 76 Percent Growth in EPS, 58 Percent Growth in Sales," PR Newswire, July 24, 2000; "CDW Named a Finalist for National Better Business Bureau Award for Outstanding Marketplace Ethics," PR Newswire, August 8, 2000; "CDW Named to Fortune List of 100 Fastest-Growing Companies," PR Newswire, August 22, 2000; "CDW Brings Compaq, Microsoft, Cisco and IDC Together to Launch Customer Technology Seminar Series," PR Newswire, June 19, 2000; Nick Turner, "Computer Retailer Michael Krasney—He Keeps the Human Touch While Selling High Tech," Investor's Business Daily, April 20, 2000; and www.cdw.com, site visited August 27, 2000; www.cdw.com, site visited February 15, 2008.

CASE 6

Accenture

On January 1, 2001, Andersen Consulting became known as Accenture. With net revenues of $19.7 billion in 2007, Accenture has positioned itself as the leading organization in the knowledge of intellectual capital with the belief that this will be the business currency of the 21st century. Perhaps best known to the general public for advertisements featuring professional golfer, Tiger Woods, the company differentiates itself from other consulting firms with a service model known as business integration. It looks at the client as a total enterprise and attempts to align the client's technology, people, and processes with an overall business strategy.

Management consulting is well over a $20 billion industry that has grown by more than 10 percent annually for almost a decade. Accenture employs more than 170,000 people in numerous countries across the globe. It serves more than 94 of the Fortune 100 largest global companies and many of the world's leading governments. That means that Accenture is larger than many of its major clients and one of the largest business-to-business professional organizations in the world.

The "Accenture Way" is to educate and train people to work in teams using very unified approaches. As consultants move from client to client, they execute projects from the same fundamental knowledge platform. This requires spending over $700 million of the company's annual revenue on employee education and development.

Knowledge is developed by learning what works in the field and applying it to new challenges. Accenture's information system collects in one centralized location nearly all the project descriptions and reports produced for clients. In this way, teams can tap into what has been done before they work on new projects. Information is applied from client to client, industry to industry, and globally. This is believed to be one of the keys to Accenture's strength.

Consulting can also be specialized, however, so that even a complex organization such as Accenture must form joint ventures with others, in some cases competitors, to satisfy a large client's needs. One alliance was put together by a major customer, J. P. Morgan. Accenture provides applications development, AT&T Solutions does network management, and Bell Atlantic Network Integration is responsible for desktop computing. Called the Pinnacle Alliance, it is an example of a new trend in team outsourcing by many corporations. In another case, DuPont formed an information technology partnership with Accenture and Computer Sciences Corporation. The DuPont contract with Accenture to handle all its data processing is worth $4 billion. Currently, Accenture is working to create a technology services joint venture with Microsoft.

Accenture and Microsoft have agreed to a $1 billion alliance. The venture, Avenade, supports Microsoft's desire to establish its products as the number-one corporate operating platform. Microsoft will benefit from Accenture's numerous top business contacts and customers.

In January, 2005, Accenture, Wal-Mart and the Retail Industry Leaders Association (RILA) completed an online Retail Supply Chain Certification (RSCC) program tailored to Wal-Mart suppliers and in-house professionals. Accenture's Supply Chain Academy (SCA) has helped Wal-Mart build better, more sophisticated supplier relationships, make better decisions and identify even more ways for leveraging supply chain excellence to increase growth, profitability and competitive differentiation.

Accenture's Supply Chain Academy also benefited Air Products, a company that provides atmospheric gases, process and specialty gases, performance materials and chemical intermediates to technology, energy, healthcare and electronics markets around the world. Completion of their four part supply chain strategy of "educate, execute, improve, and measure," has helped Air Products improve their bottom line. For example an Air Products gases plant team of 28 employees leveraged their supply chain education and quickly acquired a savings rate of $100,000 per year on raw materials in their plant alone.

To take advantage of the technology trend, Accenture is changing the way it works for and with some clients. Accenture has created a new venture that is focused on expanding the work it does with Internet start-ups and the work it does globally. Within the next three years, Accenture plans to accept stock instead of cash as exchange for consulting services. The organization's hope is that the stock will grow to be worth more than the cash it would receive. Accenture hopes to provide global expansion consulting for Internet companies. To achieve this, Accenture is opening 17 new offices throughout Europe, Asia, the United States, Africa, and South America.

1.   What types of business markets does Accenture serve? How is its business integration approach used to serve these markets?

2.   Once Accenture has identified a potential client, how do you think the organization goes about developing relationships with key buying influences within the organization?

3.   What trends are influencing the way Accenture conducts its business? How can Accenture use its knowledge base to predict trends, prepare itself for them, and take advantage of them? What do you think some future trends may be that Accenture needs to watch for?

4.   What types of issues could be addressed using Accenture's Da Vinci virtual reality simulation?

Sources: David Whitford, "Arthur, Arthur . . . ," Fortune, November 10, 1997, www.fortune.com; Esther Shien, "Outsourcing, Team Style," PC Week, November 3, 1997, pp. 84–85; Ann Marsh, "Business Services and Supplies," Forbes, January 13, 1997, www.forbes.com; Joanna Glasner, "Andersen Consulting for Stock," Wired News, February 9, 2000; Hoover's Online, "Andersen Consulting," www.hooversonline.com, visited June 18, 2000; "Andersen Consulting 1999 Annual Report/Financial Highlights," www.ac.com Web site visited on October 21, 2000; Louise Kehoe, "Microsoft and Andersen Consulting Partner Up in Venture," Financial Times, March 13, 2000; "Andersen Consulting, Sun Plan a Venture for Online Supplies," Wall Street Journal, April 26, 2000; "Andersen Consulting, Softbank Units to Invest in Incubator Network," Wall Street Journal, October 5, 2000; Jon Ashworth, "Andersen Consulting Poised for Split," The Times of London, October 14, 2000; www.accenture.com, site visited June 4, 2007. Accenture 2007 Annual Report www.accenture.com site visited February 15, 2008.

Value Orientation

When an organization focuses its resources on customer and company value, a winning customer strategy is created. Throughout this section, you will learn the importance of focusing resources on value. The following chapters are included in this section:

Chapter 7 Creating Customer Satisfaction & Loyalty
Chapter 8 Segmentation, Targeting & Positioning

CHAPTER 7

Creating Customer Satisfaction & Loyalty

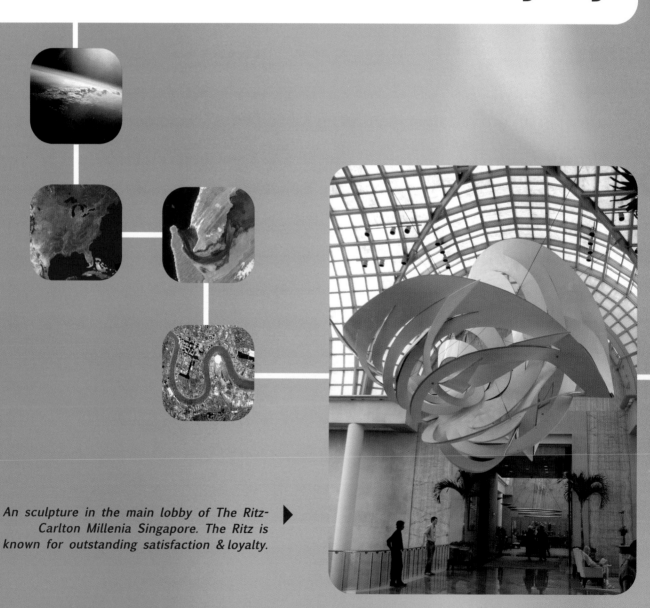

An sculpture in the main lobby of The Ritz-Carlton Millenia Singapore. The Ritz is known for outstanding satisfaction & loyalty.

Learning Objectives

1. Understand why customer satisfaction and loyalty are the focus of marketing in winning organizations.

2. Learn how consumer expectations influence satisfaction.

3. See why connecting with customers through relationships achieves outstanding satisfaction and loyalty.

4. Understand the ideas that help organizations market quality goods and services.

5. Define quality and describe how it is obtained.

Imagine you're traveling on one of many overnight business trips. You like your suit pressed by 6 a.m. sharp, and you take your coffee black with one ice cube, among other preferences. How many hotels respond to your needs with consistency and timelines, if at all? The Ritz-Carlton does. The company uses sophisticated information technology to remember your previous requests and provide them for you again and again in any of its hotels where you may be staying. For example, one customer who had regularly stayed in the Ritz-Carlton in Seoul, Korea, checked into a Ritz-Carlton in Palm Beach, Florida, to celebrate his wedding anniversary and had all of his previous requests known and carried out. The Ritz-Carlton prides itself on knowing and respecting your preferences, as well as creating loyalty and satisfaction on a one-to-one basis through its quality services and products.

In fact, the company was a multiple winner of the Malcolm Baldrige National Quality Award. Only one other company has received this award more than once, and the Ritz-Carlton is the only company in the hotel industry to have been recognized. It requires planning, a committed team of employees and management, and implementation of premium service.

How does the Ritz-Carlton Hotel Company accomplish all this? It starts at the top, with a team of senior executives who meet every week to review quality issues. This includes the company's products and services, customer satisfaction and loyalty, growth and profits, and evaluation of the competition. In fact, Ritz executives spend 25 percent of their time working on quality-related issues. Ultimately, however, the responsibility for delivering customer value (and, thereby value to the organization) depends on 32,000 employees. Employees go through a process of orientation, on-the-job training (120 hours per year per employee), and certification. Because employees are extensively trained to observe their guests, the Ritz-Carlton does not have to bother customers with surveys and questionnaires. Instead, each employee is given a "preference pad" that is used to record the personal preferences of each customer. The information is then used to provide more personalized service to the customer in future stays. Employees record the obvious, such as type of room preferred, but they also note the less obvious details, such as a request for extra towels, and note whether the guest took apples or bananas from the fruit basket.

Empowering employees to solve problems is another crucial element in the Ritz-Carlton's quest for quality. They are allowed to do "whatever it takes" to make a customer happy without first seeking management approval. No matter how large or small the problems, all employees, regardless of job description, are expected to resolve potential conflicts and fulfill customer wishes. The Ritz-Carlton believes in rewarding employees and giving recognition for commendable work. The company realizes that their employees come to work with their own personal problems and worries that can prevent the employees from doing their best possible work. To help compensate for this, the Ritz-Carlton has a system of motivation, recognition, praise, and reward.

Teamwork can be found at every level of the company. Each hotel has a "quality leader" who works to design and carry out quality plans. These plans are reviewed with all employees at the start of each shift. This person serves as a resource to coworkers and is an advocate for the company. Each area of the Ritz-Carlton Hotel has three teams, and these are responsible for both setting and implementing quality standards in their areas. Technology is also integrated in achieving objectives. Production reports provide data from 720 different parts of the hotel to indicate progress or potential problems. Automated building, safety, and reservation systems as well as the history profile technology all assist in making customer value a priority.

The Ritz-Carlton Hotel Company is very effective in the implementation of its quality program as a means to achieve customer satisfaction and loyalty. Its 121 quality-related awards in one year alone speak for themselves. With a customer satisfaction rate of up to 97 percent, the high standards are likely to pay off in repeat business.[1]

THE CONCEPTS OF CUSTOMER SATISFACTION, LOYALTY, AND QUALITY

If you want to create and capture value you must connect with customers to earn their loyalty. That means delivering goods and services worthy of their support. People have millions of choices about where to spend their money. Ultimately, the decision depends on how much value they receive for what they pay. Companies that consistently produce high value are likely to have satisfied customers who reward them with loyalty and repeat purchases. Winning organizations go to extremes to create customer satisfaction because they know that satisfaction leads to loyalty which is the single most important factor in extraordinary business performance. They also know that satisfaction and loyalty are often based on the relationship they have with customers. In this chapter we will learn that satisfaction and loyalty usually go hand in hand, but not always.

Leading companies focus a good deal of effort on satisfaction and loyalty, but how do they achieve these two goals? There is no question that the ability to produce quality goods and services is required. Without quality, it is almost impossible for goods and services to perform as expected. In order to create superior value, organizations must start with excellent products. That requires the application of management principles to assure that processes throughout the company support the creation and delivery of products that produce satisfaction. Figure 7.1 describes the relationships among all these factors.

What are customer satisfaction and loyalty? What are value and quality? How do relationships and technology play into these factors? As a marketer, you need a strong foundation in these concepts to be able to connect with customers. In this chapter, we'll take a look at each concept in more detail.

CUSTOMER SATISFACTION AND CUSTOMER LOYALTY

A significant amount of marketing research is dedicated to measuring customer satisfaction and loyalty— but especially customer satisfaction. Satisfaction ratings are a major indicator of an organization's competitiveness. Today the race to beat competitors in cus-

tomer satisfaction is a powerful business objective because satisfaction is an overall indicator of how well customers rate a company's performance. This section begins by exploring why satisfaction and loyalty are important. Next, we look at how customer expectations affect satisfaction. We then tie all of these elements together by describing how relationships promotes satisfaction and loyalty. We also examine how diversity and global competition affect efforts to build satisfaction and loyalty.

WHY SATISFACTION AND LOYALTY ARE IMPORTANT

Customer satisfaction is a customer's positive, neutral, or negative feeling about the value received from an organization's product in specific use situations.[2] In the past, product innovation was the major factor in gaining the competitive edge. That is no longer always true. Now new products are copied by rivals, often within a few weeks or months, and the life span of new products is declining rapidly. Today it is also important for organizations to conduct all aspects of business to satisfy customers. Favorable satisfaction ratings not only boost sales but can also have a dramatic effect on company performance.[3] Though the U.S. housing market slowed last year, at the same time it revealed that companies with high customer satisfaction ratings experienced little decline in their stock prices while those without good customer service had a disastrous loss. The average builder obtains 7.4

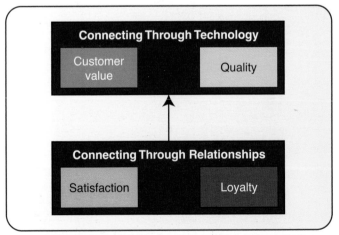

Figure 7.1   Customer Satisfaction, Customer Loyalty, and Quality: Connecting Through Relationships Formed by Organizational Systems and Actions

percent of prospects from referrals by satisfied friends and relatives. One of the nation's top builders, Pulte Homes, has more than 40 percent of its prospects referred by others. Recently, Pulte Homes has adopted energy effiecient homebuilding for increased savings and sustaiinability. It incorporates many energy effiencient practices to include "green" products in homes across the country. The additional savings and smart use of resources could create greater satisfaction ratings.[4]

Customer loyalty refers to how often, when selecting from a product class, a customer purchases a particular brand. Most business experts believe that customer satisfaction is a critical ingredient in building loyalty. The importance of loyalty cannot be overlooked. It is estimated that U.S. corporations lose 50 percent of their customers in any five-year period.[5] Thus, at this rate, few firms can achieve acceptable volume or profit without a strong base of loyal buyers. On average, 80 percent to 90 percent of a company's profits are generated by 10 percent to 20 percent of its customers.[6] A large number of satisfied, loyal customers results in strong business performance because these customers provide sales to increase revenues, have less concern about price, and help reduce the organization's costs. A recent study found that a one percent improvement in customer retention will improve firm value by five percent.[7]

Sales to Increase Revenues The revenue stream from one lifetime customer can be tremendous. A loyal Starbucks drinker will spend about $50,000, a buyer of Ralph Lauren Polo over $100,000, and a corporate buyer of Boeing aircraft equipment literally billions of dollars. When the amount a customer buys is viewed over the lifetime of a relationship, organizations understand why customer retention is so vital. In fact, many organizations develop compensation systems that tie executive and employee pay to measures of customer satisfaction and loyalty.

The importance of satisfied customers for revenue generation is magnified by their influence on other buyers. If a typical customer purchases a new car once every four years and influences one new buyer each year, the loyal, satisfied customer can be worth nearly $1 million in revenues and more than $100,000 in profit. Some companies calculate the **customer lifetime value (CLV)**, which is the amount of profit an organization expects to obtain over the course of a customer relationship. For example, assume you are a marketing manager for a large bicycle equipment manufacturer. One of your customers, Specialized, purchases about $80,000 in equipment each month. If Specialized becomes dissatisfied and selects another supplier, how much will it cost your company? At $80,000 per month for 12 months, Specialized purchases $960,000 annually. Assuming you earn a profit of 15 per-

cent, that equals $144,000 per year. Over two decades, your company would forfeit more than $2.8 million in pure profit and $19.2 million in revenue. If the same problem that dissatisfied Specialized results in the defection of other key customers, you face huge losses!

Less Concern About Price Customer satisfaction has become a key to making sales at appropriate prices. Jeff Bezos, founder of Amazon.com, commented on the role of price: "We're known for competitive prices . . . That's very important online. But we're also known for great customer experience and great customer service. If your brand is based exclusively on price, you're in a fragile position, but if your brand is about great prices and great service and great selection, that is a much better position."[8] Essentially, creating satisfied customers through service and experience is often more important and successful than trying to create satisfied customers through price. In general, customers are willing to pay more because they are certain they will receive valuable benefits. Also, they better tolerate price increases, showing little tendency to shop around. Overall, these factors lead to higher margins and profits.

Reduce the Organization's Costs The percentage of loyal, satisfied customers is a very important determinant of an organization's costs and revenues. In addition to generating sales, loyal customers affect the **cost structure**, which is the amount of resources required to produce a specific amount of sales. The cost of acquiring a new customer is usually six to ten times more expensive than keeping an existing one. A disproportionate amount of profits can be attributed to lower costs associated with loyal customers. Loyal customers no longer bear the high acquisition costs and they tell others about their satisfaction stimulating first time purchases by new buyers - some of whom are, in turn, likely to become loyal.

THE LEXUS **HYBRIDS**

Courtesy of Lexus

Lexis continues to lead competition in customer satisfaction.

CUSTOMER EXPECTATIONS

Customer expectations play an important role in determining satisfaction. **Customer expectations** are consumers' beliefs about the performance of a product based on prior experience and communications. When companies fall short of expectations, customers are dissatisfied. When companies exceed them, consumers are delighted. In both cases, customers are emotionally charged by their experience—the delighted are more likely to be loyal, and the dissatisfied are more inclined to switch.

Customer expectations are based on personal experience, observation of others, company actions, advertising, and promotion. Customers also expect companies to offer services to support their purchase decision. For example, because it is difficult for people to assess the quality of products in a catalog, companies such as Williams Sonoma and Crate & Barrel make it easy for people to return products that do not meet their expectations.

Higher and more varied expectations result when competition is intense. When Lexus entered the luxury automobile segment in 1989, expectations were high because Lexus positioned itself against such competitors as Mercedes-Benz, BMW, Cadillac, and Lincoln. Company executives knew the only way to succeed against the competition was to exceed expectations customers had for rival brands. As a result, Lexus gained significant market share at the expense of its domestic rivals. And, Lexus has frequently relieved the highest score in Customer Satisfaction with Dealer Service by J.D. Power and Associates.[9]

Each time a company delights a customer, new expectations are created. Similarly, with each change in product, price, promotion, or distribution, expectations can be affected. A major challenge for companies is to create marketing strategies that give buyers high but realistic expectations. Companies must continue to do better in light of competitors' efforts and rising consumer expectations.

CUSTOMER DEFECTIONS AND COMPLAINING BEHAVIOR

Organizations look at **customer defections,** the percentage of customers who switch to another brand or supplier. The relationship between customer satisfaction and loyalty is complex. The two often go hand in hand. Yet, loyal customers are not always highly satisfied, and satisfied customers are not always loyal. In some cases customers continue to purchase a brand that doesn't fully meet expectations because defecting would be difficult or an alternative would be no better. In other cases satisfied customers defect because they simply want to try something new. A large number of consumers have many expectations, some of which may be met and others not. Consequently, there are degrees of satisfaction; customers may be highly or only moderately satisfied. One recent study showed that 40 percent of all customers, though satisfied, would be willing to switch to a competitor, whereas highly satisfied customers are much less willing to do so.[10] The point is that just focusing on satisfaction isn't enough. You must build a bond of loyalty that is based on a relationship.

Figure 7.2 illustrates that, in a classic study completed in Sweden, 65 percent of customers defect primarily because they are dissatisfied with the way they are treated.[11] Fifteen percent defect because they are dissatisfied with the product. The remaining defect because they prefer a different product or for other reasons unrelated to the product. This is an indicator of how extremely important it is to build relationships. Treating people with respect is always important, and particularly so if you want to hold their loyalty. Loyal customers also initiate word-of-mouth marketing. Whole Foods Market only spends .5 percent of total sales on advertising and marketing, relying almost entirely on world-of-mouth recommendations from loyal customers.[12]

Companies committed to customer satisfaction will deal with any complaints they receive in a way that still leads to overall satisfaction. On average, nine of every 10

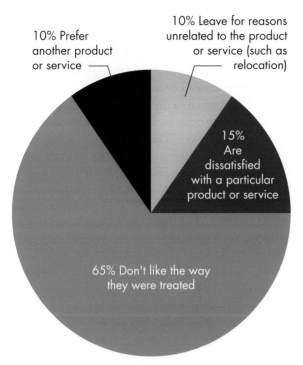

Figure 7.2   Why Customers Leave
Source: Eugene W. Anderson, Claes Fornell, and Donald R. Lehmann, "Customer Satisfaction, Market Share, and Profitability: Findings from Sweden," Journal of Marketing 58 (1994): 53.

SATISFACTION RATINGS AND MEASUREMENT

Because satisfaction contributes so much to the success of an organization, it is no surprise that marketers are very interested in measuring satisfaction. **Satisfaction ratings** provide a way for consumers to compare brands, enable testing agencies to determine how well products perform, and allow companies to monitor how satisfied consumers are with their goods and services.

You may have used a rating system to help choose a cell phone, an insurance policy, or even which college to attend. Consumers have been sensitized to the importance of satisfaction by such publications as *Consumer Reports*, which routinely rates many products, and *Motor Trend*, which rates autos. Auto advertisers and others regularly incorporate satisfaction ratings into persuasive messages. The popular press runs major stories on satisfaction ratings. For example, J.D. Power and Associates produces an annual Sales Satisfaction Index based on the responses from about 37,000 new vehicle owners about their new-vehicle purchase experiences.[14] The American Consumer Satisfaction Index (ACSI) is a quarterly rating that measures customer satisfaction in seven sectors of the economy broken down into 10 economic sections.[15] Even the U.S. government has entered the scene by sponsoring the Malcolm Baldrige National Quality Award, which is given to outstanding U.S. firms based partially on customer satisfaction.[16] We will discuss this award in more detail later in the chapter.

Competitive advantage comes to companies that can learn and adjust most quickly to market forces. One critical source of information is feedback from customers about how they behave and why they feel as they do. A **customer satisfaction measurement program** is an ongoing survey of customers (and competitors' customers) for the purpose of obtaining continuous estimates of satisfaction. Simply looking at sales data can tell us whether more or fewer products are purchased, but it does not reveal much about underlying reasons for behavior. Consequently, in addition to sales data, companies should measure customer satisfaction and loyalty rates. Marketers must not only measure their own company's performance but also that of their competitors. A company can work hard to build relationships critical to con-

customer problems that are discovered and resolved immediately will result in satisfaction and loyalty. Seven of 10 customers will do repeat business with a company that makes some sort of effort to resolve a problem. In fact, if a problem is handled satisfactorily, the average customer will tell five other people about it. A negative experience will result in nine to 20 people being told about the poor treatment or poor products and services.[13] This suggests that customers who complain and receive satisfactory attention are often more satisfied than those who don't complain at all.

It's not necessarily bad when people complain. On the contrary, research shows that soliciting complaints can be a very powerful marketing tool for satisfying customers as well as acquiring new customers. Only about half of customers that encounter problems with a product will complain. The other half are likely to be dissatisfied with the company and therefore less loyal, without the company ever knowing about the problem. When customers do complain and are subsequently satisfied, they tend to be 30 percent more loyal than someone who does not complain and 50 percent more loyal than a dissatisfied customer. Thus, encouraging feedback and responding to complaints are ways to establish a bond of loyalty based on relationships.

Marketing Vocabulary

CUSTOMER DEFECTIONS
The percentage of customers who switch to another brand or supplier.

SATISFACTION RATINGS
Ratings provided by testing agencies that compare purchase satisfaction with specified brands or with how well products perform.

CUSTOMER SATISFACTION MEASUREMENT PROGRAM
An ongoing survey of customers (and competitors' customers) for the purpose of obtaining continuous estimates of satisfaction.

sumer satisfaction, yet the level of satisfaction may decline because it is possible that competitors have improved their relationships much more quickly. Drugstores have made vast improvements in customer service including automation, softer lighting and private consultation rooms.[17]

The best consumer satisfaction program in the world is worth very little unless it feeds into the strategic and operational planning of the company. This information is then provided to all employees so that adjustments can be made to improve performance in their respective areas. Each functional area at all levels of the organization must be willing to undertake activities that lead to satisfied customers. One of the most important parts of the marketing executive's job is to get the entire organization to focus decisions on actions that affect how much customers are satisfied. So, much of a marketer's time is spent creating strategies that influence satisfaction.

RELATIONSHIPS BUILD SATISFACTION AND LOYALTY

Just a few years ago marketers were content to sell to new customers with the goal of increasing sales faster than competitors. When one company's sales rise faster than all others, that organization's market share increases. Today most companies realize that customer loyalty may be far more important than just market share.

You may try a new item for fun, but if you really like it, you will buy it again or tell others about it. The product becomes a more permanent fixture in your life and has more meaning. Without this loyalty and repeat business from customers, an organization's costs escalate, and in many cases the company fails. Very few organizations can survive on single transactions. Even companies that market products bought once in a lifetime depend on loyalty. The hospital that markets its heart surgery capa-

bilities relies on positive word of mouth from loyal customers. Likewise, a Harley-Davidson dealer who sells a customer that one and only "dream machine" still builds the relationship after the sale. This makes it evident to other potential buyers that the Harley-Davidson organization will continue to connect with its loyal users.

BabyCenter.com, a one-stop shopping and information Web site for expectant and current mothers, established a registry system. This allows the company to track children's ages, birthdays, and favorite products, and to provide relevant information regarding products, child development, and safety to the appropriate parent, based all on the child's birth date. Therefore, immediately before a child's first birthday, BabyCenter.com can automatically e-mail the mother an appropriate and exciting birthday gift, increasing the probability that the mother will remain a customer. Similarly, www.barnesandnoble.com marketed to member-only associations. It offered discounts for books and music for any of the members of a dues-paying organization. In return, www.barnesandnoble.com.com received information about each customer, including an e-mail address, demographics, and enhanced loyalty.

According to Skip Lefauvre, former CEO of Saturn Corporation, a company "must do things so astonishingly well that customers become not merely loyalists but rather outright apostles."[18] One company in particular has maintained a close relationship with its customers—Harley-Davidson. In 1983, Harley established the Harley Owners Group (H.O.G.) for Harley riders across the nation to share their passion and pride for their Harleys. Today, there are nearly a million H.O.G. members worldwide.[19] How many companies have relationships so strong that consumers are willing to tattoo the brand on their bodies - thousands of devoted customers have "Harley" tattooed on their chests, arms and elsewhere. Few companies have achieved true brand loyalty like Harley-Davidson; however, the point is clear: Connecting through relationships creates a personal bond.

That's what both Harley-Davidson and Saturn want. When you buy a Saturn, your new car is cleaned and polished to perfection and delivered to you in a special location within the dealership showroom. Your salesperson makes sure to take time, without interruptions, to discuss all of the features of your new purchase and answer any questions. And don't be surprised to find cut flowers on the driver's seat. A personal phone call from your salesperson followed by a letter shortly thereafter provides the initial follow-through to begin furthering the relationship.

CREATING A PERSONAL RELATIONSHIP

By its very nature, a relationship is personal. It reflects the connection between two or more parties. The heart of the marketing concept is to address customer needs and wants. It doesn't stop there. Customer needs and wants should be addressed in a way that produces customer satisfaction and loyalty. Although not every customer seeks a relationship with every purchase, needs and wants more often are best addressed by establishing relationships. Involvement with customers is key in relationship marketing. Chrysler bonds with buyers at its annual "Camp Jeep" weekend where thousands of Jeep vehicles and Jeep owners gather for three days of family and Jeep related activities.[20] Aside from any economic connections, relationships are socially driven as well. Figure 7.3 lists empathy, trust, commitment, and rewards as important aspects of creating personal relationships. This is true whether we are looking at consumer, B2B, or other markets.

Empathy   Empathy is the ability to understand the perspective of another person or organization. It means putting yourself in someone else's shoes and seeing the world as that person sees it. Companies that build relationships have outstanding customer empathy. They use sophisticated marketing research and create a culture within the organization that is sensitive to others. But empathy works best when customers know that they are understood—that the organization has accurate knowledge of their circumstances. Marketers communicate this empathy in nearly everything they do. For example, when you call the telephone company for information and get courteous help, even if you don't spell the name correctly, the company has communicated empathy. When a company goes out of its way to make things work just for you, you experience its empathy.

Trust   Trust is being able to rely on another party to perform as promised in the way you expect. The communications of marketers are filled with promises. For example: "Levi Strauss & Co. is committed to manufacturing products of the highest quality and ensuring the satisfaction of all our consumers. If any of our products do not meet our stringent quality standards, we want to identify the cause and take whatever corrective action is necessary."[21] Levi's backs up its promises by making it easy for you to return its products for an exchange or replacement. Companies, like people, that keep their promises

earn trust. This is a tremendously important element in building lasting connections with customers.

Commitment   Companies that are committed go out of their way to serve customers. They go beyond what is promised to make sure the customer is better off because of the relationship. When things go wrong, they work hard to fix them. This is particularly critical to relationships over time. In the $250 billion telecommunications industry, companies are committed to pleasing cus-

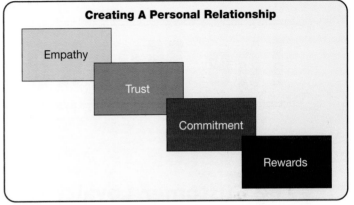

Figure 7.3 Creating a Personal Relationship

tomers. After the hurricane Katrina disaster, SBC Communications, Inc. immediately fixed its storm damage system to serve its customers and began matching employee contributions of up to $1 million for relief aid through the American Red Cross. It also provided a wide range of services valued at over $4 million a month to refugees in Houston and San Antonio, including 1000 phones with service, DSL, and computers.[22]

Rewarding Loyalty   Relationship marketing creates connections that make it unnecessary or difficult for customers to switch to competitors. In order for relationship marketing to work, companies must understand customers so well that competitors have little chance of new or unique offers that would entice a trial. This means that companies must be willing to provide superior value for their best customers. Louise O'Brien and Charles Jones, vice presidents with the successful consulting firm of Bain & Company, say that if companies want to realize the benefits of loyalty they must admit that "all customers are not equal . . . a company must give its best value to its best customers. That is, customers who generate superior profits for a company should enjoy the benefits of that value creation. As a result

www.harley-davidson.com

At the Harley-Davidson Web site, learn how the company considers environmental impact when designing its motorcycles. You can also design your own bike or sign up for a tour of its factory.

they will then become even more loyal and profitable."[23] In an effort to reward loyal customers, American Express teamed up with Starwood Hotels and Resorts to offer a credit card that earns points with each dollar spent, which can be redeemed for free hotel stays for Starwood Preferred Guests. When used to purchase a stay at any Starwood hotel, triple points can be earned. By becoming American Express cardholders and Starwood Preferred Guests, customers are rewarded for shopping anywhere that takes American Express and staying at

The Marketing Gazette™

CREATING & CAPTURING VALUE THROUGH RELATIONSHIPS

The Customer Loyalty Card Game

More and more people are discovering that there is a free lunch—or coffee, haircut, video, or even airline ticket—if you patronize certain shops and get your frequent customer card punched. The average consumer participates in 3.2 loyalty programs and spends as much as 46 percent higher with companies offering loyalty benefits. Retailers realize that building relationships with customers they already have is more profitable than luring first-timers with splashy ad campaigns or costly discounts. And for their loyalty, customers desire rewards more than anything else—from special rates in telecom and retail to frequent flyer miles in credit card companies.

Customer loyalty is in the cards. Rewards are even connected with Internet, such as the online loyalty card program at ESPRIT, an international apparel company. Nearly 55 percent of ESPRIT's retail sales worldwide come from loyal consumers that have the cards. They use it on each purchase and get discounts on what they buy, information on special sales, and exclusive shopping times. "A lot of companies in the U.S. have [loyalty programs], but they use credit card companies. We don't. We keep it ourselves," said Jerome Griffith, president of ESPRIT North America. "We have more than 5 million people on a database worldwide, and we market directly to them. That's something that's really essential for us. We know who all of our customers are and can send the right stuff to the right people." Some companies such as Starbucks has recently launched a new loyalty card with global cashless payment system. By only using one card, consumers are able to pay at outlets across the US, UK, Canada, Australia and Thailand, which also improves the speed of service.

Each time someone fills out a loyalty card, that person's name, address, and vital stats are punched into a computer. Mailings to advertise specials and new products then go to the people most likely to buy: true-blue customers. However, the government and two-thirds of shoppers with at least one frequent-shopper grocery card are concerned about the use of their personal information. On July 1, 2000, Senate Bill 926, also known as the Supermarket Club Card Disclosure Act, became effective in California. The Act allows companies to track purchases and analyze broad demographic trends but prohibits issuers of the cards from requiring applicants to provide identification such as a driver's license or Social Security card. Even outside the privacy issue, some customers are disgruntled with carrying so many cards in their wallets. And research has found that multiple loyalty card memberships of geographically close retailers will reduce consumer lifetime duration on visiting a certain retailer.

Moreover, an analysis from over 50 US retailers during the past 10 years shows that the average growth of retailers with loyalty programs was about 2.3, while that of those without loyalty programs was 4.3. And a telephone interview with 1001 adults aged 18 above indicates, though 53 percent of the interviewees regard loyalty cards as, "an excellent way of receiving vouchers or buying products at discount," 67 percent think these cards "make no difference" in encouraging them to spend money in stores. A number of incentives from loyalty cards just encourage short-term customer behaviors rather than sustainable, profitable customer relations. Therefore, an effective customer loyalty program weights much more than the small plastic card it includes.

Starwood hotels.[24] By becoming a member of AOL and AAdvantage, customers are rewarded for shopping online and for traveling. Considering that AOL and American Airlines have both had successful reward programs in the past, this program promises to reward customers above and beyond past experiences.

Building relationships may require specific incentives or rewards for loyal customers. Blockbuster offers a Blockbuster Rewards memberships to save loyal customers money. For every 5 paid new release movie rentals, the 6th rental is free. Membership also includes an e-newsletter Blockbuster uses to communicate the latest movie release information and more.[25]

It is important to remember that often competitors counter loyalty programs of rivals. For example, throughout the 1990s an explosion of miles-based incentive programs from airline industries allowed customers to get free travel after building up a certain number of paid travel miles. Because these programs were easy to copy soon most airlines were offering some sort of mileage program. Most of these programs failed to create a better customer experience, forcing competitors into bidding wars.[26]

Jollibee competes with McDonald's by tailoring its menu to local tastes.

DIVERSITY AND SATISFACTION

The diversity of tastes and preferences presents opportunities for customer-centered marketers. Diversity helps explain why companies with the highest overall sales sometimes have lower satisfaction ratings than smaller companies. The latter can design products and services for very narrowly defined segments and can focus all their attention on those customers. These companies may have lower market share but score high satisfaction points with a few customers. As companies gain share by selling to more people, their products and services must appeal to more diversified customers with a broader range of expectations. Large companies must

have the flexibility and agility to satisfy many divergent target markets while maintaining or increasing their size. Achieving satisfaction in the face of growth requires using the broadest range of marketing tools and techniques. If an organization expects impressive satisfaction scores, then it must understand all forms of diversity better than even its smallest competitors.

The success of a product or service in one market segment will not automatically transfer to consumers in another segment. The diverse nature of consumers makes universal buying preferences and behaviors very unlikely. Companies such as Coca-Cola, McDonald's, Exxon-Mobil and Levi Strauss address the individual wants and needs of people by acknowledging their unique differences. Attention to the diversity of consumers is often reflected in better market share and product sales. When McDonald's expanded to the Philippines 25 years ago, few expected the local, 11-store Jollibee fast-food chain to survive. However, Jollibee reacted by first copying McDonald's business model and then tailoring its menu to better serve the preferences of the local market. First, a slightly sweeter hamburger, then a Philippine-style chicken product, and finally a kids-oriented spaghetti plate. Today Jollibee has expanded to 24 overseas stores in seven countries, and almost unbelievably, has opened up 15 California locations to compete with McDonald's in the United States![27]

Groups based on ethnicity have such tremendous buying power that marketers have begun to recognize the

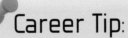

Career Tip:

Employees at Hallmark know firsthand what it means to connect with customers through relationships. Hallmark products directly promote relationships among family and friends. The employee atmosphere within Hallmark reflects this relationship philosophy. Career opportunities at Hallmark are numerous—internships, creative positions, sales, marketing, operations, corporate staff, and others. You can learn more about Hallmark career opportunities by connecting to its online job database at www.hallmark.com. Discover what positions are currently available and obtain application information for your area of interest.

advantages of addressing each group individually. Many have even created marketing positions that focus on this. At Kraft, for example, there is a director of ethnic marketing. Today most of the largest firms in the United States have created diversity management positions in an effort to modify corporate culture to reflect the growth of minority segments. After all, according to the Bureau of Labor Statistics, one third of all new workers in the past 10 years have been minorities.[28]

GLOBAL COMPETITION AND SATISFACTION

The success of global companies is highly dependent on customer satisfaction. Throughout the 1960s and 1970s, domestic firms dominated the U.S. market. By the early 1980s, U.S. businesses were under the false impression that success could be sustained by making only minor adjustments. This resulted in a real lack of focus on customer needs and satisfaction. Foreign companies spotted this weakness and entered U.S. markets quickly, putting customer satisfaction at the heart of everything they did. Some of the strongest U.S. companies saw their market shares plummet because foreign rivals gained strong customer satisfaction ratings. These foreign competitors raised consumer expectations for quality and speed of service to new levels and often at substantially lower overall prices. Essentially, foreign competitors created new levels of customer satisfaction in the U.S. market.

No one knows this better than IBM. The U.S. based IBM Corp. dominated the data systems market with large clients such as Quixtar, Shell Canada and T-Mobile Direct.[29] IBM focused on maintaining its product instead of its customers. As a result, Hitachi, a Japanese competitor, began focusing on customer satisfaction and product service. Greater customer satisfaction has made Hitachi the leading data storage vendor today.[30]

ORGANIZATIONAL SYSTEMS AND ACTIONS THAT DELIVER QUALITY

The effects of technology are absolutely phenomenal on the creation of customer value. Overall, the functionality of products is increasing while costs are staying the same or decreasing. Most leading-edge companies have systems that also deliver quality goods and services. It is this emphasis on quality—largely made possible through

technology and people—that brings more satisfaction to customers. Products work as expected, last longer, and are user friendly. This section describes some of the aspects of quality leading-edge organizations employ to help accomplish customer satisfaction and loyalty.

http://globaledge.msu.edu

Visit globalEDGE™ Online for the ultimate international marketing research tool!

globalEDGE™
Customer Satisfaction & Loyalty: Building Value with Quality

Since recent statistics indicate that the products your firm offers are not found to be satisfactory in the marketplace, your firm is currently attempting to increase customer loyalty. Part of the overall strategy determined by upper management is to reconfigure and reposition your firm's product line to be more gender-specific. Using global statistics to determine the gender ratio for each market in which your firm competes worldwide, which five countries may be best suited for a positioning strategy targeted toward females? Which five markets may find a strategy targeting males as most successful? Of these ten markets, which is the largest?

QUALITY & SATISFACTION

Quality describes the degree of excellence of a company's goods and services. It is useful to emphasize both quality in goods as well as the special case of service quality. **Service quality** is the expected and perceived quality of all of the services an organization offers. Quality is necessary for organizations that sell physical products that are manufactured as well as organizations that only sell services. Without quality, it is nearly impossible to achieve customer satisfaction. A quality good or service performs precisely according to specifications that will satisfy customers. Consequently, quality contributes to customer satisfaction. Some companies, such as Packard Electric, believe their product possesses quality to the degree that it meets or exceeds customer expectations. Elmer Reece, a former top executive at the company, introduced the "excellence concept" in a quest to deliver total quality. According to Reece, "being excellent means meeting or exceeding customer expectations in everything." Striving for excellence became a critical part of every employee's job at Packard, and Reece's philosophy turned the company into a real winner. In order to make the concept work, Reece elevated marketing from its traditional sales role to the leading force in every major decision. Reece often spoke of the problems that occurred when quality was defined from an engineering or manufacturing perspective. He said that the customer, not the company, should be the judge of quality.

No two customers are precisely alike. We all want quality goods and services—but we each may view quality as being slightly different. For example, if you get an urge for a Big Mac® and can even taste its flavor in your mouth, then you might define quality by consistency (which McDonald's has perfected). But if you get an urge for a gourmet meal at a five-star restaurant, you might define quality as uniqueness and variety. Legendary restaurants such as Spago and Lutece take very different actions from McDonald's to accomplish quality.

In many markets, a quality product is considered the price of entry. Basically, this means that quality is so important that a company must have high quality in order to even participate in a market; inferior products or services will simply not succeed. As more companies build quality into their products as a standard feature, quality alone ceases to provide a differential advantage. However, this was not always the case. For some time, many consumers bought Japanese cars because they were perceived to be of much higher quality than U.S. brands. Today most experts believe that U.S. vehicles are equal in quality to Japanese cars and that U.S. manufacturers are even beginning to take the lead in new areas of quality, such as

©iStockphoto.com/mashabuba

McDonald's burgers are known for quality by consistency.

Courtesy of Whole Foods Market

Shoppers at Whole Foods Market are willing to pay more for produce they perceive to be of high quality.

design and performance. Quality may be evaluated in two ways, subjectively and objectively. Customers are the key to understanding the subjective analysis, whereas technical specifications are the focus of objective assessments.

Assessments of Quality

Subjective assessment of quality indicates to what degree the product does what consumers want it to do. For example, the hamburger tastes good. In assessing quality, consumers tend to be subjective, whereas companies tend to be objective. After an extensive review of a number of studies, one expert defined quality as "the consumer's judgment about a product's overall excellence or superiority."[31] From this perspective, different groups may evaluate quality altogether differently. When asked, adults may say Wendy's is higher in quality than McDonald's, whereas children may have the opposite response. Health conscious people might rate both items as low in quality.

Objective assessment of quality indicates to what degree the product does consistently what it's supposed to do. McDonald's and Burger King make what many consider to be high-quality hamburgers because each time one is served it consistently meets company standards. With hamburgers and other physical objects, it's possible to develop objective assessments of quality in the form of standards, such as fat and salt content or nutrition value.

Even objective assessments are open to interpretation. This is particularly true globally. For example, German and Japanese products are manufactured to precise specifications and will not perform in excess of their rating. If a product is rated to lift 1,000 kg, it will do precisely that and no more. In contrast, a similar U.S. product in some cases has a safety factor of 1.5, so the product will lift 1,500 kg. The extra capacity is a sign of quality in the United

States but not in many other markets. Consequently, even measures of so-called objective quality are created in response to the subjective desires of various groups.[32]

Static and Dynamic Quality There are at least two types of quality. **Static quality** results when an accepted practice is perfected. Many companies have processes designed to produce to given quality standards that approach perfection. **Dynamic quality** results when a major change makes the existing standard obsolete. For example, Smith Corona once dominated the personal typewriter business with an extremely high-quality electric portable. All quality efforts at Smith Corona were directed at improving its typewriters. As consumers shifted to computers for word processing however, Smith Corona's efforts to achieve static quality became irrelevant. A revolution had taken place as software and hardware companies created value through change, a dynamic quality shift.

Focusing activities on static quality can divert resources from new ventures, and there seems little point in perfecting technology that is about to become outmoded. At the same time, dynamic quality shifts cannot be forced; the technology needs to be perfected and the market prepared. Marketers are a company's advance scouts, signaling what is new and relevant. Marketing is also critical in defining quality from the customer's perspective. Marketers develop estimates of what attributes customers use to define quality, what quality standards must be met, and what various segments are willing to pay for quality.

TOTAL QUALITY MANAGEMENT

Total quality management (TQM) is an organizational philosophy that helps companies produce products and services that deliver value to satisfy customers. TQM involves, first, assessing consumer needs and, second, developing products or services that meet those needs. The approach seeks continuous improvement, reduced cycle time, and analysis of process problems. It also includes quality function deployment, which attempts to ensure that customer desires are built into the final product offering. When implemented correctly, TQM involves many company activities that affect customer satisfaction and ends with customer service and feedback. It deals with

both deliverables (the goods and services provided) and interactions (how customers experience dealing with the provider).

Continuous Improvement **Continuous improvement** occurs as the organization strives to find better ways of satisfying customers. FedEx uses Service Quality Indications (SQI) in its efforts to achieve continuous improvement. The index measures a number of key service factors from the customer's perspective and then weights them as to how seriously the customer will view a failure in any of those areas. Based on SQI, FedEx has set the goal of scoring better year after year. Since 1987, overall customer satisfaction at FedEx has averaged more than 95 percent and is approaching the company's goal of 100 percent.

Milliken & Company, another organization known for superior quality, pays particular attention to constant improvement. It calls its "Pursuit of Excellence" program an evolving process that continuously yields new ideas for enhancing quality, increasing customer satisfaction, and improving business performance. Through Milliken's Policy Committee and Quality Council, management creates the environment and provides the leadership necessary for quality improvement. Relying heavily on employee training and an organizational structure in which employees are called associates, Milliken has instilled in every person a feeling of responsibility to find and implement quality improvement changes. Managers must respond within one day to any suggestion by an associate to enhance customer satisfaction. This form of empowerment gives each associate the opportunity to

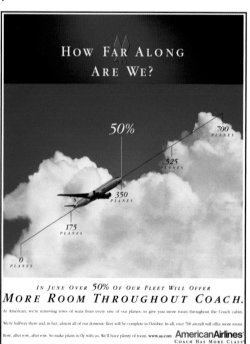

IN JUNE OVER *50% OF OUR FLEET WILL OFFER*
MORE ROOM THROUGHOUT COACH.

At American, we're removing rows of seats from every one of our planes, to give you more room throughout the Coach cabin.

We're halfway there and, in fact, almost all of our domestic fleet will be complete in October. In all, over 700 aircraft will offer more room.

Row, after row, after row. So make plans to fly with us. We'll have plenty of room. www.aa.com **AmericanAirlines**
COACH HAS MORE CLASS

American Airlines added leg room—a continuous improvement designed to increase customer satisfaction.

	Faster	Better	Cheaper
COMPANY DELIVERS	Availability Convenience	Performance Features Reliability Conformance Serviceability Aesthetics Perceived Quality	Price
CUSTOMER DESIRES	Responsiveness Access	Reliability Security Competence Credibility Empathy Communications Style	Affordability

Figure 7.4   Faster-Better-Cheaper: What the Company Delivers and What the Customer Desires

Marketing Vocabulary

REDUCED CYCLE TIME
A TQM activity that helps a company move more rapidly from product inception to final delivery of the product to the marketplace.

ANALYSIS OF PROCESS PROBLEMS
Methods designed to find and fix problems that could reduce quality.

ISO 9001
An inclusive set of standards established by the International Standards Organization (ISO) to ensure that quality requirements are met.

have a positive influence on quality.

Reduced Cycle Time   **Reduced cycle time** is a TQM activity intended to help the company move more quickly from product inception to product delivery in the marketplace. The approach pays huge dividends by reducing costs while making possible very quick shipment of products matched specifically to customer requirements. This not only allows customers more flexibility in ordering but also results in lower inventories for business customers and quicker availability of products for consumers.

A Houston-based industrial distributor of pipes, valves, and fittings, has used TQM principles to achieve reduced cycle time and has seen striking results. The company assigned a team of outside salespeople, inside salespeople (customer service and sales representatives in the home office), and accounts receivable personnel to every customer account. This allowed employees and customers to gain a great deal of familiarity with one another. Inventory turnover improved by 175 percent in five years, sales for newly introduced value-added products increased 75 percent in three years, and profits doubled.

Analysis of Process Problems   **Analysis of process problems** refers to the activities that find and fix problems in the production and delivery of products and services. For manufactured items this includes procurement of raw materials and components that go into finished goods, the manufacture of the finished products themselves, and packaging and shipping to ensure that appropriate products get to their final destination. The International Standards Organization (ISO) has established an inclusive set of standards, called **ISO 9001**, to

determine whether quality requirements are met. These standards are being introduced into laws in the European Community to ensure that firms have quality management systems in place that meet specified criteria. Individual products aren't certified. Companies must go through an arduous process to become ISO 9001 certified. Organizations such as Chrysler and Motorola require that all their suppliers be ISO 9001 certified.

An important outcome of the analysis is to establish rigid quality control, such as the Motorola six-sigma standard, which sets goals so that virtually all Motorola products perform as expected. Elaborate efforts are made in product and process design to ensure that the actual manufacturing activities efficiently produce quality items. In turn, the processes are monitored to make certain that the output is produced according to specifications.

Although quality has been the focus of manufacturing for more than a decade, the same principles are now being applied to customer service. For example, FedEx Express Canada uses the Contact Center Employer of Choice ("CCEOC") program to help identify areas of improvement in its call centers. The program helps build exceptional work environments that attract and retain high-performing employees. By using recommendations outlined in the CCEOC Summary Reporting, customer service centers have increased employee and customer satisfaction. Jeff Doran, president of CCEOC Inc. says, "Their people-focused values resonate throughout the organization and have had a profound affect on improving satisfaction, pride, commitment, respect and ultimately performance. Being recognized as a CCEOC reinforces FedEx Express Canada's customer service division as a preferred employer and FedEx Express Canada as one of the best organizations to work for in the country."[33]

Quality Function Deployment **Quality function deployment (QFD)** is used during the product or service design process to make sure that features to fulfill customer desires are built into the final offering. The three most common concerns of QFD are to make the product or service faster, better, and cheaper. Figure 7.4 shows what consumers desire in their dealings with the company and how those desires are translated into what the company delivers.

Benchmarking **Benchmarking** is the systematic evaluation of the practices of excellent organizations to learn new and better ways of serving customers. Benchmarking of **best practices**, those selected competencies for which leaders are known, has become so important that companies regularly send personnel to study and observe other organizations. Sparrow Health Systems, a leading provider in central Michigan, recently sent executives to Disney World to learn how to improve customer service. They also visited Saturn to obtain ideas for involving employees in the improvement process. Although Disney and Saturn are not in the same business, Sparrow was able to learn several new ways of ultimately improving health care delivery. By comparing its methods with those of known experts in other fields, Sparrow conducted benchmarking.

Six-Sigma is a total quality management effort focused on eliminating defects to improve processes. It equates to only 3.4 defects per million opportunities. Caterpillar Inc. is a leader in six-sigma implementation. At Caterpillar, employees are trained in six-sigma methodologies. An employee can earn a green or black belt through training. Caterpillar currently has 3,600 six-sigma black belt employees. Furthermore, Caterpillar has over 36,000 employees contributing to six-sigma projects worldwide including safety, product quality and product availability.[34]

QUALITY AWARDS

To encourage companies to improve their quality and com-

petitiveness, various governments have established awards. These are given to companies that demonstrate the most outstanding quality initiatives. Two very distinguished annual awards are the Deming Prize in Japan and the Malcolm Baldrige National Quality Award in the United States.

The Deming Prize Everyone has heard of quality inspectors—people who examine finished products as they roll off the assembly line and remove defective goods before they are sold to customers. In the early 1900s, most companies used inspectors as their main source of quality control. Little or no effort was devoted to correcting the manufacturing problems that caused product defects.

In the 1950s, Dr. Edward Deming took a new approach to the issue. He applied the idea of **statistical quality control**, a concept he learned while a statistician at AT&T's Bell Laboratories, to manufacturing. Statistical quality control involves using statistics to isolate and quantify production line problems that may cause

1. Create constancy of purpose toward improvement of product and service, with the aim to become competitive and stay in business, and to provide jobs.
2. Adopt this philosophy: We are in a new economic age created by Japan. Transformation of Western management style is necessary to halt the continued decline of industry.
3. Cease depending on inspection to achieve quality. Eliminate the need for inspection on a mass basis by building quality into the product in the first place.
4. End the practice of awarding business on the basis of price tag. Purchasing must be combined with design of product, manufacturing, and sales to work with the chosen suppliers; the aim is to minimize total cost, not merely initial cost.
5. Improve constantly and forever every activity in the company in order to improve quality and productivity and thus constantly decrease costs.
6. Institute training and education on the job for everyone, including management.
7. Institute supervision. The aim of supervision should be to help people and machines do a better job.
8. Drive out fear so that everyone may work effectively for the company.
9. Break down barriers between departments. People in Research, Design, Sales, and Production must work as a team to tackle usage and production problems that may be encountered with the product or service.
10. Eliminate slogans, exhortations, and targets for the work force that ask for zero defects and new levels of productivity. Such exhortations only create adversarial relationships; the bulk of the causes of low quality and low productivity belongs to the system and thus lies beyond the power of the work force.
11. Eliminate work standards that prescribe numerical quotas for the day. Substitute aids and helpful supervision.
12a. Remove the barriers that rob hourly workers of the right to pride of workmanship. The responsibility of supervisors must be changed from sheer numbers to quality.
12b. Remove the barriers that rob people in management and in engineering of their right to pride of workmanship. This means, among other things, abolition of the annual or merit rating and of management by objective.
13. Institute a vigorous program of education and retraining. New skills are required for changes in techniques, material, and service.
14. Put everybody in the company to work in teams to accomplish the transformation.

Figure 7.5 Edward Deming's 14 Points of Quality
Source: Reprinted from The New Economics for Industry, Government, Education by W. Edward Deming by permission of MIT and The W. Edward Deming Institute. Published by MIT, Center for Advanced Educational Services, Cambridge, MA 02139. Copyright 1993 by the W. Edward Deming Institute.

defects. The idea was to improve quality in the production process so that faulty goods would not be manufactured. The Japanese openly embraced Deming's philosophy, and this is viewed by many as one of the reasons for Japan's tremendous economic success during the 1970s and 1980s. Deming's work transformed Japan from the maker of inferior products to one of the most powerful economies in the world. To honor Deming's contributions, the Japanese created the Deming Award as their highest recognition of quality.

To help business managers implement quality initiatives within their organization, Deming outlined 14 key issues, listed in Figure 7.5. Deming insisted, moreover, that top management be involved and supportive. If quality initiatives receive only lip service, without action, they will not be successful.

The Malcolm Baldrige National Quality Award

U.S. businesses have been late to emphasize quality. During the same period that the Japanese excelled in implementing quality initiatives, U.S. firms slipped dramatically in quality. Congress finally moved to establish a quality award for U.S. firms. It was named after the late Malcolm Baldrige, an advocate for quality and a former secretary of commerce. While considering the passage of the Malcolm Baldrige National Quality Improvement Act, the U.S. Senate Committee on Commerce, Science and Technology observed: "Strategic planning for quality improvement programs is becoming more and more essential to the well-being of our nation's companies and our ability to compete effectively in the global marketplace. Such an award would parallel the prize awarded annually in Japan."[35]

The 1987 legislation was enacted by Congress to encourage U.S. businesses and other organizations to practice effective quality control in the production of goods and services. At the time of its passage, the Senate and House produced a declaration reiterating the need for an incentive program for U.S. businesses and affirming that these businesses had been considerably challenged by foreign competitors. Slow growth in productivity and in product and process quality had, in some industries, resulted in annual losses of as much as 20 percent of sales revenues. It was evident that U.S. businesses needed to learn more about the importance of quality.

The **Malcolm Baldrige National Quality Award** is widely acknowledged as having raised quality awareness and practice among U.S. companies. Some consider the Baldrige an important catalyst for transforming U.S. business because it promotes quality excellence, recognizes achievements by companies that effectively improve quality, and supplies a guideline that business, industry, government, and others can use to evaluate their quality improvement efforts.

A key criterion winners must meet is "customer driven excellence." "Performance and quality are judged by the organization's customer. Thus, the organization must take into account all product and service features and characteristics and all modes of customer access that contribute value to customers. Such behavior leads to customer acquisition, satisfaction, preference, referrals, retention, and loyalty and to business expansion. Customer-driven excellence means much more than reducing defects and errors, merely meeting specifica-

The Malcolm Baldrige National Quality Award has raised quality awareness among U.S. companies.

Marketing Vocabulary

QUALITY FUNCTION DEVELOPMENT (QFD)
A process that builds customer wants and desires into the final product offering.

BENCHMARKING
The systematic evaluation of practices of excellent organizations to learn new and better ways to serve customers.

BEST PRACTICES
The competencies of industry leaders that other organizations use as benchmarks.

STATISTICAL QUALITY CONTROL
The use of statistics to isolate and quantify production line problems that may cause product defects.

MALCOLM BALDRIGE NATIONAL QUALITY AWARD
A program designed to raise quality awareness and practice among U.S. businesses.

tions, or reducing complaints. In addition, the organization's success in recovering from defects, service errors, and mistakes is crucial for retaining customers and building customer relationships."[36] Awards are given each year in several categories: manufacturing companies or subsidiaries, service companies or subsidiaries, small business, education, and health care. Figure 7.6 lists companies that have received the Malcolm Baldrige National Quality Award.

The Ritz-Carlton Hotel Company (described in the chapter opening) was an award winner, making it the only two-time Malcolm Baldrige National Quality Award winner in the service category. The Ritz Carlton Hotel Company owns 59 luxury hotels worldwide, from Bahrain to Boston, with 28,000 employees.[37] What makes this company a total quality winner? Among many others, customer focus is a distinguishing achievement. Its outspoken goal is to "Understand Customers in Detail" by relying on extensive data gathering and the dissection of key points where customer satisfaction problems generally occur. The Ritz-Carlton maintains a database of almost a million customer files, which enables hotel staff to anticipate needs of returning guests and to make sure in advance that requests can be honored.[38]

The Ritz-Carlton is a two-time Malcolm Baldrige National Quality Award winner in the service category.

DELIVERING VALUE TO IMPROVE SATISFACTION

Customer-centered marketing requires the development of unique competencies to satisfy customers within selected target market segments and to build their loyalty. Many parties are involved in contributing to the delivery of products that benefit consumers. The value chain is used to describe the chain of activities involved in bringing products to consumers. Additionally, to improve customer satisfaction and loyalty, leading-edge companies operate ethically to fulfill commitments and involve employees and customers in performance improvement efforts.

INTEGRATED SUPPLY CHAIN

The **supply chain** is composed of all the activities that organizations undertake to deliver value to the customer, such as working with suppliers, and distribution through convenient channels. A simple supply chain starts by identifying customer needs. Most people seek products that perform as desired, portray the image they want, are easy to purchase, and are priced fairly. Companies then identi-

1998	Boeing Airlift and Tanker Programs	2002	Motorola Commercial, Government & Industrial Solutions Sector	2005	Sunny Fresh Foods, Inc.
	Solar Turbines Incorporated		Branch-Smith Printing Division		DynMcDermott Petroleum Operations Company
	Texas Nameplate Company, Inc.		SSM Health Care		Park Place Lexus
1999	STMicroelectronics, Inc.	2003	Medrad, Inc.		Jenks Public Schools
	BI		Caterpillar Financial Services Corporation -- U.S.		Richland College
	The Ritz-Carlton Hotel Company				Bronson Methodist Hospital
	Sunny Fresh Foods		Community Consolidated School District 15	2006	Premier, Inc
2000	Dana Corporation—Spicer Driveshaft Division		Boeing Aerospace Support		MESA Products, Inc.
	KARLEE Company, Inc.		Stoner, Inc.		North Mississippi Medical Center
	Clarke American Checks, Inc.		Baptist Hospital, Inc.	2007	PRO-TEC Coating Co.
2001	Pal's Sudden Service		Saint Luke's Hospital of Kansas City		Mercy Health Systems
	Chugach School District				Sharp HealthCare
	Pearl River School District	2004	The Bama Companies, Inc.		City of Coral Springs, FL
	University of Wisconsin - Stout		Texas Nameplate Company, Inc.		U.S. Army Armament Research, Development and Engineering Center (ARDEC)
			Kenneth W. Monfort College of Business		
			Robert Wood Johnson University Hospital Hamilton		

Figure 7.6   Winners of the Malcolm Baldrige National Quality Award

fy the chain of events that must occur to deliver this value to customers. It is important that quality is built into each link in the chain.

Many activities make a major difference in the amount of customer satisfaction. These include the procurement of raw materials as well as the manufacture and delivery of products to retailers and others in the channel of distribution. Each activity has the potential to deliver added value to the customer. All functional areas—purchasing, operations, manufacturing, marketing, sales, and so on—are involved in delivering customer value. Each area must clearly understand the final consumer. And many separate organizations may be linked in the chain.

Although customers have very little knowledge of these activities, they shape the quality of goods and services as well as the price that will be charged in the marketplace. For example, Nike's customers what a quality product at a good price. Nike knows that manufacturing locations make a big difference in the product cost. In the same manner, the cost of Nike's raw materials, its ability to deliver products efficiently to retail outlets, the effectiveness of its research and development, and many other activities affect the overall quality of the goods and services the company can provide to its customers. Even the quality of the ads for Nike are important, since the image of the product for users is largely shaped by the ads. Nike's competitiveness depends to a great degree on its ability, and the ability of its suppliers and distributors, to perform well on all the factors that influence the amount of value delivered to the marketplace. All organizations in the chain must behave with the intent of creating satisfaction for others in the chain in order that consumers can ultimately benefit to the greatest degree possible.

ETHICAL BEHAVIOR IN FULFILLING COMMITMENTS

Many organizations that promise satisfaction and quality think they should provide a remedy to customers when quality does not meet expectations. Fixing the problem is ethically correct and good business practice. Although "satisfaction guaranteed or your money back" usually applies to such purchases as clothes or a restaurant pizza, today some colleges believe that a promise of a quality education should be backed by a guarantee as well.

Henry Ford Community College in Dearborn, Michigan became the first school to offer a guarantee for its graduates. It provides up to 16 semester hours of further training if an employer feels a graduate lacks the expected job skills. Of course, many businesses offer satisfaction guarantees. Some pay off with little hassle, like Meijer, a regional supermarket chain with an outstanding reputation for customer service. Others pay lip service to

the offer but make it almost impossible for dissatisfied consumers to collect. Despite the satisfaction that results when a customer problem is handled well, a number of companies have tightened their rules and changed generous exchange policies. Best Buy, for example, has quit taking back goods without a sales receipt. Customers who have no receipt must pay a "restocking fee" equal to 15 percent of the purchase price of the item. Wal-Mart has changed its open-ended return policy to one with a 90-day limit.

Customers are partly responsible for these changes. Imagine people returning goods actually purchased at a garage sale or bringing back clothes worn for an entire season. Or what about customers who pull items off store shelves and bring them to the counter for a refund? Nintendo has received returned game boxes containing underwear, soap, and even a lizard. Although these are extreme examples, stores have tightened return policies to help prevent fraud. Since $16 billion is lost annually to retail fraud, the stricter policies may seem reasonable.[39] The important consideration, however, is the consumer response. If the ease of returning a defective or unwanted good is eliminated, then consumers feel negatively about the company or business. Since many aspects of satisfaction are based on how the organization and its products affect customers, it is important to make all employees aware of the importance of the customer to the overall health of the organization. That requires their involvement in knowing why products were returned and nearly every other aspect of customer evaluations.

EMPLOYEE AND CUSTOMER INVOLVEMENT

It's pretty hard to imagine making customers satisfied without having employees who are highly involved in the process. It is also hard to imagine those same employees doing a good job with customers unless they are satisfied with their organization. Satisfied employees are much more likely to produce satisfied customers than are disgruntled employees. Thus, customer satisfaction starts with the company itself. Strong companies involve the entire organization and its customers in efforts to improve performance in ways that will promote customer satisfaction. IBM integrates customers into its improvement planning process by inviting consumers from around the world to give direct input to top-level strategic planners. Executives at Procter & Gamble

Marketing Vocabulary

SUPPLY CHAIN
All the activities that organizations undertake to deliver value to the customer, such as working with suppliers and distribution through convenient channels.

take time to interview consumers at grocery stores and answer customer service calls. Hewlett-Packard recruits customers to assist in developing products that will replace current offerings. All these companies demonstrate how interaction between consumers and an organization's employees help ensure that the customer is a primary focus.[40]

The job of satisfying consumers cannot be left to the marketing or sales manager alone. According to Robert Schrandt, vice president of customer relations for Toyota Motor Sales, USA, "Achieving customer satisfaction would be impossible without a well-defined process for focusing the entire organization on the customer." As with the most important marketing functions, everyone must participate, from top management to the workers on the factory floor. In fact, most companies that are serious about improving satisfaction consider it critical to involve their top managers. They sit in on meetings about customer satisfaction and demand that everyone "walk the talk"—not just discuss issues but develop plans to address them. Compared to other organizations, managers in these companies spend more time talking with customers, and compensation structures often are based more on satisfying customers than on meeting short-term financial goals. Furthermore, all functional areas are involved, including marketing, sales, engineering, accounting, and

purchasing. Other channel members, such as manufacturers' representatives, wholesalers, and distributors, often are made part of the effort. The result is a customer-centered organization working together to create satisfied purchasers.

It isn't enough to involve members of the company and its agents. Customers also must be part of the process. Customer Review, an Internet company that establishes online communities based around sports, electronics, and the home, works to develop relationships with customers of products. An online "facilitator" directs discussion about particular products among the company's 1.2 million Web site visitors. Establishing relationships with its customers is important to the success of Customer Review. However, the quality of these relationships extends to the manufacturers of the products it reviews.[41] The quality of relationships and the accuracy of expectations that manufacturers of products establish with Customer Review's customers are reflected in the product reviews posted on its Web site.

The biggest mistake most companies make is to assume they know what their customers want without asking them. Unfortunately, most companies that guess do so incorrectly. For a true understanding of what consumers want, a company must ask them through some sort of meaningful involvement. It is important to include not only current customers but also potential purchasers and competitors' customers. Each is likely to provide unique and enlightening information. One way to achieve involvement is through formal marketing research, such as interviews or surveys. In addition, many leading companies include customers in their planning teams.

Web and E-commerce Stars
Nike - www.nike.com

Nike has created a Web site that has information about all of their products, and additional interactive links. Customers are able to view and shop for all Nike products online as well as customize their experience. At one link, "NIKEiD," visitors can create their own Nike shoe with a style and color that fits their taste. And, at "Tune Your Run with Nike+," users can enter in personal running information and check progress as well as download music that can complement a running workout.

Chapter Summary:

Objective 1: Understand why customer satisfaction and loyalty are the focus of marketing in winning organizations.

Satisfied, loyal customers generate profits because they are responsible for a large percentage of sales and are less costly to develop than new customers. Loyal, satisfied customers also influence others to buy products. Similar to product innovation, customer satisfaction has become a key to competitive advantage. In addition, satisfaction ratings help consumers compare products. Finally, loyal, satisfied customers will pay more and are less concerned about price and price increases.

Objective 2: Learn how consumer expectations influence satisfaction.

Customers form impressions about how well companies perform in relation to expectations. If performance falls short, then customers become dissatisfied. Often they defect when they don't like the way they are treated. When customers are delighted, their expectations are likely to increase. Loyal customers are not always satisfied, and they are likely to complain. If their complaint is handled quickly, then their loyalty may be even greater.

Objective 3: See why connecting with customers through relationships achieves outstanding satisfaction and loyalty.

The personal connection produces loyalty. Relationships are built, first, on empathy—the ability to understand another party and communicate that understanding. Second, trust is important, that is, behaving in line with promises you make and expectations you create. Third, commitment is also important. Commitment means making sure that the customer is better off because of the relationship.

Objective 4: Understand the ideas that help organizations market quality goods and services.

Diverse customers have different expectations. Creating satisfaction requires paying close attention to various tastes and preferences. Many companies have created units to address specific groups. The variations in customer tastes and preferences are particularly challenging for large companies that want to gain high satisfaction scores. They still need to address each specific segment to achieve high ratings. Satisfaction scores have historically been higher for some foreign companies in this country, reflecting their attention to quality. This has helped them gain a market foothold. Now that U.S. companies also are stressing quality and satisfaction, their scores are improving in marketing to foreign countries.

Objective 5: Define quality and describe how it is obtained.

Quality can be assessed objectively and subjectively. Objective assessments indicate whether the product performs as designed. Subjective assessments indicate whether the product performs according to what customers want. Businesses must be careful not to focus only on static quality. The quality of change—dynamic quality—is also important. Both build value. Total quality management (TQM) is an organizational philosophy that focuses on quality. It includes several specific actions, such as continuous improvement, reduced cycle time, and analysis of process problems. Benchmarking is also important. It refers to learning from organizations considered to be among the very best and assessing how well you perform relative to them.

Review Your Understanding

1. What is customer satisfaction? What is loyalty? What are four reasons for an organization to stress loyalty and satisfaction? Explain each.
2. How do you calculate the lifetime value of a customer?
3. What are customer expectations? Why do customers defect? Why are complainers often your most loyal customers?
4. What are the three elements that form the personal basis of relationships? Explain each. How do companies reward loyal customers?
5. What are companies doing to address satisfaction with diversified customers?
6. Why is satisfaction important in global marketing?
7. What is customer-delivered value? Explain.
8. What is the value chain? Explain.
9. What are objective and subjective assessments of quality? Static and dynamic quality?
10. What is TQM and what are its four critical components?
11. What is benchmarking?
12. What are the Deming Prize and the Malcolm Baldrige National Quality Award?

Discussion of Concepts

1. Why should companies focus on both satisfaction and loyalty? Why is satisfaction alone inadequate?
2. Imagine that you are the marketing director of a local company. How would you use the concept of customer-delivered value to improve the marketing for a product?
3. Discuss how connecting with customers through relationships relates to satisfaction and loyalty.
4. If you observed a large percentage of customer defections from a business, what might the causes be? How would you investigate?
5. Is complaining behavior good or bad? Should you encourage customers to complain?
6. What would you recommend for an organization that wishes to connect with customers through relationships?
7. What is the relationship between quality and customer value? How is quality attained?
8. Do you feel companies should allocate a great deal of effort to apply for the Malcolm Baldrige National Quality Award? Why or why not?

Key Terms And Definitions

Analysis of process problems: Methods designed to find and fix problems that could reduce quality.

Benchmarking: The systematic evaluation of practices of excellent organizations to learn new and better ways to serve customers.

Best practices: The competencies of industry leaders that other organizations use as benchmarks.

Cost structure: The amount of money required to produce a specific amount of sales.

Customer defections: The percentage of customers who switch to another brand or supplier.

Customer expectations: Consumer beliefs about the performance of a product based on prior experience and communications.

Customer loyalty: A measure of how often, when selecting from a product class, a customer purchases a particular brand.

Customer satisfaction: A customer's positive, neutral, or negative feeling about the value received from an organization's product in specific use situations.

Customer satisfaction measurement program: An ongoing survey of customers (and competitors' customers) for the purpose of obtaining continuous estimates of satisfaction.

Dynamic quality: Quality that results from a change that makes an existing standard obsolete.

ISO 9001: An inclusive set of standards established by the International Standards Organization (ISO) to ensure that quality requirements are met.

Lifetime value of a customer: The amount of profit a company expects to obtain over the course of the relationship.

Malcolm Baldrige National Quality Award: A program designed to raise quality awareness and practice among U.S. businesses.

Objective assessment of quality: An evaluation of the degree to which a product does what it is supposed to do.

Quality: The degree of excellence of a company's products or services.

Quality function deployment (QFD): A process that builds customer wants and desires into the final product offering.

Reduced cycle time: A TQM activity that helps a company move more rapidly from product inception to final delivery of the product to the marketplace.

Satisfaction ratings: Ratings provided by testing agencies that compare purchase satisfaction with specified brands or with how well products perform.

Service quality: The expected and perceived quality of all of the services an organization offers.

Static quality: Quality that results when individuals or organizations perfect an accepted practice.

Statistical quality control: The use of statistics to isolate and quantify production line problems that may cause product defects.

Subjective assessment of quality: The degree to which a product does what consumers would like it to do.

Supply chain: All the activities that organizations undertake to deliver value to the customer, such as working with suppliers, and distribution through convenient channels.

Total quality management (TQM): An organizational philosophy that helps companies produce goods and services that deliver value to satisfy customers.

References

1. Jessica Mitchell, "Journey to Excellence event in Tulsa to focus on customer service", Journal Record, March 12, 2007, p1 ; Terry R. Bacon and David G. Pugh, "Ritz-Carlton and EMC: The gold standards in operational behavioral differencetiation", Journal of Organizational Excellence, Spring 2004, p61 ; The Ritz-Carlton, www.ritzcarlton.com, visited June 15, 2007; Hoover's Online, "The Ritz-Carlton Hotel Company, LLC," www.hooversonline.com, visited June 19, 2000; "Malcolm Baldrige National Quality Award 1992 Winner: The Ritz-Carlton Hotel Company," Winners Showcase, www.quality.nist.gov, as updated May 26, 1998; www.usatoday.com; Ed Brown, "The Best Business Hotels," Fortune, March 31, 1997, www.fortune.com; Don Peppers and Martha Rogers, "Welcome to the 1:1 Future," Marketing Tools, April–May 1994, www.marketingtools.com; Laura Bly, "A Rush to Democratic South Africa," USA Today, March 25, 1997, www.usatoday.com; William C. Flannagan, "Where Executives Love to Stay," Forbes, September 23, 1996, www.forbes.com; Dave DeWitte, "Ritz-Carlton Hotel Chain Executive Speaks About Customer Service," The Gazette (Cedar Rapids), October 18, 2000, and Michael Lohs, "It Pays to Be in the Know," Business Times (Singapore), July 4, 2000, p. 32.
2. Robert B. Woodruff and Sarah F. Gardial, Know Your Customer (Cambridge, MA: Blackwell Publishers, Inc., 1996), p. 20.
3. Richard A Spreng, American Marketing Association, Conference Proceedings, Chicago: 1999. Vol. 10 pg. 208, 1 pgs
4. Paul Cardis, "Manage Your Stock in Customer Loyalty," Professional Builder, March 2007, 72(3), p.2.; www.pulte.com, Web site visited July 10, 2008.
5. "Happy Shopper," Management Accounting, July 1, 2000, pp. 28–30.
6. "Customer Care Goes End-to-End," Information Week, May 15, 2000, pp. 55–61.
7. Sunil Gupta, Donald R. Lehmann, Jennifer Ames Stuart, "Valuing Customers," Journal of Marketing Research, Vol. 41, Issue 1, February 2004.
8. "We Interrupt This Issue to Remind You That the Internet Is Big," Wired, July 2000, pp. 252–57.
9. http://www.jdpower.com/, Web site visited April 15, 2008.
10. "Beyond Satisfaction," CMA Management, March 2000, pp. 14–15.
11. Clay Carr, Front Customer Service (New York: John Wiley and Sons, 1990), p. 31.
12. www.wholefoodsmarket.com 2007 10-K. Web site visited April 7, 2008.
13. Carr, Front Customer Service, p. 19.
14. www.jdpower.com, Web site visited May 20, 2008.
15. http://www.theacsi.org/, Web site visited April 7, 2008.
16. "Judges Panel of the Malcolm Baldrige National Quality Award," Federal Register, July 21, 2000.
17. The Script for Satisfaction. Joseph Tarnowski. Progressive Grocer; Janurary 2008
18. "It's Party Time for Saturn," Sales and Marketing Management, June 1994.
19. www.harley-davidson.com, Web site visited April 7, 2008.
20. www.jeep.com, Web site visited April 7, 2008.
21. www.levistrauss.com, Web site visited May 20, 2008.
22. "SBC Foundation assists Katrina victims through $1 million in support to American Red Cross", Michigan Chronicle, Sep 21-27, 2005, Vol. 69, Iss. 1; pg. C4.
23. "Do Rewards Really Create Loyalty?" Harvard Business Review, May–June 1995, p. 75.
24. www.starwoodhotels.com/preferredguest/offers/index.htm Web site visited April 7, 2008
25. www.blockbuster.ca, site visited May 20, 2008.

26. "What Price Loyalty", Customer Relationship Management, Mar 2005, Vol. 9, Iss. 3; pg. 14.

27. www.jollibee.com.ph/default.htm, site visited March 6, 2007

28. "Are You in the Minority on Diversity Hiring?," Stores. New York: July 2005 Vol. 87, Iss. 7; pg. 109

29. IBM Systems case studies, www.ibm.com/software/success, site visited July 11, 2007

30. Hitachi Data Systems Supercharges High-performance NAS Platform, Eclipses Competition," Business Wire, New York, February 27, 2007.

31. "Consumer Perceptions of Price, Quality and Value: A Means-End Model and Synthesis of Evidence," Journal of Marketing, July 1988, p. 2; Sandra Vandermerwe, "How Increasing Value to Customers Improves Business Results," Sloan Management Review, Fall 2000, pp. 27–37.

32. Michael R. Czinkote, Masaki Kotabe, and David Mercer, Marketing Management (Cambridge, MA: Blackwell, 1997), p. 273.

33. "FedEx Express Canada Achieves Gold & Platinum CCEOC® Certification In 2007," CRM Today, June 11, 2007.

34. www.cat.com, Web site visited April 7, 2008

35. Malcolm Baldrige National Quality Improvement Act of 1987, report of the Senate Committee on Commerce, Science and Technology on HR 812 (Washington, DC: U.S. Government Printing Office, 1987).

36. Malcome Baldrige National Quality Program, "Criteria for Performance Excellence," 2007, p. 1.

37. www.ritzcarlton.com, last visited April 24, 2007.

38. www.quality.nist.gov/PDF_files/RCHC_Application_Summary.pdf site visited May 12, 2007.

39. "Retailers Rein in Returns" The Detroit News, February 3, 2005.

40. Earl Naumann, Customer Value Toolkit (Boise, ID: Thomson Executive Press, 1994).

41. "Get Sticky with Your Customer," Sales and Marketing Management, May 2000, pp. 26–27. Thomas Lee, "Constraint-Based Ontology Induction from Online Customer Revies," Group Decision and Negotiation Vol. 16, May 2007, p. 255.

The Marketing Gazette:

Jordan K Speer, "ESPRIT's Expanding Enterprise," Apparel, Jun 2007, 48(10), p.14-17; "Starbucks To GO Cashless With Top-Up Loyalty Cards," Caterer & Hotelkeeper, Oct 26-Nov 1, 2006, 196(4448), p.9; Lars Meyer-Waarden, "The Effects of Loyalty Programs on Consumer Lifetime Duration and Share of Wallet," Journal of Retailing, Apr 2007, 83(2), p.223-236; Michael Evans, Jeffrey Schumacher, and Marc Singer, "Keeping the Store," Customer Relationship Management, Feb 2007, 11(2), p.48; "Retail Week Loyalty Card Survey", May 19-26, 2006, http://www.icmresearch.co.uk/reviews/2006/RW%20May/Retail%20 Week.asp, website visited June 15, 2007.

CASE 7

J.D. Power and Associates

It's not uncommon to hear companies brag about their J.D. Power and Associates award for best in quality or service but what is J.D. Power and why our it's ranking's so important to companies? J.D. Power and Associates is a global marketing information company that administers independent and unbiased surveys of customer satisfaction, product quality and buyer behavior. Founded in 1968 by J.D. Power III, the firm's services include industry-wide studies, commissioned studies, media studies, forecasting, training, customer satisfaction consulting and business operations analyses. J.D. Power and Associates employs more than 750 professional analysts, statisticians, economists and other consumer behavior experts that work for companies across the globe in locations such as India, Japan, South Africa, France and the United States.

Perhaps best known for its work in the automotive industry, J.D. Power and Associates has expanded to other industries including healthcare, homebuilding, consumer electronics and financial services. It conducts research based on responses from millions of consumers and business customers and publicly announces the results. It also funds all of the research in order to deliver the most unbiased results possible. J.D. Power and Associates has established industry benchmarks for measuring and tracking quality and customer satisfaction. "Understanding customer data and turning it into usable information is challenging, primarily because quality and customer satisfaction mean different things to different people. Our clients leverage our proven benchmark standards and research expertise to support their business success," said J.D. Power and Associates Founder, J.D. Power III.

As one of the most trusted sources on the quality of new vehicles, consumers often use the J.D. Power and Associates Initial Quality Study as a tool when purchasing a new car or truck. However, J.D. Power revealed after conducting a study that automobile buyers found many problems in new vehicles, especially when it comes to newly introduced technology, that has been overlook in its previous annual studies. The result—J.D. Power decided to get a quality update of its own. "We found that in fact there were quite a few problems that customers reported that we had not made a special focus on in the past," said Joe Ivers, Executive Director of Quality and Customer Satisfaction with J.D. Power. So J.D. Power expanded its Initial Quality Survey to include 60 percent more questions. Its automotive research goes beyond the in-depth Initial Quality Study of new-vehicles. J.D. Power also examines the complete vehicle ownership process from the shopping experience to initial quality, service satisfaction, durability and brand loyalty.

Its research findings not only identify problems, it also isolates the cause and makes recommendations for improvements. And when J.D. Power makes a recommendation, the automakers listen. It wasn't long ago that U.S. automakers ranked far behind their Japanese competitors in quality. Many Americans began buying brands such at Honda and Toyota. By undertaking problems exposed by J.D.'s Initial Quality Survey, domestic automakers significantly narrowed the gap and improved processes in design, engineering and manufacturing. Recently, General Motors' vehicles secured five of 18 top-quality awards in the Initial Quality Study, and GM swept the awards for best quality vehicle assembly plants in North and South America. Jim Wiemels, Vice President of Manufacturing and Engineering at General Motors said, "GM's determination to lead the industry on quality in each of our vehicle segments has produced results that we are truly proud of. Most importantly, we are satisfying customers coast to coast and around the world. But, we're also gratified that industry studies conducted by J.D. Power and other independent research companies are verifying the levels that GM quality is attaining today."

Recently, J.D. Power developed the "Alternative Powertrain Study (APS)" to list environmentally friendly vehicles. The study combines U.S. Environmental Protection Agency information with voice-of-the-customer data related to fuel economy, air pollution and greenhouse gasses to rank vehicles. The most recent APS study was dominated by hybrid innovators Honda and Toyota. "High gas prices, coupled with consumers becoming more familiar with alternative powertrain technology, are definitely increasing consumer interest in hybrids and flexible fuels," said Mike Marshall, director of automotive emerging technologies at J.D. Power and Associates.

It is clear that due to the work of J.D. Power and Associates, companies in a wide-range of fields must continually strive to achieve the highest quality product possible and increase customer satisfaction in order to become or remain industry leaders. J.D. Power III stated, "To survive and, more importantly, to thrive in today's business environment, companies must become increasingly sophisticated at integrating the voice of the customer into their daily opera-

tions. Organizations that are fast and nimble enough to truly understand and respond to the needs of their customers will enjoy a greater advantage now than ever before."

1) In this chapter, requirements for creating and delivering customer value were discussed. How does J.D. Power and Associates help companies meet those requirements?

2) The increasing globalization of companies creates challenges in satisfying the tastes and preferences of diverse groups. Define metrics that J.D. Power and Associates could use to provide companies with superior satisfaction ratings for global consumers.

Sources: Michael Ellis, "Consumers to get more details on car quality: Study expands to gadgets, design," Knight Ridder Tribune Business News, Washington, May 11, 2006. pg. 1; General Motors Corp. at JPMorgan Harbour Auto Conference, Final Fair Disclosure Wire, Waltham, August 7, 2006; www.jdpower.com/corporate/automotive/ site visited July 12, 2007; www.jdpower.com/corporate/about/over-view, site visited July 12, 2007.

CHAPTER 8

Segmentation, Targeting & Positioning

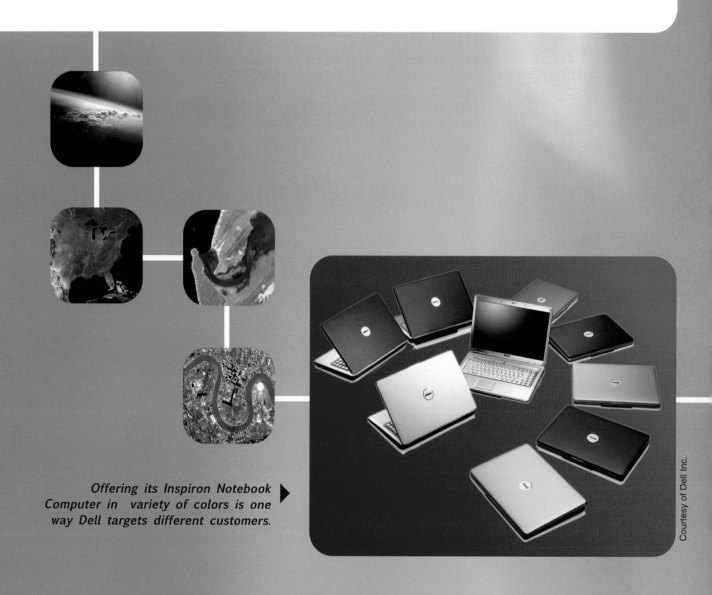

Offering its Inspiron Notebook
Computer in variety of colors is one
way Dell targets different customers.

Courtesy of Dell Inc.

Learning Objectives

1. Understand the advantages of target marketing and how it differs from mass marketing and product differentiation.

2. Describe how to do market segmentation and select target markets.

3. Explore three basic target marketing strategies: undifferentiated, differentiated, and concentrated marketing.

4. Know how to do positioning and describe several approaches marketers use to create valuable, lasting images of their products.

Small businesses are big business for Dell Computer, a leading personal computer company in the United States. Michael Dell was a premed student when he started selling PCs and components from his dorm room. He dropped out of college when monthly sales topped $80,000 and founded Dell Computer to sell PCs and related equipment to consumers and businesses via direct marketing. Now the company, based in Austin, Texas, employs 88,100 worldwide and uses the Internet to ring up half of its $57.5 billion in annual sales. In addition to desktop PCs, Dell sells high-powered workstations, notebook computers, servers for network use, and data storage systems.

Michael Dell and his team understand that different kinds of customers have different computing requirements. For example, families buy lower-priced, basic PCs for daily household needs such as homework and entertainment, whereas corporations need more sophisticated workstations for computer-aided design and other tasks. Similarly, an entrepreneur with a single webpage does not need the high-end server that a large hospital requires to power its sprawling, multiuser Web site. With these differing needs in mind, Dell's marketers use geographic, demographic, and behavioristic variables to segment the consumer and organizational markets for computers and servers.

Using the geographic variable of national boundaries, Dell has segmented the world market and created product offerings sold through Web sites for dozens of countries. Each country's Web site, presented in the local language, features hardware, software, services, and online content specifically geared to that market's interests and requirements. In addition, Dell divides its overall market into consumer, business, government, and institutional segments. The consumer segment, which Dell calls "home and home office," consists of consumers who buy for personal and home-office use. This is the segment Michael Dell originally targeted during his college days, and it remains both lucrative and highly competitive.

In June 2007, Dell departed from its strictly direct to customer sales approach and began selling its computers at Wal-Mart. Since then, Dell has partnered with retailers to sell its products at more than 10,000 locations worldwide, including Best Buy and Staples. This new strategy has been implemented in response to the company losing market share to competitor HP who recently overtook Dell as the market leader.

Dell launched its IdeaStorm Web site in 2007. This Web community allows Dell users to post technological ideas and suggestions which are reviewed and commented on by site moderators and other users. Since its birth, IdeaStorm has generated more than 9,000 ideas and has provided Dell with a new, important channel for customer feedback.

Within the business segment, Dell uses company demographics and product orientation to define specific customer groups. These customers are also invited to set up Premier Pages, Web pages they can customize for purchasing and tracking orders from Dell. To stay abreast of this segment's unique needs, Dell periodically brings small business owners to Austin for meetings with top management and factory tours. It also sends the Dell on Wheels mobile showroom to bring the latest technology to small business customers in dozens of cities across the United States. During the day, the Dell salespeople show off their state-of-the-art hardware and software in the showroom, then talk bits and bytes with small business customers over dinner in the evening.

Dell targets the prized big business segment—customers whose annual hardware purchases may total millions of dollars—with a slightly different marketing mix. Customized Premier Pages are an even more important part of the marketing mix for this segment. Ford, for example, had Dell set up its Premier Page so employees can place and track online orders for computers, servers, and other Dell equipment built to the automaker's specifications. Its Premier Page also gives Ford employees access to customized technical

support services when they need help installing or troubleshooting Dell products.

Other segments targeted by Dell are the health care industry, government agencies, education, and e-commerce. Dell has forged alliances with a number of specialized suppliers to offer a well-rounded menu of goods and services to large hospitals for staff and administrative use. Within the government market, Dell targets federal government agencies (in the United States and other countries) separately from state and local government agencies. Within the education market, Dell targets K-to-12 schools and faculty members separately from administrators, faculty, and students of colleges and universities. Within the world of e-commerce, Dell targets Internet service providers separately from companies that need goods and services for Web-based sales.[1]

THE CONCEPT OF SEGMENTATION, TARGETING, AND POSITIONING

In the early days, the philosophy of General Motors (GM) was "a different auto for every need." At that time, each GM division focused its creative energies and economic might on satisfying loyal customers in separate market segments. They connected with customers by targeting clearly designated groups of buyers defined primarily by social class. Today, GM's 12 lines of cars and trucks (Chevrolet, Pontiac, Buick, Cadillac, GMC, Saturn, Hummer, Saab, Holden, Opel, Vauxhaul) have several models each. In fact, GM markets over 80 different models of both cars and trucks.[2] When GM was founded, the members of each American social class had a good deal of upward mobility and GM had a brand targeted at each class. Typically, a young family might buy a Chevy, followed by a Pontiac. Years later, a Buick or Oldsmobile would be purchased. Finally, as a mark of economic accomplishment came the ultimate in status and prestige—a Cadillac. America is no longer defined largely by social class, so although the relative costs of GM models still reflect, to some degree, the pricing hierarchy of previous years, their target markets are vastly different.

Why would strong companies such as General Motors and Procter & Gamble develop so many brands? Among other products, Procter & Gamble (P&G) markets 10 laundry detergents, six bar soaps, 10 shampoos, four types of dishwashing soaps, and five oral care brands.[3] How many of them can you name?[4] Do these compete with one another or primarily take on rival brands? The answer is that each brand is designed for a different market segment. A market segment is a homogeneous group of customers with similar needs, wants, values, and buying behavior. Each segment is an arena for competition. Both GM and P&G have a tradition of building marketing strategies around strong brands that match the uniqueness of diverse segments. And you can bet there's some competition among the organization's own products, but that's minor in comparison to other brands. The approach has worked well—GM and P&G are the leaders.

Through **segmentation**, the market can be divided into several groups of people with similar characteristics. Each segment will vary in size and opportunity. Because it may be difficult to appeal successfully to each segment, companies select certain ones for emphasis and try to satisfy them more than competitors, which is called **target marketing**. For example, Great Lakes Crossings, an outlet mall with many entertainment destinations was opened in Auburn Hills, Michigan. The mall appeals to the entire family with stores such as Bass Pro Shop's Outdoor World and Neiman Marcus LAST Call. In addition to the shopping, the mall has many family-oriented entertainment options including Game Works, a high-tech indoor playground, Star Theatres, and Jeepers, an indoor amusement park and restaurant. It is targeting value-conscious families who want to make shopping an experience enjoyed by all members.

Positioning means creating an image, reputation, or perception in the minds of consumers about the organization or its products relative to competition. The company appeals to customers in the target segments by adjusting products, prices, promotional campaigns, service, and distribution channels in a way consistent with its

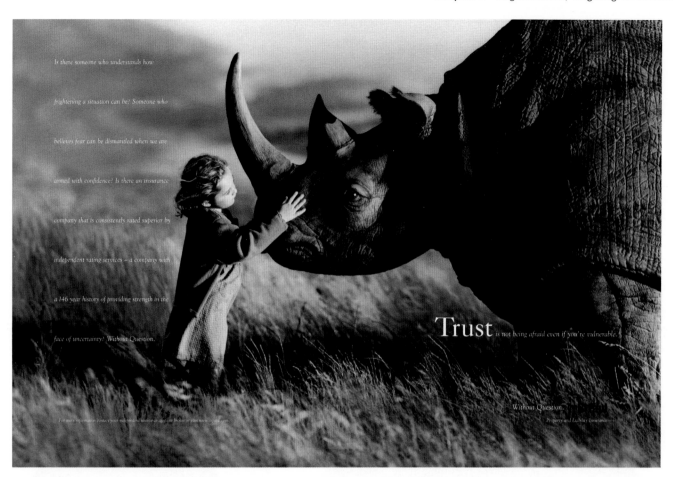

Is there someone who understands how

frightening a situation can be? Someone who

believes fear can be dismantled when we are

armed with confidence? Is there an insurance

company that is consistently rated superior by

independent rating services — a company with

a 146 year history of providing strength in the

face of uncertainty? Without Question.

Trust *is not being afraid even if you're vulnerable.*

Without Question.

Property and Liability Insurance

This ad shows St. Paul's positioning based on "Trust."

positioning strategy. Great Lakes Crossing has identified a segment of value-conscious families and positioned itself by creating a total entertainment experience for the entire family in its 200 stores and attractions.[5]

Segmentation, targeting, and positioning give organizations the means to connect with customers by identifying and understanding their characteristics, by focusing resources to meet their needs and wants, and by establishing how customers will view the organization. Let us say a company simply compiles data on consumers, averages them, and tries to develop one brand that appeals to the average consumer. In the U.S. marketplace alone, there are over 300 million people.[6] You can find the average for certain demographic characteristics—age, gender, income, location, and so forth—but what about ethnic origin, home life, or taste in music, clothing, and food? The "average" American represents few, if any, real people. Efforts to connect with this mythical average consumer probably wouldn't have appeal for any customer. Thus, marketers generally cannot use averages. Instead, they use segmentation, targeting, and positioning to define unique consumer groups, select those they wish to serve, and then integrate the marketing mix to establish a unified image of the product relative to the competition.

To be a leader, companies know that they must connect with customers by identifying, selecting, and relating to them in highly innovative ways. That's why segmentation, targeting, and positioning— three sequential stages summarized in Figure 8.1—are critical. You simply can't be a leading-edge marketer without these steps. The activities required to accomplish each stage are described in the sections that follow. Under market segmentation, we include descriptions of mass marketing and prod-

Marketing Vocabulary

MARKET SEGMENT
A homogeneous group with similar needs, wants, values, and buying behavior.

SEGMENTATION
Division of a market into homogeneous groups with similar needs, wants, values, and buying behavior.

TARGET MARKETING
The selection of specific homogeneous groups (segments) of potential customers for emphasis.

POSITIONING
Creating an image or perception in the minds of consumers about the organization or its products relative to the competition.

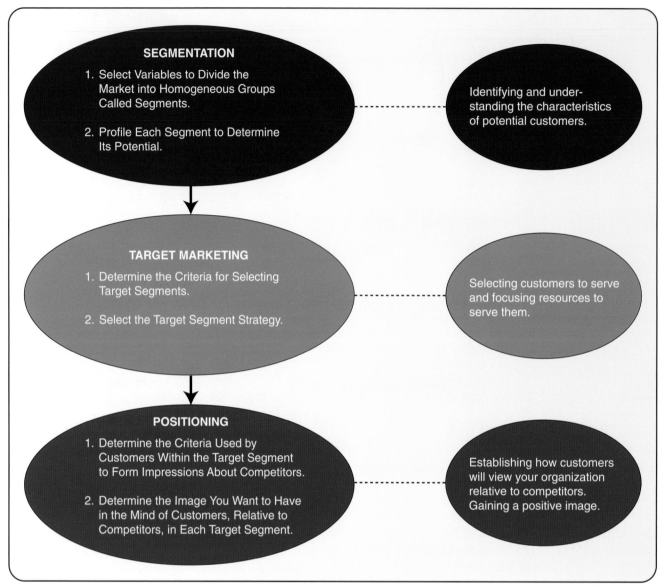

Figure 8.1   Connecting with Customers by Identifying, Selecting, and Relating to Them

uct differentiation as general marketing approaches that are contrasted with the more preferred segmentation methods. We also introduce several ways to identify diverse market segments. The section on target marketing describes how to select targets and focus resources where they will accomplish the most. The last section looks at positioning. It also describes how to reposition when things change.

MARKET SEGMENTATION

Today most leading-edge companies take great care to focus on specific market segments. It is among the most powerful weapons in the marketing arsenal. Competitors can leave themselves open to attack when their products or services lump together groups of customers with different needs or wants. Identifying key segments offers unique opportunities for innovations based on meeting specific

customers' needs more precisely.[7] Historically, there has been a movement from mass marketing, to product differentiation, to market segmentation, targeting, and positioning. In the following sections you'll explore how these approaches differ.

SEGMENTATION VERSUS MASS MARKETING

We know from Chapter 1 that many companies once pursued mass marketing, which is the mass distribution and mass promotion of the mass product to all potential customers. The objective of mass marketing is to reach as many people as possible with the same marketing approach. Coca-Cola, introduced in 1886, pioneered this strategy, and was successful in reaching most consumers with the same product formula, price, promotion, and distribution strategy. Today, however, Coca-Cola's success depends on recognizing the tremendous diversity of the

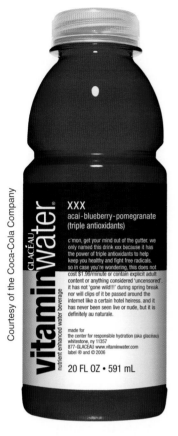

market. In an effort to expand its presence in the water and energy drink markets, Coke acquired Glaceau, maker of the popular Vitaminwater and Vitaminenergy, in 2007 in a deal valued at more than $4 billion.[8]

Although mass marketing was useful decades ago, competition that appeals to consumer diversity prevents this from being a viable strategy for most organizations to use today. While tools are constantly being developed that can reach the mass markets, these tools must be used carefully to get the greatest benefit. Today about 37 percent of all Americans own an MP3 player and there are over 166 million wireless subscribers in the United States alone, while the global wireless market is has about two billion subscribers. According to a recent study from ABI Research, by 2011, advertising to mobile subscribers will reach $19 billion in the U.S.[9] One study estimates that about 90 percent of all major brands will be attempting to reach consumers with this medium and very shortly, for many, mobile devices will be preferred ways to browse the Web, shop and read books. [10] Certainly marketing to this large number of people provides an opportunity for mass marketing as well as the use of segmentation. If marketers simply tried to reach all of these users in the same way, this could be construed as mass marketing. However, what makes it interesting is that this wireless group of consumers may have many unique qualities. These qualities can be organized into specific segments that can be addressed with varying approaches.

Be sure not to confuse mass customization, discussed in chapter 1, with mass marketing. They have nothing in common except the word "mass." Later in this chapter we will see that mass customization is a form of target marketing that takes advantage of many technologies to uniquely serve customers.

SEGMENTATION VERSUS PRODUCT DIFFERENTIATION

Eventually, companies realized that mass marketing didn't provide enough variety and they began to follow a product differentiation strategy. **Product differentiation** makes a product appear unique relative to others, whether produced by the same company or the competition. This uniqueness is then used as a major factor in appealing to customers. The belief is that by offering choices, the company will attract more of the mass market. Notice that product differentiation implies a recognition that consumers may seek variety. But unlike market segmentation, the leading dynamic is a difference in the product, not in buyer characteristics. The pain reliever market is dominated by product differentiation. Aspirin comes in plain formula or with caffeine, buffered or not, with and without sleep aids, with or without a cold remedy, and in standard or extra strength. You can also find it in caplet, liquid, tablet, chewing gum, or capsule form, coated or noncoated, flavored or not. The objective is to offer an aspirin for every preference imaginable. And hundreds of millions of dollars are spent each year by companies such as Bayer to promote its different product configurations.

It is important to keep the distinction between product differences and market segments in mind. Market segments should not be defined by product names or characteristics. Markets are made up of people and organizations. Consequently, market segments are described according to their characteristics, not according to the products they buy. Misunderstanding this distinction is a common and often deadly flaw for the marketing strategist. For example, a marketing consultant once asked the chief engineer of an air-conditioning manufacturer to describe the company's target segments. The engineer responded with product categories: heavy, medium, and light-duty units. When asked questions about the characteristics of current and potential buyers, the engineer had little knowledge. The consultant knew immediately that this client did not fully understand market segmentation, a key reason customers were buying fewer of the engineer's new-product introductions. When executives equate product categories with market segments, they tend to focus attention on what they want to make, which may not meet customer requirements. The result is often products that please the people who make them but disappoint customers.

SEGMENTATION VARIABLES

The total market is **heterogeneous,** meaning it has many types of buyers. Market segmentation divides the total mar-

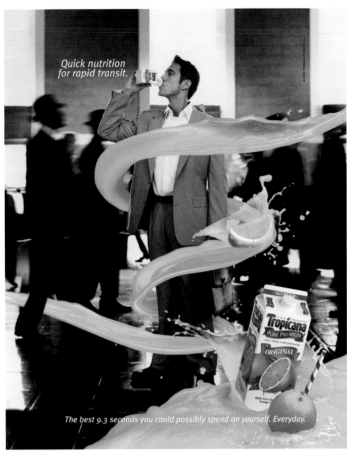

Quick nutrition for rapid transit.

The best 9.3 seconds you could possibly spend on yourself. Everyday.

Tropicana strives to differentiate each of its varieties of juices.

ket into **homogeneous** subgroups or clusters with similar characteristics. We then can inspect each subgroup in greater detail. Without a well-focused picture of the market, it's virtually impossible to create a powerful marketing strategy. Essentially, segmentation allows marketers to focus on relevant aspects of potential buyers. It's a critical step in connecting with customers.

How is segmentation done? First, the marketer must select a way to categorize potential customers into subgroups. A **segmentation variable** is any descriptive characteristic that helps separate all potential purchasers into groups. Examples include gender, age, and income. Variables are then subdivided into categories. For example, within the gender variable, the two categories are male and female. Categories may be very broadly or very narrowly defined. Income can be classified generally as low, moderate, and high, or more specifically as, for example, up to $10,000, $10,001 to $30,000, $30,001 to $50,000, $50,001 to $70,000, and above $70,000.

Think about how colleges segment students for recruiting and admissions. Like companies, they do this to gain a better understanding of potential customers. At the most basic level, the segmentation variables are grade point average in

high school, SAT or ACT scores, and high school class rank. These variables can be subdivided into categories, as shown in Figure 8.2. The categories then can be grouped together in various ways to form several market segments, which often are named descriptively. For example, the market segment in the third categories column of Figure 8.2 might be called the "cream of the crop." Or students with above average SAT/ACT scores but in the bottom of their class and with a low GPA might be the "underachiever" market segment.

Most colleges add other variables, and these can dramatically change the segmentation structure. For example, what seems to be a fairly uniform market turns out to be a lot of segments. From our example in Figure 8.2, 27 market segments emerge (3 GPA categories, 3 SAT/ACT categories, 3 class rank categories). Adding just two residence categories (in and out of state) would produce 54 segments.

Variables need to be chosen with care because each segment must meet certain criteria in order to be useful to a marketer. Figure 8.3 outlines guidelines for effective market segmentation. Segmentation typically is based on geographic, demographic, diversity, psychographic, and behavioristic factors and benefits sought. Figure 8.4 lists the variables and categories commonly used to segment. All of these apply to consumer markets. Additional variables and categories that are primarily useful to segment business markets are provided in chapter 6 on B2B marketing.

Geographic Segmentation One of the most common ways to analyze a market is by geography. It can reveal some interesting facts. For example, consider this odd statistic about the difference in the size of men's suits. In New York the most typical size is 42 regular; in Paris, 40 regular; in San Francisco, 38 regular; and in Chicago, a strapping 44 long.[11]

Segmentation by city is often used by global companies. Coke knows that soft-drink consumption relates to population size. With the exception of New York City and Los Angeles, all metropolitan areas of more than 10 million are located outside the United States. So it's no mystery why Coke markets globally. A city's population size alone doesn't always provide enough segmentation information, so marketers think about other factors. Some metropolitan areas are known for their industry expertise:

Variable	Categories		
High School GPA	Below 2.0	2.0–3.5	3.6–4.0
SAT/ACT Score	Below average	Average	Above average
High School Class Rank	Lowest 25%	Middle 50%	Top 25%

Figure 8.2 Segmenting the College Market.

Effective Market Segmentation

→ Members should have similar needs, wants, and preferences, because these are what marketers want to understand and influence.

→ Members should have similar information-gathering and media usage patterns, because these allow marketers to communicate with the segment.

→ Members should have similar shopping and buying patterns, because marketers then can find efficient places to sell and service their products.

→ The number of members should be large, because marketers need to generate a profit.

→ Data about the segments should be available, because marketers need to know about customers in order to build marketing strategies.

Figure 8.3 Effective Market Segmentation

Marketing Vocabulary

HOMOGENEOUS GROUP
Buyers with similar characteristics.

SEGMENTATION VARIABLE
Any distinguished market factor that can vary, such as gender, age or income.

GEODEMOGRAPHY
Combining geographic information with demographics, to identity segments with common consumption patterns.

ZIP CODE SEGMENTATION
Division of a market into specific geographic locations based on the demographic makeup of the zip code area.

In Hollywood it's movies; in Silicon Valley, computer software; and in Philadelphia, pharmaceuticals. Auto components suppliers, such as Bosch and Eaton Corporation, know that virtually all major buying decisions are made in fewer than 20 cities located in a handful of countries. A presence in Stuttgart, Detroit, Los Angeles, Wiesbaden, Paris, Osaka, and Seoul gives the supplier substantial global coverage.

Computer techniques allow researchers to cluster consumers in groups based on numerous variables. Using a small number of variables to explain consumer purchases in product categories, organizations develop site strategies for grocery stores, drugstores, department stores, big-box retailers, and apparel companies. An understanding of segments in regions is used to adjust merchandising and identify local challenges to customize product offerings.[12]

Geodemography combines geographic information with data on consumer expenditures and demographics to identify segments with common consumption patterns. A geographic information system (GIS) employs computer mapping to identify targets. It uses data from the Bureau of the Census, which provides computerized street maps that contain economic and population data per city block. For a relatively low price you can buy maps and data covering the entire United States. For considerably less, you can buy information for a smaller region of the country. Staples uses GIS data to carefully consider more than 5,000 sites a year for future store locations. The process begins with a real estate model that analyzes thirty factors that affect site selection. These factors include the presence of competitors and the demographics of the local consumers for segmentation purposes. This information is critical to the success of the corporation because one failed store can cost more than $1 million in losses.[13]

According to Michael Marvin, an executive at MapInfo Corporation, with GIS technology, "Quaker Oats found that 80 percent of their ethnic customers lived in 18 of their 55 sales territories."[14] The information allows Quaker to develop highly targeted segment strategies. Many colleges and universities are making use of this type of data to better target prospective students. Information is gathered from questionnaires on the SAT and ACT exams, as well as from former students from the different high schools. Profiles are created and colleges and universities can then target prospective students based on characteristics such as religion, preferred major, and computer savvy.[15]

Zip code segmentation divides the market according to the demographic makeup of the zip code area. Claritas, Inc is a leader in the use of zip codes for consumer segmentation. It uses many customer characteristics to describe geographic locations even deep within zip codes in more specific neighborhoods and in some cases to individual households. As the population shifts, Claritas and other similar firms adjust their data and the descriptive names they give to specific segments. For example the most important city residents no longer are the older, mostly white "Urban Gold Coast" people in neighborhoods like Chicago's Lakeshore Drive and Boston's Beacon Hill. Instead, young, tech-savvy, highly educated singles and couples are driving the vitality of cities and live in places like sections of Chicago's Lincoln Park. These young professionals are reading fewer newspapers and magazines but going online, so they are no longer called the "Young Literati." Now, they're called the "Young Digerati." According to Claritas the three most affluent population segments are suburban homeowners: couples age 45 and older ("Upper Crust"), middle-age executives with children ("Blue Blood Estates") and mid-

	Variable	Examples of Categories
Geographic	World region	Pacific Rim, Europe, North America
	Economic stage	Advanced, developing, subsistence
	Nation	U.S., England, Japan, Mexico
	City	Tokyo, Paris, Mexico City
	City size and density	Large and dense, small and spread out, suburban, rural
	Region	New England, Mid-Atlantic, South Atlantic, East South Central, Midwest, Mountain Pacific
	Climate	Northern Equator, Southern Equator
	Zip Code	10001, 10002, etc.
Demographic	Gender	Female, male
	Age	1–5, 6–11, 12–19, 20–34, 35–49, 50–64, 65–72, 721
	Income	Poverty, up to $15,000, up to $20,000, up to $30,0000, up to $50,000, up to $100,000, $100,0001
	Family size	1, 2, 3, 4, 5, 6
	Family life cycle	Young single, young married no children, young married with children (under 6), young married with children (over 6), older married full nest, older married empty nest, retired, middle-aged, single, divorced, sole survivor
	Occupation	Unemployed, homemaker, student, retired, clerical, blue collar, white collar, professional, proprietor
	Education	Grade school (or less), some high school, high school graduate, some college, college graduate, postgraduate degree
Diversity	Religion	Protestant, Catholic, Jewish, Muslim
	Race	Anglo, African, Asian, Hispanic, Native American
	Social class	Lower-lower, upper-lower, lower-middle (working class),middle, upper-middle, lower-upper, upper-upper
Psychographic	Lifestyle	Actualizer, Fulfilled, Achiever, Experiencer, Believer, Striver, Maker, Struggler
	Personality	Compliant, aggressive, detached, sensory, intuitive, thinking, feeling
Behavioristic	Readiness	Unaware, aware, interested, knowledgeable, desirous, intend to buy, trial
	Ability and experience	None, novice, expert, professional, nonuser, first-time user, regular user, former user
	Loyalty	Switcher, moderate, high
	Media and shopping habits	Magazine subscriber, cable user, mall, convenience stores
	Usage	Daily, weekly, monthly
	Rates	Heavy, medium, light
Benefit Sought	Delivery	Convenience, speed, flexibility
	Service	No questions asked returns
	Price	Low, medium, high

Figure 8.4 Ways to Segment Consumer Markets
Source: Adapted from Philip Kotler, Marketing Management: Analysis, Planning, Implementation, and Control, 12th ed. ©2007. Adapted by permission of Prentice Hall, Inc., Upper Saddle River, NJ.

dle-age couples, often entrepreneurs ("Movers & Shakers"). These people are mostly white, but some are Asians. Claritas can tell you specifically which geographies, by zip codes, contain each market segment.[16] The make-up of families by zip-code and close to home geographic segmentation offers segmentation opportunities for nearly every type of consumer marketer.

Several companies adjust messages and other tactics to reflect zip code differences. EProject.com uses zip code data to tailor its online radio advertisements to specific groups. For example, an 18-year-old female in Philadelphia might hear an ad for Gap at her local mall while a 25-year-old male in Boston hears a pitch for a J.Crew store down his block. This custom tailoring of advertisements based on zip codes produces a much more effective advertising campaign for eProject.com's clients.[17]

If you need to get even more specific, similar methods can be used to identify customers by city block based on street addresses. The LEXIS®-NEXIS® electronic information database now provides a service called REZIDE, which segments customers by any variable the user requests (zip code, area code, city, and so forth) and supplies the information electronically.

Demographic Segmentation

Characteristics such as gender, family life cycle, household type, and income are used in **demographic segmentation**. This type of information is readily available. Demographics are very useful in categorizing different tastes and preferences. An added benefit is that it's relatively easy to project the composition and size of demographic segments for the next five, 10, or even 15 years. Consequently, this kind of segmentation is an excellent tool for long-range strategic planning as well as short-term marketing.

Segmentation by Gender The buying behavior of men and women is unique. Some of this uniqueness can be attributed to the roles each performs. Marketers need to be able to adapt their techniques in order to reach one particular gender. NikeWomen does just that - women can go to NikeWomen.com, select a language and find the closest place that sells NikeWomen products. Users can also visit NIKEiD to design a custom Nike product.[18] Nike is opening Nikewomen stores in many cities around the world. By focusing on the specific values and lifestyles that women have, marketers can more effectively reach an entire gender of the population. Women are, in many ways, a prime segment for thousands of products. Even in early years auto companies targeted women. A 1907 ad for a Franklin showed women in long skirts behind the wheel and the caption "Notice how much room there is to get in or out of the driver's side." In 1930 Chrysler research found women to be a "potent factor" in 75 percent of new car purchases, and themes focusing on them were credited with raising company sales by 33 percent. By 1948, all major automakers were advertising in Women's Home Companion, the number-one magazine targeted at women. The issue has never been whether to segment by gender—only how to address women. Chrysler formed a Women's Advisory Committee composed of 30 women from disciplines such as finance, manufacturing, and marketing. The company pioneered driver's side sliding doors and integrative child seats on its minivan.

Men are also a unique segment. Traditional products include sports tickets, hunting and fishing equipment, and auto supplies. Sometimes men buy products traditionally sold to women. Market researcher Datamonitor expects the men's grooming market to reach $14 billion in the United States by 2008.[19] A survey conducted by WSL Research showed that among men ages 18-55, 55 percent stated that they currently buy some skin care products,

This Gillette product is made for middle-class young women.

and 16 percent said they were spending more than they did the proceeding year.[20] The growth in these markets is attributed to a redefinition of masculinity and mens concern for their appearance. Anthony is a cleansing facial bar for men and part of the price for each purchase goes to fight the devastating male disease, prostate cancer.[21]

Segmentation by Family Life Cycle Families pass through stages, from young single adults, to marriage, to childbearing, to later life. The next chapter describes the specific categories in depth. For now, it is important to note that these family stages are excellent segmentation categories. Several of the wireless service providers are marketing second and third wireless phones to families. They are targeting parents with teens in particular. Being able to stay in touch with their children and knowing where they are is comforting to parents. But cell phones are used for much more than keeping in touch with parents. According to a study by Context, a company that uses anthropologists to study consumer trends, the cell phone has become a primary mode of socializing for teens and they will often avoid contact with peers that don't have cell phones. "Next time a teenager says, 'Mom if I don't have a phone,' or 'Dad, if I don't have a phone, I'm going to be a nobody,' they are being serious," said Robbie Blinkoff, Context's principal anthropologist.[22] Organic food manufacturers are also seeing the importance of targeting health-conscious parents by offering "fun" healthy meals for children.

These companies target parents of babies, in hopes of keeping them as the children mature. Marketers like the Hain Celestial Group, of Melville, N.Y., hope that parents who start their infants on Earth's Best baby food will stick with Hain brands

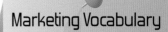

Marketing Vocabulary

<u>DEMOGRAPHIC SEGMENTATION</u>
Division of the market according to such characteristics as gender, family life cycle, household type, and income.

through the childhood years, including Arthur cookies and Earth's Best whole-grain bars. Freemont, Michigan-based Gerber's organic Tender Harvest line recently added "first foods" in single flavors and "third foods" in toddler textures. Both Tender Harvest and Earth's Best are free of genetically modified ingredients.And Fran's Healthy Helpings, of Burlingame, Calif., positions its Dino Chicken Chompers and Twinkle Star Fish in the gap between healthy products that kids deem yucky and kid-oriented products full of additives, fat and sodium.[23] By directing attention specifically to families, these companies have gained leadership in this important segment.

Segmentation by Age Age cohorts are people of similar age and life experience. Heroes, music, and even economic times are somewhat unique for each generation. Tastes, preferences, and product choices reflect those differences. Other generational similarities include physical capacity and earning power. You've probably heard of baby boomers, and baby busters. Figure 8.5 describes various age cohorts frequently discussed today.

In 2006 the baby boomers, the largest generation, began to turn 60 years old. Some of the notable personalities in this group include Donald Trump, Sylvester Stallone, and Presidents George W. Bush and Bill Clinton. Approximately 8000 people turn 60 each day or about 330 each hour. There are currently about 78 million baby boomers and approximately 60 million will still be living in 2030. The precise year the baby boomers began is debatable, but is generally estimated to be about 1946, when WWII had ended and post war prosperity began with troops returning home from the war. Population grew at an increasing rate, creating a large number of consumers with increasing incomes and standards of living.[24]

People with higher spending power, born before World War II, are sometimes called WOOFS (Well-Off Older Folks). This age cohort is often the target of major marketers. JC Penney has a clothing line called Easy Dressing, which uses velcro fasteners instead of buttons and zippers. Barnes & Noble carries large-print paperbacks, and travel agencies market special trips for the elderly.

As for Gen X, the baby busters, their purchasing power will peak about the time the boomers retire. A survey of 3,000 U.S. citizens has shown that Generation X has done a much better job saving for retirement at a much earlier age. Part of this could be attributed to their lack of confidence in the social security system. Compared to 58 percent of baby boomers, 75 percent of Generation Xers believe that most of their retirement will come from sources other than social security, such as savings and 401(k) plans.[25] Social security payments made over the years by baby boomers were not invested for them. These payments were used to pay benefits to cur-

rent social security recipients, so little of what they actually paid will remain when they retire. That issue is spurring efforts to change the social security system in the United States. Generation X-ers have a lower net worth at the same stage in life than their parents had at the same age. Because of income limitations, this generation stays home more and spends less.[26] As the boomers retire, there is concern that the more frugal busters will consume less, and will be burdened by the need to support the aging boomers, who will require retirement subsidies and help with health care.

Generation Y, sometimes referred to as Millenials, were born since the early 1980's. These people are young, smart and sometimes brash. They come to work wearing flip-flops and listen to iPods at their desks, according to USA Today.[27] Members of this generation include Britney Spears, Shawn White, Alicia Keys and perhaps you. Research suggests that Generation Y people get involved in social and civic issues, such as education, poverty and the environment. Thanks to the Internet this group is very aware of global issues.[28]

Generation Y's likely grew up fairly affluent or witnessed affluence on televisions and in the movies. They are aware of huge incomes of athletes, some executives and coaches. Perhaps the biggest difference with this generation is that it grew up with technology and feels very comfortable around it.[29] Consequently, marketers often

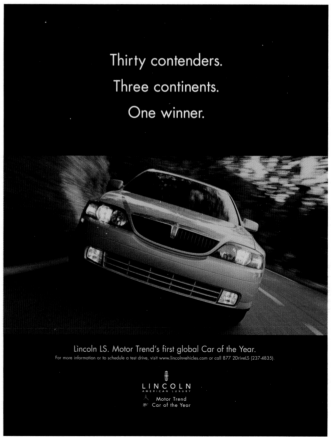

Lincoln targets the baby boomers market segment.

Cohort	Age in 2007	Approximate Average Age Today	Factors
Depression	86 - 95	90	Frugal - Came through hard times
World War II (Sometimes called the Greatest Generation)	80 - 85	83	Fought in WWII - Patriotic
War & Post War	62 - 79	70	Experienced optimism from post-war prosperity
Baby Boomers Leading Edge Generation Jones	53 - 61 42 - 52	57 47	Population explosion group Vietnam War Energy crisis
Generation X (Baby Busters)	31 - 41	36	Poorer economic times AIDs awarness
Generation Y (Millenials)	30 & Under	20	Economic prosperity, Internet generation

Figure 8.5   Geoffrey E. Meredith, Charles D. Schewe & Janice Karlovich, "Defining Markets, Defining Moments: America's 7 Generational Cohorts, Their Shared Experiences, and Why Businesses Should Care," Wiley; 1st edition, December 15, 2001.

connect with this segment through web-based media.

The buying power of the teen segment has seen steady increases over the past decade. JupiterResearch reports that teenagers spent over $158 billion in 2005 and are expected to spend $205 billion in 2008.[30] Marketers are recognizing the importance of targeting this young savvy group of consumers, a segment that was largely ignored in the past.[31] And they're spending their money online. About 80 percent of online teens age 12-17 visit retail sites. This represents an audience of between 12 to 15 million teen shoppers. For example, eBay saw 6.4 million teen users in April 2006, while Amazon saw 3.5 million and Apple saw 3 million.[32]

The teen population, a subset of generation Y represents the most multicultural age group to date. It is growing at about 17 percent annually with about 32 million consumers. As teens age, their yearly discretionary income increases from nearly $1,500 at age 12 to 13 to nearly $4,500 by age 16 to 17. With a significant amount of income at their discretion, teens display financial sophistication — a significant proportion have access to financial services to manage their money. Nearly four out of ten teens have a savings or checking account in their own name. Since, on average teens spend $46.80 per visit to a shopping mall, they are prime targets. Interestingly, parents consult the computer-savvy teens in their households for large and small purchases.[33]

Age is a useful segmentation variable for high-tech-nology services. As you would expect, most Internet users have high levels of income and education. Women actually outnumber men online and their habits vary by age. Women ages 24 to 35 spend most of their time on sites that provide information and advice, whereas girls ages 2 to 11 visit television and learning Web sites most often. The growth rate of the female population online has outpaced the overall online growth rate. All categories except females ages 18 to 24 saw a significant increase in their numbers online. Because of this shift in online usage, sites must start to target women, keeping in mind the age-specific differences in their use of the Internet.[34]

Segmentation Based on Diversity Some people hesitate to segment markets based on ethnic heritage, race, or religious factors. Yet a wonderful fact of life is the world's tremendous diversity. Marketers know that the character of many markets is dramatically influenced by these factors. It's important to remember that ethnic segments are not homogeneous. There are demographic differences within ethnic groups. For many people of color, race has nothing to do with their buying behavior. Consequently, other forms of segmentation may work much better.

African Americans, Hispanics, and Asian Americans account for much of the current population growth in the United States. Within 25 years, each is estimated to be approximately the same size—about 42 million people.

City	Origin
Atlanta	Vietnam, South Korea
Baltimore	South Korea
Chicago	Mexico, Philippines, South Korea
Denver	Mexico, Vietnam
Dallas	Mexico, Vietnam, India
Jersey City	Cuba
Los Angeles	Mexico
Miami	Cuba
Minneapolis/St. Paul	Laotians
New York City	all immigrants
Seattle	Philippines, Vietnam, South Korea

Figure 8.6 New Ethnic Populations in Selected Cities

Compared to the general population, African Americans will grow at about twice the overall rate, Hispanics at 4.5 times the rate, and Asians at more than 8 times the rate. Whites will increase at about 60 percent the rate of other groups.[35] Many people will maintain their high ethnicity by living among and associating within these groups. High ethnicity results in attractive market segments.

Minorities represent approximately one third of the U.S. population, and the Bureau of the Census estimates that figure will rise to nearly 64 percent by 2020.[36] Minorities are now a majority in one of every six U.S. cities. Most immigrants settle in urban areas along with people from their home country. This produces concentrations of new ethnic populations, as the examples in Figure 8.6 show.[37]

Currently, the U.S. Hispanic market consists of approximately 43 million individuals, making up 13.3 percent of the U.S. population. With a 3.3 percent increase per year they are the fastest growing also. The second largest group is blacks (40 million) followed by Asians (14 million), American Indians and Alaska natives (4.5 million and Hawaiians/Pacific Islanders (1 million).[38] Total spending power of Hispanics is a whopping $686 billion, a number that is growing at twice the annual rate of non-Hispanics. So, marketing to this group can be especially profitable for companies. Gateway, Inc. has begun targeting the Hispanic segment since it is expected to make up approximately 25 percent of the U.S. population by 2050. To reach this market, Gateway has begun marketing its products in the Spanish language, including running TV and radio advertisements, and hiring customer service and sales people who are fluent in Spanish.[39]

De-ethnicization occurs when a product heavily associated with one ethnic group is targeted at other segments. Products such as salsa, and egg rolls have become favorites of many people other than Mexicans or Chinese. Kikkoman soy sauce was originally marketed to Chinese groceries and restaurants. Now that ethnic foods have become more mainstream, Kikkoman products are sold in grocery chains to consumers from many different backgrounds.

Psychographic and Lifestyle Segmentation Psychographic and lifestyle segmentation links geographic and demographic descriptors with a consumer's behavioral and psychological decisions. Psychographic variables used alone are often not very useful to marketers; however, they can be quite powerful when joined with demographic, geographic, and other data. **Lifestyle** is a person's distinctive mode of living. It describes how time and money are spent and what aspects of life are important. The choice of products, patterns of usage, and the amount of enjoyment a person gains from being a consumer are all part of lifestyle. Consider the difference between people who are physically fit from exercise and proper nutrition and those who are out of shape from high-fat diets, smoking, and sedentary living. Messages such as "Just Do It!" or "No pain, no gain" are received very differently by these two groups. Of course, since there are so many lifestyles, the trick is to identify them in the context of your company's marketing strategy.

Psychographics are marketing approaches and tools used to identify lifestyles based on measures of consumer values, activities, interests, opinions, demographics, and other factors. Classifying lifestyles emerged from a Roper/Starch Worldwide survey of about 2,000 Americans for insights into views about money. Seven distinct profiles were discerned: hunter, gatherer, protector, splurger, striver, nester, and idealist. The hunter takes risks to get ahead and equates money with happiness. The gatherer is better safe than sorry, a conservative investor. The protector puts others first and uses money to protect loved ones. The splurger is self-indulgent. The striver believes that money makes the world go around and equates it with power. The nester isn't very interested in money except to take care of immediate need. The idealist believes there is more to life than money; material things aren't all that important.[40]

There are many ways to define lifestyles using psychographics, so marketers must use a combination of research and creativity to develop useful segments. The best psychographic segmentation approaches are based on accepted consumer psychology and sound research methods. One of the most popular systems is SRI Consulting Business Intelligence's (SRIC-BI's) VALS™ systems. This second version of earlier research segments consumers into groups that think and act differently. VALS research found three major categories of consumers, each with a different primary motivation. Ideals-motivated consumers follow their own beliefs; achievement-motivated consumers are influenced by others, and self-expression-motivated consumers seek variety, action, and risk taking. In addition, VALS considers a consumer's resources, which are education, age, income, energy, self-confidence, eagerness to buy, and health. Figure 8.7 illustrates the VALS™ segmentation system and Figure 8.8 provides summary descriptions of the segments. The VALS battery of attitude items is used in survey research to discover the product choices, media preferences, and leisure activities of each of the VALS consumer groups. Marketers, advertisers, media planners, and new-product designers use VALS to discover who is naturally attracted to their product or service and then to design communication strategies, advertising, and distribution plans that will be attractive to their particular consumer target. VALS refreshes its product media database twice a year. GeoVALS™ estimates the percentage of each VALS™ group living in each U.S. residential zip code. VALS systems have also been developed for Japan and the United Kingdom.

The Connected: Surfing the Net box describes how you can obtain your profile. If you answer the questions on the VALS™ questionnaire, you can find out whether you are an Innovator, Thinker, Believer, Achiever, Striver, or Experiencer. Additionally, you can explore the types of media, products, and services your profile prefers. This is just an example of how psychographic segmentation helps companies connect with customers.

Using sophisticated computer technology, GeoVALS™ allows marketers to profile a city, metropolitan area, and zip code.[41] It has been adjusted for use in other countries. The Japanese version shows categories of buyers according to product adoption as well as the VALS™ two categories.[42]

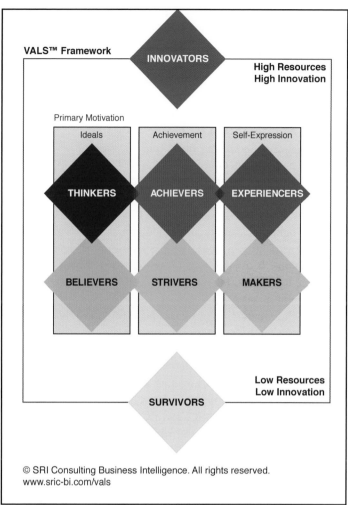

Figure 8.7   The VALS™ Segmentation System
Source: Printed with permission from SRI Consulting Business Intelligence (SRIC-BI), Menlo Park, CA.

VALS™ Segment	Primary Motivation	Description	Portion of U.S. Adult Population
Innovator	Can express all three	High self-esteem, sophisticated, open to new ideas	10%
Thinker	Ideals	Information-seeking, reflective	13%
Believer	Ideals	Traditional, respect authority, risk-averse	16%
Achiever	Achievement	Goal-oriented, focus on career and family	13%
Striver	Achievement	Trendy, low self-esteem, resource constrained	11%
Experiencer	Self-expression	Stimulation-seeking, highly social	13%
Maker	Self-expression	Self sufficient in a hands on way, practical	12%
Survivor	No particular	Not active consumers, quiet, older	12%

Figure 8.8 Brief Descriptions of the U.S. VALS Groups
Source: SRI Consulting Business Intelligence (SRIC-BI); www.sric-bi.com/VALS

Marketing Vocabulary

DE-ETHNICIZATION
The result of targeting a product heavily associated with one ethnic group to other segments.

LIFESTYLE
A person's distinctive mode of living.

PSYCHOGRAPHICS
Marketing approaches and tools used to identify lifestyles based on measures of consumers' values, activities, interests, opinions, demographics, and other factors.

Behavioristic Segmentation Behavioristic segmentation categorizes consumers based on people's awareness, product and media uses, and actions. Past behavior is one of the best predictors of future behavior, so these variables require an understanding of what consumers have previously done. The variables include purchase volume, purchase readiness, ability and experience, loyalty, media habits, and shopping behaviors.

Segmentation by Usage Rates You have probably heard about the 80-20 rule: 20 percent of buyers purchase 80 percent of the volume of any product. It is amazing how true this is for many products. Heavy users can be extremely important to companies. Consequently, most marketers divide the market into heavy, moderate, and light users, and then they look for characteristics that may explain why some people consume vastly greater amounts. It usually costs no more to reach heavy users than light users. Therefore, the marketing costs are lower per unit of sales.

Still, marketing strategists need to realize that competition for heavy users can be extreme. If medium or light users are being ignored, they may provide a marketing opportunity. For example, giants such as Coke and Pepsi are always targeting the college crowd. They spend big bucks to be represented on campus in order to capture students. Royal Crown Cola avoids this segment altogether because of the stiff competition. Instead, it concentrates on older adults, who tend to be lighter users of cola.

Segmentation by Readiness For many products, potential users go through a series of stages that describe their readiness to purchase. These stretch all the way from being unaware of a product, through trial, leading up to loyalty. Readiness is a useful segmentation variable particularly for newer products. This scheme is often used in adjusting the communications mix.

Segmentation by Ability and Experience The performance of products is determined by the ability and experience of its user. Consequently, ability is an excellent segmentation variable for almost any skill-based product. For example, the marketing of skis, tennis racquets, golf clubs, and most other sports equipment is targeted to ability segments. This is due in large part to the performance requirements of these products. As performance requirements increase, new technologies produce products with higher performance capabilities but generally require more skill. UpLink Corporation, the fastest growing GPS golf solutions provider, recently announced its INOVA GPS Golf Business Solution. The device serves two purposes, it displays the entire course on a high-resolution screen providing the golfer with information about the course, and it gives the course managers the ability to monitor the speed of play and course traffic. This will lead to a more efficiently run course, higher revenue, and

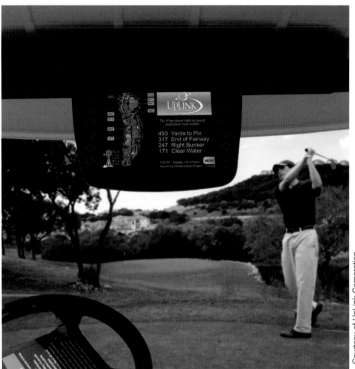

Courtesy of UpLink Corporation

a more satisfied customer.[43] An accurate rendering of a course is particularly useful for better golfers who want to fine-tune their game.

Segmentation by Loyalty As we have discussed, a key goal of firms is to create brand loyalty. Some consumers are naturally loyal to particular product categories. There are many ways to look at loyalty, but the most popular seems to be the most straightforward. It looks at switchers, moderately loyal, and highly loyal categories. Switchers may select a separate brand with nearly every purchase. They may actually seek variety or they simply don't care which brand they buy. Moderately loyal customers have a preference for a brand but will switch if it is convenient to do so. Loyal buyers have strong preferences. Not all buyers are loyal to a single brand within a product class. Some people have two or three that are equally acceptable. This type of segmentation may include more than the three categories described.

Segmentation by Media and Shopping Habits A broad range of media and shopping habits can be used to categorize shoppers. For example, some people subscribe to cable, others don't; some prefer shopping in malls, others online; and so forth. These variables focus on the accessibility of target customers. Those who shop only in mall settings are accessed differently from those who prefer catalog or online shopping at home. Shopping habits in the United States changed dramatically with the advent of E-commerce. For example, the average shopper will go from spending two hours shopping online to spending closer to five hours online in the near future.[44] Online shopping will continue to increase as consumers become accustomed to larger selections, lower prices, and the convenience of shopping from home.

Segmentation by Benefit

Benefit segmentation divides the market into homogeneous groups based on the attributes consumers seek from a particular product class. Russell Haley popularized this method in the 1960s by dividing the toothpaste market into segments based on whether the consumer wanted flavor, brightness of teeth, dental health, or low price. A benefit segmentation of auto buyers might group them according to the importance they place on economy, performance, styling, or reliability. When a lot is known about the attitudes and perceptions of buyers, it is possible to develop a benefit profile of what product attributes are considered most important. This can be a useful step in segmentation because customers in a benefit segment are likely to have other identifiable characteristics. For example, people who desire convenience are likely to be members of a dual-career family or single-parent household.

When only benefits are addressed, this technique is not always consistent with good segmentation procedures. Because the benefits are often described according to product characteristics, we learn very little about the buyers themselves. For example, you could say that Apple addressed the user-friendly computer benefit segment. Then again, you could say that Apple products are user friendly. A good rule of thumb is that segments should not be defined solely by product characteristics. In fact, when benefit segmentation is based on product attributes, it may be confused with product positioning, which will be discussed later in this chapter.

Nevertheless, benefit segmentation can be useful when it leads to descriptions of the consumers who prefer each benefit. In order to create these descriptions, researchers generally start with benefit segments and then use the other segmentation schemes to define each group. In this way, the focus is ultimately on buyers, not products.

BUSINESS MARKET SEGMENTATION

Although the business market is segmented using procedures much like those used to segment the consumer market, its distinctive characteristics are used to categorize business consumers along different dimensions—by company demographics, geographic scope, buying

approach, and product/technology—as outlined in Figure 8.9.

Basis	Example
Company Demographics	
Industry	food, mining, automotive, computer
Company size	large, medium, small
Financial stability and profitability	strong, medium, weak
Channel	distributor, OEM, first tier, second tier
Ownership	private, public
Industry leadership	leader, close follower, laggard
Geographic Scope	local, regional, national, international, global
Buying Approach	
Centralization	centralized, decentralized
Functional involvement	finance, marketing, manufacturing
Partnering approach	bid, relationship oriented, contracts
Product/Technology	
Level of technology	high, medium, low
Configuration purchased	components, modules, subsystem
Design source	internal, external

Figure 8.9 Segmenting the Business Market

Segmentation by Company Demographics In describing a company, we usually think first about its demographics: industry, size, financial stability, place in the distribution channel, and ownership. Industry is defined by the company's products. Ford, GM, and Honda are in the automotive industry, whereas Mack and International are in the heavy truck industry. Large companies may have strategic business units (SBUs) in different industries. Johnson & Johnson, for example, makes consumer health care products as well as medical supplies for professionals. The federal government's Standard Industry Classification (SIC) codes can help identify a company's industrial category. Industry classification reveals a great deal about an organization—the types of problems it is likely to face, the kinds of products it purchases, its economic cycles and regulatory environment, and the types of competitive practices it is likely to encounter.

Company size is based on dollar amount or volume of sales, number of employees, or units produced. Size affects purchase procedures and requirements such as delivery schedules and inventory capacity. Large firms often do much of their own engineering, and their purchasing department uses formal buying arrangements. Medium-sized companies may be interested in value-added services a seller can provide. Small firms often use less formal procedures and may want the seller's help with tracking and restocking inventory.

Another demographic characteristic is financial stability and profitability. Marketing to a company in difficulty may not be worth the effort and risk. If sales volumes are substantial, delays in payments can cause the seller financial hardship. The profitability of a company is often used as an indication of its ability to pay as well as other characteristics.

Channel membership refers to whether the organization is a distributor, original equipment manufacturer (OEM), or one of the tier suppliers. Each type has significantly different needs. Distributors acquire to resell, OEMs want to develop a final product, and tiers typically have unique needs as well.

Ownership influences how organizations buy. Since private companies can set policies as they see fit, we find many purchasing strategies. In the public sector, governmental units and utilities must follow very strict guidelines.

Segmentation by Geographic Scope

When we discussed geographic segmentation previously, it was in terms of locating clusters of targeted consumers. In the case of businesses, however, we are concerned with the geographic scope of the customer's business, whether local, regional, national, international, or global. The range of operations clearly affects how an organization buys. Pepsi has a global scope, so sellers must be able to think in terms of manufacturing plants around the world—and of reaching buyers who may come from various cultures.

Segmentation by Buying Approach

Organizations also can be differentiated according to their buying approach. This takes into account their degree of centralization, what functional areas are involved, and what kind of partnering arrangements they have. A centralized organization generally has one purchasing unit with very set policies, whereas a decentralized organization is likely to allow local buying decisions using various procedures and policies. Functional involvement refers to a company's orientation—manufacturing firms use one set of criteria, whereas a financial institution or a consulting firm may use others. Partnering can range from simple bid purchases to a long- or short-term contract that may or may not contain detailed specifications and other requirements, such as an exclusivity clause.

Segmentation by Product/ Technology

Product/technology can affect purchasing in numerous ways, but three of the more important are level of technology, configuration purchased, and design orientation.

First, firms vary dramatically in technological capability. This is primarily due to their hiring, training, retention, and technical practices. A high-tech firm has very different expectations from a low-tech firm. Consequently, marketing to each group is different. Second, buying configurations differ. Some companies want to purchase only components and base their decisions on price and delivery specifications. Others buy modules that already combine many components and make it easier to add the supplier's product at the time of manufacturing. Yet others prefer to purchase a system that enhances the functionality of their products, as when Chrysler buys traction-control products from Tevis. This variable is related in some ways to design. Some organizations want to do their own, some want suppliers to do it, and some work closely with suppliers to develop a design. A company such as Delphi Automotive Systems has extensive design capabilities but sometimes relies on suppliers for the design of certain components, modules, and systems.

TWO COMMON SEGMENTING METHODS

Segmentation can be quite complicated because most markets are complex. There are many different types of customers and, as we have seen, literally thousands of variables can be used to segment them. Marketers typically use one of two approaches in selecting variables and grouping customers.

The **take-down segmentation method** starts with all consumers and seeks meaningful variables for subdividing the entire market. For example, a health and beauty or cosmetic company may segment by gender. It may choose to target women, believing they have a significantly greater buying potential than men. It then may further segment women by age, type of user, or skin shade. When Dove launched its "Campaign for Real Beauty," it put the spotlight on older women, going so far as to photograph them nude for magazine advertisements and billboards. Choosing to photograph the women naked is a way to look at their "real beauty" and a new way of portraying the middle-aged woman - previously much ignored in advertising campaigns - as sexy.[45]

The **build-up segmentation method** starts with a single potential customer and adds others with similar characteristics. Anyone without those characteristics is placed in a new segment, and the process continues. In other words, rather than the whole market, the focus is on one segment at a time. For example, Fancl, a Japanese line of natural hair and skin care, is extremely successful with environmentally conscious women in Japan. To expand, it began marketing to Japanese women living in the United States. Now, Fancl is targeting American women by marketing both the idea of using natural products and by proving benefits. Fancl has expanded its product line to include make-up free of additives and preservatives, suitable for all skin tones.[46] The build-up segmentation method is helping Fancl expand its business.

TARGET MARKETING

While segmentation is an analytical process, target marketing is a decision-making process. The company must choose the segment(s) on which it will focus its energy. At one extreme, all segments may be selected; at the other, only one. Clearly, most companies would like everyone to buy its product. But even giants such as Coca-Cola and Pepsi must battle for customers, and each devotes different effort to specific market segments. Pepsi has a long history of concentrating on youth. It has spent billions trying to woo the young and nearly young, implying that Coca-Cola is for the older generation. Similarly, The Limited focuses on young, trendy women; Gerber on infants and young toddlers; McDonald's on families; and Lexus on quality-conscious, high-income adults. The relationships feature, "Credit Card Co-Branding: New Shortcut to Hitting the Target Market," discusses a new spin on target marketing.

SELECTING TARGET SEGMENTS

How do companies decide which market segments to target? Once the segmentation scheme is developed, you need to describe, or profile, each group in more detail. The **market segment profile** compiles information about a market segment and the amount of opportunity it represents. The profile may include (1) the number of current and potential buyers; (2) the potential number of products these buyers may purchase; (3) the amount of revenue the segment may provide; and (4) the expected growth rate. In addition to size and growth, other criteria used to select targets include competitive factors, cost and efficiency factors, the segment's leadership qualities, and the segment's compatibility with the company's vision, objectives, and resources.

Size and Growth   Market segments vary considerably by size and growth rate. Although a segment must be large enough to generate revenues and profits, the biggest is not always the most attractive. Competition may be very tough there. A slightly smaller segment may have enough revenue to ensure a satisfactory profit. In the 1990s, Korean companies gained strong footholds in many countries (including the United States) by targeting smaller segments that were being ignored. These were large enough to support sustained marketing efforts and included people whose spending power would increase over time.

Competitive Factors   In general, the less competition within a segment, the better. Marketers must be aware not only of who is currently serving the segment but also of who is likely to do so in the future. A company may decide not to serve a particular segment in order to avoid competitors known for their aggressiveness and strength. In

Read about the credit card industry's new approach to target marketing in the relationship feature.

Marketing Vocabulary

TAKE-DOWN SEGMENTATION METHOD
Method that starts with a set of variables and assigns all consumers to one of them.

BUILD-UP SEGMENTATION METHOD
Method that starts with a single potential customer's characteristics and adds a segment for each new characteristic found in the other.

MARKET SEGMENT PROFILE
Compiles information about a market segment and the amount of opportunity it represents.

other cases, a company may choose to challenge rivals. Church & Dwight decided to take on Procter & Gamble and Colgate-Palmolive by introducing its Arm & Hammer baking soda toothpaste. It felt the product was just different enough to be successful with certain segments.

The Marketing Gazette™

CREATING & CAPTURING VALUE THROUGH RELATIONSHIPS

Credit Card Co-Branding: New Shortcut to Hitting The Target Market

Credit card issuers are finding it a lot easier to target someone else's loyal customers than to inspire loyalty in their own. After all, with the flood of cut-rate cards filling mailboxes and the ease of transferring balances, consumers have little incentive to stick with a particular one. But what if a card gives something back? That's the principle behind credit card co-branding, a marketing strategy that's taken the business world by storm since it appeared in 1990.

Co-branding works like this: An issuer such as MasterCard or Visa teams up with a partner. It can be a retailer, a mail-order company, an airline, a university, or a nonprofit group. In a typical co-branding program, the issuer develops a marketing campaign that targets the partner's customers. The issuer also contributes about 1 percent of its sales to the partner's reward program, which may be merchandise discounts, cash rebates, gift certificates, or donations to a particular cause. In today's Internet-intensive marketplace, FreeShop.com and NextCard are teaming up with Visa to co-brand a credit card designed to give patrons of Internet commerce perks for utilizing the medium. "Our alliance with NextCard will provide great value to FreeShop.com customers, while creating a significant new revenue opportunity for FreeShop," says Tim Choate, CEO of FreeShop.

Co-branding flourishes because it's a win-win-win situation. The card issuer can easily target and reach a new base of customers and net a steady stream of revenue from transaction fees. The partner gains increased customer loyalty, higher average orders, and more frequent purchases. And the consumer gets free toys, air miles, or a host of other perks for using the co-branded card. In 2007, Mastercard offered a "backyard retreat sweepstakes" promotion to go with its "Priceless" advertising campaign. The program joined with The Home Depot to offer a chance of winning a $100,000 backyard retreat every time a Home Depot customer used their Mastercard.

Of course, perks only draw customers if the brand appeals to them in the first place. The co-branding relationship taps into consumer loyalty or emotional ties to a co-brand sponsor, says Leslie Dukker Dory, senior vice president and director of marketing for Sun Trust BankCard of Orlando, Florida. "A well-established, well-identified, easily reached target, if provided the right perks," says Dory, "will gravitate to a card."

Sun Trust's own specialty is co-branding cards that target leisure-activity niches. Two of the cards it issues are the Cool Country Visa, aimed at fans of 11 major country music artists, and the Daytona USA MasterCard, aimed at motor sports enthusiasts. Sun Trust reaches these people through direct mail as well as promotions, special event tie-ins, album inserts, and take-one dispensers.

Although country music fans and motorcycle mavens represent rather narrow niches, they can be very profitable. Co-branded cards that target populations likely to carry balances can pull in substantial revenues even among a small customer base.

Mastercard also teamed up with Citibank to create The Citi Drivers Edge Mastercard for College Students. The card allows students to redeem rebates toward the purchase of any new or used vehicle, maintenance on their current vehicle and gas cards.

Career Tip:

Interested in a career with PepsiCo? Visit the Pepsi Web site and learn more about the opportunities available in different geographic locations within the Frito-Lay North America, Pepsi Bottling Group, PepsiCo Corporate, Pepsi-Cola North America, or Tropicana North America companies. You can perform a search of the job database and apply online.

Marketing Vocabulary

TARGETING STRATEGY
The number of market segments and the relative amount of resources targeted to each group.

Cost and Efficiency Factors It is more efficient to target some segments than others. When Citibank set its sights on chief financial officers of several worldwide corporations, costs ran into the millions for research, product development, and personal selling. This sounds expensive, but it was a very efficient use of funds. This extremely compact segment consists of a few known and very influential people, so all the marketing dollars could be aimed directly at the targets. If the message reaches all sorts of consumers, then the result is higher cost and reduced efficiency. For example, alcohol abuse prevention advertisements are seen by responsible drinkers and teetotalers, not just the target audience.

Segment Leadership Qualities Some segments set the trend for adopting new ideas and products. Professional sports teams influence the dress and equipment of college athletes, who, in turn, influence high school teams. Marketers often choose a target segment with leadership qualities, hoping that other segments will follow suit.

Compatibility Factors Companies often select segments they believe are particularly compatible with the company's vision, objectives, and resources. Thus, to a significant degree, target segments reflect the qualities and character of the company. In the early 1980s, Honda recognized that Harley-Davidson was attracting customers who didn't appeal to much of the general population. Honda took advantage of this by targeting younger, well-educated buyers with the theme: "You meet the nicest people on a Honda." This segment was consistent with Honda's image. Other Japanese motorcycle companies, such as Yamaha and Kawasaki, did the same and captured a large number of U.S. customers. In the past few years Harley-Davidson has been trying to erase its Hell's Angels

image. The old image of tough bikers is definitely a fading emphasis.[47] Today the Harley-Davidson emphasis is on a lifestyle, and buyers include a broad range of responsible individuals. Harley-Davidson executives make the point that "Nobody Needs a Harley" so they attempt to market all of the factors that promote the excitement of a Harley.

FINDING NEW MARKETS TO TARGET

A major innovation occurs when companies discover new market segments. You can probably think of many examples. PocketCard discovered a novel way to market debit cards. The cards are designed specifically for parents of teenagers. The parents can track all of their teenager's purchases online and revoke privileges at any time. These cards free up parents' time because they aren't constantly running to the ATM to get cash for their children and it gives teenagers a sense of freedom. Banks and credit unions now offer debit and credit cards aimed at teenagers, and 31.8 percent of high school seniors use a credit card on a regular basis.[48] Thus, a new segment has been discovered.

TARGET MARKETING STRATEGIES

A **targeting strategy** defines the number of target markets and the relative amount of resources allocated to each. Strategies usually fall within one of the three categories shown in Figure 8.10: undifferentiated marketing,

2004 Honda VTX1800 Neo-Retro Model

differentiated marketing, and concentrated marketing. Two others are used less frequently: niche marketing and micromarketing. Mass customization may be the wave of

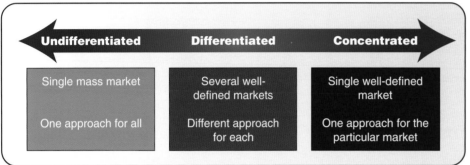

Figure 8.10   Target Market Strategies

the future. Figure 8.11 illustrates the way the marketing mix is targeted in each of the three most common strategies.

Undifferentiated Marketing   Similar to mass marketing, **undifferentiated marketing** treats all customers the same. Companies look for desires that are common to most potential customers and then try to design products that appeal to everyone. By focusing internally on a single or a few products, companies can streamline manufacturing, distribution, and even promotion in order to improve quality and gain cost efficiencies. But the standardized product may fail to meet individual customer needs. For years United Parcel Service (UPS) used this strategy. Users benefited from the cost-effective operations but were upset by the company's inability to fulfill unique customer requirements.

As long as companies keep the price relatively low and competitive alternatives are unavailable, an undifferentiated marketing strategy can be successful. Today, however, competition is tough. Companies that once thrived are being threatened by rivals that use more targeted approaches, such as differentiated or concentrated marketing.

Differentiated Marketing
Differentiated marketing serves each segment with marketing mix elements matched specifically to its desires and expectations. When Federal Express and others entered the market with differentiated strategies, UPS executives had

to make a choice. Should the company settle for slowly eroding sales, or should it choose the risk, hard work, and uncertainty of a new course? UPS decided on a differentiated marketing strategy. It carefully selected targets and designed services to meet their different needs. Some of its operations are applicable to all segments, such as its computerized tracking system and extensive aircraft fleet. Other elements differ, such as product mix, personal selling, and pricing. This approach allows UPS to serve all its customers better.

The advantage of differentiated marketing is that needs and wants are better satisfied for each targeted segment. The disadvantage is that it may also cost more than undifferentiated marketing because several marketing mix strategies are typically required. Differentiated marketing requires decentralized decision making. **Centralized decision making** involves a small group of executives who make all the major decisions for the whole company. **Decentralized decision making** permits numerous groups, each dedicated to a specific segment, to make the decisions for their particular segment. This gives marketers a lead role in the company, as they need to ensure that customers' needs and wants are considered in every decision. When

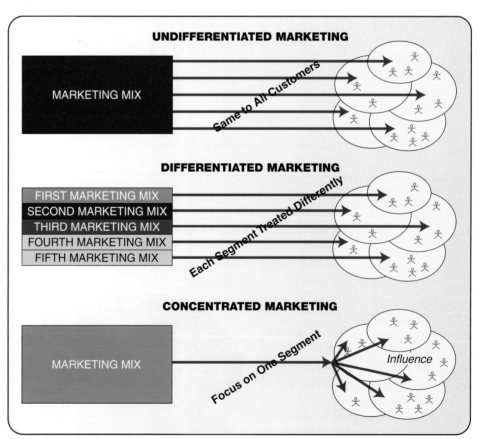

Figure 8.11   How the Marketing Mix Is Used in Common Targeting Strategies

No nuts.

Sandies
SIMPLY SHORTBREAD

See ingredient statement
for allergen information.

The Keebler Company utilizes differentiated marketing.

UPS decided to engage in differentiated marketing, the first step was to create a much stronger role for marketing. This meant educating large numbers of executives about the latest marketing techniques.

Concentrated Marketing   Focusing the organization's marketing mix on one or two of the many possible segments is called **concentrated marketing**. Companies must make sure they have a great deal of knowledge about their core market segment, as this major target is called. Although most of the marketing is aimed at the core, substantial revenues and profits may be gained from other segments. This is because segments with leadership qualities are often selected for concentrated marketing in the hope that they will influence the behavior of others. Ralph Lauren has used concentrated marketing successfully to target high-income, well-educated professionals and their families. Wanting to emulate them, consumers in the noncore segment are drawn to Lauren products as well.

Concentrated marketing has worked extremely well for new companies or companies entering new areas of the world. By gaining a foothold in a core market, a company can build the financial strength, experience, and credibility needed for expansion. When Tower Records opened its first music store in Thailand, it concentrated on young people. Success in

this segment is leading to further expansion in Thailand, including a host of additional outlets catering to listeners of all types.

Niche Marketing and Micromarketing
Niche marketing and micromarketing are two other strategies worth mentioning. A **niche** is a very small market that most companies ignore because they do not perceive adequate opportunity. For example, local grocers such as Virginia-based Ukrop compete against big chains, such as Wal-Mart and Costco by offering products such as prepared foods, ethnic foods, better quality produce and meats, and other signature items to smaller segments.[49]

The smallest possible niche is the individual. Marketing to one customer is called **micromarketing**. Advances in technology have made it possible to adjust marketing strategies to meet individual needs. "Tell me someone's zip code, and I can predict what they eat, drink, drive—even think," claims Jonathan Robbin. He is creator of the PRIZM cluster system, which matches census data and consumer surveys with the 36,000 zip codes in the United States. Consumers are partitioned into 40 lifestyle groups, which in turn are matched with buying behaviors. The information can be used to predict everything from a person's automobile choice to a preference for croissants over Kellogg's Pop-Tarts.[50] Additionally, some retail outlets market directly to niche customers. The Bass Pro Shop in Gurnee, Illinois, allows customers to try out products such as fishing polls in the store's indoor trout stream. Companies are also using computers to sift through billions of bytes and come up with sets of variables and patterns that boggle the mind.

Imagine the possibilities of micromarketing. Printing technology is so flexible that neighbors can receive the same magazine with differ-

Marketing Vocabulary

UNDIFFERENTIATED MARKETING
A strategy that views all potential customers as though they were the same.

DIFFERENTIATED MARKETING
Marketing to each of several segments with a marketing mix strategy matched specifically to its desires and expectations.

CENTRALIZED DECISION MAKING
Management process in which a small group of executives make all the major decisions for the whole company.

DECENTRALIZED DECISION MAKING
Management process in which numerous groups, each dedicated to a specific segment, make decisions about their segment.

CONCENTRATED MARKETING
Focusing the organization's marketing mix strategy on one or only a few of many possible segments.

NICHE
A very small market that most companies ignore because they do not perceive adequate opportunity.

MICROMARKETING
Marketing to an individual customer.

ent pages targeted to their own consuming patterns. For example, if the people next door shop at discount stores and you do not, then they may receive a copy with ads featuring price promotions, whereas your copy features upscale items with no mention of price. Even more impressive is the work done to pinpoint loyal customers. By linking a publisher's subscription list with a company's customer list, marketers can substitute special ads for loyal customers in place of the general ad being carried in the magazine.

Mass Customization Probably the most important technological development for marketing is the personalization of mass merchandise. As mentioned previously, mass customization serves one or several markets while efficiently responding to the needs and desires of individual consumers. By creating a process that can respond to uniquely defined needs of targeted consumers, mass customization gives customers tremendous individualized attention. Companies can make affordable, high-quality products tailored to a customer's needs—but with the short cycle time and low costs associated with mass production.[51]

Nike introduced Nike ID, a custom shoe the consumer creates on its Web site. The consumer starts with a basic shoe and works from there choosing the base and the accent colors. In addition, Nike allows each person to put their own "ID" on the back of the shoe. Dell uses mass customization by allowing customers to build their dream computer system. There are 20 or so product features that make up every computer (RAM, processor speed, disk space, etc.); the customer can pick and choose between all 20 of these, resulting in a computer that is customized exactly to the individual's specifications. After the order is processed, the machine is assembled and shipped within 24 hours.[52]

Dell Computers uses mass customization to provide computers with exact customer specifications.

ETHICAL DIMENSIONS OF TARGETING

It makes sense that manufacturers should want to target age segments, but this creates trouble for some companies. The alcoholic beverage industry frequently is criticized in this regard. When Anheuser-Busch introduced Spykes, two-ounce bottles of malt liquor designed to be drink mixers or consumed as a shot, they were specifically targeting the young adult market to help increase beer sales over liquor. Sold in individual bottles and served in a variety of fruity flavors, Spykes contain 12 percent alcohol by volume. Anheuser-Busch has drawn criticism of this new product. The National Center on Addiction and Substance Abuse believes "Spykes is a predatory move to attract underage drinkers." They and other critics cite their size, portability and flavors that mask the taste of alcohol as characteristics that will appeal to young drinkers.[53]

Similarly, the tobacco industry has come under intense fire due to targeting. With more than 400 cigarette brands and styles available in the United States, many of the products could not survive without appeal to very specific consumer groups. Lorillard, Inc. aims Newport Stripes specifically at women. Cartier Vendome is promoted by Philip Morris as a cigarette for the wealthy or aspiring rich. These brands effectively target subsets of the larger population. When R. J. Reynolds introduced a menthol cigarette for African Americans called Uptown, the result was public scrutiny and condemnation by the U.S. secretary of health and human services and numerous African American and community groups. There were demands that the government bar tobacco companies from designing and promoting cigarettes targeted at this market segment. The fight stopped short of litigation when Reynolds agreed to cancel the brand at an estimated cost of $5 million to $7 million. Not all businesspeople believe this should have happened. Caroline Jones, president of her own advertising agency in New York, a company owned predominantly by blacks, said that it is insulting to ignore the African American community and not target it. "Marketers could and should advertise products to blacks, and that includes cigarettes and alcohol as well as bread and candy."[54]

Are there differences between products such as Uptown cigarettes and Kmart's line of private-label health and beauty care items aimed specifically at African Americans? There are varying opinions among consumer groups and industry manufacturers. One thing is certain. Tobacco and alcohol companies find it increasingly difficult to introduce, position, and market their products to ethnic consumers.

GLOBAL TARGETING

Major U.S. companies have expanded efforts to reach carefully targeted foreign market segments. Vast amounts are being spent to create a presence in areas where middle-class consumers are growing by leaps and bounds.[55] Frito-Lay is changing the snack food business in Thailand by marketing its traditional potato-based products. It also is changing agriculture. Potatoes weren't traditional food in Thailand, so it is teaching farmers to grow special seeds and educating them on all aspects of potato culture.[56]

Domino's Pizza focuses on various global segments by tailoring its service to different cultural needs. Consider that in Iceland most households are without a telephone, the British consider it rude for a delivery person to knock on the door, and Japanese homes are not numbered sequentially. These cultural differences require Domino's to adjust its strategies. To find addresses in Japan, wall maps up to three times the size of those used in the United States were developed. In Iceland, Domino's paired up with drive-in movie theaters: Employees bring cellular phones to cars with a flashing turn signal, and customers

then order pizzas for delivery right to their vehicle.

PepsiCo has been testing the Chinese market, which finds the cheese flavor undesirable, with such Cheeto flavors as Peking duck, fried egg, and dog. Procter & Gamble provides Japanese mothers with thin diapers, since they change their babies twice as often as Americans do. Green Giant advertisements picture corn falling off the cob into salad and pasta in France but being sprinkled over ice cream in Korea.[57]

POSITIONING STRATEGIES

Once the segmentation process gives a clear picture of the market and the target marketing strategy is selected, the positioning approach can be developed. Positioning is the process of creating in the mind of consumers an image, reputation, or perception of the company and its products relative to competitors. Positioning aligns a marketing strategy with the way the marketer wants buyers in a given target market to perceive the value they will receive from the company's products.

Positioning helps potential customers understand what is unique about the company and its products relative to competitors. Most important, it helps buyers connect mentally with the brand by understanding the brand. **Product position** refers to the characteristics that consumers associate with a brand. For example, Snickers is positioned as the snack to give energy, while Three Musketeers can be shared with a friend. BMW is positioned on prestige performance, while Mercedes projects prestige luxury.

THE POSITIONING MAP

A **positioning map** is a diagram of how consumers in a segment perceive specific brand elements they find important. This gives marketers a picture of how their products are viewed. Essentially, the idea is to graph where each brand falls regarding important attributes relative to other brands. To understand this, follow the process used to complete a perceptual map of television talk shows (the product) based on input from executives attending a seminar. They were asked to give their perceptions of talk shows. The anchors for the graph were social enlightenment and

Marketing Vocabulary

PRODUCT POSITION
The characteristics consumers associate with a brand based on important attributes.

POSITIONING MAP
A diagram of how consumers in a segment perceive brands based on specific elements they consider important.

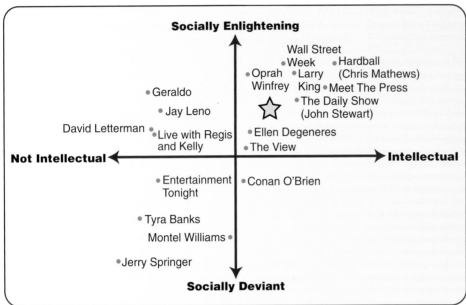

Figure 8.12   Examples of a Positioning Map: TV Talk Shows

intellect. The combined results are shown in Figure 8.12. You can probably think of other talk shows. How do you perceive them relative to the ones listed in the figure?

Once the perceptions are plotted, most marketers want to know the consumer's ideal position. The ideal position is the one most preferred by each consumer. In one example, the star near Larry King marks the positioning many executives preferred. Oprah Winfrey faced a dilemma when she realized that her own show had migrated toward the lower left quadrant, which she felt was out of alignment with her own values. Shows such as Jerry Springer's show have a sensationalism that appeals to many viewers, but many believe their value to society is questionable. Oprah decided to move her show back to its original position in the upper right quadrant. Oprah's Book Club, health features, and showcasing her charitable contributions in South Africa helped to cement her as educated and socially responsible in the minds of her viewers.   Now, when Oprah endorses a product or book, America responds.

www.delphiauto.com

Learn how Delphi markets its products that combine performance with environmental sensitivity.

ing methods used by consumer marketers, business marketers look at three other product classifications: commodity, differentiated, and specialty. Commodity products have no uniqueness. These classifications are shown in Figure 8.13. Buyers make selections according to the lowest price and reliable delivery. The differentiated position requires buyers to evaluate, compare, and contrast the products from various suppliers. The specialty position is for a unique product that can be customized to user needs.

Delphi markets auto components to various GM groups such as GMC, Cadillac, and Opel, as well as to manufacturers around the world. BMW, Renault, and Ford buy components from Delphi. Depending on the product line and target segment, Delphi uses all three positioning strategies. In some cases it positions products as commodities, such as simple wire harnesses that connect parts of the electrical system. For these commodities Delphi tries to keep costs low by using standard technologies. Delphi also markets break systems that are differentiated from those of competitors and require state-of-the-art technology. Delphi's specialty products are unique. By working closely with the designers of drive trains (engines and transmissions) in its customers' companies, Delphi produces engine fuel systems tailored to specifications. These products ensure compliance with EPA standards while producing the performance demanded by consumers.

STEPS FOR POSITIONING

Consumers' perceptions are influenced by the categories people use to sort through the massive amounts of product information. Music, for example, is categorized

POSITIONING BUSINESS PRODUCTS

In addition to the same position-

Category	Commodity	Differentiated	Specialty
Product Characteristics	No hidden qualities, similar to other suppliers	Comparisons with other suppliers show advantages	Unique
Technology	Standard	State-of-the-art	Customized

Figure 8.13   Positioning of Business Products

globalEDGE™
Segmentation, Targeting & Positioning

Segmentation allows your firm to better target and position its products to particular groups within a general market. One such method of segmentation is by ethnic groups. Your firm is currently attempting to develop a global segmentation strategy in all of the major markets in which it offers a product line. According to a source that permits you to compare various statistics, what is the overall ethnic background of the US population? How does this compare with the ethnic composition of Brazil, Germany, Japan, and the UK? Based on the criteria previously mentioned, in which market might you expect a uniform segmentation strategy? In which market would you expect an elaborate segmentation strategy?

as rock, country western, jazz, classical, and so forth, whereas other dimensions help differentiate one artist or group from another. Consumers also evaluate a brand relative to others based on their impression of whether it is more or less similar. Finally, they look at a brand according to their preferences—or how close it comes to their ideal position. The following steps can be used to position a brand.

1. Identify the attributes or characteristics used by buyers in a segment to understand brands.
2. Diagram the most important dimensions on a grid (map).
3. Locate the brand relative to others based on how it is perceived by buyers.
4. Identify the ideal position for buyers in the segment.
5. Determine the fundamental way to position the product.
6. Develop the marketing mix that supports the positioning strategy selected.

BASES FOR POSITIONING

Two noted marketing scholars have identified the following seven fundamental bases that can be used to position products.[58] Each base is described in more detail next.

Positioning by Benefit Benefits (attributes) can be used to describe the appeal of a product. For example, Procter & Gamble uses medical testimony to position Crest as a cavity-fighting toothpaste. SmithKline Beecham positions Aqua Fresh as a cavity fighter and a breath freshener. Glad trash bags are positioned to be more durable than the competition. Fisher-Price toys are positioned as safe and educational. Energizer batteries are positioned to keep going and going.

You must carefully select the benefits to associate with your product. Describing benefits that satisfy wants tends to work better than merely describing product attributes because consumers can relate the benefits to themselves.

Positioning by Price or Quality Sam Walton made $25 billion by identifying underserved geographical market segments and then positioning Wal-Mart as being consistently lower priced than competitors. Other retailers, such as Neiman Marcus, position themselves as high priced to signal higher quality. Positioning by price is common in the pharmaceutical industry. Typically, branded drugs (usually marketed by firms that first develop them) are priced much higher than generics (usually marketed by companies that copy drugs when the patent expires). The product is basically the same. The generics are positioned on price, whereas the branded products are positioned on quality.

Positioning by Time of Use or Application Marketers frequently position products on the basis of how they are used or applied. Gatorade, Powerade, and All-Sport are positioned for drinking while exercising. Wrigley's positions its gum for use by smokers when smoking is not permitted—on airplanes, in carpools, or in nonsmoking workplaces.

Often sales can be increased by positioning a product for more than one use or application. For example, McDonald's discovered a huge opportunity when breakfast service was added. Arm & Hammer expanded bak-

Coke is subtly positioning its product for use similar to Starbucks or other coffee drinks.

Positioning Basis	EXAMPLE OF USE	
	Description	Brand/Product
Benefit (Attribute)	Safety	Volvo
Price/Quality	Value	Wal-Mart
Time of Use	After a workout	Gatorade
Product User	Mature	Colgate
Direct Comparison		Verizon vs. Alltel
Product Class	Thirst quencher	Aquafina
Country of Origin	Jamaica	Jamaican rum

Figure 8.14   Examples of Positioning

ing soda sales by positioning the product as an odor fighter in the refrigerator, auto, or cupboard, in addition to its uses in toothpaste, laundry detergent, and baking. V-8 juice, originally consumed at breakfast, is now the "Wow, I could have had a V-8!" anytime beverage.

Positioning by Product User or Spokesperson

In the mind of some people, products take on meanings associated strongly with the spokesperson. For example, Nike uses Tiger Woods to position Nike as extraordinary. Andre Agassi and John McEnroe, both considered tennis rebels, were used to help position Nike athletic shoes as an alternative to the conservative models sold by competitors.

Sometimes spokespersons are not even real, such as Betty Crocker and Mr. Goodwrench. At other times, the person's area of expertise may be more significant than the unknown individual. Cat or dog breeders are shown in ads for pet food. The Club, a device to prevent auto theft, was introduced in a national ad campaign by actual police officers.

Positioning by Direct Comparison

Nearly all customers create impressions about a brand by comparing it to another. Marketers need to determine how they want their brand to be evaluated relative to the competition. In a few cases, competitors are named, although many believe they should not be given "free" publicity. More

often, the comparison is general—one brand is stronger, brighter, and so forth than "the others." For example, Ads by Alltel Wireless depict its hip spokesperson Chad embarrassing the spokespeople of competitors by highlighting their flaws and emphasizing its superior service features.

Positioning by Product Class or Category

Cereals can be categorized as natural or sweetened. Consumers are likely to position the natural cereals, such as All-Bran or granola, relative to one another. They tend not to consider sweetened cereals, such as Froot Loops or Frosted Flakes, at the same time. When determining a positioning strategy, it is important to understand how consumers categorize products.

Web and E-commerce Stars
www.fao.com

FAO Schwarz has specialized in unique, hard-to-find, and exclusive toys and collectibles from around the globe for many years. This Web site was launched in 1995, and became the fastest-growing facet of the company, allowing it to become the "ultimate" online toy retailer. In the Web site you can search toys by categories and also create your own toys. Moreover you can use 'my gift finder' to receive an idea for the "perfect" gift from a toy expert. At last, in 'Extraordinary Finds' section, people can find more interesting information about toy auditions, store events, and magical parties they can throw at the store. FAO Schwarz is the ultimate in toys both in-store and on the Internet.

Positioning by Country of Origin A company's image can be affected by the mental association people make with its country of origin. We think of German precision engineering, Japanese cost and quality, Italian fashion, French taste, and U.S. technology. Certain countries are associated with certain products: the United States with movies, Germany with beer, Japan with electronics, the Netherlands with chocolate, France with wine, and Italy with shoes. Companies may create a subsidiary in a nation associated with a product, or they may use a brand name that sounds like it's from that country. For example, Little Caesar's is a U.S. pizza company with an Italian-sounding name.

REPOSITIONING

Introduced in 1927, Naturalizer used to target their line of shoes at mature women who preferred comfort over style. Over the past eight years, it has succeeded in winning over younger women by embarking on brand repositioning that involved overhauling the product line, updating its logo, redesigning stores, and giving its catalog and Website a makeover. Today its average customer is 40-45 years old -- 15-20 years younger than the average customer a decade ago -- and seeking footwear that is stylish as well as comfortable.[59] Repositioning may become necessary over time as competitive forces, customer tastes and preferences, and the marketing environment change. Hyundai will increase its price bases and reposition itself as a European mid-level brand, not as a cheap automaker. The brand repositioning allows Hyundai to become a competitor with Western European brands, and to avoid price competition with soon-to-be-released vehicles from Chinese automakers. Hyundai's Santa Fe SUV is now attracting buyers that typically prefer to purchase top-ranked premium brands.[60] Repositioning can be difficult and very expensive because it's hard to alter old impressions and create new ones. Whether a company is positioning a new product or repositioning an old one, the ultimate goal of its decision making is to persuade the targeted consumer to make a decision as well—the decision to purchase the product.

Chapter Summary:

Objective 1: Understand the advantages of target marketing and how it differs from mass marketing and product differentiation.

Mass marketing treats all customers as though they have the same needs and wants. A single marketing strategy is designed to appeal to all potential customers. This strategy does not generally work well because customers with differing characteristics have different needs and wants. Product differentiation is a strategy that alters products to stress their uniqueness relative to competitors. It recognizes that customers have differing needs and wants, but it doesn't start with an understanding of them. Target marketing focuses on select groups of customers so marketers can more clearly understand their specific needs and wants and adjust accordingly.

Objective 2: Describe how to do market segmentation and select target markets.

Market segmentation separates potential customers into several groups or segments with distinctive characteristics. Customers within a segment should have similar needs, wants, and preferences; they should have similar media habits and shopping and buying patterns; the group should be large enough to justify attention; and data about individuals in each segment should be available.

Typical segmentation variables are geographic and demographic factors, ethnic and other diversity-related factors, psychographic and behavioristic factors, and benefits desired. Two common segmenting methods are the take-down method and the build-up method. The take-down method begins by selecting segmentation variables and assigning customers to the category in which they fit. The build-up method starts with the unique characteristics of one potential customer. Each time someone with unique characteristics is discovered, a new segment is added.

Segments are selected as target markets based on such factors as their size and growth potential, competition, cost and efficiency, leadership qualities, and compatibility with the organization.

Objective 3: Explore three basic target marketing strategies: undifferentiated, differentiated, and concentrated marketing.

Undifferentiated marketing treats all customers alike and is similar to mass marketing. In order for this strategy to work, companies generally must have significant cost advantages. Differentiated marketing involves serving several segments but adjusting the marketing mix for each. It usually requires decentralized decision making. Concentrated marketing focuses on one segment or only a few. Companies can use all their resources to gain advantage within that group. Because differentiated and concentrated strategies consider customer needs and wants, they are far superior to an undifferentiated strategy.

Objective 4: Know how to do positioning and describe several approaches marketers use to create valuable, lasting images of their products.

Positioning creates in the mind of consumers an image, reputation, or perception of the company and its products relative to competitors. It helps customers understand what is unique about a company and its products. Marketers can use a positioning map to depict how customers perceive products according to certain characteristics. For business products, a commodity, differentiated, or specialty positioning strategy can be used. Products are often positioned by benefit, by price and quality, by the time of use or application, by user or spokesperson, by direct comparison with a competitor, by product class, or by country of origin.

Review Your Understanding

1. Define mass marketing, segmentation, and targeting. How are they different?
2. What are the steps in segmentation, targeting, and positioning?
3. What variables are used to segment markets? Give examples of each.
4. What are the three basic marketing strategies associated with segmentation?
5. What is VALS™ 2? What major categories of consumers does it profile?
6. What is the difference between the take-down and the build-up segmentation methods?
7. What characteristics are used to select target markets?
8. What is micromarketing and how does it differ from mass customization?
9. What are positioning strategies? List three used in business markets.
10. What is a positioning map and how do organizations use it to position products?

Discussion of Concepts

1. Why do marketers use market segmentation to summarize information about large numbers of consumers? Why not just use averages?
2. Are segmentation techniques used by companies that follow a mass marketing strategy? A product differentiation strategy?
3. Imagine that you are the marketing manager for a company that wants to produce a new line of men's and women's dress shirts. Which segmentation variables would be relevant for this market? What categories would you use? Describe five or six market segments that may emerge.
4. What is a segment profile? Develop one for each market segment you listed in question 3.
5. Which segments in question 3 would you select as target markets?
6. Once target markets are chosen, what different strategies are available? Which would work best for your target markets?
7. Why is positioning important? What are some of the different ways to position dress shirts in your target markets?
8. Positioning is typically done relative to the competition. If you have no important competitors, then how can the concept still be useful?

Key Terms And Definitions

Build-up segmentation method: Method that starts with a single potential customer's characteristics and adds a segment for each new characteristic found in other customers.

Centralized decision making: Management process in which a small group of executives makes all the major decisions for the whole company.

Concentrated marketing: Focusing the organization's marketing mix strategy on one or only a few of many possible segments.

Decentralized decision making: Management process in which numerous groups, each dedicated to a specific segment, make decisions about their segment.

De-ethnicization: The result of targeting a product heavily associated with one ethnic group to other segments.

Demographic segmentation: Division of the market according to such characteristics as gender, family life cycle, household type, and income.

Differentiated marketing: Marketing to each of several segments with a marketing mix strategy matched specifically to its desires and expectations.

Geodemography: Combining geographic information with demographics to identify segments with common consumption patterns.

Heterogeneous group: Buyers with diverse characteristics.

Homogeneous group: Buyers with similar characteristics.

Lifestyle: A person's distinctive mode of living.

Market segment: A homogeneous group with similar needs, wants, values, and buying behavior.

Market segment profile: Information about a market segment and the amount of opportunity it represents.

Niche: A very small market segment that most companies ignore because they fail to see any opportunity.

Positioning: Creating an image or perception in the minds of consumers about the organization or its products relative to the competition.

Positioning map: A diagram of how consumers in a segment perceive brands based on specific elements they consider important.

Product differentiation: A marketing strategy with which companies attempt to make their products appear unique relative to the competition.

Product position: The characteristics consumers associate with a brand based on important attributes.

Psychographics: Marketing approaches and tools used to identify lifestyles based on measures of consumers' values, activities, interests, opinions, demographics, and other factors.

Segmentation: Division of a market into homogeneous groups with similar needs, wants, values, and buying behavior.

Segmentation variable: Any distinguishing market factor that can vary, such as gender, age, or income.

Take-down segmentation method: Method that starts with a set of variables and assigns all consumers to one of them.

Target Marketing: The selection of specific homogeneous groups (segment) of potential customers for emphasis.

Targeting strategy: The number of market segments and the relative amount of resources targeted at each.

Undifferentiated marketing: A strategy that views all potential customers as though they were the same.

Zip code segmentation: Division of a market into specific geographic locations based on the demographic makeup of the zip code area.

References

1. Chet Dembeck, "Dell Builds a Better Dot-Com Model," E-Commerce Times, April 6, 2000, www.ecommercetimes.com/news/viewpoint2000/view-000406-2.shtml; Daniel Lyons, "Make the Little Guys Feel Big," Forbes, April 17, 2000, pp. 208+; Michael Dell, "E-Business: Strategies in Net Time," speech at e-business forum at University of Texas, Austin, Texas, April 27, 2000; Dell Computer Web site (www.dell.com), August 22, 2000; Erica Ogg, "Dell to Sell PCs at Best Buy," Dec. 06, 2007, www.news.com, site visited May 01, 2008; Barry Levine, "HP Trumps Dell in 2007 PC Sales," Jan. 17, 2008. www.newsfactor.com, site visited May 01, 2008; www.dellideastorm.com/about, site visited May 01, 2008.
2. General Motors, "The Fleet," www.gm.com, site visited April 09, 2008.
3. Procter & Gamble, "P&G Products," www.pg.com, site visited April 09, 2008.
4. Bounce, Cheer, Downy, Dreft, Dryel, Era, Gain, Ivory Snow, Oxydol and Tide; Camay, Ivory, Old Spice, Olay, Safeguard, and Zest; Head and Shoulders, Daily Defense, Pantene Pro-V, Physique, Pert Plus, Herbal Essence, Aussie, Infusium 23, and Vidal Sassoon; Cascade, Dawn, Joy, Ivory; Crest, Crest Glide, Fixodent, Scope, and Gleem.
5. "Great Lakes Crossing—Michigan's Ultimate Family Entertainment Destination for Summer Fun," PR Newswire, June 1, 2000.
6. Population Reference Bureau, www.prb.org, site visited April 09, 2008.
7. Michael E. Raynor and Howard S. Weinberg, "Beyond Segmentation - Does your company want to satisfy a niche or gain a foothod in the market?," Marketing Management, November/December, 2004.
8. Harry R. Weber, "Coca-Cola to Buy Vitaminwater Maker," Associated Press, May 25, 2007.
9. "Mobile Marketing and Advertising to be Worth $3 Billion by 1Q 2008", NEW YORK, April 10, 2007; Arbitron/Edison Media Research, "The Infinite Dial 2008: Radio's Digital Platforms," April 9, 2008, www.edisonresearch.com/2008%20Infinite%20Dial%20Press%20Release.pdf, site visited May 07, 2008.
10. "Mobile Marketing," Marketing News, April 1, 2006,p. 4.; Nathan Kurtyka, "WEB 3.0: GET PREPARED FOR THE MOBILE REVOLUTION, Marketing News, Chicago, March 15, 2007. Vol 41, Issue 5; pg. 18.
11. Chicago, March 1996, p. 22.
12. Darrell K. Rigby, Vijay Vishwanath, "Localization: The Revolution in Consumer Markets," Harvard Business Review, April 1, 2006.
13. Gary H Anthes, "Beyond ZIP Codes," Computerworld. (Framingham: Sep 19, 2005) Vol.39, Iss. 38; pg. 56.
14. David Churbuck, "Geographics," Forbes, January 6, 1992, pp. 262–266.
15. "Colleges Go All Out in Increasing Effort to Gain Attention," Omaha 5World-Herald, July 30, 2000, p. 9a.
16. Haya El nasser and Paul Overberg, "Old labels just don't stick in 21st century," USA TODAY, December 17, 2003.
17. Rebecca Gardyn, "High Frequency," American Demographics, July 2000, pp. 32–36.
18. www.nikewomen.com, site visited April 09, 2008.
19. "Potential in Men's Arena Unknown," Business and Industry, March 7, 2005, Vol. 22, No. 5, Pg. 19
20. American Men Get More Savvy, Business and Industry, Vol. 22, No. 6; Pg. 21, March 21, 2005.
21. www.anthony.com, site visited April 09, 2008.
22. Elisa Batista, "She's Gotta Have It: Cell Phone," Wired, May 15, 2003.
23. Lisa Everitt, "What's Best for Baby? Parents go to four corners of the store to shop for their pride and joy", National Grocery Buyer, January/February 2003 Issue.
24. U.S. Census Bureau, Public Information Office, Last updated February 07, 2007, www.census.gov, site visited April 09, 2008.
25. Diane E. Lewis, "Gen X Seen Better at Saving Income," The Boston Globe, October 29, 2000, p. J2.
26. Kimberly Palmer, "Gen X-ers: Stingy or Strapped" U.S. News and World Report,February 14, 2007.
27. Stephanie Armour, "Generation Y: They've arrived at work with a new attitude," USA TODAY, November 6, 2005.
28. Sharon Jayson, "Generation Y gets involved," USA TODAY, October 24, 2006.
29. Deborah Rothberg, "Generation Y for Dummies," EWeek IT Journal, Aug. 24, 2006.
30. Lisa Picarille, "The Lure of Youth," Revenue Today, July/August 2006 Issue.
31. Parija Bhatnagar, "More Cheese For the 'Mall Rats'," CNNMoney.com, February 4, 2005.
32. "Teens and E-Commerce: Selling to the Teen Shopper," www.ecommerce-guide.com, visited January 22, 2007.
33. U.S. Census Bureau, 2003 Yankelovich Youth Monitor
34. "Women Outpace Men Online in Number and Growth Rate According to Media Matrix and Jupiter Communications," Business Wire, August 9, 2000.
35. U.S. Census Bureau, www.census.gov, site visited April 09, 2008.
36. U.S. Census Bureau News, May 10, 2006.
37. Michael J. McDermott, "Marketers Pay Attention! Ethnics Comprise 25% of the U.S.," Brandweek, July 18, 1994, p. 26.
38. "The World Factbook, 2003," www.bartleby.com/151/us.html#People, site visited May 16, 2007.
39. Dana James, "Lingua Franca," Marketing News, January 3, 2000, p. 17.
40. Robert Sullivan, "Americans and Their Money," Worth, June 1994, p. 60.
41. "The Best 100 Sources for Marketing Information," American Demographics, January 1995, p. 29.
42. Lewis C. Winters, "International Psychographics," Marketing Research, September 1992, pp. 48–49.
43. "New Generation Widescreen GPS Debuts for Any Golf Cart on Any Golf Course," www.golfbusinesswire.com, January 27, 2006; www.uplinkgolf.com, site visited April 09, 2008.
44. Enid Burns, "Shoppers Shift to Online," Nov. 16, 2005. ClickZ Network, www.clickz.com, site visited April 09, 2008.
45. Dianne Rinehart, "Bursting the beauty myth bubble; Just try averting your eyes from the middle-aged - and naked! -- women in Dove's new "pro-age" campaign. Impossible!," The Hamilton Spectator, February 24, 2007.
46. "Beauty Flash," South China Morning Post,October 29, 2006.
47. Associated Press, "Biker Sues Harley-Davidson for Trying to Yank Business," State News, Michigan State University's Independent Voice, April 10, 1996, p. 6.
48. Caren Weiner,"Educating teens about credit," Campbell Bankrate.com, site visited April 22, 2007.
49. Stacy Perman, "Indie Grocery Stores Beat Back the Bigs," Business Week Online, November 8, 2006.
50. Michael J. Weiss, The Clustering of America (New York: Harper & Row), p. 1.
51. Christopher Hart, "Mass Customization: Conceptual Underpinnings, Opportunities and Limits," International Journal of Service Industry Management 6, no. 2 (1995), pg. 36–45.
52. www.dell.com, site visited April 09, 2008.
53. "Anheuser-Busch criticized for drink critics say appeals to teens," The Associated Press State & Local Wire, April 6, 2007.
54. Judann Dagnoli, "RJR's Uptown Targets Blacks," Advertising Age, December 18, 1989, p. 4.
55. G. Zachary, "Strategic Shift," Wall Street Journal, June 13, 1996, A1.
56. Ibid.
57. Tara Parker-Pope, "Custom Made: The Most Successful Companies Have to Realize a Simple Truth: All Customers Aren't Alike," Wall Street Journal, September 26,1996, pp. R22–23.
58. David A. Aaker and J. Gary Shansby, "Positioning Your Product," Business Horizons, May–June 1982, p. 56.
59. Heather Retzlaff, "Naturalizer's brand makeover lifts sales," Multichannel Merchant, November 1, 2006.
60. Jason Stein, "Hyundai plans price increase in 2008; Korean automaker doesn't want to be known as 'cheaper brand'," Automotive News Europe, January 8, 2007.

The Marketing Gazette
    Kelly Shermach, "Cobranded Credit Cards Inspire Consumer Loyalty," Marketing News, September 9, 1996, p. 12; Kate Fitzgerald and Mark Gleason, "Wal-Mart Leaps into Credit Cards," Advertising Age, September 30, 1996, pp. 1, 62; Kathleen Kiley, "Branded!" Catalog Age, June 1996, pp. 77–80; Renee Covino Rouland, "Toys 'R' Free," Discount Merchandiser, October 1995, p. 70; "Freeshop.com and NextCard Offer Co-branded Credit Card," Direct Marketing, July 2000, p. 12; "Mastercard Offers 'Priceless' Summer Vacation," Bank Advertising News, June 12, 2000, p. 1; and Mary Vanac, "Sears Switches Credit Card to MasterCard," The Plain Dealer, August 15, 2000, p. 6c.; www.priceless.com, site visited June 16, 2007; www.mastercard.com, site visited June 16, 2007.

CASE 8

Tommy Hilfiger

In 1984, Tommy Hilfiger launched his line of menswear with an ad campaign that communicated his vision. It proclaimed: "The 4 Great American Designers for Men are: Ralph Lauren, Perry Ellis, Calvin Klein, Tommy Hilfiger." It was a big joke with the New York designer crowd but Hilfiger is now one of fashion's hottest designers. With 2006 revenue of almost $1.8 billion, he has found tremendous success with his original target—young professional men. Recently, he entered new market segments—hip-hop teens, women, children, and babies.

In the early years, companies such as Calvin Klein, Ralph Lauren, and Bill Blass targeted high-income professionals, so Hilfiger went after younger professionals of more modest means. Now U.S.-based companies Calvin Klein Inc, Gap Inc, and Polo Ralph Lauren Corporation are key competitors. Tommy Hilfiger uses two formats, outlet stores and specialty stores in the U.S., Canada, and Europe to distribute its products. He positioned his clothing as classic casual wear, with just enough new style to make it modern, at an affordable price. This meant building in the quality young professionals desired and adding a slight twist to differentiate his product line. The "twist" might be striped fabric lining the inside of polo shirt collars or colored fabric on a traditional oxford shirt. Thanks to the integration of design and manufacturing, Hilfiger could cash in on the Lauren trend with similar quality but for a more price-sensitive market.

The Tommy Hilfiger Corporation was formed in 1989 in partnership with Silas Chou, a member of one of Hong Kong's oldest textile and apparel families. The Chou family had built a fortune on private-label contracting but was beginning to lose business to lower-wage countries such as India, China, and Vietnam. Teaming with former Ralph Lauren executives, Lawrence Stroll and Joel Horowitz, Chou and Hilfiger integrated design, manufacturing, and marketing. By 1995, the Hilfiger vision was realized; the Council of Fashion Designers of America voted Tommy Hilfiger menswear designer of the year.

Since 1997, Tommy Hilfiger Group has had a Code of Conduct, outlining Tommy's expectations of working conditions in factories that produce its products. Printed in more than 35 languages, it's required to be displayed in all factories authorized to make Tommy products. Third-party inspectors routinely visit these locations to ensure manufacturing processes are in compliance with the code.

Hilfiger often uses a red, white, and blue theme and visualizes his clothes as "celebrating the individuality and creativity that define America." He puts a spin on the classics. Hilfiger positions his designs as an extension of himself. "I want people to feel comfortable yet unique. It's new-age funk combined with traditional style that give my clothing an edge. This enhances people's individuality and enables them to stand out." He notes that "preppy kids started wearing classics in a different way, very oversized. City kids took it another level by going giant sized." So Hilfiger created yet another size category, giant, which is considerably larger than XXL. In keeping with the theme, Hilfiger made his logos bigger and extremely graphic.

Hilfiger is worn by a diverse range of public figures. For example, Bill Clinton, Harry Connick Jr., and Mick Jagger all sport his logo. Hilfiger brings together a crossover market of young professionals, preppies, and the urban hip-hop crowd. The prep-urban style runs through many of his lines. Hilfiger says: "I think it's very cool that I can walk down Fifth Avenue and see a messenger wearing my rugby shirt five times too big, and then go to Wall Street and see an investment banker wearing my pinstripes." Hilfiger's street popularity was boosted when Snoop Dogg wore a red, white, and blue rugby shirt on Saturday Night Live. Hilfiger has even been labeled "hip-hop's favorite haberdasher."

In advertising, Tommy always wants his models to seem spirited and fun. Referencing to a typical Hilfiger ad, Adweek wrote: "Notice the group of wet and wild funsters just up from a dunk in their local quarry, their big ol' WASP prepster style Tommy underwear soaked to the eh—groin. There must be something about the large white teeth gleaming in the mouths of all these nice, clean, young 'ammuri-cans' that makes the otherwise revealing image seem spirited, as if people pose for their dentist in their underwear."

Russell Simmons, the founder of Def Jam Records, says that "Tommy's clothing represents the American dream to black kids. They're not interested in buying holey jeans; they want high-quality merchandise." Although Hilfiger has been successful in a variety of markets, of particular interest to many is his success among urban youth. Hilfiger focuses on true "hip-hoppers," a group that may seem too small and too poor to target. But millions of suburban kids follow inner-city trends—ranging from music to clothing. Hilfiger has used hip hop to tap into the inner-city market.

Although Tommy has done well in this market, the company is now attempting to move back to its more classical styles. Joel Horowitz, CEO of Tommy Hilfiger, states, "Improvements in our product design and assortments have been at the heart of our repositioning efforts this year, supported by new marketing and advertising programs.

The company is also using a partnership and new product line to help return to the classic heritage of Tommy. Tommy introduced a line of watches in a licensing deal with Movado. The watch collection includes 230 styles, which range in price from $55 to $175. For the first year of advertising, Movado contributed more than $6 million, which promoted the new line of watches. And Hilfiger's lifestyle campaign featured models Jason Shaw, Tyrone, and Maggie Rizer. "Images are very Kennedy-esque, very nautical, preppie with a twist," Hilfiger said. "It coincides with our return to our classical heritage."

In response to displeasure from animal-loving customers and Hilfiger's own values, Tommy announced that it would discontinue the use of fur in its apparel in 2007. In accordance with the company's guidelines for humane treatment of animals, all Tommy products will be made with faux fur.

Hilfiger has expanded into the professional women's market with a positioning strategy very similar to that used for men. This could be a very smart move given the strong trend among women toward casual dress. Hilfiger also has started to jump into the accessory market, such as footwear, eyewear, and handbags. And all of its accessories are preppy in style and classically designed using red, white and blue as the main colors in the logos and designs. They are also able to target a specific cohort of women, those with very young children and expectant mothers, with a line of Tommy clothes for babies. This line features onesies, body-suits, overalls, cardigans, pants, and accessories designed like traditional clothing but, of course, with that unexpected twist. Hilfiger gives a face-lift to the very traditional onesie with a large star logo chest motif and contrasting navy and red shoulder, neck, and cuff stitching. He also spruces up the classic bodysuit, adding lap shoulder styles for boys and girls, as well as polo styles for boys and petal-collar styles for girls.

1. *Identify the core target markets of Tommy Hilfiger, historically and today. What subsegments are targeted within each core target?*
2. *Develop an overall segmentation scheme using variables and categories that describe the Tommy Hilfiger market. How do the Hilfiger target market segments differ from those of Calvin Klein?*
3. *Describe the traditional positioning strategy Hilfiger used for the professional men segment. Use a positioning map to represent it. Why did you select each of the axes? How is Tommy Hilfiger differentiated from Calvin Klein and Bill Blass?*
4. *How is Tommy positioned in the women's target market segment? What are the similarities and differences with Tommy Hilfiger's positioning with men?*

Sources: Justin Doebele, "A Brand Is Born," Forbes, February 26, 1996, pp. 65–66; Elaine Underwood, "Tommy Hilfiger on Brand Hilfiger," Brandweek, February 5, 1996, pp. 23–27; Joshua Levine, "Badass Sells," Forbes, April 21, 1997, www.forbes.com; Shelley Reese, "The Quality of Cool," Marketing Tools, July 1997, www.marketingtools.com; Marc Speigler, "Marketing Street Culture: Bringing Hip-Hop Style to the Mainstream," American Demographics, www.marketingtools.com; Woody Hocksvender, "Prep-Urban," Esquire, March 1996, pp. 131–132; Martha Duffy, "H Stands for Hilifiger: The Former Menswear Laughing Stock Expands into the Women's Market," Time, September 16, 1996, p. 66; and Barbara Lippert, "Beyond Critical," Adweek, March 18, 1996; Tommy Hilfiger Corporation Reports Fiscal 2001 Second Quarter Results, PR Newswire Association, Inc., Financial News, November 1, 2000; Tommy's Quality Time With Movado, DNR, v.30, no. 130, November 6, 2000; "Tommy Hilfiger : 2006 company profile edition 1 : Company Dossier", Just-Style, August 2006, p1; http://usa.tommy.com/, site visited June 16, 2007; http://www.thinkfashion.com/accessories/tommy-hilfiger.aspx, visited June 16, 2007; Tommy Hilfiger Code of Conduct, www.tommy.com, site visited May 01, 2008; "Tommy Hilfiger Goes Fur-Free," Corporate Press Release, www.tommy.com, site visited May 01, 2008.

SECTION 4

Create Value

In this section of Concepts of Marketing: Creating and Capturing Value, you will learn the process of value creation. Value is created through the goods and services offered by an organization. The following chapters are included in this section:

Chapter 9   Brand Management & Product Decisions
Chapter 10 Goods, Services & Nonprofit Marketing
Chapter 11 Product Innovation & Management

Brand Management & Product Decisions

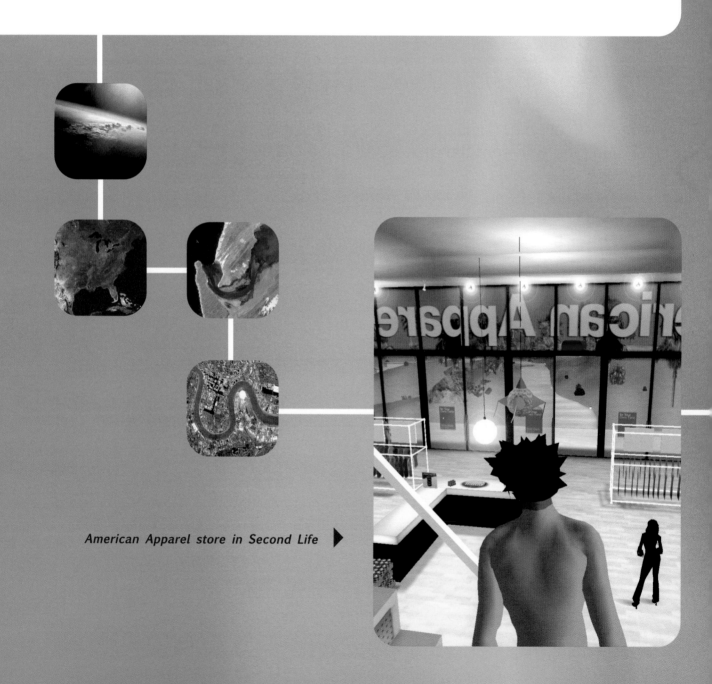

American Apparel store in Second Life ▶

Learning Objectives

1. Describe the major dimensions used by marketers to differentiate products from competitors. Understand bundling and unbundling.

2. Understand consumer and business product classifications based on how and why products are purchased and consumed.

3. Know how organizations make product line decisions that determine what will be sold, including the degree of standardization chosen for global markets.

4. Recognize that branding and brand strategies are important aspects of building and maintaining a brand name.

5. Know how to create brand equity—the value associated with a product's name.

6. Discuss the many legal and ethical issues surrounding brand and packaging decisions.

Right now you can walk into a digital world full of virtual people, entertainment, experiences, and even opportunity. Meet Second Life - a 3-D virtual world built entirely by its nearly 8 million virtual residents. Second Life's virtual playground is more than a game, it's a new digital world where people's virtual representations, called avatars, can live, communicate, teleport and buy products and services.

Second Life, or SL, is a new method of interactive communication that is likely to become second nature to millions of people around the world. Because of it's exploding potential, hundreds of corporations are developing new marketing plans to help cultivate their brand in virtual space. American Apparel opened the first virtual store in SL. Users outfit their avatar in the same clothing available in real-life brick-and-mortar stores and compare virtual clothing to the real-life equivalent by viewing photographs with direct links to the real thing on the American Apparel Web site. Virtual prices, based on the Linden Dollar (about 250L dollars to 1 US dollar), range from 30L for T-shirts, to 300L for dresses and other trendy apparel.

Toyota simultaneously launched a redesigned 2008 Scion xB and a new model called xD in SL. Users are invited to take a free test drive directly from the showroom floor and can purchase a new Scion for only 300L dollars. Customization of styles, colors, and accessories are available to satisfy the wide variety of world-wide tastes. "We developed Scion City to connect with the trendsetters," Adrian Si, Scion's interactive marketing manager, said. "That's our target demographic - - people who do things first. Trendsetters are instrumental in promoting brands." Steve Haag, Scion corporate manager says, "We want to capture customers who would not have considered the Toyota brand. We don't want to necessarily sell them Scions. We want them to get to know our brand, and hopefully consider something in the Toyota family because they like who we are."

Mercedes-Benz opened their new Island in SL with great success by reaching the island's visitor capacity. Guests have access to a variety of visual entertainment and music downloads in addition to information on the Mercedes-Benz brand itself. Upon entering the showroom, a virtual Formula 1 racing suit and helmet, wearable by your avatar, is available as a free gift.

The new Mercedes-Benz C-class debuted in SL prior to to it's official 'real world' launch. The exclusive premiere event on Mercedes-Benz Island encouraged users to take the C-class for a test drive on the island's challenging test track. Guests were also invited to an after-show party hosted by the popular German DJ, Julian Smith. "Digital communication has been established as a permanent component of the Mercedes-Benz marketing activities. With Second Life we are consequently using a new communication platform to further address our existing and potential customers," says Dr. Olaf Gottgens, Vice President Brand Communications Mercedes-Benz Passenger Cars. "In Second Life Mercedes-Benz sets new standards, both visually and with regard to the content. At the same time we offer to experience the fascination of the brand and its products in this virtual environment," continues Mr. Gottgens.

Hundreds of other brick-and-mortar companies are cultivating the potential of the new virtual world in Second Life. IBM, AOL, 20th Century Fox, CNET, Warner Bros Music, Adidas, Reebok, Dell, Disney, Mazda, MTV, and Sun Microsystems have all established a SL foundation to sell or promote their products or services. Coca-Cola has also joined the virtual world of SL, to further pursue the teen market online. Many of these companies hire staff to manage and maintain a virtual presence in SL. Mercedes-Benz, for example, has a dedicated SL staff ready to answer any of your questions. They also hired a special press avatar to be available between 2-3 p.m. during the early phases of their launch.

Real-life companies are flocking to SL's booming population and rapidly growing economy. "There is no question that interest and demand in this space is enormous right now," said Giff Constable, vice president of business development for Electric Sheep, which counts Reuters and Sony BMG among its clients. It is difficult to predict the possibilities of SL, but forward-thinking marketers are recognizing the vast potential and leveraging it to add value to their brands.[1]

THE CONCEPT OF PRODUCTS

Product strategies excite and challenge marketers. Affecting nearly every aspect of the business, product strategies connect companies and customers. This chapter describes how products are managed from a marketer's perspective with particular attention to brand management. The next chapter focuses on services, which are a special case, and Chapter 11 addresses new-product development. A **product** is any physical object, service, idea, person, event, place, or organization that can be offered to satisfy consumers' needs and wants. Products can be combined to perform important functions for individuals, families, or organizations. In the broadest sense, anything that is purchased or sold can be considered a product. Corn, cornflakes, and Kellogg's Corn Flakes are all products. A silicon chip, a transistor, and a computer are all products. A movie, a baseball game, and airplane travel are also products. For many people, the term *product* refers to a tangible item but may be actually services, a special category of products. Services represent more than 80 percent of U.S. GDP, and nearly 75 percent of the U.S. workforce is employed in service industries, such as restaurants, lodging, health care, and law.

Figure 9.1 presents the topics covered in this chapter. First we explore the three dimensions of a product. Then we turn our attention to product classifications and global product line decisions. We will then take a look at branding, packaging, and labeling. The chapter concludes with a discussion of ethical issues surrounding product safety and liability.

Most marketing experts describe products in terms of three dimensions: core, branded, and augmented.

CORE PRODUCTS

A **core product** is the physical item or intangible service that the customer receives. It refers to functions and benefits at the most basic level. A core product can be a tennis racket, a subcompact automobile, a bowling center, a life insurance policy, or a physical examination. The core product is the essential item or service purchased and does not include the brand name, styling features, packaging, or any other descriptive aspects.

A core product is often called the *generic product,* which means it conforms to the basic description that specifies the function it performs. A bicycle has two wheels and can function as a mode of

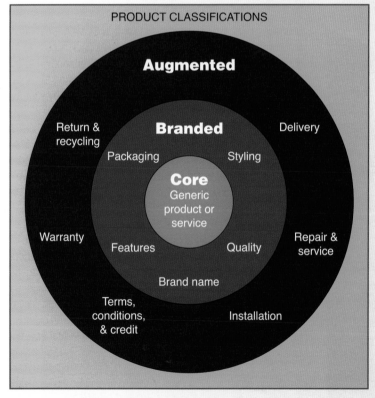

GLOBAL PRODUCT LINE DECISIONS

PRODUCT CLASSIFICATIONS

Augmented

Return & recycling

Branded

Packaging

Delivery

Core
Generic product or service

Styling

Warranty

Features

Quality

Repair & service

Brand name

Terms, conditions, & credit

Installation

Figure 9.1   Concept of a Product

transportation. Although mountain bikes have specifications different from touring bikes and racing bikes, all of them perform the generic function of transportation. One of the most common examples is generic pharmaceuticals, which are drugs sold without reference to a particular manufacturer. Usually the company that discovers or invents a drug will patent and then brand it. Once the patent expires, other companies can simply copy the pharmacological formula and sell it as a generic drug. It usually costs much less than the branded drug since its price doesn't have to reflect the research or marketing costs associated with developing and introducing new drugs.

BRANDED PRODUCTS

A **branded product** is the core product plus characteristics consumers use to differentiate it from similar products. Most important is the brand name, although styling, quality, features, and packaging are additional ways to distinguish brands. The branded product also can be called the identified product, because branding confers an identity just as a rancher's brand identifies a herd. Branded products not only carry the value of the core product but also have a distinctiveness that allows consumers to recognize and recall experiences with them. Nearly every global consumer recognizes the name Apple. In a recent international readers survey, Apple was ranked the brand with the most global impact. With its unique emphasis on innovation, simplicity and style, Apples' branded products are capturing the eyes and dollars of consumers worldwide.[2]

Some branded products are identified purely by the need for the function they perform, such as Morton's salt. Others may be identified through styling. For example, most of us easily recognize the distinctive lines of a Porsche or a Corvette. When Volkswagen dropped the popular Beetle model and used new styling, the result was confusion in the marketplace. A reintroduction of the Beetle was met with widespread consumer acceptance. Quality and reliability also tend to be associated with brands. For many decades, Maytag has promoted its product reliability by depicting the lonely repairman who never gets to visit a customer. Finally, packaging may differentiate one product from another. We all recognize immediately the distinctive script lettering of Coke.

AUGMENTED PRODUCTS

An **augmented product** has characteristics that enhance value beyond that of the core and branded products. Delivery methods, warranty conditions, and credit terms are ways to augment a product. A dishwasher from Sears can be delivered, installed, covered by a limited warranty, and paid off on credit. Many products also require extensive installation, such as an in-ground swimming pool. Once a product has been purchased, installed, and used, it may require service or repair. That's why warranty conditions and the availability of service are significant in augmenting products.

Another aspect of augmentation is product **bundling strategy** that combines many products into a single offering. Product bundling enables manufacturers to add value. Stereo equipment, for example, can be sold as a system or as individual components. Maybe in the purchasing process you find that Harman/Kardon speakers sound better, but you prefer the Pioneer receiver and a Sony CD player. In this case, you want to buy an unbundled product. Yamaha's strategy is to market a whole stereo system, with components specifically designed to work together for maximum sound quality.

The movement toward green marketing is a form of augmentation. Product disposal is becoming an extremely important issue. Many consumers want a product that can be returned for recycling at the end of its usefulness. A common example of recycling is automobiles that flow to the used car market and eventually into reclamation centers, where usable parts are extracted and such raw materials as

Courtesy of Apple

Apple's iPod Touch is an example of a branded product.

Marketing Vocabulary

PRODUCT
Any physical object, service, idea, person, event, place, or organization offered to satisfy consumers' needs and wants.

CORE PRODUCT
The essential physical item or intangible service that the customer receives.

BRANDED PRODUCT
The core product plus the characteristics that allow the consumer to differentiate it from similar products.

AUGMENTED PRODUCT
Product with characteristics that enhance its value beyond that of the core and branded products.

BUNDLING STRATEGY
A strategy in which several products are combined into a single offering.

metal and rubber are recycled. In order to promote their brand as environmentally conscientious, Staples Inc. now offers a 24 hour drop off for electronics recycling. As the first nationwide retailer to offer such a service, Staples Inc. has responded to the increasing environmental concerns of consumers.[3]

CONSUMER PRODUCT CLASSIFICATION

Marketers divide products into the five categories listed in Figure 9.2.

Unsought Products **Unsought products** are not thought about frequently nor perceived as very necessary. The need is usually felt just briefly before purchase, such as novelties, T-shirts or "over the hill" gag gifts. They also include items buyers don't like to think about, such as cemetery plots. In any case, consumers don't seek information so prominent promotions are very important. In some cases, heavy sales effort may be required to persuade potential buyers to consider the item.

Impulse items is a special category of unsought products which as the name suggests, these purchases are made on a whim, with very little thought. In most cases impulse items are relatively inexpensive and have little to

> **www.yamaha.com**
> **Yamaha has six principles that guide its approach to environmental stewardship. Learn more about how Yamaha applies these principles across its many products.**

do with need fulfillment, other than the buyer's immediate enjoyment at the time of purchase. How many times have you been grocery shopping and tossed into your cart a box of Chips Ahoy! or Twinkies?

Emergency Products **Emergency products** are purchased when an unexpected event takes place and the consumer has an urgent need for a product. When an ambulance or tow truck is needed, the buyer is unlikely to compare prices and probably has little choice about the supplier. From the marketer's standpoint, it's crucial to have telephone numbers and other means of access available to buyers when an emergency occurs. A good example is the 911 service that local police, fire, and ambulance agencies promote. American Express provides consumers with phone numbers that allow lost traveler's checks to be replaced immediately. Many automobile companies now provide toll-free numbers for emergency roadside service.

Convenience Products **Convenience products** are relatively inexpensive items that consumers purchase frequently and with minimum effort. Often they are referred to as staples because people always need them—milk, toilet paper, gum, soft drinks, and so on. Convenience items are usually bought close to home, work, or travel routes. Typically they are purchased only when the consumer's supply is low. For example, when your tube of toothpaste is almost gone, you'll probably

Classification	Repurchase Planning	Number of Comparisons Made	Frequency of Purchase	Location of Purchase	Examples
Unsought	None	Few or none	Seldom	At buyer's home or at store checkout	Cemetery plots Pet rock
Emergency	Unexpected need	None	Very rarely or once	Closest to emergency	Ambulance Towing service
Convenience	Little	Several (but over many purchases)	Often and regularly	Close to home, travel, work	Soft drinks Chewing gum Fast food
Shopping	Moderate	Many	Infrequent	In areas with many similar products	Automobiles Televisions Appliances Furniture Clothing
Specialty	Extensive	Few	Infrequent	Buyer travels to merchant's location	Fine watches Gourmet restaurants

Figure 9.2   A Product Classification Based on Consumer Purchase Behavior

buy another. Most of you won't have an inventory of three or four tubes on hand.

Brand name is very important for convenience products because buyers don't spend much time selecting their purchase. They tend to be brand loyal but will choose a substitute if their favorite is unavailable. Consider the national drugstore chain CVS. Since drugstore supplies are items that buyers want to purchase with minimum effort, CVS provides one-stop shopping for a multitude of pharmaceutical and beauty needs. CVS also offers its own brand, which reduces purchase decision time as well as cost. Marketers must ensure that convenience items are widely distributed and prominently displayed so they are noticed and easily purchased. Eye-catching packaging also can be important.

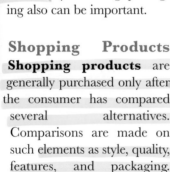

Procter & Gamble now makes laundry detergent, a shopping product, in concentrated formula to conserve materials.

Shopping Products

Shopping products are generally purchased only after the consumer has compared several alternatives. Comparisons are made on such elements as style, quality, features, and packaging. Buyers compare prices to select the product providing the best value. Most shopping products are purchased less frequently and cost more than convenience items. Automobiles, televisions, appliances, furniture, and clothing are all considered shopping goods. Although people may do some prepurchase planning at home, they are likely to visit stores to examine shopping goods. That's why stores offering similar types of shopping goods tend to be located near one another. There may be several shoe stores in the same wing of a shopping mall, or several automobile dealerships not far apart on the same street. This makes it easier for consumers to make comparisons and increases the chance that one of the outlets will make the sale.

Because shopping goods tend to be relatively durable, consumers don't want them to clash with what they already own. Selecting just the right piece of furniture to complement a room or finding an item of clothing that coordinates with one's wardrobe can require extensive shopping. Many people take along friends or family to help with the decision, and there tends to be interaction with salespeople. Most of us wouldn't purchase a car or a business suit without first consulting a salesperson. Many retailers and manufacturers recognize this and train their salespeople to identify buyers' needs and help them find exactly the right item.

Because comparisons are made among shopping goods, many manufacturers market several similar products at different price points. Apple, Inc. continually launches a range of new generation mp3 players. The iPod Touch allows users to watch movies, listen to music, and surf the internet. Apple also offers the iPod Classic, Nano and Shuffle which all have different features and storage capacities. The three units give customers more choices at multiple price points.[4]

Specialty Products

Specialty items have unique characteristics that provide unusual value to the purchaser. Most carry meanings that buyers associate with their self-image. Consequently, customers are brand loyal and often refuse to accept substitutes. They are willing to travel long distances and pay high prices to obtain particular products. Some examples are Movado watches, Gucci purses, Godiva chocolates, Louis Vuitton luggage, and Armani suits. A lobster and filet mignon dinner, a dress from Saks Fifth Avenue, a stay at the Plaza Hotel, or a luxury cruise also can be considered specialty items.

Most consumers spend a

Marketing Vocabulary

UNSOUGHT PRODUCT
An item that consumers don't think about frequently and for which they don't perceive much need.

EMERGENCY PRODUCT
A product purchased due to an unexpected event and for which the consumer has an urgent need.

CONVENIENCE PRODUCT
A relatively inexpensive item that consumers purchase frequently and with minimum effort.

SHOPPING PRODUCT
A purchase generally made only after the consumer has compared several alternatives.

SPECIALTY ITEM
A product with unique characteristics that provides unusual value to the purchaser.

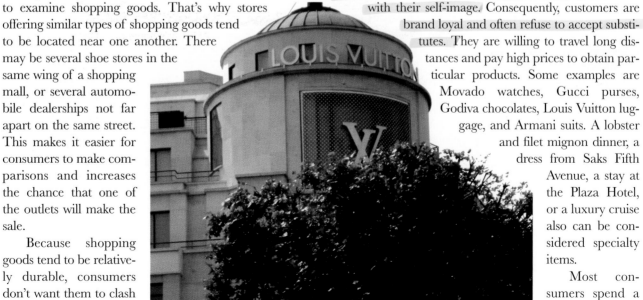

Louis Vuitton products are examples of specialty items.

considerable amount of time on prepurchase planning for specialty items. They must acquire the necessary funds and select a particular style or model of the brand. Marketing a specialty product requires heavy involvement of the retailer to ensure the right fit between the individual model and the customer's needs. To justify the expense of this service, marketers work hard to create customer loyalty. Repeat purchases generate enough profit over time to offset the cost of the first sale.

Service professionals often try to achieve the status of a specialty provider. There are physicians who practice only internal medicine, oncology, or cosmetic surgery. The specialty classification signifies a great deal more value to most customers and in turn commands a much higher price. Certain types of lawyers, architects, consultants, and accountants usually charge more than their nonspecialized counterparts. Buyers often seek these suppliers not only for their status but also because of the unique qualities of the product or service they provide.

BUSINESS PRODUCT CLASSIFICATION

Business products are purchased by an organization for its own use. The seven types listed in Figure 9.3 are grouped into three categories according to function. These are the products needed to start a company and keep it running for a long time.

several years. Capital products are subdivided into installations and equipment.

Installations house operations; examples include office buildings, factories, and distribution centers. Because they have a high cost and are intended to last for a considerable time, they are carefully selected by top management. Salespeople for these products use technical expertise to communicate with buyers. Marketing generally requires a team approach, an understanding of the prospective client's business, and customization of the product to meet the unique requirements of each customer. Providers range from a small construction firm that may put up an office for a local dentist to companies such as Bechtel, a huge multinational. It has offices in most world regions and relies on marketing skills to find opportunities and win business globally.

Equipment is movable capital goods used to manufacture or maintain other products. Drills, computers, forklifts, and die presses fit this category. ABB and AO Smith sell robotics designed for specific tasks to many types of manufacturers. General Motors (GM), Nissan, and Toyota have purchased thousands of robots for welding alone; other functions include sorting, lifting, and inspecting. Of course, products that bring information to businesses represent a huge equipment marketing opportunity. Companies such as Sun Microsystems sell com-

Category and Type	Description	Examples
Capital Products		
Installations	Facilities that contain operations	Office buildings, factories, stores, distribution centers
Equipment	Items used to manufacture products and support the business	Drills, computers, desks, robots, lifts, trucks, airplanes
Production Products		
Raw materials	Substances in natural state	Crude oil, sand, gas, water
Processed materials	Basic substances used to manufacture products	Refined oil, steel, plastic, aluminum
Component Parts and Subassemblies		
Operations products	Products that are elements of other products	Brakes, transmissions, computer chips, switches, lights, cords
Operating services	Activities purchased to help run the business	Consulting, accounting, waste removal, employee food service
Operating supplies	Consumable items used by the business	Paper, pens, file folders, cleaning products

Figure 9.3   A Classification of Business Products

Capital Products   **Capital products** are costly items that last a long time but are not part of any finished product. They usually are built or used to manufacture, distribute, or support the development of products. For accounting purposes, these items are depreciated over

puterized workstations for professional and clerical workers. These products are connected through elaborate networks that allow personnel around the globe to tie into the company system. Airline reservations in Japan, France, the United States, and the Czech Republic are likely to be made this way. It is not unusual for these

Photo courtesy of ABB.

ABB produces robots, used on automobile production lines.

equipment systems to be priced at hundreds of millions of dollars.

Production Products

Production products —raw materials, processed materials, component parts, and subassemblies—become part of other goods. Few manufacturers extract the raw materials or make all the components for a finished product. Instead, they rely on outside suppliers. Raw materials are basic substances used in the manufacture of products, such as ore or grain to produce steel or flour, or cotton and wool for textiles, or soybeans for food products. Companies such as Archer-Daniels-Midland (ADM) claim that they "feed the world" because their agricultural products go into so many food items. Processed materials undergo an intermediate treatment—such as refining, chemical combination, purification, crushing, or milling—before reaching the manufacturer.

Component parts and subassemblies are manufactured goods that are elements of other products. Brake linings are components of antilock brake systems. Since these have several components and are part of still another product—vehicles—they are called subassemblies. Companies such as Eaton and North American Rockwell make components and subassemblies. Although each part is relatively inexpensive, manufacturing companies are likely to purchase large quantities at one time, numbering thousands or even millions of units.

Quality control and delivery of component parts can be very complicated, so successful companies must perform these operations at a high level of precision. Marketers stress this aspect of their product when selling to businesses, which usually is done by highly trained sales representatives.

Operations Products

Operations products are purchased to help run the business but are not included in finished products. These range from very inexpensive items, such as paper clips, to an expensive product like nuclear waste removal from power plants. Operations products are subdivided into supplies and services. **Supplies** are consumable items that may seem relatively unimportant, but in total they can involve large sums. In banks, printed business forms alone often cost several hundred thousand dollars a year. Items such as pens, folders, and cleaning products can contribute significantly to company costs. Even with the increased use of the Internet and more offices going paperless, Xerox found that the world prints about 2.8 trillion pages each year with 45 percent of them read only once.[5]

Operations services are activities purchased to help run the business. Examples are legal, accounting, advertising, and billing services. Some companies now outsource their entire logistics operations. Accenture, EDS, and McKinsey & Company all compete for lucrative contracts involving R&D, tactical and strategic plans, and design of information systems. Companies such as ARAMARK supplies food service. Many companies have outsiders handle customer service; for example, if your Toshiba laptop computer needs to be repaired, UPS will pick it up, repair it and return it to you within three days. By having a third party, UPS, handle their customer service, Toshiba was able to greatly reduce the repair turnaround time and increase customer satisfaction.[6]

PRODUCT LINE DECISIONS

Product lines must be configured for domestic and global markets. Decisions about how many lines to carry, how many products in each line, and the degree of standardization across markets shape the overall offering of an organization. A product line consists of the closely related products marketed by an organization. A company may have one line or several, but a single line usually focuses on the same type of benefit, such as hair care. An **item** is a specific version of a product within a product line. Each item, in turn, consists of several units. A unit refers to the specific product amount, container

Marketing Vocabulary

CAPITAL PRODUCT
A costly item that lasts a long time but does not become part of any finished product.

PRODUCTION PRODUCTS
Raw materials, processed materials, component parts, and subassemblies that become part of other goods.

OPERATIONS PRODUCTS
Products purchased to help run a business and are not included in finished products.

SUPPLIES
Consumable items used for business operations.

PRODUCT LINE
Closely related products marketed by the organization.

ITEM
A specific version of a product within a product line.

size or type, and formula. Retailers call these stock-keeping units (SKUs) to identify the variations they regularly have on the shelves.

Consider a line of products in the hair care category made by Procter & Gamble, Pantene, which includes several items—mousse, styling gel, hair spray, and shampoo. Pantene's 40 SKU shampoo product line consists of five different categories based on the type of look the customer is seeking. The categories are basic, volume, smooth, curl, and color care. Each category has a shampoo, a conditioner, two hairsprays, and various other styling aids. Procter & Gamble carefully manages the entire line and Pantene is the market leader in shampoo and conditioner.

Courtesy of Procter & Gamble

Product Depth and Breadth Most companies need to consider how broad and deep their product lines should be, as described in Figure 9.4. The **depth** of a product line refers to the number of items. Since the Pantene shampoo product line consists of many items, it is said to be deep. A product line with only a few items is called shallow. **Breadth** of product lines refers to the number of different lines a company markets. Since Procter & Gamble markets many, ranging from laundry detergent to toothpaste to a variety of foods, it is considered to have a broad number of product lines. General Electric has an even broader set of product lines, marketing household products to consumers, nuclear power plants to foreign governments, and hundreds of other product lines as well.

Hershey's candies can be considered a narrow and deep product line. The products fall in a single product category, candy, and there is a wide variety of items. Hershey's produces everything from their gourmet CaCao Reserve chocolate bar to Bubble Yum. Organizations such as Dominos Pizza have a broad and shallow product line. Their menu offers a variety of products from pizza, salads and drinks with only a few choices within each category.

Most companies with a broad product line are large, although there are exceptions. Small organizations usually lack the resources for competing across diverse product categories. Brunswick is a large company that uses a broad and deep product line strategy. One of its lines, recreational boats, is marketed under the brand name Sea Ray. Sea Ray produces several different types of boats, ranging from 12 feet to more than 80 feet. It also owns Brunswick Bowling &

Billiards, which markets a line of products ranging from alleys with automatic pinsetters to bowling balls and other equipment. Another Brunswick product line is fishing equipment, marketed under the Zebco brand name, with several types of rods, reels, and related items. Brunswick also markets a number of other product lines with several items each.

Now think about 7-11. It carries a broad product line, but the variety of items within each is limited. In other words, 7-11 carries a broad and shallow product line including: beverages, cleaning supplies, food, over the counter pharmaceuticals, snack foods, auto supplies, cosmetics, and energy bars. In some instances, product lines may be too deep or too broad. Procter & Gamble continuously restructures products lines to focus on more specific lines.

GLOBAL PRODUCT DECISIONS

The globalization of business creates several product-related dilemmas. Among the most critical is determining the optimal amount of standardization for individual products and lines across market regions. Different areas of the world vary greatly in terms of consumer and business purchasing approaches, media exposure, and tastes and preferences. In addition, product standards and regulations, measurements and calibration systems, and economic factors vary immensely. Despite these differences, however, many firms like to standardize products to achieve economics of scale in R&D, production, and marketing.

Standardization plays a major role in global company strategy. In efforts to standardize the products it markets, companies often standardize its suppliers to consolidate worldwide supply purchasing, improve material quality, and reduce costs. By purchasing from a few similar suppliers, companies reduce product variations from region to region and develop relationships with its suppliers that help lead to more customer satisfaction.

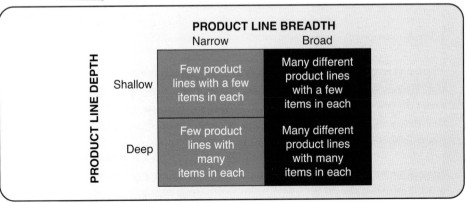

Figure 9.4   Product Line Depth and Breadth

Quaker Oatmeal is an example of a narrow and deep product line.

Although product modifications usually center around conforming to local needs, the costs can be very high. In the electronics area, Europe and the United States are different, so products made for one market simply will not work in the other. R&D costs to conform to standards run into the hundreds of millions for companies such as Siemens in Germany and General Electric.

The depth and breadth of the product line have a lot to do with successful global competition. Pepsi and Coca-Cola continually compete with each other to expand their product lines. Some believe Coke's global strategy— a narrow line with geographic variations—is one reason for its success. Pepsi, in contrast, has standardized its beverage line globally. Clearly, product line breadth doesn't determine why one company outsells another, but the issue is important in developing global strategy. Although Coca-Cola remains the number-one beverage company with a very deep product line, Pepsi is gaining in popularity through its other product lines. Pepsi recently acquired the South Beach Beverage Company, makers of SoBe, and Quaker Oaks, maker of Gatorade, to deepen its beverage offerings to include fruit blends, teas, and energy drinks, in addition to its already held Aquafina, All Sport, Lipton's Ice Tea, and Frappuccino. Coca-Cola has responded to Pepsi's expansion by purchasing Planet Java coffee, selling its own energy drink KMX, and experimenting with children's milk drinks. Coca-Cola also has its own brands of bottled water, sports drink, and root beer, in addition to other brands sold in various parts of the world. With Pepsi deriving 65 percent of its profits from its snack food line, including products such as Doritos, Cheetos, and Sun Chips, Coca-Cola must continue to promote its beverage products in ways that capture buyers.[7]

Even some companies with deep domestic product lines find additions are in order when going international. Newell Rubbermaid, known for its large number of

products, has its product lines divided to include products marketed globally, which account for approximately 28 percent of total revenues. Newell Rubbermaid implemented a global group product line strategy with four distinct product lines: cleaning, organization & decor; office products; tools & hardware; and home & family. The focus is to invest in strategic brands, reduce supply chain costs, strengthen the portfolio, and to streamline non-strategic selling, general, and administrative (SG&A) expenses.[8] Experience with a deep and broad product line in the consumer, industrial, and health care fields will be important as companies seek to connect with the needs and tastes of consumers in these diverse regions.

Emerging economies such as China present their own problems from a product standpoint because large and risky investments in design and manufacturing are often necessary. Caterpillar Inc. recently announced the opening of a components manufacturing facility in Wuxi, China. This facility will join 13 other wholly or partially owned Caterpillar plants in China. China's economic growth and lagging infrastructure has made it an ideal investment for construction equipment manufacturers such as Caterpillar Inc.[9]

BRAND MANAGEMENT

A **brand** is a distinguishing name or symbol intended to identify and differentiate products from those offered by competitors.[10] Can you name the top 10 brands in the

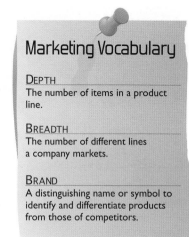

Marketing Vocabulary

DEPTH
The number of items in a product line.

BREADTH
The number of different lines a company markets.

BRAND
A distinguishing name or symbol to identify and differentiate products from those of competitors.

Rank	2000	2007
1.	Coca-Cola	Coca-Cola
2.	Microsoft	Microsoft
3.	IBM	IBM
4.	Intel	General Electric
5.	Nokia	Nokia
6.	General Electric	Toyota
7.	Ford	Intel
8.	Disney	McDonald's
9.	McDonald's	Disney
10.	AT&T	Mercedes-Benz

Figure 9.5   Top 10 Brands Worldwide
Source: Interbrand & Business Week - Best Global Brands 2007

Intel is one of the world's strongest brands.

world? Does your list match Figure 9.5? No matter what criteria are used in creating such a list, the same brands tend to emerge as leaders.[11]

Brands are very powerful concepts in business. They send strong signals about what the product represents. A brand image can make or break a company's reputation. To a consumer, a trusted brand promises high quality, but a "tainted" reputation means poor quality or bad service. One study by Pricewaterhouse-Coopers found that 80 percent of online shoppers say that their purchasing decisions are strongly influenced by the need to buy brand name products.[12]

Today, brands do far more than identify the manufacturer. They have become "personalities" with a character much greater than the products they represent. An early example of successful branding is Ivory soap, introduced in 1879 by Harvey Procter. With its claim of "99.44 percent pure," it has long been the leader. Estimates are that the Ivory brand has brought more than $3 billion in profit to Procter & Gamble over the years. In some cases the brand name becomes the product itself to many people: Xerox, Kleenex, and Rollerblade are synonymous with their functions. And such brands as Nabisco, Kellogg, Kodak, Gillette, Campbell's, and Goodyear have all outlived the specific items they represented when introduced. Although the

products themselves may have altered due to changing technology, customer preferences, and modernization, the brand name has stayed the same.

Historically, brands were used to identify a product's manufacturer. They also protected both the customer and the producer by ensuring that the products met certain quality standards and came from a reputable source. Companies with early success in building brands include Procter & Gamble (P&G), IBM, Anheuser-Busch, Sony, American Express, Volkswagen, American Airlines, Pepsi, and Kodak. Such companies created a brand perceived by consumers as having more intrinsic value.

In the 1960s, the strategy was simple: The greater the perceived value, the greater the sales. This strategy is still used today, but companies must work hard to ensure that the products themselves provide the added value communicated by the name. Brand strategies help businesses such as Coca-Cola, Disney, Gillette, and Intel develop credibility with customers. The role of brands continues to grow in importance. According to TNS Media Intelligence, a leading provider of market information, most advertising expenditures are brand related.[13]

TRADEMARKS

People tend to use the words *brand* and *trademark* interchangeably, but there are some notable differences. The brand name is the wording attached to the product. Coke, Pepsi, and Chiquita are brand names. The **trademark** (brand mark) is a distinctive form or figure that identifies the brand. A picture is called a trademark symbol; distinctively shaped letters are called a logo: IBM, HBO, GE. Coca-Cola uses white script on a red background. Burger King uses a crown, and McDonald's uses golden arches. Other examples are NBC's peacock, Fila's blue-and-red letter F, Chrysler's five-pointed star, and Nike's swoosh symbol.

An identifying mark, slogan, or set of words can provide immediate recognition and credibility even when applied to products owned by other companies. FAFSA is commonly known as Free Application for Federal Student Aid, though it is not a trademark. When a company began running a Web site, FAFSA.com, offering financial aid forms online and by phone to students, the Department of Education protested. The Department of Education said that the site deceived customers by associating itself with the government organization and implying that fees were required for financial aid services. The site's operator says that he is not trying to trick students into paying for services, while the Department of Education claims that it should have the rights to the FAFSA.com site by common law.

i'm lovin' it

Though not explicitly involving trademarks, this issue demonstrates the effectiveness of name brand association.

TRADEMARK PIRACY

The brand name and the trademark symbol or logo are protected by law if they are registered. That gives the owner sole right to use them any way he or she chooses. Just as most people want to protect their reputation, companies are careful to protect a brand. It is property they own and competitors may not use or imitate it. For example, a federal court in Milwaukee ruled that the Hog Farm, a motorcycle parts and repair shop, had to change its name. It infringed on the rights of Harley-Davidson, whose motorcycles are widely known as "hogs."

Often a company protects materials associated with its brand by copyrighting. DaimlerChrysler sued General Motors, saying the grille of the Hummer H2 looked like the grill on a Jeep. GM said that changing the grille design would cost $100 million had the court decided that it violated the DaimlerChrysler trademark design. Fortunately for GM, the Federal District Court ruled that "nothing in record indicates any intent on General Motors part to palm off the H2 as a Jeep, or to exploit consumers' association with Jeep."[14]

In the entertainment industry, property rights and

reputation are no less important. The wording, "Dreamworks presents," is used to brand the company's popular movies Shrek, Shrek 2 and Shrek the Third. Dreamworks also brands products such as Shrek clothing, dolls and videogames.[15]

Securing trademarks globally can be very tricky. People throughout the world recognize Mickey Mouse and Donald Duck as Disney characters, but a court in Indonesia ruled that the duck's picture could be used by a local company. This situation occurs frequently, particularly in developing countries where more pressing problems command government attention. In advanced economies, trademark protection is considered essential for sound competitive industrial policy. Elsewhere trademarks may be viewed as merely a tool to stimulate commerce. No single world policy has yet been developed that takes into account the perspectives of all nations.

No one knows exactly how big the market for counterfeit goods is but trade associations generally agree that it is an estimated $200 billion to $250 billion-a-year business.[16] Counterfeiting has become so widespread that *Fortune* has coined the term brandnapping for copying products and affixing illegal labels. This represents huge losses to legitimate owners of the brands. Pirated products range from computer software and designer goods to soaps and candies. Packaging closely resembles that of the American-made counterpart, and often logo designs are stolen and used. Individual firms may or may not choose to file an international suit against offenders.

Many problems with brand counterfeiting are occurring in China. In fact, China accounts for nearly 2/3 of all counterfeit goods. Recent raids in China have turned up everything from fake Sony PlayStation game controllers to Cisco Systems router interface cards, and even counterfeit elevators. When these components leave China they sometimes end up in the products legitimate supply chain, and can force companies to initiate expensive recalls. However, many fakes today are getting so good that even company executives say that it takes a forensic scientist to distinguish them from the real thing.[17]

Unfortunately, some fakes can have very serious consequences. For example, its estimated that in a single year fake drugs led to the deaths of 192,000 patients in China who were given ineffective treatments. According to the World Health Organization, counterfeit drugs account for more than 10 percent of the total global supply and can run as high as 50 percent in parts of Africa and Asia. Merck, a large pharmaceutical company, exclusively funded Global Pharma

The MGM Grand Lion is a distinctive figure that identifies the hotel.

Health Fund in an effort to derail the counterfeit drug market. The organization will work in conjunction with various governmental and world health agencies.[18] U.S. trade negotiations have lessened the occurrence of infringements, but developing countries have little incentive to enforce laws. Efforts continue through such organizations as GATT and the United Nations to develop international norms.

BRAND STRATEGIES

There are a number of brand strategies, as shown in Figure 9.6. In addition to a generic or nonbranded approach, the most common types are individual, family, manufacturer (national), private, and hybrid.

Generic Strategy   A **generic brand strategy** uses no brand name whatsoever. Firms generally select

The Marketing Gazette™

CREATING & CAPTURING VALUE THROUGH TECHNOLOGY

Intel Makes Customers Care About the Inside

Before 1992—when it wasn't cool to be a cybergeek—not many computer users knew or cared about the microprocessor powering their PC. Then Intel Corporation gave them a reason to care. The company began one of the most revolutionary corporate branding campaigns in history with its "Intel Inside" marketing campaign. Never before had an electrical component company tried to create brand identity with the end user, especially in a commodity market such as computer chips. So far, Intel's share of the microprocessor market has climbed to about 80 percent.

The biggest branding brainstorm was Intel's offer of co-op advertising money for every PC maker who put the "Intel Inside" sticker on its products or in its ads. Intel pays up to 5 percent of the ad costs, and now the logos are as common as Windows. The move shook up the whole industry, and the microprocessor has become a consumer product. Said Al Ries, chairman of a consulting firm, "'Intel Inside' will go down in history as one of the more magnificent campaigns of the century. It's brilliant and, in a sense, it preempted the branding of personal computers."

There were skeptics when Intel first tried to make consumers care about technology. One analyst asked: "If you buy a BMW, who cares about the spark plugs?" Ironically—and to the distress of PC makers—the consumer now often cares more about the "spark plugs" than the name on the disk drive. Intel has beefed up its brand identity even more by designing and building entire motherboards, the circuitry at the heart of PCs. Dozens of computer companies, including IBM, Dell, Hewlett-Packard and even Apple are selling machines with Intel chips. They were forced to march to Intel's beat since they couldn't produce their own motherboard designs as quickly.

Furthermore, as a leader in microprocessor technology, Intel is positioned to improve computer energy requirements and emissions, and last year the company took advantage of it. Developed jointly with Google, The Climate Saves Computing Initiative is making efforts to significantly reduce PC emissions and increase energy efficiency by uniting industry, consumers, and government and conservation organizations. The Initiative's goal is to reduce global computer greenhouse gas emissions by 54 million tons per year, the equivalent of 11 million cars on the road, by the year 2010.

Type	Description	Reasons for Use	Examples
Generic	No brand name is used.	Lower cost. Commodity position.	Pharmaceuticals Vegetables
Individual	Unique brand name for each major product or line.	Company has dissimilar products. Each product is matched to a segment. Products compete against one another.	Procter & Gamble's Tide, Bold, Cheer, Dreft, Era, Gain, Ivory, Oxydol, and Solo laundry detergents.
Family	Umbrella name covers all products in the line.	Economical way to create one brand identity for all existing and new products. Increase awareness and market presence by using one image for all.	Dole Sony Campbell's Sara Lee Black & Decker
Manufacturer (national)	Brand name synonymous with the owner.	Ties R&D, manufacturing, and company reputation to the product.	McDonald's Kodak Fisher-Price Johnson & Johnson General Motors General Electric
Private (labels)	Brand name applied to supplier's product by wholesaler or retailer.	Lower cost. Builds on and enhances reputation of firm. Enhances firm's buying power.	Meijer A&P: Aunt Jane Wal-Mart: Sam's American Choice ACE Hardware IGA Stores Spartain Stores Sears: Kenmore
Hybrid	Two or more approaches are used.	Merger and acquisition. Gain benefits of all approaches.	Kraft

Figure 9.6   Types of Brand Strategies

this approach when they want to gain a low-cost commodity market position. As mentioned before, pharmaceutical companies often adopt this strategy. Some grocery stores devote entire aisles exclusively to generic products, packaged in plain black and white. Many consumers prefer generics because they cost so much less than name brands.

Individual Brand Strategy An **individual brand strategy** assigns a unique brand name to each major product or product line. There are three situations in which this approach is likely to be used. First, companies may have different product lines that compete against one another. For example, General Motors builds total market share with several individual brands: Chevrolet, Cadillac, Pontiac, Buick, and Oldsmobile. Second, products within one line may be matched with unique market segment needs. For example, Procter & Gamble's nine laundry detergents appeal to different segments. Third, a company may make highly dissimilar products. For example, Kellogg markets breakfast cereals under its name, toaster pastries under the Pop-Tarts

brand, and pies under the Mrs. Smith's label.

Family Brand Strategy A **family brand strategy** uses a single brand name for the entire group of products in the company's line(s). This can be very cost-effective because advertising, promotion, and distribution resources can be focused to create a single image in the marketplace. The result is increased consumer awareness of the company and its products, such as Black & Decker tools.

The family brand strategy is used when products are similar. Dole markets more than 20 mainstream fruits and vegetables as well as numerous exotic fruits under one name. The Sony

Marketing Vocabulary

GENERIC BRAND STRATEGY
Strategy in which no brand name is used.

INDIVIDUAL BRAND STRATEGY
Strategy in which there is a unique name for each major product or product line.

FAMILY BRAND STRATEGY
Strategy in which a single brand name covers the entire group of products in the comapany's line(s).

name covers hundreds of products, from high-priced stereos to inexpensive alarm-clock radios. The family brand approach has allowed Sony to introduce and eliminate products fairly rapidly while almost guaranteeing that its new products will at least be tried. Both Dole and Sony have sought to make their names synonymous with quality, regardless of the specific product.

Manufacturer's Brand Strategy

Manufacturer's brands, as the term implies, are named after the maker. Sometimes they are called national brands, since the products often are found throughout the country. We've already mentioned a few in this chapter, such as Kodak and General Electric, but manufacturer's brands also can be local, such as Hanover pretzels. The company's reputation is closely tied to the product. Benetton, McDonald's, and Johnson & Johnson use public relations, advertising, and other means to ensure that the public connects their products with the policies of the firm. Usually this means creating a singular image for the company and the products it makes. Kodak's brand name revolves around imaging; Fisher-Price is known for products that relate to child development and safety; and Gerber is famous for baby food.

Private Brand Strategy

When wholesalers or retailers place their own name on a product, it's called a **private brand** (or private label). Since these are promoted locally rather than nationally, they can be sold at a lower price than manufacturer's brands. Private labels allow the reseller to build and enhance its own reputation. By carefully selecting suppliers and developing quality control mechanisms, Wal-Mart can promote Sam's American Choice products as being high quality at a low price. This strategy increases Wal-Mart's buying power, since the company can shop among competing suppliers for the best price and pass on some of the savings to con-

sumers. In addition, private brands enable retailers and wholesalers to differentiate themselves from competitors.

Companies that use private labels believe they understand consumers better than national marketers in several key respects, especially in their knowledge of local or regional consumer needs and shopping habits. Yet they do not have the resources to innovate far beyond current brands.[19] Their goal is to increase in-store brand sales. For their national brand competitors, the challenge is to persuade consumers not to be drawn by the low prices.[20]

The rivalry between in-store and national products has come to be known as the "battle of the brands." The private label market is growing in supermarkets as consumers become more cost-conscious and as private label brands rival the quality of national brands. The "battle" started when large manufacturers gained power by selling products through a broad range of distribution channels, and their size allowed them to place many demands on retailers. Large retailers retaliated by creating private labels.

Courtesy of Kodak

With a brand strategy based on imaging, Kodak is appealing to customers by improving energy efficiency and material use in its digital cameras.

Hybrid Brand Strategy

Many firms employ a **hybrid brand strategy**, which is a combination of two or more approaches. Often this happens when mergers and acquisitions join organizations using different strategies. In these cases, executives must decide whether to blend the acquired brands into the company's portfolio or let them maintain their identity.

General Motors uses a strategy mix. The individual brand approach generally applies for Chevrolet, Pontiac, Buick, Hummer, Saturn, and Cadillac. Saturn cars were introduced as a family brand with loose ties to GM. The company also promotes the manufacturer brand—General Motors automobiles. At the same time, many GM products, such as spark plugs, are sold under the Delco name or to resellers for private branding.

BRAND EQUITY: CONNECTING WITH A SUCCESSFUL BRAND

Brand equity refers to the assets linked with the brand name and symbol that add value to the product or service.[21] It indicates how valuable the brand is to the parent company. Be aware that a brand carries denotative and connotative meanings. It denotes (identifies) what the brand is, such as Head & Shoulders or Selsun Blue shampoo. It also connotes (produces an image of) the brand's relationship to the consumer's lifestyle. Connotative meanings grow over time and become tremendously valuable. Ideally, brands will achieve enough connotative meaning to endure forever if they are supported properly. Names such as Gillette, Morton's salt, and Betty Crocker predate your grandparents. When people gradually purchase their home from the mortgage company, we say that they are earning or gaining equity. The homeowner is investing in the property. In a similar fashion, companies must invest in developing brands. Through sustained communication of the brand's connotative qualities, value is increased. Brand equity is an intangible asset with five dimensions, as shown in Figure 9.7. Let's look at each dimension in more detail.

Brand Awareness **Brand awareness** is the extent to which consumers recognize the name and are likely to include it among the set of brands they consider. High awareness means a greater probability of purchase. If consumers are familiar with a brand and like it, they will have positive attitudes about the product(s) with that name. Consider the warmth and no-fail reliability of the

Betty Crocker mother figure or Pillsbury's Poppin' Fresh baker. Because strong brands are often global, they may be recognized around the world and provide traveling consumers with ready access to a familiar item. High brand awareness also represents the commitment of the company to maintaining long-term standards of excellence for the consumer.

Even established companies work to sustain brand awareness. One way Kraft does this is through their Web site, www.kraftfoods.com, which provides information on nutrition, cooking for specific occasions, mealtime tips, a personal recipe box, and even allows visitors to find recipes based on what main ingredient they wish to use. Online customers who choose to add their address to a marketing list will receive product information, promotions, a quarterly magazine and coupons through the mail.[22] This increased accessibility to Kraft's brand name is intended to heighten brand awareness.

Brand Loyalty **Brand loyalty** occurs when consumers select a particular brand over others on a regular basis. In effect, the firm's customers are an asset. Brand loyalty leads to lower overall marketing costs because it's much less expensive to persuade repeat buyers than to create new ones. Distribution channel members are more likely to provide a good location within their outlet for the

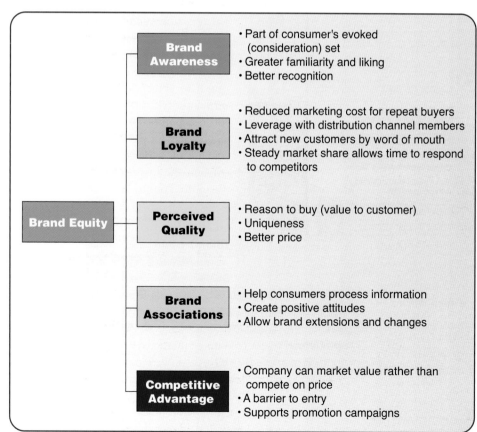

Brand Equity

Brand Awareness
- Part of consumer's evoked (consideration) set
- Greater familiarity and liking
- Better recognition

Brand Loyalty
- Reduced marketing cost for repeat buyers
- Leverage with distribution channel members
- Attract new customers by word of mouth
- Steady market share allows time to respond to competitors

Perceived Quality
- Reason to buy (value to customer)
- Uniqueness
- Better price

Brand Associations
- Help consumers process information
- Create positive attitudes
- Allow brand extensions and changes

Competitive Advantage
- Company can market value rather than compete on price
- A barrier to entry
- Supports promotion campaigns

Figure 9.7   The Five Dimensions of Brand Equity
Source: Adapted from David A. Aaker, Managing Brand Equity (New York: The Free Press, 1991), inside cover.

Marketing Vocabulary

MANUFACTURER'S BRAND (NATIONAL BRAND)
Brand named after the manufacturer.

PRIVATE BRAND (PRIVATE LABEL)
The name wholesalers or retailers attach to products they resell for numerous suppliers.

HYBRID BRAND STRATEGY
A combination of two or more brand strategies.

BRAND EQUITY
The assets linked with the brand name and symbol that add value to the product.

BRAND AWARENESS
The extent to which consumers recognize the brand and are likely to include it among the set of brands they consider.

BRAND LOYALTY
A dimension of brand equity that causes consumers to choose one brand over others available.

sale of an item with high brand loyalty. Furthermore, companies with faithful customers tend to be less susceptible to economic downturns or new competitors. Loyal buyers are not immediately inclined to look at other options, staying with the product even in times of economic hardship.

Brand loyalty is highest among more mature segments who tend to find a brand they like and stick with it, whereas younger generations are more willing to experiment with various brands. Studies show that brand loyalty may begin as early as the age of two. The nine-10 age group, usually referred to as "tweens," is the transitional generation, when "collective individualism" is a big trend; while kids 13-15, are more aware of what is cool and less affected by other advertisers.[23] Loyalty produces sales that enhance the earning power of the company. Cheerwine, created in 1917, is a nonalcoholic, carbonated drink produced by Carolina Beverage Corporation and sold mainly in the Southeast. Although Cheerwine does not even register in national market share polls, it has established itself as a southern icon and has found its way of creating loyal customers. Cheerwine uses it's Web site to promote it's southern ties through a Cheer-watch news team which covers clever stories about the product. One story reports northerners "hoarding" Cheerwine by buying large quantities of Cheerwine to bring back north and "illegally" distributing it to friends and relatives. The site also boasts the news team's slogan: "Protecting Your (southern) Right to Drink.... Cheerwine." Carolinians are so loyal to the drink that those who relocate often write the company asking where Cheerwine can be bought. Loyalists tell others about their favorite brand, often referred to as the "Nectar of the Tarheels."[24]

Even Mother Nature's own fruits have been branded—bananas by Chiquita and oranges by Sunkist. Why buy these rather than just any banana or orange? Why are names such as Kodak and Coca-Cola so well received in every part of the globe? Customers don't merely know them but prefer them. For a brand to be valuable to a company, a significant number of customers must prefer it over competitive brands.

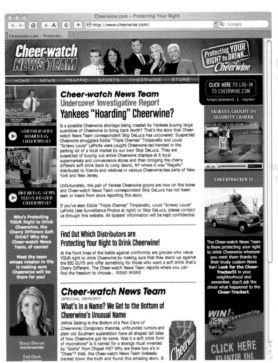

Cheerwine has such a following of loyal customers that some have the beverage shipped to them in foreign countries.

The best kind of loyalty for a company is when consumers insist on the company's brand. **Brand insistence** means that buyers are not willing to accept substitutes. This degree of loyalty is more likely for specialty items, such as polo shirts or branded pharmaceuticals. Brand insistence is an enviable position and gives the company a valuable asset that will produce significant future cash flows. In recent years, some unlikely products have gained brand insistence status. It used to be that technology products, such as electrical components, did not have much brand awareness to say nothing of brand loyalty. Intel Corporation, the pioneering semiconductor company, gave technology branding a boost. Through an innovative marketing campaign, it has persuaded consumers to insist on Intel microprocessors in their PCs. See the technology feature, "Intel Brands the Soul in the Machine."

Perceived Brand Quality The third dimension of brand equity is **perceived brand quality**, the degree to which brands consistently produce satisfaction by meeting customer expectations. This is one of the most important reasons consumers buy a product. The high or unique quality of a brand is directly related to what consumers are willing to pay and to whether the firm can charge a premium. For example, having and using a major accounting firm is associated with premium audit fees. However, a number of companies are willing to pay higher fees for the perceived higher quality of a Big Four audit, even though the identical service could be carried out by another firm.

Brand Associations Brand equity also involves establishing **brand associations** that evoke positive attitudes and feelings in consumers' minds. This enables firms to create messages that gain consumers' attention more easily. It also allows the brand equity to be extended to additional products. Procter & Gamble marketed only 13 advertised brands in 1950. By 1991, there were more than 100, not counting minor variants of major brands and now there were more than 300 brands.[25] In a hard-hitting campaign against Yamaha motorcycles, Honda used brand associations with its automobiles. It quickly produced a great number of motorcycles of every type in an effort to crowd Yamaha out of the market. This was a feasible strategy because consumers already had a positive feeling about the Honda brand name.

Brand associations also can facilitate product changes. For example, Tide gradually altered its detergent from a bulky powder to concentrated powder and liquid forms. Positive brand associations help consumers make the transition. Buyers are more willing to try these products and accept them with different features or in new forms.

Competitive Advantage Finally, brand equity can lead to **competitive advantage**, since a company can sell value rather than compete on the basis of price alone. The firm can charge a premium for many of the intangible dimensions associated with the brand. Brand equity also creates competitive advantages by serving as a barrier to entry. In other words, it may be too risky or expensive for another company or brand to compete in the same market. In the 1980s, a battle of the brands among beer companies created an environment in which only the strong survived. Within only 10 years, hundreds of small and local breweries were put out of business by such companies as Anheuser-Busch, Strohs, Miller, and Coors. Nearly every beer company that relied on product processing and procedures rather than building brand equity fell out of contention.

MAINTAINING BRAND VALUE

How many times have you requested a Coke in a restaurant and been asked whether a Pepsi would be okay? Coca-Cola has gone to great lengths to make sure that the Coke brand name does not become a generic name. This is always a danger. Believe it or not, the following used to be brand names: aspirin, escalator, kerosene, nylon, and zipper. To prevent brand names from becoming available for general use, a company must continuously inform the public about its exclusive ownership. Consequently, Coca-Cola waged court battles against retailers who substituted Pepsi when Coke was ordered. Without such efforts, Coke could have lost its trademark exclusivity. Similarly, General Foods, owner of the Jell-O brand, tries to keep the name proprietary.

Often, the first manufacturer of a new technology or product becomes synonymous with the entire product class. How many times has a friend invited you to go Rollerblading, when in fact

you would be in-line skating? Did you grow up believing that Kleenex was another name for facial tissue? Do you ask for a Band-Aid when you want an adhesive bandage? Many people say they are going to Xerox something, but they may be using a Canon or some other brand of copier. To avoid the loss of its exclusivity, Xerox runs advertisements explaining that "Xerox" is its registered trademark and should be used only when referring to the company and its products as opposed to a general process.

Marketing Vocabulary

BRAND INSISTENCE
A dimension of brand equity that makes consumers unwilling to accept substitutes for the brand.

PERCEIVED BRAND QUALITY
The degree to which a brand consistently produces satisfaction by meeting customer expectations.

BRAND ASSOCIATIONS
The positive attitudes and feelings a brand evokes in consumers' minds.

COMPETITIVE ADVANTAGE
A dimension of brand equity that permits the product to be sold on a value basis rather than a price basis and may serve as a barrier to entrance against competitive products.

DEVELOPING A SUCCESSFUL BRAND NAME

Choosing a brand name may not be easy. Americans file over 300,000 trademark applications each year, a number that continues to increase. To keep pace, the U.S. Patent and Trademark Office staff includes over 400 trademark examining attorneys.[26] This poses a challenge to companies that want a memorable and meaningful brand name. Name Lab, Inc., a specialist in this area, recommends choosing global eliminating cultural associations that may translate negatively across linguistic borders. Names like Sony, Kodak and Acura are superior to natural words suggestively based in a particular language.[27] Names should be easy to remember, distinctive, and viewed as positive in any language.

Some firms have chosen brand names that communicate product attributes or benefits. For example, Wheaties describes the ingredients of the cereal. When "Breakfast of Champions" is added, we get an image of wholesomeness or goodness. The name Weight Watchers communicates a direct consumer behavior, and it carries strong associations with weight control and health. Figure 9.8 identifies several products

Product/Service	Brand Name
Exercise equipment	Soloflex
Vegetables	Green Giant
Batteries	Eveready
Fabric softener	Stay Fresh
Refrigeration trucks	Thermo King
Sweetener	NutraSweet
Oil change service	Jiffy Lube
Reclining chair	La-Z-Boy
Mufflers	Midas
Internet stock trades	eTrade
Internet travel	Travelocity.com

Figure 9.8   Brand Names That Communicate Benefits

whose brand names are related to particular benefits.

Brand names must represent quality and commitment. That's why extensive research is usually conducted to identify whether the name is appropriate and can be used internationally. Standard Oil tested Exxon in 54 languages and more than 150 foreign markets before making a final decision. Marketers must be acutely aware that not all brand names carry the same meaning when translated. For example, the new General Mills cereal, Fringos, designed to be eaten with your fingers, translates into a less than appetizing word for Hungarians. Also consider Chevy Nova, which in Spanish-speaking countries meant "no va" or "no go."

Some brand names are successful because of what they say about the user. Many convey a personality trait that makes the connection directly. Magazines such as *Playboy, Cosmopolitan,* and *Glamour* represent attributes readers consider desirable.

JOINT MARKETING OF BRANDS

Joint marketing is cooperation between two companies to sell their brands. A common form of partnership occurs between two goods manufacturers. Since coupons and short-term promotions (such as refund certificates) often cause disloyalty and confusion among customers, replacing those tactics with joint marketing can build business for the cooperating companies. It is important for marketers to develop an awareness of how a consumer perceives how one product and brand fits with a potential co-branding products. Even more so, it is crucial to create a positive impression before marketing a co-branded product.[28] Researching and taking care to understand this can make or break the partnership. Consider the Nike and Apple partnership that brings sports and music together with its innovative Nike+iPod products. The Nike+iPod Sport Kit allows you to track your run in real time on your iPod Nano. Time, distance, pace, and calories burned is all recorded and can be shared online with other Nike+iPod users. Music and audio training sessions made specifically for this system are available for download on the Apple iTunes music store. Nike CEO Mark Parker says "Nike+iPod is a partnership between two iconic, global brands with a shared passion for creating meaningful consumer product experiences through design and innovation...

Nike+iPod will change the way people run."[29]

When you buy concert tickets at ticketmaster.com, they frequently offer free Apple iTunes downloads. By establishing this partnership, ticketmaster.com was encouraging customers to purchase tickets through their venue by promoting Apple iTunes. This type of cooperation is expected to become more frequent.[30]

PACKAGING AND LABELING

"People don't buy spray paint, they buy spray paint cans." That statement was made in a marketing research report for a major manufacturer in the industry to dramatize the importance of packaging. The research found that most buying decisions were made at the point of purchase. By looking at the color and design of the cans and by reading labels, consumers quickly determined which spray paint would best suit their needs.

Packaging and labeling once served simply to protect and identify the product inside. Now their role has been expanded to seven functions:

- Contain and protect items
- Be environmentally friendly
- Communicate messages to customers
- Contain product codes
- Make the product more convenient to use
- Protect against misuse
- Facilitate product storage

The **labels** on a package inform consumers and help promote the product. The Fair Packaging and Labeling Act of 1966 requires that consumer products carry clear and easily understood labels. They should contain the brand name and symbol, the manufacturer's name and address, the product content and amount, and recommended uses. The law also requires adequate information when value comparisons are made among competitive products.

In 1990 Congress passed the Nutritional Labeling and Education Act, which applies to food.[31] Excluded are meat, poultry, and eggs (covered by U.S. Department of Agriculture regulations) as well as restaurants, delicatessens, and infant formulas. Additional legislation that year required the FDA to develop standard definitions of terms commonly found on products, such as *reduced calories, high fiber,* and *low fat.*[32] These laws affect about 15,000 U.S. food packagers as well as many importers. Food labels must say how much fat and satu-

Fits in your Nike+ shoe

Plugs into your iPod nano

NIKE + iPod

Courtesy of Apple

rated fat, cholesterol, carbohydrate, and protein the product contains. They also must specify vitamin content and the percentage of the daily recommended allowances a serving represents. European standards on "diet" claims are even more strict than in the United States. Research shows that the people most likely to read food labels are women who have more education, live with others, are more knowledgeable about nutrition, are concerned about the quality of food they purchase, and believe that current dietary recommendations are important to their health. Less likely readers are men who have less education, live alone, are less concerned about food quality, are less knowledgeable about nutrition, and believe that the current dietary recommendations are unimportant.[33]

The Labeling of Hazardous Art Materials Act (LHAMA) of 1990 addresses another product category. The U.S. Public Interest Research Group (PIRG) lobbied for this legislation because it believed that a wide variety of suppliers inadequately warned consumers of chronic and long-term health risks related to certain chemicals used in their products.[34]

Marketers must take care to ensure that packages are properly labeled. Both consumers and marketers benefit, particularly when health and safety issues are involved.

ETHICAL ISSUES SURROUNDING PRODUCT SAFETY AND LIABILITY

The Consumer Product Safety Act of 1972 created the Consumer Product Safety Commission (CPSC) to police consumer goods. It has broad authority over the end product, can require recalls and redesigns, and even inspects production facilities. For example, a massive recall was issued in 2007 for high lead content in the paint on children's toys imported from China. In response, toymakers such as Mattel, instated a comprehensive safety protocol for all of it's products.[35] Of significance is its ability to bring criminal charges against companies and individuals who develop unsafe products.

Product liability refers to the fact that marketers and manufacturers are held responsible for injuries and damages caused by a faulty product. In one case the

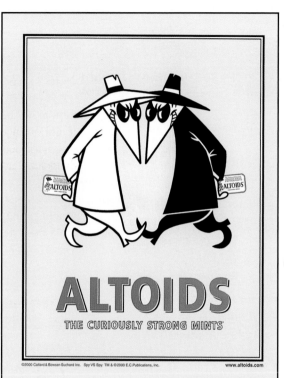

Altoids packaging prominently displays information to inform consumers and help promote the product.

CPSC found that more than 7,000 people were being injured monthly on three-wheel all-terrain vehicles (ATVs), most of them made by Honda and Kawasaki. Although the number of accidents was well known to dealers and distributors, only when the CPSC applied pressure did the makers agree to stop marketing the product in the United States. Many people believe consumers had the right to know about the ATV injuries. Clearly, wider publicity about the hazards would have meant lost sales.

The liability issue involves the right to safety and the manufacturer's responsibility for designing safe products and for informing the public about any dangers. Most companies fulfill this obligation through the product warranty and, in extreme cases, product recalls.

PRODUCT WARRANTIES

Warranties are written or implied expectations about product performance under use conditions. An express warranty is a written statement about the content or quality of a product and the manufacturer's responsibility to repair or replace it if it fails to perform. For example, an express warranty may indicate that an item is handcrafted in the United States, or may use such general terms as "unconditionally guaranteed" or "fully guaranteed," or may be a technical description of the goods. In the past, when consumers made claims under a warranty, some unethical manufacturers made it very difficult for them to receive satisfaction. General warranty statements came to lack meaning in many cases.

To combat this

Marketing Vocabulary

JOINT MARKETING
Cooperation between two companies to sell their products, which tend to be complementary.

LABELS
Information printed on a product's package to inform consumers and help promote the product.

PRODUCT LIABILITY
The responsibility of marketers and manufacturers for injuries and damages caused by a faulty product.

WARRANTIES
Implied or written expectations about product performance under use conditions.

problem, Congress passed the Magnuson-Moss Warranty–Federal Trade Commission Improvement Act in 1975. Essentially, the law requires that express warranties be written in clear language and indicate which parts or components are covered and which are not. If repair is included in the express warranty, it must occur within a reasonable time, free of charge. A full warranty states that either the merchandise will be repaired or the purchase price refunded if the product does not work after repair.

Many retailers pressure their suppliers to take back any product a customer returns for any reason. Companies such as Wal-Mart have a very liberal return policy. This provides feedback on product performance and builds good customer relations, which in turn helps gain market share.

An implied warranty is an unwritten guarantee that the product or service will do the job it is intended to do. All products, even if not accompanied by a written statement, have an implied warranty based on the Uniform Commercial Code (UCC). Adopted in 1952, the UCC is a federal statute affecting the sale of goods and giving consumers the right to reject a product if it does not meet their needs. Many states also have laws protecting consumers.

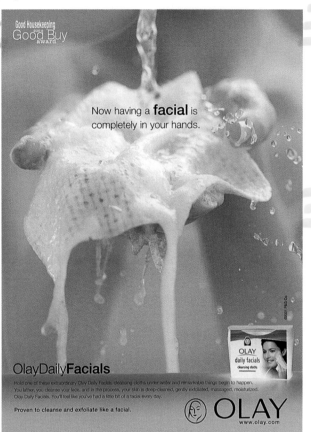

Procter & Gamble's Oil of Olay skin care products display labels/information to inform consumers and help promote the product.

PRODUCT RECALLS

A **product recall** is the withdrawal of a potentially harmful product from the market, by either a manufacturer or the federal government, for its repair, replacement, or discontinuation. The Consumer Product Safety Commission (CPSC) is the federal agency responsible for protecting consumers from product-related injuries. It establishes standards for product design and instructions. It also requires manufacturers to meet safety standards through product testing. Manufacturers and retailers are required by law to notify the CPSC if they find a defective product that may result in injury.

When a manufacturer realizes a product is defective, its response can inspire consumer confidence and actually promote sales. In chapter 2 we described the actions of Johnson & Johnson during the Tylenol scare in 1982. The unprecedented recall brought tremendous positive publicity to the company. When Tylenol went back on the shelves, consumers made it the top-selling pain reliever.

Just because a recall is made does not guarantee that consumers do not remain at risk. Consumers do not

globalEDGE™
Brand Management & Product Decisions

http://globaledge.msu.edu

Visit globalEDGE™ Online for the ultimate international marketing research tool!

Your firm must make a decision concerning its product portfolio for the coming years. As you are a manager in this leading medical components company, you have been asked to investigate the fastest-growing firms in your industry. Typically, such a company profile requires a commitment to business innovation. Since your analysis will be the basis for the cooperative development of products in the future, identify the five firms in your industry that would be the most suitable candidates for a marketing alliance. Where are each of these firms located? Is there a particular region in which they are clustered?

Marketing Vocabulary

PRODUCT RECALL
The withdrawal from the market, by either a manufacturer or the federal government, and repair, replacement, or discontinuation of a potentially harmful product.

always respond to product recalls. Sears recall proclaimed in large red letters: "Important Safety Notice. Dishwasher Rework—Potential Fire Hazard. Please Give This Your Immediate Attention." Within three days the response rate was 20 percent.[36] Even when a company meets its legal obligations, consumer awareness and other factors may have a lot to do with ethical considerations that must be addressed.

Throughout this chapter we have explored a wide range of strategies—from bundling products into special value units to assuring product safety—that marketers employ to build strong brand equity and give appeal to existing products. In Chapter 10 we will take a look at the characteristics of goods, services, and nonprofit marketing.

Web and E-Commerce Stars
Apple - www.apple.com

Apple creates highly innovative products, and it fits that their Web site is equally innovative. Like a typical site, a visitor can review product information. But, unlike many sites, the visitor can also access free downloads that aid in the use of Apple products such as downloading iTunes for use with an iPod.

Apple.com also provides a wide array of support services and resources, so the customer not only purchases and researches products, they know to revisit the site for support later on. By creating an innovative site that serves many purposes, Apple is able to build a strong relationship with their customers.

Chapter Summary:

Objective 1: Describe the major dimensions used by marketers to differentiate their products from competitors. Understand bundling and unbundling.

Products can be core, branded, and augmented. The core product represents the most basic functions and benefits. Some call this the generic product. The branded product adds characteristics that help consumers differentiate it from others. The augmented product includes such features as delivery, warranty, and customer service. A bundling strategy combines several products into one offering sold together. When products are bundled, they provide more value to the buyer than if each were sold separately.

Objective 2: Understand consumer and business product classifications based on how and why products are purchased and consumed.

Five categories are used to classify consumer products. Unsought products are bought on the spur of the moment. They include novelty, impulse, and low-involvement items. Emergency products are bought because of unexpected events, such as an accident or theft. Convenience products are inexpensive and are usually purchased near home. Brand name and wide distribution are very important for these items. Shopping items are selected after comparisons are made. They tend to be carefully chosen

and are kept for a long time. Specialty products have unique characteristics and value. They are often high-involvement purchases.

Business products are divided into capital, production, and operations products, depending on their primary use. Capital products include installations, such as offices and factories, and equipment, such as delivery vans and computers. These products last for a long time. Production products become part of other products. This category includes raw and processed materials, components, and subassemblies. Operations products help run the business. These include services such as accounting and waste removal, and office supplies such as business forms and cleaning products.

Objective 3: Know how organizations make product line decisions that determine what will be sold, including the degree of standardization chosen for global markets.

A product line may comprise one item or a number of related products. Companies may have one or more product lines, each with many or few items. The term *depth* refers to the number of items in a product line; the term *breadth* refers to the number of lines the company offers. Most companies with broad lines are relatively large; those with narrow lines may be large or small. The degree to which products should be standardized is a major consideration for global firms. Some organizations pursue standardization to benefit from the resulting scale economies whereas others use a local strategy to respond to local needs.

Objective 4: Recognize that branding and brand strategies are important aspects of building and maintaining a brand name.

A brand is distinguished from the product in general or other brands. Brands signify the "personality" of a product. The brand name and trademark can provide immediate recognition and credibility. Consequently, companies must register and protect trademarks. This is particularly challenging in global markets because stolen brand names and counterfeit products are so prevalent. There are several brand strategies. The generic approach involves no brand name. The individual strategy uses a unique name for each product line. The family brand is one name that covers all products in the line. Manufacturer brands are synonymous with the company that owns them. Private label brands are names used by wholesalers or retailers for products supplied to them. Combining two or more of these strategies is called a hybrid approach.

Objective 5: Know how to create brand equity—the value associated with a product's name.

A strong brand name is extremely valuable, but developing that name is not simple. First, the name must be selected with care. It should be acceptable globally, represent quality and commitment, and be protected legally. A good brand can easily be extended to additional products as they are developed. Second, brand equity must be created by devoting company resources to each of its five dimensions: brand awareness, brand loyalty, perceived quality, brand associations, and competitive advantage. Third, care must be taken to protect the brand so it does not become a generic name for the product.

Objective 6: Discuss the many legal and ethical issues surrounding brand and packaging decisions.

Federal laws and codes require that labels clearly identify the brand and manufacturer and warn consumers of safety hazards associated with use. Product liability holds marketers responsible for injuries and damages caused by a faulty product. Warranties refer to how products perform when used. In many cases, manufacturers are legally obligated to replace or repair faulty products. Express warranties are in writing. An implied warranty is unwritten. Essentially, a product should perform as it was designed. A product recall is instituted by the government or manufacturer to withdraw or modify a product. This occurs when a product is defective, especially if the potential for injury exists.

Review Your Understanding

1. What is a product? Give several examples.
2. What are core, branded, and augmented products?
3. What are bundling and unbundling?
4. What are five categories of consumer products? What are three categories of business products? Give examples.
5. What is a product line? Unit? SKU?
6. What is a broad and deep product line? What is a narrow and shallow product line? Give examples.

7. What are global products and brands?
8. What is joint marketing of products? Give an example.
9. What is brand equity? How is it developed?
10. Why is it important to secure trademarks?
11. Name and describe five brand categories.
12. What are the functions of packaging?
13. What is product liability?

Discussion of Concepts

1. Imagine that you are a marketing manager at IBM responsible for the sale of personal computers to individual consumers. How would you describe your product in terms of core, branded, and augmented characteristics? Which of these do you feel is most important?
2. What are some advantages of a bundling strategy over an unbundling strategy? Disadvantages?
3. Name the five categories of products based on consumer buying behavior. Why is it so important for marketers to understand the category of their product?
4. Discuss the differences between product line breadth and depth. What are some advantages and disadvantages of each combination of breadth and depth?
5. Classify each of the following companies in terms of product line breadth and depth and explain your reasoning: Sears, 7-Eleven, Hallmark Cards, Wal-Mart, Kmart, Victoria's Secret.

6. If you were the marketing manager at a company with a broad product line, which of the six brand strategies would you likely select? What factors would affect your decision? What if the product line were narrow?
7. What are the most important activities involved in developing a successful brand name? Once the name is developed, how is brand equity formed?
8. Name the key functions of packaging. Which do you feel is most important? Does this vary by product?
9. The Consumer Product Safety Commission is a government entity with the power to bring criminal charges against companies and individuals who develop and market unsafe products. Is it fair to consider marketers criminals if consumers are injured by their company's products? Why or why not?

Key Terms And Definitions

Augmented product: Product with characteristics that enhance its value beyond that of the core and branded product.

Brand: A distinguishing name or symbol to identify and differentiate products from those of competitors.

Brand associations: The positive attitudes and feelings a brand evokes in consumers' minds.

Brand awareness: The extent to which consumers recognize the brand and are likely to include it among the set of brands they consider.

Branded product: The core product plus the characteristics that allow the consumer to differentiate it from similar products.

Brand equity: The assets linked with the brand name and symbol that add value to the product.

Brand insistence: A dimension of brand equity that makes consumers unwilling to accept substitutes for the brand.

Brand loyalty: A dimension of brand equity that causes consumers to choose one brand over others available.

Breadth: The number of different lines a company markets.

Bundling strategy: A strategy in which several products are combined into a single offering.

Capital product: A costly item that lasts a long time but does not become part of any finished product.

Competitive advantage: A dimension of brand equity that permits the product to be sold on a value basis rather than a price basis and may serve as an entry barrier to competitive products.

Convenience product: A relatively inexpensive item that consumers purchase frequently and with minimum effort.

Core product: The essential physical item or intangible service that the customer receives.

Depth: The number of items in a product line.

Emergency product: A product purchased due to an unexpected event and for which the consumer has an urgent need.

Family brand strategy: Strategy in which a single brand name covers the entire group of products in the company's line(s).

Generic brand strategy: Strategy in which no brand name is used.

Hybrid brand strategy: A combination of two or more brand strategies.

Individual brand strategy: Strategy in which there is a unique name for each major product or product line.

Item: A specific version of a product within a product line.

Joint marketing: Cooperation between two companies to sell their products, which tend to be complementary.

Labels: Information printed on a product's package to inform consumers and help promote the product.

Manufacturer's brand (national brand): Brand named after the manufacturer.

Operations products: Products purchased to help run a business that are not included in the finished products.

Perceived brand quality: The degree to which a brand consistently produces satisfaction by meeting customer expectations.

Private brand (private label): The name wholesalers or retailers attach to products they resell for numerous suppliers.

Product: Any physical object, service, idea, person, event, place, or organization offered to satisfy consumers' needs and wants.

Product liability: The responsibility of marketers and manufacturers for injuries and damages caused by a faulty product.

Product line: Closely related products marketed by the organization.

Product recall: The withdrawal from the market, by either a manufacturer or the federal government, and the repair, replacement, or discontinuation of a potentially harmful product.

Production product: Raw materials, processed materials, component parts, and subassemblies that become parts of other goods.

Shopping product: A purchase generally made only after the consumer has compared several alternatives.

Specialty item: A product with unique characteristics that provides unusual value to the purchaser.

Supplies: Consumable items used for business operations.

Trademark (brand mark): A distinctive form or figure that identifies the brand.

Unsought product: An item that consumers don't think about frequently and for which they don't perceive much need.

Warranties: Implied or written expectations about product performance under use conditions.

References

1. Valerie Seckler, "Yahoo Mounts Custom Shopping Feature," WWD, July 11, 2000, p. 13; "Yahoo's Got Mail," Computer Reseller News, July 10, 2000, p. 8; Brent Schlender, "How a Virtuoso Plays the Web," Fortune, March 6, 2000, pp. F-79–F-83; Jeffrey M. O'Brien, "Behind the Yahoo!" Brandweek, June 28, 1999, pp. IQ17+; Becky Ebenkamp, "Not Waiting for Anybody," Brandweek, September 27, 1999, p. 48; Stephanie Francis Ward, "Fantasy Life, Real Law: Travel into Second Life--the virtual world where lawyers are having fun, exploring legal theory and even generating new business," ABA Journal, March, 2007; "Coca-Cola to launch on virtual world Second Life," Marketing Week(London), April 19, 2007, p 6; Claire Murphy, "Another world of opportunity", Marketing, March 14, 2007, p 18; www.zimbio.com/Mercedes-Benz/articles/; www.freshtakes.typepad.com/sl_communicators/2007/02/mercedesbenz_se.html, sites visited June 23, 2007.

2. "What's in a name?" Even Apple's branding just plain works. John Gruver. Macworld. April 2008.

3. "Staples stores to recycle e-waste.(News)." Waste News 13.2 (May 28, 2007): 4. InfoTrac OneFile. Thomson Gale. Michigan State University Libraries. June 7, 2007.

4. http://www.apple.com/itunes/ Web site visited April 4, 2008.

5. Dave's Eco-nomics: Stop the paper chase. Dave Waller. Management Today. February 1, 2008.

6. Friedman, Thomas L. The World is Flat. New York: Farrar, Straus and Giroux. 2006.

7. www.pepsico.com, Web site visited April 4, 2008.

8. http://ir.newellrubbermaid.com/annuals/cfm, 2007 Annual Report.

9. Caterpillar Paves the Future of Its Customers in China; Chairman and CEO Owens visits China to Reinforce Commitment. PR Newswire. New York: April 2, 2008.

10. David A. Aaker, Managing Brand Equity (New York: The Free Press, 1991), p. 7.

11. Interbrand, 2007 Report.

12. Diane Crispell and Kathleen Brandenburg, "What's in a Brand?" American Demographics, 1993, pp. 26–29, 31–32; Glenda Shahso Jones, "Your New Brand Image," Catalog Age, July 2000, pp. 175–178.

13. http://www.tns-mi.com/ Web site visited April 4, 2008.

14. "Company News, Judge Rule's in GM's Favor in Trademark Dispute," The New York Times, March 1, 2002.

15. www.dreamworks.com, Web site visited April 4, 2008.

16. Pirated Products are Big Business. Liza Casabona. WWD December 6, 2007.

17. Fakes!, Business Week. New York: Feb 7, 2005., Iss. 3919; pg. 54

18. Merck Fights Counterfeit Drugs. Chemical Week. July 4, 2007.

19. Gerry Meyers, "Another View on Private Labels: They're Not Going to Fade Away," Advertising Age, April 25, 1994, p. 26.

20. Jonathon Berry, "Attack of the Fighting Brands," Business Week, May 2, 1995, p. 125.

21. Adapted from Aacker, Managing Brand Equity, p. 4.

22. www.kraftfoods.com, site visited April 4, 2008

23. Rob Gray, "Stages of Youth," Campaign, May 5, 2006, p.4-5.

24. www.cheerwine.com Web site visited May 12, 2008.

25. William M. Weilbacher, Brand Marketing (Lincolnwood, IL: NTC Business Books, 1993), p51; P&G Corporate Biographical Information www.pg.com,Web site visited April 4, 2008.

26. www.uspto.gov, site visited April 4, 2008.

27. www.namelab.com, site visited April 12, 2007.

28. Bernd Helmig, Jan-Alexander Huber, Peter Leeflang, "Explaining Behavioral Intentions Toward Co-Branded Products," Journal of Marketing Management, Vol. 23, No. 3-4, April 2007, pp. 285-304.

29. "Nike and Apple team up to Launch Nike+iPod", May 23, 2006, www.apple.com.

30. www.ticketmaster.com, site visited June 8, 2007.

31. Chris Baum, "NLEA Compels Food Packagers to Redesign," Packaging, May 1994, p. 21.

32. Andrea Dorfman, "Less Bologna on the Shelves," Time, November 5, 1990, p. 79.

33. Pam Demetrakakes, "Packaging Field Gears up for New Labeling Rules," Packaging, January 1993, p. 3.

34. Mark Hartley, "For the Sake of Invisible Ink," Occupational Health & Safety, December 1993, p. 4.

35. Safety Zone: Massive Toy Recalls Have Rocked the Industry This Year--but Is Some Good Coming Out of the Bad? Josephine Collins. License. December, 2007.

36. Recall letter from Sears, on file with authors.

The Marketing Gazette

Michael Treacy and Fred Wiersema, The Discipline of Market Leaders (Reading, MA: Addison-Wesley, 1995), pp. 103–121; "Apple to Use Intel Microporcessors Beginning in 2006," www.apple.com; Mike Rogoway, "Intel Regains Turf lost to AMD," Knight Ridder Tribune Business News, Apr 18, 2007, p.1; Camille Alarcon, "Intel Begins Next Generation Marketing Push," B&T Weekly, May 4, 2007, p.6.

CASE 9

Gap

Gap was founded in 1969 in San Francisco with only one store. Today, there are over 3,100 stores throughout the United States and internationally in locations such as Canada, France, Germany, Japan, and the United Kingdom. Gap employs over 150,000 employees within its online, in-store, and corporate operations.

Composed of four different brands—Banana Republic, Old Navy, Piperlime and Gap, which includes GapKids, BabyGap, Gapmaternity and Gapbody— Gap strives to "deliver style, service, and value to everyone." That goal extends throughout all of Gap's enterprises; however, specific goals and branding techniques differ for each of the three brands. The four brands are separately housed in different locations in San Francisco to more easily keep the focus and goals of each entity distinct.

Gap purchased Banana Republic in 1983, when it consisted of only two stores that specialized in safari-inspired clothing. Since then, Banana Republic has become the brand for "the modern, versatile wardrobe." Banana Republic boasts the most expensive product line of the three brands, with clothing made from superior fabrics. The product line includes women's and men's clothing, shoes, accessories, personal care products, intimate apparel, jewelry, and home accessories.

Old Navy was created by Gap in 1994. Old Navy has become the brand for "fun, fashion, family, and value." The goal is for Old Navy to be the shopping destination for value for the entire family. This division offers clothing at a lower price point than Gap and Banana Republic for men, women, children, and babies. Old Navy stores have been using what has recently been termed enter-tailing, the combination of entertainment and retailing. By playing loud, energetic music, Old Navy hopes to bring younger generations into the stores—and maybe have them bring their parents along.

The Gap brand sits somewhere in between Banana Republic and Old Navy with pricing and quality. Its goal is to "offer a balance of modern and seasonal styles" to men, women, children, and babies in a pleasant and calm shopping environment. Gap specializes in basics such as T-shirts, jeans, and khakis, but it attracts customers by showcasing the latest trends. Many companies would be nervous about having three brands that have similar products. After all, it is possible that Gap customers would decide to purchase lower-priced clothing at Old Navy. That means a decrease in revenues for Gap. While some clothing companies actually market an image (youth, sex, money, power, etc.), Gap brands actually market the products they sell: T-shirts, khakis, and sweaters. Drexler also wants to make Gap a global brand, which is as easily recognized in Germany as it is in Japan, San Francisco, and New York City.

Piperlime is an online shoe shop launched in 2006. It offers an assortment of the leading brands in footwear for women, men and kids as well as tips and trends from leading stylists.

Recently, Gap has focused on bringing the brands to the consumer via Internet sites. The results have been good. Toby Lenk, President of Gap Inc. Direct, the e-commerce division of Gap Inc., hypothesized, "if Internet sales are projected to swell to 20 percent of all retail by 2021, store sales driven by the Internet could add up to another 40 percent," which is good news for The Gap. The future of Gap's products will depend on it providing a product assortment that meets customers' needs with an effective marketing plan. Additionally, Gap will need to continue its focus on creating customer satisfaction and loyalty through its marketing campaigns. With brands that cover many price points and meet the differences in customer needs, Gap should be able to continue its success well into the future.

Future success for the Gap also relies on its recently implemented environmental sustainability efforts. The company's philosophy is that its business operations should not come at the expense of the environment. Over the past few years, The Gap has substantially reduced energy in stores, warehouses and distribution centers. It has also constantly looking for innovative ways to use sustainable fabrics and products. With the majority of it's clothing made from cotton, the company has joined the Better Cotton Initiative to promote environmentally, socially and economically sustainable cotton cultivation and practices worldwide.

1. How has Gap achieved global status and brand equity, especially in an industry that relies so heavily on trends? Do you think that one brand will be more successful globally than the others? Why?
2. How can Gap maintain equity in its brands in the future? What are some of the obstacles it will face? Are the obstacles the same for each brand?
3. What do you think would happen if the three brands were marketed together? What are some ways that Gap could market them together successfully?
4. Which brand do you think is the easiest to market? Why?
5. Gap also has discount outlet stores across the United States. Where do those stores fit in with the others?

Sources: Nina Munk, "Gap Gets It," Fortune, www.fortune.com, August 3, 1998; Gap Web site, www.gap.com, visited June 18, 2007; Hoover's Online, "The Gap, Inc.," www.hooversonline.com, visited June 18, 2007; Stacy Permna, "Mend That GAP," Time, www.time.com, February 14, 2000; Julie Creswell, "The Next Big Things," Fortune, www.fortune.com, December 20, 1999; Erin Clack, "The New Online Challenge," Gap Inc. Direct's Internet Marketing, Footwear News, May 14, 2007, p16.; "2006 Annual Report," www.gapinc.com, site visited February 25, 2008.

CHAPTER 10

Goods, Services & Nonprofit Marketing

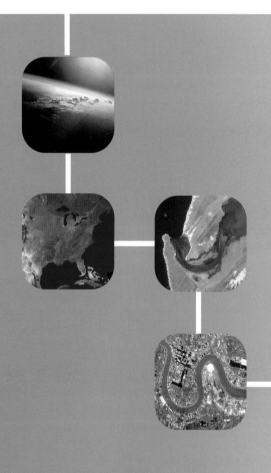

"Thank you for calling Patagonia. We're normally here if the surf's not up..." - Patagonia corporate answering machine.

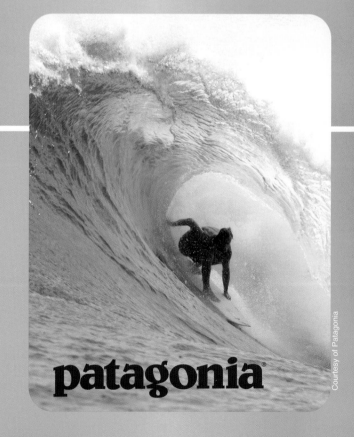

patagonia®

Learning Objectives

1. Identify the forces that have produced and will continue to create tremendous growth in the service economy.

2. Understand which characteristics of services must be adjusted for successful marketing.

3. Know how to develop the service mix.

4. Explore the expanded concept of services.

5. Appreciate the importance of nonprofit marketing and the uniqueness of this important marketing arena.

When he wasn't surfing the coast of California, Patagonia founder, Yvon Chouinard, spent his time as a young man between Yosemite, the Alps, and the high mountains of Canada rock climbing. He supported himself by selling hand-forged climbing equipment out of the back of his car. By 1965, demand for Chouinard's equipment exceeded what he could produce by hand. Partnering with Tom Frost, a fellow climber as well as an aeronautical engineer, he purchased machines and began improving his climbing tools, making them stronger, simpler and more functional. By 1970, Chouinard Equipment was the largest supplier of climbing equipment in the United States.

As climbing grew in popularity, the partners began to notice the destruction that climbers were causing to the mountains they loved. In a risky business move, they decided to phase out the destructive pitons traditionally hammered in and out of rock cracks, and replaced them with aluminum chocks that could be wedged into the rock by hand, leaving the mountain unscathed. This was the beginning to Chouinard's environmental innovations that are carried out today through Patagonia.

In the 1970s the company began selling clothing tailored to climbers. As clothing sales soared, the partners decided that rather than diluting the name of Chouinard Equipment as an equipment company, they would create a new name for their clothing line. They wanted to associate their brand with outdoor living without limiting it to climbing. They chose Patagonia for the image it invoked of a far-off, mysterious and beautiful place.

With annual sales of more than $275 million today, Patagonia has grown into a company recognized around the world for its dedication to product quality and environmental activism. Its catalog consists of hundreds of items geared towards outdoor enthusiasts, including climbers, hikers, fishers, and surfers. Patagonia is constantly improving its products, testing new materials and increasing functionality.

Nearly three-fourths of it products are composed of green materials, such as hemp and chlorine-free wool. It uses only organically grown cotton in its clothing, and more than half of its products are recyclable. In fact, Patagonia recently launched Common Threads Garment Recycling Program in which it takes back used polyester and nylon clothing from customers, recycling them into material used in new products. This approach uses 70 percent less energy than creating the materials from scratch.

Started in 1985, its Environmental Grants Program has donated $30 million to grassroots environmental activists at more than 1,000 organizations. As a member of One Percent for the Planet, it contributes one percent of all sales to grassroots groups. Through Patagonia's Employee Internship program, more than 350 employees have taken up to two months off to volunteer fulltime for environmental groups of their choosing. While away, these employees receive full pay and benefits from Patagonia.

Patagonia makes quality products, treats its employees and the environment well, and has a unique attitude towards business. When you call its corporate office (805-643-8616) and the machine picks up, it says, "Thank you for calling Patagonia. We're normally here if the

THE CONCEPT OF SERVICES

Products can be either goods or services. Goods are physical objects. **Services** are intangible ideas, tasks, experiences, performances, or activities that one party can offer another. A major difference between a service and a good is that services generally involve suppliers connecting directly with consumers for performance of the service. Your barber, your doctor, and your professor all require your involvement in order to perform their service. They connect with you personally. When you think about it, even goods are more valuable when accompanied by excellent service. Consequently, goods and services often go hand in hand.

To serve means to benefit a receiving party through personal acts. The marketing of services, by its very nature, concerns the development of beneficial relationships. Interpersonal skills are critical, because for a service to be performed well, these skills must help support the customer relationship. And the marketers of services are likely to fail if they do not embody all the principles of good marketing in their activities.

For more than a quarter century, the dollar volume of services in the U.S. economy has grown at nearly four per-cent annually, approximately double the growth rate for products. This torrid pace is expected to continue. Developed countries such as the United States rely on the marketing of services for domestic growth.

Trade in services is also very important globally, representing about 60 percent of all trade among nations. The United States has emerged as the world leader in services. Foreign countries spend more on U.S. services than Americans spend on foreign services.[2] Global marketing, therefore, is particularly important for many U.S. service providers. The Carlson Company is a good example of how U.S. service companies have gone international. Carlson owns T.G.I. Friday's, a popular "all-American" restaurant chain with a casual format that has done well at home and abroad, including the Far East. Sales volume in Seoul, Korea, for example, has set records since the early nineties, where the atmosphere is the same, the walls are decorated with remnants of American culture, and the staff has the same lively persona as in the States.[3]

Figure 10.1 provides an overview of this chapter. We begin by looking at forces that will continue to produce explosive growth for services. This is followed by a section that explores service characteristics in depth. It will show

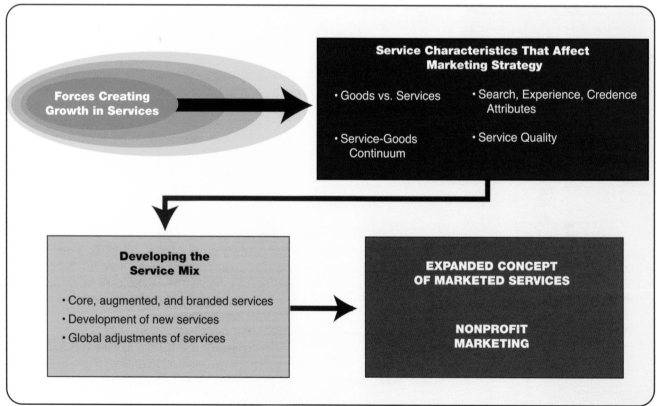

Figure 10.1   The Concept of Services

how services are differentiated, their relationships to goods, the attributes consumers use to judge them, and elements of service quality. Next, we will describe the aspects marketers consider when developing the service mix. You will extend what you learned in Chapter 9 to services by looking at core, augmented, and branded services and the development of new offerings. Keep in mind that services are as important in business-to-business marketing as they are in consumer marketing. Such traditional services as health care, insurance, energy, telecommunications, garbage and snow removal, accounting and tax preparation, auto service, and restaurants have been the backbone of the service economy for a long time. The first part of the chapter provides an understanding of how these kinds of services are marketed. The next sections discuss the expanded concept of services, which includes person, entertainment, event, place, political, cause, and internal marketing. We conclude by looking at the important area of nonprofit marketing.

TGI Friday's is an international service provider that has done especially well in the Far East.

GLOBAL FORCES CREATING GROWTH IN SERVICES

The service economy is not unique to the United States. In developed countries around the globe, more and more of total economic well-being is based on services. As nations become more sophisticated, the demand for services grows. The Industrial Revolution brought about productivity gains through the substitution of machines for human and animal labor. The technology revolution that followed went far beyond the mere substitution of labor. It resulted in the creation of products that exceeded human and animal capabilities. A century ago, who would have imagined that millions of business travelers would routinely fly six miles above the earth and use plastic cards to charge phone calls while in flight? Air transportation and telecommunications, including the explosion of the Internet as a means of global communication, are examples of services that have brought us closer to the reality of a global community. Figure 10.2 depicts the global forces that are influencing growth in services.

TECHNOLOGY

Technology is producing more sophisticated services more rapidly. Until recently, even advanced nations were dedicated to the production of goods. The technologies of today can't be used by consumers without the services of highly trained professionals. For example, jet aircrafts produced in the 1960s still carry millions of passengers annually, and planes being produced today are likely to still be flying halfway through the 21st century. Smaller percentages of the population are now able to produce greater quantities of more valuable goods, thereby shifting the emphasis to value-added services. Some of these services in the consumer sector include entertainment, travel,

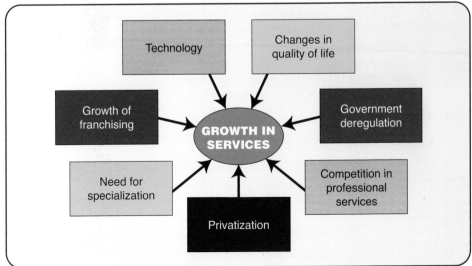

Figure 10.2 Global Forces Creating Growth in Services

Marketing Vocabulary

SERVICE
An idea, task, experience, or activity that can be exchanged for value to satisfy the needs and wants of consumers and businesses.

health, and education and consulting and environmental controls in the B2B sector.

The technological revolution is making an information revolution possible, which facilitates nearly every human endeavor. Computer technology is increasing exponentially. Moore's law states that the number of transistors on a microchip doubles every two years.[5] Each generation of microprocessors are replaced by technologies that operate millions of times faster, continually altering the commercial landscape. Technology continues to eliminate the need for face-to-face interaction between a buyer and seller. For example, the number of commercial banks has declined from 14,210 in 1986 to about 7,500 today due to consumer preferences for automated teller machines, online banking, and other services.[4] Yet, the same technology has provided greater personalization through one-to-one connections. Electronic banking allows consumers the freedom to sit in their favorite coffee shop and conduct all of their banking including making real time communications with customer service representatives. At tax time, the same systems provide financial information categorized for seamless integration into tax reporting programs.

Online shopping is growing about 20 percent a year and is putting added pressures on traditional brick-and-

Technological advances have reduced the need for customer contact.

mortar stores. Total online sales, excluding travel, were estimated at around $175 billion in 2007, growing nearly 20 percent from the previous year.[6] Jay McIntosh, director of consumer products with Ernst & Young says, "Online retailing as a group is the second largest retailer after Wal-Mart in terms of annual sales."[7]

QUALITY OF LIFE

Quality of life is defined more by how people feel and experience life than by how much they consume. For example, our thinking about basic services such as health, education, and mobility has expanded dramatically. Health once meant the absence of sickness but today's perception of health has expanded to include fitness, increased physical performance, and enhanced mental well-being. Education, once the domain of the elite few, has become accessible to a significant percentage of the population. This is particularly true in emerging nations like China and India. Today people find expenditures at a theatre as valuable as the purchase of a microwave oven was in the 1970s. In fact, a patron of a broadway play can be expected to spend more on a single performance than the cost of a microwave at Home Depot. Mobility, expressed in the 1950s by a high-performance car, now includes psychological mobility provided by movies, cellular phones, and the Internet. Internet cafes illustrate yet another change in the quality of life, providing customers with two popular services in one—specialty coffees and the worldwide computer network.

The fast pace of life has placed a tremendous premium on services of all types. There is less time available for traditional responsibilities such as child care and cooking. Nearly all women who entered the workplace in the last three decades have joined the service sector, which has increased the demand for services. Most people would prefer to use their leisure time for activities other than shopping and cooking. Today, Americans' eating patterns are changing from three square meals a day to five smaller meals. An increasing percentage of these meals are consumed in the car. So, convenient food options for on-the-go consumers proliferate; today the average person age 24 or younger spends 8 percent of their salary on food prepared outside the home.[8]

GOVERNMENT DEREGULATION OF SERVICES

Another factor profoundly influencing growth in services is industry deregulation that has occurred over the past 20 years. This trend, started in the United States, has now spread throughout Europe and Asia. Understanding that competition provides vast opportunities for economic growth, legislators have deregulated many services that were traditionally controlled by government agencies. As expected, numerous private companies have stepped in to seize and create opportunities. For example, the spectacular growth in personal communication devices was stimulated by deregulation of the telephone industry. In fact, the deregulation of the telephone industry led to competitive phone wars. Some of the smaller companies, however, bought each other out to emerge as larger, more consolidated telecommunications companies. With more resources at their disposal, they were able to compete with older companies for customers. Most of these companies, such as Verizon, sell services as a part of a total package, a "bundle" that appeals to a particular group, such as business customers to attract customers. The realignment of companies and services can sometimes be difficult for consumers, as companies stretch resources to attract more cus-

People are spending more time on quality of life

tomers. Due to deregulation, the telecommunications industry has become one of the three fastest-growing industries in the United States. According to a Veronis Suhler Stevenson study, total spending on communications in the U.S. will exceed $1 trillion in 2008, and is projected to reach $1.2 trillion by 2011.[9] But consumers should eventually emerge as winners in the midst of increasing competition due to improved services and lower prices. Major deregulation also has occurred in:

- Transportation— air freight, airlines, trucking, and shipping
- Finance— banking, securities, and insurance
- Telecommunications—radio, television, and telephones
- Energy—electricity and gas

Competition stimulated by deregulation results in a better selection at a better price, which improves demand and creates jobs. For example, when the government deregulated the airline industry, companies expanded the number, location, and pricing approaches of flights, among other changes. The result has been better prices, better schedules, and overall improved service levels for consumers. Increased competition has made it necessary for companies to deliver greater value to consumers, which in turn has stimulated demand for these services.

COMPETITION IN PROFESSIONAL SERVICES

Not long ago, doctors, lawyers, and other professionals were prohibited from marketing their services in the media. Only subtle means were allowed, such as sports team sponsorships or word of mouth. All of this changed in 1974, when the Supreme Court ruled that a ban on lawyer marketing was unconstitutional. Today, nearly every profession engages in some form of marketing. Health care is a good case in point.

Hospitals, preferred provider organizations, and health maintenance organizations compete vigorously for patients, and there are elaborate educational campaigns designed to teach doctors how to market services. The availability of information via technology has enhanced marketers' opportunities to promote health care services. Users will be able to access medical specialists and information as well as interact with visuals and audio. Marketers must exercise care in the promotion of health goods and services. Since the health care industry is complex and often confusing, consumers usually know very little about products and services offered. Without this knowledge and expertise about the industry, consumers must rely, to some degree, on marketers to inform them. This places great emphasis on the importance of truthful and reliable information, even with well-known and trusted Web sites such as WebMD. The recent explosion of drug companies advertising on television has caused some problems. For example, Pfizer and Pharmacia Corporation, the makers of Celebrex, an arthritis drug, were ordered to pull an advertisement from television by the FDA. The ad showed "Bill," a person with "arthritic knees," zipping around a park on a scooter. The FDA claimed that this ad overstated to consumers the actual efficacy of the drug.[10]

The legal profession also promotes itself. The largest section in most urban Yellow Pages is Attorneys. Although prestigious law firms still tend to use community activities as their main source of promotion, many attorneys use all forms of promotion, pricing, and distribution approaches.

PRIVATIZATION

Privatization occurs when government services are contracted to private organizations for them to manage. The concept originated in the United Kingdom as an effort to revitalize the economy by shifting many bureaucratic services to aggressive private firms. The British railroad, telecommunications, and transportation industries were privatized, among others. Privatization also occurred in

Privatization occurred after the fall of the Berlin Wall in 1989.

East Germany when the Berlin Wall came down and in Russia when the Soviet Union was dissolved. Both countries immediately began to transfer ownership of huge, government-controlled service institutions to private companies. Consulting organizations from the United States, Europe, and Japan worked diligently to help these private companies succeed. The Chinese government, for example, has recently privatized many state companies in ener-

gy, manufacturing, telecommunications and financial services. Finding the entirely state-owned companies inefficient and, therefore, more expensive, China decided that privatization and allowing competition between companies would increase efficiency and lower prices for the consumer.[11]

In the United States there is a definite trend toward privatization of local, state, and federal government services. Many hospitals and jails, once owned and maintained by cities and counties, are now operated by private companies. Likewise, prisons are often run more economically by private firms than by governments. Last year, a quiet milestone in the movement to privatize government services was marked when America's oldest and most well-known national laboratory, Los Alamos, the birthplace of the atomic bomb and one of the nation's most important national security facilities, was handed off to a private contractor.[12]

THE NEED FOR SPECIALIZATION

Specialization occurs when an organization chooses to focus its resources on core business activities. In order to utilize resources and build strength in the core business, many organizations rely on service providers for basic support of their business. Most companies find it economical to farm out some of the services they previously performed themselves. Personnel agencies hire and assess employees, accounting firms do the books, systems consultants set up the computers, and so forth. ARAMARK is one of the world's largest service companies. It has chosen the strategy of marketing services that are not core to their clients' business. For example, ARAMARK offers security, cleaning, grounds maintenance, catering, and snow removal services. For large stadiums and amusement parks, it handles everything from parking lots to food, maintenance, and cleaning. The firm even supplies hospitals with physicians for emergency rooms, a particularly difficult area of hiring and management for hospitals. Companies realize that just as they specialize in a certain aspect of business, there are service providers who do the same.

ACCESS TO KNOWLEDGE

Today, fundamental competencies required to run many service businesses are accessible to individuals or small groups of experts. At one time, these competencies were only available to large corporations. Through subscription services on the Internet, experts everywhere have access to vast quantities of information.

GROWTH OF FRANCHISING

A **franchise** is a contractual agreement in which an entrepreneur pays a fee and agrees to meet operating requirements in exchange for the franchise name and marketing plan. Franchising is another major trend influencing the service industry. National and international franchisers have developed aggressive growth strategies, particularly in the sectors of fast food, fitness and auto service. Franchising allows companies such as McDonald's, Subway, Service Master, and Jiffy Lube to increase quickly the number of locations where customers can purchase their services. McDonald's has more than 31,800 flagship restaurants in over 100 countries. Only a small portion are company-owned and more than 70 percent of its locations are run by franchisees.[13]

Another area of franchise growth is in the distribution channels for car sales. Since customers value pressure-free shopping when purchasing an automobile, online car sales have become increasingly popular. These alternatives have taken a fixed-price approach without aggressive sales tactics. However, most consumers shop for cars online to decide what models they are interested in buying and still visit showrooms to buy a car. It is apparent that cars are still a commodity that people like to touch, feel and drive for themselves.

SERVICE CHARACTERISTICS THAT AFFECT MARKETING STRATEGY

Several aspects of services are considered when marketing strategies are developed. First, services can be clearly

Subway understands it's the small things that can make a big difference such as using napkins made from 100 percent recycled fiber. Learn more about how Subway franchises are going green at the Subway Web site.

contrasted from goods in several ways. Second, services should be looked at from the perspective of a service–goods continuum, not simply as services. Some products are all service, others are a combination of each, and still others are pure goods. Third, consumers evaluate a service by looking at its attributes to find clues about its expected performance. Fourth, service quality plays a key role in success.

CONTRASTS BETWEEN GOODS AND SERVICES

When marketers refer to products, they are talking about both goods and services. Marketing strategies that work for one generally work for the other. In fact, as we will soon see, a company's product mix usually has both goods and services. Even so, there are six sharp distinctions between the two. The uniqueness of services lies in their intangibility, the relationship with the consumer, the importance of the service encounter, their simultaneous production and consumption, their perishability, and the type of quality controls required for services.

Marketing Vocabulary

FRANCHISE
A contractual agreement whereby an entrepreneur pays a fee for the franchise name and agrees to meet operating requirements and use the organization's marketing plan.

Marketing Intangibles Physical goods have form and mass; they can be seen and touched. Prior to sale, services exist primarily as an offer or promise of some experience that will occur in the future. They only become "real" when performed. Insurance is a good example of an intangible product. The paper on which the policy is printed describes the promise the company makes to the person paying the premiums. Only when the consumer suffers a loss is the product delivered—in the form of money or a replacement for an insured item.

Many services take shape in unexpected ways over time. Think about a computerized dating service. The purchaser may have high expectations, but it may be weeks, months, or even years before the potential benefit is realized. This intangibility makes it difficult

Career Tip:

ARAMARK is the world's leading managed services provider with a portfolio of career opportunities in nearly every service area. Since ARAMARK has units in thousands of locations, it can offer companywide, nationwide, and worldwide opportunities. Check out current employment listings and submit your qualifications online at www.aramark.com/careers/submit.htm.

to assess the value of services or compare alternatives prior to purchase. After the service is performed, it is too late to change the decision. Consider bungee jumping. Until you step onto the platform, have the cord attached, and jump, you cannot experience the sensation. Once you leave the platform, it is too late to reject the service.

Relationship of Provider to Customer

Services are performed on customers personally or entities in their care—children (day care, youth sports camps), animals (vets, stables, feedlots), things (lawn care, car wash, auto repair), and so forth. Whereas most goods are manufactured at a plant far from customers, most services are created in their presence or with their personal knowledge of how they were performed. Consequently, there is an inseparable relationship between the provider and the user. In some cases this interaction may be very personal, such as the relationship between parents and the provider of their child's care. Consumers may develop a strong preference about who performs the service. Most of us have a favorite barber or hair stylist and dread trying someone new. In fact, we may be willing to pay extra to have our usual stylist cut our hair. Much the same holds true for the family dentist, lawyer, and doctor.

The Service Encounter Connection

One of the most important aspects of service marketing is the **service encounter**, the contact between the consumer and the seller. Jan Carlzon, former president of Scandinavian Airline Systems (SAS), spoke of service encounters as "moments of truth." Carlzon led SAS toward a strong customer focus, pointing out that the airline came face-to-face with consumers 65,000 times each day. He estimated that each passenger had contact with five SAS employees over the course of a

year. Although the typical service encounter lasted only about 15 seconds, the outcome of each one ultimately translated into success or failure for the company. His fervent conviction has made SAS one of the most customer-oriented carriers in the industry.

The service encounter concept reinforces the importance of customer relationships in marketing a service. Employees not only must have the interpersonal skills to treat consumers well but also must be oriented toward solving the customer's problem. At the most elementary level, salespeople need to be cordial and gracious. At a more fundamental level, they have to be helpful in discovering and meeting service needs during the encounter. Each moment contributes to the customer's experience with the service. If these moments are positive, then satisfaction with purchase and service delivery is likely to be positive as well.

At SAS, Carlzon realized that in order to satisfy a customer in 15 seconds, employees had to have the tools and the authority necessary to make certain decisions. He rearranged the organization so that frontline personnel could quickly serve any customer. Managers, who typically hold power and responsibility, became supporters for those employees. Similarly, Wal-Mart managers support employees in efforts to maintain exceptional service encounters. At Wal-Mart, the company receives letters daily from customers pleased with their service encounter, which may include an associate who remembers their name or carries out a purchase for them. Some customers write letters in appreciation of a simple smile. Sam Walton, the company founder, insisted that associates practice "aggressive hospitality" in order to offer better

Wal-Mart offers eco-friendly alternative to paper or plastic bags.

service, and the People Greeter program at Wal-Mart is one example of this. The greeters have the job of handing out shopping cars, greeting customers with a smile as they enter the store, and letting them know they're glad they came to Wal-Mart.

Simultaneous Production and Consumption

The fact that many services are made and used at the same moment creates interesting situations. First, the buyer and seller have to cooperate. In some cases this involves power dynamics. When you tell your stylist how you want your hair cut, you accomplish a managerial act. Second, since buyers vary and services depend on the recipient, the same service may be dramatically different from one situation to the next. A provider may operate one way with one consumer and then adjust the service considerably to meet the needs of another. Consider the role of a personal fitness trainer. Since people have different goals and varying personal needs, a trainer must adjust a fitness program to suit each individual. Finally, since the buyer must be present in order for at least part of the service to be performed, consumers invest time. This places a premium on the speed of delivery and the importance of correct performance the first time. For example, satisfaction with automobile repair services depends largely on whether the car is ready when promised, or think about how annoying it is to wait in a physician's crowded office when you have other things to do.

No Storage and Inventory

Although goods can be stored until needed, services cannot. Services are extremely **perishable**—their value exists for a short time. When an airplane takes off with several empty seats, those fares can never be recovered. Therefore, accurate forecasting and the need to match supply with demand are important. When the demand for a service is stable, there is little difficulty in meeting supply requirements, but most services have erratic demand. For example, on very hot days almost all consumers turn on their air conditioners, creating a surge in energy demand. Should the utility company build enough capacity to supply its peak load or its average load? In the first case, there will be many periods when resources are unused; in the latter case, blackouts can result. When you telephone on

Mother's Day or Thanksgiving, it may be difficult to get through right away because of an unusually high demand for connections. At peak hours of Internet demand, the speed at which you can access information decreases significantly. Similarly, cellular phone users often have problems during rush hour, when everyone tied up in traffic decides to make calls. If the service provider cannot meet the peak load, then customers are likely to go elsewhere. This is the major theme of AT&T's "Fewest Dropped Calls" campaign.

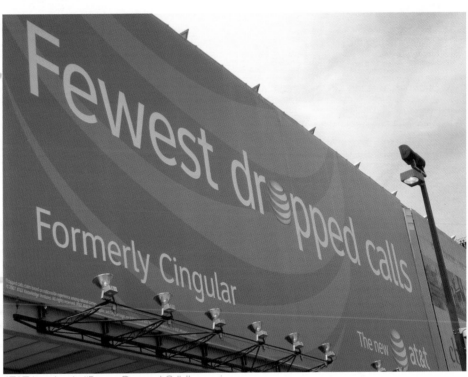

AT&T launches its "Fewest Dropped Calls," campaign.

Service Quality Control

The quality of goods is usually monitored by human inspectors or the electronic eye of machinery. That close monitoring is virtually impossible in the case of services. Unique quality control techniques, which are discussed in detail later in the chapter, are necessary for services. For now, it is important to remember that many services cannot be performed again if a mistake is made. An 18-year-old who emerges from high school poorly educated is unlikely to start all over again. In addition, because services are so people intensive, quality can depend directly on service suppliers.

Globally, training

Marketing Vocabulary

SERVICE ENCOUNTER
The interaction between the consumer and the seller.

PERISHABLE
The temporal nature of services, whose value exists for only a short time.

ALMOST PURE GOODS	GOODS WITH SERVICES	HALF GOODS, HALF SERVICES	SERVICES WITH GOODS	ALMOST PURE SERVICES
Physical products that are purchased and consumed with little or no service	Products supported with repair, mainten-ance, add-ons, and advice	Products that consist of both goods and services	Intellectual property or equipment to make goods work	Experiences that are consumed during delivery
Groceries Gasoline (self-serve) Steel	Autos Auto repair Video games	Restaurants Bookstores Movie theaters Prepared food delivery	Rental movies Training books Software Electronic mail Fax service	Health clubs Medical care Consulting Legal services Day care

Figure 10.3   Continuum of Goods and Services
Source: Valarie A. Zeithaml, "How Consumer Evaluation Processes Differ between Goods and Services," in Marketing of Services, eds. James H. Donnelly and William R. George.

methods often need to be adjusted to ensure quality service. For example, sales reps in China often sell products solely on price, fail to ask consumers business-related questions, and demonstrate little product knowledge. They also have little training or marketing support. In the United States, sales reps are trained to understand customer's needs and emphasize product benefits, have extensive product knowledge, and help the customer understand the value of the potential purchase. The Chinese and American training methods produce two distinct types of service. Differences in culture also play an important role in consumer perceptions of quality service. French salespeople, for example, are traditionally rude, show little knowledge of the product, and are generally unhelpful to the customer. However, some French companies import American consultants to retrain sales staffs in the American style.

Service quality control is monitored by trained observers during and after service delivery. Chances are that you have phoned a company and heard a recording saying the call may be monitored to be sure you receive appropriate service. This type of feedback lets the organization know whether service is being performed consistently as intended. When there are difficulties, most customer-oriented service providers give employees additional training, supervision, and help.

THE SERVICE–GOODS CONTINUUM

Although there are differences in marketing goods and services, there are also many similarities. In fact, few organizations market only one or the other. Most purchases fall somewhere along the continuum between almost pure goods and almost pure services, as illustrated in Figure 10.3.

Notice the word *almost* at each end of the continuum. Even in their purest form, goods and services still contain some aspect of the other. Almost pure goods are physical products that can be described by their form, mass, and function. There are thousands of types, ranging from computer chips to ocean liners. A gym supplies several different products that can be considered almost pure goods, such as clothes, equipment, and health food.

Next along the continuum are goods with services. These are physical products accompanied by the supportive services required to make them work. For example, automobiles play a major role in our economy not only because of their sales revenues but also because of the services they require. Saturn's success has been due in part to its policy of involving the customer in many steps of the production process. Gateway Inc. remains a very profitable computer company because of the extensive customer service support it offers to consumers.[14]

Half goods and half services are products that require both elements equally to succeed. Restaurants provide a certain level of service, which includes the wait staff, and goods such as food and beverages. Customers want to anticipate as well as enjoy their dining experiences, so marketers appeal to customer expectations about entertainment, a unique atmosphere, or opportunities to interact with others. Bookstores provide not only products (books) but also guidance in searching out unique topics. In addition, their spatial arrangement, background music, and atmosphere all contribute to the "feelings" that sell. Coffee and beverage shops have been added to most leading bookstores to encourage customers to spend hours on a self-actualizing experience.

Services with goods often entail intellectual properties and equipment required to make goods work. Examples include rental movies, training books, and software. Microsoft's introduction of Vista has presented some interesting marketing problems. Unlike earlier releases of Microsoft operating systems, Vista requires hardware enhancements to be fully functional. Therefore, Microsoft's marketing stresses the adoption of Vista simultaneously with hardware changes. This is one reason, early adopters of the software were not waiting in lines to obtain the first releases of the highly touted software.

Almost pure services provide consumers with experiences that are consumed during the delivery process. Among the many items in this category are health clubs, legal services, and education. Although a haircut is considered the classic example of a pure service, even that ordinarily takes place in an establishment selling styling and beautification products. Services such as air and train travel involve such goods as meals and soft drinks as well as tickets that can be exchanged. Even though Southwest Airlines does not offer meals or assigned seats, consumers still have a very high perception of quality and service value. How can this be? When asked, customers usually cite the great service, such as frequent departures, on-time arrival, friendly employees, and low fares. Southwest has achieved the highest level of on-time arrivals and the fewest complaints of any airline.[15] This is an almost pure service that passengers value highly, which contributes to customer loyalty at Southwest.

CONSUMER EVALUATION OF SERVICES

Product Qualities Affecting Consumer Evaluation Products can be viewed as having three types of qualities—search, experience, and credence—that affect consumer evaluation. Search qualities can be evaluated prior to purchase. Experience qualities can be assessed only during or after consumption. Credence qualities are almost impossible to evaluate even after purchase and consumption. As Figure 10.4 illustrates, most goods are high in search and experience qualities, whereas most services are high in experience and credence qualities.[16]

Search Qualities Search qualities are found mostly in goods. They make it easy for consumers to judge one product relative to another. People can use their senses of smell, hearing, sight, touch, and taste to note differences in attribute quality. Many products are compared and studied in detail before a selection is made. For example, if you are shopping for new stereo speakers, you can listen to different models at the retail store to decide which pair sounds best. Similarly, you can test-drive different cars or try out a pair of in-line skates in the store parking lot. Even after purchase, items high in search qualities allow the consumer to assess their value. Best Buy, the nation's leading volume specialty retailer, offers demonstrations of video games and other products in their

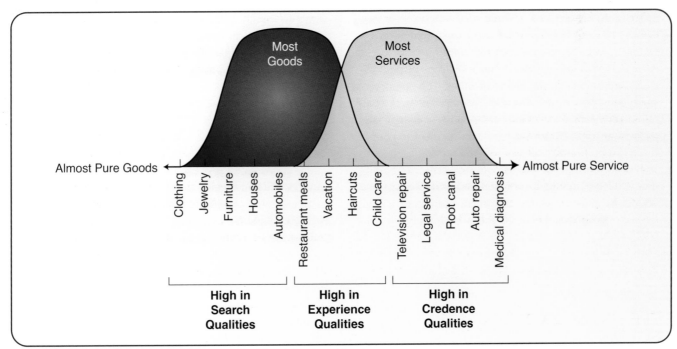

Figure 10.4   Search, Experience, and Credence Qualities of Goods and Services
Source: Valarie A. Zeithaml, "How Consumer Evaluation Processes Differ between Goods and Services," in Marketing of Services, eds. James H. Donnelly and William R. George.

stores. These are meant to increase the customer's knowledge of product features. Since Best Buy offers a number of items high in search qualities, its format enables consumers to compare and contrast products easily.

Experience Qualities The combined categories --goods with services, half goods and half services, and services with goods -- are high in experience qualities. Consumers cannot assess the amount of pleasure derived from them until they have used them. Then they can decide whether the product met or exceeded their expectations and can describe desired improvements or changes. As the name suggests, products high in experience qualities involve the customer, and promotional efforts usually depict people taking part in the experience. Cruises are a good example. Advertising campaigns for Carnival Cruise Lines often display consumers participating in a wide variety of activities. Carnival attracts more clients than any other line— more than a million per year from all over the world. These consumers can assess their experience only after the cruise has ended, but more than 98 percent of Carnival customers say they were well satisfied.[17]

Credence Qualities The credence qualities are found only in services and cannot be evaluated before, during, or after consumption. A medical diagnosis, for example, is almost impossible for consumers to assess, since most people have little or no knowledge of pathology and must trust in the ability of others. The outcomes of credence qualities are largely unobservable to the customer until indirect benefits emerge, such as higher sales as the consequence of hiring a consultant. Of course, there can be negative effects from the service, such as an IRS audit because of an accountant's error. The more intangible the result, the higher the credence qualities involved. In other words, customers must have a high degree of confidence that the exchange has been worthwhile.

Consumer Evaluation and Buying Behavior Because services are high in credence qualities, consumer buying behavior tends to be different for services than for goods. Specific differences, described next, range from the more personal nature of the information sources relied upon to the fact that the customer is often a competitor of the service provider.

Carnival possesses experience qualities that cannot be assessed until consumers have used the service.

The Personal Factor In selecting services, buyers rely more on information from personal sources. Because services tend to be personal, this is not surprising. Suppose you are going to court in an important lawsuit. Would you select your lawyer from an ad on television or a recommendation from a knowledgeable friend? Consumers not only relate better to personal information sources but also give them more credence.

Postpurchase Evaluation Because services are not easily evaluated before purchase, most assessments are made during or after the fact. Lawn care companies are careful not only to do a good job of mowing and trimming but also to clean away the clippings, leaving a well-manicured look with very little the consumer can criticize.

Surrogates for Judgment When a product is high in credence quality, consumers use surrogate cues to make judgments. One such cue is price. Many people equate high-priced services with greater value. Another cue is physical features, such as how the service provider dresses or the appearance or location of offices. The quality of car service may be judged by such a small thing as the cleanliness of the shop's restroom. An inefficiently run physician's office with new furniture may send off more positive cues than one that is better run but has poor lighting, outdated furniture, and clutter. In this case, the cues are used to make judgments about the quality of medical treatment the consumer will receive, and the office decor is a surrogate for measuring the skill and success of the physician.

Small Sets of Acceptable Brands or Suppliers Because services are personal and difficult to judge, consumers are likely to consider a small set of providers when seeking a service. Since services have no search qualities, consumers will not benefit from elaborate comparisons. Furthermore, their personal sources of information are likely to yield relatively few options. And once a reliable provider is found, customers tend to be loyal. For example, most of us use only one or perhaps two dry cleaners all the time. The same is probably true for hair stylists, tailors, party planners, and other types of providers. Some business travelers limit their choice when selecting a hotel, booking only Marriott or Sheraton because they are confident they will receive acceptable service.

Slow Adoption Because prepurchase evaluation is almost impossible, the risk of buying a service is greater than for goods. Therefore, many new services are adopted very slowly by consumers. People want to wait and see how the new service performs. Many consumers were initially reluctant to use the automatic teller machines (ATMs). They anticipated problems such as lost deposits or theft and preferred contact with a human being. Over time these fears diminished, and many consumers now do all their banking through ATMs. Shopping on the Internet caused similar security concerns among consumers, but several Web sites and credit card companies developed new security devices to ensure consumer safety while shopping on the Web.[18]

Strong Brand Loyalty Services have a built-in loyalty factor. People are more loyal to other people than to things. They also tend to stick with who they know. In addition, because consumers participate in the service, they may attribute any problems that occur to their own behavior, relieving the provider of some responsibility. For example, if your hairdresser cuts your bangs too short, you may partially blame yourself for not being explicit about what you wanted. Furthermore, the high degree of credence qualities in services makes it difficult to know whether the provider has done a poor job unless something goes wrong, such as your car failing to start the day after it was repaired. Without a negative signal, consumers are likely to assume that the provider did at least a good job. In general, there is less complaining behavior from consumers about services as opposed to goods. We know from earlier chapters, however, that it is very important to seek out and respond to consumer complaints about any type of product.

The Customer as Competitor Services usually involve activities that consumers can do for themselves. Parents may elect to stay home with their young children or have relatives take care of them, in which case, they are "competing" with day care centers. People can mow their own lawns, clean their own cars or homes, prepare their own tax returns, or prepare food for their own parties. Or they may select a service provider to do it for them. In many instances the trade-off is between time and money. This is why so many providers stress the amount of time their services will save consumers. For example, the United States Postal Service now offers Pickup On Demand, a time specific service giving customers the opportunity to conveniently schedule a pickup at their home or office through the Internet or a toll-free number.[19]

SERVICE QUALITY

Since service quality plays a significant part in the purchase decision for most consumers, it is crucial for marketing success. One study shows that service is "irrelevant" to customer perception of quality in only 15 percent of markets.[20] The Marketing Science Institute, through international conferences and research with major corporations, has identified how consumers assess overall service quality. The results, outlined in Figure 10.5, indicate that assessments have three aspects: dimensions of service quality, consumer factors, and quality perception. Dimensions of service quality are elements that consumers are most likely to perceive when making judgments, such as reliability and responsiveness. Consumer factors refer to customer needs and information acquisition. Quality perception depends on how closely the buyer's expectations are matched (or exceeded) by the service actually delivered, a concept very similar to customer satisfaction. Each of these is discussed next.

Dimensions of Service Quality The dimensions of service quality fall into five categories: tangibles, reliability, responsiveness, assurance, and empathy. It's important for marketers to consider each of these as they

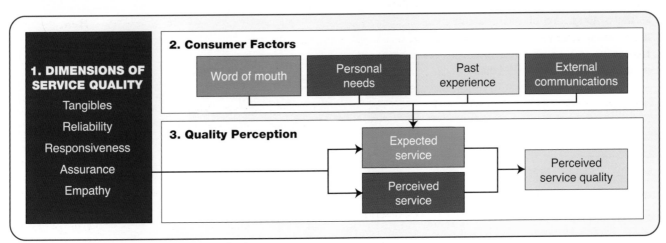

Figure 10.5   The Customer's View of Service Quality

Source: Adapted from Valarie A. Zeithaml, A. Parasuraman, and Leonard L. Berry, Delivering Quality Service, Balancing Customer Perceptions and Expectations (New York: The Free Press, 1990), p. 26.

evaluate the quality of the services they provide to consumers.

Tangibles It has been noted already that services are intangible but often are associated with physical facilities, equipment, personnel, and promotional materials. These tangibles have a very significant effect on customers. Organizations that provide tangibles of high quality communicate an impression of their nontangible offerings as well. For example, the way an office is designed and equipped, its cleanliness, and the personal appearance of employees all play a major role in conveying quality.

Reliability The ability to perform the promised service dependably and accurately is critical to service quality. Reliability involves, for example, returning calls and meeting deadlines. It also means performing activities precisely as outlined, such as sticking to the script in training programs, producing credit card statements free of errors, and doing a task correctly the first time. Research has shown that completing all car repairs when promised is more important than the quality of the work itself.

Responsiveness The willingness of providers to be helpful and give prompt service is very important to buyers. Waiting time is critical to buyer satisfaction and evaluation of service quality. What managers view as a short wait may seem long to customers. It is important to respond in a timely manner to customer requests and needs. If the customer finds an error on a financial statement, is it resolved quickly and with an adequate explanation? Are salespeople willing to answer questions about what to expect from a service? Do they help resolve difficulties if they arise?

Assurance The knowledge and courtesy of employees and their ability to convey trust and competence are essential for services which have high credence qualities. A very important factor is whether customers are treated with dignity and respect. Another is credibility— whether the provider conveys sufficient knowledge, experience, and trustworthiness to perform the service. Finally, assurance is related to security, the belief that the services will be performed safely and confidentially and that a free exchange of ideas between the provider and the consumer is possible. Providing assurance is a major component in a company's ability to build and maintain these relationships.

Empathy The caring, individualized attention that a firm provides its customers encompasses a number of dimensions. It is particularly important for serv-

ice providers to convey that they understand the customer. It is through their ability to listen, communicate clearly, and relate well to the client that they transmit empathy.

Consumer Factors Factors that influence the consumer's view of service quality include word of mouth, personal needs, past experience, and external communication. Word of mouth is particularly important because services are not readily observable and must be described verbally. Because they lack search qualities, they are likely to be discussed with friends when consumers are seeking a provider. These discussions tend to carry considerable credibility. Personal needs are also important. These deal with the motives that determine the nature and strength of what a consumer wants from a service. Past experience refers to what consumers have learned through personal interaction with a service provider. This is particularly important in shaping expectations, a topic covered next. The final element is external communication, that is, such marketer-dominated sources as personal selling and advertising. How a service is positioned and what is communicated through paid messages can influence consumer perceptions.

Quality Perception Because perceptions of service quality depend on the service meeting or exceeding customer expectations, service providers must take care in shaping those expectations. Because the product is intangible and people cannot readily observe for themselves what to expect, the messages and examples from service providers contribute much to developing expectations. To ensure high perceived quality and a loyal customer base, providers need to be accurate and reasonable about what they lead customers to expect. They also need to do a

Steak 'N' Shake promotes a higher-quality alternative to competitors

good job in the areas of tangibles, reliability, responsiveness, assurance, and empathy. Because the personal nature of services makes them very difficult for competitors to emulate, those companies that invest resources and energy in building strong service quality are most likely to be winners. Steak 'N' Shake, recognizing consumer interest in quality service, promotes the atmosphere of its restaurants as a higher-quality, more personal alternative to "fast-food" establishments. The friendly, prompt service encourages revisits.

DEVELOPING THE SERVICE MIX

Services, like goods, usually occur as a mix. They often rely on branding to communicate uniqueness. At the same time, several qualities must be considered when developing a new service. These include the service itself, the brand, and factors that enhance the fundamental service. This section explores these dimensions more extensively.

CORE, AUGMENTED, AND BRANDED SERVICES

Products have core, augmented, and branded dimensions. Let's relate these concepts to services. We can use the example of birthing in a hospital, as depicted in Figure 10.6. The **core service** is the basic benefit, in this case delivery of a healthy baby and safety for the mother. That is the main objective of the service. But, in today's competitive health care arena, the augmented and branded product also plays a key role. The augmented service is the package of bundled goods and services that differentiates one provider from another. It has a

great deal to do with how well service providers connect with customers. Since the core service is the same for all providers, the augmented features are critical.

Because a service is intangible, a customer comes to know its value through the symbols and cues around it. McDonald's has achieved name recognition not only because of the reliability of its goods but also because of its customer service, personnel management, cleanliness, child-oriented image, and so forth. Its brand equity reflects the interactive service element as well as the functional dimensions of the physical goods sold. Consider the growing brand equity of FedEx Kinko's, it has expanded to over 1,100 branches in the United States, Canada, the Netherlands, Japan, South Korea, Australia, the United Arab Emirates, China, Mexico and Great Britain. Others provide copy services, but FedEx Kinko's has become synonymous with a customer-oriented philosophy. It has expanded services to include desktop publishing, computer rental with high-speed ISDN Internet access, shipping, worldwide network videoconferencing, among others. Customers rely on the FedEx Kinko's name for value and service.[21]

Marriott extended its branded line by developing three chains with lower complexity than the original service. Courtyard has become an identifiable service mark associated with high-quality motel accommodations and limited services. Fairfield Inns are positioned as the least complex, no-frills part of the chain. Residence Inns cater to an extended stay of five days or more, with business travelers making up the majority of their guests. With these three brand names, the company has developed services consistent with the target markets for which each is intended.

DEVELOPING NEW SERVICES

Certain functional and interactive elements are important when new services are created. The **functional element** is about accomplishing what is intended. (Does the orthodontist straighten a patient's teeth? Does a shoe get repaired?) The **interactive element** involves the

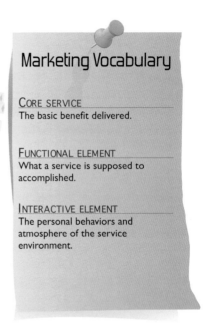

Marketing Vocabulary

CORE SERVICE
The basic benefit delivered.

FUNCTIONAL ELEMENT
What a service is supposed to accomplished.

INTERACTIVE ELEMENT
The personal behaviors and atmosphere of the service environment.

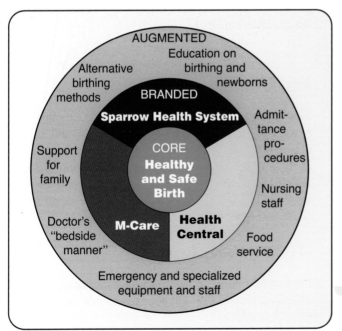

Figure 10.6 Example of a Core, Augmented, and Branded Service

personal behaviors and physical atmosphere of the service environment.

Functional Elements in Service Development   The functional element is influenced by the complexity and divergence of the service. **Service complexity** is the number and intricacy of steps involved in producing a service. For example, a muffler shop that adds brake lining and transmission repair to its services is increasing complexity. The service a defense lawyer provides a murder suspect is much more complex than a house cleaner's activities. **Divergence** is the amount of routine procedure involved. A very customized service has high divergence, such as a consultant who tailors staff development advice to each person in a company. A standardized service has low divergence. For example, Fred Pryor Seminars, Inc. (www.pryor.com) gives a set presentation on various topics to groups representing many organizations.[22]

Figure 10.7 illustrates complexity and divergence for four services. Since most local barbershops do approximately the same thing, and cutting hair is not highly complicated, divergence and complexity are very low. Dentistry has low divergence due to standardized procedures, but it tends to be high in complexity. House cleaning is highly customized (divergent) but low in complexity, whereas litigation tends to be high in both divergence and complexity.

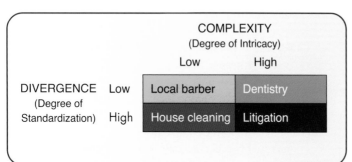

Figure 10.7 Complexity and Divergence in Services

Interactive Elements in Service Development   The interactive element is often more important than the functional aspect in creating service excellence. Walt Disney Enterprises has attempted to produce a strong interactive service by using a stage (the environment) with actors (Disney employees) to involve the audience (consumers). Through extensive role-playing, the Disney people have learned to connect in a way that produces strong customer satisfaction. One part of this interaction is simply the desire to help customers have fun.

Many companies use atmospherics, the environment in which the service is performed, to enhance the interactive element.[23] Originally applied to retail stores, atmospherics has important implications for all types of services outside the consumer's home. Such features as color, music, and layout are all part of the atmosphere. It not only influences the selection of a service provider but also, and more important, determines whether service outcomes are satisfying.

The physical components of atmosphere have an emotional dimension. The mood created greatly influences whether consumers want to enter and explore the environment, communicate with personnel, and gain satisfaction from the service encounter.[24] Retail stores such as Banana Republic, Victoria's Secret, and Eddie Bauer emphasize music as a way to increase sales. DMX, a service provider to many retailers, researches the demographics and psychographics of a store's customers and then creates suitable sound. The music is designed to encourage customers to shop longer and also creates an atmosphere for each retailer.[25] The next time you visit a Nine West, Coach, or Victoria's Secret outlet, note the music program created especially to appeal to you.

Structuring New Services   The functional and interactive aspects of services affect how organizations structure new offerings. Marketers determine where each new service attribute fits on the continuum from low complexity/divergence to high complexity/divergence. Figure 10.8 shows an example of structural alternatives in the restaurant business. The standard restaurant can be viewed as falling in the middle. The restaurant's marketing manager can choose to move in one of two directions for each area shown: more upscale (higher complexity/divergence) or more downscale (lower complexity/divergence). By conducting this type of analysis, the organization can make clear choices in developing new services.

AN EXPANDED CONCEPT OF SERVICES

In addition to the traditional offerings, service marketing is used to promote people, entertainment and events, places, political candidates and ideas, and different causes. It can even be used within an organization, through internal marketing, to promote one group's capabilities to another. The following sections give more detail about additional types of service.

PERSON MARKETING

Person marketing involves promoting an individual's character, personality, and appeal, which in turn may be used to promote a service or product. Tiger Woods,

Lower Complexity/Divergence	Current Process	Higher Complexity/Divergence
No reservation	← Take reservation →	Specific table selection
Self-seating; menu on blackboard	← Seat guest, give menu →	Recite menu; describe entrees and specials
Eliminate	← Serve water and bread →	Assortment of hot breads and hors d'oeuvres
Customer fills out form	← Take orders; prepare orders →	Taken personally by maitre d' at table
Prepared; no choice	← Salad (4 choices) →	Individually prepared at table
Limited to 4 choices	← Entree (15 choices) →	Expand to 20 choices; add flaming dishes; bone fish at table; prepare sauces at table
Sundae bar; self-service	← Dessert (6 choices) →	Expand to 12 choices
Coffee, tea, milk, and sodas	← Beverage served (6 choices) →	Add exotic coffees; wine list; liqueurs
Serve salad and entree together; bill and beverage together	← Serve orders →	Separate course service; sherbet between courses; hand-grind pepper
Cash only; pay when leaving	← Collect payment at table →	Choice of payment, including house accounts; serve mints

Figure 10.8   Structural Alternatives in the Restaurant Business
Source: Adapted with permission from G. Lynn Shostack, "Service Positioning through Structural Change," Journal of Marketing 51 (January 1987): 34–43.

whose endorsements may have a lifetime value of more than a billion dollars, is one of the most notable sports figures to date. The multiethnic appeal and charisma of Tiger Woods have struck a chord with diverse customers across the globe, creating opportunities for companies to market Tiger's image to promote many products. This includes Nike. Nike has Woods wearing its gear even when he's representing products from other sponsors such as American Express, Accenture, General Motors, Buick, Electronic Arts and Tag Heuer watches. Notice that Tiger is wearing gear with the Nike swoosh clearly visible, whether in print and television ads for non-Nike products. This is free promotion to Nike. Nike is piggybacking on the dollars spent by other sponsors. "I suspect that the nature of the relationship is such that he's obligated to wear Nike in any public appearance," says Gary Singer, chief strategy officer at Interbrand, a branding consultancy. "Tiger is so closely associated with Nike that whether you see [other] brands or not, you think of Nike."[26]

Tiger Woods has agents who help market their exceptional appeal to various companies and to consumers. For them and other Olympic or professional athletes, much of their attraction is due to their skills and character. In addition, however, service providers who market sports personalities contribute a great deal. Person marketing is often a two-way process in which promotion of the individual increases his or her value as a product endorser. Public exposure that enhances reputation leads to more lucrative endorsements, contracts, and vice versa.

Marketing Vocabulary

SERVICE COMPLEXITY
The number and intricacy of steps involved in producing a service.

DIVERGENCE
The degree to which a service involves customization beyond routine or standardized procedures.

PERSON MARKETING
Promoting an individual's personality, character, and appeal, which in turn may assist in the promotion of a product.

ENTERTAINMENT AND EVENT MARKETING

Dreamworks' sequel *Shrek The Third* opened at theaters with great success. It brought in $121.6 million, the third-highest grossing debut weekend on record. Every aspect of the movie was the result of careful planning, from promotion to the precise timing of its introduction. Mike Myers, Cameron Diaz and Eddie Murphy are huge draws in their own right, and the addition of Justin Timberlake and Larry King added appeal to the two target audiences. Young children and their parents were both drawn in by the star power of the movie.[27]

Television and radio also thrive on sophisticated marketing. Mark Burnett, creator and producer of the *Survivor* and *The Apprentice* has a knack for marketing. His programs are successful because viewers can relate to the people cast as participants as well as the individual and team tasks that separate winners and losers. His shows are heavily promoted to inform viewers about each new series and careful monitoring makes sure that from week to week a show reaches the audiences advertisers desire.

Event marketing is the promotion of an event in order to generate revenues and enhance the reputation of an organization. It has become a huge factor in the entertainment world, with sporting events at the forefront. Ohio State University characterizes its athletic department as being in the entertainment business; the university has an annual athletics budget exceeding $100 million.[28] University sports are big business. They generate the revenues that support student athletes and contribute positively or negatively to the university's reputation. College athletics are a multibillion-dollar industry, with revenues from stadium attendance, television and radio, concessions, apparel, and signage at stadiums. Michigan State University earns several million in royalties annually.

One of the most successful event marketers is the National Basketball Association. Although most NBA games are played in the United States, the 2008 All-Star Game was broadcasted in 215 countries in over 40 languages.[29] The NBA has assisted in basketball theme movies as well: Coach Carter starring Samuel L. Jackson, Finding Forester starring Sean Connery, White Men Can't Jump starring Wesley Snipes, Space Jam starring Michael Jordan, and Kazzam starring Shaquille O'Neal.

Sponsorships allow companies to link their names with the outstanding experience people associate with the

Justin Timberlake at the Shrek The Third London premiere.

event. Coke, Pepsi, and General Motors are likely to be seen supporting college athletics. A great example is Coca-Cola's sponsorship of the 2000 Summer Olympics torch relay. Aside from seeing the torch, few spectators could forget the sponsor. Coca-Cola lined the streets with posters announcing when the relay would arrive, while advance trucks sold bottles of Coke. The company also gave out posters and stickers to kids and handled press coverage.

PLACE MARKETING

Place marketing enhances a location in order to appeal to businesses, investors, and tourists. Check out "The Smart State For Business" at www.smart.state.ia.us and you'll learn about Iowa's cutting-edge business environment, such as technology centers at the University of Iowa, Iowa State University, and the University of Northern Iowa. With the theme "Pride and Prosperity," Iowa is marketed as "the smart state for business." Partners in the endeavor are Pella Windows and Doors, Maytag, the Principal Financial Group, MidAmerican Energy, Monsanto, John Deere, Rockwell, and Amana. Other possibilities include Alliant Energy, CertainTeed, EAI, Fisher Controls, Lennox, Pioneer, Quaker Oats, and Wells Fargo Mortgage (www.smart.state.ia.us/industry). Iowa is also trying to persuade other businesses, cities, and counties to join in.[30]

Vacation places receive tremendous marketing attention. Countries, states, cities, and resorts all participate. Few put it all together as well as Disney does. "It's a small world after all" in any one of several unique resort hotels at Walt Disney World near Orlando, Florida. You can walk from country to country experiencing, for example, a British pub or German restaurant. The Theme Parks and Resorts division of Disney had revenues of nearly $4 billion in recent years. This includes Disneyland near Paris and Tokyo, two newer developments.

POLITICAL MARKETING

Political marketing involves the promotion of an individual or idea with the aim of influencing public policy and voters. Politicians use political marketing in order to present themselves and their ideas in the best possible way. All of the tools of excellent marketing play a rolls in sophisticated political campaigns. The internet has pro-

Chapter 10 - *Goods, Services & Nonprofit Marketing*

vided an outstanding venue for political communication, often called web campaigning. As the 2008 presidential campaign began to heat up, new-age candidates like Barack Obama developed an outstanding web presence with unique capabilities. Obama's Web site shows the many one-way and two-way communication opportunities available. A constituent can create an individual profile called "My.BarackObama.com" which powers a custom dashboard to find supporters, plan events, network with friends, become a fundraiser, and manage a blog. The site also contains "BarackTV" which gives up-to-date video footage of his campaign and an online store where you can purchase t-shirts, bumper stickers, or other Obama goods.

CAUSE MARKETING

Cause marketing involves gaining public support and financing for a cause in order to bring about a change or a remedy. You are familiar with many of the marketing campaigns to combat AIDS, drunk driving, drugs, domestic violence, and smoking among teens; to promote the use of seat belts; and to prevent cruelty to animals, to name a few. Cause marketing is used for blood drives, Community Chest drives, and charities that feed and clothe the homeless or combat various diseases. The overall objective is to remedy a situation by gaining public support for change.

Cause marketing is challenging because it usually confronts two very difficult tasks: raising money and changing harmful behavior. For example, The American Cancer Society has been successful in educating people about the disease and how to mini-

mize their chances of infection. Cancer survivor and 6 time Tour de France winner Lance Armstrong has helped raise awareness with his LiveStrong campaign, selling 40 million of the yellow bracelets which are worn by politicians, celebrities, athletes, musicians, and cancer survivors across the world.[31]

INTERNAL MARKETING

Internal marketing occurs when one part of an organization markets its capabilities to others within the same firm. For example, imagine that you are a human resources manager. Your job, among other responsibilities, is to provide training and career development for employees in all the company's different divisions and departments. An effective approach is to use marketing concepts. The only difference is that you are aiming your efforts at internal customers—the employees of the firm—rather than end users of the company's products. This is not the same as internal communications, which are also important; all the marketing tools and techniques tend to be used, even marketing plans.

Marketing Vocabulary

EVENT MARKETING
Promoting an event in order to generate revenues and enhance the reputation of an organization.

PLACE MARKETING
Promoting a geographical location in order to appeal to businesses, investors, and tourists.

POLITICAL MARKETING
Promoting an individual or idea motivated by the desire to influence public policy and voters.

CAUSE MARKETING
Gaining public support and financing in order to change or remedy a situation.

INTERNAL MARKETING
The marketing of a business unit's capabilities to others within the same firm.

Lance Armstrong's LiveStrong Campaign raises awareness of cancer.

THE MARKETING OF NONPROFIT SERVICES

Marketing of nonprofit services is a huge area. According to the National Center for Charitable Statistics, there are more than 1.4 million non-profit organizations in the US. Simply through donations, these organizations raised almost $300 billion in 2006. Nearly 70 percent of US households donate to charity, and the average household donates more than $1,800.[32] Nonprofit services account for more than 6 percent of all economic activity in the United States. As you can see from Figure 10.9, the United States has the highest percentage of nonprofit workers to total employment and to total service employment in the world. The U.S. nonprofit sector employs 10.2 million people, compared to 1.4 million in Japan and about one million in France.

	Percentage of Total Employment	Percentage of Nonprofit Service Employment
United States	6.8	15.4
France	4.2	10.0
United Kingdom	4.0	9.4
Germany	3.7	10.4
Average	3.4	8.9
Japan	2.5	8.6
Italy	1.8	5.5
Hungary	0.8	3.0

Figure 10.9 Nonprofit Jobs as a Percentage of Total and Service Employment
Source: Stephen Greene, "Nonprofits Group Expanding World," Chronicle of Philanthropy, June 28, 1994, pp. 1, 28–29. Reprinted with permission of Chronicle of Philanthropy.

Nonprofit marketing is performed by an organization that is not motivated by profit and is exempt from paying taxes on any excess revenues over costs. Marketing has many applications in the nonprofit sector. Churches, museums, foundations, hospitals, universities, symphonies, and municipalities regularly create marketing plans in an effort to gain funds and public support. Nonprofit organizations often use person marketing, entertainment and event marketing, and place marketing. Nearly all political and cause marketing, as well as marketing of the arts, fits the nonprofit description. Most nonprofit organizations have begun advertising and soliciting donations and volunteers on the Internet, in an effort to maximize fund-raising at little cost.[33]

TYPES OF NONPROFIT SERVICE PROVIDERS

Figure 10.10 shows several categories of nonprofit service providers and gives examples of each. As you can see, marketing skills are required by a very broad range of nonprofit organizations. For example, your university probably has a fairly elaborate marketing plan, and chances are that many of the administrators have attended American Marketing Association seminars on how to promote higher education. Many athletic directors and university presidents are currently being advised to view their positions as similar to that of a CEO of a major corporation.

THE NEED FOR EXCESS REVENUES

Nonprofit service organizations are usually tax exempt and may appear to be less concerned about pricing and cost structures. Yet they need to generate revenues in excess of costs for several reasons. First, their revenues (money for services and from contributions) tend to fluctuate from year to year. For example, the Museum of Fine Arts in Boston relies on blockbuster shows every few years to boost revenues. For their all-star game, the NBA partners with local schools and youth serving community-based organizations in the host city to raise money. Thus, tying a nonprofit event to a profit-making organization, especially a well-known one such as the NBA, can provide fund-raising opportunities.[34]

Second, you can't raise money if you aren't solvent. The United Way wants the organizations it supports to

Category	Example	Product
Arts/Culture/Humanities	Metropolitan Museum of Art, New York Chicago Symphony	Exhibits Musical programs
Education/Instruction	Michigan State University Executive Education University of Southern California Undergraduate Program	Executive programs Classes, degrees
Environmental Quality/ Protection/Beautification	Smokey the Bear (U.S. Forest Service) Greenpeace	Fire safety Saving the environment
Animal Related	San Diego Zoo People for the Ethical Treatment of Animals (PETA)	Species preservation Animal rights
Health	Listening Ear Alcoholics Anonymous (AA)	Cure for AIDS Stop alcoholism
Consumer Protection	Consumer Hotline	Legal aid
Crime Prevention	Neighborhood Watch Crime Tip Hotline	Discourage criminals Catch criminals
Employment/Jobs Public Safety	U.S. Army State of Michigan State of Florida	Volunteer recruitment Drive safely Wear seat belts
Recreation/Sports	Silverdome American Youth Soccer Organization	Football Youth sports programs
Youth Development	Boy Scouts of America Big Sister/Big Brother programs	Scouting jamborees Companionship and role models
Community/Civic	Bring Your Company to . . . Kiwanis Club	Community enhancement Economic development
Grant Agencies	Rockefeller Foundation Robert Wood Johnson Foundation	Arts development Medical research
Religious Organizations	Catholic Church Evangelists	Membership Spirituality
Other Cause-Based Groups	National Organization of Women (NOW) American Civil Liberties Union (ACLU)	Women's rights Individual rights

Figure 10.10 Types of Nonprofit Service Providers

have at least a three-month safety net. That means a full quarter's expenses have to be earned and set aside—no small task for most organizations! Fund-raising operations must be run in a financially sound manner in order to gain support from large donors. That requires efficiency and documentation identifying the costs of items as well as the revenues received.

Third, nonprofits hire professionals to help the organization grow. Similar to any business, growth generally requires capital and the ability to access funds from financial institutions. Lenders look at nonprofits much the same way they look at any other organization. The Red Cross makes significant positive cash flows. This type of financial performance not only attracts managerial talent but also affords the company access to all the services required by a for-profit company.

FUND-RAISING AND REVENUE GENERATION

Nonprofit organizations may raise revenues in two ways. First, they acquire funding from third parties, such as governments, private and public agencies, and individual contributors. Second, they may expand into a number of business operations.

A considerable amount of funding comes from donations by individuals, families, or businesses. Microsoft CEO Bill Gates is recognized for making contributions to non-profits. The Bill & Melinda Gates Foundation works to

Marketing Vocabulary

NONPROFIT MARKETING
The activities performed by an organization not motivated by profit in order to influence consumers to support it with a contribution.

reduce inequities and improve lives around the world.[35] Warren Buffet, the world's richest man, pledged to give away 85 percent of his wealth a little at a time. The majority of this money will be donated to the Bill & Melinda Gates Foundation.[36]

Understanding donor profiles helps nonprofit groups target fund-raising efforts. Figure 10.11 lists six categories of donors, the types of charities they most often support, and why they give. The largest group, communitarians, believe in supporting their community. As government has decreased its support of social services and the arts, nonprofits in these areas must compete against one another for private dollars. Just as new ventures need a well-honed marketing strategy and innovative approach to entice venture capitalists, new nonprofits need to do the same to capture the attention of donors besieged by requests. The Point Community Development Corporation in the Hunt's

The Marketing Gazette ™

CREATING & CAPTURING VALUE THROUGH RELATIONSHIPS

Michiganders Preach Al Gore's Global Warming Gospel
They traverse the state presenting slide shows that warn of dangers

"A planetary emergency" is how former U.S. Vice President Al Gore describes global warming. In his recent film, "An Inconvenient Truth" Gore methodically describes the overwhelming evidence that earth is becoming dangerously warm due to the greenhouse gas emissions created by humans. The message of the Academy Award winning documentary is being carried further by thousands of Gore supporters across the country.

Personally trained by Gore, these followers are armed with copies of his climate change slide show. Their mission is to motivate audiences to insist on action by their leaders.

After years of scientific study, people are now starting to understand the significance of the global warming—due in part to Gore's efforts. Created from burning fossil fuels, the excess carbon dioxide in the atmosphere is capturing the sun's energy and heating the earth. According to Henry Pollack, a retired University of Michigan geology professor and one of Gore's science advisers, the temperature of the earth has risen 1.5 degrees in the past century. The increase in temperature has resulted in glacial melting, warmer oceans, rising sea levels and violent storms. "We can see the human effects," Pollack said.

Al Gore continued his effort to raise awareness about global warming by supporting the production of Live Earth. Featuring performers such as Madonna, Kelly Clarkson and the Red Hot Chili Peppers, Live Earth took place on July 7, 2007 and was the biggest charitable concert ever. With stages in New York, London, Sydney, Tokyo, Shanghai, Rio de Janeiro, Johannesburg and Hamburg the concert was broadcasted by more than 100 television networks around the world and streamed digitally on Microsoft's MSN. Reaching an estimated 2 billion people world-wide, Live Earth delivered a call to action and solutions to the global warming crisis. Kevin Wall, founder of Live Earth, described the event. "Live Earth is committed to continuing to provide our global audience with ways to 'Answer the Call' and individually make a difference to help solve the climate crisis…By providing the opportunity to view the shows in their entirety online coupled with our unique solutions campaign, we're able to communicate our message on a mass-scale in a way that engages people and inspires them to act," said Wall.

Gore, along with the UN's Intergovernmental Panel on Climate Change, was awarded the 2007 Nobel Peace Prize for their efforts to educate the world about global warming. He plans to donate his half of the $1.5 million prize to the Alliance for Climate Protection, a non-profit organization dedicated to changing the world's opinion about the urgency of climate change.

Category	Percentage of All Major Donors	Who They Are and What They Support	Why They Give
Communitarians	26%	91% male Local charities, cultural, religious, and educational concerns	To improve the community Good for business relationships
Devout	21%	80% male and business owners Religious organizations	Moral obligation
Investors	15%	87% male, 75% business owners Wide variety	Rather support them than the government No moral obligation
Socialites	11%	62% female Arts, education, and religious projects	Believe that giving is part of personality and provides entry into a desirable social circle
Repayers	10%	65% male Educational institutions and medical facilities	Loyalty or obligation due to an event that happened later in life
Dynasts	8%	50% male, 50% female Many have inherited wealth and give to wide range of groups	Believe everyone should support nonprofits Family traditionally supports nonprofits

Figure 10.11   Categories of Donors to Nonprofit Groups
Source: Adapted from "One Study's Analysis of 7 Types of Wealthy Donors," Chronicle of Philanthropy, March 8, 1994, p. 14.

Point section of New York's South Bronx has rustled up a significant amount of funding. It uses "out of the box" thinking and cultivates relationships within both the neighborhood and the nonprofit community. See the relationships feature, "The Point: Celebrating the Life and Culture of the South Bronx."

In addition to fund-raising, many organizations develop business ventures that provide substantial revenues. These are often unrelated to the basic nature of the core activity. Your high school band, drama club, or sports team probably has used some type of retail operation at one time or another—a car wash, a food stand at the local fair, or a candy sale—to raise money for uniforms or a special trip. We all are familiar with Girl Scout cookie sales. In fact, these activities often compete with the for-profit sector. Because the service labor is donated, the price charged by the nonprofit group can be substantially lower than the normal retail price. In some cases, for-profit businesses simply cannot compete while the fund-raiser is going on. At the same time, nonprofits are good customers for many for-profit businesses.

Sometimes the revenue-generating venture fits nicely with the core activity of the nonprofit. For example, private schools and universities have bookstores and other merchandising operations. Museums and musical organizations (symphonies, opera companies) may have shops and mail-order catalogs. Some groups license their name or logo for a fee. Zoos, museums, sports teams, and others often charge admission.

Finally, membership fees represent a large source of revenue. Most associations are formed for the benefit of members, whether individuals or organizations. For example, a member of the American Marketing Association pays $195 annually to the AMA in addition to chapter dues. Students are given a special rate. This entitles the member to obtain AMA publications and attend conferences at substantially reduced rates. The AMA is the world's largest professional society of marketers, with more that 38,000 members in 92 countries; there are 500 chapters in North America. The association works to promote education and assist in career development among marketing professionals.[37]

Most professions have a similar organization, and in many cases companies can be members. For example, firms interested in service quality are likely to join the Center for Services Leadership (CSL) at Arizona State University. It is North America's leading university-based program for the study of services marketing and management. The center conducts research, offers specialized education and training, and works to provide firms with applicable principles, concepts, and tools.[38]

PROVIDING POSITIVE SOCIAL BENEFITS

Another challenge for nonprofits is to provide maximum positive social benefits to their constituency. This can be difficult because constituents may have differing objectives and needs. For example, the San Diego Zoo must balance the public's desire to see certain animals with the interests of environmentalists in species preservation. Expenses to house, care for, and in some cases help rare animals reproduce can be very high. Likewise, groups concerned with spouse or child abuse must allocate funds to serving families as well as to promoting their cause.

Having a good understanding of constituent needs is not always easy. The Internet is a particularly useful marketing tool for nonprofit groups. Many use it to communicate, share information, educate, collaborate, and interact. It is an excellent format for publishing, sharing perspectives on issues, assisting in community development, and increasing participation.[39]

A good example of the importance of serving constituency needs can be found in the arts. These include a long list of services—museums, theaters, opera, symphonies, dance companies, exhibitions, public radio and television, and others. A major indicator of the quality of life in many communities is the availability of the arts. Numerous cities have a symphony orchestra, which can be an important factor in attracting businesses and people to the area.

Customers for the arts are called patrons. Attracting them is a critical aspect of marketing the arts, but that is only part of the challenge. Equally important is finding sponsors of all types, since revenues from ticket sales seldom generate enough money. Yet patrons may have many choices about which arts events to attend, and sponsors may have a broad range of requests for donations. Ultimately, successful organizations are those that can show the benefits they bring to their constituents.

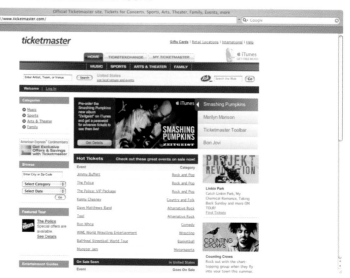

Web and E-Commerce Stars
Ticketmaster - www.ticketmaster.com

Ticketmaster is the one of the world's top ticketing companies. It operates in 20 global markets, and offers ticket sales, ticket resale services, marketing and distribution through its Web site. It provides exclusive ticketing services for hundreds of leading arenas, stadiums, performing arts venues, museums, and theaters. It also has an Auction section to allow venues, promoters, and artists to sell tickets straight to fans at a reasonable market price. It delivers tickets at once via email, so this system lets customer print tickets with any standard printer. Additionally, TicketAlert is a section where information is posted on upcoming tours and events, special ticket offers, pre-sales and so on. Once a means to an end for ticket sales, Ticketmaster.com now provides the customer with a more robust experience.

ETHICAL ISSUES SURROUNDING NONPROFIT ORGANIZATIONS

Today, many types of organizations claim nonprofit status, which entitles them to tax exemption. While a majority of these benefit society, a growing number have little or no resemblance to traditional charities. In fact, of the 45,000 new organizations that apply for tax-exempt status each year, many make a considerable profit. This raises the question of whether it is ethical for money-making nonprofits to pay no taxes. Consider professional golfing's PGA Tour, which grosses $180 million a year. It could afford to pay its commissioner $4.2 million over the last year, partly at the expense of the American taxpayer. The PGA Tour, Inc., is a nonprofit organization and is not required to pay federal tax on tour operations. Some nonprofits are very rich, indeed. The J. Paul Getty Trust in Los Angeles has $8 billion in assets.

Although nonprofits are taxed on income from businesses unrelated to their function, fewer than 5 percent report such income. The revenue for most nonprofits comes from investments and business operations. Nonprofit executives say they have shifted toward profit-making schemes in order to survive. Many others feel that there are too many nonprofits taking advantage of tax-exempt status, but efforts to change the law have failed repeatedly in Congress.

You may be familiar with many nonprofit organizations, such as National Geographic, the Academy of Motion Picture Arts and Sciences (which presents the Oscars), and the Humane Society. Nonprofits are not limited to charity, however. Many are found in retail, restaurant, hotel, insurance, and even laundry services. Most nonprofits do not pay taxes on investment income as well. Competitors of these organizations find the tax exemptions unfair and unethical. Nonprofits in competition with for-profit companies have a clear financial advantage. Consider the difference between a nonprofit hotel operated by George Washington University and other tax-paying hotels in the area. In fact, Washington, DC, houses 1,800 nonprofits. If they were to pay taxes on the land and buildings they use for operations, then approximately $94 million a year would flow to the city. Critics point out that they use city services just as other organizations do.

The nation's nonprofit sector generates amazing revenues every year and controls a large percentage of all assets. While many of these organizations directly benefit Americans, for others the tax-free status remains an ethical issue.

Chapter Summary:

Objective 1: Identify the forces that have produced and will continue to create tremendous growth in the service economy.

The service economy is growing at about twice the rate of the sale of goods. First, technological advances and the accompanying information revolution are creating vast opportunities in the service sector. Technology often can only be used with the help of service specialists who have the necessary knowledge and skills. Second, the quality of life is being measured by how people feel and experience life. Third, governments around the world have deregulated services. Fourth, professional service providers such as lawyers are turning to marketing as a way to conduct their business operations. Fifth, privatization of government functions is opening up service opportunities. Sixth, there is a need for outside specialists by companies that want to concentrate resources on their core business. Finally, there is a strong growth in franchising, which tends to focus on service-based products.

Objective 2: Understand which characteristics of services must be adjusted for successful marketing.

Services are differentiated from goods on five key dimensions that must be considered in successful marketing. First, services are intangible, so evidence of benefits may occur long after purchase and may be difficult to assess. Second, there is a unique relationship between the service provider and customers, who are either present when the service is performed or have knowledge of how it was performed. Third, the service encounter is a crucial point of connection between provider and consumer, in which each moment must contribute to meeting customer needs. Fourth, since production and consumption often occur simultaneously, the same service may be different each time it is performed and may be adjusted to the unique circumstances of each consumer. Fifth, because there is no storage or inventory with a service, demand forecasting is important so that service providers are ready when needed. Finally, service quality control is extremely important but it is complicated. It requires thorough training of personnel and careful monitoring.

Most products contain elements of both goods and services and can be placed on a service–goods continuum. Consumers tend to evaluate services differently from goods. Generally, services are high in credence qualities, which means it is difficult to evaluate them even after they have been consumed. Therefore, consumers tend to rely on personal references for information, engage in postpurchase evaluation, develop surrogates for judging quality, select providers from a small set of choices, and actually serve as a competitor to the service provider. They are slow to adopt new services but eventually develop strong brand loyalty.

Judgments of service quality usually have three aspects: the dimensions of service quality, consumer factors, and quality perceptions. The dimensions of service quality include tangibles, reliability, responsiveness, assurance, and empathy. Customer factors—word of mouth, personal needs, past experience, and external communication—help form customer expectations. Quality perception is based on the difference between what is expected and what is received.

Objective 3: Know how to develop the service mix.

Service mix development requires understanding in two areas. First, services have core, augmented, and branded dimensions similar to goods. Brand equity is equally if not more important for services than for goods. Second, when developing new services, marketers must give careful consideration to both functional and interactive elements. The functional element is influenced by the complexity and divergence of a service, which must provide benefits that match customer needs and wants. The interactive element involves such concerns as the consumer's personal behaviors and the atmosphere in which the service will be performed.

Objective 4: Explore the expanded concept of services.

There are many types of service marketing including person marketing, entertainment and event marketing, place marketing, political marketing, cause marketing, and internal marketing. Person marketing promotes an individual, often a sports figure or movie personality, who in turn generally helps market another product. Entertainment marketing promotes movies, television programming, and the like. Event marketing, like that for sporting events and concerts, is a major category. Through sponsorships of events, companies also market other products. Place marketing promotes a geographic location, such as a city, state, or country. It is often connected to investment or travel products. Political marketing promotes politicians or political ideas and policy issues. Cause marketing attempts to gain support for a cause, such as research on HIV and AIDS. Internal marketing occurs when one business unit markets its capabilities to others within the same firm.

Objective 5: Appreciate the importance of nonprofit marketing and the uniqueness of this important marketing arena.

Nonprofit marketing accounts for more than 7 percent of economic activity in the United States and is growing. It is performed by organizations that are tax exempt, such as churches, museums, foundations, hospitals, universities, and orchestras. Even nonprofits need revenues in excess of their costs. These revenues provide serv-ice continuity from year to year and allow nonprofits to access the talent and funding required to serve their constituents. Consequently, fund-raising and revenue generation from donors, patrons, and members are often a focal point. At the same time, nonprofits must provide benefits to all constituents, which can be difficult because different parties have varying expectations and needs. Ethically, there is a question about tax-exempt status for at least some nonprofits, especially when they compete with for-profit organizations.

Review Your Understanding

1. List the seven forces that are producing explosive growth in services. Very briefly describe each.
2. What are the differences between goods and services?
3. What is the service–goods continuum? What are the categories of the continuum?
4. What are search, experience, and credence attributes of services? List a product example in each attribute category.
5. What are the five dimensions of service quality, the four consumer factors, and the three elements of quality perception that shape the customer's view of service quality?
6. What are the functional and interactive elements of services?
7. List three examples of person marketing.
8. What is entertainment and event marketing?
9. Give an example of cause marketing.
10. What is internal marketing?
11. What differentiates nonprofit services?
12. Why do nonprofit organizations need excess revenues over costs?

Discussion of Concepts

1. List three of the seven forces driving the explosive growth of the service economy. How will each force influence the nature of college education?
2. Select two differences between services and goods and detail how each affects marketing strategy development.
3. Do you think it is possible for a product to be either a pure good or a pure service? Why or why not?
4. What are the differences between search, experience, and credence qualities of products? How does each affect marketing strategy development?
5. Name a service high in credence quality. What type of buyer behavior would you expect to encounter?
6. Imagine that you are the marketing manager for a major hotel chain. What steps would you recommend to help ensure success in each of the five dimensions of service quality?
7. Select a target market and design the core, augmented, and branded aspects of a restaurant.
8. Do you consider it appropriate for politicians to develop sophisticated marketing campaigns in order to be elected to office?

Key Terms And Definitions

Cause marketing: Gaining public support and financing in order to change or remedy a situation.

Core service: The basic benefit delivered.

Divergence: The degree to which a service involves customization beyond routine or standardized procedures.

Event marketing: Promoting an event in order to generate revenues and enhance the reputation of an organization.

Franchise: A contractual agreement whereby an entrepreneur pays a fee for the franchise name and agrees to meet operating requirements and use the organization's marketing plan.

Functional element: What a service is supposed to accomplish.

Interactive element: The personal behaviors and atmosphere of the service environment.

Internal marketing: The marketing of a business unit's capabilities to others within the same firm.

Nonprofit marketing: The activities performed by an organization not motivated by profit to influence consumers to support it with a contribution.

Perishable: The temporal nature of services, whose value exists for only a short time.

Person marketing: Promoting an individual's personality, character, and appeal, which in turn may assist in the promotion of a product.

Place marketing: Promoting a geographical location in order to appeal to businesses, investors, and tourists.

Political marketing: Promoting an individual or idea motivated by the desire to influence public policy and voters.

Service: An idea, task, experience, or activity that can be exchanged for value to satisfy the needs and wants of consumers and businesses.

Service complexity: The number and intricacy of steps involved in producing a service.

Service encounter: The interaction between the consumer and the seller.

References

1. "Patagonia Is Awarded 'Eco Brand of the Year' at the Volvo EcoDesign Forum" February 4, 2008. Press Release. Source: Patagonia Inc; www.patagonia.com, site visited May 01, 2008.
2. World Trade Organization, www.wto.org, site visited April 07, 2008.
3. TGIFridays.com, site visited April 07, 2008.
4. www.fdic.gov, site visited April 07, 2008.
5. Michael Kanellos, "Myths of Moore's Law," June 11, 2003. Cnet, www.news.com, site visited April 07, 2008.
6. "Online Sales Spike 19 Percent," May 14, 2007. www.cnnmoney.com.
7. Parija Bhatnagar, "Why big retailers are shuttering stores," CNNMoney.com, January 24, 2006.
8. Carolyn Bigda, "Toting a Lunch To Work May Be More Savvy Than You Think," Chicago Tribune, March 27, 2005.
9. "VSS Projects Total Communications Spending Will Top $1 Trillion Next Year," Aug. 07, 2007. B-to-B Media Business. www.btobonline.com, site visited April 07, 2008.
10. www.healthaffairs.org, site visited April 07, 2008.
11. http://rru.worldbank.org, site visited April 07, 2008.
12. "Privatization Gets an Endorsement from Smart Folks," Knight Ridder Tribune Business News, June 6, 2006, p.1.
13. www.hoovers.com, site visited April 07, 2008.
14. www.gateway.com, site visited April 07, 2008.
15. Keith L. Alexander, "Other Airlines Suit Up To Play Southwest's Game," Washington Post, July 18, 2006, Page D01.
16. Valarie A. Zeithaml, "How Consumer Evaluation Processes Differ between Goods and Services," in Marketing of Services, eds. James H. Donnelly and William R. George (Chicago, IL: American Marketing Association, 1981).
17. Patty Lamberti, "Theme cruises for golf, music, cooking and other passions," Satisfaction Magazine, September/October 2006.
18. www.palgrave-journals.com, site visited April 07, 2008.
19. www.usps.gov, site visited April 07, 2008.
20. Sandar G. Bharadwaj and Anil Menon, "Determining Success in Service Industries," Journal of Services Marketing, 7, no. 4 (1993); pp. 19-40.
21. www.kinkos.ca/companyinfo/history.html, site visited April 07, 2008.
22. www.pryor.com, site visited April 07, 2008.
23. Philip Kotler, "Atmospherics as a Marketing Tool," Journal of Marketing 40 (Winter 1973–1974): 50.
24. M. Mehrabian and J. A. Russel, An Approach to Environmental Psychology (Cambridge, MA: MIT Press, 1974).
25. www.dmx.com, site visited April 07, 2008.
26. Lisa DiCarlo, "Six Degrees Of Tiger Woods," www.forbes.com, March 18, 2004.
27. "Shrek Reclaims Crown with Third Movie," Brandon Gray, May 21, 2007. www.boxofficemojo.com, site visited April 07, 2008.
28. John Weinbach, "Inside College Sports' Biggest Money Machine," Oct. 19, 2007. Wall Street Journal.
29. John Consoli, "NBA All-Star Game Gets Int'l Push," Feb. 11, 2008. www.mediaweek.com, site visited April 07, 2008.
30. "Iowa," Fortune, March 4, 1996, special edition section.
31. www.laf.org site visited April 09, 2008.
32. Independent Sector – www. independentsector.org/programs/research/gvresources.html, site visited April 09, 2008.
33. Alessandra Bianchi, "The New Philanthropy," Inc., October 2000, pp. 23–25.
34. www.nba.con, site visited April 09, 2008.
35. gatesfoundation.org, April 09, 2008.
36. Carol J. Loomi, "Warren Buffett gives away his fortune", Fortune, June 25, 2006.
37. www.marketingpower.com, site visited April 09, 2008.
38. http://wpcarey.asu.edu/csl, site visited April 09, 2008.
39. "Establishing a Presence: Local Nonprofits Online," www.uwm.edu/People/mbarndt/npdev.htm, site visited April 09, 2008.

Marketing Gazette
   Edited and condensed: Tina Lame, "Michiganders Preach Al Gore's Global Warming Gospel," Detroit Free Press, February 19, 2007; "Gore 'Deeply Honored' by Nobel Win," USA Today, Oct. 12, 2007.

CASE 10

TICKETMASTER

Get tickets to the next Justin Timberlake show, and while you're at it, order Jimmy Buffett tickets for your parents, and send your little brother and sister to Sesame Street Live. Ticketmaster has something for everyone, regardless of age and taste, and its website is a one-stop resource for finding tickets to concerts, sporting events, and theatre near you.

Ticketmaster knows what it means to serve customers through the development of beneficial relationships. It is the world's leading computerized ticketing service, with more than 9,000 clients—including 6,500 outlets in 20 global markets. The company generates revenues by adding $1.50 to $7.00 to the more than 75 million tickets it sells to hundreds of thousands of events each year. In 2006, the company sold more than 128 million tickets that valued at over $7 billion on behalf of its clients. It employs over 6,400 employees worldwide. Its customers fill hundreds of leading arenas, stadiums, performing arts venues, and theaters.

Not long ago, buying tickets for a major event was often associated with a long drive, standing in an endless line, and sometimes even camping out overnight. In 1985, Time magazine wrote a story about computerized ticketing, which was quickly becoming the industry standard: "Queuing for hours in the subfreezing cold to buy a pair of hard-to-get tickets may have once been a mark of theater-going dedication, but increasingly, it is a mere sign that you are behind the times." Ticketmaster, formed in 1978 by two Arizona State University students, had a competitive drive to be at the forefront of improvements in its industry. Arenas often had poor inventory control, and concert organizers could not accurately predict demand for shows. Ticketmaster helped change all this and became the industry benchmark.

Ticketmaster's computerized operating system is upgraded approximately five times a year. Buyers can order by phone, through ticket centers, from box offices, or via the Internet. Ticketmaster Online enables customers to check event schedules and seating charts, chat with celebrities, shop for tour merchandise, or check on breaking tour information. Through the Ticketmaster system, customers can obtain the best available tickets, no matter where they live.

Ticketmaster has expanded from its core ticketing business into related entertainment and marketing opportunities through the creation of sponsorship and promotional programs. The company publishes Live!, a monthly event guide, and sells merchandise through Entertainment to Go.

It continually looks for new markets and new ways to serve customers with a wider variety of events.

It introduced its Mobile Ticket Van, donated by General Motors. This specially equipped vehicle gives the company yet another way to reach consumers who may not live near a Ticketmaster outlet. Ticketmaster believes "there is an unlimited number of promotional tie-ins we could initiate. [We think we will] find so many uses for this that one won't be nearly enough to cover L.A., and wouldn't be surprised if we roll them out in major cities throughout the country."

Ticketmaster's alliances and ventures are numerous. In addition to ventures with Intel and MasterCard, the company has paired up with Samsung Electronics, Calvin Klein, R. J. Reynolds, Microsoft, Pepsi, Ford, Apple, and others. The aggressive pursuit of marketing opportunities has sometimes been perceived as monopolistic, especially since Ticketmaster has acquired at least 12 of its closest competitors in the past decade and controls approximately two-thirds of major stadiums, arenas, and amphitheaters in urban centers.

Ticketmaster Online-CitySearch, Inc., purchased a competitor, Ticket Web, Inc., in a stock deal valued at $35.2 million. Ticket Web, which has about 700 of its own customers, including New York's Bowery Ballroom and the San Diego Zoo, is maintained as a separate entity from Ticketmaster. Ticketmaster itself is owned by USA Networks. Other subsidiaries include CitySearch, the Home Shopping Network, and the Hotel Reservations Network. This group of entertainment companies is now being bought by Seagram, a family-owned liquor business. It is through such purchases that the parent company hopes to develop an entire entertainment network.

The company has an exclusive section called TicketExchange, where users can re-sell legitimately. In this section, you can be offered a safe, secure and legitimate sub-stitute to unofficial secondary ticketing sites like StubHub and CraigsList. It is its new online services that allows safe and secure fan – to – fan transactions. Sellers are guaranteed payment for tickets. Ticketmaster even sends the tickets to your buyer and deposits your payment directly into your checking account.

1. Discuss how the forces creating growth in services may have affected Ticketmaster's business over time. Which has probably been the most significant influence?

2. How does Ticketmaster address each of the five dimensions of service quality? Make assumptions when necessary.

3. What are some other ways that Ticketmaster can reach more customers? What will be some potential obstacles for Ticketmaster to overcome to reach these additional customers?

Sources:

http://www.ticketmaster.com/ visited June 19, 2007; "T in the park selects Ticketmaster TicketExchange for authorized Ticket Resale", PR Newswire Europe including UK Disclose(New York), June 19, 2007; Steve James, "Vivendi-Seagram Merger Looks a Good Deal for Diller," Yahoo! Finance, biz.yahoo.com, June 15, 2000; Reuters, "Ticketmaster Online Buys Ticket Web in $35Mln Deal," www.reuters.com, May 30, 2000; Hoover's Online, "Ticketmaster Group, Inc.," www.hooversonline.com, visited June 18, 2000; Doug Reece, "Ticketmaster Offers Sales on Wheels," Billboard, August 30, 1997, p. 74; "Ticketmaster and Intel Jointly Developing Advanced Online Ticketing Service," September 30, 1997, mkt-news.nasdaq.com; United Press International, "Ticketmaster to Issue Credit Card," USA Today, November 3, 1997, www.usatoday.com; Ticketmaster Web site, www.ticketmaster.com, site visited May 01, 2008; and Linda Himelstein and Ronald Grover, "Will Ticketmaster Get Scalped?" Business Week, June 26, 1995, pp. 64–68;

CHAPTER 11

Product Innovation & Management

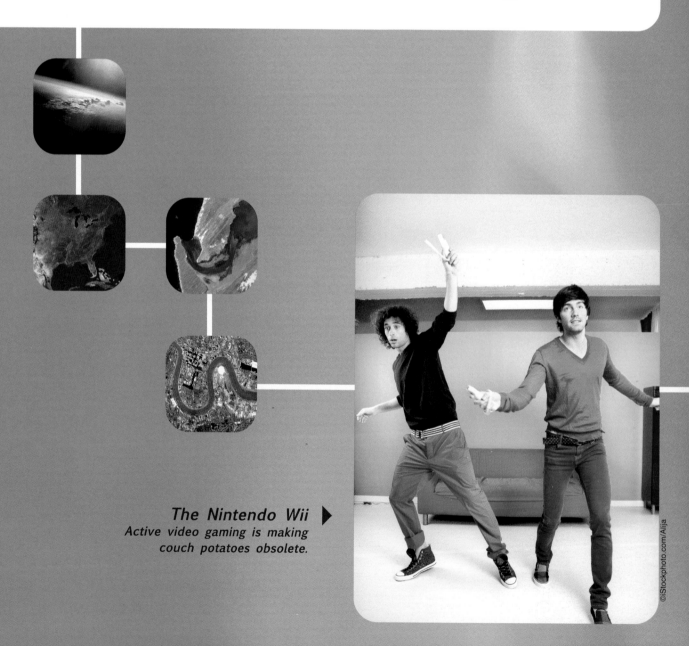

The Nintendo Wii ▶
Active video gaming is making couch potatoes obsolete.

©iStockphoto.com/Alija

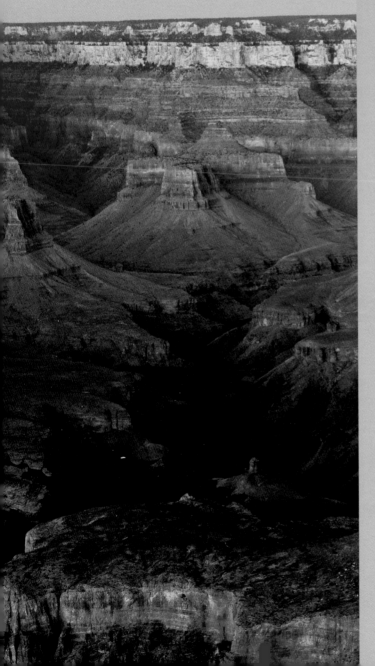

Learning Objectives

1. Provide a framework to evaluate the extent to which existing or new products are marketed to existing or new market segments.

2. Understand how the characteristics of innovation influence the speed with which product innovations are accepted.

3. Know the steps used to develop new products from the initial idea through commercialization.

4. Show how the product life cycle concept can be used to build and adjust marketing strategies over time.

5. Recognize how innovations are adopted by consumers by being spread from group to group.

The U.S. market for video games was valued at about $18 billion in 2007, according to NDP Group, and its game console market is dominated by only three players--Sony, Microsoft and Nintendo. In the last generation of video games, Sony led the market with PlayStation 2, followed by Microsoft's X-box and Nintendo's Game Cube respectively. The latest generation of consoles has led to a complete reversal of market shares for these companies. Fueled by the Wii, Nintendo has made its way to the top for the first time since the days of Super Nintendo. Microsoft maintained its spot in second place with its X-box 360, while Sony's PlayStation 3 slipped all the way to third.

Starting business in 1889 in Kyoto, Japan, Nintendo is widely known as a pure video game company. It sells hardware products and video game systems under other brand names such as DS and Wii. But Nintendo traditionally stayed away from many of the most violent games, including the popular Grand Theft Auto, which created the perception that Nintendo games were primarily for young kids.

However in November 2006, Nintendo shocked the gaming market with the launch of its new console – Wii. The Wii's development was headed by Satoru Iwata, a former game developer and recruiter for the company. He took over as company President and Director in 2002, as Nintendo engineers were already looking to affordably differentiate the next-generation console, code-named "Revolution." Iwata knew there was a gap between his own perception toward a game and players' response to it. He had seen test users overlook a feature he was excited about or become absorbed with one he had considered trivial. The overall message he got from listening to testers was that games are getting too intimidating and aren't fun, unless users devote hours to learn how to play them.

The Wii appeals to a wider audience than its competitors. With powerful processors and impressively realistic graphics, Microsoft and Sony went after their existing market of established gamers. Nintendo went in a different direction, focusing on simplicity and creating a system drastically different from any video game the world had seen. Rather than pushing complex button combinations, The Wii's wireless, motion-sensitive controllers allow users to mimic real movements, from sports like bowling and baseball to actions like sword-fighting. Games include training sessions that quickly teach players the motions required to play. This simple learning curve has contributed to the Wii's widespread popularity, from young children to the elderly. Educational games like Big Brain Academy and My Word Coach, as well as the innovative Wii Fit, which enables users to do yoga, aerobics, strength training, and balance games by standing on a balance board, have contributed to Nintendo's success among nontraditional gamers.

Product name is also crucial for product success and Nintendo was savvy enough to know that the name would raise eyebrows and generate discussion. Why Wii? Sounding like "we" the name emphasizes that the console is for everyone. It spells "Wii" with two "i"s to imply an image of player interaction. Released at a price of $250, the Wii was considerably cheaper than the low end versions of X-box 360 and PS3. This served as an advantage initially, but Nintendo's competitors have since lowered their prices to remain competitive.

Nintendo has sold more than 20 million Wiis and demand still exceeds supply more than a year since its release. This Wii shortage has prompted creative buying strategies by customers, including early morning camp-outs and stalking of UPS delivery drivers. While retailers and industry analysts estimate that Nintendo is giving up $1 billion in potential sales, the company feels they have done nothing wrong in terms of planning. Some analysts believe Nintendo is keeping supply low intentionally to prolong its buzz. "It's a good problem to have," said senior vice president for marketing at Nintendo America, George Harrison. He attributes the shortage to the difficulty of projecting future demand as well as a worldwide shortage of disk drives. Nintendo has increased production multiple times since mid-2007 in attempt to better satisfy demand. Harrison anticipates the success of the Wii to continue, with hopes of reaching a 40 percent market share in the next five years.[1]

THE CONCEPTS OF PRODUCT DEVELOPMENT AND PRODUCT MANAGEMENT

A winning company doesn't rest—it innovates. New products invigorate organizations. They create enthusiasm among employees even before they excite the market. They are absolutely essential to competitive advantage. Companies that fail to innovate usually fail, period. Even those that are slower than competitors will find their customer connections strained or broken as leading-edge organizations step in and step ahead. At the same time, winning companies don't prematurely abandon their existing products. They nurture and support them like old friends. Organizations make direct connections with customers through products. Without these, no relationship can exist. Products form the fundamental substance of all business exchanges. Whether these connections remain solid depends largely on the ability of marketers to introduce and manage products. This chapter explores how long-term, tight connections are made through technological innovations and product management that fulfill market potential.

Speed and responsiveness - the ability to develop products quickly is extremely important in gaining a competitive advantage. Companies are compressing the amount of time required to turn an idea into a marketable product. This is multiplying the number of products offered as well as shortening the life of products. Today innovation is a key aspect of corporate cultures. In a Boston Consulting Group, Inc. poll, 81 percent of chief executives listed innovation as one of their top three priorities.[2] Because of these trends, executives are emphasizing the firm's **product mix**—all the product lines and products a company offers. They also are adjusting the depth and breadth of product lines in response to rapidly changing market forces. Excellent product management is considered essential for creating superior customer value.

Organizations must continue to manage existing products, and they must have the ability to identify, find, or create new ones. In a classic study, the consulting firm of Booz, Allen & Hamilton found that 28 percent of company growth comes from products introduced in the past five years. Yet, new-product development is risky and expensive. About 56 percent of introductions fail within five years, and about 45 percent of new-product development resources are spent on failures. In fact, companies usually have to come up with 13 new-product ideas before they hit on one that works.[4] With the right strategy products can provide sufficient profits necessary to reach the organization's objectives and cover the costs of developing and growing new products.

The main objective of product management is to ensure a steady flow of products that supports the company's mission. Important elements to consider in product development and management are shown in Figure 11.1.

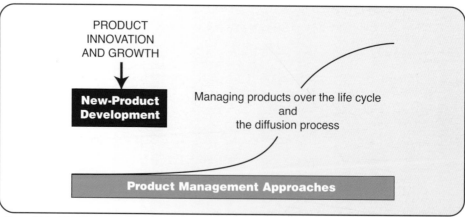

Figure 11.1   The Concepts of Product Development and Management

This chapter begins with a look at how the product mix affects growth. Organizations sometimes grow by focusing on existing products and segments, but much more growth comes from innovation in products and markets. Next we explore types of innovations and factors that affect how rapidly they are accepted by potential customers. Once a company decides the role of new products for accomplishing objectives, it employs a new-product development process. We explore a successful process—from formulation of new-product strategy to

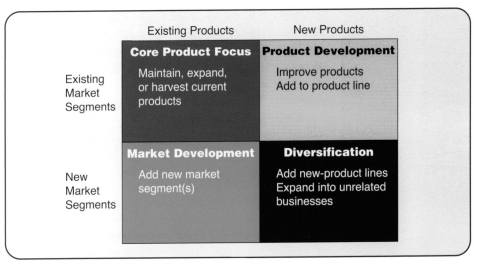

Figure 11.2   Product Planning Options

product launch. This is followed by a section on product management approaches, particularly the policies and organizational structures that foster innovation. Finally, we examine how the product life cycle and the diffusion process relate to decisions ranging from introduction to discontinuation.

PRODUCT PLANNING AND TYPES OF INNOVATION

PRODUCT PLANNING

Every business needs to develop a product plan consistent with its overall marketing strategy. **Product planning** outlines the focus given to core businesses (current products in current segments), market development (new segments for current products), product development (new products for current segments), or diversification (products totally new to the company for new segments).

Product planning decisions are influenced by market segment strategies. Marketers must decide how much emphasis to place on the existing product lines and segments and how much on developing new products and markets. Figure 11.2 depicts these fundamental choices.

Core Business Focus A core business focus emphasizes the marketing of existing products to existing market segments. Even this requires careful decisions about whether to maintain, expand, or eliminate current products, depending on market conditions, the age of the product, and competitive factors. Firms that do not make these adjustments usually must retreat. This may become evident in plant consolidations, fewer and fewer products, divestment of lines of business, and withdrawal from certain markets.

Many strong companies achieve success by focusing on their core products and market segments. This doesn't mean that all avenues for expansion are closed. The core

business can provide earnings to support other options, such as Coke's aggressive global strategy. Sometimes companies extend their core business to take advantage of additional product offerings supported by a unique competency. For example, Amazon.com's core focus is web-based marketing. The company developed unique web-based competencies, originally focusing on book and music sales. Today, it uses those competencies to sell everything from books to patio equipment. The broader array of products have significantly increased revenues for Amazon providing it with a 38.5 percent growth in sales in the year 2007.[5]

Market Development **Market development** occurs when existing products are offered to new segments. Firms may sell directly to these or use new channels of distribution. They also may expand from local markets to regional, national, international, or global markets. Many clothing companies and department stores are diversifying their product lines with plus-size clothing for women. I.N.C. label clothing, sold in Macy's and Bloomingdale's, is offering plus-size clothing that is designed exactly like regular-sized clothing, and also styles designed to provide more coverage. Ralph Lauren has extended its products to include marketing to big and tall consumers through the Rochester Big and Tall retailing outlets.[6]

Product Development **Product development** occurs when companies make new products for existing market segments. This may take the form of simple improvements to older products or extensions of the product line. Most companies are continuously introducing improved versions. For example, Microsoft has upgraded its popular Word software several times and Vista is simply the latest new product.

Ralph Lauren markets existing products to new segments through Rochester Big & Tall

Whether in the consumer or business market, product lines are continuously expanding. Pizza Hut is always developing new products and recently added yet another item to its innovative recipes – the "Cheezy Bites Pizza." This pizza has a outer crust made of 28 individual cheese-filled bites.[7] **A line extension** is an innovation closely related to other products in the line. Internet companies also expand their product lines to keep with a demanding market. Apple's iPod strategy includes the development of new models which provide alternative functionalities at several price points. Apple's objective is to meet the needs of many different groups of customers through a clearly delineated product line. Apple's iPhone combines a revolutionary mobile phone, a widescreen iPod with touch controls, and a breakthrough Internet communications device with desktop-class email, web browsing, maps, and searching — into one small and lightweight handheld device.[8]

Diversification Diversification occurs when new products are introduced into new market segments. Sometimes this is done with extensions of the current business, and sometimes it occurs with new ventures. Under Armour, the maker of athletic apparel, recently engaged in product diversification through the release of athletic shoes and cleats. The company's traditional product is its trademark moisture-wicking fabric often worn underneath athletic jerseys. [9]

Apple's introduction of the iPod is an example of diversification that worked. Apple ventured away from its computer arena and into uncharted areas. The result has been dramatic. Because of this venture Apple is growing exponentially and could surpass Microsoft's projected US$65 billion earnings as early as 2010.[10]

TYPES OF PRODUCT INNOVATION

Marketers classify innovations according to the effect they are likely to have on consumers. **Continuous innovation** is a minor change in an existing product, such as a new style or model, that can be easily adopted without significant alterations in consumer behavior. The product usually is familiar. Campbell's soup improved on its already easy-to-open ready to serve soup by adding microwave-safe heating. Soup at Hand, comes in a microwaveable cup that lets you enjoy sippable soup on the go, and will soon be available in 20 different varieties. Since the product was introduced, it has driven significant sales for Campbell's convenience platform. [11]

A **dynamically continuous innovation** endows a familiar product with additional features and benefits that require or permit consumers to alter some aspect of their behavior. When auto companies introduced the antilock braking system (ABS), consumers needed to adjust driving habits. Rather than pump the brakes in an emergency, they had to learn that ABS works best when the brakes are totally compressed. Manufacturers were careful to educate drivers about the benefits and requirements of ABS so that reaction to the new system would be positive. Another example is small printers designed to produce store quality photos at home. Users no longer need to take their digital files to photo print shops. Microsoft's Bill Gates is focusing attention on IPTV (Internet Protocol TV), a way of delivering standard TV over the internet. This will even allow integration of TV with cell phones, and PC level computing.[12]

A **discontinuous innovation** is an entirely new product with new functions. Sometimes called "new to the world," these products require behavioral changes by users. The high degree of novelty makes consumers think about the product's benefits and costs prior to adoption. Examples include cellular phones, satellite-transmitted maps for autos, and heart pumps. When automobile airbags were introduced, buyers had to evaluate the benefits carefully before committing the additional funds for the optional purchase. Eventually airbags became standard equipment and were included in the vehicle price.

The speech technologies industry is another example. Though speech recognition programs have promised beneficial results, most customers have not yet been completely satisfied. However, new innovations are still being made and could prove to be very popular. SpeechMail, for instance, would allow individuals to receive their e-mail by telephone, and SpeecHTML would allow people to receive information from a Web site by telephone.[13] These revolutionary programs are not widely available yet, but once their benefits become apparent to consumers, they may be as commonplace as the Internet.

WHY INNOVATIONS SUCCEED

Research reveals novelty alone does not ensure new-product success. What matters most is how well innovation meets customer needs.[14] Several specific factors influence consumer acceptance of new products: relative advantage, compatibility, complexity, trialability, and observability.

Relative Advantage   Relative advantage is the amount of perceived superiority of the new product in comparison to existing ones. Marketers must make it easy for consumers to recognize the benefits of switching from the old product. Often this entails a trade-off. A new word-processing program may be easier to use but requires additional training. Consumers need to be persuaded that the training investment will yield benefits, such as time savings and ease of use. Otherwise, they probably won't purchase the new program.

To increase the perceived superiority of its upgraded software versions, Microsoft offers online support that explains product updates and how the upgrade will meet user needs. It's especially important for computer software to have a relative advantage, considering the overwhelming number of offerings. Microsoft's Windows Vista, offers more system responsiveness for your everyday tasks. It's enhanced performance coupled with more security, a new desktop appearance, and Windows Media Center make the upgrade more enticing for existing Windows XP users.[15]

Compatibility   Compatible products fit easily into the consumer's current thinking or system. To succeed, a new product should be consistent with the values and beliefs of target consumers. Furthermore, if additional products are required to make a product usable, they should be included in the package. Consumers who have to seek out these additions or who find installation difficult are likely to reject the product. This is one reason many organizations now have 800 numbers to answer questions.

Most people consider safety important when deciding to purchase an automobile. Understanding that this is of value, companies are working on high-tech ways to make driving safer. For example, GM's Delco division has created a blind-spot radar to warn drivers when it's unsafe to change lanes. Texas Instruments has developed a thermal-image camera that eliminates glare from oncoming headlights. These innovations provide consumer value. Since the products are included in the vehicle purchase, the issues of installation and additional purchase are avoided.

Product Complexity   Complexity is the degree to which a new product is easy to understand and use. User-friendly items have a great advantage over products with many parts and difficult instructions. It's important for designers to keep the user in mind, a major factor in the success of Macintosh computers. Many people have sat down at a Macintosh, followed the simple instructions, and quickly learned to use elaborate programs. It wasn't until Microsoft developed its Windows interface that the DOS platform provided similar ease of use.

For complex products, understandable owner's manuals and directions are essential. The streamlined layout of switches, buttons, and knobs is also important. A major innovation in cameras was the automation of complicated focusing and lighting mechanisms in traditional cameras. Digital cameras now

Marketing Vocabulary

LINE EXTENSION
A new product closely related to others in the line.

CONTINUOUS INNOVATION
A minor alteration in an existing product, such as a new style or model, that can be easily adopted without significant changes in consumer behavior.

DYNAMICALLY CONTINUOUS INNOVATION
A familiar product with additional features and benefits that require or permit consumers to alter some aspect of their behavior.

DISCONTINUOUS INNOVATION
An entirely new product with new functions.

The LCD screens on digital cameras help reduce product complexity.

©iStockphoto.com/Giorgio Fochesato

come with bright LCD screens to help users easily align their target subject matter without the need of a viewfinder. By designing a product that matches the photographic needs of most people, companies substantially reduced the complexity and promoted huge growth in traditional and digital equipment.

Tivo Inc. pioneered an exciting new category in home entertainment that is rapidly changing the way the world watches TV. They have created an emerging market where subscribers have the ability to record and control live TV with the freedom to skip past commercials and watch replays in slow motion. The Tivo box can easily be connected to a home network to access the viewer's music and image files through the TV, and can be programmed through the Internet to record shows from anywhere in the world. This complex technology is controlled through a user-friendly remote control and simple on-screen instructions, making it a huge success with consumers.

Trialability Trialability refers to the ease with which potential users can test a new product at little or no expense. New-product acceptance can be speeded up through free samples, low-cost trials, interactive showroom techniques, or loaners. Computer retailers usually place equipment on display so consumers can interact

with it. Nearly every car buyer test-drives an automobile before purchasing it. General Motors offers an overnight test drive option on almost all of their vehicles to qualified drivers, providing the consumer doesn't drive over 100 miles or leave the state. This promoted increased trialability of their products in a setting that's comfortable for the consumer.

Trialability is critical for software vendors, because only through use can potential buyers understand the features they would gain. Several software programs can be downloaded for free from the Web, used a few times or in a limited way, and then purchased. In the magazine world, free trial issues are common. Food companies often provide free samples in supermarkets.

Observability Observability means that the product's benefits can be easily seen by potential buyers. It is particularly useful to be able to see others using the product. New products with obvious advantages are adopted rapidly. When benefits are more subtle, it's more difficult to gain acceptance. Weight-loss plans that show quick results are popular because users can see the results and acquaintances are likely to make positive comments. In comparison, the effects of fitness training may not become apparent for some time, so it's more difficult to gain consumer acceptance.

The benefits of camera phones have exploded into the cellular phone market. By 2009 camera phones will grow to account for 89 percent of all mobile phones, and over 227 billion images will be captured on them. The continued growth of phones will be driven by improvements in imaging functions like image sensors, zoom and auto focus, as well as rapid declines in prices and higher speed wireless bandwidth. The easily observable benefits of taking and instantly sharing a picture wirelessly are among the reasons these products have become so successful.[16]

THE NEW-PRODUCT DEVELOPMENT PROCESS

Success with new products depends on translating the organization's core competencies into goods or services that provide superior value to the customer. The competitiveness of most markets requires a stream of new products, processes, and ventures. It's difficult to pinpoint exactly why some organizations are more innovative than others. Nevertheless, researchers have suggested the following will improve the chances of bringing innovations to market successfully:

- A champion who believes in the new idea
- A sponsor high enough in the organization to provide access to major resources

Rocher is perfect for fall gatherings:
It comes in harvest colors.

This Ferrero Rocher ad includes a coupon that increases the trialability factor of their product.

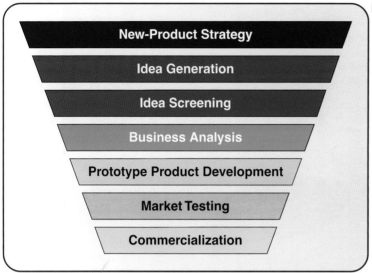

New-Product Strategy

Idea Generation

Idea Screening

Business Analysis

Prototype Product Development

Market Testing

Commercialization

Figure 11.3   The New-Product Development Process

- A mix of creative minds (to generate ideas) and experienced operators (to keep things practical)
- A team process that moves ideas through the system quickly so that they get top-level endorsement, resources, and attention early in the game
- A focus on customers at every step

Executives must be objective about the chances of product success. Since the costs of new product development increases as the product moves toward commercialization, companies will often implement a stage-gate method to prevent further investment on a product likely to fail.[17] Figure 11.3 describes the elements in the new-product development process.

NEW-PRODUCT STRATEGY

Leading-edge companies have a strategy for new-product development. In forming that strategy, top executives must answer a number of questions: Will the organization be a market leader, close follower, or also-ran? Will it have broad or deep product lines? How rapidly must the product stream flow, given competitive conditions and market expectations? How much will be invested in R&D over time? The business vision discussed in Chapter 2 is the beginning point, since most company missions require that new technologies and innovative processes be used to create superior customer value. Shiseido's R&D vision is a core part of its overall business strategy.

Companies that do the best job of new product development have excellent market knowledge including an understanding of customers and the competition.[18] They also use crossfunctional collaboration among marketing, research and development, and other areas of

the company.[19]

Fulfilling the company mission requires that marketers have the courage to bring out newer and more advanced technologies. The value statements of many corporations recognize the social responsibility of providing more functional, cost-effective, environmentally sound, and safe products. How do those goals become a reality?

IDEA GENERATION

Organizations need idea generation systems to find an adequate number of significant new-product ideas. **Idea generation** is the use of a range of formal and informal methods to stimulate new product concepts from a number of sources.[20] Among the many possible sources are employees, customers, technology analysis, distributors and suppliers, competitors, R&D, environmental trend analysis, and outside consultants. Marketers must ensure that ideas flow continuously from these groups. Often a reward is provided to individuals who make significant contributions.

A system based on four general principles seems to work quite well:

- Systematically seek and ask for new-product ideas.
- Make sure that all ideas, no matter how trivial or elaborate, reach the individual or group responsible for collecting them.
- Provide timely feedback to all people contributing ideas.

SHISEIDO Research and Development Vision

Our R&D people combine their scientific and sensory skills to innovate cosmetics that deliver new values to our customers.

We propose a "new value" to our customers, which integrates "functionality" that realizes beautiful and youthful skin, "sensitivity" that leads to comfort, and "safe and reliable quality."

We develop products with a high quality of international standards and tailored to the various regional characteristics by creatively integrating the power of research and development of our R&D bases around the world.

We try to give our customers the best satisfaction by integrating and synergistically increasing the knowledge, skills, abilities, and drive of each and every person involved in research and development.

We provide a wide variety of solutions that make our customers" dream about "beauty and health" come true.

• Build rewards and recognition into the organization scaled according to the number and quality of ideas.

Employees, who work with products every day, are likely to identify many minor improvements that can result in cost savings, better quality, and higher sales. They should constantly be encouraged to submit ideas. The 3M company breeds a culture of creativity among its employees. First is a requirement in the company that 40 percent of its sales come from products developed within the last four years. Beyond this, the company ensures that its employees do not become static by allowing them to change jobs and move into areas that they find more interesting. Moreover, each employee is encouraged to devote 15 percent of his or her time to any product idea that could benefit the company.[21] Company salespeople are in the field where they can learn about new trends or ideas that may lead to the development of a new product.

Customers are a logical source of new-product ideas. This is particularly true in business-to-business marketing, since customers rely on suppliers to improve their own products and processes. By training salespeople to explore customer problems, and creating a system for feedback, companies are likely to discover numerous new concepts. Surveys, focus groups, and other marketing research techniques can be used.

A technology analysis forecasts the speed of advances as well as possible areas of application. The result can be novel products to improve the standard of living. Any number of products have changed the way people live, from indoor plumbing and telephones to four-wheel-drive automobiles and MP3 players. True innovations such as the Internet are rare, but in the consumer and services sector they tend to be in areas where the bulk of exploration is focused, such as electronics or pharmaceuticals.

Distributors and suppliers have a personal interest in

www.3m.com

At the 3M Web site, learn how the company's innovative products are protecting the environment.

the number of products a company makes. They often are asked to serve on the council that many organizations establish to generate new-product concepts. At semiannual meetings, ideas are exchanged, and concrete lists of innovations and new approaches are developed. Sun Microsystems involves suppliers at the idea stage and allows them to qualify as providers of the new product. These suppliers help Sun introduce new technology into its own workstations.[22]

Competitors can be a major source of ideas. It's not enough for marketers simply to compare products and prices. They need to anticipate rivals' innovations by systematically monitoring and projecting the approach the competition is likely to take. For example, by recognizing progressive changes in miniaturization, Allen-Bradley Corporation has been able to surpass competitors and develop new robotics that leapfrog entire generations. Japanese firms often imitate and improve on the products of U.S. companies rather than develop their own.

R&D personnel—scientists, engineers, designers, and others—have a clear interest in new-product development, since that's a large part of their job. Companies that encourage innovation make sure they provide ample opportunity for scientists to explore on their own. When a percentage of their time is free from routine tasks, R&D staff often identify major breakthroughs. As mentioned previously, one company famous for this is 3M. In addition to allowing employees to work on projects they choose, management urges them to seek new-product ideas from everywhere, even failed experiments. The classic example, Post-it notes, were invented this way. Scientists were trying to invent a strong adhesive but kept failing. Rather than scrap the research, a way was found to use the less sticky glue.

An environmental trend analysis estimates how major social forces may affect an industry. The organization then can project ways in which it can provide timely products. One example is to identify pollutants in a current product, find substitute ingredients and components, and develop a new version that will appeal to "green" consumers. Seventh Generation is a company that sells bathroom tissue made from 100 percent recycled paper rather than trees.[23]

Outside consultants specializing in new-product development obviously focus much of their work on idea generation. They use a broad

---

Sources of New Product Ideas

- Employees
- Customers
- Technology Forecasts
- Distributors
- Suppliers

- Competitors
- R&D Groups
- Environmental Trend Analysis
- Consultants

Figure 11.4 Sources of New Product Ideas

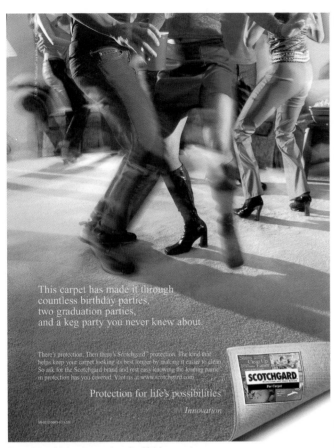

Scotchgard is an example of a 3M innovation.

competition, required resources, technology, the environment, legal and liability issues, and financial factors.[24] Multiple scales measure how well a product performs on each dimension.

Usually, a cross-functional team examines the limited information about the idea, using both experience and subjective judgment. The team may weight certain factors more than others, and a summary total is provided with qualitative comments to support the evaluation. Once this is completed, the team looks at the scores for all new products under consideration. As a rule, those with higher scores are chosen for further development. The team then provides feedback to everyone who contributed an idea, including an explanation of why it was accepted or rejected. The various team members take different responsibilities over the course of a new-product project. Involving several functions at the idea stage greatly increases the likelihood of picking the best ideas and developing a great product. Each member of the team has specific skills (engineering, marketing, manufacturing) that contribute to product success.[25]

BUSINESS ANALYSIS

A **business analysis** assesses the attractiveness of a product from a sales, cost, profit, and cash flow standpoint. Business analysis starts with the **product concept**, which refines the idea into written descriptions, pictures, and specifications. Marketing and R&D work diligently to define the benefits, form, features, and functions the product will have. The product concept is then presented to consumers, distributors, and retailers, who provide input regarding the product's potential as well as its description and visual representations. In the process, the description is likely to undergo changes. **Concept testing** helps identify the facilitators and inhibitors to a product's success. While testing concepts to sell its new cake batters, Duncan Hines stumbled on the theme of moistness. After hundreds of hours of concept

range of techniques to help companies develop concepts: surveys, brainstorming, focus groups, and others. Each method provides a structured way of discovering innovative products. The consulting firm Booz, Allen & Hamilton has gained a global reputation for its ability to identify commercially viable solutions to customer problems.

IDEA SCREENING

A good system will provide hundreds of new-product ideas each year. The **idea screening** process identifies those with the strongest potential for success. Companies usually apply certain criteria to judge each concept. The criteria generally fall into several categories: the market,

Marketing Vocabulary

IDEA SCREENING
Identifying the new-product ideas that have the most potential to succeed.

BUSINESS ANALYSIS
Assessment of the attractiveness of the product from a sales, cost, profit, and cash flow standpoint.

PRODUCT CONCEPT
A product idea that has been refined into written descriptions, pictures, and specifications.

CONCEPT TESTING
Testing the new-product concept to evaluate the likelihood of its success.

testing, one homemaker said the cake was so moist, it stuck to the fork. From this, a successful campaign emerged.

Once the concept has been fully defined, an initial marketing strategy is developed. Success depends not only on the product but also on the strategy for marketing it. This includes examining the opportunities for segmentation, product positioning, and other aspects of the marketing mix. It's also important to look at production and materials acquisition needs as well as the time required before launch. A key feature of strategy development is to project long-term profitability under different scenarios. At this point, the likelihood of success or failure becomes more apparent. Doubtful products must be weeded out because the next stages can be very expensive.

PROTOTYPE PRODUCT DEVELOPMENT

A prototype is a working model of the product, usually created by a team of marketing, manufacturing, engineering, and R&D personnel. Prototypes can be extremely expensive because handwork rather than automation is used. They may cost 10 or even 100 times more than a product made on the production line. Although costly, these models are necessary for the all-important next step, market testing. Openness among team members and a clear sense of direction, led by a product champion, greatly increase the chances for prototype success regardless of the competitive situation.[26]

Among the difficulties of developing new products is changing customer's preferences and uncertainty about competitive products. When there is high uncertainty, organizations need to maintain flexibility in defining specific product characteristics. Often a core team of professionals is used to create product descriptions and frequent repeated interactions with customers, help evolve product prototypes which meet latest marketing needs.[27]

MARKET TESTING

Test marketing is a limited trial of the strategy for the product under real or simulated conditions. Up to this point, champions may be able to push a weak product through the system. Now reality sets in. **A test market** is a small geographical area, with characteristics similar to the total market, where the product is introduced with a complete marketing program. Test marketing allows companies to implement the product strategy on a limited basis under real conditions. In fact, a test

Rank	Place	Population Rank
1.	Albany, NY	56
2.	Rochester, NY	46
3.	Greensboro, NC	36
4.	Birmingham, AL	54
5.	Syracuse, NY	59
6.	Charlotte, NC	33
7.	Nashville, TN	38
8.	Springfield, OR	123
9.	Wichita, KS	77
10.	Richmond, VA	50
11.	Davenport, IL	114
12.	Lexington, KY	85
13.	Charleston, SC	76
14.	Macon, GA	124
15.	Jacksonville, FL	45
16.	Greenvill, SC	51
17.	Little Rock, AR	73
18.	Evansville, IN	131
19.	Harrisburg, PA	66
20.	Cincinnati, OH	23

Figure 11.5 Top 20 Test Markets
Source: Kristen Bremner, "Albany Ranked No. 1 Test Market in Acxiom Study", DM News, May 24, 2004.

may involve trying two or more marketing strategies in separate areas to identify which works better.

In carefully designed test marketing, consumers are unaware that they are part of an experiment. Retailing, distribution, and promotion activities are similar to what would occur at the national or international level. When the results are in, marketers can forecast how long it will take for the product to be adopted in the general market.

Test market sites are selected very carefully to represent the segments that eventually will be targeted. For example, manufacturers testing toys would avoid Sarasota, Florida, which has a large elderly population. Snowshoes are more likely to be tested in Wyoming than in Georgia. A popular site is Boise, Idaho, where there may be up to 15 test products on the shelves at once. Pillsbury tried its All Ready pie crust there. The idea of selling kitchen towels and oven mitts in supermarkets was tested in Boise. Audit services in more than 125 cities throughout the United States monitor test market results. Figure 11.5 lists the top 20 test markets with a population of 50,000 or more.

By the time an organization enters a test market, substantial funds have been

Toyota's Lexus line mirrors the design and features of the German luxury cars.

spent on the new venture. There is a very strong probability of committing to a full-scale product launch—unless the test is a total failure. The results mainly help predict adoption rates among consumers and channel members. Testing products can also be very beneficial to companies that do not have large amounts of money to spend on research, however. Experiments also help identify factors that facilitate or hinder product adoption and may yield surprises about who the users will be.

There are several drawbacks to using test markets. First, it takes time, and product development costs rise with every delay in full-scale launch. Second, competitors become aware of the new product, and the element of surprise is lost. Sometimes a rival will jump in with a similar product or use tactics that spoil the results. For example, when a competitor test-marketed a new item, Vicks pulled all its similar products off the shelves, leaving no basis for judging whether the test was successful. Other tactics are flooding the market with unusual promotions, point-of-purchase displays, and price cuts. Third, it's impractical to use test marketing for many products because prototypes are too costly. Automobiles are an example. Fourth, it is extremely expensive to make the trial products, stock stores, train salespeople, run ads, and so forth.

A **controlled test market** uses consumer panels or other techniques to attempt to gain the same type of information obtained from real test markets. AC Nielsen's Scantrack and IRI's BehaviorScan monitor consumer behavior on new products. By combining information about consumer demographics and TV viewing behaviors with purchase data, it is possible to forecast product success. A controlled test market is often less expensive than conducting regular test marketing.

A **simulated product test** is an experiment in artificial conditions. This may be done before or instead of a full test. GHI, the most authoritative product testing center in Great Britain, performed tests on vacuum cleaners by comparing consumer use performance by cleaning carpets and hard flooring covered with measured amounts of a sand and flour mixture that simulated actual conditions.[28] This simulated product testing helps identify flaws and provides feedback. It can also be used to make evaluations against competitors. The food industry often sets up a replica of a supermarket, asks consumers to shop as if they were in a natural environment, and interviews them afterward. Although simulations are not as effective as a test market, they do provide useful information at

www.fritolay.com

Learn how Frito-lay makes Sun Chips using energy from the sun! Search for all of your favorite snacks and find great recipes too.

dramatically reduced costs. Furthermore, competitors are less likely to find out about a company's plans prior to product launch.

COMMERCIALIZATION

During the final stage of the process, **commercialization** introduces the product to the market. Launching consumer products requires heavy company support, such as advertising, sales promotions, and often free samples and price promotions. Consider the $30 million commercialization of Frito-Lay's Sunchips brand, which included television spots and the company's largest ever direct-mail sampling program to more than 6 million households. After a decade of development, Sunchips breezed through test marketing in six months, indicating to Frito-Lay executives that this multigrain snack had the potential for overnight success. In this industry new products rarely achieve even $40 million in sales, but Sunchips topped $100 million in the first year and continues to bring in huge profits. Years later, Frito-Lay continues to develop the market for Sunchips. Currently it hopes that consumers believe that Sunchips are not "junk food." David Radar, executive vice president and chief financial officer, spoke at the University of Texas at Austin stating that Sunchips, which is high in wholegrain and wheat, can be considered a healthy product. Interestingly, Cheerios contains more sodium than some of Frito-Lay's chips.[29]

THE ETHICS OF PRODUCT IMITATION

Some argue that since companies make substantial investments in new products, they should be the only ones allowed to market them. Recognizing this, intellectual property laws and patent laws afford some protection. Others argue that imitation results in healthy competition. It forces market leaders to keep up with technology, contend with lower-priced sub-

Marketing Vocabulary

TEST MARKET
A small geographic area, with characteristics similar to the total market, in which a product is introduced with a complete marketing program.

CONTROLLED PRODUCT TECHNIQUES
Consumer panels or other technique to gain similar information obtained from real test markets.

SIMULATED PRODUCT TEST
Experimentation with the marketing strategy in artificial conditions.

COMMERCIALIZATION
Final stage in the new-product development process, when the product is introduced into the market.

Gore-tex Fabrics are often used in winter sportswear to protect against the extreme cold.

stitutes, and respond to smaller and faster challengers. Organizations that want to remain competitive need to keep a keen eye on competitors' new products. Many times it helps to emulate their products, a totally ethical approach under many circumstances.

Protecting a firm's products from imitation is increasingly difficult. This tactic has become a recognized part of business strategy across the globe. Software development giant and market leader Microsoft has greatly benefited from the inventions of others. Its Windows operating system, which has become the standard program that runs nearly all personal computer operations, is considered very similar in user friendliness and visual format to Apple's Macintosh system.

Not all imitations are created equal. Some are illegal duplicates of popular products, and some are truly innovative products merely inspired by a pioneering brand.[30] The makers of knockoffs or clones often copy original designs but may leave off important attributes. In the computer industry, reproductions of IBM PCs carry their own brand names. The clones are often the same basic product, but they retail at lower price and without the prestigious IBM label. Clones are legal because protective patents, copyrights, and trademarks are absent or have expired.

Some copies play on the style, design, or fashion of a popular product. This type of imitation is common in the automobile industry. In the 1980s several Japanese automakers introduced lines to challenge Mercedes-Benz and BMW. Toyota's Lexus, Nissan's Infiniti, and Honda's Acura closely mirror the design and features of the German luxury cars. When technical products are copied, reverse engineering is often used to learn how the original was designed or made. Today, Hyundai is using the same approach but is now copying Toyota and other Japanese models.

Creative adoptions innovate beyond an existing product. These may occur as a technological development or as an adaptation to another industry. Initially, DuPont developed Teflon for the nose-cones of spacecrafts but soon extended its uses to coatings for consumer products. W.L. Gore, who was researching Teflon uses, left DuPont in 1958 and eventually developed Gore-Tex Fabrics. The fabric is best known for being water and windproof. Gore-Tex fabric is frequently used in high-end sports clothing, and has become the industry standard for outerwear comfort and protection.[31]

ORGANIZATIONAL STRUCTURES AND PRODUCT MANAGEMENT

Simultaneous new-product development occurs when people from a number of functional areas work together. Marketing coordinates the team, which usually represents R&D, engineering, production, procurement, legal and human resources, financing, and so on. This approach has many advantages over the old technique of **sequential new-product development**, which passes responsibility from one functional area to the next. Companies can produce better products at lower cost and gain returns more quickly when operating simultaneously. Consequently, the marketing function should attempt to ensure teamwork across all major departments of the business.

RECENT ORGANIZATIONAL TRENDS

There are many ways to manage existing and new products. Today, companies make creative use of computer and communications technologies to support a flexible organizational structure. This enables them to respond quickly to buyer demands. It also provides access to global technologies and the ability to adapt to competitive forces. There are three notable organizational trends.

1. *Downsizing.* Several product lines are brought under a single management team, or product offerings are reduced to those that generate strong and increasing revenues.
2. *Delayering.* The number of personnel and positions between top executives and those who manage market activities is reduced.
3. *Fewer functional silos.* When one function works in iso-

lation from others, it is called a functional silo. Organizations are stressing cross-functional synergy and personnel with experience in multiple areas.[32] Marketers no longer work only with other marketers or accountants only with other accountants.

FUNDAMENTAL STRUCTURES

There are many acceptable organizational structures. Today, most companies prefer a structure that supports strategy changes. As strategies alter to meet new challenges, organizational structures need to change with them. The most fundamental structures for new-product development are the product or market manager, the new-product department, the new-product committee, and the venture team. Companies may combine elements of several of these and may use consulting organizations as well.

Product or Market Managers Some of the most successful organizations have used the product manager or market manager structure. **Market managers** are responsible for one or several similar product lines targeted at defined market areas. **Product managers** oversee one or several products targeted at all market segments. In either case the structure is similar. The manager works closely with individuals from a range of functions to build integrated strategies. The system was pioneered by Procter & Gamble, which developed teams of experts loosely tied but headed by a very strong manager. Each team was responsible for building the equity of a given brand. Product managers compete almost as strongly with other teams in the organization as they do with competitors on the outside. For example, the Crest product manager is in competition with the Gleem product manager, and the Tide product manager is in competition with all product managers for the other detergents made by Procter & Gamble. However, since each product is positioned to address a particular benefit—Crest for tooth decay prevention and Gleem for brightness—competition may not be direct.

Product managers or market managers have the following specific responsibilities:

- Achieve the sales, profit, market share, and cash flow objectives for the product line.
- Develop the market strategy for the product.
- Prepare a written marketing plan, develop forecasts, and maintain timely updates of progress.
- Integrate all functions necessary to implement a synergistic marketing strategy.

One difficulty with this system is that the manager has responsibilities beyond the traditional lines of authority. The product manager can be described as the hub of a wheel. Notice that the spokes are all the functional areas that help make a good marketing strategy work. Product managers have no formal authority over these people, who report directly to managers in their own functional area.

What makes the system work? First, the product or market manager must have the necessary interpersonal and business skills to gain the team's respect. In fact, the lack of direct authority is what makes this system effective. Through team play and networking, strong product or market managers can tap into very specialized talents from a range of people. Second, the manager must report to someone high enough in the organization to obtain the status required. Although unable to govern the activities of team members, product and marketing managers can make their presence felt through communication with top executives and across functional areas of the company.

The system's strength is also its weakness. Product managers must rely on functional managers from various areas of the organization to help them build a strong team. New-product prospects may receive low priority from managers in the spokes. Their reward structures may inhibit working on innovations. Experience has shown that without proper attention by top management, the product or marketing manager may be relegated to relatively mundane tasks. When there is appropriate executive leadership, the system can be a flexible way to address numerous market situations.

New-Product Department The **new-product department** is responsible for identifying ideas, developing products, and preparing them for commercialization. The members generally report directly to top executives and include individuals with experience in many aspects of the business. This structure separates the responsibility of new-product development from the rest of the organization. It helps eliminate redundancies that occur when the same ideas are developed in different product areas. These personnel have a firm grasp of the methods and risks involved in developing new products. In reality, these departments are often formed with great expectations but some quickly become a functional silo neglected by top management. This is particularly the case when top management is preoccupied with current products or when the new-product department does not set aggressive goals regarding commercializable products. Such a department usually operates best when it has strong executive involvement and concentrates its efforts on finding strategies to make product ideas commercial successes.

New-Product Committee The **new-product committee** consists of key functional personnel who are brought together from time to time to develop new products. Because this activity is often not considered a strong factor in building a career, participants may give it less attention than required. Furthermore, the committee often lacks the authority to make things happen. However, ideas and expertise can be contributed by many different key people, and committee members can be brought into a project as needed.

Venture Team A **venture team** (sometimes called a task force) is a group formed for a set period to accomplish a set objective. A venture team is headed by a manager who reports very high in the organization. The manager selects team members from various areas of the company, and each is given release time for the assignment. Because the venture team has very specific objectives and a limited time frame, it tends to focus on getting the job done. Strong leadership and decision-making power allow the team to commit resources in a timely fashion. And the release time enables members to devote attention to the project. Unfortunately, in many organizations managers are unwilling to permit their best people to participate. In addition, the team is dissolved once a given task is completed. The new venture team must start over without the benefit of experience. Hewlett-Packard used this approach to develop the first low-cost laser printer.

Consulting Organizations Full service or specialty consulting firms can be hired to set up new-product development systems, facilitate the process, or conduct all or part of the development task. In many cases, consulting groups have outstanding talent with experience in the area of new products. Because of that experience, companies can save vast amounts of time and money in the innovation process. Unfortunately, employees sometimes resist implementing consulting firm recommendations because they were not involved in the decision-making process. Consulting organizations such as Booz, Allen & Hamilton, and McKinsey and Company often make strong efforts to involve their clients in all phases of their new-product consulting.

PRODUCT LIFE CYCLES

One of the oldest and most useful concepts for marketers is the product life cycle, depicted in Figure 11.6. Like living organisms, products move from birth through infan-

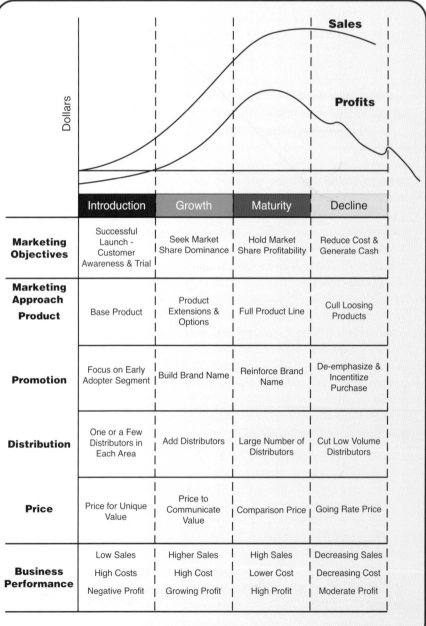

	Introduction	Growth	Maturity	Decline
Marketing Objectives	Successful Launch - Customer Awareness & Trial	Seek Market Share Dominance	Hold Market Share Profitability	Reduce Cost & Generate Cash
Marketing Approach **Product**	Base Product	Product Extensions & Options	Full Product Line	Cull Loosing Products
Promotion	Focus on Early Adopter Segment	Build Brand Name	Reinforce Brand Name	De-emphasize & Incentitize Purchase
Distribution	One or a Few Distributors in Each Area	Add Distributors	Large Number of Distributors	Cut Low Volume Distributors
Price	Price for Unique Value	Price to Communicate Value	Comparison Price	Going Rate Price
Business Performance	Low Sales / High Costs / Negative Profit	Higher Sales / High Cost / Growing Profit	High Sales / Lower Cost / High Profit	Decreasing Sales / Decreasing Cost / Moderate Profit

Figure 11.6 Traditional Life Cycle Curves and Marketing Approaches

cy, adolescence, maturity, old age, and on to death. The **product life cycle** consists of four stages: introduction, growth, maturity, and decline. It's important to recognize that this is only a conceptual tool, and not all products move through a complete life cycle. Some marketers question the usefulness of the idea, but it remains one of the most common notions in marketing strategy. It has been applied to generic products, suppliers, industries, and individual brands.

Figure 11.6 illustrates the sales and profits for a typical product as it moves through its life cycle. Before introduction, large sums are likely to be expended on development. In the pharmaceutical industry, it may take 15 years or more for R&D, testing, and FDA approval. Eli Lilly, a leading pharmaceutical company, says that it spends $2 billion annually in the research and development of new drugs.[33] Much of this budget is spent on products that are newly introduced.

STAGES IN THE PRODUCT LIFE CYCLE

Each of the four stages in the product life cycle is associated with its own opportunities, costs, and marketing strategies. In this section we examine each stage in more detail.

Stage 1: Introduction During the introductory phase of the product life cycle, sales slowly take off and grow. Shipments from the factory may be high, and channels of distribution are filled as wholesalers and retailers stock the item. Since the product is new, marketers scramble to create consumer awareness and encourage trial. This often involves heavy advertising campaigns, samples, and educational sales techniques. During this critical period, marketers attempt to build share quickly to gain first-mover advantages. As numerous studies have shown, whoever introduces a product is likely to become the future industry leader in that area. Chrysler introduced minivans and now controls more than half the market. Yet, Chrysler as a whole accounts for only 10 percent of the car market. The first products on the market often are so dominant that they become generic names: Kleenex, Jell-O, Xerox, Formica, and Gore-Tex.[34]

Typically, there are few competitors during introduction, so marketers concentrate on achieving customer acceptance of the entire product class. Less emphasis is placed on gaining competitive advantage through differentiation. When car phones were introduced, most advertising focused on selling the idea.

Later advertising attempted to distinguish the various products from one another. Most organizations introduce only one or two items in a new-product line so they can gain experience and monitor progress. Furthermore, global markets offer such vast opportunities for new products that some rivals may elect to avoid confrontations by selecting an untapped area.

As a rule, introductions represent advances in technology, manufacturing, and service. Product design also tends to be very innovative. Firms should make sure, however, that the design is easy to try and to use. It's also important to have flexible manufacturing that can match production to highly uncertain demand. Distributors don't want to be left with unsold units. But if demand is not met, buyers may lose interest, or competitors may enter the market. Finally, customer service efforts must seek out and correct problems.

Profits may be negative during all or most of the introductory phase. Sales usually grow slowly, and consumers need to be made aware of the product's existence, which requires relatively costly promotion. It can also be very expensive to develop distribution channels and to educate people about the product's use.

Stage 2: Growth During the growth stage, the pace of consumer acceptance and sales quickens. This is an especially critical time because rivals, noticing the increase in sales, will develop competitive products and aggressively pursue distribution channels. Consumers begin to make comparisons among the various products, so companies attempt to gain preferred status and brand loyalty. Strong companies such as Microsoft and Dell Computers seek dominance during this period. Many organizations believe that if they don't emerge from the growth stage as number one or two, then they should abandon that line of business. Competition is extremely aggressive. Honda, an automobile company which began in 1959 as a motorcycle company, has continued to grow beyond its original product line. Honda is now famous for its automobiles, motorcycles, power equipment, marine motors, and even jet airplanes.[35]

Product technology often enters its second generation during the growth stage. The first-generation technology applied to the original products is improved as companies gain experience. Usually, second-generation technology produces greater customer satisfaction through both cost savings and enhanced functionality. The first car phones had to be mounted permanently, and an antenna was attached to the outside. The next generation included bag phones that could be transferred from vehicle to vehicle. Now, handheld phones fit in your pocket, or simply attach to the car.

With growth comes product designs that differ substantially from one manufacturer to the next. Building on the technology of short-range wireless connections and electronics, many companies like Hewlett-Packard have developed a Bluetooth capability which allows data to be transferred from mobile phones, computers, personal digital assistants, and networked peripheral devices such as printers and scanners by short-range wireless connections. This is making it easy to synchronize multiple gadgets into personalized computer communication systems.

To expose its eco-friendly stainless steel canteen to potential customers like fans of Dave Matthews Band and Modest Mouse, Klean Kanteen sponsored sustainable musical festival Rothbury, helping free the festival of plastic bottles.

Manufacturing processes undergo change during the growth phase. The flexibility of the previous stage gives way to assembly lines and more automation. Higher sales volumes mean that standardized production can be used to achieve economies of scale and cost savings. Since markets are more predictable, just-in-time delivery and advanced quality control systems are possible.

Promotion and sales take on a whole new dimension during growth. Aggressive, head-to-head competition forces organizations to show their uniqueness, and the augmented product becomes extremely important. Financing, installation, and training in product use are critical promotion activities. Advertising shifts to substantive messages that describe the benefits, functions, and features of the product relative to competitors' offerings.

The companies that emerge as leaders tend to provide uncompromising customer service. They build trust in the distribution channel and with end users. Sometimes repeat purchases are based more on service satisfaction than on product performance and styling. Most consumers expect problems with any product. How they are handled makes the difference. If service is performed correctly the first time, then consumers are likely to feel an affinity toward the supplier. In fact, loyalty may be strengthened when problems occur and are handled well.

Stage 3: Maturity As products mature, sales level off and may remain flat for long periods. Overall market growth is relatively small, so a sales increase for one company usually comes at the expense of another. That's why firms with loyal buyers tend to have the greatest longevity. Yet, loyalty also indicates that consumer interest in the product is subsiding, which makes it very difficult and costly to build market share. Most firms are happy if they simply hold their own in this phase. Weaker competitors are likely to lower prices, while stronger rivals may sacrifice market share to maintain a satisfactory profit level. Strong rivals also engage in dramatic cost containment to preserve profits. Often this results in a standardized product design with less costly components and more efficient manufacturing.

At maturity, weaker rivals may drop out and use resources on more promising products. Even strong companies may exit if profit margins suffer too much, as GE did with its consumer line of light bulbs. The maturity phase may last several months, years, or even decades, and a low-cost position is critical for long-term success. This is particularly true if low-cost foreign competitors enter the business.

Product line size becomes especially important during the mature phase. Companies need to drop products with low-volume sales, high production costs, or little competitive viability. But many buyers want to deal with a supplier who offers a full product line. This leads many organizations to employ outsourcing; that is, they purchase certain items from other companies and affix their own label. In this way they continue to mass-produce the lower-cost standardized items while depending on smaller firms to make the rest. Competitors may even buy from one another during the mature stage in order to gain an overall cost advantage, sometimes called co-competition.

The technology used for mature products tends to be older. Many firms have invested so heavily in the past technology that they resist committing more resources to an aging product. The primary focus is on improving the manufacturing process. For example, some organizations move from assembly-line and batch-oriented production to a continuous-flow system. This integrates people, paperwork, computerization, and manufacturing into a seamless operation that maintains production at the greatest level of efficiency.

Promotional campaigns focus more on reminder

advertising than on new themes, since most buyers are now loyal to a particular brand or company. Sometimes companies resurrect messages that were used to build the brand's name. By adding a novel twist, the firm can keep its product in the forefront. For example, Wheaties, the traditional "Breakfast of Champions," regularly updates its package to show the latest sports superstars or to pay tribute to past champions. The objective is to create a link to younger consumers while maintaining its strong brand identity.

Service usually is standardized for mature products. In many cases, new service firms are formed to specialize in a particular product area. Even though Otis or Westinghouse installs most of the elevators we use, it is private service companies that keep them in tip-top condition. Many organizations elect to hire local service firms to perform repairs. The marketing of replacement parts may become extremely profitable at this stage. During economic recessions, customers often prefer to fix an existing product rather than buy a new one. In the United States, movable furniture systems from such companies as Steelcase, Herman Miller, and Haworth have entered the maturity phase. Local firms are now purchasing and refurbishing the units for resale.

The rapid sales increase in the growth stage peaks during early maturity. Profits are likely to decline because of price competition, both domestically and internationally. This is particularly true in industries with high exit barriers. That means it costs companies a lot of money to leave the line of business because of their high fixed investment. Since it is costly to stop making the product, prices often are lowered to main-

tain demand. Furthermore, such trade promotions as point-of-purchase sales and discounting may be used. By the end of the maturity phase, a product may be losing money or have a very thin profit margin because of low demand.

Stage 4: Decline   In the decline stage of the product life cycle, sales of new units diminish. For some products, such as earlier models of computers, the decrease may be very rapid. For others, it may be slow and steady, as with black-and-white television sets. Or it may be slow and then rapid, which was the case with vinyl records. Their sales dropped gradually and then plummeted as more and more titles became available on CDs. The speed of decline is related to the types and value of substitute products.

Most companies with a declining product want to maintain the lucrative replacement market but are willing to give up market share in exchange for earnings. Fierce price wars are likely to result in losses for all competitors. Low-cost producers that minimize new activities are in a much better position than high-cost competitors. Product design is nearly always standardized. Changes are intended to reduce the cost of components, which helps the company maintain earnings.

Companies are likely to return to a much shallower product line at this stage, focusing on the products that generate adequate cash flow. Old technology is kept in place, and manufacturing runs are limited, which frees up production capacity for more profitable items. To keep costs down, very little promotional activity occurs, so buyers may have to seek out the product themselves. Service is likely to be handled by independent companies. Because replacement parts still generate a profit, the firm is likely to maintain a supply that affords some level of earnings.

The profit life cycle implies that companies should have products in all stages at all times. Firms with only mature and declining products can expect dwindling profitability. Yet product development and the introductory stage are likely to absorb much of the profit generated from growing and mature products. Strong companies plan ahead and add products at various stages in the life cycle to ensure a viable business. This is particularly important for companies whose products are patented. Pfizer faces such a challenge when the patent on its biggest drug, Lipitor, expires in 2011, opening the door for generics. Analysts speculate that the company doesn't have enough new drugs in the works to

Wheaties tributes Bill Russell for his career achievements with the Boston Celtics.

offset the sales decline that is sure to occur. Pfizer has many new experimental compounds in early stages of development and has recently launched a cancer drug and anti-smoking drug. It is awaiting FDA (Federal Drug Administration) approval on many drugs in hopes they will fill the sales void left by the company's mature products.

VARIATIONS IN PRODUCT LIFE CYCLES

By looking at extinct products, we know that several kinds of life cycles are possible as depicted in Figure 11.7. By understanding the different types, marketers can make general predictions about the challenges they face. The first curve is typical of high-tech products, such as computer software. Just when sales achieve a healthy pace, another generation hits the market. General acceptance of the product grows with each wave, however, which explains the successively higher peaks. Each generation usually lowers the cost to consumers.

The second curve illustrates the life cycle of a fad. Sales rise sharply in the introductory and growth phases and then quickly fall. Marketers of such products are careful not to base the longevity of their company on one

The Marketing Gazette™

CREATING & CAPTURING
VALUE THROUGH TECHNOLOGY

Microsoft Sync

Developing a successful new product is hard enough, but what about creating one as innovative as Microsoft Sync? Sync is a voice activated in-car communication and entertainment system that fully integrates music and mobile phone technology. The technology, which was developed and Powered by Microsoft Auto, is available on most 2008 models of Ford, Lincoln and Mercury vehicles and is included as standard equipment on high-end models. "Since we know a lot of people spend a lot of time every day in their car, we need to bring the car into the equation," said Microsoft chairman Bill Gates.

Sync is the first technology to allow drivers the hands-free ability to call any contact in their phone, receive phone calls and text messages or listen to any song on their digital music player using their vehicles' in-car microphone and sound system. The technology is compatible with most Bluetooth enabled mobile phones and popular digital music players such as the Apple iPod and will even play files from most USB storage devices. The software is fully upgradeable, allowing flexibility as new technology in digital music and telecommunications emerge. Being voice-activated and hands-free means drivers have fewer distractions. Sync can even receive commands in multiple languages. "We regard this as an innovative and new approach for the automotive industry," said Mark Spain, Microsoft's automotive business director.

Ford's confidence in the software system has led the company to develop and entire marketing campaign around it. TV, radio, print and online ads, as well as dealership training have been designed to market the software system as its own product, rather than as part of a vehicle. "We have an entire communication plan around a feature, just like a product," says John Emmert, Sync marketing manager. "That is not what we have historically done."

But what's the best thing about Sync in the mind's of most consumers? You don't need to own a luxury vehicle to enjoy it. It's available in nearly every model of Ford, Lincoln and Mercury, including the Ford Focus. This means that for a price of only $395, the technology is available to everyday people in one easy package.

or two items. They realize the fad is likely to be a passing windfall. The Rubik's Cube gained immediate success in America, selling over 100 million in the first 2 years. The success of the product quickly made it a global icon, but variations where quickly introduced. There have been approximately 30 brand puzzles manufactured since the first 3x3 cube and many vintage versions are now collector items.[36]

Clothing fashions follow yet another kind of curve. When a style is first introduced, it is likely to experience relatively fast growth and then trail off, only to be resurrected a few years later. The width of neckties has gone from narrow, to medium, to wide, and back to narrow. Skirt lengths rise and fall. Marketers of these products must be aware of constantly changing consumer preferences and build strategies accordingly.

Although the product life cycle gives marketers a rule of thumb, it is not an exact science. To obtain more precise forecasts, researchers have developed mathematical and statistical models that examine market size, the number of initial buyers, and the time between first and repeat purchase. These can be very useful, particularly for products that behave similarly to those modeled.

EXTENDING THE PRODUCT LIFE CYCLE

Firms that resist change sometimes keep products going far beyond their usefulness. But there are times when it's good business to extend the product life cycle. The four most common ways to do this are to sell to new market segments, to stimulate more frequent use, to encourage more use per occasion, and to promote more varied use.

Selling to New Segments One way to give a product a new lease on life is to find new buyers. For example, in-line skates were originally used primarily by males to simulate ice hockey, but now they have been adopted widely by females. The cosmetic surgery industry is no longer geared toward only women but now must direct itself also to men. Procedures like Botox and laser hair removal is becoming common place for men as it becomes socially acceptable and even encouraged behavior to surgically enhance one's appearance. The numbers of men having cosmetic surgery in North America has been steadily increasing for the past 10 years, and is expected to keep growing.[37] The diversity feature centers on how Mattel entered the market segment of CD-ROM games for girls.

Stimulating More Frequent Use After a decade of declining sales nationwide, the milk industry needed a marketing campaign to stimulate use. From this the well-known "Got Milk?" campaign was born. Research indicated that the product played only a peripheral role in people's lives. The only time they gave it a second thought was when they didn't have any. The campaign theme chosen was "milk deprivation"— a man agonizing over a milkless bowl of cereal, deciding whether to rob his baby's bottle or his cat's dish. Or Santa entering a home, eating a brownie, finding no milk, and taking the Christmas presents away. Recently, the ads have appealed to potential milk drinkers by showing celebrities such as Britney Spears, the Dixie Chicks, and Serena and Venus Williams, and even have a Web site selling "Got Milk?" paraphernalia. These award winners not only heightened awareness by over 90 percent but also increased the frequency of use of milk.[38]

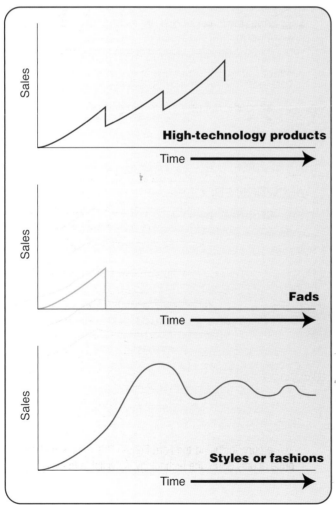

Figure 11.7 Life Cycles for Various Types of Products

Encouraging More Use per Occasion

Have you ever purchased a Snickers bar offering 20 percent more candy for free? That is one way to encourage more use per occasion. Many companies promote on this basis. For years McDonald's offered a "Super Sized®" meal, with a larger order of french fries and a larger beverage. Recently, McDonald's has shifted away from supersizing, perhaps because of public obesity concerns. Coca-Cola encourages greater consumption with 20-ounce sizes in vending machines. Claussen, a division of Campbell's, sells a giant crinkle-cut pickle slice to "blanket" hamburgers. The 69 percent of Americans who enjoy pickles on their burgers have a bigger option.

Promoting More Varied Use

Arm & Hammer dramatically extended the life cycle of baking soda by using it as an ingredient in toothpaste, laundry products, room fresheners, and deodorant. Furthermore, ads recommend it for absorbing odors in refrigerators and closets. Once used only for cooking, today baking soda has far more applications. Even when it is being disposed, it helps sanitize the drain. Another example is the "I could have had a V-8" campaign, which popularized the traditional breakfast drink as a refreshment for any time of day. And Yellowstone Park, traditionally viewed as a summer attraction, now advertises snowmobile trips in the winter.

THE PRODUCT LIFE CYCLE IN INTERNATIONAL MARKETS

A product's stage in the life cycle has important implications for international trade, not only in terms of marketing but also in terms of design and manufacture.

New products tend to be designed, manufactured, and sold first in advanced economies, where there is sufficient wealth to underwrite development costs, and where markets accept innovation more readily. For example, personal computers were developed largely in the United States and sold primarily in the more upscale U.S. and Western European markets. As sales grew, however, Pacific Rim manufacturers developed clones, produced them with lower-cost labor, and became important competitors in Western markets. The lower prices that resulted in turn opened up new international markets in less advanced economies such as Russia and Eastern Europe.

A product at the peak of its popularity, with many brands competing for market share, may be manufactured far from its primary market if it can gain a competitive advantage through lower manufacturing costs. Athletic shoes, for example, were pioneered in the United States—which remains their largest single market. But as product sales burgeoned and new competitors entered the market, both Nike and Reebok moved their production to low-wage countries to reduce costs.

Maturing products tend to be exported to less advanced economies looking for lower-priced goods. As these markets grow, companies are likely to establish production facilities there, using their already standardized processes. We see this in Mexico, where both Nissan and Volkswagen have assembly plants that produce for the local market—and export to the United States as well. As manufacturing skills and processes are absorbed locally, local companies may set up their own plants and begin producing for the home market, thereby increasing competition.

Products that have reached the end of their life cycle in one economy may still be needed in another. Few U.S. households still do their laundry with washboards and tubs, but in poorer parts of the world, particularly in rural areas that have no access to electricity, such products remain useful and desirable.

Some countries are more suitable markets early in a product's life and others are more suitable later. Where products are made and marketed depends on their stage in the life cycle and on the economic characteristics of the location.[39]

CONSUMER ACCEPTANCE OF INNOVATION

ADOPTION PROCESS

The **adoption process** comprises the five steps that consumers go through in making a product choice: knowledge, persuasion, decision, implementation, and

globalEDGE™

http://globaledge.msu.edu

Visit globalEDGE™ Online for the ultimate international marketing research tool!

Product Innovation & Management

An important aspect of successful product development and management is innovation. Your firm is aiming to enter the telecommunications industry in the next five years and is planning to develop a line of products based on your core competency: heavy machinery. After consulting a magazine of innovation, which three firms may be considered the most innovative in the telecommunications industry? Since their current areas of focus may act as a guide for your future product portfolio, what are the specialties for each of these three firms? Contrast these firms with the three listed as least innovative. As such, in which areas will you propose your firm to avoid future product development?

confirmation. First, the consumer becomes aware of the product and learns about it. Second, the person forms a favorable or unfavorable attitude toward the product. Third, the product is chosen or rejected. Fourth, the consumer tries the product. Fifth, experience confirms or disconfirms the wisdom of the choice and whether the item will be purchased again.[40]

The major point is that product adoption takes time. The speed of adoption depends on buyer characteristics and other factors. Because people are different, it is possible to categorize them according to how long it will take them to adopt an idea. We know, moreover, that product acceptance is passed from one group of consumers to the next. To explain this process, marketers have developed a concept similar to the product life cycle except it focuses on consumers: the diffusion process.

DIFFUSION PROCESS

The **diffusion process** describes the spread of innovations from one individual or group to another over time. Marketers are keenly aware of how diffusion affects the introduction and long-term adoption of goods and services. We know that sales are influenced dramatically by the interaction of buyers, through word of mouth, as well as by promotions and messages from marketers. Often managers focus only on organizing the firm to develop new or improved products. Yet they must also pay attention to understanding how consumers evaluate innovations. Otherwise even very beneficial products may not be diffused throughout the market.[41]

Figure 11.8 illustrates the five groups of consumers who can be expected to purchase a product over time. The approximate distribution is 2.5 percent innovators, 13 percent early adopters, 34 percent early majority buyers, 34 percent late majority buyers, and 16 percent laggards. The illustration is based on standard deviations, but the proportions may differ with various products.

Innovators The first consumers to purchase a new product are **innovators.** As you can guess, they are more adventurous than most of the population. They are technically competent and in some cases are almost obsessed with the

Courtesy of Apple

details of new products. At the same time, many innovators are rather eccentric. This small group has only minor influence over others, but it provides proof that the product functions properly. Marketers can point to that experience in attempting to educate other buyers. The marketer of a new computerized vision system for detecting manufacturing flaws first installed the system at a small innovative firm that makes electronic parts. The company later cited successful use there in selling the product to a leader in the industry.

Early Adopters **Early adopters** are the second group to purchase new products and are critical to marketers. They have higher incomes and, thus, can afford to try relatively expensive introductions. They are the key to good word-of-mouth publicity and wider acceptance. They are well respected in their community, so other categories of buyers are likely to emulate them. Apple, for example, sold 1 million iPhones within three months of its initial release to early adopters. The innovative device packs the features of a cellphone, iPod, and mobile Internet device in one. Later, Apple dropped the price of the device to increase the adoption rate. [42]

Early Majority Buyers **Early majority** consumers tend to be more risk averse than innovators and early adopters. They wait to see how something new works for others before purchasing it themselves. They also tend to read extensively about various products and compare different brands before

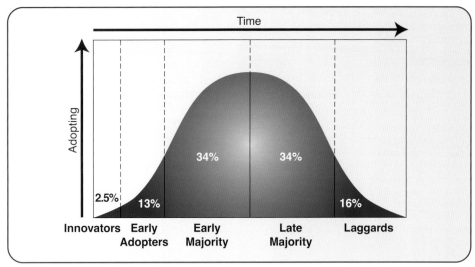

Figure 11.8   The Product Diffusion Cycle

reaching a decision. For the most part, these consumers are followers rather than leaders. For this reason, early majority consumers are likely to wait for Apple's iPhone to work out potential drawbacks before adopting it. While the benefits of this revolutionary product are exciting, early versions only provide five hours of battery life for talk time and internet browsing.[43] Early majority consumers are expected to wait until the battery life is expanded before making the purchase, despite the extensive benefits it offers.

Late Majority and Laggards

The more skeptical consumers tend to fall into the **late majority** group. They have little faith in new products, so they wait until half the population has purchased it before they do. However, even more resistant to new products is the last group of consumers to purchase, the **laggards**; little, if anything, can be done to convince laggards to purchase a new product.

U.S. farmers can be viewed using the diffusion cycle. Innovators and early adopters stay current on all developments in agriculture. They go to trade shows and read everything they can get their hands on. These consumers are the first to buy a new piece of equipment or pesticide. At the other extreme lie the laggards. They feel "if it ain't broke, don't fix it" and tend to stay brand oriented. They influence little or none of the market. Marketers have used different strategies to reach each group. The

innovators and early adopters prefer advertising with a lot of good information or copy. Laggards, on the other hand, need attention-grabbing ads and coupons as an incentive to purchase new products.[44] Since laggards often have low incomes and are a relatively small group, many marketers simply avoid marketing to this group

Web and E-Commerce Stars
www.verizonwireless.com

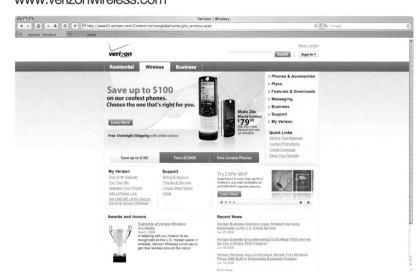

Verizon Wireless markets itself as the most reliable wireless network, and verizonwireless.com is a reliable and easy to use site for both new and potential customers. Visitors to the Web site can not only explore new phones and accessories, but browse plan offerings and coverage maps. At the features and downloads section, customers can download ringtones, music, games, video clips and more. Text messaging, picture and video messaging, mobile IMing and mobile emailing features are also available. And, to make it easy for customers to check account information, there is a special zone to view personal information, pay a bill, change a calling plan, check minutes, and more in one easy Web spot.

completely. The fact that they have low education and low income often makes them bad credit risks as well.

Here is an example of applying the diffusion cycle to the pharmaceutical industry. A pharmaceutical firm introduced a new pain reliever. Salespeople were asked to identify physicians who fit the early adopter profile: younger, heavy prescribers, on hospital boards, with modern offices and equipment. Special attention was given to these physicians through direct mail, sampling, and sales calls. Because early adopters are more cosmopolitan than average, they are more inclined to accept information and interact with innovative firms. They agreed to test and evaluate the new product, quickly gave it their support, and set in motion rapid diffusion throughout the medical community.

When we think of product innovation and new-product introductions, our tendency is to think in terms of manufactured goods. Remember that services, too, are products—as you are aware from the marketing definition in Chapter 1 and the many examples of services encountered thus far.

Chapter Summary:

Objective 1: Provide a framework to evaluate the extent to which existing or new products are marketed to existing or new market segments.

Every organization needs to develop a product mix consistent with its overall strategy. It must match current and new products with current and new segments. This produces four basic options for marketing mix management. A core business focus maintains, expands, or harvests current products in current markets. Market development seeks new market segments for existing products. Product development improves or adds new products for sale to current segments. Diversification introduces new products into new market segments. Organizations can use this framework to help allocate resources to obtain the best overall performance.

Objective 2: Understand how the characteristics of innovation influence the speed with which product innovations are accepted.

Product innovations are of three types. Continuous innovations are minor changes in existing products that require no alterations in how consumers use them. Dynamically continuous innovations have added features and benefits that require minor changes in behavior. Discontinuous innovations are new to the world and may require major changes.

How rapidly a product is accepted depends on several factors. If its relative advantage over other products is high, then faster acceptance can be expected. If the product is compatible with current thinking, then quick adoption is likely. Also, less complex products and those that can be easily tried are more readily accepted. Finally, if the product can be observed in use by others, then it is more likely to be adopted rapidly.

Objective 3: Know the steps used to develop new products from the initial idea through commercialization.

The new-product development process has seven steps. First, a strategy is outlined by top management. This indicates the importance of new products to the organization. Second, idea generation provides a list of possibilities. These can come from numerous sources, especially if they are actively sought. Third, idea screening narrows the list to those most compatible with the organization's need. Several criteria are used in screening. Fourth,

business analysis develops a product concept and performs a financial analysis to assess feasibility and estimate profitability under numerous assumptions. Fifth, prototype product development involves all the steps leading up to and including the creation of a working model. Sixth, test marketing provides a limited trial of the marketing strategy under real or simulated conditions. The objective is to see whether the strategy will work or needs to be refined before full-scale launch. Seventh, commercialization occurs when the product is formally introduced into the market.

Objective 4: Show how the product life cycle concept can be used to build and adjust marketing strategies over time.

Products can be viewed as moving over a life cycle with several stages. In the introduction phase, sales usually take off slowly despite heavy promotion. Marketers concentrate on getting consumers to be aware of and accept the product class. During the growth stage sales increase, and product technology often enters its second generation. Manufacturing and promotion are adjusted. Leading producers focus on customer service. At maturity, sales begin to slow and level off. Gains in market share for one company come at the expense of another. A few companies exit at this point. Low cost really counts now in manufacturing and marketing. The decline stage is marked by a downward sales trend. Although a good replacement parts market may exist for some products, many companies choose to exit or harvest.

Objective 5: Recognize how innovations are adopted by consumers by being spread from group to group.

People go through a series of steps in adopting a new product. The speed depends on personal characteristics. Individuals can be grouped into five categories that comprise the diffusion process. Innovators are the first to adopt. They are usually a small group and tend to be eccentric. Early adopters, a larger group, are next. They have high income and education levels, and others respect them. This group is key to the success of new products. The third category is early majority buyers, a larger segment that generally follows the leadership of the early adopters. The last two categories, late majority buyers and laggards, are the last to adopt. The late majority group is numerous, so it is important.

Review Your Understanding

1. What are the four product mix options? Describe each.
2. What are the three product innovation categories? What are the characteristics of each?
3. What product characteristics speed the adoption of an innovation?
4. What are the steps in new-product development? Describe each.
5. What are test markets?
6. List five organizational structures for new-product development.
7. What are the differences between simultaneous and sequential methods of new-product development?
8. What is the difference between a product manager and a market manager?
9. What are the stages in the product life cycle? Describe them.

Discussion of Concepts

1. Explain the differences among continuous innovation, dynamically continuous innovation, and discontinuous innovation. What are the main activities for marketers when introducing each type?
2. Assume you are senior vice president of marketing for General Electric. What four product mix management options might you consider? Give specific examples of each.
3. Describe the typical profit scenario as a product moves through its life cycle. Do you think it's important for companies to have products in all stages? Why or why not?
4. What are some problems with using the product life cycle concept to make marketing decisions? Why do you think so many companies use the concept?
5. What are some ways to extend the product life cycle? Can you think of any companies that have used these techniques?
6. Many marketers use the diffusion cycle concept and the product life cycle concept. How are they different?
7. When introducing a new product, how may a marketer facilitate consumer acceptance?
8. Describe each organizational structure for new-product development. What factors would influence your decision to select one structure over another?

Key Terms And Definitions

Adoption process: The steps an individual consumer goes through in making a product choice.

Business analysis: Assessment of the attractiveness of the product from a sales, cost, profit, and cash flow standpoint.

Commercialization: Final stage in the new-product development process, when the product is introduced into the market.

Concept testing: Testing the new-product concept to evaluate the likelihood of its success.

Continuous innovation: A minor alteration in an existing product, such as a new style or model, that can be easily adopted without significant changes in consumer behavior.

Diffusion process: The spread of innovations from one group of consumers to another over time.

Discontinuous innovation: An entirely new product with new functions.

Dynamically continuous innovation: A familiar product with additional features and benefits that require or permit consumers to alter some aspect of their behavior.

Early adopters: The second group of consumers to purchase new products.

Early majority: The third group of adopters, who are more risk averse in purchase decisions than innovators and early adopters.

Idea generation: The gathering of suggestions for new products from a number of sources using a range of formal and informal methods.

Idea screening: Identifying the new-product ideas that have the most potential to succeed.

Innovators: The first group of consumers to purchase a new product.

Laggards: Consumers who resist new products the longest.

Late majority: The more skeptical consumers who purchase products after the early majority.

Line extension: A new product closely related to others in the line.

Market development: Offering existing products to new market segments.

Market manager: A manager responsible for one or several similar product lines targeted at specific market segments.

New-product committee: A group of key functional personnel who are brought together periodically to develop new products.

New-product department: The organizational unit responsible for identifying product ideas and preparing them for commercialization.

Product concept: A product idea that has been refined into written descriptions, pictures, and specifications.

Product development: Offering new products to existing market segments.

Product life cycle: The four stages a product goes through: introduction, growth, maturity, and decline.

Product manager: A manager who oversees one or several products targeted at all market segments.

Product mix: All the product lines and products a company offers.

Product planning: The focus given to core businesses, market development, product development, and diversification.

Sequential new-product development: People from various functional areas work on different stages of product development.

Simulated product test: Experimentation with the marketing strategy in artificial conditions.

Simultaneous new-product development: People from all functional areas work together to develop products.

Test market: A small geographic area, with characteristics similar to the total market, in which a product is introduced with a complete marketing program.

Venture team: Personnel from various areas of the company who are given release time to work on a specific assignment.

References

1. Michael Bush, "Distinct Marketing Derines Console Battle," PR Week, Oct 23, 2006, 9(42), p. 8; "Wii Demand Still Outpaces Supply," CNN News, July 2, 2007, www.cnn.com, website visited July 3, 2007; "Nintendo Wii; A Gesture Toward Broader Entertainment," PC Magazine, Nov 1, 2006, 25(21), p.1; N'Gai Croal, "Playing with Gaming," Newsweek, May 29, 2006; Joseph Pereira and Nick Wingfield, "Wii!Wii!Wii! This Holiday Season Has Been a Wild Ride for Nintendo," Wall Street Journal, Dec 12, 2006, p. B1.

2. Michael Arndt, "Turning Ideas Into Dollars," Business Week, New York, February 26, 2007. Issue 4023 p. 126.

3. Booz, Allen & Hamilton, New Product Management for the Eighties (New York: Booz, Allen & Hamilton, 1982).

4. Christopher Power, "Flops—Too Many New Products Fail. Here Is Why—And How to Do Better," Business Week, August 16, 1993, pp. 76–82.

5. Amazon.com Inc. Hoover's Company Records. www.hoovers.com, Web site visited March 15, 2008

6. www.rochesterclothing.com, Web site visited March 31, 2008.

7. www.pizzahut.com, Web site visited May 13, 2008.

8. www.apple.com, Web site visited March 31, 2008.

9. www.underarmour.com Web site visited March, 31, 2008.

10. John Martellaro, "Apple Growth Rate Beats Microsoft," The mac Observer, January 30, 2007.

11. Campbell's 2007 Annual Report www.campbellsoup.com,Web site visited March 26, 2008.

12. Tom Giles, "TechTrends for 2007, Business Week, January 29, 2007.

13. Tony Dawe, "Hello, Is Anybody There," The Times of London, October 27, 2000, p. 1DD.

14. R. J. Calantone, C. A. DiBenedetto, and S. Bhoovaroghaven, "Examining the Relationship between Degree of Innovation and New Product Success," Journal of Business Research 30 (1994): pp. 143–148.

15. www.microsoft.com/windows/products, Web site visited March 31, 2008.

16. http://web3.infotrac.galegroup.com, site visisted March 22, 2007

17. Jeffery B. Schmidt & Roger Calantone, "Are Really New Product Development Projects harder to Shut Down?," Journal of Product Innovation Management, 1998:15, p. 111-123; Jeffery B. Schmidt & Roger Calantone, "Escalation of Commitment During New Product Development," Journal of the Academy of Marketing Science, Spring 2002; Power, "Flops"; and Howard Schlossberg, "Fear of Failure Stifles Product Development," Marketing News, May 14, 1990, pp. 1, 16.

18. Roger Calantore, Jeffrey Schmidt, Michael Song, "Controllable Factors of New Product Success: A Cross-National Comparison," Marketing Science, 1986-1998.

19. "Market Knowledge Dimensions and Cross-Functional Collaboration: Examining the Different Routes to Product Innovation Performance." By: Luca, Luigi M. De; Atuahene-Gima, Kwaku. Journal of Marketing, January 2007, Vol. 71 Issue 1, p95-112.

20. Janice Griffiths-Hemans & Rajivl Grover, Journal of the Academy of Marketing Science; Winter2006, Vol. 34 Issue 1, p27-39.

21. A Century of Innovation: The 3M Story, 3M Company, 2002.

22. James Carbone, "Sun Shines By Taking Time Out," Purchasing, September 19, 1996, pp. 34–35.

23. "Seventh Generation, Inc.," Marketing News, April 25, 1994, p. E8.

24. Roger J. Calantone, C. Anthony Di Benedetto, and Jeffrey B. Schmidt, "Using the Analytic Hierarchy Process in New Product Screening," Journal of Product Innovation Management, 1999:16, p. 65-76.

25. R. Calantone, S. Vikery, and C. Droge, "Business Performance and New Product Development Activities: An Empirical Investigation," Journal of Product Innovation Management 12 (June 1995): pp. 214–223.

26. T. Haggblom, R. Calantone, and C. A. DiBenedetto, "Do New Product Managers in Large or Hi-Market Share Firms Perceive Marketing R&D Interface Principles Differently?" Journal of Product Innovation Management 12 (September 1995): pp. 323–333.

27. Shantanu Bhattacharya, V. Krishnan, Vijay Mahajan, "Managing New Product Definition in High Dynamic Environments", Management Science, Vol. 44, No. 11, Part 2, November, 1998, pp. S50-S54.

28. "Consumer: Suck It and See: Dyson Has Triumphed over Hoover in the Great Vacuum Cleaner Legal War, but Which Are the Best Dust-Busters?" The Guardian, October 5, 2000.

29. Jennifer Lawrence, "The Sunchip Also Rises," Advertising Age, April 27, 1992, p. S2; and Jennifer Lawrence, "Big Push for Sunchips," Advertising Age, February 24, 1992, p. 2.; Sandie Taylor, "Changing Perceptions of Frito-Lay Products Biggest Strategic Opportunity, Says Rader," Presentation at University of Texas at Austin, September 21, 2006.

30. Steven P. Schnaars, Managing Imitation Strategies (New York: The Free Press, 1994), p. 5.

31. W.L. Gore & Associates, Inc. Hoover's Company Records. Austin: March 15, 2008. p. 40531

32. X. Michael Song, mitzi M. Montoya-Weiss, and Jeffrey B. Schmidt, "Antecedents and Consequences of Cross-Functional Cooperation: A Comparison of R&D, Manufacturing, Marketing Perspectives," Journal of Product Innovation Management, 1997:14, p. 35-47.

33. www.lilly.com/reserach/index.html

34. Al Ries and Jack Trout, The 22 Immutable Laws of Marketing (New York: Harper Collins, 1993), pp. 6–7.

35. www.honda.com, Web site visited March 31, 2008.

36. www.rubiks.com, Web site visited May 13, 2008.

37. www.apple.com, Web site visited March 31, 2008.

38. Paula Mergenhagen, "How 'Got Milk' Got Sales," American Demographics, September 1996, www.marketingpower.com/publications/MT/96 MT/9609_MT/9609MD02.HTM.

39. Raymond Vernon, "International Investment and International Trade in the Product Life Cycle," Quarterly Journal of Economics (May 1986), p. 199.

40. Evertt M. Rogers, Diffusion of Innovations, 3rd ed. (New York: The Free Press, 1982), pp. 164–175.

41. R. Olshavsky and R. Spreng, "An Exploratory Study of the Innovation Evaluation Process," Journal of Product Innovation Management 13 (November 1996): pp. 512–529.

42. Apple Sells One Millionth iPhone, www.apple.com/pr, site visited June 18, 2008

43. Ibid.

44. Brian F. Blake, "They May Be Innovative, But They're Not the Same," Marketing News, April 15, 1991, p. 12.

Marketing Newspaper:
"Ford Gives Sync its Own Marketing Campaign," Automotive News, November 12, 2007; Sarah A. Webster, "Ford-Microsoft Sync is the Dawn of Digital Driving Era: Voice-Operated Computer is for Everyday Folks," Knight Ridder Tribune Business News, Washington: September 19, 2007; Tim Moran, "Is it Windows on Wheels? Ford, Microsoft 'Sync' it is," Automotive News, Detroit: January 15, 2007. Vol. 81, Iss. 6238; pg. 38; "2008 Ford Focus Demonstrated Ford's Commitment to Small Cars," PR Newswire, New York: January 7, 2007;

CASE 11

Innovation at Minnesota Mining and Manufacturing (3M)

Innovation and invention is the foundation on which 3M is built. The company, which started in 1902 as sandpaper manufacturer, as grown to a into a globally diversified, technology based enterprise that sells products in over 200 countries. 3M's products are found in multiple markets including office supplies, health care, electronics and industrial manufacturing. The company has become a global leader in innovation, invention, financial performance and its strong commitment to ethics.

3M leverages its technology to boost market leadership. The strategy is to get to the market first with one-of-a-kind products that can be premium-priced to support strong profit margins. It's well known brands include Scotchgard fabric protectors, Post-it Notes, and Scotch tapes. The company is looking to drive growth by utilizing its core competencies and through acquisitions. It has undergone a number of acquisitions, including the purchase of dental supplies company, OMNII Oral Pharmaceuticals, and JJ Converting, a packaging company.

3M'S ESPE Dental Products Division has been the leader in the development and innovation of dental products. The company's groundbreaking ideas in dentistry come, in part, from the ongoing insight from dental practitioners. 3M often has a consultant view dental appointments and receive feedback on how to improve its products. With an average of 45 dental innovations per year, the company has been named "Most Innovative" by Dental Industry Review for multiple years running. "At the heart of the company's culture lies 100+ years of research and development expertise, making discovery a way of life at 3M ESPE. With more than 6,500 scientist's companywide, it's no surprise that innovation is fostered at every level within the organization – from the lab to the sales force," Said Jeff Lavers, division Vice President of 3M ESPE. "Our people understand that innovation, in and of itself, is not enough. It's only when we combine that spirit of discovery with customer insights that we are able to apply our deep knowledge and technological expertise for the betterment of dentistry."

Innovation has also turned sustainable at 3M. The company produces an array of products designed to minimize environmental impact in production and use and help its customers obtain their sustainability goals. "Sustainability is the responsibility of everyone. Together with customers, 3M hopes to continue to meet today's needs while allowing the next generation to meet its needs," wrote 3M CEO George Buckley. 3M has been a leader in emissions and waste reduction and has implemented a sustainability strategy aimed at obtaining customer satisfaction and financial success within a framework of environmentally friendly principles.

3M certainly has great talent to create market innovations. Its R&D personnel have backgrounds in chemistry, electronics, biochemistry, microbiology, genetics, pharmacology, and material sciences in 3M, as well as marketing. They are found in 71 R&D laboratories around the world, the largest of which houses approximately 4,000 at 3M's Maplewood campus in Austin, Texas. Many new-product ideas emerge from scientists working closely with customers who have specific needs. 3M also gives scientists the freedom to pursue their own projects with the corporate "15 percent rule". This rule says that scientists can spend up to 15 percent of their time working on individual initiatives, which has resulted in many new products for the company.

3M spends a good deal of time making sure that market conditions support a new product. The risks are gigantic, given the large number of people and huge budgets involved, but 3M personnel are taught to understand and assume risk.

The safe environment for risk-taking entrepreneurship is one key reason 3M has been able to obtain 30 percent of sales from young products. Today 3M is raising the bar by including representatives from R&D with marketing teams all the way through sales. This helps even unarticulated customer needs in support of its platforms. "Our unstoppable commitment to innovation, creating new technologies and products, places us exactly where our customers need us."

1. *Imagine you are in charge of product development at 3M. Explain why innovation is a critical part of your company's strategy.*
2. *How is 3M able to apply customer demand to its R&D?*
3. *How does 3M manage risk? Suggest additional ways the company can promote risk-taking entrepreneurship.*
4. *How might 3M use the product life cycle concept to build and adjust its marketing strategies over time?*

Sources: "3M ESPE Receives 'Most Innovative' Designation," RDH, Jun 2007, 27(6), 18; "3M Among World's 10 Most Respected Firms," Business World, Feb 24, 2003; Jennifer Bjorhus, "3M Unveils Drastic Shakeup of Research & Development Division," Knight Ridder Tribune Business News, Sep 27, 2003; www.3m.com, site visited February 25, 2008.

SECTION

5

Communicate Value

Communicating value to customers is vital to create and capture value. In this section you will learn about the different approaches marketers take to reach their target audience. The following chapters are included in this section:

Chapter 12   Integrated Marketing Communications
Chapter 13   Mass Communication
Chapter 14   Personal Selling & Sales Force Management

CHAPTER 12

Integrated Marketing Communications

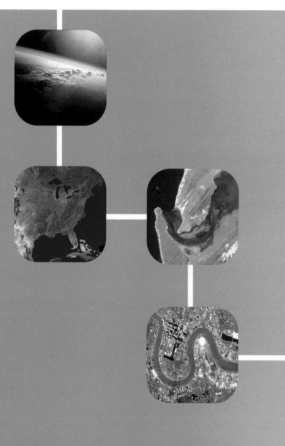

Oprah Winfrey is worth an estimated $1.4 billion, and involves herself in multiple media outlets, including television, radio, and print.

Learning Objectives

1. Understand the objectives of integrated marketing communications.

2. Learn how the communication process provides the intended information for the market.

3. Learn about the communication mix, including personal selling, advertising, sales promotion, sponsorships, and public relations.

4. Know the factors that influence the communication mix.

5. Describe the steps in developing an integrated marketing communication plan.

6. Address diversity, ethics, and technology in communications.

Known as the superstar talk show host with a passion for people, Oprah Winfrey shares compassionate style of communicating with 48 million viewers a week around the world. "The Oprah Winfrey Show" has been number one in the U.S. for 20 consecutive years, and won 35 Emmy Awards before Oprah chose to stop submitting it for further Emmy consideration. Now, the show provides a platform for Oprah's other business. As one of the best self-marketers in the industry, she is building equity in the Oprah brand with her entertainment empire ranging from publishing, film production, and more.

Now on the Forbes list of the 400 richest Americans, Oprah is worth $1.4 billion. Her successes include Harpo Inc., the production company behind "The Oprah Winfrey Show." The company comprises Harpo Films, Harpo Radio for the new Oprah & Friends channel, and Harpo Print for the "O, Oprah Magazine" and "Oprah at Home." Oprah took the show's better life message and transferred it to print when she started the "O, Oprah Magazine." It is the most successful magazine launch in publishing history with a circulation of 2.4 million and a readership of 16.3 million per month. She now reaches out to an audience of radio listeners with her Oprah & Friends satellite station that showcases such names as Maya Angelou, Gayle King and Jean Chatzky. Oprah is successful in these media ventures because she sticks to her core message of challenging her followers to live their best lives.

With her strong influence, Oprah has set a standard that others hope to follow. She holds more influence in making or breaking an individual, a business, a book, or an industry than arguably anyone in the nation. Through her Book Club, the books she recommends usually have a greater effect on sales than anything else in the history of modern publishing. "Oprah is getting people who were not particularly reading, to read," said Sara Nelson, editor-in-chief of "Publishers Weekly." Oprah gets hundreds of other books moving as well. One author, Kerry McCloskey, went on "The Oprah Winfrey Show" to promote her new diet book. The week after her appearance, McCloskey's book sales shot up 1,260 percent, according to Nielsen Bookscan. Another author, Harville Hendrix, enjoyed an 849 percent increase in his book sales following a visit with Oprah.

Oprah's magic tough extends to products other than books. She spreads her passion for her "favorites," and promotes what she thinks is important and useful. For most vendors, there is nothing like an Oprah blessing, said Rob Walker, the consumer columnist for "The New York Times Magazine." "If you have a product, there's no better environment to be in than on Oprah. You're being treated as almost a religious artifact." Oprah has recently incorporated green products such as energy saving power strips and organic household cleaners into her "favorites". "The Oprah Winfrey Show" has increasingly included episodes that encourage viewers to make going green a part of their everyday lives. Oprah encourages viewers to make eco-friendly choices at the grocery store. Viewers can even purchase canvas grocery bags at Oprah.com. "O, Oprah Magazine," also commonly features tips and ideas on how to reuse and recycle products."

Oprah.com extends Oprah's self-marketing beyond the show. "When Oprah does something, there is an immediate 'click' impact," said Heather Dougherty, senior analyst at Nielsen/Net Ratings. "She has a very deep site" with 2.2 million unique visitors, and "the deeper the site, the better the engagement."[1]

THE CONCEPT OF INTEGRATED MARKETING COMMUNICATIONS

Which do you think would sell better—a poor product supported by great marketing communication or a great product supported by poor marketing communication? Actually, the product probably would not do well in either case. A good product that is poorly communicated is unlikely to be perceived appropriately by consumers. And a poor product, no matter how well it is promoted, will quickly become known for its lack of value. This is because social connections among people get the word around.

Marketers need to ensure that all elements of the marketing mix—product, price, promotion (communication), and place—are working together. This chapter deals with communication, which is broader than promotion but includes it within its scope. Recall from Chapter 5 that a product's position is its image relative to competition in the minds of consumers. It would not make sense for Payless shoe stores to carry expensive brands. Nor would it make sense for Campbell's to charge less for its premium soup than its regular soup. Both would seem inconsistent in the minds of consumers. Nearly everything about a product communicates something to consumers. The gold label on Campbell's premium soups communicates quality. The very name *Payless* translates into lower-price shoes. Even where you buy a product says something. Doctors' offices appearances are important - patients will skip the medical procedure or change physicians if they feel uneasy in the office. Medical Centers often hire interior decorators to include carpeted patient areas, art, and other elements that communicate a professional and caring environment.

Communication is the exchange of meaning between or among parties. It involves sharing points of view and is at the heart of forming relationships. You simply cannot connect with customers unless you communicate with them. **Promotion** is the process whereby marketers inform, educate, persuade, remind, and reinforce consumers through communication. It is designed to influence buyers and other publics. Although most marketing communications are aimed at consumers, a significant number also address shareholders, employees, channel members, suppliers, and society. In addition, we will see that effective communication is a two-way street: Receiving messages is often as important as sending them.

Integrated marketing communication (IMC) is the coordination of advertising, sales promotion, personal selling, public relations, and sponsorships to reach consumers with a powerful unified effect. These five elements should not be considered separate entities. In fact, each element of the communication plan often has a multiplier effect on the others. The strategic use of television, newspaper, radio, direct mail, and the Internet can produce an extreme-

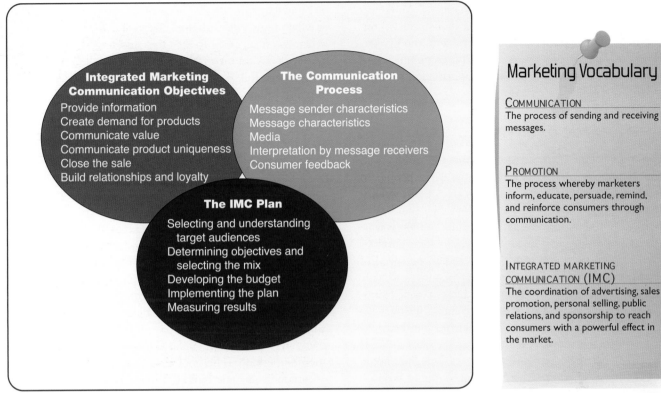

Figure 12.1 The Concept of Integrated Marketing Communications (IMC)

ly successful communication. The Coca-Cola Company has utilized nearly every form of media including television, print ads and the internet to market their products. They also maximize brand awareness, especially in growing markets, through sponsorships such as the 2008 Olympic Games in Beijing, China.[2]

The IMC concept has three parts, as depicted in Figure 12.1. First, it is important to consider the objectives of IMC, which are related to the overall marketing strategy. Second, marketers utilize the communication process characteristics to improve communications. Third each type of communication in the mix accomplishes a unique task. The key is to put several types of communication together to achieve goals; this requires planning, budgeting, implementation, and feedback. We end the chapter with a look at diversity, ethics, and technology issues pertaining to IMC.

Two important goals of IMC are to establish a one-to-one relationship with consumers and to encourage meaningful communication between a firm and its customers. Many companies try to achieve these goals by orchestrating various elements of the promotion mix and creating a brand experience directly with consumers. Oprah creates exceptional experiences that really connect with millions of customers.

OBJECTIVES OF INTEGRATED MARKETING COMMUNICATIONS

Integrated marketing communications has numerous objectives. The most notable are to provide information, create demand, communicate value and product uniqueness, close the sale, and build loyal customer relationships.

PROVIDE INFORMATION

Ultimately, all communication is designed to provide some form of information. It gives consumers what they need to know to make informed choices within a reasonable time frame. Objectives differ depending on the target audience's familiarity with a particular product. If it is relatively unknown, then marketers need to inform and educate the target audience. Often this communication introduces consumers to the product's benefits and uses. When it is working most effectively, information helps consumers make the buying decision. It provides data on a broad range of topics, including product characteristics, uses, availability, prices, and methods of acquisition. Yet, the tremendous number and variety of sources challenge consumers to select and process the most useful information. In many cases, information is purely descriptive. For example, on World AIDS Day 2006, MTV aired 24 advertisements created by six advertising agencies to raise HIV/AIDS awareness.[3] Marketers are challenged to create communications which contribute to the consumer's search for value in the marketplace or marketspace. Consequently, communications should be designed with consumer information needs in mind.

CREATE DEMAND FOR PRODUCTS

Communication helps create demand for products in global and domestic markets. It stimulates people to desire what they do not have and inspires them to earn the money to acquire items that improve their standard of living. Communication helps assure that products will be purchased in sufficient quantities to justify their development, production, and distribution. Today, the speed of communication allows companies to obtain worldwide demand in a short period. Many products marketed globally have coordinated IMC campaigns supported by high-tech information systems. The Internet and company networks make it possible for companies to see what demand is being created by communication in various geographic areas and adjust product availability accordingly. WiFi networks are growing at an unprecedented pace throughout Europe. The demand for WiFi has created collaboration among providers. Trustive, a wireless hotspot access provider, and The Cloud, a wholesale WiFi network operator, agreed to allow Trustive's 3,800 retail customers the ability to access The Cloud's locations.[4] Communication infrastructures provide growing platforms for messages that build demand within society.

COMMUNICATE VALUE

The search for value is complicated because consumers need to assess the benefits of a product relative to thousands of others. Marketers compete to provide value in keeping with consumers' willingness to pay. Consequently, much communication uses creative messages that help convey benefits. For example, Cutler-Hammer technical sales representatives learn about a broad range of sophisticated electronic products. They are taught how to communicate the benefits, functions, and features of each product to the consumer. But to communicate value they must first identify how the customer will use a product. In the case of equipment sold to contractors, they find out how it will be installed. They can then point out cost-saving product attributes due to easy installation and reliable design.

Advertisers are often careful to depict scenes of consumers clearly benefiting from products. Samsung Upstage (SPH-m620) was released in the cell phone mar-

ket to enlarge the music phone niche by Sprint Nextel. It is a flip phone style with dual face; one side is a phone and when you turn it over to the other side, it turns to a music player or TV. In the magazine advertisement, it has a big head line, "Talk, Listen" with the successive photos of a flipping phone, carrying out uses and benefits at once. The ad conveys the benefits available at a reasonable cost.[5]

COMMUNICATE PRODUCT UNIQUENESS

Marketers attempt to communicate uniqueness in order to differentiate their product from others. Burger King is broiled; McDonald's is fried; Southwest Airlines is less expensive because it has no frills; Titleist is used by more professional golfers than any other ball, and so on. In each case marketers are attempting to distinguish their particular product from those of competitors. Marketers also use persuasive communication to convince consumers to switch from one brand to another. Messages compare a product's benefits, functions, and features to the competition. The goal is to illustrate their brand's unique value and build brand preference.

Dr. Martens, a shoe manufacturer, attempts to persuade consumers by using marketing communications that tell the company's history. The campaign describes how Dr. Klaus Martens, the founder, injured his foot while skiing. He then invented a rubber-soled shoe that provides comfort to people on their feet all day. The message is that Dr. Martens, having suffered foot pain himself, knows how to build a shoe superior to that of competitors.

Samsung Upstage (SPH-m620)

CLOSE THE SALE

Communication also helps close the sale. Marketers want their product to be purchased. If the experience is good, chances are it will be repurchased. Thus, IMC seeks to move buyers to action the first time and then reinforce their positive experience so they will buy again and again. Today, customers are selective when they want to receive communications, and often that is just prior to purchase. Many people use the Web to look up ads. Newspaper, magazine, and television ads also are including Web site information so consumers can learn more or refresh their memory about what they have seen. These Web sites are interactive so communication is more personal and involves the consumer. Purchasing is made easy when customers are told just where and how to buy. Numerous Web & Ecommerce Stars highlighted in the text, for example Nike, eBay and Amazon.com, do precisely that.

BUILD RELATIONSHIPS AND LOYALTY

Once consumers have tried a particular brand, marketers remind them why they chose it in the first place and reinforce that behavior. In other words, communication helps maintain brand loyalty. Reminder communications reinforce the popularity of existing goods by reassuring loyal customers that they have made the correct choice. Because consumers tend to pay more attention to ads for products that they currently use, advertising is often meant to reinforce. For example, American Express builds loyalty and relationships with their cardholders by establishing "rewarding relationships" with them.

THE COMMUNICATION PROCESS

The basic communication process is outlined in Figure 12.2. As you can see, messages move from the sender (marketer) to the receiver (consumer). Traditionally, communication has been seen as a one-way process. With the advent of one-to-one marketing through technologies such as the Internet, it is more useful to envision a two-way or continuous flow. Marketers need to start with a clear understanding of the target market, the objectives of the communication, and how to meet those objectives. They should also be aware that proactive customers have their own objectives and use the same process in reverse.

Let's look at the process. Effective communication can be difficult because consumers are bombarded daily by thousands of conflicting messages. Once marketers decide what to communicate, they must encode the message for the target market. It can be spoken, written, illustrated through pictures or diagrams, or conveyed by a combination of these. The encoded message then must be sent to consumers via one or more media: television, radio, newspapers, magazines, telephone, fax, personal contact, the Internet, and others.

Customers must decode, or interpret, the message that marketers send. Each customer's reaction will depend on personal background and experiences. One of

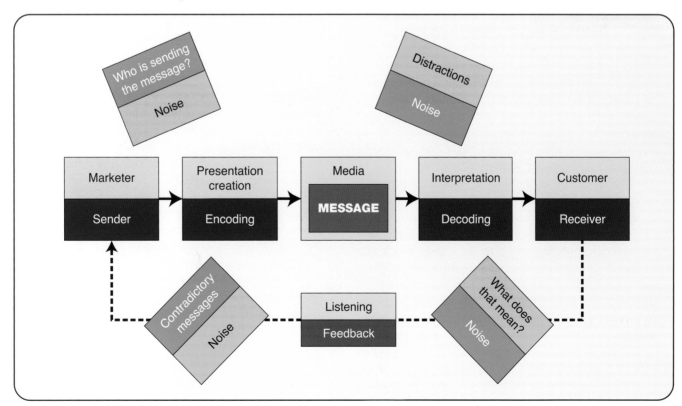

Figure 12.2 The Communication Process

the most important aspects of the communication process is feedback from the target audience. Sometimes it comes in the form of an action by the consumer. For example, if a campaign is designed to encourage product awareness, then positive feedback is an increase in the number of consumers who know about the product, and negative feedback is a flat or declining awareness. Such information is vital because it helps marketers judge whether the message accomplished its goal or needs to be adjusted.

One final element marketers must deal with when communicating to consumers is noise, that is, anything that interferes with a message being received. For example, after talking to a salesperson about a new sports car, you may want to buy it. But then a friend says, "It's a piece of junk." Your friend obviously interferes with the marketer's message. Noise can also occur if you are distracted from receiving the message or if you're not sure who sent the message. We will now look at each element of the communication process shown in Figure 12.2.

THE MESSAGE SENDER

Once marketers have determined that communication is in order, they initiate the process by formulating a message. As the sender, it is the marketer's responsibility to make sure the message is received by the targeted audience, is understood as intended, helps the audience become knowledgeable, and elicits an appropriate response.

Communications take valuable time from the receiver, so it is up to the sender to provide relevant information. Generally, a series of contacts is required. Once a relationship is created between the two parties, communication is much easier for two reasons: The sender learns the most useful information to supply, and the receiver is more inclined to listen. Effective communications obtain consumer responses that contribute to a company's goals. In some cases the message simply identifies the product so potential customers are more likely to include it in their set of possible choices. In other cases it may move consumers to act immediately.

The reputation of the sender—whether a person, a company, or some other organization—influences how consumers receive a message. In fact, when several sources communicate precisely the same message, it is received differently depending on the source. That's why marketers must select exactly the right person to carry their message. EAS launched a $10 million TV and print campaign that featured model Cindy Crawford and her mother to promote its nutritional product. The advertisements, aimed at women with busy lifestyles, appealed to these women by showing Crawford and her mother, Jenny Moluf, as people who lost weight with exercise, proper nutrition and AdvantEdge products. By showing

Crawford as a "soccer mom" who balances motherhood, work, fitness, and nutrition, EAS is shown as smart nutrition for active women.[6] One person usually does not have high credibility with all segments of the population. Different consumers respect, admire, trust, and identify with different types of people. Even within one segment, it's difficult to identify a single spokesperson to whom everyone relates. That is why the famous milk mustache appears on so many faces. For Example Dove Soap's "Campaign for Real Beauty" features advertisements that celebrate everyday women.[7]

What makes a source credible with a target audience? Generally spokespersons are judged according to their expertise, trustworthiness, and attractiveness.

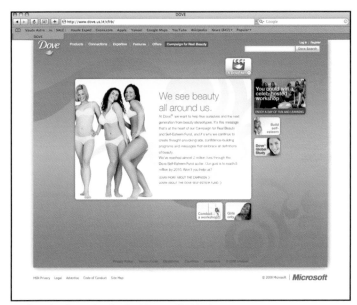

Dove's "Campaign for Real Beauty" Web site

Expertise Consumers attribute expertise to a spokesperson for many reasons. They may believe he or she has specialized training, a great deal of experience, or exceptional knowledge. Some companies hire engineers for industrial sales positions, believing that their academic degree lends special credibility. Doctors are highly credible spokespersons in messages for pain relievers. Children's Tylenol, for example, is promoted as "the first choice of pediatricians." Robitussin notes that it is recommended by physicians, pharmacists, and "Dr. Mom." Both campaigns are based on the credibility of its sources.

Consumers also tend to rely on someone with a lifestyle similar to their own, which accounts for the surge in advertising featuring "average" people. Luvs advertises that not only do average people use its product, but also that "smart moms know that Luvs helps stop leaks."[8] Also, companies use star appeal. Reebok selected NHL star Sidney Crosby as a representative to launch Reebok's

Rbk Edge Uniform system for hockey. Reebok chooses young stars in popular sports to revamp its image among younger consumers.[9]

Trustworthiness Organizations such as the Underwriter's Laboratory, American Medical Association, American Dental Association, Good Housekeeping Institute, and Consumer's Union have gained a great deal of credibility because of their trustworthiness. Not only do they have considerable technical knowledge, but also most consumers perceive them as unbiased. People tend to trust messages from "objective" sources. They also tend to discount messages from sources that stand to benefit in some way. Imagine that you are purchasing an MP3 player and the salesperson constantly emphasizes the importance of an extended warranty. If you know the salesperson gets a commission on warranty sales, you are less likely to believe what he or she is telling you. If no commission is involved, you are more inclined to trust the person.

Attractiveness (Personal Demeanor and Appeal) It's not surprising that attractive, pleasant, likable spokespersons have influence. That's why they are selected to deliver messages. Attractiveness is not about good looks. A source is more attractive if he or she is reliable, pleasant to be around and helpful.

Often celebrities gain credibility in areas outside their careers. For example, some movie stars have influenced political campaigns. When famous endorsers are also informed, their power can be substantial. Actor Leonardo Dicaprio has been involved in raising awareness of environmental issues, in particular, global warming. To set an example, Dicaprio is often seen driving a Toyota Prius, a low-emissions, environmentally friendly vehicle to celebrity events. He also created a short film, "The 11th hour," regarding global warming which premiered at the 2007 Cannes Film Festival.[10] Athletes are obvious choices for promoting sports equipment and

apparel, but the fame they have acquired on the court or playing field translates to other areas.

It's important to note that attractiveness involves all aspects of the source, whether sales personnel or any others who represent an organization. A company's general reputation also applies.

PRESENTATION CREATION: ENCODING

Encoding is the process of translating a message into terms easily understood by the target audience. We know from Chapter 6 that information processing is a complex but very important aspect of the purchase decision. Marketers must encode messages so they are interpreted appropriately by the people for whom they are intended. For example, marketers of fine jewelry have traditionally encoded their messages to reach men—once the main purchasers of engagement rings and other gems as gifts. Today, however, women have higher disposable incomes and increasingly buy expensive "presents" for themselves. Also, as the baby boomer generation reaches milestone anniversaries and birthdays, jewelers expect them to celebrate with the purchase of jewelry. The Diamond Trading Company's adiamondisforever.com Web site allows visitors to create their own diamond engagement rings, encoding the message that buyers can be actively involved in creating their own dream jewelry.[11]

Many messages are screened out by consumers. Although some people seek information on their own, it is up to the sender to stimulate the consumer's interest in receiving a message. This involves grabbing attention and keeping it while the information is

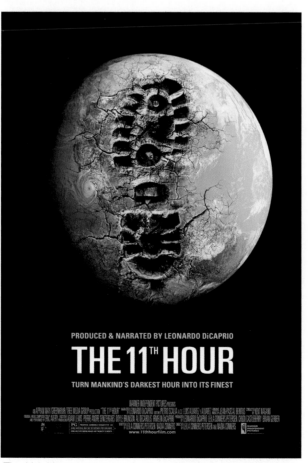

The 11th Hour was produced and narrated by Leonardo Dicaprio.

processed. Messages that are boring, uninteresting, or irrelevant are tuned out. In order to facilitate consumer understanding, communications should limit the amount of information conveyed at one time. We know that consumers take in only a little and that comprehension is based on their life circumstances and experiences. Consequently, effective messages present carefully selected topics in a context relevant to the target audience.

MESSAGE CHARACTERISTICS

There are countless ways to communicate a given message. One viewpoint or several can be presented. Recommendations or conclusions may or may not be included. Key points can be made at the beginning, middle, or end. Humor or fear can be used. And messages may or may not compare a product to those of competitors.

One-Sided and Two-Sided Messages   A **one-sided message** presents only arguments favorable to the source. A **two-sided message** recognizes the arguments against a position and provides the recipient with why reasons are invalid. For example, a message for a fast-food chain might mention only the positive aspects of the ingredients and cooking methods. Or it might present both sides in response to a competitor's charge. When the source and receiver have relatively similar views, a one-sided message is more appropriate. When there is disagreement, a two-sided message often is more useful.

Recommendations or Conclusions   A message can make recommendations or offer conclusions or leave that task to the receiver. Messages with conclusions are more easily understood, but when the audience draws its own conclusion, there is a stronger likelihood of acceptance. This is particularly true for highly educated consumers. If an advertising message is repeated, then the absence of any stated conclusion is likely to make the ad more effective. Repeated exposures give the target audience an opportunity to reach its own conclusions. If the marketer wants the message to have immediate effect, then the communication probably should draw direct conclusions. Rubbermaid launched a new campaign in response to smaller competitors that were rapidly gaining market share. Since Rubbermaid

wanted to influence consumers quickly, its ads were designed to focus on the numerous solutions its products provide to everyday problems. The campaign was reinforced with an 89-page book, *1001 Solutions for Better Living*.[12] Moreover, these days Rubbermaid's Web site, www.rubbermaid.com, provides a "Tips & Solutions" tab containing information to help customers organize life-situations with Rubbermaid products. Visitors can also register for the Rubbermaid Club to receive free promotional coupons.[13] This type of promotional effort draws direct conclusions for customers about product benefits.

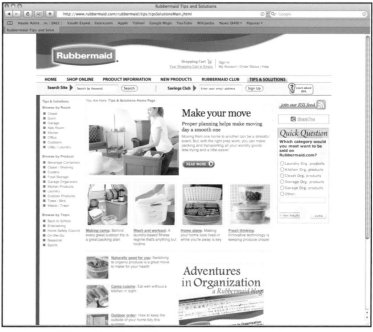

Rubbermaid's "Tips & Solutions" helps customers organize life-situations.

Order of Presentation   The placement of the key point of a communication affects how the message is interpreted and later recalled by buyers. More is remembered about the beginning and end of a message than its middle. Therefore, effective presentations usually open and close with strong statements. Weaker arguments are most often placed in the middle.

Humor   Viewers like humorous ads because they are novel and enjoyable. But advertisers must be careful not to let humor obscure the message. There are several things to keep in mind.

- Be sure to mention the brand name within the first 10 seconds. Otherwise, the communication runs the risk of inhibiting recall of key selling points.
- Subtle humor is more effective than bizarre humor.

Madeline Shoes uses humor in advertising to sell its shoes.

- Humor must be relevant to the brand or the key selling point. Without this linkage, recall and persuasion are diminished.
- It is best not to use humor that belittles or makes fun of the potential user. Jokes about the brand, the situation, or the subject matter are usually more effective.[14]

Evidence is still inconclusive as to whether a humorous approach is more effective than a serious one. Although humor tends to increase attention, it also may distract from or decrease acceptance of the message. Humorous commercials for Bud Light won the Super Bowl XL 18th Annual Ad Meter of USA Today. The "magic fridge" advertisement featured a man with unwelcome guests hiding his refrigerator - full of Bud Light - through a rotating wall. The neighbors loved the fridge of Bud Light that kept appearing as if by magic.[15] TBS runs an annual special at which it counts down the funniest advertisements of the year from around the world. Its www.veryfunnyads.com Web site allows users to stream the nominees and offers additional ad exposure for companies.

Humor is constantly utilized to create a viral message. The intention of humor is to make people laugh enough to tell their friends, which is an efficient way to pass around the message. Budweiser's "Whassup" campaign from the early 21st century is one of the legendary paragons of viral advertising. Widespread high-speed Internet access and online video sites like YouTube are facilitating the growth of viral advertising.

Fear Appeals Marketers sometimes use fear to gain the attention and interest of their audience. Campaigns by the American Dental Association warn that poor dental hygiene can result in tooth decay, gum disease, and loss of teeth. In some instances, advertisers play on fear for the safety of loved ones. A Michelin spot shows a baby floating in a tire and reminds parents, "You have a lot riding on them." An advertisement for seat belt use by the Michigan Association for Traffic Safety pictures a wheelchair: "It's your choice."

In many instances fear appeals are very effective. They can create higher attention and interest in the message. By Petty and Cacioppo's theory of persuasion, fear appeal works more successfully in a high involvement product than in a low involvement product. Moreover there is no different outcome between customers of different or even contrary cultural background since fear is one of the basic human emotions. [16]

Comparative Messages In the 1970s, the Federal Trade Commission began allowing advertisers to name competitors in ads. Since then, many companies have chosen to compare their products with those of rivals. There have been sneaker wars, hamburger wars, beer wars, and cola wars. In each case, claims and counterclaims have been used in comparative messages. Do these techniques work? They certainly draw attention. Even though comparative messages allow marketers to present clear, objective arguments in favor of their product, many companies hesitate to use the technique. References to the competition may inadvertently cause the consumer to recall that product at the time of purchase. In addition, competitors may legally challenge claims of superiority or respond with comparative ads of their own.

In general, comparative messages may be more useful for companies with a lower market share, since they have little to lose by confronting the leader. For them, the potential gain in consumer awareness outweighs the likelihood that a large competitor will

Life insurance isn't for the people who die.
It's for the people who live.

Sara's father died of cancer. He didn't live to see all the important moments in his daughter's life. But because he had enough life insurance, she'll have the kind of life he always wanted for her.
It you died today, where would the money come from for your family to live on? To pay the mortgage? To educate the kids? Would your financial plan guarantee a secure future like Sara's?
That's what life insurance is for. To find out more, talk to a life insurance agent or other financial advisor

LIFE
LIFE AND HEALTH INSURANCE FOUNDATION FOR EDUCATION & NONPROFIT ORGANIZATION

For a free consumer's guide to insurance, call 888-LIFE-777 or visit us on the Internet at http://www.life-line.org

Sometimes life insurance marketing builds public awareness by using fear appeals to persuade customers to act on the message.

launch a counterattack. Centennial Wireless, a wireless communications company, uses this tactic by featuring dim-witted "employees" from other wireless networks such as Verizon Wireless and Sprint. The intent was to give consumers the perception that Centennial Wireless is superior to their larger and better known competitors. [17]

MEDIA

Media are the means for transmitting messages from the sender to the receiver. There are three categories—personal, mass, and mixed—each with its advantages and disadvantages, as summarized in Figure 12.3.

Personal media involve direct contact, such as face-to-face communication or telephone conversations. These two-way exchanges allow for creative solutions to the consumer's problem. There is ample opportunity for relationships to form. Each party can assess the characteristics of the other. Although the telephone does not provide physical contact, it has dramatic cost advantages over personal encounters. Hot lines are an effective way to support customers after a sale. They not only help when problems arise with a product but also offer all kinds of advice that ultimately can maintain customer loyalty. Dell users have access to technical support 24 hours a day via its 1-800 number, through e-mail, or by means of real time online chat.[18] The disadvantage of personal media is its expense. Each representative can only have a limited number of conversations, and the costs associated with hiring, training, and motivating people can be very high.

Mass media include television, radio, magazines, billboards, brochures, and one-way Internet. Services are readily available to help plan for and acquire space in most markets around the world. CIO Communications, Inc., for instance, offers a resource center on the Web to assist with media planning.[19] Messages can be developed prior to being communicated through a range of nonpersonal sources. Since there are many media choices, nearly all customers can be contacted at a reasonable cost. The downside of using the mass media is the lack of interactive or two-way communication. Because it is

	Examples	Advantages	Disadvantages
Personal Media	Face-to-face Telephone	Two-way communication Allows for creative problem solving Flexible tailoring of messages Immediate response	Expensive Time-consuming Parties must be brought together at one time
Mass Media	Television Radio Magazines Newspapers Billboards Brochures	Messages can be developed prior to sending Low cost Many media choices Reaches most customers inexpensively	Messages tend to be one-way Preparations are expensive Harder to obtain feedback
Mixed (personal and mass combined)	Fax Internet Answering machine	Delayed or interactive Two-way communication Low cost	Receiver needs technology Lack of consumer experience

Figure 12.3   Media Advantages and Disadvantages

impossible to get quick feedback, a great deal is spent beforehand on research that listens to the customer. Furthermore, ad preparation can be expensive and take a long time.

The mixed media approach combines personal and mass communication and has many of the benefits of both. First, material can be developed well in advance and offered in both print (fax) and audio (via Internet) formats. Technology now allows for faxes to be sent over the Internet. Fax.com lets users send an e-mail to any fax machine and send faxes via its website. It provides subscribers with a unique fax number, eliminating the cost of a fax line, and sends incoming faxes straight to their e-mail as .pdf files. This use of mixed media provides effective two-way communication at a low cost.[20] Second, because mixed media can reach large numbers simultaneously, the technique is very cost-effective. A possible disadvantage is that fax and voice mail numbers are the property of the receiver, so the sender must be careful to respect privacy. A definite disadvantage is that many consumers lack the necessary technology or the experience to use it.

INTERPRETATION BY RECEIVERS: DECODING

Strong communications begin with an understanding of target audiences. People are not passive receivers of communications. In fact, they resist persuasion by refuting arguments, attacking the source, distorting messages, rationalizing, and tuning out. Many consumers regard marketing messages as "tricks" to make them purchase a particular product.

Refuting arguments is one way consumers resist persuasion. Weak messages may backfire as consumers create stronger counterarguments in their own mind. Another defense mechanism is to attack the source. Consumers may discount claims of comfort, prestige, or gas mileage because they don't trust the automobile company. All messages are automatically rejected. Attacking the source rather than the ideas being communicated is common in politics. When politicians don't have a very convincing case, they are likely to strike out at the people who reject their arguments.

Intelligence and self-esteem have a lot to do with susceptibility to persuasion. Highly intelligent people are more likely to be influenced by logical, precise, and complex information. Others have to be very carefully led through an argument. Depending on the audience, marketers should let some people draw their own conclusions. It is not surprising that people with low-self esteem tend to be easily persuaded. They often rely on others in developing attitudes and making choices. Messages designed for such people should avoid complex arguments.[21]

> ### Marketing Vocabulary
>
> **MEDIA**
> The channels through which messages are communicated.
>
> **PERSONAL SELLING**
> Face-to-face or other individual communication between a buyer and a seller.

CONSUMER FEEDBACK

Listening is an important way to learn what consumers think. Feedback is essential to a customer-focused company, and it helps the marketer adjust communications. Today, many organizations consider listening to be the first step in the communication process, even before the message is created. By listening to the consumer they determine needs and wants as well as how to structure communication.

THE COMMUNICATION MIX

TYPES OF COMMUNICATION ACTIVITIES

The five main types of communication activities are personal selling, sales promotion, advertising, public relations, and sponsorship. Figure 12.4 describes some characteristics of each type.

Personal Selling **Personal selling** requires person-to-person communication between buyer and seller. Generally, this occurs

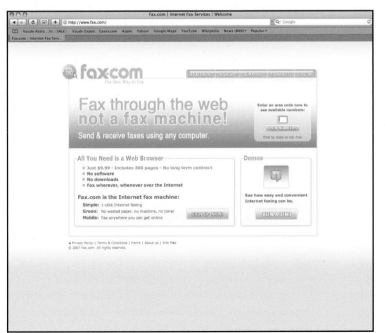

Fax.com provides inexpensive two-way communication.

	Personal Selling	**Sales Promotion**	**Advertising**	**Public Relations**	**Sponsorship**
Focus	Person-to-person interaction	Support of sales activity	Mass communication directed at target segments	Unpaid publicity that enhances the company and its products	Cash or resources in support of an event
Objective	Develop business relationship resulting in loyal customers	Obtain immediate sale and remind after the sale	Position the product and/or increase sales	Gain a favorable impression	Be associated with influential groups
Example	Pharmaceutical salesperson	Point-of-sale displays	Billboards	Press releases	Team sponsorship
	Computer and tele-communications sales	T-shirts with company name	TV ads	Charitable projects	Sport tournaments
	Retail sales	Special sales	Magazine ads	Civic leadership	Arts events
	Consulting sales	2-for-1 offers	Direct mail	Company spokesperson gives association speech	Association events
Appeal	Personal	Move buyer to action	Mass	Mass	Market segment
Cost per customer	Very high	Low	Low to high	Very low	High to low
Amount and speed of feedback	A lot and immediately	A little and fairly fast	A little and delayed	A little and fairly fast	A lot and fast

Figure 12.4   The Characteristics of Communication Activities

face-to-face, although it also may involve the telephone, videoconferencing, or interactive computer linkages. Despite its relatively high cost, personal selling continues to be the most important part of business-to-business marketing and is also significant in sales of big-ticket consumer items, such as autos, computers, and housing. The objective of most personal selling is to build loyal relationships with customers that result in profitable sales volume. For example, physicians say that pharmaceutical salespeople are the most effective when they develop personal relationships and build rapport through their personal selling techniques. Since personal selling provides two-way communication, it is possible to engage in a dialogue that leads to problem solving, consulting and relationship building. Because this is generally the most expensive form of contact, salespeople are trained to do the best possible job of helping a customer find solutions through use of their goods and services.

Advertising   **Advertising** is paid, nonpersonal communication from an identified sponsor using mass media to persuade or influence an audience. It includes newspapers, television, radio, magazines, direct mail, bill-boards, the Internet, and point-of-sale displays. It is con-

sidered mass communication because the same message is sent throughout the targeted audience and the rest of the market. A major objective of advertising is to support product positioning. The same basic theme usually is sent through all advertising channels. Television ads for Charmin have been reinforced by point-of-sale displays featuring Mr. Whipple, the "don't squeeze the Charmin" grocery clerk. Depending on audience size, cost per consumer can be very low. In 2008, it was estimated that 97.5 million people watched the Super Bowl. Companies paid as much as $3 million for a 30-second ad, or $100,000 a second. However, these figures average out to a low cost per viewer, around $0.03 per person.[22] Because advertising plays a supportive role, it is sometimes difficult to determine just how well it works, in relation to other parts of the marketing mix. For example, the effects of accompanying shifts in product distribution and pricing often are felt more quickly.

Sales Promotion   **Sales promotion** is communication designed to stimulate immediate purchases using tools such as coupons, contests, and free samples. Since the approach generally is designed to stimulate immediate purchases, its effectiveness can be easily measured.

Sometimes sales promotion is meant to remind customers after the sale, which contributes to relationship building. For example, a box of cookies may contain a discount coupon for the next box. Sales promotions usually last a short time. Mrs. Field's used all of the following promotions to celebrate its 30th birthday. Its coupons were on the newsletters of iVillage.com's Home & Food Channel; product boxes contained promotional materials; a tasting event and vote for favorite cookie was held at Mrs. Fields stores and NBC properties; the top five cookies were offered as samples across the US. [23]

Public Relations **Public relations (PR)** is the use of publicity and other nonpaid forms of communication designed to present the firm and its products positively. Because they are not paying for space, companies do not have total control over what is disseminated. The most common public relations channel is the news media. Of course, publicity can be negative. For example, news media broadcast a lot of negative information about the Ford Explorer when Firestone tires failed on the vehicle. Ford executives launched a massive public relations campaign, issuing statements to the press to counteract the negative press after the recall of over 6 million tires. Despite the PR campaign, Ford decided to launch a paid-for national mail campaign to assure owners of the vehicles' safety.[24]

Sponsorships A major form of communication is sponsorships, which are reaching 10 to 15 percent of promotion budgets. A **sponsorship** is the exchange of money (or some other form of value) in return for a public association with an event. Automobile companies sponsor many Professional Golfers' Association tournaments. There are 34 PGA Tour events with a title sponsor or a presenting sponsor, and almost one-third, 11 events, are sponsored by them.[25] Coca-Cola, PepsiCo, General Motors, Anheuser-Busch, United Parcel Service, and Nissan are among the largest sponsors of sports. Corporate sponsorship is everywhere in NASCAR, from sponsors of individual drivers to official NASCAR products. A study by James Madison University found that NASCAR fans have an impressive awareness of the sport's sponsors. Unaided awareness for official sponsors averaged almost 50 percent. More than 50 percent of fans surveyed said they feel like they are contributing to the sport when they purchase the products of a sponsor.[26] Virtually all sporting events are sponsored now by either major products or corporations or dot-com companies. The 2008 college football bowl season featured games such as the Tostitos Fiesta Bowl, the Allstate Sugar Bowl, the FedEx Orange Bowl, and the Rose Bowl was presented by Citi, each explicitly showcasing its sponsor's name.[27]

Sponsorships usually are integrated with all other aspects of the communications mix. General Motors takes its key dealers and business customers to the NASCAR racing events it sponsors, features the races in its magazine ads, and cites testimonials from NASCAR drivers. This benefits both parties of the sponsorship.

Marketing Vocabulary

ADVERTISING
Paid communication through non-personal channels.

SALES PROMOTION
A communication designed to stimulate immediate purchase using such tools as coupons, contests and free samples.

PUBLIC RELATIONS (PR)
Unpaid promotion designed to present the firm and its products in a positive light in the buyers mind.

SPONSORSHIP
The exchange of money (or some other form of value) in return for a public association with an event.

NASCAR fans have strong awareness of sponsors.

The Marketing Gazette™

CREATING & CAPTURING VALUE THROUGH GLOBAL RELATIONSHIPS

Multinationals Target China's "Little Emperors" with Ads and Promotions

"We used to go to dim sum on Sunday morning with the old folks," laments a Chinese mother, "but now my son is nine, he insists we go to McDonald's. Otherwise, he stays at home. What can we do?" This complaint is typical of mothers in China's cities. In urban areas, where a government policy of one child per family is strictly enforced, the one and only exerts a lot of influence on household purchasing decisions, especially if that child is a boy. These "little emperors" are also beneficiaries of the "six-pocket syndrome," with as many as six doting adults—parents and grandparents—to indulge every whim. It is easy to understand why multinational companies are aiming their promotional efforts straight for children and teenagers quickly approaching adulthood.

Danone S.A. of France, Nestlé of Switzerland, and U.S.-based H. J. Heinz Company have set up shop in China, marketing such foods as yogurt, milk, and cheese. Toy and technology companies such as Bandai, Lego, VTech Holdings, and IBM have stepped up their sales efforts. For multinationals, Chinese children are the key that will open the door to a burgeoning market. Even companies with products that are not sold to children have redirected their promotional efforts to the younger set. General Electric sponsors China's version of Sesame Street in the hopes of instilling its corporate name in the mind of a future generation.

Many spoiled Chinese youth spend their free time in front of the television. Companies have been taking advantage of this, which is one reason why TV advertising is booming in China. And although the Chinese are less familiar with sales promotions, companies will need to provide coupons and point-of-purchase samples to spur parents to buy what they see on TV. Not much is known about the buying habits of little emperors and their parents, but advertisers have discovered several guidelines.

- Education is a key value. In China it is not uncommon for pregnant women to play English and Chinese tapes to their bellies to give their budding babies a linguistic head start. Mothers pay over $70 for a VTech English alphabet desk, even though it costs more than they earn in a week. With only one child to assure the family's future, parents of little emperors are receptive to ads that emphasize learning.

- Kids covet Western goods. Nike shoes and Western blue jeans are seen as status symbols by Chinese kids. As the first generation to grow up in a consumer society, they are tuned in to messages of Western ads and do not want to "buy Chinese." Still, as consumer culture develops, advertisers will need to differentiate their products rather than just feature the "Western" label.

- Chinese culture cannot be ignored. For thousands of years, Confucian tradition has emphasized respect for authority and family harmony. Ads in China uniformly portray happy families. Smart-aleck teens arguing with parents would not appeal to Chinese consumers. Advertisers must walk a thin line in marketing Western goods with a Chinese flavor. Coca-Cola China, Ltd., spent two years on market research before introducing a new fruit drink. Not only does Tian Yu Di (heaven and earth) feature a Chinese name, but also the attractive container has an image of China's Yellow Mountain and calligraphy by a Chinese master.

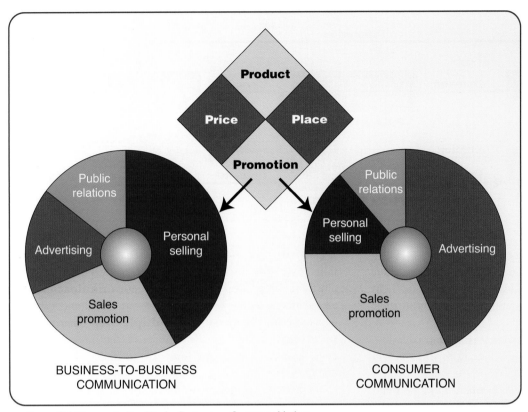

Figure 12.5 Communication Mix for Business vs. Consumer Markets

FACTORS AFFECTING THE COMMUNICATION MIX

Marketers must consider several factors in selecting the communication mix. The most important are whether the audience is the business-to-business or consumer market, whether a push or pull strategy is desirable, the product's stage in the life cycle, and whether opinion leaders will play a role.

Business Versus Consumer Markets All forms of marketing communication are important in both business-to-business and consumer marketing. Yet, the emphasis is different in each area, as seen in Figure 12.5. Personal selling is most important in marketing to businesses, whereas advertising dominates in the consumer products arena. Sales promotion is equally important in both and outweighs advertising in business markets. Public relations is relatively less important in both. One reason for these differences is costs. Mailing a catalog can cost $1 per customer; a personalized e-mail can Internet advertising revenue was estimated at about $21 billion in 2007, a 25 percent increase from 2006.[28] Per exposure, television advertising can cost less than a few cents; a print ad slightly more; direct mail, a dollar or two; a telephone call, about $10; and face-to-face personal selling, more than several hundred dollars. Although public relations involves no such expenditure, it cannot com-

pare to the other forms in terms of effectiveness and the degree of message control.

Pull Versus Push Strategies Marketers attempt to influence the market through either a push or pull strategy, as illustrated in Figure 12.6. In many cases they use both. A **pull strategy** attempts to influence consumers directly. Communication is designed to build demand so consumers will "pull" the product through the channel of distribution. In other words, consumers ask retailers for the product, who in turn ask wholesalers, who in turn contact the manufacturer. Many service firms use price discounts as pull strategies. But effectiveness of price discounts as a pull strategy has been suspicious.[29] For an airline company, dynamic pricing was proven to be the starting point for a competent pull strategy.[30]

Although pull strategies tend to be used often for consumer products, they also have a place in business-to-business marketing. For example, marketers of electrical control and distribution equipment often target the purchasing agent with their messages. Sales representatives call on design firms, which then specify that particular electrical equipment in the engineering design.

The **push strategy** involves communicating to distribution channel members, which in turn promote to the end user. This is particularly common in industrial or business-to-business marketing. Marketers often train distribution channel members on the sales techniques they believe are most suited to their products. The push technique is also used in retail marketing. For example, many manufacturers who sell to

Marketing Vocabulary

PULL STRATEGY
An attempt to influence consumers directly so they will "pull" the product through the distribution channel.

PUSH STRATEGY
Communication to distribution channel members, which in turn will promote or "push" the product to the end user.

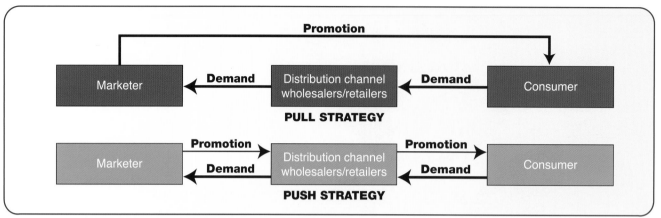

Figure 12.6   Pull Versus Push Strategies

Home Depot, such as cabinet manufactures, train Home Depot in-store sales people on the best way to sell their brand. They provide sales aids and literature to help Home Depot representatives entice consumers to their brands.[31]

Often, a **push-pull strategy** is appropriate. The combination approach markets directly to the channel and to the end user. This can speed product adoption and strengthen market share. Conflicts often occur between the marketing organization and its distributors. For example, in the food industry, retailers want to carry products that yield the greatest profitability. Since these may not be brands with the strongest pull, retailers may charge marketers for shelf space. Essentially, they are being paid to push the product to the end user. Using a pull strategy to create strong demand at the consumer level makes channel members more willing to handle the product.

Product's Stage in the Life Cycle   The appropriate use of the communication mix is related to the product's stage in the life cycle. Consumers need to be informed and educated about new products, whereas they may need to be persuaded to purchase during growth and early maturity. Reminders and reinforcement are most appropriate in the mature and declining phases of the life cycle. Think about how companies advertise clothing styles. Most department stores or clothing stores do not advertise or promote swimwear in the winter, nor do they promote wool coats in July. Other products also have life cycles and advertisers adapt their methods to the cycles. As the Tickle Me Elmo doll began to sell out in stores at the height of its popularity, Tyco temporarily pulled its television ads. Today, the product is not marketed because its life cycle has greatly declined. In other words, communications were adjusted to match the stages of the product life cycle.

Opinion Leadership   Marketing communications reach consumers directly and indirectly. Figure 12.7 illustrates both paths. In **one-step communication**, all members of the target audience are simultaneously exposed to the same message. **Multiple-step communication** uses influential members of the target audience, known as **opinion leaders**, to filter a message before it reaches other group members, modifying its effect positively or negatively for the rest of the group.[32]

Because of their important role, opinion leaders have often been called gatekeepers to indicate the control they have over ideas flowing into the group. Marketers interested in maximizing communication effectiveness nearly always attempt to identify opinion leaders. Opinion lead-

Career Tip:

The Web is an abundant source for information regarding advertising, public relations, personal selling, and other career opportunities. You'll have an opportunity to explore your career of interest or research a specific company. You will also discover links to networks allow you to post a résumé, receive daily news briefs, or access a job information service. Popular career sites include www.monster.com, www.careerbuilder.com, or search within your desired industry for professional associations that post jobs in a particular field.

ers are open to communications from all sources. They are more inclined to be aware of information regarding a broad range of subjects. They read a lot and talk with salespeople and other people who have information about products. Opinion leaders can have a sort of multiplier effect, intensifying the strength of the message if they respond positively and pass it on to others. Consequently, the resources used to gain support from opinion leaders are probably well spent.

Public figures are often opinion leaders. Consider the sales boost for several titles after Oprah Winfrey introduced her "book of the month club" feature. She

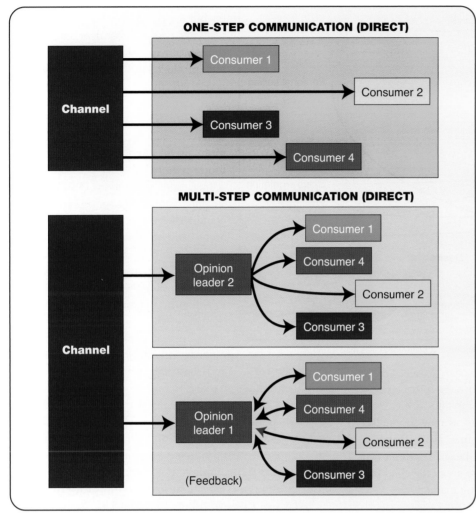

Figure 12.7 Opinion Leadership

nication plan is built. The steps are outlined in Figure 12.8. The IMC plan should never be developed in isolation from the strategic marketing plan. It's the responsibility of strategic marketing personnel to define the role of communication in the overall marketing strategy. The IMC plan is designed to position the organization and its products in a manner consistent with that strategy.

has influenced so many consumers with her highly regarded opinion that her selections have become best-sellers.[33]

DEVELOPING THE INTEGRATED MARKETING COMMUNICATIONS PLAN

Now that we have examined the factors influencing the process, let us see how an integrated marketing commu-

SELECTING AND UNDERSTANDING TARGET AUDIENCES

Understanding the target audience is the most important part of communications planning. First, remember that the overall market needs to be segmented, and each segment should be treated uniquely. For every target audience, communications experts need to understand all aspects of consumer behavior: where, how, and why they

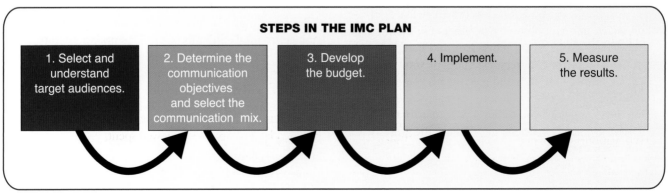

Figure 12.8   Developing the Communication Plan

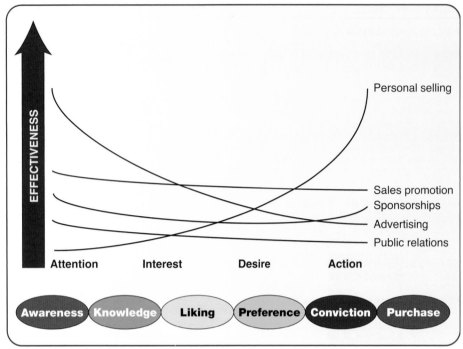

Figure 12.9 Effectiveness of Main Types of Communication at Different Stages in the Consumer Buying Process

buy as well as how they obtain and process information. In new and developing markets, companies sometimes must operate more by trial and error as they gradually come to know buying habits. For instance, as the People's Republic of China encourages more businesses to set up shop, multinationals are learning more about the children and youth segments of this burgeoning market.

DETERMINING OBJECTIVES AND SELECTING THE IMC MIX

Consumers move from a lack of awareness about brands to purchase and loyalty. This process of increasing involvement can be described by hierarchical models. The most straightforward of these is AIDA, which stands for attention, interest, desire, and action.[34] Figure 12.9 depicts AIDA and a more detailed version that includes awareness, knowledge, liking, preference, conviction, and purchase. For example, imagine that an in-line skater suddenly crosses your path and breaks your concentration (awareness). Next, you ask friends how they like their in-line skates, and you observe how others use the product (knowledge). Perhaps you rent a pair and have so much fun that you consider purchasing skates of your own (liking). By talking to friends and reading ads you develop a brand preference. Elaborate in-store displays and product guarantees convince you to buy a particular brand (conviction). Finally, you decide to purchase the skates with your credit card.[35]

As marketers plan their communication activities, they must keep the objective in mind. Is it to create awareness, build brand preference, or encourage purchase? The IMC mix will vary considerably depending on the objective. To create awareness and product knowledge, advertising is very effective. It gains attention and even can lead to liking and brand preference. Once desire is created, however, sales promotion may be more useful. At this point the customer is more influenced by personal selling, sales promotions, and sponsorships. Attending a sponsored event could make the product so immediately salient that the consumer decides to buy. Sales promotions involving coupons, price incentives, or in-store samples may move buyers to action by reinforcing their conviction to try the brand. The effectiveness of personal selling increases dramatically in the later stages of the buying process. This is especially true for high-priced items in consumer markets, but in some business markets personal selling may be necessary just to gain attention. Although public relations appears to be least useful—because it tapers off after the attention stage and remains low compared to the others—keep in mind the lower cost. Other than the fairly minor expense of creating the public relations message, there is no cost for delivering it.

AT&T's VP-advertising, Wendy Clark, said, "We believe in taking a very robust approach to our media plan, with a full array of broadcast, online, print, and outdoor, as well as some unexpected media elements," when it launched a new campaign on December 31, 2005. An enormous billboard on the building from which the ball dropped on New Year's Eve in Times Square and an online roadblock on January 9, that was seen by a likely 50 percent of the total Internet audience. AT&T also spotted itself during the Super Bowl, Academy Awards, and college playoff telecasts. [36]

DEVELOPING THE COMMUNICATION BUDGET

The communication budget falls within expenditures for the entire marketing mix. Consequently, establishing the specific amount for IMC requires an understanding of the overall marketing strategy, the financial resources available, and the contribution communication is expected to make. In allocating IMC money it must be remembered that some activities can be started or stopped quickly, such as advertising and sales promotion. Personal selling often must be adjusted more slowly, since time is required to hire, train, and deploy the sales force.

The IMC budget is usually determined in two steps.

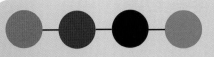

globalEDGE™
Integrated Marketing Communications

Your firm has decided that the most efficient way to decide which markets are most ready for an integrated and seamless marketing campaign is to assess the level of global information technology of each market. Review a recent study on the topic and provide a report concerning the ten markets most prepared for your firm's planned marketing campaign. In which region(s) is each market located? As a result of these findings, is it possible to organize your campaign to be less expensive? Provide justification for your proposal(s).

First, the total allocation is decided. Second, the amount for each type of communication is assigned.

Determining the Overall Budget The first issue is how much it will cost to accomplish the objective. Generally, communication objectives are established once a year. Two-thirds of advertising budgets for the following year are submitted to top marketing management during September or October, and nearly 80 percent are approved by November.[37] Most IMC budgets are based on one of the following: percentage of sales, competitive budgeting, payout plan, or cost of tasks that must be performed to accomplish objectives.

Deciding precisely how much to invest in communication requires a lot of financial calculations. It is important to establish the contribution of IMC to volume objectives and determine resulting profits and cash flows. In doing these calculations, most organizations forecast sales levels based on total expenditures. The latter include all costs that can be realistically allocated to the communication campaign such as special training and compensation for the sales force. The forecasts are based on marketing research about consumer responses to communications, expected IMC spending by competitors, and product demand estimates. The percentage of sales method simply estimates the sales level and then allocates a certain percentage of sales to communications. Often the percentage is set at the industry average. Sometimes it is based on the previous year's sales. In either case, the problem is that sales are used to create the communications budget, whereas IMC should

be used to create sales. Because the method is very easy to administer, however, it is used widely.

Competitive budgeting involves determining what rivals are spending and setting the budget accordingly. The deregulation of the telecommunications industry probably influenced the budgeting strategies of large companies such as AT&T and Sprint. In order to maintain a strong presence in the market, such companies must be able to keep up with the IMC spending of competitors.

The payout plan method is generally used for new products that require high communication expenditures. The marketer estimates future sales and establishes the budget required to gain initial acceptance and trial of the product. Generally, IMC costs are very high relative to sales, in some cases even greater. The early expenditures are deemed reasonable because of the payback expected in later years. This is similar to investing money in product development.

The task method sets specific sales targets or other

Web and E-commerce Stars
MySpace - www.myspace.com

MySpace.com is the most visited Web site by teenagers and college students. This site allows a visitor to create their own page to share items such as photos and personal interests with mutual friends. Since so many people are connected through MySpace, it is a great advertising opportunity for events, products and companies. The popularity of MySpace continues to rise as it is featured in films, videos, and music. Beyond connecting with friends, MySpace provides a classified section where users can find information on job opportunities, housing, and local services. The social network of MySpace is limitless, and as long as users are creating their personal pages and conversing with friends across the world, there will continue to be a medium for marketers.

objectives and then determines what activities and amounts are required to accomplish them. This approach can be very complex and tends to be used by large organizations in highly competitive environments. Marketers must have very accurate information and considerable experience in order to develop the extensive models necessary. The task method is superior to the others because so much detailed attention is paid to how IMC contributes to accomplishing objectives.

Allocating the Budget Communication works synergistically. In other words, investments in one type of communication may help other types accomplish their objectives. A salesperson benefits tremendously from awareness created by advertising and from purchase incentives due to sales promotion. The integrated aspect of marketing communication needs to be kept in mind when deciding the allocation for each activity. This process requires considerable and continuous dialogue among marketing team members. In many cases, data are fed into computer simulations that help determine the best allocations. In other cases, the team simply estimates what is required. In companies with major brands, many executives are usually involved, including senior management media and advertising staff, marketing personnel, brand marketing management, and sales personnel. The allocations may be determined by very specific objectives. When Nike wanted to increase traffic in retail outlets, it budgeted more for signage. When Westinghouse process control wanted to increase name recognition, it shifted resources from the sales force to advertising.

IMPLEMENTATION

Implementation of an IMC plan tends to be done by functional specialists with considerable experience in their field. There are ample career opportunities in these areas—such as personal selling, advertising, and public relations—because each is multifaceted and challenging. Marketers strive to obtain uniquely talented employees and suppliers to carry out communication programs. No matter how good the plan, without creative and professional implementation, all is lost.

The first decision is how much to do in-house and how much to outsource. For example, personal selling can be done by company personnel, manufacturer representatives (private salespeople), or distributors. Likewise, companies must decide whether to do their own advertising and sales promotion or hire outsiders. Most large and medium-sized firms outsource much of their IMC implementation. Often representatives from these advertising and promotion agencies work on-site with the client's marketing executives and personnel.

MEASURING IMC RESULTS

It was John Wanamaker, a famous 19th-century retailer, who first said: "I know that half of the money I spend on advertising is wasted, but I can never figure out which half." He was referring to the fact that many messages may never reach much of the target audience. Important questions are: Who is reached by a communication, and what does it accomplish relative to the goals established in the plan?

Why is it difficult to estimate the results of communication? The major problem is isolating the effects of one part of the IMC plan to determine its relative influence on product performance. Most marketers start by identifying criteria or measures. Performance measures are variables or factors that tell us how well the organization or product is doing. Common measures are market share, sales level, and profitability. Other factors are often used, such as number of loyal customers, amount of brand recognition, brand image, and knowledge of the product.

Once performance measures are selected, the task of assessing IMC influence can begin. Very seldom is only one part of the IMC mix adjusted at a time, and competitors' activities are virtually never stable. So determining the precise effect of communication is rarely possible. When Nike introduces a new model, how much of its success can be attributed to pricing, product distribution, customer service, or promotion? Still, by monitoring IMC expenditures and performance measures for a large number of companies and then applying statistical analysis, researchers can get a good idea of the overall effect of IMC. This information is very useful in determining whether objectives are being met and whether changes are required.

Creative, professional employees are essential in implementing an IMC plan.

ISSUES IN COMMUNICATION

DIVERSITY

Effective communications are carefully targeted. The vast differences among consumers create opportunities for a wide variety of promotions to meet their needs. For example, 54 million Americans have some form of disability, and marketers are changing the way they communicate with these consumers. Long ignored, these Americans with disabilities represent several substantial target segments.[38] Marketers now have a new vehicle for communicating with many of these consumers—the Internet.

Until recently the Web was not very user friendly for people with limited vision or dexterity. The American Federation for the Blind (AFB) and Interliant, Inc. recently redesigned the AFB's Web site, www.afb.org, to better accommodate Internet users with disabilities. Previous assistive technologies such as screen magnifiers or screen readers did not properly read site content, but the new site allows for a much more completely accessible site. Graphics are now labeled with text that can be read by screen readers and all audio on the site is now available in text form so that it can be read by the hearing impaired. The AFB's site, serves as a model for other government sites, which are required by the 1998 Rehabilitation Act to make the information they provide on their sites accessible to those with disabilities.[39]

Disability-online.com is a content and commerce Internet site for people with disabilities. Visitors to the site can find relevant news articles, information on technology that can make living easier, issues related to schools and child disabilities, and health and medical information. In addition, site visitors can find stories about other people with disabilities who continue to enjoy doing many things. Visitors can also become members of the site and receive e-mail updates and articles based on their interests. The site aims to assist people with disabilities in independent living.[40]

Promotions in general are becoming more inclusive by depicting people with disabilities. Public tolerance of insensitivity toward people with disabilities is decreasing. When Nike ran ads that claimed its trail running shoes would prevent a jogger from running into a tree and becoming a "drooling, misshapen, non-extreme-trail-running husk of my former self," it met with swift opposition and Nike removed the advertisement with a formal apology.

ETHICS

Marketers must be careful about how they communicate. The American Marketing Association Code of Ethics states that acceptable standards include, "avoidance of false and misleading advertising, rejection of high-pressure manipulations, or misleading sales tactics, and avoidance of communications that use deception or manipulation." Despite these guidelines, the ethical boundaries for promotion are not always clear.

Communications targeting children have long faced public scrutiny. Under pressure from consumer groups and the federal government, R. J. Reynolds agreed to stop using the hip Joe Camel in its tobacco advertisements. Just a few years ago, Philip Morris Company said it would pull its tobacco ads from magazines with teenage readership of more than 15 percent, or more than 2 million teenage readers. This decision removed ads from *Sports Illustrated* and *Rolling Stone*. The alcohol industry has also been accused of knowingly pushing products to minors. The Federal Trade Commission issued a report asking that beer, liquor, and wine companies stop the promotion of alcohol in ads that would appeal to minors, including "promotional placement" in PG and PG13 films, TV programs aimed at younger audiences, and on college campuses. At the same time, Anheuser-Busch launched its "We All Make a Difference Campaign" that salutes those who have made a difference in fighting alcohol abuse.

Americans have voiced much concern about violence being marketed to children either through gun companies, violent video games, or violence on television. Former U.S. Surgeon General David Satcher found that exposure to violent entertainment in childhood leads to aggressive behavior throughout life.[41] In response to attacks on the entertainment industry for marketing violence to children, ABC launched public service announcements featuring stars of the network's television series urging children to not become violent.

TECHNOLOGY THAT BUILDS RELATIONSHIPS

In communication, marketers often use technology to reach consumers and establish relationships. New advances like Internet and cell phones make it possible to connect with customers quickly. Almost every company has developed their own Web site to give consumers information about themselves and their product, and also to use effective promotions.

Today e-mail is an essential new form of personal communication. E-mail communications can be targeted more directly to a select audience, providing information that will be useful for making a purchase. Microsoft has invented its own e-mail advertising application in a frantic race to catch Google's online advertising revenue with its own software.[42] However, one survey showed that 63 percent of people erased e-mail advertising without reading it, as 56 percent thought they receive e-mail promotions excessively.[43] Therefore, marketers must be aware that sending messages indiscreetly could bring a negative effect.

Cell phone communication can also be aimed directly to consumers, especially to the younger generations, by sending text messages. For an example the message could be a special discount coupon on a consumer's birthday, giving a good impression and helping to build relationships. Mobile advertising via text message is growing in the United States, but it is far more widespread and accepted in other markets of the world. An ABI Research study projects that by 2012 mobile advertising expenditures will reach $1.2 billion in Japan, the world's leader in mobile advertising. Europe's leading cellular providers have teamed up, sharing information and pooling resources to define common measurement processes for mobile advertising.[44]

E-mail can be useful for electronic billing and online shopping. The invoice appears on the screen, and the consumer need only enter a credit card number to pay. People can buy anything from movie tickets to televisions in the comfort of their home. Most sites with something to sell offer this type of service to customers, and many even allow customers to create a profile so they do not have to enter their personal information every time they make a purchase. Customers may establish loyal relationships with companies that can provide this type of convenience.

Clearly, the Internet offers exciting new targeting opportunities that will increasingly affect the way marketers combine and orchestrate various communications activities to create the most effective IMC mix.

Chapter Summary:

Objective 1:   Understand the objectives of integrated marketing communication.

Integrated marketing communication (IMC) is the coordination of all information to the market in order to provide consistent, unified messages. Since each aspect of IMC—personal selling, advertising, sales promotion, public relations, and sponsorships—tends to work synergistically, integration is very important. Marketing communication has six objectives. First, it should provide useful information that improves customer decision making and consumption. Second, it creates demand to ensure that products will be consumed in sufficient quantities to justify their development, production, and distribution. Third, it supplies knowledge about the value of products, such as their benefits, features, and functions. Fourth, it helps differentiate products by describing their uniqueness. Fifth, it helps close the sale by moving customers to action. Finally, it is critical in building the all-important relationship with customers and in securing their loyalty.

Objective 2:   Learn how the communication process provides the intended information for the market.

Traditionally, communication was seen as a one-way process—from seller to buyer—without a feedback loop. Today, a two-way process is more realistic. The sender needs to specify objectives, as discussed previously. The sender's characteristics are important determinants of how well messages will be received. Source credibility is determined by expertise, trustworthiness, and attractiveness (or appeal). Encoding requires translating the message into terms that will be easily understood. Since message interpretation depends on consumer life experiences, a thorough comprehension of consumer behavior is required to do an adequate job of encoding. Message characteristics also play a major role. Marketers need to decide whether a one-sided or two-sided message is better; whether to supply conclusions; the order in which information will be presented; whether to use humor or fear appeals; and whether to use comparative messages. The choice of media—mass, personal, or mixed—also influences communications. Today, mixed media such as the Internet are becoming more important. Audiences are not passive receivers; they interpret information by processing it. Their intelligence and self-esteem are important factors here.

Objective 3:   Learn about the communication mix, including personal selling, advertising, sales promotion, sponsorships, and public relations.

The communication mix has five major components. Each has particular advantages. Personal selling involves face-to-face contact or two-way technology linkages, such as the telephone or Internet. This allows dialogue and interactive problem solving. Advertising is paid, nonpersonal communication. It reaches all members of the audience with the same "mass" message. Sales promotion uses a one-way message to motivate purchase, usually in the form of short-term incentives to buy. Sponsorship is paid support of an event. It associates the sponsor with the event and its participants. Public relations is nonpaid communication (publicity) about a company and its products. These messages are sometimes broadcast by sources considered to be unbiased so they can have considerable credibility.

Objective 4:   Know the factors that influence the communications mix.

The communication mix is influenced by several factors. First, business-to-business and consumer markets use different mixes. The former are dominated by personal selling, whereas the latter are dominated by sales promotion and advertising. Second, marketers use a push or pull communication strategy. A push strategy communicates to channel members, who in turn communicate to end users. A pull strategy communicates with end users, who in turn demand products from channel members. Third, communications must be suited to the product's stage in the life cycle in order to have the greatest effectiveness. Finally, marketing communications do not always work directly on consumers. There is often a two-stage process whereby opinion leaders filter information before it reaches others in the market.

Objective 5: Describe the steps in developing an integrated marketing communication plan.

The IMC plan is an outgrowth of the marketing plan. It has five steps. First, select and understand target markets. Second, determine communication objectives and select the IMC mix. Third, develop the IMC budget in line with the overall strategic marketing plan. Fourth, implement the plan. Fifth, measure communication results and adjust accordingly.

Objective 6: Address diversity, ethics, and technology in communications.

Many media are not accessible to physically impaired individuals, and other avenues must be used. One is the Internet, especially through innovative software. Marketers must be careful not to cross ethical boundaries in their communications. They should avoid false and misleading ads and sales tactics as well as high-pressure manipulation. Targeting children is a questionable practice because they may easily be misled or manipulated. Communication technology is providing better ways to connect with consumers and create relationships. E-mail is one example. Software makes interactive communication easier and more rapid than ever before.

Review Your Understanding

1. What is integrated marketing communication?
2. What are the six objectives of integrated marketing communication?
3. What is the one-way communication process? How does it differ from the two-way process?
4. What are message sender characteristics and why are they important?
5. What is encoding?
6. What message characteristics should be considered? How does each influence effectiveness?
7. What are personal, mass, and mixed media? What are the characteristics of each?
8. What factors influence how messages are interpreted? Describe each.
9. What are the main categories in the communication mix?
10. What factors influence the communication mix? Describe each.
11. What are the steps in building an integrated communication plan?
12. How does diversity offer an opportunity and a challenge to communication?
13. What aspects of communication are covered by the American Marketing Association Code of Ethics?
14. Name one way that communication technology is helping to build relationships with consumers.

Discussion of Concepts

1. Describe the various goals of communication. What helps determine communication objectives?
2. Why is it so important for marketers to understand the communication process? How does that process affect the development and implementation of a campaign?
3. The way in which a message is communicated to consumers is critically important to its success. Name some of the issues involved in developing a message.
4. How do consumers distort messages? Have you ever distorted a message directed at you? How can marketers combat this problem?
5. Why is the source of a message so important? What are the three characteristics of a good spokesperson? Do you think one spokesperson can communicate effectively with the entire market? Why or why not?
6. Briefly describe the five steps in developing a communication plan. How are the plan and the company's overall marketing strategy related?
7. List the pros and cons of each type of communication activity: personal selling, sales promotion, advertising, sponsorship, and public relations. What factors help determine the appropriate one to select?

References

1. Hazel Trice Edney, "Tearful Oprah Tells Howard Grads: 'Know Who You Are'," New Pittsburgh Courier, May 23-May 29, 2007, 98(21), p.A3; Carmen Wong Ulrich, "The Oprah Effect," Essence, Oct 2006, 37(6), p.190-192; Tanisha A Sykes, "Oprah Winfrey: America's Ultimate Brand," Black Enterprise, Jul 2005, 35(12), p.28; www.oprah.com, website visited July 10, 2007.
2. Lenovo forges 2008 Olympics link with Coca-Cola.(Brief article). Marketing (August 2, 2006): p03. From InfoTrac OneFile.
3. ADWEEK 47.44 (Nov 27, 2006): p4(1). From InfoTrac OneFile.
4. Trustive establishes in-bound roaming agreement with The Cloud.(Brief article), Internet Business News (Jan 19, 2007): pNA. From InfoTrac OneFile.
5. http://www.mobiletracker.net/archives/2007/03/26/samsung-upstage,

Sprint/Samsung Upstage advertisement in Entertainment # 931/932 April 27/May 4 2007.
6. Sonia Reyes, "EAS taps Crawford and mom," Brandweek Vol. 43, April 1, 2002, pg. 7.
7. http://www.campaignforrealbeauty.com site visited March 31, 2008.
8. www.luvs.com, site visited March 31, 2008.
9. http://www.rbkedgeuniform.com site visited March 31, 2008.
10. DiCaprio's global warning: '11th Hour' a ticking clock: wants viewers 'to be scared' by film.(festival de cannes), Hollywood Reporter 399.34 (May 21, 2007): p28(2). From InfoTrac OneFile.
11. www.adiamondisforever.com, site visited March 31, 2008.
12. Raju Narisetti, "Rubbermaid Opens Door to TV, Hoping to Put Houses in Order," Wall Street Journal Interactive Edition, February 4, 1997.

13. www.rubbermaid.com, site visited March 31, 2008.
14. Harold L. Ross, Jr., "How to Create Effective Humorous Commercials Yielding Above Average Brand Preference Change," Marketing News, March 26, 1976, p. 4.
15. Bruce Horovitz, " 'Magic fridge' of Bud Light ices an advertising win", USA Today January 26 2007.
16. Lucy Cochrane, Pascale Quester, "Fear in Advertising : The influence of Consumers' Product Involvement and Culture," Journal of International Consumer Marketing (New York) Vol. 17, 2005, pg. 7.
17. www.centennialwireless.com, site visited March 31, 2008.
18. www.support.dell.com, site visited March 31, 2008.
19. www.cio.com/feeds, site visited March 31, 2008.
20. www.fax.com, site visited March 31, 2008.
21. M. Zelner, "Self-Esteem, Self-Perception, and Influenceability," Journal of Personality and Social Psychology 25 (1973): 87–93.
22. Gillian Wee, "Fox Network Sells Last Super Bowl Ad, Earliest Ever," Jan. 29, 2008. www.bloomberg.com, site visited April 5, 2008.
23. Irene Chang, "Mrs. Fields seeks the ultimate recipe to mark 30th birthday", PRweek, April 16, 2007, p 3.
24. Paul Wenske, "Reaching Out to Customers," The Kansas City Star, January 10, 2001, p. C1.
25. http://www.golftoday.co.uk/news/yeartodate/news03/carindustry.html, site visited June 10, 2007.
26. "NASCAR Fans Have Unparalleled Awareness of Sport's Sponsors, New Study Finds," Feb. 07, 2005. www.jmu.edu/kinesiology/pdfs/NASCAR.pdf, site visited April 05, 2008.
27. www.bcsfootball.org/bcsfootball/, site visited April 05, 2008.
28. "Internet Advertising Revenues Again Reach New High…" Feb. 25, 2008. www.iab.net, site visited April 05, 2008.
29. Hsin-Hui Hu, HG Parsa, Maryam Khan, "Effectiveness of Price Discount levels and formats in service industries", Journal of Service Research, July 2006, p 17.
30. Beat Burger, Matthias Fuchs, "Dynamic pricing – A future airline business model", Journal of Revenue and Pricing Management(London), p. 39.
31. www.homedepot.com, site visited April 05, 2008.
32. Jagdish N. Sheth, "Word-of-Mouth in Low Risk Innovations," Journal of Advertising Research 11 (1971): 15–18.
33. Carmen Wong Ulrich, "The Oprah Effect," Essence(New York) Vol. 37, October 2006, pg. 190.
34. E. K. Strong, The Psychology of Selling (New York: McGraw-Hill, 1925), p. 9.
35. Robert J. Lavidge and Gary A. Steiner, "A Model for Predictive Measurements of Advertising Effectiveness," Journal of Marketing, October 1991, p. 61.
36. "Credit Cards on Campus," The New York Yimes, July 28, 2001, p A.10; http://www.mastercard.com/us/personal/en/findacard/home.html, site visited April 05, 2008.
37. J. Tom Russell, Ronald Lane, Karen King, Kleppner's Advertising Procedure, ed 17, (Prentice Hall, 2007)
38. www.ncd.gov, site visited April 05, 2008.
39. www.afb.org, site visited April 05, 2008.
40. www.halftheplanet.com, site visited April 05, 2008.
41. Jeff Leeds, "Surgeon General Links TV, Real Violence Entertainment," Los Angeles Times, January 17, 2001, p. A1; and "Youth Violence on the Decline but Surgeon General Warns of Complacency," The Hartford Courant, January 18, 2001, p. A10.
42. Nick Buchan, "Global dispatches," B&T Weekly (Sydney), June 9, 2006, pg. 11.
43. Greg Brooks, "Overcrowded Inbox", Marketing (London), July 13, 2005, pg. 40.
44. Dusan, "ABI Research: Japan and South Korea Leading in Mobile Advertising," December 18, 2007, www.intomobile.com, site visited May 06, 2008; "Leading Mobile Operators Work Together to Measure Mobile Advertising," February 12, 2008, www.intomobile.com, site visited May 06, 2008.

The Marketing Gazette

Helen Johnstone, "Little Emperors Call the Shots," Asian Business, September 1996, pp. 67–70; Sally D. Goll, "China's (Only) Children Get the Royal Treatment," Wall Street Journal, February 8, 1995, p. B1; "Wooing Little Emperors," Business China, July 22, 1996, pp. 1–2; and Gary Jones, "China's Little Emperors," The Independent (London), November 12, 2000, pp. 28, 29, 30, 32;"China's Children Article Market to Grow at 12.4% Every Year", SinoCast China Business Daily News(London), February 13, 2006, p 1; "Son Preferences and Educational Opportunities of Children in China—"I wish you were a boy!"" Gender Issues, Spring 2005, p 3.

CASE 12

Nike

In 1964, Phil Knight and his former track coach, William Bowerman, began selling shoes made by a Japanese company, Onitsuka Tiger Co., out of the back seat of Knight's car. To gain more control of their marketing efforts, Knight and Bowerman developed the Nike brand, named after the Greek goddess of victory. A Portland State University design student created the famous "swoosh" for $35. It represents a wing, to "embody the spirit of the winged goddess who inspired the most courageous and chivalrous warriors." From the onset, Knight's philosophy has been that people root for a favorite team or athlete, not a product. So Knight sold "the athletic ideals of determination, individuality, self-sacrifice, and winning." Beginning in 1973 with track star Steve Prefontaine, Nike has actively sponsored athletes with these attributes. Today, it invests hundreds of millions annually to gain sponsorship of world-class teams and players.

Nike is now the world's largest sport-shoe maker. With its subsidiary brands, Nike controlled 81.8 percent of the U.S.'s $2.6 billion basketball sneaker market in 2006. Knight attributes success to a number of factors.

- The company is based on one brand, which has a genuine and distinct personality, and tangible, emotional connections to customers the world over.

- It is rooted in sports, the fastest-growing culture, growing so fast that it is becoming the one, true international language.

- Nike has been around for over 25 years and has grown each year because "our horizon is more than 12 months away."

- It is made up of 21,800 teammates who "stood this industry on its head."

- They include the brightest, most committed, most sought-after people in the industry.

Nike's ability to coordinate integrated marketing communication that really connects with customers is outstanding. For example, the "swoosh" is so familiar that the name no longer needs to appear along with it. The company's interactive Web site is updated constantly, announcing new products and offering more sales opportunities for the company.

Nike strategically coordinates its television and print ads, sponsorships, Web site, an 800 number, billboards, and other media to form an effective mix of communications. The athletes who deliver its message are a major factor. For example, Michael Jordan is generally considered to be the best basketball player in the history of the game. At a time when Nike profits were sinking, Knight selected Jordan to reestablish the company's image. Spike Lee filmed spots depicting Jordan as the basketball player whose talent (and Nike shoes) enabled him to fly. Now, Nike's Air Jordan franchise remains the best-selling sneaker line in history.

A number of other famous athletes have elicited a tremendous response from customers, including tennis players Roger Federer and Maria Sharapova, baseball players Derek Jeter and Alex Rodriguez, football's LaDainian Tomlinson, track stars Carl Lewis and Alberto Salazar, basketball players Kobe Bryant and Vince Carter, and golf's Tiger Woods. Nike made its biggest bet in basketball in 2003 when it signed LeBron James, an 18-year-old phenom, to a $90 million deal even before he was drafted by the Cleveland Cavaliers. However, James's signature shoe has been a strong seller for the company. "It's hard to build an identity for your brand around a team," says Charles Denson, Nike brand president. "We built our brand around the athlete and his or her personality, creativity and innovation. I think that's what gives the Nike brand the edge it has today."

And Nike is expanding its total market with integrated marketing communication. Partnering with Apple, Nike added new products like Nike+iPod Sport Kit that enables runners to use special Nike sneakers and the iPod nano to track things like the number of calories burned in a workout. Besides, it produced its largest soccer campaign during the World Cup last year, when, according to Nike CEO Mark Parker, its "joga bonito" soccer community was a success and the company obtained $1.5 billion in soccer sales.

Through its NIKEiD website, Nike allows customers to design their own custom sneakers, choosing from dozens of colors and styles. Users can also add a personalized nickname or team number, ensuring a truly unique pair of shoes.

Nike also reaches consumers globally with various strategies. In China, where its younger generation is forming their own styles but don't think they need to learn from the West, Nike shifts away from its traditional marketing platform of attracting youth through sports heroes. Instead, it encourages these internet-savvy kids to submit their own stories on the site and watch different films created by Wieden-colorful, energetic montages of young Chinese playing sports in recognizable, often gritty locales. In addition, Nike is a co-founder of ninemillion.org, a global campaign for saving the estimated nine million young refugees around the world. It even created specially designed and culturally sensitive sport apparel for Muslim girls in the Dadaab camp in Kenya; it produced ninemillion.org T-shirts to help raise awareness and funds; and its stores also devoted retail space to the ninemillion.org story.

Nike sees sustainability as a source of innovation. Its sustainable product innovation team educates designers on sustainable design guidelines. It now uses environmentally preferred rubber in more than half of all Nike footwear, and plan for a minimum of 5 percent organic cotton in all cotton materials by 2010. Nike hopes its increasing use of green materials will motivate its suppliers to develop more sustainable materials. Since 2006, all Nike Air products are made with climate change-neutral nitrogen. Nike is currently working on a strategy to increase packaging efficiency and reduce excess waste, in hopes of implementing it early next decade.

Through its Let Me Play campaign, Nike will invest $315 million in worldwide sports initiatives by 2011. It aims to give hope to the millions of children across the globe that haven't had the chance to play sports because of unsafe fields, and lack of coaches and equipment. The Reuse-a-Shoe program collects used athletic shoes of all brands and recycles them into athletic surfaces like basketball and tennis courts, as well as running tracks and playgrounds.

As Nike continues to face new competition, it will need to be the leader in not only shoes but also in integrated marketing communication.

1. *Discuss how Nike uses IMC to position the company in a manner consistent with its strategy. Give examples.*

2. *How does Nike use athletes to influence the communication process? What characteristics of message senders do you think Nike considers the most important? Why?*

3. *This chapter discussed 21st-century forces affecting communication. Based on what you have read in the case and what you know about Nike, discuss how the company addresses these forces with its marketing communications.*

Sources: Normandy Madden, "Nike Drops its American Idols," Advertising Age, Mar 20, 2006, 77(12), p.12; Stephanie Kang, "Nike Profit Falls," The Wall Street Journal, Sep 22, 2006, p. B3; Mike Esterl and Stephanie Kang, "Adidas Extols 'We Over Me' as It Aims at Shoe King Nike's Cult of Personality," The Wall Street Journal, Oct 16, 2006, p. B1; "Case Study: Ninemillion.org & Nike Save the World One Child at A Time by Telling Their Stories in A New, Unique Way," PR News, Feb 12, 2007, 63(6), p.1; www.letmeplay.com, site visited May 01, 2008; Nike CR Report, www.nikeresponsibility.com, site visited May 01, 2008; www.nike.biz/responsibility, site visited May 01, 2008.

CHAPTER 13

Mass Communications: Advertising, Sales Promotions, & Public Relations

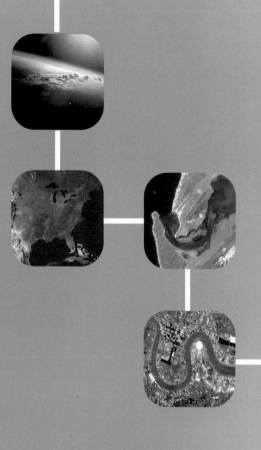

Product placement in movies, television and video games has become a popular method of advertising. ▶

Learning Objectives

1. Understand the concept of mass communications, including the relative use of advertising, sales promotion, and public relations.

2. Learn how technology, globalization, and ethics are playing major roles in mass communications.

3. Know the objectives, advantages, and disadvantages of advertising, as well as the sequence of steps in creating an advertising campaign.

4. Understand sales promotion objectives and what types of promotions are used to stimulate sales in business, trade, retailer, and consumer markets.

5. Understand the use of public relations in marketing.

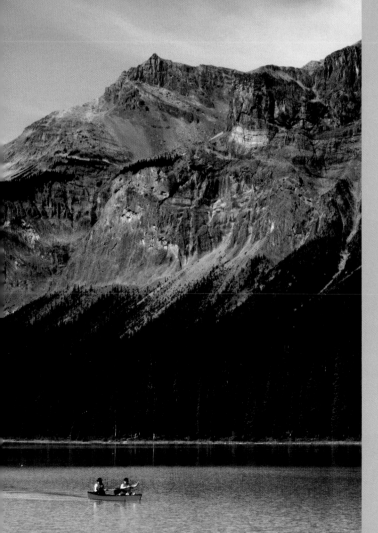

Product placement in movies, television and video games are a huge part of advertising. Disney Pixar's blockbuster animated movie "WALL-E," set in the year 2815, is about a garbage collecting robot left on earth to clean up the mess humans left behind. Can you name the five brands featured in WALL-E? It was no accident that WALL-E powers up using Apple's boot-up chime. How about as the robot rummages though the garbage left behind by humans? He finds many products familiar to us today including a Zippo lighter, Rubik's cube and iPod. Five product placements is minuscule compared to the Warner Brother's film "Get Smart" staring actor Steve Carell. The film featured 32 product placements including notables like Nike, Verizon Wireless, and Dell. These products were carefully placed in the movies as part of the elaborate advertising plans. Product placement is used as a reinforcement or reminder that the product is popular among celebrities and even animated characters in a movie.

Product placement took off back in 1982 when ET hit planet earth and discovered Reeses Pieces. Reeses Pieces soon dramatically cut into sales of M&M, whose maker rejected the offer to be featured in the now classic Spielberg film. Since then, cinema has become a major marketing medium. Many products have made their debut in highly anticipated movies and were then released to the public shortly thereafter. Marketers have found that this is an excellent way to create excitement about a newly released product. In 2008, Apple was the top featured brand in film with eleven appearances. Apple products can be seen in films such as "National Treasure: Book of Secrets" and "Sex and the City." Ford was also at the top of the list with vehicles appearing in "Hancock," "Indiana Jones," and "The Incredible Hulk."

Product placement became a trend in the film industry and eventually found its way into television. Wardrobe placements are the most common. The actresses of ABC's "Desperate Housewives" can often been seen wearing designers such as Halston. In recent years, it is reality television that has been a favorite outlet for product placements. The NBC reality show "The Biggest Loser" had the highest number of product placements in 2008 followed closely by FOX's "American Idol". Coca-Cola, which was featured on "American Idol" 2,380 times in 2008, was the leading product placement brand on television. American Idol judges are often seen sipping on Cokes.

Video games are an emerging way to introduce products and reinforce product usage. When Nissan decided to release a new version of its GT-R sports coupe in the United States, the company struck a deal with Sony Computer Entertainment and Electronic Arts to create a GT-R in downloadable video games. Nissan's approach is just one example of a shift in the advertising budgets across many industries. Videogames can provide marketers with an advanced and inexpensive form of product placement because they can digitally create images and instantly transform products.

Product placement is just one example of how marketing is helping to create and capture value for customers through popular media like movies and television. While traditional means of advertising such as television and radio commercials are still popular, the Internet, cell phones, and other portable innovations are providing interesting new ways for marketers to advertise new products.[1]

THE CONCEPT OF MASS COMMUNICATIONS: ADVERTISING, SALES PROMOTION, & PUBLIC RELATIONS

Today, mass communication helps companies connect with customers by providing information in exciting and creative formats. It adds tremendous value by informing people about the goods and services available in today's global markets. It's so pervasive that every few seconds most of us are exposed to a message designed to influence our behavior.

Spending in the United States for mass communication is about $628 billion, with growth of 7 percent annually. Much of the spending is on advertising (about $262 billion) but even slightly more for sales promotion (about $366 billion). Public relations is a distant third. The United States accounts for about one-third of the planet's spending on mass communication. Mass communication in the rest of the world totals about $1.2 trillion, for a combined global figure of nearly $2 trillion. About two-thirds is devoted to consumer products, and one-third is spent by businesses marketing to other businesses.[2]

Much of the increase in mass communication is due to competitive factors, particularly the battle for brand strength. Familiar examples are Coke versus Pepsi, Kellogg versus General Mills, Proctor & Gamble versus Unilever, Verizon versus AT&T, Barnes & Noble versus Borders, and Staples versus Office Max. Although the battle of the brands started in the United States, it has become global. Burger King and McDonald's no longer just compete at home but also in most cities around the world. And Pepsi and Coke are notorious for their vigorous rivalry in Brazil, Taiwan, and France.

Mass communication is composed of advertising, sales promotion, and public relations, as shown in Figure 13.1. Historically, techniques have changed according to advances in technology. Another recent influence is the need for standardization in global markets. Because mass communication is persuasive and powerful, there are many ethical issues for marketers to consider, but it is still a key way to connect with diverse customers. This chapter first looks at technology, global aspects, and ethics. Discussion then turns to advertising and its purposes. We describe the various categories of advertising, the agencies that create and place it, and the media that carry it to the consumer. Next, sales promotion is described as a means to get trial, stimulate immediate sales, and build customer relationships. Finally, a section on public relations and publicity addresses their role in corporate communications.

In order to understand mass communication, we start with a look at the role technology has played historically and is playing today. Second, we will see how mass communication is occurring globally. Third, we will explore several serious ethical aspects of mass communication.

TECHNOLOGICAL PERSPECTIVE

The history of mass communication mirrors a number of technological advances. Before the age of printing, street criers shouted merchants' messages, and shop signs often used pictures to identify their trade to a largely illiterate public. Movable type was invented around 1440, helping to spread literacy, and 32 years later an advertisement for

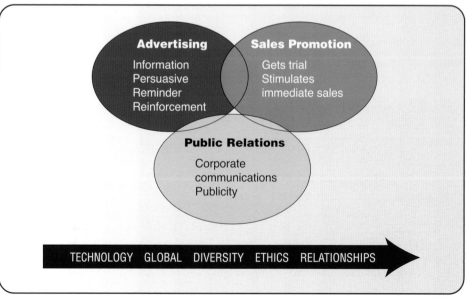

Figure 13.1   The Concept of Mass Communication in Marketing

a prayer book was tacked to church doors. The word *advertisement* appeared in about 1665, when it was used as a header to describe announcements of commercial significance. By the mid-1700s, newspapers were popular and carried publicity and ads.

By the 1800s, mass communication through newspapers and handbills was abundant. When magazines were introduced in the mid-1800s, they provided an excellent way to communicate commercial messages. Professionals who did copywriting and advertising emerged because of this medium. By the mid-1930s, great ad agencies such as J. Walter Thompson, Rubicam, and BBDO were successful. During that era, the growth of radio provided yet another medium for promotion and quickly surpassed magazines as the leading vehicle.

Although television came along in 1939 when NBC was established, not until the 1950s did television begin to surpass radio as a promotional medium. The combination of voice and video offered greater opportunities to reach consumers with a creative message. Ronald Reagan, later President, was one of the most popular spokespersons in the early days of television. Television now dominates, but magazines, newspapers, radio, and the Internet still carry a significant proportion of promotional messages.

Whereas the traditional media revolutionized advertising and public relations, in recent years information systems based on computer technology have contributed dramatically to sales promotion growth. Computers have made it possible to track product sales globally, thus enhancing the usefulness of all forms of sales promotion. Clearly the Internet has shaped communication in even more exciting ways - as a two-way exchange of value, is doing for mass communication what the telephone did for interpersonal communication.

GLOBAL MASS COMMUNICATIONS

Global advertising, sales promotion, or public relations occurs when a marketing team standardizes key elements of these activities across national boundaries. Since campaigns are usually used to support global brand strategies, companies such as Coca-Cola, PepsiCo, Procter & Gamble, BMW, Nike, Toyota, and Nestlé are leaders in this arena. Today, all the large advertising agencies have offices worldwide to support clients who seek global coordination. Due to cultural differences, marketers need to assess the benefits of standardized versus localized promotion. Global strategies can occur when

organizations employ a global strategy with local implementation which is an adjustment to local market dynamics.

Because standardization provides numerous economies, the cost of developing creative promotions can be shared across many markets. For example, when Gillette introduces a new product, a world wide campaign often uses the same actors dubbed in various languages. Lebron James' fantastic slam dunks cost millions to produce, but they have the same appeal when used in Italy or Russia as in the United States to promote Nike.

Global standardization works best when customers, not countries, are the basis for identifying segments and when the product is compatible across cultures. It is also important for the firm to have similar competitors and an equivalent competitive position in most of the markets. Finally, promotion management should be somewhat centralized so that global marketing can occur.[3] A company such as Kodak fits these criteria fairly well, although the imaging business does have regional differences. In Japan, Fuji is exceptionally strong. Consequently, Kodak uses a standardized approach with adjustments for these local competitive conditions.

There are some serious drawbacks to global standardization. Cultural attitudes toward promotion differ. Although changing, Singaporeans tend to regard it negatively, whereas Russian consumers are even more positive about it than Americans.[4] In addition, local audiences have certain cultural traditions. For example, when the National Football League created an international division to market outside the United States, it had to customize its programs to appeal to different cultures. To ensure marketing success, the NFL educated foreign consumers about U.S.-style football using a region-by-region strategy. The NFL Europe Web site has results from both the American and European leagues both in English and the home country's language (e.g., the Amsterdam Admirals results are given in Dutch). The NFL had also instituted one game per season called the World Bowl that pits two NFL teams in a country into which the NFL has attempted to expand. The 2007 World Bowl was played in London. Today, the NFL has six international Web sites so fans across the world can follow their favorite NFL team.[5]

Sales promotion and publicity often have a very local flavor. Each country has a unique promotion style, and most have legal as well as other restrictions. For example, Procter & Gamble (P&G) found it was legal to mail free

www.fujifilm.com

Go behind the scenes at Fuji and find out what it takes to be a leader in imaging, information, and environmental sustainability.

samples to consumers in Poland, a practice prohibited in many countries. What surprised them was that thieves stole the samples from mailboxes before they reached intended recipients. In Germany, however, the government regulates the size of samples sent through the mail; another law prohibits advertising as a personal letter.[6] And in England, Hoover Ltd. gave away free round-trip airplane tickets to New York or Orlando with the purchase of £250 in merchandise. The company underestimated demand and spent several million pounds more than it had budgeted.

ETHICAL ISSUES IN ADVERTISING, SALES PROMOTION, AND PUBLIC RELATIONS

The most serious ethical issue surrounding advertising, sales promotion, and public relations is deception. These communication methods are designed to be persuasive, but too much of the wrong type of persuasion can be misleading.

Deception occurs when a false belief is created or implied and interferes with the ability of consumers to make rational choices.[7] Purely descriptive information is seldom deceptive. But what about embellishment? Or what about the things left out? At what point does deception occur? Marketers must use a great amount of judgment to avoid being deceptive. An ad may show Michael Jordan soaring hundreds of feet to make a slam dunk in his Nikes, but no one is likely to believe that shoes make this possible. The exaggerated message is that Nike shoes will significantly improve the performance of the common athlete. But Nike lets you know that playing basketball well is also based on ability, training, and skill building. Nike campaigns have featured athletes as role models for children, not as superstars. By depicting the athletes as serious, compassionate and hardworking, Nike is able to convey that being an athlete is about more than just the sport. How exciting would it be to see Nike or Reebok simply describe the materials and design for their shoes? The outlandish puffery sometimes used by Nike would not be considered deceptive by most.

Marketers must walk a fine line between producing creative, stimulating messages and being deceptive. Even company slogans can come into question when they evoke strong emotions or make comparative comments. Pantene used to urge: "Don't hate me because I'm beautiful." Hanes said: "Gentlemen prefer Hanes." Can shampoo really create jealousy, and do men really care about what brand of stockings women wear? Most consumers probably would not think these slogans seriously interfere with their ability to make informed choices. Are these catchy phrases fun and provocative or misleading?

When false information or exaggerated claims are used, deception is clear—and illegal. Kentucky Fried Chicken (KFC) used deceptive communication by leaving some information out: FTC charged that KFC gave a wrong information about the relative nutritional value and healthiness of KFC fried chicken in a national television advertising campaign. KFC publicized that its fried chicken, in particular two Original Recipe fried breasts, is better than a Burger King Whopper in total fat and saturated fat aspect. But its product has more than three times of trans fat and cholesterol, more than two times of sodium and more calories.[8]

ADVERTISING

Advertising is paid, nonpersonal communication from an identified sponsor using mass media to persuade or influence an audience. The word is derived from the Latin *advertere*, "to turn toward."[9] Notice that advertising is paid for by an identified sponsor, so the audience knows the source of the message. In addition, it is a form of nonpersonal communication through mass media, such as newspapers, magazines, radio, television, and the Internet. This allows advertising to be directed at relatively large audiences. Traditionally there was no opportunity for the receiver to ask questions or for the advertiser to obtain immediate feedback. Advertising on the Internet has changed that by allowing potential customers to directly contact sponsors with questions and in some cases make orders for goods and services. Consequently, planning is extremely important in order to create a successful ad the first time.

THE MULTIPLE PURPOSES AND ROLES OF ADVERTISING

Although advertising itself is powerful, it also plays an important support role for other forms of communication. In a famous McGraw-Hill Publishing Company ad, a grumpy purchasing agent stares directly at the viewer, saying: "I don't know who you are. I don't know your company. I don't know your company's product. I don't know what your company stands for. I don't know your company's customers. I don't know your company's record. I don't know your company's reputation. Now— what was it you wanted to sell me?" The ad goes on to explain that the sales effort starts before a salesperson calls—with business publication advertising. Whether alone or in support of other promotion methods, advertising informs, persuades, reminds, or reinforces.

Informative Advertising Informative advertising is designed to provide messages that consumers can store for later use. For example, an art museum may place an informative advertisement to make the

INTRODUCING THE 200-HP MAZDA TRIBUTE LX-V6

WHAT IF AN SUV WERE RAISED BY A FAMILY OF SPORTS CARS?

If the company that created the legendary RX-7 and Miata decided to build an SUV, what would you expect? Rapid acceleration? Taut, agile handling? Pure push-you-back-in-your-seat exhilaration?

Well, here it is. The vehicle only Mazda could have created. The Mazda Tribute. The SUV with the soul of a sports car. At prices that start at just $17,750 for the Mazda Tribute DX. LX-V6 model shown $21,565.

• 200-horsepower 3.0-liter DOHC 24-valve V6 engine.
• Electronically controlled 4-speed automatic.
• 16" alloy wheels with P235/70R16 all-season tires.
• Sport-tuned MacPherson strut front suspension and multilink rear suspension.
• Available Anti-lock Brake System (ABS) with Electronic Brakeforce Distribution (EBD).
• Available on-demand 4-wheel drive.

To learn more, hit our Web site or call us at (800) 639-1000.
MSRP excludes tax, title and license fee. © 2001 Mazda North American Operations.

MazdaUSA.com

This ad for the 200-HP Madza Tribute is designed to be a persuasive ad.

community aware that a particular exhibit is on display. Often, the more information an ad provides, the better the response will be. A 6,450-word ad for Merrill Lynch brought 10,000 inquiries from interested investors. An 800-word ad for Mercedes-Benz was headlined: "You give up things when you buy the Mercedes Benz 230S. Things like rattles, rust and shabby workmanship." Sales rose from 10,000 to 40,000 cars. Many consumers want to be provided with as much information as possible about items that interest them. The Internet is a great format for informative advertising.

Persuasive Advertising **Persuasive advertising** is designed to change consumers' attitudes and opinions about products as well as create attitudes where none exist. These ads often list the product's attributes, pricing, and other factors that influence the buying decision. They attempt to make the product choice important so consumers will think about the subject. In this way, the message recipient is asked to form an attitude first and then buy. For example, a Land Rover ad emphasizes the ability of its Discovery and Range Rover to handle well under all conditions. The ad notes: "Weather is also a concern—no matter where you live. Whether it's snow, rain, wind, or ice, Land Rover's state-of-the-art traction technologies will help your Discovery or Range Rover

stay sure-footed in all kinds of weather. Regardless of the terrain you drive or the weather you face, your Land Rover serves as a layer of comfort and stability between you and the harsh environment you're navigating."[10]

Reminder Advertising **Reminder advertising** keeps the product at the forefront of the consumer's mind. In some cases these ads simply draw a connection between the brand and some aspect of life. In other cases they reinforce past consumer behavior to encourage the next purchase. One major medium for reminders is outdoor advertising. McDonald's tried to move consumers into

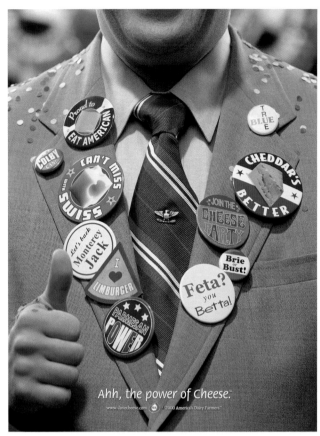

A reminder ad for cheese.

ond network TV spot in prime time reaches on average 12 million households. At current rates, that's less than 1 cent per household of coverage. No other promotional method comes close to accomplishing that kind of exposure at such low rates.

The availability of such advertising media as television, radio, newspapers, magazines, and billboards makes it easy to reach most audiences. And because advertising is used so much, it's easy for marketers to find excellent agencies that can help research markets, develop campaigns, and manage the entire process. The advantages can be summarized as follows:

- Controls the content, presentation, and placement of messages.
- Builds brand position and equity over time.
- Is cost-effective for large audiences.
- Serves many communication needs—awareness, information, reminder.
- Is easy to reach most audiences.
- Is easy to find professionals to create effective advertising.

Advertising does have a downside. It's difficult to direct an ad at only the target audience—many others will be exposed to it. Because many consumers distrust ads and try to avoid them, advertising campaigns may need to

its restaurants with the slogan: "You deserve a break today." The next campaign phases asked: "Have you had your break today?" and "Did somebody say McDonald's?" "I'm lovin' it" is the most recent reminder slogan, and is created as an international branding campaign mainly targeting people aged 15-24.[11] The reminder was intended to spur more action from the consumer.

Reinforcement Advertising To encourage repeat buying behavior, **reinforcement advertising** calls attention to specific characteristics of products experienced by the user. The key here is to communicate with the consumer about product features that created the greatest amount of satisfaction. These ads also reassure customers that they made the right choice. For example, classic ads for Dial asked, "Aren't you glad you used Dial . . . don't you wish everyone did?"

ADVANTAGES OF ADVERTISING

Advertising has many advantages. By controlling what is said, how it is said, and where it is said, marketers can develop standardized campaigns that run for extended periods. Over time, these help build a strong brand equity position. Moreover, advertising is a very cost-effective way to reach large audiences. For example, one 30-sec-

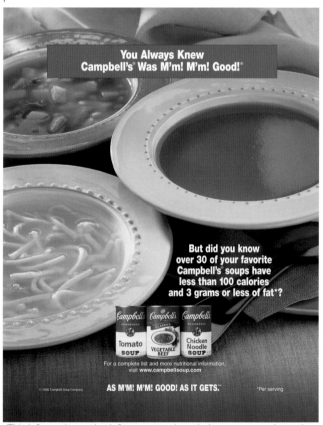

This informative and reinforcement ad reminds consumers about the good taste and nutrition of Campbell Soup.

Category	Description
National and Global (Brand) Advertising	Focuses on brand identity nationwide (globally). Aims to develop a distinctive brand image.
Retail (Local) Advertising	Focuses on local retail areas. Emphasizes positive attributes of retail outlets.
Directory Advertising	Company listings in a directory. Important to most businesses and retailers. Uses a short differentiating message.
Business-to-Business Advertising	Directed at professionals. Often communicates technical content. Common media include business publications and professional journals.
Institutional Advertising	Communicates corporate identity and philosophy. Describes social and ecological responsibilities of a company.
Direct-Response Advertising	Appeals directly to individual consumers. Usual delivery methods are telephone and mail.
Public Service Advertising	Supports public issues. Usually created for free and media donate space and time.
Political Advertising	Aimed at obtaining votes for issues or political candidates.

Figure 13.2   Categories of Advertising

run for a long time to repeat the message. It is not unusual for some companies or industries to spend hundreds of millions of dollars on advertising. Total money spent on advertising was estimated at $148 billion in 2007.[12] The disadvantages of advertising can be summarized as follows:

- Reaches many nonusers.
- Has high level of audience avoidance.
- Contains brief one-way messages.
- Can be costly in total.

CATEGORIES OF ADVERTISING

Advertising falls into various categories depending on its objectives, target audience, and type of message. Most marketers use one or more of the eight types described in Figure 13.2.

National or brand advertising, as the name implies, focuses on brand identity such as Delmonte or Pepsi and positioning throughout the country. The aim is to develop a distinctive brand image in the mind of the consumer. Although this is often called national advertising, it is also the objective for global advertising.

Retail (local) advertising focuses attention on nearby outlets where products and services can be purchased such as ads for Dusty's Wine Bar, a local restaurant. The emphasis is on attributes that will stimulate people to shop there, such as price, location, convenience, or customer service.

Directory advertising is a listing of businesses, their addresses, phone numbers, and sometimes brief descriptions in a publication such as the Yellow Pages. A short, differentiating message can be critical since so many competitors also advertise there. Businesses usually consider directories extremely important because most consumers use them only when they are ready to buy a product. The United States Postal Service recently began selling stamps and postal products online, in the hopes of making it easier for consumers to buy their products. **Business-to-business advertising** sends messages to a variety of organizations, ranging from health care providers to accountants, lawyers, and manufacturers. Often, technical content is communicated. In the health care field, for example, publications such as the *Journal of the American Medical Association* carry extensive advertising of pharmaceutical products of all types.

Marketing Vocabulary

REINFORCEMENT ADVERTISING
Messages that call attention to specific characteristics of products experienced by the user.

NATIONAL OR BRAND ADVERTISING
Advertising that focuses on brand identity and positioning throughout the country.

RETAIL (LOCAL) ADVERTISING
Advertising that focuses attention on nearby outlets where products and services can be purchased.

DIRECTORY ADVERTISING
A listing of businesses, their addresses, phone numbers, and sometimes brief descriptions in a publication.

BUSINESS-TO-BUSINESS ADVERTISING
Advertisements to businesses and professionals.

Institutional advertising is designed to communicate corporate identity and philosophy rather than messages about individual products. It describes the company's social and ecological responsibilities. For example, Toyota promotes its involvement in U.S. communities.

Direct-response advertising targets individual consumers to get immediate sales. Sales are stimulated through appeals by telephone, mail, and the Internet, and TV informercials; the product is then delivered to the customer's home or business. Companies such as Federal Express and UPS have helped facilitate the dramatic increase in sales from direct response advertising.

Public service advertising support societal issues like the prevention of child abuse or smoking cessation. These announcements are usually created free by advertising agencies, and the space or airtime is donated by the media. Sometimes they are partially supported by charitable organizations or the government.

Political advertising is aimed at influencing voters in favor of individuals or particular ballot issues. It has come under harsh criticism for mudslinging, negative and sometimes false accusations against political candidates, and the lack of focus on substantive issues.

ADVERTISING AGENCIES

Advertising agencies are independent businesses that develop, prepare, and place advertising in the appropriate media. Most companies outsource some or all of these services. In fact, more than 90 percent of all advertising is placed through outside agencies. Even very large corporations such as General Motors outsource. The cost-effectiveness of outside agencies makes this a good choice for most companies. There are more than 10,000 ad agencies in the United States alone and probably an equal number around the world. As in any industry, there are several large agencies and many smaller ones. Big companies, such as WPP Group (UK) or Omnicom, have offices in nearly every major country to provide the services required for global marketers.

In addition to full-service agencies, many specialize in certain advertising functions or in selected industries. For example, Creative Boutiques focuses primarily on developing ideas for advertising. In many cases, industries have certain unique needs. The health care industry is a good example. Durot, Donahoe, and Purohit of Rosemont, Illinois, is an expert in that kind of advertising, which requires knowledge of extensive regulation of health care ads by the Federal Drug Administration. Some agencies focus on certain target groups. Burmudez and Associates have expertise in the Hispanic market, and others specialize in various minorities.

THE ADVERTISING PLAN

The six major steps in developing a strong advertising plan are outlined in Figure 13.3. The process begins by setting objectives and next determining the budget. Then the theme and message are developed. The theme is the creative concept and the art and copy are used to convey the message. Next, media are selected and a schedule is set. This is followed by creation of the ads. Finally, their effectiveness is assessed.

SETTING OBJECTIVES

Each objective should be developed in such a way that its accomplishment can be measured. Remember that advertising should support the communications plan, which in turn supports the strategic marketing plan. As Figure 13.4 suggests, the goals of informing, persuading, remind-

Marketing Vocabulary

INSTITUTIONAL ADVERTISING
Messages designed to communicate corporate identity and philosophy as opposed to product information.

DIRECT-RESPONSE ADVERTISING
Targets individual consumers to get immediate sales.

PUBLIC SERVICE ADVERTISING
Free advertising that supports societal issues.

POLITICAL ADVERTISING
Advertising to influence voters.

ADVERTISING AGENCY
A business that develops, prepares, and places advertising for sellers seeking to find customers for their products.

Figure 13.3   Steps in the Advertising Plan

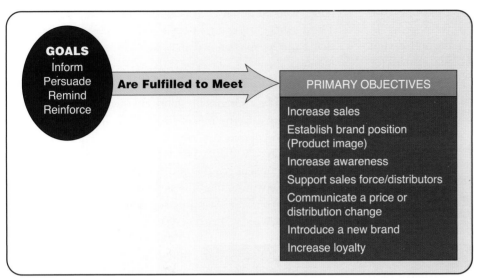

Figure 13.4   Advertising Objectives

Marketing Vocabulary

PERCENTAGE OF SALES METHOD
Allocating a percentage of estimated sales to advertising.

COMPETITIVE BUDGETING METHOD
Setting the advertising expenditures relative to what competitors spend.

PAYOUT METHOD
Setting the ad budget to gain initial acceptance and trial.

TASK METHOD
Setting the advertising budget based on activities required to accomplish objectives.

CREATIVE STRATEGY
The strategy that governs and coordinates the development of individual ads and assures that their visual images and words convey precisely and consistently what the advertiser wants to communicate.

ing, and reinforcing should be accompanied by specific objectives, such as increase sales, establish brand position, increase awareness, support the sales force or distributors, maintain awareness, or introduce a new brand.

DEVELOPING THE ADVERTISING BUDGET

As we mentioned before, advertising can be expensive in total although quite cost-effective on a per person basis. In setting the budget, the first question to answer is how much it will cost to accomplish the objective. Most advertising budgets are determined using one of the following methods: percentage of sales method, competitive budgeting method, payout plan method, or task method.

The **percentage of sales method** for developing the advertising budget involves simply estimating the desired sales level and then allocating a certain percentage of sales to advertising. Often this percentage is equal to the industry average. In some cases, the percentage of sales method is performed by taking a percentage of the previous year's sales and allocating it to advertising. The problem with this method is that sales are used to create the advertising budget when, in fact, advertising should be used to create sales. However, the method is used widely because it is very easy to administer.

The **Competitive budgeting method** involves determining what competitors are spending and setting the advertising budget accordingly. Large companies use this method in order to maintain a strong presence in the eye of the consumer. In 2007, financial services ranked the top spending category with over $9 billion spent.[13]

The **payout method** is generally used for new products that require high advertising expenditures. In this case, the marketer estimates future sales and establishes the advertising budget required to gain initial acceptance and trial of the product. Generally, these expenditures are very high relative to sales and in some cases even exceed sales. The large expenditures are deemed reasonable because of the payback that occurs in later years. This is similar to investing money in product development.

The **task method** sets specific sales targets or other objectives and then determines what advertising activities and amounts are required to accomplish those objectives. This approach can be extremely complex. Advertisers who use the task method rely on very accurate information experience, and extensive models developed for the purpose. It tends to be used by large organizations in highly competitive environments. It's superior to the other methods because so much attention to detail is paid in determining how advertising contributes toward accomplishment of objectives.

DEVELOPING THE THEME AND MESSAGE

Once objectives are in place and the budget has been established, it is time to develop the theme and message—the **creative strategy** that will govern and coordinate the development of individual ads and assure that their visual images and words convey precisely and consistently what the advertiser wishes to communicate. Be careful not to confuse this overall strategy with the creative work in putting a specific ad together. The message is a fairly straightforward outgrowth of the marketer's understanding of consumer behavior, information processing, and the advertising objectives. Kodak jumped into a very competitive inkjet-printer and cartridge market with active "think ink" marketing strategy. This strategy has lower cost ink compared to the conventionally expensive ink, and starts to advertise with online viral marketing before their "think" campaign appears in existing media as TV, print and online. In the hub of viral marketing, there are two men who print a lot but cry for the high expenditure of ink. They have their own Web site which provided viral videos that have been propagated on YouTube and MySpace where they express their thoughts of ink.[14]

An **advertising campaign** is a series of different ads with the same creative strategy. Because one ad tends to have very little effect, campaigns are required to sustain the message and accomplish the objectives. There is usually an element of continuity, such as similar characters, music, or settings. The pink Energizer bunny keeps going and going through any number of ads. Other examples are Geico's "caveman" commercials for car insurance and Aflac's "duck" commercials for disability insurance.

To be effective, the theme and message must reach the consumer and must be creative, understandable, and memorable.

Reaching the Consumer

An ad must first reach its target audience. **Exposure** is the process of putting the ad in contact with the market. Then it's up to the ad to communicate the message. A good advertisement addresses nearly every aspect of consumer behavior in a package that grabs interest and keeps it until the message is absorbed. Exposure does not ensure attention. As we learned in chapter 5, the perceptual process filters out a great deal. The ad must have what marketers call **stopping power**—the ability to gain and hold attention. Ads with stopping power are so attention getting that they interrupt whatever the person is doing. The best ads gain and hold attention because the consumer finds them interesting and relevant. They are often consistent with the buyer's lifestyle. Sometimes catchy music, humor, or an association with a celebrity works. Some phrases may gain immediate attention from certain people: weight loss, quick cash, retire early, pay off your

debts, work at home, free, new, amazing, now, and easy. These catch phrases have been so overused by advertisers that many people immediately tune out messages containing them.

Creativity Originality and uniqueness are very important in advertisements. On the one hand, ads that are too unusual may not work because people have difficulty relating to them. On the other hand, creative, humorous, upbeat ads that provide some novelty tend to gain more attention than the same old thing. Coca-Cola also captured viewers with its computer-animated polar bears, considered a "heartwarmer, creative, and upbeat."

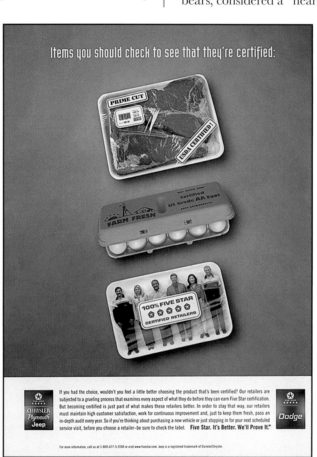

Stopping power is the key to this ad for Dodge.

"Whassup?" was the catch phrase started by a series of Budweiser commercials. Bud's Web site has files you can click to hear "whassup" in several different languages.

Once attention is gained, consumers are likely to become aware of the message and internalize it. **Pulling power** holds the interest of the consumer to the end of the message. Most advertisers insist that the message must relate to some aspect of the individual's life. Celebrities, for example, have reference group appeal. 'Proactiv' acne skin-care system ads in recent years featured entertainers such as Kelly Clarkson, Jessica Simpson, and Lindsay Lohan and had enormous pulling power. They talked about their own hard time with acne and even revealed their imperfect facial photos.[15]

Understandability Although most ads don't attempt to say everything about a product, it's important that the information selected for communication be clearly understood. Otherwise, it will not be remembered. Procter & Gamble communicated the benefits of its portable stain removal pen, 'tide to go,' through a series of ads featuring an "immediate results with a remarkable handy touch." Viewers have a clear understanding of what the product can do when the items are pulled stain free from the application of 'tide to go'.[16]

Memorability It's important that ads be memorable so that they are retained for some time. A high initial effect is useless if forgotten quickly. Consumers must remember ads until they actually purchase the product. One way to achieve this is through repetition. An ad usually must be seen at least three times before it moves into long-term memory. Jingles, slogans, and tag lines also help ensure recall. How many of the popular slogans listed in Figure 13.5 do you recognize?

SELECTING AND SCHEDULING MEDIA

Media Options **Media** are the channels through which messages are transmitted from the sender to the receiver. Each medium has unique advantages and disadvantages, as described in Figure 13.6.

Newspapers A highly credible and flexible medium, newspapers offer wide exposure to upscale adults. Many newspapers have prestige because of their positive impact on communities. They reach 90 percent of homes in a typical location, allowing for widespread coverage. Newspapers can also facilitate coordination between local and national advertising. Some effectiveness is being lost, however, because television and the Internet have become increasingly important news sources. Newsprint consumption declined 11.5 percent from 2006 to 2007.[17] The advent of the Internet in early 1990s caused the circulation to slide down by taking readership to the Internet. Newspaper companies have started their own online newspapers which accounts for a large percentage of their entire readership. This leads their online advertising to collect more revenue that print advertising.

Television Television is also a credible source and is extremely cost efficient per person. It provides the creative flexibility to use both video and audio, allowing an unlimited range of spokespersons and themes. The disadvantages are high production costs and low recall of messages. Television is filled with advertising, which makes it difficult to gain the viewer's attention, and many consumers change the channel when commercials air. Consequently, television ads need to be rerun often to be effective. Due to increased Internet usage, television viewing may decline. However a new system of TV, iDTV (interactive digital Television), has been developed, and it will bring a new phase in television advertising. As it says, It makes people be able to interact with TV. It works like the internet, but the only difference is that this happens in TV in your living room. Comcast, America's leading provider of cable, entertainment, and communications service, has started the next wave of television; It is called Comcast Spotlight products, including Searchlight. It offers the information of automotive, real estate, careers, education, and so on.[18]

Radio Very low production costs make radio an

Slogan	Product or Brand
Where's the Beef?	Wendy's Restaurants
Reach Out and Touch Someone	AT&T
Don't Leave Home Without It	American Express
Just Do It	Nike
Generation Next	Pepsi
Enjoy the Ride	Nissan
Breakfast of Champions	Wheaties
We Bring Good Things to Life	General Electric
Did Somebody Say McDonald's?	McDonald's
I Love What You Do For Me	Toyota
Good to the Last Drop	Maxwell House
Obey Your Thirst	Sprite
Sometimes You Feel Like a Nut	Almond Joy
Fly the Friendly Skies	United Airlines

Figure 13.5 Successful Advertising Slogans

attractive medium. Furthermore, marketers can be extremely selective in targeting U.S. consumers because each market area averages 30 stations, each aimed at a specific audience. The problem has been limited research on local radio markets, but new computer systems are changing that. Software is available to assist with postbuy analysis so that ad agencies can estimate the ratings for stations and specific airtimes. Lacking visual content, radio spots require more repetition than television ads. As methods for audience rating improve, however, it should be possible to use fewer spots and evaluate more accurately their effect on selected segments.

Magazines Magazines also target well-defined consumer segments, and professional journals reach very specific groups. Although about 90 percent of adults read at least one magazine per month, overall magazine readership is declining. Most adults (about 79 percent) consider magazine ads to be positive and helpful for making purchase decisions. In fact, there is evidence that consumers pay more attention to this advertising medium than to television.[19] In the past few years, many "small" magazines have been introduced to appeal to unique tastes, which makes more finely tuned tar-

Marketing Vocabulary

ADVERTISING CAMPAIGN
A series of advertisements with a main theme running through them.

EXPOSURE
The process of putting the ad in contact with the customer.

STOPPING POWER
The ability of an ad to gain and hold the consumer's attention.

PULLING POWER
The ability to maintain the interest of the consumer to the end of the advertising message.

MEDIA
The channels through which messages are transmitted.

	Advantages	**Disadvantages**
Newspapers	Wide exposure for upscale adults. Flexible; timely; buyers can save for later reference. High credibility.	Few ads are fully read. Young adults don't read them. Costs are rising. Alternate media are becoming more important news sources.
Television	Creative and flexible. Cost efficient. Credible.	Message is quickly forgotten. High production cost. Difficult to get attention.
Radio	Selective targeting possible. Mobile—goes with listeners. Low production costs.	No visual content. High frequency is required to reach many people. Audience research has traditionally been difficult.
Magazines	Target narrowly defined segments. Prestigious sources. Long life—can be passed along.	Audiences declining. Long lead times to develop ads. Need to use many different magazines to reach a lot of buyers.
Outdoor Ads	Low cost per exposure. Good to supplement other media. With color, lighting, and mechanization gets attention.	Can't communicate much. Difficult to measure results.
Internet	Considerable potential. Medium for relationship marketing. Customer driven and dialogue oriented. Increasing number of users.	Little research to indicate proven effectiveness. Relies on consumers accessing the necessary technologies. Revenues still small. Difficult to target a specific audience. Difficult to measure results.

Figure 13.6   Advantages and Disadvantages of Various Media
Source: J. Thomas Russell and W. Ronald Lane, Kleppner's Advertising Procedure, 13th ed. © 1996.

geting possible. The disadvantages of magazines are long lead times and high production costs for ads. In efforts to target more finely, new techniques for producing special ads are being designed that will bring costs down. Ultimately, the goal is to get as close to unique customers as possible. To reach a large number of buyers, however, ads in many different magazines may be required.

Outdoor Advertising Outdoor advertisements, primarily billboards, are very inexpensive per exposure, so they provide an attractive supplement to other media. With color, lighting, and mechanization, some billboards have fantastic stopping power. Even though advertising in general has been declining, outdoor advertisements have increased steadily. Moreover, digital has arrived in outdoor advertising and this medium is expected to broaden vividly for several years. Digital outdoor advertising is managed by the Internet, and has the benefit that ads can be changed in a short period of time; therefore it is expected to be more useful than standard outdoor adver-

tising to do strategic promotions.[20] However, outdoor advertisements can be so eye-catching that they distract motorists. Consider the 32-foot painting of the colorful former basketball star, Dennis Rodman, displayed on a warehouse along the Kennedy Expressway in Chicago. It attracted so much attention in rush hour that it was removed in response to traffic officials. Despite their flashiness, outdoor ads can't communicate a great amount of information because people move past them so quickly. It's often difficult to measure the results of outdoor advertisements.

The Internet The Internet provides a medium that is both customer driven and dialogue oriented. More than two-thirds of the U.S. uses the Internet and research of the products on the Internet controls almost half of all retail purchases. This gives companies another way to develop relationships with customers through Web sites that provide many messages about their products or services, and other information that builds a good, solid relationship with customers. Oral-b's Web site has a learning center section; customers are able to access not only product information but also tips for good oral care habits and so on.[21] And, the Internet allows advertising to occur in forms of banners, pop-up ads, pop-under ads, interstitials, and so forth.[22] Google Analytics and Google AdWords are two services that track visitors to a company's Web site and online banner advertisements. It helps determine what keywords attract your most desirable prospects, what advertising copy pulled the most responses, and what landing pages and content make the most money for you.[23]

A major disadvantage of Internet marketing is low click-through rates, as people are ignoring the banner ads for the most part. The Internet is the key tool in **viral marketing**. Viral marketing is diffusing the marketing messages across people, just like the flu virus's trait. Marketers need a few people to pick up on and start their message, and wait for it to go viral. However as viral marketing develops, measures of its effectiveness must be developed. So, marketers are eagerly paying attention to the effect of the transient media and to the unwilling buzz.[24] A legendary example of viral marketing is Burger King. In February 2004, Burger King ran the most creative campaigns with the Subservient Chicken Web site. This Web site had an interactive video clip, "Have chicken their way," that the customers could control the actions of a person in a chicken suit. This hilarious video clip became the source of viral marketing and led to more than 500 million visits at www.burgerking.com over the following 18 months.[25]

Mobile Mobile advertising means delivering text and video messages of ads to cell phones. Marketers are expecting to extend their messaging from offline to online and mobile handsets. Many Internet advertisers have already tried mobile messaging marketing. It is estimated that by the year 2013, over $24 billion will be spent on mobile marketing. Therefore marketers look for the most effective message formats and combinations with current marketing strategies.[26] Marketers expect this medium will be especially valuable to younger generations.

Media Popularity Which media do the major advertisers select? Figure 13.7 illustrates advertising expenditures for the top 100 companies. The four types of television media account for about two-thirds, followed at a great distance by magazines, newspapers, radio, and outdoor advertising.

The Media Schedule Media scheduling can be looked at as a plan within the advertising plan. This very exacting work involves a number of considerations: target audience analysis; reach, frequency, and continuity balance; media timing; and budgeting.

Target Audience As you know, the marketing plan is always directed at specific market segments. Media planning begins by addressing those segments. Marketers have developed very detailed methods for defining target markets. For example, Claritas Corporation has developed PRIZM, which uses such variables as socioeconomic status, ethnicity, family life cycle, education, employment, type of housing, and location of housing to describe 40 audiences. In turn, these data are correlated with media usage patterns. The information helps determine which media are likely to influence the respective segments at various times and locations.

Media scheduling usually is done geographically and demographically. For example, Taco Bell, McDonald's, and Burger King all compete for the fast-food dollar in the United States. But Taco Bell targets males age 19 to 24, whereas the other two include families with children.

Once decisions are made about target audience and geographic considerations, media planners calculate the cost of communicating with the audience through various media. Media costs are generally expressed in units of cost per thousand, abbreviated as CPM (M is the Roman numeral for 1,000). The CPM for reaching the target audience is calculated as follows:

$$CPM = \frac{\text{Advertising cost} \times 1{,}000}{\text{Circulation to target audience}}$$

For example, suppose we are interested in reaching women with children under two years of age. We know that McCall's has 600,000 readers in this category, and an advertisement there will cost $60,000. The CPM of reaching our target audience is $100 ($60,000 × 1,000 ÷ 600,000 = $100). We can then determine the cost per person by dividing CPM by 1,000. In this case it is $0.10 ($100 ÷ 1,000 = $0.10).

Reach, Frequency, and Continuity Balance Once media planners know the target audience and the cost of reaching it, they consider the reach, frequency, and continuity of the advertising campaign. **Reach** is the number of consumers in the target audience who can be contacted through a given medium. In the preceding example the reach through McCall's is 600,000. **Frequency** is the number of times the audience is contacted during a given period, usually over four weeks. **Continuity** is the length of time the advertising campaign will run in a given medium. It is important to select

Marketing Vocabulary

VIRAL MARKETING
Diffusing a marketing message across people.

REACH
The number of consumers in the target audience who can be contacted through a given medium.

FREQUENCY
The number of times the audience is reached in a given period, usually per day or per week.

CONTINUITY
The length of time the advertising campaign will run in a given medium.

2008 Global Advertising Expenditure		
Media	**Annual Expenditure**	**Percent of Total**
Newspapers	$ 127.3 billion	26.8
Magazines	$ 56.4 billion	11.9
Television	$ 180.3 billion	37.9
Radio	$ 37.7 billion	7.9
Cinema	$ 2.1 billion	0.4
Outdoor	$ 27.1 billion	5.7
Internet	$ 44.5 billion	9.4
Total	$ 475.4 billion	100.0

Source: ZenithOptimedia

Figure 13.7   Global Advertising Expenditure

a medium with enough reach, frequency, and continuity to gain the desired effect. At the same time, agencies do not want to waste funds. **Overexposure** refers to reaching a prospect either after a purchase decision has been made or so frequently that the campaign actually wastes money.

Media Timing Products may be seasonal or purchased more frequently on certain days of the week. For example, suntan lotions are bought mainly during the summer and especially on weekends. Products such as soaps and cosmetics are purchased frequently all year round and may require constant advertising. Consider the importance of media timing for advertising weight loss products. About half of all dieters initiate programs between January and April. Companies such as Weight Watchers, Curves and Jenny Craig, Inc., spent millions of dollars on television and print ads every January.

The Marketing Gazette™

CREATING & CAPTURING VALUE THROUGH DIVERSITY

Targeting Gay, Lesbian, Bisexual, & Transgender Consumers

Since 1991, Atlantis Events has been serving the GLBT (gay, lesbian, bisexual, and transgender) market, customizing exclusive vacations for 20,000 gay and lesbian travelers each year. Outreach efforts representing the West Hollywood, CA-based travel company's cruises and resort getaways have always included editorial opportunities in a variety of gay-media outlets. It is estimated that the GLBT market in the US has reached $690 billion with more than 15 million GLBT adults.

Ten years ago, the number of mainstream advertisers openly targeting the gay and lesbian market was rather low, including a few open-minded companies like Subaru, Absolut Vodka, and American Airlines. But today, things have changed. With a median household income of over $60,000 a year, gay Americans exhibit significant purchasing power. Companies that once neglected this segment are now willing to risk boycotts from groups like the American Families Association in order to gain favor with GLBT buyers. The buying power of gay and lesbian consumers is expected to grow by nearly $30 billion this year and top $835 billion by 2011.

According to a study from Packaged Facts, a division of MarketResearch.com, more than 90 percent of gay and lesbian consumers would more likely purchase from companies that marketed directly to them. They want to feel as if companies truly want their business and want to see themselves reflected in marketing efforts. As a result, companies are using words like "partner" and "sexual orientation" instead of "husband" and "preference." They could establish corporate marketing efforts by affiliating a brand with nonprofits or issues that matter to GLBT consumers. In 2007, the first edition of Boulder Colorado's Mountain Pride Connections directory hit the tables and counters of local businesses. The free guide lists almost 140 gay-friendly businesses and resources that would be huge in building stronger relationships among GLBT business owners.

Since 2003, Delta has been a PRIDE Festival sponsor, supporting diversity that extends well beyond airports and aircraft. "Delta embraces its position as a global corporation – from the places we fly to the community events and organizations we support that reflect the diverse interests of our customers and Delta people," said Cherie Caldwell, Delta's director of Global Diversity. "Delta's sponsorship of PRIDE and Gay Days is one example in which Delta Employee Networks involve themselves annually."

To complicate matters, it's important to look at the activity of competitors. It may be necessary to counteract their campaigns or take advantage of times when they tend to promote less. Tactics include selecting media that competitors are not using or making adjustments to the scheduling, timing, and frequency of various advertisements.

Media Budget Generally, the media budget is set according to the strategic marketing and communication plans. Marketers attempt to maximize the advertising effort within budget constraints, using one or a combination of media to achieve the most influence in the market. As part of the media plan, it's important to determine whether messages will be visual, verbal, or both. The amount of information to be communicated will influence the choice of media and, consequently, the budget. Recently, the costs of all forms have been escalating, so careful attention must be paid to the trade-offs among them. Fortunately, media competition helps the situation. Marketers from magazines, newspapers, television, and radio are constantly promoting their own vehicle. To accommodate clients, they are willing to provide help in media selection and scheduling.

CREATING ADS

This step in the ad plan involves both science and art. Creating ads can be as complicated as making a movie. The key is to know your objectives and the constraints imposed by the media, scheduling, and budget. What makes an ad outstanding and memorable? As with any creative process, it's difficult to determine precisely what people will like. To help answer that question, *Marketing*, a British journal, conducts a survey each month called "ad watch." British consumers are asked whether or not they remember a specific advertisement.

There are certainly many classics. The California raisins who "heard it through the grapevine" combined humor, visual novelty, and a great rock beat that caught the attention of millions in the 1980s. Most of the older generations still remember Mikey, who willingly ate Life cereal. And nearly everyone (if old enough) can recall the little boy sharing his Coke with Mean Joe Greene of the Pittsburgh Steelers after the game.

When diverse segments are part of the target audience, the advertisement must be created in such a way that it appeals to various tastes and preferences. Marketers also need to be aware of language differences, acceptable behaviors, ethnicity, and cultural norms. Many promotional efforts are now for a global audience, and that means communicating in a huge number of languages and dialects. To avoid costly mistakes, it is critical for marketers to research and understand the language(s) of a target market segment before they advertise to it. For

example, "Pepsi Brings You Back to Life" was chosen by the company as the promotional theme in China, but the slogan translated into "Pepsi Brings Your Ancestors Back from the Grave." Coca-Cola selected Chinese characters (letters) that sound like its name but which mean "bite the wax tadpole." Imagine Chevrolet's surprise when it was reported that Nova in the Spanish market translates as "It won't go." In Italy, a campaign for Schweppes tonic water referred to the product as Schweppes toilet water, Kentucky Fried Chicken's slogan in China became "eat your fingers off" rather than "finger lickin' good."[27]

Of course, not all diversity is ethnic or linguistic. Gays and lesbians, for example, may be unresponsive to ads that employ only heterosexual couples to represent the warm, loving relationships associated with use of the product. The diversity feature discusses Subaru's advertisements targeting gays and lesbians.

ASSESSING ADVERTISING EFFECTIVENESS

The effect of advertising can be assessed at two different points: before running the ad campaign and afterward. This kind of measurement is extremely important to determine what does and doesn't work so that the campaign can be adjusted.

Individual ads and campaigns may be tested beforehand to evaluate effectiveness before committing more funds. Various tests are used on the sample audience to determine whether the ad content has been stored in the consumer's memory. Both recall and recognition are considered important by advertising researchers. One test asks the audience what it remembers about an ad after a limited run in a particular medium. Two aspects usually are measured. **Unaided recall** asks the viewer to identify any advertisements he or she can recall, such as "What commercials do you remember seeing for automobiles?" **Aided recall** refers to content that can be remembered without seeing the particular ad. An example is: "Do you recall seeing a commercial for Honda?" By questioning several respondents, researchers determine both the unaided and aided recall scores. These tests may be conducted immediately following exposure to the ad or up to several

Marketing Vocabulary

OVEREXPOSURE
Continuing to reach a prospect after a buying decision has been made or to the point that the campaign becomes tedious and actually turns off some potential buyers.

UNAIDED RECALL
The viewer is asked to identify any advertisements he or she can remember.

AIDED RECALL
The viewer is given some specific piece of information about the ad before being asked if he or she recalls having seen it.

days thereafter.

Recognition means that you remember the ad when you see it again. This kind of remembrance is typically adequate for low-involvement products such as chewing gum or soup. To test recognition, audience members are shown an ad and later are asked if they remember it. In other words, the ad is a stimulus during the testing procedure. One of the most popular types of recognition test is the Starch test, which is usually conducted after an ad has been run. Respondents leaf through a magazine containing the ad and are then asked if they remember seeing it. Next, a series of questions determines whether they associated the ad with the advertiser's name or logo and whether they read at least half of the copy. Because Starch tests have been run on so many ads, marketers can compare the scores of their ad to similar types.

When persuasion is the objective of the advertisement, it is very important to go beyond simple memory tests and determine whether the ad influences attitudes or behavior. For this, marketers use persuasion tests, which essentially measure attitude change. For example, respondents may be asked to preview a particular television show with ads imbedded in it. They are then questioned about the program itself as well as brand preferences. Comparing the answers to measures taken beforehand, it's possible to determine the amount of attitude change.

SALES PROMOTION

Sales promotion is communication designed to stimulate immediate purchases using tools such as coupons, contests, and free samples.[28] It is used frequently by most companies and it accounts for about $366 billion in annual expenditures in the United States.[29] Notice that the definition focuses on immediate results and changes in the behavior of consumers or other channel members. In addition to its value as a short-term incentive, there is no doubt that sales promotion for many brands has a lot to do with long-term brand equity. This is particularly true of frequently purchased consumer items, such as Coke and Pepsi. Sales promotion plays an important role in reinforcing continuous usage and offsetting gains made by competitors. When brand switching occurs, sales promotion is a valuable way to regain consumer loyalty.

Sales promotion also stimulates trial. Many times buyers are reluctant to try a new product because it may not perform as well as their existing one. Sales promotion reduces the risk by lowering the price or creating other incentives. Most consumers are now accustomed to having a trial opportunity at little or no cost. Car dealers offer test drives, and some companies provide free samples.

Whereas advertising and public relations increase

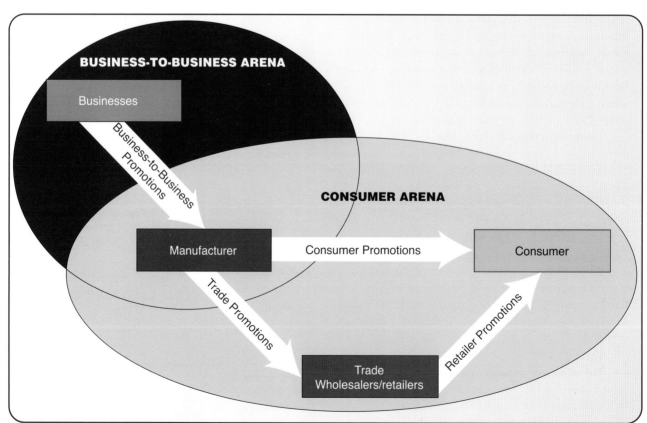

Figure 13.8   Types of Sales Promotions

awareness, sales promotion prompts people to action, resulting in immediate sales. By either increasing the perceived value of a product or reducing its price, sales promotion motivates customers to make an immediate purchase decision. Value is increased by providing a free gift, an unusual warranty, or some type of prize. Price may be lowered directly, with an introductory offer, or through coupons and rebates. In any case, the consumer recognizes an immediate opportunity and acts on it.

Although sales promotion generally has an immediate result, its long-term effects are less clear. It is most commonly used in conjunction with other forms of promotion, such as advertising, public relations campaigns, or personal selling. Consequently, it is usually seen as part of the total promotion package designed by the marketing communication strategists.

TYPES OF SALES PROMOTION

Figure 13.8 depicts four different types of sales promotion: business-to-business, consumer, trade, and retailer promotions.

Figure 13.9 lists typical activities in each category. Business-to-business promotions usually involve trade shows, conventions, sales contests, and specialty deals, such as volume discounts and price sales. Sales promotion in the consumer market is directed at gaining a behavioral change by way of trial or actual purchase. Manufacturers use two basic approaches to influence the consumer—the sales pull and the sales push. **Consumer promotions** are manufacturer incentives offered directly to consumers, largely bypassing the retailer. They are designed to pull the product through the retail establishment with coupons, rebates, and other means that the manufacturer can control from headquarters.

Trade promotions are provided by manufacturers to distribution channel members. The objective is to give wholesalers and retailers an incentive to sell the manufacturer's brand. Essentially, these promotions make it worthwhile for the channel member to push the product to the consumer. Common incentives are advertising allowances and price reductions. For example, Ralston Purina may offer a 3 percent discount on Cat Chow to retailers. They may pass the savings on to the consumers in order to increase trade or may pocket the difference in order to increase profit.

Retailer promotions are directed at the consumer by the retail outlet. They are often confined to a local area, although large chains such as Best Buy may run many of the same promotions at all locations. This provides a sales level sufficient to obtain quantity discounts from suppliers, which enables prices to be kept low.

Normally, the push and pull elements of the sales promotion strategy should work hand in hand. Trade promotions are usually coordinated with the firm's other sales activities. The sales force works to persuade customers (retailers or wholesalers) to purchase greater volume and push to consumers through retailer promotions. At the same time, consumer promotions are usually coordinated with ad messages about coupons

Marketing Vocabulary

SALES PROMOTION
Communications designed to stimulate immediate purchases using tools such as coupons, contests, and free samples.

CONSUMER PROMOTION
Offer designed to pull the product through the retail establishment.

TRADE PROMOTION
An offer from a manufacturer to channel members, such as wholesalers and retailers.

RETAILER PROMOTION
An offer to the consumer that is sponsored by a retailer.

Business-to-Business Promotions	Manufacturer Trade Promotions	Manufacturer Consumer Promotions	Retailer Consumer Promotions
Trade shows	Discounts	Coupons	Price cuts
Conventions	• off invoice	Rebates (refunds)	Displays
Sales contests	• off list	Samples	Free goods ("trials")
Specialty items	Allowances	Price packs ("cents off")	Retailer coupons
Virtual trade shows	• advertising	Value packs ("2 for 1")	Feature advertising
	• display	Premiums (gifts)	Patronage awards
	Financing incentives	Sweepstakes (prizes and contests)	
	Contests	Point-of-purchase displays	
	Spiffs	Cross-promotion	
		Continuity programs	

Figure 13.9   Major Types of Sales Promotion Activities

and point-of-purchase displays tied into the advertising theme. This kind of one-two punch can produce dramatic results.

THE SUCCESS OF SALES PROMOTION

Sales promotion has become increasingly successful due to changing consumer lifestyles, better technology, and the changing structure of the retail industry.[30] Today's busy consumers are looking for ways to simplify purchase choices in order to save time. In addition, they want value, and they view sales promotion as a way of getting more for their money. Bundle promotions grant consumers a discount when they buy a given number of units. Many manufacturers have found that promoting products in this way increases brand line sales.[31]

Technology helps marketers target sales promotions more precisely than ever before. Checkout scanners tell immediately which brands are purchased. Sorting machines identify which coupons and other redemption items are used, and tracking devices identify where purchases are made and by whom. It's now very easy for marketers to measure the effect of specific promotion activities on unit sales and profitability. The Internet has also begun to track consumer spending patterns.

Another influence on the use of promotions is the changing structure of the retail industry. As large establishments such as Wal-Mart gain market power, they can compete more effectively with manufacturers' brands. To counteract this power, manufacturers use sales promotion to create a pull through the channel to maintain their customer base. At the same time, they are engaged in competitive battles to maintain market share. A company that wants to hold share is almost compelled to use sales promotions commensurate with those of other major competitors, whether retailers or other manufacturers.

CREATING CUSTOMER RELATIONSHIPS AND LOYALTY THROUGH SALES PROMOTION

Sales promotion is an excellent tool for organizations that want to connect with customers through relationships. The purpose of relationship marketing is to create loyal, satisfied customers. Consumers can be very fickle, however, and marketers must keep that constantly in mind. Relational marketing and customer relationship manage-

ment have received considerable attention by managers. One research finds that, among business managers, relationship marketing is becoming institutionalized. That is, relationship marketing has been so widely discussed that managers now perceive it is a standard practice to implement relationship marketing in business-to-business exchange relationships.[32] Figure 13.10 describes the four main categories of buyers and strategies for marketing to each group.

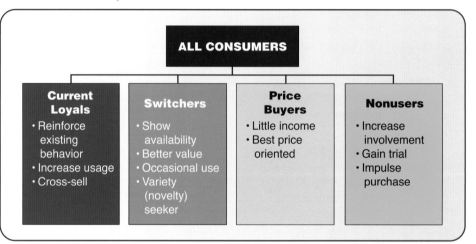

Figure 13.10   Types of Buyers

Current Loyals   As the name implies, current loyals are presently purchasing a company's brand. They range from intensely loyal users who buy because of their relationship with the company to people who are loyal because of simple convenience or price factors. It's difficult to persuade them to switch. One strategy used to maintain these customers is to reward their loyalty with personally targeted one-to-one promotions. This encourages them to continue using the brand and reminds them about the product they have been purchasing. Many retail establishments send out e-newsletters and coupons, particularly for special occasions such as birthdays. Others will provide loyalty cards that reward the customer for making purchases.

Loyal consumers also may respond to sales promotions by buying a product in larger quantities or at a time when they normally do not purchase. For example, loyal users of Cheerios will likely view a promotion as an opportunity to stockpile the product. Users of Starkist tuna may buy several cans when the brand is on sale. Once it is available at home, it is likely to be used more often.

When a manufacturer owns two or more brands, current loyal customers are excellent candidates for **cross-selling,** promoting another of the brands or using one product to boost sales of another, often an unrelated product. Different companies also may work together to cross-sell. Many hotels now offer higher end toiletries. Marriott provides guests with travel size beauty products by Bath & Body Works, and also offers both travel size and full size bottles for sale.[33] This campaign appeals to loyal customers of all the partners, building relationships synergistically.

Switchers Switchers purchase a number of different brands. Loyalty has decreased in recent years, and the percentage of consumers in the switcher category has become somewhat larger. Consequently, many manufacturers and retailers focus on this group. In many cases, switchers cut their overall expenditures by finding the best deal at the time. They may switch regularly or only when they see an opportunity to increase value or decrease price.

Switchers are not likely to wait for an out-of-stock brand. Trade promotion aimed at maximizing inventory levels and store space works well with this group. Since they are interested in price and value, they respond to even fairly complex purchase offers. For example, several units of the same product can be bundled together, the amount of product can be increased for the same price, or the price can be reduced.

Some switchers are occasional users, purchasing infrequently or according to season. This is even true of churchgoers. In England, the Churches Advertising Network launches a series of ads targeted at this group around holiday time.[34]

Other switchers are simply seeking novelty or variety and change brands to alleviate boredom or monotony. Sales promotions work particularly well on them, since they are responsive to novel purchase opportunities. If the product is noticed at the precise time the variety seeker is interested in buying, then the manufacturer benefits. 7-Up positioned itself in a way that distinguishes it not only from colas but also from other uncolas. "Make 7-Up yours" is intended to reach buyers looking for a novel purchase opportunity.

Price Buyers The price buyer's only concern is cost. Most in this category want low prices, but a few choose only the most expensive brand. People in the latter category tend to ignore nearly all sales promotion, and they consider clipping coupons a total waste of time. In contrast, buyers after low prices are likely to purchase opportunistically, when they have funds and the product is on sale. They respond very well to price promotions: cents-off, two for one, buy a second one for a penny, limited time offers, and so forth.

Nonusers Nonusers do not currently purchase a particular brand. Sales promotions are designed to create involvement, which may stimulate purchase. Again, cross-selling works to gain trial. For example, many Barnes & Noble bookstores have Starbucks coffee stands in their cafes. In this case, sales promotion encourages nonusers to try a new drink. Some companies mail samples to nonusers' homes. Rather than throw the product out, consumers are usually willing to try it. In other cases, nonusers are supplied a trial under captive circumstances. An example is the complimentary snacks offered on airlines, such as branded peanuts, pretzels, and sodas.

BUSINESS-TO-BUSINESS PROMOTIONS

The four main types of business-to-business promotion are trade shows, conventions, sales contests, and specialty items. Often volume discounts and price sales occur in conjunction with these four activities.

Trade Shows Trade shows are designed to bring marketers and customers together at a given location for a short period. They occur around the world and are an opportunity for companies to display existing and new product

Approximately 80 million people attend trade shows in the United States each year.

©Robert Wertheimer

lines in ways that are convenient for customers. Nearly 75 percent of all firms use trade shows as a major promotion mechanism.[35] In the United States, nearly 6,000 trade shows take place every year, attended by approximately 80 million people.

Companies set up booths that are staffed by key personnel and salespeople, and it's not unusual for retailers and distributors to select the merchandise they will carry during the coming year. Consequently, business marketers may invest a large percentage of their promotional budget in trade shows. This is a very cost-effective way to meet a great number of potential purchasers. The cost of closing a trade show sale is estimated at around $500, compared to over $1,500 for a regular business-to-business sale.[36]

Today, trade show information is heavily promoted and accessed on the Internet. The Biz Trade Shows Web site is the largest directory of business events and trade fairs on the Internet. Companies can quickly identify and select the event that will be the most beneficial in reaching potential customers.[37] Companies can quickly identify and select the event that will be the most beneficial in reaching potential customers.

Conventions   Conventions provide another opportunity for marketers and buyers to meet. They are often sponsored by professional groups, such as the American Hospital Association, the American Medical Association, or the International Association of Certified Public Accountants. It is important to note that conventions are held around the world, giving marketers the chance to assess the level of global competition and gather ideas for new strategies. Although companies attend primarily to stimulate immediate sales, they also can take the opportunity to do long-range assessments of customer and industry trends. Marketing researchers often attend conventions and trade shows because so many qualified buyers

are concentrated in one place. This provides a pool of readily available respondents, and schedules often permit in-depth interviews, focus groups, and surveys. These events are considered prime opportunities for data collection.

Sales Contests   Sales contests for salespeople and dealers offer prizes for accomplishing specific goals. Most companies sponsor some type of sales contest from time to time and award trips, gifts, or cash, often at an annual sales convention. This type of sales promotion is designed to elicit immediate action by giving short-term rewards for short-term behavior. When incentives are tied to measurable and achievable sales objectives, they can be highly motivating. Sales contests frequently are specific to product lines or market segments and are integrated into the overall selling and promotion strategy. Volkswagen rewards top sellers of its featured models with free trips to destination vacation spots.[38]

Specialty Items   **Specialty items** are gifts for customers, usually sent through the mail or handed out by salespeople, with the organization's name imprinted on them. These include such items as pens, calendars, memo pads, T-shirts, sun visors, or hats. Generally there is no purchase requirement. Specialty items create good will with customers and allows brand exposure in a variety of places.[39]

TRADE PROMOTIONS

Trade promotions are offered by the manufacturer to wholesalers or retailers. Trade promotions are becoming prevalent worldwide. The Dubai World Trade Centre in the United Arab Emirates has become a focal point for international trade promotions by hosting a range of industry events including the Middle East International Motor Show.[40] You can expect nearly every type of trade promotion to be offered by the suppliers. Five common types are discounts, allowances, financing incentives, sales contests, and spiffs.

Discounts   One of the most popular trade promotions is discount or price-off arrangements, which reduce either the invoice or the list price. The invoice price is what the manufacturer charges to the distributor, whereas the list price is what the end customer is charged. If distributors choose to pass the price cut on to consumers, demand may increase. If not, distributor profit margins increase. Like all trade promotions, discounts encourage distributors to handle more of the company's product and to stimulate sales to consumers.

Allowances   **Allowances** are funds given to retailers and wholesalers based on the amount of product they

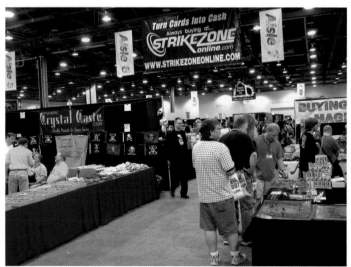

Gamers gather at the Origin Game Fair, one of North America's largest gaming conventions.

buy. Two typical allowances are for advertising and display purposes. For example, a retailer who purchases $5,000 worth of product may receive a $500 allowance to help pay for advertising. Display allowances work the same way, except that the funds must be used for point-of-purchase displays in the retail outlet.

Financing Incentives

Financing incentives help reduce the retailer's inventory carrying cost. This is commonly referred to as financing the "floor plan," which is the retailer's stock of inventory. For example, in the automobile business, dealers do not have to pay immediately for all the cars shipped to them. Instead, they pay a fee for having them in their showroom. Financing incentives come in a broad variety, but all are designed to get the manufacturer's product into the retail establishment.

Patronage awards are very useful promotions.

Sales Contests and Spiffs

Two other types of trade promotion are sales contests and "spiffs." In this context, sales contests reward the retailer for selling a certain level of product and often extend to the salespeople within the retail establishment. Spiffs are like a commission paid to salespeople in retail outlets who sell the manufacturer's product rather than a competitor's brand. These cash incentives are not uncommon for such items as cameras, televisions, mobile homes, and cellular telephones. Many people consider spiffs unethical because they encourage the promotion of one brand over others irrespective of its value to the customer. Because consumers are not aware of the spiff, they may believe the salesperson's motives are more "pure" than is actually the case.

RETAILER PROMOTIONS

Retailer promotions are directed specifically at the end customer and originate within the retailing organization. They seek to encourage consumers to purchase a product from a given location. Consequently, retailer promotions are often in-store or specific with regard to where the promotion can be exercised. Manufacturers may help with retailer promotions. Sony's "Modern Rock Live" Campaign was one of the biggest promotions ever undertaken by the company. It is a real value for consumers and a great sales builder for retailers, because Sony provided kits to help outlets develop local tie-ins to the national promotion campaign by using TV, radio, print ads, and consumer Web sites.

The most common type of retailer promotion is price cuts. Retailers are likely to use these regularly to stimulate sales of certain product lines or to reduce inventory of older products. Also common are display promotions to direct attention to particular goods. Large national retailers are likely to send teams to work with local outlets in developing similar displays across the country. These teams are likely to be dispatched on a seasonal basis. Gap takes this approach for displays. Free trials are another type of retailer promotion. Local copy shops, for example, often offer a free color copy to induce customers to try their services. Retailer coupons are used relatively frequently and are often placed in local newspapers. Also popular is feature advertising on radio or television of discounted items, such as automobiles and mobile homes. It's not unusual for the retailer to be the spokesperson in these types of ads. Finally, patronage awards are very useful promotions. Generally, a card is punched or stamped each time the consumer shops at the retail outlet. When the card is filled, it's redeemed for free merchandise. The Cappuccino Cafe in Okemos, Michigan, redeems not only its own loyalty card but also those of competitors as a way to get new trials. Patronage awards, which stimulate loyalty to a given outlet, are particularly useful in local markets for creating a bond between regular customers and the retailer.

CONSUMER PROMOTIONS

Manufacturers use consumer sales promotions to influence their market share across all retailing outlets. There are several popular forms: coupons, rebates, samples, sweepstakes, price and value packs, point-of-purchase displays, and continuity programs.

Coupons **Coupons** are certificates that entitle a

Marketing Vocabulary

SPECIALTY ITEMS
Gifts with the organization's name that are provided to customers, usually given through the mail or by the sales force.

ALLOWANCES
Funds given to retailers and wholesalers based on the amount of product they buy.

FINANCING INCENTIVE
An offer to finance the retailer's inventory prior to its sale.

COUPON
Certificate that entitles a consumer to an incentive to buy the product, usually a price reduction or a free sample.

consumer to an incentive, usually a price reduction or free sample. Trade coupons are redeemable only at a particular store or chain, whereas manufacturer coupons are redeemable at any outlet. They are particularly appealing to manufacturers because they can make a direct connection with consumers. Since manufacturers' coupons create work for retailers, they may be given incentives for handling them.

Coupons are one of the most popular forms of consumer sales promotion. Some consumers purchase a large percentage of their nondurable products through coupons; and many plan their shopping lists around coupons. Other consumers do not want to take the time to search for and cut coupons, especially those who are loyal to particular brands and stores.

Coupons are generally distributed as freestanding inserts (FSIs) in newspapers or magazines. They also may be sent in special mailings or as bill stuffers. Another technique is an on-shelf dispenser at the retail outlet, placed near the manufacturer's brand. Only about 2 percent of regular coupons are redeemed, 8.5 percent of checkout coupons, 9.8 percent of electronic coupons, and 13 percent of on-shelf coupons. Marketers try to identify the level of price reduction that will stimulate coupon use. If a 25-cent incentive will do as much as a 50-cent reduction, then the 25-cent incentive should be used.

Rebates **Rebates** are refunds given to consumers for the purchase of particular items. Psychologically, rebates make a larger impression than price reductions. For example, let's say an automobile manufacturer offers a $1,500 rebate or a 10 percent reduction in price for a $15,000 car. Although the discount may be precisely the same, consumers are likely to see the rebate as greater. The reason is that the price discount from $15,000 to $13,500 is a perceptually smaller decrease than the $1,500 rebate. Since consumers usually have to mail a form to the manufacturer to get the rebate, they often will not bother if the amount is small. They also may lose or forget about the rebate. In those cases the company gets the sale without paying the incentive. Another advantage of rebates is that they leave higher margins for intermediaries.

Rebates tend to be particularly effective in stimulating trial of brands that are priced higher than those of competitors. Hewlett-Packard frequently runs rebate offers on its printers and other electronic devices. To get the rebate, customers have to submit a completed rebate coupon in addition to a proof-of-purchase sticker. They receive their rebate six to eight weeks after the purchase.[41]

Samples Generally, samples are distributed via direct mail, door-to-door, or in stores.

Sometimes coupons may be redeemed for free samples. This method is effective with new products or when targeted at people who lack experience with the brand. Occasionally, manufacturers attempt to renew an older product by providing samples. American Sampling, Inc., sends gift packs to 3.8 million new mothers annually, and companies such as Market Source provide samples to college freshmen.

This kind of sales promotion requires very careful attention to detail because the cost of samples is high. One study found that 51 million coupons for a free product distributed through freestanding inserts (FSIs) cost $7 per thousand, whereas 5 million samples distributed through direct mail cost $80 per thousand. But the FSIs only converted 367,200 people ($0.97 per convert), whereas the mail samples converted 800,000 ($0.50 per convert.)[42]

Sweepstakes A sweepstakes is a contest in which participants' names are pooled, and the winner is drawn randomly. Most of you have experienced a twinge of anticipation upon receiving an envelope stating that you may have won millions of dollars. The objective of the contest is to get buyers to purchase the products included in the sweepstakes offer. Laws prevent the sponsor from requiring a purchase in order to participate. Sweepstakes promoters must provide full disclosure of the requirements for entering as well as the probabilities of winning.

Johnson & Johnson Vision Care offered a chance to attend the 2008 Beijing Olympic Games for four winners and their guests. The sweepstakes was part of a campaign to promote vision care and eye health.[43]

Price and Value Packs Price and value packs are cents-off or two-for-one offers. The cents-off variety is easier to administer and receives a great deal of attention. The value pack, while more difficult to administer, gets more product in the hands of the consumer in a shorter period. Both are very flexible and relatively easy sales promotions to consumers. Value packs are different from premiums or gifts, which may

This display at check out has a lot of attention-getting power and can increase consumer interest in a product.

not be related directly to the product. For example, in real estate sales it's not uncommon for the purchaser of a home to receive a free airline ticket to a vacation spot.

Point-of-Purchase Displays Point-of-purchase (POP) displays exhibit products at retail locations. Since up to 70 percent of purchase decisions are made in the store, the displays can be very important. Companies spend huge amounts annually on POP. More than 52 percent of carbonated beverage sales, 26 percent of candy/mint sales, and 22 percent of beer/ale sales have been attributed to such displays.[44] They work best when tied directly to other messages or advertising campaigns. Generally, POP displays need to have a lot of attention-getting power and must focus the consumer's interest on the sales promotion and product at hand.

Many stores are using POP to connect with customers in an interactive and exciting environment. For example, customers at Niketown can hear the sounds of bouncing tennis balls and squeaking tennis shoes.

Continuity Programs Continuity programs reward people for continued and frequent use of a particular product. A good example is the frequent flyer miles offered in the airline industry. Although these usually don't stimulate more air travel, they are an incentive for a purchaser to travel with a particular carrier. The programs also are a recognized tool for increasing customer satisfaction. Nearly every airline offers frequent flyer miles, and most hotel chains now have similar programs. Hyatt, for example, offers free room stays after a certain number of regular stays. Continuity programs tend to run longer than other types of sales promotion because their basic objective is to promote long-term usage.

PUBLIC RELATIONS AND PUBLICITY

PUBLIC RELATIONS

Public relations (PR) is the use of publicity and other nonpaid forms of communication designed to present the firm and its products positively. A disadvantage is that the communication is not always controlled by the company. It can determine when to issue press releases and hold events, but it cannot control the press that independently decides whether to run the communication. Nevertheless, public relations offers several advantages not found with other types of promotion vehicles. Because gatekeepers—editors and news reporters—screen company issued communication to ensure its accuracy, the public can have some confidence that the information it receives through public relations is truthful. In addition, PR provides editorial-type messages that can break through advertising clutter. Public relations can be used to establish the social responsibility of a good corporate citizen. Because of the typical content and source of messages, it is possible to reach upscale opinion leaders, who in turn spread the message. Furthermore, there are few legal restrictions on PR activities, making it a way to address numerous issues in a more balanced light than may be possible with advertising.

Public relations is likely to focus on many publics, including employees, shareholders, community members, news media, and government. Rather than directly promote a particular product or brand, most PR messages have the appearance of objectivity. Many PR promotional campaigns center on social issues. For example, Avon supports breast cancer awareness in the United States, the prevention of violence against women in Malaysia, child nourishment in China, and AIDS prevention in Thailand. Toys "R" Us and Reebok offer gift certificates in exchange for guns. There has been a recent resurgence in cause marketing. Spending on cause-marketing campaigns and sponsorships of non-profits

> ## Marketing Vocabulary
>
> REBATE
> Refunds given to consumers for the purchase of particular items,
>
> PUBLIC RELATIONS (PR)
> The use of publicity and other nonpaid forms of communication to present the firm and its products positively.

rose to $1.34 billion in 2006, up from $120 million in 1990. One of the more visible recent examples was Nike Inc.'s pairing with the Lance Armstrong Foundation to sell yellow "LiveStrong" wristbands, which raised money for cancer research and created a brief, yet memorable, international fashion statement.[45] These cause marketing campaigns are generally supported by major PR activities including visibility of company executives and other spokespersons.

The Washington Apple Commission supported the North American Free Trade Agreement (NAFTA) because its defeat would have cost the industry $150 million a year. It developed a PR strategy with a target market of 11 members of Congress. First, it started a letter-writing campaign by sending packets to almost 4,000 apple growers and shippers. The packet contained a sample letter to editors and congressional delegates as well as a fact sheet on NAFTA. Then 51 agricultural producers in Washington State signed a letter endorsing NAFTA. Next, one apple grower went to Washington State with 150 other pro-NAFTA groups to meet with the president. This resulted in some free publicity on the television networks and the national wire services, which liked the idea of an apple grower talking to the president. The commission continued its show of public support but also focused its efforts on press conferences. Once again, two national wire services wrote stories on the industry. The PR effort resulted in a 10–1 vote in favor of NAFTA by the targeted congressional delegates. It also won an award from the National Agri-Marketing Association. Public relations supports the marketing function in several ways.

- *Corporate communication.* Messages promote a better understanding of the organization among employees, shareholders, and other relevant publics.
- *Media relations.* Newsworthy information, such as new activities and personnel promotions, are provided to the media on a timely basis.
- *Lobbying.* Communication with legislators and government officials to promote or defeat legis-

lation is a major activity for heavily regulated industries.

- *Product publicity.* Newsworthy innovations or new attributes of products can be promoted at little cost through the media.

PUBLICITY

Publicity is what is communicated about an organization in the public news media. Publicity can be positive or negative. Negative publicity detracts from the organization's image and can have serious effects on its market position. Most PR groups attempt to generate positive publicity through news stories and public service announcements. The more common avenues are press releases, news conferences, and event sponsorship. The Internet increasingly is being used by marketers, both to spread publicity and to respond to crisis situations.

Press Releases and News Conferences A **press release** is a statement written by company personnel and distributed to various media for publication at their discretion. It includes information about the organization or product that marketers believe will be of interest to the public. The advantage of a press release is that the marketer has control over what information is provided. Many large organizations issue press releases regularly. This type of communication is used almost invariably when negative publicity needs to be countered. Rather than leave it to the media to track down the facts, companies provide the same information to all members of the press simultaneously. Press releases must be accurate, to the point, and based on hard evidence. If not, then the media will become skeptical about any material the company issues.

http://globaledge.msu.edu
Visit globalEDGE™ Online for the ultimate international marketing research tool!

globalEDGE™
Mass Communications: Advertising, Sales Promotions, & Public Relations

Due to the emergence of text messaging with cellular telephones, the global system for mobile communications (or, GSM) is an important measure to assess the accelerated nature of mass information access in certain markets. However, even though your firm is globalizing at a phenomenal rate, the wireless technologies available in different markets around the world are diverse. Therefore, to maximize your firm's efficiency, you must cluster the markets in which your firm operates based on particular wireless technologies. How many wireless technologies are currently in use worldwide? Which has had the most growth over the past two years? Which has had the least growth over the same time period?

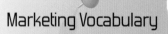

Marketing Vocabulary

PRESS RELEASE
A statement written by company personnel and distributed to various media for publication at their discretion.

News or press conferences occur when reporters are invited to a meeting at which company officials make a public statement and usually respond to questions. As with press releases, companies have some control over news conferences.

Sponsored Events or Activities A very popular type of publicity is sponsored events or activities, especially for local promotion. Many companies sponsor rock or symphony concerts, sports teams, or youth groups. This gets their name before the public while contributing to the community. Various nontraditional activities are becoming popular publicity opportunities. Guinness recently opened a museum in the stout's hometown of Dublin, complete with brewery tour, free samples, merchandise, and a restaurant, to overturn its stodgy image and appeal to younger customers. Coca-Cola, to relaunch the brand in Belgium after a bottling accident left hundreds ill, participated in community events by sponsoring games with Coca-Cola products as the prizes. Nowadays sponsorship goes beyond having a logo postered on a property. A growing trend with some brands, particularly mobile phones, is to own the event, which enables limitless opportunities in terms of engaging with customers, but also no competition. However, James Ralley, account manager at integrated agency, Space, spent five weeks at the 2006 World Cup in Germany, visiting every tournament venue and conducting 1,500 supporter interviews on behalf of a client. What he discovered was fans becoming disaffected with sponsors. Fans were concerned that the corporate money is becoming more important to football than the fan supporters' money. Supporters are increasingly unhappy at the commercialization of what they regard as their game.[46]

The Internet The Internet can be an ideal medium for publicity. In fact, it has spawned a new group of PR companies. Edelman Public Relations Worldwide is a leading creator of Web sites. Its services can be especially helpful when companies need to minimize negative publicity. For example, several bottles of Odwalla apple juice were found to contain E. coli bacteria. In less than three hours, Edelman created a site to provide consumers with information. Ford has also utilized the Internet to aid in the recall of defective tires.

Other companies use the Internet to host chat sessions, which serve as a form of positive publicity. Recent PR nightmares for Menu Foods, JetBlue, Turner Broadcasting, Dell Computers and KFC-Taco Bell demonstrate that as the "social Web" evolves, the focus for brands needs to be less on digital marketing and more on digital brand management.[47]

Marketers who skillfully blend public relations and publicity into their communications mix can underscore and intensify the positive feelings created by other mass communications activities. In Chapter 18 we will turn our attention to the most personal and individualized form of marketing communication—personal selling. Although one-on-one relationship building is key to effective personal selling, mass communication provides important support. It lays the groundwork for personal sales by creating deeper receptivity toward the company and its products.

Web and E-commerce Stars
DreamWorks - www.dreamworks.com

DreamWorks is a well known animation and production company. Dreamworks.com allows the visitor to choose from movies, home video, television and animation. The movie section shows trailers, posters and even provides a link for users to purchase tickets to see new DreamWorks films. The home video and television sections showcase new DVD releases, including trailers and previews, links to the film or TV show's Web site, and a link to purchase through amazon.com. Site interactivity allows for a one stop shop for the customer interested in researching a particular film and making the final decision to purchase a ticket or DVD.

Chapter Summary:

Objective 1: Understand the concept of mass communication including the relative use of advertising, sales promotion, and public relations.

Mass communication helps companies connect with customers around the world. It adds value by providing information about the goods and services available. Expenditure on mass communication—advertising, sales promotion, and public relations—is increasing at about 7 percent annually in the United States and at a slightly higher rate globally. Roughly the same amount is spent on sales promotion and advertising, but sales promotion is slightly ahead and is growing faster. Public relations is a distant third.

Objective 2: Learn how technology, globalization, and ethics are playing major roles in mass communication.

The history of mass communication coincides with the development of communications technology, particularly print, radio, and television. Today, the Internet is adding an interactive medium. Global mass communication occurs when key elements of messages are standardized across regions and nations. Standardization has cost advantages when the same customer segments are found in many countries, but it has several limitations. The primary ethical issue in mass communication is deception. Puffery may be used to make a point, but care must be taken not to be deceptive. Some countries have very strict legislation that does not allow exaggerations of any sort.

Objective 3: Know the objectives, advantages, and disadvantages of advertising, as well as the sequence of steps in creating an advertising campaign.

Advertising is highly controllable and works over time to build brand equity. It is cost-effective for reaching large audiences. Its primary objective may be to inform consumers, to persuade them to buy, to remind them of the product, or to reinforce buying behavior and positive feelings about the brand. Advertising media are readily available, and it's easy for marketers to find help in creating effective campaigns. But advertising reaches many people outside the target audience, encounters a high level of avoidance, and can be costly. It also can communicate only brief, one-way messages. There are several different types of advertising: national, retail (local), directory, business-to-business, institutional, direct response, public service, and political. Generally, there are five steps in developing the advertising plan: set objectives, establish the budget, create the theme and message, select and schedule media, create the ads, and assess effectiveness.

Objective 4: Understand sales promotion objectives and what types of promotions are used to stimulate sales in business, trade, retailer, and consumer markets.

Sales promotion is used to prompt consumers to action, resulting in immediate sales results. It is generally used with other forms of promotion, such as advertising, public relations, or personal selling. There are four types of sales promotion: business-to-business, trade, retailer, and consumer. Business-to-business promotions include trade shows, conventions, sales contests, and specialty deals. Trade promotions, which are offered by manufacturers to wholesalers or retailers, include discounts, allowances, financing incentives, sales contests, and spiffs. Retailer promotions, offered to consumers, include price cuts, displays, free tri-als, coupons, and patronage awards. Consumer promotions are manufacturers' offers, including coupons, rebates, free samples, sweepstakes, price and value packs, POP displays, and continuity programs.

Objective 5: Understand the use of public relations in marketing.

Public relations activities are used primarily to influence feelings, opinions, or beliefs about a company or its products. An attempt is made to develop messages that at least have the appearance of objectivity. PR supports the marketing function in the following ways: corporate communication, press relations, lobbying, and product publicity. Common publicity-generating activities are press releases, news conferences, and sponsorship of events or activities. Because public relations messages are placed through public channels, the messages tend to be more credible and believable. They also tend to break through the advertising clutter and are relatively low in cost. Public relations can publicize the social responsibility of a good corporate citizen.

Review Your Understanding

1. Why is global standardization of mass communication useful?
2. How do deception and puffery relate?
3. What is advertising? What is its overriding goal?
4. What are the objectives of advertising, which also describe types of ads?
5. What are some of the advantages and disadvantages of advertising?
6. List the eight types of advertising. What is the focus of each?
7. Name the six types of advertising media. What are the advantages and disadvantages of each?
8. What is sales promotion? How is it different from advertising?
9. Briefly describe the four different types of sales promotion. What are the most common promotional activities within each category?
10. How does sales promotion help build relationships?
11. What is public relations? How is it unique from other forms of mass communication?
12. What are the pros and cons of public relations?

Discussion of Concepts

1. Describe the five steps in developing an advertising plan. On which ones would you most enjoy working? Least enjoy? Why?
2. Why is it important to develop a creative strategy before creating specific ads?

3. Which techniques are most commonly used to determine the advertising budget? Which one do you believe should be used and why?

4. What are the critical issues in selecting and scheduling the appropriate advertising media?

5. As with any creative process, it's difficult to determine precisely what people will like. When it comes to developing an advertisement, what are some of the characteristics that will tend to make the ad successful? Why?

6. In business, it's important to measure how well the organization performs certain tasks in order to make adjustments as necessary. How do marketers measure the effectiveness of advertising campaigns?

7. Marketers sometimes divide consumers into four categories of buyers. Briefly describe each type and the promotional activities that are likely to be successful with each.

8. List the most popular types of trade promotions. When is each type appropriate?

9. How do the advantages and disadvantages of public relations compare to those of other forms of promotional activities?

Key Terms And Definitions

Advertising: Paid communication through nonpersonal channels.

Advertising agency: A business that develops, prepares, and places advertising for sellers seeking to find customers for their products.

Advertising campaign: A series of advertisements with a main theme running through them.

Aided recall: The viewer is given some specific piece of information about the ad before being asked if he or she recalls having seen it.

Allowances: Funds given to retailers and wholesalers based on the amount of product they buy.

Business-to-business advertising: Advertising to business and professionals.

Competitive budgeting method: Setting the advertising expenditures relative to what competitors spend.

Consumer promotion: Offer designed to pull the product through the retail establishment.

Continuity: The length of time the advertising campaign will run in a given medium.

Coupon: Certificate that entitles a consumer to an incentive to buy the product, usually a price reduction or a free sample.

Creative strategy: The strategy that governs and coordinates the development of individual ads and assures that their visual images and words convey precisely and consistently what the advertiser wants to communicate.

Cross-selling: Promotion in which the manufacturer of one brand attempts to sell another brand to the same customers, or the purchase of one product is used to stimulate the selection of another, often unrelated product.

Deception: When a false belief is created or implied and interferes with the ability of consumers to make a rational choice.

Directory advertising: A listing of businesses, their addresses, phone numbers, and sometimes brief descriptions in a publication.

Direct response advertising: Targets individual consumers to get immediate sales.

Exposure: The process of putting the ad in contact with the consumer.

Financing incentive: An offer to finance the retailer's inventory prior to its sale.

Frequency: The number of times the audience is reached in a given period, usually per day or per week.

Informative advertising: Messages designed to provide information that consumers can store for later use.

Institutional advertising: Messages designed to communicate corporate identity and philosophy as opposed to product information.

Media: The channels through which messages are transmitted.

National or brand advertising: Advertising that focuses on brand identity and positioning throughout the country.

Overexposure: Continuing to reach a prospect after a buying decision has been made or to the point that the campaign becomes tedious and actually turns off some potential buyers.

Payout method: Setting the advertising budget to gain initial acceptance and trial.

Percentage of sales method: Allocating a percentage of anticipated sales to advertising.

Persuasive advertising: Messages designed to change consumers' attitudes and opinions about products, often listing product attributes, pricing, and other factors that may influence consumer decisions.

Political advertising: Advertising to influence voters.

Press release: A statement written by company personnel and distributed to various media for publication at their discretion.

Public relations (PR): The use of publicity and other non-paid forms of communication to present the firm and its products positively.

Pulling power: The ability to maintain the interest of the consumer to the end of the advertising message.

Reach: The number of consumers in the target audience who can be contacted through a given medium.

Reinforcement advertising: Messages that call attention to specific characteristics of products experienced by the user.

Reminder advertising: Messages that keep the product at the forefront of the consumer's mind.

Retail (local) advertising: Advertising that focuses attention on nearby outlets where products and services can be purchased.

Retailer promotion: An offer to the consumer that is sponsored by a retailer.

Sales contest: A competition for salespeople and dealers that awards prizes for accomplishing specific goals.

Sales promotion: Communications designed to stimulate immediate purchases using tools such as coupons, contests, and free samples.

Specialty items: Gifts with the organization's name that are provided to customers, usually given through the mail or by the sales force.

Stopping power: The ability of an ad to gain and hold the consumer's attention.

Task method: Setting the advertising budget based on activities required to accomplish objectives.

Trade promotion: An offer from a manufacturer to channel members, such as wholesalers and retailers.

Unaided recall: The viewer is asked to identify any advertisements he or she can remember.

Viral marketing: Diffusing a marketing message across people.

References

1. www.brandchannel.com Web site visited July 11, 2008; The Nielsen Company. Nielsen Media Research. www.nielsen.com May 5, 2008; www.disney.com Web site visited July 11, 2008; www.fox.com Web site visited July 11, 2008; Effects of Product Placement in On-line Games on Brand Memory, Mira Lee, Ronald J Faber. Journal of Advertising. Armonk: Winter 2007. Vol. 36, Iss. 4; pg. 75, 16 pgs; You've Played the Videogame, Now Buy the Car Amy Chozick. Wall Street Journal. (Eastern edition). New York, N.Y.: Oct 24, 2007.

2. Projected based on Ian P. Murphy, "Yearly 7% Growth Seen for Communications Spending," Marketing News, October 7, 1996, p. 8; "Marketing Communications and Promotion Strategy," www.pcola.gulf.net/tonypitt/mk15.htm, site visited on February 20, 1997; Kip D. Cassino, "A World of Advertising," American Demographics, November 1997, pp. 57–60; and Robert J. Coen, "Ad Revenue Growth Hits 7% in 1997 to Surpass Forecasts," Advertising Age, May 18, 1998, p. 50.

3. Subhash C. Jain, "Standardization of International Marketing Strategy: Some Research Hypotheses," Journal of Marketing 53 (January 1989): 70–79.

4. William K. Darley and Denise M. Johnson, "An Exploratory Investigation of the Dimensions of Beliefs toward Advertising in General: A Comparative Analysis of Four Developing Countries," Journal of International Consumer Marketing 7, no. 1 (1994): 5–21; and J. Craig Andrews, Srinivas Durvasula, and Richard G. Netemeyer, "Testing the Cross-National Applicability of U.S. and Russia Advertising Belief and Attitude Meaures," Journal of Advertising 23 (March 1994): 21.

5. www.nfl.com/international, site visited March 18, 2008.

6. David Wessel, "Memo to Marketers: Germany wants to Import American Junk Mail," Wall Street Journal, December 10, 1999, p. B1.

7. John R. Boatright, Ethics and the Conduct of Business (Upper Saddle River, NJ: Prentice Hall, 1997), p. 277.

8. Anonymous, "KFC Plucked, Gently,, Multinational Monitor, May/June 2004. Vol.25, Iss 5/6; pg. 45.

9. Wells, Burnett, and Moriarty, Advertising, p. 10.

10. www.rangerover.com, Web site visited May 28, 2008.

11. www.mcdonalds.com, Web site visited March 30, 2008.

12. Kate Maddox, "Ad ratios and budgets grow," B to B, July 10, 2006, Vol.91, Issue 9, pg. 12.

13. TNS Media Intelligence Reports U.S. Advertising Expenditures Grew 0.2 percent in 2007. Business Wire. New York: March 25, 2008.

14. Beth Snyder Bulik, "Kodak develops new model:expensive printer, cheap ink,",Advertising Age Vol. 78, March 12 2007, pg. 4.

15. Brian Steinberg, "Marketing Success of Proactiv leads to new directions," Wall Street Journal, April 18 2007, pg. B3C.

16. http://business.maktoob.com/News-20050613155801-.aspx

17. Newspaper Association of America: Newsprint Consumption. www.naa.org. Web site visited March 28, 2008.

18. www.comcastspotlight.com, Web site visited March 28, 2008.

19. Mediamark Research, Inc., Doublebase 1988 Study: 19, cited in "Study of Media Involvement," Audits & Surveys, March 1988.

20. David Benady, "OUTDOOR ADVERTISING: Take it outside", Marketing Week(London), March 22, 2007, pg. 31.

21. www.oralb.com/us/learningcenter/, site visited May 12, 2007.

22. Chun-Yao Huang, Chen-Shun Lin, "Modeling the Audience's banner ad exposure for internet advertising planning", Journal of Advertising Vol. 35, Summer 2006, pg. 123.

23. www.google.com/analytics, site visited June 30, 2007.

24. Ducan J Watts & Jonah Peretti, "Viral Marketing for the Real World", Harvard Business Review Vol. 85 , May 2007, pg. 22.

25. "Burger King: King of the world", Brand Strategy(London), November 2 2005, pg. 20.

26. Mobile. Alice Cuneo. Advertising Age. Chicago. March 17, 2008.

27. "International Marketing Nightmares," Marketing Update Newsletter, exton.com, site visited on August 15, 1996.

28. Adapted from Peter D. Bennett, Dictionary of Marketing Terms (Chicago: American Marketing Association, 1988), pg. 179.

29. Projected based on "Marketing Communications and Promotion Strategy."

30. Robert D. Buzzell, John A. Quelch, and Walter J. Salmon, "The Costly Bargain of Trade Promotions," Harvard Business Review, March–April 1990, pg. 141–149.

31. Shopper Reponse to Bundle Promotions for Packaged Goods. Bram Foubert, et al. Journal of Marketing Research. Chicago: November 2007.

32. Regina C. McNally and Abbie Griffin, "An Exploratory Study of the Effect of Relationship Marketing Institutionalization and Professional and Organizational Commitment in Business-to-Business Exchanges," Journal of Business-to-Business Marketing, 2005, 12(4), p.1-39

33. www.shopmarriott.com, Web site visited March 31, 2008.

34. www.churchads.org.uk/, website visited June 26, 2007.

35 Business/Professional Advertising Association, 1992.

36. Projected to 2001 based on data in Pat Friedlander, "When Is It Time to Get a New Booth?" Business Marketing, February 1993, p. 48.

37. http://www.biztradeshows.com Web site visited March 31, 2008.

38. Vincent Alonzo, "Showering Dealers with Incentives," Sales and Marketing Management, October 1999, pp. 24–26.

39. Free Gifts Work as a Marketing Tool. Andrea Hernandez. McClatchy-Tribune Business News. Washington: December 18, 2007.

40. Dubai World Trade Centre Recieves Trade Promotion Award. Al Bawaba. London: November 28, 2007.

41. www.hp.com, Web site visited May 17, 2008.

42. Lefton, "Try It: You'll Like It."

43. Experience a Close-Up View of the Beijing Olympic Games; The importance of vision in performance inspires Johnson & Johnson Vision Care Sweepstakes for ACUVUE Brand Contact Lenses. PR newswire. New York: March 19, 2008.

44. Rebeca Piirto Heath, "Pop Art," Marketing Tools, April 1997, www.marketingtools.com.

45. Colleen DeBaise, "Small Business (A Special Report); Cause and Effect: Linking a national franchiser to a charity can both unify an organization and help businesses stand out in their local markets," Wall Street Journal (Eastern Edition), April 30, 2007, pg. R.9.

46. "Sponsorship: Onus on product ownership," marketing Week, Marcy 29, 2007, pg. 45.

47. Marc Schiller, "Crisis and the Web," Adweek, March 5, 2007, Vol. 48, Issue 10, pg. 16.

The Marketing Gazette:
Randi Schmelzer, "Connecting With an Influential Market," PR Week, Jun 4, 2007, 10(22), p.18; Alicia Wallace, "Area Gay and Lesbian Business Owners Network Through Directory, Leads Group," Knight Ridder Tribune Business News, Apr 2007; "Delta, Official Airline of 2007 U.S. PRIDE Festivals, Supports Diversity", New York Beacon, Jun 7-Jun 13, 2007, 14(23), p.22; Atlantis Events, Company Overview, www.atlantisevents.com, site visited May 01, 2008; Gay and Lesbian Consumer Census, www.glcensus.com, site visited Jan. 30, 2008.

CASE 13

Superbowl Advertising

At the end of January every year, people all over the world gather around the television for one of the biggest events of the year: Super Bowl commercials. With some exceptions, the commercials often outweigh lopsided games for pure entertainment value and companies pay top dollar to put their best advertising efforts forth. Fox sold 30-second ad slots for as much as $3 million each during Super Bowl XLII in 2008. It's come a long way from the $40,000 networks were charging for spots during Super Bowl I in 1967. Bob Scarpelli, senior vice president and chief creative officer of DDB Needham, Chicago, said: "Super Bowl day is the Super Bowl of advertising. The Super Bowl has evolved to the point where people watch the ads more than the game." Networks take full advantage of their Super Bowl coverage. Between the opening kickoff and the end of the game, Fox aired more than 45 minutes of advertisements during Super Bowl XLII, a Super Bowl record.

One of the statistics that sets Super Bowl Sunday so far apart from most other television programs is its holding power. The 2008 Super Bowl between the New York Giants and the New England Patriots kept almost 99 percent of its viewing audience during commercial breaks. That means that the advertisements annually have the highest exposure of any other television event. It also pulled in a Super Bowl record 97.5 million viewers, making it one of the most viewed programs of all time, second only to the finale of M-A-S-H in 1983.

Most Super Bowl ads are stand-alone spots, but a cost of up to $3 million requires more than just a typical commercial. The advertising industry sees the event as a chance to showcase talent, and risks are often taken with content and even the timing of ads. However, focusing on being the most clever or humorous commercial sometimes causes spots to lose their main objective: to convey a message to the customer.

Advertisers may be falling into the trap of chasing the unattainable ad: the "1984" Apple Macintosh computer ad. The 60-second commercial that ran during Super Bowl XVIII is thought by many to be the most innovative and effective spot of all time. It used drama, brilliant positioning, and a simple message to introduce its relatively new product

as a competitor to the already established IBM. It subtly preyed on people's fears of being controlled by technology and moved them to do something while being visually appealing at the same time. Many unsuccessful ads obtain either one or the other of these factors in grand fashion but miss the other completely. With the high costs of time slots for the Super Bowl spots and high production costs for many of the more attention-grabbing commercials, one ad could send an upstart company spiraling to its doom. However, it can also be a launching pad to introduce a business or revitalize a struggling company.

In the past, many Super Bowl ads aired only once. Some companies questioned whether it was really worth the multi-million dollar investment for an ad that would be seen one time. Increased access to high speed internet and online video sites like YouTube are changing that. Viewers can easily find their favorite commercials online. In 2008, Fox added an extra incentive for advertisers. Through sister company Myspace, it created an official Super Bowl Ad site where consumers can re-watch all the commercials aired during the game and vote for their favorites. One day after the big game, 90,000 Myspace users had already befriended the group.

Anheuser-Busch has crafted a deal with the NFL that allows it to run the only beer ads during the Super Bowl until 2012. It reportedly spent $16 million for four minutes of time during 2008, devoting 6 of 7 slots to Bud Light, the most ever dedicated to one brand during a Super Bowl. The company originally created a dozen potential ads, later narrowing them down through a series of consumer tests.

Yet, many experts believe that Super Bowl advertising may not be a smart buy. Ted Bell, vice chairman, world wide creative director of Young & Rubicam, New York, says: "It's become advertising's in-joke, all these agency guys trying to outdo each other. It's about who can have the coolest commercial. It's self-indulgence on the part of the ad industry." According to Bob Scarpelli at DDB Needham, "Many clients want to be on the Super Bowl just to be on the Super Bowl. The CEO wants his name on the Super Bowl. It's almost like bragging rights."

1. *What should a marketer consider in deciding whether to advertise at the Super Bowl? Would this differ for a smaller organization versus a larger company?*
2. *What qualities must an ad possess in order to gain attention at the Super Bowl?*
3. *Recall one of your favorite Super Bowl ads and describe what elements made it successful from your perspective.*

Sources: Ellen Newborne and Roger Crockett, "More Bang for the Super Bowl Bucks," Business Week, February 2, 1998, p. 70; Eleftheria Parpis, "Playing for the Ring," AdWeek, January 19, 1998, p. 29; Steve Hamm, "This Year's Super Bowl Hero?" Business Week, January 19, 1998, p. 6; Scott Andron, "Volvo Trucks Buys Super Bowl Ad," Greensboro (North Carolina) News & Record, November 16, 1997, p. E1; Kyle Pope, "NBC Scores Big with the Super Bowl; Game Is Among Most Watched Ever," Wall Street Journal Interactive Edition, January 27, 1998; Michael Kraus, "The Season Ahead; Back to Branding Basics," Marketing News, September 11, 2000, pp. 11–12; Terry Lefton, "Rescuing Reebok," Brandweek, September 18, 2000, pp. 1, 61; John Dempsey, "Top Spex Nearly Zap-Proof," Variety, October 16–October 22, 2000, p. 123; Gillian Wee, "Fox Network Sells Last Super Bowl Ad, Earliest Ever," Jan. 29, 2008. www.bloomberg.com, site visited 4/05/08; TNS Media Intelligence, "Super Bowl XLII 2008 Creative Log," http://www.tns-mi.com/resources/creativeSuperBowl2008.htm, site visited May 01, 2008; Theresa Howard, "Anheuser-Busch Brews Up Batch of Bowl Ads," USA Today, Jan. 21, 2008; Associated Press, "Redcord 97.5 Million Watch Super Bowl XLII," MSNBC, Feb. 04, 2008.

CHAPTER 14

Personal Selling & Sales Force Management

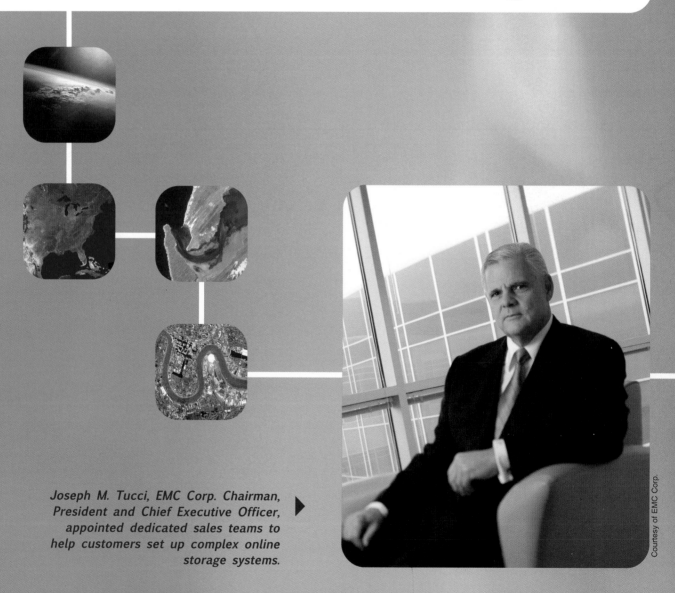

Joseph M. Tucci, EMC Corp. Chairman, President and Chief Executive Officer, appointed dedicated sales teams to help customers set up complex online storage systems.

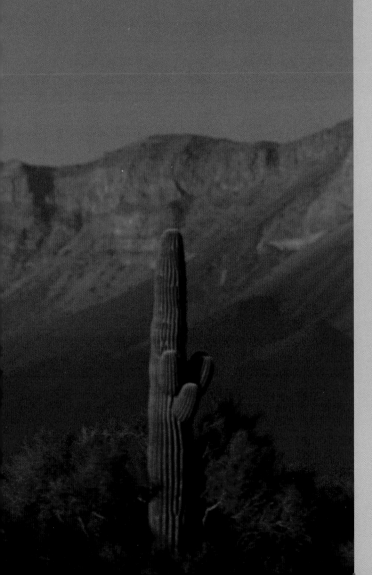

Learning Objectives

1. Understand the evolution of selling to a focus on relationships and the elements that result in strong customer relationships.

2. Know the responsibilities of salespeople and sales managers.

3. Identify and understand the steps in personal selling.

4. Learn the characteristics of strong salespeople.

5. Understand how to develop a diverse sales organization.

6. Explore how to implement sales actions from setting quotas and compensating salespeople to evaluating and adjusting plans.

The list of customers who buy high-powered electronic data storage systems from EMC Corporation reads like a who's who of the corporate world. Traditional businesses such as Delta Air Lines, Visa International, and e-businesses such as Amazon.com, are just some of the hundreds of companies that rely on EMC products to keep their valuable data on customers, transactions, products, and Web pages safe and accessible.

EMC, based in Hopkinton, Massachusetts, was founded in 1979 to make memory devices for minicomputers. Building its reputation as a maker of storage systems for the world's biggest companies, EMC focused on large-scale storage systems for mainframe computers and added specialized software for data storage, management, and recovery. Today EMC holds an impressive share of the data storage market, which is growing around 35 percent per year.

EMC's salespeople make multiple sales calls to forge a close working relationship with the chief information officer of each prospect firm. As the relationship develops, the sales rep learns more about the firm's data storage requirements and then recommends the appropriate combination of hardware and software components. The EMC sales force is structured according to segment, so reps become knowledgeable about the industries they service and the storage challenges their customers face. EMC's customer-focused approach to personal selling requires meticulous attention to detail and a thorough understanding of how different EMC products fit in a broad range of systems configurations. The company sets aggressive sales goals but provides a rich package of financial incentives for peak performance.

In recent years, EMC has also targeted the small and mid-sized business market, believing that this segment has much greater growth potential. Those small businesses are usually Internet firms that have fewer than 100 employees and their sales are less than $15 million. Data are the lifeblood of these growing e-businesses; any disruption in the availability of information would be extremely costly. As a result, data storage and protection devices are must-haves for e-businesses. So firms in this segment turn out to be ideal prospects for EMC's sales staff.

EMC has also made environmental responsibility as a top priority among its sales force and employees. The company actively raises awareness of environmental issues within its offices through training. EMC implemented an ambitious recycling program within its offices which includes recycling everything from aluminum cans to paper products. It is estimated that since the beginning of the program, EMC has saved over 17 thousand trees, 7 million gallons of water, and 4 million kilowatts of electricity.

EMC continues to increase reliance on its sales force, "We have a great company system now that allows our sales force, actually encourages our sales force, to work with others," according to Joe Tucci, EMC chairman, president and CEO. "You create this ecosystem that's not only the 27,000 people we have out there. If our partners have 20,000, 30,000 or 40,000 people, we get all that help." EMC also appointed dedicated teams of sales personnel to help Internet service providers, network providers, and other e-business customers set up complex online storage systems. Although these actions add another level of complexity to the sales process, they also open new opportunities for EMC's sales professionals. In the future, EMC may go further down-

market and finally provide products for consumers, because computer users who like storing hundreds of gigabytes of videos, music, and photographs will soon need the kind of sophisticated data management systems now used in business.[1]

THE CONCEPTS OF PERSONAL SELLING AND SALES MANAGEMENT

Successful people nearly always "sell" their ideas. Broadly speaking, any time one party attempts to motivate the behavior of another party through personal contact, some form of selling takes place. When was the last time you tried to influence someone by expressing your point of view? Did you try to convince a friend to go to a movie you wanted to see or to a restaurant you wanted to visit? Whether intentional or not, you were engaged in the kind of communication that is at the heart of personal selling. It is through interpersonal contact that leaders influence the behavior of others. Although an attempt to influence people is not always labeled personal selling, it has the same characteristics. What makes personal selling a profession and not just interpersonal influence? It focuses on creating the economic exchange that is at the center of marketing. Salespeople sell customers on products.

Personal selling is one of the most prevalent and highest-paid occupations in the United States. For every person employed in advertising, there are many more jobs in sales. The sales and marketing sector is expanding at a great rate—by 2012, employment in sales and related occupations is expected to increase by 12.9 percent or by 2 million additional workers.[2] Furthermore, personal selling pays well, and compensation is rising dramatically. Top sales executives on average earn more than $152,700 a year. Average incomes vary according to industry and position. In 2008, the median base salary before bonuses and commission for pharmaceutical sales representatives in the US was $56,425; bio-medical equipment and supplies reps averaged almost $60,000; and eCommerce sales managers made more than $80,000 on average.[3] It is not unusual for salespeople to make hundreds of thousands or more than a million dollars annually.

Whether you are planning a professional sales career or simply want to sell your ideas more effectively, you'll find this chapter very helpful. We begin by describing the different types of sales personnel and selling situations. Next, a comparison of various selling approaches emphasizes the importance of relationship selling. This is fol-lowed by a section on the responsibilities of the salesperson, both to the customer and to the company. We then walk through each of the steps involved in personal selling—from planning and prospecting to closing the sale and providing follow-up service. The final personal selling section, which describes the four characteristics of strong salespeople, may help you determine if sales would be a good career choice for you.

Although a salesperson in a small start-up company may work fairly independently, as a company grows its management must begin to think in terms of a sales force, sales teams, and sales managers. Good sales force management is needed to coordinate and inspire the efforts of these personnel and to integrate their efforts with the overall marketing plan. In the second half of the chapter we examine the five key functions of sales management: organizing the sales force, developing diverse sales teams, preparing forecasts and budgets, implementing sales actions, and overseeing sales force activities. We conclude with information about sales force automation.

PERSONAL SELLING

Figure 14.1 diagrams the topics in personal selling. We will examine each of these in turn.

TYPES OF SALES PERSONNEL AND SELLING SITUATIONS

The many titles for sales positions tend to describe the type of activity performed: sales executive, sales engineer, sales consultant, sales counselor, representative, account executive, account representative, territory representative, management representative, technical representative, marketing representative, agent, and sales associate. Many times the title of vice president is conferred on top-level salespeople who have important sales responsibilities but may have few if any people reporting to them.

Some common categories of salespeople are described in Figure 14.2. **Direct sales** occur when a salesperson interacts with a consumer or company in order to make a sale. **Missionary sales** are made by

Types of Sales Personnel	Relationship Selling	Responsibilities of Salespeople	Steps in Personal Selling	Characteristics of Salespeople
• Executive and team • Field • Over the counter • Inside • Global	• Customer as an asset of the firm • Understanding customer's business strategy • Partnering • Win-win opportunities • Commitment over time	• Implement company's marketing strategy • Communicate company policy • Provide feedback • Make ethical decisions	• Planning • Prospecting • Organizing information and developing a call plan • Approach • Presenting and building relationships • Managing objections and closing the sale • Servicing	• Goal directed • Empathetic • Applications knowledge • Ethics/trustworthy

Figure 14.1   The Concept of Personal Selling

people who do not take orders but influence purchase by recommending or specifying a product to others. For example, textbook salespeople influence professors, who then require students to purchase a particular book for a class. Likewise, physicians prescribe drugs, golf professionals recommend a brand of clubs, and travel agents help select vacation packages.

The circumstances in which selling occurs can be categorized as executive and team selling, field selling, over-the-counter selling, inside sales, and global sales. Because each category involves a different setting, the activities of salespeople differ accordingly.

Executive and Team Selling

Although many people are employed in personal selling, the statistics don't count the numerous individuals with non-sales titles who spend much of their time on sales activities. Many executives, irrespective of their area, view personal selling as one of their primary functions. They not only communicate with the board of directors and employees in order to "sell" corporate policies but also frequently interact with major customers and suppliers.

Team selling involves people from most parts of the organization, including top executives, who work together to create relationships with the buying organization. In 2006, Boeing had 1050 airplane orders with 729 net orders in its 737 pro-

gram. Corporate executives were deeply committed to the effort, although most of the responsibility still remained with the sales force. In a high-technology business such as aircraft manufacturing, nearly every function gets involved in the sales process. At Boeing it is the sales-

www.boeing.com

Learn more about the world's leading producer of commercial airplanes and its successful team-selling effort. Also read about how the company is trying to reduce its carbon footprint.

Marketing Vocabulary

DIRECT SALES
Sales that result from the salesperson's direct interaction with a consumer or company.

MISSIONARY SALES
Sales made indirectly through people who do not obtain orders but influence the buying decision of others.

TEAM SELLING
Selling that involves people from most parts of the organization, including top executives, working together to create a relationship with the buying organization.

person's job to coordinate contact between the company and the technical, financial, and planning personnel from the airline. Even if the CEO is brought in, it is not unusual for the salesperson to remain in charge of the sale using the CEO when appropriate. The salespeople perform the leadership function because they know all aspects of their customers' business. They also must be thoroughly

	ACTIONS	EXAMPLE
Telemarketing Representative (Direct)	Uses telephone to contact customers to receive orders.	People who respond to callers of 800 numbers (Gateway 2000).
Inside Sales Support (Missionary)	Works inside the seller's company to support the sales representatives who make face-to-face calls on customers. Uses telephone and other non-face-to-face communication to help customers.	Westinghouse salesperson who sells without traveling to a customer's site.
Field Salesperson (Direct)	Meet face-to-face with customers.	Nike salesperson calling on retail sporting goods chain.
Technical Salesperson (Direct)	Meets face-to-face with customers to sell very technical products that need to be customized or explained in technical ways.	Square D salesperson (engineering background) calling on an electric utility.
Detail Person (Missionary)	Meets with people who influence the sale of a company's products but may not purchase directly.	Eli Lilly salesperson who calls on doctors to increase prescription rate for Lilly products.
Service Salesperson (Direct)	Sells intangible products, such as insurance and real estate, to a broad range of customers.	Prudential salesperson who sells a life insurance policy.
Retail Salesperson (Direct)	Associates or clerks selling items in a retail outlet.	Saturn salesperson working in showroom.

Figure 14.2   Types of Sales Personnel

familiar with Boeing's services. This includes cost-per-seat calculations, computerized route simulations, and many other analysis tools Boeing uses to show how it can fulfill customer needs.[4]

Field Selling   Field selling occurs at a consumer's residence or at a customer's place of business. Field representatives spend most of their time, as the name implies, away from their company and near customers. Their job is to discover prospects, make contact, and create relationships. By working with customers in their own environment, field reps have ample opportunity to understand the customer's circumstances in depth. The best

performers in field selling are often skilled at learning about the customer's situation and problems. Field sales in consumer markets include products such as real estate, home building and remodeling, landscape maintenance, and even computers. For example, Hand Technologies sells personal computers in the home, where sales consultants can provide individual attention and have plenty of uninterrupted time.[5]

Field selling to businesses and distributors is also common. It is used for nearly every imaginable industrial product, for pharmaceutical sales to physicians and hospitals, and for selling consulting, accounting, and business management services to manufacturers and retailers.

Merck, a leader in health care products, sends sales reps to hospitals, clinics, government agencies, drug wholesalers, and retailers, among others. In the 2007 fiscal year, Merck salespeople sold $24.1 billion in goods and services to other businesses and organizations.[6]

Over-the-Counter Selling Over-the-counter selling occurs in a retail outlet. Examples include furniture, clothing, and jewelry stores as well as auto dealerships. Customers are drawn to the salesperson by the attraction of the store itself or by advertising and sales promotion. Salespeople need to be skilled at identifying the customer's requirements quickly, often in a single encounter, and at providing the appropriate service at the point of sale. Helping consumers the first time brings them back, which provides the opportunity to gain a loyal customer. It also creates good word of mouth, which brings in friends and relatives of satisfied customers. Successful over-the-counter salespeople tend to build loyal relationships by becoming knowledgeable about the unique tastes of customers. This occurs while working with them on numerous transactions over a long period.

Inside Sales Inside sales involve one-to-one contact with the customer via the telephone and Internet. Mail-order companies are a good example. At L.L. Bean, sales representatives know the products, how they fit, how to ship them quickly, and how to repair and care for them. "L.L.Bean Live Help" in its website offers customers the opportunity to chat with salespeople online to provide them with a helpful, pleasant experience so that they will be likely to use the service again.[7] Another example is the banks of telephone sales representatives who take orders in response to advertisements and infomercials. Sometimes they perform only a clerical function, since the consumer already is sold on the product, but many of these people do an excellent job of answering questions and selling additional items. A variation is telephone mar-

keters who solicit business by calling people at home or at work. Usually the intent is to sell products, but sometimes the purpose is to obtain a home visit for field salespeople.

Another form of inside sales is to work with established clients primarily by phone. Stock brokerage firms conduct much of their business this way. Many manufacturers and distributors have field reps and inside salespeople who work together with large customers. The reps solicit business at the customer's site, and inside sales personnel are ready at all times to provide technical support and take orders via the phone. This form of inside sales can be critical for industrial companies.[8] These inside sales people are increasingly more educated and trained about products, acting more as consultants for the customer. This service is crucial for recruiting and retaining customers. It is also a first job for many technical salespeople, since they can learn about company policies and products while receiving plenty of help with their first customer contacts. Once experience is gained inside, these people often take a field sales position.

Global Sales It is difficult to overstate the importance of personal selling in global markets. Many of these sales involve millions or even billions of dollars. For example, YTL Corporation selected Siemens AG of Germany and General Electric of the United States, among others, as bidders on a $750 million order for power generation turbines. One reason GE lost was its failure to send a top executive to help make the sale. YTL's managing director said: "I wanted to look them in the eye to see if we can do business."[9] Even as today's communication becomes increasingly more technological, many cultures adhere to personal relationships as the foundation of business.

In the domestic arena, companies and their representatives often become accepted in a short period, but this may take years in a foreign environment. To overcome this resistance, many companies use domestic personnel from the host country to represent them. But this can

Field sales occur in a customer's place of business or in a consumer's home.

cause problems if personal selling is not considered a prestigious occupation in that culture. Furthermore, finding and training qualified people can be challenging and expensive. Yet salespeople from the home office are less knowledgeable about the local business climate.

As a compromise solution, companies often rely on nationals to provide information and make initial customer contact but send salespeople from headquarters on regular visits to establish relationships and negotiate larger contracts. Pete Macking, vice president of sales for UPS, made a career traveling abroad for that purpose. Although he has considerable overseas experience, he still worked with foreign nationals affiliated with UPS.[10]

Some companies find a local partner to facilitate their business abroad. Trade.com, affiliated with BlueStone Capital Partners, tried to establish its financial network worldwide, but found it impossible to do without working with financial institutions that were familiar to the local culture.[11] For tips on global etiquette, see the global diversity feature, "A Few Do's and Taboos for the Round-the-World Rep."

RELATIONSHIP AND OTHER SELLING APPROACHES

All employees are important in building and maintaining customer relationships, but salespeople are critical because that is their primary responsibility. There is an increasing trend to move from building short-term sales to building long-term satisfaction and loyalty. By establishing personal, long-term and loyal relationships with customers, salespeople can increase the competitive advantage for their company through increased customer retention and repeat sales. If salespeople do not have the competencies and desire to build relationships one customer at a time, then no amount of support from all the other company employees will make up the deficit.

Business strategies should focus on creating relationships rather than simply selling products. Companies are entering into joint activities in record numbers, and selling organizations must work closely with customers to help them accomplish their goals.

Sellers must understand the consumer's lifestyle or how the customer's business works. Consequently, sales organizations are shifting from traditional ways of doing business to a new emphasis on building relationships. The three basic sales approaches are shown in Figure 14.3 - traditional sales, consultative sales, and relationship selling.

The Traditional Sales Approach The **traditional sales approach** focuses on persuading consumers to buy a company's products, thereby raising sales volume. Remember that the Industrial Revolution produced goods in record quantities. Output grew more rapidly than demand. During the first half of this century, the purpose of personal selling was to stimulate sales. Firms no longer needed to find ways to produce more in order to keep up with demand. Instead, they had to sell more in order to keep up with increased production. The salesperson's focus was on pushing the company's products, especially features and functions, to increase the sales volume. Prospects were persuaded to buy. Techniques for persuasive selling, which taught salespeople how to negotiate, were often the dominant subject of sales training courses. Essentially, sellers and buyers tried to see who could get the best deal.

The Consultative Sales Approach For many organizations, the traditional sales era continued well into the 1970s. As the marketing function became more important, however, the sales function also took on new responsibilities. Marketing began to focus on serving customers, and selling had to change with it. **Consultative selling** means working closely with customers to help solve their problems. Salespeople are expected to understand how their company's products can do that. Essentially, the

	Traditional Sales	**Consultative Sales**	**Relationship Selling**
Focus	Understand your product	Understand customer's problems	Understand customer's business or lifestyle
Role of the customer	Prospect	Target	Asset of the business
Salesperson focus	Persuasion	Problem solving	Partnering
Salesperson role	Obtain sales volume	Advise customers	Building win-win circumstances
Objective	Profit through sales volume	Profit through problem solving	Profit through strategic relationships and customer satisfaction

Figure 14.3 Major Sales Approaches

The Marketing Gazette™

CREATING & CAPTURING VALUE THROUGH GLOBAL DIVERSITY

A Few Do's and Taboos For the Round-the-World Rep

Many selling skills that work in the United States also work overseas, but knowing how to act in certain cultures can make the difference in closing a sale. For instance, the simple thumbs-up sign that Americans use every day may offend a customer in the Middle East. And while health nuts often sip seltzer at a U.S. business lunch, in Japan it is bad manners to refuse a stronger drink. Here are a few global p's and q's gathered from a number of international business experts:

China
- Negotiating is an art, and there is no such thing as a quick sale. Chinese negotiator is a mixture role of Maoist bureaucrat in learning, Confucian Gentleman, and Sun Zi-like strategist.
- The more sales reps know about the culture the better. Foreigners who exert themselves to learn about Chinese society are more accepted by Chinese business people.
- Chinese regard modesty as a moral virtue and part of their integrity. They may display modesty by humbling or downplaying themselves, which does not mean they are not professional.

Japan
- Business is about relationship. Japanese may prolong the relationship building time until they reach consensus, so clinching a deal in Japan is time-consuming that may take months or even years.
- Gift giving at a first meeting is the norm; business card should be presented with both hands and a slight bow, and the card received should be scrutinized carefully.
- The ever-accommodating Japanese will rarely say no. Instead, they will say "maybe" or "that would be very difficult" – both of which essentially mean no

France
- When in dinner, never mention business before discussing the menu and choosing the wine. Better still hold off until after the second or third course of the dinner.
- The traditional elite networks are powerful. Once a foreigner taps into such networks, doors will open.
- Hierarchy is important. The more formal "vous" remains the rule with any boss, often addressed as Mr. Chairman even after several years.
- Meetings are not for decisions, for it is hard for French to compromise. The only way to get things done is to have one-on-one meetings.

United Arab Emirates
- Punctuality is not considered a virtue but often treated casually. Be patient in waiting before or during meetings; take time to chat and establish good working relationships.
- Business is frequently conducted over lunch or dinner, often in a lavish hotel or restaurant, and it is polite to return the invitation.
- Foreigners are expected to abide by local standards of modesty, but not expected to adopt native clothing; traditional clothes on foreigners may be considered offensive.

Oceania
- Emotions and trust are important elements in the buying process. No one purchases unless they are absolutely comfortable with the salesperson.
- Brazilians do not like to get straight to the point. They tend to want to get to know you, and for you to get to know them, before they do business with you; small-talk, chit-chat and other social skills are crucial before starting Brazilian business adventure.
- In New Zealand, it is a bad manner to discuss business during the meal; a conservative business dress code is considered to be appropriate.
- You are expected to shake hands with New Zealand business associates both at the beginning of the meeting and the end; and maintain eye contact throughout the handshake.
- Australians are generally friendly and open, but directness and brevity are valued during business communication.

Latin America
- Scheduling more than two appointments per day is unwise. Attitudes about time are casual.

salesperson becomes an advisor to customers rather than a negotiator seeking the best deal. In order for this type of selling to be successful, salespeople must work closely with the customer over an extended period. Customers on all levels, from individuals to businesses, are extending the buying cycle through spending more time in the decision-making process.[12] At some companies, salespeople act as consultants to their customers and may even suggest a competitor's product if it would better suit the customer. Consultative selling stops just short of relationship selling.

Relationship Selling
Relationship selling attempts to forge bonds between buyers and sellers in an effort to gain loyalty and mutual satisfaction.[13] Because it promotes loyalty, it is in tune with the strategic nature of marketing. It recognizes that sellers and buyers benefit from one another's success. In today's consumer markets, people want to buy based on relationships with companies that can be counted on to enhance their lifestyle. Businesses are looking for partners who will help them compete. Relationship selling recognizes that the salesperson's role is to create value for the customer as well as the company. Typically, a great deal of work on both sides goes into building and maintaining relationships. The main aspects of relationship selling are discussed in more detail next.

Understanding the Customer's Business Strategy The focus of relationship selling is to uncover strategic needs, develop creative solutions, and arrive at mutually beneficial agreements.[14] Salespeople must recognize that companies buy products to help them run their businesses more efficiently. By understanding the customer's business, salespeople are more likely to communicate in meaningful ways with the potential buyer. Delphi Corporation, a supplier of engines and fuel systems to the global automotive industry, "lends" sales engineers to clients to assist with product and program development. They help create product strategies and are very familiar with confidential aspects of the client's business.

In effect, they become an integral part of the customer's marketing team. Cisco Systems showed its customer-focused structure when in entered into a deal with Wachovia, the parent company of the nation's fourth-largest bank and third-largest brokerage firm. Wachovia wanted to improve their key business drivers including business growth, higher productivity and employee engagement. Cisco provided their TelePresenece system to Wachovia to enhance collaboration by providing ultra-high-definition "in person" virtual communications, ultimately saving on travel expenses and increasing individual productivity.[15]

The Customer as an Asset Loyal customers should be viewed as an asset by the firm. Long-term contracts and repeat sales produce predictable sources of revenue. In fact, the worth of many businesses can be calculated by the size of the customer base, such as the number of subscribers of a cellular phone company. Customers are not viewed as prospects for a single sale or as targets for problem solving. Rather, they are partners in a relationship that produces long-term cash flows for the seller. In the highly competitive hotel industry, Marriott International restructured its sales program to make it possible for individuals to earn reward points at one hotel and then take their families on vacation at another. Marriott executives' belief that this would increase customer loyalty and frequency of stays proved to be true. The role of the salesperson is increasingly becoming one of service to the customer over a long time period and in many situations rather than simply selling a product.[16]

Partnering Under the traditional approach, salespeople use persuasion to obtain orders, whereas consultative selling emphasizes the ability to solve customers' problems. In contrast, relationship selling focuses on partnering. Some partnerships are contractual, established through long-term written agreements. Some are noncontractual; that is, the buyer and seller enter into an implied agreement to do business together over time. In either case, a sharing of power occurs. In traditional sales, the balance of power is typically with the salesperson; in consultative selling it is with the customer. Relationship selling involves a symmetrical relationship—both parties have equal authority and responsibility. Both share information to help the other party succeed.[17]

Relationship selling replaces short-term thinking with a perspective that ensures value long after the sale is made. Consequently, just as much work is needed after the sale as before. A strong follow-through makes certain that partnerships are honored.

Building Win-Win Circumstances Historically, buying and selling have involved negotiation. **Negotiation** can be defined as discussions by two or more parties to arrange a transaction. It requires give and take. To some it means that each party tries to maximize its own benefit relative to the other through a power position obtained during the interaction. To others, negotiation is a way to build relationships. As mentioned earlier, in Japan and other cultures it is viewed as a long process that should involve every decision maker. Instead of being seen as conflict or struggle, negotiations can be regarded as information sessions that lead to win-win opportunities.[18]

	Buyer Gains	Buyer Loses
Seller Gains	Win-Win	Buyer negotiates poorly
Seller Loses	Seller negotiates poorly	Lose-Lose

Figure 14.4 Buyer-Seller Negotiations

Figure 14.4 describes the negotiating possibilities. When any party loses, the foundation for building a relationship diminishes greatly. And when one party gains a great deal more than the other, a relationship will not grow or will dissolve over time. A sound relationship requires that each party perceives it has gained value. In other words, lasting relationships involve win-win situations. Even in early meetings with customers, both parties need to win.

Managing Strategic Relationships Account management refers to the activities of a salesperson or sales team to build and support the relationship with a customer. To become more customer-focused, many companies assign an account manager to each large customer. Consulting firms, advertising agencies, and manufacturers often have account managers. Delphi assigns them to work with the Ford, Toyota, Volkswagen, and BMW accounts as well as with GM assembly divisions. These managers concentrate their energies on maintaining the bonds between Delphi and the client. Account managers are particularly effective when the product supplied is important to the overall strategy of the buying company. For example, Delphi's components are critical to their customers' product designs. For some auto brands, Delphi produces most of the electrical systems, brake systems, and other components. Account managers spend considerable time with customers and carefully monitor satisfaction with products and delivery.

UPS sells third-party logistical support. Some clients want only basic services, such as low-cost shipping or warehousing. Others want more. According to the company's senior vice president of business development, John Sutthoff:

> Account managers are trained to understand the business strategies of our customers and to provide solutions that contribute to the success of these strategies. Often our account managers help customers build totally new strategies that result in stronger bonds with their customers. Consequently . . . account managers need to comprehend all aspects of business strategy as well as the competitive world our clients experience.[19]

THE RESPONSIBILITIES OF A SALESPERSON

Salespeople do not simply increase sales volume. Today, most view themselves as the marketing manager of a territory. This can be a geographical area, such as a city or region, or a single large account. Essentially, a **sales territory** is all the actual and potential customers for whom the salesperson has responsibility. As marketing manager of a territory, the salesperson has several functions. The first is to implement the company's marketing strategy in that territory. The second is to communicate company policy to clients and potential customers. The third is to provide the company with feedback about the marketing environment, including the competition and customer needs and wants. Finally, salespeople must operate ethically.

Implement the Marketing Strategy In order to translate the company's marketing strategy into action, the sales force needs to have a basic understanding of all marketing functions. In many companies, salespeople have considerable leeway in applying the entire marketing mix to their territory, including which products to emphasize, which prices and discounts to offer, and which promotional materials to distribute. In other words, although their primary responsibility is to carry out the company's strategic marketing plan, they can use considerable judgment about how that will be done. Constant communication between sales teams and marketers is essential to success. Salespeople

Marketing Vocabulary

RELATIONSHIP SELLING
Forging bonds between buyer and seller to gain loyalty and mutual satisfaction.

NEGOTIATION
Discussion between two or more parties to arrange a transaction.

SALES TERRITORY
All the actual and potential customers, often within a specified geographic area, for which the salesperson has responsibility.

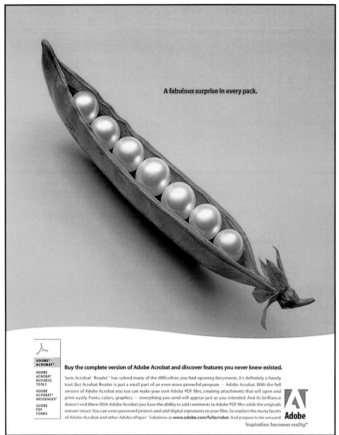

A fabulous surprise in every pack.

Buy the complete version of Adobe Acrobat and discover features you never knew existed.

Sure, Acrobat™ Reader™ has solved many of the difficulties you had opening documents. It's definitely a handy tool. But Acrobat Reader is just a small part of an even more powerful program — Adobe Acrobat. With the full version of Adobe Acrobat you too can make your own Adobe PDF files, creating attachments that will open and print easily. Fonts, colors, graphics — everything you send will appear just as you intended. And its brilliance doesn't end there. With Adobe Acrobat you have the ability to add comments to Adobe PDF files while the originals remain intact. You can even password protect and add digital signatures to your files. So explore the many facets of Adobe Acrobat and other ePaper™ Solutions at www.adobe.com/fullacrobat. And prepare to be amazed.

Adobe

Inspiration becomes reality.™

Adobe Acrobat offers features to manage strategic relationships.

are able to provide the customer with information gathered by the marketing team's surveys and focus groups. Sales calls are often made by representatives from both marketing and sales divisions.

Communicate Company Policy
As agents of their organization, salespeople are responsible for communicating company policies to customers. A policy is a guide or set of rules the company uses in conducting business. Foot Locker's policy of total customer satisfaction means that products can be returned for a refund within 30 days.[20] Salespeople must honor this policy no matter what the circumstance. Although company policies are relatively straightforward in most consumer sales situations, they can be extremely complex in business-to-business selling. For example, pharmaceutical sales representatives usually educate doctors about the proper use of certain drugs or medical equipment, and sometimes they are present when surgeons operate in order to answer questions about products should the need arise.

Companies are likely to specify exactly what salespeople can communicate. Also common are policies on appropriate product use, warranty issues, delivery, and pricing. By communicating such policies and enforcing them, salespeople help shape customer expectations, create goodwill, and maintain positive customer relationships.

Provide Feedback
Another important role of the sales force is to provide their company with information about customers, competitors, and market conditions. Salespeople are in constant contact with the market, and many companies have formal systems for collecting their information rapidly. Examples are portable personal computers with elaborate, user-friendly programs or arrangements with customers to contact their computer systems directly.

Most salespeople have an array of sophisticated communication capabilities, including voice mail, e-mail, facsimile and satellite linkages, cellular phones, and pagers. This keeps them in touch 24 hours a day, seven days a week. Customer inventory levels (stock on hand), purchase orders, price quotations, shipping data, and promotional offers can be transmitted in both directions online. In addition, salespeople usually help forecast opportunities by describing the plans of current and potential customers that may affect future sales. Many times these estimates require careful analysis of a client's strategic plan.

Salespeople also provide valuable information about competitors. By collecting and assembling this input from around the globe, Kodak can identify nearly every initiative competitors make. Let us say a salesperson in Austria identifies a rival's product introduction, new promotional campaign, or altered pricing strategy in that territory. The information can be evaluated at Kodak headquarters to determine the likelihood that markets elsewhere will be affected. In one case, Fuji strategies in one area of the world soon appeared in other areas. Because salespeople had provided an early warning, Kodak marketing executives were able to create a counterstrategy rapidly.

Make Ethical Decisions
Salespeople must exhibit excellent ethical judgment. With little supervision, they often have considerable freedom in what they do and say. Because performance evaluation frequently is tied to sales levels, there are strong pressures to put their own interests ahead of those of customers. Salespeople are likely to face ethical dilemmas regarding the company they represent and the customers they serve. It helps immensely if their company's philosophy is value creation for the customer as well as the organization. Let's look at these ethical dilemmas in greater depth.

Why does independence from supervision pose ethical issues? The company usually goes to great expense to hire, train, and support a salesperson. If he or she does not work hard, then the company may be denied sales. The amount of time spent selling is an issue of personal ethics. Most employers recognize that the job may require spending time on evenings or weekends with customers or doing paperwork. To compensate, there tends to be some flexibility regarding working hours, but an unethical salesperson may take advantage of the situation. For example, it may be relatively easy to shorten the workweek without being missed or to play golf repeatedly with clients, more with an eye to a low handicap than to building a relationship. A salesperson may add another job rather than devote full energy to the primary employer. And what about taking an MBA class during work hours without telling the company?

Other ethical issues arise with regard to performance objectives. Most salespeople are evaluated at least partially on sales volume or profitability. This creates several temptations, including overstocking, overselling, or pushing brands that yield higher commissions. Overstocking occurs when customers purchase more than is required for a given period, which results in unnecessary inventory carrying charges. Imagine that you are a few thousand dollars short of your monthly sales objective. Suppose there is a distributor who relies on your estimates to restock inventory. If you put in an order for more than is needed, then you may gain a better performance evaluation, but you have behaved unethically. Overselling occurs when customers request a lower-priced product that suits their needs and budget, but the salesperson supplies a much more expensive and more profitable product. Similarly, some companies offer spiffs for selling their product rather than a competitor's. Another unethical practice is to promise delivery when the salesperson knows the product will be late. The customer is prevented from ordering a competitor's brand, and when the delay becomes apparent, it is too late to obtain a substitute.

What salespeople communicate can also be an ethical issue. Puffery, or sales rhetoric so obviously excessive that customers recognize it as such, may not be in good taste but rarely is considered dishonest. Misrepresentation is far more serious. Salespeople are unethical when they give incorrect information, such as claiming their product is the same as another when it is not. Selling often involves verbal communication, and there may be little documentation other than an invoice after the sale. Whether spoken or written, intentional misrepresentation is illegal and can result in criminal or civil suits. Unintentional misrepresentation is at best a sign of incompetence in the salesperson and is grounds for canceling a contract. Ethical salespeople say, "I don't know, but I'll find out," rather than guess at the facts.

THE STEPS IN PERSONAL SELLING

Personal selling can be divided into seven stages, as outlined in Figure 14.5. Each step is explained in more detail next.

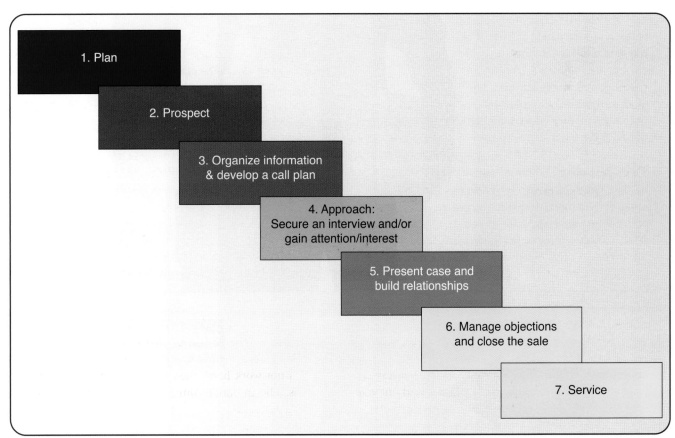

1. Plan
2. Prospect
3. Organize information & develop a call plan
4. Approach: Secure an interview and/or gain attention/interest
5. Present case and build relationships
6. Manage objections and close the sale
7. Service

Figure 14.5   Steps in Personal Selling

Planning Sales planning translates the company's marketing strategy into territory plans and account plans. Territory management is extremely important. Salespeople must determine how the company's target marketing and positioning can best be applied in their territory. Because each area is different, it is important to make adjustments based on local conditions. Exceptional sales skills are of little use if calls are not made on the appropriate accounts with the right frequency and intensity. **Territory planning** determines the pool of customers, their sales potential, and the frequency with which they will be contacted about various products. The fundamental objective is to allocate sales time and use company resources to obtain the best results. Territory management is so important that many companies calculate to the minute what their salespeople do with their time.

Account planning establishes sales goals and objectives for each major customer, such as the sales volume and profitability to be obtained. Increasingly, account objectives include customer satisfaction, often measured by loyalty (repeat business). Account plans are based on an understanding of the customer's business and how the seller's products contribute to it. Elaborate account plans for major customers are common. For example, the AT&T sales team responsible for Ford Motor Company has a detailed description of its entire communication picture. This required a massive effort to develop, but the millions of dollars in revenues make it worthwhile. The plan provides all the information necessary to build and maintain the AT&T relationship with Ford.

Prospecting As the name implies, **prospecting** is seeking out new customers within the company's target markets. As illustrated in Figure 14.6, it involves three steps: obtain leads, identify prospects, and qualify them. **Leads** are the names of all those who might have a need for the product, a large pool that must be narrowed down to the most likely buyers. **Prospects** are potential customers who have an interest in the product. They may currently buy from a competitor, are former customers, or have shown interest in some way. **Qualifying** is the process of determining which prospects have the authority and ability to buy the product. It also determines whether they are desirable customers. A **qualified prospect** is a potential buyer interested in the product and likely to be a reliable customer.

A number of methods are used in prospecting: cold calls (canvassing), referrals, exhibiting at trade shows, networking, telemarketing, secondary data, and coupons and ads. These

Salespeople must perform a variety of tasks and must possess the skills to do so in a timely manner.

©iStockphoto.com/Eric Hood

Marketing Vocabulary

TERRITORY PLANNING
Identifying potential customers, their sales potential, and the frequency with which they will be contacted about various products.

ACCOUNT PLANNING
Establishing sales goals and objectives for each major customer.

PROSPECTING
Seeking potential customers within the company's target market.

LEADS
All those that may have need for a company's products.

QUALIFYING
Examining prospects to identify those with the authority and ability to buy the product.

PROSPECT
A potential customer interested in the seller's product.

QUALIFIED PROSPECT
A potential buyer interested in the seller's product who possesses the attributes of a good customer.

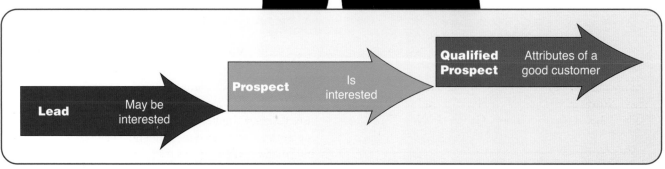

Figure 14.6 Potential Customers

Cold Calls (Canvassing)	Going door-to-door
Center of Influence	Identify opinion leaders and contact them for leads.
Referrals	Get customers or prospects to provide names of others.
Exhibitions and Demonstrations	Exhibit at trade shows or give speeches.
Networking	Contact friends, relatives, and associates to obtain leads.
Telemarketing	Phone people on lists.
Secondary Data	Obtain lists from companies such as Dun & Bradstreet.
Coupons and Ads	The prospect responds to an ad or redeems a coupon.

Figure 14.7 Prospecting Methods

Marketing Vocabulary

COLD CALLING
Contacting a lead for the first time.

CENTER OF INFLUENCE
An opinion leader who can be quickly qualified as a potential customer because of his or her standing in the community.

REFERRAL
A lead provided by a qualified prospect.

NETWORKING
Contacting friends, relatives, and associates to obtain leads.

TELEMARKETING
Making telephone calls to leads provided by marketing services or from other lists.

are shown in Figure 14.7.

Cold calling (canvassing) is contacting the lead for the first time, either by telephone, fax, or in person. The salesperson has no idea whether the person will be interested. A few prospects are likely to be found, some of whom may be qualified. Cold calling is warranted when there is little information about the market or when the product is likely to have universal appeal. Many consumer products are sold door-to-door, and cold calling is also used in business-to-business selling. It is not very popular with customers, but it can be a useful method if not abused.[21]

A variation of cold calling is the **center of influence** method, which identifies leads by contacting opinion leaders. Opinion leaders are open to communications with salespeople and are considered reference group models. It is common knowledge that the pharmaceutical industry has profiled every physician in the country according to opinion leadership. The leaders are more open to new products and also are more likely to influence colleagues.

Referrals are names of leads provided by a qualified prospect. This method can be very effective, since qualified prospects tend to associate with those who have similar attributes. Furthermore, compared to cold calling, the referral is likely to be receptive when the salesperson mentions the name of someone they both know.

Exhibitions are an important way to obtain leads. About 85 percent of attendees significantly influence buying within their firm. This also is an inexpensive method. It costs 70 percent less to close a sale with these leads than with others.[22] In 2008, over 700,000 people attended the Detroit Auto Show.[23] Annually, over one million are drawn to the Greater Los Angeles Auto Show. Participants included both domestic and foreign automakers as well as specialty manufacturers and retailers.[24] Nearly every industry sponsors a trade show. Large halls such as Madison Square Garden in New York City, the Omni in Atlanta, and McCormick Place in Chicago provide facilities for thousands of organizations to display their products and obtain leads. Despite increasing networking through the Internet, trade shows continue to play an important role.[25]

Networking involves contacting friends, relatives, and associates to obtain leads. Successful salespeople in most fields find this an important part of their business. Amway Corporation, a part of the Alticor family of companies, has had great success obtaining sales through networking. The company uses a system of independent agents who sell home care products directly to consumers. The agents obtain from customers the names of additional leads to contact.[26] Amway has had incredible success globally and has distributors in Asia, Africa, Latin America, and North America. Its worldwide sales are over $6 billion annually.[27]

Telemarketing uses phone calls to contact lists of leads provided by marketing services and various directories. Organizations, such as Dun & Bradstreet and Information Resources, Inc., provide listings of nearly every private and public organization as well as the name and title of executives, managers, and buying influencers. Many marketing services contact these leads to determine the types of products they purchase and other information. These interviews are then turned into lists of prospects and sold to various marketing organizations. For example, AT&T has its own staff of telemarketers to find small business prospects for its products. Increased use and accessibility of the Internet are changing the nature of telemarketing. Marketing services still make phone calls, but some also use real-time Internet conversations and e-mail responses to consumer inquiries.

Secondary data sources can provide thousands of lists. Chapter 4 noted categories of secondary data, ranging from local libraries to company databases. Today, the information highway provides access to the names of

©iStockphoto.com/Zsolt Nyulaszi

Telemarketing uses phone calls to contact lists of leads provided by marketing services and various directories.

nearly all U.S. companies and most international organizations. By using database technologies, companies can effectively qualify prospects. In some cases, the selling organization manages the database, but this is a highly specialized field. Because of the very costly technology and expertise required, most secondary data searches are outsourced.

Coupons and ads are another method for obtaining leads. Generally, coupons are placed in newspapers or magazines or sent through the mail. People who take the time to respond tend to be very interested and may have the attributes of a qualified prospect. A trend in magazine advertising is response cards that consumers mail in for free information after circling a number that corresponds to a specific ad. These cards give the seller a list of leads to pursue.

Organizing Information and Developing a Call Plan

Preapproach refers to preparing for the initial meeting by learning about the prospect. For consumers, just their address can yield socioeconomic information, such as the likelihood of sufficient income to purchase the product and even some general idea of tastes and preferences. Columbia TriStar Home Video has developed its own software for its sales force to use in learning about the large retail chain outlets they visit. In the case of businesses, the salesperson can obtain copies of the organization's literature and annual reports. These contain data on the firm's financial strength, organizational structure, objectives, plant locations, and sometimes even its purchasing philosophy. The salesperson's goal is to obtain enough information to develop an initial strategy for each call.

Once the preapproach phase is completed, a call plan is developed to save time and minimize travel expenses. The **routing schedule** identifies which prospects will be called on and when. There are computerized programs to help with routing, or it can be done informally.

Approach   The **approach** is the first formal contact with the customer. The objective is to secure an initial meeting and gain customer interest. It's usually a good idea to schedule an appointment; that will save time and puts the prospect in the frame of mind for a sales call. Many times, a letter of introduction before calling to schedule will help in obtaining the first appointment.

Many techniques have been developed for the initial approach. The most successful ones focus on the potential customer's business, such as a brief explanation of how or why the seller's product can help. It also is important to determine not just when the meeting will take place but how long it will last and its objective. Organizations with a strong reputation generally have an advantage in the approach stage. For example, Xerox or Kodak salespeople will have more success gaining an initial interview than will representatives of an unknown company.

Making the Case and Building Relationships

The sales **presentation** is a two-way process: The salesperson listens in order to identify customer needs and then describes how the company will fulfill them. The most important part of any good presentation is listening. In fact, it is often said that successful selling is 90 percent listening and 10 percent talking. Unfortunately, many salespeople believe their role is to tell prospects about products. Instead, by asking questions, they should put the customer first and demonstrate that they have the customer's best interest in mind. The first contact is the first opportunity to connect with a customer.

Organizations generally have to train their sales force to be good listeners. This is a trait few people possess naturally. The training identifies ways to learn about the prospect's situation. It also teaches how to communicate that the salesperson is listening and is concerned about the customer's needs and wants. **Empathy** occurs when salespeople know precisely how prospects feel. Only when prospects know that the seller understands their needs and wants are they receptive to solutions the salesperson offers.

A popular technique for interfacing with customers is SPIN selling. It stands for situation, problem, implication, and need payoff.[28] The approach resulted from research into what makes people successful at large sales. More than 35,000 sales calls were investigated. Companies such as Xerox, IBM, and Kodak supported the study and have used the system successfully for years. Considerable training is required for people to become proficient with the technique. Essentially, it employs a sequence of probing questions that enlighten the salesperson and the client at the same time.

Situation questions help discover facts about the buyer's condition. Much of this can be learned before the interview so these questions should be limited. Problem questions identify dissatisfaction with the current circumstances.[29] For example, the salesperson may ask: "What makes it difficult to use this type of product?" Implication questions follow, and these are crucial. They unearth the consequences of current problems and are likely to reveal important needs. For example, in response to questions about product safety, one customer began to realize that high insurance costs, low morale, and ethical issues were consequences or hidden costs.[30] Need payoff questions then explore why it is important to solve the problem. In the SPIN process, the buyer and seller establish the need for a product and the benefit of its ownership.

The first contact not only is an opportunity for the salesperson to make a case for a product but also may be the first step in building a relationship. Although sales sometimes are made on the first visit, most occur later. Over time, the salesperson assumes different roles as the relationship develops.

cases this is simple, such as asking directly if someone wants to buy the product or whether they will use cash or credit. In other cases, it involves elaborate contracts. Good salespeople know how important it is to help the buyer toward the final decision. You have probably tried on a suit or dress and heard the

This ad by Dovebid illustrates their selling power.

salesperson say: "Shall I have that measured for alterations?" or "Shall I wrap that for you now?" In business-to-business situations, the salesperson may ask if the purchaser is ready to make a decision or would like to discuss the issue more thoroughly. It is important to use caution in regards to closing.[31] If a buyer is not ready to make the commitment, then asking for an order prematurely can make the salesperson appear pushy and unconcerned with the buyer's needs. A great deal of sensitivity is required for an accurate reading of the buyer's state of mind.

Managing Objections and Closing the Sale One of the most important sales skills is the ability to overcome a buyer's objections. These may be raised subtly in many cultures. In the United States, for example, they often are disguised questions. A consumer may say, "I can't afford to purchase that automobile," but he or she really is asking what financing is available, or how much it costs, or what the trade-in terms are. Assertive salespeople do not let the first objection stop the dialogue; they use it to advance the discussion. Most organizations have training programs to teach salespeople how to manage objections.

Closing means getting the first order. In many

Service There is a big difference between making a sale and gaining a customer. One sale equals one sale. The word customer implies something more than a single sale. In order to maintain relationships, salespeople spend significant time servicing accounts. They make sure products are delivered on schedule and operate to the buyer's liking. When there is a problem, the salesper-

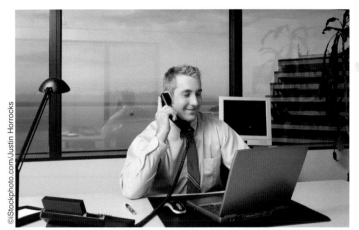

Follow-up occurs when a salesperson ensures after-sale satisfaction in order to obtain repeat business.

son makes sure that it is resolved quickly and satisfactorily.

Follow-up occurs when a salesperson ensures after-sale satisfaction in order to obtain repeat business. Good follow-up reduces buyer's remorse. A bad feeling about spending a lot of money can be alleviated if a salesperson provides information that supports the decision. If that evidence is not forthcoming, then customers may quickly become dissatisfied. Follow-up also offers a way to identify additional sales opportunities. After the first step is taken, the second is easier. The salesperson who continues to work closely with the buying organization can uncover other needs to supply. Good service builds strong customer loyalty, which is the goal of partnership selling.

CHARACTERISTICS OF STRONG SALESPEOPLE

Hundreds, perhaps thousands, of studies have been done to determine what makes a good salesperson. Figure 14.8 describes the characteristics noted most often: goal direction, empathy, strong knowledge of applications, and ethics.

First, strong sales performers tend to be goal directed. They spend adequate time on planning and then work according to the plans. They use their time effectively, which allows them to manage their territory efficiently. They are also highly competitive and obtain results in the face of stiff competition.

Second, because strong salespeople are empathetic, they are aware of the concerns and feelings of others. This means they can understand buyer behavior and have a customer focus. They see things from the customer's per-

spective. Most have very good listening and questioning skills that help them obtain this information.

Third, strong salespeople know how their products apply to the customer's situation. This requires technical competency as well as a good understanding of the customer's business.

That combination allows the salesperson to solve problems for the customer creatively. Since each customer has a specific set of needs, each requires special attention. A salesperson must customize or assemble a mix of products that offers the best possible answer. In essence, the strong salesperson works with the customer to tailor a solution.

Fourth, salespeople must be ethical. The nature of the job often places them in difficult situations. Since good salespeople build relationships, they must be viewed as totally trustworthy, a requisite for creating partnerships. They seek out information when they don't know the answer to a question. They provide pertinent information. They try to help customers solve problems, whether or not a sale is involved. They have a record of keeping customers informed, of facing up to mistakes, and of not promising what they can't deliver.

Relationship selling requires that salespeople be more versatile, creative, and visionary than ever before. A strong salesperson works to harness all company resources for the customer's benefit.

SALES FORCE MANAGEMENT

The sales organization connects directly with customers. Personal relationships are what it's all about. Managers develop and guide the sales organization to make sure the connections are made in the right ways with the right customers. They lead others in order to carry out the overall personal selling portion of the

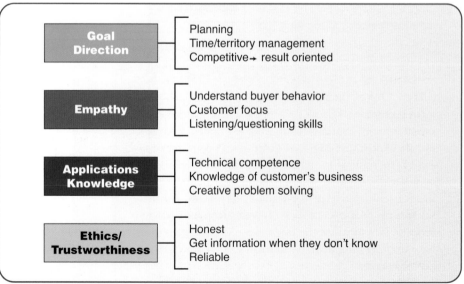

Figure 14.8 Characteristics of Successful Salespeople

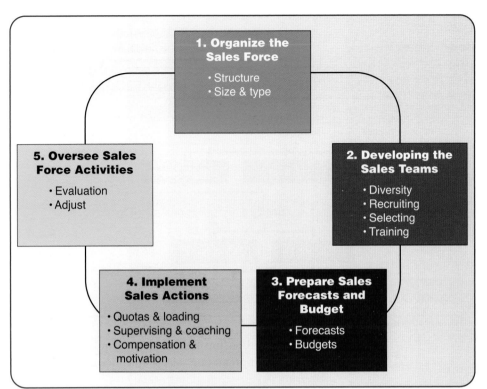

Figure 14.9 Sales Management Functions

communications mix. **Sales force management** is the marketing function involved with planning, implementing, and adjusting sales force activities. It is a tremendously important function for companies that stress customer relationships. Nearly every dimension of how salespeople behave with customers is influenced by how they are managed. Sales management teams keep this in mind when they recruit, train, and motivate salespeople. And sales force management helps salespeople create lasting connections with customers by directing company resources to support relationship building.

Sales managers are responsible for the leadership and management of salespeople in order to accomplish the sales objectives established in the marketing plan. Sales managers make things happen through other people. They are not simply supersalespeople. They are vital in implementing the marketing strategy in companies such as General Electric, Intel, Xerox, Kodak, Eaton Corporation, and thousands of others. Many marketing executives, especially in technology-driven firms, have made their way up through the sales manager route. To do an effective job, sales managers need a full understanding of marketing strategy and planning, each aspect of the marketing mix, and personnel management in addition to the principles of selling and sales management.

Sales force managers perform many functions in support of the marketing strategy. Figure 14.9 describes the key functions: organize the sales force, develop diverse sales teams, prepare sales forecasts and budgets, implement sales actions, and oversee the sales force. These functions may be performed alone in a smaller organization or by a team of people in a larger company. The sales management team is comprised of representatives from personnel, who help with recruiting, training, and personnel records; from marketing (management) information systems, who provide necessary sales data; and from customer service, who connect the sales force and their customers with manufacturing and logistics. Yet the overall responsibility for all the functions described in Figure 14.9 belongs to sales management.

ORGANIZING THE SALES FORCE

The characteristics of sales managers and the chain of command are important considerations in organizing the sales force. These and other concerns are of particular importance in global settings. The sales force may be structured by geography, by division or product line, or by market segment. Both the structure and the size of the sales group have a lot to do with sales coverage.

Sales Manager Types   The sales manager position can be executive, midlevel, or first line, depending on responsibilities and scope of operations. At the top are national and international sales executives, often with the title of vice president. They usually report to the top marketing executive. In most companies, only one or a few people are in this position. Their management scope covers several products across a broad territory. In large companies, executive sales managers may have several other sales managers reporting to them, and they ultimately are responsible for several thousand salespeople. Midlevel managers, called regional managers when the sales force structure is geographic, supervise several other managers, called district managers or first-line managers, in a large area, such as New England or several countries. First-line managers oversee several salespeople who handle certain products or types of accounts in a limited geographic area. First-line managers who supervise field reps and retail salespeople usually have a sales force of eight to twelve; those who supervise inside sales or telemarketing personnel are likely to have more. As a first assignment, some sales managers supervise only three or four people.

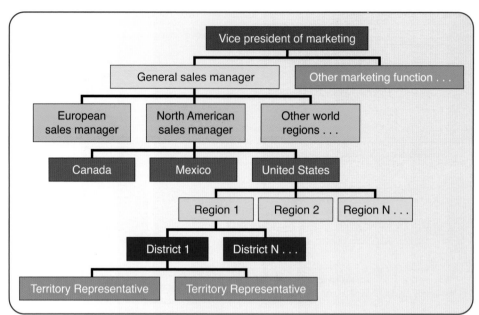

Figure 14.10 A Geographic Sales Force Structure

Sales Force Structures A **sales structure** is the organization of the reporting relationship between sales managers and salespeople. Sales organizations can be structured by geography, by product or division, by market segment, or by individual account. In some cases, all four are used. Figure 14.10 shows a typical geographical structure, topped by a general sales manager who reports to the vice president of marketing. Sales managers in the various geographical areas report to the general sales manager. Below them may be sales managers at the regional and district level, then territory representatives (salespersons).

Figure 14.11 illustrates the division or product line structure. Many companies are organized into divisions, and each may have a sales organization. Companies with very technical products are likely to use this sort of structure. For example, GM's Delphi division has a sales organization structured according to the components of an automobile: interior, exterior,

electronics, and so forth. Each area requires a great deal of interaction among salespeople, designers, manufacturing personnel, and individual customers.

The third approach is to structure the sales force by market segment, as shown in Figure 14.12. Salespeople are focused on a given target segment, as outlined in the marketing plan. IBM has historically operated in this manner. It has one sales organization that sells to the financial community, another for universities, and yet another for manufacturing firms. The advantage is that salespeople focus on and truly understand the needs of a particular market segment. A company with a limited product line that has differing applications by segment would prefer this arrangement.

Many companies have a few customers who represent extremely large volume, called key accounts, house accounts, national accounts, or global accounts, depending on how they are managed. Major accounts may fit the 80-20 rule: About 80 percent of a company's sales volume comes from only 20 percent of its accounts. Although the percentages may differ considerably, the point is that major accounts are large, usually have unique sales needs, and are so important to volume and profitability that they require special emphasis. Major accounts are often managed by a separate sales group of a few very experienced people who report to the top sales executive. In other cases, they may be allocated to the midlevel area in which they are located. In some companies major accounts are assigned to sales man-

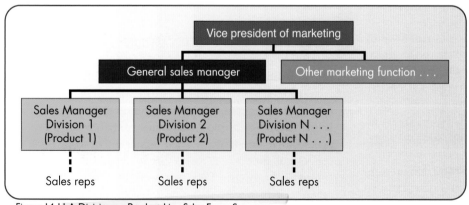

Figure 14.11 A Division or Product Line Sales Force Structure

agers who split their time between these customers and their management duties.

DEVELOPING THE SALES TEAM

In order to develop the sales team, a good sales force must first be recruited, selected, and trained. Recruitment is the activity of attracting qualified prospects for the sales job. Selection involves choosing the strongest recruits for employment in the sales force. Training provides education and preparation to sales-people. In the United States it is a manager's responsibility to comply with the federal Equal Employment Opportunity Act. Hiring discrimination based on age, sex, race, national origin, religion, ethnic background, and physical handicap is strictly forbidden. Many countries have similar requirements that must be carefully followed.

Diversity in the Sales Force Although the structure and size of the sales force are important, nothing is more critical for relationship marketing than the diversity of the sales organization. Managers must take care to develop a sales force that represents various groups. This enhances the ability of the organization to be sensitive to the needs of individual customers, thereby improving its relationship-building capacity. A diverse sales force provides a variety of insights, ideas, and perspectives, all of which make it easier to accommodate a dynamic and multicultural customer base.[32] Strong managers consider diversity in all stages of their sales force development, particularly during recruitment, selection, and training. The Columbus GA-based insurance company Aflac has a program called Diversity Development Grant, whose goals are to increase minority sales force recruitment and hence overall account development; its regional sales coordinators in Los Angeles, Baltimore and Miami received one-year grants of up to $20,000 each for their teams.[33]

Although men traditionally have dominated the sales profession, many managers are finding that women have excellent relationship skills and often are more successful at selling. The mostly male readership of *Sales and Marketing Management* was asked: "Who is better at sales, women or men?" Although 70 percent ranked the sexes as equal, 17 percent said women were better, compared to 13 percent who ranked men higher. Gender-balanced sales forces were the focus of a more recent study that concluded few gender differences existed.[34]

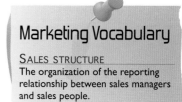

Marketing Vocabulary

SALES STRUCTURE
The organization of the reporting relationship between sales managers and sales people.

Many companies organize committees or task forces to promote diversity in the sales force and across all levels of the organization. Pfizer implemented a data tool called the Diversity Dashboard, which provides an up-to-the-minute demographic snapshot of the organization. "It's very powerful when you see visually how the gap widens from the recruiting level to the senior level," says Shinder Dhillon, Pfizer's global director of diversity. "We have had an increase in the number of women in senior to mid-level management."[35]

Recruiting Effective recruitment attracts a qualified pool of candidates to fill the sales positions. The first step is to develop a job description specifying activities and qualifications. This written document spells out organizational relationships, responsibilities, and duties of the position.

The convenience of the recruiting site is important, which is why college campuses are often chosen. Many organizations use recruiting companies to find experienced candidates. Strong organizations spend a good deal of time identifying a pool of candidates. Many companies have increased college hiring through aggressive e-recruiting through the Internet. Some companies also offer mock interviews, career fairs, and resume critiques on university campuses. To find out more, contact your college placement office or visit company Web sites directly.

Selecting Because good sales talent is in high demand, not only the company but also the candidate does the choosing. Sales managers must demonstrate sound judgment in selecting from a broad range of talents, and they also need to sell top candidates on opportunities with their organization. FedEx sales managers see recruitment and selection of sales

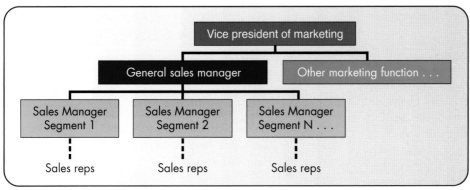

Figure 14.12 A Market Segment Sales Force Structure

candidates as one of their most important functions. FedEx is considered to have one of the best global sales forces. It selects candidates who can build relationships with a dynamic customer base spread over 220 countries.[36]

Although there is no definitive list of attributes that define those likely to become successful salespeople, the attitudes, skills, and knowledge of some individuals set them apart. Important personality traits include empathy, which allows a salesperson to understand problems from another's perspective; ego drive, which ties self-image and identity to job performance; and resilience, which allows a salesperson to bounce back from defeat. Also important is the ability to communicate, think analytically, and effectively organize and manage time. Knowledge of and experience with a product, industry, competitor, or company territory are also valuable qualities. Others include self-discipline, intelligence, creativity, flexibility, self-motivation, persistence, a personable nature, and dependability.

Thingamajob.com serves as a recruiting and job search tool.

Training Even the most qualified salespeople need continuous education. New hires need the most, but seasoned veterans also can benefit from advanced training and formal practice. Many sales executives believe training is critical for developing individual and team skills. Many companies found that it increased morale, reduced turnover, improved relationship-building skills and developed a stronger sense of teamwork, all of which combined to increase sales dramatically. The US market for corporate training was valued at $58.5 billion in 2007.[37] Training programs are usually conducted regarding company policies and procedures, product and customer applications knowledge, sales skills, and territory and account planning.

Company policies and procedures can be very elaborate, specifying the exact relationship that salespeople are expected to have with customers. Policies range from mundane matters, such as sales account and entertainment budgets, to complicated issues, such as the types of special customer requests the company will honor. In today's sales environment, procedures often are highly complex. Among other things, they may involve understanding how to enter orders, how to service accounts, and how to create and maintain reporting systems between the selling and buying organizations.

Training is necessary to understand the product's attributes and benefits. In technical sales jobs, products are often very sophisticated. In some cases training builds background information, such as a knowledge of electricity for electrical products or pharmacology for drug products. Salespeople learn not only about the technologies behind the product but also about how the product works. Teaching salespeople about new items is critical to the success of a pharmaceutical company such as Merck. There is very little time between a product's FDA approval and its introduction to customers.

Most organizations train new hires in basic relationship selling skills and experienced salespeople in more advanced techniques. The objective is to help the sales force do a better job of working with customers, listening, and finding ways to develop profitable relationships for each party. Sales certification programs enhance the skills and credibility of a sales force. These programs are usually provided by companies or associations that specialize in sales training. In this form of training, salespeople must attend classes or in some cases take distanced learning courses offered over the Internet. Certificates are given according to the competency level attained. More than 50 percent of managers believe that a certification program would benefit their company, and 66 percent of consumers believe certified salespeople are more credible. Certification is thought to demonstrate a defined level of competency and skill. Although such training is expensive, many organizations consider it a good investment.[38]

SALES FORECASTING AND BUDGETING

Forecasting and budgeting are important steps in allocating sales resources. The forecast estimates demand based on likely responses of buyers to future market conditions, sales force, and other promotional activities and marketing actions. Sales force budgets are generally set with the sales forecast in mind. Accuracy in the forecast and budgets is important, since production is scheduled to meet demand. When forecasts are lower than actual demand, customers go unserved. When they are higher than demand, high inventory carrying costs dramatically reduce profitability. Estimation methods vary from elaborate computer programs to fairly simple questioning of potential buyers. Even small companies, which are known for their ability to adjust quickly, depend on accurate forecasts.

Sales Forecasting Most companies go through three basic steps in estimating demand—an environmental forecast, an industry forecast, and a company sales forecast. The **environmental forecast** examines the economic, political, and social factors likely to affect the level of spending for a product. Factors include unemployment, consumer spending, interest rates, business investments, and inventory levels. In general, information of this type helps determine whether economic conditions for the company's products are likely to be positive or negative. Environmental forecasting can estimate not only global, international, national, and regional trends but also very localized trends. Every year Sales and Marketing Management prints a "Survey of Buying Power," a tool that helps marketers predict sales of products based on environmental conditions, consumer age and wealth, and distribution channels.

Sales forecasts often use the industry outlook as a key element. An **industry forecast** estimates the amount of overall demand expected based on such factors as the industry business condition, amount of spending, number of new products, and communications budgets anticipated for competitors. In other words, this forecast projects the level of sales and marketing activity for the industry as a whole as well as for competitors likely to affect the company most directly.

The **company sales forecast** is based on the overall marketing strategy. It forecasts unit sales and must be in line with marketing, financial, and operations plans. If not, then adjustments must be made to the sales forecast. The marketing plan is particularly critical. For example, a product positioned as a high-priced specialty item may have a low expected sales volume. For a product positioned as a low-priced commodity, the sales volume estimate probably will be higher. In addition, in order to do a good job of developing objectives, it is important to estimate demand with other departments in mind. Sales managers communicate about forecasts with many areas of the company to reconcile any differences. Since various departments may have specific objectives, such as cost containment, brand growth, and financial targets, this interaction is necessary. Estimates may be made for the entire company, a particular product, a geographic region, a market segment, or on some other basis.

It's important to remember the more dynamic the situation, the more difficult the prediction is likely to be. Consequently, businesses in new fields may have to spend more time estimating demand than do businesses with mature product lines. Yet, even in innovative, highly competitive industries it is important to obtain reliable forecasts.

Some marketers mistakenly associate good forecasting with strong marketing. In fact, there are many examples of organizations that have forecast low sales volume and, thus, created less aggressive marketing strategies. Although they met their forecasts, they probably would have reached much higher sales levels if they had pursued an aggressive strategy. Most organizations recognize that perfect sales projections may mean the company is operating much too conservatively. Whirlpool Corporation believes a perfect forecast is possible only when a marketing group is performing below potential.

Forecasts are very important in deciding how to allocate company resources. Divisions that foresee high levels of sales are often given ample resources, such as additional salespeople, large advertising and promotion budgets, and lots of attention from product development and manufacturing. Consequently, the forecast can become a self-fulfilling prophecy. When forecasts are low, fewer resources are provided, and lower sales result.

Sales Force Budgets One of the most important tasks of the sales manager is to create and administer the sales budget. The three most common methods for setting the budget are a percentage of overall sales, in relation to competitors in the industry, and as projected costs for the sales tasks. The first method establishes the sales budget as a percentage of the historical sales level. Although simple to use, this method has a major flaw. The estimated increase over past sales results in a larger sales budget, but perhaps the situation should be the reverse. A larger sales budget should result in improved sales volume. Despite this problem, many sales organizations base the budget on past performance. Essentially, a sales force that produces more is rewarded more resources in the future for its past success. A variation

---

Marketing Vocabulary

ENVIRONMENTAL FORECAST
An estimate of the economic, political, and social factors likely to affect the level of spending for the types of products or services being forecasted.

INDUSTRY FORECAST
An estimate of the amount and type of competitive activity likely to occur in an industry.

COMPANY SALES FORECAST
A prediction of unit or dollar sales for a given period, in total or broken down by product, segments, or other categories, and based on the marketing strategy that will be put in place.

on this is to use the sales forecast to establish the budget. This is more acceptable because it looks at the future rather than the past.

The second way to determine the sales budget is through comparison with a competitor's budget. Industry data provide the number of salespeople and sales offices as well as sales expenditures for other companies. The sales budget is then set accordingly. One advantage of this method is that it emphasizes competitive activity in the marketplace. A disadvantage is that it is not based on an understanding of the actual costs of one's own sales activities.

Task-based budgeting looks at the tasks salespeople must perform in order to accomplish objectives. Careful thought is given to each aspect of the sales process and to estimating the associated costs. The items usually considered are salaries, recruiting, training, travel, sales promotion, staff and clerical expenses, dues, and supplies.

IMPLEMENTING SALES ACTIONS

Once the sales forecast and budget have been established, sales activity can take place. Sales managers set quotas, measure performance, determine compensation, and supervise, coach, and motivate the sales organization in such a way that objectives are accomplished.

Quotas **Quotas** are quantitative performance standards used to direct sales force activity. They also provide a way to evaluate performance. Whereas forecasts estimate results, quotas provide guidelines. They are one of the most important methods sales managers use to set and meet objectives. When quotas are exceeded, we would say that the sales force has produced beyond objectives; when quotas are not met, we would say that the sales force has fallen short of objectives. Overall, quotas are set in line with the strategic marketing plan. Most sales organizations use one of three types: sales volume, profit, or activity quotas.

Sales volume quotas establish unit or dollar objectives. Usually these are set for a market segment, product or service line, and average volume per customer. Typically, a quota for the entire sales organization is determined and then divided among the various sales regions and salespeople. During this process, salespeople and others are likely to provide feedback to sales executives regarding potential in their territory, the level of competition, and their belief about what is possible to accomplish. That information is combined with the sales forecast.

Sales profit quotas establish profitability objectives for customers, products, and market segments. Rather than volume, the focus is on the overall profit that can be made. This kind of quota is particularly important when sales actions such as price negotiations or repeat versus new customers influence profit. It is also important when different products yield different profit.

Activity quotas encourage salespeople to engage in certain tasks, such as prospecting calls, service calls, sales calls, demonstrations, and visiting new accounts. The focus is on customer contacts that will allow the company to implement its overall marketing strategy.

Quotas are generally used to determine some portion of a salesperson's compensation. The simplest procedure is to set the same quota (such as amount of sales) for all salespeople and provide bonuses to those who exceed it. This tends to be inequitable, however, because sales potential and competition are likely to differ from one sales territory to another. Consequently, sales quotas usually vary for different parts of the organization and different salespeople. Compensation is covered in more detail in a later section.

Performance Measures Volume, profit, and activity quotas can be combined to measure performance, as shown in Figure 14.13. In this example the quota is based on sales volume, profit margin percentage, number of new accounts obtained, percentage of accounts

	(1) Weight	(2) Quota	(3) Performance	(4) % of Quota	(5) Contribution to Total Quota: (4) 3 (1)
Sales in dollars	40%	$500,000	$525,000	105%	42%
Profit margin	20%	30%	33%	110%	22%
Number of new accounts	15%	25%	20%	80%	12%
Number of accounts retained	20%	100%	120%	120%	24%
Number of new leads	5%	25%	50%	200%	10%
					TOTAL: 110%

Figure 14.13   Quotas as a Measure of Performance

retained, level of customer satisfaction, and number of new leads. Each factor is weighted in terms of importance. At the end of the sales period, the percentage of quota reached in each category is multiplied by the weight to determine the contribution of that category to achieving the total quota. In the example, sales are weighted at 40 percent, the quota is $500,000, and performance is $25,000 above that, leading to 105 percent of quota on that item. Multiplying by the weight, we get a 42 percent contribution to the total quota. Notice that when all these items are put together, this particular salesperson achieved 110 percent of quota (exceeded objectives by 10 percent). Performance exceeded the quota in all areas except the number of new accounts.

The performance measurement shown in Figure 14.13 can be used for several purposes. First, this person maintains loyal customers but seems to do little to increase the number of new accounts. The sales manager should discuss the situation to see whether training is needed or whether the territory has minimal potential for new customers. Second, since quotas can be used to motivate the sales force, the salesperson could be compensated for performing so well. Third, although the example provided here focuses on dollar volume, organizations often use this method to emphasize certain products or market segments consistent with their overall marketing strategy and positioning plan.

Compensation

A well-designed compensation plan should be geared toward the needs of both the company and the sales force. It should be developed with the overall sales strategy in mind. A compensation system not only helps motivate salespeople but also is important in keeping loyal employees. For obvious reasons, turnover is harmful in relationship marketing. Furthermore, satisfied salespeople work hard to develop loyal customers. It is almost impossible to build customer loyalty with a dissatisfied sales force.

The three basic elements of sales force compensation are salaries, commissions, and bonuses. A **salary** is a fixed amount paid regardless of specific performance. Salaries are usually based on education, experience, longevity, and overall professionalism. A **commission** is an amount paid in direct proportion to the accomplishment of specific short-term sales objectives. It usually is given for meeting or exceeding a broad range of criteria, including volume and profit by product, or according to customer type and loyalty. A **bonus** is a percentage of salary or fee paid in addition to other compensation for meeting long-term or unique goals. Bonuses are often given to the entire sales team for an outstanding effort, usually quarterly or annually. Compensation plans can be based on salary only, commission only, or both, and sometimes bonuses as well.

Supervision and Coaching

Supervision and coaching are face-to-face interactions between the sales manager and a salesperson. Most managers spend considerable time working with their people in the field. Good managers communicate well and help salespeople determine appropriate sales actions. They provide guidance to keep the sales force operating according to the company's philosophies, policies, and marketing plans.

The three components to central coaching are: "supervisory feedback, role modeling, and salesperson trust in managers."[39] Essentially, sales coaching occurs when the manager aids in the development of skills. Similar to a voice coach or athletic coach, the sales manager gives advice and demonstrations that enable salespeople to do a better job. Feedback should be an objective, and positive incentives should be used as progress is made. Coaching usually involves visits with customers by the manager and salesperson. The sales manager observes and gives pointers afterward on sales techniques. Good coaches also address all aspects of selling—from time management to customer sales support or even interaction with other company employees. In some cases coaching is done through role-playing. Henry Mueller, former vice president of new business partnerships at American Express, said: "The sales manager's role is to add value, whether it's with the customer or whether it's helping your salespeople prepare for their next round of sales calls. It's keeping an eye out for those common problems and opportunities that are coming up . . . you're always coaching, coaching, coaching."[40]

There are many appropriate coaching styles, but good coaches usually don't simply take over. They observe, ask questions, and listen. They communicate clearly and provide positive reinforcement for the activ-

Marketing Vocabulary

QUOTAS
Quantitative objectives used to direct sales force activity and evaluate performance.

SALES VOLUME QUOTAS
Unit or dollar objectives, usually set by market segment, product or service line, and average volume per customer.

SALES PROFIT QUOTAS
Profitability objectives for customers, products, and market segments.

ACTIVITY QUOTAS
Action objectives that encourage salespeople to engage in certain tasks, such as prospecting calls, service calls, sales calls, demonstrations, and visiting new accounts.

SALARY
The fixed amount of compensation paid regardless of performance.

COMMISSION
A form of sales force compensation in which the amount paid is in direct proportion to the accomplishment of specific objectives.

BONUS
A percentage of salary or a fee paid in addition to other compensation for meeting long-term or unique goals.

ities that salespeople carry out well. Feedback from sales managers is invaluable because it helps salespeople understand their strengths and weaknesses.

Motivation Most top salespeople are motivated by the very nature of the job. They find selling fascinating and want to excel in a competitive environment. Still, good sales managers can add to motivation by providing a positive organizational climate as well as financial and career incentives. Since many salespeople spend little time under direct supervision, the systems for motivation must work well without the constant presence of the sales manager. A positive organizational climate exists when salespeople feel good about their opportunities and rewards. A positive climate also helps salespeople perform at the highest professional level.

Telcordia Technologies promotes the fact that they are an employee-owned company to attract new associates.

Many companies use financial incentives. Money is a strong motivator, but companies are increasingly incorporating different forms of incentives. Carlson Marketing Group's (CMG) employee motivation and loyalty programs include employee rewards to each other, seminars on personal growth, and day care facilities. CMG's program "Ovation" personalizes a sales

target for each salesperson, which provides incentive without creating an atmosphere overly competitive with coworkers.[41]

Ethical Issues in Motivation and Compensation In striving to produce peak performers, sales managers may use several motivational approaches. If they push too hard in the wrong ways, then salespeople may be pressured to compromise ethical standards. When performance is poor, rewards may be withheld, or in extreme cases punishment may be used. Motivational techniques generally reward people for good performance. A key part of the management job, however, is to establish expectations not only in terms of sales volume but also regarding acceptable behavior. When managers focus exclusively on sales volume objectives, they are telling salespeople that the ends justify the means. This lack of attention to appropriate behavior in combination with pressure to perform can be considered unethical in itself. Let's look at three questionable practices.

- *Family pressure.* Salespeople are required to attend the annual sales meeting with their spouse (and perhaps other family members). Those performing well are rewarded publicly with free trips, gifts, or a large bonus. For the others, it is obvious to the family that they are low producers. Essentially, the company is interfering in family relationships with the intent of elevating sales.

- *Peer pressure.* The sales manager broadcasts performance results to all salespeople or, in announcing sales contest winners, points out a few low producers. Rather than private communications between the manager and the salesperson, overt peer pressure is being used to gain behavior changes. This would be like posting student names along with grades in the student newspa-

per. Is that an ethical way to motivate you to learn? Could this increase the pressure on students to cheat?

- *Termination.* All salespeople are rank ordered, and the lowest performers are asked to leave even though they may be performing very profitably for the company. This keeps all salespeople pushing for fear of losing their job. Since termination is devastating for most people, to avoid it they may put undue or unscrupulous pressure on buyers.

Even quotas, though less extreme than these scenarios, can be troublesome. They are generally considered useful tools, but some sales managers believe they lead to high-pressure tactics and, thus, are harmful to relationship building. That is why Saturn moved away from quotas in favor of salary incentives.

OVERSEEING SALES FORCE ACTIVITIES

Once sales operations are in effect, management needs to evaluate them and in some cases make adjustments. Evaluation and control are the final steps in the management process. Sales activities nearly always can be improved. In fact, some of the strongest sales organizations are very flexible in meeting business challenges and competitive situations. This is particularly important in industries in which changes occur rapidly. In general, most evaluation programs look at efforts and results, assess the company's influence in supporting performance, identify problems and opportunities, and take corrective action.

Salesperson performance can be evaluated behaviorally or by outcome. Behavioral performance is based on skills and the ability to meet the demands of the job. This includes such aspects as sales presentation, planning, teamwork, relationship selling, and technical knowledge. Outcome performance is measured by such customer-related factors as sales volume, market share, customer loyalty and satisfaction, and number of new accounts.[42]

In addition to evaluating individual salespeople, managers must regularly assess the entire sales force. This tells whether overall performance is strong. It may result in territory shifts, the addition of people, or other adjustments. The process gives both field reps and management an opportunity to learn whether the level of activity has produced the expected results. This often means doing productivity analysis to determine whether sales volumes have been reached, market shares have been accomplished, and the appropriate product mix has been sold to targeted segments. Usually, good evaluation requires looking behind the numbers to determine where the strongest and weakest results occurred and under what conditions.

Today, many companies use 360-degree evaluations; that is, salespeople are asked to evaluate their sales managers as well. This supports the team concept and helps break down the old barriers to joint progress. It is instrumental in helping sales managers improve. Since managerial success depends on working through others, this type of feedback is seen as absolutely critical in many companies.

Web and E-commerce Stars
www.llbean.com

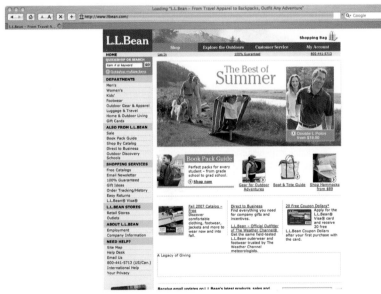

It was in 1911 when Leon Leonwood Bean returned from a hunting trip with cold, damp feet and an innovative idea. L.L. Bean started as a local shoe store in Maine and has grown to be a leader in apparel and outdoor equipment. It has also become a leader in inside sales. Its Web site, www.llbean.com, includes a full list of shopping departments. Visitors can also "explore the outdoors" by researching outdoor tips, gear and even register for outdoor discovery schools. L.L. Bean's Live Help, available on its Web site, allows customers to chat with a customer service representative online. Making customer service easily accessible has helped create a loyal customer base for L.L. Bean.

SALES FORCE AUTOMATION

All sorts of high-tech tools are revolutionizing selling and sales management. **Sales force automation** is the use of technology to improve personal selling and sales management effectiveness. When Oracle Corps found demand exceeding its ability to supply, it spent millions of dollars to develop a Web-centered selling system in which customers can do the ordering themselves. Although salespeople still do the selling, they have more time to focus on the customer's needs and act as consultants. Nick Ward, former CEO at MOHR Development, concluded, "People who are successful today are holding back on that sale and being careful to craft a total solution for the customer." The Oracle Web site allows salespeople to demonstrate the software immediately, and the client may also try out the product. Oracle salespeople are able to deal with a larger workload and in 2006, its revenue approximately doubled to $18 billion in five years.[43]

Sales personnel commonly use the following technologies: sales automation software, notebook and desktop computers, contact management/calendaring systems, cell phones, the internet, paging, wireless communication, and handheld date recorders.

Gateway Systems Corporation of East Lansing, Michigan, has been a pioneer in sales force automation software. According to the director of marketing, Karen Griggs:

> Gateway's product, SYNERGIST Sales Portfolio (SSP), is designed to increase sales effectiveness on two levels. At the sales representative level, SSP facilitates the tracking of key account information, helps representatives monitor competitive inroads, and streamlines paperwork. At the sales management level, SSP allows managers to electronically collect critical pieces of information from the person closest to the customer—the sales representative. Furthermore, this information can be aggregated, analyzed, and provide indicators of the organization's performance within key target markets and accounts. And finally, SSP can serve as a communication vehicle from sales managers to their field sales representatives.[44]

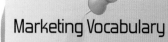

Marketing Vocabulary

SALES FORCE AUTOMATION
The use of technology to improve personal selling and sales management effectiveness.

Sales force automation facilitates communication and gives salespeople fast access to necessary information. The use of notebook computers, updated software, and other technologies has improved the overall effectiveness of personal selling and sales management. Managers and salespeople alike can coordinate, plan, and interact more efficiently than ever before. This helps develop stronger relationships within the sales force and with customers.

Personal selling, like the mass communication activities we explored in the previous chapter, is a forceful means of implementing the promotion strategy element of the marketing mix. We have now examined three of the four basic elements in the mix: product, place, and promotion.

Chapter Summary:

Objective 1: Understand how selling evolved to a focus on relationships and what elements are involved in building them.

Personal selling techniques have moved through three distinct modes: the traditional persuasive approach, consultative selling, and relationship selling. The latter is strategic in nature and involves developing long-term relationships that are mutually beneficial for buyer and seller. It requires that the selling organization understand the customer's business or lifestyle and treat loyal customers as assets of the firm. Typically this leads to partnering that creates value for the customer and the selling organization. The objective of relationship selling is to create steady profit through customer loyalty and satisfaction. Interactions with customers focus on win-win situations.

Objective 2: Know the responsibilities of salespeople and sales managers.

Most professional salespeople view themselves as the marketing manager of a territory. As such, they are responsible for implementing the company's marketing strategy within the territory. They also communicate company policy to customers and potential customers. They are important sources of feedback and have a responsibility to convey this information to their organization. Salespeople must have excellent ethical judgment since they often operate without much direct supervision, are under pressure to boost volume, and have leeway in what they say to customers.

Sales force management is the marketing function involved with planning, implementing, and adjusting sales force activities. First, sales managers work with others in their company to organize the sales force, including its structure, size, and type. Second, they develop diverse sales teams through recruiting, selecting, and training. Third, they prepare forecasts and budgets. Fourth, they implement actions by establishing quotas, assessing performance, determining compensation, and supervising, coaching, and motivating the sales force. Finally, they evaluate sales activities and make any necessary changes.

Objective 3: Identify and understand the steps in personal selling.

The seven steps in personal selling are planning, prospecting, organizing information and developing a call plan, approaching a prospect, presenting a case and building relationships, managing objections and closing, and service. Sales planning translates the company's marketing strategy into territory and account plans. Prospecting involves seeking out new customers within the company's target markets. Next, sales personnel organize information and develop a call plan. To do this, they learn about prospects and prepare a routing schedule to identify which prospects will be called on and when. The approach is the first formal contact with the customer. The objective is to secure an initial meeting and gain customer interest. The next step is making the case and building relationships. This is done through the sales presentation. Sales personnel then manage objections and close the sale. One of the most important sales skills is the ability to overcome business objections. Closing means getting the first order. Service follow-through is essential for developing customer loyalty.

Objective 4: Learn the characteristics of strong salespeople.

First, strong salespeople are goal oriented. They use time well, manage their territory efficiently, and like to compete to obtain results. Second, they are empathetic; they understand buyer behavior, are customer focused, and possess excellent listening and questioning skills. Third, they have applications knowledge. They are technically competent, know their customers' business, and are good at creative problem solving. Fourth, excellent salespeople are ethical and trustworthy; they are honest, seek additional information when they don't know the answer, and make reliable partners.

Objective 5: Understand how to develop a diverse sales organization.

Once the sales structure is determined, the sales organization is developed. Diversity is one of the most important aspects of a sales force because of its role in building relationships with multicultural customers. Strong attention must be paid to diversity when recruiting, selecting, and training salespeople. Recruitment seeks a pool of exceptional candidates and often takes place on college campuses. Selection is a choice process for the company and candidates alike, as both seek a good match. Training involves educating salespeople about company policies and procedures, product and customer application knowledge, relationship selling skills, territory and account planning, and diversity.

Objective 6: Explore how to implement sales actions, from setting quotas and compensating salespeople to evaluating and adjusting plans.

Implementing sales actions involves several steps. Quotas establish the sales volume, profit, and activities expected from each salesperson. They are used to direct action and evaluate performance. Supervision and coaching, which involve working with salespeople to improve performance, build self-esteem and skills. Motivation is also part of the sales manager's job. It depends on a positive organizational climate in which employees feel rewarded for the effort they make. Sales force compensation is developed with the overall marketing strategy in mind. It is designed to support the development of loyal salespeople, who in turn help create loyal customers. Salaries, commissions, and bonuses are used singly or in combination. Several significant ethical issues surround motivation and compensation. Managers must be careful not to use techniques that lead to unethical actions by salespeople. The final step in sales force management is evaluation and adjustment. Organizations must be flexible in order to maintain competitive advantage. This requires an assessment of individual salespeople and each part of the sales organization. Companies are beginning to use 360-degree feedback techniques to evaluate sales managers as well as the sales force.

Review Your Understanding

1. List several types of personal selling situations. Give an example of each.
2. What is relationship selling?
3. List the responsibilities of a salesperson.
4. What are the seven steps in personal selling?
5. What characterizes a strong salesperson?
6. What does closing mean?
7. Give three reasons why ethics are important to salespeople.
8. What are the five sales management functions?
9. List the types of sales forecasting. Briefly describe each.
10. What are three methods for setting a sales force budget?
11. What are quotas?
12. What is coaching?
13. What are three ethical issues surrounding sales force management?

Discussion of Concepts

1. What are the key differences among the traditional, consultative, and relationship sales approaches? Which do you feel is most appropriate in a majority of circumstances? Why?
2. List the seven types of sales personnel. Under what circumstances would it make sense to have each type?
3. Why is it important for the salesperson to support the company's strategic marketing plan?
4. What is most important about each of the seven steps in personal selling? How do they form a process?
5. Describe some of the ways salespeople seek out new customers. Under what circumstances might each be appropriate?
6. Do you have the characteristics of a strong salesperson? Do you believe people are born with these, or can they be learned?
7. The job of the sales manager is to support the strategic marketing and communications plan of the organization. What are the key responsibilities of a sales manager?
8. Describe the methods a sales manager can use to set the sales budget. Which one do you feel is most effective? Why?
9. Training is now considered one of the most important factors in developing a strong sales team. What are the four major areas of training programs?
10. What is sales force automation, and how does it help sales managers and salespeople?
11. Is it acceptable to use family pressure to motivate salespeople? Why or why not?

Key Terms And Definitions

Account planning: Establishing sales goals and objectives for each major customer.

Activity quotas: Action objectives that encourage salespeople to engage in certain tasks, such as prospecting calls, service calls, sales calls, demonstrations, and visiting new accounts.

Approach: The salesperson's first formal contact with the potential customer.

Bonus: A percentage of salary or a fee paid in addition to other compensation for meeting long-term or unique goals.

Center of influence: An opinion leader who can be quickly qualified as a potential customer because of his or her standing in the community.

Closing: The point at which the salesperson obtains the first order from the customer.

Cold calling: Contacting a lead for the first time.

Commission: A form of sales force compensation in which the amount paid is in direct proportion to the accomplishment of specific objectives.

Company sales forecast: A prediction of unit or dollar sales for a given period, in total or broken down by product, segments, or other categories, and based on the marketing strategy that will be put in place.

Consultative selling: An approach to selling in which sales personnel work closely with customers to help solve problems.

Direct sales: Sales that result from the salesperson's direct interaction with a consumer or company.

Empathy: An interpersonal connection in which the salesperson knows precisely how the prospect feels and communicates that understanding.

Environmental forecast: An estimate of the economic, political, and social factors likely to affect the level of spending for the types of products or services being forecast.

Follow-up: After-sales service to ensure customer satisfaction in order to obtain repeat business.

Industry forecast: An estimate of the amount and type of competitive activity that is likely to occur in an industry.

Leads: All those who may have need of a company's product.

Missionary sales: Sales made indirectly through people who do not obtain orders but influence the buying decision of others.

Negotiation: Discussion by two or more parties to arrange a transaction.

Networking: Contacting friends, relatives, and associates to obtain leads.

Preapproach: Preparation by the salesperson for the initial meeting with a prospect.

Presentation: A two-way process in which the salesperson listens to the customer to identify needs and then describes how the product will fulfill them.

Prospect: A potential customer interested in the seller's product.

Prospecting: Seeking potential customers within the company's target markets.

Qualified prospect: A potential buyer interested in the seller's product and with the attributes of a good customer.

Qualifying: Examining prospects to identify those with the authority and ability to buy the product.

Quotas: Quantitative objectives used to direct sales force activity and evaluate performance.

Referral: A lead provided by a qualified prospect.

Relationship selling: Forging bonds between buyer and seller to gain loyalty and mutual satisfaction.

Routing schedule: A travel plan for calling on prospects that is developed to save time and minimize expenses.

Salary: The fixed amount of compensation paid regardless of performance.

Sales force automation: The use of technology to improve personal selling and sales management effectiveness.

Sales force management: The marketing function involved with planning, implementing, and adjusting sales force activities.

Sales manager: The person responsible for the leadership and management of salespeople in order to accomplish the sales objectives established in the marketing plan.

Sales profit quotas: Profitability objectives for customers, products, and market segments.

Sales structure: The organization of the reporting relationship between sales managers and salespeople.

Sales territory: All the actual and potential customers, often within a specified geographic area, for which the salesperson has responsibility.

Sales volume quotas: Unit or dollar objectives, usually set by market segment, product or service line, and average volume per customer.

Team selling: Selling that involves people from most parts of the organization, including top executives, working together to create a relationship with the buying organization.

Telemarketing: Making telephone calls to leads provided by marketing services or from other lists.

Territory planning: Identifying potential customers, their sales potential, and the frequency with which they will be contacted about various products.

Traditional sales approach: Emphasizing persuasive techniques to get consumers to buy a company's products.

References

1. Hiawatha Bray, "Hopkinton, Mass.–Based Data Storage Giant Faces Challenge from Alliance," Knight Ridder/Tribune Business News, July 7, 2000; John Madden, "Removable Storage: While IT Has Been Slow to Outsource Data Management, More Vendors Enter the Fray," eWeek, May 22, 2000, pp. 23+; Tim McLaughlin, "Rapid Expansion in Store for EMC Corp.," Boston Herald, March 6, 2000; Paul C. Judge, "EMC: High-Tech Star," Business Week, March 15, 1999, www.businessweek.com; "Ruettger: Focus on Execution," PC Week, July 26, 1999, Vol. 16 Issue 30, pg. 20; Joseph F. Kovar, "Back Up to the Future—EMC Is Quietly Becoming a Top E-Business Supplier," Computer Reseller News, December 6, 1999, pp. 208+; EMC Web site, www.emc.com, site viewed May 22, 2008.

2. United Sates Department of Labor, "Tomorrow's Job," Occupational Outlook Handbook 2004-2005, New York: VGM Career Books, 2005, pg. 5.

3. Average Sales Job Salaries and Sales Pay Scale. www.salary.com, site visited March 26, 2008.

4. "Boeing Sets Records for Airplane Orders in 2006," Jan 4, 2007, Boeing News Release at www.boeing.com/news/releases/2007/q1; Bill Kelly, "How to Sell Airplanes, Boeing-Style," Sales and Marketing Management, December 9, 1985, Vol. 135 Issue 8 pg. 32–34.he Lazy Bee' a Bad Rap Question," Fortune, January 25, 1993, p. 10.

5. www.handtech.com, site visited March 26, 2008.

6. Merck & Co., Inc., Hoovers Company Records, May 6, 2008.

7. www.llbean.com, site visited March 26, 2008.

8. Brett A. Boyle, "The Importance of the Industrial Inside Sales Force: A Case Study," Industrial Marketing Management Vol. 25, Issue 5 (September 1996): 339–348.

9. Marcus W. Brauchli, "Looking East: Asia, on the Assent, Is Learning to Say No to 'Arrogant' West," Wall Street Journal, April 13, 1994, pp. A1, A8.

10. Interview by the author.

11. Ferranti, "Navigating the Depths of Global Commerce."

12. John R. Graham, "Successful Selling: Learn the Customer's Buying Cycle," The American Salesman, March 2000, Vol. 45, Issue 3 pg. 3–9.

13. See Joe Chapman and Stephanie Rauck, "Relationship Selling: A Synopsis of Recent Research," in Developments in Marketing Science, no. 18, ed. Roger Gomes (Coral Gables, FL: Academy of Marketing Science, 1995), p. 163.

14. Edward R. Del Gaizo, Keven J. Corcoran, and David J. Erdman, The Alligator Trap (Chicago: Irwin Professional Pub, 1996), pg. 21.

15. "Wachovia Chooses To Innovate With Cisco TelePresence" CiscoNews Release, www.newsroom.cisco.com, June 27, 2007.

16. Ibid.

17. For more information, see Lisa M. Ellram, "Partnering Pitfalls and Success Factors," International Journal of Purchasing and Materials Management Vol. 31, Issue 2 (April 1995) pg. 35–44.

18. Dean Allen Foster, "Negotiating and 'Mind-Meeting,'" Directors and Boards, Fall 1992, Vol.17, Issue 1 pg. 52–54. See also Sandra J. Allen, "Tactics for Success," Communication World, September 1999, Vol. 16. Issue 8, pg. 34–37.

19. Personal interview with John Sutthoff in Atlanta, GA, 1997.

20. www.footlocker.com, site visited March 26, 2008.

21. Mark J. Astarita, "Cold Calling Rules and Procedures," 1995, www.seclaw.com/ coldcall.htm, site visited May 22, 2007.

22. Roger S. Peterson, "Go Modular, Be Flexible to Control Exhibit Costs," Marketing News, December 2, 1996, Vol. 30, Isue 25, pg. 11.

23. "Auto Show Attendance Numbers Released." www.clickondetroit.com/ autoshow/15151960/detail.html, site visited March 26, 2008.

24. Jeremy Rosenberg, "Auto Show Draws More Than 1 Million Visitors," Jan 16, 2004, www.cars.com, site visited May 22, 2007.

25. Alan Test, "Trade Show Selling," The American Salesman, September 2000, Vol. 45, Issue 9, pg. 15–18.

26. "Amway Business Opportunity," www.amway.com, site visited March 26, 2008.

27. Alticor News Release, www.amyway.com, January 31, 2007.

28. Neil Rackham, SPIN Fieldbook: Practical Tools, Methods, Exercises, and Resources (New York: McGraw-Hill, 1996).

29. Ibid, pgs. 11-12.

30. Role-playing with executives witnessed by the author.

31. Jon M. Hawes, James T. Strong, and Bernard S. Winich, "Do Closing Techniques Diminish Prospect Trust?" Industrial Marketing Management Vol. 25, Issue 5 (September 1996), 349–360.

32. Kenneth Labich, "Making Diversity Pay," Fortune, September 9, 1996, Vol. 134, Issue 5, pg. 177–179; and Louisa Wah, "Diversity at Allstate: A Competitive Weapon," Management Review, July/August 1999, Vol. 49, Issue 3, pg. 24–30.

33. Steven Tuckey, "Companies Push Recruitment of Minority Agents," National Underwriter, May 9, 2005, 109(18), p.14.

34. William C. Moncrief, et al., "Examining Gender Differences in Field Sales Organizations," Journal of Business Research, September 2000, Vol. 49, Issue 3, pg. 245–257.

35. "The National Association for Female Executives Announces its 2007 Top Companies," www.nafe.com, site visited March 26, 2008.

36. Geoffrey Brewer and Christine Galea, "Best Sales Forces: The Top 25."; www.fedex.com/us/about/overview/worldwide/, site visited June 26, 2007.

37. Bersin & Assoc. "2008 Corporate Learning Factbook Values U.S. Training Market at $58.5B, with Companies Spending an Average of $1,202 Per Employee," January 29, 2008.

38. Earl D. Honeycutt, Jr., Ashraf M. Attia, and Angela R. D'Auria, "Sales Certification Programs," Journal of Personal Selling and Sales Management Vol. 16, Issue 3 (Summer 1996), pg. 59–65.

39. Gregory A. Rich, "The Constructs of Sales Coaching: Supervisory Feedback, Role Modeling, and Trust," The Journal of Personal Selling and Sales Management, Volume 18, Issue 1 Winter 1998) pg. 53–63.

40. Geoffrey Brewer, "Meeting of the Minds," Sales and Marketing Management, Nov 1996, Vol. 148, Issue 11, pg. 72-74.

41. www.carlsonmarketing.com, site visited June 27, 2007; Chad Kaydo, "A Motivation Master Class," Sales & Marketing Management, August 2000, Vol. 18, Issue 1, p. 88-94.

42. Ken Grant and David W. Cravens, "Examining Sales Force Performance in Organizations That Use Behavior-Based Sales Management Processes," Industrial Marketing Management Vol. 25 (September 1996) pg. 361–371.

43. Philip B Clark and Sean Callahan, "Sales Staffs: Adapt or Die," B to B, April 10, 2000, Vol.85, Issue 3, pg. 0-1.; www.oracle.com/ corporate/about, site visited June 27, 2007.

44. Interview with Karen Griggs, March 4, 1997.

The Marketing Gazette

Tony Fang, "Negotiation: the Chinese Style," The Journal of Business and Industrial Marketing, 2006, 21 (1), p.50-60; Daniel D Ding, "An Indirect Style in Business Communication," Journal of Business and Technical Communication, Jan 2006, 20 (1), p.87-100; Mariko Sanchanta, "Japanese Value Relationships and Quality time," Financial Times, Apr 2, 2007, p.4;Peggy Hollinger, "Business Etiquette: Excuse My French, But Pleasure Before Business?" FT.com, Feb 13, 2007; Abigail Stevens, "When in Rome…A Glimpse of Global Business Etiquette," Accountancy Ireland, Feb 2007, 39(1), p.70-71; Robert Eugene DiPaolo, "Doing Business in Brazil Is First of All an Adventure," Brazzil, Sep 11, 2006.

CASE 14

Whole Foods

Whole Foods Market has been a pioneer in the organic food industry. Founded in 1980, Whole Foods Market has become the world's leading retailer of natural and organic foods with over 265 stores in North America. The company's growth has been substantial amidst rising awareness of environmental sustainability among consumers. Sales have consistently increased over the past few years as the company has opened multiple new stores annually. The company's core values include selling the highest quality natural and organic products available while satisfying and delighting customers through extraordinary customer service.

Whole Foods targets customers looking to enhance the quality of their lives through quality organic foods. The company believes quality is a never-ending process and evaluates its products based on nutrition, freshness, appearance, and taste. Highlighting foods free of artificial preservatives, sweeteners, and hydrogenated fats the company supports health and well-being.

In order to ensure a positive experience in its stores, Whole Foods extensively trains each employee about organic food and healthful living. Customers receive personal attention and friendly service. As a result, Whole Foods relies almost entirely on word-of-mouth recommendations, allocating less than 1 percent of its budget to advertising. The company motto discusses how employees are empowered to make decisions and suggestions for improvement to current company policies. Employees are assigned to a self-managed team such as produce, groceries or prepared foods with an average of 10 teams per store. The teams are carried through upper management with regional managers and even to executives forming teams. The company believes that teamwork promotes information sharing, cooperation, and even competition. Teams often compete against each other in quality, service and profitability. Teams are also given the authority to approve new hires. "Whole Foods is a social system. It's not a hierarchy. We don't have lots of rules handed down from headquarters in Austin. We have lots of self-examination going on. Peer pressure substitutes for bureaucracy. Peer pressure enlists loyalty in ways that bureaucracy doesn't," said John Mackey, Whole Foods' CEO.

Whole Foods has a broad selection of products with emphasis on perishable products designed to appeal to both natural foods and gourmet shoppers. In order to fulfill the demand for fresh, perishable foods, Whole Foods has empowered individual store and regional buyers to seek out locally grown products that meet the quality, and environmental standards of the company. Space is each store is allocated specifically for locally grown foods. The company believes in the importance of offering local foods in its stores because it is the freshest. But Whole Foods does not limit itself to local products. The company has launched a global buying initiative to search for quality organic products from developing countries that promote fair wages and working conditions. Whole Foods also offers a large selection of prepared foods to its shoppers. Teams of chefs provide a constantly changing variety of quick entrees and side dishes such as sesame-crusted salmon and couscous salad made with natural ingredients for customers on the go.

Knowing that intangible elements, such as organically grown food through environmentally sustainable practices, have contributed to the perception of quality, Whole Foods continues to innovate the retail food marketplace. This is the kind of innovation, along with a combination of goods and services, has made the company a leader in the natural and organic food industry.

1. What are the benefits and downfalls to Whole Foods Corporation's approach to sales structure?

2. Identify the effective tactics used by Whole Foods' employees in over-the-counter selling.

Sources: www.wholefoods.com, site viewed February 25, 2008; John Egan, "The Whole of Whole Foods," Retail Traffic. Atlanta: Nov 2007. Vol. 36, Iss. 11; pg. 69, 6 pgs; Hoovers Company Records, Whole Foods Market, Inc. June 17, 2008.

SECTION

6

Deliver Value

This section covers the methods in which marketers deliver value to customers. Delivering value is reflected by an organization's ability to deliver products and services to customers. The following chapters are included in this section:

Chapter 15 Supply Chain Management & Marketing Channels
Chapter 16 Retailing, Direct Marketing & Wholesaling

CHAPTER 15

Supply Chain Management & Channels

Nokia is renowned for its supply chain practices, including a nework of suppliers that conform to strict environmental and social obligations.

Learning Objectives

1. Understand supply chain management activities and objectives and how they improve business performance.

2. Learn why companies frequently use intermediaries to reach targeted customers.

3. Attain insight into how channel relationships should be managed over time.

4. Appreciate the economic importance of wholesalers.

5. Know the different types of wholesalers and the distinct roles they play.

6. Identify what physical distribution entails and why it is critical for any business organization.

7. Learn the steps in the order management process.

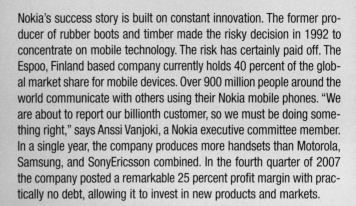

Nokia's success story is built on constant innovation. The former producer of rubber boots and timber made the risky decision in 1992 to concentrate on mobile technology. The risk has certainly paid off. The Espoo, Finland based company currently holds 40 percent of the global market share for mobile devices. Over 900 million people around the world communicate with others using their Nokia mobile phones. "We are about to report our billionth customer, so we must be doing something right," says Anssi Vanjoki, a Nokia executive committee member. In a single year, the company produces more handsets than Motorola, Samsung, and SonyEricsson combined. In the fourth quarter of 2007 the company posted a remarkable 25 percent profit margin with practically no debt, allowing it to invest in new products and markets.

Nokia's global success would not be possible without an outstanding supply chain. In fact, the company was ranked number 1 by Boston consultancy AMR Research's survey of top supply-chain operators. The company's ability to link supply, demand and product management has given it an advantage over competitors in the world's fastest growing markets, which include China, Southeast Asia, India and Africa. Its success in these markets has been made possible by the ability to efficiently deliver entry-level phones with practical features to low-income customers. The company has made substantial investments in building distribution systems and retailer networks in developing countries. Its customers include those in most rural parts of India and China. Aside from an extensive distribution network, Nokia's ability to maintain strong profit margins in the entry-level market segment has also been aided by standardization of parts among different device models and designing phones that have fewer inputs than the competition.

Further contributing to Nokia's outstanding supply chain is the company's supply network. Nokia developed a set of global Nokia Supplier Requirements, which include specified environmental and social obligations. Nokia establishes collaborative relationships with its suppliers through face-to-face meetings, assessments, training programs, and supplier-focused events to enhance corporate responsibility. Nokia also expands its supply network through supplier developments programs. The company spends nearly $20 million a year on supplier diversity programs in the United States. Nokia actively supports the creation and growth of minority owned suppliers and strives to increase the amount of business conducted with them.

Nokia views its efficient supply network as an opportunity to reduce its environmental impact. Nokia requires the mobile device components promote waste reduction, energy efficiency and recycling. As a result, each supplier must have an environmental management system that complies with environmental legislation and includes continuous improvement. Nokia suppliers must measure the environmental impact of their operations including air, water, and soil waste emissions, and energy efficiency. The supplier must then identify options to minimize its impact and provide statistical evidence to Nokia of its improvements.

Nokia's supply chain has made it one of the most successful companies in the world today. Supply chain management has a growing importance in business as more and more companies are going global and making efforts to reduce their environmental impact.[1]

THE CONCEPT OF SUPPLY CHAIN MANAGEMENT AND CHANNELS

Supply chain management helps companies link upstream suppliers of raw materials, components, and expertise required to make a product; and all of the downstream distribution of products by wholesalers, retailers and other organizations. Our discussion of supply chain management is followed by an understanding of marketing channels used to distribute and sell products. Historically, marketers focused primarily on channels. Today, information systems provide the data required to manage the entire supply chain to create outstanding customer value. For example, when you buy a product from Wal-mart, at the time of check out a supplier from as far away as China, knows the product has left the store – and that companies suppliers and all of the other members of the chain that produce and ship that product have the same information. So that product can be replaced in the quickest and most efficient way possible.

Figure 15.1 depicts supply chain management and channels in the most elementary way. Notice that supply chain management deals with the total chain, while channels is a very important part of the chain. The idea of a value chain discussed in B2B marketing chapter is useful in discussions about supply chain management. We will use the same idea in this chapter extending it to include the consumer. Channels is included in two places in figure 15.1 because channel strategies are equally important in B2B (business to business) and B2C (business to consumer) marketing.

It is useful to look at the value chain depicted in figure15.2, which shows the linkage of actions preformed by suppliers, producers and all channel members to create and deliver value to customers. Members of the value chain extend from the environment, including all of the natural resource,s to society which consumes and disposes of products. Members include extractors, suppliers, OEMs, distributors,

providers, users and society are described along the chain. At each link in the chain marketing helps connect the specific organizations by forming beneficial relationships. These are the value added interfaces along the chain. The types of organizations that are linked for a particular product form the supply chain for the product's industry. An individual company generally refers to its supply chain as that part of the value chain which is most important to its overall business. In some cases it only refers to upstream elements, but should include both upstream and downstream members.

SUPPLY CHAIN MANAGEMENT, LOGISTICS, AND PHYSICAL DISTRIBUTION

Supply chain management incorporates all of the activities concerned with planning, implementation, and control of sourcing, manufacturing, and delivery for products and services.[2] The development of a network of supply and distribution organizations involved in acquiring and moving products, as well as the flow of information about these activities within and across different firms is important because these business activities impact customer satisfaction and profitability. First, we will discuss supply chain management. We will then cover integrated logistics management which deals mostly with the physical

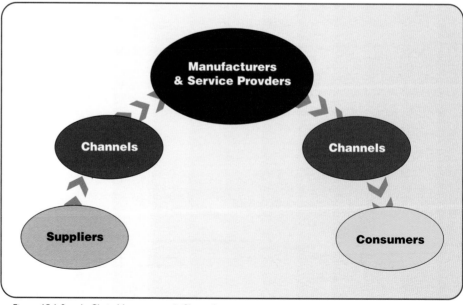

Figure 15.1 Supply Chain Management & Channels

412

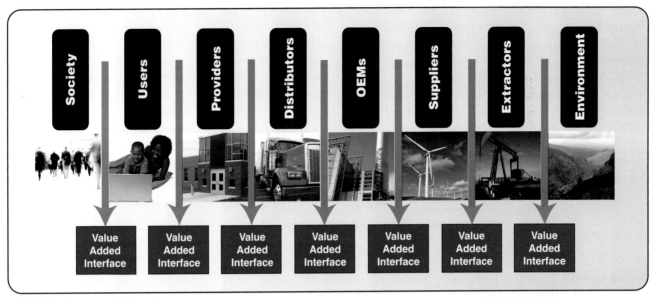

Figure 15.2 Elements of a Value Chain

management of raw materials, components and finished products. Finally, we will address physical distribution in detail.

SUPPLY CHAIN MANAGEMENT

Supply chain management can typically lower a company's costs by 3–7 percent and increase cash flow as much as 30 percent.[3] One important aspect of supply chain management is the development of a supply network. The **supply network** consists of the organizations from which components, semi-finished products, and services are purchased. It is important to develop a network of suppliers that can provide the support required to develop excellent products. Ford has a supply network of more than two thousand companies, not including a large set of independent Ford dealers.

Firms employ different strategies to obtain a competitive advantage in supply chain management. Many firms form strategic alliances with suppliers and distributors to optimize performance and increase customer satisfaction.[4] Raytheon uses a program to

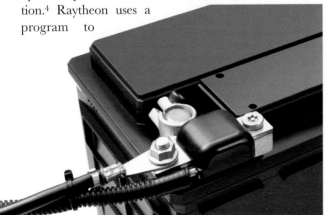

Delphi IVT sensor on a battery monitors voltage and temperature.

help its suppliers reduce costs and increase efficiency. This may or may not lead to a larger profit margin for Raytheon, but it invariably results in a lower cost for its end customers. This reduction in costs promotes customer loyalty.[5]

Some companies use vertical integration to control the supply chain. **Vertical integration** occurs when the buyer controls or owns the supplier or customer. This allows for great control over the supply chain, but it is expensive and leaves the firm with less flexibility. The automotive companies were vertically integrated in the past but have started to spin off different divisions to form new companies. General Motors spun off Delphi, the world's largest auto supplier, and Ford spun off Visteon, the nation's second largest auto supplier. Now General Motors and Ford have no direct management responsibilities for these spin-offs and as a result are more inclined to source some components from other suppliers. At the same time, in order to achieve objectives, Delphi and Visteon must now aggressively market components to other auto manufacturers such as Volkswagen, Daimler-Chrysler, and Nissan.

Marketing Vocabulary

SUPPLY CHAIN MANAGEMENT
Incorporation of all activities concerned with planning, implementation, and control of sourcing, manufacturing, and delivery of products and services.

SUPPLY NETWORK
All of the organizations from which components, semi-finished products, and services are purchased.

VERTICAL INTEGRATION
Ownership or control of suppliers by a buying company.

Supply Chain Mangement Activities and Objectives Figure 15.3 shows supply chain management activities, objectives, and business performance elements. The activities are movement of products and information management. The objectives include increased efficiency and improved customer service. The resulting business performance improvements are described in the four cells.

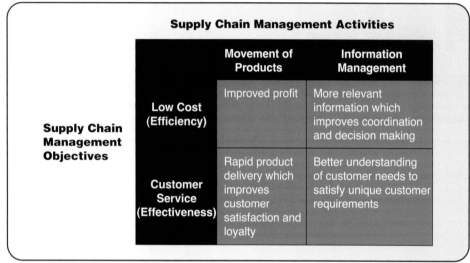

Figure 15.3 Supply Chain Activities, Objectives, and Business Performance Improvements

Business Performance Improvement Overall there are four types of business performance improvements: decreased costs which improves profit; more relevant information which improves coordination and decision making; rapid product delivery which improves customer satisfaction and loyalty; and better understanding of customer needs to satisfy unique customer requirements.

Activities—Movement of Products and Integration of Information The movement of goods in the supply chain starts with raw materials and ends with the final consumption of the product. An important part of this process is the selection of suppliers. In the case of cereal, the chain would start with the farmer and end with the family that finally consumes the cereal. Information management includes the collection, storage, and processing of data from different departments and across firms to provide real time knowledge of the flow of goods from all sources. It also provides feedback on whether schedules are being met and the types of problems that occur as well as their remedies. This information links all parties; therefore, integration provides consumers with what they want, when they expect it, in a location that is most convenient, and at a reasonable cost.

Objectives—Efficiency and Customer Service Better efficiency occurs when unnecessary steps are avoided, delays are eliminated, and the actions of all companies are coordinated at the lowest cost while producing precisely what is intended. Customer service is all of the actions taken to meet customer expectations. This includes rapid and fair care of any problems that might occur. A firm that focuses on customer service will better meet customer needs. The initial increase in costs to the firm to meet those needs will allow the firm to capture greater rewards in the future through customer loyalty.

LOGISTICS

Logistics is the movement of raw materials, components, and finished products within and between companies. Physical distribution is the part of logistics that involves only finished products. **Integrated logistics management** coordinates all parts of the process. If the movement of inputs is not properly managed, then physical distribution to customers will be hindered. Coordination is equally important when goods move between plants, distribution centers, warehouses, wholesalers, and retailers. A firm must excel at integrated logistics management to have superior supply chain management.[6] Integration requires effective communications among companies, departments, and people whose decisions affect logistics. Even within the company, there can be problems. Salespeople may be so worried about late deliveries that they pad their forecasts. Concerned about costs, purchasing, and production departments are conservative in their projections. In many companies, the people deepest in the organization and farthest from the customer—production planners—develop the final estimates used to hire workers and build inventory.[7]

Integrated logistics management is only as strong as a company's understanding of its customers and the ability of its people to work together. Cross-functional teams in purchasing, production-warehousing, marketing, and sales often produce excellent results. By sharing information on purchasing, production schedules, marketing and sales plans, customer service standards, and customer preferences, the team can make logistical decisions that are truly integrated and beneficial to the company. Even without teams, integration can occur if communication from and about customers flows throughout the company in the form of market research reports, sales activity, forecasts, and orders. This information can be refined into specific purchasing and manufacturing plans.

PHYSICAL DISTRIBUTION

Physical distribution is the movement of finished products to customers. Although the concept is simple, accomplishing this task effectively and efficiently is often complex. The primary objective of physical distribution is to get the right products to the right locations at the right times at the lowest total cost. An effective distribution system can contribute to customer satisfaction and, in turn, increased sales revenues. A poor performance will alienate customers, who will switch allegiance to competitors.[8]

While revenue generation is important, no less significant is careful control of the costs of processing orders, maintaining warehouses, carrying and handling inventory, and shipping products. Physical distribution can account for up to 40 percent of total cost and more than 25 percent of each sales dollar.[9] Achieving high customer service levels at the expense of company profitability makes no sense. Therefore, physical distribution management involves a delicate balance between effective customer service and efficient operations.

Toyota's Lexus division is an excellent example of striking the right balance. The typical car dealer has more than $200,000 in parts inventory, a heavy financial burden. At the same time, stockouts frequently occur.

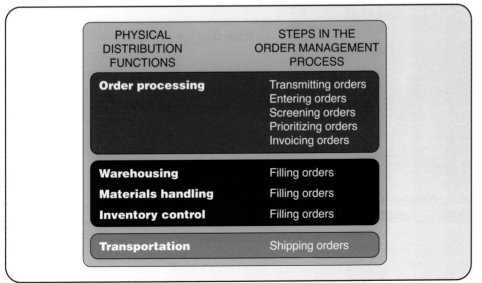

Yellow Freight System promotes their excellent capabilities for physical distribution.

Understanding this, Lexus designed a system that better serves the company, its dealers, and its customers. Lexus requires dealers to have AS400 computers and satellite dishes that connect them to company headquarters in Torrance, California. Specialized inventory control software helps dealers have the right parts on hand. If an item is unavailable in inventory, then it can be ordered electronically one day and received by air freight the next. Although Lexus dealers have only $100,000 tied up in parts inventory, there are few stockouts, and customer satisfaction levels are higher.[10] The systemwide costs of computers, satellite dishes, software, and air freight are more than offset by lower inventory costs and increased sales through better customer service.

Order Management refers to how the company receives, fills, and delivers orders to customers. The design of the physical distribution system—including order processing, warehousing, materials handling, inventory control, and transportation functions—determines how well the company manages orders, as outlined in Figure 15.4. New technologies, such as electronic data interchange and bar coding, have had a remarkable effect on system

PHYSICAL DISTRIBUTION FUNCTIONS	STEPS IN THE ORDER MANAGEMENT PROCESS
Order processing	Transmitting orders
	Entering orders
	Screening orders
	Prioritizing orders
	Invoicing orders
Warehousing	Filling orders
Materials handling	Filling orders
Inventory control	Filling orders
Transportation	Shipping orders

Figure 15.4 Order Management

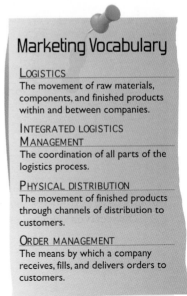

Marketing Vocabulary

LOGISTICS
The movement of raw materials, components, and finished products within and between companies.

INTEGRATED LOGISTICS MANAGEMENT
The coordination of all parts of the logistics process.

PHYSICAL DISTRIBUTION
The movement of finished products through channels of distribution to customers.

ORDER MANAGEMENT
The means by which a company receives, fills, and delivers orders to customers.

design, which in turn has improved the effectiveness and efficiency of order management. **Electronic data interchange (EDI)** is an intercompany computer-to-computer exchange of orders and other business documents in standard formats.

Customer service standards will have a major bearing on the design of the physical distribution system. Companies that want high marks on order fill rate, order cycle time, delivery reliability, and invoice accuracy must be prepared to invest heavily in network design. Often, managers find they must lower desired standards somewhat because the costs of achieving an ideal level are prohibitive. One approach is to recognize that all customers are not equal. As a general rule, a small percentage of a company's customers, often 20 percent or less, provide over 80 percent of its revenues. Customer service standards can be set higher for the firm's most important customers. Scarce resources can be saved by lowering customer service standards, at least to some extent, with less important customers.

Order Processing

The distribution of products cannot begin until the company receives an order. Order processing includes all the activities and paperwork involved in transmitting and entering, screening and prioritizing, and invoicing orders.

Orders received from customers, channel members, or company personnel are entered into the company's record-keeping system. Traditionally, salespeople wrote the orders by hand and delivered them to the office in person or by mail, phone, or fax. New technologies have dramatically changed all that. EDI connects many companies directly with customers, who key in the order and submit it electronically. Order cycle time is significantly reduced. Furthermore, since no one has to reenter the information,

errors are minimized, and invoice accuracy is improved. Labor and material costs for printing, mailing, and handling paper-based transactions are lower. An EDI system helped Texas Instruments reduce order cycle time by 57 percent, resource requirements by 70 percent, and shipping errors by 95 percent.[11] Companies such as Marshall Industries and Motorola supply their outside salespeople with laptop computers. They can access price information instantly rather than check price lists or call the office. They can enter an order, plug into phone lines, and transmit it electronically. Inside salespeople input telephone orders directly into the system. Order cycle time, invoice errors, and order processing costs are all reduced.

Caller ID integrated with computer IT systems enables an inside salesperson to know who is calling before picking up the phone. A variety of information about the caller appears on a computer screen, including payment history and credit information. If a problem is apparent, then the salesperson can notify the customer before entering the order. This avoids a good deal of wasted time on everyone's part. After screening, many companies prioritize orders based on the importance of the customer or the order cycle time requested. For example, often customers can request same-day delivery on orders at a premium price. The computer system transmits these orders to distribution ahead of next-day orders. Bills are prepared once it is known how much of the order can be filled from available inventory. Today, advanced electronic systems keep track of inventory and the latest prices continuously. Invoices are automatically printed out. Order cycle time is reduced, while invoice accuracy is dramatically improved. And interestingly, invoices are becoming a hot promotion tool. They have a 100 percent readership rate, and companies are including special information and offers on them.

Benetton Group ships 130 million items each year directly to 5,000 stores in 120 countries with an order cycle of as little as seven days because most items are sent from a single automated distribution center.

Warehousing **Warehousing** is the storage of inventory in the physical distribution system. Many companies perform this function with a mix of distribution centers and warehouses. **Distribution centers** are where the bulk of a company's finished-goods inventory is maintained before being routed to individual sales outlets or customers. These are of two types: **Private warehouses** are owned and operated by the company, and **public warehouses** rent space to store products. Preferences for fixed versus variable costs help determine a company's mix of private and public warehousing.

With technology, many companies can provide better customer service with fewer warehouses. Benetton Group, Italy's integrated fashion manufacturer and retailer, ships 150 million items each year directly to 5,000 shops in 120 countries with its unique, the Automated Distribution System. It is spread out in 20,000 square meters, with an overall capacity of 400, 000 boxes. And in here, daily 40,000 incoming/outgoing boxes with workforce of only 24 which is only 6 percent of normally required in a traditionally organized operation are able to handle.[12]

Cross-docking involves sorting and reloading an incoming shipment from a supplier for delivery to customers without its being stored in any warehouse. The method is used most frequently in truck transport. EDI and specialized information systems allow for the close coordination that makes cross-docking efficient. This practice is on the increase because it reduces inventory carrying costs and order cycle time. Furthermore, the fewer times the product is handled, the lower the potential for damage. Wal-mart, for example, relies on cross-docking at its distribution centers. The technique affects warehousing design: Larger parking lots are needed for transferring products from truck to truck, and buildings are smaller.

Materials Handling

Materials handling is the moving of products in a warehouse in the process of filling orders. Traditionally, the facility manager would receive the paperwork and assign it to a worker. With a handcart or motorized forklift, the worker would go through the warehouse, picking up products and checking them off on the order forms. If some were unavailable, that would be noted on the form, and a back order would

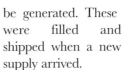

www.benetton.com

Explore the Benetton Web site, where you can learn the details of its distribution network as well as the role of information systems in its business practices. You can also read about how the company evaluates suppliers based on ethical requirements.

be generated. These were filled and shipped when a new supply arrived.

Bar codes, radio frequency technology, and handheld scanning devices are having a remarkable effect on materials handling. Bar code labels for identification purposes can be placed on everything from cardboard boxes to plywood sheets. Handheld scanners with display panels receive orders directly from the mainframe computer through radio waves and guide workers to the appropriate locations. Workers then scan in the bar codes to make sure the right product and quantity are selected. If not, the scanner will beep. Errors and order cycle time are reduced. Back orders are processed much more quickly. This system is a must for any company interested in boosting quality control and customer satisfaction.

RFID or Radio-frequency identification is one of the most useful automatic identification methods. It is used in supply chain management because it allows users to store and retrieve data remotely. Its speed and accuracy has provided significant cost savings for companies. Wal-Mart has invested significant amounts of money to improve RFID technology and increase its usage across suppliers.

Marketing Vocabulary

ELECTRONIC DATA INTERCHANGE
Intercompany computer-to-computer exchange of orders and other business documents in standard formats.

WAREHOUSING
The storage of inventory in the physical distribution system.

DISTRIBUTION CENTER
A location where inventory is maintained before being routed to individual sales outlets or customers.

PRIVATE WAREHOUSE
A storage facility owned and operated by the company.

PUBLIC WAREHOUSE
A storage facility owned and operated by businesses that rent space.

CROSS-DOCKING
Sorting and loading an incoming shipment from a supplier for delivery to customers without it being stored in any warehouse.

MATERIALS HOLDING
The moving of products in and around a warehouse in the process of filling orders.

Automated distribution centers reduce errors in filling orders and other cycle times.

Inventory Control **Inventory control** is the management of stock levels. For each product, company management must decide how much inventory will be carried in each distribution center and warehouse. Carrying too little inventory leads to poor order fill rates, too many back orders, and poor customer service. Carrying too much leads to higher than necessary costs. Many companies fail because they have too much capital tied up in inventory; this reduces cash flow, which means that bills cannot be paid.[13]

Inventory levels are often determined with the help of the ABC classification approach. Stockkeeping units (SKUs) are divided into three categories based on their sales volume and profitability. Inventory levels are kept relatively high for the A category, moderate for B, and relatively low for C. The trap to avoid is a large inventory of less profitable SKUs purchased by fringe or noncore customers.

Part of inventory control is to determine reorder points and order quantities. A reorder point is the inventory level at which a replenishment order is generated. The standard formula is

Reorder point = Demand or usage rate × Order cycle time + Safety stock

In other words, there should be enough inventory to supply customers during the time required to get more stock, plus a margin of safety. More formally, safety stock is the inventory kept on hand in case of forecasting error or delayed delivery of replenishment stock. For example, if the average daily demand rate is 50 units, order cycle time is 4 days, and safety stock is 20 units, then the reorder point is (50 x 4) + 20 = 220 units. Whenever inventory drops to that level, a replenishment order should be made.

The **economic order quantity (EOQ) model** is a method for determining how much product to order each time. It compares ordering costs to inventory carrying costs, with the objective of minimizing total costs. The standard formula is where :

CO = Cost per order
D = Annual sales volume in units
CI = Annual inventory carrying cost
U = Unit cost

The cost per order is calculated by determining purchasing costs, computer costs, and accounts payable costs associated with placing individual orders. Annual inventory carrying costs are calculated by summing expenses associated with warehouse space, insurance, taxes on inventory, obsolescence and shrinkage, materials handling (including wages and equipment), and costs of money invested. The lower the cost per order relative to inventory carrying costs, the lower the order quantity.

The EOQ method should be used only as a guide-line. It works particularly well for products with consistent demand patterns throughout the year. For seasonal items or for products on which suppliers give discounts at certain order quantities, EOQ estimates need some adjustment. A just-in-time (JIT) system also skews the EOQ method. In a JIT system the necessary unit is delivered in the necessary quantity at the necessary time. The fundamental objective is to eliminate waste of all sorts, especially excess inventory. Products are delivered in just enough quantity to cover demand for a short period. Shipments are made frequently and are scheduled precisely; 100 percent delivery reliability is sought because little safety stock is carried. Total cost of ownership is stressed. Per-unit price is less important than the costs associated with extra handling, warehousing, and inventorying. JIT requires companies to meet specific deadlines, supply exact quantities, and adjust deliveries and quantities to meet changing needs, all with a minimum of paperwork. Strong relationships between the companies, including high trust, are critical to the success of such systems.

The Japanese popularized JIT delivery for materials and parts used in manufacturing, but it is now used for a variety of consumer and business-to-business products. If done well, JIT can reduce inventory carrying costs by well over half.[14] The increase in transportation costs is offset by inventory reductions. Saturn, and Wal-Mart are among the companies that rely on JIT today.

Transportation In a physical distribution system, transportation is the movement of goods to channel members and customer locations. That is the largest distribution expense for many manufacturers, especially if heavy, bulky products are involved, since transportation fees are charged by the pound. The cost of transporting weight-training equipment and exercise bicycles, for example, might approach the cost of equipment itself. Deregulation of the transportation industry increased competition among carriers, which has led to greater efficiency and real cost savings for U.S. manufacturers, wholesalers, retailers, and consumers.

The methods for moving products are motor vehicles, railroads, airlines, water carriers, and pipelines. Figure 15.5 contrasts the advantages and disadvantages of the various modes of transportation. Managers choose among them based on customer service versus cost trade-offs. Different modes can be used to serve different clients. For example, orders to core customers may go via fast, reliable air service, whereas orders to noncore customers may be delivered by less expensive ground transportation.

Trucks The major advantages of trucks are door-to-door service and speed. Trucks also are dependable and widely available, making frequent shipments possible. Their major disadvantage is cost. Given these characteristics, trucks are ideally suited for high-value manufac-

	Trucks	Railroads	Air	Water Carriers	Pipeline
Transportation cost	high	average	very high	very low	low
Door-to-door service	high	average	average	low	high
Speed of service	high	average	very high	very low	low
Dependability in meeting schedules	high	average	very high	average	high
Availability in different locations	very high	high	average	low	very low
Frequency of shipments	very high	low	average	very low	high
Need for intermodal transfer for door-to-door service	no	often	almost always	often	often
Primary advantage	door-to-door service and speed	low cost for long hauls of bulk commodities	fastest and highest quality	low cost for long hauls of bulk commodities	low cost and dependability

Figure 15.5   Comparison of Different Modes of Transportation

tured products. Companies can purchase and operate their own fleet of trucks or use the services of independent companies. The trade-offs have to do with level of control and fixed versus variable costs. When uncertainty is high, the use of independents is preferable.

Railroads Railroads represent the most efficient mode of land transportation for bulky commodities, such as chemicals, coal, grain, iron ore, lumber, sand, and steel. Major U.S. railroads haul more than 40 percent of all freight, more than any other mode of transportation. Coal is the most distinct commodity carried by rail, accounting for about 20 percent of revenue for Class I

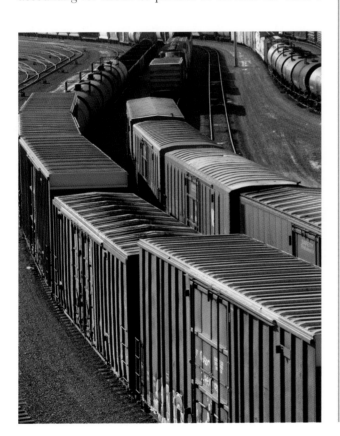

railroads.[15] The major disadvantages of railroads are transit time and lack of door-to-door service, although rail spurs can be built to some customer locations. Unit trains run back and forth between a single loading point, such as a coal mine, and a single destination, such as a power plant, to deliver one commodity. Leading U.S. companies providing rail transportation include Burlington Northern, CSX, and Union Pacific.

Air Transport Air transport is offered by the airlines and cargo service companies. Speed and dependability in meeting schedules are very high relative to the other modes. Air is the most costly, however. Fashion merchandise, fragile and highly perishable items, emergency shipments, and expensive industrial goods account for the majority of products shipped air freight.

Water Carriers Water carriers include transoceanic ships as well as barges used on inland waterways. Their transportation cost is the lowest among the various options. However, only channel members and customers in port cities can be reached directly. Water carriers are used for bulky commodities, such as cement and petroleum. Ore barges, for example, are a common sight on the Great Lakes. The mode also is used to carry mass-produced products, such as automobiles and toys, overseas.

Pipelines Pipelines transport natural gas and petroleum by land from production fields to refineries. Up to 40 different grades of product can be shipped through the same pipeline simultaneously and separated at destination points. Pipelines are very dependable and offer door-to-door service.

Marketing Vocabulary

INVENTORY CONTROL
Management of stock levels

ECONOMIC ORDER QUANTITY (EOQ) MODEL
A method of determining the amount of product to be ordered each time.

They are the least labor intensive of any mode, and maintenance expenses are low. They can be used only for a narrow range of products, however, and delivery speed—less than five miles per hour—is slow.

Intermodal transportation, the combination of two or more modes in moving freight, is gaining popularity. The objective is to exploit the major advantages of each. Piggybacking truck trailers on rail cars, for example, joins the benefits of long-haul rail movement with the door-to-door service of trucks. Express delivery often uses trucks and air to rush shipments from source to destination. Federal Express, the pioneer in overnight delivery, has developed a thriving business running transportation services for such clients as National Semiconductor, Laura Ashley, and Vanstar. Other companies offer a variety of intermodal options. For example, CNF Transportation, headquartered in Palo Alto, California, owns and operates Conway Transportation Services, which focuses on trucking services, and Emery Worldwide, which offers global air freight, ocean transport, and air charter.

The transportation modes used by companies is sometimes influenced by laws and government pressure. Some companies use three-wheeled motorbikes for deliveries in Shanghai, China, because truck use is restricted during daylight hours. New York City, Tokyo and many metro areas have strict laws about truck deliveries because of extreme traffic congestion. Many companies use bicycles to deliver products in Europe because of pollution concerns, and a few cities in the United States have begun delivering goods in this way for the same reason.

New technologies are influencing how the transportation function is being performed. Progressive trucking companies install on-board computers in vehicles. UPS, which provides transportation services to companies globally, gives its drivers electronic data which informs the driver exactly where to go, which route to take, and how much time to spend getting there.

Satellite communication systems also have an important role, providing a fast and high-volume channel for information movement around the globe. Many companies use a real-time global positioning system in its fleet of delivery trucks. The drivers and dispatchers can contact each other while the truck is in transit, and dispatchers always know where a truck is on the delivery route. The real-time interaction provides up-to-date information to customers regarding location and delivery time. Furthermore, dispatchers can redirect trucks in response to need or traffic congestion. Federal Express, UPS, Roadway, and DHL are among the many companies that track shipments electronically to ensure

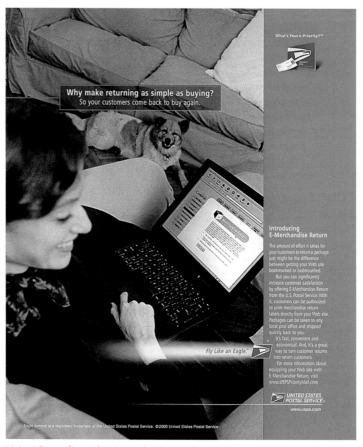

Why make returning as simple as buying? So your customers come back to buy again.

Fly Like an Eagle.™

Introducing E-Merchandise Return

UNITED STATES POSTAL SERVICE®
www.usps.com

United States Postal Service makes it easy for Internet customers to return their goods.

that all customers remain fully informed about deliveries.

Efficient Customer Response **Efficient consumer response (ECR) programs** are designed to improve the efficiency of replenishing, delivering, and stocking inventory while promoting customer value. Enhanced cooperation among channel members in order to eliminate activities that do not add value is a primary goal. A study found that ECR could yield as much as $24 billion in operating cost reductions and $6 billion in financial savings. Potential savings ranged from about 3 percent for manufacturers to 12 percent for retailers.[16]

Traditionally, retailers and wholesalers have used professional buyers to decide what and when to order from suppliers.

Suppliers frequently offered buyers price deals. Forward buying became commonplace: a large order for a product at a special price per carton and then a long delay until the next order. This led to a wide variation in order patterns for manufacturers and great uncertainty. Because of inefficiencies, stockouts occurred much too frequently, even though inventory levels for many products were high throughout the channel.

ECR requires a change in the roles played by channel members. Wholesalers and retailers give up some of their buying authority. On a daily basis, they send information on stock levels and warehouse shipments to their suppliers over EDI networks. Personnel in the supplier organizations use this information to decide what and when to ship. Order quantities are determined with the objectives of providing sufficient safety stock, minimizing total logistics costs, and eliminating excess inventory in the channel. Before shipments go out, wholesalers and retailers can review and edit orders if they desire via EDI. Fewer special prices are offered by suppliers to reduce the incentive for forward buying, which is disruptive to ECR. Instead, everyday low pricing may be used.

If done effectively, ECR can reduce inventory costs and stockouts in the channel. Furthermore, wholesalers and retailers can reduce the number of professional buyers they employ, since suppliers assume more ordering responsibilities.

Procter & Gamble has been a leader in developing and implementing ECR programs with supermarket customers. In a recent five-year period, it more than doubled inventory turnover for such products as Crest, Pampers, Tide, and Prell, and order fill rates rose from 90 to 99 percent. P&G's overall sales were up 33 percent, with more than 40 percent of orders shipped automatically based on withdrawals from customer warehouses. Such moves helped the company cut its annual production and distribution costs by $1.6 billion, or about 8 percent.[17]

GLOBAL PHYSICAL DISTRIBUTION

When doing business abroad, the challenge is multiplied. Uncertainty increases because of greater transport distances, longer lead times, and complex customs requirements and trade restrictions. The most important factor from a physical distribution perspective, however, is a country's infrastructure, which influences how products are stored and transported.

With the extremely high economic growth rate, China now is the worlds' second largest economy after the United States. Introducing free markets and private ownership 20 years ago, China joined the World Trade Organization in 2002, initiating an international "gold rush," and many foreign companies jumped at the chance to establish supply relationships with China. The infrastructure in China is well developed in the large coastal cities, providing a significant advantage over other areas of the world.[18] However, the entire infrastructure still couldn't catch up with the pace of China's continued economic growth. Aware of this, the Chinese government has spent billions of dollars building and updating road and rail access, and water treatment plants. Moreover, the government is increasingly establishing e-commerce and Internet business-to-business links, and many practical and logistical problems have been solved while China's potentially huge market is becoming fully open to non-Chinese businesses.

Of course, a major challenge for many companies is moving products into other countries. **Freight forwarders** are cargo specialists, and their services are often used. Domestically, they pick up partial shipments at the customer location, consolidate all these into truckload or carload size, and arrange for delivery at destination points. Their gross margin is the difference between the rates they charge customers and what they pay carriers. Many exporters rely on freight forwarders to handle the documentation, insurance, and other aspects of delivery abroad. For example, they ensure that letters of credit are issued at the buyer's bank and properly transferred into the seller's account. Leading global freight forwarders include Nippon Express and Kintetsu World Express (Japan), Schenker (Germany), Lep International and MSAS (United Kingdom), and Burlington Air Express. The trend in air freight has been consolidation into a few large companies. For example, DHL, although owned by a German national company, serves Switzerland, Sweden, and the United States, because it bought out smaller companies based in those countries.[19]

Regardless of geographic location, the ultimate goal of distribution is to make the product

readily available to the consumer or end user. For the majority of consumer products, this has traditionally meant delivering goods to the retail outlets where consumers shop. Today, however, direct marketing - including sales via the Internet - is a growing force in consumer as well as business-to-business sales.

MARKETING CHANNELS

A **Marketing channel** is a set of interdependent organizations that help make a good or service available for purchase by consumers or businesses. The distribution channel serves to connect a manufacturer, such as Coach, or a service provider, such as AT&T, with consumers or users. In simple terms, a distribution channel is a pipeline or pathway to the market.

Distribution channels are needed because producers are separated from prospective customers. Mattel's star product, Barbie, is made available to consumers in countries around the world through a host of different retail establishments. Wal-Mart, Toys "R" Us, and Target account for nearly 45 percent of Mattel sales. [20] These retailers are members of Mattel's distribution channel and they are customers of Mattel.

A distribution channel consists of at least a producer and a customer. Most channels, however, use one or more intermediaries to help move products to the customer. **Intermediaries** are independently owned organizations that act as links to move products between producers and the end user. The primary categories are brokers, wholesalers-distributors, and retailers. **Brokers** do not purchase the goods they handle but instead actively negotiate their sale for the client. A familiar example is real estate brokers, who negotiate the sale of property for their customers. Companies have more control over the activities of brokers, including the final price to the customer, because brokers do not own the goods they sell. **Wholesalers** (also referred to as distributors) take title to products and resell them to retail, industrial, commercial, institutional, professional, or agricultural firms, as well as to other wholesalers. A good example is Ingram Micro, Inc. The company, based in Santa Anna, California, is the worlds largest wholesale distributor of computer hardware and software. With over 159,000 customers worldwide, Ingram Micro distributes to retailers such as Wal-mart.com, Staples, and Office Depot.[21] **Retailers** take title to products for resale to the ultimate consumer. These range from discounters such as Wal-Mart and large department stores to specialty chains such as The Limited and local boutiques.

CHANNEL STRUCTURE, DYNAMICS AND FUNCTIONS

Direct and Indirect Channels There are two fundamental types of channels. In **direct channels** (also called integrated channels) companies use their own employees (e.g., salespeople) and physical assets (e.g., warehouses, delivery vehicles) to serve the market. For example, IBM's sales force sells information technology systems directly to large companies such as Bank of America. Sherwin-Williams owns and operates a majority of the outlets where its paint is sold. In **indirect channels** (also called nonintegrated channels) companies make use of independent agents to serve markets. General Motors sells aftermarket components through a variety of channels such as independent parts distributors, auto body repair shops, and independently owned dealerships.

Distribution channels can be described by the number of **channel levels** or the number of distinct units (producers, intermediaries, and customers) in a distribution channel. A direct channel has two levels: the producer and its targeted customers. Indirect channels are longer with at least three levels. Figure 15.6

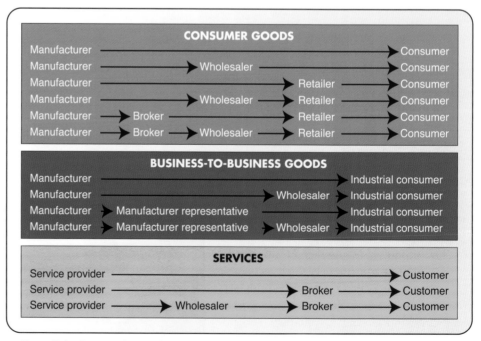

Figure 15.6 Common Channel Configurations

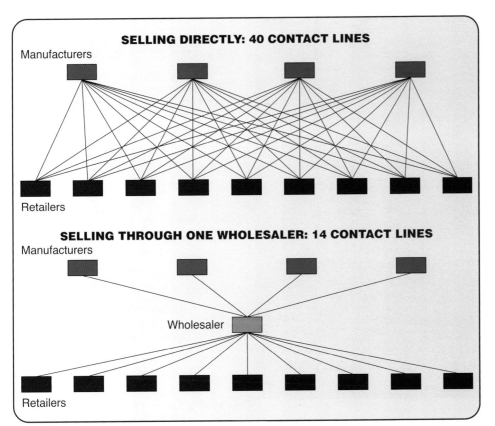

Figure 15.7   Contractual Efficiency
Source: Louis Stern, Adel El-Ansary, and Anne Coughlan, Marketing Channels, 6th ed. © 2001.

Marketing Vocabulary

MARKETING CHANNEL
A set of interdependent organizations that help make a good available for purchase.

INTERMEDIARY
Independently owned organization that acts as a link to move products between the producer and the end user.

BROKER
A firm that does not take title to the goods it handles but actively negotiates the sale of goods for its clients.

WHOLESALER
A firm that takes title to products for resale to businesses, consumers, or other wholesalers or distributors.

RETAILER
A firm that takes title to products for resale to ultimate consumers.

DIRECT CHANNEL
A distribution channel in which the producer uses its own employees and physical assets to distribute the product directly to the end user.

INDIRECT CHANNEL
A distribution channel in which the producer makes use of independent organizations to distribute the product to end users.

CHANNEL LEVELS
The number of distinct units (producers, intermediaries, and customers) in a distribution channel.

illustrates common channel arrangements for consumer goods, business-to-business goods, and services.

Companies must decide whether to use direct channels or intermediaries. Direct channels are more attractive when the following conditions obtain:

- Customers and orders are large, especially if concentrated in a few geographical areas.
- Resource constraints are not severe.
- Environmental uncertainty is low to moderate.
- Investments in direct distribution will produce a high return.
- Significant value-added activity is required in the channel, including specialized investments.
- Customers prefer or demand to deal directly with manufacturers, Wal-Mart being a prime example.

Many markets are simply too small to make it economically feasible for companies to establish a direct channel. Consider independently owned convenience stores, whose average order from a company such as Procter & Gamble or Gillette would be tiny relative to supermarket or discount chains. The manufacturer's costs of selling, processing orders, and delivering products to mom-and-pop stores would be larger than the revenues generated. The problem is intensified because convenience stores are so geographically dispersed.

Intermediaries assemble merchandise from a variety of manufacturers and sell in smaller lots at a regional or local level. Therefore, an order from a small convenience store represents a relatively larger sale to a wholesaler than to an individual manufacturer. Moreover, wholesalers often have greater cost efficiencies than manufacturers due to their smaller size (lower overhead) or proximity to customers (lower selling and logistics costs). The result is that wholesalers can make money serving smaller customers whereas manufacturers cannot. The same rationale applies to retailers. Figure 15.7 shows that four manufacturers selling directly to 10 retailers would need to make 40 contacts to conduct business. Each one consumes resources. That compares to four contacts if they do business with one wholesaler, who in turn makes 10 contacts with the retailers for a total of 14.

Intermediaries tend to require less of the company's resources. Intermediaries make investments in inventory, offer credit to customers, and manage accounts receivable. They also pay for sales personnel and other employees, allowing the producer to avoid these costs. More and

Courtesy of UPS

UPS uses technology to offer supply chain solutions to other companies.

Channel Dynamics and Technology Companies continually evaluate whether their channels need adjustment to deal with changing conditions. If this is ignored, the foundation of the company can be weakened. Alterations are required as products progress through the life cycle. For example, Intel introduces new microprocessors about every two years. In the introductory phase, only a direct channel is used. The supply of new chips is limited until production is slowly scaled up. Large computer manufacturers get them first, as a reward for being very important customers. In the growth and maturity phases, both direct and indirect channels are used; wholesalers sell to smaller manufacturers and the replacement market. Finally, Intel relies primarily on indirect channels in the decline stage. Then the next generation of microprocessors is launched and the cycle repeats.

Technology is also having a tremendous influence on channel operations. Many companies now send orders electronically rather than have salespeople submit handwritten sheets. Caller-identification systems give inside salespeople updated information on customers when they phone in orders. Handheld computers let sales reps take inventory on retail shelves and submit orders to manufacturers via satellite. Automated conveyor systems and robots have brought enormous efficiencies to many companies. Fax machines, toll-free numbers, e-mail, and the Internet have made it much easier and more efficient for all companies to reach customers all over the world. Technology that improves sales and distribution capability is helping to level the playing field for smaller competitors.

more companies such as General Electric, Intel and Texas Instruments are relying on the use of intermediaries rather than company-owned or direct channels.

The use of intermediaries is attractive to companies when it is difficult to make accurate predictions about the future. This lowers the risk level for the company because the intermediary is sharing the investment burden. Adapting to change is also easier, since companies have less fixed investment and, therefore, more financial flexibility. Warehouse facilities are an obvious example. If owned by the company, then the building, equipment, and personnel are a significant drain on resources when the economy takes a downturn.

Multiple Channel Systems Many manufacturers want to connect with customers in as many ways as possible. **Multiple channel systems** make use of more than one channel to access markets for the same product. For example, Ben & Jerry's distributes its premium ice cream through company-owned stores, wholesalers that resell to supermarkets and convenience stores, and franchised outlets.

Most distribution channels flow from the manufacturer to the end user, but goods sometimes move in the opposite direction. A **reverse channel** flows from the end user to the wholesaler or the manufacturer. An example is the recycling of bottles and cans.

Channel Functions Tasks that must be performed within a distribution system to facilitate sales with ultimate customers. Common channel functions that help sell goods are illustrated in Figure 15.8, broken down into four categories: selling, financing, order management, and postsales service.

Based on the nature of the target market and products, the company must determine the functions to be performed in the channel. For example, Timex does not have to worry much about the product repair function, since its watches are priced so low that customers merely discard them once they stop working. Rolex, in contrast, must ensure that customers have access to reliable repair services.

CHANNEL ALIGNMENT

In a **conventional channel system,** efforts to coordinate actions are seen as unimportant by channel members. Loosely aligned and relatively autonomous manufacturers, wholesalers, and retailers bargain aggressively with one another over each transaction.[22] Once a deal is reached, there is not much concern about what others in the channel are doing. Most giftware, furniture, and motion pictures move through conventional channels, where channel members tend to follow traditions.

In contrast, **vertical marketing systems (VMS)** are networks that emphasize channel coordination. VMS have grown in importance over the past two decades. More and more companies realize that customer satisfaction is impossible without efficient and effective distribution. There are three types of VMS: administered, contractual, and corporate.

Administered Channel Systems Members of an **administered channel system** coordinate with others in the channel and facilitate activities. Marketing programs, such as cooperative advertising and sales training, are developed and offered to channel members.[23] Black & Decker, General Electric, and Sealy (the mattress company) are among the manufacturers known for their administered channel systems. Wal-Mart has invested heavily in coordinating relationships with its suppliers. The Internet has selling spaces in which companies and wholesalers can develop strong relationships, such as the shopping sites in Yahoo! or America Online. When channel members have roles that are rather complex and challenging, greater coordination is needed.

Contractual Channel Systems In a **contractual channel system**, relationships are formalized, often with a written contract. Retail cooperatives, wholesaler-sponsored voluntary chains, and franchises are three common forms.

Selling
- Advertising
- Generating leads
- Qualifying leads
- Personal selling (face-to-face)
- Personal selling (over the phone)
- Customer education

Financing
- Offering credit
- Collecting accounts receivable

Order Management
- Holding inventory
- Transmitting and entering orders
- Screening and prioritizing orders
- Filling orders
- Invoicing
- Loading
- Delivering

Postsales Service
- Training in product use
- Installing
- Assisting with applications
- Handling product returns
- Repairing product

Figure 15.8   Common Channel Functions

Marketing Vocabulary

CONVENTIONAL CHANNEL SYSTEM
A channel system in which efforts to coordinate the actions of channel members are seen as unimportant.

VERTICAL MARKETING SYSTEM (VMS)
A system in which channel members emphasize coordination of behaviors and programs.

ADMINISTERED CHANNEL SYSTEM
A vertical marketing system in which channel members devote effort to coordinating their relationships.

CONTRACTUAL CHANNEL SYSTEM
A vertical marketing system in which relationships among channel members are formalized in some fashion, often with a written contract.

RETAIL COOPERATIVE
An alliance of small retailers for wholesaling purposes.

WHOLESALER-SPONSORED VOLUNTARY CHAIN
A group of retailers that have been united by a wholesaler.

FRANCHISE SYSTEM
A type of distribution channel in which the franchiser holds the product trademark and licenses it to franchisees who contract to meet certain obligations.

A **retail cooperative** unites a group of small retailers into a wholesaling operation to increase buying power. Compare a hardware retailer who buys 20 Black & Decker power drills a year to 100 stores that buy 2,000. Obviously, the group will have more clout in bargaining on price. Ace Hardware and SERVISTAR are examples. Retail cooperatives also are common in the grocery industry, such as Associated Grocers and Topco Associates.

In a **wholesaler-sponsored voluntary chain**, a wholesaler takes the initiative to unite a group of retailers. Again, enhanced buying power is the main objective. Such channels are prominent in the automotive accessory market (Western Auto), the grocery trade (Independent Grocers Alliance, Red and White, and Super Value), and the hardware arena (Pro, Sentry). More than 40,000 neighborhood drug stores, retail chains, and healthcare facilities are aligned with McKesson Drug Co., a wholesaler of pharmaceuticals and health care products.[24]

In a **franchise system**, a formal contract ties the franchiser to franchisees. The franchiser holds the product trademark and licenses it to franchisees. They pay royalty fees and promise to conform to standards and guidelines laid out in the contractual agreement. This usually covers such issues as the fees required, rights and responsibilities of both parties, transfer of the franchise, and grounds for termination.

There are two types of franchise systems. In product and trade-name franchising, the franchisee acquires some of the identity of the franchiser. Automobile dealerships, gasoline stations, motorcycle dealerships, and soft-drink bottlers are a few examples. Business format franchising involves not only the product and trademark but also the entire business concept—marketing, strategy, training, merchandising, and operating procedures.[25] This is especially prevalent in the service arena: fast-food restaurants (McDonald's and Burger King), hotels and motels (Holiday Inn), diet programs (Nutri-Systems), real estate (Century 21), travel services (Uniglobe), and vehicle rental (Hertz).

About 760,000 franchise outlets in the United States account for more than $1.5 trillion in annual sales. About 40 percent of all U.S. retail sales flow through a franchise system, and a new franchise is opened every 8 minutes of every business day.[26] Business format franchising is growing at a phenomenal rate. U.S. franchisers have been particularly successful in establishing indirect channels in global markets. For example, Coca-Cola has a long relationship with independent franchised bottlers in each market, who buy the syrup concentrate and then carbonate, package, and sell the product to retailers. Its anchor bottlers, a breed of regional intermediaries, have deep local ties, huge capital budgets, and finely tuned distribution system. On a broader scale, McDonald's has developed an excellent program for recruiting and developing a diverse mix of franchisees. See the diversity feature, "McDonald's: Serving Diverse Communities in More Ways Than One."

In a **corporate channel system**, the corporation runs and operates organizations at other levels in the channel. It is very similar to a direct channel, and great emphasis is placed on coordinating activities. Examples are Goodyear, Sherwin-Williams, and Tandy, which operate such systems in whole or in part.[27]

EXTENSIVE, SELECTIVE AND EXCLUSIVE DISTRIBUTION

The number of locations through which a company sells its products in a given market area is an important strategic consideration. There are three strategic options. **Intensive distribution** uses many outlets in each geographical area. **Selective distribution** uses several outlets per area. **Exclusive distribution** uses only one outlet in each trading area.

The choice is driven to some extent by the nature of the product. Many consumer and business-to-business products are relatively low price and are purchased frequently, requiring little value-added activity in the channel. Commonly referred to as convenience goods, they require intensive distribution. Numerous sales outlets per trade area will minimize travel time and acquisition costs for customers. Examples are most brands of coffee, detergent, chewing gum, motor oil, soft drinks, and toilet tissue. Other products, referred to as shopping goods, require some search on the part of the customer. Different brands are compared on price, quality, and other features at the time of purchase. Selective distribution is appropriate for these goods, which include bicycles, cameras, and motorcycles. Finally, specialty goods have unique qualities that induce high customer loyalty. Since people are willing to exert considerable effort to seek out and purchase them, exclusive distribution can be used. Luxury items and top-of-the-line cosmetics are examples.

The brand strategy of the company also will influence the decision. Different brands of the same product can have widely differing distribution patterns. Brands positioned for high quality and price, and requiring significant value-added activity in the channel, require more selective distribution to protect them against rampant price competition.[28] Generally, the more prestigious the brand, the fewer the number of outlets used by the manufacturer.

When a company uses independent wholesalers and retailers in its channel system, selective and especially exclusive distribution breeds considerable loyalty. For example, Caterpillar uses only 80 dealers in North

http://globaledge.msu.edu

Visit globalEDGE™ Online for the ultimate international marketing research tool!

globalEDGE™

Supply Chain Management Channels

You have been asked to begin tracking urgent domestic and international shipments to and from your firm. Using global statistics to assist in monitoring these valuable and critical deliveries, a key component of this assignment is to identify the five largest cargo airports in the US. This information will allow you to focus your attention on certain domestic locations to better track your firm's shipments and enhance its supply chain management. Are the five largest cargo airports in the US geographically close? Which two cargo airports are the closest?

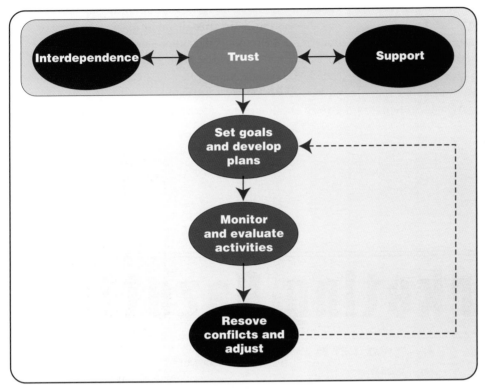

Figure 15.9   A Process for Managing Channel Relationships

America and about 200 worldwide. Some dealers have two or three entire states as their exclusive domain. They are like extensions of Caterpillar, willing to support the company in any way they can.

Companies that use independent intermediaries must be careful in moving from a selective to a more intensive strategy. The loyalty of traditional channel members can quickly vanish. For example, Vidal Sassoon hair care products used to be distributed only in beauty salons. When the company decided to distribute through major supermarket and drugstores, the salons dropped the line in a flash. Similarly, when Gitano Group made its jeans and sportswear available to discount stores such as Wal-Mart and Kmart, full-priced retailers no longer wanted to carry the line for fear of hurting their store images.[29] Calvin Klein sued licensee Warnaco for selling goods bearing his name to discount outlets such as Costco; he was trying to prevent his own brand from being devalued in a similar fashion.[30] Also, wider distribution is likely to increase price competition and, thus, reduce profit margins of current channel members.

STRATEGICALLY MANAGING CHANNEL RELATIONSHIPS

Companies must think strategically about relationships with intermediaries. Interdependence, trust, and support are important elements in managing channel relationships. Figure 15.9 outlines these guidelines for channel management.

Interdependence Each channel member depends to some degree on other channel members to achieve desired goals. This need is high when a large amount of a channel member's sales and profits can be attributed to the arrangement.[31] High interdependence means that each has the potential to influence the decisions of another. Gaining attention and support is easier in that case because each party has a vested interest in continuing the relationship. For example, Pepsi and Wal-Mart have a highly dependent relationship, and both commit considerable effort and resources to ensuring that it works smoothly.

When a channel relationship is unbalanced, one firm is more dependent on the other for success. The firm that is less dependent has a power advantage. If the producer has the advantage, then the buyer is likely to be very receptive to its salespeople and their plans. In the semiconductor industry, Intel has that kind of power over wholesalers such as Arrow Electronics and Hamilton-Hallmark. When the supplier is dependent, because for example the buyer purchases most of its output, the supplier is likely to suffer. The buyer is likely to demand very low prices.

When dependence is low for all parties, each lacks power in the channel relationship. All are unconcerned about the others and offer little or no support. Therefore, producers need to establish channel systems in which the dependence of associated firms is reasonably high.

Trust   Another important factor in channel relationships is trust, or confidence in the reliability and integrity of channel members.[32] High trust is the belief that words and promises can be relied upon. It makes the coordination of channel relationships much easier. The credibility of information exchanged need not be questioned. Lack of trust creates serious problems. Intentions and basic honesty are likely to be questioned. When Anthony Conza, a cofounder of Astor Restaurant Group, discovered he was losing the trust of many of his 600 Blimpie franchisees, he responded by improving communications. He established a franchisee advisory council, a newsletter called No Baloney News, and a toll-free hot line for franchisees. These changes increased trust—as well as sales growth and franchisee satisfaction.[33]

The Marketing Gazette™

CREATING & CAPTURING VALUE THROUGH SUSTAINABILITY

The Buzz about Burt's Bees

Roxanne Quimby and Burt Shavitz first met in Maine in 1984. Roxanne came across Burt, an amateur bee keeper at the time, selling honey on the side of the road. She instantly fell for Burt's products and they soon teamed up to sell candles made from his beeswax at local craft shows. Their popularity grew quickly. Armed with a 19th century personal care recipe book and with orders pouring in from New York boutiques, they hired 40 employees and set up shop in an old bowling alley in 1989. They incorporated in 1991, and soon after, Burt's Bees moved to North Carolina, leaving candle making behind to focus exclusively on personal care products.

Today, Burt's Bees is the world's leading manufacturer of environmentally-friendly personal care products, with global sales in 2006 of more than $250 million. It makes over 150 products in categories including facial, hair and lip care. On average, its products are composed of 99 percent natural ingredients like beeswax, botanical oils, herbs and flowers. Burt's Bees refrains from using artificial preservatives and sells its products in recycled and reusable packaging. In recent years, the company purchased enough carbon offsets through wind power to compensate for 100 percent of its electricity use and aspires to eliminate all waste by 2020. In response to its pledge to produce products that are safe for users and the environment, Burt's Bees has received dozens of awards from health, cosmetic, and environmental publications.

Burt's Bees donates 10 percent of website sales revenue to green "well-being" partners. It formed a partnership with Habitat for Humanity to create an affordable green housing development in North Carolina. The company hopes to inspire others to build in sustainable ways while providing housing for local residents in need. It has donated $2 million to the Nature Conservancy to help protect nearly 200,000 acres of forest in remote Maine. It's also a member of the Conservation Alliance, an organization of outdoor businesses with a mission of protecting and conserving natural habitats. Partnering with the National Arbor Day Foundation, Burt's Bees has planted more than 4,000 trees across the country. These trees will absorb enough carbon to offset the emissions of more than 100 million miles of automotive travel.

Recently purchased by the Clorox Company, Burt's Bees pledges to continue its commitment to the greater good. Concerned with the number of personal care products labeled "natural" that contain chemicals with suspected health risks and no natural ingredients, the company created Burt's Bill for "Setting the Natural Standard." For the safety of customers and the environment, it feels there should be regulation on what can be called a "natural" personal care product. The bill proposes adding a packaging seal to help customers easily identify products that meet the highest levels of being natural and safe. Burt's Bees is working with the Natural Products Association to make this happen and encourage customers to log on to www.burtsbees.com and sign the bill.

Support A company may lack power with an intermediary because of low dependence, but it can grab attention with the right kind of support. Cooperative advertising is a common means. The producer reimburses intermediaries for expenses when they submit proof of the ad along with media invoices. Usually, certain standards must be met. For example, motorcycle manufacturers do not reimburse dealers if ads mention more than one brand. For eligible ads, half the expense is normally reimbursed, although limits are set on the amount per year, which are ordinarily based on the intermediary's percentage of

Blimpie improved communications to increase trust and franchisee satisfaction

annual sales for a product. Many manufacturers supply prepared advertising material to ensure quality.

Another form of support is to invite intermediaries to sales conferences to mingle and attend sessions devoted to new products or marketing techniques. Although some business is conducted at these events, the main purpose is to socialize and build personal relationships. As another way to foster goodwill, many companies help fund sales conferences sponsored by intermediaries. Support also may be offered through inventory management and sales training programs, hot lines, and toll-free numbers.

Set Goal and Develop Plans Channel management is facilitated when members meet formally to set joint goals and develop plans for the coming year. This works best when interdependence and trust are high. During these sessions, intermediaries make a commitment to a set of goals, often including accounts and products that will get special emphasis. Specific business plans are developed regarding the activities and investments intermediaries will make to help achieve the goals. At the same time, the producer agrees to assist intermediaries through support programs and marketing efforts.

Monitor and Evaluate Performance Once the business plan is in place, company sales personnel must keep abreast of the marketing and selling efforts of each intermediary. Deviations from the plan must be noted. How well the intermediary is doing in reaching the goals established must be constantly evaluated.

For example, McDonald's has company personnel

visit franchisee locations and order food as a regular customer. They rate the facility on a variety of dimensions, including friendliness of the staff, quality of the food, and cleanliness. Similarly, Holiday Inn evaluators stay overnight and rate performance. Monitoring such as this gives a company leverage in channel relationships.

Conflict Resolution Channel conflict occurs when members disagree about the course of their relationship. It often arises due to business pressures, policy changes, and the use of coercion. Some conflict is inevitable. Channel members recognize that some policies will not be changed and get on with their business. Sometimes company sales personnel can help by explaining policies to intermediaries. In other cases, companies recognize they made a mistake and try to correct it.

LEGAL AND ETHICAL ISSUES IN CHANNEL MANAGEMENT

U.S. antitrust laws and other regulations designed to promote competition and consumer welfare affect distribution practices. Legislation in other countries varies widely.

Resale Price Maintenance Resale price maintenance is an attempt by companies to compel channel members to charge certain prices. The practice is illegal when title to the product changes hands. Since wholesalers and retailers normally purchase the products they sell, they can charge any price they choose. If manufacturers cross the line between persuasion and coercion, then legal problems can arise. For example, a manufacturer should never threaten to take a product line away if prices are not raised.

Collusion among channel members to pressure a wholesaler or retailer to charge higher prices is against the law. Therefore, company personnel should never consult with channel members to find out whether any are discounting prices. They also should not solicit the support of intermediaries in persuading another channel member to maintain a certain price level.

Differential Pricing and Support Programs

A company must give prices and support programs on proportionally equal terms to competing channel members unless two conditions are met. First, a price differential is justified if it costs less to serve one channel member versus another. Costs are usually lower in dealing with large distributors and retailers due to economies of scale. Therefore, quantity discounts are justified. Second, variations are legal if they are required to meet a competitive offer.

Companies can provide differential pricing and support programs to intermediaries who are not in competition. For example, a computer manufacturer can charge one price to a local wholesaler in San Diego and another to a local wholesaler in Seattle. Whether this makes good business sense is another matter.

Territorial and Customer Constraints

A territorial constraint exists when a company assigns an intermediary a specific geographic area in which to sell its products. That is, it can sell there but nowhere else. Such constraints are legal, as they are seen as protecting the investment of all neighboring intermediaries who sell the company's products.

A class-of-customer constraint is a company limit on the customer groups to which an intermediary can sell its product. For example, a manufacturer of medical equipment may direct a wholesaler to sell to physicians and nursing homes in New York City but not to hospitals. This constraint is illegal, as the courts have found that it limits competition and harms consumer welfare. A company is allowed to suggest that an intermediary focus on certain targets: "We are looking for you to cover primarily these customer groups."

Exclusive Dealing

Exclusive dealing occurs when a company restricts intermediaries from carrying competitive lines. Such constraints are legal, unless they are proved to be a substantial limit on competition in the marketplace. Furthermore, terminating intermediaries for failure to perform can be difficult if exclusive dealing is a requirement. The intermediary may have passed up opportunities to add other lines and may be very dependent on the channel relationship as a result.

Tying Arrangements and Full-Line Forcing

A **tying arrangement** exists when a company conditions the purchase of a superior product on the purchase of a second and less desirable product. For example, a copier company may refuse to sell a high-quality machine unless the customer buys a service agreement. Such arrangements are illegal.

Full-line forcing occurs when a company requires intermediaries to carry and sell its complete line. This practice has been generally upheld in the courts, especially when it is common within an industry. It may be challenged, however, if it entails quantities to be purchased and inventory

Web and E-Commerce Stars
UPS - www.ups.com

UPS is one of the most acknowledged and valued brands in the world, who enables commerce around the globe. It was grown into $42.6 billion Corporation. Fundamentally, this website allows people to track their packages and freight and give them information how to ship their objects to all over the world. It also has a section where UPS provides Business Solutions to many businesses. Companies can find advices to streamline their supply chain, to manage both their domestic and international shipment, and so on.

levels to be maintained. It also may be challenged as an illegal tying arrangement if it involves unrelated product lines.

Intermediary Termination   In many channel systems, agreements commonly allow either party to terminate the relationship with 30 days' notice. In franchise systems, contracts are more complex. Whatever the case, companies need to document the reasons for termination. Usually, the intermediary fails to meet standards or is a poor credit risk. The termination may be challenged if based on intermediary noncompliance with illegal restraints on trade.

Ease of termination varies considerably by state. Wisconsin has a very strict law. If a company's product comprises 12 percent or more of an intermediary's sales volume, then the company cannot terminate it. This has led many manufacturers to establish direct channels in Wisconsin, though they generally use indirect channels elsewhere.

Ethics   It is illegal for companies to impose certain constraints on channel members. Other practices may not be against the law but are ethically questionable. For example, franchisers often confront the issue of how close to place outlets. Market coverage improves with a greater number, but existing franchisees may be hurt. They have committed time and money to building their business, and they do not want to be crowded out by competition from their own company.

Another ethical issue arises when companies set territorial constraints and then choose to ignore them. They lack the courage to confront large intermediaries for selling outside their assigned territory. Such intermediaries often claim they will drop the product line and switch to competitors if they cannot broaden their market area.

Every company must take a deep look at itself. Competitive pressures aside, what is good, ethical business practice and what is not must be carefully spelled out to all employees. Companies must recognize that short-term sales increases make no sense if they weaken existing channel members. And policies must be enforced. To maintain the integrity of the entire channel system, violators must be terminated.

> ### Marketing Vocabulary
>
> EXCLUSIVE DEALING
> Restricting intermediaries from carrying competitive lines.
>
> TYING ARRANGEMENT
> The purchase of a superior product is conditioned on the purchase of a second product of lower quality.
>
> FULL-LINE FORCING
> Requiring intermediaries to carry and sell the company's complete line.

Chapter Summary:

Objective 1:   Understand supply management activities and objectives, and how they improve business performance.

Supply chain management involves acquiring suppliers and moving products, as well as the flow of information about these activities within a firm and across different firms. The movement of goods in the supply chain starts with raw materials and ends with the final consumption of the product. An important part of this process is the selection of suppliers. Information management includes the collection, storage, and processing of data from different departments within and across firms to provide real time knowledge of the flow of goods from all sources. The objectives of supply chain management are low cost and customer service. Business performance improvements include: better profit; more relevant information; rapid product delivery; and better understanding of customers.

Objective 2:   Learn why companies frequently use intermediaries to reach targeted customers.

Indirect channels involving independent intermediaries are frequently used, especially when the targeted market is small and geographically dispersed, companies face severe resource con-

straints, environmental uncertainty is high, the anticipated return from investments in direct channels is low, the level of value-added activities is low, and customers prefer dealing with intermediaries. Deciding whether to use direct or indirect channels in foreign markets is especially challenging, but culture, market structure, entrenched channels, and legal regulations have a significant effect on the choice.

Objective 3:   Attain insight into how channel relationships should be managed over time.

Coordinating relationships within the distribution channel is a challenge. The company must think strategically and develop a management plan. Interdependence, trust, and support will influence the success of coordination. Joint goal setting and planning, monitoring, the use of influence, conflict resolution, and performance appraisals are steps that need to be taken.

Objective 4:   Appreciate the economic importance of wholesalers.

Wholesalers are intermediaries who take title to the products they carry and make the majority of their sales to businesses. Wholesalers purchase large amounts of merchandise from a variety of suppliers and offer it for resale in smaller quantities. They often provide credit, extensive information on product benefits, training on product use, and technical assistance. They are needed because small to medium-sized companies in many industries do not buy in sufficient quantity to deal directly with manufacturers. Many large companies also buy from wholesalers because of convenience, lower personnel costs, and better customer service.

Objective 5: Know the different types of wholesalers and the distinct roles they play.

A wide range of functions is performed for customers by full-service wholesalers, a category that includes general line wholesalers, specialty wholesalers, and rack jobbers. In contrast, limited-service wholesalers perform only some of the traditional channel functions. In this category are cash-and-carry wholesalers, drop shippers, truck jobbers, and mail-order wholesalers.

Objective 6: Identify what physical distribution entails and why it is critical for any business organization.

Physical distribution, the movement of finished products through channels of distribution to end customers, entails order processing, warehousing, materials handling, and transportation. The primary objective is to get the right product to the right customer location at the right time at the lowest total cost. Physical distribution management involves a delicate balance between effective customer service and efficient operations. Order fill rate, order cycle time, delivery reliability, and invoice accuracy are four commonly used measures of customer service proficiency.

Objective 7: Learn the steps in the order management process.

Order management is concerned with how the company receives, fills, and delivers orders to customers. New technologies have dramatically changed the way orders are transmitted, entered, screened, prioritized, invoiced, and filled. Many orders are now sent electronically. Handheld scanners with display panels often are used by warehouse workers in filling orders. There are automated distribution centers with mechanized picking equipment controlled by computers in conjunction with conveyor systems. Inventory control is essential to assure maximum fill rates at minimum cost. In transporting orders to customers, the major advantage of trucks and airplanes is speed, but they are relatively costly. Railroads and water carriers are the most efficient modes for the movement of bulky commodities. Gaining in popularity is intermodal transportation, the combination of two or more modes in moving freight.

Efficient consumer response programs attempt to eliminate activities that do not add value in distribution channels. Wholesalers and retailers give up some of their buying authority. They send daily information via EDI to their suppliers on stock levels and warehouse shipments. Personnel in the supplier organization then decide what and when to ship.

Review Your Understanding

1. What are intermediaries? List three primary categories of intermediaries.
2. What is a reverse channel? Give an example.
3. What is a conventional channel system? Give an example.
4. What do members of an administered channel system do?
5. List three common forms of contractual channel systems. Briefly describe each.
6. What are the guidelines for managing channel relationships?
7. What is a wholesaler? Briefly explain why wholesalers are important.
8. What is a full-service wholesaler? A limited-service wholesaler? List three types for each.

9. What is integrated logistics? What is physical distribution? Name the primary objective of physical distribution.
10. What is order management? Name a technological advance that has improved its effectiveness and efficiency.
11. What is warehousing? Name two types of distribution centers.
12. What is economic order quantity? What is its formula?
13. List five modes of transportation used in a physical distribution system.
14. What is efficient consumer response?
15. Name an important factor in global physical distribution.

Discussion of Concepts

1. What is a distribution channel? Why are distribution channels so important to companies and consumers?
2. How do direct channels differ from indirect channels? Under what conditions are indirect channels preferred to direct channels?
3. Why do channels vary in length or number of levels? What are multiple channels? Why are they being relied on by more and more companies today?
4. What are vertical marketing systems? Discuss the three types of VMS.
5. Describe the three distribution intensity options available to companies and give examples of each.
6. What is interdependence? Why is it such an important concept in managing channel relationships? What role do support programs play in the distribution channel?

7. Explain how conflicts can be resolved in channel relationships.
8. Compare the businesses of limited-service and full-service wholesalers. Can limited-service wholesalers be just as successful financially as full-service wholesalers?
9. What is EDI? How is it influencing the effectiveness and efficiency of order processing?
10. Explain how bar codes, radio frequency technology, and scanning devices are improving the effectiveness and efficiency of the materials handling function.
11. How are efficient consumer response programs changing the way business is conducted between manufacturers and retailers?
12. What is the major challenge to integrated logistics management? How can companies overcome this challenge?

Key Terms And Definitions

Administered channel system: A vertical marketing system in which channel members devote effort to coordinating their relationships.

Broker: A firm that does not take title to the goods it handles but actively negotiates the sale of goods for its clients.

Channel levels: The number of distinct units (producers, intermediaries, and customers) in a distribution channel.

Contractual channel system: A vertical marketing system in which relationships among channel members are formalized in some fashion, often with a written contract.

Conventional channel system: A channel system in which efforts to coordinate the actions of channel members are seen as unimportant.

Corporate channel system: A vertical marketing system in which a company owns and operates organizations at other levels in the channel.

Cross-docking: Sorting and loading an incoming shipment from a supplier for delivery to customers without its being stored in any warehouse.

Direct channel: A distribution channel in which the producer uses its own employees and physical assets to distribute the product directly to the end user.

Distribution center: A location where inventory is maintained before being routed to individual sales outlets or customers.

Distribution channel: A set of interdependent organizations involved in making a product available for purchase.

Distribution intensity: The number of locations through which a company sells its product in a given market area.

Economic order quantity (EOQ) model: A method of determining the amount of product to be ordered each time.

Efficient consumer response (ECR) programs: Programs to improve the efficiency of replenishing, delivering, and stocking inventory in the distribution channel, while promoting customer value.

Electronic data interchange (EDI): Intercompany computer-to-computer exchange of orders and other business documents in standard formats.

Exclusive dealing: Restricting intermediaries from carrying competitive lines.

Exclusive distribution: Distributing a product through only one sales outlet in each trading area.

Franchise system: A type of distribution channel in which the franchiser holds the product trademark and licenses it to franchisees who contract to meet certain obligations.

Freight forwarders: Service companies specializing in the movement of cargo from one point to another, often country to country.

Full-line forcing: Requiring intermediaries to carry and sell the company's complete line.

Indirect channel: A distribution channel in which the producer makes use of independent organizations to distribute the product to end users.

Integrated logistics management: The coordination of all logistical activities in a company.

Intensive distribution: Making the product available through every possible sales outlet in a trade area.

Intermediary: Independently owned organization that acts as a link to move products between the producer and the end user.

Intermodal transportation: The combination of two or more modes in moving freight.

Inventory control: Management of stock levels.

Logistics: The movement of raw materials, components, and finished products within and between companies.

Materials handling: The moving of products in and around a warehouse in the process of filling orders.

Multiple channel systems: The use of more than one channel to access markets for the same product.

Order management: The means by which a company receives, fills, and delivers orders to customers.

Physical distribution: The movement of finished products through channels of distribution to customers.

Private warehouse: A storage facility owned and operated by the company.

Public warehouse: A storage facility owned and operated by businesses that rent space.

Retailer: A firm that takes title to products for resale to ultimate consumers.

Retail cooperative: An alliance of small retailers for wholesaling purposes.

Reverse channel: A distribution channel that flows from the end user to the wholesaler and producer.

Selective distribution: The use of a limited number of sales outlets per trade area.

Supply chain management: Incorporation of all activities concerned with planning, implementation, and control of sourcing, manufacturing, and delivery of products and services.

Supply network: All the organizations from which components, semi-finished products, and services are purchased.

Tying arrangement: The purchase of a superior product is conditioned on the purchase of a second product of lower quality.

Vertical marketing system (VMS): A system in which channel members emphasize coordination of behaviors and programs.

Warehousing: The storage of inventory in the physical distribution system.

Wholesaling: Selling goods for resale or use to retailers and other businesses.

Wholesaler: A firm that takes title to products for resale to businesses, or other wholesalers or distributors, and sometimes consumers.

Wholesaler-sponsored voluntary chain: A group of retailers that have been united by a wholesaler.

References

1. Jack Ewing and Nandini Lakshman, "Why Nokia is Leaving Moto in the Dust," July 30, 2007, BusinessWeek; "The Next Billion; Nokia Covers the Globe, but it's Phones are a Flop in the U.S. and it a Weakling on the Web. There's a Plan to Change All That," Forbes Inc. November 12, 2007; Nokia Corporate Responsibility, www.nokia.com, site visited January 25, 2008.
2. Donald J. Bowersox, David J, Closs and M. Bixby cooper, supply chain logistics management, (McGraw-Hill; 2005)
3. Ibid.
4. Donald J. Bowersox, David J. Closs, and Theodore P. Stank, 21st Century Logistics: Making Supply Chain Integration a Reality, Council of Logistics Management, 1999, p. 6.
5. Collin Reeves, Raytheon, from a talk given on March 12, 2001, at Michigan State University.
6. Donald J. Bowersox, David J, Closs and M. Bixby cooper, supply chain logistics management, (McGraw-Hill; 2005)
7. Benson Shapiro, V. Kasturi Rangan, and John Sviokla, "Staple Yourself to an Order," Harvard Business Review, July–August 1992, pp. 113–122.
8. Bowersox and Closs, Logistical Management.
9. Stern, El-Ansary, and Coughlan, Marketing Channels, p. 119.
10. Federick F. Reichheld, Thomas Teal, The loyalty effect; the hidden force behind growth, profits, and lasting value, (Harvard business school press; 2001), p 263
11. Clay Youngblood, "EDI Trial and Error," Transportation and Distribution 4 (1993): 46.
12. www.benettongroup.com/en/whoweare/distribution.htm, Web site visited March 17, 2008
13. Graham, Distributor Survival ; Federick f. Reichheld, Thomas teal, The loyalty effect; the hidden force behind growth, profits, and lasting value, (Harvard business school press; 2001), p 25B
14. Rosenbloom, Marketing Channels.
15. American Association of Railroads, www.aar.org, Web site visited march 17, 2008 .
16. Stern, El-Ansary, and Coughlan, Marketing Channels, p. 119.
17. Schiller, "Make It Simple."
18. William H Wiersema, "Is Doing Business in China for Everyone?" Electrical Apparatus, Jan 2006, 59(1), p.36-37; The World Fact Book www.cia.gov Web site visited March 18, 2008

19. Toby G. Gooley, "Air Carriers: The Urge to Merge," Logistics Management and Distribution Report, July 2000, p. 74
20. Hoover's Company Records. March 1, 2008.
21. www.ingrammicro.com About Ingram Micro. Web site visited March 17, 2008
22. William Davidson, "Changes in Distribution Institutions," Journal of Marketing (January 1970): 7.
23. Bert Rosenbloom, Marketing Channels, 8th ed., Cincinnati, Ohio: South-Western College Pub, February 1, 2007.
24. www.mckesson.com Corporate Profile. Web site visited March 17, 2008.
25. Anne Coughlan, Erin Anderson, and Louis W. Stern, Marketing Channels, 7th ed., Upper Saddles River, NJ: Prentice Hall, December 29, 2005
26. www.franchise.org International Franchise Association. March 19, 2008.
27. Bert Rosenbloom, Marketing Channels, 8th ed., Cincinnati, Ohio: South-Western College Pub, February 1, 2007.
28. Frazier and Lassar, "Determinants of Distribution Intensity."
29. Gretchen Morgenson, "Greener Pastures," Forbes, July 6, 1992, p. 48.
30. Lauren L. Rublin, "Retailers on Sale," Barron's, October 23, 2000, p. 23.
31. Gregory Gundlach and Ernest Cadotte, "Exchange Interdependence and Interfirm Interaction: Research in a Simulated Channel Setting," Journal of Marketing Research 31 (November 1994): 516–53
32. Robert Morgan and Shelby Hunt, "The Commitment-Trust Theory of Relationship Marketing," Journal of Marketing 58 (July 1994): 20–38.
33. Laurel Touby, "Blimpie Is Trying to Be a Hero to Franchisees Again," Business Week, March 22, 1993, p. 70.

The Marketing Gazette
   www.burtsbees.com, site visited June 5, 2008; Andrew Farrell, "Clorox to Buy Burt's Bees," October 31, 2007, Forbes.com Market Scan.

CASE 15

The Limited Brands

The shopping mall just wouldn't be the same without The Limited Brands stores. With a wide range of brands including Express, Bath & Body Works, C.O. Bigelow, Henri Bendel, La Senza, The Limited, The White Barn Candle Co., Diva London and their most lucrative holding, Victoria's Secret, the Limited Brand sells women's and men's apparel, lingerie, beauty and personal care products through its more than 3,700 stores. The company recorded net sales of 9.46 billion in 2007 and employs more than 100,000 associates throughout the United States. The Victoria's Secret brand accounted for $3 Billion in sales alone.

However, success for The Limited Brands has not always been so sweet. In 2002, some 400 tractor-trailers showed up unexpectedly in a distribution center parking lot built for 150 vehicles. That moment sparked an initiative within the company to renovate their logistics and distribution channels. "It was one of our worst supply chain disasters ever," said Paul Matthews, senior vice president of Limited Logistics Services. To this day no one knows what caused the scheduling nightmare that clogged streets, crashed computer systems and ticked off neighbors for blocks. But the Limited Brands it determined to prevent it from happening again.

The Limited Brands, like many companies, outsource their manufacturing. Their transformation began by recognizing they needed greater visibility into the supply chain. Visibility pertains not just to a company's internal operations but to its global network. And getting it isn't easy. "You can't do it alone, and you can't do it on a whim," Matthews said.

For retailers like the Limited Brands, it is important to keep the customer focus firmly in mind while developing and implementing a sophisticated supply chain solution. The first step was to move procurement from a transaction-based activity to a tactical activity. The Limited Brands consolidated procurement for its many brands into one function. The second step was to bring in the right technology. As a result of acquiring many stores and brands, the Limited Brands had a complex assortment of information-technology systems and software which included 60 major systems running hundreds of applications, many of them redundant and on numerous platforms. The Limited Brands started consolidating it's IT by integrating it's suppliers online to give them the ability to access data. They also gained the ability to track customer information as they moved from store to store. The system was user-friendly, easily accessible, high-speed and most importantly it was contained in a central database. Increased access to information was not the only change the Limited Brands made. It put into practice policies and discipline to make sure all aspects of it's business including logistics, finance, marketing and planning were receiving what they needed when they needed it.

Integrating suppliers is no small task for the Limited Brands. It buys merchandise from over 1,000 suppliers and sells through multiple channels - retail stores, the Internet, catalog and third-party. Radio frequency identification technology will play a role in deeper collaboration and transport cycle reduction time. Although, Matthews said, "The fashion retail business will not be a leader in RFID; we will absolutely be a fast follower." With a project involving such a large number of suppliers and advanced technology, implementation is still occurring.

Aside from technological integration of suppliers, the Limited Brands also encourages environmental stewardship. Believing that effective management is established through the thoughtful procurement of supplies, The Limited Brands began demanding lean and recyclable packaging as well as fuel efficient transportation from it's suppliers.

Investing in supply chain renovations will help the Limited Brands further their commitment to building a family of the world's best fashion brands offering captivating customer experiences that drive long-term loyalty and deliver sustained growth. The retailer's ultimate goal: a supply chain that begins and ends with the customer.

1. *How will greater visibility into the supply chain create cost savings for The Limited Brands?*
2. *Would it be beneficial for The Limited Brands to consolidate their supplier base? Why or why not?*
3. *The Limited Brands is a vertically integrated supply chain—they control almost every aspect from start to finish. What would the benefits of having a third party such as UPS control their logistics and distribution be?*

Sources: "A Clothes Call," Baseline. New York: Apr 2006. Vol.1, Iss. 57; pg. 1; William Hoffman, "Managing a Logistics Makeover," Traffic World. Newark: Feb 6, 2006. pg. 1; Lamont Wood, "Adding Visibility to the Demand Chain," Chain Store Age. New York: May 2006; www.limtedbrands.com, site visited January 25, 2008.

CHAPTER 16

Retailing, Direct Marketing & Wholesaling

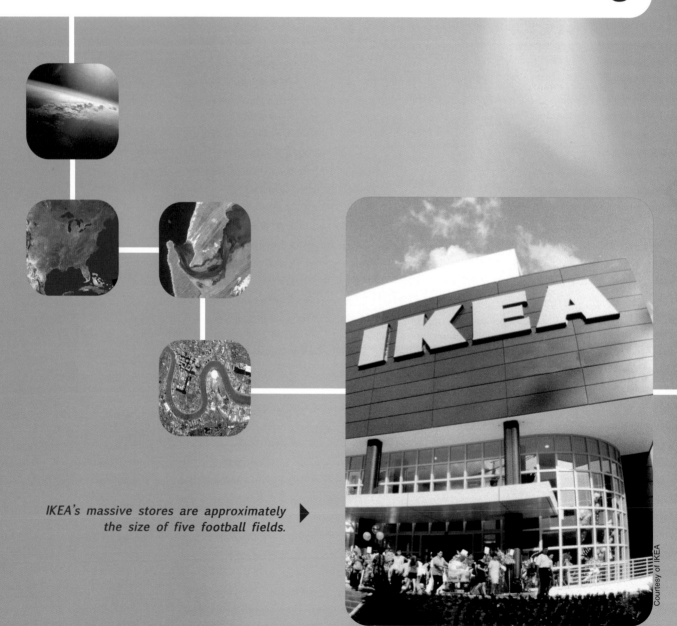

IKEA's massive stores are approximately the size of five football fields. ▶

Learning Objectives

1. Appreciate the important role retailers play in our economy and society.

2. Understand strategy issues confronted by retailers when making marketing decisions.

3. Recognize the diverse array of retailers that compete with one another.

4. Learn what direct marketing entails, its value, and how it differs from mass communication.

5. Be familiar with the different types of direct-response media.

6. Understand the marketing decisions made by direct-marketing companies.

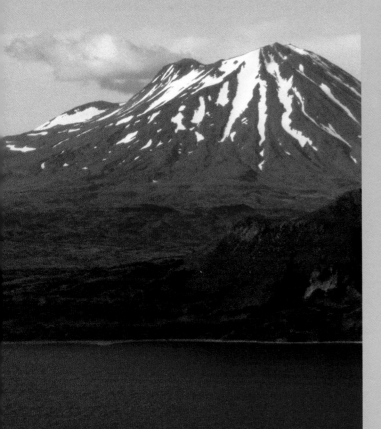

Retail giant IKEA has a retailing formula geared for growth. Its concept of "offering a wide range of well designed, functional home furnishing products at prices so low that as many people as possible will be able to afford them," has over 500 million annual visitors purchasing more than $22 billion in products each year. As one of the world's top furniture retailers, IKEA sells well designed home furnishings in over 30 countries. To keep prices affordable, IKEA uses flat packaging and customers assemble the products at home. With more than 250 stores world wide, each is massive in scale with an average of 300,000 square feet or equal to about five football fields.

Targeting the global middle class, IKEA has found success by creating a culture built for a community of trendy shoppers. With a quintessential cult brand, IKEA has become a global phenomenon. Using clever stunts, IKEA creates frenzy with each new store opening. Before the Atlanta opening, IKEA managers accepted essays from locals on why they deserve $2,000 in store vouchers. Five winners would each receive $2,000, but not until after they lived in the store for three days before the opening and slept in the bedroom department. IKEA's press generated enough buzz to draw in even more shoppers than expected on opening day.

With sales blazing at over 20 percent increases each year, IKEA continues to grow at an incredible pace. This kind of growth is partially due to the accelerated store rollouts. In 2008, IKEA plans to open 23 new stores in 11 different countries. CEO Anders Dahlvig expects to continue the expansion of the IKEA brand throughout the states. "We have 25 stores [in the United States] in a market the size of Europe, where we have more than 160 stores," says Dahlvig. Goals are set at 50 U.S. stores by 2010.

IKEA's commitment to the environment has aided its impressive growth. Renewable and biodegradable, the company uses wood in its products whenever possible. It's very selective in obtaining timber for products, refusing to buy materials logged from intact natural forests and from others it considers to have high conservation value. Unused wood from the creation of one product is used in the production of new ones. IKEA also promotes energy efficient light bulbs. These bulbs use 80 percent less energy than traditional incandescent lights and last up to 10 times longer. Consumers can be sure these bulbs are disposed of properly by returning them to an IKEA outlet for free recycling. IKEA's "Bag the Plastic Bag" campaign, started in 2008, aims at reducing the use of plastic bags in stores by 50 percent. The company charges 5 cents for every "throw-away" plastic bag and donates the proceeds to American Forest, a non-profit conservation organization.

Selling products through its huge superstores across the world is not the only way IKEA reaches its target market. Catalogs are used as a primary marketing channel and distributed to more than 174 million homes world wide. The catalogs are produced in 55 editions and 27 languages. IKEA also uses the Internet effectively to reach even more potential customers. IKEA attracts more than 278 million hits around the world each year as online sales continue to be a growing proportion of total sales.

IKEA's success did not come easily in the US. Steen Kanter, a former IKEA employee said "We got our clocks cleaned in the early 1990s because we really didn't listen to the consumer." U.S. managers were not paying close enough attention to details. "Americans want more comfortable sofas, higher-quality textiles, bigger glasses, more spacious entertainment units," says Pernille Spiers-Lopez, head of Ikea North America. There is no doubt, with revised products in the US and closer attention to other regional markets, consumers will continue to make IKEA one of the most successful retailers in the world.[1]

THE CONCEPTS OF RETAILING, DIRECT MARKETING & WHOLESALING

Retailing and direct marketing touch our lives daily. Retailing is involved whenever you purchase a burger at McDonald's, rent a movie at Blockbuster, or buy a pair of jeans at Gap. Direct marketing is involved whenever you receive a catalog from Dell Computer, watch QVC, or place an order for Justin Timberlake's latest release on iTunes. Wholesalers enter the picture by supporting retailers and direct marketing with product assortments that match the needs of the vast array of target customers. Retailers, direct marketers, and wholesalers help connect us with the goods and services that support our diverse lifestyles.

Operating a retailing organization in today's fast-paced world is challenging. Competition is intense, with different types of sellers going after many of the same customers. Retailers must make decisions about target markets, service levels, pricing, merchandise assortment, store locations, image, and the use of direct marketing, among others. They must stay abreast of new technologies that affect the efficiency and effectiveness of store operations. They must decide whether to follow increasing numbers of retailers into global markets.

More and more companies like Apple and Best Buy are using direct marketing to connect with customers. Direct marketing plays an important role in selling to consumers as well as in the business-to-business market. As technologies continue to advance, direct marketing will increase in importance.

Wholesalers are important because they take title to products from manufacturers and sell them to retailers and direct marketers. They help retailers and direct marketers by delivering products where and when needed to satisfy their customers' requirements.

RETAILING

Retailing refers to selling products directly to consumers for personal or household use. It does not include the sale of products to other resellers, which is the domain of wholesaling. Best Buy sells primarily to consumers while retailers like Staples have a large business clientele. Home Depot does significant business with each group. So typically, a retailer is a firm that makes the majority of its sales to consumers. Many discounters and warehouse clubs sell to small businesses as well, such as restaurants and small independent stores. Office Max and Staples are also examples of retailers that have a significant amount of sales to business customers.

Many retailers use direct mail and catalogs to supplement their store sales. Texas-based Neiman Marcus sends out a Christmas Book every October to its credit card customers. Over the years it has included exotic products such as camels, his-and-her airplanes, mummy cases, windmills, and submarines. In 2006, the Neiman Marcus Christmas Catalog featured a $1.7 million chartered trip for six to space with an all-inclusive 4-night stay at Virgin Chairman Richard Branson's private retreat in the British Virgin Islands.[2]

With about 8 percent of all retail sales throughout the Web, it is a key part of most retailing businesses.[3] Companies can increase customer profits through add-on services that encourage multi-channel shopping. For example, customers that order a product online but pick it up offline are exposed to multiple services and therefore expected to be more satisfied.[4]

www.ikea.com

Check out how IKEA effectively sells on the Internet by visiting its Web site. Also learn how the company uses innovative packaging to reduce waste!

THE IMPORTANCE OF RETAILERS

Retailers are vital to our economy. Sales in the United States through retail stores are more than $4 trillion annually. Retailing also is one of the largest U.S. industries in terms of employment. About 15 million people work in retailing— approximately one out of every seven full-time workers.[5]

Retailing is the final stage in the distribution channel for the majority of products sold to consumers, everything from chewing gum to insurance to automobiles. As retailing practices develop and become more refined, better products are provided to consumers at better prices. Retailers perform a variety of functions described in Figure 16.1 that increase the value of products to consumers. Similar to wholesalers, they play two critical roles in the mix of goods. They perform an allocation function by purchasing products in large quantities from suppliers (manufacturers, wholesalers, or brokers) for resale to consumers in smaller quantities. They perform an assortment function by purchasing merchandise from a variety of suppliers and offering it for sale in one location. Therefore, retailers make a broad variety of goods available to consumers in amounts they can afford and effectively handle.

Although packaged goods such as cereal, detergent, milk, and toothpaste are purchased off the shelf by consumers, retailers still provide information about such products through advertising, displays, and unit prices posted on the shelves. Other consumer products, especially durable goods and services such as insurance, require that retailers use salespeople to provide information and answer questions about product benefits.

Well-located stores increase the convenience of shopping for customers through physical locations and integrated Web-based e-tailing. Furthermore, many retailers facilitate transactions by investing in scanner technology and offering credit. They also may customize products, as do clothing retailers who alter suits or insurance agents who develop specialized packages. Repair services are provided by retailers such as Sears, Circuit City, and Radio Shack.

Without retailers, acquiring the basic necessities would be difficult in terms of both time and money. Time, place, possession, and form utilities are provided to consumers. Retailers help make the lives of consumers more pleasant and managable.

Some manufacturers, such as Sherwin-Williams in the paint industry and Liz Claiborne in the apparel industry, own their outlets, at least in part. Others, such as Dell Computer, sell directly to consumers, bypassing retailers. For a majority of consumer good manufacturers, however, retailers are essential for product distribution. Most producers cannot afford to access consumer markets themselves. Their capital is tied up in operations, and it makes no sense for even large manufacturers such as Procter & Gamble to open up outlets. Retailers do this for them, investing in land,

buildings, fixtures, and personnel. Furthermore, retailers typically take title to the goods they resell, incurring the inventory carrying costs and sales risks otherwise held by the manufacturer. Retailers often sell goods

to consumers on credit, assuming the risks associated with accounts receivable and bad debts. Retailers also promote the products they carry. In other words, retailers make it economically feasible for manufacturers of consumer goods to operate.

The **wheel of retailing** is one way to describe how retailers emerge, evolve, and sometimes fade away. According to the theory, new retailers locate their no-frills stores in low-rent areas to keep costs down. Those that succeed start to change. They add more services, move to more expensive real estate, upgrade facilities, and raise prices. This makes them vulnerable to new low-price entrants, and the wheel goes round and round. The wheel can be broken if retailers carefully develop a strategy. They must choose a target market and create a marketing mix that satisfies it. Upgrading services, locations, and prices can be defended only if that is what the target market demands.

RETAIL STRATEGY

The steps in formulating a retail strategy are shown in Figure 16.2. Invariably, successful retailers have a sound retail strategy.

Target Markets and Positioning Like any business, retailers must understand their customers to be truly successful. As a first step, they carefully analyze the general market and decide the segment or segments to target.

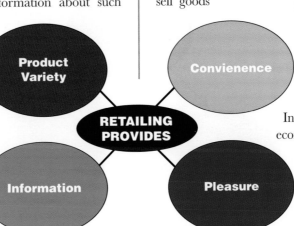

Figure 16.1 Functions of Retailing

Home Depot is a successful retailer to both consumers and business clientele.

For example, Autozone, based in Memphis, is an auto parts retailer that targets lower-income consumers who repair their own cars. Nordstrom's, headquartered in Seattle, is a department store chain that targets middle- to high-income households desiring superior service. Wet Seal, Inc., based in Irvine, California, operates over 400 hundred apparel stores throughout the country targeting young women ages 13 through 18.

Whatever the overall targeting strategy, individual outlets may face different mixes of customers. The primary trade area is the geographic territory in which the majority of a store's customers reside. The trade area can vary in circumference from less than one mile for a convenience store to 20 miles for a specialist such as Toys'R'Us. Each store manager must understand primary trade areas and react accordingly. For example, Wal-Mart uses AC Neilson and Census information to locate stores in areas with large multicultural populations and tailors merchandise for these locations specifically to these customers. [6]

Retailer positioning is the mental picture consumers have of the retailer and the shopping experiences it provides in relation to competitors. Retailers decide what image they want to establish with customers—high prestige, superior service, friendly atmosphere, low prices, etc. Then they must determine how to instill this image in the minds of their customers. Decisions on service level and pricing, merchandise assortment, and store location all influence the retailer's image.

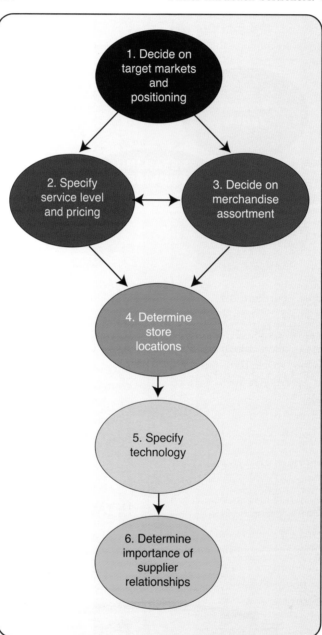

Figure 16.2 Developing a Retail Strategy

ity at low prices. The objective is to keep service costs and overhead down in order to make prices competitive. Lucky Stores is a supermarket chain in southern California that offers low prices and few amenities. Wal-Mart and Kmart have a discount-oriented strategy. Crown Books offers a standard 10 percent discount in addition to discounts up to 40 percent on New York Times hardback bestsellers. Competitors such as Barnes & Noble and Borders may provide coffee shops or sell compact disks as well as offering sales and special discounts.

A service-oriented strategy emphasizes quality products and value-added functions with prices to match. It is successful to the extent that this is what the target market wants. In the jewelry business, Italian jeweler Bvlgari offers unique jewelry, and its well-trained sales force caters to the specific needs of each customer. Nordstrom is well known in the Northwest for its quality of service, such as ironing shirts for customers immediately after purchase. A store's environment can also contribute to its success in competing against large competitors.

Other retailers follow a hybrid strategy, combining quality products, value-added services, and low pricing in some manner. Autonation, Carchoice, and Carmax (a division of Circuit City) offer huge inventories of used cars marked with low, no-haggle prices. Their stores have such amenities as child care centers, coffee bars, and touch-screen computers. The well-known bookseller Borders offers more services than just selling books. The stores also feature coffee shops, sell music, have special promotions, and even coordinate products, contests, and in-store events with special events such as the Ken Burns

Service Level and Pricing The target market and positioning will influence decisions on service level and pricing. Many retailers follow a discount-oriented strategy, offering products and service of acceptable qual-

project on jazz music. For example, visitors to the store found many jazz-related items, a limited edition Jazz Fusion Blend coffee, and could participate in workshops to learn more about the music. Borders offers the Borders Rewards program, Seattle's Best Coffee cafes, and Paperchase gift and stationery shops to enhance customer loyalty and distinguish them from their competition.[7]

Merchandise Assortment

Retailers must take great care in deciding what merchandise to offer. Those with the right assortment have greater sales revenues and customer satisfaction. Merchandise breadth, the variety of product lines offered, and merchandise depth, the number of products available within each line, must be determined.

Jewelry stores such as Bvlgari offer unique jewelry and a sales force catering to specific customer needs.

Department stores have considerable breadth but only moderate depth. Retailers such as Circuit City and CompUSA have limited breadth but great depth.

A **scrambled merchandising** strategy means that the product lines carried seem to be unrelated. The goal is to facilitate one-stop shopping for customers and achieve competitive advantage. For example, in the new "Super Kmart" stores, traditional goods are combined with a well-stocked supermarket of food products. Meijer, a chain in the Midwest, has used this strategy since its inception.

Part of the assortment of many retailers is **private label merchandise.** JCPenney's St. John's Bay jeans

and Sears, Roebuck & Company's Canyon River Blues jeans are two examples. Private labels are especially common in the apparel, food, home appliance, and drug industries. In apparel, private labels serve to build the image of the retailer rather than the manufacturer. Ann Taylor and Gap have taken this a step further to vertical retailing. These companies design, manufacture, and market their own products in their own stores. Private label sales are growing in supermarket chains that are increasingly featuring their own products. Notice the Kroger brand orange juice placed next to the popular Tropicana brand with the prices clearly displayed. Once supermarket retailers realized customers would buy private label products if they believed they were of good quality, the quality and marketing of these products improved. Private label sales in supermarkets total about $65 billion, 25 percent of total sales. Each year, private label brands increase their share. As these labels continue to grow in acceptance and contribute to customer loyalty, it seems the trend will continue to grow.[8]

Globally, private label products represent more than 20 percent of grocery sales and are expected to grow to 30 percent by 2020.[9] In markets like the US, the United Kingdom, Belgium, and Germany, private label brands gain market share during times of recession. However, national brands regain some of their share during stronger economic periods.[10]

Store Location The location decision is very important for any retailer. Among other things, it affects how convenient shopping will be for customers. The target market dictates the choice to some degree. Autozone, for example, places its stores directly in low-income neighborhoods.[11] In contrast, specialty toy stores and clothing boutiques locate in well-to-do suburbs or high end urban shopping districts such as the Gold Coast Miracle Mile in Chicago. The location decision can be a source of competitive advantage if it preempts competitors from moving to an area with high sales and profit potential.

Kroger strategically places its own brand of orange juice next to its competitors.

Wal-Mart's strategy was to establish stores in small towns that could not support more than one large discount operation. It froze out competition while building a strong sales base. Wal-Mart then spread to larger suburban areas.[12]

Some retailers use a destination location strategy; that is, stores are put in low-rent areas off highways and some distance from other retailers. Because the store is off the beaten path, consumers make it their destination when they want to shop there. In contrast, a competitor location strategy puts stores near those of major competitors. The rationale is that even more consumers will be drawn to the area. For example, Borders is likely to place its superstores as close as possible to a Barnes & Nobles outlet. They often compete for the same retail site.[13] Wherever you find McDonald's you are very likely to see Burger King. Diamond Merchants cluster along 47th Street in New York City, antique stores line the Place du Grand Sablon in Brussels, and a Planet Hollywood usually can be found near a Hard Rock Cafe. In general, retailers with large stores, a large amount of merchandise, and attractive pricing can use a destination location strategy effectively. Retailers selling goods that consumers want to compare on quality and price are usually wise to locate close to competitors.

Of course, many retailers choose a local or regional shopping mall rather than a freestanding location. A shopping mall or center is a group of retail stores in one place marketed as a unit to shoppers in a trade area. Shopping malls, especially regional ones, have immense pulling power. The diverse mix of stores offers a wide array of merchandise. Merchants can pool resources to

Cosmetics and perfumes generally have a high markup in the retail arena.

provide entertainment, such as pianists or clowns or even a supervised indoor playground, as at the huge Mall of America in Minneapolis. This supermall has 2.5 million square feet of retail space, equivalent to four regional shopping malls, features more than 520 specialty stores and brings in over 42.5 million visitors annually, including many who charter flights from all over the world. The mall is scheduled to double in size with a new addition scheduled to open in 2011.[14] The West Edmonton Mall in Alberta, Canada, is another example of a supermall.

Supplier Relationships

Developing strong relationships with suppliers is a strategic imperative for many retailers. Partners go out of their way to serve one another. Supplier loyalty pays off when the retailer gets the goods it needs in a quick and efficient manner. Wal-Mart has long been known as a retailer that values close partnerships with its major suppliers.[15] Whatever the strength of a relationship, tough bargaining issues are likely to arise between suppliers and retailers.

Cost and pricing issues are the most common areas of friction. Retailers have a targeted **markup**, the difference between merchandise cost and the retail price. For example, if Wet Seal buys blouses from California Concepts, a manufacturer in Gardena, at $12 each and prices them in stores at $20 each, the markup is $8, or 40 percent of the selling price ($8 / $20 = .40). The formula is:

$$\text{Markup Percentage} = \frac{\text{Amount added to cost (markup)}}{\text{Selling price}}$$

Goods that do not sell as expected require a **markdown**, a reduction in the original retail price. Wet Seal may sell some of the blouses at $20 but then lower the price to $15 in order to sell the rest. The markdown in this case is $5, and the markdown percentage is 25 percent ($5 / $20). That is the discount amount typically advertised for a sale item, and it is computed as follows:

$$\text{Markdown Percentage} = \frac{\text{Amount of markdown}}{\text{Previous selling price}}$$

The retailer typically goes back to the supplier and asks for markdown money, a credit to the retailer's account to adjust for the unanticipated price reduction.

Shopping malls have immense pulling power, especially when they are as large as the Mall of America in Minneapolis.

Limited Line	General Merchandise
Specialty stores	Department stores
Franchises	Convenience stores
Category killers or superstores	Supermarkets
Automatic vending retailers	Warehouse clubs
	Discount stores
	Variety stores
	Hypermarkets

Figure 16.3 Classification of Retailers

TYPES OF RETAILERS

There are several ways to classify retailers. Form of ownership distinguishes between small independents (often called mom-and-pop stores) and **chain stores,** which are a group of centrally owned and managed retail outlets that handle the same product lines. Level of service can be used, whether full, limited, or self-service. Price level can be used as well. However, the most informative classification is based on the merchandise assortment, whether retailers sell a limited line or general merchandise. Within each category, different types of retailers exist based on their service level and pricing strategy, as outlined in Figure 16.3. A number of successful companies have stores of more than one type, such as Macy's and Wal-Mart.

Limited-Line Retailers Limited-line retailers focus on one product category. The four types are specialty stores, franchises, superstores, and automated vending retailers.

Specialty stores offer merchandise in one primary product category in considerable depth. Examples are Wet Seal, The Limited, Florsheim, Women's Foot Locker, Champ's Sports, and Roller Skates of America. Goods are of moderate to high quality. Prices tend to be high and comparable to department stores.

Many specialty stores are run by franchisees, who sign a contractual agreement with a franchiser organization to represent and sell its products in particular retail locations. Examples include Blockbuster Video stores, the vast majority of fast-food restaurants (some outlets are company owned), and automobile dealerships.

Superstores, sometimes called category killers, focus on a single product category but offer huge selection and low prices. They tend to range in size from 50,000 to 75,000 square feet. Service levels are normally low to moderate. Examples include Barnes & Nobles, Home Depot, IKEA, Staples, and Sportsmart. Superstores have been particularly successful in taking business away from traditional discount stores as well as wholesalers.[16]

Automated vending retailers use machinery operated by coin or credit card to dispense goods. The placement of machines is critical, and airports, hospitals, schools, and office buildings are among the most popular locations. Traditionally, vending has focused on beverages, candy, cigarettes, and food, but the industry is expanding into new areas, such as life insurance policies in airports, movie rentals in supermarkets, and lottery tickets. ARAMARK and Canteen Corporation are two leading automatic vending retailers.

In Japan, vending machines are more important in retail trade. Homes and apartments are small, with little storage space, and consumers often travel on foot or by mass transit. The convenience of location and small quantities is appealing, and a wider variety of products can be bought. Roboshop Outlets allow customers to look through displayed items, punch in the desired product's number, and then receive their purchases through a trap door. More than a dozen of these shops exist in Tokyo alone, and the Vending Machine Manufacturers Association of Japan reports that there is one vending machine for every 23 people in Japan. These vending machines sell everything from alcohol to pagers and underwear.[17]

www.staples.com

Staples has pioneered the office products Superstore industry. Staples has also made recycle solutions easy for offices small and large. To learn more, connect to the company's Web site.

Marketing Vocabulary

MARKUP
The difference between merchandise cost and retail price.

MARKDOWN
A reduction from the original retail selling price of a product.

CHAIN STORE
One of a group of centrally owned and managed retail stores that handle the same product lines.

SPECIALTY STORE
A retailer offering merchandise in one primary product category in considerable depth.

SUPERSTORE
A retailer that focuses on a single product category but offers huge selection and low prices; also called a category killer.

AUTOMATED VENDING RETAILER
The use of machinery operated by coins or credit cards to dispense goods.

General Merchandise Retailers General merchandise retailers carry a number of different product categories. There are seven types: department stores, convenience stores, supermarkets, warehouse clubs, discount stores, variety stores, and hypermarkets.

Department stores carry a broad array and varying depth of merchandise, and the level of customer service is relatively high. Merchandise is grouped into well-defined departments. Both soft goods, such as apparel and linens, and hard goods, such as appliances and sporting goods, are normally sold. The intention is to provide one-stop shopping for most personal and household items. While often situated in downtown areas at a stand-alone location, department stores also are prevalent in shopping malls, where they are considered anchor tenants that draw customers.

Target markets and pricing strategies vary considerably among department stores. Some seek the upscale customer such as Bloomingdale's, Neiman Marcus, and Saks Fifth Avenue. Their decor is plush, with an ambiance and prices to match. Others such as Kohl's and Target appeal to a somewhat broader middle-income clientele and focus on mainstream tastes, increasingly offering popular brands at lower prices.[18] Yet others, such as JCPenney and Sears, seek an even broader array of customers. Finally, department stores such as Mervyn's, Upton, and Byron's focus primarily on low-income households, featuring low prices and frequent promotions.[19] Specialty stores provide the most competition to upscale department stores, whereas at the lower end there is intense rivalry from discounters.

Convenience stores are small and have moderately low breadth and depth of merchandise. Sandwiches, soft drinks, snack foods, newspapers and magazines, milk, and beer and wine are among the most popular products carried. They are open long hours, prices are high, and their location is their primary advantage. Some are part of large corporate chains, including 7-Eleven, Circle K, and Dairy Mart. Some large oil companies have established their own operations, such as Arco's AM/PM stores and Texaco's Food Mart. Many convenience stores are mom-and-pop businesses, family owned and operated.

Supermarkets are large, departmentalized, food-oriented retail establishments that sell beverages, canned goods, dairy products, frozen foods, meat, produce, and such nonfood items as health and beauty aids, kitchen utensils, magazines, pharmaceuticals, and toys. Many have in-store bakeries and delicatessens. Merchandise breadth and depth are moderately high. Since gross margins are generally low, supermarkets attempt to maximize sales volume. In the United States, regional chains dominate, such as Hughes, Kroger, Safeway, and Winn-Dixie.

Warehouse clubs are large, no-frills stores that carry a revolving array of merchandise at low prices. They are typically 60,000 square feet or more. Consumers must become members before shopping in the clubs. Brands carried vary by day and week, depending on the deals arranged with suppliers so product selection is somewhat limited. By carrying only the most popular items in a merchandise category, clubs strive for high asset turnover (net sales divided by total assets) with gross margins as low as 8 percent. There are approximately 3,400 warehouse clubs and superstores in the United States, accounting for $191 billion.[20] These retailers give supermarkets stiff competition.

Discount stores offer a broad variety of merchandise, and low prices. Merchandise depth is low to moderate. Service levels are minimal. Operating costs, including payroll, are normally 20 percent or less of total sales.[21] Discounters concentrate on low- to middle-income consumers. The goal is asset turnover and sales volume per store. Wal-Mart and Kmart are the major U.S. discount stores.

There are two specialized types of discounters. **Off-price retailers** sell brand-name clothing at low prices. Their inventory frequently changes as they take advantage of special deals from manufacturers selling excess

Whole Foods Market is a specialty supermarket that offers a large selection of organic foods.

Courtesy of Whole Foods Market

merchandise. Examples are Loehmann's, Marshall's, Men's Warehouse, and T. J. Maxx.

Variety stores offer an array of low-priced merchandise of low to moderate quality. There is not much depth. These retailers are not as numerous as they used to be because of intense competition, mainly from larger discounters. Examples of variety stores are Everything's A Dollar and Pic'N'Save.

Hypermarkets are giant shopping facilities offering a wide selection of food and general merchandise at low prices. They have at least 100,000 square feet of space, some of them three times that. The concept was developed by a French company, Carrefour, which is very successful throughout Europe and Latin America. Hypermarkets have not thrived in the United States, partly because there is so much competition. Furthermore, consumers often complain about too much walking and limited brand selections. The costs of operating the giant facilities are high.[22] Nevertheless, hypermarkets might become more popular in the United States because they offer one-stop shopping. Existing hypermarket operations include Super Kmart Centers and Hypermarket USA.

Fred Myer stores carry a wide array of products and are considered to be a hypermarket.

ISSUES IN RETAILING

Retailing changes rapidly. Retailers must address such important factors as diversity, legal and ethical issues, and global retailing.

Diversity and Retailing   Because retailers deal directly with consumers, most of them realize that staffing and marketing programs must reflect the nature of the population they serve. Recognizing diversity and its implications for business practice is a must for top-performing retailers. Sears Roebuck and Co. is at the forefront in connecting with diverse markets. Some of their stores in Florida have a customer base that is 90 percent Hispanic, and Sears has bilingual signs, sales staff, in-store posters featuring minority models and four apparel lines designed for multicultural women.[23] With the Spanish-Language media market growing at twice the pace of the rest of the market, companies are investing great amounts of money in advertising geared toward the Hispanic population.[24]

In another approach to diversity, Marriott International has a program in the inner cities called Pathways to Independence, which recently reached its 10-year anniversary. It recruits, screens, and trains individuals on public assistance. To qualify, applicants must have a sixth-grade reading ability, pass a drug test, and demonstrate a desire to work. Initially a program in the Atlanta Marriott Marquis hotel, the program now exists in 40 locations. The six-week program includes 60 hours of classroom instruction and 120 hours of occupational skills instruction. Over 2,700 people have graduated from the program since its inception and have assumed responsible positions in the hotel chain. Graduates of the program have among the highest retention rates in the hospitality industry. The Pathways to Independence program has been used as a model for other similar programs.[25]

Legal and Ethical Issues in Retailing
Retailers face a range of legal and ethical issues. It is important that they understand and comply with the applicable laws. For example, title companies perform a variety of services in consumer real estate transactions. Some California title companies were found guilty of giving kickbacks, such as cash payments, computers, and free printing of sales literature, to real estate brokers in exchange for recommending them to customers. Under federal law, no one may receive or charge any fee, kickback, or thing of value for referring business in mortgage transactions. Because of kickback violations in mortgage transactions in California, nearly 82,000 households were eligible for refunds averaging $300.[26]

Ethical dilemmas often arise over the goods sold by retailers. Consumer action groups often lobby them to stop carrying certain products. Over 10 years ago, Target eliminated all cigarette sales in its stores. The decision was influenced by the growing stigma attached to smoking and mounting pressure to comply with laws barring the sale of tobacco to minors.[27] Depending on community standards, many stores do not carry certain magazines, or keep them under the counter, away from children. Wal-Mart stopped carrying guns in its stores in 1994. It still sells them through catalogs and sells many shooting accessories such as gun cases, which offends many consumer advocates.

Employee relations are another area in which ethical questions arise, such as steps taken to prevent unionization or reduce employee theft. Whatever the issue, if employees are not treated with fairness and respect, then major problems can result. One recent survey found that a two-way performance review is an excellent way to retain good workers. This way both the management and the employee can comment on the employee's performance, as well as on the management's performance. Thus, the review can be just that, a "review," and not a "criticism." This plan aims to confront problems in the employee-employer relationship before they cause problems for the company.[28]

Global Retailers For years, a number of US retailers have had successful ventures in global markets. Kodak has had successful retail establishments in nearly every major city for over 30 years and McDonald's, along with KFC and Burger King have brought fast food retailing to most mature and emerging markets for the past couple of decades. Each of these retailers uses a similar approach with adjustments to local requirements. For example, Kodak in China features black and white film – a product seldom promoted in Western Europe or the US – and, you will find beer in McDonald's in Germany and Cadbury chocolate sticks in its ice cream cones in the UK.

Today, retailers from other countries are finding the US to be an excellent market, as well. Uniqlo is Japan's largest casual apparel retailer, with 733 outlets primarily in Asia and Britain. Now it has unveiled a new global flagship store on Manhattan in New York City. The store is the area's second-largest retail showroom (after Bloomingdale's) and dominates a block packed with rivals like Banana Republic. Uniqlo's objective is to become the largest global clothing retailer by 2010.[29] As with most growth oriented companies, leading edge retailers emphasize the global nature of business.

Similar to other businesses, retailers are entering emerging markets like China and India. More than 30 of the world's top 250 retailers operate in China, but only five currently operate in India. These retailers are looking for growing middle income markets which characterizes many emerging markets.[30] Wal-Mart, with over 20 percent in sales outside the U.S. is increasingly looking to its worldwide operations to drive growth, which is slowing in its U.S. stores. Wal-Mart president and chief executive officer H. Lee Scott has cited emerging markets in Russia and China, along with India, as major future opportunities.[31]

Developed markets are also new targets of some U. S. retailers. Well-known U.S. names such as Office Depot and Circuit City are moving into Europe, Asia and other areas while attempting to grow at home.[32]

DIRECT MARKETING

Direct marketing uses various methods to communicate with consumers, generally calling for a direct response on their part. Direct marketing is both a form of communication and a channel of distribution. Direct mail and catalogs have been used for many years. Telemarketing is another prominent method. Advertisements in print media or on television and radio that include toll-free numbers for placing orders have become very popular. The field is being revolutionized by technology—fax machines, e-mail and voice mail, electronic catalogs, infomercials, home television shopping channels, and the Internet.

Many organizations can benefit from direct marketing. A growing number of companies, called direct marketers, conduct business primarily or solely in this way. Excellent examples are CDNow on the Internet and Dell Computer. This kind of direct marketing is most powerful when it communicates product and pricing information, along with guidance for placing orders. The sale is completed by delivery of products via computer (such as software) or through services such as UPS, DHL, and FedEx.

According to the Direct Marketing Association, direct marketing expenditures of approximately $160 billion generate about $1.85 trillion in sales annually. That represents about 7 percent of all U.S. sales. Sales attributed to direct marketing are increasing at about 6.4 percent annually, which is faster than all sales in general. Clearly direct marketing is very significant in generating sales and is increasing in importance. It is estimated that, on average, for each dollar companies spend on direct marketing they receive about $11.50 in increased sales.[33]

Approximately, 1.2 percent of all U.S. workers are employed in direct marketing and about 8 percent of the workforce is in some way supported by direct marketing sales. For each employee in a direct marketing job you can expect about 5 other employees to be directly supported by those activities.[34] As a comparison, total direct marketing expenditures are approximately equal to total expenditures for mass advertising. About 52 percent is spent by B2C businesses and the remaining 48 percent is directed at the B2B arena. However, the B2B expenditures are growing fastest. Because the B2B arena is larger, direct marketing represents about 4.4 percent of business sales and about 12 percent of consumer sales. And, direct marketing is slightly more productive in generating sales for consumer businesses:

- $1 spent on consumer direct marketing yields $12.66 in sales
- $1 spent on business direct marketing yields $10.10 [35]

Direct marketing offers consumers a convenient way to shop from the comfort of their home or office. The fast-paced lifestyle of many people leaves little time or energy for shopping trips. Driving costs keep increasing. Traffic congestion and parking are problems. Checkout lines are growing as many retailers reduce staff to cut costs. All these factors have increased the importance of convenience. The widespread availability of credit cards, toll-free numbers, internet connectivity, and overnight delivery service has made direct marketing to consumers even more viable. Convenience is also important in business-to-business markets. Direct marketing allows business customers to gain information on products and place orders efficiently. It requires much less time than meeting with a variety of salespeople.

Direct marketing also can improve the quality of products offered to customers. For example, mail-order florist Calyx & Corolla claims that its flowers have superior blooms that last 5 to 10 days longer by eliminating long truck or retail cooler times. Instead, they partner with growers to send flowers direct using UPS.[36] Another advantage of direct marketing is competitive prices. A company can operate out of an unadorned warehouse in an inexpensive location, keeping overhead low. Many Japanese consumers save money by ordering from U.S. catalog companies such as L.L. Bean.

Direct marketing is of increasing value to many entrepreneurs as retailers cut back on inventory. For example, many music stores feature only the more mainstream artists and compilations. Music fans can, however, often find exactly what they are looking for through Internet sites such as iTunes. Wholesalers are overloaded as well. Even if they agree to add a product, there is no guarantee the product will get much support from salespeople.

Direct marketing allows small businesses to access markets without the assistance of retailers, wholesalers, or a company sales force. Consequently, the investment required for product launch is relatively low. For example, Ziff-Davis Publishing in New York City puts out a large monthly catalog, *Computer Shopper*, in which companies can advertise. A full-page ad can reach 3.34 million customers per month through the printed magazine. In addition, companies can advertise on the Web site www.zdnet.com/computershopper. *Computer Shopper* has enabled several small companies to start and successfully maintain their businesses.

Large organizations also benefit from direct marketing. Some use it as their primary means of doing business. Others use it in combination with other channels. Victoria's Secret, a division of The Limited, Inc., has retail stores in major shopping malls throughout the country and also mails out several catalogs per year.

DIRECT MARKETING DATABASES

All direct-marketing companies maintain a database with customer name, address, and purchase history. These are often supplemented with lists purchased from market research companies such as Zeller's and Dun's. Some direct marketers have taken the art of database management to a new level. Access Innovations has a software called Data Harmony, which helps publishers, corporate libraries, and online directory producers design and manipulate databases. The company's Thesaurus Master allows users to tag their own phrases and keywords in a databases' thesaurus, and it gives searchers more accurate results by using individualized terms relevant to a specific company, industry, and scientific discipline.[37]

DIRECT MARKETING MEDIA

Direct marketers use many media; some choose only one, but many combine several media in attempts to connect with customers. Figure 16.4 identifies the most popular media which are described in this section. The fol-

Marketing Vocabulary

DIRECT MARKETING
Uses various methods to communicate with consumers, generally calling for a direct response on their part.

Figure 16.4 Direct-Marketing Media

DIRECT-MARKETING MEDIA

- Direct Mail
- Internet
- Catalogs
- Telemarketing
- Print & Broadcast Media
- Televised Home Shopping

lowing sections describe each type of direct marketing media in more detail. In the U.K., where direct marketing now generates about 9 percent of consumer sales, sales attributed to direct marketing activity are believed to total $107 billion a year, with $67 billion derived from consumer sales and $40 from business-to-business.[38]

Direct Mail With more than three-quarters of marketers using it, direct mail is the most popular method of direct marketing (compared with 64 percent who use e-mail), according to the Direct Marketing Association.[39] Each year, billions of paper-based pieces are sent to prospective customers through the U.S. Postal Service. Usually, a cover letter and brochure are included but CDs and DVDs are also popular. America Online mails out CDs so consumers can try the service. Orders can be placed by calling a toll-free number, filling out and mailing back an order form, or faxing the order form.

Mail contact is popular because it hits a select market at a reasonably low cost. Selective mailing lists can be developed or purchased. Direct mail also can be personalized, is flexible, and allows early testing and response measurement. Most market research projects that direct mail will continue to grow, but not as fast as it did in the 1990s. Direct mail is the US's second largest ad medium after TV. The Robert J Coen's annual Universal McCann media survey shows that US direct mail volume grew 15 percent over the past five years to a current annual total of over 115 billion pieces. Internet advertising grew 25 percent in 2006, while direct mailing increased by only 8 percent. However, only $1 is spent on internet advertising for every $4 spent on direct mail. It is estimated that at current growth rate, Internet spending will not overtake direct mail until 2016.[40]

Three forms of mechanized mail are becoming popular with marketers. Fax mail is sent from one fax machine to another. Fax numbers are published in directories that can be purchased from market research companies. This method has the advantage of speed, as do the two others. E-mail is sent from one computer to another. Messages arrive almost instantly and are stored until individuals access the files. Voice mail is a verbal message sent via telephone and stored until it is retrieved. The public is less enthusiastic than direct marketers about these techniques. Many people resent paper being used to print unsolicited messages, or the time wasted reading, listening to, and deleting messages. These forms of direct mail are best used to communicate with regular customers or people who express an interest in a product. For example, it is appropriate to send customized e-mail to people who regularly access a company's Web site or who request to be included on e-mailing lists.

Internet Many companies have e-commerce Web sites, allowing consumers to make purchases directly on the Web site. Consumers are already comfortable with other types of direct-response media, which helps make them receptive to the Net. Security is an issue, however. Many people are reluctant to provide credit card numbers online. Furthermore, as more and more households own computers, e-commerce is now less limited than before. And beyond our borders, the Web's heavy U.S. accent grates on many cultures. As the Web becomes more global, however, this problem also provides an opportunity for enterprising marketers who can operate across boundaries in many languages.

Companies must decide whether to set up their own Web operation or turn to a provider. The trade-off is between greater control and no fees to outside Internet resellers, on one hand, and expertise and an existing subscriber base on the other. An annual fee plus some percentage of the company's online sales, typically two percent, is paid to the online service.

Individuals who do not have their own Web sites, or who wish to sell their items through larger sites, can use sites such as eBay, which allows users to bid on items and then charges the seller a set amount based on the purchase price.

In the consumer market, Amazon.com is an Internet reseller offering books, music, movies, clothing, and millions of other goods. Amazon.com owns no inventory; instead it relies on a network of wholesalers to ship orders, normally within 24 hours.

The Internet is a great interactive medium. Many companies' profits are coming increasingly from Internet sales. The new uSwitch research shows that on average in the U.K., 8 million households spend two hours per day shopping online. And it predicts online shopping is going to occupy nearly 40 percent of all U.K.'s retail sales and reach $162 billion by 2020.[41] Nowadays the booming of Internet in direct marketing has led to a growth of digital printing with personalized targeting possibilities. The Target Marketing's first Media Usage Forecast indicates that of the top 15 media channels used in direct marketing, e-mail is the second best ROI generator (22 percent) after direct mail (32 percent). And when asked to choose the media method for driving ROI on customer retention contract, 35 percent of the responsive marketers list e-mail as their top choice.[42]

Catalogs **Mail-order catalogs** publish product and price information in paper form. Annually, more than 12 billion copies of more than 8,000 different paper-based catalogs are sent through the U.S. Postal Service. Some feature general merchandise, such as those by JCPenney. Others focus on a narrow range of products. Omaha Steaks sells beef, seafood, pork, lamb, chicken, pastas, and desserts in its catalog.[43] Eddie Bauer catalogs include men and women's apparel, luggage, footwear, and accessories.

Some companies, such as airlines and hotels, assemble products from various sources and hire third parties to publish paper-based catalogs. United Airlines provides SkyMall to passengers. It is a collection of upscale, unique merchandise from a number of catalogs, including Brookstone, Disney, Healthrider, Hammacher Schlemmer, and Sharper Image. Customers call an 800 number or visit www.skymall.com to order.

A major disadvantage of catalog marketing is the expense. Paper and postage prices are so high that many entrepreneurs find it impossible to issue their own, and it's very hard to get products included in brand-name catalogs. The Good Catalog Company has filled a need by partnering with producers who can't afford to publish and distribute on their own.

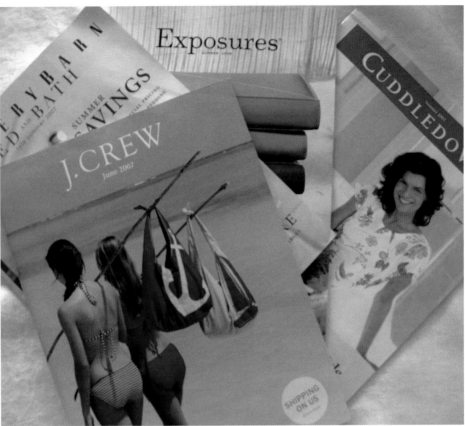

Mail-order catalogs reach customers. J. Crew gives a 10 percent discount to students with a valid ID.

Electronic catalogs are a popular way to store product information, especially in business-to-business markets. iPlanet E-Commerce Solutions, a company formed by the blending of America Online and Sun Microsystems, seeks to meet the needs of the B2B world by providing services to aid companies in becoming Internet savvy. The company collaborated with J. D. Edwards to develop "B2B in a Box," a program and electronic catalog that allows online purchasing and electronic trading.

Telemarketing **Telemarketing** occurs when salespeople make telephone calls to leads provided by marketing services or from other lists. The timing of calls is very important. Late morning and early afternoon are normally the best times for reaching businesses, while evenings between 7:00 and 9:00 are best for contacting households—from the marketer's standpoint. You probably have had more than a few interruptions at that time from telemarketers. When people are out, messages are often left on voicemail.

Telemarketing has a higher cost per contact than direct mail or catalogs. Furthermore, many consumers view unsolicited telephone calls as an annoyance and resent unwanted clutter on voice mail. Salespeople often are poorly trained and cannot answer questions. In fact, they may be instructed not to deviate from prearranged scripts regardless of what they are asked.

Automated telemarketing uses machines to dial numbers, play recorded messages, and take orders either via answering machines or by forwarding calls to live operators. Outbound automated calls meet with strong resistance, and the system is better used for incoming calls—that is, consumers are reached by other means and then place orders through the automated systems.

Precise list selection and development are critical for telemarketing. The sales message must be simple and strong. Salespeople must receive at least some training on how to make calls and handle customer concerns. Person-to-person telemarketing is best used in the consumer market with current customers who prefer this mode of communication. In business-to-business markets, especially when targeted at employees outside the purchasing area, telemarketing is not very successful. But some professional buyers prefer it to face-to-face dealings because less time is involved. In the business setting, it is especially important that telemarketers be carefully selected, well trained, and adequately compensated.

Marketing Vocabulary

MAIL-ORDER CATALOG
A collection of product and price information that is published in paper form.

TELEMARKETING
Using the telephone to contact leads (potential customers) from a list.

Print and Broadcast Media Print ads in magazines and newspapers are used a great deal in direct marketing. Along with information on products and prices, toll free numbers are given. For example, Horizon Instruments of Fullerton, California, sells digital engine tachometers and other instrumentation to owners of private planes through ads in leading aviation magazines.

Direct marketers also rely on television and radio spots, usually ranging from 10 to 60 seconds. Exercise equipment from NordicTrack and Bowflex, publications such as *Sporting News* and *Sports Illustrated,* and music CDs are among the products frequently advertised on television. Oreck Corporation of New Orleans uses radio ads to sell vacuum cleaners.

Infomercials are long advertisements that resemble documentaries. They range from 15 to 60 minutes and often include celebrity endorsers and testimonials from satisfied customers. Such products as smoking cessation, weight-control programs, cosmetics, and exercise equipment are promoted this way. Established companies such as Chrysler and Mattel are beginning to use the technique to communicate in depth about product benefits. Some direct marketers use it to obtain distribution in retail stores. For example, Pitchman Billy Mays started selling cleaning products like OxiClean for Orange Glo International on the Home Shopping Network in the 1990s. By 2006, sales were nearly $200 million and Orange Glo products were available at retailers across the country.[44]

Televised Home Shopping In the past several years, home shopping via cable television has come into prominence. The two largest marketers are Quality Value Channel (QVC) and the Home Shopping Network (HSN), with others including the Home Shopping Mall, Teleshop, and Value Club of America. Themed programs are telecast 24 hours a day, seven days a week, to more than 248 million households worldwide. Program hosts, including such celebrities as Suzanne Somers and Tori Spelling, offer products ranging from books to computers, jewelry to lamps, clothing to power tools. Customers send orders over toll-free lines, enabling companies to adjust inventory minute by minute, not just season by season. Orders are usually shipped within 48 hours. In 2007, HSN reported sales of $3 billion and QVC's net sales totaled more than $7 billion. QVC and HSN also have Web sites that allow customers to shop online, track purchases, and chat with other users.[45]

Videotext links a consumer's television with a seller's computerized catalog of products by cable or telephone lines. Consumers can place orders through special keyboard devices. The use of videotext in direct marketing has not yet been successful, partly because the systems are costly to install and are available in only a few markets.

DIRECT-MARKETING DECISIONS

Direct marketers make several decisions when developing a marketing strategy. The most important relate to target markets, database management, merchandise assortment, pricing, choice of media and other channels, message design, and payment methods and delivery. The steps are depicted in Figure 16.5.

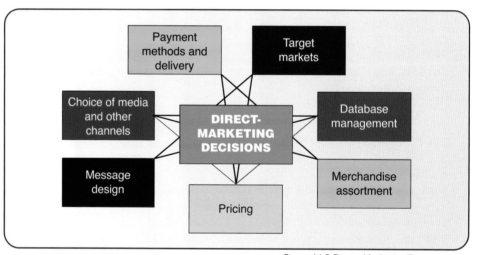

Figure 16.5 Direct-Marketing Decisions

Target Markets Every excellent marketing strategy begins with an understanding of the intended audience, whether baseball hobbyists, newlyweds, cooking buffs, or outdoor enthusiasts. Therefore, the first decision is which customers to target.[46] Many direct marketers are small companies content to serve a narrow group of customers in their home territory. Others expand nationally or globally once a strong business foundation is established. Dell Computer Corporation began in 1983 by serving small and medium-sized businesses in Austin, Texas, that needed upgrades on IBM-compatible computers. Dell branched out to serve large businesses and government agencies throughout the United States in the mid-1980s. Today, Dell has regional business units in all over the world : 10 regional offices in America, 12 regional offices in Asia Pacific, and 41 regional offices in Europe, Middle East and Africa.[47]

Database Management Maintaining a strong customer database is essential. Addresses and preferences must be current. Duplicate names must be removed. Those with poor credit histories must be flagged, and inactive customers must be noted. A record must be kept of those who do not want to be contacted.

Another critical function of a database is tracking. For example a retailer of sports-oriented hats developed a database that tracks individual stores' performances and shows which are falling short of company goals. Because of the stores' limited product line, the company could not afford to overlook missed opportunities for improvement.

Merchandise Assortment   The choice of target markets goes hand in hand with decisions on merchandise assortment. Baseball enthusiasts will be attracted to fantasy baseball camps and memorabilia. Cooking buffs are interested in exotic ingredients and hard-to-get equipment. Companies need to review and adjust the assortment in light of economic trends, competition, and changes in preferences of the target market. Omaha Steaks initially sold beef but responded to the trend toward lower-fat foods by offering seafood, lamb, and chicken. Dell computer, which focused on desktop computers for years, had to add laptops and local area network (LAN) servers when it expanded to many user segments and began selling numerous handheld devices. It has also started to produce storage, appliance severs, and network switches.[48]

Pricing   Direct-marketing companies often follow a low-price strategy, facilitated by their low overhead. Dell, the nation's largest producer of personal computers, ensures that customers receive quality products at low costs by eliminating unnecessary retailers. Customers can purchase custom-built computers directly through the Web site or by calling the company.[49]

In contrast, some companies emphasize merchandise quality and follow a premium price strategy. Brigandi Coin Company in New York City has a strong direct-marketing business in baseball cards, team-signed baseballs, and autographs. It has developed a reputation for selling only the finest-quality, authentic memorabilia. This is important, since fraud is a major problem in the industry. Many collectors will pay Brigandi's high prices because of their confidence in the company.

Media and Channels   Direct-marketing companies normally start with one promotion medium. QVC started with a home television shopping channel. Over time, many branch out to multiple media. Lands' End now uses the Internet as well, and QVC not only has a Web site but also sends out catalogs.

Some direct marketers continue to use traditional channels though they also operate large Internet sites. Omaha steaks has established over 80 company-owned retail stores in 22 states in addition to its Internet-based business, including a Japanese Web site.[50]

Message Design   Whatever medium is used, message design and presentation are most important. For paper-based mail, attention must be paid to the envelope, the cover letter, and the product brochure. Envelopes of standard size and appearance are often discarded unopened, especially when mailing labels are used. An illustration or an important reason for opening the envelope often helps. The cover letter should be short and clear, using bold type to identify key product or service benefits. Brochures must be of high quality in appearance and content.[51]

Catalogs vary in quality of production depending on the company, its merchandise, and its targeted customers. For example, Victoria's Secret sells high-quality lingerie and women's apparel, targeted to an upscale market. Paper, design, and photographs are of high quality. Hello Direct sells telephone productivity tools, such as cordless headsets and speakerphones, to businesses. It emphasizes low prices, and its catalog is produced at low cost.

> **Marketing Vocabulary**
>
> INFOMERCIAL
> A programmatic advertisement of considerable length that resembles a documentary.

Dell Direct Kiosk in Brisbane, Australia

On the Web, the home page must be eye-catching and provide different categories of information the user can access. Sites must be easy to navigate. One rule of thumb is that content should never be more than three clicks away. Getting back to the home page must be simple. One guideline in creating content is to think of how the best salesperson would sell the company and its products. The site must provide a clear overview of the company and why its products are a good buy. Testimonials from satisfied customers are a good idea. Finally, sites must be updated regularly so that users will keep coming back to see what's new.[52] A recent study indicates that the use of lifelike characters, or avatars, can have a significant impact on customers during their online shopping experience. Lifelike characters can engage users and enhance perceptions of social interaction often missed in online

The Marketing Gazette™

CREATING & CAPTURING VALUE THROUGH DIVERSITY

Direct Marketing Association (DMA)

As the leading trade association of business and non-profit organizations around the globe, the Direct Marketing Association (DMA) seeks to advance all forms of direct marketing including mail, email, telephone, radio and television. Originally established in the United States, the DMA is present in 46 other nations. With 3,600 members including the majority of Fortune 100 Companies, their purpose is to advocate industry standards for responsible marketing, promote relevance as the key to reaching consumers with desirable offers, and provide cutting-edge research, education, and networking opportunities to improve results throughout the entire direct marketing process.

For companies, direct marketing is a high priority. According to the DMA, in 2006, commercial and non-profit marketers spent $166.5 billion on direct marketing in the United States. Compared to the total US sales, these advertising expenditures produced $1.93 trillion in incremental sales. Last year, direct marketing accounted for 10.3 percent of total US GDP. There are 1.7 million direct marketing employees today in the US alone, and their collective sales efforts directly support 8.8 million jobs. Each dollar spent on direct marketing yields, on average, a return on investment of $11.65, versus ROI of $5.29 from non-direct marketing expenditures.

Members of the DMA include marketers, vendors and suppliers to the direct marketing community, and nonprofit organizations. Their goal is to maintain long-term consumer and community relationships that are based on fair and highly ethical standards. Peter Johnson, VP-senior economist for research and market intelligence at the DMA stresses the importance of long-term relationships. "Generally speaking, direct marketers have found that you're more likely to get more of your revenue from existing customers," Johnson says. In order to maximize profits, it is an objective of the DMA to obtain loyal customers for their members.

The DMA also emphasizes the importance of cultivating business relationships. Member organizations get unparalleled opportunities to share ideas with the best marketers in the community and connect with their peers through workshops, round-tables and seminars.

DMA's Committee on Environment and Social Responsibility helps companies develop strategies that reduce their impact on the environment. In 2007 it developed the "Recycle Please" logo for use on printed materials, which promotes the recycling of catalogues and direct mail. The logo directs consumers to its www.recylceplease.org website which offers tips and resources for going green. The DMA Board of Directors recently passed a resolution urging members to implement the "Green 15," 15 environmentally friendly practices in areas such as paper use, packaging, and pollution reduction.

shopping, which leads to positive feelings and higher perceptions of value.[53]

Finally, the diversity of a company's customers must be considered when designing direct-marketing messages. A study by Skunkworks of New York said that companies can average a 20 percent increase in sales simply by advertising on Spanish-language network television instead of on English-language broadcast networks. By directly targeting Hispanic communities in ways that appeal to them, companies can increase their sales and increase customer loyalty.[54]

Payment Methods and Delivery Direct-marketing companies serving the consumer market often offer several different payment methods—check, money order, or credit card. Installments also may be possible, especially when the product is relatively expensive, although the final cost to the consumer is greater under that option. Oreck Corporation allows a free trial period of two weeks for its vacuum cleaners.

In business-to-business markets, customers often have an account with the direct marketer, and a monthly bill is sent. Typically, if the invoice is paid within 10 days, a 2 percent credit will be applied to the next bill. Payment is normally due within 30 days.

Customers usually have several delivery options. The standard mode at Sharper Image is Federal Express second-day air; the delivery charge is based on the dollar value of the order. For an extra fee, customers can select next-day air or Saturday delivery. Eddie Bauer offers standard delivery (3 to 5 days), express (3 days), or express plus (2 days) at progressively higher charges.

ETHICS IN DIRECT MARKETING

There are a number of ethical problems that confront direct marketers and consumers, including important issues involving fraud, the right to privacy and confidentiality of personal information. Misrepresentation happens often. For example, contests and sweepstakes are sometimes worded so people believe they have won a prize only to find out that their call to a 900 number has rung up a big bill with no prize in sight. In other cases, products are misrepresented or sales are made and shipments don't occur. Every time you enter a sweepstakes, buy a magazine subscription or register you name online, chances are your name goes into a database that could be

Pepsi's homepage is eye-catching and easily navigated.

accessed by many organizations. In some cases these data bases have been stolen and fall into the hands of people interested in identity theft. All of these ethical issues, make it difficult for legitimate direct marketers and consumers. Consequently, the Direct Marketing Association has developed a rigorous set of guidelines for ethical business practice. If you read the guidelines in total, you will probable recognize many situations where someone has tried to use direct mail to violate your rights. The guidelines provide 53 articles that should be followed. Figure 16.6 shows some ethical guidelines.

Additional ethical guidelines fall in the following categories:

- Advance Consent Marketing -- guidance for credit card usage, advance payments, reminders, refunds, etc.
- Marketing to Children – suitable communications, parental involvement, information from and about children, marketing by age (ie, under 13),
- Special Offers and Claims – the meaning of free, price comparisons, and guarantees
- Use of Test or Survey Data -- valid, reliable including source and methods
- Sweepstakes -- prizes awarded by chance (no skill required) without participants rendering anything (including no purchase required), can't represent that the participant has already won, clear representation of prizes vs. premiums, and disclosure of all of the rules
- Fulfillment – no shipments without permission, product availability and free test periods
- Collection, Use and Maintenance of Marketing Data – consumer must be told if their information will be rented, sold or exchanged, upon request by individual provided with source of data, confidential maintenance of data, health related data use guidelines, promotion and sale of lists, who in the firm sees and uses data, and information security
- Online Marketing – notice of online listeners, honoring time of contact, online access for problems, online data security, age restrictions, accountability procedures, commercial e-mail

THE TERMS OF THE OFFER

HONESTY AND CLARITY OF OFFER: All offers should be clear, honest, and complete. Before publication of an offer, marketers should be prepared to substantiate any claims or offers made. Claims that are untrue, misleading, deceptive, or fraudulent should not be used.

ACCURACY, CONSISTENCY AND CLARITY: Simple and consistent statements or representations of all the essential points of the offer should appear in the promotinal material. Representations which, by their size, placement, duration, or other characteristics are unlikely to be noticed or are difficult to understand should not be used.

ACTUAL CONDITIONS: All descriptions, promises, and claims of limitation should be in accordance with actual conditions, situations, and circumstances existing at the time of the promotion.

DISPARAGEMENT: Disparagement of any person or group on grounds addressed by federal or state laws that prohibit discrimination is unacceptable.

DECENCY: Solicitations should not be sent to consumers who have indicated to the marketer that they consider those solicitations to be vulgar, immoral, profane, pornographic, or offensive in any way and who do not want to receive them.

PHOTOGRAPHS AND ART WORK: Photographs, illustrations, artwork, and the situations they describe should be accurate portrayals and current reproductions of the products, services, or other subjects they represent.

DISCLOSURE OF SPONSOR AND INTENT: All marketing contacts should disclose the name of the sponsor and each purpose of the contract. No one should make offers or solicitations in the guise of one purpose when the intent is a different purpose.

ACCESSIBILITY: Every offer should clearly identify the marketer's name and street address or telephone number, or both, at which the individual may obtain service. If an offer is made online, the marketer should provide its name, an Internet-based contact mechanism, and a street address. For e-mail solicitations, marketers should comply with Article #38 (Commercial Solicitations Online).

SOLICITATION IN THE GUISE OF AN INVOICE OR GOVERNMENTAL

NOTIFICATION: Offers that are likely to be mistaken for bills, invoices, or notices from public utilities or governmental agencies should not be used.

POSTAGE, SHIPPING, OR HANDLING CHARGES: Postage, shipping, or handling charges, if any, should bear a reasonable relationship to actual costs incurred.

Figure 16.6 Summary of Direct Marketing Association Guidelines for Ethical Conduct
Source: "Terms of the Offer," Direct Marketing Association

solicitation restrictions and information required, e-mail authentication, use and installation of software on others computers, getting online leads from people, appending e-mails to consumer records

- Telephone Marketing – calling during reasonable hours, taping only with notice (and a beeping device), not calling unlisted numbers, interfacing with caller-id, limited ring time on automated dialing equipment, diary of call success, appropriate use or prerecorded voice messaging so consumers can gain feedback, use of Facsimile machines, promotion with toll free and pay-per-call numbers, disclosures, fundraising and compliance with all laws.[55]

WHOLESALING

Wholesaling affects our lives every day, but we rarely notice. We may buy aspirin at Good Neighbor retail pharmacies, not knowing it was purchased from Bergen Brunswig Corporation, a large pharmaceutical wholesaler. We order a pepperoni pizza at a small neighborhood restaurant, not knowing most of the ingredients were acquired from SYSCO, a large wholesaler of food products, or FoodGalaxy.com, a new Web marketplace that allows independent restaurants and other food distributors to buy their supplies online.[56] ToyDirectory.com, Inc. provides a web service that helps 26,500 retail stores access toys from 2,200 toy importers (wholesalers) and manufacturers. One reason parents and kids can find a broad range of toys at many price points including the latest dolls or Spiderman miniatures, is because organizations like ToyDirectory.com or WholesaleCentral.com, a business-to-business service, provide information for retailers about the vast number of toy wholesalers.[57] Most of us never see these intermediaries, but they are very important to us. **Wholesaling** is selling goods for resale or use to retailers and other businesses. Producers have a number of options in making sales to retailers and other businesses, including company-owned sales branches, brokers, and wholesalers.

Many wholesalers are relatively small, filling a certain niche. Others are multibillion-dollar companies serving global markets. Wholesalers help thousands of companies connect with millions of customers. Whatever their size or scope, they all face competition. Their ability to make decisions about target markets, service level, pricing, business locations, merchandise assortment, credit management, use of technology, and image will influence their survival.

A wholesaler is an intermediary that takes title to the products it carries and makes a majority of sales to retailers or other businesses. Many wholesalers make no sales directly to consumers. For others, these sales may be a significant part of revenue. For example, Smart and Final, Inc., sells food products and related merchandise to small businesses and to some consumers. Since more than half of its sales come from small businesses, it is classified as a wholesaler. A pure wholesaler organization does not manufacture any goods. Only firms that sell goods they purchase from manufacturers or other intermediaries are considered part of wholesale trade. As a marketing ploy, many retailers that sell mostly to the general public present themselves as wholesalers. For example, "wholesale" price clubs, factory outlets, and other organizations are retail establishments, even though they sell their good to the public at wholesale prices.[58]

For wholesalers of consumer goods, the primary customers are retailers and service businesses, such as restaurants, hospitals, and nursing homes. In business-to-business markets, the primary customers are manufacturing organizations and service firms, such as accountants or contractors.

THE IMPORTANCE OF WHOLESALERS

Wholesalers play an important role in the economy. The roughly 375,000 such organizations in the United States employ approximately six million people. Annual sales approach $2 trillion.[59] Wholesalers are prominent in a wide variety of product categories, including beverages, climate control equipment, computer hardware and software, electrical products, electronic components, fabrics, flowers and florist supplies, food, giftware, medical supplies, movies, pharmaceuticals, telecommunications, tools, and toys. They provide value to customers and suppliers, as depicted in Figure 16.7. We will also see that they provide value for one another.

able in amounts that can be afforded and handled effectively.

Wholesalers also perform other functions, depending on customer needs. They may provide credit, education on product benefits, training in product use, and technical assistance. Hamilton-Hallmark recently opened a Technical Support Center staffed by electrical engineers, near Phoenix. Customers call an 800 number if they have questions about specific applications for semiconductors.[60]

Wholesalers are needed because small or medium-sized companies in many industries cannot buy directly from manufacturers. Either direct channels are unavailable or minimum orders are too large. For example, approximately 100,000 original equipment manufacturers (OEMs) in the United States purchase semiconductors to incorporate into products such as automobiles, computers, televisions, and videocassette recorders. Roughly 96,000 of these buy from wholesalers such as Arrow Electronics, Hamilton-Hallmark, and Wyle Laboratories because manufacturers cannot afford to serve them directly.[61]

Some believe that wholesalers only add to the price of goods. Actually, their price is lower than what individual manufacturers would have to charge on most orders if they were made directly. Wholesalers get a discount for buying in quantity, and part of that is passed on to consumers. Furthermore, overhead is normally lower for wholesalers than for manufacturers. Therefore, wholesalers can serve small or medium-sized companies and still make a profit, whereas most manufacturers cannot.

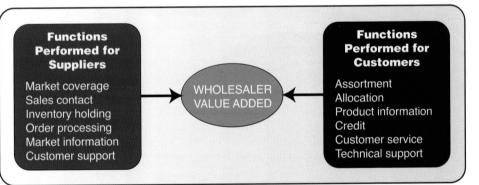

Figure 16.7 Wholesalers Add Value for Suppliers and Customers by Performing Important Channel Functions
Source: Adapted from Bert Rosenbloom, Marketing Functions and the Wholesaler-Distributor (Washington, DC: Distribution Research and Educational Foundation, 1987) p. 26.

Wholesalers are important for product assortment and allocation. They fulfill their **assortment** function by purchasing merchandise from a variety of suppliers for resale. This makes a range of products available in one place for the convenience of customers. They fulfill their **allocation** function by purchasing large quantities to resell in smaller amounts. This means savings for customers in both purchase price and storage costs. In essence, wholesalers make a wide variety of goods avail-

Wholesalers often do business with one another. Sometimes this is just a matter of courtesy. A wholesaler may need a Black & Decker power drill for an important customer and can get it most quickly by calling a nearby wholesaler. In other cases, the transactions are systematic. Small wholesalers may find it easier to do business with large wholesalers than with manufacturers. As a result, in a number of industries other wholesalers are a primary target market.

Master distributors are wholesaling companies given the right by manufacturers to develop certain geographical areas and recruit other distributors. These, in turn, are called subdistributors. All sales to subdistributors go through the master distributor. The system is often used by manufacturers entering a global market, especially if they lack the resources to serve it directly.

TYPES OF WHOLESALERS

Full-service wholesalers perform a wide range of tasks for their customers. **Limited-service wholesalers** provide only some of the traditional channel functions, either eliminating others entirely or passing them on to someone else to perform. Within each category, several types of wholesalers can be identified. Figure 16.8 summarizes the functions performed by different types of wholesalers.

Rack jobbers set up product displays for Krispy Kreme and keep them stocked with goods.

Full-Service Wholesalers

General Line Wholesalers General line wholesalers carry a wide variety of products and provide a full range of services. Bosler Supply of Chicago and W. W. Grainger are good examples. They stock thousands of different industrial products, provide technical advice on product applications, and expedite shipments when necessary. Another example is SYSCO, which sells a broad array of frozen, dry, and refrigerated products to the food industry. It can provide special packaging and delivery schedules. Its cruise ship customers, for example, can receive plastic-wrapped pallets of food at any time of day or night.

Specialty Wholesalers Specialty wholesalers focus on a narrow range of products, carry them in great depth, and provide extensive services. Ryerson is the

www.sysco.com

Visit the SYSCO Web site to learn more about the largest marketer and distributor of food service products in North America. Also learn how the company is making its warehouses and distribution centers green.

largest metals wholesaler in the world, with 50 distribution centers across the United States. It performs a variety of specialized services for customers, such as cutting metals to specification. Ingram-Micro and Tech Data focus on computer hardware and software products, while providing many customer services.

Rack Jobbers Rack jobbers, who sell single product lines to retail stores on consignment, set up product displays and keep them stocked with goods. Retailers pay for the goods only after they are sold to consumers. Krispy Kreme doughnuts are distributed this way. Rack jobbers are common in the music industry. They have had to take back new albums with offensive language. For example, Wal-Mart learned that one of the singer's lyric suggesting that it sold guns to children and pulled the album from the shelves. These days, in Wal-Mart and Sam's club, HDTV is one of the most common products who use the rack jobbers.[62]

Type of Wholesaler	Personal Selling	Carry Inventory	Product Delivery	Offer Credit	Specialized Services
Full Service					
General line	yes	yes	yes	yes	yes
Specialty	yes	yes	yes	yes	yes
Rack jobbers	yes	yes	yes	yes	yes
Limited Service					
Cash and carry	yes	yes	no	no	no
Drop shippers	yes	no	no	yes	no
Truck jobbers	yes	yes	yes	no	no
Mail order	no	yes	no	sometimes	no

Figure 16.8 Functions Performed by Different Wholesalers

Marketing Vocabulary

FULL-SERVICE WHOLESALER
An intermediary who performs a wide range of functions or tasks for its customers.

LIMITED-SERVICE WHOLESALER
An intermediary who performs only some of the traditional channel functions, either eliminating others or passing them on to someone else.

Limited-Service Wholesalers

Cash-and-Carry Wholesalers
Cash-and-carry wholesalers are located near customers. They do not extend credit and do not use an outside sales force. Customers perform certain functions for themselves, such as bagging their own goods and delivery. Costs are tightly controlled in order to offer excellent prices.

Drop Shippers Drop shippers arrange for shipments directly from the manufacturer to the customer. They do not physically handle the goods but take title to them, assuming all associated risks (such as damage and theft) while in transit. They do offer credit terms. Drop shippers are prominent in the lumber, chemicals, and petroleum industries, where goods are bulky and sold in large quantity.

Truck Jobbers Truck jobbers specialize in the speedy delivery of perishables or semiperishables, such as candy, bakery goods, fresh fruits, potato chips, and tobacco products. They use their own vehicles and offer virtually all services except credit. They focus on smaller cus-

tomers that full-service wholesalers tend to ignore.

Mail-Order Wholesalers Mail-order wholesalers sell through catalogs distributed to retailers and other businesses. They are most popular among small businesses in outlying areas that are not regularly contacted by salespeople. These wholesalers are prominent in the clothing, cosmetics, hardware, office supply, jewelry, sporting goods, and specialty food industries.

WHOLESALING RELATIONSHIPS

Wholesalers are successful to the extent they develop strong customer loyalty. Sometimes relationships with other wholesalers are used to serve their customers. For example, W. W. Grainger has developed alliances with a number of specialty wholesalers. The relationships feature explains Grainger's program and the special efforts of its internal sourcing group to satisfy customer needs.

Developing strong connections with suppliers is also important to more effective and efficient business operations. Southwestern Supply, an industrial products wholesaler in Las Vegas, and Milwaukee Electric Tool, a manufacturer of portable power tools, have developed an outstanding working relationship. Southwestern relies on Milwaukee to develop annual business plans, identify potential customers, develop new marketing strategies, and train its sales force. In exchange, Southwestern employees promote Milwaukee over other brands car-

Web and E-commerce Stars
IKEA - www.ikea.com

IKEA provides a wide range of well-designed, functional home furnishing products at retail stores around the world at low-prices. As indicated in its company vision, it strives to create a better everyday life for over six decades. You can shop IKEA's vast assortment of products in three ways; online, catalog, and massive brick-and-mortar stores. Through its expansive Web site, products are searchable through well organized categories and its exceptional design makes the shopping experience enjoyable for even first-time visitors. It also offers tips and ideas to design, furnish and decorate your house fashionably.

ried by the company.[63]

The decision to add new suppliers can sometimes alienate current partners. For example, when the Atlanta-based Apex Supply Co. was acquired by Home Depot, Grohe America terminated all sales relationships with Apex Supply. Grohe only sells to wholesalers; when it was bought by Home Depot, Apex no longer fit Grohe's preferred customer base.[64] In such a situation, the wholesaler must weigh the pros and cons to determine which supplier is a better match for the future.

Chapter Summary:

Objective 1: Appreciate the important role retailers play in our economy and society.

Retailing is the final stage in the distribution channel for a majority of products sold to consumers. Time, place, possession, and form utilities are provided to consumers by retailers. In addition, retailers may promote the general welfare of society through efforts to recruit a diverse workforce. A number of U.S. retailers have been very successful in global markets by understanding important variations in consumer tastes across cultures.

Objective 2: Understand strategy issues confronted by retailers when making marketing decisions.

Retailing strategy must cover a variety of issues. Each retailer must decide on the target market(s) and positioning, then adopt a distinct service level and pricing approach, and decide what type of merchandise assortment it will offer. The geographical location of stores is a very important decision. Some retailers locate stores in low-rent areas off highways and at a distance from other retailers, whereas others place stores close to competitors. Well-run shopping centers have immense pulling power and are good locations for many retailers. New technologies, such as sophisticated computer systems that allow merchandise to be tailored in individual stores, help improve retailer performance. Furthermore, effectively managing relationships with suppliers—whether manufacturers, wholesalers, or agents—is critical.

Objective 3: Recognize the diverse array of retailers that compete with one another.

Limited-line retailers include specialty stores, superstores, and automated vending operations. General merchandise retailers include department stores, convenience stores, supermarkets, warehouse clubs, discount stores, variety stores, and hypermarkets. An understanding of each type is useful in tracking and predicting competitive trends. A number of successful retailers have stores of different types.

Objective 4: Learn what direct marketing entails, its value, and how it differs from mass communication.

Direct marketing is a powerful selling approach, especially when media are used to communicate information on products and prices and how to place orders. Growth in sales through direct-marketing channels is outpacing growth in U.S. retail sales by about two to one. Direct marketing offers consumers and businesses a convenient way to shop. It enables many small companies to access markets they could not reach through traditional retail and wholesale organizations. It is popular in many parts of the world. In fact, the largest direct-marketing companies are based in foreign countries. International direct-marketers must adjust their strategies to the unique characteristics of each country they serve.

Objective 5: Be familiar with the different types of direct-response media.

A large number of direct-response media are available. Paper-based mail, fax mail, e-mail, and voice mail are options. Mail-order catalogs are used by many companies, and electronic versions are gaining popularity. Telemarketing is a major force, especially in business-to-business markets. Advertisements in print and broadcast media are important in direct-marketing activities. Infomercials can be used effectively to sell products and gain distribution through retailers. Television shopping channels have done well. The Internet is an intriguing medium still in its infancy. Each medium has its strengths and weaknesses that must be considered by companies choosing which one or which mix to use.

Objective 6: Understand the marketing decisions made by direct-marketing companies.

Direct marketers make a number of decisions when developing a marketing strategy. They must carefully select the target market(s). Strong customer databases must be developed and maintained. In particular, direct marketers can put database marketing to great use. Decisions on target markets go hand in hand with merchandise assortment and pricing. Multiple direct-response media should be used with great attention paid to the content of messages in each medium. Each medium has unique challenges with regard to message content. Finally, payment methods and delivery options must be selected.

Review Your Understanding

1. What is retailing? What is a retailer? List two reasons retailers are important.
2. What are the steps in developing a retail strategy?
3. What is a markup? Markdown?
4. What are the four types of limited-line retailers? What are the seven types of general merchandise retailers?
5. List three ethical issues in retailing.
6. What is direct marketing?
7. List several ways direct marketing provides value to customers.
8. List several media used in direct marketing.
9. List the seven decisions direct marketers make when developing a marketing strategy.
10. What are two ethical problems in the direct-marketing industry? Briefly explain each.

Discussion of Concepts

1. Explain the Pathways to Independence program of Marriott International, Inc. What are its main benefits?
2. Is following a hybrid strategy on service and price more difficult for a retailer than either a discount-oriented or service-oriented strategy? Explain.
3. What are the pros and cons of following a destination location strategy? Under what conditions would locating stores close to the competition be preferable?
4. Among the various types of limited-line and general merchandise retailers, which have the strongest competitive position? Why?
5. Some experts view electronic shopping over the Internet as a major threat to retailers. Do you agree or disagree?
6. What are the major reasons for the growing importance of direct marketing in the United States?
7. What are the pros and cons of using fax mail, e-mail, and voice mail? Would you recommend their use to a direct-marketing company? Why or why not?
8. What are infomercials? Can they be misused? How?
9. Explain how effective database management can improve the performance of a direct marketing company.
10. Are the efforts of the Direct Marketing Association to promote ethics among its members worthwhile? What else can be done to encourage ethical behavior in the industry?

Key Terms And Definitions

Allocation: A wholesaler function that entails purchasing products in large quantities and reselling them in smaller quantities.

Assortment: A wholesaler function that entails selling a range of merchandise from a variety of sources.

Automated vending: The use of machinery operated by coins or credit cards to dispense goods.

Catalog showroom: A discount retailer whose customers shop from catalogs and can view floor samples of items held in stock.

Chain store: One of a group of centrally owned and managed retail stores that handle the same product lines.

Convenience store: A small retailer with moderately low breadth and depth of merchandise.

Department store: A retailer with merchandise of broad variety and moderate depth and with a relatively high level of customer service.

Direct marketing: The use of various communication media to interact directly with customers and generally calling for them to make a direct response.

Discount store: A retailer offering a broad variety of merchandise, limited service, and low prices.

Full-service wholesaler: An intermediary who performs a wide range of functions or tasks for its customers.

Hypermarket: A giant shopping facility with a wide selection of food and general merchandise at low prices.

Infomercial: A programmatic advertisement of considerable length that resembles a documentary.

Limited-service wholesaler: An intermediary who performs only some of the traditional channel functions, either eliminating others or passing them on to someone else.

Mail-order catalog: A collection of product and price information that is published in paper form.

Markdown: A reduction from the original retail selling price of a product.

Markup: The amount added to the cost of acquiring a product that determines its retail selling price.

Off-price retailer: A seller of brand-name clothing at low prices.

Retailing: The activities involved in selling products and services directly to end users for personal or household use.

Scrambled merchandising: A retail strategy that entails carrying an array of product lines that seem to be unrelated.

Specialty store: A retailer offering merchandise in one primary product category in considerable depth.

Supermarket: A large, departmentalized, food-oriented retail establishment that sells beverages, canned goods, dairy products, frozen foods, meat, produce, and such nonfood items as health and beauty aids, kitchen utensils, magazines, pharmaceuticals, and toys.

Superstore: A retailer that focuses on a single product category but offers a huge selection and low prices; also called a category killer.

Telemarketing: Using the telephone to contact leads (potential customers) from a list.

Variety store: A retailer offering a variety of low-priced merchandise of low to moderate quality.

Warehouse club: A large, no-frills store that carries a revolving array of merchandise at low prices.

Wheel of retailing: A descriptive theory about how retailers emerge, evolve, and sometimes fade away.

References

1. IKEA Group Stores, www.ikea-group.ikea.com; IKEA Social & Environmental Responsibility, www.ikea.com; www.hoovers.com; www.businessweek.com/magazine/content/05_46/b3959001.htm, sites visited May 05, 2008;
2. "A space ride for Christmas," December. 04, 2006, CNNMoney.com, site visited March 12, 2008.
3. www.dmnews.com/CMS/dm-news/catalog-retail/35345.html, site visited March 12, 2008.
4. Rajkumar Venkatesan, V. Kumar, & Nalini Ravishanker, "Multichannel Shopping: Causes and Consequences," Journal of Marketing, Vol. 70, No. 2, April, 2006.
5. www.retailindustry.about.com/od/abouttheretailindustry/p/retail_industry.htm, site visited March 17, 2008.
6. CNW Group, "For the First Time Wal-Mart Canada Stores Add Authentic Merchandise to Help Asian Customers Ring in the New Year," February 4, 2008, www.newswire.ca/en/releases/archive/February2008/04/c6692.html, visited March 17, 2008.

7. Borders 2006 Annual Report, www.bordersgroupinc.com, site visited June 22, 2007.
8. "Store Brands Achieving New Heights of Customer Popularity and Growth", Private Label Manufacturers Association, http://plma.com/storeBrands/sbt07.html, site visited March 17, 2008.
9. Not Your Father's Store Brand David Phillips. Dairy Foods. Troy: Jun 2006. Vol.107, Iss. 6; pg. 8, 1 pgs viewed June 22, 2007
10. Lien Laney, Bar "How Bus Cycles Continue..." Journal of Marketing, January, 2007, Vol. 71, Number 1, p1-15.
11. Bolotsky and Fassler, Hard Goods Specialty Retailing, pp. 2–4.
12. Levy and Weitz, Retailing Management, p. 258.
13. Patrick Reilly, "Where Borders Group and Barnes & Noble Compete, It's a War," Wall Street Journal, September 3, 1996, pp. A1, A6.
14. "Mall of America to Double in Size", March 22, 2007 - Chicago Sun Times.
15. More challenges from Wal-Mart.(management of Wal-Mart Stores Inc)(Brief article); Advertising Age 77.17 (April 24, 2006): p18. From InfoTrac OneFile. Viewed June 22, 2007.
16. John Cortez, "Kmart Unleashes Its Category Killer Chains," Advertising Age, February 1, 1993, pp. S4, S5.
17. www.japan-guide.com/e/e2010.html, site visited March 17, 2008.
18. Robert J. Frank, Elizabeth A Mihas, Laxmar Norasimlar, and Stacry Rant, "Competing in a Value Driven World", McKinsey & Company Report, February, 2003.
19. Levy and Weitz, Retailing Management, p. 40.
20. 2006 U.S. Industry & Market Outlook by Barnes Reports
21. Stern, El-Ansary, and Coughlan, Marketing Channels, p. 43.
22. Walter Levy, "Are Department Stores Doomed?" Direct Marketing, May 1991, pp. 56–60.
23. Joyce Smith and Knight Ridder, "Chain stores change focus," Tribune Business News, Washington, pg. 1, April 8, 2006.
24. Laurel Wentz, "Expect More Growth in '07," Advertising Age. (Midwest region edition). Chicago, Vol.78, Iss. 17; pg. S1, 2 pgs, April 23, 2007.
25. Bill Marriott, "Marriott on the Move – Pathways to Independence," www.blogs.marriott.com/default.asp?item=509040, site visited March 17, 2008.
26. California Department of Insurance - Press Release, July 20, 2005.
27. George White and Myron Levin, "Target Stores to Stop Selling Cigarettes," Los Angeles Times, August 29, 1996, pp. A1, A28.
28. Jules Steinberg, "Worker Performance Reviews Can Be a Two-Way Street," Twice, September 4, 2000, p. 28.
29. Elizabeth Woyke, "Hipster Appeal, Mall Prices; In a bid to be No. 1 globally, Japan's top retailer opens a flagship Uniqlo store in Manhattan," Business Week, New York., Iss. 4021; pg. 68, February 12, 2007
30. India, China shine bright on global retail majors' radar, Knight Ridder Tribune Business News. Washington, pg. 1, March 12, 2007
31. Katherine Bowers, "Wal-Mart Acquisition Builds China Presence," WWD, New York, Vol.193, Iss. 44; pg. 4, February 28, 2007
32. Expect new stores as firms go global, Sue Stock and Nichole Monroe Bell. Knight Ridder Tribune Business News. Washington: Dec 31, 2006. pg. 1.
33. "U.S. Direct Marketing Today," Direct Marketing Association, New York, New York, 2006, p. 6.
34. Ibid.
35. Ibid.
36. www.calyxandcorolla.com, site visited March 17, 2008.
37. Hoover's Company Records, Jun 15, 2007, p. 99161; "Access Innovations Enhances Thesaurus Master," Information Today, Jul/Aug 2005, 22(7), p.38
38. Robert Gary, "Targeted, Personal, Effective," Marketing, Mar 7, 2007, p.39
39. Michael Fielding, "Direct mail still has its place; Marketers find it works best as part of integrated campaigns," American Marketing Association, Direct marketing; Pg. 31, November 1, 2006.
40. "Direct Mailings Still Welcome on The Mat," Precision Marketing, Jan 12, 2007, p.9
41. Hayley Pinkerfield, "Broadband Fuelling Online Shopping Boom," Revolution, May 2007, p.27
42. Hillie Mummert, "Media Usage Forecast 2007," Target Marketing, Mar 2007, 30(3), p.42-48
43. "Rare Philosophy," Marketing Management, Summer 1995, pp. 4–6; www.omahasteaks.com, site visited March 17, 2008.
44. Business Wire, "Church & Dwight to Acquire Orange Glo International for $325 Million Brands Include OxiClean, Orange Glo and Kaboom Products," July, 17, 2006.
45. www.qvc.com/qic/qvcapp.aspx/main.html, site visited June 22, 2007; www.hsn.com/corp/info/, site visited March 19, 2008.
46. Robert Stone, Successful Direct Marketing Methods (Lincolnwood, IL: NTC Business Books, 1994).
47. www.dell.com, site visited June 22, 2007
48. Ibid.
49. Ibid.
50. www.omahasteaks.com, site visited March 19, 2008.
51. Stone, Successful Direct Marketing Methods.
52. Judson, NetMarketing.
53. Liz C. Wang, Julie Baker, Judy Wagner, & Kirk Wakefield, "Can a Retail Web Site Be Social?," Journal of Marketing, Vol. 71. No. 3, July, 2007.
54. Dwight Cunningham, "One Size Does Not Fit All," Media Week, November 15, 1999, p. 54.
55. Summarized from: "Direct Marketing Association's Guidelines for Ethical Business Practice," Direct Marketing Association, New York, September, 2006.
56. www.foodgalaxy.com, site visited March 19, 2008.
57. www.toydirectory.com; www.wholesalecentral.com, sites visited March 19, 2008.
58. Bureau of Labor Statistics, U.S. Department of Labor, Career Guide to Industries, 2006-07 Edition, Wholesale Trade, www.bls.gov/, site visited April 14, 2007.
59. Ibid.
60. Based on consulting experience in the computer industry.
61. Ibid.
62. Brent Felgner, "Wal-Mart testing various new CE Initiatives", June 18, 2007, p 4
63. "Quality . . . A Critical Part of a Successful Distributor Partnership," Today's Distributor, June 1995, pp. 4–5.
64. Pat Lenius, "Grohe Stops Selling to Apex After Home Depot Acquisition," Contractor, June 2000, p. 3.

The Marketing Gazette
www.dma.org, site visited June 29, 2007; Carol Krol, "DMA: Direct response gets larger share of b-to-b marketing." (News)(Report). B to B 92.6 (May 7, 2007): p3. From InfoTrac OneFile.

CASE 16

Costco Wholesale Corporation

Low prices and quality products have made Costco Wholesale Corporation the top wholesaler in the United States. The company, which was founded in 1983 by Jim Sinegal and Jeffrey Brotman, has nearly 500 wholesale stores in 40 states. With nearly 50 million members, it has grown to become the fourth largest retailer in the United States. Costco also has operations internationally including 6 countries with plans to expand.

Costco's membership only policy with emphasis on customer satisfaction has led to strong customer loyalty. Customers can buy anything from name-brand handbags to electronics, clothing and fine wines. The company believes that its members love to shop there because they can get unmatched quality and value. Costco experiences a remarkable 87 percent member renewal rate, indicative of the high level of customer satisfaction it provides.

Costco is able to execute its effective wholesaling strategy in part due to its ability to buy merchandise directly from manufacturers. The company buys bulk shipments and routes them either directly to the warehouses or to a cross-docking facility where the products are allocated to an individual warehouse. This has given the wholesaler the capability to maximize freight volume and handling efficiencies which leads to the elimination of costs associated with multiple step distribution channels. A lower cost in the distribution channels means lower costs for customers.

Costco's merchandise assortment policy is also a source of effective wholesaling. The company offers a limited selection of products in a wide range of categories at consistently lower prices to its customers. The merchandise assortment is designed to produce high sales volumes and rapid inventory turnover. Costco will limit items in a given product line to fast-selling models, sizes and colors. Each warehouse only carries an average of 4,000 products, compared to 40,000 found in the average retailer. When combined with the operating efficiencies achieved by volume purchasing, efficient distribution and self-service warehouse facilities, this merchandise assortment strategy permits the company to operate profitably while offering significantly lower prices to its customers.

Costco's expansion into groceries has led the company to become the third-largest grocer in the United States. Grocery products accounted for nearly half of all sales in Costco stores in 2007. In the produce department alone, Costco sold an astonishing 100 million pounds of grapes and $100 million in fresh blueberries. This success has motivated Costco to increase its premium private label, Kirkland Signature, from 330 products to nearly 500 products by 2011 which includes organic product offerings. The Kirkland Signature brand offers organic products such as cereal, peanut butter and olive oil. The brand plans to expand to offer a greater number of organic fresh fruits and vegetables.

Expanding its product line is not the only changes Costco is undergoing. At a 2008 annual shareholder meeting, CEO Jim Sinegal announced the company is making a concerted effort to minimize its carbon footprint. Many Costco Warehouses are getting a facelift with new skylights and solar panels. The company is also making small changes that have a big impact. Simply converting from round to rectangular tubs of cashews saved the company 400 truckloads annually because they can be stacked more efficiently. "We recognize, like all businesses, that we must continue to conserve and save the planet," Singeal said. "This is not something that's just nice to do anymore. It's imperative."

1. *How does Costco Wholesaling Corporation engage in the important wholesaling activities of assortment and allocation?*
2. *What type of wholesaling relationships has Costco established to help develop strong customer loyalty?*

Sources: "Martha Stewart Living Omnimedia Introduces 'Kirkland Signature Martha Stewart' Prepared Food Program," PR Newswire, New York: Dec 7, 2007; Costco Wholesale Corporation 2007 Annual Report, www.costco.com, site visited January 28, 2008

Pricing Strategies

Pricing strategies and objectives are methods in which marketers capture value. An organization's ability to capture value is built upon its proficiency in executing the previous concepts of marketing covered in this book. The following chapters are included in this section:

Chapter 17   Pricing Objectives & Influences
Chapter 18   Pricing Strategies

CHAPTER 17

Pricing Objectives & Influences

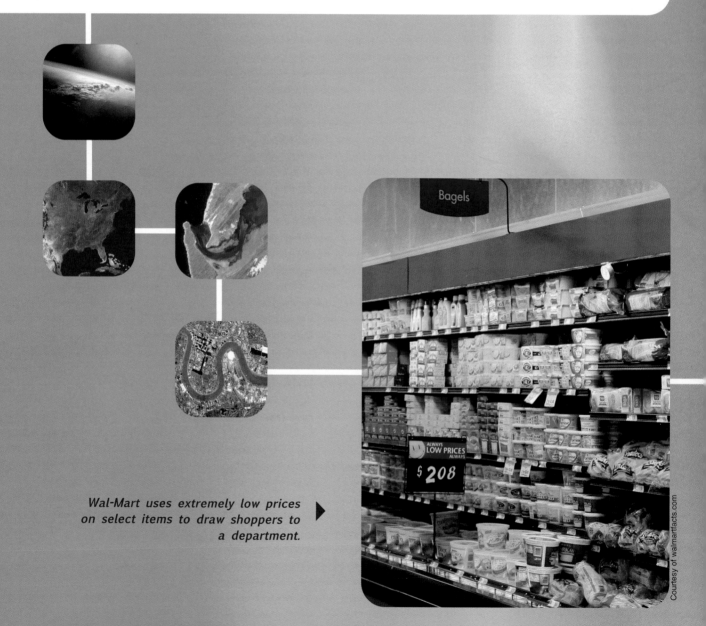

Wal-Mart uses extremely low prices on select items to draw shoppers to a department. ▶

Courtesy of walmartfacts.com

Learning Objectives

1. Describe how pricing works with the other parts of the marketing mix.

2. Learn how economic factors such as demand and supply influence prices.

3. Understand the legal and ethical constraints on pricing decisions.

4. Use industry structure concepts to understand how competitors in different types of industries price.

5. Use competitive factors surrounding industry structure concepts to understand how pricing works in different types of industries.

6. Recognize the conditions that make international pricing complex.

"Always low prices" has made Wal-Mart the leader of the discount chain and supermarket world. As the nation's biggest retailer, Wal-Mart has 6,000 global suppliers, 15 billion imports per year, and 127 million Americans shop for 120,000 items in a Wal-Mart store each week. Wal-Mart has more than 1.9 million employees worldwide and over 7,000 stores and wholesale clubs across 14 countries.

What matters most to Wal-Mart? Prices! Wal-Mart uses the buy-cheap, sell-for-less strategy to generate a profitable business serving price-sensitive consumers, and makes profit on high volume and fast turnover. Over the years, Wal-Mart continues to build on its pricing strategy through its world leadership in logistics. It revolutionized how goods are produced by creating a shift from a "push production" model in which the manufacturer decides what it's going to produce and then attempts to get retailers to buy and sell it, to a "pull production" model where retailers collect information on what is being sold and then tell manufacturers what and when to produce. Wal-Mart reversed a 100 year history that had the retailer dependent on the manufacturer, and dramatically changed the balance of power in the business world. Now the retailer is the center, the power, while the manufacturer becomes the subordinate who has to do the bidding of the retailers.

Another key pricing strategy Wal-Mart utilizes is opening price point. It's the lowest price that Wal-Mart showcases in special displays, usually along the aisles. Wal-Mart puts tremendous amount of planning, organization, and thinking into what their opening price point is going to be based on their last year's sales and customer requests. "The opening price points are clearly the foundations of who we are and how we interact with our customers," said Ray Bracy, Wal-Mart Vice President. "We think they need tap the best product, best value, and the best price we can achieve." Every line of goods has an alluring and unbeatable "opening price point" item – whether TV sets or bathing suits. The low price functioned to catch the consumer's eye and create the perception of value across the higher price points further up the aisle. When customers go to that department, they will find and buy what they really want, which however may be not the lowest price in town.

Prices are not the only thing that matters to Wal-Mart. The retail giant has also become a leader in environmental sustainability initiatives. The company believes that merchandise should be both affordable and sustainable. As a result, it has set goals such as selling 100 million energy efficient compact fluorescent light bulbs in the United States during 2008. Wal-Mart has also issued a packaging reduction goal of 5 percent to all it's suppliers by the year 2013. This goal would reduce waste and remove nearly 213,000 trucks from the road. Lastly, Wal-Mart's sustainability efforts have carried over to the store floor. The company has adopted a state-of-the-art daylight harvesting systems that relies on hundreds of rooftop skylights connected to sensors. The sales floor lighting changes based on the availability of natural light streaming through the skylights during the day. Additionally, Wal-Mart freezer cases are now installed with motion-activating lights that turn on as a customer approaches and turn off as they walk away.

Wal-Mart was twice recently named "Most Admired Company In America" by Fortune. Wal-Mart's managers believe that the company's careful strategy of low pricing, continuous innovation and sustainability will keep customers loyal for the long term.[1]

THE CONCEPT OF PRICING

You can purchase a totebag for as little as $2, but you can also purchase the trendy Louis Vuitton bag for about $5,000. A scarf can cost as little as $10, but a luxury Hermes, may cost over $1000. A remarkably broad range of prices is charged for items that have similar functions. Ginseng roots grown for tea in Korea and other Pacific Rim nations sell for a few dollars, but a couple of ounces found in the wild will cost nearly $50,000. New cars range from $20,000 for a Saturn Aura to almost $400,000 for a Rolls-Royce Phantom.[2] Even four years of college tuition can cost from several thousand dollars to well over $100,000 at a select private school or a prestigious foreign university.

Pricing plays a critical role in the allocation of resources in free market economies. Since prices fluctuate according to competitive forces, their rise and fall directly influence the amount of goods and services consumers are willing to purchase. Pricing is also critical for the firm. The amount consumers purchase times its price determines the total revenue a company receives. Long before a sale is made, marketers forecast consumer demand at varying prices. This influences the allocation of resources used to create, promote, and distribute products. Prices have a dramatic effect in determining the overall profitability of the firm. Consequently, pricing is one of the most important and complex areas of marketing.

Seldom do we find one concept described by so many names. These "soften" the unpleasant feeling people may have when making payment. How many can you think of? Tuition is what you pay to go to school. Rent is what you pay for your apartment. An honorarium is paid for a speech. A retainer is paid to a lawyer. A fee is paid to a doctor. A premium is charged for insurance. Highways charge a toll. Dues are charged for membership. Assessments are used to calculate property taxes, the ongoing price for real estate ownership. A wage or salary is the price paid for work, and interest is the price paid for using money. Fares are charged for public transportation. Salespeople receive a commission for achieving a certain level of sales, and a bonus is the price paid for extraor-

dinary performance. Whatever the name, price still signals that an amount is given up for the right to own or use something.

We have mentioned before that value comes from both the marketing organization and the buyer. In each case value is given up and received. **Price** is the exchange value of a good or service in the marketplace. We tend to think of price as a set amount of money that can be exchanged for a particular product. Yet, a good or service can also be exchanged for a different product through trading or bartering. Bartering simply bypasses the monetary system.

PRICE AS PART OF THE MARKETING MIX

We have discussed many of the decisions concerning the elements of the marketing mix. Products, logistics, and promotion create value for buyers. Price captures value from buyers for the firm. It is how the firm recovers its costs for other parts of the marketing mix. All parts of the mix interact to establish the firm's positioning. In fact, good pricing decisions require analyzing what target customers expect to pay even before products are developed, distributed, and promoted. Marketers need to understand ahead of time what customers perceive to be good value. If too much is charged, customers perceive that they are losing value, and they will spend their money on other

Payless Shoe Source is known for its low priced footwear.

products or purchase the minimum amount necessary. If too little is charged, the firm can lose money, eventually become uncompetitive, and go out of business.

OBJECTIVES OF PRICE SETTING

Prices are set with profit, volume, competitive, and customer objectives in mind. Businesses need to charge enough to make a profit, which satisfies owners (shareholders) and creates the financial resources needed to grow. Even nonprofits must have excess revenues over costs in order to keep pace with inflation and expand operations. Second, prices directly influence the quantity sold. Like profit, volume maintains or increases the size of the business. In addition to pleasing owners, financial health creates opportunities for employees to progress and prosper. Third, price can prevent competitors from taking your customers. Finally, proper pricing helps build customer relationships.

As with the chicken and the egg, it is difficult to determine what comes first; similarly profit, volume, competitive, and customer objectives are all linked. Figure 17.1 shows that the satisfaction of all parties to the business is in some way affected by price. Most important, when relationship objectives are met, we have satisfied, loyal customers who consistently produce revenues and profit. Yet it takes satisfied shareholders, contented employees, and a strong competitive position to make customers happy. Let's look at each set of objectives in turn.

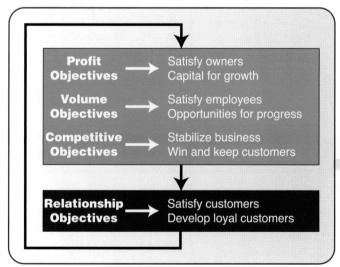

Figure 17.1 Prices Serve Several Objectives

PROFIT OBJECTIVES

Profit is critical for every business. Without it, investors will take their money elsewhere, and the business will cease to exist. In other words, you always need to price in order to make money. How do you do that? Simply stated, revenue minus cost equals profit. Price dramatically affects revenue. In fact, price times volume equals revenue. Later, we will see how price affects volume, which in turn affects cost. The point is that price

plays a role in all the major factors that influence profit. To change profit, you simply increase or reduce price, volume, or cost. Since these three elements are so closely connected, the situation is very intriguing. Exactly how they interact is a big issue for marketers. For many businesses, a small change in price has a huge effect on profit. Let's say a business makes a 10 percent profit on sales. If nothing else changes, then a three percent price increase means that profits soar by 30 percent. A similar price decrease will have the opposite effect.

Price sometimes is designed to create maximum profits, but often satisfactory profits are the objective. Essentially, satisfactory means that the expectations of investors are met or exceeded. Satisfactory profits are based roughly on how much the company has historically made, plus how much similar companies make, plus the risks involved in the business. Profits are usually stated in terms of return on sales, a return on investment, or profit margin. A minimum return on investment is the amount you make when you put your money in a financial institution and earn interest. Since risks are involved in marketing a product, profits must be high enough to cover them. Companies with significant profit margins will typically have increased success. Satisfactory profit goals are designed to reflect what shareholders, management, employees, and customers believe are fair for all parties involved.

Profit maximization is often stated as the goal of pricing, but what price will achieve this? Since price interacts with volume and cost, it is hard to say. Furthermore, there are limits to what people will pay. Theoretically, to maximize profit you would increase unit price until just before unit volume declines, and that is the point at which profit is maximized. In other words, the greatest quantity is being sold at the highest price the market will bear. Economists call this marginal analysis. But marginal analysis needs to take into account the long-term picture. Customer demand fluctuates due to economic conditions and shifts in the marketing mix. Competitive pressures also make it difficult to know exactly which price maximizes profit in dynamic markets.

VOLUME (SALES) OBJECTIVES

The price charged often affects the number of units purchased. Firms must price in such a way that production is maintained at a stable or growing level. Too high a price may result in layoffs, and too low a price may cause difficulty in meeting demand, which means lost sales and damage to the company's reputation. In either situation, employees will be unhappy. In the first case they will lose income or a job; in the second case they can't serve customers adequately. As you have learned, too low a price can even reduce the units demanded. Because it influences the overall amount to be consumed, price must be carefully set.

COMPETITIVE OBJECTIVES

Volume translates into market share, which creates market power. Many firms have specific market share objectives and price accordingly. Of course, many factors other than price contribute to high share. Although lowering price to increase share may reduce profits in the short run, it may cause competitors to restrict activities or withdraw from markets. Prices sometimes can be raised later in the absence of competition. But certain predatory pricing is illegal, as discussed later in this chapter.

Aside from gaining share, pricing also can help the organization maintain its market position. Leaders try to establish the market price. Followers react to what the leaders charge. If either party wants to prevent pricing from being used to adjust demand, then it may choose one of two strategies. **Status quo pricing** maintains the same relative position: Every time a competitor makes a price change, rivals follow suit. **Nonprice competition** leaves price at a given level and adjusts other parts of the marketing mix, adding or subtracting value when appropriate. For example, advertising may be increased or decreased, extra products may be piggybacked on packages, or container size may be reduced. Of course, in the short term it is always easier to adjust price than alter other marketing mix variables.

RELATIONSHIP (CUSTOMER) OBJECTIVES

Prices can be established with customer loyalty in mind. This is at the heart of relationship marketing. The objective is to create sufficient value over time to develop repeat business. In this case, pricing signals the relationship the company desires with customers. This is called value-based pricing and is a major topic in the next chapter. Fundamentally, prices are set to provide value for the customer in both the short term and the long run. Your most loyal customers should benefit to some degree from the extra profit generated through the relationship. This can be accomplished by lowering the price to loyal buyers or by adding value to the product they receive. Most important, you must understand your customers thoroughly in order to learn what they value.

MAJOR FACTORS INFLUENCING PRICE

Pricing according to value concepts requires a grasp of several elements, as outlined in Figure 17.2. First, economic factors explain how the demand for and supply of products relate to price. Second, legal and ethical constraints affect pricing decisions. Since price plays a major role in determining how economic resources are distributed, the government and courts have taken a particular interest in pricing. Third, the competitive environment influences price. Marketers must understand how competitors differentiate their products and the effect that substitutes have on price. Fourth, understanding how the company's cost structure is influenced by price decisions is very important. Finally, numerous global factors affect pricing in domestic and international markets. Each of these areas is addressed in the following sections.

ECONOMIC FACTORS: DEMAND AND SUPPLY

Economists have developed elaborate theories about the effect of consumer demand and product supply. Both have a significant influence on pricing.

Saks Fifth Avenue

Stopping power.

Somebody had to stop them. The visible signs of aging: lines, age spots.

A job for Clinique's Stop Signs Visible Anti-Aging Serum. And our newest addition: Stop Signs Hand Repair, which even addresses hand crepiness.

Powered by the same patent-pending formula* of collagen boosting ingredients. Select botanicals.

And a proven mix of vitamins and antioxidants.

Real time-stoppers on your side. Helping prevent past damage from becoming visible. Even forestalling future damage caused by the environment.

You might say, the power is in your hands.

Clinique.

Allergy Tested. 100% Fragrance Free.

www.clinique.com

Clinique Cosmetics uses non-price competition and increases its advertising for promotional purposes.

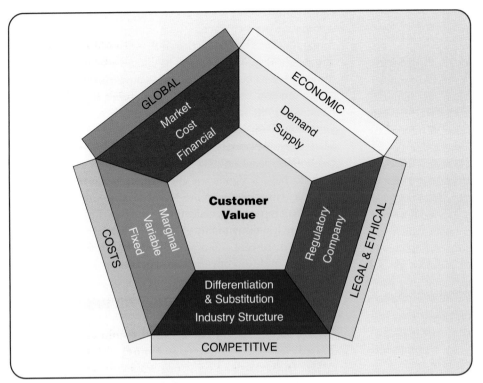

Figure 17.2   Factors Influencing Price

The Demand Curve   Demand is determined by the amount of product customers need, plus their willingness and ability to buy. Demand has a major influence on price. It is usually depicted by a **demand curve**, which is a graph showing quantity along the horizontal axis and different prices along the vertical axis. Marketers use the curve to estimate changes in total demand for a product based on differing prices. The demand curve describes the price elasticity of a given product. Price elasticity is the extent to which changes in what is charged affect the number of units sold. The formula for calculating it is:

Price elasticity is used to forecast responses to price changes and to define market segments. Knowing the price elasticity for company and competitor products is important in determining a pricing strategy.[3]

When price has a major effect on demand, the product is price elastic. When price has little effect on demand, the product is price inelastic. Figure 17.3 shows two demand curves, one for a price-elastic product (CD-ROMs) and the other for a price-inelastic product (heart surgery). CD-ROMs are useful and entertaining but are not a necessity. If their average price is high, then consumers will demand very few; if the price goes down, then demand will increase dramatically. In contrast, most consumers who need heart surgery do not care about the price, especially if government or private insurance will cover the cost. Price changes in heart surgery are not likely to influence the total demand to any large degree.

When demand is elastic, prices tend to decrease over time. As Figure 17.3 shows, when the price of CD-ROMs drops from about $250 down to $50, sales increase from 1,000 units to more than 7,000 units, reflecting elastic demand. For heart surgery, as the price drops from $2,000 to $1,000, demand stays roughly the same. There are also effects on total revenue. In the elastic case it rises from $250,000 to $350,000 as increased volume more than compensates for the lower price. In the inelastic

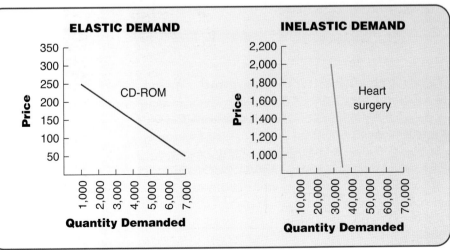

Figure 17.3   Demand Curves

case, revenue declines from about $60 million to $35 million.

Demand Sensitivity by Market Segment

In addition to the type of product, differences in market segments explain some of the variation in demand. Because the airline industry believes that the overall demand for business travel is less sensitive to price than the demand for leisure travel, pricing policies are designed specifically for each segment. Business travelers often purchase tickets at the last minute and are likely to pay full fare, whereas vacationers can plan well in advance and pay discounted rates. Fares are also lower for trips that include at least one weekend night, which seldom applies to business travelers. Their demand is inelastic because a certain amount of travel is required for the functioning of the firm. Leisure travelers not only have more elastic demand but also are more sensitive to price differences among airlines. Just before spring break, student newspapers are full of ads offering trip packages at greatly reduced prices. Yahoo Travel, for example, has cruise vacations for as low as $299 per person.[4]

Cross-Price Elasticity of Demand

We find **cross-price elasticity of demand** when the quantity demanded of one product changes in response to price changes in another product. For example, an increase in the cost of lumber in the building industry increases the demand for substitute products made of plastic and steel. At the brand level, an increase in the price of Coke increases the demand for Pepsi. Marketers use demand curves to describe price elasticity for a product class (all brands) or for a single brand. Price elasticity may differ for the total industry (that is, for all brands) versus an individual brand. Because gasoline is a necessity, variations in the average price charged by all producers may not affect demand dramatically. But British Petroleum-Amoco may find that its demand is elastic if it charges a lot more than the industry average. In other words, cross-elasticity refers to the amount of demand for one company's product based on its difference from the average price. Therefore, the concept of elasticity applies to the total industry, whereas cross-elasticity applies to preferences for individual brands or substitutes. Several marketing factors are likely to have a significant effect on cross-elasticity. For example, customers who are brand loyal to a particular gasoline company, especially those who buy the premium grade, are less likely to buy gasoline elsewhere because of a two- or three-cent difference in price; those with little or no loyalty, and who buy the lowest grade, are more likely to shop around.

Many marketing plans are designed to produce inelastic cross-elasticity for the brand. That means price is less important to buyers than brand attributes, so price competitors cannot lure them away. Consider Lucky jeans, which typically retail for more than $100 per pair, whereas Levi's often sell for less than $40. Many consumers are willing to pay more for the Lucky brand for prestige reasons or because they like its features.

To reduce the cross-price elasticity of their products, marketers may use any of the following approaches:[5]

- *Position the product relative to costly substitutes.* General Motors attempted this when it priced its Aurora to be competitive with BMW, Audi, Lexus, and Infiniti in the $40,000 price range.
- *Focus attention on unique features.* Boston Whaler commands a premium for its line of recreation craft due to the company's reputation for safety. The boats can't sink, which is a major reason the U.S. Coast Guard selects the brand.
- *Make it costly or difficult to switch.* ABB Robotics trains users of its systems in programming and maintenance. Retraining on another system is expensive and time consuming.
- *Make cross-brand comparisons difficult.* Prudential says "get a piece of the rock," implying that its size is an asset in financial planning.
- *Use price to signal status, image, or quality.* The name Mercedes is synonymous with high price. One dealer says: "If customers have to ask the price, they can't afford it."
- *Put price in the context of high value.* Volvo emphasizes family protection. Assuring the safety of loved ones is a benefit that customers are likely to value more highly than the money they could save by purchasing a cheaper brand.

The Supply Curve

Price, which influences profit,

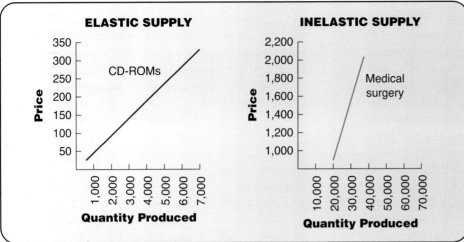

Figure 17.4 Supply Curves

also has an important influence on the willingness to produce. When price is higher, producers are willing to supply more. When profit margins are low, companies are likely to produce less. The supply curves shown in Figure 17.4 depict these relationships. In the elastic curve, an increase in unit price from $30 to $280 causes a dramatic increase in CD-ROM production, from 700 units to 6,500 units. In the inelastic curve, price hikes cause only a moderate increase in supply; there are relatively few trained heart surgeons, and they can squeeze only so many procedures into each day's schedule.

The **supply curve** reveals the amount that producers are willing to provide at each price. Theoretically, it operates very much like a demand curve, but different factors are at work. For example, companies with high fixed investment find it extremely difficult to exit the industry, so supply is inelastic. Another example is lawyers, who are generally reluctant to switch careers because they have invested heavily in education. When the price of legal services drops dramatically because of competition, lawyers are still willing to produce the same amount, reflecting the highly inelastic supply curve. When industry entry and exit are easy, supply tends to be more elastic. As prices rise, firms are willing to produce more; as prices decline, firms produce less or switch to other products

Equilibrium Price

In theory, price plays a role in balancing supply and demand. In Figure 17.5, the equilibrium price for CD-ROMs—the point at which the supply and demand curves cross—is $150. At prices below that point, producers are increasingly reluctant to supply CD-ROMs; at prices above it, consumers are increasingly reluctant to buy. Market forces work to help balance supply and demand so that products do not go unused and customers do not pay more than is required. Economic theory suggests that, over time, most product

prices are somewhat elastic. When prices are high, supply is likely to outstrip demand. Suppliers then lower prices until supply and demand come into equilibrium. When prices are too low, less is produced. Consumers are willing to pay more for scarce products, so supply increases until it is in balance with demand. In other words, supply and demand are related because changes in price affect how both suppliers and consumers respond. For example, in 2000 the price of cranberries fell to $11 per barrel from a high of $80 in 1996. The demand for cranberries rose sharply after 1994 after a Harvard University study showed that cranberry juice soothed urinary tract infections, and cranberry growers increased their acreage by 176 percent over the next few years to match the new demand. In 1999, however, the new acreage yielded a record harvest and the supply of cranberries surpassed the demand, resulting in the low price of $11 a barrel. Some cranberry farmers went out of business because the price of their product does not cover the costs of growing it, much less produce a profit. With cranberry production thus scaled back, in the year of 2003 its price rebounded up to $38.[6]

It is important to remember that supply and demand

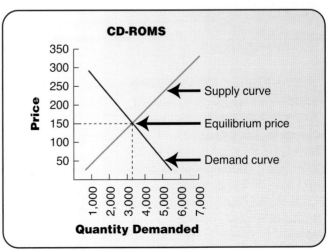

Figure 17.5 Supply and Demand Equilibrium

curves work perfectly only in economic theory, which assumes that most variables are held constant. In reality, the marketplace changes rapidly. Indeed, a main purpose of marketing strategy is to alter the supply and demand characteristics of an industry in the company's favor. Unfortunately, this does not always work positively for all competitors. For example, Toyota, Honda and Ford have increased their hybrid car production; environmental concerns among consumers and increasing gas prices have made these models in higher demand. As a result, vehicles with poor gas mileage have slowed in sales.[7] In many industries the tremendous diversity in market segments and individual firms introduces more variables than can reasonably be taken into account. Furthermore, it is very difficult to forecast demand and to predict what competitors will do. For all these reasons, attempts to influence elasticities through marketing strategies may not be very effective in practice.

LEGAL AND ETHICAL INFLUENCES ON PRICING

Both federal and state laws affect pricing decisions. In fact, pricing is one of the most legally constrained areas of marketing. Most regulations are designed to allow prices to fluctuate freely so that market forces can work. Some, however, protect consumers from unfair prices—those that are higher than the value created due to the manipulation of market forces. Pricing practices that are legislatively restrained or regulated include price-fixing, price discrimination, minimum prices (unfair sales), price advertising, dumping, and unit pricing, each of which is described later. Figure 17.6 summarizes federal legislation on pricing.

Although marketers certainly must take care to avoid outlawed pricing practices, many companies are equally concerned to avoid unethical pricing that could tarnish their reputation and erode consumer trust. "Pricing Ethics," the last topic in this section, describes a number of questionable practices.

Price-Fixing **Price-fixing**

occurs when one party attempts to control what another party will charge in the market. There are laws against vertical and horizontal price-fixing. **Vertical price-fixing** is an attempt by a manufacturer or distributor to control the final selling price at the retail level. The Consumer Goods Pricing Act of 1975 made all interstate use of

Preprinted-prices on products is one common legal practice for controlling retail prices.

unfair trade or resale price maintenance illegal. Retailers cannot be required to use the list price (suggested retail price) set by manufacturers or resellers. Freedom for retailers to adjust prices enhances competition, thereby reducing the overall average price to consumers. The passage of this law was controversial because manufacturers and wholesalers often want to control retail prices in order to maintain consistent positioning. Several practices for controlling retail prices are legal. The manufacturer or distributor may do any of the following:

- Own the retail outlet and establish its pricing policy
- Suggest and advertise a retail price
- Preprint prices on products
- Sell on consignment (own items until they are sold)

Act	Key Aspects
Sherman Antitrust Act 1890	Restricts predatory pricing (to drive competitors from the market) and makes it illegal to price fix.
Federal Trade Commission Act 1914	Set up the Federal Trade Commission, which is responsible for limiting unfair and anticompetitive practices in business.
Clayton Act 1914	Restricts price discrimination and purchase agreements between buyers and sellers.
Robinson-Patman Act 1936	Restricts discriminatory pricing that diminishes competition, particularly among resellers.
Wheeler-Lea Act 1938	Allows the Federal Trade Commission to investigate deceptive pricing practices and to regulate advertising of prices to help ensure that it does not deceive consumers.
Consumer Goods Pricing Act 1975	Eliminates price controls vertically and horizontally in the market so that channel members cannot set prices and so that retailers do not have to sell according to manufacturer or other channel member price schedules.

Figure 17.6   Major Federal Price Legislation

- Screen channel members, choosing only those with a history of price maintenance in their retail outlet

Horizontal price-fixing is an agreement among manufacturers and other channel members to set prices at the retail level. The Sherman Act and the Federal Trade Commission Act outlaw these practices even if the prices are "reasonable." Violations of either statute can be severely punished with steep fines and prison sentences. For example, the Department of Justice investigated several corporations for price-fixing through business-to-business exchanges. The largest controversy surrounded the online exchange for car suppliers, called Covisint. A joint venture among Ford, General Motors, DaimlerChrysler, and Renault/Nissan, the exchange hoped to become the preferred place for carmakers' suppliers to sell their parts to the Big Three. Some in the car industry claimed that staff at one of the four car firms implied that suppliers have no choice but to do business through this one exchange. The exchange also put pressure on suppliers not to work with other exchanges. This set of circumstances could imply a monopoly and horizontal price-fixing.[8]

Signs of price-fixing include cooperation among competitors on discounting, credit terms, or conditions of sale; any discussions about pricing at association meetings; plans to issue price lists on the same date or on given dates; plans to withhold or rotate bids on contracts; agreements to limit production in order to increase prices; and any exchange of information among competitors on pricing. The intent is to prohibit communication among competitors about pricing or any aspects of the business that may influence pricing levels.

On the international level, there are few antitrust sanctions to ensure fair competition. For example, in most countries impartial bidding processes are required, but in others the winners are secretly predetermined. In Japan this practice is called *dango* and is frequently used. In the United States and many other nations, it is known as *bid rigging*. U.S. trade officials estimate that substantial business is lost as a result of this practice. For example, U.S.

builders have been prevented from competing for their share of the $500 billion Japanese construction market. The United States hired a Japanese law firm to file for $35 million in damages against 140 Japanese companies accused of rigging bids. This action resulted in a $32.6 million settlement.

Price Discrimination

Price discrimination occurs when a manufacturer or other channel member charges different prices to retailers competing in the same marketplace. The Robinson-Patman Act of 1936 was designed to enhance competition by protecting small retailers against discounters or larger retailers that might obtain favorable treatment from suppliers. Today, this law is a major restriction on how manufacturers price. Essentially, the Act permits manufacturer discounts only if the seller can demonstrate that they are available to all competing channel buyers on the same fair basis. Price fluctuations must be developed in such a way that both small and large buyers can qualify for discounts, or the discounts must be cost justified. The law specifies that it is illegal not only for sellers to engage in unfair practices but also for retailers to purchase products when they know that discrimination toward other retailers is occurring.

The Robinson-Patman Act involves a relatively complex issue. Differential pricing is allowed in many circumstances in which manufacturers are competing to gain or hold business. The law was designed to enhance competition by preventing restraint of trade. Essentially, violation occurs when manufacturers or other channel members charge differential prices that inhibit the ability of one retailer to compete with another. Acceptable price discrimination occurs when the differences are based on time, place, customer characteristics, or product distinctions. In other words, any time the marketing mix has been altered, price

Marketing Vocabulary

PRICE- FIXING
An attempt by one party to control what another party will charge in the market.

VERTICAL PRICE- FIXING
An attempt by a manufacturer or distributor to control the final selling price at the retail level.

HORIZONTAL PRICE- FIXING
Agreement among manufacturers and channel members to set prices at the retail level.

PRICE DISCRIMINATION
A legally restricted practice in which a manufacturer or other channel member charges different prices to different retailers in the same marketplace.

may reflect those changes.

Consider the annual fees associated with different credit cards. The issuer may charge affluent customers $100 a year for premium gold cards but suspend all fees for students. Discounts for senior citizens, such as a percentage off on a particular day of the week, are another acceptable form of price discrimination. These practices demonstrate how price deviates among consumer segments.

Minimum Prices Laws against so-called minimum prices, often called unfair sales acts, have been enacted in a number of states. These prevent retailers from selling merchandise for less than the cost of the product plus a reasonable profit. Many states have such laws in order to protect smaller retailers and agricultural industries from larger competitors. **Predatory pricing** occurs when large firms cut prices on products in order to eliminate small local competitors. Wal-Mart was recently accused of violating predatory pricing laws when it began offering $4 generic prescription drugs. However, other competitors such as Costco and Kroger were able to match Wal-mart's low price.[9] At the national level, the Sherman and Clayton acts prevent this. Other laws apply to intrastate commerce.

Loss leaders are items priced below cost to attract customers. In some states this practice is restricted. In others it is legal, particularly when it is not designed to injure specific local competitors. Most loss leaders are heavily advertised brands with strong appeal. For example, supermarkets may feature a special on brand-name laundry detergents that have wide appeal. Once in the store, customers are likely to purchase additional goods at normal or even elevated prices. McDonald's and other fast-food chains can lower prices on burgers to increase traffic because their margins on soft drinks and fries make up the difference. Even investment companies use loss leaders; many waive fees on money funds to attract business, hoping that customers will later invest in other areas.

Marketers must be careful in using loss leaders. According to Donald Hughes, a former research manager at Sears, "You have to ask yourself how much money are you willing to spend to bring people into the store, because you have the problem of cherry picking, where people come in and buy only the loss leader, which foils your strategy."[10]

Items such as milk and bread are often priced as loss leaders.

Price Advertising The Federal Trade Commission has set up permissible standards for price advertising. Essentially, these guidelines prohibit marketers from communicating price deceptively. Firms may not claim that a price is reduced unless the original price has been offered to the public regularly and recently. Price comparison with the competition cannot be made unless verification is provided. And premarked prices cannot be artificially increased as a point of comparison unless products are actually sold at that price in substantial quantities. In addition, a retailer cannot continuously advertise the same product as being on sale when that price has become standard at that outlet.

Bait-and-switch promotions are specifically outlawed by the Federal Trade Commission Act and various state statutes. **Bait and switch** occurs when the seller advertises items at extremely low prices and then informs the customer these are out of stock, offers different items, or attempts to sell the customer more expensive substitutes. In other words, when there is no intent to sell the advertised item, retailers are being dishonest.

Dumping In the international market, one of the most common regulations relates to dumping, which is a form of price discrimination. **Dumping** occurs when a product is sold in a foreign country at a price lower than in the producing country and lower than its actual cost of production. Why do companies do this? It can be a very effective way to maximize profits, since global organizations cover many of their fixed costs through product pricing in the home market; they then price according to only their variable costs in other parts of the world. Dumping is illegal because it puts manufacturers in the local foreign market at a disadvantage. The U.S. Department of Commerce recently placed and anti-dumping tariff on certain steel products imported from China and the United Arab Emirates. The importers were penalized as much as 118 percent of the products value. Often, emerging economies are the source of dumping in the United States because of lower labor costs.[11]

Predatory dumping is pricing designed to drive local firms out of the market. Strong market share is gained, competitors are put out of business, and then higher average prices are charged.[12]

Unit Pricing Container sizes for the same item can vary considerably. In some cases the package may have similar wording, such as "giant" or "large economy" size. This makes it difficult for consumers to compare the price of products based on the size and type of packaging. The unit pricing legislation enacted two decades ago requires that certain types of retail outlets, especially food stores, display price per unit of measure as well as total price. For example, a 4-ounce can of tuna selling for $1.00 is also priced at 25 cents per ounce. In this way consumers can clearly see whether a larger size makes a price difference. The law is designed to help cost-conscious consumers make wise decisions at the retail level. In fact, according to a survey of customers, the most important attribute in stores is unit pricing signs on the shelves.[13]

Pricing Ethics Ethical issues in pricing abound. For price-sensitive products they revolve around the creation of demand and delivery of value based on price. For price-inelastic products, particularly because of the captive audience, gouging is an issue.

Although laws protect customers against unscrupulous pricing, we still find questionable ways of using price to increase demand. For example, an ad for dramatically reduced airfares states (in tiny print) that some restrictions may apply. When you call, you learn that so many restrictions apply that your choices are limited to a few seats and times. Italy's airline Alitalia was fined EUR30,000 for misleading consumers with an advert on round-trip flight fares showing only the one-way ticket cost. And the Philippine Civil Aeronautics Board is finalizing a new set of rules that seeks to sanction airline carriers for releasing false information to customers, such as misleading fares exclusive of tax and other surcharges, or with unclear requirements, terms and conditions.[14]

Another way to increase demand is to make the product seem less expensive than it really is. Sometimes all costs are not clearly communicated. For example, you go to a car dealer and receive a price. After deciding to purchase, you notice a charge for administration expenses on the invoice. The salesperson tells you that this is standard and was stated in small print on the sheets you were shown previously.

Perhaps you have noticed that your favorite brand of paper towel or pudding seems to disappear faster than it once did. Check the package. There is a good chance that the price remained the same but the size was reduced. Rather than pass on increased costs to customers, some manufacturers reduce the amount of product contained in a package. To obscure the issue, words like "new convenience package" are printed in small type. You're getting less value but may not be aware of it, because basic package design and price stay the same.

The captive customer creates a tempting target for some marketers. Because demand is already there, the question is how much to charge. Consider the cost of automobile parts. After an accident, you find that replacing one door will cost 20 percent of what you paid for the car. Are you likely to scrap it? It is true that handling and stocking inventory has to be included in prices, but it is a known fact that many companies make a much greater percentage on replacement items than on the original product.

Another way to reduce the amount delivered is to price on an all-you-want basis and then limit the supply. For example, a golf course or tennis club has a monthly fee for unlimited usage, but there are so many customers that you must wait an exorbitant amount of time for space. Some e-retailers experienced a similar circumstance during Christmas,

Marketing Vocabulary

PREDATORY PRICING
Price-cutting by large firms to eliminate small local competitors.

LOSS LEADERS
Items priced below cost to attract customers.

BAIT AND SWITCH
An unethical practice in which sellers advertise items at extremely low prices and then inform the customer that the items are out of stock, offer different items, or attempt to sell the customer more expensive substitutes.

DUMPING
Selling a product in a foreign country at a price lower than in the producing country and lower than its cost of production.

PREDATORY DUMPING
Pricing below cost to drive local firms out of business.

Airlines have been known to use unethical pricing practices.

when many online stores did not have enough products, or an efficient system of delivery, to deliver items already bought and paid for by consumers. A number of orders arrived late or did not arrive at all, and hence the Federal Trade Commission fined stores that failed to make good on their delivery promises. As a result, during the next Christmas season, many online retailers improved ordering and shipping practices to meet the consumer demand for their products and services.

COMPETITIVE FACTORS THAT INFLUENCE PRICE

When making pricing decisions, marketers must take the competitive environment into consideration. More specifically, it's important to look at industry structure and the potential for differentiating products through pricing strategies.

Industry Structure Industry may be defined broadly or narrowly for marketing purposes. It refers to a group of firms offering similar products. For example, Pizza Hut executives may view their industry as only establishments that sell pizza or as all restaurants in a particular price range. As with most other tools, marketers must make sure that the industry concept they use is relevant to the situation at hand.

To understand how competition affects price, we must look at industry structure as well as the behavior of individual firms. Industry analysis examines such aspects as the number of firms, whether products are differentiated, and the freedom of firms to enter and exit. Economists have identified four basic industry structures—perfect competition, monopoly, oligopoly, and monopolistic competition. Figure 17.7 shows how each type is likely to affect pricing and other forms of competition.

Perfect Competition In an industry with perfect competition each firm has little if any control over prices. None is large enough relative to others to control factors of production or market demand. Usually, many small firms produce precisely the same product. Because they cannot dictate prices, their primary decisions revolve around how much to produce and how to produce it. Since firm size is small, it is generally easy to enter and exit the market. Profits tend to be generated not through price but economies of scale and cost reductions.

Monopoly At the opposite end of the spectrum from pure competition is monopoly, an industry structure in which one organization makes a product with no close substitutes. As the only firm in the market, the monopolist has a great deal of freedom in establishing price. Most monopolies exist because there are barriers to entry for competing firms. For example, governments in many countries establish sole providers for certain services, such as communications or public transportation. Generally, these are heavily regulated to prevent abuses, and prices are set by governing boards rather than company executives. Public utilities that are established as monopolies usually must have their rates approved by a commission whose job is to protect the public interest.

From time to time private enterprises can achieve monopoly status through control of a patent or scarce raw material. Sometimes entry barriers, such as the sheer size of initial investment, may keep competitors out. Intel has been called a monopoly because of its dominance as a technology supplier. Legal experts often refer to companies such as Microsoft and Intel as essential facilities because customers have to buy their products. However, in 2000 federal court judges decided that Microsoft constituted a monopoly because the company illegally tied its Internet browser to the Windows operating system, making it difficult for consumers to buy separate operating

Type of Structure	Number of Firms	Product Differentiated or Homogeneous	Firms Have Price-Setting Power	Free Entry	Distinguishing Characteristics	Examples
Perfect Competition	Many	Homogeneous	No	Yes	Price competition only	Wheat farmer Textile firm
Monopoly	One	A single unique product	Yes	No	Constrained by market demand	Public utility Brewery in Taiwan
Oligopoly	Few	Either	Yes	Limited	Strategic behavior	Cereal maker Primary copper producer
Monopolistic Competition	Many	Differentiated	Yes, but limited	Yes	Price and quality competition	Restaurants Music industry

Figure 17.7 Industry Structure and Competition

Whirlpool Corporation uses differentiation in this ad to stress product value.

and Internet systems.

Wanting lower concert prices for fans, Pearl Jam contended that Ticketmaster inflated the cost with an unwarranted charge, which added as much as 30 percent to the face value. The company argued that the service charge was used to secure venue arrangements, to guarantee performances, and sometimes for marketing purposes. It claimed that its activities may be misconstrued as anticompetitive because small-scale ticket services are unable to duplicate them. Increased competition, however, has not led to an elimination of the service charge. A number of Web sites sell concert and event tickets, such as TicketWeb.com, Ticketmaster.com, and Tickets.com, and charge a service fee. The fee has fallen, although, from the almost 30 percent Ticketmaster was charging in the early 1990s to a price as low as $2. Most ticket sellers now charge a variable fee based on the event, the face value, the demand for the tickets, and the delivery method chosen.[15]

Oligopoly An oligopoly exists when an industry has a small number of companies competing for the same customers. Firms may behave in unusual ways to gain business, such as introducing a new technology, or they may combine a number of factors that can affect their use of price as a strategic tool. They tend to be large, and

old rivals engage in strategies and counterstrategies over long periods. The global auto industry is a good example. Seven major companies around the world produce nearly all motor vehicles, and each firm is large enough to commit considerable resources to differentiate itself. Each gains competitive advantage over the others from time to time. A few small firms in a local market also can be considered an oligopolistic situation.

Because oligopolies are usually well established and have strong market position, it is difficult for new firms to enter. The incumbents also get to know one another well. Through intelligence gathering, they learn about their competitors' cost structure. Their detailed market knowledge gives them insight into the amount of profitability rivals are likely to generate based on various pricing decisions. Because members of oligopolies engage in moves and countermoves, planning is essential.

Monopolistic Competition The industry structure, monopolistic competition, occurs when many firms compete for the same customers by differentiating their products. It falls somewhere between monopoly and pure competition but is much closer to the latter. Companies create brand loyalty to gain some of the benefits of monopoly. They control price by creating unique market offerings, such as nonfast-food restaurants in urban areas. Both price and quality are important in attracting customers and differentiating the product. Often there are numerous firms that are small or similar in size. Entry and exit are relatively easy, and the success of incumbents invites additional competitors. That's why several similar restaurants are likely to spring up when one starts doing well.

Strong marketing plans help organizations gain monopolistic-like advantages in highly competitive markets. They do this by creating subtle product differentiation. Rock groups are in this category. Stylistic differences enable you to differentiate between Radiohead, Green Day, Coldplay, and Modest Mouse. And each commands a price differential for concerts. Monopolistic competition also is the structure of the athletic footwear industry.

Marketing Vocabulary

PERFECT COMPETITION
The industry structure in which no single firm has control over prices.

MONOPOLY
The industry structure in which one organization makes a product with no close substitutes.

OLIGOPOLY
The industry structure in which a small number of firms compete for the same customers.

MONOPOLISTIC COMPETITION
The industry structure in which many firms compete for the same customers by differentiating their products and by creating unique offerings.

DIFFERENTIATION
A strategy in which product attributes that provide value are stressed.

Nike, Reebok, New Balance, Adidas, and a few others compete more or less on subtle differences in products.

Differentiation and Price Competition

Nonprice competition usually involves a differentiation strategy. **Differentiation** occurs when product attributes are stressed. Marketers try to demonstrate value and avoid any price reductions. In its purest form, a differentiation strategy relies on little or no mention of price. The relationships feature in this chapter, "Paying a Premium for Pet Care Nets Pampering, Too," focuses on ways in which quality pet products are differentiated beyond price considerations for many pet lovers.

Price competition adjusts prices to gain more customers or to establish a dominant position in the market. Recall that nonprice competition occurs when other marketing mix variables, such as product quality and promotion, are adjusted in response to competitors' pricing practices. Marketers need to understand the general approaches to price taken by their key competitors. This helps them anticipate overall market prices and what rivals are likely to do in response to price competition.

Marketing strategists study competitors in order to predict what they are likely to do under various conditions. Most companies respond in fairly consistent ways to price situations. Those that can produce at lower cost are more inclined to engage in price competition. Southwest Airlines cut costs by removing services such as in-flight meals and, therefore, is able to charge less per ticket than other airlines. Furthermore, it sells most of its tickets on the Internet; this cuts out the travel agency fees that further inflate airline ticket prices. Even at lower prices Southwest Airlines can sustain a profit, whereas companies with higher costs are likely to lose money as prices drop. In countries where wage rates are low, such as Korea and Taiwan, production costs are low for many types of goods.

COST FACTORS THAT INFLUENCE PRICE

Although prices should never be determined solely by cost, cost is critical information in making profitable pricing decisions. By understanding costs, marketers can judge profitability in advance. They can move resources to the highest-profit opportunities, avoid losing money, and gain better control of internal processes. By comparing costs with those of competitors, it is possible to assess production efficiency and estimate the relative profits each competitor can expect at various prices. This, in turn, helps anticipate the pricing choices available to competitors.

Types of Costs Costs are categorized in several ways. Most simply, accountants look at fixed and variable

McDonald's Egg McMuffin improves the effectiveness of fixed costs.

costs. Marketers also should consider marginal and incremental costs.

Fixed and Variable Costs Most **fixed costs** do not change in the short run. These are expenditures for items such as production facilities, equipment, and salaries. Often these are called sunk costs because, once committed, nothing can be done to lower them. They do not change very much no matter how many units of a product are sold. In service industries, salaries account for a large portion of fixed (sunk) costs. For example, hospitals pay nurses irrespective of the number of patients served. For airlines, payments for aircraft and hanger space as well as salaries are fixed costs. The best you can do is use these costs more effectively. McDonald's introduced the Egg McMuffin so its facilities could produce revenues during more hours. That improved the effectiveness of the fixed costs.

Variable costs change depending on how much is produced or sold. They are usually calculated for each unit of production. These costs include raw materials, warranty costs, and the aspects of payroll (such as commissions) that rise or fall depending on the units sold. In the airline industry, for example, variable costs include the commissions paid to travel agents and food served on planes.

Total costs (*TC*) for a given period are calculated by multiplying the variable cost (*VC*) per unit times the quantity (*Q*) of units and adding the fixed costs (*FC*):

$$TC = VC \times Q + FC$$

Total revenues (*TR*) for a period are calculated by multiplying the price (*P*) per unit times the quantity (*Q*) of units sold:

$$TR = P \times Q$$

Profits (*PR*) are the difference between total revenues (*TR*) and total costs (*TC*):

$$PR = TR - TC$$

The average cost (*AC*) of each unit is the total cost (*TC*) divided by the quantity (*Q*) of units:

$$AC = TC/Q$$

The average cost of each unit doesn't provide very much useful information for pricing decisions, however, because average costs are sensitive to volume. The more units sold, the lower is the average cost.

Marginal Costs Unlike accountants, economists look at marginal costs and marginal revenues. Marginal costs (MC) are expenditures incurred in producing one additional unit of output. These costs often go down with each unit sold and stabilize at a volume of production near full capacity. **Marginal cost** then increases because additional fixed costs must be added, such as more production machinery. Imagine an airline with a plane that normally flies half full. It would not cost much to add one passenger—the cost of another meal and the commission paid to the travel agent who sells the ticket.

Yet any price the airline can get that is greater than that marginal cost adds to profit. The price of the new ticket sold would be the **marginal revenue** (MR), the income from one more unit of the product sold, usually the product price. But let's say the plane is full. Would you add another aircraft to take one more passenger? Obviously not, unless that passenger is willing to pay a huge price.

Economic theory shows that profits are maximized—total revenues (*TR*) minus total costs (*TC*) are greatest—when *MR* equals *MC*. In the airline example, we can continue to lower the price until all seats are gone, or *MC* (the price of food and commissions) equals the price of a ticket. Airlines do this to a degree by offering a few discount seats. But selling a ticket for the cost of food and the agent commission (about $35) is impractical. In reality, you won't often find many marketing executives sitting in their offices looking at graphs of marginal revenues and costs. Yet, like most good theories, this concept provides useful insights.

It was noted that fixed costs do not change with prices and sales volume. Many people assume that these are the costs of being in business. Also called overhead, these fixed costs may be higher or lower for different competitors. For example, the pharmaceutical industry has high fixed costs because of the research and development necessary to yield one profitable drug; of the 5,000 compounds tested in the laboratory, only five make it to the clinical trials, which are expensive and time-consuming to conduct. Of those five drugs, only one is approved by the FDA for patient use. Fixed costs are extremely important in determining the profitability of a firm.

In practice, companies with high overhead may justify high prices if these reflect added value. Often they do not, yet decision makers push prices higher in an effort to obtain maximum revenue. The result may be even lower volume or reduced profit. If fixed costs do not add value for customers, they probably should not be a factor in pricing decisions. This is very difficult for many execu-

Each extra seat an airline can fill is considered marginal revenue.

Marketing Vocabulary

PRICE COMPETITION
A strategy that employs price adjustments to gain more customers or to establish a dominant position in the market.

FIXED COST
A cost that does not vary with changes in volume produced.

VARIABLE COST
A cost that changes depending on volume.

MARGINAL COST
The expenditures incurred in producing one additional unit of output.

MARGINAL REVENUE
The income from selling one additional unit of output.

tives to accept because pricing to cover all costs (cost-based pricing) has been so prevalent.

Incremental Costs Relevant costs for pricing decisions are **incremental costs**, costs that go up or down based on volume. Like variable costs, incremental costs are related to pricing because the price can affect the volume sold. Variable costs are always incremental. Only some fixed costs are incremental. For example, if a low price will increase demand to the extent that a new factory will have to be added to satisfy it, then the factory is an incremental cost and becomes a factor in the decision whether to lower the price. Once the factory is built, the cost becomes fixed or sunk. It has to be paid for no matter how much is produced. Pricing decisions that increase volume, thus, influence fixed costs, which in turn greatly influence the firm's cost structure.

Cost-Oriented Pricing
Both cost-plus and rate-of-return pricing are based on the company's costs. Cost-oriented pricing adds an amount to the product cost, called a markup, which is designed to yield a profit. A percentage markup can be added directly, or additional calculations can be made to determine what percentage rate of return the seller will receive. Either approach has serious problems because each tends to ignore the customer and, to varying degrees, the competition as well.

Cost-Plus Pricing Because of its simplicity, the cost-plus approach is popular. But, as the following example shows, it doesn't necessarily assure a profit. A local furniture store pays $750 to a wholesaler for a sofa and sells it to the consumer for $1,500, a markup of 100 percent. On the surface, it appears that the store has gained $750. But it has many costs to meet, such as salaries and overhead. When these are taken into account, and depending on overall sales volume, the retailer might actually lose money on this sofa and other items. Clearly, to determine whether the sale is profitable and precisely how much is made on the sofa a portion of the retailer's costs has to be allocated to each of the products sold.

Markups are popular because they are perceived to be fair or equitable for both the buyer and the seller. Standard markups have evolved in many industries to help indicate what amount is "fair." Manufacturers or wholesalers often suggest prices to retailers, or retailers form their own conventions. For example, an auto parts dealer may mark up brake assemblies by 40 percent and consumables such as oil by 25 percent. Since all similar retailers use the same basic markup structure, all have approximately the same retail price. Notice that the calculation is based on the wholesale price, which itself is a markup on the manufacturer's price.

Government contracts and some industrial contracts often specify that the seller must use cost-plus pricing. This is full-cost pricing because the markup is based on all costs, including allocations of overhead and other fixed costs. Sellers are expected to provide an accounting upon request. The difficulty lies in determining which costs to assign to which products. Again, even full-cost pricing largely ignores the value of the product to the customer.

Rate-of-Return Pricing A variation on cost-plus pricing, rate-of-return pricing is based on the break-even point. Essentially, the method determines how many units must be sold at a particular price in order to cover fixed costs plus a profit on the investment made. The break-even point is the amount sold at a given price on which the business neither makes nor loses money. Any volume beyond that point makes money.

The break-even point is calculated by dividing the total fixed cost (FC) by the difference between the selling price (P) of one unit and the variable cost (VC) of one unit:

$$\text{Break-even point} = FC/(P - VC)$$

The difference between the price and the variable cost of a unit $(P - VC)$ is called the contribution margin. It tells how much the sale of one unit contributes to covering fixed costs. Once these costs are covered, any remaining contribution is profit. Figure 17.8 shows the break-even concept graphically.

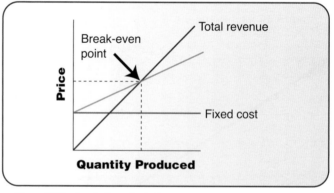

Figure 17.8   Break-Even Analysis

As an example of rate-of-return pricing, assume that you decide to start a small business that will offer house-painting services to homeowners during summer vacation. You calculate that you will have to invest $10,000 in fixed (sunk) costs, including advertising and promotion, insurance, equipment, truck rental, and a salary for yourself. You feel that you should earn a 20 percent return

Marketing Vocabulary

INCREMENTAL COST
Costs that go up or down based on volume, including variable costs and certain fixed costs.

Market Factors	Cost Factors	Financial Factors
Local demand	Distance and transportation	Exchange rates
Competitive conditions	Tariffs and homologation	Inflation
Availability of substitutes	Export duties, subsidies, and controls	Government price controls
Gray marketing	Transfer pricing	

Figure 17.9   Influences on Global Pricing

($10,000 x 20% = $2,000) for having the idea, taking the initiative, and assuming the risk of losing your invested capital. Furthermore, you estimate that labor, paint, and other variable costs for each house will average $2,100, and with four workers your company can paint eight houses in four months. What is the average price you should charge for each house?

To answer this question, you first add your desired return to your fixed costs ($2,000 + $10,000 = $12,000) to determine the total revenue contribution required. Then you divide that sum by the number of houses (units) to find the amount that each unit must contribute ($12,000 / 8 = $1,500). Since the variable cost to paint a house is $2,100, you determine that you must charge $2,100 + $1,500 = $3,600 per house.

Notice in this example that profit is treated much like a fixed cost. This is because if you break even in a strict sense—that is, neither make nor lose money—then your project will not accomplish its profit objective.

Also notice that rate-of-return pricing ignores the customer and the competition. If homeowners consider $3,600 to be too expensive, then they may hire someone who charges less or choose to do the work themselves. If they believe the price is very low, then they may be willing to pay even more. The pricing of competitors is important. Whether competitors are willing to paint a house for $3,000 or $9,000 will influence how consumers perceive your price.

Rate-of-return pricing also tends to ignore the scale of operations you could have. For example, if eight painters rather than four were employed, the fixed costs could be spread across 16 houses rather than eight. That would lower the price, but you would have to supervise more workers while not making more profit. A major problem with the rate-of-return approach is that price will increase when demand goes down. For example, if only six houses are painted, the price for each rises by $500, to $4,100. Does this make sense? In the 1990s, U.S. auto companies lost share dramatically to foreign rivals. As demand for U.S. cars declined due to competitive pressure, Detroit increased prices to try to make up for lost unit sales, further reducing demand.

INTERNATIONAL PRICING

Pricing in global environments is affected by several factors not experienced in domestic markets. Also, because markets vary greatly among countries, international pricing is complex. Marketing executives must be knowledgeable about many issues and remain flexible in adjusting to unforeseeable circumstances. The major influencers on global pricing are market, cost, and financial factors, as outlined in Figure 17.9.

GLOBAL MARKET FACTORS

Market factors such as local demand, tastes and preferences, competitor activities, and gray marketing are important. All of these elements must be considered in international pricing.

Local demand can vary dramatically due to demographic, geographic, and political conditions. For example, China is the world's most populous country and is experiencing economic growth at a staggering rate. Yet few Chinese have enough income or even the space for most of the durable goods so common in the West. Consequently, many products for the Chinese market must be designed to be priced very low.

Subtle competitive differences can influence demand, even in fairly similar economic environments. With the advent

In Brussels, jeans are 43 percent cheaper than in Paris.

The Marketing Gazette™

CREATING & CAPTURING VALUE THROUGH RELATIONSHIPS

Paying a Premium for Pet Care Nets Pampering

63 percent of U.S. households own a pet and 62 percent of those households buy gifts for their pets. Pet owners easily drop $100 at the local pet supply store. Americans want the best for their pets and lavish $38.5 billion a year on them for things such as food, supplies, grooming, medicine, and veterinary services.

A Barron's survey showed that seven out of ten people spend money on their pets as if they were their children. Pet care businesses are cashing in on this spending with steep prices. For instance, Colgate once sold its premium Hill's Science Diet exclusively through veterinarians. Now it is one of dozens of brands available at the vast number of pet supply and specialty stores popping up all over the country. Huge national chains such as Petco and PetSmart, as well as regional competitors, stock up to 12,000 items, with premium pet foods accounting for more than half their sales.

Grocery stores are losing out on this valuable product category not only because they cannot carry the huge variety but also because pet supply stores give customers added value by providing information to consumers willing to buy premium items for their pet. Customers want to know why a product is good and what it is going to do for their pet. They want knowledgeable salespeople to help them. Many specialty shops hold continuing education programs for employees to make sure they are up on topics such as premium pet food versus standard grocery store pet food. These specialty stores also host events for owners and their pets.

In this business, building customer relationships means reaching out to poodles, gerbils, iguanas, and guppies. It is not uncommon for a specialty store to conduct costume shows, pet trick contests, and portrait sessions. Sometimes even the owners take center stage. One store located in Minneapolis hosted singles night on Valentine's Day, and 200 people showed up with their pets. Aunt B's Pet Resort & Spa in DeForest, Wisconsin, is another example of the lengths pet owners will go in order to ensure the comfort and happiness of their pets. Guests from as far away as California, Florida, and

Oklahoma have come to be pampered and treated to such luxuries as massages, manicures, heated floors and furniture, and poochie Jacuzzi time.

In 2007, Proctor & Gamble and NBC Universal teamed up to launch Petside.com, a Web site for pet owners and the marketers that love them. The site resembles a Yahoo for pet owners, offering news stories, animal training and health information, shopping, and even funny animal videos. Visitors are encouraged to register for its social network to meet other pet lovers. The site draws information from many reputable sources like the American Society for the Prevention of Cruelty to Animals, with the idea that compiling useful pet information in one convenient location will offer new marketing opportunities. Procter & Gamble is using the site to market its Iams pet food and Febreze air fresheners to pet lovers.

Pet owners can also buy pet medical insurance. Veterinary Pet Insurance (VPI), the nation's number- one provider of pet insurance policies, recently announced new marketing relationships with two leading websites geared toward pet owners. Through various efforts, VPI and the participating sites will spread awareness about the benefits of quality pet care. While many companies offer pet health insurance, Progressive is now coupling Pet Injury Coverage with its auto insurance in attempt to attract pet owners. This is included free with standard collision coverage and will pay up to $500 in expenses for a pet injured in a car accident. In addition, it has teamed up with several pet insurance companies to get Progressive customers discounts on pet insurance policies.

"The point is that people are taking owning a pet as a real part of their lives," says Bill Lechner, general merchandise manager of Pet Food Warehouse, now owned by Petco. "The idea of just going down to the corner and picking up a can of cat food has changed, and now there's an emotional and social aspect of pet ownership. We realize it, and we promote it, foster it, and cater to it, because if you can get the pets in the store with the owners, they are going to stay in the store a lot longer than if they simply walk in, go to the food, get it, and go out."

of the Euro, for example, price gaps have narrowed between euro-area countries in the past years. Though some items like electrical goods, which are easily shipped across borders, have the smallest price ranges, Madrid still has the cheapest total shopping basket in euro. In Amsterdam, a bottle of whiskey costs almost 80 percent more than in Rome; in Brussels, Pampers cost 56 percent more than in Frankfurt, and a cinema ticket costs 170 percent more than in Madrid, but Brussels is the place for Levi jeans - 43 percent cheaper than in Paris.[16]

Globally, tastes and preferences also vary dramatically. A nationalistic bias for domestic products can make them less cross-price elastic in relation to imports. Generally, people in countries where domestic brands are preferred have high incomes and tend to be much less price sensitive across the board. That means more latitude for premium pricing. For example, companies selling consumer food products in Europe have found themselves in a difficult position recently. The economic unification of the European Union means that many global food retailers want to reduce the number of brands to streamline production processes and lower prices. The customers, however, tend to want to continue to buy specific brands and products, irrespective of price, as when British consumers protested Heinz's decision to stop manufacturing salad cream, a type of salad dressing popular among older Britons. However, the advent of the euro has caused more shoppers in the United Kingdom to become price sensitive in their selections.

The availability of substitute products also varies widely. The most obvious case is the substitution of automation for labor. Japan—with its high education level, high labor rates, and low unemployment—is highly automated, while Chinese producers use readily available low-cost human labor whenever possible. The market for high-priced robotics is mature in Japan, where many competitors are constantly seeking an edge, but demand is weak in China.

GRAY MARKETING

A notable feature of many foreign economies is the gray market, which has a significant effect on pricing. Many global companies manufacture in local markets so they can sell at lower prices there, but this also may lead to gray marketing.[17] **Gray marketing** occurs when pirated products made in a foreign country are imported back to the company's home market without approval. They

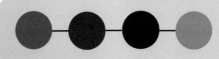

globalEDGE™
Pricing Objectives & Influences

http://globaledge.msu.edu
Visit globalEDGE™ Online for the ultimate international marketing research tool!

Your retailing firm has just received a shipment of apparel from Russia. However, before stocking the shelves with these products, you must first assess its overall value. The invoice accompanying the delivery indicates that the shipment has been valued at 10 million Russian roubles. Use current currencies rates found on foreign exchange markets to determine its value in US dollars.

are then sold at reduced prices, usually by unauthorized channel members. The importation of gray market goods is prohibited in the United States by a law that forbids bringing products into the country without permission of the trademark owner. Elsewhere in the world, restrictions vary, may not exist, or may not be well enforced. Many times the foreign-made product is of a different quality but bears the company label, so consumers are confused. In other cases, prices differ because of manufacturing costs, exchange rates, or other reasons.

Gray markets can disrupt the best-laid plans of companies desiring selective or exclusive distribution. Any brand with some consumer following may find itself in this situation.

Companies that want to ensure selective or exclusive distribution must take steps to eliminate gray market problems. If not, then the strength and motivation of the authorized channel will be seriously impaired. The company must clearly communicate to all members of the authorized channel the importance of following policy and upholding contracts. Their activities must be monitored, especially when significant gray market activity exists. Contracts with those who violate agreements must be terminated. Some companies even team up with gray importers to reduce the harm from gray markets. For example, HP recently signed up eXpansys as an authorized UK HP channel partner to assist its anti-gray marketing efforts in the European Economic Area (EEA) after the Manchester-based e-tailer admitted importing iPaqs from outside the EEA.[18]

GLOBAL COST FACTORS

In calculating the costs

Marketing Vocabulary

GRAY MARKETING
Importing products made in a foreign country back to the company's home market without approval.

of doing business internationally, it is not just distance that matters but the expense of moving goods from one country to another. Transportation and insurance costs escalate when borders are crossed, as do tariffs and red tape. Risks also increase, so prices must cover potential adverse circumstances.

Tariffs—taxes levied against incoming goods—contribute to costs and are sometimes added to price. They affect imports in nearly every country. Vehicle prices in Turkey are elevated nearly threefold by tariffs. In the United States, importers pay an average of less than 10 percent on all items, much more for some. Recently the World Trade Organization ruled against the European Union's import tariffs for bananas from African and Latin American countries. The World Trade Organization serves as a regulatory body for importing and exporting.[19]

Bureaucratic red tape often makes it difficult and expensive to enter a market. The Japanese use it as a barrier to foreign competitors. For example, they lock out international construction companies by claiming that Japan's dirt is unique, or they require considerable testing at border entry points for all sorts of products. Vietnam rescinded hundreds of bureaucratic procedures and tariffs that prevented foreign firms from doing business in the country. Multinational companies that had tried to do business in Vietnam pulled out of the country because red tape made doing business almost impossible. In the end though, Vietnamese officials decided that the country needed the investments more than they needed to protect their own industries. Some European pharmaceutical companies claim that FDA regulations impede their access to the U.S. market. The US federal health agency has streamlined its system, cutting to months rather than years the time needed to help speed the approval process to bring certain new drugs to market.[20]

The opposite of a tariff is an **export subsidy** paid by a government to encourage businesses to export. When you compete against these companies, essentially you're competing against their government as well. When they target a certain market, their prices can be more competitive because the subsidy covers much or all of their export costs. This may put nonsubsidized exports and domestic products at a pricing disadvantage. In other cases, governments may restrict exports by adding costly duties, which raises prices in importing countries. Many countries in the world subsidize big national industries; Canada, Brazil, France, and Great Britain all subsidize their aircraft manufacturers, for example.

Risk is also a factor in international business. When risk is high, prices must be raised. For example, selling in Russia is risky because of an unstable economy and the possibility of political takeovers. Anywhere in the world, a change in government can affect economic regulations and market access. Furthermore, a weak or indifferent government may permit greater corruption or lawlessness, which can mean that warehousing and distribution channels are insecure.

Transfer prices are the amounts that companies charge their foreign affiliates for products. This causes some interesting price variations across countries. By altering the transfer price, both local prices and profits can be dramatically affected. In this way, companies can manipulate their price in markets globally, affecting competition and their sources of revenues. For example, Japanese auto supply

Web and E-commerce Stars
Google - www.google.com

Google is an Internet search engine. Its popularity is such that "to google" became part of the English vocabulary. "To google" means to look up someone using the Google search engine. Google has 380 million users per month and ranks as the top search engine in 14 countries, making it the world's most popular portal into the Internet. It organizes World Wide Web information and makes it easily accessible to everyone. Google also offers specialty services such as Gmail e-mail services, Google Maps, online books, blogs, news feeds, Google earth, just to name a few. It also promotes AdWords and AdSense for web marketers as an alternative advertising means to pop-ups and banners, and sells products with its logo on them. Google is an excellent example of diversifying and expanding all while staying true to the original business model and providing the end user with what they need and want.

companies can charge higher transfer prices for components going to assembly plants in the United States. This practice yields more profit in Japan and less profit in the United States. In turn taxes are paid in Japan, where the rate may be lower than in the United States. Ultimately, the tax savings mean that a lower price can be charged for the product in the United States.

GLOBAL FINANCIAL FACTORS

The primary financial factors influencing international prices are exchange rates, inflation, and government price controls. Exchange rates and inflation alter the value of currencies, whereas government price controls prohibit companies from moving prices upward at will. Controls are particularly troublesome when a rapid shift in exchange rates or inflation devalues the price put on a product.

Even money has a price, which is reflected in the exchange rate. The **exchange rate** is how much one currency is worth relative to another. If the Chinese yuan has risen about 5 percent against the U.S. dollar over the past 18 months, Chinese goods will be more expensive in America. Currency exchange rates can fluctuate considerably over time, affecting prices for imported and exported products.

Inflation is the tendency of a currency to be worth less over time. When inflation occurs, product prices along the supply chain increase. These are passed on in higher prices, so consumers have to spend more money to buy the same item. Most advanced nations now have low inflation rates, often around 3 percent or even less per year. In some countries inflation is extremely high and escalates monthly or even weekly. In extreme cases, companies may need to raise prices twice a month, by 20 or 30 percent, just to keep up with inflation.

Governments often use **price controls** in an attempt to keep inflation in check. Essentially, the maximum price increase allowable is set by law. Sometimes the controls are applied to all goods, sometimes they are selective, and sometimes they apply only to imports. In any case, they can make it difficult to earn a profit, so companies may not want to sell in that market. It is not uncommon for people to buy key raw materials, such as coal, cheaply on the local price controlled market and sell them on the world market for a huge profit, instead of selling the products locally at a price controlled by the state.

Companies use many factors when making pricing decisions locally or globally. All of these factors are likely to influence price. However, as we will see in the next chapter, the actual pricing strategy must be well grounded in an understanding of how pricing captures value from the market. This requires knowing how customers define value.

Marketing Vocabulary

TARIFF
A tax levied against a good being imported into a country.

EXPORT SUBSIDY
Funding by a government to encourage businesses to export goods.

TRANSFER PRICE
The amount a company charges its foreign affiliate for a product.

EXCHANGE RATE
The worth of one currency relative to another.

INFLATION
The tendency of a currency to be worth less over time.

PRICE CONTROLS
Government restrictions on the price that can be charged for a product.

Chapter Summary:

Objective 1: Describe how pricing works with the other parts of the marketing mix.

Pricing is an important element of the marketing mix. Price decisions are made along with product, promotion, and logistics decisions. Pricing is influenced by profit, volume, competitive, and customer relationship objectives. Consequently, pricing is important for nearly all aspects of the business.

Objective 2: Learn how economic factors such as demand and supply influence prices.

The demand curve helps us understand how price influences the amount of a product customers buy. The availability of substitutes, necessity, the portion of income spent on the product, and the timing of price changes affect the price sensitivity of demand. The supply curve tells how much product firms will provide at various prices. Usually, more is produced when prices are expected to rise. By analyzing the supply and demand curves, it is possible to get some idea of future prices in an industry.

Objective 3: Understand the legal and ethical constraints on pricing decisions.

Both legal and ethical factors affect price. Laws prohibit both vertical and horizontal price-fixing by U.S. firms. It is also illegal for manufacturers to sell to different parties at different prices, although some forms of price discrimination are acceptable. To control unfair price competition, many states regulate pricing minimums and the use of loss leaders. The Federal Trade Commission sets permissible standards for price advertising. For example, you cannot advertise a sale price unless it is really a sale and the items are available. International firms must sell at a high enough price to avoid violating antidumping laws. Finally, unit pricing regulations help consumers make comparisons. To be ethical, prices should reflect a fair exchange of value, and marketers must be careful not to misrepresent the terms of an exchange. This requires clear communication of both price and value.

Objective 4: Use industry structure concepts to understand how competitors in different types of industries price.

The four basic industry structures are perfect competition, monopoly, oligopoly, and monopolistic competition. In perfect competition, many firms vie to provide goods at the going price. A firm with a monopoly can set prices as high as the market will bear, although pricing by public utility monopolies is generally regulated in the public interest. In an oligopoly, a small number of competitors make pricing decisions based on their knowledge of one another's cost structures. Monopolistic competition tends to be based on product differentiation rather than price.

Objective 5: Use competitive factors surrounding industry structure concepts to understand how pricing works in different types of industries.

Pricing decisions must consider variable and fixed costs, marginal costs, and incremental costs. Incremental costs, which are the most important, include variable costs and, often, some fixed costs, such as the cost of building a new factory to meet increased demand. Cost-oriented methods, such as cost-plus pricing and rate-of-return pricing, have serious drawbacks because they tend to ignore the consumer and competitors.

Objective 6: Recognize the conditions that make international pricing complex.

Market, cost, and financial factors unique to global business must be considered in pricing. Market factors include local demand, competitive conditions, tastes and preferences, the availability of substitutes, and gray marketing. Important cost factors are transportation distance, tariffs, red tape, and export subsidies. Major financial considerations are inflation, exchange rates, and price controls. Risk is another influence on international pricing.

Review Your Understanding

1. List 10 names for price.
2. Which constituents of a firm can be pleased with profit objectives, volume objectives, competitive objectives, and relationship objectives?
3. What are the major factors that influence price?
4. What is elastic demand? Inelastic demand?
5. What factors influence price elasticity?
6. What is supply and demand equilibrium?
7. What are the laws that affect pricing practices? Describe the restrictions.
8. Describe dumping.
9. What are two ethical issues regarding pricing? Explain.
10. What is industry structure? What are four structures that have price implications?
11. What are fixed and variable costs?
12. What are incremental costs?
13. What is cost-plus pricing?
14. What factors influence pricing in global settings?

Discussion of Concepts

1. Prices are set with several objectives in mind. What are they, and how are they important to a company?
2. A company's pricing strategy is influenced by many factors: legal and ethical issues, economic conditions, the company's costs, the global environment, and competitors. What major effect does each category have on pricing decisions?
3. Product demand is influenced by price elasticity. What does this mean, and what effect does it have on a marketer's pricing policy?
4. Federal and state laws in the United States prohibit unfair pricing. What is meant by "unfair"? Give specific examples of laws and briefly describe their objectives. Is this true of all countries?
5. How does the type of competition within an industry affect a company's ability to set prices? Briefly describe the major competitor-based pricing approaches.
6. What types of costs are relevant for pricing decisions? Which are irrelevant? Why? What are some of the main problems with cost-oriented pricing?
7. Despite its drawbacks, cost-oriented pricing is still used by many companies. Briefly describe the two types.

Key Terms And Definitions

Bait and switch: An unethical practice in which sellers advertise items at extremely low prices and then inform the customer that the items are out of stock, offer different items, or attempt to sell the customer more expensive substitutes.

Cross-price elasticity of demand: The extent to which the quantity demanded of one product changes in response to changes in the price of another product.

Differentiation: A strategy stressing product attributes that provide value.

Demand curve: A depiction of the price elasticity demand for a product.

Dumping: Selling a product in a foreign country at a price lower than in the producing country and lower than its cost of production.

Exchange rate: The worth of one currency relative to another.

Export subsidy: Money paid by a government to encourage businesses to export goods.

Fixed cost: A cost that does not vary with changes in volume produced.

Gray marketing: Importing products made in a foreign country back to the company's home market without its approval.

Horizontal price-fixing: Agreement among manufacturers and channel members to set prices at the retail level.

Incremental costs: Costs that go up or down based on volume, including variable costs and certain fixed costs.

Inflation: The tendency of a currency to be worth less over time.

Marginal costs: The expenditures incurred in producing one additional unit of output.

Marginal revenue: The income from selling one additional unit of output.

Monopolistic competition: The industry structure in which many firms compete for the same customers by differentiating their products and by creating unique offerings.

Monopoly: The industry structure in which one organization makes a product with no close substitutes.

Nonprice competition: Price is unchanged but adjustments are made to other parts of the marketing mix in response to competitor's price changes.

Oligopoly: The industry structure in which a small number of firms compete for the same customers.

Perfect competition: The industry structure in which no single firm has control over prices.

Predatory dumping: Pricing below cost to drive local firms out of business.

Predatory pricing: Price-cutting by large firms to eliminate small local competitors.

Price: The exchange value of a good or service in the marketplace.

Price competition: A strategy that employs price adjustments to gain more customers or to establish a dominant position in the market.

Price controls: Government restrictions on the price that can be charged for a product.

Price elasticity: The extent to which changes in price affect the number of units demanded or supplied.

Price-fixing: An attempt by one party to control what another party will charge in the market.

Status quo pricing: When a competitor makes a change, rivals follow suit.

Supply curve: A depiction of the price elasticity of supply for a product.

Tariff: A tax levied on a good being imported into a country.

Transfer price: The amount a company charges its foreign affiliate for a product.

Variable cost: A cost that changes depending on volume.

Vertical price-fixing: An attempt by a manufacturer or distributor to control the retail selling price.

References

1. "Corporate Facts: Wal-Mart By the Numbers,"; Sustainability Report 2008. www.walmart.com, March 21, 2008; Sam Hornblower , "Is Wal-Mart Good For America?", www.pbs.org/wgbh/pages/frontline/shows/walmart/view, web site visited July 5, 2007; Sam Hornblower, "Always Low Prices," http://www.pbs.org/wgbh/pages/frontline/shows/walmart/secrets/pricing.html, site visited July 6, 2007; Wal-Mart Sustainability Report, February 18, 2008, www.walmart.com.
2. Kelly Blue Book www.kbb.com Web site visited March 21, 2008.
3. James Stotter, "Applying Economics to Competitive Intelligence," Competitive Intelligence Review, Winter 1996, pp. 26–36.
4. www.travel.yahoo.com, Web site visited March 21, 2008.
5. See Thomas T. Nagle and Reed E. Holder, The Strategy and Tactics of Pricing (Upper Saddle River, NJ: Prentice Hall, 1995), pp. 78–95.
6. Greg Winter, "Growers Sue Ocean Spray, Seeking Possibility of Sale," New York Times, November 29, 2000, Section C; p. 6; Column 5; Robin Lord, "Cape Code, Mass. – Area Cranberry Season Is Off to Slow Start," Knight Ridder Tribune Business News, October 7, 2003, p.1.
7. Green Means GO. Paul Ferriss. Marketing. Toronto. Feburary 11, 2008.
8. "A Market for Monopoly?" The Economist, June 17, 2000, Vol. 355, Issue 8175, pg. 59.
9. $4 Generic Drugs Often Loss Leaders for Big Retailers. Barry Shlachter. McClatchy-Tribune Business News. Washington. March 1, 2008.
10. Gene Koprowski, "The Price Is Right," Marketing Tools, September 1995.
11. Nail Dumping Tariffs Approved. Bill Addison. New York. Feburary 11, 2008.
12. Associated Press, "Japanese Company Defends Sale of Supercomputers," USA Today, May 12, 1997.
13. "Consumers Are Skeptical Again," Progressive Grocer, April 1996, pp. 40–46.
14. "Alitalia Fined for Misleading Advertising," Airline Industry, December 14, 2005, pg.1; Maricel E. Estavillo, "Regulator Prepares Guidelines for Airlines' Fare Promotions," BusinessWorld, Manila, May 23, 2007, pg.1.
15. www.ticketmaster.com, site visited June 27, 2007.
16. "Finance and Economics: The Flaw of One Price; Price Differences in Europe," The Economist, Oct 18, 2003, Vol. 369, Issue 8346, pg. 97.
17. Paul Lansing and Joseph Gabriella, "Clarifying Gray Market Gray Areas," American Business Law Journal, September 1993, pp. 313–337.
18. Based on the author's consulting experience in these industries; Paul Kunert, "HP Signs Up Former Grey Importer as Registered Partner," MicroScope, Nov 6, 2006, pg. 1.
19. WTO Rules Against EU on Banana's. Wall Street Journal. New York: Feburary 9, 2008.
20. Jason Gertzen, "Official Promises at Biotech Convention to Help Speed Up Drug Approval Process," Knight Ridder Tribune Business News, June 8, 2004, pg. 1.

The Marketing Gazette
Doug Desjardins, "Pets live in lap of luxury with new high-end goodies," DSN Retailing Today (Vol. 44), September 12, 2005, p 16; http://www.appma.org/, visited June 19, 2007; Jerry Minkoff, "Perking Up Pet Supplies," Discount Merchandiser, July 1995, pp. 30 32; Jerry Minkoff, "Pet Supply Depot: Netting a Share of the Animal-Lover Market," Discount Merchandiser, November 1995, pp. 46, 48; Jay Palmer, "Well, Aren't You the Cat's Meow?," Barron's, April 1, 1996, pp. 29 34; and Jerry Minkoff, ?Pampering Pets = Persistent Profits,"Discount Merchandiser, November 1995, p. 47; www.petinsurance.com, press release, February 21, 2000," Veterinary Pet Insurance Announces Co-Marketing Efforts with Leading Pet-Related Web Sites"; Rick Barrett, "Pets Enjoy Music, Treats at DeForest, Wis. Spa," The Wisconsin State Journal, June 29, 2000; Louise Story, "A Web Site for Pet Lovers, and Marketers Who Love Them," November 19, 2007, New York Times; Progressive Pet Injury Coverage, www.progressive.com, site visited June 09, 2008.

CASE 17

Webkinz

If you aren't around kids, chances are you haven't heard of them, but ask any 6 to 8 year old and they can surely tell you about Webkinz. Webkinz are plush toys that virtually live in the online Webkinz World created in 2005 by a Canadian toy company called Ganz. There are over 60 of these plush toys available including frogs, ponies, and dogs; imagine Beanie Babies in cyberspace. Each toy comes with a tag that includes a registration code for the Webkinz.com Web site. Here customers can create a special environment just for their Webkinz stuffed animal. While they hold the stuffed animal, it comes to life on the screen, ready to be adopted. The customers give each toy a name and gender. They can also use "Kinzcash" to buy clothes, food, furniture or any other necessities by playing games, winning quizzes and taking on virtual jobs.

Webkinz are a hit with children, parents and even educators. "I believe the popularity of the pets is based on the fact that kids can combine their love of plush pets and the nurturing and make-believe elements of play, with the appeal of the Internet," said Susan McVeigh, communications manager for Ganz. "Now, younger kids can play games, learn to budget and care for their pets, have responsibility for raising and decorating their pets' rooms, 'chat' with friends and more." She said the pets appeal to kids as young as 3 to 5, although the most popular age range seems to be 7 to 12, both boys and girls. With increased internet access, these kids are growing up in wired households where both parents are usually very familiar with the web. A 2005 report by Packaged Facts concluded that there are nearly 29 million U.S. kids ages 8 to 14, with a combined annual purchasing power of $40 billion. With 90 percent of these children having internet access, this means there's a lot of money to be made by websites that can capture their attention. "This will be an increasing trend going into the future, as toy manufacturers attempt to use what is appealing about the internet (engagement and interactivity) to keep their products as current and relevant to today's `digi-native' kids as possible," says Anita Frazier, analyst for the marketing firm NPD Group.

Webkinz success is in part because they are affordable. They sell for $10 to $12.50 apiece, and Ganz recently added Lil' Kinz to its product line, a slightly smaller and cheaper version of the plush toys with all the features kids love about the full size Webzinz. With many stores receiving shipments that sell out within hours, some customers have turned to the internet to acquire these scarce toys. The seasonal Love Puppy can be found on Amazon.com selling for nearly $200. Highly demanded Webkinz, like the retired Cheeky Dog, have sold on eBay for more than $500.

Ganz reports that toy buyers have purchased more than 2 million Webkinz pets since April 2005 and more than 1 million users have registered at their Web site. The privately held toy maker will not reveal their sales figures but experts estimate they are high.

As for the future, although the actual number may vary a bit, according to McVeigh, Webkinz plans to release a new pet every month. Ganz is also seeking to extend Webkinz from a single toy line into a larger brand. In fact, they have already begun creating pursues, backpacks and other accessories children can use to carry their Webkinz pet. "We're certainly exploring a lot more customer-demand driven accessories," McVeigh says. "We're looking to develop that side of things-both things for the pets and products for the kids themselves."

1. *How has Ganz used demand and supply to influence the sale of Webkinz?*

2. *Most Webkinz sales come from small retailers. If Ganz had decided to sell their Webkinz Pets to large retailers such as Toys "R" Us and Wal-Mart, what effect might this have had on price and demand for the toy? Is Ganz's distribution strategy effective? Why or why not?*

3. *In this chapter you learned that prices serve several objectives. How has Ganz fulfilled relationship (customer) objectives?*

Sources: Eugenia Levenson, "NEW 'KINZ ON THE BLOCK," Fortune 155.4 (March 5, 2007): p18. From InfoTrac OneFile; Denise Pappalardo, "Fuzzy logic: How Webkinz is getting young kids hooked on the Web; Webkinz marries the Internet with soft, plush animal toys; even some adults are biting," Network World (April 2, 2007): pNA. From InfoTrac OneFile; Carleen Hawn , "Time to Play, Money to Spend.(What Works: The People and Companies that Get It; Social Networks)(Webkinz, Club Penguin)," Business 2.0 8.3 (April 2007): p43. From InfoTrac OneFile; Beth Synder , "THIS FROG SPEAKS VOLUMES ABOUT WORD-OF-MOUTH; Webkinz sell by the millions-without advertising,"(News) (Webkinz.com) (Web site overview); Bulik, "Small wonders," Advertising Age 78.4 (Jan 22, 2007): p4. From InfoTrac OneFile; "Playthings" 104.11 (Nov 1, 2006): p8. From InfoTrac OneFile.

CHAPTER 18

Pricing Strategies

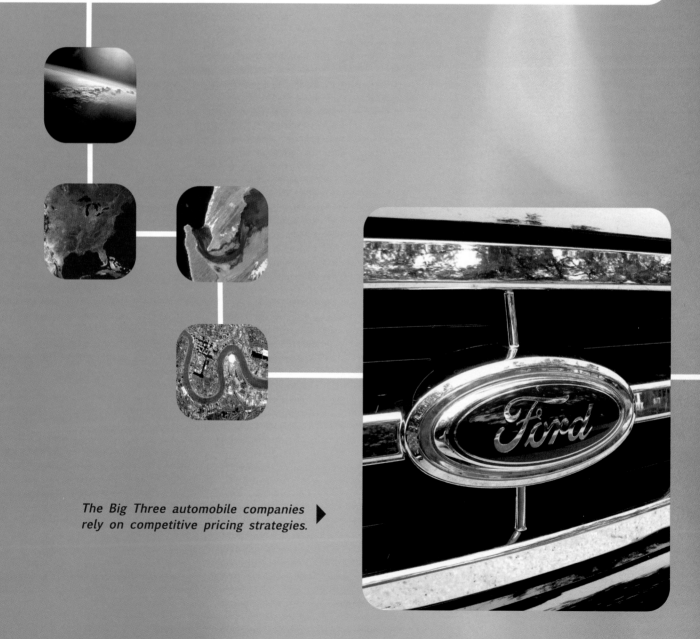

The Big Three automobile companies ▶ rely on competitive pricing strategies.

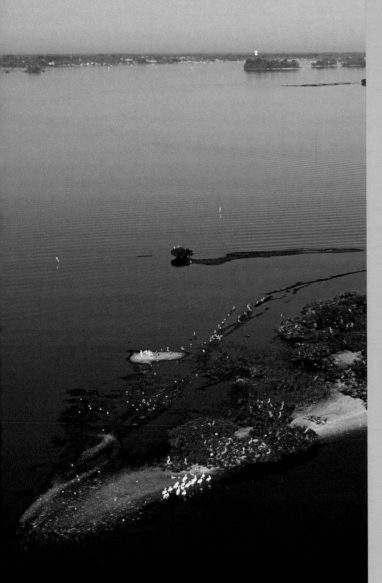

Learning Objectives

1. Understand why an appropriate customer value proposition is a useful guide to pricing strategy.

2. Know what factors to consider when using customer- and competitor-oriented pricing methods.

3. Learn how pricing strategy is implemented by setting prices and communicating them to the market.

The past few years have been dramatic for the auto industry in North America. Lagging sales, intense foreign competition, and high fuel prices caused increased inventories for General Motors, Ford, and DaimlerChrysler. Several years ago, falling sales led the Detroit companies to introduce huge employee pricing sales that quickly cleared dealer lots but significantly hurt profits and, in the longer run, discouraged new car sales because the resale values of their cars plummeted. The employee pricing programs mistakenly seemed like a big success, boosting summer sales for domestic auto makers substantially. However, foreign makers continued with their strategies of relying less on price incentives to sell cars. The U.S. companies have insisted that they do not plan to revive that strategy in 2008, no matter how bad the market becomes.

The problem with deep discounting was that is was neither sustainable nor profitable. Despite sales jumps, the domestic automakers actually lost profit. The price wars that GM began certainly helped to clear out some inventories, but hurt the long-term success of the company due to consumer expectations of lower prices. New products, like G.M.'s newly designed Chevrolet Malibu and Cadillac CTS sedans and the Ford Edge crossover vehicle, have sold exceptionally well, but they are not enough on their own to keep the companies from continuing to lose market share to foreign competitors. "We have some fairly severe headwinds: the weaker economy, high commodity and steel prices, and energy prices," Rick Wagoner, CEO of GM said. "Frankly, more headwinds, especially from the first two, than I would have hoped. We're going to be in soupy water for a while."

The deep discounting has also hurt the North American automaker's reputation. Customer loyalty is a key measure of success; last year Toyota was No. 1, with 65 percent of buyers trading in a Toyota for a new one, with Chevrolet at 56 percent and Pontiac at a dismal 28 percent, according to a J.D. Power survey. But Wagoner has made impressive progress. Before he took over North America, customers listed rebates and incentives as the number one reason to buy a GM vehicle. Today exterior styling is the biggest selling point.

Despite GM's recent woes, the automaker is planning to improve its current product line and strengthen its ability to manage increasing fuel prices and environmental issues. By 2010, GM plans to introduce the Chevrolet Volt, a four-passenger car powered by lithium-ion batteries. It is designed to run on those batteries for 40 miles, enough to satisfy the commuting needs of most Americans. Unlike current hybrids such as the Toyota Prius, the Volt will be capable of being recharged overnight when plugged into a household current and carries a small gasoline engine on board to recharge the batteries while underway, giving it a theoretical range of 640 miles. In the meantime, GM, and the other North American Automakers, must find a way to turn sales into profit and compete with foreign automakers.[1]

THE CONCEPT OF PRICE STRATEGY

This chapter could just as well be titled "Managing Customer Value." Pricing and value are so intertwined that you cannot talk about one without the other. Customers should receive an excellent value for the price they pay, and marketers should earn a satisfactory return. The objective of marketing is not simply to sell a product but to create value for the customer and the seller. Consequently, marketers should price products to reflect the value produced as well as received. Innovative marketers create value by offering, for example, a better product, faster delivery, better service, easier ordering, and more convenient locations. The greater the value perceived by customers, the more often they demand a company's products, and the higher the price they are willing to pay.

The firm is likely to incur higher costs when producing increased value. For example, it often costs more to make better products, create better distribution systems, or develop service facilities. Gillette can command higher prices because it invests in regular innovations in razor

tomers are willing to pay and the costs associated with the strategy. Essentially, the price charged is what marketers think their product is worth. The price paid is what the customer thinks the product is worth. If both parties have a similar price in mind, there is a strong likelihood that each party will believe it is worthwhile to trade.

It is not easy to establish precisely what price both buyers and sellers agree is appropriate. We need to look at how customer value is derived, recognizing that people place different values on the products they buy as well as the relationships they have with companies. Several pricing strategies may work. It all depends on how price is perceived, how competitors act, and how a strategy is designed and implemented. This chapter will deal with these issues. First, we will explore using value as the basis for pricing. We will learn how critical it is for relationship marketing. Next, we will discuss the methods used for customer, competitor, and global pricing. Finally, we will see how marketers implement the pricing strategy.

VALUE AS THE BASIS FOR PRICING

To arrive at the proper balance between the needs of the market and the needs of the firm, it is important to understand a marketing decision approach called value-based pricing. **Value-based pricing** recognizes that price reflects value, not simply costs. This is contrasted with cost-based pricing in Figure 18.1. Traditionally, firms assessed the costs of doing business, added a profit, and arrived at the price. Once it was set, the marketer's job was to convince customers that the product was worth it. If the marketer was not successful, then the price was lowered. If demand turned out to be higher than anticipated, then the price was raised. An important point is that the customer was the last person to be considered in this chain of events.

Value-based pricing begins by understanding customers and the competitive marketplace. The first step is to look at the value customers perceive in owning the product and to examine their options for acquiring similar products and brands. In other words, how much is the

Figure 18.1 Value-Based vs. Cost-Based Pricing

blades. In some cases, companies produce value by reducing their costs relative to those of competitors so that they can pass savings on to the customer in lower prices. That's how Wal-Mart became a leading retailer. It developed very focused marketing strategies that allowed dramatic cost reductions compared with rivals. By passing most of the savings on to customers, Wal-Mart gained considerable competitive advantage.

Whether a company improves its position through innovative products, distribution, communication, or cost cutting, the trick is to find a balance between what cus-

satisfaction gained from owning the product worth to them compared with what similar items or substitutes cost? Next, the marketer estimates the costs of production and necessary profit. To the extent possible, a similar analysis is usually done for each major competitor. Finally, product, distribution, and promotion decisions can be made. Notice that price is defined before developing the rest of the marketing mix. That way the marketer has a better chance of producing products at a volume competitive with rivals and of earning profits that satisfy the firm's financial objectives.

Although cost-based pricing is easier, it ignores the customer and the competition. Marketers know that it is impossible to predict demand or competitors' actions simply by looking at their own costs. Consequently, cost-based pricing is becoming less popular.

SOURCES OF VALUE

What is value? Generally there are two sources: value in use and value in exchange. **Value in use** is the customer's subjective estimate of the benefits of a particular product. **Value in exchange** is the product's objective worth in the competitive marketplace. Figure 18.2 describes these two concepts. Value in use is what economists call utility. The use value of a product is based on the buyer's needs and his or her understanding of the marketplace at a given time. For example, under normal circumstances a Snickers candy bar may sell for 75 cents. But after working several hours in a location where food is unavailable, a person may be willing to pay two or three dollars for it. In this case, the use value is high because of the buyer's circumstances. The exchange value is still 75 cents, the price established by competitive forces in the market.

Although general prices are based on value in exchange, companies also need to manage buyer percep-

www.volvo.com

Learn more about the Volvo Saved My Life Club by visiting the company's Web site. There is also information about hybrid technologies and renewable fuels.

tions of the value of their products in use. Volvo has captured buyers at relatively high prices for years because of a reputation for durability and safety. The Volvo Saved My Life Club is not an advertising gimmick. On their own initiative, Volvo owners who had survived a wreck wrote to the company about their real-life stories. Volvo then developed a campaign of testimonial print and television ads to promote the safety and reliability of the car and enhance value-in-use perceptions of consumers.[2] Volvo continues to take vehicle safety very seriously. It has a team of accident investigators that collect data on real-life accidents and this information is used in the development of new features.[3] Volvo's Safety Center developed the first "pregnant" crash-test dummy to analyze how they can make cars safer for pregnant women and their unborn children.[4]

CUSTOMER VALUE IN PRICING

Because prices send powerful messages, it is extremely important that they reflect the customer value the company delivers. Customer value is derived from the product itself, the services surrounding it, the company–customer interaction, and the image the customer associates with the product. First, we will examine the connection between price and customer value. Second, we will find out how market leaders create customer value.

Price and Customer Value Strategies The relationship between price and customer value is illustrated in Figure 18.3. FedEx, with its reputation for delivery 100 percent of the time by 10:00 a.m. the next day, is perceived by many consumers as having a high price and high customer value. The U.S. Postal Service (USPS) scores low on both dimensions. When FedEx introduced

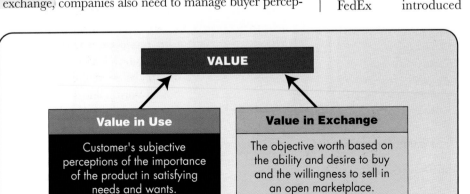

Figure 18.2 Sources of Value

VALUE

Value in Use
Customer's subjective perceptions of the importance of the product in satisfying needs and wants.

Value in Exchange
The objective worth based on the ability and desire to buy and the willingness to sell in an open marketplace.

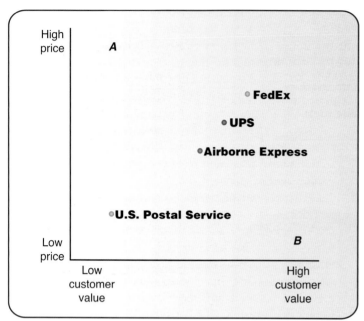

Figure 18.3 Price and Customer Value Strategies Example

overnight delivery, it charged 25 times more than the USPS. Rather than undercut price, it redefined expectations of high customer value.

Two hypothetical price strategies are indicated in Figure 16.3. Would it be practical for any company to use strategy A—high price and low perceived value? Clearly, few buyers would want to purchase from this company; they would give up more in price than they would gain in value. How about strategy B—low price and high value? Buyers would leap at the opportunity, but the company would be pricing at less than buyers are willing to pay. A strategy of this sort is called **buying market share**, that is, setting prices low in order to pull buyers away from competing brands. "Two Buck Chuck" is a wine that one consumer says is, "better than the box wines we drank in college for the same prices."[5] The wine brand is owned by a distant relative of the famous Gallo wine family. Basically, the $2 price is so low that it is taking market share from other labels. The potential profit that could come from a higher price is given up to gain market share. The payoff - the company has sold over 100 million pallets of wine.[6]

The strategy selected depends on the company's target market and the number of buyers who desire to purchase at

each value/price position. Any price strategy has the potential to produce profit or loss depending on the volumes it obtains and the marketing costs associated with it.

Customer Value Propositions Product leadership, operational excellence, and customer intimacy are the three strategies to deliver customer value. Because different customers buy different kinds of value, it is not necessary to be the best in all these areas. However, an organization should be excellent in one area and good enough in the other two to deliver what buyers want. Essentially, the customer value proposition for each of the three areas is (1) customers want the best products (product leadership); (2) customers want the best price (operational excellence); and (3) customers want the best solution (customer intimacy).[7] Figure 18.4 describes how companies gain leadership in customer value by matching their strategy with what buyers want.

Product Leadership The **product leadership** strategy builds customer value by differentiating the product. Nike and Intel come to mind. Both the design and functionality of their products are seen as offering high customer value. Both companies invest heavily in R&D, and they stay ahead of the pack in innovation. Customers have grown to rely on their leadership and are willing to pay extra, knowing they will benefit from the product's supremacy. At the same time, these leaders can cut prices on old models, keeping even price competitors in check. For example, Intel's release of new products like the Z series Atom processors will result in lower prices for older ones like the Quad-core Xeon processor series.[8] Each company has very good operations which keep costs in line, but neither is striving for the absolute lowest cost producer. Both also have good customer relationships, but few would describe them as pursuing customer intimacy strategies.

Operational Excellence An **operational excellence** strategy is designed to produce lower costs than competitors while achieving high quality. Why can Casio sell a calculator more cheaply than Kellogg can sell a box of cornflakes? For one thing, Casio's operational competencies translate into some of the lowest costs imaginable for manufacturing small objects. This means that no one can offer a lower price and sustain the same margins as Casio. Casio leads with price, its

Diabolo de Cartier Steel Writing Instruments. From $280.
www.cartier.com · 1-800-cartier

Cartier's pricing strategy reflects value, not just cost.

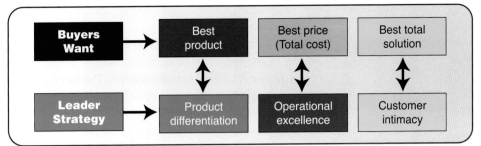

Figure 18.4 Leadership in Customer Value

product design is adequate, and its customer service is equitable.

Stat-A-Matrix has trained employees on Six Sigma, a program to help companies achieve operational excellence. The rigorous standards of Six Sigma, a program pioneered by Motorola, begins with setting goals such as less than two late deliveries per month, one customer complaint per year, and manufacturing all parts within design tolerances. It was introduced at Bank of America and has helped the company capture about $500 million in revenue gains and cost savings annually. These projects range from back office processes, to customer greeting, to fraud management.[9]

Customer Intimacy The **customer intimacy** strategy is about creating very close relationships. DHL has grown faster than rivals FedEx and UPS. It acquired Xerox Corporation as a client with a customer intimacy strategy. By carefully targeting a few accounts and working closely with them to identify and serve their specific needs, DHL has eliminated services the customers do not really want, while customizing services they desire. The company shares the rewards of intimacy by passing some of the savings on to customers. Both parties win.

CUSTOMER, COMPETITOR, AND GLOBAL PRICING

Customer-oriented, competitor-oriented, or global pricing describe the three ways to set prices.

CUSTOMER-ORIENTED PRICING

Marketers should keep in mind the effect of prices. Customers can't purchase everything they want, so they have to determine what will give them the "best value"—or, at least satisfactory value—for the money. But value is relative, not absolute. That is why exact prices are not nearly as important as price differences. Among the most important influences on customers are reference prices, price awareness, the association between price and quality, the perception of odd-even prices, and limited offers. Also discussed at the end of this section is target pricing.

Reference Prices Consumers try to obtain satis-

factory value, not necessarily the best value. They try to determine how much satisfaction will be gained by comparing the benefits and price of one product relative to another. In most situations it is simply not worth the time to make all the calculations necessary to identify the absolute best value. Instead, buyers use reference prices and a price range. The **reference price** is what consumers expect to pay, and the **acceptable price range** is all prices around the reference point that consumers believe reflect good value.

In many airports the price of food so far exceeds consumers' reference points and acceptable range that they are dissatisfied with purchases. The Greater Pittsburgh Airport Authority requires concessionaires to use prices consistent with those in "typical" retail settings. The result is a unit volume of sales and a percentage of satisfied customers much higher there than in many other airports. An important point is that consumers respond more to price differences than to absolute prices. A reference price is often used to establish that difference. It represents the basis for judging value. For example, if a brand price is greater than a reference price, then the consumer perceives a loss in purchasing that product. If the brand price is less than the reference price, then the consumer perceives a gain.[10]

Researchers have found that consumers are likely to accept a price range for products and adjust their reference price accordingly. The brands lying outside the range will be rejected, and their prices won't be used in creating the reference price.[11] For example, you are looking for a mountain bike and expect to pay about $500 to $600. You find several bikes similar to what you want with price tags from $375 to $450. Your range shifts to about $400 to $500, and your reference price drops to around $425. You also see bikes at $200 and $800 (a midpoint of

Marketing Vocabulary

BUYING MARKET SHARE
A strategy in which prices are set low for the short run to pull buyers away from competing brands.

PRODUCT LEADERSHIP
The value strategy that builds value by differentiating the product.

OPERATIONAL EXCELLENCE
The value strategy designed to produce lower costs than competitors while achieving high quality.

CUSTOMER INTIMACY
The value strategy designed to create close relationships with customers.

REFERENCE PRICE
The amount that consumers expect to pay for a product.

ACCEPTABLE PRICE RANGE
All prices around the reference price that consumers believe reflect good value.

$500), but those extremes do not figure in your calculations.

The reference price gives consumers an idea about the value they can expect. They can formulate the reference price in several ways:

- The last price paid
- The going price (amount paid most frequently)
- The believed fair price
- The average price
- The price limit (what most buyers will pay)
- The expected future price (price based on trends)[12]

Marketers also look at the differentiation value of their product's attributes to determine whether their brand is seen favorably or unfavorably. The buyer looks at the relative price and relative quality. If consumers tend to evaluate a product as better than others, then it has a positive differentiation value. This means that it may have higher demand or command a price on the upper end of the range. The opposite is true if a brand has a negative differentiation value.

Marketers often help consumers establish reference prices. How many times have you seen ads with the original price (manufacturer's suggested retail or list price) and a sale price? In this way, marketers attempt to create favorable differential price impressions. Other methods are "cents off," "everyday low prices," "new low prices," or promotions such as "2009 models at 2008 prices." Marketers must be careful, however, about price changes. If the frequency, length, and level of price promotions are not carefully managed, consumers' reference prices can be affected. As a result, consumers may lower their reference price.[13]

Price Awareness Business-to-business customers must be very price conscious. Each item they buy contributes to their costs and, thus, to their profits and competitiveness. Many businesses keep extensive records using formalized purchasing systems designed to obtain the best value for the price. Consumers tend to be less aware of actual prices. Studies of grocery shoppers have found that people are inaccurate about the exact price

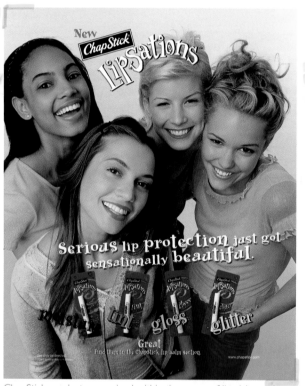

ChapStick products are priced within the range of lipstick products.

they paid for an item 90 percent of the time, and they err by approximately 20 percent.[14]

Price/Quality Association and Product Categorizations When buyers have little information about a product, they often assume a relationship between its price and its quality. In other words, price is a surrogate for quality. A traveler who doesn't know the local hotels may select a medium-priced unit, expecting an average room, or the highest-priced hotel, expecting luxury accommodations. Ordinarily, the product delivered should be consistent in quality with its price relative to the competition.

Sometimes putting a very low price on a high-quality item may reduce demand by signaling low quality. Nike found that higher prices on many of its signature lines increased sales because consumers perceived that the price tag matched the company's image. Would it make sense to price Michael Jordan signature shoes the lowest? Prices that are inconsistent with perceived value can confuse buyers. Price indicates not only what we expect to give up or pay but also what we expect to gain. If these two are highly inconsistent, we distrust the seller, our own judgment, or both. Nike decided not to do business with Sears Holdings, the combination of Sears and Kmart, because it might hurt its image. Kmart and Sears are discounters, which could undermine the premium image that Nike holds. Although Nike does sell to Wal-Mart, it only sells its swoosh-free Starter brand.[15]

Marketers refer to the top end of a price range as the **price ceiling.** Many companies establish ceiling prices from which reductions can be bargained.[16] In a product line with several levels of quality, there may be several ceiling prices. When consumers make few or no comparisons among brands, companies can charge prices at or near the ceiling. Companies with strong brands also can charge at the upper end. That is why Fuji is likely to price cameras at just under a $150 ceiling (or just under a $200 ceiling). It would be less profitable to charge $142.99 rather than $149.99. The $7 difference can add a lot to revenues but doesn't change the consumer's perception of value.

We know from experiments that price comparisons

are made on a ratio rather than an absolute basis. If a Toyota RAV4 has a sticker price of $20,000 and is sold for $1,000 less, then that is seen as roughly a five percent discount. The same discount on a RAV4 with a sticker price of $15,000 is seen as slightly larger, approaching seven percent. Although consumers may not actually compute the percentages, their perception works as if rough calculations were made.[17] Pricing policy must take this into account.

Consider the error made by a discount copying service that didn't understand how prices are perceived. Major copy centers had established copy prices of approximately four cents per page. The discount firm offered the same service for three cents a page. This attracted a lot of customers and produced a substantial amount of sales. The difference of "approximately 25 percent" was enough to entice many students. When the major centers increased price to five cents and then six cents, however, the discounter followed with two one-cent increases. At six cents per page, the one-cent differential was perceived as much smaller—only about 17 percent. The discounter's sales volume declined with each price increase, although the one-cent absolute differential in price was maintained.

Performance Pricing   Performance pricing provides a warranty that the product will perform as expected. It is generally used with new and uncertain products. Johnson and Johnson has negotiated with Britain's national health service using performance pricing, offering money back if its cancer drug Velcade doesn't work. If a patient on the $48,000 per year drug doesn't obtain expected results, Johnson and Johnson will refund the cost. Like in the U.S., British medicare providers are looking for new ways to justify spending great amounts on products that promise outstanding

value in use. Likewise, providers like Johnson and Johnson are looking for ways to charge higher prices for extremely innovative, high value products.[18]

Odd-Even Price Perceptions   Prices that end in odd numbers tend to be perceived differently from even-numbered prices. Consumers have learned that discounters tend to use prices ending in a nine, seven or five. Before sophisticated computer systems and inventory control systems were available, retailers used these endings as a code: nine identified a markdown, seven a second markdown, and five a third markdown. Early discounters adopted the odd numbers for all their products to suggest sales prices. Today, odd numbers connote lower quality and price, whereas even numbers connote higher quality and price.[19]

Limited Offers   Limited offers are often used by marketers to encourage consumers to buy types or quantities of products they had not planned to purchase. The special prices are meant to persuade consumers to stock up. Consider for example, the psychology behind a limit on sales. A special promotion for sugar may read "limit four." Why? A study has found that people are more likely to buy an item that has a limit. This is similar to children who want candy because they are told they cannot have any. Furthermore, one study showed that shoppers are more likely to buy an item with a limit of four rather than two.[20]

Target Pricing   Customer-oriented pricing focuses on buyers' psychological information processing and their perceptions of value in use and value in exchange. **Target pricing**, which uses price to reach a particular market segment, is a very important strategy. It is a way of matching price with the value perceived by each segment. Burton manufactures and sells snowboards that are marketed towards various types of snowboarders. Distinct lines are priced in relation to an individual's level of interest, ability and income. The Clash and the Bullet are value boards priced at $299.95 for beginners and price sensitive customers. Freestyle riders can choose from more than a dozen boards including the modestly priced Custom and Jussi models which sell for $499.95. For the ultimate enthusiasts in need of the latest and best in snow-

Courtesy of Sam's Club

Sam's Club is associated with low prices, which for some equates to lower quality.

Marketing Vocabulary

PRICE CEILING
The top end of a price range.

TARGET PRICING
The use of price to reach a particular market segment.

The Marketing Newspaper ™

CREATING & CAPTURING VALUE THROUGH RELATIONSHIPS

Banks Coddle Some Customers and Make Others Pay their Way

The retail banking industry has taken a sharp turn in some markets from focusing on serving its customers to focusing on its bottom line. Feeling the effects of this trend perhaps closest to home are clients of the New England banks that are being taken over by the New Jersey–based FleetBoston Financial Corp.

The general feeling of smaller account customers of these recently acquired banks is that they now need to pay for the services they may have previously enjoyed for free, while the big fish are treated like royalty. John S. Reed, the retired chairman of Citigroup, expressed his concerns by stating that financial institutions, "are poorly serving their customers."

The evidence? In the past, banks made their profit on the difference between interest paid to account holders and interest charged to borrowers. However, over the last few years, as interest rates fell and competition for loan customers increased, banks started to rely more on another stream of income: ATM and overdraft charges. While many banks offer free cash withdrawals from their ATMs, customers are often double charged for using other ATMs. After fees from their own bank and the owner of the ATM, customers pay nearly $3 on average for a single withdrawal. Many customers are unhappy with the growing expense of accessing their own money, something that was almost undoubtedly free in the past. In 2006, FDIC-Insured banks earned almost $220 billion in non-interest income, such as service charges and ATM fees, a number more than twice what it was a decade earlier.

Since most of a large commercial bank's, such as Fleet's, profits come from the big-ticket clients, the attention of the tellers and staff is focused on keeping those people happy, while perhaps neglecting or charging the little guy. Because of this, banks such as Fleet look to possibly lose many customers to smaller banks that can provide the services that people are seeking.

Not all banks, however, are concerned only with the big-ticket clients. Commerce Bank, the winner of a 2006 Consumers Report customer satisfaction survey, has emphasized convenience and customer service. "Smart bank executives realized their customers were comparing the way they were treated at their bank with their experiences at places like Nordstrom and Starbucks," says Jim Eckenrode, managing director of banking and payments for TowerGroup, an industry research firm. So Commerce Bank responded by investing in branches that stay open until 7:00 p.m., seven days a week. Commerce has also added door greeters and placed its tellers at concierge desks, instead of the traditional booth. With smaller customers in mind, Commerce offers a credit card with no late fee, no annual fee, and no balance-transfer fee. Better yet, it recently announced to rebate the fees its customers are charged by other banks for using those banks' ATMs

So the point remains that in order to effectively determine a bank's pricing policy, keeping each of its customers in mind is vitally important to success.

boarding technology, Burton offers the Vapor for $999.99. Burton also markets boards designed especially for women, such as the Feelgood at $499.95, and boards for kids priced at $249.95 and less.[21] As with most forms of customer-oriented pricing, target pricing requires a good understanding about what price communicates to potential buyers.

COMPETITOR-ORIENTED PRICING

Competitor-oriented pricing focuses primarily on prices set by rivals. Leader-follower, going rate, discount or premium, and competitive bids are all price schemes of this type. Carried to its extreme, competitor-oriented pricing can lead to mutually destructive price wars.

Leader-Follower Pricing Recently, manufacturers of major household appliances, also known as white goods, were faced with rising commodity costs from oil and steel shortages. As a result, Whirlpool decided to raise prices by up to 10 percent. Competitors like Maytag and Electrolux followed by increasing prices. Although material and energy costs were squeezing profits, all were able to produce additional profits through retail prices which more than compensated for price increases.[22]

Competitor-oriented pricing often involves scenarios such as this. The leader-follower situation tends to occur in oligopolistic industries whose products have relatively inelastic derived demand. The leader usually has considerable strength—high market share, a loyal customer base, an efficient cost structure, moderate inventory, and a technological edge. Gas stations use price leadership to determine prices. The stations with the largest share of the market dictate the price.[23] Leaders generally can exercise power, but often that is not necessary. The reason is that they create competitive environments, which benefit followers by providing fair profits for all. Good followers can also help create a positive industry pricing climate. In banking, most small and medium-sized institutions copy the products and pricing policies of larger competitors.

Price leaders must show a willingness to defend their position when price becomes an issue. Yet, across-the-

board cuts may hurt larger companies more, so it's important to be selective. After the Spanish government began taking anti-smoking measures, Spanish-French tobacco company Altadis raised prices in order to pass tax increases on to consumers. However, Phillip Morris' response to the government measures was a price drop on Marlboro cigarettes. Altadis was then forced to lower its prices by 20 percent taking a huge hit to its profits, and declared that it was the manufacturers' responsibility to price higher in order to maintain a virtuous cycle. Competition drove cigarette prices in Spain down to about a quarter of those in the UK.[24]

Discount or Premium Pricing Discount or premium pricing positions the company relative to competitors based solely on price. In most markets there are buyers who seek the cheapest products and those who seek the most expensive. Consider the sale of store-brand hair coloring at very low prices and L'Oréal at a higher prices. L'Oréal says its hair coloring is the more expensive "because I'm worth it." The Meijer food chain establishes the lowest price possible and asks: "Why pay more?"

Going Rate Pricing The **going rate** price evolves over time when no competitor has power over others so all price at a similar level. This is often the case in monopolistic competition when product differentiation is very minor and firms attempt to gain loyalty while pricing at the going rate. For example, lawyers often charge the going rate per hour, which will vary considerably from one community to another. The going rate tends to avoid price wars. Because all providers charge approximately the same, and these prices are broadly communicated, buyers' price expectations are usually met. When Connecticut Light & Power experiences more demand than anticipated, ener-

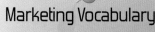
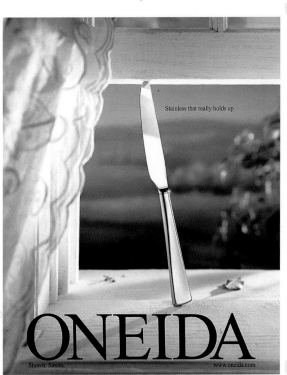

Oneida sells its flatware at higher prices than competitors because it offers high quality and value to customers.

gy is purchased at an auction for a price that creates enough supply to meet demand. However, natural gas sets the going rate because it produces about 40 percent of the region's electricity and is also the most expensive source.[25]

Competitive Bids   We tend to think of bids as related to the purchasing function, but they also are a prevalent form of competitive pricing. Sealed bids are opened at a certain time, and the low price usually is the winner. An alternative is for buyers to look at bids as they are received and perhaps give feedback to sellers indicating they are too high. This is called open bidding, and it is intended to get suppliers to lower prices.

By understanding competitors, a company can greatly enhance its ability to win contracts at the highest possible price while still being the low bidder. Competitors often scale prices up or down to meet their own volume or cost objectives. By knowing competitors' capacity and cost structure, marketers can adjust their own bids. At priceline.com, a commonly used web auction site, customers can "name their own price" for airline tickets, home financing, hotel rooms, rental cars, cruises, and vacation packages. The customer's price is either accepted or rejected. Upon rejection, the customer is able to submit another bid at a higher price. [26]

Price Wars   **Price wars** occur when price cuts by one company spur similar reductions by competitors. These price-slashing battles can substantially lower profit margins. The consumer benefits, since products can be purchased below their value. The company most successful at cutting costs is usually the victor—if it can survive despite the meager profit margins. Large organizations with ample reserves have an obvious advantage.

Price wars have been especially common in the airline industry, with the success of low cost carriers like Southwest and JetBlue. One day after JetBlue announced a flight from Boston to New York for $69 round trip, American and Delta followed suit by cutting prices by as much as 80 percent. This heavy discounting technique was pioneered by Southwest and has been very successful. If these price wars continued to different routes, profits for American and Delta would undoubtedly take a large tumble. JetBlue, on the other hand, experienced positive moves in market share with better than expected results.[27]

Some price wars are especially damaging. Historically, phone companies have experienced price wars. However, the telecom climate has moved away from cutthroat competition to consolidation. The joining of Verizon with MCI, Sprint with Nextel, and AT&T with SBC and Cingular may allow the newly formed companies to raise prices slightly. However, this will not

last long as they continue to add more and better services. With new opportunities, such as Voice over IP as well as wireless services, the competition is sure to heat back up. The push for new technology is forcing companies to look at the effects of the price war. Maintaining a lion's share of the market will require continuous improvement in performance and service to keep up with the needs of customers and still make a profit.[28] It can be advantageous for a company not to participate in a price war. Heinz typically will not participate in price wars and has not suffered major losses as a result.

GLOBAL PRICING

Global pricing is complicated by many factors. One of the most important is when a government mandates that imported products cannot be paid for with cash; **countertrade** requires companies from the exporting nation to purchase products of equivalent value from the importing nation. Countertrade affects up to 30 percent of all world trade. When a nation's banking system is poor, countertrade may be the best form of pricing. It also provides governments with a mechanism for stimulating exports. For example, until a few years ago all trade between Eastern Europe and Russia was done through countertrade. Eastern Europe paid for Russian gas and oil with pharmaceuticals from Hungary, machine tools from former Czechoslovakia and East Germany, food products from the Balkans, and textiles from Poland.[29] In other words, countertrade is a simple barter, the exchange of one good for another.

Although technically the term refers to government-regulated exchanges, countertrade also may be initiated by trading partners. There are many arrangements similar to barter that can benefit both parties. There may be tax advantages to not using cash. Agreements to purchase like values but without exchanging money can increase demand. A countertrade deal that covers an extended period can provide a lot of flexibility in scheduling, manufacturing, and shipping. Japanese and Dutch trading companies may have hundreds of these arrangements going at one time. The Japanese keiretsu system relies on cross-ownership, cross-ties in banking, and discrimination against outside buyers and sellers to form huge trading organizations.[30] By locking suppliers into the organization, enormous cost savings result. The major keiretsu are Mitsui, Mitsubishi, Sumitomo, Fuyo, Sanwa, and Daiichi. However, these arrangements between closely knit manufacturers, suppliers, and distributors are eroding in Japan.[31]

International pricing also is complicated by the need to transfer funds. Payment is seldom direct, and generally a bank must be involved. This often requires a letter of credit that specifies the bank will pay a seller under various conditions. Because a good deal of time may pass between the settlement of an international deal and the transfer of products and funds, financing is critical. If it is poorly executed, then a lot of money can be lost.

Exchange fluctuations also influence global pricing. Companies that use value-based pricing tend to treat these fluctuations differently from those that use cost-plus pricing. As exchange rates go up and down, profit margins tend to vary. The cost-plus method simply increases or decreases price to keep the same margins, which changes what buyers pay. The value-based method tends to leave prices the same, varying instead the level of profit. Japanese companies exporting to the United States tend to maintain stable prices, reflecting their tendency to keep them in line with the market as well as profit objec-

tives.[32] This works unless exchange rates fluctuate widely. For example, if the Japanese Yen depreciated in relation to the dollar, Japanese companies such as Honda, Sony, and Nissan could lower prices on their U.S. products. Many companies benefit when the dollar is strong because foreign made products and components are cheaper. However, this can also create challenges for domestic companies attempting to keep up with the lower prices offered by foreign competitors.

IMPLEMENTING THE PRICING STRATEGY

Once the overall pricing strategy has been chosen, it must be implemented. Since prices are easier to adjust than any other part of the marketing mix, they tend to fluctuate. Even companies with consistent pricing based on customer value make changes. Whether initiating a new strategy or adjusting an existing one, the first step in implementation is to set prices. The second step is to communicate them to the market. At both stages, ethical issues are involved.

SETTING PRICES

Fundamental Strategies for Price Setting Price strategies are often categorized according to the following six approaches: skimming, penetration, sliding down the demand curve, the price umbrella, everyday low prices, and promotional pricing. Companies can price high, low, or in between. Whatever the decision, it is sure to affect buyers and competitors. Figure 18.5 describes the funda-

Strategy	Objective	When Typically Used
Skimming	High short-term profit without concern for the long run	No competitive products Innovation or fad Block competitor entry due to patent control, high R&D costs, high fixed costs, control of technology, government regulation, or high promotion costs Uncertain demand and/or cost Short life cycle Price-insensitive buyers
Sliding Down the Demand Curve	Gain short-term profits before competitors become entrenched without sacrificing long-term market share	Launch of high-technology innovations Slight barriers to competitive entry Medium life cycle
Price Umbrella Leadership	Encourage competitors to promote the product category to stimulate purchase of all brands and encourage competitors to follow the price leader	Several comparable competitors Growing market Stable competitors One or a few dominant competitors
Everyday Low Prices or Value Pricing	Appeal to buyers willing to shop for the "greatest" benefits for the money	Component parts in industrial markets Repurchased consumer products Mass merchandisers Established products
Promotional Pricing	Stimulate demand to introduce or reintroduce a product, neutralize a competitor, or move excess inventory	Demand fluctuates seasonally or for a certain period Marketing "wars" or head-to-head competition Mass merchandisers Fashion items
Penetration Pricing	Stimulate market growth and capture market share; become entrenched to produce long-term profits	Large markets Products of broad appeal Long product life cycle Very price-elastic demand

Figure 18.5 Fundamental Strategies for Price Setting

Marketing Vocabulary

PRICE WAR
A cut by one company spurs similar reductions by competitors, resulting in price slashing that can lower profit margins

COUNTERTRADE
Government mandates that imported products can't be paid for with cash; the exporting country must purchase goods of equivalent value from the importing nation.

mental strategies for price setting.

Skimming and Penetration Pricing These two approaches are discussed together because they are opposites. **Price skimming** is designed to obtain a very high price from relatively few consumers with the desire to buy irrespective of price. The name is taken from the practice of dairy farmers, who once skimmed the valuable cream off the top of nonhomogenized milk and discarded the remainder or fed it to farm animals. Today, skimming is used by companies with certain innovations or fads. Marketers charge a very high price, thereby attracting only a small part of the total market. Because use value is high in a product's introductory period, a premium can be obtained. When more producers enter the market, prices tend to move downward as exchange value declines.

If companies perceive they can obtain a monopoly position for a short time, then they might skim to generate profits that provide investment capital for further innovations. To sustain skimming, companies must offer unusual products of the highest quality or artistic value. Many times this strategy does not produce loyal customers, since subsequent entrants eventually will offer a better value at lower price. In contrast to skimming, **penetration pricing** seeks the maximum number of buyers by charging a low price. This approach is used for products that are very price elastic. If costs are sensitive to volume, then these will drop dramatically as share increases relative to competitors. This is a way to keep rivals from entering the market, since many companies avoid situations in which overall prices are extremely low.

The problem with penetration pricing is that losses are likely, especially in the short term. Because profit margins tend to be very small, demand must meet expectations in order to generate enough earnings. Furthermore, when customers buy only because of price, loyalty tends to be low. They are likely to switch to competitors offering an even lower price or innovations of higher value at a higher price.

Figure 18.6 summarizes the main features of skimming and penetration pricing, which are opposite ends of a spectrum. Because neither is likely to achieve strong buyer loyalty in competitive markets, most companies use pricing approaches that fall somewhere between these extremes.

Sliding Down the Demand Curve To **slide down the demand curve** means to descend from higher to lower prices when competitors enter. When launching its industrial control products, Texas Instruments has been known to use this strategy. First, management establishes a high price for an innovative product to skim the market. Second, when a major competitor follows with its version, Texas Instruments drops its price—sometimes only slightly, often considerably. This aggressive strategy discourages or delays market entrants, and Texas Instruments obtains high short-term profit margins without sacrificing its long-term objective of penetrating the market.

The Price Umbrella DuPont is known for its leadership in innovations. It produces innumerable plastics, fibers, and chemicals used to create thousands of products, and is doing so in more and more sustainable ways. Because of its strength, the company is in a perfect position to use the **price umbrella**; that is, the leader prices high. Competitors can make fair profits at that level or even lower, especially if their costs are relatively low. Price leadership occurs when one or two companies price in such a way that others follow them. In DuPont's case, marketers launch innovations after careful study of the product's likely contributions to customers and society. By assessing the use value relative to substitutes and other brands, DuPont establishes a price commensurate with the high value it typically offers. Along with the product, buyers receive DuPont's uncompromising customer support, which is based on an advanced distribution system, consultative and relationship selling, and service.

Generally, DuPont's price is high enough to encourage other healthy companies to participate in the market. At the same time, because several competitors are promoting a similar product, demand is stimulated for the product category. DuPont even licenses its products to rivals in exchange for a percentage of sales revenue. Since these competitors do not have to engage in basic R&D, DuPont's leadership in product innovation is protected.

Everyday Low Prices Wal-Mart is famous for its **everyday low prices**, which on average are consistently lower than those of competitors. Sometimes this strategy is called value pricing (not to be confused with value-based pricing). In order for it to work, retailers need to develop extremely efficient (low-cost) operations. Wal-Mart has the most advanced computerized restocking system imaginable. Rapid turnover (products don't sit on the shelves for long) and aggressive purchasing power provide the basis for keeping prices low. Wal-Mart has approxi-

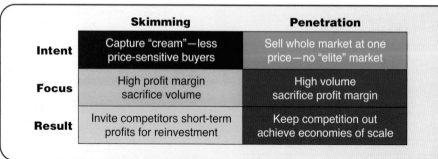

	Skimming	Penetration
Intent	Capture "cream"—less price-sensitive buyers	Sell whole market at one price—no "elite" market
Focus	High profit margin sacrifice volume	High volume sacrifice profit margin
Result	Invite competitors short-term profits for reinvestment	Keep competition out achieve economies of scale

Figure 18.6 Skimming vs. Penetration Pricing

mately $375 billion in sales annually and is the largest retailer in the world.[33] Target and Toys "R" Us also use this strategy—and pledge to meet or beat any competitor's price on any item. In this way, they maximize volume and keep customers from shopping around. Another example is Riesbeck Food Market, an independent supermarket chain in Ohio and West Virginia. Reisbeck moved to an everyday low price strategy several years ago after noticing the rise in popularity of supercenters and dollar stores. As a result, the company has been quite successful, but it is set to face one of its biggest challenges in the coming year as Wal-Mart stores in its area will nearly double.[34]

Everyday low pricing can be highly competitive on an international scale as well. For example, Zellers, Canada's low-price leader, used the slogan "lowest price is the law." Its profit margins shrank when Wal-Mart entered the Canadian market, and the two now compete intensely with their value-pricing strategies. The Zellers slogan is "there's more than low prices," while Wal-Mart continues to implement cuts in order to offer the lowest regular prices to consumers. In an effort to keep its customers and lure customers from its rival, Zellers became the first retailer in the world to seek and gain from the International Organization for Standardization in Geneva its certification that it meets world-class standards of efficiency and quality. Wal-Mart has run into problems with price controls, strict labor laws, tough zoning regulations, and fierce competition. Mature rivals, such as Aldi and Lidl are more than ready to compete on low prices and are familiar with thin profit margins.[35]

Promotional Pricing
Companies such as Coca-Cola and PepsiCo, Burger King and McDonald's, and Toyota and Nissan are nearly always engaged in some form of **promotional pricing**. These battles serve three purposes. First, the price discount is a way to make consumers notice the product. Second, immediate purchase is encouraged because promotional pricing gives consumers the impression that the price is likely to rise in the near future. Third, consumers are kept aware of the

www.target.com

What other pricing approaches does Target use? Visit its Web site and find out. While you're there, be sure to read up on the company's environmental policies.

entire product category. The "wars" between Coke and Pepsi keep buyers loyal to cola at the expense of other soft drinks. Marketers in these two companies expect continuous challenges from one another as price interacts with other parts of the marketing mix to stimulate demand and produce minor market share shifts.

One kind of promotional pricing is loss leaders, used by retailers to lure consumers into their store. As you'll remember from the previous chapter, these products are priced at or below the retailer's cost. For example, the Midwest grocery chain Meijer often prices milk very low compared with competitors. Because this item is purchased regularly by most consumers, its price tends to be remembered. For that reason, milk and similar repeat purchases provide shoppers with a ready source of comparison among rivals. At the same time, shoppers can benefit from the price reduction on most trips. Retailers make up for loss leaders by increased volume or higher prices on other items.

There are many other forms of price promotion. Although we usually assume that price reduction is most likely to stimulate demand, sometimes any message drawing attention to the prod-

Burger King partnered with Visa to offer their joint customers promotional pricing.

Marketing Vocabulary

PRICE SKIMMING
A strategy designed to obtain a high price from relatively few consumers with the resources to buy irrespective of price.

PENETRATION PRICING
A strategy seeking the maximum number of buyers by charging low prices.

SLIDE DOWN THE DEMAND CURVE
A strategy that involves setting a high price when a product is introduced and lowering it significantly as competitors enter the market.

PRICE UMBRELLA
The leader maintains the price at a high enough level that competitors can earn a profit at the same price or lower levels.

EVERYDAY LOW PRICES
Prices, on average, are consistently lower than those of competitors.

PROMOTIONAL PRICING
A strategy in which price discounts are used to gain attention and encourage immediate purchase.

uct, including a price differential, will lead to purchase. Marketing research by a major pharmaceutical company revealed some surprising news. For many years, price promotions had been used to boost sales of selected prescription drugs. Each time the product was promoted at a reduced price by sales representatives, physicians prescribed it more. The assumption was that these products were price elastic for doctors, but the research found that most of them didn't know the price of these drugs and did not much care. Then why the increase in prescriptions? The study found that the price reduction gave salespeople a reason to discuss the product with physicians; drawing their attention to the product was what increased prescriptions. Subsequent research revealed that nearly any relevant sales message led to a rise in sales because, for established and commonly used drugs, many doctors prescribe the brand that first comes to mind—often the one discussed most recently with a sales rep. The point is that price decreases often stimulate sales, but the attention drawn to a product by price promotions also may be a factor.

PRODUCT LINE PRICING STRATEGIES

Consumers tend to use all products in a company's line as a way of making comparisons. Consequently, marketers use several strategies: product array, bundled, optional product, and captive product pricing.

Product Array Pricing Most companies sell several products. These may be offered within the same brand, such as different GMC trucks, or in several lines, such as Chevy, Pontiac, and Cadillac. Prices need to be established across the entire product array. Although digital photography has significantly reduced the sale of film, photo stores still carry a deep line of film. The difficulty arises because products are often substitutes for one another. Kodak film is sold at different prices depending on the shutter speed used to take pictures. Many speeds will work well enough for most amateur photographers, although a certain speed may be preferred for a certain shot. Many consumers select Kodak film at a premium price over rivals because of its reputation for lasting quality. They then must choose among film type and speed. Pricing often plays a major role in precisely which product is bought, since all the Kodak films are likely to be displayed close together. If price differences cause confusion, then consumers may become dissatisfied. Kodak is careful to price each product so that the differences help the photographer select differing value—what is best for action photos, landscapes, or flash shots. The various price points offer value for nearly every photographer. If one average price were used for all Kodak film, then competitors would quickly take share with dramatically lower prices.

Bundled Pricing Products can be bundled or unbundled for pricing purposes. The bundled approach, which gives a single price for the entire offering, is used for standardized products, whereas unbundling is often used for customized products. For example, home builders use each method depending on the offering. Houses in a subdivision usually are priced to include carpeting, fixtures, and landscaping, whereas various items will be listed separately for custom homes. Even property and land preparation cost will be specified. The unbundling helps custom buyers assess the value to them of each item and make choices according to tastes and budgets. Comcast offers packages that bundle digital cable, high-speed Internet and Comcast Digital Voice®. Other telecom companies also offer discounts to customers that buy more than one service.[36]

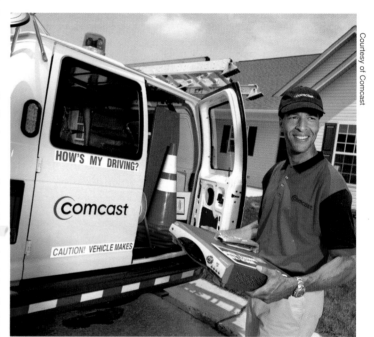

Courtesy of Comcast

Comcast provides bundled pricing for its cable, phone and internet packages.

Optional Product Pricing Many products are sold as a base unit with optional add-ons. Cars are an obvious example. Dodge's Charger has a base price of $22,020 but customers can add over $4,000 in options.[37] Add-ons for automobiles include satellite radios, sunroofs, security features, and alloy wheels. Companies often price the base product low as a platform for selling other items. Telephone companies also use this method. When you sign up for service, you also can buy caller ID and call waiting.

Captive Product Pricing It is pretty obvious why Gillette prices its razors low. Once you own one, you will buy blades—perhaps for years. In a sense, you're a captive customer, but since razors and blades are not very expensive, the cost to escape is minor. But how about the cost of moving from XBOX to PlayStation video games? You will need to purchase a new system (at a price of $350 or more), and your current games no longer will be useful. The average consumer might find that switching console systems is far too costly and continue to purchase XBOX brand products. The captive product strategy is used by many marketers. Internet-access cellular phone companies price with a variation on the captive theme. They have an installment fee, then a fixed rate plus a variable usage charge. Often the fixed rate is set very low in order to obtain the more profitable usage fees.

price are these:

- Finance charges
- Installation fees
- Warranty charges
- 800-number assistance
- Replacement parts inventory
- Shipping and handling
- Training

It is important to communicate clearly the components that are included within a price quotation. If buyers are hit with unexpected charges for items they thought were included within the original price, dissatisfaction is likely. This is because many consumers believe this is unethical behavior on the part of the seller.

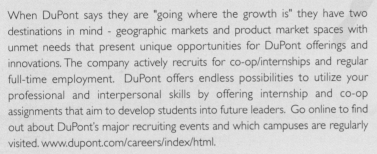

Career Tip:

When DuPont says they are "going where the growth is" they have two destinations in mind - geographic markets and product market spaces with unmet needs that present unique opportunities for DuPont offerings and innovations. The company actively recruits for co-op/internships and regular full-time employment. DuPont offers endless possibilities to utilize your professional and interpersonal skills by offering internship and co-op assignments that aim to develop students into future leaders. Go online to find out about DuPont's major recruiting events and which campuses are regularly visited. www.dupont.com/careers/index/html.

COMMUNICATING PRICE

An important step in price implementation is to communicate with the market. This involves more than just advertising a figure. The price may have several components that are quoted in differing ways, and various kinds of price reductions can be offered.

Price Components Let's say that Joan Martin purchased Rossignol skis, poles, and boots at the California Ski Company outlet. The package cost $800, and the total including tax was $848. Her roommate purchased the same package at a Winter Sports Equipment store for $800, but the total including tax was $893. She was charged $30 extra for binding installation and $15 for tuning the skis. Whether the buyer or seller pays for "extras" can make a substantial difference in price.

In consumer markets, there is wide variation in what is included in the price. Foot Locker will return your money if a shoe does not meet your expectations. If the support breaks down before you think it should, then you can take the shoes back for a refund or a new pair, no questions asked. Although the Foot Locker price may be similar to that of other retailers, others may not provide the same level of customer service. Foot Locker's return policy is added value. The most common additions to

Price Quoting Price quoting is how prices are communicated to buyers. Some companies offer price quoting service. For example, Progressive Auto Insurance uses online comparative shopping by showing quotes from their competitors as well as their own. This establishes rapport with consumers and makes them feel confident they are getting a fair and reliable price.[38] Sometimes prices are stated clearly and directly, but often an indirect method is used. The **list price** (or suggested retail price) set by the manufacturer usually provides the reference point by which consumers judge the fairness of the market price. The **market price** is the actual amount buyers must pay for the product. Often the list price is much higher than the market price. For example, when Sony introduces a product the list price may be over double the market price. The market price is likely to result from several types of reductions, including discounts and rebates.

Price Reductions Discounts are often given for cash payment, for purchasing large quantities, or for loyalty. Cash discounts are offered to consumers, business-to-business customers, and nearly all channel members. Many buyers look at the undiscounted price as a penalty for delayed payment. Discounts are incentives to speed cash flow from buyer to seller, and they are standard in many

Marketing Vocabulary

LIST PRICE
The price set by the manufacturer and used by consumers as a reference point. Also called suggested retail price.

MARKET PRICE
The actual price buyers must pay for a product.

industries. It is common for cash discounts to be quoted in terms of a percentage reduction and a specific time for payment, most often 2/10, net 30. This says the buyer has a two percent discount if paid in 10 days, and full payment without a discount is due in 30 days. Many buyers pay within the first 10 days because a two percent discount figured over the remaining 20 days is equivalent to an interest rate of about 36 percent on an annual basis. Sellers use the discounts to speed payment and reduce losses due to bad debts. Many industries have increased their prices by nearly two percent to offset these cash discounts.

Quantity discounts, which are reductions for large purchases, are justified because the seller has lower costs when handling larger orders. That is, selling, order processing, billing, shipping, and inventory carrying costs are averaged over a greater volume. It is common for a supplier to use quantity discounts to entice buyers to purchase more and to achieve economies of scale for transportation and processing costs.[39] These can be offered at one time or on a cumulative basis. Eddie Bauer sells Foot-Cushioning socks for $7.50 per pair, but when a customer buys three pairs or more, they can save $1 per pair.[40] Another example is mutual funds, which often charge differing commissions, or "loads," depending on the amount purchased. One popular fund charges 4.25 percent for orders less than $50,000, 3.5 percent for $50,000 to $100,000, and 2.5 percent for more than $100,000. The buyer has up to one year to meet the commitment.

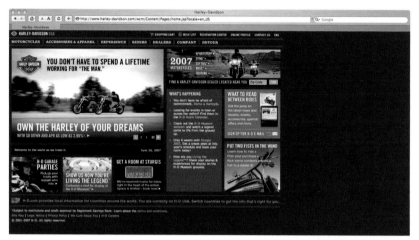

Web and E-Commerce Stars
Harley-Davidson - www.harleydavidson.com

The Harley-Davidson Company designed their Web site for consumer's to have the complete Harley experience. More than just a retail outlet for their motorcycles and accessories, visitors can join the Harley Ownership Group (H.O.G.) and read about motorcycle education and safety. For the avid Harley riders, the website offers information about great riding roads in the United States as well as a trip planner. And if a visitor is interested in buying a Harley, www.harley-davidson.com includes a side-by-side spec sheet and a complete list of accessory pricing, making it an easy way to shop.

Patronage discounts are very similar to cumulative quantity discounts and they reward buyer loyalty. An example is a café that stamps a card for each cup of coffee bought and then gives a free cup when the card is full. Another variation is Sam's Club, a no-frills retail buying center developed by Wal-Mart, which offers discounts only to fee-paying members. Discounts should not be used, however, as the sole means for achieving customer loyalty. Customers who buy your product because of price are likely to switch to a competitor for the same reason.

Rebates reduce prices through direct payments, usually from the manufacturer to the consumer. In today's competitive car market, rebates are a popular way to move cars off the lot. Rebates may have a greater psychological effect on customers than discounts. The buyer perceives a rebate as a large amount of money. In contrast, the discount is seen as a small percentage of the total price. Remember that price differentials make the largest impression on buyers. With rebates manufacturers also are more assured that the rebates will not be partially absorbed by dealers. Sometimes, when discounts are

http://globaledge.msu.edu

Visit globalEDGE™ Online for the ultimate international marketing research tool!

globalEDGE™
Pricing Strategies

A component of offering value to customers is to offer high quality while keeping prices low. Currently, your firm manufactures precision components in the Riverside and San Bernadino areas in California. However, to give your firm competitive alternatives, you have performed some regional and city comparisons concerning the costs of producing precision manufacturing products. Since your firm would like to keep operations in North America, which location has the lowest cost structure for your firm's particular industry? If your firm was willing to internationalize production, would the decision for manufacturing re-location change? Provide sufficient information to justify your position(s).

given to dealers with the idea that they be passed along to consumers, part of the difference is kept by the dealer.

UNETHICAL PRICING PRACTICES

When marketers develop a pricing strategy, it should reflect the value perceived and received. This does not always happen. Abuses can occur through manipulation of the consumer's reference price, quoting overcharged or misleading prices, or using discriminatory pricing practices. Unethical pricing can have legal repercussions, not to mention the risk of losing valuable customers.

As mentioned earlier, the reference price serves as a guideline to consumers. What happens when marketers manipulate that price in order to change the consumer's perception of what is "fair"? Three studies have addressed this issue.[41] When a reference price is set at an implausibly high level, it can influence perceptions about a fair price as well as the highest price. Another study indicates that plausible reference prices can strongly influence customers' estimates of the highest and lowest prices for a given item, but implausible reference prices have little impact on their estimates.[42] Therefore, it is important for marketers to establish reference prices with care.

Another unethical practice is to quote unclear or misleading prices, which can have serious legal consequences. After Hurricane Charlie in Florida, Days Inn in West Palm Beach and Crossroads Motor Lodge in Lakeland charged substantially higher rates than normal to customers trying to get out of the storm. A billboard close to the Days Inn reportedly advertised rooms for under $50 per night. However, consumers were forced to pay over $100 per night. Civil suits were filed to the Attorney General against the two establishments, which were subject to penalties of $1000 per violation and up to $25,000 for multiple violations.[43]

Discriminatory pricing practices are often very controversial. Is it fair to charge a woman more than a man for dry-cleaning a shirt or for a haircut? This depends on a number of circumstances. Are the shirts similar, or is the service more difficult to perform for one gender versus another? Since most women have longer hair than men, perhaps it is more difficult or time-consuming to cut. Nevertheless, studies have found that women do pay more than men for products ranging from haircuts to cars.[44] In 1995, with the Gender Tax Repeal Act, California became the first state to prohibit gender discrimination in pricing for similar services. Even so, a number of California businesses continue to use different prices. Three years after the passage of the act, the California Public Interest Research Group reported that many dry cleaners and hairdressers continued to charge higher prices for services to women than to men. Because of the small amounts involved in these price differences, however, very few women have chosen to take costly legal action against businesses that violate the law.[44]

Chapter Summary:

Objective 1: Understand why an appropriate customer value proposition is a useful guide to pricing strategy.

Pricing strategies are complex and must balance the needs of both the customer and the firm. Value-based pricing, which includes the concepts of value in use and value in exchange, is increasingly popular. Since customers seek differing types of value and competitors have a broad range of choices in how to price, other strategies are viable as well. In devising a pricing strategy, it is important to identify a customer value proposition that matches the capabilities of the organization. The three types of capabilities are product leadership, operational competence, and customer intimacy.

Objective 2: Know what factors to consider when using customer- and competitor-oriented pricing methods.

Pricing strategies may focus on customers, competitors, or global factors. Customer-oriented pricing requires an understanding of reference prices, price awareness, price/quality association, odd-even perceptions, limited offers, and target pricing.

Competitor-oriented pricing considers leader-follower scenarios, going rates, discounting, and competitive bids. Some companies engage in price wars that can seriously affect industry and company profits. On a global scale, pricing may include countertrading or barter. Funds transfer and exchange rates also affect international pricing.

Objective 3: Learn how pricing strategy is implemented by setting prices and communicating them to the market.

Implementing a price strategy requires setting and communicating prices. One of six fundamental approaches can be used to set prices: skimming, sliding down the demand curve, price umbrella, everyday low prices, promotional pricing, and penetration pricing. Product line pricing complicates matters. Options are product array, bundled, optional product, and captive product pricing. When prices are communicated, various components may be specified or only the overall price, and various reductions may be offered. Price communication must be done carefully to avoid unethical practices, such as false impressions about price or unfair discrimination.

Review Your Understanding

1. What is value-based pricing? How does it differ from cost-based pricing?
2. What is value in use? Value in exchange?
3. What three leader strategies match what buyers want?
4. What are reference prices? Give several categories.
5. What is a ceiling price, and how is it used in setting prices?
6. How are odd and even prices perceived?
7. When is going rate pricing used?
8. How is pricing used to attract senior citizens?
9. What are price skimming and penetration pricing?
10. What is umbrella pricing?
11. List three aspects of product line pricing.
12. How are prices quoted?
13. What is discriminatory pricing?

Discussion of Concepts

1. How are price and value related? What are the advantages of value-based pricing over the traditional cost-based approach?
2. What is the difference between value in use and value in exchange? How could a marketer use these concepts to improve profitability?
3. What is required if a company wants to use product leadership, operational competence, or customer intimacy as the basis for establishing a customer value proposition? Give examples of each.
4. How does competition affect a company's prices? Briefly describe the major competitor-based pricing approaches.
5. We know that several factors influence consumer responses to prices. What psychological factors should marketers keep in mind when using consumer-oriented pricing? Describe each.
6. How is a company's market position related to price leadership? What does this have to do with price wars?
7. Describe the six fundamental ways to set price. In what situations is each strategy typically used?
8. How does the communication of price present ethical dilemmas? Give examples of several questionable practices.

Key Terms And Definitions

Acceptable price range: All prices around the reference price that consumers believe reflect good value.

Buying market share: A strategy in which prices are set low for the short run to pull buyers away from competing brands.

Countertrade: Government mandates that imported products cannot be paid for with cash; instead, companies from the exporting nation are required to purchase products of equivalent value from the importing nation.

Customer intimacy: The value strategy designed to create close relationships with customers.

Everyday low prices: Prices that, on average, are consistently lower than those of competitors.

Going rate: The price that evolves over time when no competitor has power over others and all price at a similar level.

List price: The price set by the manufacturer and used by consumers as a reference point. Also called suggested retail price.

Market price: The actual price buyers must pay for a product.

Operational excellence: The value strategy designed to produce lower costs that competitors while achieving high quality.

Penetration pricing: A strategy that seeks the maximum number of buyers by charging low prices.

Price ceiling: The top end of a price range.

Price skimming: A strategy to obtain a very high price from relatively few consumers, who have the resources and desire to buy irrespective of price.

Price umbrella: The leader maintains the price at a high enough level that competitors can earn a profit at that or lower levels.

Price war: A cut by one company spurs similar reductions by competitors, resulting in price slashing that can lower profit margins.

Product leadership: The value strategy that builds value by differentiating the product.

Promotional pricing: A strategy in which price discounts are used to get attention and encourage immediate purchase.

Reference price: The amount consumers expect to pay for a product.

Slide down the demand curve: Set a high price when a product is introduced and then lower it significantly as competitors enter the market.

Target pricing: The use of price to reach a particular market segment.

Value-based pricing: A strategy that reflects value, not just cost.

Value in exchange: The objective worth of a product in the competitive marketplace.

Value in use: The consumer's subjective estimate of the benefits of a particular product.

References

1. "Auto Makers Return to Deep Discounts; GM's Problems Prompt Price Cuts of up to $10,000; Ford, Chrysler Likely to Follow", Wall Street Journal, Nov. 15, 2005. "Editorial: GM in a Battle for Survival", Knight Ridder Tribune Business News, Nov. 20, 2005. "Carmakers & apos: Year in Review: Last Reminder of 2005 to be Unveiled Today: Industry to Move on After Sales Report", Knight Ridder Tribune Business News, Jan. 4, 2006. "Auto Makers Return to Deep Discounts; GM's Problems Prompt Price Cuts of up to $10,000; Ford, Chrysler Likely to Follow", Wall Street Journal, Nov. 15, 2005; 2007 GM statement of earning for 2006; Taylor, Alex, III. "Gentlemen, Start Your Turnaround. (Features)(Interview)." Fortune. 157.1 (Jan 21, 2008); Nick Bunkley, "Final Darker 2008 For Detroit's Automakers," January 1, 2008, The New York Times

2. www.volvocars.com/us/footer/about/VolvoSavedMyLifeClub, site visited March 19, 2008.

3. "Volvo Traffic Accident Research Team Continues to Revolutionize Passenger Safety After 30 Years," PR Newswire, December 20, 2000, ptg.djnr.com.

4. www.popularmechanics.com/technology/industry/1286406.html, site visited March 19, 2008.

5. CBS Evening News Los Angeles, June 2003, Accessed April 18, 2007.

6. Jean Marbella, "Two buck chuck adds its own mystique to wine market," The Baltimore Sun, December 12, 2003.

7. Michael Treacy and Fred Wiersema, The Discipline of Market Leaders (Reading, MA: Addison-Wesley, 1995).

8. Intel Microprocessor Quick Reference Guide, http://www.intel.com/pressroom/kits/quickrefyr.htm, site visited May 12, 2008.

9. "BofA Praises Workers for Achievements", Knight Ridder Tribune Business News, July 2005.

10. Praveen Kopalle, Ambar G. Rao, and L. Joao Assoncao, "Asymmetric Reference Price Effects and Dynamic Pricing Policies," Marketing Science, 15, no. 1 (1996): 60–85.

11. Joel E. Urbany, William O. Bearden, and Dan C. Weilbaker, "The Effects of Plausible and Exaggerated Reference Prices on Consumer Perceptions and Price Search," Journal of Consumer Research 15 (June 1988): 95–110.

12. Michael H. Morris and Gene Morris, Market Oriented Pricing (Lincolnwood, IL: NTC Business Books, 1990), pp. 5–8.

13. "Consumers' Reference Prices: Implications for Managers," Stores 78 (April 1996): RR4.

14. Joel E. Urbany and Peter R. Dickson, Consumer Knowledge of Normal Prices: An Exploratory Study & Framework (Cambridge, MA: Marketing Science Institute, 1990), pp. 7–8.

15. "Nike, with little explanation, has decided not to do business with Sears. Who's image suffers?", New York Times, May 5, 2005.

16. Yongmin Chen and Robert W. Rosenthal, "On the Use of Ceiling Price Commitments by Monopolies," Rand Journal of Economics 27 (Summer 1996): 207–220.

17. Gilbert D. Harrell, Consumer Behavior (New York: Harcourt Brace Jovanovich, 1986), p. 68.

18. Andrew Pollack, "Performance Pricing: Drug Company Offering a Money Back Guarantee," New York Times, July 14, 2007, p. B1.

19. Gilbert D. Harrell, Consumer Behavior (New York: Harcourt Brace Jovanovich, 1986), p. 68.

20. Vince Staten, "Can You Trust a Tomato in January?" Library Journal, July 1993, p. 179.

21. www.burton.com, site visited March 24, 2008.

22. "Whirlpool lifts prices to offset commodity costs", Financial Times, February 4, 2005.

23. "Gas Stations Sometimes Follow the Price Leader, Execs Say," Associated Press Newswires, July 7, 2000, as retrieved from the World Wide Web: ptg.djnr.com.

24. Delphine Strauss, "Altadis Enters Spain's Cigarette Price War," February 1, 2006. Financial Times. www.ft.com visited March 24, 2008.

25. "Deregulation benefits soften Connecticut Light & Power rate hike", Knight Ridder Tribune Business News, January 2006.

26. www.priceline.com, site visited March 24, 2008.

27. "American, Delta cut JFK air fares to match JetB", Knight Ridder Tribune Business News, October 2005.

28. "Telecom mergers will end price wars", Kiplinger Forecasts, Nov. 2005. "Convergence makes rivals out of cable companies and telecoms", Knight Ridder Tribune Business News, October 2005.

29. "Eastern Europe considers more trade with Russia," New York Times, July 8, 2005.

30. Genay Hesna, "Japan's Corporate Groups," Economic Perspectives 15 (January–February 1991): 20–30.

31. "Japan: Just the facts," Journal of Commerce, June 2005.

32. Onkvisit and Shaw, International Marketing, p. 614.

33. "Wal-Mart Reports Record Fourth Quarter Sales and Earnings," www.walmartfacts.com/articles/5675.aspx site visited March 24, 2008.

34. "Pricing model; Rural independent keeps customers coming back with everyday low prices in grocery aisles", Supermarket News, February 2006.

35. "How big can it grow," The Economist, March 2004.

36. www.comcast.com, site visited March 24, 2008.

37. www.dodge.com/en/2008/charger, site visited March 24, 2008.

38. www.progressive.com, site visited March 24, 2008.

39. W. C. Benton and Seungwook Park, "A Classification of Literature on Determining the Lot Size under Quantity Discounts," European Journal of Operational Research, July 19, 1996, pp. 219–238.

40. www.eddiebauer.com, site visited March 24, 2008.

41. Tracy A. Suter and Scot Burton, "Believability and Consumer Perceptions of Implausible Reference Prices in Retail Advertisements," Psychology and Marketing 13 (January 1996): 37–54.

42. Bruce L. Alford and Brian T. Engelland, "Advertised Reference Price Effects on Consumer Price Estimates, Value Perception, and Search Intention," Journal of Business Research, Vol. 28, No. 2, May 2000, p. 96.

43. "Florida hotels charged with price gouging," www.consumeraffairs.com, August 2004.

44. Gerry Myers, "Why Women Pay More," American Demographics 18 (April 1996): 40–41.

45. Emily Bazar, "Women Pay More for Services, Study Finds," The Nando Times, October 29, 1998, www.techserver.com/newsroom/ntn/nation/102998/nation15_24075_body.html, visited December 15, 2000.

The Marketing Gazette:
Siow Li Sen, "Jostling for the Lucrative Consumer Business," Business Times (Singapore), May 24, 2000, Banking and Finance, p. 6, retrieved November 12, 2000 from the World Wide Web: www.web.lexis-nexis.com; Geoffrey Smith, "Bigger Isn't Better for Fleet's Customers," Business Week, July 10, 2000, p. 64; and Don Stancavish, "Boston-Based Bank Reassures New Jersey Residents About Buyout," The Record (New Jersey), retrieved November 11, 2000 from the World Wide Web: web.lexis-nexis.com/universe; "Customer service is getting new attention, but watch out for those sneaky fees," Consumer Reports, September 2006 www.consumerreports.org June 20, 2007; FDIC: Historical Statistics on Banking Report, Table CB07, Noninterest Income and Noninterest Expense, www.fdic.gov, site visited May 01, 2008; Greg McBride, "Checking Survey: ATM Fees Hit a Record High," www.bankrate.com, site visited May 01, 2008.

Harley-Davidson

In 1903, the first Harley-Davidson was sold—a single-cylinder, belt-driven two-wheeler. It was ridden for 100,000 miles by four owners without replacement of a single major component. The company still enjoys the reputation of producing outstanding, high-quality, high-value motorcycles. In the early days, there were 151 motorcycle manufacturers, but only Harley-Davidson and Indian came through the Great Depression, and by 1953 Harley was the sole survivor. Today, Harley dominates the domestic market and international sales comprised 22 percent their global retail volume. Harley retailers sold more than 330,000 new motorcycles worldwide in 2007.

Much of the value of a Harley resides in its tradition—the look, sound, and heritage that have made it an all-American symbol. Customers include people like the CEO of Southwest Airlines, Forbes magazine founder Malcolm Forbes, and Tonight Show host Jay Leno. The Harley V-twin engine designed in 1909 still turns heads across America with its throaty rumble, and the bikes are easily recognized by their teardrop gas tank and oversized instruments. According to Jeffrey Bleustein, a Harley owner, the bikes "represent something very basic—a desire for freedom, adventure, and individualism."

Harley-Davidson CEO Richard Teerlink foresees continued growth. He believes that the Harley buyer is getting older, more affluent, and much better educated. A recent study showed that the average Harley rider is now 47 years old and has a salary of over $82,000 per year. The company is no longer dependent on the Hell's Angels crowd, and it has an audience that can really afford the higher-priced products. "There's a high degree of emotion that drives our success," says Teerlink. "We symbolize the feeling of freedom and independence that people really want in this stressful world."

Harleys are expensive compared to other brands, ranging from $6,595 for an 883 Sportster to the custom models price as high as $33,495. Furthermore, used bikes may cost far more than their original selling price due to limited edition models and collectors items. How is it possible to command such premium prices for a product that is slower and less fuel efficient than many of the performance bikes from Europe and Asia? Clearly, the competition has technological superiority.

Even if you were willing to pay $25,000 for a top-of-the-line Harley, until recently you would likely have to wait more than a year for delivery. However, with increased production, customers have a chance to receive their bikes more quickly. Despite the fact that rivals such as Yamaha have started creating look-alikes, Harley enjoys brand recognition and loyalty experienced by few other products.

With supply finally catching up to demand, Harley may have some interesting marketing challenges, particularly in the area of pricing. Forbes asks, "Is Hog Going Soft?"

Although Harley's share of its class of bikes has recently held steady near 50 percent, a few years ago it exceeded 70 percent. Before recent efforts to improve its supply chain, dealers could obtain premium prices for bikes they did not yet have. Now that the machines are immediately available, prices are negotiable. Dealers now have plenty of new and used bikes in stock, including some of the models traditionally hard to find. The amount of stock may mean demand has been satisfied and may present problems for future pricing. Harley continues to fine-tune its distribution system by working with dealers to ensure they have the right mix of products, in the right markets at the right time. Also, retail sales drive wholesale shipments which in turn could drive company growth.

The price competition is also getting tougher. For example, Honda's American Classic lists for under $10,000, whereas Harley's similar Dyna Low Rider starts at about $14,595. And Yamaha has made technical improvements, such as an easy-to-maintain shaft instead of a belt drive. Does that matter to bikers who wear T-shirts that say "I'd rather push a Harley than drive a Honda?" Sales of lower-priced models, such as Harley's Sportster, which enters the market at around $6,595, have declined due to inroads by Suzuki's Intruder, Kawasaki's Falcon, and Honda's American Classic, which sell between $6,500 and $11,000. According to Gil Steward, sales manager of Harleys "R" Us, "Bikes are still selling, but the price is coming down." That means reduced profit margins.

"We don't just deliver bikes, we deliver experiences," says Jay Dabney, dealer at Skip Fordyce Harley-Davidson located in Riverside, CA. A few years back, Harley-Davidson requested retailers upgrade their showrooms to include better locations, décor and more room to accommodate for increased accessories, clothing and motorcycle inventory. These upgrades, along with the reduced profit margins, challenged retailers to maintain profitability but in 2006, retail sales increased by 5.9 percent, proving the upgrades were worthwhile. "Harley-Davidson dealers have the tools they need to ensure an extraordinary retail experience. This year, my sales staff attended a Harley-Davidson University course to learn about and ride competitors' products. Because of a thorough training like that, we are prepared to answer any customer question," Dabney says.

Recently, Harley-Davidson has begun a full range of marketing outreach activities, new events, and new strategies to connect with emerging customer markets. Harley began hosting Garage Parties at local dealers. These free women-only events offer information to non-riders with little motorcycle knowledge. Through efforts like this, Harley-Davidson has been able to grow in unexpected markets. In fact, in a 2006 company study, 12 percent of U.S. retail motorcycle sales of new Harley-Davidson motorcycles were to female buyers.

Harley experienced a slight slip in revenue during 2007 due to low sales in the US, but international sales were up more than 17 percent from the prior year. International shipments now compose more than 25 percent of the company's total sales. However, with the majority of sales revenue generated by domestic sales, its strong international year was not enough to offset the 14 percent decrease in US sales. While sales have slowed at home, Harley expects earnings to improve in 2008, fueled by a continued increase in international market share.

1. Describe the Harley-Davidson pricing strategy. What does the company's positioning have to do with its pricing strategy?

2. How does the fact that Harley has a relatively deep line of heavy bikes influence the pricing of each product within the line?

3. Create the customer value proposition that would allow Harley-Davidson to continue using a premium pricing strategy.

4. Should Harley alter its price, given strong price pressures from rivals? If not, what strategy should it pursue in light of industry developments?

Sources: www.harley-davidson.com; Gary Strauss, "Harley Working to Stay Leader of the Pack," USA Today, November 5, 1997, www.usatoday.com; "Harley Davidson Plans Marketing Tactics after Indiana Headquarters Opening," Knight-Ridder/Tribune Business News, November 12, 1996, pp. 11–12B; Gina Fann, "Nashville, Tenn., Cycle Shop Finds a Niche Renting Harley-Davidson Bikes," Knight-Ridder/Tribune Business News, April 25, 1997, p. 42B; Dyan Machan, "Is Hog Going Soft?" Forbes, March 10, 1997, www.forbes.com; Gary Hamel, "Killer Strategies That Make Shareholders Rich," Fortune, June 23, 1997, www.fortune.com; Ronald B. Lieber, "Selling the Sizzle," Fortune, June 23, 1997, www.fortune.com; www.harley-davidson.com, November 15, 2000; Steve Watkins, "Harley Vrooms Through Wall Street with Hog Lovers, Restless Boomers," Investor's Business Daily, September 1, 2000; Tony Kennedy, "Victory's Slow Start Surprises Polaris, Which Ups Incentive and Advertising," Star Tribune (Minneapolis, MN), August 13, 2000; and Angela Daidone, "With Baby Boomers Fueling Growth, Harley Davidson Hogs the Motorcycle Market," The Record (New Jersey), September 24, 2000; 2006 Annual Report, Harley-Davidson. www.Harley-Davidson.com June 20, 2007; Rich Rovito, "International Roar: Harley Looking Overseas for Sales Recovery," Feb. 01, 2008, Business Journal of Milwaukee;

credits

Photo credits are listed throughout the text adjacent to the appropriate image. Images not credited in the text are cited below, property of the author, or deemed public domain.

Ad and Image Credits:

Chapter 1 **5** ©istockphoto.com/Oksana Perkins; **11** ©istockphoto.com/Lise Gagne; **15** ©istockphoto.com/Mark Evans; **18** Courtesy of Microsoft; **20** Courtesy of Coca-Cola; **25** Barbie ad courtesy of Mattell, Inc.; **26** ©istockphoto.com/Kenneth C. Zirkel.

Chapter 2 **40** Courtesy of Texaco, Inc.; **43** courtesy of UPS; **44** Courtesy of E.I. Dupont Corp.; **54** Used with permission of Wal-Mart. **55** licensed under Creative Commons by Douglas Whitaker.

Chapter 3 **65** ©istockphoto.com/Jerry McElroy; **72** Courtesy of Phoenix Wealth Management.

Chapter 4 **103** Oren Jack Turner, Princeton, N.J.

Chapter 5 **121** ©istockphoto.com/ranplett; **148** Courtesy of Merle Norman Cosmetics; **134** Courtesy of Allstate/Lapiz; **137** licensed under Creative Commons by Festival Eurockéennes; courtesy of JC Penney; **137** Courtesy of Bozell Worldwide; **140** 2000 American Baby Group. A division of Primedia Magazines, Inc.

Chapter 6 **149** ©istockphoto.com/laughingmango; **153** Courtesy of Principle Financial Group; **154** Courtesy of Timken; **156** Courtesy of CNF; **157** Courtesy of Zurich-American Insurance Group; **158** ©istockphoto.com/Ben Blankenburg; **159** Courtesy of Siemens AG; **164** Used with permission of 3M; **165** Courtesy of the American Arbitration Association.

Chapter 7 **186** Courtesy of American Airlines.

Chapter 8 **199** ©istockphoto.com/Rafal Belzowski; **201** Courtesy of the St. Paul Companies, Inc.; **204** Courtesy of Tropicana Products Inc.; **207** Courtesy of Gillette Company; **208** Courtesy of Ford Motor Company; **219** ©2000 Keebler Corporation. Used with Permission; **221** ©istockphoto.com/Lisa F. Young.

Chapter 9 **242** Courtesy of McDonald's; **243** Courtesy of MGM Grand; **251** ©2000 Callard & Bowser-Suchard Inc.; **252** Courtesy of Proctor & Gamble Company.

Chapter 10 **259** ©istockphoto.com/Bettina Ritter; **261** courtesy of TGI Friday's; **262** courtesy of walmartfacts.com.

Chapter 11 **289** ©istockphoto.com/Kimberly Deprey **294** ©2001 Ferrero. Photographer: Victor Schrager; **297** Courtesy of 3M.

Chapter 12 **326** courtesy of Rubbermaid; ©istockphoto.com/Andyd; **327** Courtesy of Consolidated Shoe Co.; **328** Courtesy of Life and Health Insurance Foundation.

Chapter 13 **345** ©istockphoto.com/Tashka; **349** Courtesy Mazda; **350** Courtesy of America's Dairy Farmers; **350** Courtesy of Campbell's Soup; **354** Courtesy of Daimler Chrysler Corporation.

Chapter 14 **386** Courtesy of Adobe; **391** Courtesy of Dovebid; **396** Courtesy of Thingamajob.com; **400** Courtesy of Telcordia Technologies.

Chapter 15 **411** ©istockphoto.com/Tammy616; **413** Courtesy of Delphi; **415** Courtesy of Yellow Freight Systems; **419** ©istockphoto.com/Rick Sargeant; **420** Courtesy of United States Postal Service. **420** ©istockphoto.com/thecarlinco; **421** Courtesy of Schenker; **429** Courtesy of Blimpie.

Chapter 16 **442** Courtesy of Dior. **439** courtesy of Home Depot;

Chapter 17 **465** ©istockphoto.com/Danny Warren; **477** courtesy of McDonald's; **468** Courtesy of Clinique Cosmetics; **477** Courtesy of Whirlpool Corporation; **481**©istockphoto.com/Lori Lee Miller.

Chapter 18 **494** Courtesy of Diablo de Cartier; **496** Courtesy of ChapStick; **499** Courtesy of Oneida.

index

A

A.C. Neilson, 102, 103, 440

AARP, 12, 130

Abell, Derek, 46

Accenture, 169, 275

Acceptable price range, 495

Access to more customers, 86

Account planning, 388

Action groups, 68

Active learning, 123

Activity quotas, 398

Adero Incopororated, 24

Administering surveys, 107

Adoption process, 308

Advanced Micro Devices Inc., 50

Advertising agencies, 352

Advertising campaign, 354

Advertising, 330, 348

Advocates, 163

African Americans, 26, 135

Age cohort, 76

Agility, 8

Aided recall, 359

Air transport, 419

Allen-Bradly Corporation, 296

Allocation, 455

Allowances, 364

Allstate Insurance, 125

Alltel Wireless, 224

Alternatives evaluation, 124

America Online, 24

American Airlines, 242

American Express, 23, 182, 242, 275, 323

American Marketing Association, 6, 83, 112, 278, 281

Americans with Disabilities Act, 26

Analysis of process problems, 187

Anheuser-Busch, 242, 249, 331

Apple, 6, 10, 11, 42, 45, 47, 52, 143, 150, 153, 213, 237, 250, 292, 300, 309, 310, 345

Approach, 390

Approach-approach conflict, 126

Approach-avoidance conflict, 127

ARAMARK, 44, 149, 153, 239, 264, 444

Armstrong, Lance, 277

Asian Americans, 26, 134

Assessing SBUs, attractiveness-strength matrix, 42

Assessing SBUs, growth-share matrix, 42

Associative reference groups, 137

Assortment, 455

AT&T, 27, 45, 47, 66, 267, 336, 337, 346, 388, 389, 422

Attitude, 130

Augmented product, 235

Automated vending retailers, 443

Aveda, 15, 24

Avoidance-avoidance conflict, 126

B

Bait and switch, 474

Bargaining power, 70

Bargaining, 166

Base technology, 44

Baxter, 8

Behavioral, 130

Behavioristic Segmentation, 212

Belief, 130

Ben & Jerry's, 27, 142

Benchmarking, 188

Benetton Group, 416

Best Buy, 52, 269, 361

Best practices, 188

Better information, 85

Better prices, 86

Blockbuster, 183

BMW, 178, 347, 470

Boeing, 8, 380

Bonus, 399

Booz, Allen & Hamilton, 101, 290, 302

Borden, Neil, 11

Boston Consulting Group, 42

Brand associations, 248

Brand awareness, 247

Brand equity, 246

Brand insistence, 248

Brand loyalty, 247

Brand, 241

Branded product, 235

Breadth, 240

Brokers, 422

Buick, 81

Build-up segmentation method, 214

Bundling strategy, 235

Burger King, 57, 100, 107, 357

Burt's Bees, 428

Business analysis, 297

Business definition, 39

Business-to-business advertising, 351

Business-to-Business marketing, 9

Business-to-Consumer e-commerce, 83

Buyer's market, 16

Buying center, 162

Buying decisions, 154

Buying market share, 494

C

Calloway, 131

Campbell's Soup Company, 112, 308, 320

Canon, 44

Capital products, 238

Carnival Cruise Lines, 270

Cartel, 80

Case analysis, 106

Cash cows, 42

Cash-and-Carry wholesalers, 457

Caterpillar, 188, 426

Causal research, 107

Cause marketing, 277

CBS, 153

CDW, 160

Cental Intelligence Agency, 66

Center of influence, 389

Centralized decision making, 218

Chain stores, 443

Channel levels, 422

Chapstick, 132

Cheerwine, 248

Cingular, 47

Classical conditioning, 129

Closing, 391

Coach, 51

Coca-Cola, 6,8, 12, 20, 28, 84, 103, 122, 128, 161, 183, 202, 215, 235, 241, 242, 248, 249, 276, 291, 308, 321, 331, 346, 359, 369

Cognitive, 130

Cold calling, 389

Commercial market, 151

Commercialization, 299

Commission, 399

Commitment, 181

Communication, 320

Company sales forecast, 397

Competition, 69

Competitive advantage, 249

Competitive behavior, 8

Competitive bidding, 156

Competitive budgeting method, 353

Components of the strategic marketing plan, 48

ConAgra, 129

Concentrated marketing, 219

Concept testing, 297

Consolidated Metropolitan Statistical Area, 76

Consultative selling, 383

Consumer behavior, 122

Consumer decision making, 124

Consumer marketing, 9

Consumer promotions, 361

Continuity, 357

Continuous improvement, 186

Continuous innovation, 292

Contractual channel system, 425

Control process, 54

Control review meeting, 54

Controlled test market, 299

Convenience products, 236

Convenience samples, 110

Convenience stores, 444

Conventional channel system, 425

Conway, 420

Core competencies, 43

Core product, 234

Core service, 273

Core values, 37

Corporate channel system, 426

Cost structure, 177

Costco Wholesale Corporation, 219, 427, 461

Cost-plus pricing, 480

Countertrade, 500

Coupons, 365

Courtship phase, 159

Crate & Barrel, 178

Creative strategy, 353

Credence qualities, 270

Cross-docking, 417

Cross-functional planning team, 46

Cross-price elasticity of demand, 470

Cross-selling, 362

Culliton, James, 11

Cultural environment, 76

Culture, 132

Customer defections, 178

Customer expectations, 178

Customer intimacy strategy, 47

Customer intimacy, 495

Customer lifetime value, 177

Customer loyalty, 177

Customer marketing era, 17

Customer orientation, 7

Customer satisfaction measurement program, 179

Customer satisfaction, 176

Customer value, 14

CVS, 237

D

DaimlerChrysler, 102, 159, 181, 187, 207, 243, 303, 450, 473, 491

Data, 99

Database, 100

Decentralized decision making, 218

Deception, 348

Decision makers, 163

De-ethnicization, 210

Dell, 85, 87, 159, 199, 303, 328, 369, 438, 450

Deloitte & Touche, 112

Delphi Corp., 222, 384, 385, 394

Demand curve, 469

Deming prize, 188

Demographic environment, 74

Demographic segmentation, 206

Department of Defense, 22

Department stores, 444

Depth interviews, 105

Depth, 240

Derived demand, 150

DHL, 13, 420, 446, 485

Diassociative reference groups, 137

Differentiated marketing, 218

Differentiation strategy, 47

Differentiation, 478

Diffusion process, 309

Direct channels, 422

Direct export intermediaries, 56

Direct Marketing Association, 452, 453

Direct sales, 378

Directory advertising, 351

Direct-response advertising, 352

Discount stores, 444

Discontinuous innovation, 292

Discretionary income, 72

Discrimination, 129

Disney, 35, 36, 41, 45, 50, 242, 274, 276, 345

Disney, Walt, 35

Disposable income, 71

Distribution centers, 416

Distribution channel, 20, 52

Divergence, 274

Diversity segmentation, 209

Domino's, 221, 240

Dow Chemical, 150

Dreamworks, 276

Drop Shippers, 457

Drucker, Peter, 9

DSL, 181

Dumping, 474

DuPont, 44, 68

Dynamic quality, 186

Dynamically continuous innovation, 292

E

Early adoptors, 309

Early majority, 309

East Asia, 73

Ebay, 65

Ecomagination, 5

Economic environment, 71

Economic order quantity, 418

EDS, 154, 239

Effective, 130

Effectiveness, 8

Efficiency, 8

Efficient consumer response programs, 420

Einstein, Albert, 103

Electronic Arts, 80

Electronic data interchange, 416

Eli Lilly, 36, 38, 40, 45, 303

EMC, 377

Emergency products, 236

Empathy, 181, 390

Encoding, 131, 325

Environmental forecast, 397

Environmental Protection Agency, 81, 222

Environmental scanning, 66

Ernst & Young, 262

Ethical environment, 82

Ethics, 26

Ethnic background, 25

Ethnicity, 25

Europe, 73

European Union, 72

Event marketing, 276

Everyday low prices, 502

Evolution of Marketing, 15

Exchange rate, 485

Exchange, 11

Exclusive dealing, 430

Exclusive distribution, 426

Experience qualities, 270

Experiments, 107

Exploratory research, 104

Export and import intermediaries, 56

Export subsidy, 484

Exports, 56

Exposure, 354

External research, 112

Extractor market, 151

Exxon-Mobil, 152, 183

F

Family brand strategy, 245

Family decision making, 138

Family life cycle, 139

Family purchasing roles, 138

Family, 138

Federal Trade Commission, 80, 81

FedEx, 10, 13, 43, 45, 154, 187, 273, 446

Field selling, 380

Financing incentives, 365

Fixed costs, 478

Fluctuating demand, 151

Focus group, 104

Follow-up, 392

Food and Drug Administration, 79

Forces important to create and capture value, 21

Ford, 16, 49, 58, 68, 81, 111, 388, 413, 473, 491

Ford, Henry, 16

Foreign Licensing, 57

Forestry Systems, Inc., 55

Form Utility, 12

Forrester Research Group, 100

Franchise system, 425

Franchise, 265

Franchising, 57

Frequency, 357

Freight forwarders, 421

Frito-lay, 161, 299

Fuji Film, 40

Full nesters, 140

Full-line forcing, 430

Full-service wholesalers, 456

Functional element, 273

Functional managers, 162

G

Gannett Co., 100

Gap, 256

Gatekeeper, 162

Gateway, Inc., 268

Gatorade, 10, 68

GATT, 74

General Electric, 5, 6, 36, 40, 44, 48, 67, 100, 150, 304, 393, 424

General line wholesalers, 456

General Mills, 9, 58

General Motors, 413

General Motors, 13, 28, 40, 57, 58, 150, 200, 243, 246, 275, 276, 293, 352, 413, 473, 491, 504

Generalization, 129

Generic brand strategy, 244

Geodemography, 205

Geographic scope, 55

Geographic segmentation, 204

Gillette, 56

Global macroenvironment, 70

Global marketing research, 114

Global scope, 56

Global targeting, 221

Globally, 24

Going rate, 499

Google, 39, 85, 104, 113, 119, 340, 356

Gore, Al, 68, 280

Gortex, 68, 300

Government markets, 154

Gray marketing, 483

Greater convenience, 85

Green Marketing, 27

Grocery Manufacturers of America (GMA), 9

Gross domestic product (GDP), 72

Gucci, 72

Guinness, 369

H

Hall, Edward, 77

Harley-Davidson, 180, 243, 510

Hershey's, 240

Heterogeneous, 203

Hewlett-Packard, 9, 302, 304, 483

High-involvement purchases, 122

Hispanic Americans, 26

Hispanics, 133

Homogenous, 204

Honda, 46, 58

Horizontal price-fixing, 473

Household, 138

Hybrid brand strategy, 246

Hypermarkets, 445

Hypothesis, 106

Hyundai, 225

I

IBM, 8, 72, 155, 184, 191, 242, 300, 391, 394

Idea generation, 295

Idea screening, 297

IKEA, 437, 443

Imports, 56

Incremental costs, 480

Indirect channels, 422

Indirect export intermediaries, 56

Individual brand strategy, 245

Industry forecast, 397

Inelastic demand, 151

Inflation, 485

Infomercials, 450

Information processing, 131

Information search, 124

Information seekers, 163

Information systems, 45

Information, 99

Informative advertising, 348

Inktomi Corporation, 24

Innovators, 309

Institutional advertising, 352

Institutions, 153

Integrated logistics management, 414

Integrated marketing communication, 320

Integrated marketing mix plans, 50

Intel Corp., 71, 244, 393, 424, 427, 494

IntelliQuest Research, 98

Intensive distribution, 426

Interactive element, 273

Intermediaries, 68, 422

Intermodal transportation, 420

Internal data, 100

Internal marketing, 10, 277

International scope, 55

Internet marketing economy, 84

Internet searches, 113

Internet surveys, 109

Internet, 22

Inventory control, 418

ISO 9001, 187

Items, 239

J

J.C. Penney, 101

J.D. Power and Associates, 111, 115, 179, 195

Jimmy Au's, 11

JIT, 418

Jobs, Steven, 71

Johnson & Johnson, 9, 26, 36, 38, 31, 132, 213, 252, 366

Joint venture, 57

Jollibee, 183

Jones, Lafayette, 25

JPMorganChase, 70

Judgment samples, 110

K

Kellogg's, 58, 218, 245

Kennedy, John F., 17, 37

Kmart, 159, 427, 440, 444

Koch, 57

Kodak, 40, 393, 504

Kohl's, 444

Kraft, 53, 184, 247

Krauss, Michael, 85

Kroger, 441

L

L.L. Bean, 13, 22, 39, 447

Labels, 250

Laggards, 310

Land Rover, 12, 349

LARABAR, 13

Late majority, 310

Leads, 388

Learning, 129

Legal/regulatory environment, 79

Levi-Strauss, 87

Levitt, Ted, 39

Lexus, 178

Lifestyle, 210

Likert scales, 107

Limited Brands, 435

Limited-service wholesalers, 456

Line extension, 292

Linking pins, 163

List price, 505

Live Earth, 69

Logistics, 414

Loss leaders, 474

Louis Vuitton, 237

Low-cost strategy, 47

Low-involvement purchases, 122

Loyalty, 14

M

Maastricht Treaty, 74

Macro-marketing, 9

Magazines, 355

Mail surveys, 109

Mail-order catalogs, 448

Mail-order wholesalers, 457

Make-or-buy decision, 155

Malcolm Baldridge Award, 179, 189

Mall Intercepts, 108

Management information systems, 98

Manufacturer's brands, 246

Marginal costs, 479

Marginal revenue, 479

Markdown, 442

Market development, 291

Market managers, 301

Market price, 505

Market segment profile, 215

Market segmentation, 202

Market, 9

Marketing channel, 422

Marketing decision support system, 99

Marketing environment, 66

Marketing ethics, 26

Marketing information systems, 98

Marketing mix decisions, 19, 101

Marketing mix, 11

Marketing myopia, 39

Marketing research, 98

Marketing research, ethics, 115

Marketing strategy process, 18

Marketing, definition of, 6

Marketing, exchanging, 11

Marketing, for customers, clients, partners, and society, 14

Marketing, partners, 14

Marketing, processes, 10

Marketing, set of institutions, 9

Marketing, society, 15

Marketing, the activity, 7

Marketing, your involvement, 28

Marketspace, 22

Markup, 442

Marriott, 273, 445

Mars, 24

Maslow's Hierarchy, 125

Mass customization, 21, 220

Mass marketing, 16

Materials handling, 417

Mattel, 68, 251, 307, 450

McDonald's, 8, 12, 28, 43, 44, 50, 57, 77,
78, 107, 129, 183, 185, 224, 265, 273,
308, 322, 340, 446, 478,

McKesson, 425

McKinsey Company, 56, 239, 302

Media budget, 359

Media timing, 358

Media, 355

Memory, 132

Mercedes-Benz, 178, 349

Merck, 70, 243

Merrill Lynch, 70, 349

Metropolitan Statistical Area, 76

Microenvironment, 67

Micromarketing, 9, 219

Microsoft, 18, 22, 26, 40, 52, 70, 71, 269,
279, 291, 293, 300, 306, 476

Midas, 126

Milliken & Company, 186

Minnick, Mary, 12

Missionary sales, 378

Mobile, 357

Modified rebuy, 156

Monitoring performance, 102

Monopolistic competition, 477

Monopoly, 476

Motivation, 125

Motivational conflict, 126

Motorola, 45, 71, 72, 155, 187

MTV, 18

Multinational scope, 55

Multiple channel systems, 424

Multiple-step communication, 334

N

Nabisco, 51

NAFTA, 73, 368

NASCAR, 331

National and brand advertising, 351

National Basketball Association, 91, 276

National Football League, 347, 373

Natural resources, 74

NBC, 133

Needs, 7

Negotiation, 385

Networking, 389

New couples, 140

New task situation, 156

New-product committee, 302

New-product department, 301

Newspapers, 355

Niche, 219

Nike, 6, 9, 19, 87, 131, 191, 220, 250,
275, 342, 347

Nintendo, 42, 52, 289

Nissan, 473

Nokia, 45, 411

Nonprice competition, 468

Nonprobability samples, 110

Nonprofit marketing, 10, 278

O

Objective assessment of quality, 186

Observation, 105

Offprice retailers, 444

Oligopoly, 477

Olympic Games, 5, 44, 48, 275, 321, 366

One-sided message, 326

One-step communication, 334

Operant conditioning, 129

Operational excellence, 494

Operations products, 239

Opinion leaders, 334

Order management, 415

Order processing, 41

Oreck, 453

Organizational vision, 37
Our Common Future, 27
Outdoor advertising, 356
Outsourcing, 155
Overexposure, 358
Over-the-counter selling, 381
Ownership utility, 13

P

Pacific Rim, 73
Palmer, Arnold, 53
Panera Bread Company, 67
Partnership phase, 159
Passive learning, 123
Patagonia, 259
Pavlov, 129
Payout method, 353
Pella Windows, 276
Penetration pricing, 502
People systems, 45
Pepsi, 8, 103, 115, 221, 241, 276, 331, 346
Perceived brand quality, 248
Percentage of sales method, 353
Perception, 127
Perceptions of time, 77
Perfect competition, 476
Perishable, 267
Person marketing, 274
Personal interviews, 108
Personal selling, 329
Personalized and Customized Products, 86
Persuasion, 166
Persuasive advertising, 349
Pfizer, 264
PGA Tour, Inc., 282
Philip Morris, 499
Physical distribution, 20, 52, 415
Pilot study, 104
Pipelines, 419
Pizza Hut, 292, 476
Place decisions, 101
Place marketing, 276
Place utility, 13
Place, 20

Planning team, 46
Playboy Enterprises, 42
Playstation, 52
Plunkett, Warren, 25
Political advertising, 352
Political marketing, 276
Politicking, 166
Population density, 75
Population, 75, 109
Portfolio planning tools, 42
Positioning map, 221
Positioning, 19, 49, 200
Postpurchase evaluation, 270
Potential competitors, 70
Preapproach, 390
Predatory dumping, 474
Predatory pricing, 474
Presentation, 390
Press release, 368
Price ceiling, 496
Price competition, 478
Price components, 505
Price controls, 485
Price discrimination, 473
Price elasticity, 469
Price skimming, 502
Price umbrella, 502
Price wars, 500
Price, 20, 466
Price-fixing, 472
Pricewaterhouse-Coopers, 242
Pricing plans, 54
Primary data, 100
Private brand, 246
Private label merchandise, 441
Private warehouses, 416
Probability sample, 110
Problem recognition, 124
Problem solving, 166
Process technology, 44
Procter & Gamble, 9, 25, 27, 97, 116, 200, 216, 240, 242, 245, 301, 347, 421, 423, 239
Product concept, 297
Product decisions, 101
Product development, 291
Product differentiation, 203
Product factors, 164

Product leadership, 494
Product liability, 251
Product life cycle, 303
Product line, 51, 239
Product managers, 301
Product mix, 290
Product plans, 51, 291
Product position, 221
Product recall, 252
Product technology, 21, 44
Product, 19, 234
Production era, 16
Production orientation, 16
Production products, 239
Projective techniques, 105
Promotion decisions, 102
Promotion plans, 53
Promotion, 20, 320
Promotional pricing, 503
Prospects, 388
Psychographics, 210
Psychological needs, 125
Public relations, 331, 367
Public warehouses, 416
Public-service advertising, 352
Pull strategy, 333
Pulling power, 354
Purchase decision, 124
Purchase evaluation, 124
Purchase, 124
Purchasing agents, 162
Push strategy, 333
Push-pull strategy, 334

Q

Quaker Oats Company, 56, 241
Qualified prospect, 388
Qualifying, 388
Quality awards, 188
Quality function deployment, 188
Quantitative research, 104, 106
Quotas, 398

R

R.J. Reynolds, 81, 339

Rack jobbers, 456

Radio, 355

Railroads, 419

Ralph Lauren Company, 50, 54, 177

Rate-of-return pricing, 480

Raytheon, 413

Reach, 357

Realplayer, 23

Rebates, 366

Reduced cycle time, 187

Reebok, 324

Reference groups, 137

Reference price, 495

Referrals, 389

Regional scope, 55

Reinforcement advertising, 350

Relationship marketing, 12

Relationship selling, 384

Relationship-building phase, 159

Relationships, 23

Reminder advertising, 349

Rent, 54

Research design, 104

Resellers, 152

Retail (local) advertising, 351

Retail cooperative, 425

Retailer promotions, 361

Retailers, 422

Retailing and direct marketing, 20

Retailing, 438

Retired empty nesters, 140

Reverse channel, 424

Revlon, 137

Rewarding loyalty, 181

RFID, 417

Ritz-Calton, 175, 190

Roadway express, 420

Robb Report, 123

Robinson-Patman Act, 473

Routing schedule, 390

Rowling, J.K., 85

Rubbermaid, 326

S

S.C. Johnson & Sons, 15, 28

Salary, 399

Sales contests, 364

Sales era, 16

Sales force automation, 402

Sales force management, 393

Sales managers, 393

Sales orientation, 16

Sales profit quotas, 398

Sales promotion, 330, 360

Sales structure, 394

Sales territory, 385

Sales volume quotas, 398

Sample, 110

Sampling frame, 110

Sampling, 109

Satisfaction ratings, 179

Satisfaction, 14

Saturn, 180

Scandinavian Airline Systems, 266

Scientific method, 106

Scrambled merchandising, 441

Sea Ray, 240

Search qualities, 269

Sears, 439, 441

Second life, 233

Secondary data, 100

Segmentation by age, 208

Segmentation by family life cycle, 207

Segmentation variable, 204

Segmentation by ability and experience, 212

Segmentation by benefit, 213

Segmentation by buying approach, 214

Segmentation by gender, 207

Segmentation by geographic scope, 214

Segmentation by loyalty, 212

Segmentation by media and shopping habits, 212

Segmentation by product technology, 214

Segmentation by readiness, 212

Segmentation by usage rates, 212

Segmentation, 200

Selective attention, 128

Selective comprehension, 128

Selective distribution, 426

Selective exposure, 127

Selective retention, 128

Self-reference criterion, 76

Seller's market, 16

Sequential new-product development, 300

Service complexity, 274

Service encounter, 266

Service quality, 184

Service-goods continuum, 268

Services, 260

Sherman Antitrust Act, 79

Shisheido, 295

Shopping products, 237

Simple random sampling, 110

Simulated test market, 299

Simultaneous new-product development, 300

Situation analysis, 18, 48

Skycat, 42

Smith Corona, 186

Smith Klein Beecham, 15

Social class, 135

Social responsibility, 27

Sole survivors, 140

Sony, 235, 242, 345

Southwest Airlines, 14, 269

Specialty items, 237, 364

Specialty stores, 443

Specialty wholesalers, 456

Spending power, 72

Sponsorship, 331

Stakeholder, 67

Staples, 236

Starbucks, 32, 43

Starwood Hotels, 182

Static quality, 186

Statistical quality control, 188

Status quo pricing, 468

Stewart, Martha, 62

Stopping power, 354

Straight rebuy, 155

Strategic Alliances, 23

Strategic business units (SBUs), 41

Strategic direction, 40

Strategic Environmental Initiative, 74

Strategic infrastructure, 40

Strategic marketing plan, 36, 45

Strategic window, 46

Strategy, 46

Stratified random sampling, 110

Subculture, 133

Subjective assessment of quality, 186

Subliminal information, 128

Substitute product, 70

Subway, 51, 265

Supermarkets, 444

Superstores, 443

Suppliers, 68

Supplies, 239

Supply chain costs, 87

Supply chain management, 412

Supply chain, 154, 190

Supply curve, 471

Supply network, 413

Sustainability, 15, 27

Sustainable competitive advantage, 47

SWOT analysis, 48

SYSCO, 454

T

Tactics, 50

Tag Hauer, 275

Take-down segmentation method, 214

Take-Two, 80

Tantau Software, 98

Target audience, 357

Target marketing, 19, 49, 200, 215

Target pricing, 497

Targeting strategy, 217

Tariffs, 484

Task method, 353

Team selling, 379

Technological environment, 70

Technology and e-commerce, 21

Telemarketing, 398, 449

Telephone surveys, 108

Television 355

Territory planning, 388

Test market, 298

Texas Instruments, 416, 424

The American Cancer Society, 277

The concept of the strategic marketing planning process, 36

The Home Depot, 121, 262, 458

The Marketing Science Institute, 271

The Red Cross, 8

3M, 296, 314

Ticketmaster, 285

Tier, 154

Time utility, 13

Tommy Hilfiger, 228

Toshiba, 58

Total quality management, 186

Toyota, 40, 161, 192, 300, 325, 347, 415

Toys "R" Us, 102, 367, 440

Trade industries, 152

Trade promotions, 361

Trademark, 242

Trading blocs, 72

Trading companies, 57

Traditional sales approach, 382

Transaction-based information system, 99

Transfer prices, 484

Transportation and telecommunications, 153

Truck Jobbers, 457

Trucks, 418

Trust, 181

Two-sided message, 326

Two-way communication, 87

Tying arrangement, 430

Tylenol, 38

U

U.S. Census Bureau, 66, 72

U.S. Patent Office, 66, 249

Unaided recall, 359

Undifferentiated marketing, 218

Union Pacific, 153, 419

United Airlines, 8

United States Postal Service, 10, 351, 494

Unsought products, 236

UPS, 10, 13, 42, 43, 70, 158, 218, 382, 420, 446, 495

Urbanization, 75

Users, 163

Utilities, 153

V

Value in exchange, 493

Value in use, 493

Value proposition, 50

Value-based pricing, 492

Value-driven organizations, 18

Values, 133

Variable costs, 478

Variety stores, 445

Venture team, 302

Verizon Wireless, 263, 328, 500

Vertical integration, 413

Vertical marketing systems, 425

Vertical price-fixing, 472

Viacom, 146

Viral marketing, 356

Viral trade shows, 84

Volkswagan, 22, 58, 235, 242

Volvo, 493

W

Wal-Mart, 69, 70, 85, 102, 219, 252, 266, 412, 423, 427, 440, 442, 444, 446, 457, 465, 492

Wants, 7

Warehouse clubs, 444

Warehousing, 416

Warranties, 251

Water carriers, 419

Web auctions, 156

Web marketers, 84

Web portals, 84

Web product-service providers, 85

Webkinz, 488

WebMD, 263

Webster, Frederick, Jr., 45

Westinghouse Process Control, 55

Wheel of retailing, 439

Whirlpool, 133, 397, 477

Whole Foods Market, 37, 38, 406

Wholesalers, 422

Wholesaler-sponsored voluntary chain, 425

Wholesaling, 454

Wider selection and customization, 86

Williams Sonoma, 178

Winfrey, Oprah, 222, 310

Woods, Tiger, 19

Working empty nesters, 140

World Commission on Environment and
  Development, 27

Wyndham Worldwide, 53, 62

X

Xerox,   14, 239, 242, 390, 393, 495

Y

Young singles, 140

Z

Zappos, 38

Zip code segmentation, 205

notes

notes

notes

notes

notes